Handbook of Dividend Achievers

2000

VICKI PEARTHREE RAEBURN, *President*

HOWARD G. KIEDAISCH, *Publisher*

SUZANNE WITTEBORT, *Asst. Vice Pres.*

BRAD A. ARMBRUSTER, *Editor*

Associate Editors

REGGIE D. CAIN   STACY M. CLEELAND
KEVIN HECKERT

Senior Business Analysts

CHRISTALYN Y. DANIEL   RICHARD K. DEE, JR.
MELISSA A. FRANCIS

Business Analysts

GARY DEGENNARO   SAMANTHA HASTINGS
GEOFFERY K. FORSYTH   ANTHONY MAGNARINI
FATIMA M. GADDY   AVA J. OSZLANYI
TROY GAUNT   SHANNON R. TANSKY
TALVI S. YOUNG

Published By:

A MERGENT COMPANY

TABLE OF CONTENTS

Page

The Handbook of
DIVIDEND ACHIEVERS

Since 1979, Mergent FIS, formerly the Financial Information Services division of Moody's Investors Service, has been singling out companies that have increased their cash dividends annually for at least the past ten consecutive calendar years. Mergent has dubbed these distinctive companies Dividend Achievers. Mergent is proud to present the first Dividend Achievers of the new millennium in this volume.

Each year, Mergent compiles its list of Dividend Achievers from more than 10,000 companies in its U.S. equity database. For a company to be eligible for inclusion, its stock must be actively traded on the New York Stock Exchange, Nasdaq's National Market or the American Stock Exchange.

Mergent's Dividend Achievers list is based on the concept that certain equity investments can provide a rising cash return over the long run, while offering the additional benefit of potential price appreciation. Annual total return, income plus price appreciation, for some stocks may compare favorably with some other investment alternatives, particularly during times of low interest rates. In addition, dividends can also serve as signals from companies' managements about the future. When directors increase dividends they're saying, in effect, that they believe that future earnings will be able to sustain the higher payouts.

Mergent's 2000 survey has identified 320 companies that have increased their per-share cash dividends annually for at least the past ten consecutive calendar years. Internet and other technology stocks were the market darlings in 1999, and that trend touched even the diversified Dividend Achiever universe. *Cohu Inc.*, a San Diego-based manufacturer of semiconductor testing equipment and other electronic products, led the Dividend Achievers in one-year total return to investors, with a total return of 184.7% in 1999. In second place was *Telephone and Data Systems, Inc.*, a diversified Chicago-based telecommunications company, which racked up a total return of 182.0% in 1900. Total return rankings begin on page 13a.

Altogether, of the 28,000 publicly-held issues (including mutual funds and small-cap companies) tracked by Mergent, 1,703 increased their dividends in 1999, a decrease from 2,162 in 1998. Dividend decreases also fell, to 135 from 182.

The list of Dividend Achievers follows, ranked by average annual compound dividend growth rate over the ten-year period of calendar 1989-99. *Paychex, Inc.*, the Rochester, NY-based payroll, tax-preparation and employee-benefits services provider, held the top spot for the second year in a row, with an annual average compound dividend growth rate over ten years of 42.91%. The second-highest growth rate, 35.58%, belongs to *Home Depot, Inc.*, the Atlanta-based home-improvement retailer with 960 warehouse stores. Newcomer *Charles Schwab Corp.*, the discount brokerage firm that has expanded powerfully into on-line trading, took third-place honors with a ten-year annual average dividend growth rate of 34.00%. *Citigroup Inc.*, the financial giant with $716.94 billion in assets created by the merger of Travelers Group and Citicorp in 1998, ranked fourth with 32.56%. *Raymond James Financial, Inc.*, the St. Petersburg, Florida-based brokerage, investment banking and money management firm, scored fifth with 26.68%.

In a major shift, the longest record of annual dividend increases has been seized by *Ohio Casualty Corp.* The Hamilton, Ohio-based property and casualty insurer has increased its dividends for 54 consecutive years. Long-time record-holder Winn-Dixie Stores, Inc., did not raise its dividends in 1999, after 55 consecutive years of increases. Raising its dividends for the 48 consecutive year was *Aon Corp.*, the Chicago-based insurance holding company.

Ranking the 2000 Dividend Achievers

Companies are listed by the ten-year average annual compound growth rate of their dividends.

Rank	Company	Growth Rate %	No. of Yrs.	Rank	Company	Growth Rate %	No. of Yrs.
1.	[2] Paychex, Inc. (NS)	42.91	11	49.	Park National Corp. (AM)	16.14	12
2.	[1] Home Depot, Inc. (The) (NY)	35.58	12	50.	[1] Schering-Plough Corp. (NY)	16.06	14
3.	[1] Schwab (Charles) Corp. (NY)	34.00	10	51.	[2] Analysts International, Inc. (NS)	16.00	11
4.	[1] Citigroup Inc. (NY)	32.56	13	52.	[1] Firstar Corp. (NY)	15.98	21
5.	[1] Raymond James Finl. Inc. (NY)	26.68	13	53.	[1] Automatic Data Processing (NY)	15.86	24
6.	Sovereign Bancorp, Inc. (NS)	26.16	11	54.	[1] Reynolds & Reynolds Co. (NY)	15.46	10
7.	[1] Fannie Mae (NY)	25.86	14	55.	[2] LESCO, Inc. (NS)	15.44	14
8.	Pacific Capital Bancorp (NS)	25.15	30	56.	[1] Valspar Corp. (NY)	15.38	21
9.	[1] Sysco Corp. (NY)	24.06	23	57.	Federal Signal Corp. (NY)	15.32	12
10.	[1] Washington Mutual Inc. (NY)	23.52	10	58.	[1] ConAgra, Inc. (NY)	15.28	22
11.	[2] Jones Pharma Inc. (NS)	23.16	10	59.	[1] UNUMProvident Corp. (NY)	15.27	12
12.	Mercury General Corp. (NY)	22.96	13	60.	[1] Wells Fargo & Co. (NY)	15.24	12
13.	[2] Cintas Corp. (NS)	22.74	17	61.	Associated Banc-Corp. (NS)	15.19	26
14.	T. Rowe Price Associates (NS)	22.52	13	62.	M & T Bank Corp. (NY)	15.13	19
15.	[1] Wal-Mart Stores, Inc. (NY)	22.12	18	63.	[1] Merck & Co., Inc. (NY)	14.94	16
16.	[1] Medtronic, Inc. (NY)	21.73	22	64.	[1] McCormick & Co., Inc. (NY)	14.87	13
17.	[1] DQE, Inc. (NY)	21.70	10		[1] Pall Corp. (NY)	14.87	19
18.	[1] Hewlett-Packard Co. (NY)	21.67	13		[1] State Street Corp. (NY)	14.87	19
19.	[1] Franklin Resources, Inc. (NY)	21.61	10	67.	1st Source Corp. (NS)	14.73	11
20.	Charter One Financial, Inc. (NY)	21.15	11	68.	[1] Leggett & Platt, Inc. (NY)	14.69	30
21.	Virco Manufacturing Corp. (AM)	20.76	17	69.	[1] Pitney Bowes, Inc. (NY)	14.65	16
22.	Trustco Bank (NS)	20.64	23	70.	[1] Campbell Soup Co. (NY)	14.62	17
23.	[1] Archer Daniels Midland Co. (NY)	20.58	25	71.	[1] Abbott Laboratories (NY)	14.61	27
24.	[1] Eaton Vance Corp. (NY)	20.40	18	72.	[1] Johnson & Johnson (NY)	14.56	37
25.	S&T Bancorp, Inc. (NS)	20.20	10	73.	[1] BB&T Corp. (NY)	14.52	28
26.	[1] Brady Corp. (NY)	20.19	15	74.	[1] Golden West Financial Corp. (NY)	14.43	16
27.	Corus Bankshares, Inc. (NS)	19.01	13	75.	[1] Albertson's, Inc. (NY)	14.40	28
28.	Alliance Cap. Mgmt. Holdg. (NY)	18.71	11	76.	[1] Baldor Electric Co. (NY)	14.37	16
29.	[1] Disney (Walt) Co. (The) (NY)	18.55	14	77.	Raven Industries, Inc. (NS)	14.35	12
30.	[1] Synovus Financial Corp. (NY)	18.44	23	78.	[1] Coca-Cola Co. (The) (NY)	14.18	37
31.	[1] Tootsie Roll Industries, Inc. (NY)	18.32	36	79.	[1] First Union Corp. (NY)	14.16	22
32.	[1] Kaydon Corp. (NY)	18.22	12	80.	[1] AFLAC Inc. (NY)	14.14	17
33.	[1] Hasbro, Inc. (NY)	18.05	18	81.	[1] Warner-Lambert Co. (NY)	14.13	47
34.	[1] SLM Holding Corp. (NY)	17.95	19	82.	[1] Avery Dennison Corp. (NY)	13.87	24
35.	[2] Cohu Inc. (NS)	17.87	12		[1] Hannaford Bros. Co. (NY)	13.87	28
36.	[1] MBIA Inc. (NY)	17.84	12		[1] Legg Mason, Inc. (NY)	13.87	16
37.	[1] Fidelity National Financial (NY)	17.36	12	85.	Superior Uniform Group Inc. (AM)	13.67	16
38.	WestAmerica Bancorporation (NS)	17.35	10	86.	[1] SunTrust Banks, Inc. (NY)	13.47	14
39.	[2] Fifth Third Bancorp (NS)	17.32	27	87.	[2] Schulman (A.), Inc. (NS)	13.40	23
40.	F.N.B. Corp. (NS)	17.19	15	88.	[1] Old Republic International (NY)	13.29	18
41.	[1] Gillette Co. (The) (NY)	17.17	22	89.	[1] PepsiCo, Inc. (NY)	13.28	28
42.	[1] Cooper Tire & Rubber Co. (NY)	17.15	20	90.	Compass Bancshares Inc. (NS)	13.27	16
43.	[1] Nucor Corp. (NY)	16.85	27	91.	[2] First Security Corp. (NS)	13.11	12
44.	[1] Illinois Tool Works, Inc. (NY)	16.65	37	92.	Wausau-Mosinee Paper Corp. (NY)	13.05	15
45.	[2] Northern Trust Corp. (NS)	16.60	14		[1] American Int'l Group (NY)	13.05	14
46.	[1] Superior Industries Int'l. (NY)	16.50	14	94.	Huntington Bancshares, Inc. (NS)	13.04	33
47.	[1] Philip Morris Cos., Inc. (NY)	16.35	31	95.	[1] Wrigley (Wm.) Jr. Co. (NY)	13.00	19
48.	[1] Omnicare Inc. (NY)	16.23	10	96.	[1] Bank of America Corp. (NY)	12.90	22

Rank	Company	Growth Rate %	No. of Yrs.	Rank	Company	Growth Rate %	No. of Yrs.
97.	Hilb, Rogal & Hamilton Co. (NY)	12.88	13		Protective Life Corp. (NY)	10.38	10
98.	[1] Family Dollar Stores, Inc. (NY)	12.83	23	152.	[2] Block Drug Co., Inc. (NS)	10.31	28
	[1] Pfizer Inc. (NY)	12.83	32	153.	[1] KeyCorp (NY)	10.03	20
	[2] Lancaster Colony Corp. (NS)	12.83	30	154.	[2] Regions Financial Corp. (NS)	10.02	28
101.	[2] Myers Industries Inc. (AM)	12.76	23	155.	[1] AmSouth Bancorporation (NY)	9.95	29
102.	[1] Teleflex Inc. (NY)	12.66	22	156.	[1] McDonald's Corp. (NY)	9.94	23
103.	[1] Bank One Corp. (NY)	12.57	29	157.	[1] Clorox Co. (NY)	9.83	23
	[1] General Electric Co. (NY)	12.57	24		[1] Worthington Industries (NY)	9.83	17
105.	First Tennessee National (NY)	12.54	22	159.	[1] Pep Boys (NY)	9.80	22
106.	[1] Jefferson-Pilot Corp. (NY)	12.46	32	160.	[1] Bandag, Inc. (NY)	9.74	23
107.	[2] Sigma-Aldrich Corp. (NS)	12.41	18		Weyco Group, Inc. (NS)	9.74	19
108.	[1] Old Kent Financial Corp. (NY)	12.38	19	162.	SAFECO Corp. (NS)	9.71	24
109.	[2] Cincinnati Financial Corp. (NS)	12.32	39	163.	[1] Grainger (W.W.) Inc. (NY)	9.68	28
110.	[1] HON Industries Inc. (NY)	12.22	11	164.	[1] First Virginia Banks Inc. (NY)	9.67	22
111.	Donegal Group Inc. (NS)	12.18	10	165.	[1] Dover Corp. (NY)	9.66	44
112.	[2] Tuscarora, Inc. (NS)	12.08	10	166.	[1] Hubbell Inc. (NY)	9.58	39
113.	[1] Hillenbrand Industries, Inc. (NY)	12.05	29	167.	Citizens Banking Corp. (NS)	9.48	16
114.	[1] Wallace Computer Services (NY)	12.01	28	168.	[2] Kimball International, Inc. (NS)	9.43	16
115.	[2] Modine Manufacturing Co. (NS)	11.99	13	169.	[1] Cedar Fair, L.P. (NY)	9.33	12
116.	SouthTrust Corp. (NS)	11.91	29	170.	[1] NiSource, Inc. (NY)	9.28	11
117.	[1] Interpublic Group of Cos. (NY)	11.90	18	171.	[1] Hanna (M.A.) Co. (NY)	9.26	12
118.	[1] Bemis Co., Inc. (NY)	11.86	16	172.	Banta Corp. (NY)	9.25	21
119.	First Commonwealth Fin'l (NY)	11.84	15	173.	[1] ABM Industries, Inc. (NY)	9.24	35
120.	[1] Gallagher (Arthur J.) & Co. (NY)	11.76	15	174.	WesBanco, Inc. (NS)	9.22	14
121.	Harleysville Group, Inc. (NS)	11.73	13	175.	Pentair, Inc. (NY)	9.15	23
122.	[1] Colgate-Palmolive Co. (NY)	11.71	37	176.	[1] Morgan (J.P.) & Co., Inc. (NY)	9.08	23
123.	First Financial Bancorp (NS)	11.69	16	177.	[1] Int'l Flavors & Fragrances (NY)	9.04	38
124.	[1] Hormel Foods Corp. (NY)	11.61	32	178.	Keystone Financial, Inc. (NS)	9.02	13
	[2] Nordson Corp. (NS)	11.61	18	179.	[1] American Greetings Corp. (NY)	8.98	10
126.	[1] Walgreen Co. (NY)	11.45	24		[1] Belo (A.H.) Corp. (NY)	8.98	12
	[1] Wachovia Corp. (NY)	11.45	22	181.	[1] Bestfoods (NY)	8.93	13
128.	[2] Berkley (W.R.) Corp. (NS)	11.40	14	182.	CCB Financial Corp. (NY)	8.83	35
129.	[1] Procter & Gamble Co. (NY)	11.36	46	183.	[1] American Water Works Co. (NY)	8.80	24
130.	City Holding Co. (NS)	11.34	12	184.	[1] Millipore Corp. (NY)	8.76	29
131.	Mercantile Bankshares Corp. (NS)	11.30	23	185.	Community Trust Bancorp (NS)	8.75	11
132.	BancorpSouth, Inc. (NY)	11.26	13	186.	Stepan Co. (NY)	8.74	33
133.	[1] Anheuser-Busch Cos., Inc. (NY)	11.23	25	187.	[1] Emerson Electric Co. (NY)	8.72	43
134.	[1] Alberto-Culver Co. (NY)	11.19	15	188.	[1] Carlisle Companies Inc. (NY)	8.71	23
135.	[1] Lockheed Martin Corp. (NY)	11.14	15		[1] Pacific Century Financial (NY)	8.71	22
136.	[1] Comerica, Inc. (NY)	11.09	16	190.	RLI Corp. (NY)	8.59	23
137.	Wilmington Trust Corp. (NY)	10.83	18	191.	[1] Kellogg Co. (NY)	8.36	43
138.	[1] Heinz (H.J.) Co. (NY)	10.81	36	192.	Fulton Financial Corp. (NS)	8.35	26
139.	[1] Sara Lee Corp. (NY)	10.76	23	193.	[1] Chubb Corp. (NY)	8.34	35
140.	[2] Liqui-Box Corp. (NS)	10.74	21	194.	[1] Air Products & Chemicals (NY)	8.31	17
141.	Trustmark Corp. (NS)	10.70	26	195.	[2] Apogee Enterprises, Inc. (NS)	8.26	25
142.	One Valley Bancorp, Inc. (NY)	10.67	18	196.	Midland Co. (NS)	8.24	13
143.	[1] Sherwin-Williams Co. (NY)	10.62	20	197.	[1] GATX Corp. (NY)	8.20	14
144.	[2] Alfa Corp. (NS)	10.60	14		[1] Liberty Corp. (NY)	8.20	10
145.	[2] Commerce Bancshares, Inc. (NS)	10.59	31	199.	[1] Diebold, Inc. (NY)	8.05	46
146.	[1] Lilly (Eli) & Co. (NY)	10.55	32	200.	[1] Bard (C.R.) Inc. (NY)	8.04	28
147.	[1] Becton, Dickinson & Co. (NY)	10.52	27	201.	[1] Target Corp. (NY)	7.92	28
148.	[1] ReliaStar Financial Corp. (NY)	10.49	28	202.	[1] Sonoco Products Co. (NY)	7.90	16
149.	[1] Hershey Foods Corp. (NY)	10.45	25	203.	[1] American General Corp. (NY)	7.87	16
150.	Marshall & Ilsley Corp. (NY)	10.38	26	204.	[2] Fuller (H.B.) Co. (NS)	7.84	32

Rank	Company	Growth Rate %	No. of Yrs.
205.	[1] ALLTEL Corp. (NY)	7.81	39
206.	[1] Bear Stearns Cos. Inc. (The) (NY)	7.80	13
207.	[1] Fleetwood Enterprises, Inc. (NY)	7.77	17
208.	[1] Flowers Industries, Inc. (NY)	7.74	27
	[1] Brown-Forman Corp. (NY)	7.74	15
210.	[1] GPU, Inc. (NY)	7.73	12
211.	[1] RPM Inc. (NY)	7.72	26
212.	North Pittsburgh Systems (NS)	7.70	37
213.	[1] Dean Foods Co. (NY)	7.69	27
214.	FirstMerit Corp. (NS)	7.59	17
215.	[1] PPG Industries, Inc. (NY)	7.46	28
216.	[1] Marsh & McLennan Cos. Inc. (NY)	7.39	38
217.	[2] Kelly Services Inc. (NS)	7.37	28
218.	[2] United Fire & Casualty Co. (NS)	7.25	14
219.	[1] Aon Corp. (NY)	7.20	48
220.	[1] Lowe's Cos., Inc. (NY)	7.18	22
221.	[1] Genuine Parts Corp. (NY)	7.17	43
222.	[1] Harcourt General, Inc. (NY)	7.05	32
223.	Health Care Prop. Investors (NY)	6.97	14
224.	[1] Donnelley (R.R.) & Sons Co. (NY)	6.93	30
225.	[1] SUPERVALU Inc. (NY)	6.88	27
226.	[1] Du Pont (E.I.) De Nemours (NY)	6.80	17
227.	Old National Bancorp (NS)	6.79	16
228.	[1] May Department Stores Co. (NY)	6.78	24
229.	[1] St. Paul Cos., Inc. (NY)	6.72	13
	Susquehanna Bancshares (NS)	6.72	29
231.	[1] Rohm & Haas Co. (NY)	6.71	22
232.	Quaker Chemical Corp. (NY)	6.70	28
233.	[1] VF Corp. (NY)	6.45	27
234.	Mine Safety Appliances Co. (AM)	6.42	29
235.	[1] American Home Products (NY)	6.38	47
236.	[1] Household International (NY)	6.35	47
237.	[1] La-Z-Boy Incorporated (NY)	6.32	18
238.	[2] American National Insurance (NS)	6.29	26
239.	CFW Communications Co. (NS)	6.26	11
240.	[1] Weis Markets, Inc. (NY)	6.18	25
241.	F&M National Corp. (NY)	6.07	17
242.	[1] Masco Corp. (NY)	6.05	41
243.	[1] Lincoln National Corp. (NY)	5.90	16
244.	[1] Progressive Corp. (NY)	5.89	30
245.	[1] Chevron Corp. (NY)	5.88	12
246.	[2] Ohio Casualty Corp. (NS)	5.87	54
	Telephone & Data Systems (AM)	5.87	25
248.	[1] Lee Enterprises, Inc. (NY)	5.84	39
249.	United Dominion Rlty. Trust (NY)	5.83	14
250.	[1] Kimberly-Clark Corp. (NY)	5.77	25
251.	[1] Piedmont Natural Gas Co. (NY)	5.65	20
252.	[1] Johnson Controls, Inc. (NY)	5.60	24
253.	[1] Minnesota Mining & Mfg. Co. (NY)	5.59	41
254.	[1] Bristol-Myers Squibb Co. (NY)	5.57	27
	[1] McGraw-Hill Cos., Inc. (NY)	5.57	26
	[1] TECO Energy Inc. (NY)	5.57	40
257.	[1] Universal Corp. (NY)	5.54	29
258.	[1] Stanley Works (NY)	5.49	32
259.	Washington R.E.I.T. (NY)	5.46	38
260.	[1] HSB Group, Inc. (NY)	5.45	34
261.	[1] Ingersoll-Rand Co. (NY)	5.17	12
262.	Frisch's Restaurants, Inc. (AM)	5.16	16
263.	[2] Semco Energy Inc. (NY)	4.94	21
264.	Bowl America Inc. (AM)	4.91	27
265.	Haverty Furniture Cos., Inc. (NY)	4.70	29
266.	[1] NICOR Inc. (NY)	4.57	12
267.	[1] ServiceMaster Co. (NY)	4.50	29
	[2] Kenan Transport Co. (NS)	4.50	16
269.	Black Hills Corp. (NY)	4.41	19
270.	EnergyNorth, Inc. (NY)	4.39	16
271.	[1] TRW Inc. (NY)	4.38	28
272.	[1] Indiana Energy, Inc. (NY)	4.36	24
273.	[1] Crawford & Co. (NY)	4.34	19
274.	[1] National Service Industries (NY)	4.30	38
275.	[1] Houghton Mifflin Co. (NY)	4.29	17
276.	[1] Energen Corp. (NY)	4.26	17
277.	Wesco Financial Corp. (AM)	4.23	28
278.	[1] SBC Communications Inc. (NY)	4.15	15
279.	[1] Gannett Co., Inc. (NY)	4.14	28
	[1] KeySpan Energy Corp. (NY)	4.14	23
281.	[1] CenturyTel, Inc. (NY)	4.09	26
282.	Northwestern Corp. (NY)	4.03	16
283.	[1] NACCO Industries Inc. (NY)	3.99	16
284.	Atmos Energy Corp. (NY)	3.96	12
285.	UNITIL Corp. (AM)	3.95	14
286.	[1] Exxon Mobil Corp. (NY)	3.80	17
287.	[1] Wisconsin Energy Corp. (NY)	3.68	38
288.	[1] Questar Corp. (NY)	3.55	20
289.	Clarcor Inc. (NY)	3.53	19
290.	[1] Carolina Power & Light Co. (NY)	3.48	11
	[1] National Fuel Gas Co. (NY)	3.48	28
292.	Gorman-Rupp Co. (AM)	3.47	27
293.	Health Care REIT, Inc. (NY)	3.43	10
294.	Florida Public Utilities Co. (AM)	3.34	31
295.	[2] Tennant Co. (NS)	3.29	27
296.	[1] SIGCORP, Inc. (NY)	3.26	40
297.	[1] CLECO Corp. (NY)	3.19	18
298.	[1] LG&E Energy Corp. (NY)	3.12	45
299.	Valley Resources, Inc. (AM)	3.09	19
300.	[1] UGI Corp. (NY)	2.97	12
301.	[1] Kansas City Power & Light (NY)	2.88	14
302.	[1] Northern States Power Co. (NY)	2.87	24
303.	[2] Middlesex Water Co. (NS)	2.86	27
304.	SJW Corp. (AM)	2.80	33
305.	[1] St. Joseph Light & Power Co. (NY)	2.78	19
306.	[2] Otter Tail Power Co. (NS)	2.68	24
307.	Federal Realty Invest. Trust (NY)	2.67	32
308.	[1] California Water Service Co. (NY)	2.59	32
309.	Florida Progress Corp. (NY)	2.40	47
310.	[1] Washington Gas Light Co. (NY)	2.28	23

Rank	Company	Growth Rate %	No. of Yrs.	Rank	Company	Growth Rate %	No. of Yrs.
311.	[1] WPS Resources Corp. (NY)	2.26	41	316.	[1] Peoples Energy Corp. (NY)	2.13	16
312.	[1] Consolidated Edison, Inc. (NY)	2.21	25	317.	CH Energy Group, Inc. (NY)	2.07	11
313.	Commercial Net Lease Realty (NY)	2.17	10	318.	[1] Western Resources, Inc. (NY)	2.03	39
	Universal Health Rlty. Inc. (NY)	2.17	12	319.	[2] Madison Gas & Electric Co. (NS)	1.56	24
315.	American States Water Co. (NY)	2.15	46	320.	[2] Connecticut Water Service (NS)	1.27	24

[1] Mergent's Handbook of Common Stocks. [2] Mergent's Handbook of Nasdaq Stocks.
(NY) New York Stock Exchange. (NS) Nasdaq Stock Market. (AM) American Stock Exchange.

Longest Records of Dividend Achievement

The following Dividend Achievers boast the longest records of consecutive annual dividend

Rank	Company	No. of Yrs.	Rank	Company	No. of Yrs.
1.	Ohio Casualty Corp.	54		Colgate-Palmolive Co.	37
2.	Aon Corp.	48		Illinois Tool Works, Inc.	37
3.	American Home Products	47		Johnson & Johnson	37
	Florida Progress Corp.	47		North Pittsburgh Systems, Inc.	37
	Household International, Inc.	47	35.	Heinz (H.J.) Co.	36
	Warner-Lambert Co.	47		Tootsie Roll Industries, Inc.	36
7.	American States Water Co.	46	37.	ABM Industries, Inc.	35
	Diebold, Inc.	46		CCB Financial Corp.	35
	Procter & Gamble Co.	46		Chubb Corp.	35
10.	LG&E Energy Corp.	45	40.	HSB Group, Inc.	34
11.	Dover Corp.	44	41.	Huntington Bancshares, Inc.	33
12.	Emerson Electric Co.	43		SJW Corp.	33
	Genuine Parts Corp.	43		Stepan Co.	33
	Kellogg Co.	43	44.	California Water Service Co.	32
15.	Masco Corp.	41		Federal Realty Invest. Trust	32
	Minnesota Mining & Mfg. Co.	41		Fuller (H.B.) Co.	32
	WPS Resources Corp.	41		Harcourt General, Inc.	32
18.	SIGCORP, Inc.	40		Hormel Foods Corp.	32
	TECO Energy Inc.	40		Jefferson-Pilot Corp.	32
20.	ALLTEL Corp.	39		Lilly (Eli) & Co.	32
	Cincinnati Financial Corp.	39		Pfizer Inc.	32
	Hubbell Inc.	39		Stanley Works	32
	Lee Enterprises, Inc.	39	53.	Commerce Bancshares, Inc.	31
	Western Resources, Inc.	39		Florida Public Utilities Co.	31
25.	International Flavors & Frags.	38		Philip Morris Cos., Inc.	31
	Marsh & McLennan Cos. Inc.	38	56.	Donnelley (R.R.) & Sons Co.	30
	National Service Industries	38		Lancaster Colony Corp.	30
	Washington R.E.I.T.	38		Leggett & Platt, Inc.	30
	Wisconsin Energy Corp	38		Pacific Capital Bancorp	30
30.	Coca-Cola Co. (The)	37		Progressive Corp.	30

Dividend Achiever Arrivals and Departures

The following companies, which recorded ten consecutive years of dividend increases in 1999, mark their debut as Dividend Achievers.

American Greetings Corp.
Commercial Net Lease Realty
Donegal Group Inc.
DQE, Inc.
Franklin Resources, Inc.
Health Care REIT, Inc.
Jones Pharma Inc.
Liberty Corp.

Omnicare Inc.
Protective Life Corp.
Reynolds & Reynolds Co.
S&T Bancorp, Inc.
Schwab (Charles) Corp.
Tuscarora, Inc.
Washington Mutual Inc..
WestAmerica Bancorporation

According to Mergent's database, the following former Dividend Achievers did not increase their regular cash dividends in 1999 and dropped from the list.

Bell Atlantic Corp.
Chemed Corp.
CSX Corp.
Duke Energy Corp.
Engelhard Corp.
Fluor Corp.
General Binding Corp.
Golden Enterprises, Inc.
Graco Inc.
Hawaiian Electric Industries, Inc.

Helmerich & Payne, Inc.
Hickory Tech Corp.
Northwest Natural Gas Co.
Potlatch Corp.
SCANA Corp.
United Asset Management Corp.
Universal Foods Corp.
Watts Industries, Inc.
Winn-Dixie Stores, Inc.

The following former Dividend Achiever companies have been merged or acquired.

Aliant Communications, Inc.
American Business Products, Inc.
American Heritage Life Investment Corp.
American Stores Company
Ameritech Corp.
Analysis & Technology, Inc.
CNB Bancshares, Inc.
Colonial Gas Company
Connecticut Energy Corp.

Frontier Corp.
Honeywell, Inc.
Mobil Corp.
North Carolina Natural Gas Corp.
Public Service Co. of N.C.
Pulitzer Publishing Co.
Republic New York Corp.
WICOR, Inc.

Dividend Achiever Name Changes

The following companies have changed their names in the last year.

Old Name	New Name
Alliance Capital Management L.P.	Alliance Capital Management Holding L.P.
Central Hudson Gas & Electric Co.	CH Energy Group, Inc.
Dayton-Hudson Corp.	Target Corp.
Exxon Corp.	Exxon Mobil Corp.
UNUM Corp.	UNUMProvident Corp.

Top 20 by Total Assets

Rank	Company	Assets ($Mil.)	Rank	Company	Assets ($Mil.)
1.	Citigroup Inc.	716,937.0	11.	Bear Stearns Companies	153,894.3
2.	Bank of America Corp.	632,574.0	12.	Exxon Mobil Corporation	144,521.0
3.	Fannie Mae	575,167.0	13.	American General Corp.	115,447.0
4.	General Electric Co.	405,200.0	14.	Lincoln National Corp.	103,095.7
5.	Bank One Corp.	269,425.0	15.	SunTrust Banks, Inc.	95,390.0
6.	American Int'l Group	268,238.0	16.	KeyCorp.	83,395.0
7.	Morgan (J.P.) & Company	265,627.0	17.	SBC Communications, Inc.	83,215.0
8.	First Union Corporation	254,762.0	18.	Firstar Corporation	72,787.8
9.	Wells Fargo & Company	218,102.0	19.	Wal-Mart Stores, Inc.	70,349.0
10.	Washington Mutual, Inc.	186,513.6	20.	Wachovia Corporation	67,352.5

Top 20 by Return on Equity

Rank	Company	Return on Equity %	Rank	Company	Return on Equity %
1.	Campbell Soup Company	308.1	11.	Merck & Co., Inc.	44.5
2.	NiSource, Inc.	187.4	12.	Hershey Foods Corporation	41.9
3.	Alliance Cap. Manag. Hldg.	144.1	13.	Kellogg Company	41.6
4.	Sara Lee Corporation	91.7	14.	Gillette Company (The)	41.2
5.	Bestfoods	76.4	15.	Schering-Plough Corporation	40.9
6.	SLM Holding Corporation	59.6	16.	Pitney Bowes Inc.	40.5
7.	Colgate-Palmolive Company	51.1	17.	Millipore Corporation	36.4
8.	Lilly (Eli) & Company	50.8	18.	Pfizer Inc.	36.0
9.	Philip Morris Companies	50.1	19.	Anheuser-Busch Companies	35.8
10.	Bristol-Myers Squibb Co.	48.2	20.	Warner-Lambert Company	34.0

Top 20 by Return on Assets

Rank	Company	Return on Assets %	Rank	Company	Return on Assets %
1.	Alliance Cap. Manag. Hldg.	140.7	11.	Jones Pharma Incorporated	16.3
2.	Bristol-Myers Squibb Co.	24.3	12.	Pfizer Inc.	15.5
3.	T. Rowe Price Associates, Inc.	24.0	13.	Superior Industries Int'l	15.4
4.	Schering-Plough Corporation	22.5	14.	Warner-Lambert Company	15.1
5.	Liqui-Box Corporation	20.2	15.	Eaton Vance Corporation	14.6
6.	Wrigley (William) Jr. Co.	19.9	16.	Kaydon Corporation	14.5
	Lilly (Eli) & Company	19.9	17.	Johnson & Johnson	14.3
8.	Lancaster Colony Corporation	17.3	18.	Hershey Foods Corporation	13.8
9.	Abbott Laboratories	16.9	19.	Home Depot (The), Inc.	13.6
10.	Merck & Co., Inc.	16.5	20.	Tootsie Roll Industries	13.5

Top 20 by Current Yield

Rank	Company	Current Yield %	Rank	Company	Current Yield %
1.	Health Care REIT, Inc.	14.6		Wisconsin Energy Corp.	7.4
2.	Commercial Net Lease Realty	11.5	12.	Philip Morris Companies	7.3
3.	Universal Health Realty Inc. Trust	11.3	13.	Madison Gas & Electric Co.	7.0
4.	Health Care Property Investors	10.9		Kansas City Power & Light Co.	7.0
5.	United Dominion Realty Trust	10.0		UGI Corporation	7.0
6.	Federal Realty Investment Trust	8.0	16.	CH Energy Group, Inc.	6.7
7.	GPU, Inc.	7.7		Consolidated Edison, Inc.	6.7
	Western Resources, Inc.	7.7	18.	Wallace Computer Services	6.6
9.	Cedar Fair, L.P.	7.5		Alliance Cap. Management Hldg.	6.6
10.	Washington R.E.I.T.	7.4		Northern States Power Co.	6.6

Highest Price/Earnings Ratios

Rank	Company	P/E Ratio	Rank	Company	P/E Ratio
1.	Du Pont (E.I.) De Nemours	612.5	11.	Millipore Corporation	51.3
2.	Flowers Industries, Inc.	258.0	12.	Schwab (Charles) Corp.	50.1
3.	Paychex Inc.	76.1	13.	Jones Pharma Incorporated	49.2
4.	Disney (Walt) Company (The)	73.6	14.	Home Depot (The), Inc.	48.8
5.	Medtronic, Inc.	66.2		EnergyNorth, Inc.	48.8
6.	Warner-Lambert Company	61.7	16.	General Electric Company	48.3
7.	CFW Communications Co.	61.0	17.	Cintas Corporation	46.8
8.	Pfizer Inc.	57.1	18.	Wal-Mart Stores, Inc.	46.4
9.	Coca-Cola Company (The)	54.5	19.	Automatic Data Processing	43.7
10.	Apogee Enterprises, Inc.	51.6	20.	Marsh & McLennan Cos. Inc.	41.8

Lowest Price/Earnings Ratios

Rank	Company	P/E Ratio	Rank	Company	P/E Ratio
1.	Fleetwood Enterprises, Inc	5.3	11.	Fidelity National Financial, Inc.	6.9
2.	American National Insurance	5.4		Bear Sterns Companies, Inc. (The)	6.9
3.	NACCO Industries Inc.	5.7	13.	National Service Industries	7.2
	Bowl America Inc.	5.7	14.	Health Care REIT, Inc.	7.3
5.	Sovereign Bancorp, Inc.	5.8	15.	Community Trust Bancorp	7.4
6.	Wallace Computer Services	6.1	16.	Midland Co.	7.6
7.	Universal Corporation	6.5	17.	Schulman (A.), Inc.	7.7
8.	Virco Manufacturing Corp.	6.6		GPU, Inc.	7.7
	Ohio Casualty Corp.	6.6	19.	Superior Uniform Group, Inc.	7.9
10.	Cooper Tire & Rubber Co	6.8	20.	Philip Morris Companies	8.2

Highest Long-Term Price Scores

Definitions of price scores may be found on page 25a.

Rank	Company	Price Score	Rank	Company	Price Score
1.	Schwab (Charles) Corp.	202.1	11.	Northern Trust Corp.	141.6
2.	Home Depot (The), Inc.	162.7		Citigroup Inc.	140.2
3.	Wal-Mart Stores, Inc.	152.6	13.	Medtronic, Inc.	138.5
4.	Eaton Vance Corporation	152.4	14.	Hewlett-Packard Company	134.7
5.	Jones Pharma Incorporated	151.5	15.	Walgreen Company	131.7
6.	Paychex Inc.	148.5	16.	American Int'l Group	131.2
7.	Warner-Lambert Company	145.7	17.	Interpublic Group of Cos.	130.8
8.	Target Corporation	145.4	18.	Legg Mason, Inc.	129.4
9.	Cohu, Inc.	143.0	19.	SJW Corp.	129.0
10.	General Electric Company	141.8	20.	Telephone & Data Systems	127.3

Highest Short-Term Price Scores

Definitions of price scores may be found on page 25a.

Rank	Company	Price Score	Rank	Company	Price Score
1.	Millipore Corporation	144.9	11.	Medtronic, Inc.	123.8
2.	Warner-Lambert Company	135.3	12.	Gallagher (Arthur J.) & Co.	123.4
3.	State Street Corporation	131.0		Northern Trust Corp.	123.4
4.	Omnicare, Inc.	129.5	14.	Hewlett-Packard Company	120.2
5.	Disney (Walt) Company (The)	127.5	15.	Marsh & McLennan Cos. Inc.	119.9
6.	Cohu, Inc.	127.2	16.	EnergyNorth, Inc.	119.7
7.	Paychex Inc.	127.0	17.	Jones Pharma Incorporated	118.3
8.	Alliance Cap. Management Hldg.	126.7	18.	General Electric Company	117.0
9.	CFW Communications Co.	126.4	19.	Dover Corporation	116.9
10.	Valley Resources, Inc.	124.9	20.	Citigroup Inc.	115.2

Top 20 by Revenues

Rank	Company	Rev. ($Mil.)	Rank	Company	Rev. ($Mil.)
1.	Exxon Mobil Corporation	185,527.0	11.	Albertson's, Inc.	37,478.0
2.	Wal-Mart Stores, Inc.	166,809.0	12.	Bank of America Corp.	37,323.0
3.	General Electric Company	111,630.0	13.	Fannie Mae	36,968.0
4.	Citigroup Inc.	82,005.0	14.	Chevron Corporation	36,586.0
5.	Philip Morris Companies	78,596.0	15.	Target Corporation	33,702.0
6.	SBC Communications, Inc.	49,489.0	16.	Merck & Co., Inc.	32,714.0
7.	Hewlett-Packard Co.	42,370.0	17.	Du Pont (E.I.) De Nemours	27,892.0
8.	Home Depot (The), Inc.	38,434.0	18.	Johnson & Johnson	27,717.0
9.	Procter & Gamble Company	38,125.0	19.	Lockheed Martin Corp.	25,530.0
10.	American Int'l Group	37,751.0	20.	ConAgra, Inc.	24,594.3

Top 20 by Net Income

Rank	Company	Net Inc. ($Mil.)	Rank	Company	Net Inc. ($Mil.)
1.	General Electric Co.	10,717.0		Johnson & Johnson	4,167.0
2.	Citigroup Inc.	9,994.0	12.	Fannie Mae	3,921.0
3.	Exxon Mobil Corporation	7,910.0	13.	Procter & Gamble Company	3,763.0
4.	Bank of America Corporation	7,882.0	14.	Wells Fargo & Company	3,747.0
5.	Philip Morris Companies	7,675.0	15.	Bank One Corporation	3,479.0
6.	SBC Communications, Inc.	6,573.0	16.	First Union Corporation	3,223.0
7.	Merck & Co., Inc.	5,890.5	17.	Pfizer Inc.	3,199.0
8.	Wal-Mart Stores, Inc.	5,575.0	18.	Hewlett-Packard Company	3,104.0
9.	American Int'l Group	5,055.0	19.	Lilly (Eli) & Company	2,546.7
10.	Bristol-Myers Squibb Co.	4,167.0	20.	Abbott Laboratories	2,445.8

Ranking the Dividend Achievers
by Total Returns

For information about total returns, please see page 20a.

1999 Rank	Company	1999 Tot. Return %	3-yr. Tot. Return %	3-yr. Rank	5-yr. Tot. Return %	5-yr. Rank
1.	Cohu Inc.	184.7	174.8	23	477.3	12
2.	Telephone & Data Systems	182.0	257.0	6	186.0	79
3.	SJW Corp.	110.6	185.8	17	366.8	28
4.	EnergyNorth, Inc.	100.0	190.7	16	340.9	33
5.	Valley Resources, Inc.	88.4	137.7	34	155.3	108
6.	Eaton Vance Corp.	84.1	231.7	10	598.3	5
7.	Jones Pharma Inc.	79.1	79.6	75	2160.1	1
8.	Wal-Mart Stores, Inc.	70.5	518.7	2	573.7	8
9.	Citigroup Inc.	70.1	185.2	18	737.6	3
10.	Home Depot, Inc. (The)	68.9	522.8	1	584.6	7
11.	Hewlett-Packard Co.	67.8	132.4	38	377.0	26
12.	Marsh & McLennan Cos. Inc.	67.5	198.4	13	319.6	36
13.	Avery Dennison Corp.	64.4	117.0	45	353.2	30
14.	General Electric Co.	53.6	227.1	11	567.3	9
15.	CFW Communications Co.	51.4	66.2	86	86.4	186
16.	Gallagher (Arthur J.) & Co.	51.3	131.0	40	138.1	119
17.	UNITIL Corp.	48.5	112.8	46	198.4	74
18.	Hilb, Rogal & Hamilton Co.	46.3	135.8	36	182.0	87
19.	Sysco Corp.	46.0	153.4	30	231.4	57
20.	Interpublic Group of Cos.	45.7	274.7	5	470.7	13
21.	Colgate-Palmolive Co.	41.6	194.2	15	349.1	31
22.	Minnesota Mining & Mfg. Co.	41.2	27.4	167	117.0	136
23.	ALLTEL Corp.	40.6	184.6	19	217.6	65
24.	American International Group	40.2	183.0	21	372.5	27
25.	Millipore Corp.	38.2	-3.1	251	69.0	213
26.	American States Water Co.	37.9	90.9	59	167.6	97
27.	Middlesex Water Co.	37.7	120.1	43	161.6	102
	Rohm & Haas Co.	37.7	59.3	97	139.5	117
	Worthington Industries, Inc.	37.7	1.5	237	-3.7	297
30.	Schwab (Charles) Corp.	36.3	443.5	3	1417.3	2
31.	Target Corp.	36.2	284.2	4	566.6	10
32.	Automatic Data Processing	35.3	157.6	28	285.2	42
33.	LESCO, Inc.	33.0	5.2	224	37.8	247
34.	Hannaford Bros. Co.	32.3	112.0	47	193.0	77
35.	Brady Corp.	28.8	47.3	116	132.3	126
36.	Nucor Corp.	28.1	10.6	213	2.9	290
37.	Gannett Co., Inc.	27.9	126.6	41	233.8	54
38.	Bear Stearns Cos. Inc. (The)	27.6	85.6	68	291.2	39
39.	Du Pont (E.I.) De Nemours	26.9	49.4	112	165.0	100
40.	Hormel Foods Corp.	26.1	60.3	95	82.7	193
41.	Dover Corp.	25.3	86.0	67	274.6	47
42.	Alliance Capital Mgmt. Holding L.P.	25.2	182.0	22	377.4	25
43.	Morgan (J.P.) & Co., Inc.	24.4	43.1	131	170.1	94
44.	Connecticut Water Service, Inc.	23.6	90.4	61	177.6	89
45.	McGraw-Hill Cos., Inc.	22.9	183.1	20	314.7	37

Total Returns (cont.)

1999 Rank	Company	1999 Tot. Return %	3-yr. Tot. Return %	3-yr. Rank	5-yr. Tot. Return %	5-yr. Rank
46.	Northern Trust Corp.	22.7	203.4	12	559.3	11
47.	Pacific Capital Bancorp	22.5	136.2	35	---	---
48.	Kimberly-Clark Corp.	22.2	45.4	121	189.9	78
49.	Haverty Furniture Cos., Inc.	21.9	134.6	37	138.4	118
50.	Procter & Gamble Co.	21.5	111.8	48	282.3	43
51.	St. Joseph Light & Power Co.	20.2	56.8	100	90.2	178
52.	Fuller (H.B.) Co.	18.0	24.4	178	77.5	200
53.	Ingersoll-Rand Co.	17.9	93.2	57	183.6	83
54.	Illinois Tool Works, Inc.	17.5	73.7	81	224.4	60
55.	Paychex, Inc.	17.3	168.5	26	677.7	4
56.	Lowe's Cos., Inc.	17.0	239.4	8	252.0	51
57.	Grainger (W.W.) Inc.	16.4	23.8	183	76.9	202
58.	Legg Mason, Inc.	15.8	157.8	27	383.2	24
59.	Weis Markets, Inc.	15.0	48.5	114	107.7	151
60.	North Pittsburgh Systems, Inc.	14.9	-32.4	304	23.3	269
61.	Valspar Corp.	13.8	53.7	105	167.8	96
62.	Exxon Mobil Corp.	12.6	76.7	78	207.8	71
63.	Johnson & Johnson	12.5	94.7	56	265.8	48
64.	Stanley Works	12.0	20.0	187	92.3	172
65.	First Security Corp.	11.8	82.9	71	335.7	34
66.	Aon Corp.	10.7	53.9	104	217.6	65
67.	PPG Industries, Inc.	10.4	19.8	190	90.7	174
68.	Golden West Financial Corp.	10.3	62.0	93	194.3	76
69.	Warner-Lambert Co.	10.2	239.1	9	595.7	6
70.	Anheuser-Busch Cos., Inc.	9.8	88.1	64	222.6	61
71.	Marshall & Ilsley Corp.	9.2	90.5	60	265.6	49
72.	T. Rowe Price Associates, Inc.	9.0	75.2	79	424.2	20
73.	Bard (C.R.) Inc.	8.7	100.5	52	116.9	137
74.	Gorman-Rupp Co.	8.4	42.0	135	16.3	280
75.	AFLAC Inc.	8.2	126.0	42	363.4	29
76.	Chevron Corp.	7.4	45.4	121	127.9	128
77.	National Fuel Gas Co.	7.1	27.0	168	127.8	129
78.	Washington Gas Light Co.	6.8	40.0	138	110.6	146
79.	CenturyTel, Inc.	5.7	251.9	7	276.6	46
80.	United Dominion Realty Trust	5.6	-18.3	283	0.1	291
81.	McDonald's Corp.	5.4	80.7	73	183.9	81
82.	Lancaster Colony Corp.	5.1	13.6	199	84.2	189
83.	State Street Corp.	5.0	131.7	39	440.9	16
84.	SouthTrust Corp.	4.7	73.4	82	258.1	50
85.	Bowl America Inc.	4.3	24.2	181	13.6	282
86.	Fifth Third Bancorp	4.1	173.0	24	460.3	15
87.	RLI Corp.	3.9	33.2	151	183.7	82
88.	Associated Banc-Corp.	3.6	32.1	157	109.3	150
89.	Lee Enterprises, Inc.	3.5	46.0	120	106.0	152
90.	Sigma-Aldrich Corp.	3.3	-1.2	245	90.0	179
	Wells Fargo & Co.	3.3	97.2	55	288.6	40
92.	Weyco Group, Inc.	2.8	100.3	53	132.5	125
93.	Florida Public Utilities Co.	2.2	88.0	65	172.1	93
94.	First Commonwealth Financial	1.9	44.1	128	115.5	140
95.	Franklin Resources, Inc.	0.8	42.9	134	178.9	88

Total Returns (cont.)

1999 Rank	Company	1999 Tot. Return %	3-yr. Tot. Return %	3-yr. Rank	5-yr. Tot. Return %	5-yr. Rank
96.	Bestfoods	0.6	43.4	130	118.5	133
	California Water Service Co.	0.6	64.0	90	142.8	115
98.	Walgreen Co.	0.4	196.5	14	462.6	14
99.	Park National Corp.	0.3	103.8	50	168.1	95
100.	Lincoln National Corp.	0.1	64.8	89	166.7	98
	St. Paul Cos., Inc.	0.1	25.2	174	74.8	207
102.	Reynolds & Reynolds Co.	-0.1	-8.8	266	94.6	166
103.	American General Corp.	-0.5	99.7	54	210.1	69
	Dean Foods Co.	-0.5	30.5	160	52.8	228
	Florida Progress Corp.	-0.5	54.7	102	94.1	167
106.	Leggett & Platt, Inc.	-1.0	29.3	163	164.6	101
107.	Otter Tail Power Co.	-1.2	36.1	145	49.2	234
108.	Medtronic, Inc.	-1.5	117.3	44	437.3	17
109.	CLECO Corp.	-1.7	36.2	144	82.4	195
110.	Disney (Walt) Co. (The)	-1.8	28.3	164	97.0	162
	Pentair, Inc.	-1.8	25.2	174	95.8	164
112.	Johnson Controls, Inc.	-2.1	44.6	127	157.5	105
113.	Alberto-Culver Co.	-2.3	10.4	215	98.3	161
114.	F&M National Corp.	-2.4	44.7	126	109.7	149
	Superior Industries Int'l, Inc.	-2.4	19.9	189	5.8	288
116.	Trustmark Corp.	-2.5	79.3	76	173.6	92
117.	Bristol-Myers Squibb Co.	-2.9	146.9	32	401.6	21
118.	Community Trust Bancorp, Inc	-3.0	8.4	220	7.5	287
	Emerson Electric Co.	-3.0	26.1	172	105.5	153
120.	Belo (A.H.) Corp.	-3.1	13.1	201	42.7	242
121.	Liqui-Box Corp.	-3.5	58.9	99	59.8	220
122.	Energen Corp.	-3.9	32.4	156	100.9	158
123.	La-Z-Boy Incorporated	-4.0	80.7	73	75.8	205
124.	One Valley Bancorp, Inc.	-4.3	11.2	209	95.1	165
125.	Kenan Transport Co.	-4.5	65.6	87	91.7	173
	Nordson Corp.	-4.5	-20.5	289	-13.5	305
127.	Household International, Inc.	-4.6	26.5	171	229.0	58
128.	TRW Inc.	-4.9	12.9	202	78.3	199
129.	Raven Industries, Inc.	-5.4	-29.1	296	-15.4	307
130.	Bemis Co., Inc.	-5.6	1.2	239	62.5	216
	Madison Gas & Electric Co.	-5.6	19.3	192	25.0	264
132.	Wrigley (Wm.) Jr. Co.	-5.9	54.6	103	83.0	192
133.	First Virginia Banks Inc.	-6.0	45.3	123	133.5	123
134.	Old National Bancorp	-6.3	52.5	107	90.4	177
135.	HON Industries Inc.	-6.8	38.4	141	76.9	202
136.	BancorpSouth, Inc.	-7.1	26.7	170	122.6	131
	Kellogg Co.	-7.1	1.2	239	19.4	276
138.	Jefferson-Pilot Corp.	-7.2	92.0	58	232.6	55
139.	SBC Communications Inc.	-7.4	101.8	51	177.5	90
140.	Merck & Co., Inc.	-7.5	77.1	77	287.8	41
141.	Hanna (M.A.) Co.	-7.7	-45.5	314	-21.7	310
	Tuscarora, Inc.	-7.7	-30.6	300	8.0	286
143.	Clarcor Inc.	-7.8	31.3	159	45.3	239
	Mine Safety Appliances Co.	-7.8	27.5	166	57.8	225
145.	UGI Corp.	-7.9	9.8	216	37.2	249

Total Returns (cont.)

1999 Rank	Company	1999 Tot. Return %	3-yr. Tot. Return %	3-yr. Rank	5-yr. Tot. Return %	5-yr. Rank
146.	Crawford & Co.	-8.0	-1.8	247	50.0	231
	GATX Corp.	-8.0	52.1	109	79.8	198
148.	Trustco Bank	-8.1	60.0	96	154.2	109
149.	SunTrust Banks, Inc.	-8.2	46.9	117	216.9	67
150.	Baldor Electric Co.	-8.5	3.7	230	46.9	238
151.	WesBanco, Inc.	-9.1	31.5	158	89.6	180
152.	Fulton Financial Corp.	-9.3	37.4	142	96.6	163
153.	Compass Bancshares Inc.	-9.5	37.0	143	166.7	98
154.	Houghton Mifflin Co.	-9.6	55.4	101	101.9	156
155.	Harcourt General, Inc.	-9.9	7.1	221	44.7	240
	Kimball International, Inc.	-9.9	-12.1	272	49.6	233
	Stepan Co.	-9.9	22.7	184	75.5	206
158.	McCormick & Co., Inc.	-10.1	34.9	150	82.7	193
159.	Masco Corp.	-10.3	48.6	113	148.7	112
160.	Huntington Bancshares, Inc.	-10.4	30.0	161	146.7	113
161.	Raymond James Finl. Inc.	-10.6	44.1	128	221.5	63
162.	SLM Holding Corp.	-10.7	65.6	87	399.8	22
163.	Chubb Corp.	-11.1	10.9	211	61.3	219
164.	Peoples Energy Corp.	-11.4	15.8	196	69.8	212
165.	International Flavors & Fragrances	-11.7	-7.4	260	-4.9	298
166.	FirstMerit Corp.	-11.8	40.1	137	116.1	139
167.	Black Hills Corp.	-11.9	35.3	148	98.9	160
168.	Coca-Cola Co. (The)	-12.1	13.8	197	138.1	119
169.	Pall Corp.	-12.2	-8.4	265	29.9	256
170.	Clorox Co.	-12.4	110.7	49	279.5	45
171.	PepsiCo, Inc.	-12.5	36.0	146	126.5	130
172.	Gillette Co. (The)	-12.7	9.5	217	132.7	124
	Piedmont Natural Gas Co., Inc.	-12.7	46.7	118	101.3	157
174.	Liberty Corp.	-12.8	13.4	200	83.5	191
	Tootsie Roll Industries, Inc.	-12.8	84.9	69	156.4	106
176.	Midland Co.	-13.0	67.6	84	53.3	227
	Northwestern Corp.	-13.0	46.1	119	111.9	144
178.	Cincinnati Financial Corp.	-13.3	52.3	108	122.0	132
	S&T Bancorp, Inc.	-13.3	-20.0	288	23.7	268
180.	ReliaStar Financial Corp.	-13.5	43.0	132	198.9	73
	Washington R.E.I.T.	-13.5	4.4	228	28.4	259
182.	Federal Realty Invest. Trust	-13.7	-13.9	275	31.6	255
183.	Bank of America Corp.	-14.0	11.0	210	155.9	107
	HSB Group, Inc.	-14.0	24.1	182	59.4	221
185.	Fannie Mae	-14.2	74.5	80	279.7	44
	Frisch's Restaurants, Inc.	-14.2	-40.9	312	19.1	277
187.	Health Care Property Investors	-14.3	-13.0	273	15.7	281
188.	Air Products & Chemicals	-14.4	2.3	232	64.5	214
189.	F.N.B. Corp.	-14.7	20.9	185	104.3	154
	Mercantile Bankshares Corp.	-14.7	62.1	92	183.2	85
191.	Commerce Bancshares, Inc.	-15.0	32.9	153	161.4	103
192.	Banta Corp.	-15.5	4.7	225	22.8	270
193.	Synovus Financial Corp.	-15.8	45.3	123	302.7	38
194.	Tennant Co.	-16.5	26.8	169	52.5	229
195.	First Financial Bancorp	-16.7	89.3	62	114.6	141

Total Returns (cont.)

1999 Rank	Company	1999 Tot. Return %	3-yr. Tot. Return %	3-yr. Rank	5-yr. Tot. Return %	5-yr. Rank
196.	Commercial Net Lease Realty	-16.9	-18.8	285	25.4	263
197.	1st Source Corp.	-17.0	59.2	98	150.6	110
	Quaker Chemical Corp.	-17.0	-0.7	244	-5.0	299
199.	Universal Health Realty Inc. Trust	-17.6	-6.5	259	41.0	244
200.	Ohio Casualty Corp.	-17.7	3.2	231	41.7	243
201.	May Department Stores Co.	-17.9	10.9	211	84.8	188
202.	DQE, Inc.	-18.2	35.2	149	118.3	134
	Kelly Services Inc.	-18.2	1.7	235	5.5	289
204.	MBIA Inc.	-18.4	8.5	219	103.2	155
	Old Kent Financial Corp.	-18.4	82.8	72	239.4	53
206.	Protective Life Corp.	-18.9	66.3	85	184.3	80
207.	National Service Industries	-19.3	-13.3	274	35.8	253
	Wilmington Trust Corp.	-19.3	33.2	151	150.1	111
209.	M & T Bank Corp.	-19.4	47.6	115	220.2	64
210.	Questar Corp.	-19.5	-9.5	267	29.8	257
211.	American National Insurance	-19.7	-4.5	255	61.8	218
	Susquehanna Bancshares, Inc.	-19.7	12.9	202	90.5	176
213.	NICOR Inc.	-19.8	2.0	233	75.9	204
214.	Sara Lee Corp.	-20.1	25.3	173	93.8	170
	Wachovia Corp.	-20.1	29.6	162	142.5	116
216.	Kansas City Power & Light	-20.2	-7.5	261	27.5	261
	KeySpan Energy Corp.	-20.2	---	---	---	---
218.	Hasbro, Inc.	-20.6	12.9	202	53.6	226
219.	Cedar Fair, L.P.	-20.7	24.4	178	77.5	200
	Pacific Century Financial	-20.7	-2.7	249	71.1	209
221.	Sonoco Products Co.	-20.8	4.5	227	35.9	252
222.	Cooper Tire & Rubber Co.	-21.2	-15.6	278	-27.6	311
223.	Virco Manufacturing Corp.	-21.3	67.8	83	211.9	68
224.	Pfizer Inc.	-21.5	141.0	33	437.1	18
225.	CCB Financial Corp.	-22.0	35.7	147	183.6	83
	CH Energy Group, Inc.	-22.0	24.6	177	70.3	210
227.	Hershey Foods Corp.	-22.2	13.7	198	114.5	142
228.	WestAmerica Bancorporation	-22.4	52.8	106	208.2	70
229.	Schering-Plough Corp.	-22.6	171.1	25	396.8	23
230.	Brown-Forman Corp.	-23.1	32.7	154	110.5	147
231.	Genuine Parts Corp.	-23.2	-8.1	263	20.8	274
	Semco Energy Inc.	-23.2	-18.0	280	-1.4	294
233.	WPS Resources Corp.	-23.5	7.0	223	28.6	258
234.	First Tennessee National	-23.6	62.4	91	221.9	62
235.	Block Drug Co., Inc.	-23.9	-19.3	286	9.8	285
236.	Corus Bankshares, Inc.	-24.2	-21.9	292	58.9	223
	Lilly (Eli) & Co.	-24.2	89.2	63	342.7	32
238.	Cintas Corp.	-24.3	83.1	70	206.0	72
	Indiana Energy, Inc.	-24.3	10.5	214	44.6	241
240.	Archer Daniels Midland Co.	-24.6	-34.0	307	-21.0	309
241.	Abbott Laboratories	-24.7	50.0	111	143.2	114
242.	Family Dollar Stores, Inc.	-25.2	149.1	31	329.1	35
243.	Northern States Power Co.	-25.3	0.8	241	17.9	278
244.	Pitney Bowes, Inc.	-25.6	86.6	66	240.6	52
245.	Charter One Financial, Inc.	-25.8	12.2	207	174.2	91

Total Returns (cont.)

1999 Rank	Company	1999 Tot. Return %	3-yr. Tot. Return %	3-yr. Rank	5-yr. Tot. Return %	5-yr. Rank
	ConAgra, Inc.	-25.8	-2.2	248	62.7	215
	Hubbell Inc.	-25.8	-31.4	301	24.3	266
248.	Schulman (A.), Inc.	-25.9	-28.4	295	-34.3	314
249.	SUPERVALU Inc.	-26.8	51.9	110	88.9	182
250.	Sherwin-Williams Co.	-27.1	-21.2	290	36.6	250
251.	Heinz (H.J.) Co.	-27.7	20.5	186	87.8	184
252.	Campbell Soup Co.	-28.2	1.6	236	94.1	167
	KeyCorp	-28.2	-3.6	253	111.0	145
254.	GPU, Inc.	-28.7	4.1	229	50.3	230
	Modine Manufacturing Co.	-28.7	1.5	237	-1.3	293
256.	American Home Products	-29.1	42.0	135	182.7	86
	Carlisle Companies Inc.	-29.1	24.3	180	116.5	138
258.	Comerica, Inc.	-29.9	43.0	132	231.9	56
259.	TECO Energy Inc.	-30.1	-10.4	270	17.1	279
260.	Teleflex Inc.	-30.4	24.7	176	88.3	183
261.	BB&T Corp.	-30.6	61.6	94	227.5	59
	Washington Mutual Inc.	-30.6	-4.1	254	160.9	104
263.	Wesco Financial Corp.	-30.7	32.5	155	118.2	135
264.	Alfa Corp.	-30.8	39.5	139	70.1	211
265.	Firstar Corp.	-30.9	156.1	29	435.4	19
266.	United Fire & Casualty Co.	-31.0	-31.9	302	36.0	251
267.	Consolidated Edison, Inc.	-31.3	38.7	140	80.1	197
268.	Citizens Banking Corp.	-31.5	-23.0	293	-8.8	301
269.	Flowers Industries, Inc.	-31.6	19.5	191	130.1	127
270.	Carolina Power & Light Co.	-31.7	-3.0	250	48.2	236
271.	Universal Corp.	-32.1	-21.2	290	38.4	246
272.	Kaydon Corp.	-32.2	17.8	193	138.0	121
273.	Diebold, Inc.	-32.5	-40.8	311	40.6	245
274.	Wausau-Mosinee Paper Corp.	-32.8	-33.6	306	-31.0	312
275.	SIGCORP, Inc.	-33.1	12.2	207	62.3	217
276.	Analysts International, Inc.	-33.2	-29.9	297	100.1	159
277.	Atmos Energy Corp.	-33.5	-3.3	252	47.8	237
278.	RPM Inc.	-34.1	-18.0	280	-1.2	292
279.	VF Corp.	-34.5	-5.7	257	37.7	248
	Wisconsin Energy Corp.	-34.5	-14.6	276	-1.6	295
281.	Health Care REIT, Inc.	-34.8	-18.2	282	21.7	272
282.	AmSouth Bancorporation	-34.9	45.0	125	196.9	75
	Wallace Computer Services	-34.9	-48.1	315	27.6	260
284.	LG&E Energy Corp.	-35.0	-17.1	279	22.3	271
	Superior Uniform Group Inc.	-35.0	-25.3	294	-13.9	306
286.	American Water Works Co.	-35.1	12.7	205	86.2	187
	Bandag, Inc.	-35.1	-42.7	313	-53.7	316
288.	Bank One Corp.	-35.2	-10.1	268	81.2	196
289.	Regions Financial Corp.	-35.9	4.7	225	86.6	185
290.	Becton, Dickinson & Co.	-36.2	27.9	165	137.1	122
291.	Berkley (W.R.) Corp.	-37.5	-35.5	308	-10.7	303
	Old Republic International	-37.5	-18.7	284	59.0	222
293.	NiSource, Inc.	-38.7	1.8	234	48.3	235
294.	Fleetwood Enterprises, Inc.	-38.8	-19.4	287	24.0	267
	NACCO Industries Inc.	-38.8	7.1	221	21.6	273

Total Returns (cont.)

1999 Rank	Company	1999 Tot. Return %	3-yr. Tot. Return %	3-yr. Rank	5-yr. Tot. Return %	5-yr. Rank
296.	Myers Industries Inc.	-38.9	16.7	194	58.1	224
297.	Federal Signal Corp.	-39.3	-32.0	303	-9.7	302
298.	SAFECO Corp.	-39.7	-30.5	298	12.7	283
299.	ABM Industries, Inc.	-39.8	16.5	195	94.0	169
300.	American Greetings Corp.	-40.7	-11.0	271	-2.3	296
301.	Keystone Financial, Inc.	-40.8	-6.4	258	26.6	262
302.	Donnelley (R.R.) & Sons Co.	-41.7	-15.2	277	-6.1	300
303.	Pep Boys	-42.0	-69.8	318	-69.6	317
304.	Harleysville Group, Inc.	-43.0	0.7	242	33.9	254
	ServiceMaster Co.	-43.0	12.6	206	93.3	171
306.	Hillenbrand Industries, Inc.	-43.1	-8.1	263	24.7	265
307.	First Union Corp.	-43.3	-1.6	246	89.4	181
308.	UNUMProvident Corp.	-44.3	-7.7	262	83.9	190
309.	Western Resources, Inc.	-44.8	-33.1	305	-17.9	308
310.	Lockheed Martin Corp.	-46.9	-49.2	316	---	---
311.	Sovereign Bancorp, Inc.	-47.2	0.1	243	90.7	174
312.	Mercury General Corp.	-47.7	-10.2	269	71.2	208
313.	Albertson's, Inc.	-48.6	-5.2	256	20.2	275
314.	Fidelity National Financial, Inc.	-52.1	20.0	187	109.8	148
315.	Apogee Enterprises, Inc.	-53.9	-73.2	319	-36.2	315
316.	Philip Morris Cos., Inc.	-54.7	-30.5	298	49.9	232
317.	City Holding Co.	-55.2	-40.4	309	-33.4	313
318.	Progressive Corp.	-56.7	9.3	218	112.4	143
319.	Donegal Group Inc.	-57.7	-40.4	309	-11.6	304
320.	Omnicare Inc.	-65.2	-62.2	317	11.6	284

Note: Five-year total returns for Lockheed Martin Corp. and Pacific Capital Bancorp. and three- and five-year total returns for KeySpan Energy Corp. do not appear as sufficient pricing data were not available.

About Total Return

Total return represents one of the best measures of how well an investor in any given stock has fared because it reflects both dividend payments and price appreciation. Mergent has calculated total return for each Dividend Achiever company on the basis that cash dividends on each stock were reinvested in that company's shares at the end of the month in which the dividends were paid. Thus the preceding table demonstrates the effect of compounding as well as each stock's performance and the level of dividends paid. Figures have been adjusted for splits, stock dividends and spin-offs. In the case of a spin-off, shares in the spun-off company were assumed to be converted to cash and reinvested in the original company's stock.

How to read the rankings: On the preceding pages the Dividend Achiever companies are listed by one-year total return for calendar 1999. For example, an investor who bought shares at the end of December, 1998 in Cohu Inc., and sold them at the end of December, 1999, would have realized a 184.7% gain on the original investment. Following each company's 1999 total return is its three-year total return and ranking and five-year total return and ranking. The three-year total return is based on an investment made at the end of December, 1996, and the five-year total return on an investment made at the end of December, 1994. The three- and five-year total-return percentages represent cumulative totals. Thus an investment made in Cohu Inc. at the end of December, 1996, would have increased 174.8% if the stock were sold at the end of December, 1999. If an investor had bought shares in Cohu at the end of December, 1994, and sold them at the end of December, 1999, his investment would have grown by 477.3%.

ADVERTISING
* Interpublic Group of Companies, Inc.

AMUSEMENTS
Bowl America Inc.
Hasbro, Inc.

APPAREL
* Superior Uniform Group, Inc.
* VF Corp.

AUTOMOBILE PARTS
Clarcor Inc.
* Genuine Parts Corp.
* Myers Industries, Inc.
* Superior Industries International, Inc.

BANKS - MID-ATLANTIC
City Holding Co.
Community Trust Bancorp, Inc.
F & M National Corp.
* First Commonwealth Financial Corp.
* First Virginia Banks, Inc.
* F.N.B. Corp.
* Fulton Financial Corp.
* Keystone Financial Corp.
* Marshall & Ilsley Corp.
* Mercantile Bankshares Corp.
* One Valley Bancorp, Inc.
* Sovereign Bancorp, Inc.
* Susquehanna Bancshares, Inc.
WesBanco, Inc.

BANKS - MIDWEST
* Associated Banc-Corp.
* Bank One Corp.
* Charter One Financial, Inc.
* Citizens Banking Corp.
* Comerica, Inc.
* Commerce Bancshares, Inc.
Corus Bankshares, Inc.
* Fifth Third Bancorp
* First Financial Bancorp
1st Source Corp.
* FirstMerit Corp.
* Firstar Corp.
* KeyCorp
Northern Trust Corp.
* Old Kent Financial Corp.
* Old National Bancorp
* Park National Corp.
* Wells Fargo & Co.

BANKS - NORTHEAST
* Huntington Bancshares, Inc.
* M&T Bank Corp.
* Morgan (J.P.) & Co., Inc.
S&T Bancorp, Inc.
* State Street Corp.
* Trustco Bank
* Wilmington Trust Corporation

BANKS - SOUTH
* AmSouth Bancorporation
* Bancorp South Inc.
* Bank of America Corp.
* BB&T Corp.

* CCB Financial Corp.
* Compass Bancshares, Inc.
* First Tennessee National Corp.
* First Union Corp.
* Regions Financial Corp.
* Southtrust Corp.
* SunTrust Banks, Inc.
* Synovus Financial Corp.
* Trustmark Corp.
* Wachovia Corp.

BANKS - WEST
* First Security Corp.
Pacific Capital Bancorp
* Pacific Century Financial Corp.
* WestAmerica Bancorporation

BREWING
* Anheuser-Busch Companies, Inc.

BUILDING MATERIALS & EQUIPMENT
Apogee Enterprises, Inc.

CANDY & GUM
* Hershey Foods Corporation
* Tootsie Roll Industries, Inc.
* Wrigley (Wm.) Jr. Co.

CHEMICALS
* Air Products & Chemicals, Inc.
Brady Corp.
* Du Pont (E.I.) de Nemours & Company
* Fuller (H.B.)
* PPG Industries, Inc.
Quaker Chemical Corp.
Rohm & Haas Co.
Sigma-Aldrich Corporation
Stepan Co.

COMPUTERS - SERVICES
Analysts International, Inc.
Automatic Data Processing, Inc.

CONGLOMERATES
* Carlisle Companies, Inc.
* Hillenbrand Industries, Inc.
* Minnesota Mining & Manufacturing Co.
* TRW Inc.

COSMETICS & TOILETRIES
Alberto-Culver Co.
* Gillette Co.
* International Flavors & Fragrances, Inc.

DEFENSE SYSTEMS & EQUIPMENT
* Lockheed Martin Corp.

DISTILLING
* Brown-Forman Corp.

DRUGS
* American Home Products Corp.
* Block Drug Co. Inc.
* Bristol-Myers Squibb Co.
Jones Pharma Incorporated
* Lilly (Eli) & Co.
* Merck & Co., Inc.
* Pfizer Inc.

* Schering-Plough Corp.
* Warner-Lambert Co.

ELECTRIC POWER - CENTRAL & SOUTHEASTERN REGIONS
* Carolina Power & Light Co.
* CLECO Corp.
* Florida Progress Corp.
* Kansas City Power & Light Co.
* LG&E Energy Corp.
* Madison Gas & Electric Co.
* NiSource, Inc.
* St. Joseph Light & Power Co.
* SIGCORP, Inc.
* TECO Energy, Inc.
* Wisconsin Energy Corp.
* WPS Resources Corporation
* Western Resources, Inc.

ELECTRIC POWER - NORTHEASTERN REGION
* CH Energy Group, Inc.
* Consolidated Edison, Inc.
* DQE, inc.
* GPU, Inc.
* UNITIL Corp.

ELECTRIC POWER - WESTERN REGION
* Black Hills Corp.
* Northern States Power Co. (Minn.)
* Northwestern Corp.
* Otter Tail Power Co.

ELECTRICAL EQUIPMENT
* Baldor Electric Co.
  Cohu, Inc.
* Emerson Electric Co.
* General Electric Co.
  Hewlett-Packard Co.
* Hubbell Inc.
* Raven Industries, Inc.

ENGINEERING & CONSTRUCTION
* Masco Corp.

FINANCE
* Fannie Mae
* Household International, Inc.
  SLM Holding Corp.

FINANCIAL SERVICES
  Alliance Capital Management Holding, L.P.
* Eaton Vance Corp.
  T. Rowe Price Associates, Inc.
* Citigroup Inc.

FOOD - GRAIN & AGRICULTURE
  Archer Daniels Midland Co.
* ConAgra, Inc.

FOOD PROCESSING
* BestFoods Inc.
* Campbell Soup Company
* Dean Foods Co.
* Flowers Industries, Inc.
* Heinz (H.J.) Co.
* Hormel Foods Corp.

* Kellogg Co.
* Lancaster Colony Corp.
* McCormick & Co., Inc.
* Sara Lee Corp.

FOOD WHOLESALERS
* SUPERVALU Inc.
* Sysco Corporation

FURNITURE & FIXTURES
  Kimball International
* La-Z-Boy Incorporated
  Leggett & Platt, Inc.
  Virco Mfg. Co.

GROCERY CHAINS
* Albertson's Inc.
* Hannaford Bros. Co.
* Weis Markets, Inc.

HARDWARE & TOOLS
* Illinois Tool Works Inc.
* The Stanley Works

HEALTHCARE MANAGEMENT & SERVICES
* Omnicare, Inc.

INSURANCE - BROKERAGE
  Gallagher (Arthur J.) & Co.
  Hilb, Rogal & Hamilton Co.
* Marsh & McLennan Companies, Inc.

INSURANCE - COMBINED
  American International Group, Inc.
* American General Corp.
* Aon Corp.
  Berkley (W.R.) Corp.
* Cincinnati Financial Corp.
  Crawford & Co.
* Jefferson-Pilot Corp.
* Lincoln National Corp.
* Midland Co.
* Old Republic International Corp.
  The Progressive Corp.
* SAFECO Corp.
* UNUMProvident Corp.

INSURANCE - LIFE
* AFLAC Inc.
  American National Insurance Co.
  Liberty Corporation (The)
  Protective Life Corp.
* ReliaStar Financial Corp.

INSURANCE - PROPERTY & CASUALTY
* Alfa Corp.
* The Chubb Co.
* Donegal Group Inc.
  Harleysville Group, Inc.
* HSB Group, Inc.
  Mercury General Corporation
* Ohio Casualty Corp.
* RLI Corp.
* St. Paul Cos., Inc.
* United Fire & Casualty Co.

INSURANCE - SPECIALTY
* Fidelity National Financial, Inc.
  MBIA Inc.

MACHINERY & EQUIPMENT
Dover Corp.
* Federal Signal Corp.
* Ingersoll-Rand Co.
  Kaydon Corp.
* Modine Manufacturing Co.
  NACCO Industries Inc.
* Nordson Corporation
* Tennant Co.

MAINTENANCE & SECURITY SERVICES
ABM Industries, Inc.

MEASURING & CONTROL INSTRUMENTS
* Gorman-Rupp Co.
* Johnson Controls, Inc.
* Millipore Corp.
* Teleflex, Inc.

MEDICAL & DENTAL EQUIPMENT & SUPPLIES
* Abbott Laboratories
* Bard (C.R.), Inc.
* Becton, Dickinson & Co.
* Johnson & Johnson
* Medtronic, Inc.
* Mine Safety Appliances Co.

METAL PRODUCTS
* Worthington Industries, Inc.

MOBILE HOMES
Fleetwood Enterprises

NATURAL GAS
* National Fuel Gas Co.
* Peoples Energy Corp.
* Valley Resources, Inc.

NATURAL GAS - DISTRIBUTORS
* Atmos Energy Corp.
* Energen Corp.
* EnergyNorth, Inc.
* Florida Public Utilities Co,
* Indiana Energy, Inc.
* KeySpan Energy Corp.
* NICOR Inc.
* Piedmont Natural Gas Co., Inc.
* Questar Corp.
* Semco Energy Inc.
* UGI Corp.
* The Washington Gas Light Co.

NEWSPAPERS
Belo (A.H.) Corp.
* Gannett Co., Inc.
  Lee Enterprises, Inc.

OFFICE EQUIPMENT & SUPPLIES
* Avery Dennison Corp.
* Diebold, Inc.
  HON Industries Inc.
* Pitney Bowes Inc.
* Reynolds & Reynolds Company
* Wallace Computer Services, Inc.

OIL
* Chevron Corp.
* Exxon Mobil Corp.

PAINTS & RELATED PRODUCTS
* RPM Inc.
* Sherwin-Williams Co.
  The Valspar Corp.

PAPER
* Bemis Co., Inc.
* Kimberly-Clark Corp.
* Pentair, Inc.
* Sonoco Products Co.
* Wausau-Mossinee Paper Corp.

PLASTICS & PLASTIC PRODUCTS
* Hanna (M.A.) Co.
* Liqui-Box Corp.
  Schulman (A.), Inc.
  Tuscarora Incorporated

POLLUTION CONTROL/ENVIRONMENT
* LESCO Inc.
* Pall Corp.

PRINTING & ENGRAVING
* Banta Corp.
* Donnelley (R. R.) & Sons Co.

PUBLISHING
* American Greetings Corp.
* Houghton Mifflin Co.
* McGraw-Hill Companies, Inc.

RAILROAD EQUIPMENT
GATX Corp.

REAL ESTATE INVESTMENT TRUSTS
Commercial Net Lease Realty
* Federal Realty Investment Trust
  Health Care Property Investors, Inc.
  Health Care REIT, Inc.
* Washington Real Estate Investment Trust
* United Dominion Realty Trust, Inc.
* Universal Health Realty Inc. Trust

RECREATION
* Cedar Fair, L.P.
* Disney (Walt) Co.

RESTAURANTS
Frisch's Restaurants, Inc.
* McDonald's Corp.

RETAIL DEPARTMENT STORES
* May Department Stores Co.
* Target Corp.

RETAIL - DISCOUNT & VARIETY STORES
Family Dollar Stores, Inc.
* Wal-Mart Stores, Inc.

RETAIL - DRUG STORES
* Walgreen Co.

RETAIL - SPECIALTY STORES
* Harcourt General, Inc.
  Haverty Furniture Companies, Inc.
* Home Depot, Inc.

* Lowe's Companies, Inc.
* Pep Boys-Manny, Moe & Jack

SAVINGS & LOAN
Golden West Financial Corp.
Wesco Financial Corp.
* Washington Mutual, Inc.

SECURITIES BROKERAGE
Bear Stearns Cos., Inc.
* Franklin Resources, Inc.
Legg Mason, Inc.
Raymond James Financial, Inc.
* Schwab (Charles) Corporation

SERVICES
Cintas Corporation
Kelly Services, Inc.
* National Service Industries, Inc.
* Paychex, Inc.
* ServiceMaster Co.

SHOE MANUFACTURING
Weyco Group, Inc.

SOAPS & CLEANERS
* Clorox Co.
* Colgate-Palmolive Co.
* Procter & Gamble Co.

SOFT DRINKS
* The Coca-Cola Co.
* Pepsico, Inc.

STEEL
* Nucor Corp.

TELECOMMUNICATIONS
* ALLTEL Corp.
* CenturyTel, Inc.
* CFW Communications Co.
North Pittsburgh Systems, Inc.
* SBC Communications Inc.
* Telephone & Data Systems, Inc.

TIRES & RUBBER GOODS
* Bandag, Inc.
Cooper Tire & Rubber Co.

TOBACCO
* Philip Morris Companies, Inc.
* Universal Corp.

TRUCKING
Kenan Transport Co.

WATER COMPANIES
* American States Water Co.
* American Water Works Company, Inc.
* California Water Service Co.
* Connecticut Water Service, Inc.
* Middlesex Water Company
SJW Corp.

WHOLESALERS - DISTRIBUTORS - JOBBERS
Grainger (W.W.), Inc.

*Designates companies offering dividend reinvestment plans

HOW TO USE THIS BOOK

The Handbook of Dividend Achievers is a compact, easy-to-use reference for people who recognize that investing wisely in stocks with increasing annual dividend payments can be a profitable endeavor. This valuable investment tool provides basic financial and business information on 320 companies that have increased their dividends consistently over the past 10 years. The presentation of background information plus current and historical data provides the answers to three basic questions:

1. What does the company do?
   (See H)
2. How has it done in the past?
   (See B, D, E, G, J, K)
3. How is it doing now?
   (See D, E, F, G, I)

The following common terms are used throughout *The Handbook of Dividend Achievers*:

A. CAPSULE STOCK INFORMATION – Shown are the stock symbol, plus the approximate yield afforded by the indicated dividend based on a recent price, and the price/earnings ratio, based on the most recent four quarters' earnings.

B. LONG-TERM PRICE CHART – The chart illustrates the pattern of monthly stock price movements, fully adjusted for stock dividends and splits. Monthly stock trading volume is also included.

C. PRICE SCORES – Below each company's price/volume chart are its *Mergent Price Scores*. These are two basic measures of the stock's performance. Each stock is measured against the New York Stock Exchange Composite Index. A score of 100 indicates that the stock did as well as the New York Stock Exchange Composite Index during the

time period. A score of less than 100 means that the stock did not do as well; a score of more than 100 means that the stock outperformed the NYSE Composite Index.

Thus, **Mergent Price Scores** allow the user to make easy, across-the-board comparisons of various stocks' historical price performance. All stocks, regardless of exchange, are measured against the NYSE Composite Index so that their scores may be compared with any other stock.

The *7 YEAR PRICE SCORE* mirrors the common stock's price growth over the previous 7 years. The higher the price score, the better the relative performance. It is based on the ratio of the latest 12-month average price to the current 7-year average. This ratio is indexed against the same ratio for the market as a whole (the New York Stock Exchange Composite Index), which is taken as 100.

The *12 MONTH PRICE SCORE* is a similar measurement but for a shorter period of time. It indicates the recent vigor or sluggishness of a stock's price movement. It is based on the ratio of the latest 2-month average price to the current 12-month average. As was done for the Long-Term Price Score, this ratio is also indexed to the same ratio for the market as a whole.

In both cases, all prices are adjusted for all stock dividends and splits.

D. INTERIM EARNINGS (Per Share) – This figure essentially is what has been reported by the company. Figures are reported before extraordinary items, discontinued operations and effects of accounting changes (unless otherwise noted). Prior to 12/15/97, primary earnings per share are shown. After that date, diluted earnings per share are dis-

ILLUSTRATIVE INC.

YIELD	0.5%
P/E RATIO	10.9

B 50% STK / 10% STK

TRADING VOLUME
Thousand Shares

| 1986 | 1987 | 1988 | 1989 | 1990 | 1991 | 1992 | 1993 | 1994 | 1995 | 1996 | 1997 | 1998 | 1999 | 2000 |

C *7 YEAR PRICE SCORE 122.8   *12 MONTH PRICE SCORE 86.2
*NYSE COMPOSITE INDEX=100

D INTERIM EARNINGS (Per Share):

Qtr.	Apr.	July	Oct.	Jan.
1996-97	0.06	0.09	0.10	0.10
1997-98	0.17	0.16	0.17	0.16
1998-99	0.28	0.25	0.27	0.26
1999-00	0.47	0.46	0.34	0.25
2000-01	0.53	...	...	...

E INTERIM DIVIDENDS (Per Share):

Amt.	Decl.	Ex.	Rec.	Pay.
10% STK	1/08/99	1/15/99	1/20/99	2/04/99
0.04S	4/02/99	4/13/99	4/15/99	4/30/99
0.04S	9/23/99	10/02/99	10/06/99	10/30/99
10% STK	12/17/99	12/23/99	12/28/99	1/11/00
0.04S	3/17/00	4/07/00	4/09/00	4/30/00

Indicated div.: $0.08

F CAPITALIZATION (1/31/00):

	($000)	(%)
Long-Term Debt	138,793	20.0
Capital Lease Obligations	56,801	8.2
Common & Surplus	498,512	71.8
Total	694,106	100.0

G DIVIDEND ACHIEVER STATUS:
Rank: 350   10-Year Growth Rate: 2.56%
Total Years of Dividend Growth: 24

RECENT DEVELOPMENTS: For the year ended 1/31/00, net income before an extraordinary gain improved to $46.8 million compared with net income of $22.3 million the year before. Total revenues increased to $1.15 billion from $614.1 million the year before. Revenues are improving as a result of increasing margins at Bill's Burgers, Salads a Go Go, and Pizza Galore chains. Revenues from Company-owned restaurants climbed to $867.0 million from $712.8 billion. Revenues from franchised and licensed restaurants rose to $159.8 million from $127.2 million. Operating income jumped to $168.2 million from $86.2 million.

H BUSINESS

ILLUSTRATIVE INC., through its subsidiaries and franchisees, owns and operates 1,256 Bill's Burgers restaurants, featuring the Company's patented vegetarian Bill Burgers. The restaurants are located in all 50 states. In addition, the Company owns 435 Salad a Go Go restaurants and take-out facilities in 14 eastern and southeastern states. The Company also owns and operates 121 Pizza Galore restaurants. It recently opened three Seafood Symphony restaurants in North and South Carolina.

REVENUES

(01/31/00)	($000)	(%)
Co.-operated		
restaurants	1,022,453	88.9
Franchised &		
licensed	127,206	11.1
Total	1,149,659	100.0

J ANNUAL FINANCIAL DATA

	1/31/00	1/31/99	1/31/98	1/31/97	1/31/96	1/25/95	1/27/94
Earnings Per Share	0.88	0.60	0.32	0.04	0.13	d0.09	0.40
Cash Flow Per Share	1.76	1.34	0.95	0.71	0.81	0.68	1.20
Tang. Book Val. Per Share	8.86	5.34	3.01	2.67	2.72	2.58	2.76
Dividends Per Share	0.07	0.06	0.05	0.04	0.03	0.02	0.01
Dividend Payout %	7.5	7.3	13.6	56.2	23.1	N.M.	2.5
INCOME STATEMENT (IN MILLIONS):							
Total Revenues	1,149.7	614.1	465.4	443.7	460.4	502.6	533.6
Costs & Expenses	1,017.1	545.0	418.3	412.4	427.0	484.7	487.0
Depreciation & Amort.	46.4	27.1	21.4	22.8	22.8	25.2	26.6
Operating Income	86.2	42.0	25.7	8.6	10.5	d7.3	20.0
Net Interest Inc./(Exp.)	d16.9	d9.9	d10.0	d9.2	d10.4	d13.6	d16.7
Income Before Income Taxes	76.6	36.7	18.0	2.4	6.3	d7.3	18.9
Income Taxes	29.9	14.4	7.0	1.1	1.8	cr4.2	5.8
Net Income	46.8	22.3	11.0	1.3	4.4	d3.1	13.0
Cash Flow	93.2	49.4	32.3	24.0	27.3	22.1	39.6
Average Shs. Outstg. (000)	52,934	36,801	33,902	33,971	33,699	32,732	33,018
BALANCE SHEET (IN MILLIONS):							
Cash & Cash Equivalents	30.4	39.8	25.9	18.2	26.1	44.4	36.7
Total Current Assets	92.2	72.9	56.8	56.8	69.4	90.6	83.8
Net Property	674.6	242.9	155.7	163.8	146.8	150.6	175.0
Total Assets	957.4	401.2	246.8	244.3	242.1	268.9	292.6
Total Current Liabilities	176.5	83.9	61.3	71.6	66.6	91.4	92.3
Long-Term Obligations	195.6	81.9	70.6	69.9	63.3	80.3	102.1
Net Stockholders' Equity	498.5	214.8	101.2	88.5	92.1	84.7	89.7
Net Working Capital	d84.3	d11.0	d4.5	d14.7	2.9	d0.9	d8.5
Year-end Shs. Outstg. (000)	56,293	40,195	33,632	33,133	33,899	32,835	32,521
STATISTICAL RECORD: **K**							
Operating Profit Margin %	7.5	6.8	5.5	1.9	2.3	...	3.8
Net Profit Margin %	4.1	3.6	2.4	0.3	1.0	...	2.4
Return on Equity %	9.4	10.4	10.8	1.4	4.8	...	14.5
Return on Assets %	4.9	5.6	4.4	0.5	1.8	...	4.5
Debt/Total Assets %	20.4	20.4	28.6	28.6	26.1	29.8	34.9
Price Range	37½-15³⁄₁₆	19-7	9¹⁵⁄₁₆-3½	7¹⁵⁄₁₆-3⁹⁄₁₆	5⁷⁄₈-3³⁄₄	6¹⁄₈-3³⁄₄	5⁷⁄₁₆-3¹⁄₈
P/E Ratio	42.4-17.2	33.1-13.2	30.5-10.8	202.1-91.4	44.4-28.2	...	13.7-7.8
Average Yield %	0.3	0.3	0.7	0.4	...	...	...

Statistics are as originally reported. Adj. for stk. splits: 10% div., 1/99, 2/98; 3-for-2, 1/97

HOW TO USE THIS BOOK (Continued)

played, as set out in Financial Accounting Standards Board Statement 128.

E. INTERIM DIVIDENDS (Per Share) – The cash dividends are the actual dollar amounts declared by the company. No adjustments have been made for stock dividends and splits. **Ex-Dividend Date**: a stockholder must purchase the stock prior to this date in order to be entitled to the dividend. The **Record Date** indicates the date on which the shareholder had to have been a holder of record in order to have qualified for the dividend. The **Payable Date** indicates the date the company paid or intends to pay the dividend. The cash amount shown in the first column is followed by a letter (example ''Q'' for quarterly) to indicate the frequency of the dividend.

Indicated Dividend is the annualized rate (fully adjusted) of the latest regular cash dividend. Companies with dividend reinvestment programs are indicated.

F. CAPITALIZATION – These are certain items in the company's capital account. Both the dollar amounts and their respective percentages are given.

Long-term Debt is the total amount of debt owed by the company due beyond one year.

Capital Lease Obligations is shown as a separate caption when displayed on the balance sheet as such.

Deferred Income Taxes represents the company's tax liability arising from accelerated depreciation and investment tax credit.

Preferred Stock and/or Preference Stock is the sum of equity issues, exclusive of common stock, whose holders have a prior claim, ahead of the common shareholders, to the income of the company while it continues to operate and to its assets in the event of dissolution.

Minority Interest in this instance is a capital item reflecting the share of ownership by an outside party in a consolidated subsidiary of the company.

Common and Surplus is the sum of the stated or par value of the common stock, plus additional paid-in capital and retained earnings less the dollar amount of treasury shares.

G. DIVIDEND ACHIEVER STATUS – The company's rank among the dividend achievers is given. Also included is the company's average annual compound dividend growth rate for the latest 10 year period and the number of consecutive calendar years the cash payment increased.

H. COMPANY BUSINESS – This is what a company does: its products and services, its markets and production facilities.

I. RECENT DEVELOPMENTS – This section focuses on the current position of each company. In addition to analysis of recently released sales and earnings figures, items covered include, where applicable (if available), new product introductions, capital expenditures, expanded operations, acquisitions, labor developments, equity or debt financing, the rate of incoming orders, the level of backlog and other operating statistics.

J. PER SHARE ANNUAL FINANCIAL DATA – These figures are displayed as originally reported, and are fully adjusted for all stock dividends and stock splits.

Earnings Per Share are as reported by the company except for adjustment for certain items as footnoted. Prior to 12/15/97, primary earnings per share are shown. After that date, diluted earnings per share are indicated, in accordance with Financial Accounting Standards Board Statement 128.

Cash Flow Per Share is net income minus preferred dividends plus depreciation and amortization, divided by average shares outstanding.

Tangible Book Value Per Share is common shareholders' equit y minus preferred stock and intangibles, divided by year-end shares outstanding.

Dividends Per Share represent the sum of all cash payments on a calendar year basis. Any fiscal year ending prior to June 30, for example, is shown with dividends for the prior calendar year.

Dividend Payout % is the percentage of cash paid out of **Earnings Per Share**.

K. INCOME STATEMENT, BALANCE SHEET AND STATISTICAL RECORD –

Shares outstanding and per-share data have been adjusted for all splits and stock dividends. In order to preserve the historical relationships between prices, dividends and earnings, income statement and balance sheet figures are presented as originally reported and not restated to reflect subsequent events.

Total Revenues is the total income from operations including non-operating revenues.

Costs and Expenses are the total of all costs related to the operation of the business – including cost of sales, selling, and general and administrative expenses. Excluded items are depreciation, interest and non-operating expenses.

Depreciation and Amortization includes all non-cash charges such as depletion and amortization as well as depreciation.

Operating Income is the profit remaining after deducting depreciation as well as all operating costs and expenses from the company's net sales and revenues. The figure is *before* interest expenses, extraordinary gains

and charges, and income and expense items of a non-operating nature.

Income Before Income Taxes is the remaining income *after* deducting all costs, expenses, property charges, interest, etc. but *before* deducting income taxes.

Income Taxes are as reported by the company and include both the amount of current taxes actually paid out and the amount deferred.

Equity Earnings/Minority Interest in the income statement is that portion of *profits* of a consolidated subsidiary that is allocated to a minority owner of that subsidiary who shares in the results of its operations.

Net Income is as reported by the company, before extraordinary gains and losses, discontinued operations and adjustments for changes in accounting principles.

Cash Flow is net income minus preferred dividends, plus depreciation and amortization.

Average Shares Outstanding is the weighted average number of shares including common equivalent shares outstanding during the year, as reported by the company, adjusted for stock dividends and splits.

BALANCE SHEET:

Cash and Cash Equivalents comprise unrestricted cash and temporary investments in marketable securities, such as U.S. Government securities, certificates of deposit and short-term investments.

Net Property is total fixed assets, including all property, land, plants, buildings, equipment, fixtures, etc., net of depreciation and amortization.

Long-term Obligations is the total long-term debt (due beyond one year) reported by the company, including bonds, capital lease obligations, notes, mortgages, debentures, etc.

28a

Net Stockholders' Equity is the sum of all capital stock accounts – stated values of preferred and common stock, paid-in capital, earned surplus (retained earnings), etc., net of all treasury stock.

Total Assets represent the sum of all tangible and intangible assets as reported.

Total Current Assets are all of the company's short-term assets such as cash, marketable securities, inventories, etc., as reported.

Total Current Liabilities are all of the obligations of the company due within one year, as reported.

Net Working Capital is derived by subtracting Current Liabilities from Current Assets.

Year-end Shares Outstanding are the number of shares outstanding as of the date of the company's annual report, exclusive of treasury stock and adjusted for subsequent stock dividends and splits.

STATISTICAL RECORD:

Operating Profit Margin indicates the operating profit as a percentage of revenues.

Net Profit Margin is the percentage of revenues realized as net profit.

Return on Equity, a measure of profitability, is the ratio of net income to net stockholders' equity, expressed as a percentage.

Return on Assets is the ratio of net income to total assets, expressed as a percentage.

Debt/Total Assets is the ratio, expressed as a percentage, of long-term debt to total assets.

Price Ranges are shown for calendar years, regardless of the fiscal reporting period.

Price/Earnings Ratio is shown as a range. The figures are calculated by dividing the stock's highest price for the year and its lowest price by the year's earnings per share. Prices are for calendar years.

Average Yield is the ratio, expressed as a percentage, of the annual dividend to the mean price of the common stock (average of the high and low for the year). Both prices and dividends are for calendar years.

L. ADDITIONAL INFORMATION on each stock includes the officers of the company, date and state of incorporation, its address, telephone number, fax number and website when available, investor relations contact, annual meeting date, the number of employees, the number of stockholders, institutional holdings, and transfer agent.

Institutional Holdings – indicates the number of investment companies, insurance companies, bank trust and college endowment funds holding the stock and the total number of shares held as last reported. The percentage of shares outstanding held by institutions is also provided.

ABBREVIATIONS
AND
SYMBOLS

A	Annually
d	Deficit
E	Extra
M	Monthly
N.M.	Not Meaningful
P.F.	Pro Forma
Q	Quarterly
r	Revised
S	Semi-annual
Sp	Special Dividend

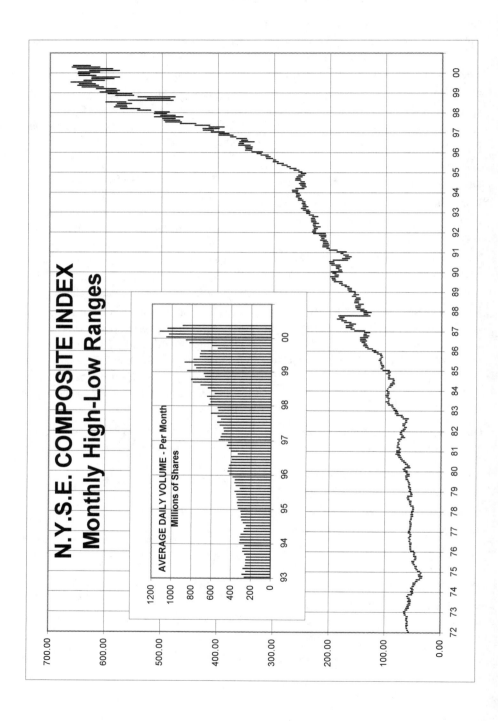

N.Y.S.E. COMPOSITE INDEX
Monthly High-Low Ranges

AVERAGE DAILY VOLUME - Per Month
Millions of Shares

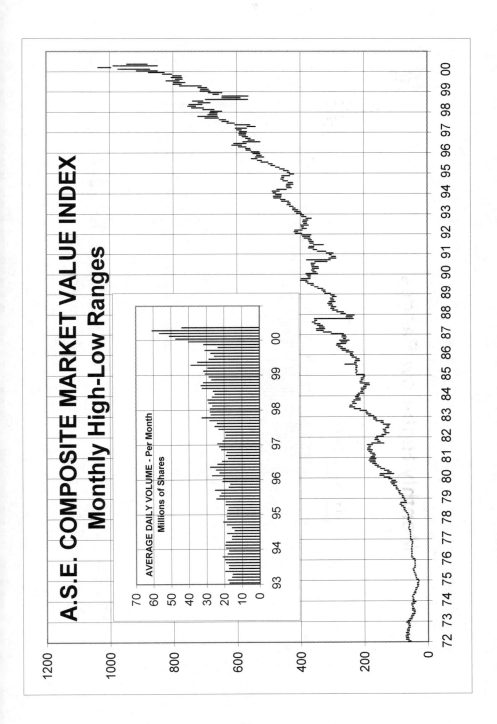

A.S.E. COMPOSITE MARKET VALUE INDEX
Monthly High-Low Ranges

AVERAGE DAILY VOLUME - Per Month
Millions of Shares

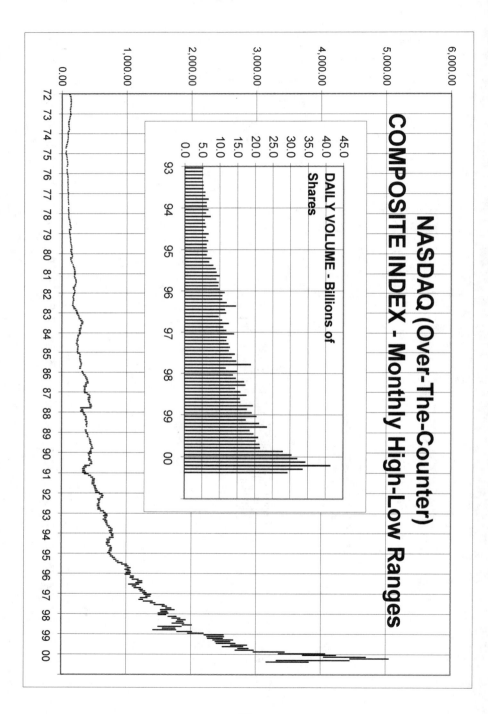

NASDAQ (Over-The-Counter)
COMPOSITE INDEX - Monthly High-Low Ranges

DAILY VOLUME - Billions of Shares

ABBOTT LABORATORIES

YIELD	1.9%
P/E RATIO	24.5

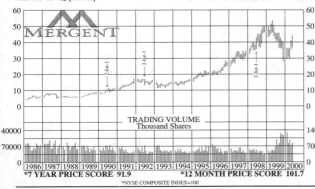

INTERIM EARNINGS (Per Share):

Qtr.	Mar.	June	Sept.	Dec.
1996	0.31	0.30	0.27	0.33
1997	0.35	0.34	0.31	0.37
1998	0.38	0.38	0.34	0.41
1999	0.43	0.42	0.38	0.43

INTERIM DIVIDENDS (Per Share):

Amt.	Decl.	Ex.	Rec.	Pay.
0.17Q	6/11/99	7/13/99	7/15/99	8/15/99
0.17Q	9/10/99	10/13/99	10/15/99	11/15/99
0.17Q	12/10/99	1/12/00	1/14/00	2/15/00
0.19Q	2/11/00	4/12/00	4/14/00	5/15/00

Indicated div.: $0.76 (Div. Reinv. Plan)

CAPITALIZATION (12/31/99):

	($000)	(%)
Long-Term Debt	1,336,789	15.2
Deferred Income Tax	23,779	0.3
Common & Surplus	7,427,595	84.5
Total	8,788,163	100.0

TRADING VOLUME
Thousand Shares

7 YEAR PRICE SCORE 91.9   **12 MONTH PRICE SCORE 101.7**
*NYSE COMPOSITE INDEX=100

DIVIDEND ACHIEVER STATUS:
Rank: 71   10-Year Growth Rate: 14.61%
Total Years of Dividend Growth: 27

RECENT DEVELOPMENTS: For the year ended 12/31/99, net income rose 4.8% to $2.45 billion from $2.33 billion in 1998. The 1999 results included a nonrecurring pre-tax charge of $168.0 million relating to a FDA consent decree. Net sales increased 5.3% to $13.18 billion. Sales in the diagnostic products segment grew 8.9% to $3.04 billion, while sales in the hospital products segment jumped 14.4% to $2.20 billion. Meanwhile, sales in the pharmaceutical products segment fell 6.0% to $2.44 billion.

PROSPECTS: Results should be favorably affected by the FDA's approval to market PRECEDEX™, a sedative for use in patients hospitalized in intensive care settings, and an agreement to obtain the U.S. marketing rights to OMNICEF®, a cephalosporin antibiotic, from Warner Lambert Company. On 12/16/99, Abbott announced that ABT's proposed acquisition of Alza Corporation was terminated as the two companies were unable to come to terms with the FTC to satisfy certain concerns relating to the merger.

BUSINESS

ABBOTT LABORATORIES' principal business is the discovery, development, manufacture, and sale of a broad and diversified line of human health care products and services. Pharmaceutical and nutritional products, 57.1% of 1999 sales, include a broad line of adult and pediatric pharmaceuticals and nutritional vitamins. This segment also includes consumer products, agricultural and chemical products, and bulk pharmaceuticals. Hospital and laboratory products, 42.9% of sales, include diagnostic systems, intravenous and irrigating fluids and related administration equipment, anesthetics, critical care equipment, and other specialty products.

ANNUAL FINANCIAL DATA

	12/31/99	12/31/98	12/31/97	12/31/96	12/31/95	12/31/94	12/31/93
Earnings Per Share	☐ 1.57	1.51	1.34	1.21	1.06	0.94	0.85
Cash Flow Per Share	2.10	2.02	1.81	1.64	1.42	1.25	1.14
Tang. Book Val. Per Share	3.78	2.88	2.54	2.48	2.69	2.52	2.24
Dividends Per Share	0.66	0.58	0.53	0.47	0.41	0.37	0.33
Dividend Payout %	42.0	38.7	39.2	38.6	38.7	39.6	39.0
INCOME STATEMENT (IN MILLIONS):							
Total Revenues	13,177.6	12,477.8	11,883.5	11,013.5	10,012.2	9,156.0	8,407.8
Costs & Expenses	9,200.2	8,575.7	8,305.3	7,710.3	7,062.9	6,501.3	5,999.8
Depreciation & Amort.	828.0	784.2	727.8	686.1	566.4	510.5	484.1
Operating Income	3,149.4	3,117.9	2,850.4	2,617.1	2,382.9	2,144.2	1,924.0
Net Interest Inc./(Exp.)	d81.8	d104.1	d86.8	d50.9	d17.7	d12.8	d16.5
Income Before Income Taxes	3,396.9	3,240.6	2,949.9	2,669.6	2,395.3	2,166.7	1,943.2
Income Taxes	951.1	907.4	855.5	787.5	706.6	650.0	544.1
Net Income	☐ 2,445.8	2,333.2	2,094.5	1,882.0	1,688.7	1,516.7	1,399.1
Cash Flow	3,273.8	3,117.5	2,822.2	2,568.1	2,255.1	2,027.2	1,883.2
Average Shs. Outstg. (000)	1,557,655	1,545,658	1,561,462	1,562,494	1,590,724	1,624,472	1,657,976
BALANCE SHEET (IN MILLIONS):							
Cash & Cash Equivalents	723.3	383.3	259.0	123.1	315.7	315.3	378.8
Total Current Assets	6,419.8	5,553.1	5,038.2	4,480.9	4,226.7	3,876.3	3,585.5
Net Property	4,770.1	4,738.8	4,569.7	4,461.5	4,249.5	3,920.9	3,511.0
Total Assets	14,471.0	13,216.2	12,061.1	11,125.6	9,412.6	8,523.7	7,688.6
Total Current Liabilities	4,516.7	4,962.1	5,034.5	4,343.7	3,790.3	3,475.9	3,094.9
Long-Term Obligations	1,336.8	1,339.7	938.0	932.9	435.2	287.1	306.8
Net Stockholders' Equity	7,427.6	5,713.7	4,998.7	4,820.2	4,396.8	4,049.4	3,674.9
Net Working Capital	1,903.0	591.0	3.7	137.2	436.4	400.5	490.6
Year-end Shs. Outstg. (000)	1,547,020	1,516,063	1,528,188	1,548,898	1,574,614	1,606,560	1,642,260
STATISTICAL RECORD:							
Operating Profit Margin %	23.9	25.0	24.0	23.8	23.8	23.4	22.9
Net Profit Margin %	18.6	18.7	17.6	17.1	16.9	16.6	16.6
Return on Equity %	32.9	40.8	41.9	39.0	38.4	37.5	38.1
Return on Assets %	16.9	17.7	17.4	16.9	17.9	17.8	18.2
Debt/Total Assets %	9.2	10.1	7.8	8.4	4.6	3.4	4.0
Price Range	53⁵/₁₆-33	50¹/₁₆-32⁹/₁₆	34⁷/₈-24⁷/₈	28¹¹/₁₆-24⁷/₁₆	22³/₈-15³/₁₆	17-12¹¹/₁₆	15⁷/₁₆-11³/₁₆
P/E Ratio	34.0-17.8	33.2-21.5	26.0-18.6	23.8-15.8	21.1-14.4	18.2-13.6	18.3-13.4
Average Yield %	1.6	1.4	1.8	1.9	2.2	2.5	2.5

Statistics are as originally reported. Adj. for 2-for-1 stock split, 5/98. ☐ Incl. a nonrecurring pre-tax charge of $168.0 million relating to an FDA consent decree.

OFFICERS:
M. D. White, Chmn., C.E.O.
R. L. Parkinson, Pres., C.O.O.
G. P. Coughlan, Sr. V.P., Fin., C.F.O.
G. W. Linder, V.P., Treas.

INVESTOR CONTACT: Catherine V. Babington, Vice-Pres., (847) 938-5633

PRINCIPAL OFFICE: 100 Abbott Park Road, Abbott Park, IL 60064-6400

TELEPHONE NUMBER: (847) 937-6100
FAX: (847) 937-1511
WEB: www.abbott.com

NO. OF EMPLOYEES: 57,100 (avg.)

SHAREHOLDERS: 106,766

ANNUAL MEETING: In Apr.

INCORPORATED: IL, Mar., 1900

INSTITUTIONAL HOLDINGS:
No. of Institutions: 922
Shares Held: 805,277,611
% Held: 52.4

INDUSTRY: Pharmaceutical preparations (SIC: 2834)

TRANSFER AGENT(S): BankBoston, N.A., Boston, MA

ABM INDUSTRIES INCORPORATED

YIELD 2.7%
P/E RATIO 13.8

7 YEAR PRICE SCORE 84.5   **12 MONTH PRICE SCORE 97.1**
*NYSE COMPOSITE INDEX=100

INTERIM EARNINGS (Per Share):

Qtr.	Jan.	April	July	Oct.
1996-97	0.20	0.26	0.34	0.40
1997-98	0.25	0.30	0.40	0.49
1998-99	0.29	0.35	0.46	0.55
1999-00	0.32	...	...	...

INTERIM DIVIDENDS (Per Share):

Amt.	Decl.	Ex.	Rec.	Pay.
0.14Q	3/16/99	4/13/99	4/15/99	5/05/99
0.14Q	6/15/99	7/13/99	7/15/99	8/04/99
0.14Q	9/22/99	10/13/99	10/15/99	11/03/99
0.155Q	12/21/99	1/12/00	1/14/00	2/03/00
0.155Q	3/21/00	4/12/00	4/14/00	5/03/00

Indicated div.: $0.62

CAPITALIZATION (10/31/99):

	($000)	(%)
Long-Term Debt	28,903	9.3
Redeemable Pfd. Stock	6,400	2.0
Common & Surplus	276,951	88.7
Total	312,254	100.0

DIVIDEND ACHIEVER STATUS:
Rank: 173   10-Year Growth Rate: 9.24%
Total Years of Dividend Growth: 35

RECENT DEVELOPMENTS: For the quarter ended 1/31/00, net income rose 8.0% to $7.5 million versus $7.0 million in the equivalent 1999 quarter. Revenues were $428.6 million, up 9.4% from $391.8 million a year earlier. The improvement in results was primarily attributed to ABM's momentum in its multi-service and national account sales. In addition, ABM benefited from outsourcing from the private sector, privatization by governmental agencies, and ABM's active acquisition program.

PROSPECTS: ABM's subsidiary, Amtech Elevator, was awarded a multi-million dollar contract from the University of Georgia to provide elevator maintenance services. Amtech is providing comprehensive elevator modernization for the University's ten elevators in Russell Hall and Creswell Hall. In April 2000, ABM's subsidiary Ampco System Parking, was awarded a multi-year, multi-million dollar contract to provide parking service for CocoWalk, located in Miami Beach, FL.

BUSINESS

ABM INDUSTRIES INCORPORATED is engaged in the business of providing commercial, industrial and institutional janitorial, window cleaning, engineering and building maintenance services. The Company is also engaged in the business of air conditioning, heating equipment, elevator and escalator installation, repair and servicing; lighting and outdoor signage installation and maintenance; parking facility operations; building security services; and janitorial supplies and equipment sales. Amtech group offers a wide range of mechanical, electrical and elevator services to retail and commercial businesses. Contributions to sales for fiscal 1999 were as follows: ABM Janitorial, 57%; Ampco System Parking, 10%; ABM Engineering, 9%; Amtech Elevator, 6%; Amtech Lighting 6%; and all other segments, 12%.

ANNUAL FINANCIAL DATA

	10/31/99	10/31/98	10/31/97	10/31/96	10/31/95	10/31/94	10/31/93
Earnings Per Share	1.65	1.44	1.33	1.11	0.93	0.83	0.73
Cash Flow Per Share	2.54	2.31	2.15	1.85	1.55	1.37	1.15
Tang. Book Val. Per Share	7.65	6.24	4.76	4.51	3.87	3.48	2.98
Dividends Per Share	0.56	0.48	0.40	0.35	0.30	0.26	0.25
Dividend Payout %	33.9	33.3	30.1	31.5	32.4	31.2	34.5
INCOME STATEMENT (IN MILLIONS):							
Total Revenues	1,629.7	1,501.8	1,252.5	1,086.9	965.4	884.6	773.3
Costs & Expenses	1,539.8	1,421.3	1,186.7	1,032.6	919.7	846.8	743.7
Depreciation & Amort.	20.7	19.6	16.1	13.7	11.5	9.3	7.2
Operating Income	69.2	61.0	49.6	40.7	34.2	28.5	22.4
Net Interest Inc./(Exp.)	d2.0	d3.5	d2.7	d2.6	d2.7	d3.5	d2.2
Income Before Income Taxes	67.2	57.5	47.0	38.1	31.4	25.1	20.2
Income Taxes	27.6	23.6	19.7	16.4	13.2	9.9	7.6
Net Income	39.7	33.9	27.2	21.7	18.2	15.2	12.6
Cash Flow	59.9	53.0	42.8	34.9	29.2	24.0	19.7
Average Shs. Outstg. (000)	23,748	23,161	20,143	19,123	19,180	17,816	17,292
BALANCE SHEET (IN MILLIONS):							
Cash & Cash Equivalents	2.1	1.8	1.8	1.6	1.8	7.4	1.7
Total Current Assets	367.6	324.3	291.5	233.8	209.9	189.4	166.9
Net Property	35.2	27.3	26.6	22.6	22.6	19.8	17.0
Total Assets	563.4	501.4	464.3	379.8	335.0	299.5	268.1
Total Current Liabilities	183.3	157.8	153.8	113.8	114.2	99.3	90.3
Long-Term Obligations	28.9	33.7	38.4	33.7	22.6	25.3	20.9
Net Stockholders' Equity	277.0	237.5	197.8	164.3	141.8	124.3	110.2
Net Working Capital	184.3	166.5	137.8	120.0	95.6	90.2	76.6
Year-end Shs. Outstg. (000)	22,407	21,601	20,464	19,489	18,732	18,098	17,556
STATISTICAL RECORD:							
Operating Profit Margin %	4.2	4.1	4.0	3.7	3.5	3.2	2.9
Net Profit Margin %	2.4	2.3	2.2	2.0	1.9	1.7	1.6
Return on Equity %	14.3	14.3	13.8	13.2	12.8	12.2	11.5
Return on Assets %	7.0	6.8	5.9	5.7	5.4	5.1	4.7
Debt/Total Assets %	5.1	6.7	8.3	8.9	6.7	8.4	7.8
Price Range	35¹/₁₆-20	37-25	31¹/₂-17⅜	20³/₁₆-13¹/₂	14¹/₄-10¹/₂	11¹⁵/₁₆-8⅝	10⁷/₈-7⁵/₁₆
P/E Ratio	21.3-12.1	25.7-17.4	23.7-13.1	18.2-12.2	15.4-11.4	14.5-10.5	15.0-10.1
Average Yield %	2.0	1.5	1.6	2.1	2.4	2.5	2.7

Statistics are as originally reported. Adj. for stk. split: 2-for-1, 8/96.

OFFICERS:
M. H. Mandles, Chmn., C.A.O.
W. W. Steele, Pres., C.E.O.
D. H. Hebble, Sr. V.P., C.F.O.
D. B. Bowlus, Treas.

PRINCIPAL OFFICE: 160 Pacific Avenue, Suite 222, San Francisco, CA 94111

TELEPHONE NUMBER: (415) 733-4000
FAX: (415) 733-7333
WEB: www.abm.com
NO. OF EMPLOYEES: 57,000 (approx.)
SHAREHOLDERS: 7,292 (approx.)
ANNUAL MEETING: In Mar.
INCORPORATED: CA, Apr., 1955; reincorp., DE, Mar., 1955

INSTITUTIONAL HOLDINGS:
No. of Institutions: 86
Shares Held: 12,884,449
% Held: 57.7

INDUSTRY: Building maintenance services, nec (SIC: 7349)

TRANSFER AGENT(S): ChaseMellon Shareholder Services, San Francisco, CA

NYSE SYMBOL AFL
Rec. Pr. 51 11/16 (5/31/00)

AFLAC INCORPORATED

YIELD 0.7%
P/E RATIO 25.0

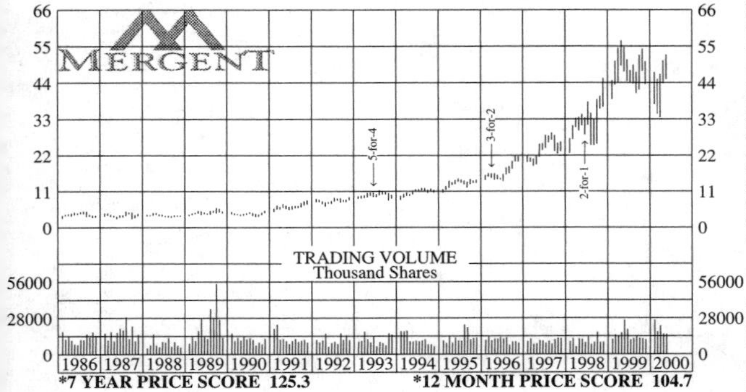

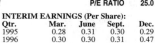

MERGENT
66
55
44
33
22
11
0
5-for-4
3-for-2
2-for-1
TRADING VOLUME
Thousand Shares
56000
28000
0
1986 1987 1988 1989 1990 1991 1992 1993 1994 1995 1996 1997 1998 1999 2000

*7 YEAR PRICE SCORE 125.3 *12 MONTH PRICE SCORE 104.7

*NYSE COMPOSITE INDEX=100

INTERIM EARNINGS (Per Share):

Qtr.	Mar.	June	Sept.	Dec.
1995	0.28	0.31	0.30	0.29
1996	0.30	0.30	0.31	0.47
1997	0.32	1.07	0.34	0.35
1998	0.58	0.37	0.39	0.42
1999	0.71	0.47	0.52	0.37

INTERIM DIVIDENDS (Per Share):

Amt.	Decl.	Ex.	Rec.	Pay.
0.075Q	5/03/99	5/18/99	5/20/99	6/01/99
0.075Q	7/27/99	8/17/99	8/19/99	9/01/99
0.075Q	10/25/99	11/16/99	11/18/99	12/01/99
0.075Q	1/27/00	2/15/00	2/17/00	3/01/00
0.085Q	5/01/00	5/16/00	5/18/00	6/01/00

Indicated div.: $0.34 (Div. Reinv. Plan)

CAPITALIZATION (12/31/99):

	($000)	(%)
Long-Term Debt	1,111,000	17.1
Deferred Income Tax	1,511,000	23.3
Common & Surplus	3,868,000	59.6
Total	6,490,000	100.0

DIVIDEND ACHIEVER STATUS:
Rank: 80 10-Year Growth Rate: 14.14%
Total Years of Dividend Growth: 17

RECENT DEVELOPMENTS: For the year ended 12/31/99, net income improved 17.3% to $571.0 million compared with $487.0 million in the corresponding year. Results included realized investment losses of $13.0 million and $2.0 million in 1999 and 1998, respectively. Total revenues were $8.64 billion, an increase of 21.6% from $7.10 billion in the previous year. Premiums revenues, principally from supplemental health insurance, jumped 22.2% to $7.26 billion.

PROSPECTS: The Company and its insurance operations remain strong and well-positioned for continued growth in fiscal 2000 and beyond. The Company anticipates particularly strong growth in the U.S. and Japan, as they are the largest life insurance markets in the world. Accordingly, the Company's goal for 2000, 2001 and 2002 is to achieve earnings per share growth in the 15.0% to 17.0% range, excluding currency fluctuations.

BUSINESS

AFLAC INCORPORATED is an international insurance organization whose principal subsidiary is American Family Life Assurance Company of Columbus. In addition to life, and health & accident insurance, AFL has pioneered cancer-expense and intensive-care insurance coverage. In 1999, AFLAC Japan accounted for 81% of revenues. U.S. insurance operations totaled 19%. AFLAC's subsidiary Communicorp specializes in printing, advertising, audio-visuals, sales incentives, business meetings and mailings. In 1997, the Company completed the sale of its broadcast business which consisted of seven network-affiliated television stations.

ANNUAL FINANCIAL DATA

	12/31/99	12/31/98	12/31/97	12/31/96	12/31/95	12/31/94	12/31/93
Earnings Per Share	**2.07**	**1.76**	**[2] 2.08**	**[2] 1.37**	**1.17**	**0.95**	**[1] 0.77**
Tang. Book Val. Per Share	**14.56**	**14.19**	**12.88**	**7.14**	**6.79**	**5.49**	**4.03**
Dividends Per Share	**0.29**	**0.25**	**0.22**	**0.19**	**0.17**	**0.15**	**0.13**
Dividend Payout %	**14.0**	**14.3**	**10.7**	**14.1**	**14.4**	**15.7**	**16.7**
INCOME STATEMENT (IN MILLIONS):							
Total Premium Income	7,264.0	5,943.0	5,873.7	5,910.0	6,070.8	5,180.7	4,225.4
Net Investment Income	1,369.0	1,138.0	1,077.7	1,022.0	1,025.0	838.8	689.3
Other Income	7.0	23.0	299.3	168.2	94.8	91.2	86.0
Total Revenues	8,640.0	7,104.0	7,250.7	7,100.2	7,190.6	6,110.8	5,000.6
Policyholder Benefits	5,885.0	4,877.0	4,833.1	4,895.5	5,034.3	4,256.5	3,423.3
Income Before Income Taxes	778.0	551.0	864.8	650.0	601.0	504.3	428.4
Income Taxes	207.0	64.0	279.8	255.6	251.9	211.5	184.5
Net Income	571.0	487.0	[2] 585.0	[2] 394.4	349.1	292.8	[1] 243.9
Average Shs. Outstg. (000)	275,423	275,872	281,596	289,024	299,080	309,304	315,604
BALANCE SHEET (IN MILLIONS):							
Cash & Cash Equivalents	616.0	374.0	279.0	261.7	236.3	348.6	190.1
Premiums Due	270.0	272.0	215.7	227.0	321.1	303.7	232.0
Invst. Assets: Fixed-term	25,248.0	21,564.0	22,437.8	20,327.7	19,675.0	15,530.7	12,137.8
Invst. Assets: Equities	215.0	177.0	146.3	136.3	108.1	84.4	82.1
Invst. Assets: Loans	...	...	16.7	17.8	22.2	25.1	57.5
Invst. Assets: Total	31,408.0	26,620.0	22,644.2	20,746.5	20,040.8	15,976.1	12,445.7
Total Assets	37,041.0	31,183.0	29,454.0	25,022.8	25,338.0	20,287.1	15,442.7
Long-Term Obligations	1,111.0	596.0	523.2	353.5	327.3	184.9	122.1
Net Stockholders' Equity	3,868.0	3,770.0	3,430.5	2,125.6	2,134.1	1,751.8	1,365.6
Year-end Shs. Outstg. (000)	265,741	265,684	266,436	289,024	299,080	298,908	310,414
STATISTICAL RECORD:							
Return on Revenues %	6.6	6.9	8.1	5.6	4.9	4.8	4.9
Return on Equity %	14.8	12.9	17.1	18.6	16.4	16.7	17.9
Return on Assets %	1.5	1.6	2.0	1.6	1.4	1.4	1.6
Price Range	56 3/4-39	45 5/16-22 11/16	28 15/16-18 3/4	22-14 1/8	14 15/16-10 5/8	12 1/16-8 7/16	11 5/16-8 1/4
P/E Ratio	27.4-18.8	25.7-12.9	13.9-9.0	16.1-10.3	12.8-9.1	12.7-8.9	14.7-10.7
Average Yield %	0.6	0.7	0.9	1.1	1.3	1.5	1.3

Statistics are as originally reported. Adj. for stk. splits: 2-for-1, 6/98; 3-for-2, 3/96 [1] Bef. acctg. change credit $11.4 mill. [2] Incl. non-recurr. credit 97, $267.2 mill.; 96, $60.3 mill.

OFFICERS:
P. S. Amos, Chmn.
D. P. Amos, Vice-Chmn., Pres., C.E.O.
K. Cloninger III, Exec. V.P., C.F.O., Treas.

INVESTOR CONTACT: Kenneth S. Janke, Jr., Sr. V.P., Inv. Rel., (800) 235-2667

PRINCIPAL OFFICE: 1932 Wynnton Rd., Columbus, GA 31999

TELEPHONE NUMBER: (706) 323-3431
FAX: (706) 596-3488
WEB: www.aflac.com

NO. OF EMPLOYEES: 4,673 (avg.)

SHAREHOLDERS: 69,899 (registered); 155,900 (common) (approx.)

ANNUAL MEETING: In May

INCORPORATED: GA, 1973

INSTITUTIONAL HOLDINGS:
No. of Institutions: 360
Shares Held: 137,314,464
% Held: 51.6

INDUSTRY: Accident and health insurance (SIC: 6321)

TRANSFER AGENT(S): AFLAC Incorporated

NYSE SYMBOL APD
Rec. Pr. 34⅝ (5/31/00)

AIR PRODUCTS & CHEMICALS, INC.

YIELD 2.2%
P/E RATIO 23.7

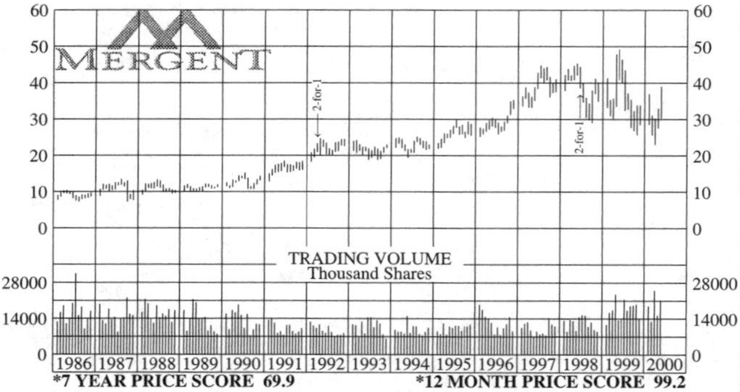
MERGENT
60
50
40
30
20
10
0
2-for-1
2-for-1
TRADING VOLUME
Thousand Shares
28000
14000
0
1986
1987
1988
1989
1990
1991
1992
1993
1994
1995
1996
1997
1998
1999
2000

***7 YEAR PRICE SCORE 69.9** ***12 MONTH PRICE SCORE 99.2**

*NYSE COMPOSITE INDEX=100

INTERIM EARNINGS (Per Share):

Qtr.	Dec.	Mar.	June	Sept.
1997-98	0.72	0.55	0.63	0.59
1998-99	0.59	0.50	0.44	0.57
1999-00	0.23	...	...	...

INTERIM DIVIDENDS (Per Share):

Amt.	Decl.	Ex.	Rec.	Pay.
0.18Q	9/16/99	9/29/99	10/01/99	11/12/99
0.18Q	11/18/99	12/31/99	1/04/00	2/14/00
0.18Q	3/16/00	3/30/00	4/03/00	5/12/00

Indicated div.: $0.72 (Div. Reinv. Plan)

CAPITALIZATION (9/30/99):

	($000)	(%)
Long-Term Debt	1,961,600	33.9
Def. Inc. Tax & Minor. Int.	858,400	14.8
Common & Surplus	2,961,600	51.2
Total	5,781,600	100.0

DIVIDEND ACHIEVER STATUS:
Rank: 194 10-Year Growth Rate: 8.31%
Total Years of Dividend Growth: 17

RECENT DEVELOPMENTS: For the quarter ended 12/31/99, net income fell 60.0% to $50.6 million versus $126.4 million in 1998. Results for fiscal 2000 included a $70.6 million after-tax charge associated with a loss on a currency hedge related to the BOC Group plc acquisition. The 1998 results included a non-recurring net gain of $21.4 million. Total revenues were $1.27 billion, down from $1.28 billion in the prior-year period. Revenues in the equipment business segment dropped 57.7% to $50.6 million.

PROSPECTS: The Company confirmed that its joint preconditional offer with Air Liquide to purchase The BOC Group would not be extended. The offer was conditional on regulatory approvals in four jurisdictions. The companies had been in discussions with the Federal Trade Commission to sell BOC's U.S. assets. Going forward, the Company will continue to discuss other alternatives with Air Liquide, BOC and the Federal Trade Commission in order to complete the transaction.

BUSINESS

AIR PRODUCTS & CHEMICALS, INC. is an international supplier of industrial and specialty gas products. Principal products of the industrial gases segment are oxygen, nitrogen, argon, hydrogen, carbon monoxide, carbon dioxide, synthesis gas, and helium. The chemical business consists of polymer chemicals, performance chemicals, and chemical intermediates. The equipment and services segment designs and manufactures cryogenic and gas processing equipment for air separation, gas processing, natural gas liquefaction, hydrogen purification, and nitrogen rejection. This segment also includes the continuing businesses from the environmental/energy segment (power generation and Pure Air™).

BUSINESS LINE ANALYSIS

(09/30/99)	Rev(%)	Inc(%)
Gases	59.7	69.5
Chemicals	33.0	25.8
Equipment	7.3	4.7
Total	100.0	100.0

ANNUAL FINANCIAL DATA

	9/30/99	9/30/98	9/30/97	9/30/96	9/30/95	9/30/94	9/30/93
Earnings Per Share	**[5] 2.09**	**[4] 2.48**	**1.95**	**[2] 1.86**	**[2] 1.65**	**[3] 1.03**	**[1] 0.88**
Cash Flow Per Share	**4.53**	**4.71**	**4.04**	**3.71**	**3.35**	**2.58**	**2.40**
Tang. Book Val. Per Share	**11.39**	**11.08**	**10.00**	**11.22**	**10.34**	**9.43**	**8.92**
Dividends Per Share	**0.70**	**0.64**	**0.57**	**0.54**	**0.51**	**0.47**	**0.45**
Dividend Payout %	**33.5**	**25.8**	**29.5**	**28.8**	**30.7**	**46.1**	**50.6**
INCOME STATEMENT (IN MILLIONS):							
Total Revenues	5,039.8	4,933.8	4,662.0	4,033.0	3,891.0	3,483.8	3,355.5
Costs & Expenses	3,787.9	3,599.4	3,477.5	3,030.0	2,907.0	2,644.9	2,640.5
Depreciation & Amort.	527.2	489.4	459.1	412.0	382.0	352.8	345.7
Operating Income	724.7	845.0	725.4	591.0	602.0	486.1	369.3
Net Interest Inc./(Exp.)	d159.1	d162.8	d161.3	d129.0	d100.0	d81.6	d81.3
Income Before Income Taxes	669.0	823.7	630.4	610.0	553.0	325.3	300.8
Income Taxes	203.4	276.9	201.1	193.0	185.0	91.8	99.9
Equity Earnings/Minority Int.	d15.1	38.0	66.3	81.0	51.0	28.5	11.8
Net Income	[5] 450.5	[4] 546.8	429.3	[2] 417.0	[2] 368.0	[3] 233.5	[1] 200.9
Cash Flow	977.7	1,036.2	888.4	829.0	750.0	586.3	546.6
Average Shs. Outstg. (000)	216,000	220,100	220,100	223,400	224,000	227,200	227,800
BALANCE SHEET (IN MILLIONS):							
Cash & Cash Equivalents	132.0	61.5	52.5	79.0	87.0	99.9	238.4
Total Current Assets	1,782.4	1,641.7	1,624.3	1,375.0	1,332.0	1,177.7	1,196.3
Net Property	5,192.9	4,786.1	4,441.2	3,959.0	3,502.0	2,992.6	2,705.6
Total Assets	8,235.5	7,489.6	7,244.1	6,522.0	5,816.0	5,036.2	4,761.5
Total Current Liabilities	1,857.8	1,265.6	1,124.6	1,263.0	1,311.0	1,076.4	874.0
Long-Term Obligations	1,961.6	2,274.3	2,291.7	1,739.0	1,194.0	922.5	1,016.4
Net Stockholders' Equity	2,961.6	2,667.3	2,648.1	2,574.0	2,398.0	2,206.4	2,101.9
Net Working Capital	d75.4	376.1	499.7	112.0	21.0	101.3	322.3
Year-end Shs. Outstg. (000)	229,305	211,500	119,500	222,000	224,000	226,816	228,304
STATISTICAL RECORD:							
Operating Profit Margin %	14.4	17.1	15.6	14.7	15.5	14.0	11.0
Net Profit Margin %	8.9	11.1	9.2	10.3	9.5	6.7	6.0
Return on Equity %	15.2	20.5	16.2	16.2	15.3	10.6	9.6
Return on Assets %	5.5	7.3	5.9	6.4	6.3	4.6	4.2
Debt/Total Assets %	23.8	30.4	31.6	26.7	20.5	18.3	21.3
Price Range	49¼-25 11/16	45⅜-29	44 13/16-33 3/16	35 5/16-25 3/16	29 13/16-21 15/16	25 3/16-19⅜	24¼-18¾
P/E Ratio	23.6-12.3	18.3-11.7	23.0-17.0	19.0-13.5	18.1-13.3	24.5-18.8	27.6-21.3
Average Yield %	1.9	1.7	1.5	1.8	2.0	2.1	2.1

Statistics are as originally reported. Adj. for 2-for-1 split, 6/98. [1] Incl. wkfr. reduc. & ast wt-dwn; $120 mil. [2] Incl. $35.0 mil aft-tx gn, 1998; $41.0 mil, 1996; $6.6 mil gn gas plt. sale, 1995. [3] Bef. $14.3 mil. acct. cr. & $74.5 mil. aft-tx chg for spl items. [4] Incl. $58.1 mill. aft-tax gain. [5] Incl. $28.3 mill. net chgs. & $23.6 mill. net gain.

OFFICERS:
H. A. Wagner, Chmn., C.E.O.
J. P. Jones III, Pres., C.O.O.

INVESTOR CONTACT: Michael F. Hilton, Director, (610) 481-5775

PRINCIPAL OFFICE: 7201 Hamilton Blvd., Allentown, PA 18195-1501

TELEPHONE NUMBER: (610) 481-4911
FAX: (610) 481-5900
WEB: www.airproducts.com
NO. OF EMPLOYEES: 17,400 (approx.)
SHAREHOLDERS: 11,922
ANNUAL MEETING: In Jan.
INCORPORATED: MI, Oct., 1940; reincorp., DE, Jun., 1940

INSTITUTIONAL HOLDINGS:
No. of Institutions: 379
Shares Held: 176,623,725
% Held: 77.0

INDUSTRY: Industrial gases (SIC: 2813)

TRANSFER AGENT(S): First Chicago Trust Company of New York, Jersey City, NJ.

NYSE SYMBOL ACV
Rec. Pr. 26 5/16 (5/31/00)

ALBERTO-CULVER COMPANY

YIELD 1.1%
P/E RATIO 16.9

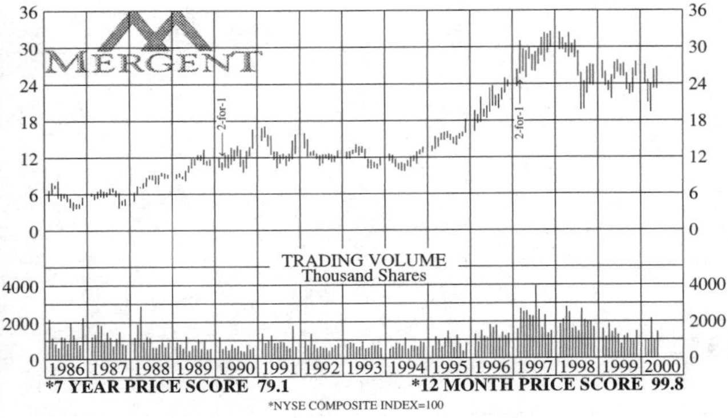
MERGENT
2-for-1
2-for-1
TRADING VOLUME
Thousand Shares
1986 1987 1988 1989 1990 1991 1992 1993 1994 1995 1996 1997 1998 1999 2000
*7 YEAR PRICE SCORE 79.1
*12 MONTH PRICE SCORE 99.8
*NYSE COMPOSITE INDEX=100

INTERIM EARNINGS (Per Share):

Qtr.	Dec.	Mar.	June	Sept.
1995-96	0.23	0.26	0.29	0.34
1996-97	0.47	0.31	0.33	0.38
1997-98	0.32	0.32	0.35	0.38
1998-99	0.32	0.35	0.40	0.44
1999-00	0.37	...	...	...

INTERIM DIVIDENDS (Per Share):

Amt.	Decl.	Ex.	Rec.	Pay.
0.065Q	4/22/99	4/29/99	5/03/99	5/20/99
0.065Q	7/22/99	7/29/99	8/02/99	8/20/99
0.065Q	10/27/99	11/04/99	11/08/99	11/20/99
0.075Q	1/27/00	2/03/00	2/07/00	2/21/00
0.075Q	4/27/00	5/04/00	5/08/00	5/20/00

Indicated div.: $0.30

CAPITALIZATION (9/30/99):

	($000)	(%)
Long-Term Debt	225,173	27.2
Deferred Income Tax	33,833	4.1
Common & Surplus	568,820	68.7
Total	827,826	100.0

DIVIDEND ACHIEVER STATUS:
Rank: 134 10-Year Growth Rate: 11.19%
Total Years of Dividend Growth: 15

RECENT DEVELOPMENTS: For the quarter ended 12/31/99, net income increased 44.1% to $26.8 million compared with $18.6 million in the prior-year quarter. Results for the current quarter included a non-recurring gain of $6.0 million from the sale of ACV's European trademark owned by its Indola professional business. Net sales were $525.8 million, up 13.2% from $464.6 million in the previous year.

PROSPECTS: Going forward, the Company will continue to focus on expanding its beauty systems group through acquisitions, new product lines, new store openings and sales force expansions. Meanwhile, results should benefit from strong growth in the Company's packaged goods business, driven primarily by the ALBERTO VO5, ST. IVES SWISS FORMULA and TRESEMME brands.

BUSINESS

ALBERTO-CULVER COMPANY and its consolidated subsidiaries operates in three principal business segments. The Company's consumer products business includes two segments, Alberto-Culver North America and Alberto-Culver International, which are engaged in developing, manufacturing, distributing and marketing branded consumer products worldwide. Alberto-Culver North America includes ACV's consumer products in the U.S. and Canada, while Alberto-Culver International sells consumer products in more than 120 other countries. ACV's third segment, Specialty Distribution - Sally, consists of Sally Beauty Company, a specialty distributor of professional beauty supplies with 2,203 stores as of 12/31/99 in the United States, Germany, the United Kingdom, Canada and Japan. Name brands sold by the Company include ALBERTO VO5 hair care products and ST. IVES SWISS FORMULA hair and skin products.

ANNUAL FINANCIAL DATA

	9/30/99	9/30/98	9/30/97	9/30/96	9/30/95	9/30/94	9/30/93
Earnings Per Share	**1.51**	**1.37**	**[1] 1.49**	**[1] 1.11**	**0.95**	**0.79**	**0.72**
Cash Flow Per Share	**2.25**	**1.94**	**2.17**	**1.70**	**1.39**	**1.16**	**1.06**
Tang. Book Val. Per Share	**5.81**	**5.75**	**5.57**	**4.33**	**5.08**	**4.93**	**4.36**
Dividends Per Share	**0.26**	**0.24**	**0.20**	**0.18**	**0.16**	**0.14**	**0.13**
Dividend Payout %	**17.2**	**17.5**	**13.4**	**16.2**	**16.9**	**17.8**	**18.1**
INCOME STATEMENT (IN MILLIONS):							
Total Revenues	1,975.9	1,834.7	1,775.3	1,590.4	1,358.2	1,216.1	1,148.0
Costs & Expenses	1,787.3	1,655.6	1,607.6	1,445.4	1,242.8	1,118.3	1,056.0
Depreciation & Amort.	42.2	38.1	38.9	32.9	24.7	20.9	19.6
Operating Income	146.5	141.0	128.7	112.1	90.8	76.9	72.5
Net Interest Inc./(Exp.)	d12.7	d8.6	d8.2	d12.1	d6.5	d5.9	d7.3
Income Before Income Taxes	133.8	132.4	136.1	100.0	84.2	71.1	65.1
Income Taxes	47.5	49.3	50.7	37.3	31.6	27.0	23.9
Net Income	86.3	83.1	[1] 85.4	[1] 62.7	52.7	44.1	41.3
Cash Flow	128.5	121.2	124.4	95.7	77.3	65.0	60.9
Average Shs. Outstg. (000)	57,162	62,420	57,202	56,426	55,698	56,084	57,360
BALANCE SHEET (IN MILLIONS):							
Cash & Cash Equivalents	57.8	73.3	87.6	71.6	147.0	50.4	73.9
Total Current Assets	645.6	591.6	580.3	512.7	536.5	401.8	401.0
Net Property	238.8	223.5	191.0	175.9	157.8	132.9	124.4
Total Assets	1,184.5	1,068.2	1,000.1	909.3	815.1	610.2	593.0
Total Current Liabilities	336.4	313.6	311.3	286.6	234.8	216.0	195.9
Long-Term Obligations	225.2	171.8	149.4	161.5	183.1	43.0	80.2
Net Stockholders' Equity	568.8	534.0	497.0	425.1	370.9	327.0	298.9
Net Working Capital	309.2	277.9	269.0	226.1	301.7	185.7	205.1
Year-end Shs. Outstg. (000)	55,726	57,210	56,142	55,630	55,458	55,360	56,730
STATISTICAL RECORD:							
Operating Profit Margin %	7.4	7.2	7.3	7.0	6.7	6.3	6.3
Net Profit Margin %	4.4	4.5	4.8	3.9	3.9	3.6	3.6
Return on Equity %	15.2	15.6	17.2	14.8	14.2	13.5	13.8
Return on Assets %	7.3	7.8	8.5	6.9	6.5	7.2	7.0
Debt/Total Assets %	19.0	16.1	14.9	17.8	22.5	7.0	13.5
Price Range	27 7/8-21 9/16	32 7/16-19 3/4	32 9/16-23 9/16	25-16 1/4	18 1/4-12 15/16	13 11/16-9 11/16	14 1/8-10 1/16
P/E Ratio	18.5-14.3	23.7-14.4	21.9-15.8	22.5-14.6	19.3-13.7	17.4-12.3	19.6-14.0
Average Yield %	1.1	0.9	0.7	0.9	1.0	1.2	1.1

Statistics are as originally reported. Adj. for stk. splits: 2-for-1, 2/97. [1] Incl. non-recurr. credit 97, $15.6 mill., 96, $9.8 mill.

OFFICERS:
L. H. Lavin, Chmn.
B. E. Lavin, Vice-Chmn., Sec., Treas.
C. L. Bernick, Vice-Chmn., Asst. Sec.
H. B. Bernick, Pres., C.E.O.

INVESTOR CONTACT: Daniel B. Stone, Vice President, (708) 450-3005

PRINCIPAL OFFICE: 2525 Armitage Ave., Melrose Park, IL 60160-1163

TELEPHONE NUMBER: (708) 450-3000
FAX: (708) 450-3419
WEB: www.alberto.com

NO. OF EMPLOYEES: 8,000 full-time (approx.); 5,400 part-time (approx.)

SHAREHOLDERS: 1,014 (cl. A com.); 1,029, (cl. B com.).

ANNUAL MEETING: In Jan.

INCORPORATED: DE, Jan., 1961

INSTITUTIONAL HOLDINGS:
No. of Institutions: 128
Shares Held: 11,360,462
% Held: 34.5

INDUSTRY: Toilet preparations (SIC: 2844)

TRANSFER AGENT(S): EquiServe L.P., Boston, MA.

NYSE SYMBOL ABS
Rec. Pr. 36⅝ (5/31/00)

ALBERTSON'S, INC.

YIELD 2.1%
P/E RATIO 36.6

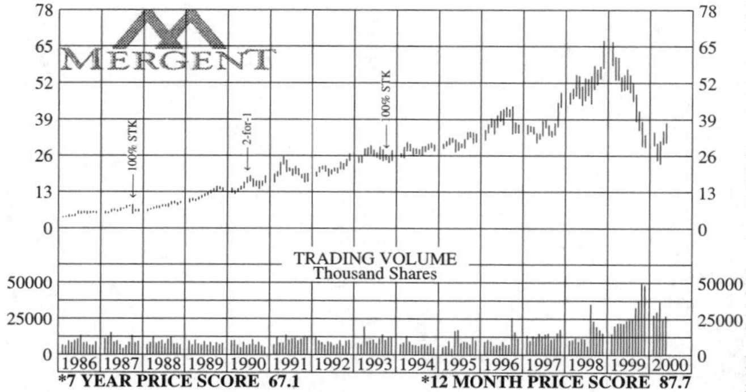

MERGENT
78
65
52
39
26
13
0
100% STK
2-for-1
100% STK
TRADING VOLUME
Thousand Shares
50000
25000
0
1986 1987 1988 1989 1990 1991 1992 1993 1994 1995 1996 1997 1998 1999 2000

*7 YEAR PRICE SCORE 67.1 *12 MONTH PRICE SCORE 87.7

*NYSE COMPOSITE INDEX=100

INTERIM EARNINGS (Per Share):

Qtr.	Apr.	July	Oct.	Jan.
1996-97	0.45	0.48	0.42	0.61
1997-98	0.44	0.44	0.50	0.71
1998-99	0.45	0.52	0.56	0.77
1999-00	0.56	d0.49	0.31	0.62

INTERIM DIVIDENDS (Per Share):

Amt.	Decl.	Ex.	Rec.	Pay.
0.18Q	5/27/99	7/13/99	7/15/99	7/30/99
0.18Q	8/31/99	10/13/99	10/15/99	11/10/99
0.18Q	11/30/99	1/12/00	1/14/00	2/10/00
0.19Q	3/17/00	4/12/00	4/14/00	5/10/00

Indicated div.: $0.76 (Div. Reinv. Plan)

CAPITALIZATION (2/3/00):

	($000)	(%)
Long-Term Debt	4,805,000	44.7
Capital Lease Obligations	187,000	1.7
Deferred Income Tax	52,000	0.5
Common & Surplus	5,702,000	53.1
Total	10,746,000	100.0

DIVIDEND ACHIEVER STATUS:
Rank: 75 10-Year Growth Rate: 14.40%
Total Years of Dividend Growth: 28

RECENT DEVELOPMENTS: For the 53 weeks ended 2/3/00, earnings before an extraordinary charge totaled $427.4 million compared with net earnings of $800.9 million in the corresponding 52-week period the year before. Results in the recent period included one-time pre-tax charges of $689.0 million, while prior-year results included one-time pre-tax charges totaling $219.7 million. Sales grew 4.5% to $37.48 billion from $35.87 billion a year earlier.

PROSPECTS: Going forward, the Company plans to slow its integration efforts. ABS will focus on integrating the Acme chain during the second quarter and the Jewel stores in the first quarter of 2001. Meanwhile, the Company is enjoying higher-than-expected cost savings from its acquisition of American Stores. During the fourth quarter, ABS achieved synergies of $60.0 million, exceeding the Company's estimate of approximately $25.0 million.

BUSINESS

ALBERTSON'S, INC. is one of the largest retail food-drug chains in the United States operating nearly 2,500 stores in 37 states under three different formats: combination food-drug, conventional, and warehouse. Combination food-drug units, ranging between 35,000 sq. ft. and 82,000 sq. ft., consist of grocery, general merchandise, and meat and produce departments, along with pharmacy, lobby/video, floral, and bakery service departments. The Company's stores are operated under the Albertson's, Jewel Osco, Acme Markets, Sav-on and Osco Drug banners, while warehouse stores are operated primarily under the ''Max Food and Drug'' banner. Retail operations are supported by 12 Company-owned distribution centers. On 6/23/99, the Company acquired American Stores Company.

QUARTERLY DATA

(2/3/00)($000)	Rev	Inc
1st Quarter	9,215,000	238,000
2nd Quarter	9,381,000	(228,000)
3rd Quarter	8,983,000	130,000
4th Quarter	9,899,000	264,000

ANNUAL FINANCIAL DATA

	[4] 2/3/00	1/28/99	1/29/98	1/30/97	2/1/96	2/2/95	2/3/94
Earnings Per Share	**[3] 1.00**	**[2] 2.30**	**2.08**	**1.96**	**1.84**	**[1] 1.65**	**1.34**
Cash Flow Per Share	**3.17**	**3.82**	**3.40**	**3.13**	**2.83**	**2.54**	**2.11**
Tang. Book Val. Per Share	**9.72**	**10.84**	**9.85**	**8.96**	**7.75**	**6.65**	**5.48**
Dividends Per Share	**0.71**	**0.67**	**0.63**	**0.58**	**0.50**	**0.42**	**0.35**
Dividend Payout %	**71.0**	**29.1**	**30.3**	**29.6**	**27.2**	**25.5**	**26.1**
INCOME STATEMENT (IN MILLIONS):							
Total Revenues	37,478.0	16,005.1	14,689.5	13,776.7	12,585.0	11,894.6	11,283.7
Costs & Expenses	35,326.0	14,656.6	13,469.1	12,632.8	11,526.4	10,925.0	10,448.2
Depreciation & Amort.	912.0	375.4	328.8	294.3	251.5	226.5	196.4
Operating Income	1,240.0	973.2	891.7	849.6	807.2	743.1	639.0
Net Interest Inc./(Exp.)	d353.0	d107.1	d82.6	d64.6	d55.6	d62.1	d51.0
Income Before Income Taxes	899.0	894.8	826.9	794.8	758.5	678.7	552.2
Income Taxes	472.0	327.7	310.1	301.1	293.5	261.3	212.5
Net Income	[3] 427.0	[2] 567.2	516.8	493.8	465.0	[1] 417.4	339.7
Cash Flow	1,339.0	942.5	845.6	788.1	716.4	643.8	536.1
Average Shs. Outstg. (000)	423,000	246,808	248,497	251,710	253,080	253,633	254,227
BALANCE SHEET (IN MILLIONS):							
Cash & Cash Equivalents	231.0	80.6	108.1	90.9	69.1	50.2	62.5
Total Current Assets	4,582.0	1,833.9	1,627.9	1,475.9	1,283.0	1,189.6	1,122.2
Net Property	8,913.0	3,974.0	3,383.4	3,054.6	2,697.5	2,309.4	2,081.9
Total Assets	15,701.0	6,234.0	5,218.6	4,714.6	4,135.9	3,621.7	3,294.9
Total Current Liabilities	4,055.0	1,378.8	1,275.5	1,055.1	1,088.5	1,095.4	990.1
Long-Term Obligations	4,992.0	1,684.5	1,130.6	1,051.8	732.3	512.3	665.0
Net Stockholders' Equity	5,702.0	2,810.5	2,419.5	2,247.0	1,952.5	1,687.9	1,389.4
Net Working Capital	527.0	455.1	352.3	420.8	194.5	94.2	132.2
Year-end Shs. Outstg. (000)	424,000	245,697	245,736	250,690	251,919	253,984	253,407
STATISTICAL RECORD:							
Operating Profit Margin %	3.3	6.1	6.1	6.2	6.4	6.2	5.7
Net Profit Margin %	1.1	3.5	3.5	3.6	3.7	3.5	3.0
Return on Equity %	7.5	20.2	21.4	22.0	23.8	24.7	24.4
Return on Assets %	2.7	9.1	9.9	10.5	11.2	11.5	10.3
Debt/Total Assets %	31.8	27.0	21.7	22.3	17.7	14.1	20.2
Price Range	66⅝-29	67⅛-44	48⅝-30½	43¾-31½	34⅝-27¼	30⅞-25⅛	29¹¹⁄₁₆-23⅜
P/E Ratio	66.6-29.0	29.2-19.1	23.4-14.7	22.3-16.1	18.8-14.8	18.7-15.2	22.2-17.4
Average Yield %	1.5	1.2	1.6	1.5	1.6	1.5	1.3

Statistics are as originally reported. [1] Bef. $17 mil ($0.07/sh) chg. for acctg. adj. [2] Incl. $24.4 mil pre-tax impairment chg. for store closures. [3] Bef. $23.3 mil ($0.05/sh) extraord. chg. & incl. one-time pre-tax chgs. totaling $689.0 mil related to the acq. of American Stores Company and a litigation settlement. [4] Refl. acquis. of American Stores Co. in 6/99.

OFFICERS:
G. G. Michael, Chmn., C.E.O.
P. Lynch, Pres., C.O.O.
A. C. Olson, Exec. V.P., C.F.O.
T. R. Saldin, Exec. V.P., Gen. Couns.

INVESTOR CONTACT: A. Craig Olson, Exec. V.P. & C.F.O., (208) 395-6284

PRINCIPAL OFFICE: 250 Parkcenter Blvd., P.O. Box 20, Boise, ID 83726

TELEPHONE NUMBER: (208) 395-6200
FAX: (208) 395-6777
WEB: www.albertsons.com

NO. OF EMPLOYEES: 235,000 (approx.)

SHAREHOLDERS: 32,000 (approx.)

ANNUAL MEETING: In May

INCORPORATED: DE, Apr., 1969

INSTITUTIONAL HOLDINGS:
No. of Institutions: 463
Shares Held: 276,912,071
% Held: 65.4

INDUSTRY: Grocery stores (SIC: 5411)

TRANSFER AGENT(S): ChaseMellon Shareholder Services, L.L.C., Ridgefield Park, NJ

ALFA CORPORATION

YIELD	3.1%
P/E RATIO	10.6

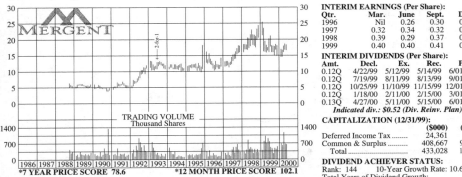

INTERIM EARNINGS (Per Share):

Qtr.	Mar.	June	Sept.	Dec.
1996	Nil	0.26	0.30	0.22
1997	0.32	0.34	0.32	0.30
1998	0.39	0.29	0.37	0.33
1999	0.40	0.40	0.41	0.39

INTERIM DIVIDENDS (Per Share):

Amt.	Decl.	Ex.	Rec.	Pay.
0.12Q	4/22/99	5/12/99	5/14/99	6/01/99
0.12Q	7/19/99	8/11/99	8/13/99	9/01/99
0.12Q	10/25/99	11/10/99	11/15/99	12/01/99
0.12Q	1/18/00	2/11/00	2/15/00	3/01/00
0.13Q	4/27/00	5/11/00	5/15/00	6/01/00

Indicated div.: $0.52 (Div. Reinv. Plan)

CAPITALIZATION (12/31/99):

	($000)	(%)
Deferred Income Tax	24,361	5.6
Common & Surplus	408,667	94.4
Total	433,028	100.0

DIVIDEND ACHIEVER STATUS:

Rank: 144   10-Year Growth Rate: 10.60%
Total Years of Dividend Growth: 14

RECENT DEVELOPMENTS: For the year ended 12/31/99, net income increased 13.8% to $64.6 million from $56.7 million in the previous year. Earnings growth reflected the continuation of favorable weather and an industry-wide improvement in automobile loss ratios. Total revenues amounted to $482.3 million, up 4.6% from $461.0 million the year before. Total premiums and policy charges grew 3.4% to $405.3 million from $391.8 million due to increased production and and an improved lapse ratio. Net

investment income amounted to $67.8 million, up 8.5% compared with $62.5 million in 1998 primarily due to an increase in invested assets resulting from positive cash flow. Realized investment gains jumped 15.1% to $5.1 million from $4.4 million a year earlier. On 4/3/00, the Company completed the acquisition of the leasing portfolio and assets of OFC Capital, an Atlanta-based business unit of First Liberty Bank for approximately $23.1 million.

BUSINESS

ALFA CORPORATION is a financial services holding company with approximately $1.42 billion in assets as of 3/31/00. The Company and its subsidiaries together with Alfa Mutual Companies comprise the Alfa Group. Alfa's primary business is personal lines of property and casualty insurance and life insurance. Alfa's subsidiaries write life insurance in Alabama, Georgia and Mississippi and casualty insurance in Georgia and Mississippi. The Company's noninsurance subsidiaries are engaged in consumer financing, leasing, real estate investments, residential and commercial construction and real estate sales.

ANNUAL FINANCIAL DATA

	12/31/99	12/31/98	12/31/97	12/31/96	12/31/95	12/31/94	12/31/93
Earnings Per Share	1.60	1.38	1.29	0.79	0.55	0.81	[1] 1.04
Tang. Book Val. Per Share	10.33	10.63	9.65	7.93	7.57	6.25	6.40
Dividends Per Share	0.47	0.44	0.40	0.39	0.38	0.34	0.28
Dividend Payout %	29.5	31.7	30.8	49.0	68.2	42.3	26.9
INCOME STATEMENT (IN MILLIONS):							
Total Premium Income	405.3	391.8	371.0	337.2	308.1	247.1	212.6
Net Investment Income	67.8	62.5	57.5	54.2	50.9	44.3	43.6
Other Income	9.1	6.6	5.5	5.0	3.8	3.6	7.8
Total Revenues	482.3	461.0	434.0	396.3	362.8	295.0	264.0
Policyholder Benefits	281.7	277.9	266.1	267.3	249.6	182.6	147.3
Income Before Income Taxes	92.1	83.3	76.8	45.9	31.0	47.8	63.3
Income Taxes	27.5	26.5	24.0	13.7	8.7	15.0	21.0
Net Income	64.6	56.7	52.8	32.2	22.3	32.9	[1] 42.3
Average Shs. Outstg. (000)	40,236	41,148	40,931	40,787	40,786	40,786	40,786
BALANCE SHEET (IN MILLIONS):							
Cash & Cash Equivalents	60.0	60.6	30.9	44.6	34.3	36.5	58.0
Premiums Due	13.0	23.4	11.5	9.5	13.8	9.0	14.0
Invst. Assets: Fixed-term	813.9	775.8	733.6	613.1	576.1	478.3	420.8
Invst. Assets: Equities	113.2	103.1	116.1	96.0	89.0	71.8	87.7
Invst. Assets: Loans	43.1	39.0	35.5	32.5	30.1	26.7	24.3
Invst. Assets: Total	1,155.2	1,084.1	1,027.7	886.0	841.1	718.1	653.8
Total Assets	1,335.3	1,246.7	1,170.1	1,019.3	965.4	846.4	766.1
Net Stockholders' Equity	408.7	423.6	382.9	323.3	308.6	255.0	261.0
Year-end Shs. Outstg. (000)	39,542	39,868	39,688	40,787	40,786	40,786	40,786
STATISTICAL RECORD:							
Return on Revenues %	13.4	12.3	12.2	8.1	6.2	11.1	16.0
Return on Equity %	15.8	13.4	13.8	10.0	7.2	12.9	16.2
Return on Assets %	4.8	4.5	4.5	3.2	2.3	3.9	5.5
Price Range	25⅜-14¹³⁄₁₆	24⅜-16	18⅛-11¼	16¼-10¼	18¼-9¾	12½-10	13⅜-10⅜
P/E Ratio	15.9-9.3	17.7-11.6	14.0-8.7	20.6-13.0	33.2-17.7	15.4-12.3	12.9-10.0
Average Yield %	2.4	2.2	2.7	2.9	2.7	3.0	2.4

Statistics are as originally reported. Adj. for stk. splits: 2-for-1, 6/2/93 [1] Bef. acctg. change credit $2.6 mill. ($0.06/sh.)

OFFICERS:
J. A. Newby, Chmn., Pres.
D. Price, Sr. V.P., C.F.O.
C. L. Ellis, Exec. V.P., Treas.
A. Scott, Sr. V.P., Sec., Gen. Couns.

INVESTOR CONTACT: John D. Holley, (334) 288-3900

PRINCIPAL OFFICE: 2108 E. South Blvd., Montgomery, AL 36116

TELEPHONE NUMBER: (334) 288-3900
FAX: (334) 288-0905
WEB: www.alfains.com

NO. OF EMPLOYEES: 477

SHAREHOLDERS: 3,700 (approx.)

ANNUAL MEETING: In Apr.

INCORPORATED: DE, 1974

INSTITUTIONAL HOLDINGS:
No. of Institutions: 39
Shares Held: 3,208,934
% Held: 8.1

INDUSTRY: Fire, marine, and casualty insurance (SIC: 6331)

TRANSFER AGENT(S): The Bank of New York, New York, NY

ALLIANCE CAPITAL MANAGEMENT HOLDING L.P.

YIELD 6.6%
P/E RATIO 17.8

INTERIM EARNINGS (Per Share):				
Qtr.	Mar.	June	Sept.	Dec.
1996	0.54	0.55	0.57	0.61
1997	0.31	d0.38	0.38	0.42
1998	0.39	0.43	0.40	0.44
1999	0.55	0.55	0.57	0.86

INTERIM DIVIDENDS (Per Share):				
Amt.	Decl.	Ex.	Rec.	Pay.
0.54Q	4/28/99	5/13/99	5/17/99	5/24/99
0.54Q	7/29/99	8/05/99	8/09/99	8/16/99
0.56Q	10/18/99	10/26/99	10/28/99	11/15/99
0.85Q	1/13/00	1/28/00	2/01/00	2/14/00
0.74Q	4/28/00	5/04/00	5/08/00	5/18/00
		Indicated div.: $2.96		

TRADING VOLUME
Thousand Shares

*7 YEAR PRICE SCORE 125.5   *12 MONTH PRICE SCORE 126.7
*NYSE COMPOSITE INDEX=100

CAPITALIZATION (12/31/99):		
	($000)	(%)
Common & Surplus	265,608	100.0
Total	265,608	100.0

DIVIDEND ACHIEVER STATUS:
Rank: 28   10-Year Growth Rate: 18.71%
Total Years of Dividend Growth: 11

RECENT DEVELOPMENTS

For the year ended 12/31/99, net income improved 30.7% to $382.8 million compared with $292.9 million in the preceding year. Total revenues increased 12.6% to $1.49 billion from $1.32 billion in the previous year. The increase in revenues was attributed to strong mutual fund sales coupled with robust sales through financial planners, U.S. banks and non-U.S. distribution channels led by sales of EPTA Funds distributed in Italy. In addition, the Company raised over $12.00 billion in new client account assets. Revenues from Alliance mutual funds climbed 11.9% to $658.6 million versus $588.4 million in the prior year. Distribution revenues jumped 17.3% to $354.2 million. Expense increased 7.1% to $1.04 billion from $975.3 million a year earlier. Income before taxes jumped 28.0% to $446.5 million compared with $348.7 million in the preceding year.

BUSINESS

ALLIANCE CAPITAL MANAGEMENT HOLDING L.P. (formerly Alliance Capital Management L.P.) is a major global investment management firm with over $368.00 billion in assets under management as of 12/31/99. AC manages retirement assets for many of the largest U.S. public and private employee benefit plans, for public employee retirement funds in 31 out of the 50 U.S. states, and for foundations, endowments, banks, and insurance companies worldwide. AC is one of America's largest mutual fund sponsors, with a diverse family of fund portfolios and approximately 5.0 million shareholder accounts at 12/31/99. As of 12/31/99, the Company owned approximately 42.0% of the outstanding Alliance Capital units, which are units of limited interest in Alliance Capital Management L.P. In 10/99, the Company reorganized by transferring its business to Alliance Capital Management L.P., a newly-formed operating partnership, in exchange for Alliance Capital units.

ANNUAL FINANCIAL DATA

	12/31/99	12/31/98	12/31/97	12/31/96	12/31/95	12/31/94	12/31/93
Earnings Per Share	2.53	1.66	①0.74	1.14	0.95	0.85	②0.48
Cash Flow Per Share	3.35	2.41	1.29	1.60	1.37	1.29	0.83
Tang. Book Val. Per Share	3.68	1.93	1.78	1.44	1.99	1.79	1.27
Dividends Per Share	2.07	1.60	1.28	1.05	0.86	0.82	0.71
Dividend Payout %	81.8	96.4	173.6	92.5	91.5	96.5	149.4
INCOME STATEMENT (IN MILLIONS):							
Total Revenues	1,491.2	1,324.1	975.3	788.5	639.3	601.0	499.5
Costs & Expenses	875.3	838.4	610.9	502.1	403.7	383.9	317.8
Depreciation & Amort.	152.6	129.4	92.8	76.9	67.4	67.7	50.5
Operating Income	463.2	356.3	271.6	209.5	168.2	149.4	131.2
Net Interest Inc./(Exp.)	d16.7	d7.6	d3.0	d1.9	d1.2	d7.6	d10.3
Income Before Income Taxes	446.5	348.7	147.8	207.6	167.0	141.8	80.1
Income Taxes	63.6	55.8	18.8	14.2	11.6	8.3	11.5
Net Income	382.8	292.9	①129.0	193.3	155.4	133.5	②68.7
Cash Flow	535.5	422.3	221.7	270.2	222.7	201.2	119.2
Average Shs. Outstg. (000)	159,673	175,143	171,876	168,968	163,116	155,882	144,170
BALANCE SHEET (IN MILLIONS):							
Cash & Cash Equivalents	...	169.9	110.9	93.4	159.6	102.0	152.9
Total Current Assets	1.9	502.0	319.3	233.7	271.9	204.8	344.3
Net Property	...	96.4	80.5	57.5	44.2	43.8	28.8
Total Assets	272.1	1,132.6	784.5	725.9	575.1	518.4	561.3
Total Current Liabilities	6.5	509.2	291.8	210.5	164.9	133.2	237.8
Long-Term Obligations	...	190.2	90.4	24.7	3.5	3.9	109.4
Net Stockholders' Equity	265.6	430.3	398.1	476.0	406.7	381.3	214.0
Net Working Capital	d4.6	d7.2	27.5	23.2	107.0	71.6	106.5
Year-end Shs. Outstg. (000)	72,260	170,366	168,976	167,566	162,320	161,108	144,372
STATISTICAL RECORD:							
Operating Profit Margin %	31.1	26.9	27.8	26.6	26.3	24.9	26.3
Net Profit Margin %	25.7	22.1	13.2	24.5	24.3	22.2	13.8
Return on Equity %	144.1	68.1	32.4	40.6	38.2	35.0	32.1
Return on Assets %	140.7	25.9	16.4	26.6	27.0	25.8	12.2
Debt/Total Assets %	...	16.8	11.5	3.4	0.6	0.7	19.5
Price Range	34-24⅛	29-18¾	19¹³⁄₁₆-12	14⅝-10¹¹⁄₁₆	11⅝-7¹¹⁄₁₆	13⁹⁄₁₆-8¼	13¹³⁄₁₆-8⅜
P/E Ratio	13.4-9.5	17.5-11.3	26.7-16.2	12.9-9.4	12.3-8.1	16.0-9.7	29.1-17.6
Average Yield %	7.1	6.7	8.1	8.3	9.0	7.5	6.4

Statistics are as originally reported. Adj. for stk. splits: 2-for-1, 4/2/98. ① Incl. $120.9 mill. reduction in value of intangible assets. ② Incl. non-recurr. chrg. $40.8 mill.; bef. acctg. change credit $900,000.

OFFICERS:
D. H. Williams, Chmn.
B. W. Calvert, Vice-Chmn., C.E.O.
A. Harrison, Vice-Chmn.
J. D. Carifa, Pres., C.O.O.

INVESTOR CONTACT: Charlotte M. Fox, Manager, Investor Relations

PRINCIPAL OFFICE: 1345 Avenue of The Americas, New York, NY 10105

TELEPHONE NUMBER: (212) 969-1000
FAX: (212) 887-2245
WEB: www.alliancecapital.com

NO. OF EMPLOYEES: 2,396 (avg.)

SHAREHOLDERS: 1,659

ANNUAL MEETING: In Dec.

INCORPORATED: DE, Nov., 1987

INSTITUTIONAL HOLDINGS:
No. of Institutions: 133
Shares Held: 10,163,916
% Held: 5.9

INDUSTRY: Investment advice (SIC: 6282)

TRANSFER AGENT(S): First Chicago Trust Company of New York, Jersey City, NJ

NYSE SYMBOL AT
Rec. Pr. 65 5/8 (5/31/00)

ALLTEL CORPORATION

YIELD 2.0%
P/E RATIO 26.7

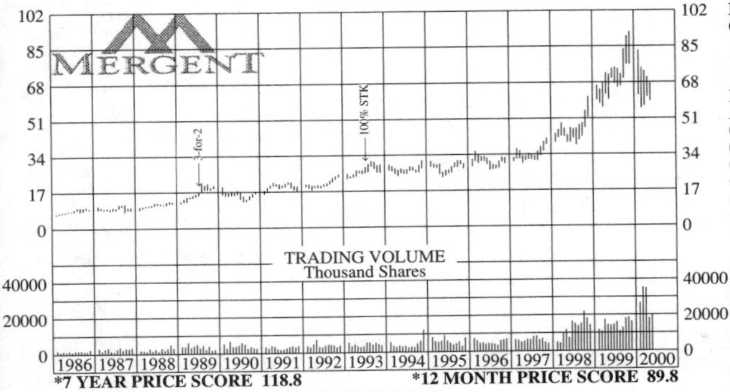

*7 YEAR PRICE SCORE 118.8 *12 MONTH PRICE SCORE 89.8

*NYSE COMPOSITE INDEX=100

INTERIM EARNINGS (Per Share):

Qtr.	Mar.	June	Sept.	Dec.
1997	0.54	0.92	0.65	0.59
1998	0.66	1.06	0.57	0.55
1999	0.59	0.67	0.47	0.73

INTERIM DIVIDENDS (Per Share):

Amt.	Decl.	Ex.	Rec.	Pay.
0.305Q	4/22/99	6/07/99	6/09/99	7/06/99
0.305Q	7/22/99	9/08/99	9/10/99	10/04/99
0.32Q	10/28/99	12/07/99	12/09/99	1/03/00
0.32Q	1/27/00	2/24/00	2/28/00	4/03/00
0.32Q	4/20/00	6/07/00	6/09/00	7/03/00

Indicated div.: $1.28 (Div. Reinv. Plan)

CAPITALIZATION (12/31/99):

	($000)	(%)
Long-Term Debt	3,750,413	41.6
Deferred Income Tax	1,056,921	11.7
Redeemable Pfd. Stock	1,491	0.0
Preferred Stock	562	0.0
Common & Surplus	4,205,175	46.6
Total	9,014,562	100.0

DIVIDEND ACHIEVER STATUS:
Rank: 205 10-Year Growth Rate: 7.81%
Total Years of Dividend Growth: 39

RECENT DEVELOPMENTS: For the twelve months ended 12/31/99, net income rose 29.9% to $783.6 million. Results for 1999 and 1998 included merger and integration expenses and other charges and a provision to reduce the carrying value of certain assets of $90.5 million and $307.0 million, respectively. Results also included a gain of $43.1 million in 1999 and $292.7 million in 1998 for the disposal of assets. Revenues and sales rose 12.0% to $6.30 billion.

PROSPECTS: On 1/10/00, AT announced that it will provide local telephone service in 17 cities in seven states during 2000. By the end of 2000, AT expects to have local telephone service in 43 cities in the Southeast and Midwest. On 2/10/99, AT announced the formation of five operating regions. The regions will be located in Charlotte, NC, Cleveland, OH, Little Rock, AR, Phoenix, AR, and Tampa, FL.

BUSINESS

ALLTEL CORPORATION provides wireline and wireless communications and information services to more than 8.0 million customers in 25 states. AT owns subsidiaries that provide wireless and wireline local, long-distance, network access and Internet services, wide-area paging service and information processing management services and advanced application software. ALLTEL Communications Products, Inc. operates nine warehouses and 23 counter-sales showrooms across the U.S. and is a major distributor of telecommunications equipment and materials. ALLTEL Communications Products supplies equipment to affiliated and non-affiliated communications companies, business systems suppliers, railroads, governments, and retail and industrial companies. On 7/2/99, the Company completed its acquisition of Aliant Communications Inc. for $1.80 billion.

ANNUAL FINANCIAL DATA

	12/31/99	12/31/98	12/31/97	12/31/96	12/31/95	12/31/94	12/31/93
Earnings Per Share	[4] **2.47**	[1] **1.89**	[2] **2.70**	[2] **1.53**	**1.86**	[3] **1.43**	**1.39**
Cash Flow Per Share	**5.19**	**4.44**	**5.10**	**3.75**	**4.02**	**3.34**	**2.84**
Tang. Book Val. Per Share	**7.03**	**5.82**	**8.67**	**8.88**	**7.64**	**5.96**	**5.53**
Dividends Per Share	**1.22**	**1.16**	**1.10**	**1.04**	**0.96**	**0.88**	**0.80**
Dividend Payout %	**49.4**	**61.4**	**40.7**	**68.0**	**51.6**	**61.5**	**57.5**
INCOME STATEMENT (IN MILLIONS):							
Total Revenues	6,302.3	5,194.0	3,263.6	3,192.4	3,109.7	2,961.7	2,342.1
Costs & Expenses	3,915.0	3,597.9	2,065.8	2,176.7	2,015.9	1,965.9	1,550.6
Depreciation & Amort.	862.2	707.1	450.8	424.1	409.8	362.0	272.4
Operating Income	1,525.1	889.0	747.0	591.6	684.0	633.9	519.0
Net Interest Inc./(Exp.)	d280.2	d263.7	d130.2	d130.8	d138.2	d137.1	d98.7
Income Before Income Taxes	1,330.9	972.3	828.7	461.4	571.8	436.5	449.9
Income Taxes	547.2	446.9	320.8	169.7	217.2	164.8	187.9
Equity Earnings/Minority Int.	d11.6	12.7	. . .	. . .	d8.7	. . .	. . .
Net Income	[4] 783.6	[1] 525.5	[2] 507.9	[2] 291.7	354.6	[3] 271.8	262.0
Cash Flow	1,644.9	1,231.7	957.6	714.8	763.3	632.5	532.9
Average Shs. Outstg. (000)	316,814	277,276	187,689	190,370	190,072	189,454	187,665
BALANCE SHEET (IN MILLIONS):							
Cash & Cash Equivalents	17.6	55.5	16.2	13.9	21.4	26.1	7.9
Total Current Assets	1,167.2	980.8	665.8	709.5	731.2	692.7	494.1
Net Property	5,734.5	4,828.1	3,190.5	3,041.5	2,972.8	2,963.2	2,676.4
Total Assets	10,774.2	9,374.2	5,633.4	5,359.2	5,073.1	4,713.9	4,270.5
Total Current Liabilities	1,194.0	1,206.5	637.3	590.7	569.3	605.6	608.6
Long-Term Obligations	3,750.4	3,491.8	1,874.2	1,756.1	1,761.6	1,846.2	1,596.0
Net Stockholders' Equity	4,205.7	3,270.9	2,208.5	2,097.1	1,935.6	1,625.4	1,554.7
Net Working Capital	d26.8	d225.7	28.6	118.8	162.0	87.1	d114.4
Year-end Shs. Outstg. (000)	314,258	281,198	183,673	187,200	189,268	187,981	187,458
STATISTICAL RECORD:							
Operating Profit Margin %	24.2	17.1	22.9	18.5	22.0	21.4	22.2
Net Profit Margin %	12.4	10.1	15.6	9.1	11.4	9.2	11.2
Return on Equity %	18.6	16.1	23.0	13.9	18.3	16.7	16.9
Return on Assets %	7.3	5.6	9.0	5.4	7.0	5.8	6.1
Debt/Total Assets %	34.8	37.2	33.3	32.8	34.7	39.2	37.4
Price Range	91 13/16-56 5/16	61 3/8-38 1/4	41 5/8-29 3/4	35 5/8-26 5/8	31 1/8-23 1/4	31 3/8-24	31 1/4-22 7/8
P/E Ratio	37.2-22.8	32.5-20.2	15.4-11.0	23.3-17.4	16.7-12.5	21.9-16.8	22.5-16.5
Average Yield %	1.6	2.3	3.1	3.3	3.5	3.2	3.0

Statistics are as originally reported. Adj. for stk. splits: 2-for-1, 7/93 [1] Incls. one-time pre-tax net chrg. of $10.8 mill. [2] Incls. non-recurr. credit 12/31/97: $189.7 mill.; chrg. 12/31/96: $74.2 mill. [3] Bef. write-dwn. of $32.0 mill on assets. [4] Incls. one-time chrgs. of $90.5 mill.

OFFICERS:
J. T. Ford, Chmn., C.E.O.
D. E. Foster, Vice-Chmn.
S. T. Ford, Pres., C.O.O.

INVESTOR CONTACT: D. A. Powell, V.P., Inv. Rel., (501) 905-8991

PRINCIPAL OFFICE: One Allied Drive, Little Rock, AR 72202

TELEPHONE NUMBER: (501) 905-8000
FAX: (501) 905-8991
WEB: www.alltel.com

NO. OF EMPLOYEES: 24,440 (avg.)

SHAREHOLDERS: 271,000 (approx.)

ANNUAL MEETING: In April

INCORPORATED: OH, Jun., 1960; reincorp., DE, 1990

INSTITUTIONAL HOLDINGS:
No. of Institutions: 502
Shares Held: 165,770,894
% Held: 52.8

INDUSTRY: Telephone communications, exc. radio (SIC: 4813)

TRANSFER AGENT(S): First Union National Bank of North Carolina, Charlotte, NC

AMERICAN GENERAL CORPORATION

YIELD	2.7%
P/E RATIO	14.5

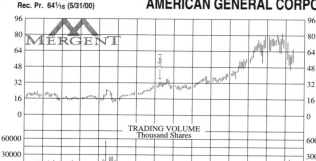

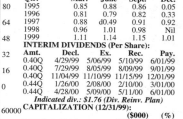

*7 YEAR PRICE SCORE 95.2   *12 MONTH PRICE SCORE 86.6

*NYSE COMPOSITE INDEX=100

INTERIM EARNINGS (Per Share):

Qtr.	Mar.	June	Sept.	Dec.
1995	0.85	0.88	0.86	0.05
1996	0.81	0.79	0.82	0.33
1997	0.88	d0.49	0.91	0.92
1998	0.96	1.01	0.98	Nil
1999	1.11	1.14	1.15	1.01

INTERIM DIVIDENDS (Per Share):

Amt.	Decl.	Ex.	Rec.	Pay.
0.40Q	4/29/99	5/06/99	5/10/99	6/01/99
0.40Q	7/29/99	8/05/99	8/09/99	9/01/99
0.40Q	11/04/99	11/10/99	11/15/99	12/01/99
0.44Q	1/26/00	2/08/00	2/10/00	3/01/00
0.44Q	4/28/00	5/09/00	5/11/00	6/01/00

Indicated div.: $1.76 (Div. Reinv. Plan)

CAPITALIZATION (12/31/99):

	($000)	(%)
Long-Term Debt	13,326,000	61.5
Redeemable Pfd. Stock	1,924,000	8.9
Preferred Stock	85,000	0.4
Common & Surplus	6,335,000	29.2
Total	21,670,000	100.0

DIVIDEND ACHIEVER STATUS:
Rank: 203   10-Year Growth Rate: 7.87%
Total Years of Dividend Growth: 16

RECENT DEVELOPMENTS: For the year ended 12/31/99, net income increased 48.0% to $1.13 billion compared with $764.0 million a year earlier. Results included realized investment losses of $12.0 million and a gain of $4.0 million in 1999 and 1998, respectively. Results also included a non-recurring charge of $36.0 million and $288.0 million in 1999 and 1998, respectively. Total revenues amounted to $10.68 billion versus $10.25 billion the year before.

PROSPECTS: On 3/13/00, AGC acquired the assets of CypressTree Investments Inc., which include the retail mutual fund operation of North American Funds. North American Funds is a sub-advised, multi-manager complex of 16 mutual funds distributed nationwide, with assets of $1 billion. Going forward, the Company should continue to benefit from the strength of its multiple distribution channels coupled with its diverse portfolio of businesses.

BUSINESS

AMERICAN GENERAL CORPORATION, with assets of $115.45 billion at 12/31/99, is one of the nation's largest consumer financial service organizations. It is a provider of retirement annuities, consumer loans, and life insurance. Variable Annuity Life Insurance Co., AGC's retirement annuity company, which contributed 37% of 1999 earnings, is a provider of retirement plans for teachers and other employees of not-for-profit organizations. The consumer finance companies, 15%, offer a wide range of credit-related products and services. The life insurance segment, 48%, emphasizes the sale and service of both traditional and interest-sensitive life insurance and annuities. On June 30, 1997, AGC acquired USLIFE Corp. During 1998, AGC acquired Western National Corp.

ANNUAL FINANCIAL DATA

	12/31/99	③12/31/98	12/31/97	12/31/96	12/31/95	12/31/94	12/31/93
Earnings Per Share	①4.40	①2.96	①2.19	2.75	2.64	2.45	②1.15
Tang. Book Val. Per Share	19.48	28.67	28.07	24.53	25.61	14.09	21.12
Dividends Per Share	1.60	1.50	1.40	1.30	1.24	1.16	1.10
Dividend Payout %	36.4	50.7	63.9	47.3	47.0	47.3	95.6
INCOME STATEMENT (IN MILLIONS)							
Total Premium Income	3,772.0	3,605.0	3,362.0	1,968.0	1,753.0	1,210.0	1,252.0
Net Investment Income	5,232.0	5,095.0	4,020.0	3,271.0	3,095.0	2,493.0	2,437.0
Other Income	1,675.0	1,551.0	1,545.0	1,608.0	1,604.0	1,138.0	1,140.0
Total Revenues	10,679.0	10,251.0	8,927.0	6,887.0	6,495.0	4,841.0	4,829.0
Policyholder Benefits	5,313.0	5,159.0	4,332.0	3,156.0	3,047.0	2,224.0	2,311.0
Income Before Income Taxes	1,887.0	1,323.0	1,073.0	964.0	850.0	802.0	602.0
Income Taxes	664.0	459.0	447.0	347.0	286.0	289.0	352.0
Equity Earnings/Minority Int.	...	d11.0	...	40.0	43.0	...	...
Net Income	①1,131.0	①764.0	①542.0	577.0	545.0	513.0	②250.0
Average Shs. Outstg. (000)	259,200	261,500	249,200	201,000	205,000	209,000	217,000
BALANCE SHEET (IN MILLIONS)							
Cash & Cash Equivalents	970.0	995.0	569.0	309.0	264.0	254.0	73.0
Invst. Assets: Fixed-term	60,625.0	62,731.0	47,747.0	38,490.0	37,213.0	25,700.0	26,479.0
Invst. Assets: Equities	339.0	325.0	116.0	133.0	186.0	224.0	233.0
Invst. Assets: Loans	17,091.0	15,354.0	13,440.0	4,698.0	4,646.0	3,848.0	4,188.0
Invst. Assets: Total	79,365.0	69,863.0	54,589.0	44,805.0	43,311.0	30,971.0	31,876.0
Total Assets	115,447.0	105,107.0	80,620.0	66,254.0	61,153.0	46,295.0	43,982.0
Long-Term Obligations	13,326.0	11,606.0	9,182.0	9,163.0	9,193.0	8,926.0	7,529.0
Net Stockholders' Equity	6,420.0	8,871.0	7,583.0	5,621.0	5,801.0	3,457.0	5,137.0
Year-end Shs. Outstg. (000)	248,100	251,800	243,000	203,000	204,000	203,000	214,000
STATISTICAL RECORD:							
Return on Revenues %	10.6	7.5	6.1	8.4	8.4	10.6	5.2
Return on Equity %	17.6	8.6	7.1	10.3	9.4	14.8	4.9
Return on Assets %	1.0	0.7	0.7	0.9	0.9	1.1	0.6
Price Range	82³/₁₆-61⁷/₈	79-52⁵/₁₆	56¹/₄-36¹/₂	41³/₄-32⁷/₈	39¹/₈-27¹/₂	30¹/₂-24⁷/₈	36¹/₂-26¹/₄
P/E Ratio	18.7-14.1	26.7-17.7	25.7-16.7	15.2-12.0	14.8-10.4	12.4-10.2	31.7-22.8
Average Yield %	2.2	2.3	3.0	3.5	3.7	4.2	3.5

Statistics are as originally reported. ① Incl. non-recurr. chrg. 1999, $36.0 mill.; 1998, $56.0 mill.; 1997, $435.0 mill. ② Bef. acctg. change chrg. $46.0 mill. ③ Includes results of Western National Corporation, acquired on 2/25/98.

OFFICERS:
R. M. Devlin, Chmn., Pres., C.E.O.
J. A. Graf, Vice-Chmn.
J. P. Newton, Vice-Chmn.

INVESTOR CONTACT: Investor Relations, (800) 242-1111

PRINCIPAL OFFICE: 2929 Allen Parkway, Houston, TX 77019-2155

TELEPHONE NUMBER: (713) 242-1111
FAX: (713) 523-8531
WEB: www.agc.com
NO. OF EMPLOYEES: 15,800 (approx.)
SHAREHOLDERS: 36,129 (of record); 85,000 (beneficial, approx.)
ANNUAL MEETING: In Apr.
INCORPORATED: TX, July, 1980

INSTITUTIONAL HOLDINGS:
No. of Institutions: 461
Shares Held: 180,689,776
% Held: 73.1

INDUSTRY: Life insurance (SIC: 6311)

TRANSFER AGENT(S): First Chicago Trust Company of New York, Jersey City, NJ

NYSE SYMBOL AM
Rec. Pr. 18⅝ (5/31/00)

AMERICAN GREETINGS CORPORATION

YIELD 4.3%
P/E RATIO 13.6

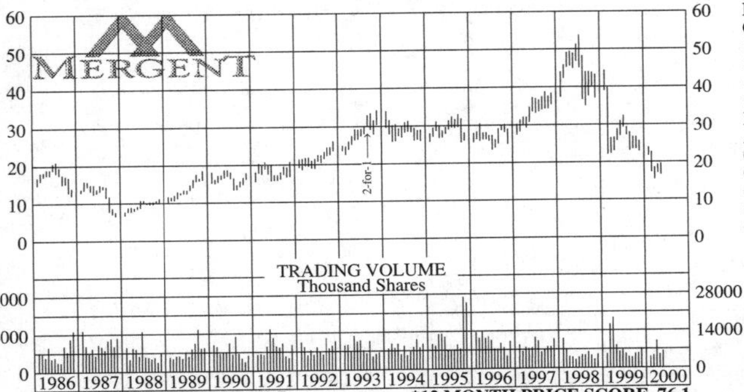

MERGENT
TRADING VOLUME
Thousand Shares
2-for-1

*7 YEAR PRICE SCORE 50.7 *12 MONTH PRICE SCORE 76.1

*NYSE COMPOSITE INDEX=100

INTERIM EARNINGS (Per Share):

Qtr.	May	Aug.	Nov.	Feb.
1996-97	0.37	0.15	1.00	0.71
1997-98	0.40	0.35	1.05	0.75
1998-99	0.47	0.20	1.04	0.82
1999-00	0.16	d0.39	0.81	0.79

INTERIM DIVIDENDS (Per Share):

Amt.	Decl.	Ex.	Rec.	Pay.
0.19Q	2/25/99	5/25/99	5/27/99	6/10/99
0.20Q	6/25/99	8/25/99	8/27/99	9/10/99
0.20Q	9/07/99	11/22/99	11/24/99	12/09/99
0.20Q	1/25/00	2/23/00	2/25/00	3/10/00
0.20Q	2/22/00	5/24/00	5/26/00	6/09/00

Indicated div.: $0.80 (Div. Reinv. Plan)

CAPITALIZATION (2/29/00):

	($000)	(%)
Long-Term Debt	442,102	25.4
Deferred Income Tax	44,997	2.6
Common & Surplus	1,252,411	72.0
Total	1,739,510	100.0

DIVIDEND ACHIEVER STATUS:
Rank: 179 10-Year Growth Rate: 8.98%
Total Years of Dividend Growth: 10

RECENT DEVELOPMENTS: For the year ended 2/29/00, net income declined 50.1% to $90.0 million compared with $180.2 million in the previous year. Earnings for fiscal years 2000 and 1999 included pre-tax restructuring charges of $38.9 million and $13.9 million, respectively. Net sales decreased 1.4% to $2.18 billion from $2.21 billion in the prior year, due to AM's decision to reduce shipments of everyday cards in an effort to increase retail inventory productivity.

PROSPECTS: Going forward, AM's U.K. operations should continue to benefit from a new greeting card and licensing program called Bubblegum, which was introduced in the U.S. in early 2000. As a result of AM's retail productivity initiative, initial sales for fiscal 2000 are expected to decrease $100.0 million. The Company estimates earnings per share of $3.20 to $3.30 for fiscal 2002. On 3/2/00, the Company acquired Gibson Greetings, Inc. for approximately $175.0 million.

BUSINESS

AMERICAN GREETINGS CORPORATION designs, manufactures and sells everyday and seasonal greeting cards and other social expression products. Greeting cards, gift wrap, paper party goods, candles, balloons, stationery and giftware are manufactured and sold in the U.S. by the Company, Plus Mark, Inc., Carlton Cards Retail, Inc. and Quality Greeting Card Distributing Company. AM also manufactures and sells its products in Canada, the United Kingdom, France, Mexico, Australia, New Zealand, and in South Africa. In March 1998, AM acquired U.K.-based Camden Graphics Corp. In May 1998, the Company acquired U.K.-based Hanson White Ltd. On 3/2/00, AM acquired Gibson Greetings, Inc.

ANNUAL FINANCIAL DATA

	2/29/00	2/28/99	2/28/98	2/28/97	2/29/96	2/28/95	2/28/94
Earnings Per Share	[4] **1.37**	[4] **2.53**	[3] **2.55**	**2.23**	[1] **1.54**	**2.00**	[2] **1.77**
Cash Flow Per Share	**2.35**	**3.48**	**3.43**	**3.10**	**2.56**	**2.92**	**2.58**
Tang. Book Val. Per Share	**14.18**	**17.53**	**18.90**	**18.16**	**16.53**	**15.61**	**14.21**
Dividends Per Share	**0.78**	**0.74**	**0.70**	**0.66**	**0.60**	**0.53**	**0.47**
Dividend Payout %	**56.9**	**29.2**	**27.4**	**29.6**	**39.0**	**26.5**	**26.3**
INCOME STATEMENT (IN MILLIONS):							
Total Revenues	2,175.2	2,205.7	2,212.1	2,172.3	2,012.0	1,878.4	1,780.8
Costs & Expenses	1,932.3	1,826.5	1,830.8	1,822.7	1,737.3	1,566.0	1,494.9
Depreciation & Amort.	64.3	67.0	65.9	64.6	75.3	68.4	59.6
Operating Income	178.5	312.2	315.4	285.1	199.3	244.0	226.3
Net Interest Inc./(Exp.)	d34.3	d29.3	d23.0	d30.7	d24.3	d16.9	d16.9
Income Before Income Taxes	140.6	281.6	292.4	254.3	175.0	227.2	209.4
Income Taxes	50.6	101.4	102.4	87.2	59.9	78.4	78.5
Net Income	[4] 90.0	[4] 180.2	[3] 190.1	167.1	[1] 115.1	148.8	[2] 130.9
Cash Flow	154.3	247.3	256.0	231.7	190.5	217.2	190.5
Average Shs. Outstg. (000)	65,592	71,104	74,546	74,819	74,529	74,305	73,809
BALANCE SHEET (IN MILLIONS):							
Cash & Cash Equivalents	61.0	144.6	47.6	35.1	30.1	87.2	101.1
Total Current Assets	1,100.7	1,145.8	1,023.2	1,004.9	970.2	893.4	850.2
Net Property	447.4	434.8	447.6	462.8	440.3	448.8	428.9
Total Assets	2,518.0	2,419.3	2,145.9	2,135.1	2,005.8	1,761.8	1,565.2
Total Current Liabilities	582.5	417.7	517.2	442.7	453.8	362.3	375.9
Long-Term Obligations	442.1	463.2	148.8	219.6	231.1	74.5	54.2
Net Stockholders' Equity	1,252.4	1,346.6	1,345.2	1,361.7	1,235.0	1,159.5	1,053.4
Net Working Capital	518.2	728.1	506.0	562.1	516.3	531.2	474.3
Year-end Shs. Outstg. (000)	77,803	77,783	71,182	74,982	74,708	74,302	74,119
STATISTICAL RECORD:							
Operating Profit Margin %	8.2	14.2	14.3	13.1	9.9	13.0	12.7
Net Profit Margin %	4.1	8.2	8.6	7.7	5.7	7.9	7.3
Return on Equity %	7.2	13.4	14.1	12.3	9.3	12.8	12.4
Return on Assets %	3.6	7.4	8.9	7.8	5.7	8.4	8.4
Debt/Total Assets %	17.6	19.1	6.9	10.3	11.5	4.2	3.5
Price Range	44 5/16-22	53¾-35	38¾-27⅜	30½-23½	33-25½	34-25⅞	34¼-22½
P/E Ratio	32.3-16.1	21.2-13.8	15.2-10.7	13.7-10.5	21.4-16.6	17.0-12.9	19.3-12.7
Average Yield %	2.4	1.7	2.1	2.4	2.1	1.8	1.6

Statistics are as originally reported. Adj. for 2-for-1 stock split, 6/93. [1] Incl. $52.1 mill. asset impairment loss. [2] Excl. $17.2 mill. cumulative effect of acct. chrgs. [3] Incl. pre-tax gain of $22.1 mill. resulting from the divestiture of Acme Frame Products and Wilhold, Inc. [4] Incl. pre-tax restructuring chrg. of $38.9 mill., 2/00; $13.9 mill., 2/99.

OFFICERS:
M. Weiss, Chmn., C.E.O.
E. Fruchtenbaum, Pres., C.O.O.
W. S. Meyer, Sr. V.P., C.F.O.
D. A. Cable, V.P., Treas.

INVESTOR CONTACT: Dale A. Cable, V.P. & Treas., (216) 252-7300

PRINCIPAL OFFICE: One American Rd., Cleveland, OH 44144

TELEPHONE NUMBER: (216) 252-7300
FAX: (216) 252-6778
WEB: www.americangreetings.com
NO. OF EMPLOYEES: 15,200 full-time (approx.); 19,000 part-time (approx.)
SHAREHOLDERS: 28,790 (approx. Cl. A); 210 (approx. Cl. B)
ANNUAL MEETING: In June
INCORPORATED: OH, Jan., 1944

INSTITUTIONAL HOLDINGS:
No. of Institutions: 192
Shares Held: 50,830,091
% Held: 84.9

INDUSTRY: Greeting cards (SIC: 2771)

TRANSFER AGENT(S): National City Bank, Cleveland, OH

AMERICAN HOME PRODUCTS CORPORATION

YIELD 1.7%
P/E RATIO ...

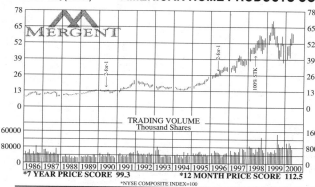

*7 YEAR PRICE SCORE 99.3   *12 MONTH PRICE SCORE 112.5
*NYSE COMPOSITE INDEX=100

TRADING VOLUME
Thousand Shares

INTERIM EARNINGS (Per Share):

Qtr.	Mar.	June	Sept.	Dec.
1996	0.39	0.31	0.39	0.40
1997	0.45	0.36	0.34	0.44
1998	0.74	0.39	0.46	0.26
1999	0.49	0.30	d2.20	0.45

INTERIM DIVIDENDS (Per Share):

Amt.	Decl.	Ex.	Rec.	Pay.
0.225Q	4/22/99	5/11/99	5/13/99	6/01/99
0.225Q	7/22/99	8/11/99	8/13/99	9/01/99
0.23Q	9/23/99	11/09/99	11/12/99	12/01/99
0.23Q	1/27/00	2/09/00	2/11/00	3/01/00
0.23Q	4/27/00	5/10/00	5/12/00	6/01/00

Indicated div.: $0.92 (Div. Reinv. Plan)

CAPITALIZATION (12/31/99):

	($000)	(%)
Long-Term Debt	3,668,643	37.1
Preferred Stock	61	0.0
Common & Surplus	6,214,686	62.9
Total	9,883,390	100.0

DIVIDEND ACHIEVER STATUS:
Rank: 235   10-Year Growth Rate: 6.38%
Total Years of Dividend Growth: 47

RECENT DEVELOPMENTS: For the year ended 12/31/99, net loss was $1.23 billion versus net income of $2.47 billion in 1998. The 1999 results included a net charge of $3.29 billion for legal action brought against AHP over the use of the anti-obesity drugs REDUX and PONDIMIN, and net special charges of $272.9 million. Earnings for 1998 included items that resulted in a nonrecurring net gain of $90.3 million. Net sales rose nearly 1.0% to $13.55 billion.

PROSPECTS: Wyeth-Ayerst Laboratories, the pharmaceutical division of AHP, announced that the FDA has accepted its submission of a new drug application to market RAPAMUNE® in a tablet formulation. Separately, despite a merger agreement between AHP and the Warner-Lambert Co., Warner entered into discussions and agreed to a merger-of-equals transaction with Pfizer, Inc. Hence, AHP is entitled to receive a ''walk-away'' fee of $1.80 billion.

BUSINESS

AMERICAN HOME PRODUCTS CORPORATION is engaged in the discovery, development, manufacture, distribution and sale of products in three segments: Pharmaceuticals, Consumer Health Care and Agricultural Products. Pharmaceuticals include branded and generic human ethical pharmaceuticals, biologicals, nutritionals, and animal biologicals and pharmaceuticals. Consumer Health Care products include analgesics, cough/cold/allergy remedies, vitamin, mineral and nutritional supplements, herbal products, and hemorrhoidal, antacid and asthma relief items sold over-the-counter. Agricultural Products include crop protection and pest control products such as herbicides, insecticides and fungicides. Pharmaceuticals accounted for 70.2% of 1999 sales; Consumer Health Care, 17.5%; and Agricultural Products, 12.3%.

ANNUAL FINANCIAL DATA

	12/31/99	12/31/98	12/31/97	12/31/96	12/31/95	12/31/94	12/31/93
Earnings Per Share	⑥ d0.94	⑤ 1.85	④ 1.56	③ 1.48	①② 1.36	① 1.24	1.18
Cash Flow Per Share	d0.42	2.35	2.09	2.00	1.90	1.49	1.38
Tang. Book Val. Per Share	...	1.23	0.31	...	...	...	2.75
Dividends Per Share	0.91	0.87	0.83	0.78	0.76	0.73	0.71
Dividend Payout %	...	47.0	53.2	52.9	55.7	59.2	60.4
INCOME STATEMENT (IN MILLIONS)							
Total Revenues	13,550.2	13,462.7	14,196.0	14,088.3	13,376.1	8,966.2	8,304.9
Costs & Expenses	14,817.0	9,875.4	10,249.9	10,453.6	10,364.6	6,655.9	6,068.1
Depreciation & Amort.	682.3	664.7	702.0	658.1	679.2	306.2	241.1
Operating Income	d1,949.2	2,922.6	3,244.1	2,976.7	2,332.3	2,004.2	1,995.7
Net Interest Inc./(Exp.)	d213.9	d207.2	d370.7	d433.0	d514.9	d8.8	42.5
Income Before Income Taxes	d1,925.6	3,585.5	2,814.7	2,755.5	2,438.7	2,029.8	1,992.7
Income Taxes	cr698.5	1,111.1	771.6	872.1	758.3	501.5	523.4
Net Income	⑥ d1,227.1	⑤ 2,474.3	④ 2,043.1	③ 1,883.4	①② 1,680.4	① 1,528.3	1,469.3
Cash Flow	d544.8	3,138.9	2,745.1	2,541.4	2,359.6	1,834.3	1,710.3
Average Shs. Outstg. (000)	1,308,876	1,336,641	1,312,975	1,270,852	1,239,340	1,229,652	1,242,672
BALANCE SHEET (IN MILLIONS)							
Cash & Cash Equivalents	2,413.3	1,301.5	1,099.7	1,544.1	2,020.1	1,944.2	2,220.3
Total Current Assets	9,738.1	7,955.6	7,361.3	7,470.4	7,986.1	7,821.2	4,807.7
Net Property	4,565.0	4,289.7	4,296.9	4,036.7	3,960.3	3,811.9	2,059.8
Total Assets	23,906.3	21,079.1	20,825.1	20,785.3	21,362.9	21,674.8	7,687.4
Total Current Liabilities	7,110.2	4,210.7	4,327.0	4,337.6	4,556.2	4,618.1	1,584.4
Long-Term Obligations	3,668.6	3,859.2	5,031.9	6,020.6	7,808.8	9,973.2	859.3
Net Stockholders' Equity	6,214.7	9,614.8	8,741.7	7,045.9	5,657.9	4,443.6	4,128.9
Net Working Capital	2,627.9	3,744.9	3,034.3	3,132.8	3,429.9	3,203.2	3,223.3
Year-end Shs. Outstg. (000)	1,303,916	1,312,399	1,300,754	1,279,966	1,254,800	1,223,924	1,241,304
STATISTICAL RECORD:							
Operating Profit Margin %	...	21.7	22.9	21.1	17.4	22.4	24.0
Net Profit Margin %	...	18.4	14.4	13.4	12.6	17.0	17.7
Return on Equity %	...	25.7	23.4	26.7	29.7	34.4	35.6
Return on Assets %	...	11.7	9.8	9.1	7.9	7.1	19.1
Debt/Total Assets %	15.3	18.3	24.2	29.0	36.6	46.0	11.2
Price Range	70¼-36½	58¾-37¾	42⁷/₁₆-28½	33¼-23⁹/₁₆	24-15⁷/₁₆	16¹³/₁₆-13⅞	17¼-13⅞
P/E Ratio	...	31.8-20.4	27.2-18.3	22.5-15.9	18.4-11.4	13.5-11.1	14.6-11.7
Average Yield %	1.7	1.8	2.3	2.8	3.7	4.8	4.6

Statistics are as originally reported. Adj. for 2-for-1 stock split, 5/98, 5/96. ① Incl. one-time chg. of $308.3 mill., 1995; & $97.0 mill., 1994. ② Incl. American Cyanamid Co., a net, non-recurr. gain of $506.4 mill. ③ Incl. net, non-recurr. gain of $8.4 mill. ④ Incl. a spec. net chg. of $180.0 mill. for product recall. ⑤ Incl. net, non-recurr. chg. of $12.8 mill. ⑥ Incl. a net spec. chg. of $53.0 mill. & a net chg. of $3.29 bill. for lit. assoc/w Pondimin & Redux.

OFFICERS:
J. R. Stafford, Chmn., Pres., C.E.O.
K. J. Martin, Sr. V.P., C.F.O.
L. L. Hoynes, Jr., Sr. V.P., Gen. Couns.
J. M. O'Conner, V.P., Treas.

INVESTOR CONTACT: Thomas G. Cavanagh, V.P., Inv. Relat., (201) 660-5706

PRINCIPAL OFFICE: Five Giralda Farms, Madison, NJ 07940-0874

TELEPHONE NUMBER: (973) 660-5000
FAX: (973) 660-5012
WEB: www.ahp.com

NO. OF EMPLOYEES: 51,656 (avg.)

SHAREHOLDERS: 61,995

ANNUAL MEETING: In Apr.

INCORPORATED: DE, Feb., 1926

INSTITUTIONAL HOLDINGS:
No. of Institutions: 914
Shares Held: 865,079,977
% Held: 66.2

INDUSTRY: Pharmaceutical preparations (SIC: 2834)

TRANSFER AGENT(S): ChaseMellon Shareholder Services, L.L.C., Ridgefield Park, NJ

NYSE SYMBOL AIG
Rec. Pr. 112 9/16 (5/31/00)

AMERICAN INTERNATIONAL GROUP, INC.

YIELD 0.1%
P/E RATIO 34.3

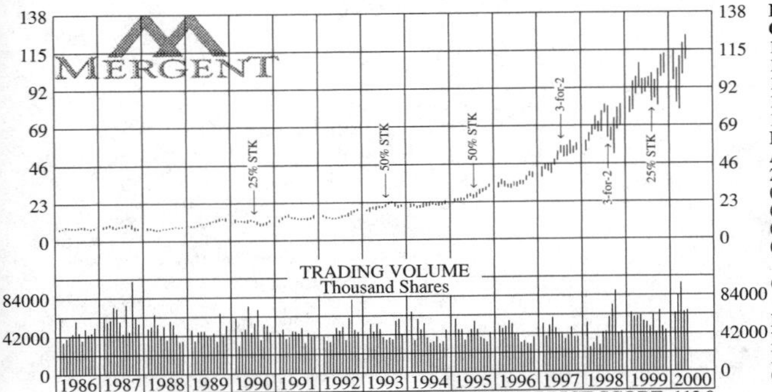

***7 YEAR PRICE SCORE 131.2** ***12 MONTH PRICE SCORE 112.9**

*NYSE COMPOSITE INDEX=100

INTERIM EARNINGS (Per Share):

Qtr.	Mar.	June	Sept.	Dec.
1995	0.34	0.38	0.38	0.40
1996	0.40	0.43	0.44	0.46
1997	0.47	0.50	0.50	0.54
1998	0.54	0.57	0.57	0.61
1999	0.62	1.01	0.81	0.84

INTERIM DIVIDENDS (Per Share):

Amt.	Decl.	Ex.	Rec.	Pay.
25% STK	5/19/99	8/02/99	6/25/99	7/30/99
0.05Q	5/19/99	9/01/99	9/03/99	9/17/99
0.05Q	9/20/99	11/30/99	12/02/99	12/16/99
0.05Q	11/22/99	3/01/00	3/03/00	3/17/00
0.05Q	3/15/00	5/31/00	6/02/00	6/16/00

Indicated div.: $0.20

CAPITALIZATION (12/31/99):

	($000)	(%)
Long-Term Debt	2,344,000	6.2
Minority Interest	1,350,000	3.6
Redeemable Pfd. Stock	895,000	2.4
Common & Surplus	33,306,000	87.9
Total	37,895,000	100.0

DIVIDEND ACHIEVER STATUS:
Rank: 92 10-Year Growth Rate: 13.05%
Total Years of Dividend Growth: 14

RECENT DEVELOPMENTS: For the year ended 12/31/99, net income jumped 18.1% to $5.06 billion from $4.28 billion in the prior year. Results include the consolidation of Transatlantic Holdings, Inc. and 21st Century Insurance Group in 1999 and in the third and fourth quarters of 1998. Total revenues were $37.75 billion versus $30.85 billlion a year earlier. Comparisons were made with restated prior-year figures to reflect the consolidation of SunAmerica Inc.

PROSPECTS: Going forward, the Company expects the primary and reinsurance markets to continue to be pressured by intense competition. Accordingly, the Company continues to focus on its disciplined underwriting approach in an attempt to help offset this pressure. Meanwhile, the Company continues to focus on expandings its operations into China and Vietnam.

BUSINESS

AMERICAN INTERNATIONAL GROUP, INC. is a holding company engaged in a broad range of insurance and insurance-related activities in the U.S. and abroad. Activities are divided among general insurance, life insurance, financial services and other services. Approximately 50% of AIG's revenues during 1999 were derived from its foreign operations. Major insurance subsidiaries are: American Home Assurance Co., National Union Fire Insurance Co. of Pittsburgh, PA., and New Hampshire Insurance Co. On 1/1/99, AIG acquired SunAmerica Inc. for $18.00 billion.

ANNUAL FINANCIAL DATA

	12/31/99	12/31/98	12/31/97	12/31/96	12/31/95	12/31/94	12/31/93
Earnings Per Share	**3.23**	**2.86**	**2.52**	**2.19**	**1.88**	**1.63**	**1 1.43**
Tang. Book Val. Per Share	**21.50**	**20.67**	**18.30**	**16.70**	**14.87**	**12.32**	**11.36**
Dividends Per Share	**0.19**	**0.17**	**0.15**	**0.13**	**0.11**	**0.10**	**0.09**
Dividend Payout %	**5.9**	**5.9**	**6.0**	**6.0**	**6.1**	**6.3**	**6.4**
INCOME STATEMENT (IN MILLIONS):							
Total Premium Income	27,486.0	24,345.0	22,346.7	20,833.1	19,443.9	17,011.2	15,312.7
Other Income	10,265.0	6,507.0	5,600.7	5,041.2	4,386.1	3,781.7	3,410.3
Total Revenues	37,751.0	30,852.0	27,947.4	25,874.3	23,829.9	20,792.8	18,723.0
Policyholder Benefits	6,919.0	6,036.0	5,607.0	5,451.1	4,936.7	4,076.5	3,640.0
Income Before Income Taxes	7,512.0	5,529.0	4,698.9	4,013.2	3,465.9	2,952.0	2,601.1
Income Taxes	2,219.0	1,594.0	1,366.6	1,116.0	955.5	776.5	683.0
Equity Earnings/Minority Int.	d238.0	d112.0	81.7	56.1	45.4	26.3	39.6
Net Income	5,055.0	3,766.0	3,332.3	2,897.3	2,510.4	2,175.5	1 1,918.1
Average Shs. Outstg. (000)	1,567,000	1,318,750	1,321,845	1,324,814	1,333,187	1,335,597	1,339,290
BALANCE SHEET (IN MILLIONS):							
Cash & Cash Equivalents	43,995.0	36,784.0	28,972.3	22,963.9	19,285.6	15,601.1	16,879.5
Premiums Due	37,898.0	35,652.0	33,109.0	29,937.1	29,610.3	27,721.5	25,576.3
Invst. Assets: Fixed-term	90,142.0	61,906.0	51,326.7	48,148.0	42,441.1	35,018.4	30,066.9
Invst. Assets: Equities	6,002.0	5,565.0	5,209.3	5,989.6	5,294.9	5,002.7	4,364.4
Invst. Assets: Loans	12,134.0	8,247.0	7,919.8	7,876.8	7,860.5	5,353.1	3,576.5
Invst. Assets: Total	152,204.0	114,526.0	94,970.6	87,696.9	76,934.5	62,796.8	53,970.4
Total Assets	268,238.0	194,398.0	163,970.7	148,431.0	134,136.4	114,346.1	101,014.8
Long-Term Obligations	2,344.0	1,620.0	13,885.4	13,299.3	9,915.3	8,194.6	5,804.6
Net Stockholders' Equity	33,306.0	27,131.0	24,001.1	22,044.2	19,827.1	16,421.7	15,224.2
Year-end Shs. Outstg. (000)	1,549,128	1,312,500	1,311,596	1,320,303	1,333,643	1,332,456	1,339,993
STATISTICAL RECORD:							
Return on Revenues %	13.4	12.2	11.9	11.2	10.5	10.5	10.2
Return on Equity %	15.2	13.9	13.9	13.1	12.7	13.2	12.6
Return on Assets %	1.9	1.9	2.0	2.0	1.9	1.9	1.9
Price Range	112 7/8-76 1/2	82 1/8-51 7/8	60 1/16-37 7/8	41 3/8-31 5/16	33 15/16-22 13/16	23 7/8-19 3/8	23 3/4-17 3/8
P/E Ratio	34.9-23.7	28.7-18.2	23.8-15.0	18.9-14.3	18.0-12.1	14.7-11.9	16.6-12.2
Average Yield %	0.2	0.3	0.3	0.4	0.4	0.5	0.4

Statistics are as originally reported. Adj. for stk. splits: 25% div., 7/30/99; 3-for-2, 7/98, 7/97, 7/95 1 Bef. acctg. change credit 1993, $20.7 mill.

OFFICERS:
M. R. Greenberg, Chmn., C.E.O.
E. M. Greenberg, Pres., C.O.O.

PRINCIPAL OFFICE: 70 Pine Street, New York, NY 10270

TELEPHONE NUMBER: (212) 770-7000
FAX: (212) 344-6828
WEB: www.aig.com

NO. OF EMPLOYEES: 55,000

SHAREHOLDERS: 26,000 (approx.)

ANNUAL MEETING: In May

INCORPORATED: DE, Jun., 1967

INSTITUTIONAL HOLDINGS:
No. of Institutions: 1,041
Shares Held: 870,337,737
% Held: 56.2

INDUSTRY: Fire, marine, and casualty insurance (SIC: 6331)

TRANSFER AGENT(S): First Chicago Trust Company of New York, Jersey City, NJ

AMERICAN NATIONAL INSURANCE COMPANY

YIELD 5.3%
P/E RATIO 5.4

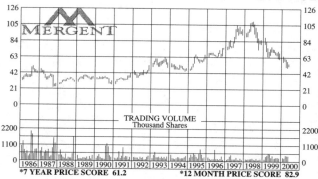

INTERIM EARNINGS (Per Share):

Qtr.	Mar.	June	Sept.	Dec.
1996	1.61	1.75	2.03	2.75
1997	2.37	1.66	2.10	3.25
1998	2.50	1.78	1.54	1.63
1999	4.20	1.55	1.73	2.60

INTERIM DIVIDENDS (Per Share):

Amt.	Decl.	Ex.	Rec.	Pay.
0.69Q	4/30/99	6/02/99	6/04/99	6/18/99
0.69Q	7/29/99	9/01/99	9/03/99	9/17/99
0.71Q	10/28/99	12/01/99	12/03/99	12/17/99
0.71Q	2/24/00	3/01/00	3/03/00	3/17/00
0.71Q	4/28/00	5/31/00	6/02/00	6/16/00

Indicated div.: $2.84 (Div. Reinv. Plan)

TRADING VOLUME
Thousand Shares

CAPITALIZATION (12/31/99):

	($000)	(%)
Deferred Income Tax	221,341	6.7
Common & Surplus	3,063,146	93.3
Total	3,284,487	100.0

*7 YEAR PRICE SCORE 61.2   ***12 MONTH PRICE SCORE 82.9**
*NYSE COMPOSITE INDEX=100

DIVIDEND ACHIEVER STATUS:
Rank: 238   10-Year Growth Rate: 6.29%
Total Years of Dividend Growth: 26

RECENT DEVELOPMENTS: For the year ended 12/31/99, net income increased 35.1% to $266.6 million compared with $197.4 million in the previous year. The improved earnings reflected the Company's emphasis on profitability and growth. Gross revenues increased 8.3% to $1.89 billion from $1.74 billion the year before. Operating earnings, excluding after-tax realized investment gains, grew 6.8% to $165.7 million from $155.2 million a year earlier. After-tax gains on the sale of investments soared 139.1% to $100.9 million from $42.2 million in 1998. Consolidated assets of ANAT grew to $9.09 billion at 12/31/99, compared with $8.82 billion reported on 12/31/98, an increase of 3.1%. For the fourth quarter ended 12/31/99, net income jumped 59.4% to $68.7 million from $43.1 million in 1998.

BUSINESS

AMERICAN NATIONAL INSURANCE COMPANY is licensed to do business in 49 states, the District of Columbia, Puerto Rico, Guam, American Samoa and Western Europe. ANAT offers a broad line of insurance coverages including: life, health, disability and annuities; group life and health; personal lines property and casualty and credit insurance. ANAT also offers a variety of mutual funds for sale through its licensed representatives. In addition to ANAT, the family of companies includes: Standard Life and Accident Insurance Co., American National Life Insurance Co. of Texas, American National Property and Casualty Co., and Securities Management and Research, Inc., manager and distributor for the American National group of funds.

ANNUAL FINANCIAL DATA

	12/31/99	12/31/98	12/31/97	12/31/96	12/31/95	12/31/94	12/31/93
Earnings Per Share	10.07	7.45	9.38	8.14	7.79	8.12	7.00
Tang. Book Val. Per Share	115.68	110.07	102.17	93.43	87.66	78.26	74.09
Dividends Per Share	2.78	2.70	2.62	2.54	2.40	2.24	2.08
Dividend Payout %	27.6	36.2	27.9	31.2	30.8	27.6	29.7
INCOME STATEMENT (IN MILLIONS):							
Total Premium Income	1,230.9	1,193.7	1,140.5	1,034.9	981.1	946.5	929.6
Net Investment Income	473.9	475.2	472.9	435.7	386.9	333.3	312.2
Other Income	184.7	75.7	126.5	79.4	102.9	115.7	87.2
Total Revenues	1,889.6	1,744.7	1,739.9	1,550.0	1,471.0	1,395.4	1,329.0
Policyholder Benefits	866.1	828.6	895.9	831.1	749.0	670.8	653.1
Income Before Income Taxes	388.7	273.9	373.0	305.5	306.3	315.9	289.1
Income Taxes	122.1	76.5	124.7	89.9	99.9	100.8	103.6
Equity Earnings/Minority Int.	19.9	8.0	9.3	10.8	2.2	0.4	10.9
Net Income	266.6	197.4	248.4	215.6	206.4	215.1	185.5
Average Shs. Outstg. (000)	26,479	26,479	26,479	26,479	26,479	26,479	26,479
BALANCE SHEET (IN MILLIONS):							
Cash & Cash Equivalents	947.9	833.4	732.6	547.3	511.7	115.0	64.9
Premiums Due	395.9	328.3	274.9	223.6	197.1	174.3	159.3
Invst. Assets: Fixed-term	3,636.8	3,566.0	3,605.9	3,430.7	2,966.9	2,477.1	2,022.9
Invst. Assets: Equities	963.3	1,051.9	882.9	754.0	710.7	623.7	673.0
Invst. Assets: Loans	1,326.6	1,321.8	1,403.9	1,401.9	1,227.2	1,230.9	1,216.8
Invst. Assets: Total	7,372.9	7,263.6	7,082.8	6,661.8	5,919.8	4,915.1	4,470.9
Total Assets	9,090.5	8,815.7	8,483.0	7,988.5	7,140.0	5,961.2	5,450.9
Long-Term Obligations	...	...	...	...	...	12.4	24.2
Net Stockholders' Equity	3,063.1	2,914.6	2,705.4	2,473.9	2,321.1	2,072.3	1,961.7
Year-end Shs. Outstg. (000)	26,479	26,479	26,479	26,479	26,479	26,479	26,479
STATISTICAL RECORD:							
Return on Revenues %	14.1	11.3	14.3	13.9	14.0	15.4	14.0
Return on Equity %	8.7	6.8	9.2	8.7	8.9	10.4	9.5
Return on Assets %	2.9	2.2	2.9	2.7	2.9	3.6	3.4
Price Range	89⅜-60⅝	109⅞-73	105-73	75½-63	66¾-45½	55-44¼	63¼-49
P/E Ratio	8.9-6.0	14.7-9.8	11.2-7.8	9.3-7.7	8.6-5.8	6.8-5.4	9.0-7.0
Average Yield %	3.7	3.0	2.9	3.7	4.3	4.5	3.7

Statistics are as originally reported.

OFFICERS:
R. L. Moody, Chmn., Pres., C.E.O.
G. R. Ferdinandtsen, Pres., C.O.O.
V. E. Soler Jr., V.P., Sec., Treas.

INVESTOR CONTACT: William F. Carlton,
(409) 766-6447

PRINCIPAL OFFICE: One Moody Plaza,
Galveston, TX 77550-7999

TELEPHONE NUMBER: (409) 763-4661
FAX: (409) 766-6502
WEB: www.anico.com

NO. OF EMPLOYEES: 1,300

SHAREHOLDERS: 2,213

ANNUAL MEETING: In Apr.

INCORPORATED: TX, Mar., 1905

INSTITUTIONAL HOLDINGS:
No. of Institutions: 75
Shares Held: 4,695,066
% Held: 17.7

INDUSTRY: Life insurance (SIC: 6311)

TRANSFER AGENT(S): ChaseMellon
Shareholders Services, LLC, Ridgefield
Park, NJ

NYSE SYMBOL AWR
Rec. Pr. 29 13/16 (5/31/00)

AMERICAN STATES WATER COMPANY

YIELD 4.3%
P/E RATIO 16.7

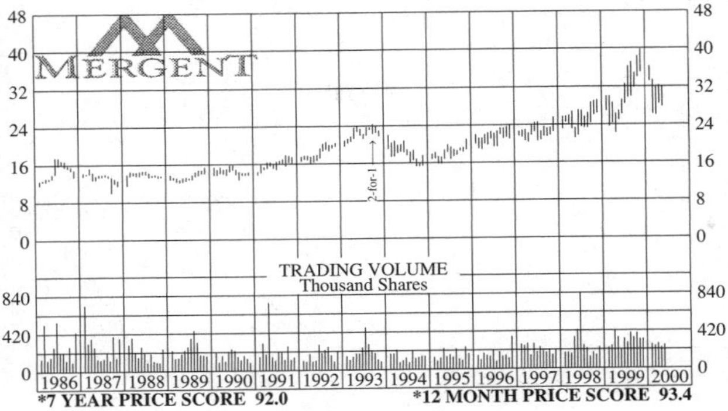

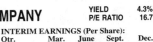

MERGENT
2-for-1
TRADING VOLUME
Thousand Shares
1986 1987 1988 1989 1990 1991 1992 1993 1994 1995 1996 1997 1998 1999 2000

*7 YEAR PRICE SCORE 92.0 *12 MONTH PRICE SCORE 93.4

*NYSE COMPOSITE INDEX=100

INTERIM EARNINGS (Per Share):

Qtr.	Mar.	June	Sept.	Dec.
1996	0.27	0.52	0.68	0.22
1997	0.14	0.34	0.67	0.41
1998	0.20	0.31	0.71	0.40
1999	0.33	0.49	0.74	0.23

INTERIM DIVIDENDS (Per Share):

Amt.	Decl.	Ex.	Rec.	Pay.
0.32Q	4/26/99	5/06/99	5/10/99	6/01/99
0.32Q	7/26/99	8/05/99	8/09/99	9/01/99
0.32Q	10/26/99	11/04/99	11/08/99	12/01/99
0.32Q	1/31/00	2/03/00	2/07/00	3/01/00
0.32Q	5/01/00	5/10/00	5/12/00	6/01/00

Indicated div.: $1.28

CAPITALIZATION (12/31/99):

	($000)	(%)
Long-Term Debt	167,363	23.7
Deferred Income Tax	50,163	7.1
Redeemable Pfd. Stock	360	0.1
Preferred Stock	1,600	0.2
Common & Surplus	487,015	68.9
Total	706,501	100.0

DIVIDEND ACHIEVER STATUS:
Rank: 315 10-Year Growth Rate: 2.15%
Total Years of Dividend Growth: 46

RECENT DEVELOPMENTS: For the year ended 12/31/99, net income climbed 10.1% to $16.1 million compared with $14.6 million the year before. Total operating expenses as a percentage of total operating revenues inched up to 83.6% from 83.1% to 1998. Operating revenues increased 17.1% to $173.4 million from $148.1 million. Water operating revenues rose 18.5% to 159.7 million due to dry, warm weather conditions throughout Southern California and general rate increases in six customer service areas. A 2.7% increase in kilowatt-hour sales, due primarily to industrial power users, caused electric operating revenues to rise 1.0% to $13.3 million in 1999. Operating income amounted to $28.5 million compared with $25.1 million in the prior year.

BUSINESS

AMERICAN STATES WATER COMPANY is a public utility engaged principally in the purchase, production, distribution, and sale of water, and distribution of electricity through its primary subsidiary Southern California Water Company (SCW). SCW is organized into three regions and one electric customer service area operating within 75 communities in 10 counties in the State of California and provides water service in 21 customer service areas. As of 12/31/99, SCW served 244,086 water customers and 21,181 electric customers. Through its American States Utility Services subsidiary, the Company contracts to lease, operate and maintain government-owned water and wastewater systems and to provide other services to local governments to assist them in the operation and maintenance of their water and wastewater systems.

BUSINESS LINE ANALYSIS

(12/31/1999)	REV (%)	INC (%)
Water-Region I	15.7	15.5
Water-Region II	40.9	37.5
Water-Region III	35.7	37.9
Electric	7.7	9.1
Total	100.0	100.0

ANNUAL FINANCIAL DATA

	12/31/99	12/31/98	12/31/97	12/31/96	12/31/95	12/31/94	12/31/93
Earnings Per Share	**1.79**	**1.62**	**1.56**	**1.69**	**1.54**	**1.43**	**1.66**
Cash Flow Per Share	**3.39**	**3.06**	**2.83**	**3.01**	**2.69**	**2.51**	**2.73**
Tang. Book Val. Per Share	**54.37**	**48.16**	**46.82**	**45.33**	**44.96**	**42.44**	**40.92**
Dividends Per Share	**1.28**	**1.26**	**1.25**	**1.23**	**1.21**	**1.20**	**1.19**
Dividend Payout %	**71.5**	**77.8**	**79.8**	**72.5**	**78.2**	**83.9**	**71.5**
INCOME STATEMENT (IN MILLIONS):							
Total Revenues	173.4	148.1	153.8	151.5	129.8	122.7	108.5
Costs & Expenses	130.5	110.1	118.9	117.7	99.4	95.3	80.8
Depreciation & Amort.	14.4	12.9	11.4	10.4	9.0	8.5	7.7
Operating Income	28.5	25.1	23.5	23.4	21.4	18.9	20.1
Net Interest Inc./(Exp.)	d12.9	d11.2	d10.2	d10.5	d9.6	d7.8	d8.4
Income Before Income Taxes	16.1	14.6	14.1	13.5	12.2	11.3	12.0
Net Income	16.1	14.6	14.1	13.5	12.2	11.3	12.0
Cash Flow	30.4	27.4	25.4	23.8	21.1	19.7	19.6
Average Shs. Outstg. (000)	8,958	8,958	8,957	7,891	7,845	7,842	7,186
BALANCE SHEET (IN MILLIONS):							
Cash & Cash Equivalents	2.2	0.6	4.2	3.8	0.3	2.3	1.7
Total Current Assets	44.3	39.3	44.5	43.8	43.0	40.1	34.5
Net Property	449.6	414.8	383.6	357.8	335.0	314.9	295.0
Total Assets	533.2	484.7	457.1	430.9	406.3	383.6	358.5
Total Current Liabilities	55.0	63.8	56.2	44.7	46.5	46.6	32.7
Long-Term Obligations	167.4	120.8	115.3	107.2	107.5	92.9	84.3
Net Stockholders' Equity	488.6	433.0	421.0	404.4	354.3	334.6	321.0
Net Working Capital	d10.6	d24.5	d11.7	d0.9	d3.6	d6.5	1.9
Year-end Shs. Outstg. (000)	8,958	8,958	8,958	8,886	7,845	7,845	7,805
STATISTICAL RECORD:							
Operating Profit Margin %	16.4	16.9	15.3	15.5	16.5	15.4	18.5
Net Profit Margin %	9.3	9.8	9.1	8.9	9.4	9.2	11.1
Return on Equity %	3.3	3.4	3.3	3.3	3.4	3.4	3.7
Return on Assets %	3.0	3.0	3.1	3.1	3.0	3.0	3.4
Debt/Total Assets %	31.4	24.9	25.2	24.9	26.5	24.2	23.5
Price Range	39 3/4-22 3/16	29 1/4-21 1/8	25 5/8-20 1/4	24 1/8-18 3/4	21-15 3/4	22-15 1/4	24 3/8-19 5/8
P/E Ratio	22.2-12.4	18.1-13.0	16.4-13.0	14.3-11.1	13.6-10.2	15.4-10.7	14.7-11.8
Average Yield %	4.1	5.0	5.4	5.7	6.6	6.4	5.4

Statistics are as originally reported.

OFFICERS:
L. E. Ross, Chmn.
F. E. Wicks, Pres., C.E.O.
M. Harris III, V.P., Fin., C.F.O., Treas., & Corp. Sec.

INVESTOR CONTACT: McClellan Harris III, C.F.O. & Sec., (909) 394-3600

PRINCIPAL OFFICE: 630 East Foothill Blvd., San Dimas, CA 91773-1212

TELEPHONE NUMBER: (909) 394-3600
FAX: (909) 394-0711
WEB: www.aswater.com

NO. OF EMPLOYEES: 492

SHAREHOLDERS: 3,519 (approx.)

ANNUAL MEETING: In May

INCORPORATED: CA, Dec., 1929

INSTITUTIONAL HOLDINGS:
No. of Institutions: 71
Shares Held: 2,740,963
% Held: 30.6

INDUSTRY: Water supply (SIC: 4941)

TRANSFER AGENT(S): ChaseMellon Shareholder Services, L.L.C., Ridgefield Park, NJ

NYSE SYMBOL AWK
Rec. Pr. 23⅜ (5/31/00)

AMERICAN WATER WORKS COMPANY, INC.

YIELD 3.9%
P/E RATIO 16.3

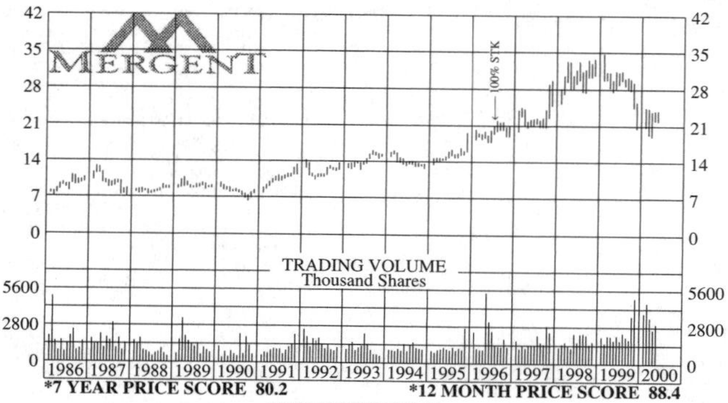

MERGENT
100% STK
TRADING VOLUME
Thousand Shares
1986 1987 1988 1989 1990 1991 1992 1993 1994 1995 1996 1997 1998 1999 2000

*7 YEAR PRICE SCORE 80.2 *12 MONTH PRICE SCORE 88.4

*NYSE COMPOSITE INDEX=100

INTERIM EARNINGS (Per Share):

Qtr.	Mar.	June	Sept.	Dec.
1996	0.24	0.35	0.45	0.27
1997	0.22	0.39	0.54	0.31
1998	0.26	0.42	0.57	0.33
1999	0.23	0.33	0.54	0.33

INTERIM DIVIDENDS (Per Share):

Amt.	Decl.	Ex.	Rec.	Pay.
0.215Q	4/01/99	4/21/99	4/23/99	5/17/99
0.215Q	7/01/99	7/21/99	7/23/99	8/16/99
0.215Q	10/14/99	10/27/99	10/29/99	11/15/99
0.225Q	1/06/00	1/26/00	1/28/00	2/15/00
0.225Q	4/06/00	4/26/00	4/28/00	5/15/00

Indicated div.: $0.90 (Div. Reinv. Plan)

CAPITALIZATION (12/31/99):

	($000)	(%)
Long-Term Debt	2,393,097	51.6
Deferred Income Tax	610,460	13.2
Redeemable Pfd. Stock	74,020	1.6
Preferred Stock	19,791	0.4
Common & Surplus	1,542,337	33.2
Total	4,639,705	100.0

DIVIDEND ACHIEVER STATUS:
Rank: 183 10-Year Growth Rate: 8.80%
Total Years of Dividend Growth: 24

RECENT DEVELOPMENTS: For the year ended 12/31/99, net income declined 7.6% to $138.9 million versus $150.4 million in the corresponding 1998 period. Results for 1999 included net charges of $3.6 million. Operating revenues totaled $1.26 billion, an increase of 5.1%, versus $1.20 billion last year. Revenues for the year were pressured by usage limitations, one-time costs associated with contract management activities and incremental expenses.

PROSPECTS: The Company has received approval from the Pennsylvania Public Utility Commission (PUC) for an 8.7% overall rate increase which will generate $24.6 million in revenue. Meanwhile, the acquisitions of SJW Corp. and certain assets of Citizens Utilities, are still underway. On 2/7/00, the Company finalized its purchase of Anglian Water's interest in AmericanAnglian.

BUSINESS

AMERICAN WATER WORKS COMPANY, INC. is engaged in the ownership of utility companies providing water supply service. The Company and its subsidiaries constitute the American Water System, which has been functioning for over 50 years. The American Water Works Service Company, a subsidiary, provides professional and staff services to affiliated companies. AWK established American Commonwealth Management Services Company to provide management services to water and sewer systems. Its subsidiary operating companies provide water service to 10.0 million people in more than 870 communities in 23 states.

ANNUAL FINANCIAL DATA

	12/31/99	12/31/98	12/31/97	12/31/96	12/31/95	12/31/94	12/31/93
Earnings Per Share	**② 1.40**	**1.58**	**1.45**	**1.31**	**① 1.32**	**1.17**	**1.15**
Cash Flow Per Share	**3.11**	**3.20**	**2.88**	**2.68**	**2.62**	**2.43**	**2.35**
Tang. Book Val. Per Share	**15.85**	**15.32**	**14.28**	**13.49**	**12.07**	**11.23**	**10.49**
Dividends Per Share	**0.86**	**0.82**	**0.76**	**0.70**	**0.64**	**0.54**	**0.50**
Dividend Payout %	**61.4**	**51.9**	**52.4**	**53.4**	**48.5**	**46.1**	**43.7**
INCOME STATEMENT (IN MILLIONS):							
Total Revenues	1,260.9	1,017.8	954.2	894.6	802.8	770.2	717.5
Costs & Expenses	675.6	528.1	507.8	498.7	471.6	456.9	422.1
Depreciation & Amort.	165.6	129.8	112.5	101.9	87.0	80.6	75.1
Operating Income	419.6	359.9	333.9	294.0	244.3	182.8	172.5
Net Interest Inc./(Exp.)	d170.4	d150.5	d142.7	d133.1	d108.7	d106.7	d95.7
Income Taxes	91.4	83.3	74.7	63.8	57.6	49.9	47.9
Net Income	② 138.9	131.0	119.1	101.7	① 92.1	78.7	75.4
Cash Flow	300.6	256.8	227.7	199.6	175.0	155.3	146.5
Average Shs. Outstg. (000)	96,544	80,298	79,144	74,609	66,764	63,836	62,278
BALANCE SHEET (IN MILLIONS):							
Gross Property	6,143.7	4,945.0	4,527.7	4,188.9	3,510.6	3,219.6	2,969.4
Accumulated Depreciation	1,152.6	848.5	755.4	682.8	590.8	535.1	484.2
Net Property	5,084.5	4,153.2	3,828.1	3,560.1	2,962.6	2,726.1	2,529.1
Total Assets	5,952.2	4,708.3	4,314.3	4,032.2	3,403.1	3,206.7	2,994.0
Long-Term Obligations	2,393.1	2,106.0	1,870.8	1,716.4	1,384.6	1,308.0	1,187.4
Net Stockholders' Equity	1,562.1	1,257.1	1,160.3	1,075.8	836.9	751.4	673.3
Year-end Shs. Outstg. (000)	97,304	80,895	79,993	78,421	67,826	65,318	62,488
STATISTICAL RECORD:							
Operating Profit Margin %	33.3	35.4	35.0	32.9	30.4	23.7	24.0
Net Profit Margin %	11.0	12.9	12.5	11.4	11.5	10.2	10.5
Net Inc./Net Property %	2.7	3.2	3.1	2.9	3.1	2.9	3.0
Net Inc./Tot. Capital %	3.0	3.4	3.4	3.1	3.5	3.2	3.3
Return on Equity %	8.9	10.4	10.3	9.5	11.0	10.5	11.2
Accum. Depr./Gross Prop. %	18.8	17.2	16.7	16.3	16.8	16.6	16.3
Price Range	34¾-20½	33¾-25¼	29 11/16-19⅞	22-17¾	19⅝-13⅜	16⅛-12⅝	16⅛-12 5/16
P/E Ratio	24.8-14.6	21.4-16.0	20.5-13.7	16.8-13.5	14.9-10.1	13.8-10.8	14.1-10.8
Average Yield %	3.1	2.8	3.1	3.5	3.9	3.8	3.5

Statistics are as originally reported. Adj. for stk. splits: 2-for-1, 8/96 ① Incl. non-recurr credit of $3.9 mill. ($0.06/sh.) ② Incl. after tax cost of $3.6 mill.

OFFICERS:
M. Lewis, Chmn.
A. P. Terracciano, Vice-Chmn.
J. J. Barr, Pres., C.E.O.
E. C. Wolf, V.P., C.F.O.

INVESTOR CONTACT: W. Timothy Pohl, Esq., Gen. Counsel and Secretary

PRINCIPAL OFFICE: 1025 Laurel Oak Rd., P.O. Box 1770, Voorhees, NJ 08043

TELEPHONE NUMBER: (609) 346-8200
FAX: (609) 346-8300
WEB: www.amwater.com

NO. OF EMPLOYEES: 4,970

SHAREHOLDERS: 43,577 com. stock

ANNUAL MEETING: In May

INCORPORATED: DE, Aug., 1936

INSTITUTIONAL HOLDINGS:
No. of Institutions: 165
Shares Held: 29,916,607
% Held: 30.9

INDUSTRY: Water supply (SIC: 4941)

TRANSFER AGENT(S): BankBoston N.A., Boston, MA

AMSOUTH BANCORPORATION

YIELD 4.4%
P/E RATIO 14.0

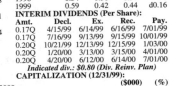

INTERIM EARNINGS (Per Share):

Qtr.	Mar.	June	Sept.	Dec.
1996	0.25	0.25	0.18	0.27
1997	0.29	0.30	0.31	0.32
1998	0.34	0.36	0.37	0.38
1999	0.59	0.42	0.44	d0.16

INTERIM DIVIDENDS (Per Share):

Amt.	Decl.	Ex.	Rec.	Pay.
0.17Q	4/15/99	6/14/99	6/16/99	7/01/99
0.17Q	7/16/99	9/13/99	9/15/99	10/01/99
0.20Q	10/21/99	12/13/99	12/15/99	1/03/00
0.20Q	1/20/00	3/13/00	3/15/00	4/01/00
0.20Q	4/20/00	6/12/00	6/14/00	7/01/00

Indicated div.: $0.80 (Div. Reinv. Plan)

CAPITALIZATION (12/31/99):

	($000)	(%)
Total Deposits	27,912,443	76.5
Long-Term Debt	5,603,486	15.4
Common & Surplus	2,959,205	8.1
Total	36,475,134	100.0

DIVIDEND ACHIEVER STATUS:
Rank: 155   10-Year Growth Rate: 9.95%
Total Years of Dividend Growth: 29

TRADING VOLUME
Thousand Shares

*7 YEAR PRICE SCORE 81.7   *12 MONTH PRICE SCORE 78.6
*NYSE COMPOSITE INDEX=100

RECENT DEVELOPMENTS: For the year ended 12/31/99, net income decreased 28.2% to $340.5 million from $474.1 million in 1998. Earnings for 1999 and 1998 included net gains on the sale of businesses of $8.6 million and $32.7 million, respectively, as well as merger-related charges of $301.4 million and $121.7 million, respectively. Net interest income rose 4.4% to $1.51 billion. Comparisons were made with restated 1998 figures.

PROSPECTS: Going forward, ASO expects improved earnings for 2000 due to its decision to exit the health care industry segment of its loan portfolio. This decision resulted from the federal government's legislation to reduce Medicare reimbursements to health care providers, which had an adverse financial effect on certain companies that were reliant on such reimbursements. On 5/15/00, ASO completed the integration of First American Corporation.

BUSINESS

AMSOUTH BANCORPORATION is headquartered in Birmingham, Alabama and as of 3/31/00, had assets of $43.58 billion. As of 12/31/99, ASO operated 661 branch banking offices and 1,343 ATMs in nine southeastern states: Alabama, Florida, Tennessee, Mississippi, Georgia, Lousiana, Arkansas, Kentucky, and Virginia. ASO's affiliates, AmSouth N.A., AmSouth Bank of Florida, AmSouth Bank of Tennessee, AmSouth Bank of Georgia and AmSouth Bank of Alabama, AmSouth Investment Services and AmSouth Leasing Corporation, provide a full line of traditional and nontraditional financial services including consumer and commercial banking, mortgage lending, trust services and investment management. On 10/1/99, ASO acquired First American Corporation.

LOAN DISTRIBUTION

(12/31/1999)	($000)	(%)
Commercial	10,003,310	38.1
Commercial real estate	4,712,006	17.9
Consumer	11,551,443	44.0
Total	26,266,759	100.0

ANNUAL FINANCIAL DATA

	[5] 12/31/99	12/31/98	12/31/97	12/31/96	12/31/95	12/31/94	12/31/93
Earnings Per Share	[4] 0.86	[3] 1.45	1.21	[2] 0.96	[1] 0.89	0.67	0.92
Tang. Book Val. Per Share	7.56	8.05	7.64	7.38	7.16	6.69	6.52
Dividends Per Share	0.67	0.53	0.50	0.47	0.45	0.41	0.34
Dividend Payout %	78.3	36.9	41.0	49.5	50.7	62.2	37.4
INCOME STATEMENT (IN MILLIONS):							
Total Interest Income	2,932.8	1,462.5	1,377.8	1,353.8	1,275.1	1,047.7	777.0
Total Interest Expense	1,424.8	763.6	701.5	701.4	679.4	480.4	314.9
Net Interest Income	1,507.9	699.0	676.3	652.4	595.7	567.3	462.1
Provision for Loan Losses	165.6	58.1	67.4	65.2	40.1	30.1	19.0
Non-Interest Income	847.6	346.6	266.0	235.3	231.8	179.0	194.4
Non-Interest Expense	1,648.5	582.1	526.2	534.2	512.1	522.9	420.1
Income Before Taxes	541.4	405.3	348.7	288.3	275.2	193.3	217.4
Net Income	[4] 340.5	[3] 262.7	226.2	[2] 182.7	[1] 175.0	127.3	146.2
Average Shs. Outstg. (000)	396,515	181,922	186,179	191,042	196,634	190,779	159,141
BALANCE SHEET (IN MILLIONS):							
Cash & Due from Banks	1,563.3	619.6	658.5	648.5	651.6	616.6	577.0
Securities Avail. for Sale	6,016.7	3,033.5	2,509.1	2,294.4	2,482.8	389.4	94.8
Total Loans & Leases	26,436.4	12,869.9	12,342.8	12,168.6	11,819.8	11,496.1	7,999.9
Allowance for Credit Losses	533.1	283.7	284.4	267.4	255.0	237.4	187.8
Net Loans & Leases	25,903.3	12,586.2	12,058.5	11,901.2	11,564.8	11,258.7	7,812.1
Total Assets	43,406.6	19,794.1	18,622.3	18,407.3	17,738.8	16,778.0	12,547.9
Total Deposits	27,912.4	13,283.8	12,945.2	12,467.6	13,408.8	13,067.1	9,567.9
Long-Term Obligations	5,603.5	3,239.8	1,633.2	1,435.7	447.8	386.1	163.1
Total Liabilities	40,447.3	18,474.1	17,237.0	17,011.4	16,355.3	15,467.5	11,457.9
Net Stockholders' Equity	2,959.2	1,427.6	1,385.2	1,395.8	1,383.5	1,310.5	1,090.0
Year-end Shs. Outstg. (000)	391,374	177,377	181,208	189,081	193,269	195,939	167,117
STATISTICAL RECORD:							
Return on Equity %	11.5	18.4	16.3	13.1	12.6	9.7	13.4
Return on Assets %	0.8	1.3	1.2	1.0	1.0	0.8	1.2
Equity/Assets %	6.8	7.2	7.4	7.6	7.8	7.8	8.7
Non-Int. Exp./Tot. Inc. %	70.0	55.7	55.8	60.2	61.9	70.1	64.1
Price Range	34 9/16-18 1/4	30 1/16-20 7/16	25 3/8-14	15 1/16-10 3/16	12 1/4-7 5/8	10 5/16-7 1/2	10 5/8-8 1/8
P/E Ratio	40.2-21.8	21.0-14.1	20.9-11.5	15.8-10.6	13.8-8.6	15.5-11.3	11.6-8.8
Average Yield %	2.5	2.1	2.5	3.8	4.5	4.6	3.7

Statistics are as originally reported. Adj. for 3-for-2 splits 5/99, 4/98 & 4/97. [1] Incl. pre-tax gain on the sale of 3rd party mtg. servicing portfolio to G.E. Capital Services, Inc. & $22.0 mill. in additional expenses related to the consolidation & workforce reduction. [2] Incl. SAIF pre-tax charge of $24.2 mill. ($0.18 sh.) [3] Incl. $28.0 mill. gain fr. sale of assets. [4] Incl. net gain fr. sale of businesses of $8.6 mill. & merger-rel. chrgs. of $301.4 mill. [5] Refl. acquis. of First American Corp. in 10/99.

OFFICERS:
D. Bottorff, Chmn.
S. D. Gibson, Vice-Chmn., C.F.O.
C. D. Ritter, Pres., C.E.O.

INVESTOR CONTACT: M. List Underwood, Jr., Exec. V.P.-Corp. Fin., (205) 801-0265

PRINCIPAL OFFICE: 1900 Fifth Avenue North, Amsouth Sonat Tower, Birmingham, AL 35203

TELEPHONE NUMBER: (205) 320-7151
FAX: (205) 326-4072
WEB: www.amsouth.com

NO. OF EMPLOYEES: 13,882

SHAREHOLDERS: 27,992 (approx.)

ANNUAL MEETING: In Apr.

INCORPORATED: DE, Nov., 1970

INSTITUTIONAL HOLDINGS:
No. of Institutions: 284
Shares Held: 152,123,958
% Held: 38.9

INDUSTRY: State commercial banks (SIC: 6022)

TRANSFER AGENT(S): The Bank of New York, New York, NY

NASDAQ SYMBOL ANLY
Rec. Pr. 8⅛ (5/31/00)

ANALYSTS INTERNATIONAL CORPORATION

YIELD 4.9%
P/E RATIO 10.4

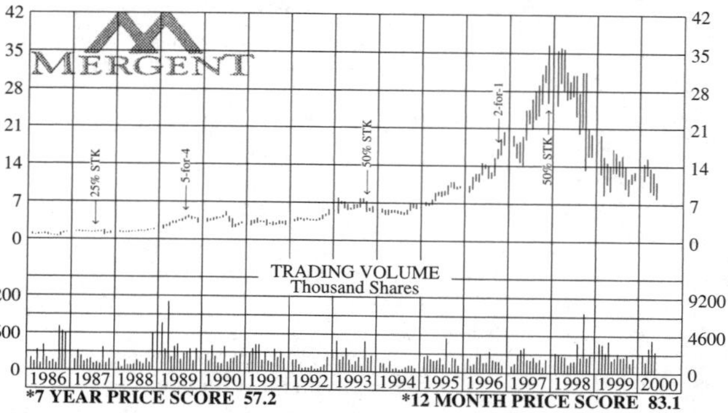

*7 YEAR PRICE SCORE 57.2 *12 MONTH PRICE SCORE 83.1

*NYSE COMPOSITE INDEX=100

INTERIM EARNINGS (Per Share):

Qtr.	Sept.	Dec.	Mar.	June
1995-96	0.13	0.13	0.15	0.15
1996-97	0.17	0.17	0.19	0.19
1997-98	0.23	0.22	0.24	0.29
1998-99	0.27	0.22	0.25	0.26
1999-00	0.17	0.10	...	...

INTERIM DIVIDENDS (Per Share):

Amt.	Decl.	Ex.	Rec.	Pay.
0.10Q	2/18/99	4/28/99	4/30/99	5/14/99
0.10Q	6/24/99	7/28/99	7/30/99	8/13/99
0.10Q	8/19/99	10/27/99	10/29/99	11/15/99
0.10Q	12/15/99	1/27/00	1/31/00	2/15/00
0.10Q	2/22/00	4/26/00	4/28/00	5/15/00

Indicated div.: $0.40

CAPITALIZATION (6/30/99):

	($000)	(%)
Long-Term Debt	20,000	16.9
Common & Surplus	98,014	83.1
Total	118,014	100.0

DIVIDEND ACHIEVER STATUS:
Rank: 51 10-Year Growth Rate: 16.00%
Total Years of Dividend Growth: 11

RECENT DEVELOPMENTS: For the second quarter ended 12/31/99, net income decreased 53.0% to $2.3 million compared with $5.0 million in the corresponding quarter the year before. Total revenues decreased 9.2% to $138.9 million from $153.0 million in the comparable quarter a year earlier. Revenues provided directly totaled $103.6 million, down 12.5% from $118.4 million due to a decrease in billable hours, which reflected the industry-wide slowdown. The decrease in billable hours was partially offset by an increase in hourly rates. Revenues provided through sub-suppliers rose 1.8% to $35.2 million from $34.6 million due to an increase in billable hours of service rendered to clients. Operating income declined to $3.8 million from $7.9 million in the equivalent 1998 quarter. On 4/13/00, the Company agreed to acquire 80.1% of Sequoia, a Michigan-based Internet professional services organization that provides strategic e-business services.

BUSINESS

ANALYSTS INTERNATIONAL CORPORATION is primarily engaged in the business of providing contract programming and related software services through its branch and field offices to users and manufacturers of computers. Software services offered by the Company include custom programming, systems analysis and design, software-related consulting and specialized software-related educational courses for computer programmers and analysts. The Company also distributes proprietary software packages. The Company maintains offices in more than 45 cities in the United States, Canada and the United Kingdom, and serves more than 900 corporate and governmental clients.

ANNUAL FINANCIAL DATA

	6/30/99	6/30/98	6/30/97	6/30/96	6/30/95	6/30/94	6/30/93
Earnings Per Share	**1.00**	**0.99**	**0.73**	**0.56**	**0.52**	**0.37**	**0.38**
Cash Flow Per Share	**1.19**	**1.15**	**0.85**	**0.66**	**0.60**	**0.44**	**0.45**
Tang. Book Val. Per Share	**4.03**	**3.54**	**2.79**	**2.44**	**2.07**	**1.71**	**1.49**
Dividends Per Share	**0.40**	**0.34**	**0.25**	**0.21**	**0.18**	**0.16**	**0.14**
Dividend Payout %	**40.0**	**34.3**	**34.8**	**37.5**	**34.8**	**44.5**	**36.4**
INCOME STATEMENT (IN THOUSANDS):							
Total Revenues	620,156	587,411	439,546	329,544	218,426	175,982	159,703
Costs & Expenses	579,859	547,292	410,542	307,641	198,842	161,788	145,259
Depreciation & Amort.	4,259	3,731	2,839	2,191	1,814	1,660	1,405
Operating Income	36,038	36,388	26,165	19,712	17,770	12,534	13,039
Net Interest Inc./(Exp.)	d178	...	...	...	...	...	...
Income Before Income Taxes	37,268	37,687	27,210	20,739	18,530	12,775	13,501
Income Taxes	14,535	15,077	10,829	8,321	7,274	4,824	5,235
Net Income	22,733	22,610	16,381	12,418	11,256	7,951	8,266
Cash Flow	26,992	26,341	19,220	14,609	13,070	9,611	9,671
Average Shs. Outstg.	22,732	22,829	22,544	22,221	21,822	21,636	21,510
BALANCE SHEET (IN THOUSANDS):							
Cash & Cash Equivalents	33,870	11,868	17,888	17,018	12,615	10,700	9,914
Total Current Assets	139,892	109,970	87,831	69,079	56,814	41,319	34,987
Net Property	29,644	10,360	6,121	5,715	5,020	4,912	5,404
Total Assets	186,216	132,661	105,370	81,445	67,533	51,210	44,907
Total Current Liabilities	60,668	42,496	32,822	21,731	17,047	9,846	8,918
Long-Term Obligations	20,000	...	...	...	...	...	...
Net Stockholders' Equity	98,014	82,994	66,104	53,718	45,134	36,571	31,673
Net Working Capital	79,224	67,474	55,009	47,348	39,767	31,473	26,069
Year-end Shs. Outstg.	22,552	22,440	22,275	21,975	21,774	21,354	21,192
STATISTICAL RECORD:							
Operating Profit Margin %	5.8	6.2	6.0	6.0	8.1	7.1	8.2
Net Profit Margin %	3.7	3.8	3.7	3.8	5.2	4.5	5.2
Return on Equity %	23.2	27.2	24.8	23.1	24.9	21.7	26.1
Return on Assets %	12.2	17.0	15.5	15.2	16.7	15.5	18.4
Debt/Total Assets %	10.7	...	...	...	...	...	...
Price Range	19¾-8⅝	36-13¼	36½-14³⁄₁₆	20⁵⁄₁₆-9¹⁄₁₆	11-6⁹⁄₁₆	6¹⁵⁄₁₆-4¹³⁄₁₆	7¹⁵⁄₁₆-5
P/E Ratio	19.7-8.6	36.4-13.4	50.2-19.5	36.3-16.2	21.3-12.7	18.8-13.2	20.7-13.0
Average Yield %	2.8	1.4	1.0	1.4	2.0	2.8	2.2

Statistics are as originally reported. Adj. for stk. splits: 50% div., 12/3/97; 2-for-1, 9/30/96; 3-for-2, 10/1/93

OFFICERS:
F. W. Lang, Chmn., C.E.O.
V. C. Benda, Pres., C.O.O.
M. R. Charpentier, V.P., Treas.

PRINCIPAL OFFICE: 3601 West 76th Street, Minneapolis, MN 55435-3000

TELEPHONE NUMBER: (612) 835-5900
FAX: (612) 897-4555
WEB: www.analysts.com

NO. OF EMPLOYEES: 4,900 (approx.)

SHAREHOLDERS: 1,300 (of record); 8,500 (beneficial)

ANNUAL MEETING: In Oct.

INCORPORATED: MN, Mar., 1966

INSTITUTIONAL HOLDINGS:
No. of Institutions: 71
Shares Held: 13,217,107
% Held: 58.6

INDUSTRY: Computer programming services (SIC: 7371)

TRANSFER AGENT(S): Boston EquiServe, Boston, MA

ANHEUSER-BUSCH COMPANIES, INC.

YIELD	1.5%
P/E RATIO	26.4

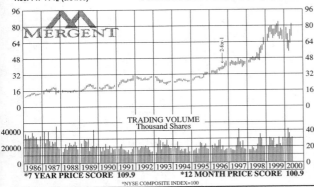

TRADING VOLUME
Thousand Shares

*7 YEAR PRICE SCORE 109.9   *12 MONTH PRICE SCORE 100.9
*NYSE COMPOSITE INDEX=100

INTERIM EARNINGS (Per Share):

Qtr.	Mar.	June	Sept.	Dec.
1996	0.54	0.70	0.75	0.30
1997	0.51	0.76	0.79	0.30
1998	0.54	0.80	0.84	0.35
1999	0.66	0.90	0.97	0.41

INTERIM DIVIDENDS (Per Share):

Amt.	Decl.	Ex.	Rec.	Pay.
0.28Q	4/28/99	5/06/99	5/10/99	6/09/99
0.30Q	7/28/99	8/05/99	8/09/99	9/09/99
0.30Q	10/27/99	11/05/99	11/09/99	12/09/99
0.30Q	1/14/00	2/07/00	2/09/00	3/09/00
0.30Q	4/26/00	5/05/00	5/09/00	6/09/00

Indicated div.: $1.20 (Div. Reinv. Plan)

CAPITALIZATION (12/31/99):

	($000)	(%)
Long-Term Debt	4,880,600	48.1
Deferred Income Tax	1,344,700	13.3
Common & Surplus	3,921,500	38.6
Total	10,146,800	100.0

DIVIDEND ACHIEVER STATUS:
Rank: 133   10-Year Growth Rate: 11.23%
Total Years of Dividend Growth: 25

RECENT DEVELOPMENTS: For the year ended 12/31/99, net income increased 13.7% to $1.40 billion from $1.23 billion in the previous year. Net sales rose 4.1% to $11.70 billion from $11.25 billion in 1998, primarily due to higher domestic beer sales volume and increased revenue per barrel. Results were positively affected by accelerating volume growth and price increases that were implemented in 72.0% of the country on certain brands and packages representing 40.0% of BUD's volume.

PROSPECTS: In 2000, the Company expects double-digit growth in earnings per share due to better demographics, high capacity utilization, and an improved pricing environment. BUD is currently implementing selected price increases and additional discount reductions on approximately 20.0% of its volume. The Company also continues to benefit from a strong economy. Separately, BUD's tenth park, Discovery Cove located in Orlando, Florida, is scheduled to open in Summer 2000.

BUSINESS

ANHEUSER-BUSCH COMPANIES, INC. is a diversified corporation whose chief subsidiary is Anheuser-Busch, Inc., the world's largest brewer. Beer is sold under brand names including BUDWEISER, MICHELOB, BUSCH and NATURAL LIGHT. BUD is also the country's second largest theme park operator. Theme park operations are conducted through BUD's subsidiary, Busch Entertainment Corporation, which currently owns nine theme parks. BUD also engages in packaging, malt and rice production, international beer and non-beer beverages. BUD owns approximately 50.0% of Grupo Modelo, S.A. de C.V., a Mexican brewer.

BUSINESS LINE ANALYSIS

(12/31/99)	REV (mill.)	INC (mill.)
Domestic Beer	10,966.8	1,395.4
Int'l Beer	763.3	145.2
Package	1,941.9	92.6
Entertainment	750.5	69.0
Other	120.2	7.6

ANNUAL FINANCIAL DATA

	12/31/99	12/31/98	12/31/97	12/31/96	12/31/95	12/31/94	12/31/93
Earnings Per Share	2.94	2.53	③ 2.36	② 2.28	① 1.72	1.96	④ 1.09
Cash Flow Per Share	4.57	4.04	3.73	3.46	2.82	3.14	2.19
Tang. Book Val. Per Share	8.50	8.85	8.30	8.10	8.73	7.64	7.04
Dividends Per Share	1.16	1.08	1.00	0.92	0.84	0.76	0.68
Dividend Payout %	39.5	42.7	42.4	40.3	48.8	38.9	62.7
INCOME STATEMENT (IN MILLIONS):							
Total Revenues	11,703.7	11,245.8	11,066.2	10,883.7	10,340.5	12,053.8	11,505.3
Costs & Expenses	8,624.4	8,382.1	8,329.5	8,260.7	7,982.0	9,527.2	9,685.1
Depreciation & Amort.	777.0	738.4	683.7	593.9	565.6	627.5	608.3
Operating Income	2,302.3	2,125.3	2,053.0	2,029.1	1,792.9	1,899.1	1,211.9
Net Interest Inc./(Exp.)	d285.3	d259.7	d211.2	d187.9	d191.7	d196.0	d165.9
Income Before Income Taxes	2,007.6	1,852.6	1,832.5	1,892.9	1,461.7	1,707.1	1,050.4
Income Taxes	762.9	704.3	703.6	736.8	575.1	675.0	455.9
Equity Earnings/Minority Int.	157.5	85.0	50.3	...	...	...	...
Net Income	1,402.2	1,233.3	③ 1,179.2	② 1,156.1	① 886.6	1,032.1	④ 594.5
Cash Flow	2,179.2	1,971.7	1,862.9	1,750.0	1,452.2	1,659.6	1,202.8
Average Shs. Outstg. (000)	476,800	487,500	499,700	505,800	515,800	528,200	548,600
BALANCE SHEET (IN MILLIONS):							
Cash & Cash Equivalents	152.1	224.8	147.3	93.6	93.6	156.4	127.4
Total Current Assets	1,600.6	1,640.4	1,583.9	1,465.8	1,510.6	1,861.6	1,795.2
Net Property	7,964.6	7,849.0	7,750.6	7,208.2	6,763.0	7,547.7	7,497.1
Total Assets	12,640.4	12,484.3	11,727.1	10,463.6	10,590.9	11,045.4	10,880.3
Total Current Liabilities	1,987.2	1,730.3	1,500.7	1,430.9	1,242.0	1,669.0	1,815.6
Long-Term Obligations	4,880.6	4,718.6	4,365.6	3,270.9	3,270.1	3,078.4	3,031.7
Net Stockholders' Equity	3,921.5	4,216.0	4,041.8	4,029.1	4,433.9	4,415.5	4,255.5
Net Working Capital	d386.6	d89.9	83.2	34.9	268.6	192.6	d20.4
Year-end Shs. Outstg. (000)	461,100	476,600	487,020	497,357	507,952	514,580	534,074
STATISTICAL RECORD:							
Operating Profit Margin %	19.7	18.9	18.6	18.6	17.3	15.8	10.5
Net Profit Margin %	12.0	11.0	10.7	10.6	8.6	8.6	5.2
Return on Equity %	35.8	29.3	29.2	28.7	20.0	23.4	14.0
Return on Assets %	11.1	9.9	10.1	11.0	8.4	9.3	5.5
Debt/Total Assets %	38.6	37.8	37.2	31.3	30.9	27.9	27.9
Price Range	84-64⁷⁄₁₆	68¼-42¹⁵⁄₁₆	48¼-38½	45-32³⁄₈	34-25³⁄₈	27¹¹⁄₁₆-23⁹⁄₁₆	30⅛-21½
P/E Ratio	28.6-21.9	27.0-17.0	20.4-16.3	19.7-14.2	19.8-14.8	14.2-12.1	27.8-19.8
Average Yield %	1.6	1.9	2.3	2.4	2.8	3.0	2.6

Statistics are as originally reported. Adj. for 2-for-1 stk. split, 9/96. ① Incl. $160.0 mill. pre-tax write off & excl. disc. oper. loss of $244.3 mill. ② Incl. $54.7 mill. gain fr. the sale of the St. Louis Cardinals & bef. disc. oper. gain of $33.8 mill. ③ Bef. acctg. change chrge. of $10.0 mill., 1997; $76.7 mill., 1992. ④ Incl. $565.0 mill. restruct. chg.

OFFICERS:
A. A. Busch III, Chmn., Pres.
W. R. Baker, V.P., C.F.O.
J. Jacob, Exec. V.P., C.O.O.

INVESTOR CONTACT: C. Ramirez, (314) 577-9629

PRINCIPAL OFFICE: One Busch Place, St. Louis, MO 63118

TELEPHONE NUMBER: (314) 577-2000
FAX: (314) 577-2900
WEB: www.anheuser-busch.com

NO. OF EMPLOYEES: 23,645

SHAREHOLDERS: 60,100

ANNUAL MEETING: In Apr.

INCORPORATED: DE, Apr., 1979

INSTITUTIONAL HOLDINGS:
No. of Institutions: 616
Shares Held: 279,872,765
% Held: 60.1

INDUSTRY: Malt beverages (SIC: 2082)

TRANSFER AGENT(S): ChaseMellon Shareholder Services, L.L.C., Ridgefield Park, NJ

NYSE SYMBOL AOC
Rec. Pr. 35 1/8 (5/31/00)

AON CORPORATION

YIELD 2.5%
P/E RATIO 27.7

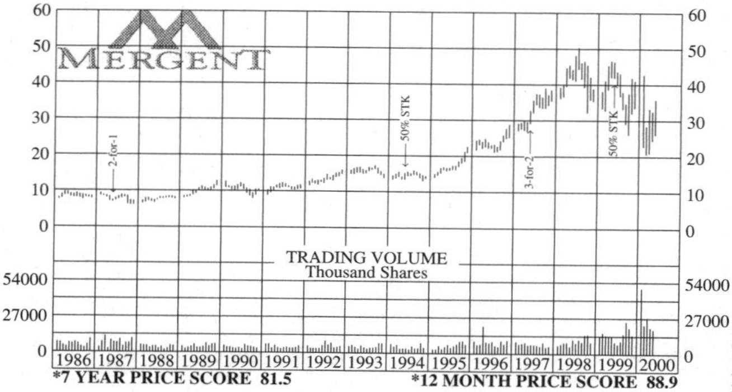

MERGENT
2-for-1
50% STK
3-for-2
50% STK
TRADING VOLUME
Thousand Shares
1986 1987 1988 1989 1990 1991 1992 1993 1994 1995 1996 1997 1998 1999 2000

***7 YEAR PRICE SCORE 81.5** ***12 MONTH PRICE SCORE 88.9**

*NYSE COMPOSITE INDEX=100

INTERIM EARNINGS (Per Share):

Qtr.	Mar.	June	Sept.	Dec.
1995	0.34	0.27	0.29	0.24
1996	0.46	0.33	0.29	0.17
1997	d0.01	0.32	0.38	0.43
1998	0.53	0.54	0.47	0.53
1999	0.13	0.57	0.52	0.05

INTERIM DIVIDENDS (Per Share):

Amt.	Decl.	Ex.	Rec.	Pay.
50% STK	3/19/99	5/18/99	5/04/99	5/17/99
0.21Q	7/16/99	7/30/99	8/03/99	8/16/99
0.21Q	10/15/99	10/29/99	11/02/99	11/15/99
0.21Q	1/21/00	2/04/00	2/08/00	2/22/00
0.22Q	4/18/00	4/28/00	5/02/00	5/15/00

Indicated div.: $0.88 (Div. Reinv. Plan)

CAPITALIZATION (12/31/99):

	($000)	(%)
Long-Term Debt	1,011,000	20.6
Redeemable Pfd. Stock	850,000	17.3
Common & Surplus	3,051,000	62.1
Total	4,912,000	100.0

DIVIDEND ACHIEVER STATUS:
Rank: 219 10-Year Growth Rate: 7.20%
Total Years of Dividend Growth: 48

RECENT DEVELOPMENTS: For the year ended 12/31/99, net income declined 34.9% to $352.0 million compared with $541.0 million a year earlier. Results for the current year included special charges of $313.0 million. Total revenue was $7.07 billion, up 8.9% from $6.49 billion in the prior year. Revenues from insurance brokerage rose 9.6% to $4.14 billion, while consulting revenue jumped 6.7% to $656.0 million. Insurance underwriting revenue climbed 8.2% to $2.11 million.

PROSPECTS: Going forward, AOC's focus will turn to improving the efficiency of its operations while growing revenues organically. However, results may be dampened by the loss of revenues from Unicover, lower income from equity investments and additional costs related to the integration of AOC's global acquisition strategy. Meanwhile, the Company expects to achieve earnings per share in the range of $2.10 to $2.20 for fiscal 2000.

BUSINESS

AON CORPORATION is a holding company whose subsidiaries operate in three distinct segments: Insurance Brokerage and Other Services, Consulting, and Insurance Underwriting. The Insurance Brokerage and Other Services segment consists principally of Aon's retail, reinsurance, specialty and wholesale brokerage operations. The Consulting segment provides a full range of employee benefits, human resources, compensation, and change management services. The Insurance Underwriting segment is comprised of direct sales life and accident and health, warranty, specialty and other insurance products. The Company is comprised of Aon Group, Inc., the holding company for AOC's commercial brokerage and consulting operations, its subsidiaries and certain other indirect subsidiaries including Aon Risk Services Companies, Inc.; Aon Holdings bv; Aon Consulting Worldwide, Inc.; Aon Services Group, Inc.; Aon Re Worldwide, Inc.; Aon Group Limited; and Alternative Market Operations.

ANNUAL FINANCIAL DATA

	12/31/99	12/31/98	12/31/97	12/31/96	12/31/95	12/31/94	12/31/93
Earnings Per Share	**[2] 1.33**	**2.07**	**1.12**	**[1] 1.10**	**[1] 1.14**	**1.40**	**1.25**
Tang. Book Val. Per Share	...	...	...	**4.93**	**4.38**	**2.88**	**3.26**
Dividends Per Share	**0.81**	**0.73**	**0.68**	**0.63**	**0.60**	**0.56**	**0.52**
Dividend Payout %	**61.1**	**35.4**	**60.7**	**57.3**	**52.1**	**40.1**	**42.0**
INCOME STATEMENT (IN MILLIONS):							
Total Premium Income	1,854.0	1,706.0	1,608.9	1,526.7	1,426.5	1,933.7	1,823.0
Net Investment Income	577.0	590.0	494.0	384.0	329.4	759.5	745.2
Other Income	4,639.0	4,197.0	3,647.7	1,977.5	1,709.8	1,463.7	1,276.6
Total Revenues	7,070.0	6,493.0	5,750.6	3,888.2	3,465.7	4,156.9	3,844.8
Policyholder Benefits	973.0	896.0	842.3	789.5	698.5	1,304.9	1,267.3
Income Before Income Taxes	635.0	931.0	541.6	445.6	458.0	537.6	479.1
Income Taxes	243.0	349.0	203.1	153.8	154.0	177.6	155.3
Equity Earnings/Minority Int.	d40.0	d41.0	d39.7	...	...	...	...
Net Income	[2] 352.0	541.0	298.8	[1] 291.8	[1] 303.7	360.0	323.8
Average Shs. Outstg. (000)	262,700	259,350	255,750	247,950	244,575	238,898	239,330
BALANCE SHEET (IN MILLIONS):							
Cash & Cash Equivalents	3,199.0	2,944.0	2,782.4	1,676.4	1,053.6	1,292.0	968.0
Premiums Due	7,346.0	6,543.0	6,183.1	4,555.2	2,844.3	2,519.7	2,100.5
Invst. Assets: Fixed-term	2,497.0	3,103.0	3,143.6	2,826.1	7,687.1	7,144.1	7,053.4
Invst. Assets: Loans	...	...	...	87.2	858.3	782.4	764.4
Invst. Assets: Total	6,184.0	6,452.0	5,922.1	5,212.8	10,639.1	9,782.5	9,651.7
Total Assets	21,132.0	19,688.0	18,691.2	13,722.7	19,735.8	17,921.9	16,279.1
Long-Term Obligations	1,011.0	580.0	637.1	521.2	554.3	561.0	593.8
Net Stockholders' Equity	3,051.0	3,017.0	2,822.1	2,832.9	2,673.7	2,257.4	2,287.8
Year-end Shs. Outstg. (000)	253,753	256,191	251,957	249,525	243,675	242,316	228,497
STATISTICAL RECORD:							
Return on Revenues %	5.0	8.3	5.2	7.5	8.8	8.7	8.4
Return on Equity %	11.5	17.9	10.6	10.3	11.4	15.9	14.2
Return on Assets %	1.7	2.7	1.6	2.1	1.5	2.0	2.0
Price Range	46 11/16-26 1/16	50 3/8-32 3/16	38 15/16-26 3/4	28 3/4-21 1/8	22 5/8-13 15/16	15 7/8-13	17 5/16-13 11/16
P/E Ratio	35.1-19.6	24.3-15.5	34.8-23.9	26.1-19.2	19.8-12.2	11.4-9.3	13.9-11.0
Average Yield %	2.2	1.8	2.1	2.5	3.3	3.9	3.4

Statistics are as originally reported. Adj. for stk. splits: 3-for-2, 5/99; 5/97; 5/94 [1] Bef. disc. oper. gain 1996, $43.4 mill.; 1995, $99.1 mill. [2] Incl. non-recurr. chrg. $313.0 mill.

OFFICERS:
P. G. Ryan, Chmn., C.E.O.
H. N. Medvin, Exec. V.P., C.F.O.

INVESTOR CONTACT: S.P. O'Neil, V.P., Fin. Rel. (312) 701-3983

PRINCIPAL OFFICE: 123 North Wacker Drive, Chicago, IL 60606

TELEPHONE NUMBER: (312) 701-3000
FAX: (312) 701-3080
WEB: www.aon.com
NO. OF EMPLOYEES: 50,000 (approx.)
SHAREHOLDERS: 13,300 (approx.)
ANNUAL MEETING: In Apr.
INCORPORATED: IL, Oct., 1949; reincorp., DE, 1979

INSTITUTIONAL HOLDINGS:
No. of Institutions: 287
Shares Held: 151,037,123
% Held: 58.9

INDUSTRY: Accident and health insurance (SIC: 6321)

TRANSFER AGENT(S): First Chicago Trust Company of New York, Jersey City, NJ

NASDAQ SYMBOL APOG
Rec. Pr. 4 1/8 (5/31/00)

APOGEE ENTERPRISES, INC.

YIELD 5.1%
P/E RATIO 51.6

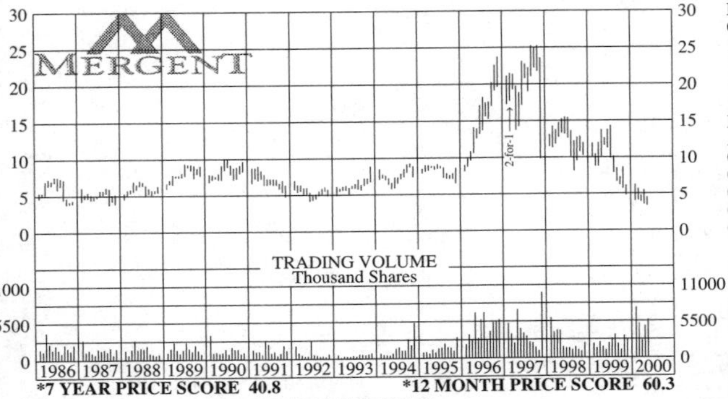

30
25
20
15
10
5
0
MERGENT
2-for-1
TRADING VOLUME
Thousand Shares
11000
5500
0
1986 1987 1988 1989 1990 1991 1992 1993 1994 1995 1996 1997 1998 1999 2000

***7 YEAR PRICE SCORE 40.8** ***12 MONTH PRICE SCORE 60.3**

*NYSE COMPOSITE INDEX=100

INTERIM EARNINGS (Per Share):

Qtr.	May	Aug.	Nov.	Feb.
1996-97	0.18	0.28	0.27	0.20
1997-98	0.24	0.34	d0.37	d2.06
1998-99	0.14	0.33	0.26	0.08
1999-00	0.16	0.18	d0.19	d0.07

INTERIM DIVIDENDS (Per Share):

Amt.	Decl.	Ex.	Rec.	Pay.
0.052Q	4/16/99	4/29/99	5/03/99	5/18/99
0.052Q	7/28/99	8/12/99	8/16/99	8/31/99
0.052Q	10/08/99	10/21/99	10/25/99	11/09/99
0.052Q	1/14/00	1/27/00	1/31/00	2/16/00
0.052Q	4/14/00	4/27/00	5/01/00	5/17/00

Indicated div.: $0.21 (Div. Reinv. Plan)

CAPITALIZATION (2/27/99):

	($000)	(%)
Long-Term Debt	165,097	55.8
Common & Surplus	130,664	44.2
Total	295,761	100.0

DIVIDEND ACHIEVER STATUS:
Rank: 195 10-Year Growth Rate: 8.26%
Total Years of Dividend Growth: 25

RECENT DEVELOPMENTS: For the year ended 2/26/00, the Company reported income of $3.1 million from continuing operations compared with income from continuing operations of $20.2 million in the previous year. Net sales rose 6.7% to $840.5 million from $788.1 million the year before. Glass Technologies sales grew 11.0% to $360.2 million from $324.5 million a year earlier. Glass Services sales rose 4.6% to $485.5 million from $464.3 million a year ago. For the fourth quarter ended 2/26/00, the Company reported a loss of $2.0 million from continuing operations compared with income of $2.3 million from continuing operations in the comparable quarter the year before. Net sales increased 6.4% to $212.7 million from $199.9 million in the corresponding quarter a year earlier due to sales growth in both the Glass Technologies and Glass Services businesses.

BUSINESS

APOGEE ENTERPRISES, INC. is a holding company that, through its subsidiaries, is primarily engaged in the design and development of value-added glass products, services, and systems. The Glass Technologies businesses are engaged in architectural glass and high-end glass coatings for the electronics markets, while the Glass Services businesses provide replacement auto glass and building glass services. On 2/24/99, the Company sold all 8 of its remaining Midas Muffler franchises. On 5/13/99, the Company completed the sale of its domestic curtainwall business, Harmon Ltd., to CH Holdings Inc.

BUSINESS LINE ANALYSIS

(02/27/99)	Rev(%)	Inc(%)
Glass Technologies	40.9	51.5
Glass Services	59.1	48.5
Total	100.0	100.0

ANNUAL FINANCIAL DATA

	2/27/99	2/28/98	3/1/97	3/2/96	2/25/95	2/26/94	2/27/93
Earnings Per Share	[3] **0.71**	[2] **d1.84**	**0.93**	**0.65**	**0.48**	[1] **0.13**	**0.17**
Cash Flow Per Share	**1.64**	**d0.97**	**1.66**	**1.26**	**1.04**	**0.72**	**0.74**
Tang. Book Val. Per Share	**2.74**	**2.15**	**4.29**	**4.76**	**4.32**	**4.21**	**4.08**
Dividends Per Share	**0.20**	**0.18**	**0.17**	**0.16**	**0.15**	**0.14**	**0.13**
Dividend Payout %	**28.5**	**...**	**18.5**	**25.0**	**31.8**	**113.9**	**77.9**
INCOME STATEMENT (IN THOUSANDS):							
Total Revenues	792,552	912,831	950,777	871,147	756,549	688,233	572,450
Costs & Expenses	724,471	944,108	883,823	822,162	717,156	665,451	550,971
Depreciation & Amort.	25,938	23,990	20,458	16,528	15,131	15,724	15,110
Operating Income	42,143	d55,267	46,496	32,457	24,262	9,352	8,244
Net Interest Inc./(Exp.)	d9,524	d7,334	d6,964	d5,697	d4,135	d2,735	d1,794
Income Before Income Taxes	32,619	d62,601	39,532	26,611	20,127	6,617	6,450
Income Taxes	11,743	cr12,425	13,802	9,820	8,101	2,634	1,936
Equity Earnings/Minority Int.	d1,189	d879	490	1,044	1,024	1,619	1,875
Net Income	[3] 19,687	[2] d51,055	26,220	17,835	13,050	[1] 3,308	4,514
Cash Flow	45,625	d27,065	46,678	34,363	28,181	19,032	19,624
Average Shs. Outstg.	27,762	27,795	28,057	27,258	27,002	26,578	26,586
BALANCE SHEET (IN THOUSANDS):							
Cash & Cash Equivalents	1,318	7,853	4,065	7,389	2,894	10,824	8,908
Total Current Assets	205,345	262,244	305,194	258,559	256,820	221,286	169,029
Net Property	180,428	129,937	118,799	78,485	75,028	64,917	66,128
Total Assets	471,191	464,121	500,964	386,136	361,928	306,188	251,456
Total Current Liabilities	115,211	177,768	176,621	142,477	135,719	140,846	99,787
Long-Term Obligations	165,097	151,967	127,640	79,102	80,566	35,688	28,419
Net Stockholders' Equity	130,664	109,601	172,149	138,921	124,629	114,063	112,335
Net Working Capital	90,134	84,476	128,573	116,082	121,101	80,440	69,242
Year-end Shs. Outstg.	27,623	27,453	27,882	27,034	26,886	26,624	26,354
STATISTICAL RECORD:							
Operating Profit Margin %	5.3	...	4.9	3.7	3.2	1.4	1.4
Net Profit Margin %	2.5	...	2.8	2.0	1.7	0.5	0.8
Return on Equity %	15.1	...	15.2	12.8	10.5	2.9	4.0
Return on Assets %	4.2	...	5.2	4.6	3.6	1.1	1.8
Debt/Total Assets %	35.0	32.7	25.5	20.5	22.3	11.7	11.3
Price Range	15 1/2-8 1/8	25 1/4-9 13/16	23 3/4-8 1/8	9 1/8-6 1/2	9 1/4-5 3/4	8 7/8-4 7/8	7-4 1/8
P/E Ratio	21.8-11.4	...	25.5-8.7	14.0-10.0	19.3-12.0	70.9-39.0	41.2-24.3
Average Yield %	1.7	1.1	1.1	2.1	2.0	2.1	2.4

Statistics are as originally reported. Adj. for stk. split: 2-for-1, 2/14/97 [1] Bef. acctg. change credit $525,000 ($0.02/sh.)but incl. non-recurr. chrg. $5.2 mill. [2] Incl. non-recurr. chrg. $96.1 mill., 2/28/98; $5.8 mill., 2/29/92 [3] Bef. income of $5.5 mill. ($0.20/sh.) from disc. ops.

OFFICERS:
R. Huffer, Chmn., Pres., C.E.O.
R. G. Barbieri, V.P., C.F.O.
M. Bevilacqua, Treas.
M. L. Richards, Gen. Couns., Sec.

PRINCIPAL OFFICE: 7900 Xerxes Ave. South, Suite 1800, Minneapolis, MN 55431

TELEPHONE NUMBER: (612) 835-1874
FAX: (612) 835-3196

NO. OF EMPLOYEES: 6,367 (avg.)

SHAREHOLDERS: 1,965 (approx.)

ANNUAL MEETING: In June

INCORPORATED: MN, Jul., 1949

INSTITUTIONAL HOLDINGS:
No. of Institutions: 68
Shares Held: 16,002,294
% Held: 57.6

INDUSTRY: Glass and glazing work (SIC: 1793)

TRANSFER AGENT(S): American Stock Transfer & Trust Company, New York, NY

ARCHER DANIELS MIDLAND COMPANY

YIELD 1.7%
P/E RATIO 37.3

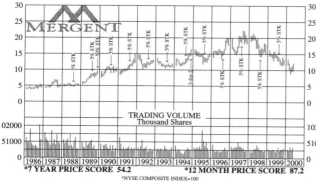

TRADING VOLUME
Thousand Shares

*7 YEAR PRICE SCORE 54.2   *12 MONTH PRICE SCORE 87.2
*NYSE COMPOSITE INDEX=100

INTERIM EARNINGS (Per Share):

Qtr.	Sept.	Dec.	Mar.	June
1995-96	0.27	0.35	0.27	0.24
1996-97	0.01	0.30	0.10	0.20
1997-98	0.21	0.23	0.11	0.10
1998-99	0.19	0.18	0.02	0.07
1999-00	0.06	0.17	...	...

INTERIM DIVIDENDS (Per Share):

Amt.	Decl.	Ex.	Rec.	Pay.
0.05Q	7/30/99	8/04/99	8/06/99	8/30/99
5% STK	7/30/99	8/19/99	8/23/99	9/20/99
0.05Q	10/21/99	11/03/99	11/05/99	11/29/99
0.05Q	12/30/99	2/02/00	2/04/00	2/28/00
0.05Q	4/28/00	5/03/00	5/05/00	6/05/00

Indicated div.: $0.20

CAPITALIZATION (6/30/99):

	($000)	(%)
Long-Term Debt	3,191,883	31.8
Deferred Income Tax	619,752	6.2
Common & Surplus	6,240,640	62.1
Total	10,052,275	100.0

DIVIDEND ACHIEVER STATUS:

Rank: 23   10-Year Growth Rate: 20.58%
Total Years of Dividend Growth: 25

RECENT DEVELOPMENTS: For the three months ended 12/31/99, net earnings totaled $101.9 million, down 7.7% compared with income, before an extraordinary charge, of $110.4 million a year earlier. Net sales and other operating income slid 12.6% to $3.42 billion from $3.91 billion the previous year, stemming primarily from lower sales of oilseed products. Net sales of oilseed products fell 19.1% to $1.87 billion, due to lower average selling prices and weak demand in Asia. Gross profit slipped 3.6% to $406.3 million from $421.3 million the prior year.

PROSPECTS: Abundant worldwide supply of agricultural commodities is continuing to hamper sales of the Company's oilseed products. This increased supply, coupled with weak demand in Asia for both protein meals and vegetable oils, is driving average selling prices lower. Meanwhile, improving conditions in several of the Company's key markets could boost near-term earnings. Results are beginning to benefit from increased sales of corn products, as demand for the Company's fuel alcohol is improving in existing and new markets.

BUSINESS

ARCHER DANIELS MIDLAND COMPANY is engaged in the business of processing and merchandising agricultural commodities. ADM is one of the largest domestic processors of oil seeds and vegetable oil, and one of the largest flour millers and corn refiners in the U.S. ADM's corn wet milling operations produce corn syrups, high fructose syrups, glucose, corn starches and ethyl alcohol (ethanol). Other operations include storage of grain, shelling of peanuts, production of consumer food products and formula feeds, production of malt products and refining of sugar. ADM Investor Services provides the Company and other commercial firms with commodity hedging services and is a futures commission merchant.

ANNUAL FINANCIAL DATA

	6/30/99	6/30/98	6/30/97	6/30/96	6/30/95	6/30/94	6/30/93
Earnings Per Share	④ 0.45	③ 0.65	③ 0.60	② 1.09	1.21	0.73	① 0.83
Cash Flow Per Share	1.45	1.55	1.36	1.75	1.83	1.29	1.28
Tang. Book Val. Per Share	10.07	10.45	9.84	9.73	9.19	7.65	7.44
Dividends Per Share	0.198	0.184	0.175	0.167	0.10	0.057	0.048
Dividend Payout %	44.0	28.3	29.2	15.3	8.3	7.8	5.8
INCOME STATEMENT (IN MILLIONS)							
Total Revenues	14,283.3	16,108.6	13,853.3	13,314.0	12,671.9	11,374.4	9,811.4
Costs & Expenses	13,130.2	14,828.3	12,752.3	11,980.4	11,052.0	10,233.9	8,727.8
Depreciation & Amort.	622.2	560.1	475.5	419.2	406.8	374.1	345.4
Operating Income	531.0	720.3	625.4	914.4	1,213.1	766.4	738.2
Income Before Income Taxes	419.8	610.0	644.4	1,054.4	1,181.5	738.3	746.0
Income Taxes	138.5	206.4	267.1	358.5	385.6	254.2	211.5
Net Income	④ 281.3	③ 403.6	③ 377.3	② 695.9	795.9	484.1	① 534.5
Cash Flow	903.5	963.7	852.8	1,115.1	1,202.7	858.1	880.0
Average Shs. Outstg. (000)	621,613	622,265	626,169	636,746	657,909	664,043	689,028
BALANCE SHEET (IN MILLIONS)							
Cash & Cash Equivalents	903.6	725.5	728.0	1,354.8	1,119.3	1,335.5	1,868.3
Total Current Assets	5,789.6	5,451.7	4,284.3	4,384.7	3,712.6	3,910.8	3,921.7
Net Property	5,567.2	5,322.7	4,708.6	4,114.3	3,762.3	3,538.6	3,214.8
Total Assets	14,029.9	13,833.5	11,354.4	10,449.9	9,756.9	8,746.9	8,404.1
Total Current Liabilities	3,840.3	3,717.3	2,248.8	1,633.6	1,172.4	1,127.0	960.2
Long-Term Obligations	3,191.9	2,847.1	2,344.9	2,003.0	2,070.1	2,021.4	2,039.1
Net Stockholders' Equity	6,240.6	6,504.9	6,050.1	6,144.8	5,854.2	5,045.4	4,883.3
Net Working Capital	1,949.3	1,734.4	2,035.6	2,751.1	2,540.3	2,783.8	2,961.5
Year-end Shs. Outstg. (000)	619,810	622,777	614,925	631,856	636,895	659,406	656,217
STATISTICAL RECORD:							
Operating Profit Margin %	3.7	4.5	4.5	6.9	9.6	6.7	7.5
Net Profit Margin %	2.0	2.5	2.7	5.2	6.3	4.3	5.4
Return on Equity %	4.5	6.2	6.2	11.3	13.6	9.6	10.9
Return on Assets %	2.0	2.9	3.3	6.7	8.2	5.5	6.4
Debt/Total Assets %	22.8	20.6	20.7	19.2	21.2	23.1	24.3
Price Range	16^{9}/$_{16}$-11^{7}/$_{16}$	21^{7}/$_{16}$-14^{1}/$_{8}$	22^{5}/$_{16}$-14^{11}/$_{16}$	19-13^{1}/$_{2}$	16^{7}/$_{16}$-11^{3}/$_{4}$	16^{9}/$_{16}$-11^{1}/$_{8}$	13^{3}/$_{4}$-10^{7}/$_{16}$
P/E Ratio	36.1-25.4	33.0-21.7	37.3-24.5	18.3-12.4	13.6-9.7	22.8-15.3	16.7-12.6
Average Yield %	1.4	1.0	0.9	1.0	0.7	0.4	0.4

Statistics are as originally reported. Adj. for all stk. divs. & splits through 9/99. ① Bef. $33 mil ($0.07/sh) chg. for acctg. adj. ② Incl. $0.04/sh net chg. ③ Incl. $48 mil ($0.07/sh) chg. for fines & litig. costs & $0.04/sh gain fr secs. transactions, 1998; & $0.19/sh net chg., 1997. ④ Excl. $15.3 mil ($0.02/sh) extraord. chg. & incl. $0.10/sh gain from secs. transactions.

OFFICERS:
G. A. Andreas, Chmn., C.E.O.
J. D. McNamara, Pres.
D. J. Schmalz, V.P., C.F.O.

PRINCIPAL OFFICE: 4666 Faries Parkway, Box 1470, Decatur, IL 62525

TELEPHONE NUMBER: (217) 424-5200
FAX: (217) 424-5447
WEB: www.admworld.com
NO. OF EMPLOYEES: 23,603 (avg.)
SHAREHOLDERS: 31,764
ANNUAL MEETING: In Oct.
INCORPORATED: DE, May, 1923

INSTITUTIONAL HOLDINGS:
No. of Institutions: 286
Shares Held: 352,231,567
% Held: 57.9

INDUSTRY: Soybean oil mills (SIC: 2075)

TRANSFER AGENT(S): Harris Trust and Savings Bank, Chicago, IL

ASSOCIATED BANC-CORP.

YIELD 5.0%
P/E RATIO 9.9

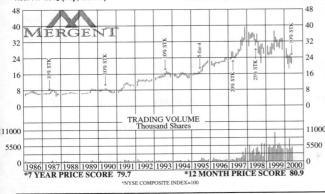

TRADING VOLUME
Thousand Shares

*7 YEAR PRICE SCORE 79.7   *12 MONTH PRICE SCORE 80.9
*NYSE COMPOSITE INDEX=100

INTERIM EARNINGS (Per Share):

Qtr.	Mar.	June	Sept.	Dec.
1995	0.39	0.42	0.45	0.45
1996	0.45	0.46	0.49	0.49
1997	0.49	0.52	0.53	d0.77
1998	0.56	0.58	0.55	0.55
1999	0.55	0.56	0.59	0.63

INTERIM DIVIDENDS (Per Share):

Amt.	Decl.	Ex.	Rec.	Pay.
0.29Q	7/28/99	7/29/99	8/02/99	8/16/99
0.29Q	10/27/99	10/29/99	11/01/99	11/15/99
0.29Q	1/26/00	1/28/00	2/01/00	2/15/00
0.29Q	4/26/00	4/27/00	5/01/00	5/15/00
10% STK	4/26/00	5/30/00	6/01/00	6/15/00

Indicated div.: $1.16 (Div. Reinv. Plan)

CAPITALIZATION (12/31/99):

	($000)	(%)
Total Deposits	8,691,829	90.3
Long-Term Debt	24,283	0.3
Common & Surplus	909,789	9.5
Total	9,625,901	100.0

DIVIDEND ACHIEVER STATUS:

Rank: 61   10-Year Growth Rate: 15.19%
Total Years of Dividend Growth: 26

RECENT DEVELOPMENTS: On 2/24/00, the Company and Citibank USA entered into a long-term agency agreement, which includes the sale of the Company's $130.0 million credit card portfolio to Citibank. For the year ended 12/31/99, net income increased 5.0% to $164.9 million compared with $157.0 million in the previous year. Toal interest income increased 5.6% to $814.5 million from $785.8 million the year before. Total interest expense grew 1.9% to $418.8 million from $411.0 million a year earlier.

Net interest income increased to $395.7 million from $374.7 million the year before. Provision for loan losses amounted to $19.2 million compared with $14.7 million in 1998. Non-interest income decreased 1.2% to $165.9 million from $167.9 million in 1998, primarily due to a decline in mortgage banking income, and to a lesser extent, a decline on the sale of investments. Non-interest expense rose to $305.1 million versus $295.0 million in the prior year.

BUSINESS

ASSOCIATED BANC-CORP is a bank holding company that owns ten commercial banks and a federally chartered thrift located in Wisconsin, Minnesota and Illinois. ASBC provides advice and specialized services to its affiliates in banking policy and operations, including auditing, data processing, marketing/advertising, investing, legal/compliance, personnel services, trust services, risk management, facilities management, security, corporate-wide purchasing, treasury, finance, accounting, and other financial services functionally related to banking. Through its affiliates, ASBC provides a wide range of banking services to individuals and small to medium-sized businesses. As 12/31/99, ASBC had total assets of $12.52 billion and owned 32 non-banking subsidiaries located in Arizona, California, Delaware, Illinois, Missouri, Nevada, and Wisconsin. On 12/19/98, ASBC acquired Citizens Bankshares Inc.

ANNUAL FINANCIAL DATA

	12/31/99	12/31/98	12/31/97	12/31/96	12/31/95	12/31/94	12/31/93
Earnings Per Share	2.34	2.24	☐ 0.74	1.89	1.72	1.56	1.40
Tang. Book Val. Per Share	13.09	12.70	11.75	12.98	11.95	10.56	9.90
Dividends Per Share	1.05	0.95	0.81	0.69	0.59	0.51	0.45
Dividend Payout %	44.9	42.4	109.5	36.5	34.3	32.7	32.2
INCOME STATEMENT (IN MILLIONS):							
Total Interest Income	814.5	785.8	787.2	311.7	264.4	211.0	200.5
Total Interest Expense	418.8	411.0	411.6	142.5	117.8	79.7	76.9
Net Interest Income	395.7	374.7	375.6	169.3	146.6	131.3	123.6
Provision for Loan Losses	19.2	14.7	31.7	4.7	3.2	2.8	5.5
Non-Interest Income	165.9	168.0	96.0	65.1	53.0	47.8	48.6
Non-Interest Expense	305.1	295.0	323.6	140.4	123.1	113.8	111.8
Income Before Taxes	237.3	233.0	116.3	89.3	73.4	62.5	54.8
Net Income	164.9	157.0	☐ 52.4	57.2	46.7	40.4	36.2
Average Shs. Outstg. (000)	70,467	70,168	70,329	30,298	27,233	26,006	25,903
BALANCE SHEET (IN MILLIONS):							
Cash & Due from Banks	284.7	331.5	288.0	236.3	206.5	196.4	157.3
Securities Avail. for Sale	2,841.5	2,357.0	2,167.7	437.4	359.0	305.9	268.3
Total Loans & Leases	8,357.9	7,272.7	7,076.6	3,159.9	2,611.2	2,277.3	2,037.2
Allowance for Credit Losses	113.2	99.7	92.7	47.4	39.1	36.4	33.9
Net Loans & Leases	8,244.8	7,173.0	6,983.8	3,112.4	2,572.2	2,240.9	2,003.2
Total Assets	12,519.9	11,250.7	10,691.4	4,419.1	3,697.8	3,284.3	2,981.6
Total Deposits	8,691.8	8,557.8	8,364.1	3,508.0	2,973.1	2,663.6	2,431.4
Long-Term Obligations	24.3	26.0	15.3	21.1	18.1	3.9	5.3
Total Liabilities	11,610.1	10,371.9	9,877.7	4,025.9	3,372.2	3,009.7	2,724.6
Net Stockholders' Equity	909.8	878.7	813.7	393.1	325.6	274.6	257.0
Year-end Shs. Outstg. (000)	69,520	69,176	69,267	30,295	27,250	26,002	25,969
STATISTICAL RECORD:							
Return on Equity %	18.1	17.9	6.4	14.6	14.3	14.7	14.1
Return on Assets %	1.3	1.4	0.5	1.3	1.3	1.2	1.2
Equity/Assets %	7.3	7.8	7.6	8.9	8.8	8.4	8.6
Non-Int. Exp./Tot. Inc. %	54.6	55.0	64.2	60.1	61.8	63.6	65.1
Price Range	40¹⁵⁄₁₆-27⁷⁄₁₆	40³⁄₁₆-23¹⁄₁₆	43¹⁄₁₆-25¹⁄₈	26½-21³⁄₈	24⁷⁄₈-16⁵⁄₈	18⁹⁄₁₆-15¹⁄₈	19⅜-14³⁄₁₆
P/E Ratio	17.5-11.7	18.0-10.3	58.1-33.9	14.0-11.3	14.5-9.7	11.9-9.7	13.8-10.1
Average Yield %	3.1	3.0	2.4	2.9	2.8	3.0	2.7

Statistics are as originally reported. Adj. for stk. splits: 10% div., 6/00; 25% div., 6/12/98; 20% div., 3/17/97; 5-for-4, 6/15/95; 10% div., 8/30/93 ☐ Incl. non-recurr. chrg. $103.7 mill. ($1.41/sh.)

OFFICERS:
H. B. Conlon, Chmn., C.E.O.
R. C. Gallagher, Pres. & C.O.O.
J. B. Selner, C.F.O.

INVESTOR CONTACT: Joseph B. Selner (920) 491-7120

PRINCIPAL OFFICE: 1200 Hansen Road, Green Bay, WI 54304

TELEPHONE NUMBER: (920) 491-7000
FAX: (920) 433-3261
WEB: www.asbc.com

NO. OF EMPLOYEES: 3,966

SHAREHOLDERS: 10,400 (approx.)

ANNUAL MEETING: In Apr.

INCORPORATED: WI, 1964

INSTITUTIONAL HOLDINGS:
No. of Institutions: 119
Shares Held: 23,222,366 (Adj.)
% Held: 33.0

INDUSTRY: Bank holding companies (SIC: 6712)

TRANSFER AGENT(S): First Chicago Trust Company of New York, Jersey City, NJ

ATMOS ENERGY CORPORATION

YIELD 6.2%
P/E RATIO 31.0

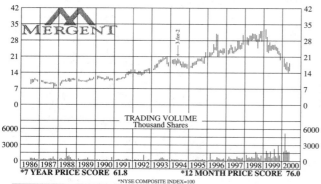

7 YEAR PRICE SCORE 61.8   **12 MONTH PRICE SCORE 76.0**
*NYSE COMPOSITE INDEX=100

INTERIM EARNINGS (Per Share):

Qtr.	Dec.	Mar.	June	Sept.
1996-97	0.55	0.90	0.03	d0.74
1997-98	0.68	1.25	0.06	d0.13
1998-99	0.50	0.94	d0.17	d0.68
1999-00	0.46	...	...	...

INTERIM DIVIDENDS (Per Share):

Amt.	Decl.	Ex.	Rec.	Pay.
0.275Q	8/11/99	8/23/99	8/25/99	9/10/99
0.285Q	11/10/99	11/22/99	11/24/99	12/10/99
0.285Q	2/08/00	2/23/00	2/25/00	3/10/00
0.285Q	5/10/00	5/23/00	5/25/00	6/12/00

Indicated div.: $1.14 (Div. Reinv. Plan)

CAPITALIZATION (9/30/99):

	($000)	(%)
Long-Term Debt	377,483	43.5
Deferred Income Tax	112,610	13.0
Common & Surplus	377,663	43.5
Total	867,756	100.0

DIVIDEND ACHIEVER STATUS:
Rank: 284   10-Year Growth Rate: 3.96%
Total Years of Dividend Growth: 12

RECENT DEVELOPMENTS: For the quarter ended 12/31/99, net income declined 6.9% to $14.3 million from $15.4 million in the same period of 1998. Results were affected by weather that was 17.0% warmer than normal and 2.0% warmer year over year. Results were also pressured by an increase in depreciation and interest expense. Operating revenues rose 6.8% to $224.5 million from $210.2 million the year before. Gross profit slipped 1.9% to $89.6 million from $91.2 million a year earlier. Operating income fell 4.9% to $30.1 million from $31.7 million in 1998.

PROSPECTS: On 4/13/00, ATO announced it has an agreement to acquire the Louisiana gas operations of Louisiana Gas Service Company and LGS Natural Gas Company for $375.0 million. This acquisition is expected to make Atmos the largest natural gas distributor in Louisiana with approximately 359,000 customers. The transaction may be accretive to earnings, excluding charges related to transaction, in the first full year of operations after closing. The transaction should be completed in early 2001 and is subject to approval by the Louisiana Public Service Commision.

BUSINESS

ATMOS ENERGY CORPORATION distributes natural gas to more than one million residential, commercial, industrial and agricultural customers in thirteen states. ATO's Louisiana distribution system is operated through Trans Louisiana Gas Company and the Kentucky distribution system is operated through Western Kentucky Gas Company. The Texas distribution system is operated through the Energas Company. The Colorado, parts of Kansas, and Missouri distribution systems are operated through Greeley Gas Company. United Cities Gas Company is a natural gas utility company engaged in the distribution and sale of natural gas to customers in Tennessee, Illinois, Virginia, Kansas, Missouri, South Carolina, Georgia, and Iowa. The Company also distributes propane to approximately 40,000 customers in Kentucky, North Carolina, Virginia and Tennessee.

ANNUAL FINANCIAL DATA

	9/30/99	9/30/98 ③	9/30/97	9/30/96	9/30/95	9/30/94 ①	9/30/93
Earnings Per Share	0.58	1.84	② 0.81	1.51	1.22	0.97	0.97
Cash Flow Per Share	2.58	3.62	2.35	2.82	2.57	2.21	1.80
Tang. Book Val. Per Share	12.09	12.21	11.04	10.75	10.20	9.78	6.93
Dividends Per Share	1.11	1.07	1.02	0.97	0.93	0.89	0.86
Dividend Payout %	191.3	58.1	125.9	64.2	76.2	91.7	89.1

INCOME STATEMENT (IN THOUSANDS):

Total Revenues	690,196	848,208	906,835	483,744	435,820	499,808	388,495
Costs & Expenses	565,142	671,635	782,995	406,430	368,852	440,511	335,599
Depreciation & Amort.	61,674	53,416	45,257	20,849	20,741	28,841	13,620
Maintenance Exp.	9,141	10,278	11,974	4,212	4,276	5,888	3,804
Operating Income	54,239	112,879	52,311	38,943	32,377	26,466	26,067
Net Interest Inc./(Exp.)	d36,298	d25,808	d28,185	d14,585	d13,504	d11,787	d10,355
Income Taxes	9,555	31,806	14,298	13,310	9,574	8,102	9,405
Net Income	17,744	55,265	② 23,838	23,949	18,873	14,679	15,712
Cash Flow	79,418	108,681	69,095	44,798	39,614	33,520	29,332
Average Shs. Outstg.	30,819	30,031	29,409	15,892	15,416	15,195	16,266

BALANCE SHEET (IN THOUSANDS):

Gross Property	1,549,258	1,446,420	1,332,672	666,438	595,359	543,692	399,404
Accumulated Depreciation	583,476	528,560	483,545	252,871	232,107	216,285	158,894
Net Property	965,782	917,860	849,127	413,567	363,252	327,407	240,510
Total Assets	1,230,537	1,141,390	1,088,311	501,861	445,783	416,678	323,694
Long-Term Obligations	377,483	398,548	302,981	122,303	131,303	138,303	85,250
Net Stockholders' Equity	377,663	371,158	327,260	172,298	158,278	149,556	118,227
Year-end Shs. Outstg.	31,248	30,398	29,642	16,021	15,519	15,297	17,063

STATISTICAL RECORD:

Operating Profit Margin %	7.9	13.3	5.8	8.1	7.4	5.3	6.7
Net Profit Margin %	2.6	6.5	2.6	5.0	4.3	2.9	4.0
Net Inc./Net Property %	1.8	6.0	2.8	5.8	5.2	4.5	6.5
Net Inc./Tot. Capital %	2.0	6.5	3.3	7.2	5.8	4.6	6.8
Return on Equity %	4.7	14.9	7.3	13.9	11.9	9.8	13.3
Accum. Depr./Gross Prop. %	37.7	36.5	36.3	37.9	39.0	39.8	39.8
Price Range	33-19⁵/₈	32¼-24³/₄	30½-22¹/₈	31-20⁷/₈	23-16¹/₈	20¼-15⁷/₈	21³/₁₆-15³/₁₆
P/E Ratio	56.9-33.8	17.5-13.5	37.6-27.3	20.5-13.8	18.9-13.2	20.9-16.4	21.9-15.7
Average Yield %	4.2	3.8	3.9	3.7	4.8	4.9	4.7

Statistics are as originally reported. Adjusted for 3-for-2 stock split, 5/94. ① Incl. results of Greeley Gas Co. ② Incl. a non-recurr. after-tax chg. of $2.8 mill. related to mgmt. changes & an after-tax charge of $12.6 mill. for merger & integration exps. ③ Incl. results of United Cities Gas Company

OFFICERS:
R. W. Best, Chmn., Pres., C.E.O.
J. P. Reddy, C.F.O., Treas., Sr. V.P.
INVESTOR CONTACT: Lynn Hord, V.P.
Investor Relations, (972) 855-3729
PRINCIPAL OFFICE: Three Lincoln Centre, Suite 1800, 5430 LBJ Freeway, Dallas, TX 75240

TELEPHONE NUMBER: (972) 934-9227
FAX: (972) 855-3075
WEB: www.atmosenergy.com
NO. OF EMPLOYEES: 2,062
SHAREHOLDERS: 35,179
ANNUAL MEETING: In Feb.
INCORPORATED: TX, Oct., 1983

INSTITUTIONAL HOLDINGS:
No. of Institutions: 85
Shares Held: 12,336,499
% Held: 39.2
INDUSTRY: Natural gas transmission (SIC: 4922)
TRANSFER AGENT(S): Bank Boston N.A., Boston, MA

AUTOMATIC DATA PROCESSING, INC.

YIELD	0.6%
P/E RATIO	43.7

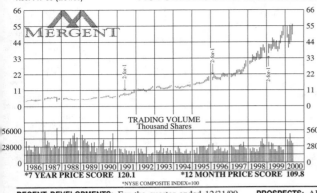

TRADING VOLUME
Thousand Shares

1986 1987 1988 1989 1990 1991 1992 1993 1994 1995 1996 1997 1998 1999 2000
*7 YEAR PRICE SCORE 120.1   *12 MONTH PRICE SCORE 109.8
*NYSE COMPOSITE INDEX=100

INTERIM EARNINGS (Per Share):

Qtr.	Sept.	Dec.	Mar.	June
1996-97	0.16	0.22	0.28	0.22
1997-98	0.18	0.25	0.31	0.26
1998-99	0.20	0.27	0.36	0.30
1999-00	0.23	0.31	...	...

INTERIM DIVIDENDS (Per Share):

Amt.	Decl.	Ex.	Rec.	Pay.
0.076Q	5/19/99	6/09/99	6/11/99	7/01/99
0.076Q	8/10/99	9/08/99	9/10/99	10/01/99
0.087Q	11/09/99	12/08/99	12/10/99	1/01/00
0.087Q	1/25/00	3/08/00	3/10/00	4/01/00
0.087Q	5/16/00	6/07/00	6/09/00	7/01/00
Indicated div.: $0.35				

CAPITALIZATION (6/30/99):

	($000)	(%)
Long-Term Debt	145,765	3.4
Deferred Income Tax	138,236	3.2
Common & Surplus	4,007,941	93.4
Total	4,291,942	100.0

DIVIDEND ACHIEVER STATUS:
Rank: 53   10-Year Growth Rate: 15.86%
Total Years of Dividend Growth: 24

RECENT DEVELOPMENTS: For the quarter ended 12/31/99, net earnings rose 29.6% to $199.5 million versus $154.0 million in 1998. Results in 1998 included net charges totaling $27.0 million. Total revenues were $1.49 billion, up 13.9% from $1.31 billion in the prior-year period. Revenues benefited from a $35.0 million contract with a single mailing company in the Brokerage Investor Communications business. Operating margins improved due to the effect of dispositions in 1998, higher interest rates, and increased operating efficiencies.

PROSPECTS: AUD's Emerging Business Services division of Employer Services announced a marketing alliance with DSL.net, Inc., a business Internet applications provider. The partnership will allow small businesses to leverage the efficiencies of AUD's on-line ezSuite℠ of applications and DSL.net's range of Internet services. Separately, AUD entered into a definitive agreement to acquire Cunningham Graphics International, Inc., a provider of time-sensitive printing to the financial services industry, for about $125.0 million.

BUSINESS

AUTOMATIC DATA PROCESS-ING, INC. is an independent computer services firm with over 450,000 clients. AUD's Employer Services group (59.7% of 1999 revenues) serves employers with payroll, human resources, tax deposit and reporting services. Brokerage Services (20.8% of revenues) provides high quality, high speed securities transaction processing, investor support tools, market data services, and investor communications related services to the financial community worldwide. ADP Dealer Services (13.4% of revenues) is the world's largest provider of computing, data and professional services to auto and truck dealers in the U.S., Canada, Europe, Asia and Latin America. Other Service groups (6.1% of revenues) include claims services and ADP international.

ANNUAL FINANCIAL DATA

	6/30/99	6/30/98	6/30/97	6/30/96	6/30/95	6/30/94	6/30/93
Earnings Per Share	③ 1.10	0.99	② 0.88	0.79	0.69	① 0.59	0.52
Cash Flow Per Share	1.52	1.37	1.27	1.14	0.99	0.86	0.77
Tang. Book Val. Per Share	3.97	2.90	2.30	1.86	2.41	1.92	1.63
Dividends Per Share	0.30	0.27	0.23	0.20	0.16	0.14	0.12
Dividend Payout %	27.7	26.8	26.1	25.5	23.4	23.6	23.6
INCOME STATEMENT (IN MILLIONS):							
Total Revenues	5,540.1	4,798.1	4,112.2	3,566.6	2,893.7	2,469.0	2,223.4
Costs & Expenses	4,163.7	3,645.2	3,136.9	2,699.8	2,162.6	1,853.5	1,676.8
Depreciation & Amort.	272.8	244.6	223.4	201.6	172.5	148.3	140.2
Operating Income	1,103.6	908.2	751.8	665.1	558.6	467.2	406.4
Net Interest Inc./(Exp.)	d19.1	d24.0	d27.8	d29.7	d24.3	d20.8	d19.8
Income Before Income Taxes	1,084.5	884.2	724.0	635.4	534.3	446.3	386.6
Income Taxes	387.7	278.9	210.5	180.7	139.5	112.2	92.4
Net Income	③ 696.8	605.3	② 513.5	454.7	394.8	① 334.1	294.2
Cash Flow	969.6	849.9	736.9	656.3	567.4	482.4	434.4
Average Shs. Outstg. (000)	636,892	620,822	581,980	577,934	570,224	563,560	565,308
BALANCE SHEET (IN MILLIONS):							
Cash & Cash Equivalents	1,092.5	897.2	1,024.9	636.2	697.6	590.6	368.2
Total Current Assets	2,194.3	1,829.3	1,805.3	1,454.3	1,211.1	985.4	771.3
Net Property	579.3	583.7	519.3	468.3	416.0	395.8	361.2
Total Assets	5,824.8	5,175.4	4,382.8	3,839.9	3,201.1	2,705.6	2,439.4
Total Current Liabilities	1,286.4	1,221.0	1,019.9	835.6	543.2	478.2	416.3
Long-Term Obligations	145.8	192.1	401.2	403.7	390.2	373.0	347.6
Net Stockholders' Equity	4,007.9	3,406.5	2,660.6	2,315.3	2,096.6	1,691.3	1,494.5
Net Working Capital	907.9	608.3	785.5	618.7	667.9	507.2	355.0
Year-end Shs. Outstg. (000)	623,627	604,212	585,698	575,242	576,336	562,796	564,476
STATISTICAL RECORD:							
Operating Profit Margin %	19.9	18.9	18.3	18.6	19.3	18.9	18.3
Net Profit Margin %	12.6	12.6	12.5	12.7	13.6	13.5	13.2
Return on Equity %	17.4	17.8	19.3	19.6	18.8	19.8	19.7
Return on Assets %	12.0	11.7	11.7	11.8	12.3	12.3	12.1
Debt/Total Assets %	2.5	3.7	9.2	10.5	12.2	13.8	14.2
Price Range	54¹³/₁₆-36¼	42³/₁₆-28¹³/₁₆	31⅜-19¾	22⅞-17¹³/₁₆	20⅝-14⅜	14¹⁵/₁₆-11¹⁵/₁₆	14¼-11¾
P/E Ratio	49.8-33.0	42.6-29.1	35.6-22.4	29.1-22.7	29.7-20.7	25.2-20.1	27.3-22.5
Average Yield %	0.7	0.7	0.9	1.0	0.9	1.0	0.9

Statistics are as originally reported. Adj. for 2-for-1 stk. split, 1/99 & 1/96. ① Excl. acctg. chg. of $4.8 mill. ② Incl. non-recur. chg. of $11.7 mill. ③ Incl. about $37.0 pre-tax gain, $40.0 mill. provision for taxes, & $14.0 mill. net non-recur. adjustment.

OFFICERS:
A. F. Weinbach, Chmn., C.E.O.
G. C. Butler, Pres., C.O.O.
R. J. Haviland, V.P., C.F.O.

PRINCIPAL OFFICE: One ADP Blvd.,
Roseland, NJ 07068-1728

TELEPHONE NUMBER: (973) 974-5000
FAX: (973) 974-5390
WEB: www.adp.com
NO. OF EMPLOYEES: 37,000 (avg.)
SHAREHOLDERS: 32,681
ANNUAL MEETING: In Nov.
INCORPORATED: DE, Jun., 1961

NYSE SYMBOL AVY
Rec. Pr. 61 1/4 (5/31/00)

AVERY DENNISON CORPORATION

YIELD 1.8%
P/E RATIO 23.1

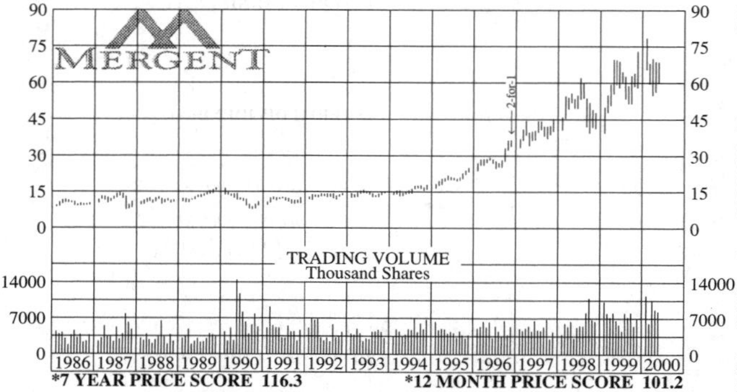

*7 YEAR PRICE SCORE 116.3 *12 MONTH PRICE SCORE 101.2

*NYSE COMPOSITE INDEX=100

INTERIM EARNINGS (Per Share):

Qtr.	Mar.	June	Sept.	Dec.
1996	0.38	0.40	0.45	0.46
1997	0.47	0.48	0.51	0.52
1998	0.52	0.55	0.54	0.54
1999	0.18	0.63	0.65	0.67

INTERIM DIVIDENDS (Per Share):

Amt.	Decl.	Ex.	Rec.	Pay.
0.24Q	7/29/99	8/30/99	9/01/99	9/15/99
0.27Q	10/29/99	11/29/99	12/01/99	12/15/99
0.27Q	1/28/00	2/28/00	3/01/00	3/15/00
0.27Q	4/27/00	6/05/00	6/07/00	6/21/00

Indicated div.: $1.08 (Div. Reinv. Plan)

CAPITALIZATION (1/1/00):

	($000)	(%)
Long-Term Debt	617,500	40.4
Deferred Income Tax	99,400	6.5
Common & Surplus	809,900	53.0
Total	1,526,800	100.0

DIVIDEND ACHIEVER STATUS:
Rank: 82 10-Year Growth Rate: 13.87%
Total Years of Dividend Growth: 24

RECENT DEVELOPMENTS: For the twelve months ended 1/1/00, net income slipped 3.5% to $215.4 million compared with $223.3 million in 1999. Results for 2000 included a $65.0 million charge for the implementation of AVY's company-wide restructuring program during the first quarter. Net sales were $3.77 billion, up 8.9% from $3.46 billion in the prior-year. Gross profit climbed 12.0% to $1.28 billion compared with $1.14 billion the year before.

PROSPECTS: The Company completed the acquisition of the Adespan pressure-sensitive materials operation of Panini S.p.A., a printing and publishing company in Italy. The acquisition strengthens AVY's base materials business in Europe. Terms of the transaction were not disclosed. Meanwhile, AVY announced a $35.0 million investment to expand its Fasson Roll North America pressure-sensitive base materials operation in Greenfield, IN. The expansion should be completed by the end of 2000.

BUSINESS

AVERY DENNISON CORPORATION is a worldwide manufacturer of pressure-sensitive adhesives and materials, office products and converted products. A portion of self-adhesive material is ''converted'' into labels and other products through embossing, printing, stamping and die-cutting, and some are sold in unconverted form as base materials, tapes and reflective sheeting. AVY also manufactures and sells a variety of office products and other items not involving pressure-sensitive components, such as notebooks, three-ring binders, organization systems, felt-tip markers, glues, fasteners, business forms, tickets, tags, and imprinting equipment. Sales for 1999 were derived: pressure-sensitive adhesives and materials, 51.1%; and consumer and converted products, 48.9%.

ANNUAL FINANCIAL DATA

	1/1/00	1/2/99	12/27/97	12/28/96	12/30/95	12/31/94	1/1/94
Earnings Per Share	**[2] 2.13**	**2.15**	**1.93**	**[1] 1.68**	**[1] 1.35**	**0.98**	**0.72**
Cash Flow Per Share	**3.61**	**3.37**	**3.03**	**2.76**	**2.36**	**1.91**	**1.54**
Tang. Book Val. Per Share	**4.18**	**6.88**	**6.87**	**6.72**	**8.91**	**6.84**	**6.98**
Dividends Per Share	**0.99**	**0.87**	**0.72**	**0.62**	**0.56**	**0.49**	**0.45**
Dividend Payout %	**46.5**	**40.5**	**37.3**	**36.9**	**41.1**	**50.5**	**62.5**
INCOME STATEMENT (IN MILLIONS):							
Total Revenues	3,768.2	3,459.9	3,345.7	3,222.5	3,113.9	2,856.7	2,608.7
Costs & Expenses	3,244.0	2,961.4	2,886.0	2,801.1	2,737.0	2,538.3	2,337.9
Depreciation & Amort.	150.4	127.2	116.8	113.4	107.9	102.5	95.4
Operating Income	373.8	371.3	342.9	308.0	269.0	215.9	175.4
Net Interest Inc./(Exp.)	d43.4	d34.6	d31.7	d37.4	d44.3	d43.0	d43.2
Income Before Income Taxes	330.4	336.7	311.2	270.6	224.7	172.9	132.2
Income Taxes	115.0	113.4	106.4	94.7	81.0	63.5	48.9
Net Income	[2] 215.4	223.3	204.8	[1] 175.9	[1] 143.7	109.4	83.3
Cash Flow	365.8	350.5	321.6	289.3	251.6	211.9	178.7
Average Shs. Outstg. (000)	101,300	104,100	106,100	105,000	106,500	111,100	115,900
BALANCE SHEET (IN MILLIONS):							
Cash & Cash Equivalents	6.9	18.5	3.3	3.8	27.0	3.1	5.8
Total Current Assets	956.0	802.0	793.5	804.5	800.1	676.9	614.6
Net Property	1,043.5	1,035.6	985.3	962.7	907.4	831.6	758.5
Total Assets	2,592.5	2,142.6	2,046.5	2,036.7	1,963.6	1,763.1	1,639.0
Total Current Liabilities	850.4	664.3	629.9	693.9	672.5	554.1	473.0
Long-Term Obligations	617.5	465.9	404.1	370.7	334.0	347.3	311.0
Net Stockholders' Equity	809.9	833.3	837.2	832.0	1,069.4	859.9	913.5
Net Working Capital	105.6	137.7	163.6	110.6	127.6	122.8	141.6
Year-end Shs. Outstg. (000)	98,800	100,000	102,400	103,600	106,100	107,100	112,385
STATISTICAL RECORD:							
Operating Profit Margin %	9.9	10.7	10.2	9.6	8.6	7.6	6.7
Net Profit Margin %	5.7	6.5	6.1	5.5	4.6	3.8	3.2
Return on Equity %	26.6	26.8	24.5	21.1	17.6	15.0	11.6
Return on Assets %	8.3	10.4	10.0	8.6	7.3	6.2	5.1
Debt/Total Assets %	23.8	21.7	19.7	18.2	17.0	19.7	19.0
Price Range	72 1/4-39 3/8	62 1/16-39 7/16	45 5/16-33 3/8	36 1/2-23 3/4	25 1/16-16 9/16	18-13 3/16	15 3/4-12 9/16
P/E Ratio	33.9-18.5	28.9-18.3	23.5-17.3	21.7-14.1	18.6-12.3	18.4-13.5	21.9-17.4
Average Yield %	1.8	1.7	1.8	2.1	2.7	3.2	3.2

Statistics are as originally reported. Adj. for 2-for-1 split, 12/96. [1] Incl. non-recur. chgs. of $2.1 mill., 1996; $1.5 mill., 1995. [2] Incl. $65.0 mill. one-time restr. chg.

OFFICERS:
P. M. Neal, Chmn., C.E.O.
D. A. Scarborough, Pres., C.O.O.
R. M. Calderoni, C.F.O., Sr. V.P., Fin.

INVESTOR CONTACT: Wayne H. Smith, V.P. & Treas., (626) 304-2000

PRINCIPAL OFFICE: 150 N. Orange Grove Boulevard, Pasadena, CA 91103

TELEPHONE NUMBER: (626) 304-2000
FAX: (626) 792-7312
WEB: www.averydennison.com

NO. OF EMPLOYEES: 17,400 (avg.)

SHAREHOLDERS: 13,817

ANNUAL MEETING: In Apr.

INCORPORATED: DE, Sep., 1946

INSTITUTIONAL HOLDINGS:
No. of Institutions: 355
Shares Held: 78,950,434
% Held: 70.1

INDUSTRY: Paper coated and laminated, nec (SIC: 2672)

TRANSFER AGENT(S): First Chicago Trust Company of New York, Jersey City, NJ.

BALDOR ELECTRIC COMPANY

	YIELD	2.6%
	P/E RATIO	15.8

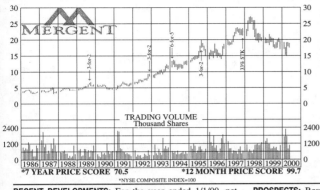

INTERIM EARNINGS (Per Share):

Qtr.	Mar.	June	Sept.	Dec.
1996	0.23	0.25	0.24	0.26
1997	0.26	0.28	0.28	0.28
1998	0.31	0.30	0.29	0.27
1999	0.29	0.30	0.30	0.30

INTERIM DIVIDENDS (Per Share):

Amt.	Decl.	Ex.	Rec.	Pay.
0.11Q	8/03/99	9/07/99	9/09/99	9/30/99
0.12Q	11/01/99	12/10/99	12/14/99	1/04/00
0.12Q	2/08/00	3/08/00	3/10/00	3/31/00
0.12Q	5/01/00	6/07/00	6/09/00	6/30/00

Indicated div.: $0.48 (Div. Reinv. Plan)

CAPITALIZATION (1/1/00):

	($000)	(%)
Long-Term Debt	56,305	16.8
Deferred Income Tax	13,153	3.9
Common & Surplus	266,109	79.3
Total	335,567	100.0

TRADING VOLUME Thousand Shares

DIVIDEND ACHIEVER STATUS:
Rank: 76   10-Year Growth Rate: 14.37%
Total Years of Dividend Growth: 16

7 YEAR PRICE SCORE 70.5   *12 MONTH PRICE SCORE 99.7*
NYSE COMPOSITE INDEX=100

RECENT DEVELOPMENTS: For the year ended 1/1/00, net income fell 2.0% to $43.7 million from $44.6 million in 1998. Earnings were pressured by an increase in the cost of sales to 69.3% of revenues versus 69.7% in the previous year before. Net sales declined 2.1% to $577.3 million from $589.4 million a year earlier. Gross profit decreased nearly 1.0% to $177.5 million from $178.7 million in the prior year. Operating profit amounted to $80.8 million in 1999 compared with $81.1 million in 1998.

PROSPECTS: Results should be favoraby affected by the Company's new stock products catalog. The expansion of the Company's sales organization by opening new sales offices and adding additional warehouses and salespeople should also contribute to results. During 2000, the Company expects to benefit from a reduction in its lead time to two weeks compared with its current three-week lead time. Results will continue to reflect the Company's ability to successfully control its operating costs and expenses.

BUSINESS

BALDOR ELECTRIC COMPANY designs, manufactures and markets a line of electric motors, adjustable speed drives and soft starters that are used with electric motors. The electric motors BEZ makes range from 1/50 HP through 700 HP D.C. and ½ HP through 800 HP A.C. The Company sells industrial control products, which include servo products, DC controls, and inverter and vector drives. BEZ's motors and drives are designed, manufactured and marketed for general purposes and individual customer requirements and specifications.

ANNUAL FINANCIAL DATA

	1/1/00	1/2/99	1/3/98	12/28/96	12/30/95	12/31/94	1/1/94
Earnings Per Share	1.19	1.17	1.09	0.97	0.84	0.70	0.52
Cash Flow Per Share	1.79	1.71	1.61	1.45	1.24	1.04	0.85
Tang. Book Val. Per Share	7.48	7.21	6.76	5.71	5.62	5.01	4.54
Dividends Per Share	0.43	0.40	0.35	0.29	0.25	0.20	0.16
Dividend Payout %	36.1	34.2	31.7	29.5	29.5	28.8	31.3

INCOME STATEMENT (IN THOUSANDS):

Total Revenues	579,262	591,425	559,783	505,372	475,699	419,820	357,993
Costs & Expenses	475,737	487,802	463,829	420,590	398,742	356,420	308,144
Depreciation & Amort.	20,767	20,511	19,337	17,277	15,583	13,121	12,220
Operating Income	82,758	83,112	76,617	67,505	61,374	50,279	37,629
Net Interest Inc./(Exp.)	d2,790	d1,721	d2,124	d2,668	d1,260	d1,279	d975
Income Before Income Taxes	70,523	71,952	65,635	57,192	52,946	43,212	32,370
Income Taxes	26,800	27,342	25,270	22,019	20,641	16,853	12,944
Net Income	43,723	44,610	40,365	35,173	32,305	26,359	19,426
Cash Flow	64,490	65,121	59,702	52,450	47,888	39,480	31,646
Average Shs. Outstg.	36,077	38,067	37,063	36,291	38,521	38,004	37,423

BALANCE SHEET (IN THOUSANDS):

Cash & Cash Equivalents	42,908	38,789	21,475	25,842	34,809	34,844	30,224
Total Current Assets	272,330	256,488	219,440	218,157	212,095	181,172	152,002
Net Property	124,802	123,137	104,097	95,364	89,071	81,502	72,396
Total Assets	423,941	411,926	355,889	325,486	313,462	283,155	237,950
Total Current Liabilities	88,374	80,362	78,172	71,182	67,026	62,622	43,401
Long-Term Obligations	56,305	57,015	27,929	45,027	25,255	26,303	22,474
Net Stockholders' Equity	266,109	264,292	243,434	199,633	208,885	183,364	162,209
Net Working Capital	183,956	176,126	141,268	146,975	145,069	118,550	108,601
Year-end Shs. Outstg.	35,592	36,677	36,029	34,935	37,160	36,620	35,696

STATISTICAL RECORD:

Operating Profit Margin %	14.3	14.1	13.7	13.4	12.9	12.0	10.5
Net Profit Margin %	7.5	7.5	7.2	7.0	6.8	6.3	5.4
Return on Equity %	16.4	16.9	16.6	17.6	15.5	14.4	12.0
Return on Assets %	10.3	10.8	11.3	10.8	10.3	9.3	8.2
Debt/Total Assets %	13.3	13.8	7.8	13.8	8.1	9.3	9.4
Price Range	21¹¹/₁₆-17	27³/₁₆-19¹/₁₆	23¹³/₁₆-18³/₁₆	18¾-13⁷/₈	19⁵/₈-12¹⁵/₁₆	13¾-10⅝	12⅜-8¹/₁₆
P/E Ratio	18.2-14.3	23.2-16.3	21.8-16.7	19.4-14.3	23.7-15.4	19.8-15.3	23.7-15.5
Average Yield %	2.2	1.7	1.6	1.8	1.5	1.6	1.6

Statistics are as originally reported. Adj. for a 3-for-2 stock split 9/95; 6-for-5, 1/94; 4-for-3, 12/97.

QUARTERLY DATA

(01/01/00)($000)	Rev	Inc
1st Quarter	143,133	10,731
2nd Quarter	152,130	11,030
3rd Quarter	144,349	11,043
4th Quarter	138,707	10,919

OFFICERS:
R. S. Boreham Jr., Chmn.
R. L. Qualls, Vice-Chmn.
J. A. McFarland, Pres.
L. G. Davis, Exec. V.P., C.F.O., Treas., Sec.

INVESTOR CONTACT: Lloyd G. Davis, V.P.-Fin., C.F.O., Sec. & Treas., (501) 646-4711

PRINCIPAL OFFICE: P.O. Box 2400, Ft. Smith, AR 72908

TELEPHONE NUMBER: (501) 646-4711
FAX: (501) 648-5752
WEB: www.baldor.com

NO. OF EMPLOYEES: 3,865

SHAREHOLDERS: 5,842

ANNUAL MEETING: In Apr.

INCORPORATED: MO, Mar., 1920

INSTITUTIONAL HOLDINGS:
No. of Institutions: 91
Shares Held: 12,002,374
% Held: 33.4

INDUSTRY: Motors and generators (SIC: 3621)

TRANSFER AGENT(S): Continental Stock Transfer & Trust Company, New York, NY.

BANCORPSOUTH, INC.

YIELD	3.4%
P/E RATIO	12.8

INTERIM EARNINGS (Per Share):

Qtr.	Mar.	June	Sept.	Dec.
1995	0.20	0.23	0.24	0.18
1996	0.23	0.27	0.25	0.27
1997	0.26	0.28	0.26	0.22
1998	0.27	0.28	0.25	0.21
1999	0.29	0.29	0.31	0.31

INTERIM DIVIDENDS (Per Share):

Amt.	Decl.	Ex.	Rec.	Pay.
0.12Q	4/28/99	6/11/99	6/15/99	7/01/99
0.12Q	7/28/99	9/13/99	9/15/99	10/01/99
0.13Q	10/27/99	12/13/99	12/15/99	1/03/00
0.13Q	1/26/00	3/13/00	3/15/00	4/03/00
0.13Q	5/04/00	6/13/00	6/15/00	7/03/00

Indicated div.: $0.52 (Div. Reinv. Plan)

CAPITALIZATION (12/31/99):

	($000)	(%)
Total Deposits	4,815,415	88.3
Long-Term Debt	138,560	2.5
Common & Surplus	497,400	9.1
Total	5,451,375	100.0

TRADING VOLUME
Thousand Shares

*7 YEAR PRICE SCORE 80.5   ***12 MONTH PRICE SCORE 93.6**

*NYSE COMPOSITE INDEX=100

DIVIDEND ACHIEVER STATUS:
Rank: 132   10-Year Growth Rate: 11.26%
Total Years of Dividend Growth: 13

RECENT DEVELOPMENTS: For the year ended 12/31/99, net income rose 18.9% to $69.0 million compared with $58.0 million in the previous year. Earnings for 1998 included after-tax merger-related charges of $3.7 million. Net interest revenue increased 6.8% to $217.5 million versus $203.7 million in 1998. Net interest margin fell to 4.28% from 4.31% in the prior year. Non-interest revenue advanced 19.8% to $79.3 million from $66.2 million a year earlier. Non-interest expense grew 9.9% to $183.0 million.

PROSPECTS: On 4/17/00, the Company announced a definitive merger agreement, under which BXS will acquire First United Bancshares, Inc. The transaction is valued at approximately $455.0 million and should be completed in the third quarter of 2000. First United, with assets of $2.70 billion, operates eleven affiliate banks and a non-bank subsidiary, First United Trust Company N.A., from 69 banking locations in Arkansas, Louisiana and Texas.

BUSINESS

BANCORPSOUTH, INC. is a bank holding company which, as of 3/31/00, had total assets of approximately $5.81 billion. The Company conducts commercial banking and trust business through 167 offices in 87 municipalities in 50 counties throughout Mississippi, Western Tennessee, and parts of Alabama. The Company, through its subsidiaries, provides a range of financial services and products to individuals and small-to-medium size businesses that include various types of checking accounts, savings accounts and certificates of deposit. Other services include safe deposit and night depository facilities. Limited 24-hour banking with automated teller machines is provided in most principal markets. In addition, the Bank operates consumer finance, credit life insurance and insurance agency subsidiaries. Its principal subsidiary is BancorpSouth Bank.

LOAN DISTRIBUTION

(12/31/99)	($000)	(%)
Commercial & Agricultural	371,169	8.9
Consumer & Installment	978,013	23.7
Real Estate Mortgage	2,514,573	60.9
Lease Financing	254,868	6.2
Other	12,795	0.3
Total	4,131,418	100.0

ANNUAL FINANCIAL DATA

	12/31/99	12/31/98	12/31/97	12/31/96	12/31/95	12/31/94	12/31/93
Earnings Per Share	1.20	1.01	1.02	1.01	0.85	0.80	① 0.75
Tang. Book Val. Per Share	8.68	8.48	8.09	7.50	6.86	6.49	5.99
Dividends Per Share	0.48	0.44	0.38	0.34	0.30	0.27	0.23
Dividend Payout %	40.0	43.6	37.4	33.7	35.5	33.7	31.4
INCOME STATEMENT (IN MILLIONS):							
Total Interest Income	414.2	383.5	307.1	277.9	252.4	173.2	158.5
Total Interest Expense	196.7	187.4	144.1	126.5	114.5	69.3	62.0
Net Interest Income	217.5	196.1	163.0	151.4	138.0	103.9	96.5
Provision for Loan Losses	14.7	15.0	9.0	8.8	6.2	5.7	7.8
Non-Interest Income	79.3	53.0	43.7	40.7	31.2	23.4	22.6
Non-Interest Expense	183.0	152.1	132.0	118.5	111.8	85.8	80.7
Income Before Taxes	99.1	82.0	65.7	64.9	51.3	35.8	30.6
Net Income	69.0	54.5	45.4	42.9	35.5	25.4	① 23.4
Average Shs. Outstg. (000)	57,524	53,871	44,788	42,426	42,030	31,668	31,276
BALANCE SHEET (IN MILLIONS):							
Cash & Due from Banks	217.3	175.4	286.3	153.1	149.9	128.0	116.4
Securities Avail. for Sale	345.3	549.8	406.2	230.7	239.8	130.5	202.5
Total Loans & Leases	4,131.4	3,561.4	2,852.9	2,554.1	2,371.7	1,795.1	1,558.7
Allowance for Credit Losses	133.4	142.3	133.7	122.1	111.2	88.9	75.2
Net Loans & Leases	3,998.0	3,419.1	2,719.2	2,432.1	2,260.5	1,706.2	1,483.6
Total Assets	5,776.9	5,203.7	4,180.1	3,617.2	3,306.2	2,518.4	2,306.7
Total Deposits	4,815.4	4,441.9	3,540.3	3,161.4	2,863.6	2,171.7	2,031.5
Long-Term Obligations	138.6	178.3	47.5	55.8	73.6	48.0	24.5
Total Liabilities	5,279.5	4,747.4	3,819.7	3,301.9	3,018.1	2,313.1	2,118.1
Net Stockholders' Equity	497.4	456.4	360.4	315.3	288.1	205.3	188.6
Year-end Shs. Outstg. (000)	57,304	53,833	44,542	42,026	41,994	31,660	31,496
STATISTICAL RECORD:							
Return on Equity %	13.9	11.9	12.6	13.6	12.3	12.4	12.4
Return on Assets %	1.2	1.0	1.1	1.2	1.1	1.0	1.0
Equity/Assets %	8.6	8.8	8.6	8.7	8.7	8.2	8.2
Non-Int. Exp./Tot. Inc. %	62.5	61.3	64.2	61.7	65.7	67.3	68.1
Price Range	19⁷/₁₆-15³/₈	24-16¹³/₁₆	23¹³/₁₆-13¼	14¼-10¹/₁₆	11¹⁵/₁₆-8¹/₁₆	9¹/₁₆-7¼	9³/₈-7³/₈
P/E Ratio	16.2-12.8	23.8-16.6	23.4-13.1	14.1-10.0	14.1-9.5	11.3-9.0	12.5-9.9
Average Yield %	2.8	2.2	2.1	2.8	3.0	3.3	2.8

Statistics are as originally reported. Adj. for 2-for-1 split 5/98, 100% stock dividend 11/95, & 15% stock dividend 11/93. ① Bef. $3.2 mill. acct. chrg.

OFFICERS:
A. B. Patterson, Chmn., C.E.O.
L. N. Allen Jr., C.F.O., Treas.

INVESTOR CONTACT: Cathy Freeman, Investor Relations, (662) 680-2084

PRINCIPAL OFFICE: One Mississippi Plaza, Tupelo, MS 38804

TELEPHONE NUMBER: (662) 680-2000
FAX: (662) 680-2570
WEB: www.bancorpsouth.com

NO. OF EMPLOYEES: 2,606

SHAREHOLDERS: 9,149

ANNUAL MEETING: In May

INCORPORATED: MS, Jul., 1982

INSTITUTIONAL HOLDINGS:
No. of Institutions: 48
Shares Held: 5,058,383
% Held: 8.8

INDUSTRY: State commercial banks (SIC: 6022)

TRANSFER AGENT(S): SunTrust Bank, Atlanta, GA

NYSE SYMBOL BDG
Rec. Pr. 24 13/16 (5/31/00)

BANDAG, INC.

YIELD 4.8%
P/E RATIO 10.4

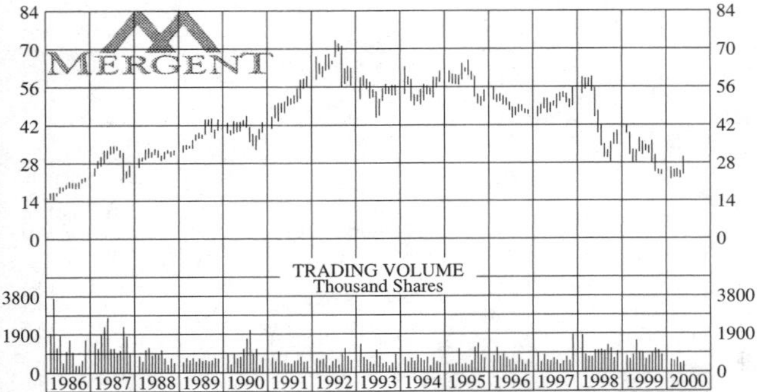

***7 YEAR PRICE SCORE 38.9** ***12 MONTH PRICE SCORE 91.1**

*NYSE COMPOSITE INDEX=100

INTERIM EARNINGS (Per Share):

Qtr.	Mar.	June	Sept.	Dec.
1996	0.65	0.83	1.02	0.94
1997	0.60	0.76	1.04	2.92
1998	0.40	0.62	0.77	0.84
1999	0.46	0.73	0.82	0.38

INTERIM DIVIDENDS (Per Share):

Amt.	Decl.	Ex.	Rec.	Pay.
0.285Q	5/04/99	6/16/99	6/18/99	7/21/99
0.285Q	8/24/99	9/16/99	9/20/99	10/21/99
0.295Q	11/09/99	12/16/99	12/20/99	1/21/00
0.295Q	3/07/00	3/27/00	3/29/00	4/20/00
0.295Q	5/02/00	6/15/00	6/19/00	7/21/00

Indicated div.: $1.18 (Div. Reinv. Plan)

CAPITALIZATION (12/31/99):

	($000)	(%)
Long-Term Debt	111,151	19.6
Deferred Income Tax	3,142	0.6
Common & Surplus	454,075	79.9
Total	568,368	100.0

DIVIDEND ACHIEVER STATUS:
Rank: 160 10-Year Growth Rate: 9.74%
Total Years of Dividend Growth: 23

RECENT DEVELOPMENTS: For the year ended 12/31/99, the Company reported net earnings of $52.3 million, a decrease of 11.8% compared with net earnings of $59.3 million in 1998. Results for 1999 included a non-recurring charge of $13.5 million. Total revenues fell 4.9% to $1.03 billion versus $1.08 billion the previous year. Globally, tread volume was down 6.0% compared with 1998. The North American restructuring program adversely affected results.

PROSPECTS: Although the Company is experiencing lower tread volumes, BDG made a few small acquisitions to maintain the strength of its TDS subsidiary. Separately, BDG plans to initiate its largest equipment launch in the past decade, unveiling three major innovative pieces of equipment designed to deliver significant improvements in productivity, finished product quality, manufacturing costs and dealer profitability.

BUSINESS

BANDAG, INC. is engaged in the manufacture of precured tread rubber, equipment, and supplies primarily for the retreading of truck and bus tires by a patented cold-bonding reaction. The Company also does some custom processing of rubber compounds. Revenues are generated by nearly 1,295 franchised dealers in the U.S. and abroad who are licensed to produce and market cold process retreads utilizing the Bandag process. BDG's wholly-owned subsidiary, Tire Management Solutions, Inc. (TMS), provides tire management systems outsourcing for commercial truck fleets. Tire Distribution Systems, Inc. (TDS), also a wholly owned subsidiary, sells and services new and retread tires.

QUARTERLY DATA

(12/31/1999)($000)	Rev	Inc
1st Quarter	224,138	10,037
2nd Quarter	252,120	16,126
3rd Quarter	273,240	18,056
4th Quarter	263,167	8,111

ANNUAL FINANCIAL DATA

	12/31/99	12/31/98	12/31/97	12/31/96	12/31/95	12/31/94	12/31/93
Earnings Per Share	**③ 2.40**	**② 2.63**	**① 5.33**	**3.44**	**3.82**	**3.51**	**2.88**
Cash Flow Per Share	**4.87**	**4.91**	**6.93**	**4.89**	**5.18**	**4.83**	**4.10**
Tang. Book Val. Per Share	**18.62**	**17.84**	**17.00**	**17.85**	**16.43**	**16.62**	**15.21**
Dividends Per Share	**1.14**	**1.10**	**1.00**	**0.90**	**0.80**	**0.70**	**0.65**
Dividend Payout %	**47.5**	**41.8**	**18.8**	**26.2**	**20.9**	**19.9**	**22.6**
INCOME STATEMENT (IN MILLIONS):							
Total Revenues	1,027.9	1,079.5	931.7	769.0	755.3	665.7	601.1
Costs & Expenses	872.3	917.8	688.6	602.4	563.6	478.4	440.6
Depreciation & Amort.	53.8	51.4	36.9	34.6	34.6	35.3	33.3
Operating Income	101.8	110.3	206.3	132.0	157.1	152.0	127.1
Net Interest Inc./(Exp.)	d9.7	d10.8	d3.3	d1.2	d2.0	d2.1	d2.2
Income Before Income Taxes	92.1	99.5	202.9	130.8	155.1	149.8	125.0
Income Taxes	39.8	40.2	80.9	49.2	58.1	55.8	46.2
Net Income	③ 52.3	② 59.3	① 122.0	81.6	97.0	94.0	78.7
Cash Flow	106.1	110.7	158.9	116.2	131.6	129.3	112.1
Average Shs. Outstg. (000)	21,764	22,559	22,908	23,746	25,420	26,801	27,337
BALANCE SHEET (IN MILLIONS):							
Cash & Cash Equivalents	60.1	47.6	198.0	33.5	40.8	83.4	83.0
Total Current Assets	428.1	439.1	599.0	341.7	328.5	344.9	316.1
Net Property	198.0	213.0	197.6	145.1	144.9	151.8	146.6
Total Assets	722.4	755.7	899.9	588.3	554.2	582.1	550.7
Total Current Liabilities	154.1	174.9	306.5	139.2	122.0	113.3	102.5
Long-Term Obligations	111.2	109.8	123.2	10.1	11.9	12.3	11.0
Net Stockholders' Equity	454.1	495.7	463.4	410.9	404.1	442.8	426.4
Net Working Capital	274.1	264.2	292.5	202.5	206.4	231.6	213.6
Year-end Shs. Outstg. (000)	20,771	21,955	22,813	22,923	24,178	26,123	27,152
STATISTICAL RECORD:							
Operating Profit Margin %	9.9	10.2	22.1	17.2	20.8	22.8	21.2
Net Profit Margin %	5.1	5.5	13.1	10.6	12.8	14.1	13.1
Return on Equity %	11.5	12.7	26.3	19.9	24.3	21.7	19.1
Return on Assets %	7.2	7.8	13.6	13.9	17.5	16.1	14.3
Debt/Total Assets %	15.4	14.5	13.7	1.7	2.1	2.1	2.0
Price Range	41 5/8-23 1/2	59 3/4-28 5/16	55 3/4-45	55 7/8-44 1/2	65 7/8-49	63 1/2-49 1/8	60 1/4-44 3/4
P/E Ratio	17.3-9.8	22.7-10.8	10.5-8.4	16.2-12.9	17.2-12.8	18.1-14.0	20.9-15.5
Average Yield %	3.5	2.5	2.0	1.8	1.4	1.2	1.2

Statistics are as originally reported. ① Incl. non-recurr. gain of $78.6 mill. on sale of secur. ② Incl. non-recurr chrg. of $4.2 mill. ③ Incl. non-recurr. chrg. of $13.5 mill.

OFFICERS:
M. G. Carver, Chmn., Pres., C.E.O.
W. W. Heidbreder, V.P., C.F.O., Sec.
L. A. Carver, Treas.

INVESTOR CONTACT: Warren W. Heidbreder, V.P., C.F.O., Corp. Sec., (319) 262-1260

PRINCIPAL OFFICE: 2905 North Highway 61, Bandag Headquarters, Muscatine, IA 52761-5886

TELEPHONE NUMBER: (319) 262-1400
FAX: (319) 262-1069
WEB: www.bandag.com

NO. OF EMPLOYEES: 4,441 (avg.)

SHAREHOLDERS: 2,179 (com.); 1,200 (Cl. A); 231 (Cl. B)

ANNUAL MEETING: In May

INCORPORATED: IA, Dec., 1957

INSTITUTIONAL HOLDINGS:
No. of Institutions: 79
Shares Held: 4,652,960
% Held: 51.2

INDUSTRY: Tires and inner tubes (SIC: 3011)

TRANSFER AGENT(S): BankBoston, NA, Boston, MA

BANK ONE CORPORATION

YIELD 5.1%
P/E RATIO 11.3

*7 YEAR PRICE SCORE 66.9   *12 MONTH PRICE SCORE 84.4
*NYSE COMPOSITE INDEX=100

TRADING VOLUME
Thousand Shares

INTERIM EARNINGS (Per Share):

Qtr.	Mar.	June	Sept.	Dec.
1996	0.70	0.73	0.74	0.77
1997	0.78	0.02	0.66	0.79
1998	0.79	0.68	0.89	0.19
1999	0.96	0.83	0.79	0.36

INTERIM DIVIDENDS (Per Share):

Amt.	Decl.	Ex.	Rec.	Pay.
0.42Q	4/20/99	6/11/99	6/15/99	7/01/99
0.42Q	7/20/99	9/13/99	9/15/99	10/01/99
0.42Q	10/19/99	12/13/99	12/15/99	1/01/00
0.42Q	1/18/00	3/13/00	3/15/00	4/01/00
0.42Q	4/18/00	6/13/00	6/15/00	7/01/00

Indicated div.: $1.68 (Div. Reinv. Plan)

CAPITALIZATION (12/31/99):

	($000)	(%)
Total Deposits	162,278,000	74.5
Long-Term Debt	35,435,000	16.3
Preferred Stock	190,000	0.1
Common & Surplus	19,900,000	9.1
Total	217,803,000	100.0

DIVIDEND ACHIEVER STATUS:
Rank: 103   10-Year Growth Rate: 12.57%
Total Years of Dividend Growth: 29

RECENT DEVELOPMENTS: For the year ended 12/31/99, net income advanced 11.9% to $3.48 billion from $3.11 billion in the prior year. Results for 1999 and 1998 included pre-tax merger-related and restructuring charges of $554.0 million and $1.06 billion, respectively. Net interest income declined 3.5% to $9.02 billion from $9.35 billion in 1998. Non-interest income increased 7.7% to $8.69 billion, while non-interest expense fell to $11.49 billion.

PROSPECTS: In 2000, ONE estimates earnings per share of $2.80 to $3.00. All lines of business, excluding the Company's credit card business, are expected to increase earnings by 10% to 12%, driven by revenue growth of 5% to 8%. As a part of the Company's strategy to return its credit card business to profitability by the end of 2000, ONE sold its Canadian retail credit card operations to Royal Bank of Canada.

BUSINESS

BANK ONE CORPORATION (formerly Banc One Corporation) with assets of more than $270.00 billion as of 3/31/00, is a bank holding company. The Company, formed on 10/1/98, is a result of the merger of First Chicago NBD Corporation with and into Banc One Corporation, and is the nation's fourth-largest bank holding company, the second-largest Visa/Mastercard issuer, and the third-largest bank lender to small businesses. ONE offers a variety of financial services to corporate, retail and trust customers. The Company operates more than 1,800 banking centers and a nationwide network of ATM's. ONE also operates affiliates that engage in data processing, venture capital, merchant banking, trust, investment management, brokerage, equipment leasing, consumer finance and insurance.

LOAN DISTRIBUTION

(12/31/99)	($000)	(%)
Commercial	96,352,000	58.8
Consumer	63,488,000	38.7
Credit card	4,037,000	2.5
Total	163,877,000	100.0

ANNUAL FINANCIAL DATA

	12/31/99	12/31/98	12/31/97	12/31/96	12/31/95	12/31/94	12/31/93
Earnings Per Share	④ 2.95	④ 2.61	④ 1.99	③ 2.94	2.65	② 2.00	① 2.42
Tang. Book Val. Per Share	17.55	17.02	14.74	16.95	16.38	14.68	14.23
Dividends Per Share	1.64	1.49	1.35	1.21	1.10	1.00	0.85
Dividend Payout %	55.6	56.9	67.6	41.2	41.5	50.1	34.9
INCOME STATEMENT (IN MILLIONS):							
Total Interest Income	17,294.0	17,524.0	9,383.2	8,044.9	7,100.9	6,437.5	5,735.1
Total Interest Expense	8,273.0	8,177.0	3,990.9	3,189.4	2,971.5	2,248.8	1,645.0
Net Interest Income	9,021.0	9,347.0	5,392.3	4,855.5	4,129.4	4,188.6	4,090.1
Provision for Loan Losses	1,249.0	1,408.0	1,211.1	788.1	457.5	242.3	368.5
Non-Interest Income	8,692.0	8,071.0	3,835.9	2,227.5	1,870.0	1,419.6	1,491.7
Non-Interest Expense	11,490.0	11,545.0	6,048.8	4,184.2	3,631.6	3,847.1	3,514.1
Income Before Taxes	4,974.0	4,465.0	1,968.3	2,110.7	1,910.3	1,518.9	1,699.1
Net Income	④ 3,479.0	④ 3,108.0	④ 1,305.7	③ 1,426.5	1,277.9	② 1,005.1	① 1,120.6
Average Shs. Outstg. (000)	1,178,000	1,189,000	655,700	480,620	476,655	492,930	455,962
BALANCE SHEET (IN MILLIONS):							
Cash & Due from Banks	16,076.0	19,878.0	7,727.4	6,350.8	5,501.3	5,073.4	4,757.5
Securities Avail. for Sale	11,324.0	12,299.0	15,306.2	14,983.9	15,075.1	13,857.6	1,747.9
Total Loans & Leases	163,877.0	155,398.0	82,052.8	74,193.9	65,328.7	61,992.9	53,845.6
Allowance for Credit Losses	2,285.0	2,271.0	1,325.9	1,075.1	938.0	897.2	918.2
Net Loans & Leases	161,592.0	153,127.0	80,726.9	73,118.8	64,390.7	61,095.7	52,927.5
Total Assets	269,425.0	261,496.0	115,901.3	101,848.1	90,454.0	88,922.6	79,918.6
Total Deposits	162,278.0	161,542.0	77,414.3	72,373.1	67,320.2	68,090.1	60,943.2
Long-Term Obligations	35,435.0	22,298.0	11,066.4	4,189.5	2,720.4	1,866.4	1,701.7
Total Liabilities	249,335.0	240,936.0	105,525.3	93,201.1	82,256.5	81,357.7	72,884.9
Net Stockholders' Equity	20,090.0	20,560.0	10,376.0	8,647.0	8,197.5	7,564.9	7,033.6
Year-end Shs. Outstg. (000)	1,113,000	1,177,000	644,500	469,989	470,416	480,353	460,632
STATISTICAL RECORD:							
Return on Equity %	17.3	15.1	12.6	16.5	15.6	13.3	15.9
Return on Assets %	1.3	1.2	1.1	1.4	1.4	1.1	1.4
Equity/Assets %	7.5	7.9	9.0	8.5	9.1	8.5	8.8
Non-Int. Exp./Tot. Inc. %	64.9	66.3	65.5	59.1	50.5	60.5	63.0
Price Range	63¹⁵⁄₁₆-29³⁄₄	65⅝-36¹¹⁄₁₆	54⁷⁄₁₆-35¹¹⁄₁₆	43¹⁄₂-28⁷⁄₁₆	33³⁄₁₆-20³⁄₄	31³⁄₈-19¹⁵⁄₁₆	36¹⁵⁄₁₆-31¹⁄₁₆
P/E Ratio	21.5-10.1	25.1-13.8	27.4-17.9	14.8-9.7	12.5-7.8	15.7-10.0	15.3-11.0
Average Yield %	3.5	2.9	3.0	3.4	4.1	3.9	2.7

Statistics are as originally reported. Adj. for 5-for-4 stock split, 8/93 & 10% stk. div. 2/98, 3/96 & 3/94. ① Bef. an acct. cr. $19.4 mill. ② Incl. $40.0 mill. chrg. for acq. of Liberty Bancorp, mtg. loan ctr. consol. & liti. costs. ③ Incl. one-time SAIF chrg. of $34.3 mill. ④ Incl. pre-tax merger-rel. & restr. chrgs.: $554.0 mill., 1999; $1.06 bill., 1998; $337.3 mill., 1997.

OFFICERS:
J. Dimon, Chmn., C.E.O.
W. P. Boardman, Vice-Chmn.

INVESTOR CONTACT: Jay S. Gould, Dir.-Investor Relations, (312) 732-4812

PRINCIPAL OFFICE: One First National Plaza Chicago, IL 60670

TELEPHONE NUMBER: (312) 732-4000
FAX: (614) 248-5624
WEB: www.bankone.com

NO. OF EMPLOYEES: 86,198

SHAREHOLDERS: 131,280

ANNUAL MEETING: In May

INCORPORATED: DE, Apr., 1998

NYSE SYMBOL BAC
Rec. Pr. 68 9/16 (5/31/99)

BANK OF AMERICA CORPORATION

YIELD 2.6%
P/E RATIO 15.3

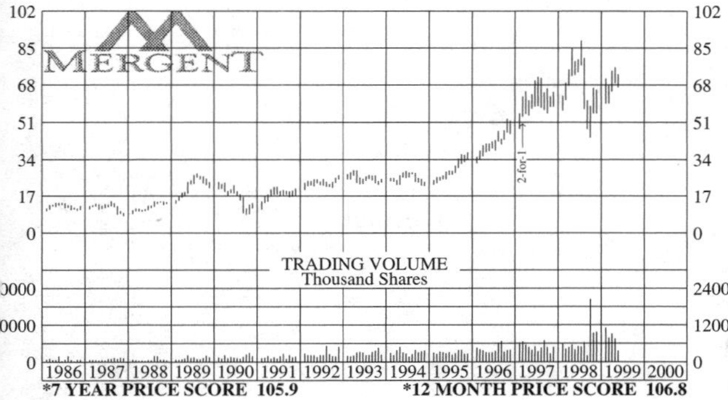
MERGENT
TRADING VOLUME
Thousand Shares
2-for-1
1986 1987 1988 1989 1990 1991 1992 1993 1994 1995 1996 1997 1998 1999 2000

*7 YEAR PRICE SCORE 105.9 *12 MONTH PRICE SCORE 106.8

*NYSE COMPOSITE INDEX=100

INTERIM EARNINGS (Per Share):

Qtr.	Mar.	June	Sept.	Dec.
1996	0.85	1.00	1.06	1.10
1997	0.97	1.05	1.11	1.12
1998	0.51	1.43	0.21	0.66
1999	1.08	1.07	1.23	1.10

INTERIM DIVIDENDS (Per Share):

Amt.	Decl.	Ex.	Rec.	Pay.
0.45Q	4/28/99	6/02/99	6/04/99	6/25/99
0.45Q	7/28/99	9/1/99	9/3/99	9/24/99
0.50Q	10/27/99	12/1/99	12/3/99	12/23/99
0.50Q	1/26/00	3/1/00	3/3/00	3/24/00
0.50Q	4/25/00	5/31/00	6/2/00	6/23/00

Indicated div.: $1.80 (Div. Reinv. Plan)

CAPITALIZATION (12/31/99):

	($000)	(%)
Total Deposits	347,273,000	77.7
Long-Term Debt	55,486,000	12.4
Preferred Stock	77,000	0.0
Common & Surplus	44,355,000	9.9
Total	447,191,000	100.0

DIVIDEND ACHIEVER STATUS:
Rank: 96 10-Year Growth Rate: 12.90%
Total Years of Dividend Growth: 22

RECENT DEVELOPMENTS: For the year ended 12/31/99, net income advanced 52.6% to $7.88 billion from $5.17 billion in the previous year. Earnings for 1999 and 1998 included after-tax charges of $358.0 million and $1.33 billion, respectively, related to the BankAmerica and NationsBank merger. Net interest income fell to $18.24 billion from $18.30 billion in the prior year. Non-interest income improved 8.4% to $14.31 billion.

PROSPECTS: Going forward, the Company's credit outlook for 2000 remains favorable, reflecting continued healthy economic conditions and growth in loans with historically lower credit risk. On 3/6/00, BAC announced its on-line banking customer base exceeded 2.0 million, reflecting increased investment by the Company and a higher acceptance by consumers. On-line services include access to account information and transfering of funds.

BUSINESS

BANK OF AMERICA CORPORATION (formerly NationsBank Corporation), is a bank holding company with $656.11 billion in total assets as of 3/31/00. The Company was formed on 9/30/98 as BankAmerica Corporation, as a result of BankAmerica merging into NationsBank. The Company adopted its present name on 4/29/99. BAC provides financial products and services to more than 30 million households and 2 million businesses, as well as providing international corporate financial services for business transactions in 190 countries. The Company maintains full-service operations in 21 states and the District of Columbia.

LOAN DISTRIBUTION

(12/31/99)	($000)	(%)
Commercial	195,779,000	52.8
Residential Mortgage	81,860,000	22.1
Home equity lines	17,273,000	4.7
Direct/Indirect consumer	42,161,000	11.4
Consumer finance	22,326,000	6.0
Bankcard	9,019,000	2.4
Foreign consumer	2,244,000	0.6
Total	370,662,000	100.0

ANNUAL FINANCIAL DATA

	12/31/99	[4] 12/31/98	12/31/97	12/31/96	12/31/95	12/31/94	12/31/93
Earnings Per Share	[3] 4.48	[3] 2.90	4.17	[2] 4.00	3.56	3.06	[1] 2.50
Tang. Book Val. Per Share	15.66	16.68	14.86	18.43	19.08	16.64	15.51
Dividends Per Share	1.85	1.59	1.37	1.20	1.04	0.94	0.82
Dividend Payout %	41.3	54.8	32.9	30.0	29.2	30.7	32.8
INCOME STATEMENT (IN MILLIONS):							
Total Interest Income	37,323.0	38,588.0	16,579.0	13,796.0	13,220.0	10,529.0	8,207.0
Total Interest Expense	19,086.0	20,290.0	8,681.0	7,467.0	7,773.0	5,318.0	3,570.0
Net Interest Income	18,237.0	18,298.0	7,898.0	6,329.0	5,447.0	5,211.0	4,637.0
Provision for Loan Losses	1,820.0	2,920.0	800.0	605.0	382.0	310.0	430.0
Non-Interest Income	14,309.0	13,206.0	5,155.0	3,713.0	3,107.0	2,584.0	2,185.0
Non-Interest Expense	18,511.0	20,536.0	7,457.0	5,803.0	5,136.0	cr12.0	48.0
Income Before Taxes	12,215.0	8,048.0	4,796.0	3,634.0	2,991.0	2,555.0	1,991.0
Net Income	[3] 7,882.0	[3] 5,165.0	3,077.0	[2] 2,375.0	1,995.0	1,690.0	[1] 9,947.0
Average Shs. Outstg. (000)	1,760,058	1,775,760	737,791	590,216	544,959	550,000	516,000
BALANCE SHEET (IN MILLIONS):							
Securities Avail. for Sale	124,945.0	124,942.0	72,120.0	32,809.0	39,578.0	20,125.0	27,559.0
Total Loans & Leases	370,662.0	357,328.0	146,417.0	125,031.0	119,020.0	105,033.0	93,262.0
Allowance for Credit Losses	6,828.0	7,122.0	5,407.0	4,716.0	4,150.0	3,848.0	3,424.0
Net Loans & Leases	363,834.0	350,206.0	141,010.0	120,315.0	114,870.0	101,185.0	89,838.0
Total Assets	632,574.0	617,679.0	264,562.0	185,794.0	187,298.0	169,604.0	157,686.0
Total Deposits	347,273.0	357,260.0	138,194.0	106,498.0	100,691.0	100,470.0	91,113.0
Long-Term Obligations	55,486.0	45,888.0	27,204.0	22,985.0	17,775.0	8,488.0	8,352.0
Total Liabilities	588,142.0	571,741.0	243,225.0	172,085.0	174,497.0	158,593.0	147,707.0
Net Stockholders' Equity	44,432.0	45,938.0	21,337.0	13,709.0	12,801.0	11,011.0	9,979.0
Year-end Shs. Outstg. (000)	1,677,273	1,724,484	712,188	573,000	549,000	552,000	542,000
STATISTICAL RECORD:							
Return on Equity %	17.7	11.2	14.4	17.3	15.6	15.3	99.7
Return on Assets %	1.2	0.8	1.2	1.3	1.1	1.0	6.3
Equity/Assets %	7.0	7.4	8.1	7.4	6.8	6.5	6.3
Non-Int. Exp./Tot. Inc. %	56.9	65.2	57.1	57.8	60.0	d0.2	0.7
Price Range	76 3/8-47 5/8	88 7/16-44	71 11/16-48	52 5/8-32 3/16	37 3/8-22 5/16	28 11/16-21 11/16	29-22 1/4
P/E Ratio	17.0-10.6	30.5-15.2	17.2-11.5	13.2-8.0	10.5-6.3	9.4-7.1	11.6-8.9
Average Yield %	2.7	2.4	2.3	2.8	3.5	3.7	3.2

Statistics are as originally reported. Adj. for 2-for-1 stk. split, 2/97. [1] Bef. acct. adj. of $200.0 mill. [2] Incl. after-tax merger-related chgs. of $77.0 mill. [3] Incl. merg.-rel. & restr. chgs. of $358.0 mill., 1999; $1.80 bill., 1998. [4] Refl. merger of NationsBank Corp. & BankAmerica Corp. on 9/30/98.

OFFICERS:
H. L. McColl, Chmn., C.E.O.
J. H. Hance Jr., Vice-Chmn., C.F.O.
K. D. Lewis, Pres.

INVESTOR CONTACT: Jane Smith, Mgr., Shareholder Relations, (704) 386-5000

PRINCIPAL OFFICE: Bank of America Corporate Center, Charlotte, NC 28255

TELEPHONE NUMBER: (704) 386-5000
FAX: (704) 386-0284
WEB: www.bankofamerica.com

NO. OF EMPLOYEES: 155,906

SHAREHOLDERS: 276,300

ANNUAL MEETING: In Apr.

INCORPORATED: NC, July, 1968; reincorp., DE, Sep., 1998

INSTITUTIONAL HOLDINGS:
No. of Institutions: 936
Shares Held: 980,826,290
% Held: 56.4

INDUSTRY: National commercial banks (SIC: 6021)

TRANSFER AGENT(S): ChaseMellon Shareholder Services LLC, Ridgefield Park, NJ

BANTA CORPORATION

YIELD 3.2%
P/E RATIO 29.8

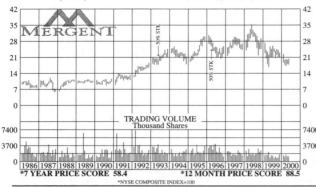

7 YEAR PRICE SCORE 58.4   **12 MONTH PRICE SCORE 88.5**
*NYSE COMPOSITE INDEX=100

INTERIM EARNINGS (Per Share):

Qtr.	Mar.	June	Sept.	Dec.
1996	0.28	0.38	0.49	0.48
1997	0.33	0.42	0.19	0.50
1998	0.37	0.45	0.55	0.43
1999	0.35	d0.97	0.65	0.59

INTERIM DIVIDENDS (Per Share):

Amt.	Decl.	Ex.	Rec.	Pay.
0.14Q	4/27/99	7/14/99	7/16/99	8/02/99
0.14Q	7/27/99	10/13/99	10/15/99	11/01/99
0.15Q	12/09/99	1/12/00	1/14/00	2/01/00
0.15Q	2/02/00	4/12/00	4/14/00	5/01/00
0.15Q	4/26/00	7/12/00	7/14/00	8/01/00

Indicated div.: $0.60 (Div. Reinv. Plan)

CAPITALIZATION (1/1/00):

	($000)	(%)
Long-Term Debt	113,520	23.3
Deferred Income Tax	20,382	4.2
Common & Surplus	353,775	72.5
Total	487,677	100.0

DIVIDEND ACHIEVER STATUS:
Rank: 172   10-Year Growth Rate: 9.25%
Total Years of Dividend Growth: 21

RECENT DEVELOPMENTS: For the twelve months ended 12/31/99, net income fell 69.8% to $16.0 million compared with $52.9 million in 1998. Results in 1999 included a $38.5 million after-tax restructuring charge. Net sales slipped 4.3% to $1.28 billion from $1.34 billion in the prior year. Sales were negatively affected by paper price reductions, changes in product mix and the closing of three facilities, partially offset by improved operating efficiencies. Operating earnings decreased 50.4% to $48.4 million compared with $97.5 million in the previous year.

PROSPECTS: The Company expects to report double-digit sales and earnings in 2000. BN will release two new web presses at its publication plants to expand its printing capacity. BN's outlook for its books and catalog and direct marketing segments are favorable. Separately, BN reached an agreement in principle with XYAN.com to provide business-to-business publishers and marketers with document management and digital delivery services. Under the agreement, XYAN will acquire certain BN assets and certain digital press assets.

BUSINESS

BANTA CORPORATION is a North American provider of printing digital imaging and global supply chain management. BN serves publishers of educational and general books, special-interest magazines, consumer and business catalogs, and direct marketing materials. The Company's other businesses offer pre-press services, computer software packages, multimedia kits, point-of-purchase displays, product labels, postage stamps and single-use products. Customers consist primarily of publishers located throughout the United States.

BUSINESS LINE ANALYSIS

(01/01/2000)	REV(%)	INC(%)
Printing	75.1	74.8
Turnkey	16.7	7.0
Healthcare	8.2	18.2
Total	100.0	100.0

ANNUAL FINANCIAL DATA

	1/1/00	1/2/99	1/3/98	12/28/96	12/31/95	12/31/94	1/1/94
Earnings Per Share	③ 0.59	1.80	① 1.44	1.63	1.75	1.56	1.36
Cash Flow Per Share	3.10	4.06	3.50	3.49	3.42	2.92	2.47
Tang. Book Val. Per Share	12.31	11.83	11.80	12.29	16.83	15.29	9.17
Dividends Per Share	0.56	0.51	0.47	0.44	0.37	0.35	0.31
Dividend Payout %	94.9	28.3	32.6	26.8	21.3	22.2	22.9
INCOME STATEMENT (IN MILLIONS):							
Total Revenues	1,278.3	1,335.8	1,202.5	1,083.8	1,022.7	811.3	691.2
Costs & Expenses	1,161.7	1,171.4	1,060.8	933.3	873.7	686.5	584.9
Depreciation & Amort.	68.2	66.9	62.1	58.3	51.1	41.5	33.7
Operating Income	48.4	97.5	79.5	92.2	97.9	83.4	72.7
Net Interest Inc./(Exp.)	d12.4	d10.8	d11.1	d10.2	d9.9	d5.9	d5.3
Income Before Income Taxes	34.6	86.1	70.8	84.2	89.1	78.7	68.7
Income Taxes	18.6	33.2	27.5	33.3	35.5	31.5	27.7
Net Income	③ 16.0	52.9	①② 43.3	50.9	53.6	47.2	41.0
Cash Flow	84.2	119.8	105.4	109.2	104.6	88.7	74.7
Average Shs. Outstg. (000)	27,177	29,475	30,113	31,249	30,624	30,366	30,220
BALANCE SHEET (IN MILLIONS):							
Cash & Cash Equivalents	27.7	26.6	16.4	57.4	27.1	0.4	8.2
Total Current Assets	355.9	354.6	365.7	347.5	310.8	248.4	197.9
Net Property	327.4	318.6	338.4	319.9	313.7	293.7	232.9
Total Assets	773.3	770.0	781.2	719.2	678.8	577.8	457.4
Total Current Liabilities	245.4	196.5	200.4	127.8	122.9	147.0	91.7
Long-Term Obligations	113.5	120.6	130.1	133.7	135.0	67.8	45.6
Net Stockholders' Equity	353.8	409.9	414.1	420.6	387.1	331.6	292.4
Net Working Capital	110.5	158.1	165.3	219.6	188.0	101.4	106.2
Year-end Shs. Outstg. (000)	23,943	28,261	29,793	30,969	20,560	20,126	29,996
STATISTICAL RECORD:							
Operating Profit Margin %	3.8	7.3	6.6	8.5	9.6	10.3	10.5
Net Profit Margin %	1.3	4.0	3.6	4.7	5.2	5.8	5.9
Return on Equity %	4.5	12.9	10.5	12.1	13.8	14.2	14.0
Return on Assets %	2.1	6.9	5.5	7.1	7.9	8.2	9.0
Debt/Total Assets %	14.7	15.7	16.6	18.6	19.9	11.7	10.0
Price Range	27⅜-16¾	35¼-21¹³⁄₁₆	29⅞-21⅝	30¹¹⁄₁₆-20½	30¹⁄₁₆-19	25¹¹⁄₁₆-18	24¹¹⁄₁₆-17¾
P/E Ratio	46.4-28.4	19.6-12.1	20.7-15.0	18.8-12.6	17.2-10.9	16.5-11.5	18.1-13.1
Average Yield %	2.5	1.8	1.8	1.7	1.5	1.6	1.5

Statistics are as originally reported. Adj. for 50% stk. div., 3/1/96. ① Incl. non-recurr. chrg. $13.5 mill. ② Incl. $8.1 mill. after-tax restr. chg. ③ Incl. $38.5 mill. after-tax restr. chg.

OFFICERS:
D. D. Belcher, Chmn., Pres., C.E.O.
G. A. Henseler, Exec. V.P., C.F.O.

INVESTOR CONTACT: Gerald A. Henseler, Exec. V.P., (920) 751-7777

PRINCIPAL OFFICE: 225 Main Street, Menasha, WI 54952

TELEPHONE NUMBER: (920) 751-7777
FAX: (920) 751-7790
WEB: www.banta.com

NO. OF EMPLOYEES: 7,200 (approx.)

SHAREHOLDERS: 2,175

ANNUAL MEETING: In Apr.

INCORPORATED: WI, 1901

INSTITUTIONAL HOLDINGS:
No. of Institutions: 117
Shares Held: 19,305,350
% Held: 72.6

INDUSTRY: Commercial printing, nec (SIC: 2759)

TRANSFER AGENT(S): Firstar Trust Company, Milwaukee, WI.

NYSE SYMBOL BCR
Rec. Pr. 45 5/8 (5/31/00)

BARD (C.R.), INC.

YIELD 1.8%
P/E RATIO 20.0

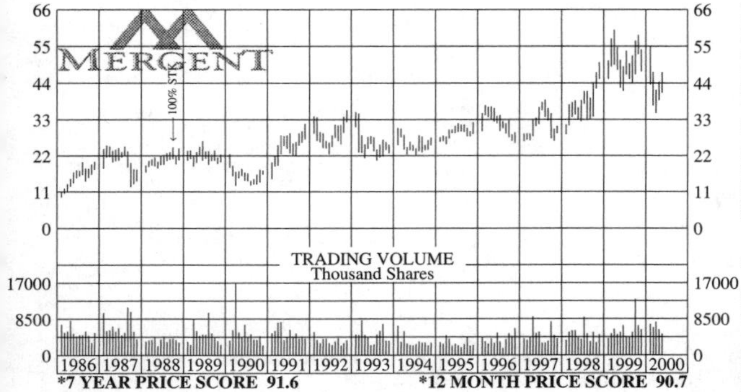

MERGENT
100% STK
TRADING VOLUME
Thousand Shares
1986 1987 1988 1989 1990 1991 1992 1993 1994 1995 1996 1997 1998 1999 2000

*7 YEAR PRICE SCORE 91.6 *12 MONTH PRICE SCORE 90.7

*NYSE COMPOSITE INDEX=100

INTERIM EARNINGS (Per Share):

Qtr.	Mar.	June	Sept.	Dec.
1996	0.48	0.44	0.20	0.46
1997	0.46	0.46	d0.07	0.42
1998	0.44	0.71	0.42	3.03
1999	0.51	0.55	0.58	0.64

INTERIM DIVIDENDS (Per Share):

Amt.	Decl.	Ex.	Rec.	Pay.
0.20Q	7/14/99	7/22/99	7/26/99	8/06/99
0.20Q	10/13/99	10/21/99	10/25/99	11/05/99
0.20Q	12/08/99	1/20/00	1/24/00	2/04/00
0.20Q	4/19/00	4/27/00	5/01/00	5/12/00

Indicated div.: $0.80 (Div. Reinv. Plan)

CAPITALIZATION (12/31/99):

	($000)	(%)
Long-Term Debt	158,400	21.6
Common & Surplus	574,300	78.4
Total	732,700	100.0

DIVIDEND ACHIEVER STATUS:
Rank: 200 10-Year Growth Rate: 8.04%
Total Years of Dividend Growth: 28

RECENT DEVELOPMENTS: For the year ended 12/31/99, net income fell 53.2% to $118.1 million from $252.3 million in 1998. Results included gains of $9.2 million in 1999 and $329.2 million in 1998 from the disposition of the cardiology business. Net sales declined 11.0% to $1.04 billion from $1.16 billion last year. Revenues for 1998 included $195.8 million in sales from products that have been divested. Diluted earnings per share amounted to $2.28 versus $4.51 in 1998.

PROSPECTS: On 1/11/00, the Company announced that it has received the FDA's approval to market the MEMOTHERM FLEXX biliary stent for treating malignant biliary obstructions. The MEMOTHERM FLEXX biliary stent will be marketed through the Company's Peripheral Technologies division and will be available immediately. Meanwhile, results will reflect BCR's ability to successfully introduce new products as well as control its selling, general and administrative expenses.

BUSINESS

BARD (C.R.), INC. is a major multinational developer, manufacturer and marketer of health care products. The Company engages in the design, manufacture, packaging, distribution and sale of medical, surgical, diagnostic and patient-care devices. Bard holds strong positions in cardiovascular, urological, surgical and general health care products. BCR products are marketed worldwide to hospitals, individual health care professionals, extended care facilities, alternate site facilities and the home, employing a combination of direct delivery and medical specialty distributors. Hospitals, physicians and nursing homes purchase approximately 90% of the Company's products. The Vascular Group accounted for 21.8% of 1999 sales, Urology, 34.1%; Oncology, 23.0%; Surgery, 16.0%; and other, 5.2%.

ANNUAL FINANCIAL DATA

	12/31/99	12/31/98	12/31/97	12/31/96	12/31/95	12/31/94	12/31/93
Earnings Per Share	[6] **2.28**	[5] **4.51**	[4] **1.26**	[3] **1.62**	[1] **1.53**	[1] **1.44**	[2] **1.19**
Cash Flow Per Share	**3.22**	**5.56**	**2.26**	**2.63**	**2.42**	**2.20**	**1.87**
Tang. Book Val. Per Share	**4.67**	**4.05**	**2.62**	**2.71**	**4.36**	**3.35**	**4.49**
Dividends Per Share	**0.78**	**0.74**	**0.70**	**0.66**	**0.62**	**0.58**	**0.54**
Dividend Payout %	**34.2**	**16.4**	**55.6**	**40.7**	**40.5**	**40.3**	**45.4**
INCOME STATEMENT (IN MILLIONS):							
Total Revenues	1,036.5	1,164.7	1,213.5	1,194.4	1,137.8	1,018.2	970.8
Costs & Expenses	797.5	947.3	991.8	976.0	947.3	827.9	806.8
Depreciation & Amort.	49.1	58.7	57.3	57.4	50.6	39.6	35.5
Operating Income	189.9	158.7	164.4	161.0	139.9	150.7	128.5
Net Interest Inc./(Exp.)	d19.3	d26.4	d32.9	d26.4	d24.2	d15.1	d11.4
Income Before Income Taxes	173.3	464.4	104.9	102.7	123.5	103.0	98.9
Income Taxes	55.2	212.1	32.6	10.2	36.7	28.1	36.8
Net Income	[6] 118.1	[5] 252.3	[4] 72.3	[3] 92.5	[1] 86.8	[1] 74.9	[2] 62.1
Cash Flow	167.2	311.0	129.6	149.9	137.4	114.5	97.6
Average Shs. Outstg. (000)	51,882	55,970	57,273	57,090	56,731	52,005	52,197
BALANCE SHEET (IN MILLIONS):							
Cash & Cash Equivalents	95.9	42.4	60.7	78.0	51.3	34.2	75.0
Total Current Assets	529.1	488.5	563.5	576.9	503.9	428.0	421.5
Net Property	169.7	172.7	206.4	226.1	214.2	199.9	168.9
Total Assets	1,126.4	1,079.8	1,279.3	1,332.5	1,091.0	958.4	798.6
Total Current Liabilities	352.5	302.8	310.6	336.2	273.3	364.6	264.3
Long-Term Obligations	158.4	160.0	340.7	342.8	198.4	78.3	68.5
Net Stockholders' Equity	574.3	567.6	573.1	601.5	564.6	439.8	383.1
Net Working Capital	176.6	185.7	252.9	240.7	230.6	63.4	157.2
Year-end Shs. Outstg. (000)	50,782	51,498	56,785	56,986	57,101	52,048	52,098
STATISTICAL RECORD:							
Operating Profit Margin %	18.3	13.6	13.5	13.5	12.3	14.8	13.2
Net Profit Margin %	11.4	21.7	6.0	7.7	7.6	7.4	6.4
Return on Equity %	20.6	44.5	12.6	15.4	15.4	17.0	16.2
Return on Assets %	10.5	23.4	5.7	6.9	8.0	7.8	7.8
Debt/Total Assets %	14.1	14.8	26.6	25.7	18.2	8.2	8.6
Price Range	59 7/8-41 11/16	50 1/4-28 1/2	39-26 3/8	37 3/8-25 7/8	32 1/4-25 1/2	30 1/2-22 1/4	35 1/4-20 1/2
P/E Ratio	26.3-18.3	11.1-6.3	30.9-20.9	23.1-16.0	21.1-16.7	21.2-15.5	29.6-17.2
Average Yield %	1.5	1.9	2.1	2.1	2.1	2.2	1.9

Statistics are as originally reported. [1] Incl. one-time chg. of $17.7 mill., 1995; & a ch$16.9 mill., 1994. [2] Incl. one-time gain of $17.6 mill. & bef. acctg. adj. of $6.1 mill. [3] Incl. net nonrecurr. chgs. of $12.9 mill. [4] Incl. pre-tax restruct chg. of $44.1 mill. & a nonrecurr. net gain of $3.9 mill. [5] Incl. net gain of $163.8 mill. fr. the sale of cardiology bus. & several nonrecur. chgs. total. $25.9 mill. [6] Incl. gain of $9.2 mill. fr. the sale of cardiology bus.

OFFICERS:
W. H. Longfield, Chmn., C.E.O.
C. P. Slacik, Sr. V.P., C.F.O.
N. C. Adler, V.P., Gen. Couns., Sec.

INVESTOR CONTACT: Earle L. Parker, V.P. & Chief Inv. Rel. Off., (908) 277-8059

PRINCIPAL OFFICE: 730 Central Ave., Murray Hill, NJ 07974

TELEPHONE NUMBER: (908) 277-8000
FAX: (908) 277-8278
WEB: www.crbard.com

NO. OF EMPLOYEES: 7,700 (approx.)

SHAREHOLDERS: 7,463 (approx.)

ANNUAL MEETING: In Apr.

INCORPORATED: NJ, Feb., 1972

INSTITUTIONAL HOLDINGS:
No. of Institutions: 239
Shares Held: 40,487,021
% Held: 79.0

INDUSTRY: Surgical and medical instruments (SIC: 3841)

TRANSFER AGENT(S): First Chicago Trust Company of New York, Jersey City, NJ

BB&T CORPORATION

	YIELD	2.7%
	P/E RATIO	15.9

INTERIM EARNINGS (Per Share):

Qtr.	Mar.	June	Sept.	Dec.
1996	0.72	0.50	0.68	0.64
1997	0.75	0.45	0.71	0.69
1998	0.39	0.42	0.44	0.46
1999	0.44	0.49	0.44	0.47

INTERIM DIVIDENDS (Per Share):

Amt.	Decl.	Ex.	Rec.	Pay.
0.175Q	2/23/99	4/14/99	4/16/99	5/03/99
0.20Q	6/22/99	7/14/99	7/16/99	8/02/99
0.20Q	8/24/99	10/13/99	10/15/99	11/01/99
0.20Q	12/14/99	1/12/00	1/14/00	2/01/00
0.20Q	2/22/00	4/12/00	4/14/00	5/01/00

Indicated div.: $0.80 (Div. Reinv. Plan)

CAPITALIZATION (12/31/99):

	($000)	(%)
Total Deposits	27,251,142	75.8
Long-Term Debt	5,491,734	15.3
Common & Surplus	3,199,159	8.9
Total	35,942,035	100.0

DIVIDEND ACHIEVER STATUS:
Rank: 73   10-Year Growth Rate: 14.52%
Total Years of Dividend Growth: 28

TRADING VOLUME
Thousand Shares

*7 YEAR PRICE SCORE 98.0   ***12 MONTH PRICE SCORE 89.5**
*NYSE COMPOSITE INDEX=100

RECENT DEVELOPMENTS: For the year ended 12/31/99, net income advanced 12.8% to $612.8 million from $543.2 million in the prior year. Earnings for 1999 and 1998 included after-tax non-recurring charges of $46.2 million and $17.9 million, respectively. Net interest income increased 10.9% to $1.58 billion from $1.43 billion in 1998. Non-interest income advanced 31.9% to $764.7 million. Non-interest expense grew 18.2% to $1.29 billion. Comparisons were made with restated 1998 figures.

PROSPECTS: On 2/7/00, BBT announced plans to acquire One Valley Bancorp, Inc., which has approximately $6.60 billion in assets and owns 123 branches in West Virginia and Virginia. As a result of the acquisition, BBT will rank sixth in deposit market share in West Virginia. On 1/13/00, BBT acquired Altanta, Georgia-based Premier Bancshares, Inc. Premier had $2.00 billion in assets, 32 banking offices in Atlanta and north Georgia, and 10 mortgage banking offices.

BUSINESS

BB&T CORPORATION is a multi-bank holding company, with assets totaling $46.60 billion as of 3/31/00, and owns 687 banking offices in the Carolinas, Virginia, West Virginia, Kentucky, Georgia, Maryland and Washington, D.C. The Company's largest subsidiary is Branch Banking and Trust Company (BB&T-NC). BB&T-NC's subsidiaries include BB&T Leasing Corp., BB&T Investment Services, BB&T Insurance Services and Prime Rate Premium Finance Corporation, Inc. BB&T-NC also owns 51.0% of AutoBase Information Systems. BBT's other subsidiaries include Branch Banking and Trust Company of South Carolina, Branch Banking and Trust Company of Virginia, Fidelity Federal Savings Bank and Virginia First Savings Bank. On 3/26/99, BBT acquired Scott & Stringfellow Financial, Inc. On 1/13/00, BBT acquired Premier Bancshares, Inc.

LOAN DISTRIBUTION

(12/31/99)	($000)	(%)
Comm. Financial & Agric.	4,593	15.2
Real Estate-Construction	3,311	11.0
Real Estate-Mortgage	16,011	53.1
Consumer	3,635	12.1
Leases	2,603	8.6
Total	30,152	100.0

ANNUAL FINANCIAL DATA

	12/31/99	12/31/98	12/31/97	12/31/96	12/31/95	12/31/94	12/31/93
Earnings Per Share	⑥ 1.83	⑤ 1.71	④ 1.30	③ 1.28	② 0.83	1.19	① 0.04
Tang. Book Val. Per Share	9.66	9.51	8.22	7.91	8.08	7.12	8.81
Dividends Per Share	0.75	0.66	0.58	0.50	0.43	0.37	0.32
Dividend Payout %	41.0	38.6	44.6	39.1	51.8	31.1	911.7

INCOME STATEMENT (IN MILLIONS):

Total Interest Income	3,115.8	2,481.2	2,122.9	1,606.6	1,548.2	578.4	547.3
Total Interest Expense	1,534.1	1,233.8	1,023.4	778.1	806.6	255.7	236.8
Net Interest Income	1,581.7	1,247.4	1,099.5	828.5	741.5	322.7	310.5
Provision for Loan Losses	92.1	80.3	89.9	53.7	31.4	7.2	31.4
Non-Interest Income	761.4	528.0	474.9	297.4	226.4	83.0	87.7
Non-Interest Expense	1,346.9	961.4	937.1	654.1	672.3	231.2	336.1
Income Before Taxes	904.1	733.7	547.4	418.2	264.2	167.3	30.6
Net Income	⑥ 612.8	⑤ 501.8	④ 359.9	③ 283.7	② 178.1	109.6	① 8.2
Average Shs. Outstg. (000)	335,298	293,571	276,440	220,972	207,964	87,658	84,662

BALANCE SHEET (IN MILLIONS):

Cash & Due from Banks	1,138.8	938.8	839.6	638.7	582.6	264.7	283.9
Securities Avail. for Sale	10,575.3	8,031.8	6,549.4	5,136.8	5,201.3	992.0	1,194.2
Total Loans & Leases	30,152.2	23,375.2	20,012.0	14,524.6	13,636.2	5,434.9	4,838.3
Allowance for Credit Losses	1,627.8	1,024.6	495.2	344.0	241.1	70.6	69.5
Net Loans & Leases	28,524.5	22,350.7	19,516.9	14,180.7	13,395.0	5,364.3	4,768.8
Total Assets	43,481.0	34,427.2	29,177.6	21,246.6	20,492.9	8,756.1	8,274.5
Total Deposits	27,251.1	23,046.9	20,210.1	14,953.9	14,684.1	6,165.1	6,394.9
Long-Term Obligations	5,491.7	4,736.9	3,283.0	2,051.8	1,383.9	197.5	479.7
Total Liabilities	40,281.8	31,668.7	26,940.0	19,517.4	18,818.9	8,123.8	7,709.6
Net Stockholders' Equity	3,199.2	2,758.5	2,237.6	1,729.2	1,674.1	632.3	564.9
Year-end Shs. Outstg. (000)	331,170	290,211	272,104	218,594	206,714	88,318	63,690

STATISTICAL RECORD:

Return on Equity %	19.2	18.2	16.1	16.4	10.6	17.3	1.5
Return on Assets %	1.4	1.5	1.2	1.3	0.9	1.3	0.1
Equity/Assets %	7.4	8.0	7.7	8.1	8.2	7.2	6.8
Non-Int. Exp./Tot. Inc. %	57.4	54.4	59.6	58.3	68.2	57.1	87.4
Price Range	40⅝-27³⁄₁₆	40¾-26¼	32½-17½	18½-12⅞	14-9⅜	11-8⁷⁄₁₆	11¾-9¼
P/E Ratio	22.2-14.9	23.8-15.3	25.0-13.5	14.5-10.1	16.9-11.3	9.2-7.1	334.8-263.5
Average Yield %	2.2	2.0	2.3	3.2	3.7	3.8	3.0

Statistics are as originally reported. Adj. for 100% stock div., 8/98. ① Bef. acct. chrg. of $27.2 mill. & incl. $49.1 mill. loss on the bulk sale of assets. ② Incl. $108.0 pre-tax merger-rel. chgs., $19.8 mill. in sec. losses, & $12.3 mill. gain on the sale of divest. deposits. ③ Incl. one-time after-tax SAIF chg. of $21.3 mill. ④ Incl. $42.7 mill. in after-tax UCB merger-rel. chgs. ⑤ Incl. after-tax merger costs of $10.9 mill. ⑥ Incl. non-recurr. chrg. of $46.2 mill.

OFFICERS:
J. A. Allison IV, Chmn., C.E.O.
K. S. King, Pres.
S. E. Reed, Sr. Exec. V.P., C.F.O.
H. G. Williamson, C.O.O.

INVESTOR CONTACT: Thomas A. Nicholson Jr, Senior Vice Pres, (336) 733-3058

PRINCIPAL OFFICE: 200 West Second Street, Winston-Salem, NC 27101

TELEPHONE NUMBER: (336) 733-2000
FAX: (336) 671-2399
WEB: www.bbandt.com
NO. OF EMPLOYEES: 13,700 (approx.)
SHAREHOLDERS: 68,703
ANNUAL MEETING: In Apr.
INCORPORATED: NC, 1897; reincorp., NC, 1968

INSTITUTIONAL HOLDINGS:
No. of Institutions: 243
Shares Held: 69,744,419
% Held: 21.1

INDUSTRY: National commercial banks (SIC: 6021)

TRANSFER AGENT(S): Branch Banking & Trust Company, Wilson, NC

NYSE SYMBOL BSC
Rec. Pr. 39 3/8 (5/31/00)

BEAR STEARNS COMPANIES, INC. (THE)

YIELD 1.0%
P/E RATIO 6.9

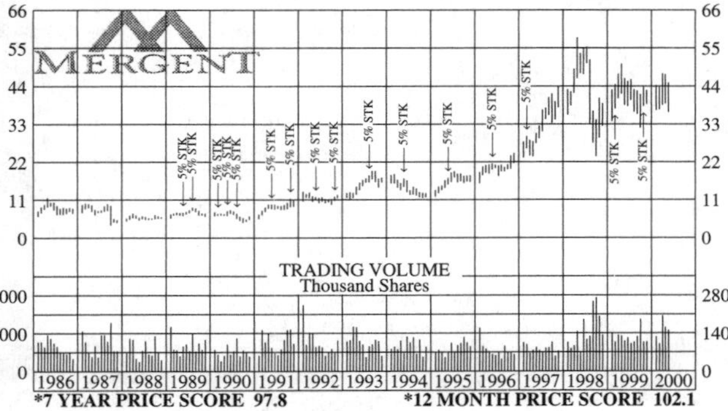

MERGENT
TRADING VOLUME
Thousand Shares
1986 1987 1988 1989 1990 1991 1992 1993 1994 1995 1996 1997 1998 1999 2000

*7 YEAR PRICE SCORE 97.8 *12 MONTH PRICE SCORE 102.1
*NYSE COMPOSITE INDEX=100

INTERIM EARNINGS (Per Share):

Qtr.	Sept.	Dec.	Mar.	June
1996-97	0.65	1.10	1.04	1.05
1997-98	1.01	1.01	1.05	1.11
1998-99	0.36	0.80	1.35	1.76
1999-00	0.95	1.64	...	...

INTERIM DIVIDENDS (Per Share):

Amt.	Decl.	Ex.	Rec.	Pay.
0.15Q	7/21/99	8/11/99	8/13/99	8/27/99
0.15Q	10/29/99	11/09/99	11/12/99	11/26/99
5% STK	10/29/99	11/09/99	11/12/99	11/26/99
0.15Q	1/19/00	2/09/00	2/11/00	2/25/00
0.10E	3/15/00	4/12/00	4/14/00	4/28/00

Indicated div.: $0.40

CAPITALIZATION (6/30/99):

	($000)	(%)
Long-Term Debt	14,647,092	72.9
Redeemable Pfd. Stock	500,000	2.5
Preferred Stock	800,000	4.0
Common & Surplus	4,155,509	20.7
Total	20,102,601	100.0

DIVIDEND ACHIEVER STATUS:
Rank: 206 10-Year Growth Rate: 7.80%
Total Years of Dividend Growth: 13

RECENT DEVELOPMENTS: For the quarter ended 12/31/99, net income advanced 80.3% to $245.1 million from $135.9 million in the corresponding period of the prior year. Total revenues grew 31.4% to $2.54 billion from $1.93 billion the year before. Revenues, net of interest expense, increased 39.7% to $1.43 billion. Interest and dividends revenues grew 21.9% to $1.30 billion. Principal transactions revenues improved 44.7% to $606.2 million.

PROSPECTS: Going forward, the Company should continue to increase the size and activity of its existing clearance accounts. In addition, BSC should continue to benefit from growth in the number of new fully disclosed and prime brokerage clients worldwide. The Company also continues to invest substantially in Clearnet™, BSC's on-line correspondent clearing service. BSC announced that it will change its fiscal year-end to November 30 from June 30.

BUSINESS

THE BEAR STEARNS COMPANIES, INC., is the parent company of Bear, Stearns and Company Inc., a worldwide investment banking, securities trading and brokerage firm. The firm's business includes corporate finance and mergers and acquisitions, public finance, institutional equities and fixed income sales and trading, private client services and asset management. Through its wholly-owned subsidiary, Bear Stearns Securities Corp., it provides professional and correspondent clearing services. The revenue breakdown for the fiscal year ended 6/30/99 was commissions, 12.9%; principal transactions, 24.5%; investment banking, 10.6%; interest & dividends, 50.9%; and other, 1.2%.

REVENUES

(06/30/99)	($000)	(%)
Commissions	1,013,909	12.9
Principal transactions	1,929,137	24.5
Investment banking	839,301	10.6
Interest & dividends	4,008,566	50.9
Other income	91,125	1.1
Total	7,882,038	100.0

ANNUAL FINANCIAL DATA

	6/30/99	6/30/98	6/30/97	6/30/96	6/30/95	6/30/94	6/30/93
Earnings Per Share	**4.27**	**[1] 4.17**	**3.81**	**2.97**	**1.40**	**2.26**	**2.24**
Cash Flow Per Share	**4.63**	**4.47**	**4.17**	**3.27**	**1.69**	**2.66**	**2.51**
Tang. Book Val. Per Share	**33.07**	**28.39**	**21.90**	**17.72**	**13.43**	**12.37**	**10.31**
Dividends Per Share	**0.56**	**0.544**	**0.538**	**0.51**	**0.48**	**0.46**	**0.43**
Dividend Payout %	**13.2**	**13.0**	**14.1**	**17.3**	**34.5**	**20.3**	**19.3**
INCOME STATEMENT (IN MILLIONS):							
Total Revenues	7,882.0	7,979.9	6,077.3	4,963.9	3,753.6	3,441.1	2,856.9
Costs & Expenses	2,853.9	2,632.3	2,165.9	1,868.8	1,449.2	1,557.5	1,346.5
Depreciation & Amort.	133.1	115.1	89.7	69.9	59.3	48.0	41.2
Operating Income	4,895.0	5,232.5	3,821.7	3,025.2	2,245.1	1,835.6	1,469.2
Net Interest Inc./(Exp.)	d3,379.9	d3,638.5	d2,551.4	d1,981.2	d1,678.5	d1,020.1	d710.1
Income Before Income Taxes	1,064.1	1,063.5	1,013.7	834.9	388.1	642.8	614.4
Income Taxes	391.1	403.1	400.4	344.3	147.5	255.8	252.0
Net Income	673.0	[1] 660.4	613.3	490.6	240.6	387.0	362.4
Cash Flow	766.7	744.6	679.2	536.0	274.7	410.3	396.5
Average Shs. Outstg. (000)	165,483	166,457	163,002	164,113	162,901	163,430	160,553
BALANCE SHEET (IN MILLIONS):							
Cash & Cash Equivalents	93,925.7	92,088.8	71,749.8	55,958.5	45,582.9	43,873.5	35,369.9
Total Current Assets	110,255.1	108,122.1	81,956.2	65,051.9	52,382.4	52,298.7	41,449.6
Net Property	486.7	448.0	379.5	331.9	312.9	271.8	238.9
Total Assets	153,894.3	154,495.9	121,433.5	92,085.2	74,597.2	67,392.0	57,439.5
Total Current Liabilities	133,791.7	136,558.4	109,686.8	83,146.1	68,034.8	61,667.4	53,779.9
Long-Term Obligations	14,647.1	13,296.0	8,120.3	6,043.6	4,059.9	3,408.1	1,883.1
Net Stockholders' Equity	4,955.5	4,291.5	3,246.4	2,745.4	2,352.5	2,227.9	1,847.6
Net Working Capital	d23,536.7	d28,436.3	d27,730.7	d18,094.2	d15,652.3	d9,368.6	d12,330.2
Year-end Shs. Outstg. (000)	125,662	123,003	129,646	130,248	142,623	144,781	146,477
STATISTICAL RECORD:							
Operating Profit Margin %	62.1	65.6	62.9	60.9	59.8	53.3	51.4
Net Profit Margin %	8.5	8.3	10.1	9.9	6.4	11.2	12.7
Return on Equity %	13.6	15.4	18.9	17.9	10.2	17.4	19.6
Return on Assets %	0.4	0.4	0.5	0.5	0.3	0.6	0.6
Debt/Total Assets %	9.5	8.6	6.7	6.6	5.4	5.1	3.3
Price Range	50 1/2-31 7/8	58 1/16-23 9/16	44 1/16-23 3/16	24 1/2-15 3/4	19 1/4-11 15/16	18 1/2-11 9/16	19 3/8-11 3/16
P/E Ratio	11.8-7.5	13.9-5.7	11.6-6.1	8.3-5.3	13.8-8.6	8.2-5.1	8.7-5.0
Average Yield %	1.4	1.3	1.6	2.5	3.1	3.1	2.8

Statistics are as originally reported. Adj. for all stk. dividends thru 11/99. [1] Includes special charges of $108.0 million related to an increase in litigation reserves.

OFFICERS:
A. C. Greenberg, Chmn.
J. E. Cayne, Pres., C.E.O.
S. L. Molinaro Jr., Sr. V.P., Fin., C.F.O.
M. Minikes, Treas.

INVESTOR CONTACT: Investor Relations, (212) 272-8188

PRINCIPAL OFFICE: 245 Park Ave., New York, NY 10167

TELEPHONE NUMBER: (212) 272-2000
FAX: (212) 272-4785
WEB: www.bearstearns.com

NO. OF EMPLOYEES: 9,808

SHAREHOLDERS: 2,744

ANNUAL MEETING: In Oct.

INCORPORATED: DE, Aug., 1985

INSTITUTIONAL HOLDINGS:
No. of Institutions: 247
Shares Held: 77,434,644
% Held: 65.0

INDUSTRY: Security brokers and dealers (SIC: 6211)

TRANSFER AGENT(S): ChaseMellon Shareholder Services LLC, New York, NY

BECTON, DICKINSON AND COMPANY

YIELD	1.3%
P/E RATIO	28.1

INTERIM EARNINGS (Per Share):

Qtr.	Dec.	Mar.	June	Sept.
1996-97	0.22	0.32	0.27	0.35
1997-98	0.25	d0.05	0.36	0.34
1998-99	0.29	0.34	0.12	0.29
1999-00	0.29	...	...	...

INTERIM DIVIDENDS (Per Share):

Amt.	Decl.	Ex.	Rec.	Pay.
0.085Q	7/27/99	9/07/99	9/09/99	9/30/99
0.092Q	11/23/99	12/10/99	12/14/99	1/07/00
0.092Q	1/25/00	3/08/00	3/10/00	3/31/00
0.092Q	5/23/00	6/07/00	6/09/00	6/30/00

Indicated div.: $0.37 (Div. Reinv. Plan)

CAPITALIZATION (9/30/99):

	($000)	(%)
Long-Term Debt [1]	954,169	34.5
Deferred Income Tax	40,711	1.5
Preferred Stock	46,717	1.7
Common & Surplus	1,721,971	62.3
Total	2,763,568	100.0

DIVIDEND ACHIEVER STATUS:
Rank: 147   10-Year Growth Rate: 10.52%
Total Years of Dividend Growth: 27

TRADING VOLUME Thousand Shares

*7 YEAR PRICE SCORE 83.4   *12 MONTH PRICE SCORE 97.1
*NYSE COMPOSITE INDEX=100

RECENT DEVELOPMENTS: For the quarter ended 12/31/99, net income fell 1.1% to $75.3 million from $76.2 million in 1998. Revenues jumped 11.7% to $859.2 million from $769.0 million in the prior year. Revenues in the medical systems segment rose 8.8% to $462.6 million. Recently acquired Clontech added to the 18.4% increase to $264.4 million in revenues in the biosciences segment. Revenues in the preanalytical solutions segment climbed 9.6% to $132.1 million.

PROSPECTS: The Company expects its gross profit margin, which declined to 47.6% in the first quarter of fiscal 2000, to improve over the remainder of the year. In fiscal 2000, BDX expects to report record earnings and a year-over-year improvement in sales. Results should receive a boost from the FDA's approval to market BDPROBETEC™ ET system for the direct qualitative detection of chlamydia trachomatis and neisseria gonorrhoeae, two of the most common causes of sexually transmitted diseases.

BUSINESS

BECTON, DICKINSON AND COMPANY is principally engaged in the manufacture and sale of a broad line of medical supplies and devices and diagnostic systems used by health care professionals, medical research institutions and the general public. The Company's operations consist of two worldwide business segments: medical supplies and devices, and diagnostic systems. Major products in the medical supplies segment are hypodermic products, specially designed devices for diabetes care, prefillable drug delivery systems, infusion therapy products, elastic support products and thermometers. Major products in the diagnostic systems segment are clinical and industrial microbiology products, sample collection products, flow cytometry systems tissue culture labware and hematology instruments.

ANNUAL FINANCIAL DATA

	9/30/99	9/30/98	9/30/97	9/30/96	9/30/95	9/30/94	9/30/93
Earnings Per Share	[4] 1.04	[3] 0.90	1.15	1.06	0.90	0.76	[2] 0.68
Cash Flow Per Share	2.02	1.78	2.08	1.91	1.66	1.47	1.31
Tang. Book Val. Per Share	2.74	3.30	4.11	4.43	3.19	2.98	2.81
Dividends Per Share	0.34	0.29	0.26	0.23	0.20	0.18	0.17
Dividend Payout %	32.7	32.2	21.5	20.9	22.9	24.3	24.4
INCOME STATEMENT (IN MILLIONS):							
Total Revenues	3,418.4	3,116.9	2,810.5	2,769.8	2,712.5	2,559.5	2,465.4
Costs & Expenses	2,714.3	2,482.7	2,150.2	2,138.0	2,108.1	2,030.7	2,005.2
Depreciation & Amort.	258.9	228.7	209.8	200.5	207.8	203.7	189.8
Operating Income	445.2	405.4	450.5	431.2	396.7	325.0	270.4
Net Interest Inc./(Exp.)	d72.1	d56.3	d39.4	d37.4	d42.8	d47.6	d53.4
Income Before Income Taxes	372.7	340.9	422.6	393.7	349.6	296.2	222.9
Income Taxes	96.9	104.3	122.6	110.2	97.9	69.0	10.1
Net Income	[4] 275.7	[3] 236.6	300.1	283.4	251.7	227.2	[2] 212.8
Cash Flow	532.0	462.7	507.2	481.3	456.8	428.2	399.8
Average Shs. Outstg. (000)	264,580	262,128	245,230	253,418	276,804	293,332	307,720
BALANCE SHEET (IN MILLIONS):							
Cash & Cash Equivalents	64.6	90.6	141.0	165.1	240.0	178.8	64.9
Total Current Assets	1,683.7	1,542.8	1,312.6	1,276.8	1,327.5	1,326.6	1,150.7
Net Property	1,431.1	1,302.7	1,250.7	1,244.1	1,281.0	1,376.3	1,403.1
Total Assets	4,437.0	3,846.0	3,080.3	2,889.8	2,999.5	3,159.5	3,087.6
Total Current Liabilities	1,329.3	1,091.9	678.2	766.1	720.0	678.3	636.1
Long-Term Obligations	954.2	765.2	665.4	468.2	557.6	669.2	680.6
Net Stockholders' Equity	1,768.7	1,613.8	1,385.4	1,325.2	1,398.4	1,481.7	1,457.0
Net Working Capital	354.4	450.8	634.4	510.7	607.5	648.2	514.7
Year-end Shs. Outstg. (000)	250,798	247,843	244,168	247,220	260,300	281,112	298,908
STATISTICAL RECORD:							
Operating Profit Margin %	13.0	13.0	16.0	15.6	14.6	12.7	11.0
Net Profit Margin %	8.1	7.6	10.7	10.2	9.3	8.9	8.6
Return on Equity %	15.6	14.7	21.7	21.4	18.0	15.3	14.6
Return on Assets %	6.2	6.2	9.7	9.8	8.4	7.2	6.9
Debt/Total Assets %	21.5	19.9	21.6	16.2	18.6	21.2	22.0
Price Range	44 3/16-22 3/4	49 5/8-24 3/8	27 13/16-20 15/16	22 3/4-17 11/16	19-12	12 1/2-8 1/2	10 3/16-8 3/16
P/E Ratio	42.5-21.5	55.1-27.1	24.2-18.2	21.7-16.8	21.2-13.4	16.4-11.2	15.0-12.0
Average Yield %	1.0	0.8	1.1	1.1	1.3	1.8	1.8

Statistics are as originally reported. Adj. for 2-for-1 stk. split, 2/93 & 8/96. [1] Incl. debentures convertible into common stk. [2] Bef. acctg. chg. of $141.1 mill. [3] Bef. inc. fr. disc. opers. of $6.9 mill. & incl. a one-time acq.-related chg. of $7.0 mill. and a spec. pre-tax chg. of $90.9 mill. [4] Incl. a one-time gain of $7.0 mill. from a favorable tax judge. in Brazil & incl. pre-tax chgs. of $103.0 mill.

QUARTERLY DATA

(9/30/99)($000)	Rev	Inc
1st Quarter	768,966	76,158
2nd Quarter	873,964	90,114
3rd Quarter	873,002	33,124
4th Quarter	902,480	76,323

OFFICERS:
E. J. Ludwig, Pres. C.E.O.
R. K. Berman, Treas., V.P.
B. M. Healy, V.P., Sec.

INVESTOR CONTACT: Investors Relations, (800) 284-6845

PRINCIPAL OFFICE: 1 Becton Drive, Franklin Lakes, NJ 07417-1880

TELEPHONE NUMBER: (201) 847-6800
FAX: (201) 847-6475
WEB: www.bd.com

NO. OF EMPLOYEES: 24,000 (approx.)

SHAREHOLDERS: 11,500 (approx.)

ANNUAL MEETING: In Feb.

INCORPORATED: NJ, Nov., 1906

INSTITUTIONAL HOLDINGS:
No. of Institutions: 369
Shares Held: 210,486,284
% Held: 83.7

INDUSTRY: Surgical and medical instruments (SIC: 3841)

TRANSFER AGENT(S): First Chicago Trust Company of New York, Jersey City, NJ

NYSE SYMBOL BLC
Rec. Pr. 16 1/16 (5/31/00)

BELO (A.H.) CORPORATION

YIELD 1.7%
P/E RATIO 10.7

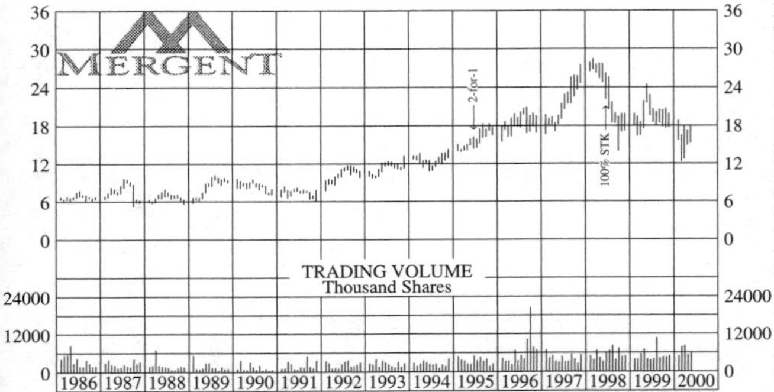

*7 YEAR PRICE SCORE 67.4 *12 MONTH PRICE SCORE 90.3
*NYSE COMPOSITE INDEX=100

INTERIM EARNINGS (Per Share):

Qtr.	Mar.	June	Sept.	Dec.
1994	0.12	0.24	0.20	0.30
1995	0.14	0.27	0.17	0.27
1996	0.17	0.30	0.21	0.39
1997	0.19	0.21	0.12	0.19
1998	0.11	0.24	0.08	0.10
1999	0.11	0.67	0.14	0.58

INTERIM DIVIDENDS (Per Share):

Amt.	Decl.	Ex.	Rec.	Pay.
0.06Q	2/12/99	5/12/99	5/14/99	6/04/99
0.07Q	7/30/99	8/11/99	8/13/99	9/03/99
0.07Q	9/24/99	11/09/99	11/12/99	12/03/99
0.07Q	12/16/99	2/09/00	2/11/00	3/03/00
0.07Q	2/11/00	5/10/00	5/12/00	6/02/00

Indicated div.: $0.28

CAPITALIZATION (12/31/99):

	($000)	(%)
Long-Term Debt	1,849,490	50.5
Deferred Income Tax	422,465	11.5
Common & Surplus	1,389,837	38.0
Total	3,661,792	100.0

DIVIDEND ACHIEVER STATUS:
Rank: 179 10-Year Growth Rate: 8.98%
Total Years of Dividend Growth: 12

RECENT DEVELOPMENTS: For the year ended 12/31/99, net income more than doubled to $178.3 million from $64.9 million in the preceding year. Results for 1999 included a gain on the sale of subsidiaries and investments of $117.8 million. Results for 1998 included non-recurring charges of $26.2 million. Total net operating revenues were $1.43 billion, up 3.0% from $1.39 billion in the prior year.

PROSPECTS: Going forward, results for the Company's television group should benefit from political advertising and the summer Olympics. In addition, retail and general advertising at BLC's newspapers should grow at impressive rates in 2000. Also, the Company anticipates an upward trend in classified employment volume at The Mornings News in fiscal 2000.

BUSINESS

A.H. BELO CORPORATION is a television broadcasting and newspaper publishing company that owns and operates 16 network-affiliated television stations; seven daily newspapers; five local or regional cable news channels; and Belo Productions, Inc. The Company also manages four television stations through local marketing agreements. Four of Belo's stations are in the top 17 U.S. television markets, seven in the top 30 and 11 in the top 50 markets. The Company's television group reaches 14.0% of all U.S. television households. In 1999, newspaper publishing accounted for 57.0% of revenues, broadcasting 41.7%, interactive media, 0.5% and other, 0.8%.

ANNUAL FINANCIAL DATA

	12/31/99	12/31/98	12/31/97	12/31/96	12/31/95	12/31/94	12/31/93
Earnings Per Share	[3] **1.50**	**0.52**	**0.71**	**1.06**	**0.84**	**0.85**	[1] [2] **0.55**
Cash Flow Per Share	**2.91**	**1.80**	**1.86**	**1.84**	**1.59**	**1.43**	**1.02**
Dividends Per Share	**0.26**	**0.24**	**0.22**	**0.20**	**0.16**	**0.15**	**0.14**
Dividend Payout %	**17.3**	**46.1**	**31.0**	**19.4**	**18.7**	**17.6**	**25.4**
INCOME STATEMENT (IN MILLIONS):							
Total Revenues	1,434.0	1,407.3	1,248.4	824.3	735.3	628.1	544.8
Costs & Expenses	1,000.5	1,014.8	872.6	593.5	539.3	450.7	417.7
Depreciation & Amort.	169.0	159.4	135.0	65.2	59.4	46.4	37.7
Operating Income	264.5	233.1	240.8	165.6	136.6	131.0	[2] 89.5
Net Interest Inc./(Exp.)	d110.6	d107.6	d90.8	d27.6	d30.0	d16.1	d15.0
Income Before Income Taxes	276.5	130.5	154.1	144.0	111.0	107.9	75.6
Income Taxes	98.1	65.6	71.2	56.5	44.4	39.0	31.1
Net Income	[3] 178.3	64.9	83.0	87.5	66.6	68.9	[1] [2] 44.5
Cash Flow	347.3	224.3	218.0	152.7	126.0	115.3	82.1
Average Shs. Outstg. (000)	119,177	124,836	117,122	83,020	79,292	80,892	80,816
BALANCE SHEET (IN MILLIONS):							
Cash & Cash Equivalents	45.6	19.5	11.9	13.8	12.8	9.3	8.9
Total Current Assets	352.0	275.8	277.0	171.9	165.3	130.3	117.4
Net Property	655.0	626.8	608.3	370.8	361.8	312.2	270.0
Total Assets	3,976.3	3,539.1	3,623.0	1,224.1	1,154.0	913.8	796.2
Total Current Liabilities	259.8	180.7	214.5	89.3	81.7	83.7	59.7
Long-Term Obligations	1,849.5	1,634.0	1,614.0	631.9	557.4	330.4	277.4
Net Stockholders' Equity	1,389.8	1,248.1	1,326.0	370.5	388.5	382.5	346.1
Net Working Capital	92.1	95.0	62.5	82.6	83.6	46.6	57.7
Year-end Shs. Outstg. (000)	118,656	118,925	124,694	72,520	76,484	79,444	80,840
STATISTICAL RECORD:							
Operating Profit Margin %	18.4	16.6	19.3	20.1	18.6	20.9	16.4
Net Profit Margin %	12.4	4.6	6.6	10.6	9.1	11.0	8.2
Return on Equity %	12.8	5.2	6.3	23.6	17.1	18.0	12.9
Return on Assets %	4.5	1.8	2.3	7.1	5.8	7.5	5.6
Debt/Total Assets %	46.5	46.2	44.6	51.6	48.3	36.2	34.8
Price Range	24 1/2-16 3/8	28 1/2-13 15/16	27 9/16-16 5/8	20 7/8-15 1/2	18 3/8-13 15/16	14 5/16-10 13/16	13 1/4-9 11/16
P/E Ratio	16.3-10.9	54.7-26.8	38.8-23.4	19.8-14.7	21.9-16.6	16.8-12.7	24.1-17.6
Average Yield %	1.3	1.1	1.0	1.1	1.0	1.2	1.2

Statistics are as originally reported. Adj. for stk. splits: 2-for-1, 6/98 and 5/95. [1] Bef. acctg. credit $6.6 mill. [2] Incl. non-recurr. chrg. $5.8 mill. [3] Incl. gain. on sale of subs. & invest. $117.8 mill.

OFFICERS:
R. W. Decherd, Chmn., Pres., C.E.O.
W. L. Huey Jr., Vice-Chmn.,
D. A. Shive, Sr. V.P., C.F.O.

INVESTOR CONTACT: Carey P. Hendrickson, V.P., Investor Relations, (214) 977-6626

PRINCIPAL OFFICE: 400 South Record Street, Dallas, TX 75202

TELEPHONE NUMBER: (214) 977-6606
FAX: (214) 977-6603
WEB: www.belo.com

NO. OF EMPLOYEES: 7,612

SHAREHOLDERS: 10,225 (approx. Series A); 615 (approx. Series B)

ANNUAL MEETING: In May

INCORPORATED: DE, May, 1987

INSTITUTIONAL HOLDINGS:
No. of Institutions: 166
Shares Held: 65,994,034
% Held: 66.4

INDUSTRY: Newspapers (SIC: 2711)

TRANSFER AGENT(S): BankBoston, NA., Boston, MA.

BEMIS COMPANY, INC.

INTERIM EARNINGS (Per Share):

Qtr.	Mar.	June	Sept.	Dec.
1996	0.41	0.47	0.45	0.57
1997	0.37	0.52	0.47	0.64
1998	0.41	0.56	0.52	0.60
1999	0.35	0.60	0.59	0.63

INTERIM DIVIDENDS (Per Share):

Amt.	Decl.	Ex.	Rec.	Pay.
0.23Q	5/06/99	5/18/99	5/20/99	6/01/99
0.23Q	7/29/99	8/09/99	8/11/99	9/01/99
0.23Q	10/28/99	11/09/99	11/12/99	12/01/99
0.24Q	2/03/00	2/16/00	2/18/00	3/01/00
0.24Q	5/04/00	5/17/00	5/19/00	6/01/00

Indicated div.: $0.96 (Div. Reinv. Plan)

CAPITALIZATION (12/31/99):

	($000)	(%)
Long-Term Debt ☐	372,267	30.3
Deferred Income Tax	89,635	7.3
Minority Interest	39,498	3.2
Common & Surplus	725,895	59.1
Total	1,227,295	100.0

DIVIDEND ACHIEVER STATUS:
Rank: 118   10-Year Growth Rate: 11.86%
Total Years of Dividend Growth: 16

TRADING VOLUME
Thousand Shares

7 YEAR PRICE SCORE 71.3   **12 MONTH PRICE SCORE 105.1**
NYSE COMPOSITE INDEX=100

RECENT DEVELOPMENTS: For the year ended 12/31/99, net income increased 13.5% to $114.8 million versus $101.1 million in 1998. Net sales were $1.92 billion, up 3.8% from $1.85 billion a year earlier. Cost of products sold advanced 2.5% to $1.49 billion versus $1.46 billion in 1998. Selling, general and administrative expenses rose 4.3% to $193.8 million compared with $185.8 million a year earlier. Comparisons were made with restated 1998 results.

PROSPECTS: The Company expects capital expenditures to decline 19.7% to approximately $110.0 million in 2000 as several large projects are completed. The reorganization of the Pressure Sensitive Materials business in North America is largely complete and BMS is optimistic about the prospects for significant improvement in the financial performance of this business unit in 2000.

BUSINESS

BEMIS COMPANY, INC. is a manufacturer of flexible packaging and specialty coated and graphics products. Flexible packaging products include coated and laminated films, polyethylene packaging, packaging machinery, multi-wall paper bags and consumer-size paper packaging, and specialty containers. Specialty coated and graphics products include pressure-sensitive materials, non-woven products and rotogravure cylinders. The primary market for BMS's products is packaging related, which accounts for about 70% of sales. Other markets include chemicals, agribusiness, pharmaceuticals, printing and graphic arts, and a variety of other industrial end uses.

ANNUAL FINANCIAL DATA

	12/31/99	12/31/98	12/31/97	12/31/96	12/31/95	12/31/94	12/31/93
Earnings Per Share	2.18	2.09	2.00	1.90	1.63	1.40	☑ 0.89
Cash Flow Per Share	4.04	3.76	3.46	3.14	2.74	2.40	1.80
Tang. Book Val. Per Share	13.91	12.83	12.08	10.83	9.76	8.16	7.24
Dividends Per Share	0.92	0.88	0.80	0.72	0.64	0.54	0.50
Dividend Payout %	42.2	42.1	40.0	37.9	39.3	38.6	56.2
INCOME STATEMENT (IN MILLIONS):							
Total Revenues	1,918.0	1,848.0	1,877.2	1,655.4	1,523.4	1,390.5	1,203.5
Costs & Expenses	1,602.1	1,550.5	1,603.1	1,413.9	1,317.1	1,209.6	1,054.8
Depreciation & Amort.	97.7	88.9	78.9	66.2	58.0	51.8	47.0
Operating Income	218.2	208.5	195.3	175.4	148.3	129.1	101.7
Net Interest Inc./(Exp.)	d21.2	d21.9	d18.9	d13.4	d11.5	d8.4	d7.2
Income Before Income Taxes	185.9	181.9	175.0	162.8	136.1	118.1	74.4
Income Taxes	71.1	70.5	67.4	61.7	50.9	45.3	28.3
Equity Earnings/Minority Int.	d4.2	d4.4	d5.4	d4.7	d3.8	d3.4	d2.4
Net Income	114.8	111.4	107.6	101.1	85.2	72.8	☑ 46.1
Cash Flow	212.5	200.3	186.4	167.3	143.2	124.6	93.1
Average Shs. Outstg. (000)	52,657	53,324	53,880	53,252	52,311	51,953	51,767
BALANCE SHEET (IN MILLIONS):							
Cash & Cash Equivalents	18.2	23.7	13.8	10.2	22.0	12.7	8.9
Total Current Assets	583.6	517.9	516.4	466.9	442.3	418.9	337.0
Net Property	776.2	740.1	685.2	583.5	534.6	461.3	414.9
Total Assets	1,532.1	1,453.1	1,362.6	1,168.8	1,030.6	923.3	789.8
Total Current Liabilities	253.3	242.8	251.2	214.4	219.2	210.8	184.2
Long-Term Obligations	372.3	371.4	316.8	241.1	166.4	171.7	123.2
Net Stockholders' Equity	725.9	670.8	639.9	567.1	512.8	418.0	370.5
Net Working Capital	330.3	275.2	265.2	252.5	223.1	208.1	152.8
Year-end Shs. Outstg. (000)	52,189	52,269	52,968	52,361	52,567	51,211	51,201
STATISTICAL RECORD:							
Operating Profit Margin %	11.4	11.3	10.4	10.6	9.7	9.3	8.4
Net Profit Margin %	6.0	6.0	5.7	6.1	5.6	5.2	3.8
Return on Equity %	15.8	16.6	16.8	17.8	16.6	17.4	12.4
Return on Assets %	7.5	7.7	7.9	8.6	8.3	7.9	5.8
Debt/Total Assets %	24.3	25.6	23.2	20.6	16.1	18.6	15.6
Price Range	40⅜-30³⁄₁₆	46¹⁵⁄₁₆-33½	47¹⁵⁄₁₆-33⅝	37⅝-25⅝		30-23	25¾-20½	27⅜-19⅞
P/E Ratio	18.5-13.8	22.5-16.0	24.0-16.8	19.8-13.5	18.4-14.1	18.4-14.6	30.8-22.3
Average Yield %	2.6	2.2	2.0	2.3	2.4	2.3	2.1

Statistics are as originally reported. ☐ Incl. capital lease obligations. ☑ Incl. restruct. chg. of approx. $13 mill. ($0.25/sh.), and bef. acctg. change chrg. $1.7 mill. ($0.03/sh.).

OFFICERS:
J. H. Roe, Chmn.
R. F. Mlnarik, Vice-Chmn.
J. H. Curler, Pres., C.E.O.
B. R. Field, III, Sr. V.P., C.F.O., Treas.

INVESTOR CONTACT: Robert F. Kleiber, Dir., Investor Relations, (612) 376-3030

PRINCIPAL OFFICE: 222 South 9th Street, Suite 2300, Minneapolis, MN 55402-4099

TELEPHONE NUMBER: (612) 376-3000
FAX: (612) 340-6174
WEB: www.bemis.com

NO. OF EMPLOYEES: 9,534

SHAREHOLDERS: 5,316

ANNUAL MEETING: In May

INCORPORATED: MO, May, 1885

INSTITUTIONAL HOLDINGS:
No. of Institutions: 175
Shares Held: 30,364,774
% Held: 58.0

INDUSTRY: Paper coated & laminated, packaging (SIC: 2671)

TRANSFER AGENT(S): Norwest Bank Minnesota, South St. Paul, MN

BERKLEY (W. R.) CORPORATION

YIELD 2.4%
P/E RATIO ...

TRADING VOLUME
Thousand Shares

7600
3800
0

1986 | 1987 | 1988 | 1989 | 1990 | 1991 | 1992 | 1993 | 1994 | 1995 | 1996 | 1997 | 1998 | 1999 | 2000

*7 YEAR PRICE SCORE 48.6   *12 MONTH PRICE SCORE 99.2
*NYSE COMPOSITE INDEX=100

INTERIM EARNINGS (Per Share):

Qtr.	Mar.	June	Sept.	Dec.
1996	0.52	0.61	0.71	0.75
1997	0.90	0.63	0.80	0.74
1998	0.78	0.70	0.36	d0.14
1999	0.07	0.22	d0.02	d1.59

INTERIM DIVIDENDS (Per Share):

Amt.	Decl.	Ex.	Rec.	Pay.
0.13Q	5/11/99	6/11/99	6/15/99	7/01/99
0.13Q	8/10/99	9/15/99	9/17/99	10/01/99
0.13Q	11/09/99	12/15/99	12/17/99	1/03/00
0.13Q	3/09/00	3/17/00	3/21/00	4/03/00
0.13Q	5/09/00	6/14/00	6/16/00	7/03/00

Indicated div.: $0.52

CAPITALIZATION (12/31/99):

	($000)	(%)
Long-Term Debt	394,792	32.5
Minority Interest	30,275	2.5
Redeemable Pfd. Stock	198,126	16.3
Common & Surplus	591,778	48.7
Total	1,214,971	100.0

DIVIDEND ACHIEVER STATUS:
Rank: 128   10-Year Growth Rate: 11.40%
Total Years of Dividend Growth: 14

RECENT DEVELOPMENTS: For the year ended 12/31/99, BKLY reported a net loss of $34.0 million compared with income of $58.8 million in 1998. Results for 1999 included a restructuring charge of $11.5 million. Revenues rose 5.8% to $1.67 billion from $1.58 billion a year earlier. Net written premiums grew 6.1% to $1.43 billion, while premiums earned climbed 10.6% to $1.41 billion. BKLY reported realized losses on investments of $6.1 million

compared with realized gains on investments of $25.4 million a year ago. The combined ratio of BKLY's insurance operations grew to 104.7% versus 99.7% a year earlier. Catastrophe losses grew 2.4% to $39.1 million from $38.2 million in the prior year. In an effort to restore profitability, BKLY restructured its regional businesses to trim expenses, and has increased their reserves. BKLY has also implemented price increases across many of its lines of business.

BUSINESS

W.R. BERKLEY CORPORATION is an insurance holding company that, through its subsidiaries, operates in all segments of the property casualty insurance business. The Company's operating units are grouped in five segments according to market served: Regional Property Casualty Insurance, Reinsurance, Specialty Insurance, Alternative Markets and International. The Company's regional insurance operations are conducted primarily in the New England, Mid-Atlantic, Midwest and Southern sections of the United States. The reinsurance, specialty insurance, and alternative insurance operations are conducted on a nationwide basis. Presently, international operations are conducted primarily in Argentina and the Philippines.

ANNUAL FINANCIAL DATA

	12/31/99	12/31/98	12/31/97	12/31/96	12/31/95	12/31/94	12/31/93
Earnings Per Share	② d1.34	① 1.76	3.02	2.56	1.91	0.96	1.91
Tang. Book Val. Per Share	20.11	29.60	29.56	27.37	28.43	21.54	18.47
Dividends Per Share	0.51	0.47	0.40	0.34	0.31	0.29	0.26
Dividend Payout %	...	26.7	13.1	13.3	16.4	29.9	13.6
INCOME STATEMENT (IN MILLIONS):							
Total Premium Income	1,414.4	1,278.4	1,111.7	981.2	803.3	655.0	420.3
Other Income	259.3	304.1	288.6	243.9	218.6	175.8	161.5
Total Revenues	1,673.7	1,582.5	1,400.3	1,225.2	1,021.9	830.8	581.8
Policyholder Benefits	1,085.8	914.8	734.4	669.2	571.0	486.1	301.2
Income Before Income Taxes	d79.2	62.8	129.2	115.0	82.7	30.8	60.4
Income Taxes	cr45.8	5.5	30.7	25.1	17.6	cr1.6	9.6
Equity Earnings/Minority Int.	d0.6	1.4	0.5	0.3	d4.3	2.8	0.8
Net Income	② d34.5	① 51.2	91.2	76.4	49.8	24.7	51.6
Average Shs. Outstg. (000)	25,927	29,115	30,185	29,792	26,121	25,773	26,919
BALANCE SHEET (IN MILLIONS):							
Cash & Cash Equivalents	20.1	16.1	21.7	19.3	10.2	5.5	9.4
Premiums Due	1,259.8	1,120.3	764.3	683.9	654.7	1,318.8	379.0
Invst. Assets: Fixed-term	2,516.5	2,866.1	2,817.1	2,517.1	2,290.1	1,618.3	1,215.8
Invst. Assets: Equities	61.4	65.9	86.2	93.9	101.6	69.3	37.6
Invst. Assets: Total	2,577.9	2,931.9	2,903.4	2,611.0	2,391.6	1,687.6	1,363.6
Total Assets	4,784.8	4,983.4	4,599.3	4,073.3	3,618.7	3,582.3	2,156.5
Long-Term Obligations	394.8	394.4	390.4	390.1	319.3	331.0	254.8
Net Stockholders' Equity	591.8	861.2	947.2	879.6	929.7	597.5	526.3
Year-end Shs. Outstg. (000)	25,617	26,504	29,568	29,454	30,252	25,167	26,006
STATISTICAL RECORD:							
Return on Revenues %	...	3.2	6.5	6.2	4.9	3.0	8.9
Return on Equity %	...	5.9	9.6	8.7	5.4	4.1	9.8
Return on Assets %	...	1.0	2.0	1.9	1.4	0.7	2.4
Price Range	36¼-19¹³/₁₆	49⅞-25¼	46⅜-28¹³/₁₆	35¹³/₁₆-26¹³/₁₆	37-23	28-21¹¹/₁₆	33¹¹/₁₆-21⁵/₁₆
P/E Ratio	...	28.3-14.3	15.4-9.5	14.0-10.5	19.4-12.1	29.2-22.6	17.6-11.2
Average Yield %	1.8	1.3	1.1	1.1	1.0	1.2	0.9

Statistics are as originally reported. Adj. for stk. splits: 3-for-2, 9/18/97 ① Bef. extraord. chrg. $5.0 mill. ($0.17/sh.) ② Incl. non-recurr. chrg. $11.5 mill.

OFFICERS:
W. R. Berkley, Chmn., C.E.O.
J. D. Vollaro, Pres., C.O.O.
E. G. Ballard, Sr. V.P., C.F.O., Treas.
C. T. Finnegan III, Sr. V.P., Gen. Couns., Sec.
INVESTOR CONTACT: Eugene G. Ballard, (203) 629-3000
PRINCIPAL OFFICE: 165 Mason St., P.O. Box 2518, Greenwich, CT 06836-2518

TELEPHONE NUMBER: (203) 629-3000
FAX: (203) 629-3492
WEB: www.wrbc.com
NO. OF EMPLOYEES: 4,181
SHAREHOLDERS: 724 (approx.)
ANNUAL MEETING: In May
INCORPORATED: DE, Jan., 1970

INSTITUTIONAL HOLDINGS:
No. of Institutions: 68
Shares Held: 19,149,580
% Held: 74.8
INDUSTRY: Fire, marine, and casualty insurance (SIC: 6331)
TRANSFER AGENT(S): ChaseMellon Shareholder Services, L.L.C., New York, NY

BESTFOODS

INTERIM EARNINGS (Per Share):

Qtr.	Mar.	June	Sept.	Dec.
1996	0.41	0.52	0.50	0.54
1997	0.40	d0.02	0.50	0.56
1998	0.44	0.58	0.56	0.57
1999	0.49	0.61	0.64	0.74

INTERIM DIVIDENDS (Per Share):

Amt.	Decl.	Ex.	Rec.	Pay.
0.265Q	9/21/99	9/28/99	9/30/99	10/25/99
0.265Q	11/16/99	12/30/99	1/03/00	1/25/00
0.265Q	3/21/00	3/29/00	3/31/00	4/25/00
0.265Q	5/16/00	6/28/00	6/30/00	7/25/00

Indicated div.: $1.06 (Div. Reinv. Plan)

CAPITALIZATION (12/31/99):

	($000)	(%)
Long-Term Debt	1,842,000	62.8
Deferred Income Tax	7,000	0.2
Minority Interest	148,000	5.0
Preferred Stock	151,000	5.1
Common & Surplus	787,000	26.8
Total	2,935,000	100.0

*7 YEAR PRICE SCORE 84.7   ***12 MONTH PRICE SCORE 106.9**

*NYSE COMPOSITE INDEX=100

DIVIDEND ACHIEVER STATUS:
Rank: 181   10-Year Growth Rate: 8.93%
Total Years of Dividend Growth: 13

RECENT DEVELOPMENTS: For the year ended 12/31/99, net income was $717.0 million, up 12.0% versus income from continuing operations of $640.0 million the year before. Results in the prior year included a pre-tax restructuring charge of $33.0 million. Net sales rose 2.7% to $8.64 billion from $8.41 billion in 1998. Operating income grew 12.0% to $1.33 billion from $1.19 billion the prior year.

PROSPECTS: In 2000, earnings growth should be fueled by increased volume stemming from new product introductions and increased marketing. Separately, BFO formed International Food Solutions, Inc., a new company with annual sales of about $230.0 million that merges the operations of Case-Swayne Co., Inc. and the Company's Milwaukee Seasonings unit.

BUSINESS

BESTFOODS (formerly CPC International, Inc.) operates in the consumer foods business. BFO was the surviving company following the 1/2/98 spin-off of CPC's corn-refining operations. BFO has operations in more than 60 countries and markets its products in 110 countries in many regions, including North America, Europe, Latin America, Africa and Asia. Well-known brands include: HELLMANN'S mayonnaise and BEST FOODS products; MAZOLA corn oil and margarine; SKIPPY peanut butter; THOMAS' English muffins; ARNOLD, BROWNBERRY, FREIHOFER'S, and OROWEAT breads; ENTENMANN'S pastries; BOBOLI Italian bread shells; MUELLER'S pasta products; KARO syrup; and KNORR soups, sauces and bouillons.

QUARTERLY DATA

(12/31/1999)($000)	REV	INC
1st Quarter	2,195	144
2nd Quarter	2,155	176
3rd Quarter	2,064	184
4th Quarter	2,223	213

ANNUAL FINANCIAL DATA

	12/31/99	12/31/98	12/31/97	12/31/96	12/31/95	12/31/94	12/31/93
Earnings Per Share	2.48	③ 2.15	①③1.43	② 1.97	② 1.72	② 1.13	1.48
Cash Flow Per Share	3.39	3.01	2.33	3.30	2.86	2.13	2.39
Tang. Book Val. Per Share	...	...	...	0.82	0.06	2.01	2.67
Dividends Per Share	1.00	0.92	0.84	0.78	0.73	0.67	0.63
Dividend Payout %	40.3	42.8	58.9	39.4	42.6	59.6	42.7
INCOME STATEMENT (IN MILLIONS):							
Total Revenues	8,637.0	8,374.0	8,400.0	9,844.0	8,432.0	7,425.0	6,738.0
Costs & Expenses	7,047.0	6,932.0	7,273.0	8,389.0	7,120.0	6,436.0	5,602.5
Depreciation & Amort.	260.0	255.0	264.0	376.0	322.0	288.0	265.8
Operating Income	1,330.0	1,187.0	866.0	1,092.0	1,007.0	712.0	883.3
Net Interest Inc./(Exp.)	...	...	d161.0	d172.0	d123.0	d92.0	d90.1
Income Before Income Taxes	1,147.0	1,021.0	704.0	917.0	877.0	615.0	790.3
Income Taxes	384.0	352.0	250.0	308.0	338.0	243.0	316.1
Equity Earnings/Minority Int.	d46.0	d29.0	d22.0	d16.0	d10.0	d16.0	d6.1
Net Income	717.0	③ 640.0	①③ 429.0	② 580.0	② 512.0	② 345.0	454.5
Cash Flow	965.0	882.0	678.0	941.0	819.0	617.0	704.6
Average Shs. Outstg. (000)	288,400	297,200	298,000	290,000	292,000	296,742	300,800
BALANCE SHEET (IN MILLIONS):							
Cash & Cash Equivalents	68.0	142.0	39.0	163.0	203.0	125.0	166.3
Total Current Assets	2,204.0	2,405.0	2,188.0	2,751.0	2,577.0	2,215.0	1,971.9
Net Property	1,964.0	1,965.0	1,941.0	3,080.0	2,898.0	2,281.0	2,120.7
Total Assets	6,232.0	6,435.0	6,100.0	7,875.0	7,502.0	5,668.0	5,060.8
Total Current Liabilities	2,368.0	2,312.0	2,347.0	2,792.0	3,066.0	2,088.0	1,583.4
Long-Term Obligations	1,842.0	2,053.0	1,818.0	1,869.0	1,333.0	879.0	775.0
Net Stockholders' Equity	938.0	981.0	1,042.0	2,084.0	1,987.0	1,749.0	1,769.1
Net Working Capital	d164.0	93.0	d159.0	d41.0	d489.0	127.0	388.5
Year-end Shs. Outstg. (000)	391,000	391,000	287,942	288,000	291,212	298,920	299,634
STATISTICAL RECORD:							
Operating Profit Margin %	15.4	14.2	10.3	11.1	11.9	9.6	13.1
Net Profit Margin %	8.3	7.6	5.1	5.9	6.1	4.6	6.7
Return on Equity %	76.4	65.2	41.2	27.8	25.8	19.7	25.7
Return on Assets %	11.5	9.9	7.0	7.4	6.8	6.1	9.0
Debt/Total Assets %	29.6	31.9	29.8	23.7	17.8	15.5	15.3
Price Range	60-45¼	60⅞-43¼	54⅜-37¹¹⁄₁₆	42⅛-32⁷⁄₁₆	37¼-25¹³⁄₁₆	27¹³⁄₁₆-22⅛	25⁹⁄₁₆-19¹⁵⁄₁₆
P/E Ratio	24.2-18.2	28.3-20.1	38.2-26.4	21.4-16.5	21.7-15.1	24.7-19.7	17.3-13.5
Average Yield %	1.9	1.8	1.8	2.1	2.3	2.7	2.8

Statistics are as originally reported. Adj. for 2-for-1 stk. split, 4/98. ① Bef. loss from disc. opers. of $11.1 mil. ② Incl. non-recur. pre-tax chg. $7 mil, 1996; & $58.3 mil chg., 1995; & after-tax chg. $137.3 mil ($0.92/sh), 1994. ③ Bef. $700,000 gain on disp. of discont. opers. & $17.2 mil ($0.06/sh) acctg. change chrg., 1998; $82.6 mil loss on disposal of disc. opers & incl. $155 mil restr. chg., 1997.

OFFICERS:
C. R. Shoemate, Chmn., Pres., C.E.O.
I. Ramsey, Sr. V.P.
R. S. Gluck, V.P., Treas.
INVESTOR CONTACT: Rainer H. Mimberg, V.P., Inv. Rel., (201) 894-2837
PRINCIPAL OFFICE: 700 Sylvan Avenue, International Plaza, Englewood Cliffs, NJ 07632-9976

TELEPHONE NUMBER: (201) 894-4000
FAX: (201) 894-2186
WEB: www.bestfoods.com
NO. OF EMPLOYEES: 44,000
SHAREHOLDERS: 22,500 (approx.)
ANNUAL MEETING: In Apr.
INCORPORATED: NJ, Aug., 1958; reincorp., DE, 1959

INSTITUTIONAL HOLDINGS:
No. of Institutions: 546
Shares Held: 181,930,527
% Held: 65.2

INDUSTRY: Dehydrated fruits, vegetables, soups (SIC: 2034)

TRANSFER AGENT(S): Equiserve, First Chicago Trust Division, Jersey City, NJ

BLACK HILLS CORPORATION

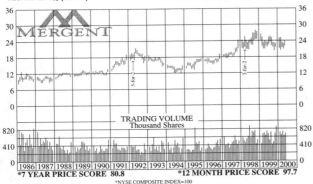

TRADING VOLUME
Thousand Shares

*7 YEAR PRICE SCORE 80.8   *12 MONTH PRICE SCORE 97.7

*NYSE COMPOSITE INDEX=100

INTERIM EARNINGS (Per Share):

Qtr.	Mar.	June	Sept.	Dec.
1995	----------	1.19	----------	
1996	0.37	0.27	0.38	0.38
1997	0.39	0.31	0.40	0.38
1998	0.39	0.35	0.44	0.01
1999	0.42	0.36	0.45	0.50

INTERIM DIVIDENDS (Per Share):

Amt.	Decl.	Ex.	Rec.	Pay.
0.26Q	4/20/99	5/12/99	5/14/99	6/01/99
0.26Q	7/20/99	8/11/99	8/13/99	9/01/99
0.26Q	10/27/99	11/09/99	11/12/99	12/01/99
0.27Q	1/28/00	2/09/00	2/11/00	3/01/00
0.27Q	4/28/00	5/10/00	5/12/00	6/01/00

Indicated div.: $1.08 (Div. Reinv. Plan)

CAPITALIZATION (12/31/99):

	($000)	(%)
Long-Term Debt	160,700	36.8
Deferred Income Tax	59,140	13.6
Common & Surplus	216,606	49.6
Total	436,446	100.0

DIVIDEND ACHIEVER STATUS:

Rank: 269   10-Year Growth Rate: 4.41%
Total Years of Dividend Growth: 19

RECENT DEVELOPMENTS: For the year ended 12/31/99, net income jumped 43.6% to $37.1 million compared with $25.8 million in the previous year. Results for 1998 included an $8.8 million after-tax non-recurring charge. Net income growth was driven by increased sales in the electric utility business unit, improved results in the independent energy business unit, partially offset by expected start-up losses in the communications business unit. Total operating revenues rose 16.6% to $791.9 million from $679.3 million in 1998. The increase in revenues reflected acquisitions and growth in the energy marketing segment of the independent energy business unit. Electric utility revenues rose 3.1% to $133.2 million from $129.2 million a year earlier. Independent energy revenues advanced 19.7% to $658.4 million from $550.0 million in 1998. Separately, the pending acquisition of Indeck Capital, Inc. is expected to close late in the second quarter of 2000.

BUSINESS

BLACK HILLS CORPORATION is an energy company consisting of three principal businesses units: regulated electric, independent energy and communications. The Company operates its public utility electric operations under the name Black Hills Power and Light Company. Black Hills Power is engaged in the generation, purchase, transmission, distribution and sale of electric power and energy to approximately 57,700 customers in western South Dakota, northeastern Wyoming, and southeastern Montana. The Company operates its independent energy businesses through direct and indirect subsidiaries: Wyodak Resources, Black Hills Exploration and Production, Enserco Energy, Inc., Black Hills Energy Resourses, Inc., Black Hills Coal Network, Inc., Black Hills Generation, Black Hills Capital, and Black Hills Energy Ventures. The communications segment is operated by Black Hills Fiber Systems, Inc. (formerly Black Hills FiberCom, Inc.), which owns 51.0% of Black Hills FiberCom LLC, which provides facilities-based communication services for Rapid City and the Northern Black Hills of South Dakota.

ANNUAL FINANCIAL DATA

	12/31/99	12/31/98	12/31/97	12/31/96	12/31/95	12/31/94	12/31/93
Earnings Per Share	1.73	① 1.19	1.49	1.40	1.19	1.11	1.11
Cash Flow Per Share	2.89	2.30	2.52	2.45	2.09	1.94	1.91
Tang. Book Val. Per Share	10.14	9.52	9.46	8.91	8.43	8.13	7.85
Dividends Per Share	1.04	1.00	0.95	0.92	0.89	0.88	0.85
Dividend Payout %	60.1	84.0	63.5	65.7	75.3	79.5	77.1
INCOME STATEMENT (IN MILLIONS):							
Total Revenues	791.9	679.3	313.7	162.6	149.8	145.4	139.4
Costs & Expenses	704.9	606.0	232.4	85.5	88.0	89.0	85.5
Depreciation & Amort.	25.1	24.0	22.3	22.8	19.7	17.6	16.1
Operating Income	61.9	49.2	58.9	54.3	42.2	38.8	37.8
Net Interest Inc./(Exp.)	d15.5	d14.7	d13.9	d13.6	d8.3	d6.4	d8.1
Income Taxes	15.8	11.7	14.3	13.6	10.7	10.4	9.0
Net Income	37.1	① 25.8	32.4	30.3	25.6	23.8	22.9
Cash Flow	62.1	49.8	54.7	53.0	45.3	41.4	39.0
Average Shs. Outstg. (000)	21,482	21,665	21,706	21,660	21,614	21,509	20,717
BALANCE SHEET (IN MILLIONS):							
Gross Property	659.9	619.5	598.3	581.5	557.6	516.8	425.9
Accumulated Depreciation	246.3	229.9	197.2	181.1	164.4	156.0	144.5
Net Property	464.2	389.6	401.1	400.4	393.3	360.8	281.4
Total Assets	674.8	559.4	508.7	467.4	448.8	436.9	352.9
Long-Term Obligations	160.7	162.0	163.4	164.7	166.1	128.9	85.3
Net Stockholders' Equity	216.6	206.7	205.4	193.2	182.3	175.4	168.1
Year-end Shs. Outstg. (000)	21,372	21,719	21,705	21,675	21,638	21,579	21,405
STATISTICAL RECORD:							
Operating Profit Margin %	7.8	7.2	18.8	33.4	28.1	26.7	27.1
Net Profit Margin %	4.7	3.8	10.3	18.6	17.1	16.4	16.4
Net Inc./Net Property %	8.0	6.6	8.1	7.6	6.5	6.6	8.1
Net Inc./Tot. Capital %	8.5	6.1	7.7	7.4	6.5	7.0	8.1
Return on Equity %	17.1	12.5	15.8	15.7	14.0	13.6	13.7
Accum. Depr./Gross Prop. %	37.3	37.1	33.0	31.1	29.5	30.2	33.9
Price Range	26½-20⁵⁄₁₆	27¹⁵⁄₁₆-20¹¹⁄₁₆	24⁵⁄₁₆-17½	19³⁄₁₆-15³⁄₁₆	17¹⁄₁₆-13³⁄₁₆	15³⁄₁₆-11¹³⁄₁₆	18¹³⁄₁₆-14⁹⁄₁₆
P/E Ratio	15.3-11.7	23.5-17.4	16.3-11.7	13.7-10.8	14.7-11.1	13.7-10.7	17.0-13.2
Average Yield %	4.4	4.1	4.5	5.4	5.8	6.5	5.1

Statistics are as originally reported. Adj. for 3-for-2 stk. split, 3/98 ① Inc. non-recurr. chrg. $8.8 mill.

OFFICERS:
D. P. Landguth, Chmn., C.E.O.
R. R. Basham, V.P.-Fin., Sec. & Treas.
M. Thies, Sr. V.P., C.F.O.

INVESTOR CONTACT: Roxann Basham, (605) 348-1700

PRINCIPAL OFFICE: 625 Ninth St., Rapid City, SD 57701

TELEPHONE NUMBER: (605) 348-1700
FAX: (605) 642-6214
WEB: www.blackhillscorp.com

NO. OF EMPLOYEES: 475

SHAREHOLDERS: 6,086

ANNUAL MEETING: In June

INCORPORATED: SD, Aug., 1941

INSTITUTIONAL HOLDINGS:
No. of Institutions: 94
Shares Held: 6,442,995
% Held: 30.2

INDUSTRY: Electric services (SIC: 4911)

TRANSFER AGENT(S): Norwest Shareowner Services, St. Paul, MN

NASDAQ SYMBOL BLOCA
Rec. Pr. 27¾ (5/31/00)

BLOCK DRUG CO., INC.

YIELD 4.6%
P/E RATIO 11.9

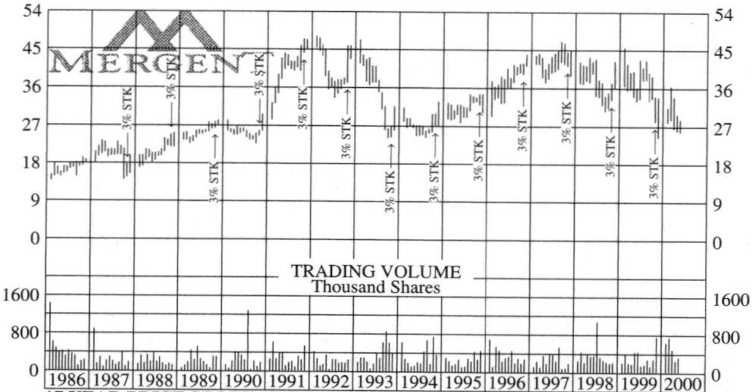

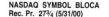

***7 YEAR PRICE SCORE 63.3** ***12 MONTH PRICE SCORE 82.7**

*NYSE COMPOSITE INDEX=100

INTERIM EARNINGS (Per Share):

Qtr.	June	Sept.	Dec.	Mar.
1996-97	0.66	0.65	0.70	d1.64
1997-98	0.66	0.67	0.49	0.42
1998-99	0.50	0.56	0.52	0.62
1999-00	0.55	0.59	0.57	. . .

INTERIM DIVIDENDS (Per Share):

Amt.	Decl.	Ex.	Rec.	Pay.
0.318Q	6/08/99	6/17/99	6/21/99	7/01/99
0.318Q	7/27/99	8/30/99	9/01/99	10/01/99
0.32Q	10/26/99	11/29/99	12/01/99	1/03/00
3% STK	10/26/99	11/29/99	12/01/99	1/03/00
0.32Q	2/01/00	2/28/00	3/01/00	4/03/00

Indicated div.: $1.28 (Div. Reinv. Plan)

CAPITALIZATION (3/31/99):

	($000)	(%)
Long-Term Debt	107,012	13.4
Deferred Income Tax	8,155	1.0
Common & Surplus	683,885	85.6
Total	799,052	100.0

DIVIDEND ACHIEVER STATUS:
Rank: 152 10-Year Growth Rate: 10.31%
Total Years of Dividend Growth: 28

RECENT DEVELOPMENTS: For the third quarter ended 12/31/99, net income increased 10.6% to $13.6 million from $12.3 million in the prior-year quarter. Revenues climbed 6.7% to $218.1 million from $204.3 million the year before. Net sales advanced 7.7% to $209.5 million from $194.5 million a year earlier. Sales for the Americas division, covering North and South America, declined 3.1% to $98.4 million from 101.5 million in 1998. Total US division sales decreased 5.6% to $75.4 million, while Latin America Sales were flat at $13.0 million. International sales, covering Europe, Asia-Pacific, Africa and the Middle East, grew 19.4% to $111.1 million, primarily due to 77.0% sales growth in Asia to $27.0 million due to the introduction of PARODONTAX toothpaste in Korea, strong sales of POLIDENT denture cleanser in Japan, a stronger Japanese yen during the year and SENSODYNE sales in Australia, and 8.0% sales growth in Europe to $84.1 million due to sales growth of denture cleansers in Germany, SENSODYNE toothpaste in France and PARODONTAX toothpaste in Holland.

BUSINESS

BLOCK DRUG CO., INC. is a worldwide manufacturer and marketer of dental products, denture care products, consumer over-the-counter medicines and specialty household products. The Company's brand names include SENSODYNE® desensitizing toothpastes, POLIDENT® denture cleansers, POLIGRIP® and COREGA denture adhesives, 2000 FLUSHES® toilet bowl cleaners, X-14® household cleaners, PHAZYME® and BEANO® anti-gas products, NYTOL® sleep aid tablets, BALMEX® diaper rash ointments, STANBACK® headache powders, CHAPET® lip balm, ATRIDOX™ periodontal treatment, and PERIOGLAS® bone grafting particulate.

ANNUAL FINANCIAL DATA

	3/31/99	3/31/98	3/31/97	3/31/96	3/31/95	3/31/94	3/31/93
Earnings Per Share	**2.19**	**2.21**	**0.37**	**1 2.29**	**1 1.96**	**2.18**	**2.81**
Cash Flow Per Share	**3.30**	**3.25**	**1.42**	**3.21**	**2.70**	**2.84**	**3.33**
Tang. Book Val. Per Share	**51.21**	**19.72**	**20.36**	**21.94**	**21.96**	**22.45**	**21.08**
Dividends Per Share	**1.18**	**1.13**	**1.02**	**0.92**	**0.86**	**0.81**	**0.71**
Dividend Payout %	**53.7**	**51.1**	**279.5**	**40.3**	**44.0**	**37.1**	**25.1**
INCOME STATEMENT (IN MILLIONS):							
Total Revenues	849.1	888.9	890.8	745.4	692.9	636.7	651.3
Costs & Expenses	755.5	794.7	855.4	658.4	612.2	565.0	561.9
Depreciation & Amort.	26.1	24.7	24.6	21.5	17.1	14.5	11.7
Operating Income	67.5	69.6	10.8	65.5	63.6	57.1	77.7
Income Before Income Taxes	67.5	69.6	10.8	65.5	63.6	57.1	77.7
Income Taxes	15.9	17.8	2.2	11.8	13.3	9.3	16.2
Net Income	51.6	51.8	8.6	1 53.7	1 45.9	47.9	61.5
Cash Flow	77.7	76.5	33.2	75.2	63.0	62.4	73.2
Average Shs. Outstg. (000)	23,551	23,492	23,449	23,406	23,358	21,997	21,952
BALANCE SHEET (IN MILLIONS):							
Cash & Cash Equivalents	78.4	61.4	38.8	29.8	37.8	28.2	32.9
Total Current Assets	409.6	380.7	393.1	312.2	295.9	249.1	254.8
Net Property	252.3	251.7	235.5	242.6	229.4	207.5	189.3
Total Assets	1,166.8	1,087.1	1,014.9	929.1	871.3	771.1	726.5
Total Current Liabilities	348.1	360.9	302.9	206.2	269.8	216.5	203.6
Long-Term Obligations	107.0	58.3	55.9	56.1	15.3	17.9	19.2
Net Stockholders' Equity	683.9	647.3	631.3	641.0	562.5	515.1	485.3
Net Working Capital	61.6	19.8	90.2	106.0	26.1	32.6	51.2
Year-end Shs. Outstg. (000)	8,672	23,515	23,472	23,429	22,703	21,980	21,962
STATISTICAL RECORD:							
Operating Profit Margin %	7.9	7.8	1.2	8.8	9.2	9.0	11.9
Net Profit Margin %	6.1	5.8	1.0	7.2	6.6	7.5	9.4
Return on Equity %	7.5	8.0	1.4	8.4	8.2	9.3	12.7
Return on Assets %	4.4	4.8	0.8	5.8	5.3	6.2	8.5
Debt/Total Assets %	9.2	5.4	5.5	6.0	1.8	2.3	2.6
Price Range	43⅜-30⅝	47⅛-37 5/16	43 15/16-29 5/16	34⅝-27 13/16	32¾-24 5/16	47⅜-24 3/16	48⅛-33 9/16
P/E Ratio	19.8-14.0	21.4-16.9	120.0-80.1	15.1-12.1	16.7-12.4	21.8-11.1	17.1-11.9
Average Yield %	3.2	2.7	2.8	3.0	3.0	2.3	1.7

Statistics are as originally reported. Adj. for stk. splits: 3% div., 1/3/00; 1/4/99; 3% div., 1/2/98; 3% div., 1/2/97; 3% div., 1/2/96; 3% div., 1/3/95; 3% div., 1/3/94 1 Bef. disc. oper. gain 3/31/96: $35.0 mill. ($1.58/sh.); 3/31/95: $4.4 mill. ($0.21/sh.)

OFFICERS:
L. Block, Sr. Chmn.
J. A. Block, Chmn.
T. R. Block, Pres.
P. M. Block, Pres.

PRINCIPAL OFFICE: 257 Cornelison Avenue Jersey City, NJ 07302-9988

TELEPHONE NUMBER: (201) 434-3000
FAX: (201) 432-6183
WEB: www.blockdrug.com
NO. OF EMPLOYEES: 3,251
SHAREHOLDERS: 438 (Cl. A approx.); 5 (Cl. B approx.).
ANNUAL MEETING: In Mar.
INCORPORATED: NJ, Mar., 1970

INSTITUTIONAL HOLDINGS:
No. of Institutions: 57
Shares Held: 6,741,068
% Held: 46.6

INDUSTRY: Toilet preparations (SIC: 2844)

TRANSFER AGENT(S): American Stock Transfer and Trust Company, New York, NY

BOWL AMERICA INC.

YIELD	6.0%
P/E RATIO	5.7

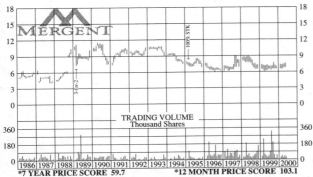

TRADING VOLUME
Thousand Shares

*7 YEAR PRICE SCORE 59.7 ***12 MONTH PRICE SCORE 103.1**
*NYSE COMPOSITE INDEX=100

INTERIM EARNINGS (Per Share):

Qtr.	Sept.	Dec.	Mar.	June
1994-95	d0.02	0.18	0.29	0.10
1995-96	d0.02	0.15	0.23	0.07
1996-97	d0.02	0.13	0.27	0.04
1997-98	Nil	0.14	0.29	0.09
1998-99	0.01	0.17	0.30	0.10
1999-00	0.64	0.21	0.34	...

INTERIM DIVIDENDS (Per Share):

Amt.	Decl.	Ex.	Rec.	Pay.
0.105Q	6/22/99	7/12/99	7/14/99	8/04/99
0.105Q	9/23/99	10/12/99	10/14/99	11/10/99
0.11Q	12/07/99	1/10/00	1/12/00	2/09/00
0.11Q	3/21/00	4/17/00	4/19/00	5/10/00
5% STK	3/21/00	6/30/00	7/05/00	7/26/00

Indicated div.: $0.44

CAPITALIZATION (6/27/99):

	($000)	(%)
Common & Surplus	35,477	100.0
Total	35,477	100.0

DIVIDEND ACHIEVER STATUS:
Rank: 264   10-Year Growth Rate: 4.91%
Total Years of Dividend Growth: 27

RECENT DEVELOPMENTS: For the third quarter ended 3/26/00, net earnings remained flat at $1.8 million compared with the corresponding quarter in the prior year. Operating revenues remained flat at $8.7 million versus the previous year. Operating revenues were negatively affected by ice and snow, which resulted in lost revenues due to closings at some locations and additional costs for removal, partially offset by tournament activity in February and March. Bowling and other revenue remained flat at $6.3 million, while food and merchandise sales remained flat at $2.4 million compared with the year before. Operating income remained constant at $2.6 million compared with a year ago. Operating expenses were $6.1 million, the same as a year earlier. For the thirty-nine weeks ended 3/26/00, net earnings totaled $3.3 million, an increase of 16.6% to $2.8 million in 1999. Operating revenues climbed 3.5% to $22.0 million from $21.3 million in the prior year.

BUSINESS

BOWL AMERICA INC. operates 13 bowling centers in the greater metropolitan area of Washington, D.C., two bowling centers in the greater metropolitan area of Baltimore, Maryland, one bowling center in the greater metropolitan area of Winterpark, Florida, three bowling centers in the greater metropolitan area of Jacksonville, Florida, and three bowling centers in the greater metropolitan area of Richmond, Virginia. These 22 bowling centers contain a total of 854 lanes. These establishments are fully air-conditioned with facilities for service of food and beverages, game rooms, rental lockers, and playroom facilities. All centers provide shoes for rental, and bowling balls are provided free. In addition, each center retails bowling accessories.

REVENUES

(06/27/1999)	($000)	(%)
Bowling & Other	19,696	71.5
Food & Merchandise		
Sales	7,851	28.5
Total	27,547	100.0

ANNUAL FINANCIAL DATA

	6/27/99	6/28/98	6/29/97	6/30/96	7/2/95	7/3/94	6/27/93
Earnings Per Share	0.58	0.51	0.42	0.43	0.54	0.63	0.65
Cash Flow Per Share	0.98	0.91	0.77	0.77	0.86	0.91	0.89
Tang. Book Val. Per Share	6.43	5.94	5.61	5.51	5.38	4.96	4.69
Dividends Per Share	0.40	0.381	0.376	0.36	0.35	0.34	0.32
Dividend Payout %	65.6	74.1	89.8	84.4	64.9	54.5	49.6
INCOME STATEMENT (IN THOUSANDS):							
Total Revenues	27,547	27,087	26,995	27,327	29,494	28,171	27,300
Costs & Expenses	20,727	20,661	21,475	21,795	23,026	20,854	20,180
Depreciation & Amort.	2,268	2,323	2,111	2,035	1,942	1,715	1,416
Operating Income	4,552	4,103	3,410	3,497	4,526	5,602	5,704
Net Interest Inc./(Exp.)	685	675	633	664	593	480	621
Income Before Income Taxes	5,237	4,778	4,042	4,161	5,119	6,082	6,324
Income Taxes	1,902	1,716	1,552	1,567	1,849	2,265	2,350
Net Income	3,335	3,062	2,490	2,594	3,270	3,817	3,974
Cash Flow	5,603	5,385	4,601	4,629	5,212	5,532	5,390
Average Shs. Outstg.	5,739	5,943	5,964	6,015	6,035	6,049	6,073
BALANCE SHEET (IN THOUSANDS):							
Cash & Cash Equivalents	9,248	9,986	8,173	8,881	7,635	8,470	9,633
Total Current Assets	10,453	11,194	9,366	10,508	9,259	9,430	11,444
Net Property	20,909	22,223	23,455	22,681	22,681	22,449	18,721
Total Assets	41,748	40,435	38,003	37,901	36,585	33,550	31,611
Total Current Liabilities	2,064	1,968	2,286	2,855	2,254	2,567	2,124
Net Stockholders' Equity	35,477	35,292	33,382	32,904	32,444	29,948	28,452
Net Working Capital	8,389	9,226	7,080	7,653	7,004	6,863	9,319
Year-end Shs. Outstg.	5,518	5,939	5,945	5,967	6,030	6,040	6,069
STATISTICAL RECORD:							
Operating Profit Margin %	16.5	15.1	12.6	12.8	15.3	19.9	20.9
Net Profit Margin %	12.1	11.3	9.2	9.5	11.1	13.6	14.6
Return on Equity %	9.4	8.7	7.5	7.9	10.1	12.7	14.0
Return on Assets %	8.0	7.6	6.6	6.8	8.9	11.4	12.6
Price Range	7 3/4-6 1/16	8 15/16-6 9/16	9 1/16-6 3/16	7 3/4-5 15/16	8 9/16-6 7/8	9 1/2-7 1/2	10 13/16-9 1/16
P/E Ratio	13.3-10.4	17.4-12.7	21.6-14.8	18.1-13.9	15.8-12.7	15.1-11.9	16.6-13.9
Average Yield %	5.8	4.9	4.9	5.3	4.6	4.0	3.3

Statistics are as originally reported. Adj. for stk. splits: 5%, 7/00; 2-for-1, 2/95.

OFFICERS:
L. H. Goldberg, Pres., C.E.O., C.O.O.
R. E. Macklin, Sr. V.P., Treas.
C. A. Dragoo, Asst. Treas., Contr.
A. J. Levy, Sr. V.P., Sec.

PRINCIPAL OFFICE: 6446 Edsall Road, Alexandria, VA 22312

TELEPHONE NUMBER: (703) 941-6300
FAX: (703) 256-2430
NO. OF EMPLOYEES: 750 (approx.)
SHAREHOLDERS: 524 (approx. Cl. A com.); 39 (approx. Cl. B com.)
ANNUAL MEETING: In Dec.
INCORPORATED: MD, July, 1958

INSTITUTIONAL HOLDINGS:
No. of Institutions: 7
Shares Held: 326,168 (Adj.)
% Held: 8.5

INDUSTRY: Bowling centers (SIC: 7933)

TRANSFER AGENT(S): American Stock Transfer & Trust Company, New York, NY

NYSE SYMBOL BRC
Rec. Pr. 30⅛ (5/31/00)

BRADY CORPORATION

YIELD 2.3%
P/E RATIO 15.3

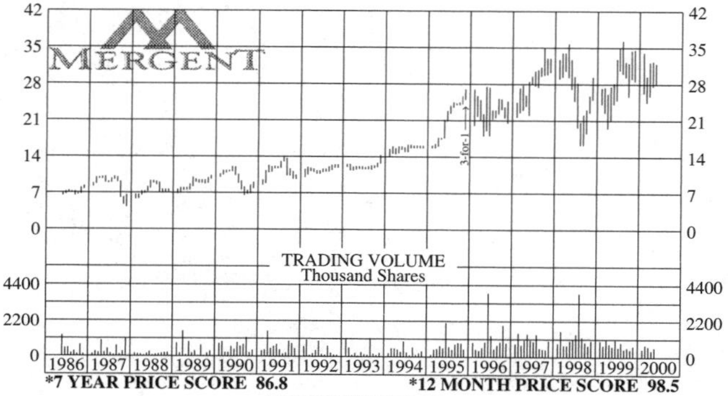

MERGENT
TRADING VOLUME
Thousand Shares
3-for-1
1986 1987 1988 1989 1990 1991 1992 1993 1994 1995 1996 1997 1998 1999 2000

*7 YEAR PRICE SCORE 86.8 *12 MONTH PRICE SCORE 98.5

*NYSE COMPOSITE INDEX=100

INTERIM EARNINGS (Per Share):

Qtr.	Oct.	Jan.	Apr.	July
1995-96	0.29	0.26	0.36	0.36
1996-97	0.30	0.31	0.43	0.40
1997-98	0.37	0.31	0.44	0.11
1998-99	0.38	0.35	0.57	0.43
1999-00	0.54	0.43	...	...

INTERIM DIVIDENDS (Per Share):

Amt.	Decl.	Ex.	Rec.	Pay.
0.16Q	5/10/99	7/07/99	7/09/99	7/30/99
0.17Q	9/14/99	10/06/99	10/08/99	10/31/99
0.17Q	11/17/99	1/05/00	1/07/00	1/31/00
0.17Q	2/22/00	4/06/00	4/10/00	4/28/00
0.17Q	5/16/00	7/06/00	7/10/00	7/31/00

Indicated div.: $0.68 (Div. Reinv. Plan)

CAPITALIZATION (7/31/99):

	($000)	(%)
Long-Term Debt	1,402	0.5
Preferred Stock	2,855	1.1
Common & Surplus	257,709	98.4
Total	261,966	100.0

DIVIDEND ACHIEVER STATUS:

Rank: 26 10-Year Growth Rate: 20.19%
Total Years of Dividend Growth: 15

RECENT DEVELOPMENTS: For the three months ended 1/31/00, net income rose 23.3% to $9.8 million from $8.0 million in the corresponding 1999 quarter. Net sales grew 15.1% to $129.2 million from $112.3 million a year earlier. U.S. sales climbed 17.3%, while international sales grew 12.6%, as sales in the Asia/Pacific region jumped 42.4% versus the prior year. Operating income totaled $15.4 million, up 17.3% from $13.1 million the year before.

PROSPECTS: On 3/22/00, BRC announced that its subsidiary, IMTC Acquisition Corp., has accepted for payment all shares of Imtec Inc. common stock. BRC expects the addition of Imtec to strengthen its position in the automatic identification and data collection market and the high-performance-label segment. On 3/3/00, BRC announced that it acquired Data Recognition, Inc., a systems integrater providing automatic identification and data collection services.

BUSINESS

BRADY CORPORATION (formerly W.H. Brady Co.) is an international manufacturer and marketer of identification and material services designed to help companies improve safety, security, productivity and performance. BRC's array of labels are used in applications ranging from marking wires and cables in facilities, electrical, telecommunication and transportation equipment to marking electronic components and printed circuit boards that require identification for purposes such as maintenance, work-in-process or asset tracking. Offerings ranging from signs, pipemakers, lockout/tagout devices, labels and tags to services including consulting, product installation and training enable companies to comply with safety and environmental regulations.

ANNUAL FINANCIAL DATA

	7/31/99	7/31/98	7/31/97	7/31/96	7/31/95	7/31/94	7/31/93
Earnings Per Share	**1 1.73**	**1 1.23**	**1.44**	**1.27**	**1.28**	**0.85**	**1 0.78**
Cash Flow Per Share	**2.41**	**1.83**	**1.05**	**0.88**	**1.71**	**1.29**	**1.25**
Tang. Book Val. Per Share	**8.87**	**7.87**	**7.64**	**6.96**	**7.69**	**6.54**	**5.79**
Dividends Per Share	**0.65**	**0.61**	**0.54**	**0.43**	**0.30**	**0.24**	**0.21**
Dividend Payout %	**37.6**	**49.6**	**37.5**	**33.9**	**23.5**	**27.8**	**26.6**
INCOME STATEMENT (IN THOUSANDS):							
Total Revenues	470,862	455,150	426,081	359,542	314,362	255,841	242,970
Costs & Expenses	391,941	395,932	361,562	307,775	264,618	216,931	207,473
Depreciation & Amort.	15,149	13,288	14,151	10,602	9,159	9,435	10,173
Operating Income	63,772	45,930	50,368	41,165	40,585	29,475	25,324
Net Interest Inc./(Exp.)	d445	d403	d256	d302	d555	d410	d54
Income Before Income Taxes	64,782	46,165	51,271	45,433	44,639	29,902	25,829
Income Taxes	25,198	18,129	19,564	17,406	16,728	11,362	8,973
Net Income	1 39,584	1 28,036	31,707	28,027	27,911	18,540	1 16,856
Cash Flow	54,474	41,065	45,599	38,370	36,811	27,716	26,770
Average Shs. Outstg.	22,683	22,602	43,816	43,694	21,681	21,678	21,585
BALANCE SHEET (IN THOUSANDS):							
Cash & Cash Equivalents	75,466	65,609	65,329	49,281	89,067	66,107	42,366
Total Current Assets	203,169	184,053	187,969	156,111	164,472	131,763	105,644
Net Property	66,984	67,165	62,442	65,649	58,573	64,343	67,362
Total Assets	351,120	311,824	291,662	261,835	230,005	202,509	179,899
Total Current Liabilities	73,285	58,667	57,245	46,423	34,534	31,740	27,703
Long-Term Obligations	1,402	3,716	3,890	1,809	1,903	1,855	1,978
Net Stockholders' Equity	260,564	233,373	206,547	189,263	170,823	145,129	128,068
Net Working Capital	129,884	125,386	130,724	109,688	129,938	100,023	77,941
Year-end Shs. Outstg.	20,835	22,496	21,941	21,863	21,831	21,738	21,618
STATISTICAL RECORD:							
Operating Profit Margin %	13.5	10.1	11.8	11.4	12.9	11.5	10.4
Net Profit Margin %	8.4	6.2	7.4	7.8	8.9	7.2	6.9
Return on Equity %	15.2	12.0	15.4	14.8	16.3	12.8	13.2
Return on Assets %	11.3	9.0	10.9	10.7	12.1	9.2	9.4
Debt/Total Assets %	0.4	1.2	1.3	0.7	0.8	0.9	1.1
Price Range	36 5/16-19½	35¾-16¼	35-21⅝	27½-18	27-15 11/16	16 5/16-14 1/16	14 5/16-11 5/16
P/E Ratio	21.0-11.3	29.1-13.2	24.3-15.0	21.7-14.2	21.1-12.3	19.2-16.6	18.4-14.6
Average Yield %	2.3	2.3	1.9	1.9	1.4	1.6	1.6

Statistics are as originally reported. Adj. for stk. splits: 3-for-1, 12/95. 1 Incl. $611,000 non-recur. pre-tax gain, 1999; $5.4 mil chrg., 1998; $1.2 mil gain, 1993

OFFICERS:
K. M. Hudson, Pres., C.E.O.
F. M. Jaehnert, V.P., C.F.O.
T. E. Scherer, V.P., Contr., Asst. Sec.
P. J. Lettenberger, Sec.

INVESTOR CONTACT: L. Spiegelberg Bernardy, V.P. Corp. Comm., (414) 438-6880

PRINCIPAL OFFICE: 6555 West Good Hope Rd., Milwaukee, WI 53223-0571

TELEPHONE NUMBER: (414) 358-6600
FAX: (414) 438-6910
WEB: www.bradycorp.com

NO. OF EMPLOYEES: 2,800 (approx.)

SHAREHOLDERS: 411 (Cl. A); 2 (Cl. B); 5,000 (ben.)

ANNUAL MEETING: In Nov.

INCORPORATED: WI, 1939

INSTITUTIONAL HOLDINGS:
No. of Institutions: 98
Shares Held: 14,259,137
% Held: 68.3

INDUSTRY: Signs and advertising specialities (SIC: 3993)

TRANSFER AGENT(S): Firstar Trust Company, Milwaukee, WI

NYSE SYMBOL BMY
Rec. Pr. $55\frac{1}{16}$ (5/31/00)

BRISTOL-MYERS SQUIBB COMPANY

YIELD 1.8%
P/E RATIO 26.7

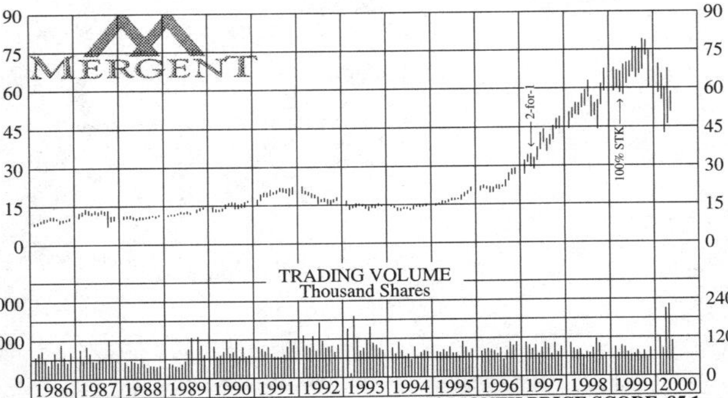

*7 YEAR PRICE SCORE 122.7 *12 MONTH PRICE SCORE 85.1

*NYSE COMPOSITE INDEX=100

INTERIM EARNINGS (Per Share):

Qtr.	Mar.	June	Sept.	Dec.
1995[1]	0.33	0.30	0.34	d0.07
1996	0.36	0.33	0.38	0.36
1997[2]	0.41	0.37	0.43	0.39
1998[3]	0.46	0.41	0.48	0.21
1999	0.53	0.47	0.54	0.52

INTERIM DIVIDENDS (Per Share):

Amt.	Decl.	Ex.	Rec.	Pay.
0.215Q	3/02/99	3/30/99	4/02/99	5/01/99
0.215Q	6/01/99	6/30/99	7/02/99	8/01/99
0.215Q	9/14/99	9/29/99	10/01/99	11/01/99
0.245Q	12/08/99	1/05/00	1/07/00	2/01/00
0.245Q	3/07/00	4/05/00	4/07/00	5/01/00

Indicated div.: $0.98 (Div. Reinv. Plan)

CAPITALIZATION (12/31/99):

	($000)	(%)
Long-Term Debt	1,342,000	13.4
Common & Surplus	8,645,000	86.6
Total	9,987,000	100.0

DIVIDEND ACHIEVER STATUS:
Rank: 254 10-Year Growth Rate: 5.57%
Total Years of Dividend Growth: 27

RECENT DEVELOPMENTS: For the year ended 12/31/99, net income rose 32.7% to $4.17 billion from $3.14 billion in 1998. The 1998 results included a nonrecurring after-tax charge of $495.0 million. Net sales climbed 10.6% to $20.22 billion from $18.28 billion a year earlier. Sales of TAXOL, grew 23.0% to $1.48 billion, while sales of GLUCOPHAGE, a medication for the treatment of non-insulin dependent diabetes, jumped 53.0% to $1.32 billion.

PROSPECTS: The Company submitted a new drug application to the FDA for a new formulation of VIDEX®. The new capsules contain enteric coated VIDEX beadlets designed to protect the medicine from degrading until it has passed through the stomach. Meanwhile, BMY received the FDA's approval to market TEQUIN™, a type of quinolone antibiotic for indications including the treatment of community-acquired respiratory tract infections.

BUSINESS

BRISTOL-MYERS SQUIBB COMPANY is a diversified worldwide health and personal care company whose principal businesses are pharmaceuticals, consumer products, nutritionals, and medical devices. Medicines, 70.8% of 1999 sales, include prescription medicines, mainly cardiovascular drugs, anti-cancer, anti-infective and central nervous system drugs, and consumer medicines, mainly analgesics. Brand names include PRAVACHOL, a cholesterol-lowering agent; TAXOL, used in the treatment for refractory ovarian cancer; ZERIT, an advanced HIV disease treatment; SERZONE, an anti-depressant; and GLUCOPHAGE, an oral anti-diabetes agent for type two non-insulin-dependent diabetes. Nutritionals, 9.1%, include infant formulas and other nutritional products. Medical Devices, 8.3%, include orthopaedic implants, ostomy and wound care products and other medical devices. Beauty Care 11.87%, includes haircoloring and hair preparations and other beauty care products.

ANNUAL FINANCIAL DATA

	12/31/99	12/31/98	12/31/97	12/31/96	12/31/95	12/31/94	12/31/93
Earnings Per Share	**2.06**	[3] **1.55**	[2] **1.57**	**1.42**	[1] **0.90**	**0.91**	**0.95**
Cash Flow Per Share	**2.39**	**1.85**	**1.86**	**1.68**	**1.12**	**1.07**	**1.10**
Tang. Book Val. Per Share	**3.61**	**3.01**	**2.82**	**2.53**	**2.28**	**2.35**	**2.81**
Dividends Per Share	**0.86**	**0.78**	**0.76**	**0.75**	**0.74**	**0.73**	**0.72**
Dividend Payout %	**41.7**	**50.3**	**48.4**	**52.8**	**82.7**	**80.7**	**75.8**
INCOME STATEMENT (IN MILLIONS):							
Total Revenues	20,222.0	18,284.0	16,701.0	15,065.0	13,767.0	11,984.0	11,413.0
Costs & Expenses	13,691.0	12,337.0	11,897.0	10,593.0	10,014.0	8,435.0	8,202.0
Depreciation & Amort.	678.0	625.0	591.0	519.0	448.0	328.0	308.0
Operating Income	5,853.0	5,322.0	4,213.0	3,953.0	3,305.0	3,221.0	2,903.0
Net Interest Inc./(Exp.)	...	d67.0	d12.0	17.0	42.0	56.0	39.0
Income Before Income Taxes	5,767.0	4,268.0	4,482.0	4,013.0	2,402.0	2,555.0	2,571.0
Income Taxes	1,600.0	1,127.0	1,277.0	1,163.0	590.0	713.0	612.0
Net Income	4,167.0	[3] 3,141.0	[2] 3,205.0	2,850.0	[1] 1,812.0	1,842.0	1,959.0
Cash Flow	4,845.0	3,766.0	3,796.0	3,369.0	2,260.0	2,170.0	2,267.0
Average Shs. Outstg. (000)	2,027,000	2,031,000	2,042,000	2,008,000	2,024,000	2,036,000	2,060,000
BALANCE SHEET (IN MILLIONS):							
Cash & Cash Equivalents	2,957.0	2,529.0	1,794.0	2,185.0	2,178.0	2,423.0	2,729.0
Total Current Assets	9,267.0	8,782.0	7,736.0	7,528.0	7,018.0	6,710.0	6,570.0
Net Property	4,621.0	4,429.0	4,156.0	3,964.0	3,760.0	3,666.0	3,374.0
Total Assets	17,114.0	16,272.0	14,977.0	14,685.0	13,929.0	12,910.0	12,101.0
Total Current Liabilities	5,537.0	5,791.0	5,032.0	5,050.0	4,806.0	4,274.0	3,065.0
Long-Term Obligations	1,342.0	1,364.0	1,279.0	966.0	635.0	644.0	588.0
Net Stockholders' Equity	8,645.0	7,576.0	7,219.0	6,570.0	5,823.0	5,705.0	5,941.0
Net Working Capital	3,730.0	2,991.0	2,704.0	2,478.0	2,212.0	2,436.0	3,505.0
Year-end Shs. Outstg. (000)	1,980,806	1,988,000	1,986,000	2,002,000	2,020,000	2,028,000	2,048,000
STATISTICAL RECORD:							
Operating Profit Margin %	28.9	29.1	25.2	26.2	24.0	26.9	25.4
Net Profit Margin %	20.6	17.2	19.2	18.9	13.2	15.4	17.2
Return on Equity %	48.2	41.5	44.4	43.4	31.1	32.3	33.0
Return on Assets %	24.3	19.3	21.4	19.4	13.0	14.3	16.2
Debt/Total Assets %	7.8	8.4	8.5	6.6	4.6	5.0	4.9
Price Range	$79\frac{1}{4}$-$57\frac{1}{4}$	$67\frac{5}{8}$-$44\frac{3}{16}$	$49\frac{1}{8}$-$26\frac{5}{8}$	$29\frac{1}{8}$-$19\frac{1}{2}$	$21\frac{13}{16}$-$14\frac{7}{16}$	$15\frac{1}{4}$-$12\frac{1}{2}$	$16\frac{13}{16}$-$12\frac{3}{4}$
P/E Ratio	38.5-27.8	43.6-28.5	31.3-17.0	20.5-13.7	24.3-16.1	16.8-13.8	17.7-13.4
Average Yield %	1.3	1.4	2.0	3.1	4.1	5.3	4.9

Statistics are as originally reported. Adj. for 2-for-1 stock split, 2/97 & 2/99. [1] Incl. a spec. after-tax chg. of $590.0 mill. & a $98.0 mill. prov. for litigation. [2] Incl. a pre-tax prov. of $225.0 mill. for restr. & a $225.0 mill. gain on the sale of a bus. [3] Incl. a spec. chg. of $800.0 mill., a pre-tax prov. for restr. of $201.0 mill., and a gain of $201.0 mill. on the sale of a bus.

OFFICERS:
C. A. Heimbold Jr., Chmn., C.E.O.
P. R. Dolan, Pres.
M. F. Mee, Sr. V.P., C.F.O.
H. M. Bains Jr., V.P., Treas.

INVESTOR CONTACT: Investor Relations, (212) 546-4000

PRINCIPAL OFFICE: 345 Park Avenue, New York, NY 10154

TELEPHONE NUMBER: (212) 546-4000
FAX: (212) 546-4020
WEB: www.bms.com

NO. OF EMPLOYEES: 54,500 (approx.)

SHAREHOLDERS: 120,358 (approximately)

ANNUAL MEETING: In May

INCORPORATED: DE, Aug., 1933

INSTITUTIONAL HOLDINGS:
No. of Institutions: 1,105
Shares Held: 1,184,886,868
% Held: 59.7

INDUSTRY: Pharmaceutical preparations (SIC: 2834)

TRANSFER AGENT(S): ChaseMellon Shareholder Services, L.L.C., Ridgefield Park, NJ

BROWN-FORMAN CORPORATION

YIELD 2.1%
P/E RATIO 18.6

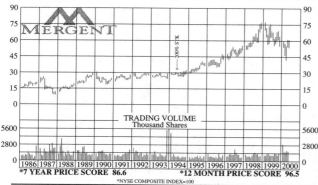

INTERIM EARNINGS (Per Share):

Qtr.	July	Oct.	Jan.	Apr.
1996-97	0.47	0.80	0.60	0.58
1997-98	0.50	0.88	0.66	0.63
1998-99	0.54	0.97	0.72	0.70
1999-00	0.56	1.06	0.80	...

INTERIM DIVIDENDS (Per Share):

Amt.	Decl.	Ex.	Rec.	Pay.
0.295Q	5/27/99	6/03/99	6/07/99	7/01/99
0.295Q	7/22/99	9/02/99	9/07/99	10/01/99
0.31Q	11/18/99	12/01/99	12/03/99	1/01/00
0.31Q	1/27/00	3/08/00	3/10/00	4/01/00
0.31Q	5/25/00	6/07/00	6/09/00	7/01/00

Indicated div.: $1.24 (Div. Reinv. Plan)

CAPITALIZATION (4/30/99):

	($000)	(%)
Long-Term Debt	53,000	4.8
Deferred Income Tax	137,000	12.4
Common & Surplus	917,000	82.8
Total	1,107,000	100.0

DIVIDEND ACHIEVER STATUS:
Rank: 208   10-Year Growth Rate: 7.74%
Total Years of Dividend Growth: 15

TRADING VOLUME
Thousand Shares

*7 YEAR PRICE SCORE 86.6   ***12 MONTH PRICE SCORE 96.5**
*NYSE COMPOSITE INDEX=100

RECENT DEVELOPMENTS: For the quarter ended 1/31/00, net income rose 11.2% to $54.8 million from $49.3 million the previous year. Net sales grew 8.0% to $558.1 million from $516.7 million the year before. Net sales for the wine and spirit segment advanced 7.8% to $393.8 million and operating income improved 15.0% to $74.0 million, due to the strong performance of BFB's beverage business in the U.S. and in numerous international markets.

PROSPECTS: Going forward, the Company expects to continue to perform well in both of its business segments. BFB's wine and spirits segment should continue to benefit from strong worldwide growth in sales and profits of JACK DANIELS TENNESSEE WHISKEY, as well as United States growth of FETZER and BOLLA wines and FINLANDIA VODKA. Prospects for continued revenue and earnings growth are favorable.

BUSINESS

BROWN-FORMAN CORPORA-TION, with assets as of 4/30/00 of $1.74 billion, operates in two business segments: wines and spirits and consumer durables. The wines and spirits segment includes the production, importing and marketing of wines and distilled spirits under brand names of JACK DANIEL's, SOUTHERN COMFORT, CANADIAN MIST, KORBEL CALIFORNIA CHAMPAGNES, and FETZER VINEYARDS CALIFORNIA WINES. The consumer durables segment manufactures and sells china, crystal, ceramic and crystal collectibles, silver, pewter and luggage. In fiscal 2000, sales (operating income) were as follows: 70.6% (85.0%), wine and spirits; and 29.4% (15.0%) consumer durables.

BUSINESS LINE ANALYSIS

(4/30/99)	Rev(%)	Inc(%)
Wine & Spirits	73.2	88.2
Consumer durables	26.8	11.8
Total	100.0	100.0

ANNUAL FINANCIAL DATA

	4/30/99	4/30/98	4/30/97	4/30/96	4/30/95	4/30/94	4/30/93
Earnings Per Share	2.93	2.67	2.45	2.31	2.15	① 2.04	1.88
Cash Flow Per Share	3.74	3.42	3.17	2.99	2.78	2.63	2.42
Tang. Book Val. Per Share	9.53	8.04	6.73	5.26	3.94	2.50	6.37
Dividends Per Share	1.12	1.08	1.04	0.99	0.95	0.91	0.81
Dividend Payout %	38.2	40.4	42.4	42.9	44.0	44.4	43.3
INCOME STATEMENT (IN MILLIONS):							
Total Revenues	2,030.0	1,924.0	1,841.0	1,807.0	1,679.6	1,628.5	1,691.7
Costs & Expenses	1,653.0	1,566.0	1,504.0	1,487.0	1,368.4	1,342.1	1,392.5
Depreciation & Amort.	55.0	51.0	50.0	46.0	43.5	46.0	43.8
Operating Income	322.0	307.0	287.0	274.0	267.8	240.4	255.4
Net Interest Inc./(Exp.)	d4.0	d11.0	d14.0	d17.0	d20.7	d13.2	d12.8
Income Before Income Taxes	318.0	296.0	273.0	257.0	247.1	257.2	242.6
Income Taxes	116.0	111.0	104.0	97.0	98.4	96.2	86.4
Net Income	202.0	185.0	169.0	160.0	148.6	① 161.1	156.2
Cash Flow	257.0	235.0	218.0	205.0	191.7	207.1	199.5
Average Shs. Outstg. (000)	68,700	69,000	69,014	68,996	68,996	78,657	82,664
BALANCE SHEET (IN MILLIONS):							
Cash & Cash Equivalents	171.0	78.0	58.0	54.0	62.5	30.5	93.1
Total Current Assets	999.0	869.0	802.0	768.0	697.9	649.9	720.3
Net Property	348.0	281.0	292.0	281.0	252.2	246.0	257.4
Total Assets	1,735.0	1,494.0	1,428.0	1,381.0	1,285.6	1,233.8	1,311.0
Total Current Liabilities	517.0	382.0	399.0	303.0	285.6	281.1	210.4
Long-Term Obligations	53.0	50.0	63.0	211.0	246.8	299.1	154.4
Net Stockholders' Equity	917.0	817.0	730.0	634.0	545.8	463.7	818.1
Net Working Capital	482.0	487.0	403.0	465.0	412.3	368.9	509.9
Year-end Shs. Outstg. (000)	68,506	68,996	68,996	68,996	68,996	70,174	82,665
STATISTICAL RECORD:							
Operating Profit Margin %	15.9	16.0	15.6	15.2	15.9	14.8	15.1
Net Profit Margin %	10.0	9.6	9.2	8.9	8.8	9.9	9.2
Return on Equity %	22.0	22.6	23.2	25.2	27.2	34.7	19.1
Return on Assets %	11.6	12.4	11.8	11.6	11.6	13.1	11.9
Debt/Total Assets %	3.1	3.3	4.4	15.3	19.2	24.2	11.8
Price Range	76⅞-51¾	55⅜-42	47½-35¼	40¾-29⅜	32½-26⅛	29⁹⁄₁₆-24⁵⁄₁₆	30-24
P/E Ratio	26.2-17.7	20.7-15.7	19.4-14.4	17.6-12.7	15.1-12.2	14.5-11.9	16.0-12.8
Average Yield %	1.7	2.2	2.5	2.8	3.2	3.4	3.0

Statistics are as originally reported. Adj. for 200% stk. div. 5/94. ① Bef. acct. chge. of $32.5 mill. ($0.41 per sh.) & gain fr. sale of bus. of $30.1 mill. ($0.67 per sh.).

OFFICERS:
O. Brown II, Chmn., C.E.O.
O. B. Frazier, Vice-Chmn.
W. M. Street, Vice-Chmn.
S. B. Ratoff, Exec. V.P., C.F.O.

INVESTOR CONTACT: John Bridendall, Sr. V.P.-Corp. Dev., (502) 774-7290

PRINCIPAL OFFICE: 850 Dixie Highway, Louisville, KY 40210

TELEPHONE NUMBER: (502) 585-1100
FAX: (502) 774-7876
WEB: www.brown-forman.com
NO. OF EMPLOYEES: 6,445 full-time; 1,155 part-time
SHAREHOLDERS: 3,150 (Cl. A com.); 4,936 (Cl. B com.)
ANNUAL MEETING: In July
INCORPORATED: KY, 1901; reincorp., DE, 1901

INSTITUTIONAL HOLDINGS:
No. of Institutions: 157
Shares Held: 27,919,891
% Held: 70.6

INDUSTRY: Wines, brandy, and brandy spirits (SIC: 2084)

TRANSFER AGENT(S): First Chicago Trust Company of New York, Jersey City, NJ

CALIFORNIA WATER SERVICE GROUP

YIELD 4.7%
P/E RATIO 14.9

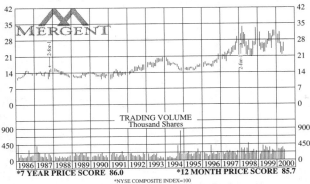

*7 YEAR PRICE SCORE 86.0   *12 MONTH PRICE SCORE 85.7
*NYSE COMPOSITE INDEX=100

INTERIM EARNINGS (Per Share):

Qtr.	Mar.	June	Sept.	Dec.
1996	0.09	0.46	0.69	0.27
1997	0.23	0.70	0.62	0.28
1998	0.12	0.28	0.72	0.33
1999	0.20	0.44	0.62	0.30

INTERIM DIVIDENDS (Per Share):

Amt.	Decl.	Ex.	Rec.	Pay.
0.271Q	4/22/99	4/28/99	5/01/99	5/15/99
0.271Q	7/21/99	7/28/99	8/01/99	8/15/99
0.271Q	10/27/99	10/28/99	11/01/99	11/15/99
0.275Q	1/26/00	1/28/00	2/01/00	2/15/00
0.275Q	4/19/00	4/27/00	5/01/00	5/15/00

Indicated div.: $1.10 (Div. Reinv. Plan)

CAPITALIZATION (12/31/99):

	($000)	(%)
Long-Term Debt	156,572	43.7
Deferred Income Tax	21,427	6.0
Preferred Stock	3,475	1.0
Common & Surplus	177,182	49.4
Total	358,656	100.0

DIVIDEND ACHIEVER STATUS:
Rank: 308   10-Year Growth Rate: 2.59%
Total Years of Dividend Growth: 32

RECENT DEVELOPMENTS: For the year ended 12/31/99, net income advanced 5.2% to $19.9 million from $18.9 million in the previous year. Operating revenues rose 8.9% to $206.4 million from $189.7 million the year before. before. The growth in revenues was primarily attributed to increased customer usage, increased rates and the addition of new customers. Total operating expenses were $175.8 million, an increase of 10.5% from $159.1 million last year.

PROSPECTS: CWT completed the acquisition of South Sound Utility Company. South Sound Utility Company and Harbor Water Company, acquired in October 1999, are expected to increase revenues by approximately $3.4 million. Separately, the California Public Utilities Commission approved the merger between CWT and Dominguez Services Corporation on 05/18/00.

BUSINESS

CALIFORNIA WATER SERVICE GROUP is a public utility water company that owns and operates 21 water systems serving 62 communities in California and Washington. CWT is the parent company of California Water Service Co., CWS Utility Services and Washington Water Service Co. The sole business of the Company consists of the production, purchase, storage, purification, distribution and sale of water for domestic, industrial, public, and irrigation uses, and for fire protection. Annual water production totals nearly 105 billion gallons with 50% derived from purchased surface sources and 50% pumped from more than 500 Company-owned wells. In September 1999, Washington Water Service Co., was formed as a new subsidiary.

REVENUES

(12/31/99)	($000)	(%)
Residential	150,326	72.8
Business	34,219	16.6
Industrial	6,947	3.4
Public Authorities	9,501	4.6
Other	5,447	2.6
Total	206.440	100.0

ANNUAL FINANCIAL DATA

	12/31/99	12/31/98	12/31/97	12/31/96	12/31/95	12/31/94	12/31/93
Earnings Per Share	1.53	1.45	1.83	1.51	1.17	1.22	1.35
Cash Flow Per Share	2.76	2.61	2.93	2.52	2.09	2.17	2.27
Tang. Book Val. Per Share	13.70	13.38	13.00	12.22	11.72	11.56	10.90
Dividends Per Share	1.08	1.07	1.05	1.04	1.02	0.99	0.96
Dividend Payout %	70.9	73.8	57.6	69.1	87.5	81.1	71.1
INCOME STATEMENT (IN THOUSANDS):							
Total Revenues	206,440	186,273	195,324	182,764	165,086	157,271	151,716
Costs & Expenses	138,669	122,056	124,036	119,265	110,686	103,353	95,707
Depreciation & Amort.	15,802	14,563	13,670	12,665	11,436	10,958	10,304
Maintenance Exp.	9,183	9,030	9,319	8,317	7,722	7,855	7,250
Operating Income	30,610	30,074	34,349	30,367	25,392	25,505	27,855
Net Interest Inc./(Exp.)	d13,201	d12,446	d11,902	d11,907	d11,462	d11,384	d12,627
Income Taxes	12,176	10,550	13,500	12,150	9,850	9,600	10,600
Net Income	19,919	18,395	23,305	19,067	14,698	14,408	15,501
Cash Flow	35,568	32,805	36,822	31,579	25,981	25,213	25,652
Average Shs. Outstg.	12,936	12,619	12,619	12,580	12,506	11,676	11,378
BALANCE SHEET (IN THOUSANDS):							
Gross Property	737,352	680,690	647,648	618,432	584,392	559,180	533,213
Accumulated Depreciation	221,998	202,385	187,241	174,844	162,217	151,285	141,510
Net Property	515,354	478,305	460,407	443,588	422,175	407,895	391,703
Total Assets	587,618	548,499	531,297	512,390	484,883	464,228	446,619
Long-Term Obligations	156,572	136,345	139,205	142,153	145,540	128,944	129,608
Net Stockholders' Equity	180,657	172,279	167,540	157,701	150,424	147,922	127,474
Year-end Shs. Outstg.	12,936	12,619	12,619	12,620	12,538	12,494	11,378
STATISTICAL RECORD:							
Operating Profit Margin %	14.8	16.1	17.6	16.6	15.4	16.2	18.4
Net Profit Margin %	9.6	9.9	11.9	10.4	8.9	9.2	10.2
Net Inc./Net Property %	3.9	3.8	5.1	4.3	3.5	3.5	4.0
Net Inc./Tot. Capital %	5.6	5.5	7.0	5.9	4.7	5.0	5.8
Return on Equity %	11.0	10.7	13.9	12.1	9.8	9.7	12.2
Accum. Depr./Gross Prop. %	30.1	29.7	28.9	28.3	27.8	27.1	26.5
Price Range	32-22⁹/₁₆	33³/₄-20³/₄	29³/₈-18⁵/₈	21⁷/₈-16¹/₄	17⁵/₈-14¹³/₁₆	20¹/₂-14¹¹/₁₆	20⁵/₈-16¹/₈
P/E Ratio	20.9-14.7	23.3-14.3	16.1-10.2	14.5-10.8	15.1-12.7	16.8-12.0	15.3-11.9
Average Yield %	4.0	3.9	4.4	5.5	6.3	5.6	5.2

Statistics are as originally reported. Adj. for stk. split: 2-for-1, 1/98

OFFICERS:
R. W. Foy, Chmn.
P. C. Nelson, Pres., C.E.O.
G. F. Feeney, V.P., C.F.O., Treas.
C. L. Breed, Contr., Asst. Sec., Asst. Treas.

INVESTOR CONTACT: Gerald F. Feeney
(408) 451-8200

PRINCIPAL OFFICE: 1720 North First Street, San Jose, CA 95112-4598

TELEPHONE NUMBER: (408) 367-8200
FAX: (408) 437-9185
WEB: www.calwater.com

NO. OF EMPLOYEES: 708 (avg.)

SHAREHOLDERS: 11,000

ANNUAL MEETING: In Apr.

INCORPORATED: CA, Dec., 1926

INSTITUTIONAL HOLDINGS:
No. of Institutions: 55
Shares Held: 2,855,313
% Held: 22.2

INDUSTRY: Water supply (SIC: 4941)

TRANSFER AGENT(S): Boston Equiserve, Boston, MA

CAMPBELL SOUP COMPANY

YIELD 2.9%
P/E RATIO 17.8

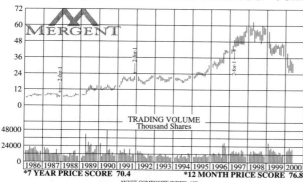

TRADING VOLUME
Thousand Shares

| 1986|1987|1988|1989|1990|1991|1992|1993|1994|1995|1996|1997|1998|1999|2000 |
*7 YEAR PRICE SCORE 70.4   *12 MONTH PRICE SCORE 76.8
*NYSE COMPOSITE INDEX=100

INTERIM EARNINGS (Per Share):

Qtr.	Oct.	Jan.	Apr.	July
1996-97	0.18	0.59	0.34	0.42
1997-98	0.58	0.67	d0.08	0.40
1998-99	0.58	0.49	0.37	0.18
1999-00	0.54	0.65	...	...

INTERIM DIVIDENDS (Per Share):

Amt.	Decl.	Ex.	Rec.	Pay.
0.225Q	6/24/99	7/07/99	7/09/99	8/02/99
0.225Q	9/23/99	10/06/99	10/08/99	11/01/99
0.225Q	11/18/99	1/05/00	1/07/00	1/31/00
0.225Q	3/22/00	4/05/00	4/07/00	5/01/00

Indicated div.: $0.90 (Div. Reinv. Plan)

CAPITALIZATION (8/1/99):

	($000)	(%)
Long-Term Debt	1,330,000	85.0
Common & Surplus	235,000	15.0
Total	1,565,000	100.0

DIVIDEND ACHIEVER STATUS:
Rank: 70   10-Year Growth Rate: 14.62%
Total Years of Dividend Growth: 17

RECENT DEVELOPMENTS: For the quarter ended 1/30/00, net earnings advanced 28.1% to $280.9 million from $219.2 million the year before. Net sales increased 4.6% to $1.92 billion from $1.83 billion the previous year. Sales of Soups and Sauces rose 6.5% to $1.36 billion. Biscuits and Confectionery sales grew 3.0% to $419.1 million, while Away From Home sales climbed 6.0% to $143.0 million. Operating earnings jumped 31.0% to $500.9 million.

PROSPECTS: Earnings are benefiting from strong U.S. soup shipments, reflecting the Company's aggressive marketing efforts and Year 2000-related stockpiling. In addition, new products rolled out during the current fiscal year are gaining strong consumer acceptance. CPB is attempting to boost soup sales to food service outlets such as cafeterias, quick-service restaurants, convenience stores and airports.

BUSINESS

CAMPBELL SOUP COMPANY is a major manufacturer of prepared convenience foods. The Company is also involved in the fresh foods, refrigerated foods, candy and mail order businesses. Well-known brand names include CAMPBELL'S, PEPPERIDGE FARM, SWANSON, V-8, PACE, PREGO, and GODIVA chocolates. Products sold by CPB under these brand names include: canned foods such as ready-to-serve soups, juices, gravies, pasta, meat and vegetables; frozen foods such as dinners, breakfasts and entrees; other items including salsa, pickles and relishes, various condiments, chocolate, salads and confectionery items. For fiscal year 1999, sales were derived: Soup and Sauces, 69.5%; Biscuits and Confectionery, 22.5%; Away From Home (including the foodservice business), 8.0%; and Other, 2.0%.

ANNUAL FINANCIAL DATA

	8/1/99	8/2/98	8/3/97	7/28/96	7/30/95	7/31/94	8/1/93
Earnings Per Share	③ 1.63	④ 1.50	③ 1.51	② 1.61	1.40	1.26	① 0.51
Cash Flow Per Share	2.20	2.07	2.21	2.27	1.99	1.76	0.99
Tang. Book Val. Per Share	...	...	...	1.64	1.20	2.78	2.36
Dividends Per Share	0.90	0.84	0.77	0.69	0.62	0.56	0.48
Dividend Payout %	55.2	56.0	51.0	42.9	44.3	44.6	95.1
INCOME STATEMENT (IN MILLIONS):							
Total Revenues	6,424.0	6,696.0	7,964.0	7,678.0	7,278.0	6,690.0	6,586.2
Costs & Expenses	4,899.0	5,187.0	6,370.0	6,035.0	5,837.0	5,408.0	5,750.4
Depreciation & Amort.	255.0	261.0	328.0	326.0	294.0	255.0	242.2
Operating Income	1,270.0	1,248.0	1,266.0	1,317.0	1,147.0	1,027.0	593.6
Net Interest Inc./(Exp.)	d173.0	d175.0	d159.0	d120.0	d105.0	d64.0	d73.8
Income Before Income Taxes	1,097.0	1,073.0	1,107.0	1,197.0	1,042.0	963.0	519.8
Income Taxes	373.0	384.0	394.0	395.0	344.0	333.0	262.6
Net Income	③ 724.0	④ 689.0	③ 713.0	② 802.0	698.0	630.0	① 257.2
Cash Flow	979.0	950.0	1,041.0	1,128.0	992.0	885.0	499.4
Average Shs. Outstg. (000)	445,000	460,000	472,000	498,000	498,000	502,000	503,800
BALANCE SHEET (IN MILLIONS):							
Cash & Cash Equivalents	6.0	16.0	26.0	34.0	53.0	96.0	69.5
Total Current Assets	1,294.0	1,440.0	1,583.0	1,618.0	1,581.0	1,601.0	1,686.2
Net Property	1,726.0	1,723.0	2,560.0	2,681.0	2,584.0	2,401.0	2,264.4
Total Assets	5,522.0	5,633.0	6,459.0	6,632.0	6,315.0	4,992.0	4,897.5
Total Current Liabilities	3,146.0	2,803.0	2,981.0	2,229.0	2,164.0	1,665.0	1,850.5
Long-Term Obligations	1,330.0	1,169.0	1,153.0	744.0	857.0	560.0	461.9
Net Stockholders' Equity	235.0	874.0	1,520.0	2,618.0	2,312.0	1,961.0	1,781.6
Net Working Capital	d1,852.0	d1,363.0	d1,398.0	d611.0	d583.0	d64.0	d164.3
Year-end Shs. Outstg. (000)	429,000	448,000	458,000	494,000	498,000	496,638	503,412
STATISTICAL RECORD:							
Operating Profit Margin %	19.8	18.6	15.9	17.2	15.8	15.4	9.0
Net Profit Margin %	11.3	10.3	9.0	10.4	9.6	9.4	3.9
Return on Equity %	308.1	78.8	46.9	30.6	30.2	32.1	14.4
Return on Assets %	13.1	12.2	11.0	12.1	11.1	12.6	5.3
Debt/Total Assets %	24.1	20.8	17.9	11.2	13.6	11.2	9.4
Price Range	55¾-37⁷⁄₁₆	62⅞-46¹¹⁄₁₆	59⁷⁄₁₆-39⅜	42⅛-28	30⅝-20½	23-17⅛	22¹¹⁄₁₆-17⅝
P/E Ratio	34.2-23.0	41.9-31.1	39.4-26.1	26.2-17.4	21.9-14.6	18.3-13.6	44.5-34.6
Average Yield %	1.9	1.5	1.6	2.0	2.4	2.8	2.4

Statistics are as originally reported. Adj. for 2-for-1 stk. split, 3/97. ① Bef. $249 mil chg. for acctg. adj. & incl. $300 mil ($1.19/sh) restr. chg. ② Incl. a $0.05/sh non-recur. gain. ③ Incl. $36.0 mil pre-tax restr. chg., 1999; & $160.1 mil ($0.34/sh) after-tax restr. chg., 1997. ④ Incl. $262 mil pre-tax restr. chg.; bef. $11 mil acctg. chg.; & bef. $54 mil loss from discont. opers.

OFFICERS:
P. E. Lippencott, Chmn.
D. W. Johnson, Pres., C.E.O.
B. L. Anderson, Exec. V.P., C.F.O.
A. P. DiSilvestro, V.P., Treas.

INVESTOR CONTACT: Leonard F. Griehs, V.P., Investor Relations, (609) 342-6428

PRINCIPAL OFFICE: Campbell Place, Camden, NJ 08103-1799

TELEPHONE NUMBER: (609) 342-4800
FAX: (609) 342-3878
WEB: www.campbellsoups.com

NO. OF EMPLOYEES: 24,500 (avg.)

SHAREHOLDERS: 38,722

ANNUAL MEETING: In Nov.

INCORPORATED: NJ, Nov., 1922

INSTITUTIONAL HOLDINGS:
No. of Institutions: 331
Shares Held: 116,861,619
% Held: 27.4

INDUSTRY: Canned specialties (SIC: 2032)

TRANSFER AGENT(S): First Chicago Trust Company of New York, Jersey City, NJ

CARLISLE COMPANIES INC.

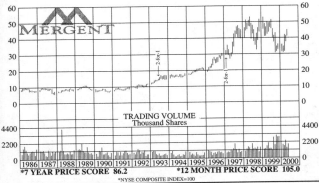

	YIELD	1.7%
	P/E RATIO	13.3

INTERIM EARNINGS (Per Share):

Qtr.	Mar.	June	Sept.	Dec.
1996	0.35	0.53	0.50	0.42
1997	0.43	0.68	0.63	0.54
1998	0.62	0.80	0.73	0.62
1999	0.71	0.91	0.81	0.70

INTERIM DIVIDENDS (Per Share):

Amt.	Decl.	Ex.	Rec.	Pay.
0.16Q	5/05/99	5/13/99	5/17/99	6/01/99
0.18Q	8/04/99	8/13/99	8/17/99	9/01/99
0.18Q	11/03/99	11/12/99	11/16/99	12/01/99
0.18Q	2/02/00	2/16/00	2/18/00	3/01/00
0.18Q	5/03/00	5/15/00	5/17/00	6/01/00

Indicated div.: $0.72 (Div. Reinv. Plan)

CAPITALIZATION (12/31/99):

	($000)	(%)
Long-Term Debt	281,744	37.1
Common & Surplus	478,133	62.9
Total	759,877	100.0

DIVIDEND ACHIEVER STATUS:

Rank: 188   10-Year Growth Rate: 8.71%
Total Years of Dividend Growth: 23

TRADING VOLUME
Thousand Shares

*7 YEAR PRICE SCORE 86.2   *12 MONTH PRICE SCORE 105.0
*NYSE COMPOSITE INDEX=100

RECENT DEVELOPMENTS: For the year ended 12/31/99, net income advanced 12.9% to $95.8 million from $84.9 million a year earlier. Total sales rose 6.2% to $1.61 billion from $1.52 billion. Sales for the Construction Materials segment grew 9.1% to $405.4 million. Industrial Components segment sales improved 3.3% to $527.9 million. The Automotive Components segment sales increased 15.6% to $314.3 million. General Industry sales were $363.7 million versus $363.2 million in 1998.

PROSPECTS: Going forward, CSL expects revenues to continue to benefit from strong automobile and light truck market and construction markets as well as the expansion of product lines. On 4/11/00, the Company acquired Extract Technologies Limited, a biotech/pharmaceutical system provider. CSL's subsidiary Carlisle FoodService Products completed the acquisition of Dura-Ware, a manufacturer of commercial cookware and servingware for foodservice and hospitality markets.

BUSINESS

CARLISLE COMPANIES INC. produces and sells a diverse line of products for industry, primarily of rubber, plastic and metal content. The Construction Materials segment manufactures membranes and accessories necessary for rubber and plastic roofing systems for non-residential flat roofs. The Industrial Components segment manufactures and distributes tire and wheel assemblies, heavy-duty friction and braking products and high-performance wire/cable and cable assemblies. The Automotive Components segment manufactures highly engineered plastic and rubber components for tier 1 suppliers and other manufacturers in the automotive industry. The General Industry consists of several businesses that produce specialty trailers, payload trailers and dump bodies, stainless steel in-plant processing equipment, food service products and cheesemaking systems. In January 1999, CSL divested its perishable cargo business. On 12/10/99, the Company acquired Marko International, Inc.

ANNUAL FINANCIAL DATA

	12/31/99	12/31/98	12/31/97	12/31/96	12/31/95	12/31/94	12/31/93
Earnings Per Share	① 3.13	2.77	2.28	1.80	1.41	1.15	0.92
Cash Flow Per Share	4.67	4.24	3.53	2.76	2.15	1.86	1.59
Tang. Book Val. Per Share	10.63	8.85	7.48	6.55	7.71	7.44	6.71
Dividends Per Share	0.68	0.60	0.53	0.47	0.42	0.38	0.35
Dividend Payout %	21.7	21.7	23.0	25.8	29.8	33.0	38.2
INCOME STATEMENT (IN MILLIONS)							
Total Revenues	1,611.3	1,517.5	1,260.6	1,017.5	822.5	692.7	611.3
Costs & Expenses	1,396.0	1,320.7	1,094.4	890.6	723.2	609.3	541.7
Depreciation & Amort.	47.4	45.2	38.8	29.8	23.2	21.9	20.7
Operating Income	174.6	151.6	127.4	97.1	76.1	61.4	48.9
Net Interest Inc./(Exp.)	d19.2	d22.7	d16.5	d9.1	d6.1	d4.6	d4.3
Income Before Income Taxes	155.5	140.3	116.8	92.0	72.9	58.8	46.9
Income Taxes	59.7	55.4	46.1	36.4	28.8	23.2	18.5
Net Income	① 95.8	84.9	70.7	55.7	44.1	35.6	28.4
Cash Flow	143.2	130.1	109.4	85.4	67.3	57.5	49.1
Average Shs. Outstg. (000)	30,635	30,674	31,025	30,953	31,266	30,960	30,956
BALANCE SHEET (IN MILLIONS)							
Cash & Cash Equivalents	10.4	3.9	1.7	8.3	3.2	71.0	51.8
Total Current Assets	541.0	478.5	417.5	345.9	281.9	273.2	236.7
Net Property	349.5	354.8	294.2	264.2	193.1	158.2	142.2
Total Assets	1,080.7	1,022.9	861.2	742.5	542.4	485.3	420.4
Total Current Liabilities	240.4	255.3	226.1	170.6	128.2	108.6	92.2
Long-Term Obligations	281.7	273.5	209.6	315.5	72.7	69.1	59.5
Net Stockholders' Equity	478.1	406.9	348.8	307.5	273.3	247.9	220.5
Net Working Capital	300.7	223.2	191.4	175.3	153.7	164.7	144.5
Year-end Shs. Outstg. (000)	30,128	30,179	30,351	30,351	30,638	30,826	30,506
STATISTICAL RECORD:							
Operating Profit Margin %	10.8	10.0	10.1	9.5	9.3	8.9	8.0
Net Profit Margin %	5.9	5.6	5.6	5.5	5.4	5.1	4.6
Return on Equity %	20.0	20.9	20.3	18.1	16.1	14.4	12.9
Return on Assets %	8.9	8.3	8.2	7.5	8.1	7.3	6.8
Debt/Total Assets %	26.1	26.7	24.3	42.5	13.4	14.2	14.2
Price Range	52¹⁵/₁₆-30⁵/₈	53¹/₁₆-32¹⁵/₁₆	47³/₄-27	30¹/₂-19	21¹³/₁₆-17¹/₄	18¹/₁₆-15¹/₈	17¹/₄-11⁹/₁₆
P/E Ratio	16.9-9.8	19.2-11.8	20.9-11.8	16.9-10.6	15.5-12.2	15.7-13.2	18.9-12.6
Average Yield %	1.6	1.4	1.4	1.9	2.2	2.3	2.4

Statistics are as originally reported. Adj. for stk. splits: 2-for-1, 1/97; 6/93 ① Incl. non-recurr. gain of $685,000.

OFFICERS:
S. P. Munn, Chmn., C.E.O.
D. J. Hall, Vice-Chmn., C.O.O.
John S. Barsanti, V.P., C.F.O.

INVESTOR CONTACT: Investor Relations, (800) 897-9071

PRINCIPAL OFFICE: 250 S. Clinton St., Suite 201, Syracuse, NY 13202-1258

TELEPHONE NUMBER: (315) 474-2500
FAX: (315) 474-2008
WEB: www.carlisle.com
NO. OF EMPLOYEES: 10,290 (approx.)
SHAREHOLDERS: 2,546
ANNUAL MEETING: In Apr.
INCORPORATED: DE, Sep., 1917; reincorp., DE, May, 1986

INSTITUTIONAL HOLDINGS:
No. of Institutions: 133
Shares Held: 13,095,355
% Held: 43.5

INDUSTRY: Tires and inner tubes (SIC: 3011)

TRANSFER AGENT(S): Harris Trust and Savings Bank, Chicago, IL

CAROLINA POWER & LIGHT COMPANY

YIELD 6.0%
P/E RATIO 13.5

INTERIM EARNINGS (Per Share):

Qtr.	Mar.	June	Sept.	Dec.
1996	0.81	0.37	1.15	0.33
1997	0.56	0.37	1.15	0.58
1998	0.60	0.45	1.28	0.42
1999	0.63	0.43	0.97	0.51

INTERIM DIVIDENDS (Per Share):

Amt.	Decl.	Ex.	Rec.	Pay.
0.50Q	9/10/99	10/07/99	10/12/99	11/01/99
0.515Q	12/08/99	1/06/00	1/10/00	2/01/00
0.515Q	3/15/00	4/06/00	4/10/00	5/01/00
0.515Q	5/10/00	7/06/00	7/10/00	8/01/00

Indicated div.: $2.06 (Div. Reinv. Plan)

CAPITALIZATION (12/31/99):

	($000)	(%)
Long-Term Debt	3,028,561	37.2
Deferred Income Tax	1,632,778	20.1
Preferred Stock	59,376	0.7
Common & Surplus	3,412,647	42.0
Total	8,133,362	100.0

TRADING VOLUME Thousand Shares

*7 YEAR PRICE SCORE 67.2   *12 MONTH PRICE SCORE 98.8

*NYSE COMPOSITE INDEX=100

DIVIDEND ACHIEVER STATUS:
Rank: 290   10-Year Growth Rate: 3.48%
Total Years of Dividend Growth: 11

RECENT DEVELOPMENTS: For the year ended 12/31/99, net income was $382.3 million, down 4.3% compared with $399.2 million in 1998. Results for 1999 included a $29.0 million one-time charge related to recovery costs and lost earnings from hurricanes Dennis and Floyd. Mild weather, hurricane expenses and the perpetual decline of industrial revenues negatively affected earnings. Operating revenues rose 5.2% to $3.36 billion from $3.19 billion a year earlier.

PROSPECTS: CPL's acquisition of Florida Progress should be completed in September 2000. As a result of the merger, future earnings are expected to benefit from increased diversity in customer base, skill sets of employees, additional resources and service territories, enhanced competitive position and optimized business practices. Near-term earnings may be adversely affected by certain damage recovery and power restoration costs.

BUSINESS

CAROLINA POWER & LIGHT COMPANY provides electric services to more than 1.2 million customers in an area of 33,667 square miles, almost half of North Carolina and one-fourth of South Carolina. Most customers live in small towns and urban centers largely in the coastal plains, although CPL also serves portions of the Piedmont and mountain sections of the two states. Major industries served include textiles, chemicals, metals, paper and electronic machinery and equipment. CPL also provides gas to about 167,000 customers through its subsidiary, North Carolina Natural Gas.

BUSINESS LINE ANALYSIS

(12/31/99)	Rev(%)	Inc(%)
Electric	93.5	110.6
Natural Gas	2.9	0.7
Other Revenues	3.6	(11.3)
Total	100.0	100.0

ANNUAL FINANCIAL DATA

	12/31/99	12/31/98	12/31/97	12/31/96	12/31/95	12/31/94	12/31/93
Earnings Per Share	② 2.55	2.75	2.66	2.66	2.48	① 2.03	2.10
Cash Flow Per Share	6.52	6.77	6.60	5.77	5.54	5.19	4.96
Tang. Book Val. Per Share	...	19.49	18.63	17.77	16.93	16.54	16.38
Dividends Per Share	2.00	1.94	1.88	1.82	1.76	1.70	1.64
Dividend Payout %	78.4	70.5	70.7	68.4	71.0	83.7	78.1
INCOME STATEMENT (IN MILLIONS):							
Total Revenues	3,357.6	3,130.0	3,024.1	2,995.7	3,006.6	2,876.6	2,895.4
Costs & Expenses	1,928.9	1,654.2	1,663.2	1,765.4	1,767.8	1,553.5	1,542.2
Depreciation & Amort.	588.1	578.3	565.2	446.5	446.7	473.5	460.1
Maintenance Exp.	...	...	...	...	...	206.7	235.4
Operating Income	840.5	897.5	795.5	783.9	792.1	642.9	657.7
Net Interest Inc./(Exp.)	d169.1	d164.7	d139.6	d167.5	d181.0	d172.6	d179.8
Income Taxes	258.4	257.5	253.0	269.8	259.2	198.5	189.3
Net Income	② 382.3	399.2	388.3	391.3	372.6	① 313.2	346.5
Cash Flow	967.4	974.6	947.5	828.9	820.9	777.0	797.0
Average Shs. Outstg. (000)	148,344	143,941	143,645	143,621	146,232	149,614	160,737
BALANCE SHEET (IN MILLIONS):							
Gross Property	11,740.2	10,796.2	10,474.6	10,196.5	9,821.6	9,545.6	9,330.0
Accumulated Depreciation	4,975.4	4,496.6	4,181.4	3,796.6	3,493.2	3,196.1	2,897.8
Net Property	6,764.8	6,299.5	6,293.2	6,399.9	6,328.5	6,349.5	6,432.2
Total Assets	9,494.0	8,347.4	8,220.4	8,369.2	8,227.1	8,211.2	8,194.0
Long-Term Obligations	3,028.6	2,614.4	2,415.7	2,525.6	2,610.3	2,530.8	2,584.9
Net Stockholders' Equity	3,472.0	3,008.7	2,878.2	2,834.3	2,718.5	2,730.0	2,775.9
Year-end Shs. Outstg. (000)	159,600	151,338	151,340	151,416	152,103	156,382	160,737
STATISTICAL RECORD:							
Operating Profit Margin %	25.0	28.7	26.3	26.2	26.3	22.3	22.7
Net Profit Margin %	11.4	12.8	12.8	13.1	12.4	10.9	12.0
Net Inc./Net Property %	5.7	6.3	6.2	6.1	5.9	4.9	5.4
Net Inc./Tot. Capital %	8.1	5.5	5.5	5.4	5.3	4.5	5.0
Return on Equity %	9.1	13.3	13.5	13.8	13.7	11.5	12.5
Accum. Depr./Gross Prop. %	42.4	41.7	39.9	37.2	35.6	33.5	31.1
Price Range	47⅞-29¼	49⅝-39³⁄₁₆	42¹¹⁄₁₆-32¾	38¾-33¾	34⅝-26⅛	30-22½	34⅝-27
P/E Ratio	18.8-11.5	18.0-14.2	16.0-12.3	14.6-12.7	14.0-10.5	14.8-11.1	16.5-12.9
Average Yield %	2.6	4.4	5.0	5.0	5.8	6.5	5.3

Statistics are as originally reported. Adj. for stk. split: 2-for-1, 2/93 ① Incl. non-recurr. chrg. $20.6 mill. ② Incl. one-time chrg. of $29.0 mill. ($0.14/sh.) related to storm damage.

OFFICERS:
W. Cavanaugh III, Chmn., Pres., C.E.O.,
P. M. Scott III, C.F.O., Exec. V.P.
R. B. McGehee, Exec. V.P., Gen. Couns.,
Chief Adm. Officer

INVESTOR CONTACT: Robert F. Drennan,
Jr., Manager-Investor Relations and Funds
Management, (919) 546-7474

PRINCIPAL OFFICE: 411 Fayetteville St,
Raleigh, NC 27601

TELEPHONE NUMBER: (919) 546-6111
FAX: (919) 546-7678
WEB: www.cplc.com

NO. OF EMPLOYEES: 7,752

SHAREHOLDERS: 66,791

ANNUAL MEETING: In May

INCORPORATED: NC, Apr., 1926

INSTITUTIONAL HOLDINGS:
No. of Institutions: 254
Shares Held: 64,817,303
% Held: 40.6

INDUSTRY: Electric services (SIC: 4911)

TRANSFER AGENT(S): Wachovia Bank &
Trust Co., N.A., Winston-Salem, NC.

CCB FINANCIAL CORPORATION

YIELD 2.5%
P/E RATIO 14.2

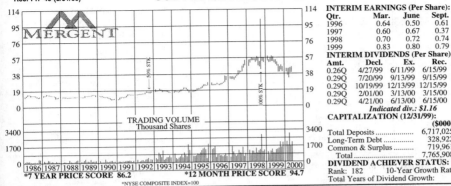

INTERIM EARNINGS (Per Share):

Qtr.	Mar.	June	Sept.	Dec.
1996	0.64	0.50	0.61	0.59
1997	0.60	0.67	0.37	0.66
1998	0.70	0.72	0.74	0.77
1999	0.83	0.80	0.79	0.83

INTERIM DIVIDENDS (Per Share):

Amt.	Decl.	Ex.	Rec.	Pay.
0.26Q	4/27/99	6/11/99	6/15/99	7/01/99
0.29Q	7/20/99	9/13/99	9/15/99	10/01/99
0.29Q	10/19/99	12/13/99	12/15/99	1/03/00
0.29Q	2/01/00	3/13/00	3/15/00	4/03/00
0.29Q	4/21/00	6/13/00	6/15/00	7/03/00

Indicated div.: $1.16

CAPITALIZATION (12/31/99):

	($000)	(%)
Total Deposits	6,717,025	86.5
Long-Term Debt	328,922	4.2
Common & Surplus	719,961	9.3
Total	7,765,908	100.0

DIVIDEND ACHIEVER STATUS:
Rank: 182   10-Year Growth Rate: 8.83%
Total Years of Dividend Growth: 35

TRADING VOLUME
Thousand Shares

*7 YEAR PRICE SCORE 86.2   *12 MONTH PRICE SCORE 94.7

*NYSE COMPOSITE INDEX=100

RECENT DEVELOPMENTS: For the year ended 12/31/99, net income advanced 24.4% to $150.8 million from $121.2 million in 1998. Earnings for 1999 included a pre-tax gain of $32.8 on the sale of credit card receivables. Net interest income climbed 2.8% to $332.1 million from $322.9 million in the previous year. Total non-interest income, including the above gain, grew 40.1% to $158.5 million. Total non-interest expense rose 6.0% to $244.0 million. Provision for loan losses fell 10.0% to $14.3 million.

PROSPECTS: On 3/20/00, CCB and National Commerce Bancorporation announced that they have entered into a definitive merger of equals agreement, under which CCB shareholders will receive 2.45 shares of National Commerce common stock. The combined company will retain the name National Commerce Bancorporation and will have assets of $15.00 billion. CCB common stockholders will own approximately 47% of the combined company. The merger is expected to close in the third quarter of 2000.

BUSINESS

CCB FINANCIAL CORPORATION is a registered bank holding company, with total assets of $8.50 billion as of 3/31/00. CCB offers a complete line of traditional banking services in North and South Carolina, as well as a full array of financial products, such as investments, insurance and trust services. Its two principal banking subsidiaries, Central Carolina Bank & Trust Co. in North Carolina and American Federal Bank in South Carolina, serve customers through 208 offices, 229 ATMs, its Telebanking Center, and on-line banking for both retail and commercial accounts. The Trust and Investment Management division has 14 offices in the Carolinas, Virginia and Florida, with trust assets managed exceeding $5.50 billion. On 10/1/99, CCB acquired Stone Street Bancorp, Inc.

LOAN DISTRIBUTION

(12/31/99)	($000)	(%)
Comm, Fin & Agric	697,776	11.7
Real Estate-Construction	1,152,081	19.3
Real Estate-Mortgage	3,406,789	57.1
Installment Loans	571,771	9.6
Revolving Credit	58,926	1.0
Lease Financing	76,424	1.3
Total	5,963,767	100.0

ANNUAL FINANCIAL DATA

	12/31/99	12/31/98	12/31/97	12/31/96	12/31/95	12/31/94	12/31/93
Earnings Per Share	③ 3.74	2.93	① 2.28	2.34	1.94	1.47	② 1.55
Tang. Book Val. Per Share	18.19	17.05	16.40	15.90	14.60	12.57	13.61
Dividends Per Share	1.07	0.96	0.86	0.78	0.70	0.65	0.61
Dividend Payout %	28.6	32.9	38.0	33.4	36.2	44.2	39.4
INCOME STATEMENT (IN MILLIONS):							
Total Interest Income	589.6	577.3	550.5	397.8	383.5	309.9	254.9
Total Interest Expense	257.5	254.6	250.1	181.3	179.4	126.4	102.0
Net Interest Income	332.1	322.7	300.4	216.4	204.1	183.5	153.0
Provision for Loan Losses	14.3	15.9	16.4	12.8	8.2	9.3	7.1
Non-Interest Income	158.5	113.2	93.4	62.6	52.3	49.0	49.6
Non-Interest Expense	244.0	230.2	226.2	161.4	160.2	147.3	129.5
Income Before Taxes	232.2	189.8	151.2	104.8	88.0	76.0	66.0
Net Income	③ 150.8	121.2	① 95.4	70.3	57.9	45.1	② 44.1
Average Shs. Outstg. (000)	40,315	41,409	41,946	30,096	29,898	30,709	28,460
BALANCE SHEET (IN MILLIONS):							
Cash & Due from Banks	300.1	250.9	277.5	201.5	189.3	204.9	191.3
Securities Avail. for Sale	1,563.1	1,284.2	1,482.1	947.1	1,021.6	766.1	553.3
Total Loans & Leases	5,963.8	5,494.4	5,099.3	3,776.3	3,350.5	3,163.8	2,162.6
Allowance for Credit Losses	86.8	80.3	73.3	53.9	48.7	46.0	30.1
Net Loans & Leases	5,876.9	5,414.2	5,026.0	3,722.4	3,301.8	3,117.8	2,132.5
Total Assets	8,186.3	7,740.4	7,138.5	5,384.1	5,089.8	4,720.7	3,257.6
Total Deposits	6,717.0	6,459.8	5,984.6	4,589.5	4,297.4	4,057.7	2,816.8
Long-Term Obligations	328.9	216.7	100.7	57.8	79.0	95.6	78.7
Total Liabilities	7,466.3	7,052.5	6,457.2	4,905.9	4,656.3	4,349.5	3,006.6
Net Stockholders' Equity	720.0	687.9	681.4	479.7	437.0	377.1	259.0
Year-end Shs. Outstg. (000)	39,580	40,345	41,552	30,164	29,922	29,994	19,035
STATISTICAL RECORD:							
Return on Equity %	20.9	17.6	14.0	14.7	13.2	12.0	17.0
Return on Assets %	1.8	1.6	1.3	1.3	1.1	1.0	1.4
Equity/Assets %	8.8	8.9	9.5	8.9	8.6	8.0	8.0
Non-Int. Exp./Tot. Inc. %	53.5	53.1	57.5	58.0	62.3	63.4	64.9
Price Range	59⅛-40	58½-43⅛	54⅛-30¹⁵/₁₆	35⅞-24⁵/₈	28¼-17	22¼-16⅜	21¼-16¼
P/E Ratio	15.8-10.7	20.0-14.7	23.8-13.6	15.4-10.5	14.6-8.8	15.1-11.1	13.7-10.5
Average Yield %	2.2	1.9	2.0	2.6	3.1	3.4	3.3

Statistics are as originally reported. Adj. for 2-for-1 split, 10/1/98. ① Incl. non-recurr. chrg. $17.9 mill. ② Bef. acctg. change chrg. $1.4 mill. ③ Incl. a pre-tax gain of $32.8 million on the sale of credit card receivables.

OFFICERS:
E. C. Roessler, Chmn., Pres., C.E.O.
E. J. McDonald, Exec. Vice-Chmn.
D. B. Jordan, Vice-Chmn.
W. J. Abercrombie Jr., Vice-Chmn.

INVESTOR CONTACT: W. Harold Parker, Jr., Sr. V.P. & Controller, (919) 683-7631

PRINCIPAL OFFICE: 111 Corcoran Street, P.O. Box 931, Durham, NC 27702

TELEPHONE NUMBER: (919) 683-7777
FAX: (919) 683-7254
WEB: www.ccbonline.com

NO. OF EMPLOYEES: 2,831

SHAREHOLDERS: 9,400 (approx.)

ANNUAL MEETING: In Apr.

INCORPORATED: NC, Nov., 1903

INSTITUTIONAL HOLDINGS:
No. of Institutions: 124
Shares Held: 14,449,885
% Held: 35.9

INDUSTRY: State commercial banks (SIC: 6022)

TRANSFER AGENT(S): Registrar and Transfer Company, Cranford, NJ

CEDAR FAIR, L.P.

YIELD 7.5%
P/E RATIO 12.2

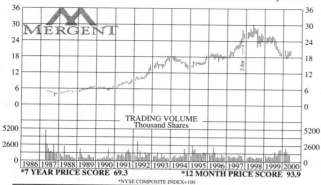

TRADING VOLUME
Thousand Shares

*7 YEAR PRICE SCORE 69.3   *12 MONTH PRICE SCORE 93.9
*NYSE COMPOSITE INDEX=100

INTERIM EARNINGS (Per Share):

Qtr.	Mar.	June	Sept.	Dec.
1996	d0.34	0.42	1.80	d0.29
1997	d0.37	0.31	1.81	d0.28
1998	d0.44	0.37	1.79	d0.14
1999	d0.41	0.37	1.83	d0.15

INTERIM DIVIDENDS (Per Share):

Amt.	Decl.	Ex.	Rec.	Pay.
0.35Q	3/08/99	4/01/99	4/06/99	5/14/99
0.35Q	6/24/99	7/01/99	7/06/99	8/16/99
0.362Q	9/17/99	10/01/99	10/05/99	11/15/99
0.362Q	12/22/99	1/03/00	1/05/00	2/15/00
0.375Q	3/06/00	4/03/00	4/05/00	5/15/00

Indicated div.: $1.50

CAPITALIZATION (12/31/99):

	($000)	(%)
Long-Term Debt	261,200	42.7
Common & Surplus	349,986	57.3
Total	611,186	100.0

DIVIDEND ACHIEVER STATUS:
Rank: 169   10-Year Growth Rate: 9.33%
Total Years of Dividend Growth: 12

RECENT DEVELOPMENTS: For the year ended 12/31/99, net income rose 2.8% to $85.8 million versus $83.4 million in 1998. Net revenues were $438.0 million, up 4.4% from $419.5 million a year earlier. For the 1999 season, combined attendance totaled 10.6 million, the second highest in FUN's history, and in-park guest per capita spending increased to $34.58 from $33.20 in 1998 on a combined basis.

PROSPECTS: The Company's subsidiary, Valleyfair Family Amusement Park, introduced the nearly $10.0 million thrill ride, Power Tower, on 5/6/00 during opening ceremonies for their 2000 operating season. Power Tower is a unique three-tower structure, with a pyramid top, that combines two thrill rides in one. Separately, FUN's $110.0 million in capital improvements slated for its five parks are well underway.

BUSINESS

CEDAR FAIR, L.P. is a limited partnership managed by Cedar Fair Management Company. The Partnership owns and operates six amusement parks: Cedar Point, located on Lake Erie in Sandusky, OH; Knott's Berry Farm, located in Buena Park, CA; Dorney Park & Wildwater Kingdom, located in South Whitehall Township, PA; Valleyfair, located in Shakopee, Minnesota; Knott's Soak City USA, located in Chula Vista, CA; and Worlds of Fun and Oceans of Fun, located in Kansas City, Missouri. The parks are family-oriented, with recreational facilities for people of all ages, and provide environments with rides and entertainment. All principal rides and attractions are owned and operated by the Partnership. The Company has two hotels: Breakers Tower at Cedar Point and the Buena Park Hotel. FUN also operates Knott's Camp Snoopy at the Mall of America in Bloomington, Minnesota under a management contract.

ANNUAL FINANCIAL DATA

	12/31/99	12/31/98	12/31/97	12/31/96	12/31/95	12/31/94	12/31/93
Earnings Per Share	1.63	1.58	1.47	1.59	1.45	1.40	1.38
Cash Flow Per Share	2.31	2.20	1.95	2.02	1.83	1.75	1.72
Tang. Book Val. Per Share	6.56	6.38	5.24	3.47	3.06	2.33	1.98
Dividends Per Share	1.39	1.28	1.26	1.18	1.13	1.03	0.94
Dividend Payout %	85.1	81.3	85.5	73.9	78.0	73.9	68.6
INCOME STATEMENT (IN THOUSANDS):							
Total Revenues	438,001	419,500	264,137	250,523	218,197	198,358	178,943
Costs & Expenses	286,194	274,827	166,306	150,330	128,442	115,382	106,990
Depreciation & Amort.	35,082	32,065	21,528	19,072	16,742	14,960	14,473
Operating Income	116,755	112,608	76,303	81,121	73,013	68,016	57,480
Net Interest Inc./(Exp.)	d15,371	d14,660	d7,845	d6,942	d6,877	d7,293	d6,601
Income Before Income Taxes	101,384	97,948	68,458	74,179	66,136	62,825	61,879
Income Taxes	15,580	14,507	...	...	...	...	...
Net Income	85,774	83,441	68,458	74,179	66,136	62,825	61,879
Cash Flow	120,856	115,506	89,986	93,251	82,878	77,785	76,352
Average Shs. Outstg.	52,390	52,414	46,265	46,116	45,214	44,534	44,504
BALANCE SHEET (IN THOUSANDS):							
Cash & Cash Equivalents	638	1,137	2,520	1,279	111	350	228
Total Current Assets	24,184	20,967	21,954	11,730	9,805	8,198	6,887
Net Property	674,640	600,044	567,137	281,638	253,840	204,331	199,611
Total Assets	708,961	631,325	599,619	304,104	274,717	223,982	218,359
Total Current Liabilities	86,559	77,231	62,426	39,241	37,648	33,602	31,592
Long-Term Obligations	261,200	200,350	189,750	87,600	80,000	71,400	86,800
Net Stockholders' Equity	349,986	341,991	285,381	169,994	151,476	115,054	99,967
Net Working Capital	d62,375	d56,264	d40,472	d27,511	d27,843	d25,404	d24,705
Year-end Shs. Outstg.	51,798	51,980	52,403	45,920	45,920	44,480	44,480
STATISTICAL RECORD:							
Operating Profit Margin %	26.7	26.8	28.9	32.4	33.5	34.3	32.1
Net Profit Margin %	19.6	19.9	25.9	29.6	30.3	31.7	34.6
Return on Equity %	24.5	24.4	24.0	43.6	43.7	54.6	61.9
Return on Assets %	12.1	13.2	11.4	24.4	24.1	28.0	28.3
Debt/Total Assets %	36.8	31.7	31.6	28.8	29.1	31.9	39.8
Price Range	26 1/8-18 7/16	30 1/8-21 3/4	28 1/8-17 11/16	19 1/2-16 1/8	18 9/16-14 1/16	18 5/16-13 3/8	18 5/16-13 1/2
P/E Ratio	15.9-11.3	19.1-13.8	19.2-12.0	12.3-10.1	12.8-9.7	13.1-9.6	13.3-9.8
Average Yield %	6.2	5.0	5.5	6.6	6.9	6.5	5.9

Statistics are as originally reported. Adj. for stk. split: 2-for-1, 11/7/97.

OFFICERS:
R. L. Kinzel, Pres., C.E.O.
B. A. Jackson, Corp. V.P., C.F.O.
T. W. Salamone, Treas.

INVESTOR CONTACT: Brian C. Witherow,
Dir., Investor Relations, (419) 626-0830

PRINCIPAL OFFICE: P.O. Box 5006,
Sandusky, OH 44871-5006

TELEPHONE NUMBER: (419) 626-0830
FAX: (419) 627-2234
WEB: www.cedarfair.com

NO. OF EMPLOYEES: 1,200 (approx.)

SHAREHOLDERS: 11,000 (approx.)

ANNUAL MEETING: N/A

INCORPORATED: MN, 1983; reincorp., DE, 1987

INSTITUTIONAL HOLDINGS:
No. of Institutions: 96
Shares Held: 10,073,383
% Held: 19.4

INDUSTRY: Amusement parks (SIC: 7996)

TRANSFER AGENT(S): ChaseMellon
Shareholder Services, Ridgefield Park, NJ

CENTURYTEL, INC.

YIELD 0.7%
P/E RATIO 15.9

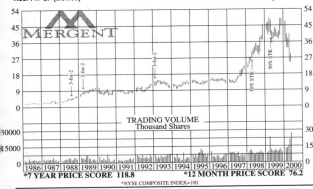

7 YEAR PRICE SCORE 118.8   **12 MONTH PRICE SCORE 76.2**
*NYSE COMPOSITE INDEX=100

INTERIM EARNINGS (Per Share):

Qtr.	Mar.	June	Sept.	Dec.
1997	0.25	0.61	0.30	0.73
1998	0.41	0.46	0.39	0.37
1999	0.43	0.38	0.46	0.43

INTERIM DIVIDENDS (Per Share):

Amt.	Decl.	Ex.	Rec.	Pay.
50% STK	2/23/99	4/01/99	3/10/99	3/31/99
0.045Q	5/25/99	6/02/99	6/04/99	6/18/99
0.045Q	8/24/99	9/01/99	9/03/99	9/17/99
0.045Q	11/18/99	12/01/99	12/03/99	12/17/99
0.048Q	2/22/00	3/03/00	3/07/00	3/21/00

Indicated div.: $0.19(Div. Reinv. Plan)

CAPITALIZATION (12/31/99):

	($000)	(%)
Long-Term Debt	2,078,311	52.9
Preferred Stock	7,975	0.2
Common & Surplus	1,840,017	46.9
Total	3,926,303	100.0

DIVIDEND ACHIEVER STATUS:
Rank: 281   10-Year Growth Rate: 4.09%
Total Years of Dividend Growth: 26

RECENT DEVELOPMENTS: For the twelve months ended 12/31/99, net income was $239.8 million, up 4.8% from $228.8 million in the previous year. Results for 1999 and 1998 included gains of $62.8 million and $49.9 million, respectively, from the sale of assets. Total revenues were $1.68 billion, up 6.3% from $1.58 billion a year earlier. Revenues from telephone operations rose to $1.14 billion from $1.09 billion, while wireless operations revenues increased 3.5% to $422.3 million.

PROSPECTS: On 2/18/00, CTL completed the sale of its interests in Alaska to Dobson Cellular Systems Inc., which is located in Oklahoma City, OK. This transaction is the final step in CTL's divestiture of its Alaska operations. This initiative should help strengthen the Company's core operations and better position CTL for future growth. These asset sales are also helping the Company reduce debt. Going forward, CTL will be focusing on increasing growth in its core wireline and wireless operations.

BUSINESS

CENTURYTEL, INC. (formerly Century Telephone Enterprises, Inc.) is a regional diversified telecommunications company that is primarily engaged in providing local exchange telephone services and wireless telephone communications services. Century's telephone subsidiaries service more than 1.27 million telephone access lines in 20 states, with the largest customer bases located in Wisconsin, Washington, Michigan, Louisiana, Colorado, Ohio, Oregon and Montana. The Company also provides long distance, security monitoring, cable television and interactive services, as well as certain local and regional printing and related services. On 12/1/97, CTL acquired Pacific Telecom, Inc. for nearly $2.20 billion.

BUSINESS LINE ANALYSIS

(12/31/99)	REV (%)	INC (%)
Telephone	68.1	69.3
Wireless	25.2	26.4
Other	6.7	4.3
Total	100.0	100.0

ANNUAL FINANCIAL DATA

	12/31/99	12/31/98	12/31/97	12/31/96	12/31/95	12/31/94	12/31/93
Earnings Per Share	③ 1.70	① 1.64	② 1.87	② 0.96	0.88	0.84	0.60
Cash Flow Per Share	4.16	3.98	3.02	1.94	1.75	1.63	1.35
Tang. Book Val. Per Share	1.39	...	...	3.61	2.95	1.71	2.03
Dividends Per Share	0.20	0.17	0.164	0.16	0.15	0.142	0.138
Dividend Payout %	10.6	10.6	8.8	16.7	16.8	17.0	23.0
INCOME STATEMENT (IN MILLIONS):							
Total Revenues	1,676.7	1,577.1	901.5	749.7	644.8	540.2	433.2
Costs & Expenses	819.8	768.7	474.3	394.4	328.2	275.1	222.2
Depreciation & Amort.	348.8	328.6	159.5	132.0	113.8	95.7	86.2
Operating Income	508.1	479.8	267.8	223.3	202.9	169.4	124.8
Net Interest Inc./(Exp.)	d150.6	d167.6	d56.5	d44.7	d43.6	d42.6	d30.1
Income Before Income Taxes	429.3	387.5	408.3	203.6	183.1	161.5	106.3
Income Taxes	189.5	158.7	152.4	74.6	68.3	61.3	37.3
Equity Earnings/Minority Int.	d0.2	20.1	22.3	20.3	12.0	15.7	6.6
Net Income	③ 239.8	① 228.8	② 256.0	② 129.1	114.8	100.2	69.0
Cash Flow	588.2	556.9	415.0	260.7	228.4	195.9	155.1
Average Shs. Outstg. (000)	141,432	140,105	137,412	134,829	130,806	120,150	115,214
BALANCE SHEET (IN MILLIONS):							
Cash & Cash Equivalents	56.6	5.7	26.0	8.4	8.5	7.2	9.8
Total Current Assets	286.1	226.2	283.5	109.2	95.3	81.2	72.5
Net Property	2,256.5	2,351.5	2,258.4	1,149.0	1,047.8	947.1	d342.7
Total Assets	4,705.4	4,935.5	4,709.2	2,028.5	1,862.4	1,643.3	1,319.4
Total Current Liabilities	309.2	304.8	322.1	144.1	139.9	286.7	179.2
Long-Term Obligations	2,078.3	2,558.0	2,609.5	625.9	622.9	518.6	460.9
Net Stockholders' Equity	1,848.0	1,531.5	1,300.3	1,028.2	888.4	650.2	532.2
Net Working Capital	d23.1	d78.6	d38.6	d34.9	d44.6	d205.4	d106.7
Year-end Shs. Outstg. (000)	139,946	138,083	136,656	134,683	133,007	120,542	115,414
STATISTICAL RECORD:							
Operating Profit Margin %	30.3	30.4	29.7	29.8	31.5	31.4	28.8
Net Profit Margin %	14.3	14.5	28.4	17.2	17.8	18.6	15.9
Return on Equity %	13.0	14.9	19.7	12.6	12.9	15.4	13.4
Return on Assets %	5.1	4.6	5.4	6.4	6.2	6.1	46.3
Debt/Total Assets %	44.2	51.8	55.4	30.9	33.4	31.6	309.5
Price Range	49-35³/₁₆	45⅛-21⁹/₁₆	27⁷/₁₆-12¹¹/₁₆	15¾-12¹¹/₁₆	14¾-12¹/₁₆	14⁵/₁₆-9¾	14¹³/₁₆-10⁵/₁₆
P/E Ratio	28.8-20.7	27.5-13.1	12.0-6.8	16.5-13.2	16.8-13.7	17.1-11.6	24.7-17.2
Average Yield %	0.5	0.5	0.9	1.1	1.1	1.2	1.1

Statistics are as originally reported. Adj. for stk. splits: 50%, 3/99 & 3/98; and 3-for-2, 1/93 ① Incls. non-recurr. pre-tax credit of $49.9 mill. ② Incls. pre-tax credit 12/31/97: $169.9 mill.; credit 12/31/96, $815,000; ③ Incls. one-time gain of $62.8 mill.

OFFICERS:
C. M. Williams, Chmn.
G. F. Post III, Vice-Chmn., Pres., C.E.O.
R. S. Brunson, Jr., Exec. V.P., C.F.O.

INVESTOR CONTACT: Jeff Glover, Director of Investor Relations, (800) 833-1188

PRINCIPAL OFFICE: 100 Century Park Dr., Monroe, LA 71203

TELEPHONE NUMBER: (318) 388-9000
FAX: (800) 789-8656
WEB: www.centurytel.com

NO. OF EMPLOYEES: 5,700 (approx.)

SHAREHOLDERS: 6,000 (approx.)

ANNUAL MEETING: In May

INCORPORATED: LA, Apr., 1968

INSTITUTIONAL HOLDINGS:
No. of Institutions: 318
Shares Held: 94,553,406
% Held: 67.7

INDUSTRY: Telephone communications, exc. radio (SIC: 4813)

TRANSFER AGENT(S): Harris Trust and Savings Bank, Chicago, IL

NASDAQ SYMBOL CFWC
Rec. Pr. 38 7/16 (5/31/00)

CFW COMMUNICATIONS COMPANY

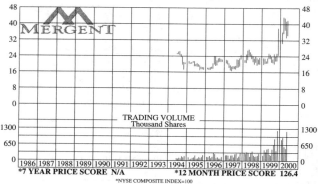

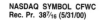

YIELD 1.2%
P/E RATIO 61.0

MERGENT
48
40
32
24
16
8
0
TRADING VOLUME
Thousand Shares
1300
650
0
1986 1987 1988 1989 1990 1991 1992 1993 1994 1995 1996 1997 1998 1999 2000

*7 YEAR PRICE SCORE N/A *12 MONTH PRICE SCORE 126.4

*NYSE COMPOSITE INDEX=100

INTERIM EARNINGS (Per Share):

Qtr.	Mar.	June	Sept.	Dec.
1996	0.18	0.18	0.18	0.19
1997	0.19	0.45	0.22	0.07
1998	0.19	0.19	0.17	0.11
1999	0.10	0.10	0.33	d0.04

INTERIM DIVIDENDS (Per Share):

Amt.	Decl.	Ex.	Rec.	Pay.
0.115Q	2/22/99	3/08/99	3/10/99	3/31/99
0.115Q	4/27/99	6/08/99	6/10/99	6/30/99
0.115Q	8/23/99	9/08/99	9/10/99	9/30/99
0.115Q	10/25/99	12/07/99	12/09/99	12/30/99
0.115Q	3/07/00	3/16/00	3/20/00	3/31/00

Indicated div.: $0.46 (Div. Reinv. Plan)

CAPITALIZATION (12/31/99):

	($000)	(%)
Long-Term Debt	37,685	20.1
Deferred Income Tax	31,605	16.9
Minority Interest	1,781	1.0
Common & Surplus	116,184	62.0
Total	187,255	100.0

DIVIDEND ACHIEVER STATUS:
Rank: 239 10-Year Growth Rate: 6.26%
Total Years of Dividend Growth: 11

RECENT DEVELOPMENTS: For the year ended 12/31/99, net income totaled $6.5 million, a decrease of 23.7% compared with $8.5 million in 1998. Earnings for 1999 included a gain of $8.3 million on the sale of tower assets and investments. The 1998 results included a nonrecurring loss of $1.0 million. Operating revenues improved 10.7% to $73.8 million. On 5/18/00, the Company and R&B Communications, Inc., an integrated communications provider, announced a binding letter agreement to merge. The transaction, which will be completed via the exchange of 3.7 million shares of the Company's common stock, is valued at approximately $131.0 million. CFW also announced a definitive agreement to acquire PrimeCo's PCS licenses, assets and operations in Richmond and Norfolk, Virginia. The R&B merger and the PrimeCo PCS acquisition are both expected to close in the third quarter of 2000.

BUSINESS

CFW COMMUNICATIONS COMPANY is an integrated communications provider, which offers a broad range of products and services to business and residential customers in Virginia, West Virginia, Kentucky and Tennessee. These products and services include digital personal communications services, dial-up Internet access, high-speed data services such as digital subscriber line and dedicated service, local telephone, competitive local telephone services to businesses, long distance, analog cellular, paging, wireless and wireline cable television, directory assistance, competitive access, and alarm monitoring services.

REVENUES

(12/31/99)	($000)	(%)
Wireline Communications	44,110	59.8
Wireless Communications	13,549	18.4
Directory Assistance	12,104	16.4
Other Comm. Services	4,028	5.4
Total	73,791	100.0

ANNUAL FINANCIAL DATA

	12/31/99	12/31/98	12/31/97	12/31/96	12/31/95	12/31/94	12/31/93
Earnings Per Share	**② 0.50**	**0.65**	**0.94**	**0.77**	**0.69**	**0.65**	**① 0.60**
Cash Flow Per Share	**1.46**	**1.45**	**1.64**	**1.38**	**1.15**	**1.01**	**0.94**
Tang. Book Val. Per Share	**6.50**	**5.73**	**5.65**	**5.65**	**5.85**	**5.53**	**4.61**
Dividends Per Share	**0.46**	**0.43**	**0.41**	**0.39**	**0.38**	**0.37**	**0.35**
Dividend Payout %	**91.8**	**66.9**	**43.8**	**50.9**	**54.9**	**56.6**	**59.2**
INCOME STATEMENT (IN THOUSANDS):							
Total Revenues	73,792	66,686	59,010	49,948	43,929	32,651	27,427
Costs & Expenses	47,646	33,556	30,402	26,124	23,230	15,372	12,169
Depreciation & Amort.	12,623	10,503	9,196	8,410	6,438	4,578	4,039
Operating Income	13,522	22,626	19,412	15,415	14,262	12,702	11,219
Net Interest Inc./(Exp.)	d11,365	107	285	587	604	594	995
Income Before Income Taxes	9,749	14,725	20,066	15,179	13,920	11,325	10,708
Income Taxes	2,868	5,639	7,398	5,162	5,006	3,550	3,767
Equity Earnings/Minority Int.	d210	d6,847	d1,207	d17	d420	d212	d21
Net Income	② 6,493	8,508	12,221	9,550	8,494	7,563	① 6,920
Cash Flow	19,116	19,011	21,417	17,959	14,931	12,141	10,959
Average Shs. Outstg.	13,113	13,094	13,056	13,056	12,934	12,016	11,600
BALANCE SHEET (IN THOUSANDS):							
Cash & Cash Equivalents	199	43	1,224	3,004	5,265	8,559	19,183
Total Current Assets	21,375	21,163	16,544	15,554	16,274	17,092	26,822
Net Property	125,881	102,860	95,671	90,034	81,093	73,354	40,304
Total Assets	218,002	155,025	148,448	142,400	143,251	123,964	98,976
Total Current Liabilities	19,096	15,366	13,090	11,596	10,575	9,683	7,203
Long-Term Obligations	37,685	19,774	24,606	24,000	20,000	20,067	20,114
Net Stockholders' Equity	116,184	93,410	90,456	86,002	89,242	75,577	52,981
Net Working Capital	2,280	5,797	3,455	3,958	5,699	7,409	19,618
Year-end Shs. Outstg.	13,060	13,017	12,987	12,980	12,983	12,677	11,486
STATISTICAL RECORD:							
Operating Profit Margin %	18.3	33.9	32.9	30.9	32.5	38.9	40.9
Net Profit Margin %	8.8	12.8	20.7	19.1	19.3	23.2	25.2
Return on Equity %	5.6	9.1	13.5	11.1	9.5	10.0	13.1
Return on Assets %	3.0	5.5	8.2	6.7	5.9	6.1	7.0
Debt/Total Assets %	17.3	12.8	16.6	16.9	14.0	16.2	20.3
Price Range	38-19 7/8	27 1/2-19 1/2	24 3/4-16 5/8	24-17 1/4	21 1/2-17	26 1/2-17 1/4	...
P/E Ratio	76.0-39.7	42.3-30.0	26.3-17.7	31.2-22.4	31.2-24.6	40.8-26.5	...
Average Yield %	1.6	1.9	2.0	1.9	2.0	1.7	...

Statistics are as originally reported. ① Bef. acctg. change credit $256,300 ② Incl. gain $8.3 mill.

OFFICERS:
J. S. Quarforth, Chmn., C.E.O.
C. A. Rosberg, Pres., C.O.O.

INVESTOR CONTACT: Shareholder Services, (888) 221-4239

PRINCIPAL OFFICE: 401 Spring Lane, Ste. 300, Waynesboro, VA 22980

TELEPHONE NUMBER: (540) 946-3500
FAX: (540) 946-3599
WEB: www.cfw.com or www.intelos.com

NO. OF EMPLOYEES: 984

SHAREHOLDERS: 2,977

ANNUAL MEETING: In Apr.

INCORPORATED: VA, Jan., 1988

INSTITUTIONAL HOLDINGS:
No. of Institutions: 44
Shares Held: 3,467,803
% Held: 26.6

INDUSTRY: Telephone communications, exc. radio (SIC: 4813)

TRANSFER AGENT(S): First Union National Bank of NC, Charlotte, NC

NYSE SYMBOL CHG
Rec. Pr. 32 3/16 (5/31/00)

CH ENERGY GROUP, INC.

YIELD 6.7%
P/E RATIO 11.3

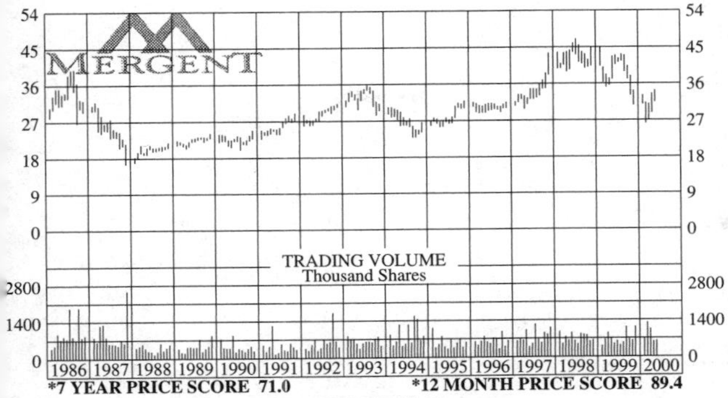

*7 YEAR PRICE SCORE 71.0 *12 MONTH PRICE SCORE 89.4

*NYSE COMPOSITE INDEX=100

INTERIM EARNINGS (Per Share):

Qtr.	Mar.	June	Sept.	Dec.
1995	1.06	0.55	0.70	0.43
1996	1.20	0.58	0.73	0.48
1997	1.18	0.55	0.72	0.52
1998	1.06	0.54	0.77	0.52
1999	1.09	0.51	0.77	0.51

INTERIM DIVIDENDS (Per Share):

Amt.	Decl.	Ex.	Rec.	Pay.
0.54Q	12/17/99	1/06/00	1/10/00	2/01/00
0.54Q	3/24/00	4/06/00	4/10/00	5/01/00

Indicated div.: $2.16 (Div. Reinv. Plan)

CAPITALIZATION (12/31/99):

	($000)	(%)
Long-Term Debt	335,451	33.2
Deferred Income Tax	199,241	19.7
Preferred Stock	56,030	5.5
Common & Surplus	420,891	41.6
Total	1,011,613	100.0

DIVIDEND ACHIEVER STATUS:
Rank: 317 10-Year Growth Rate: 2.07%
Total Years of Dividend Growth: 11

RECENT DEVELOPMENTS: For the year ended 12/31/99, net income slipped 1.5% to $48.6 million compared with $49.3 million in 1998. The decline in earnings was attributed to an increase in the costs of operations as well as higher depreciation and maintenance expenses. Total operating revenues were $521.9 million, up 3.7% from $503.5 million in the prior year. Operating income decreased slightly to $70.6 million versus $71.3 million the year before. Electric sales grew 4.0%, while sales of firm natural gas increased 8.0% from a year earlier.

PROSPECTS: Going forward, the Company plans to boost earnings growth 6.0% by 2004 through increasing its market share and customer base. CNG expects to earn a rate of return of 10.6% in the electric division and 10.0% in the gas division. The electric division should contribute about $63.8 million to offset stranded costs by year-end. In addition, CHG plans to sell the Danskammer and Roseton electric generating plants by auction during 2000. The proceeds from these sales should be realized by early 2001.

BUSINESS

CH ENERGY GROUP, INC. (formerly Central Hudson Gas & Electric Corp.) became the holding company of Central Hudson Gas & Electric Corporation and Central Hudson Energy Services, Inc. on 12/15/99. CHG generates, purchases, and distributes electricity, and purchases and distributes gas to communities along the Hudson River. The service area, serving a population of approximately 625,000 in a 2,600 square-mile area, extends from just above New York City to below Albany. Electric service is available throughout the territory, and natural gas is provided in the following cities: Poughkeepsie, Beacon, Newburgh, Kingston and the Village of Catskill. The Company's territory reflects a diversified economy, including manufacturing industries, research firms, farms, governmental agencies, public and private institutions, resorts, and wholesale and retail trade operations.

REVENUES

(12/31/99)	($000)	(%)
Electric	427,809	82.0
Gas	94,131	18.0
Total	521,940	100.0

ANNUAL FINANCIAL DATA

	12/31/99	12/31/98	12/31/97	12/31/96	12/31/95	12/31/94	12/31/93
Earnings Per Share	**2.88**	**2.90**	**2.97**	**2.99**	**2.74**	**2.68**	**2.68**
Cash Flow Per Share	**5.92**	**5.77**	**5.75**	**5.67**	**5.35**	**5.29**	**5.30**
Tang. Book Val. Per Share	**24.96**	**28.00**	**27.61**	**26.90**	**25.96**	**25.34**	**24.65**
Dividends Per Share	**2.16**	**2.15**	**2.13**	**2.11**	**2.09**	**2.07**	**2.03**
Dividend Payout %	**75.0**	**74.1**	**72.0**	**70.6**	**76.3**	**77.2**	**75.7**
INCOME STATEMENT (IN MILLIONS):							
Total Revenues	521.9	503.5	520.3	514.0	512.2	515.7	517.4
Costs & Expenses	285.8	356.3	374.3	362.1	366.5	365.2	364.4
Depreciation & Amort.	51.2	49.0	48.3	47.1	45.4	44.6	43.9
Maintenance Exp.	28.2	26.9	27.6	28.9	29.4	32.7	34.5
Operating Income	70.9	71.3	70.1	75.8	70.9	73.1	74.6
Net Interest Inc./(Exp.)	d29.6	d27.4	d26.4	d26.7	d28.4	d30.6	d31.7
Income Taxes	0.3	cr1.1	cr3.0	cr1.6	cr0.4	cr1.2	cr1.4
Net Income	48.6	52.5	55.1	56.1	52.7	50.9	50.4
Cash Flow	99.8	98.3	100.2	99.5	93.0	90.4	88.7
Average Shs. Outstg. (000)	16,862	17,034	17,435	17,549	17,380	17,102	16,725
BALANCE SHEET (IN MILLIONS):							
Gross Property	1,598.7	1,561.0	1,526.2	1,490.4	1,454.1	1,416.8	1,363.0
Accumulated Depreciation	677.3	632.8	593.4	550.7	517.0	485.8	448.2
Net Property	921.4	928.2	932.8	939.6	937.1	931.1	914.9
Total Assets	1,259.4	1,316.0	1,252.1	1,249.1	1,250.1	1,309.4	1,328.2
Long-Term Obligations	335.5	356.9	361.8	362.0	389.2	389.4	391.8
Net Stockholders' Equity	476.9	528.2	533.1	527.7	510.3	517.8	498.9
Year-end Shs. Outstg. (000)	16,862	16,862	17,285	17,555	17,496	17,238	16,953
STATISTICAL RECORD:							
Operating Profit Margin %	13.6	14.2	13.5	14.8	13.8	14.2	14.4
Net Profit Margin %	9.3	10.4	10.6	10.9	10.3	9.9	9.7
Net Inc./Net Property %	5.3	5.7	5.9	6.0	5.6	5.5	5.5
Net Inc./Tot. Capital %	4.8	4.8	5.0	5.2	4.8	4.4	4.5
Return on Equity %	10.2	9.9	10.3	10.6	10.3	9.8	10.1
Accum. Depr./Gross Prop. %	42.4	40.5	38.9	37.0	35.6	34.3	32.9
Price Range	45-30 9/16	47 1/16-38 7/8	43 9/16-29 3/4	31 1/2-28 3/4	31 7/8-25 3/8	30 3/8-22 7/8	35 3/4-28 3/8
P/E Ratio	15.6-10.6	16.2-13.4	14.7-10.0	10.5-9.6	11.6-9.3	11.3-8.5	13.3-10.6
Average Yield %	5.7	5.0	5.8	7.0	7.3	7.8	6.3

Statistics are as originally reported.

OFFICERS:
P. J. Ganci, Chmn.
C. E. Meyer, Pres., C.O.O.
S. V. Lant, C.F.O., Treas.

INVESTOR CONTACT: Investor Relations, (914) 486-5204

PRINCIPAL OFFICE: 284 South Avenue, Poughkeepsie, NY 12601-4879

TELEPHONE NUMBER: (914) 452-2000
FAX: (914) 486-5782
WEB: www.cenhud.com

NO. OF EMPLOYEES: 1,107

SHAREHOLDERS: 20,472

ANNUAL MEETING: In Apr.

INCORPORATED: NY, Dec., 1926

INSTITUTIONAL HOLDINGS:
No. of Institutions: 104
Shares Held: 6,571,341
% Held: 39.0

INDUSTRY: Electric and other services combined (SIC: 4931)

TRANSFER AGENT(S): First Chicago Trust Company of New York, Jersey City, NJ

NYSE SYMBOL CF
Rec. Pr. 22 3/4 (5/31/00)

CHARTER ONE FINANCIAL, INC.

YIELD 3.2%
P/E RATIO 14.7

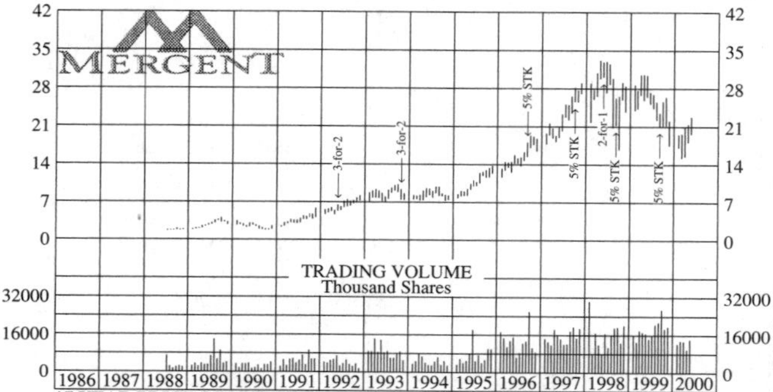

MERGENT
42
35
28
21
14
7
0
3-for-2
3-for-2
5% STK
5% STK
2-for-1
5% STK
5% STK
TRADING VOLUME
Thousand Shares
32000
16000
0
1986 1987 1988 1989 1990 1991 1992 1993 1994 1995 1996 1997 1998 1999 2000

*7 YEAR PRICE SCORE 81.9 *12 MONTH PRICE SCORE 94.1

*NYSE COMPOSITE INDEX=100

INTERIM EARNINGS (Per Share):

Qtr.	Mar.	June	Sept.	Dec.
1995	0.16	0.18	0.18	0.19
1996	0.19	0.22	0.22	0.19
1997	0.38	0.40	0.39	0.04
1998	0.45	0.48	0.48	0.26
1999	0.48	0.49	0.49	0.09

INTERIM DIVIDENDS (Per Share):

Amt.	Decl.	Ex.	Rec.	Pay.
0.16Q	7/21/99	8/04/99	8/06/99	8/20/99
5% STK	7/21/99	9/10/99	9/14/99	9/30/99
0.16Q	10/20/99	11/04/99	11/08/99	11/22/99
0.16Q	1/24/00	2/03/00	2/07/00	2/22/00
0.18Q	4/26/00	5/08/00	5/10/00	5/22/00

Indicated div.: $0.72 (Div. Reinv. Plan)

CAPITALIZATION (12/31/99):

	($000)	(%)
Total Deposits	19,073,975	62.1
Long-Term Debt	9,226,150	30.1
Common & Surplus	2,397,700	7.8
Total	30,697,825	100.0

DIVIDEND ACHIEVER STATUS:
Rank: 20 10-Year Growth Rate: 21.15%
Total Years of Dividend Growth: 11

RECENT DEVELOPMENTS: For the year ended 12/31/99, CF reported income of $335.5 million, before an extraordinary loss of $1.6 million, versus income of $305.7 million, before an extraordinary loss of $61.7 million, the previous year. Net interest income totaled $934.1 million, an increase of 5.4% from $886.2 million in the prior year. Net interest income was positively affected by reduced interest expense. Provision for loan and lease losses grew 12.5% to $35.2 million from $31.3 million a year earlier. Other income fell 15.4% to $230.6 million from $272.6 million in 1998 due to CF's commitment to sell seasoned, fixed-rate mortgage-backed securities, partially offset by increases in retail banking income and income from the Company's Bank Owned Life Insurance program. Total administrative expenses amounted to $633.3 million in 1999 compared with $665.3 million in the prior year.

BUSINESS

CHARTER ONE FINANCIAL, INC. is a bank holding company whose principal line of business is consumer banking, which includes retail banking, mortgage banking and other related financial services. With nearly $31.46 billion in total assets as of 12/31/99, Charter One is one of the 30 largest bank holding companies in the country. The Company currently has 417 branch locations in Ohio, Michigan, Illinois, western and upstate New York, Vermont and Massachusetts. Additionally, Charter One Mortgage Corp., the Company's mortgage banking subsidiary, operates 36 loan production offices across 13 states, and Charter One Auto Finance Corp., the Company's indirect auto finance subsidiary, generates loans in 10 states. On 11/30/98, the Company acquired AUBANK Financial Corporation, and in conjunction with the acquisition, converted from a unitary savings institution to a bank holding company. On 10/16/98, the Company acquired CS Financial, a privately-owned thrift holding company headquartered in Cleveland, Ohio. On 10/1/99, the Company completed the acquisition of St. Paul Bancorp, Inc., a savings and loan holding company. On 11/5/99, the Company completed the acquisition of 14 Vermont National Bank offices from Chittenden Corporation.

ANNUAL FINANCIAL DATA

	12/31/99	12/31/98	12/31/97	12/31/96	12/31/95	12/31/94	12/31/93
Earnings Per Share	[5] 1.53	[1] 1.54	[2] 1.06	1.21	[3] 0.32	[4] 1.26	1.15
Tang. Book Val. Per Share	10.56	9.88	8.98	8.44	8.00	7.09	7.09
Dividends Per Share	0.60	0.50	0.43	0.37	0.30	0.24	0.17
Dividend Payout %	39.2	32.4	40.6	30.6	93.8	19.0	14.8
INCOME STATEMENT (IN MILLIONS):							
Total Interest Income	2,128.5	1,760.4	1,377.7	1,004.5	1,087.4	395.6	358.4
Total Interest Expense	1,194.4	1,031.3	850.7	621.1	769.6	217.5	188.1
Net Interest Income	934.1	729.1	527.0	383.4	317.8	178.1	170.3
Provision for Loan Losses	35.2	29.5	40.9	4.0	1.0	2.8	5.1
Non-Interest Income	230.6	211.6	110.8	57.1	d47.8	28.1	26.2
Non-Interest Expense	633.3	492.5	373.9	244.0	215.7	102.1	97.9
Income Before Taxes	496.1	418.7	223.0	192.5	53.2	101.3	93.4
Net Income	[5] 335.5	[1] 277.0	[2] 151.1	127.7	[3] 34.0	[4] 67.6	61.4
Average Shs. Outstg. (000)	217,846	179,275	142,785	105,655	106,175	53,702	53,274
BALANCE SHEET (IN MILLIONS):							
Cash & Due from Banks	689.1	334.1	214.7	152.3	163.1	126.8	101.8
Securities Avail. for Sale	4,193.1	2,299.2	1,070.2	265.4	1,843.0	99.4	1.2
Total Loans & Leases	22,545.8	17,688.0	12,360.1	8,295.0	6,842.9	3,635.6	3,297.0
Allowance for Credit Losses	623.2	185.3	...	194.6	168.6	93.1	77.2
Net Loans & Leases	21,922.6	17,502.7	12,360.1	8,100.3	6,674.3	3,542.5	3,219.8
Total Assets	31,464.8	24,467.3	19,760.3	13,904.6	13,578.9	5,756.7	4,460.5
Total Deposits	19,074.0	15,165.1	10,219.2	7,841.2	7,012.5	4,368.2	4,179.4
Long-Term Obligations	9,226.2	6,186.1	5,370.5	3,194.3	3,163.1	1,318.7	604.2
Total Liabilities	29,421.4	22,592.1	18,383.4	12,975.9	12,734.5	5,761.1	4,845.8
Net Stockholders' Equity	2,397.7	1,875.1	1,376.9	928.7	844.4	369.1	369.6
Year-end Shs. Outstg. (000)	209,258	173,669	143,232	102,407	104,228	52,033	52,142
STATISTICAL RECORD:							
Return on Equity %	14.0	14.8	11.0	13.8	4.0	18.3	16.6
Return on Assets %	1.1	1.1	0.8	0.9	0.3	1.2	1.4
Equity/Assets %	7.6	7.7	7.0	6.7	6.2	6.4	8.3
Non-Int. Exp./Tot. Inc. %	54.4	52.4	58.6	55.4	79.9	49.5	49.8
Price Range	30 5/8-17 1/2	33 1/4-16 13/16	29-17 3/4	19 5/16-11 5/8	13 3/4-7 3/4	9 7/8-7 5/16	10 5/16-6
P/E Ratio	20.0-11.4	21.5-10.9	27.5-16.8	16.0-9.6	42.6-24.1	7.8-5.8	8.9-6.1
Average Yield %	2.5	2.0	1.8	2.4	2.9	2.8	2.0

Statistics are as originally reported. Adj. for stk. splits: 5% stk. div., 9/99; 9/98; 2-for-1, 5/98; 5% stk. div., 10/97; 5% stk. div., 9/96; 3-for-2, 11/93 [1] Incl. non-recurr. chrg. $55.7 mill. but bef. extraord. chrg. $61.7 mill. [2] Incl. non-recurr. chrg. $60.6 mill. but bef. extraord. chrg. $2.7 mill. [3] Incl. non-recurr. chrg. $37.5 mill. [4] Bef. extraord. credit $7.0 mill. [5] Excl. extraord. loss $1.6 mill.

OFFICERS:
C. J. Koch, Chmn., Pres., C.E.O.
H. G. Chorbajian, Vice-Chmn.
R. W. Neu, Exec. V.P., C.F.O.

INVESTOR CONTACT: Ellen L. Batkie, Sr. V.P., (800) 262-6301

PRINCIPAL OFFICE: 1215 Superior Avenue, Cleveland, OH 44114

TELEPHONE NUMBER: (216) 566-5300
FAX: (216) 566-1465
WEB: www.charterone.com

NO. OF EMPLOYEES: 7,055

SHAREHOLDERS: 21,379

ANNUAL MEETING: In Apr.

INCORPORATED: DE, 1987

INSTITUTIONAL HOLDINGS:
No. of Institutions: 241
Shares Held: 117,446,259
% Held: 55.4

INDUSTRY: Federal savings institutions (SIC: 6035)

TRANSFER AGENT(S): BankBoston, NA, Boston, MA

NYSE SYMBOL CHV
Rec. Pr. 92 7/16 (5/31/00)

CHEVRON CORPORATION

YIELD 2.8%
P/E RATIO 29.4

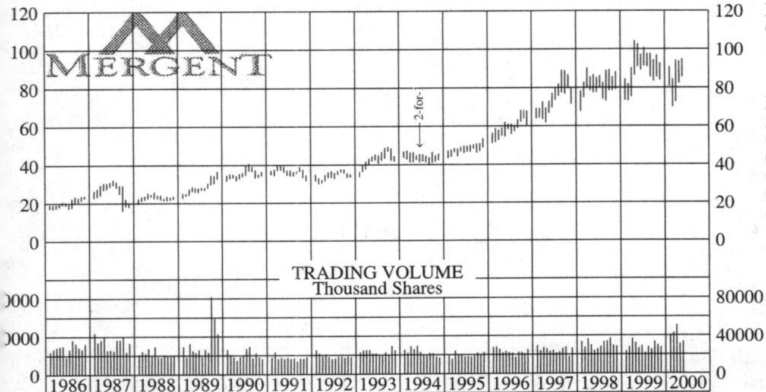

*7 YEAR PRICE SCORE 90.1 *12 MONTH PRICE SCORE 99.6

*NYSE COMPOSITE INDEX=100

INTERIM EARNINGS (Per Share):

Qtr.	Mar.	June	Sept.	Dec.
1997	1.27	1.26	1.11	1.33
1998	0.76	0.88	0.70	0.66
1999	0.50	0.53	0.88	1.23

INTERIM DIVIDENDS (Per Share):

Amt.	Decl.	Ex.	Rec.	Pay.
0.61Q	4/28/99	5/18/99	5/20/99	6/10/99
0.61Q	7/28/99	8/18/99	8/20/99	9/10/99
0.65Q	10/27/99	11/17/99	11/19/99	12/10/99
0.65Q	1/26/00	2/16/00	2/18/00	3/10/00
0.65Q	4/26/00	5/17/00	5/19/00	6/12/00

Indicated div.: $2.60 (Div. Reinv. Plan)

CAPITALIZATION (12/31/99):

	($000)	(%)
Long-Term Debt	5,174,000	18.3
Capital Lease Obligations	311,000	1.1
Deferred Income Tax	5,010,000	17.7
Common & Surplus	17,749,000	62.8
Total	28,244,000	100.0

DIVIDEND ACHIEVER STATUS:
Rank: 245 10-Year Growth Rate: 5.88%
Total Years of Dividend Growth: 12

RECENT DEVELOPMENTS: For the year ended 12/31/99, net income advanced 54.6% to $2.07 billion from $1.34 billion in the previous year. Results for 1999 and 1998 included special charges of $216.0 million and $606.0 million, respectively. Earnings benefited from a rebound in crude oil prices, higher crude oil and natural gas production and lower unit operating expenses. Total revenues increased 19.7% to $36.59 billion from $30.56 billion a year earlier.

PROSPECTS: CHV and Phillips Petroleum signed a letter of intent and exclusivity agreement to combine their worldwide chemicals operations into a 50/50 joint venture with more than $6.00 billion in assets. The joint venture plans to reduce annual costs by $150.0 million by tapping efficiencies in purchasing and logistics and enhancing organizational efficiency. The transaction is expected to close by mid-year.

BUSINESS

CHEVRON CORPORATION manages its investments in, and provides administrative, financial and management support for its U.S. and foreign affiliates that engage in petroleum, chemical and coal mining operations. CHV operates in the U.S and 100 other countries. Petroleum operations include the exploring for, developing and producing of crude oil and natural gas; refining crude oil into finished petroleum products; marketing crude oil, natural gas and the many products derived from petroleum; and transporting crude oil, natural gas and petroleum products by pipelines and marine vessels, motor equipment and rail car. Chemical operations include the development and marketing of petrochemicals, plastics for industrial uses and fuel and lube oil additives. In 1999, net proved developed reserves were: crude oil, condensate and natural gas liquids, 4,784 million barrels; and natural gas, 9,056 billion cubic feet.

ANNUAL FINANCIAL DATA

	12/31/99	12/31/98	12/31/97	12/31/96	12/31/95	12/31/94	12/31/93
Earnings Per Share	**[2] 3.14**	**2.04**	**4.95**	**[1] 3.99**	**[1] 1.43**	**2.60**	**[1] 1.95**
Cash Flow Per Share	**7.48**	**5.47**	**9.48**	**8.56**	**7.46**	**7.00**	**6.40**
Tang. Book Val. Per Share	**27.04**	**25.81**	**26.64**	**23.82**	**22.02**	**22.39**	**21.47**
Dividends Per Share	**2.48**	**2.44**	**2.28**	**2.08**	**1.93**	**1.85**	**1.75**
Dividend Payout %	**79.0**	**119.6**	**46.1**	**52.1**	**134.6**	**71.2**	**90.0**
INCOME STATEMENT (IN MILLIONS):							
Total Revenues	36,586.0	30,557.0	41,950.0	43,893.0	37,082.0	35,854.0	37,082.0
Costs & Expenses	29,600.0	25,998.0	33,836.0	36,573.0	31,511.0	30,274.0	31,887.0
Depreciation & Amort.	2,866.0	2,320.0	2,300.0	2,216.0	3,381.0	2,431.0	2,452.0
Operating Income	3,594.0	2,011.0	5,126.0	4,337.0	1,637.0	2,709.0	2,303.0
Net Interest Inc./(Exp.)	d472.0	d405.0	d312.0	d364.0	d401.0	d346.0	d317.0
Income Before Income Taxes	3,648.0	1,834.0	5,502.0	4,740.0	1,789.0	2,803.0	2,426.0
Income Taxes	1,578.0	495.0	2,246.0	2,133.0	859.0	1,110.0	1,161.0
Equity Earnings/Minority Int.	526.0	228.0	688.0	767.0	553.0	440.0	440.0
Net Income	[2] 2,070.0	1,339.0	3,256.0	[1] 2,607.0	[1] 930.0	1,693.0	[1] 1,265.0
Cash Flow	4,936.0	3,659.0	5,556.0	4,823.0	4,311.0	4,124.0	3,717.0
Average Shs. Outstg. (000)	659,500	657,100	658,400	653,000	652,000	652,000	650,000
BALANCE SHEET (IN MILLIONS):							
Cash & Cash Equivalents	2,032.0	1,413.0	1,670.0	1,637.0	1,394.0	1,306.0	2,016.0
Total Current Assets	8,297.0	6,297.0	7,006.0	7,942.0	7,867.0	7,591.0	8,682.0
Net Property	25,317.0	23,729.0	22,671.0	21,496.0	21,696.0	22,173.0	21,865.0
Total Assets	40,668.0	36,540.0	35,473.0	34,854.0	34,330.0	34,407.0	34,736.0
Total Current Liabilities	8,889.0	7,166.0	6,946.0	8,907.0	9,445.0	9,392.0	10,606.0
Long-Term Obligations	5,485.0	4,393.0	4,431.0	3,988.0	4,521.0	4,128.0	4,082.0
Net Stockholders' Equity	17,749.0	17,034.0	17,472.0	15,623.0	14,355.0	14,596.0	13,997.0
Net Working Capital	d592.0	d869.0	60.0	d965.0	d1,578.0	d1,801.0	d1,924.0
Year-end Shs. Outstg. (000)	656,346	660,000	655,900	656,000	652,000	652,000	652,000
STATISTICAL RECORD:							
Operating Profit Margin %	9.7	7.3	13.9	11.6	5.9	8.8	7.4
Net Profit Margin %	5.7	4.4	7.8	5.9	2.5	4.7	3.4
Return on Equity %	11.7	7.9	18.6	16.7	6.5	11.6	9.0
Return on Assets %	5.1	3.7	9.2	7.5	2.7	4.9	3.6
Debt/Total Assets %	13.5	12.0	12.5	11.4	13.2	12.0	11.8
Price Range	104 7/16-73 1/8	90 3/16-67 3/4	89 3/16-61 3/4	68 3/8-51	53 5/8-43 3/8	47 5/16-39 7/8	49 3/8-33 11/16
P/E Ratio	33.3-23.3	44.2-33.2	18.0-12.5	17.1-12.8	37.5-30.3	18.2-15.3	25.4-17.3
Average Yield %	2.8	3.1	3.0	3.5	4.0	4.2	4.2

Statistics are as originally reported. Adj. for 2-for-1 stk. split 5/94 [1] Incls. nonrecurr. chrg. 12/31/96: $44.0 mill.; chrgs. totaling 12/31/95: $1.03 bill.; chrg. 12/31/93: $552.0 mill. [2] Incls. special chrgs. of $216.0 mill.

OFFICERS:
D. J. O'Reilly, Chmn., C.E.O.
R. H. Matzke, Vice-Chmn.
J. N. Sullivan, Vice-Chmn.
M. R. Klitten, V.P., C.F.O.

INVESTOR CONTACT: Peter Trueblood, Manager, Investor Relations, (415) 894-5690

PRINCIPAL OFFICE: 575 Market Street, San Francisco, CA 94105

TELEPHONE NUMBER: (415) 894-7700
FAX: (415) 894-6017
WEB: www.chevron.com

NO. OF EMPLOYEES: 36,940 (avg.)

SHAREHOLDERS: 116,000 (approx.)

ANNUAL MEETING: In April

INCORPORATED: DE, Jan., 1926

INSTITUTIONAL HOLDINGS:
No. of Institutions: 876
Shares Held: 338,646,278
% Held: 51.6

INDUSTRY: Petroleum refining (SIC: 2911)

TRANSFER AGENT(S): ChaseMellon Shareholder Services, Ridgefield Park, NJ

NYSE SYMBOL CB
Rec. Pr. 69⅞ (5/31/00)

CHUBB CORPORATION (THE)

YIELD 1.9%
P/E RATIO 18.9

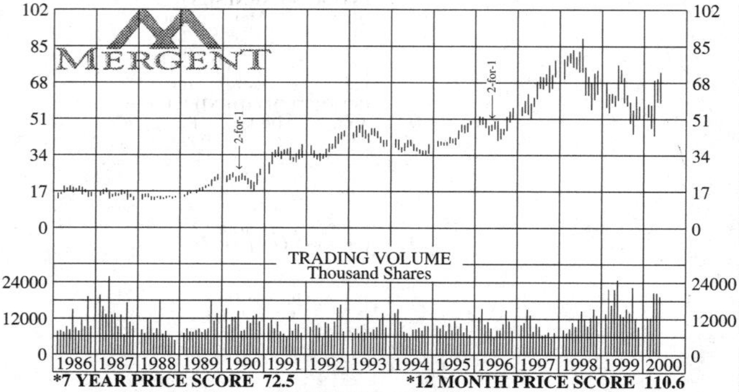

MERGENT
2-for-1
2-for-1
TRADING VOLUME
Thousand Shares

*7 YEAR PRICE SCORE 72.5 *12 MONTH PRICE SCORE 110.6
*NYSE COMPOSITE INDEX=100

INTERIM EARNINGS (Per Share):

Qtr.	Mar.	June	Sept.	Dec.
1995	0.83	1.05	0.97	1.09
1996	0.79	0.93	0.87	0.16
1997	1.09	1.09	1.12	1.13
1998	1.12	1.08	1.04	0.95
1999	1.14	1.18	0.44	0.93

INTERIM DIVIDENDS (Per Share):

Amt.	Decl.	Ex.	Rec.	Pay.
0.003RR	3/19/99	3/29/99	3/31/99	4/13/99
0.32Q	6/11/99	6/23/99	6/25/99	7/13/99
0.32Q	9/10/99	9/22/99	9/24/99	10/12/99
0.32Q	12/10/99	12/22/99	12/27/99	1/11/00
0.33Q	3/03/00	3/15/00	3/17/00	4/04/00

Indicated div.: $1.32 (Div. Reinv. Plan)

CAPITALIZATION (12/31/99):

	($000)	(%)
Long-Term Debt	759,200	10.8
Common & Surplus	6,271,800	89.2
Total	7,031,000	100.0

DIVIDEND ACHIEVER STATUS:
Rank: 193 10-Year Growth Rate: 8.34%
Total Years of Dividend Growth: 35

RECENT DEVELOPMENTS: For the year ended 12/31/99, net income declined 12.2% to $621.1 million from $707.0 million in the previous year. Results included after-tax realized investment gains of $55.8 million and $92.2 million in 1999 and 1998, respectively. Results for 1998 included restructuring charges of $40.0 million. Total revenues improved 6.0% to $6.73 billion from $6.35 billion a year earlier. Net premiums written improved 3.6% to $5.70 billion from $5.50 billion in the prior year.

PROSPECTS: Near-term results for the personal insurance segment should continue to benefit from adequate pricing and strong underwriting. However, revenues for the standard commercial insurance segment may continue to be negatively affected by losses from non-renewed accounts and underpriced business. Going forward, the Company will continue to focus on improving its pricing program in an attempt to earn higher rates while eliminating unprofitable non-renewed business.

BUSINESS

THE CHUBB CORPORATION offers commercial and personal property and casualty insurance. CB also maintains operations in life and health insurance, and real estate development. Chubb's clients are located in North America, South America, Europe, and the Pacific Rim. The Corporation operates more than 120 offices throughout North America, Europe, South America and the Pacific Rim. For the year ended 12/31/99, property and casualty accounted for 96% of total revenues; real estate, 2%; and other, 2%. In 1999, the combined loss and expense ratio after policyholders' dividends was 102.8%.

ANNUAL FINANCIAL DATA

	12/31/99	12/31/98	12/31/97	12/31/96	12/31/95	12/31/94	12/31/93
Earnings Per Share	**3.66**	**4.19**	**4.39**	**2 2.75**	**3.93**	**2.98**	**1 1.96**
Tang. Book Val. Per Share	**32.85**	**34.78**	**32.11**	**31.24**	**30.14**	**24.46**	**23.92**
Dividends Per Share	**1.27**	**1.22**	**1.14**	**1.05**	**0.96**	**0.91**	**0.84**
Dividend Payout %	**34.8**	**29.1**	**26.0**	**38.4**	**24.6**	**30.4**	**43.2**
INCOME STATEMENT (IN MILLIONS):							
Total Premium Income	5,652.0	5,303.8	5,157.4	4,569.3	4,770.1	4,612.6	4,306.1
Other Income	1,077.6	1,046.0	1,506.6	1,111.3	1,319.1	1,097.0	1,193.6
Total Revenues	6,729.6	6,349.8	6,664.0	5,680.5	6,089.2	5,709.5	5,499.7
Policyholder Benefits	3,942.0	3,493.7	3,307.0	3,010.8	3,219.2	3,271.6	3,548.5
Income Before Income Taxes	710.1	849.7	974.1	546.9	900.1	639.4	344.5
Income Taxes	89.0	142.7	204.6	60.7	203.4	110.9	0.3
Net Income	621.1	707.0	769.5	2 486.2	696.6	528.5	1 344.2
Average Shs. Outstg. (000)	169,800	168,600	176,200	174,402	179,884	180,900	181,098
BALANCE SHEET (IN MILLIONS):							
Cash & Cash Equivalents	1,223.3	352.5	736.6	280.6	496.4	816.5	535.9
Premiums Due	1,234.7	1,199.3	1,144.4	984.9	872.9	787.2	720.1
Invst. Assets: Fixed-term	14,519.1	13,318.9	12,453.4	11,158.8	12,602.8	10,722.7	10,186.5
Invst. Assets: Equities	769.2	1,092.2	871.1	646.3	587.8	642.2	930.0
Invst. Assets: Loans	...	...	...	...	212.3	202.7	194.3
Invst. Assets: Total	17,188.3	15,501.3	14,839.6	13,685.0	15,630.0	14,118.7	13,551.1
Total Assets	23,537.0	20,746.0	19,615.6	19,938.9	22,996.5	20,723.1	19,436.9
Long-Term Obligations	759.2	607.5	398.6	1,070.5	1,156.0	1,285.6	1,273.8
Net Stockholders' Equity	6,271.8	5,644.1	5,657.1	5,462.9	5,262.7	4,247.0	4,196.1
Year-end Shs. Outstg. (000)	175,490	162,267	176,200	174,861	174,602	173,642	175,418
STATISTICAL RECORD:							
Return on Revenues %	9.2	11.1	11.5	8.6	11.4	9.3	6.3
Return on Equity %	9.9	12.5	13.6	8.9	13.2	12.4	8.2
Return on Assets %	2.6	3.4	3.9	2.4	3.0	2.6	1.8
Price Range	76⅜-44	88 13/16-55⅜	78½-51⅛	56¼-40⅞	50 5/16-38 1/16	41 9/16-34 5/16	48 3/16-38
P/E Ratio	20.9-12.0	21.2-13.2	17.9-11.6	20.5-14.9	12.8-9.7	14.0-11.5	24.6-19.4
Average Yield %	2.1	1.7	1.8	2.2	2.2	2.4	2.0

Statistics are as originally reported. Adj. for stk. split: 2-for-1, 5/96 1 Bef. acctg. change chrg. $20.0 mill. 2 Bef. disc. oper. gain $26.5 mill.

OFFICERS:
D. R. O'Hare, Chmn., C.E.O.
J. J. Degnan, Pres.
H. G. Gulick, V.P., Sec.
J. L. Bober, Sr. V.P., Gen. Couns.

INVESTOR CONTACT: Mary Jane Murphy, Asst. Sec., (908) 903-3579

PRINCIPAL OFFICE: 15 Mountain View Rd., Warren, NJ 07061-1615

TELEPHONE NUMBER: (908) 903-2000
FAX: (908) 903-2003
WEB: www.chubb.com

NO. OF EMPLOYEES: 11,900 (approx.)

SHAREHOLDERS: 7,225 (approx.)

ANNUAL MEETING: In Apr.

INCORPORATED: NJ, Jun., 1967

INSTITUTIONAL HOLDINGS:
No. of Institutions: 432
Shares Held: 119,034,027
% Held: 67.7

INDUSTRY: Fire, marine, and casualty insurance (SIC: 6331)

TRANSFER AGENT(S): First Chicago Trust Company of New York, Jersey City, NJ

NASDAQ SYMBOL CINF
Rec. Pr. 40⅛ (5/31/00)

CINCINNATI FINANCIAL CORPORATION

YIELD 1.9%
P/E RATIO 26.4

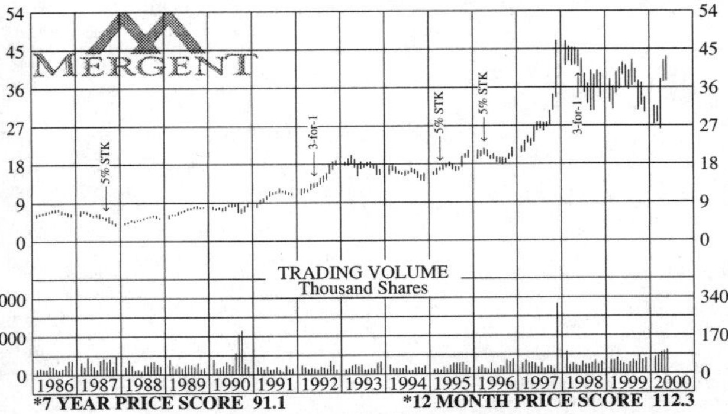

MERGENT
5% STK
3-for-1
5% STK
5% STK
3-for-1
TRADING VOLUME
Thousand Shares
1986 1987 1988 1989 1990 1991 1992 1993 1994 1995 1996 1997 1998 1999 2000

*7 YEAR PRICE SCORE 91.1 *12 MONTH PRICE SCORE 112.3

*NYSE COMPOSITE INDEX=100

INTERIM EARNINGS (Per Share):

Qtr.	Mar.	June	Sept.	Dec.
1996	0.35	0.32	0.27	0.37
1997	0.43	0.44	0.46	0.43
1998	0.49	0.35	0.31	0.27
1999	0.38	0.52	0.34	0.28

INTERIM DIVIDENDS (Per Share):

Amt.	Decl.	Ex.	Rec.	Pay.
0.17Q	5/21/99	6/16/99	6/18/99	7/15/99
0.17Q	8/20/99	9/15/99	9/17/99	10/15/99
0.17Q	11/19/99	12/15/99	12/17/99	1/14/00
0.19Q	2/05/00	3/22/00	3/24/00	4/14/00
0.19Q	5/30/00	6/21/00	6/23/00	7/14/00

Indicated div.: $0.76

CAPITALIZATION (12/31/99):

	($000)	(%)
Long-Term Debt	456,373	6.0
Deferred Income Tax	1,719,673	22.6
Common & Surplus	5,421,284	71.4
Total	7,597,330	100.0

DIVIDEND ACHIEVER STATUS:
Rank: 109 10-Year Growth Rate: 12.32%
Total Years of Dividend Growth: 39

RECENT DEVELOPMENTS: For the year ended 12/31/99, net income increased 5.4% to $254.7 million compared with $241.6 million in the previous year. Earnings for 1999 and 1998 included a net capital loss of $400,000 and a net capital gain of $42.5 million, respectively. Revenues were $2.13 billion, an increase of 3.6% from $2.05 billion in the prior year. Net operating income improved 28.1% to $255.1 million from $199.1 million. Net written premiums climbed 7.9% to $1.68 billion from $1.56 billion a year earlier. Net premiums earned advanced 7.4% to $1.66 billion from $1.54 billion the year before. Revenues from investment income rose 5.1% to $386.8 million from $368.0 million in 1998. The slower growth rate reflects reduced cash available for investment, due to costs associated with the Company's new office tower, ongoing technology initiatives and repurchase of CINF stock. Total catastrophe losses fell 60.6% to $36.8 million versus $93.5 million in the previous year. The statutory combined ratio declined to 100.0% from 103.6% in the prior year.

BUSINESS

CINCINNATI FINANCIAL CORPORATION has six subsidiary companies, operating principally in the field of insurance. The Cincinnati Insurance Company, The Cincinnati Indemnity Company and The Cincinnati Casualty Company market property and casualty insurance, the Company's main business. Life, health and accident insurance is marketed by The Cincinnati Life Insurance Company. CFC Investment Company supports the insurance subsidiaries through leasing, and finance activities. Cincinnati Financial Capital Management provides investment management services to institutions, corporations and individuals.

REVENUES

(12/31/99)	($000)	(%)
Commercial lines	1,088,039	51.1
Personal lines	569,238	26.8
Life Insurance	74,673	3.5
Investment operations	386,209	18.1
Corporate & other	10,064	0.5
Total	2,128,223	100.0

ANNUAL FINANCIAL DATA

	12/31/99	12/31/98	12/31/97	12/31/96	12/31/95	12/31/94	12/31/93
Earnings Per Share	**1.52**	**1.41**	**1.77**	**1.31**	**1.33**	**1.18**	[1] **1.19**
Tang. Book Val. Per Share	**33.46**	**33.72**	**28.35**	**18.95**	**15.90**	**11.63**	**11.70**
Dividends Per Share	**0.66**	**0.60**	**0.53**	**0.47**	**0.42**	**0.37**	**0.33**
Dividend Payout %	**43.6**	**42.3**	**30.1**	**36.1**	**31.2**	**31.7**	**27.9**
INCOME STATEMENT (IN MILLIONS):							
Total Premium Income	1,732.0	1,612.7	1,516.4	1,422.9	1,314.1	1,219.0	1,140.8
Net Investment Income	386.8	368.0	348.6	327.3	300.0	262.6	239.4
Other Income	9.5	73.6	77.4	58.5	41.5	30.8	61.9
Total Revenues	2,128.2	2,054.3	1,942.4	1,808.7	1,655.7	1,512.5	1,442.2
Policyholder Benefits	1,254.4	1,221.1	1,054.9	1,087.1	964.2	900.8	832.5
Income Before Income Taxes	321.6	307.1	394.6	282.4	295.2	249.3	267.0
Income Taxes	66.9	65.5	95.2	58.7	67.8	48.1	64.8
Net Income	254.7	241.6	299.4	223.8	227.4	201.2	[1] 202.2
Average Shs. Outstg. (000)	168,615	172,078	170,795	173,349	173,058	172,635	172,206
BALANCE SHEET (IN MILLIONS):							
Cash & Cash Equivalents	339.6	58.6	80.2	59.9	20.0	48.3	48.1
Premiums Due	358.7	332.5	299.4	304.8	285.1	225.3	206.4
Invst. Assets: Fixed-term	2,617.4	2,812.2	2,751.2	2,561.8	2,447.0	1,943.1	1,759.7
Invst. Assets: Equities	7,510.9	7,454.8	5,999.3	3,740.2	3,041.8	2,230.2	2,318.8
Invst. Assets: Total	10,194.2	10,325.0	8,797.1	6,355.0	5,528.6	4,212.2	4,116.8
Total Assets	11,380.2	11,086.5	9,493.4	7,045.5	6,109.3	4,734.3	4,602.3
Long-Term Obligations	456.4	471.5	58.4	79.8	80.0	80.0	80.0
Net Stockholders' Equity	5,421.3	5,620.9	4,717.0	3,162.9	2,658.0	1,940.0	1,947.3
Year-end Shs. Outstg. (000)	162,021	166,681	166,356	166,908	167,130	166,758	166,386
STATISTICAL RECORD:							
Return on Revenues %	12.0	11.8	15.4	12.4	13.7	13.3	14.0
Return on Equity %	4.7	4.3	6.3	7.1	8.6	10.4	10.4
Return on Assets %	2.2	2.2	3.2	3.2	3.7	4.3	4.4
Price Range	42½-30⅛	46 15/16-30½	47 1/16-20 11/16	21 13/16-17¾	21 3/16-15⅜	17⅝-13 15/16	20 3/16-15⅛
P/E Ratio	28.0-19.8	33.3-21.6	26.6-11.7	16.7-13.6	15.9-11.5	14.9-11.8	17.0-12.7
Average Yield %	1.8	1.5	1.6	2.4	2.3	2.4	1.9

Statistics are as originally reported. Adj. for stk. splits: 3-for-1, 5/15/98; 5% div., 4/30/96; 5% div., 4/28/95 [1] Bef. acctg. change credit $13.8 mill. ($0.08/sh.)

OFFICERS:
J. J. Schiff Jr., Jr. Chmn., C.E.O.
K. W. Stecher, Sr. V.P., Sec., Treas.

INVESTOR CONTACT: T.F. Elchynski, C.F.O., (513) 870-2639

PRINCIPAL OFFICE: 6200 S. Gilmore Rd., Fairfield, OH 45014

TELEPHONE NUMBER: (513) 870-2000
FAX: (513) 870-2066
WEB: www.cinfin.com

NO. OF EMPLOYEES: 2,920

SHAREHOLDERS: 11,485 (approx.)

ANNUAL MEETING: In Mar.

INCORPORATED: DE, Sep., 1968

INSTITUTIONAL HOLDINGS:
No. of Institutions: 202
Shares Held: 60,913,390
% Held: 37.1

INDUSTRY: Fire, marine, and casualty insurance (SIC: 6331)

TRANSFER AGENT(S): Cincinnati Financial Corporation, Cincinnati, OH

CINTAS CORPORATION

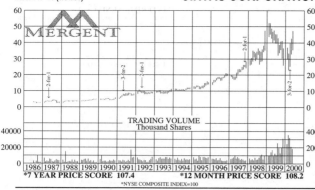

INTERIM EARNINGS (Per Share):

Qtr.	Aug.	Nov.	Feb.	May
1996-97	0.14	0.16	0.16	0.18
1997-98	0.17	0.19	0.18	0.20
1998-99	0.21	0.25	0.23	0.11
1999-00	0.25	0.29	0.29	...

INTERIM DIVIDENDS (Per Share):

Amt.	Decl.	Ex.	Rec.	Pay.
0.22A	1/19/99	2/03/99	2/05/99	3/03/99
0.28A	1/18/00	2/02/00	2/04/00	3/07/00
3-for-2	1/18/00	3/08/00	2/04/00	3/07/00

Indicated div.: $0.28

CAPITALIZATION (5/31/99):

	($000)	(%)
Long-Term Debt	283,581	23.7
Deferred Income Tax	40,717	3.4
Common & Surplus	871,423	72.9
Total	1,195,721	100.0

DIVIDEND ACHIEVER STATUS:

Rank: 13   10-Year Growth Rate: 22.74%
Total Years of Dividend Growth: 17

RECENT DEVELOPMENTS: For the third quarter ended 2/29/00, net income increased 27.0% to $49.1 million compared with $38.6 million in the prior-year quarter. Results reflected increased momentum in the Company's internal growth rate throughout all segments of its business. Total revenues were $473.9 million, up 9.3% from $433.7 million a year earlier. Rental revenues climbed 10.3% to $355.7 million, while other service revenues advanced 6.4% to $118.2 million. Comparisons were made with restated prior year figures to reflect the acquisition of Unitog in March 1999. Recently, the Company extended its marketing partnership with NASCAR through 2002, and will have new marketing and promotional initiatives to support the continued relationship. CTAS will continue to outfit officials in 12 of NASCAR's 13 divisions and is also working with employees at the NASCAR Cafe restaurants, NASCAR Thunder retail stores, NASCAR SpeedParks and NASCAR Silicon Motor Speedway.

BUSINESS

CINTAS CORPORATION designs, manufactures and implements corporate identity uniform programs. Currently, the Company occupies 200 uniform rental locations throughout the United States and Canada. The Company operates processing plants that house administrative, sales and service personnel and the necessary equipment involved in the cleaning of uniforms and bulk items. Branch operations provide administrative, sales and service functions. The Company operates six distribution facilities and has 13 manufacturing plants. The Company also provides dust control and hygiene services as well as first aid and safety products services. In March 1999, CTAS acquired Unitog Company, based in Kansas City, Missouri. In April 1999, the Company acquired Chicago-based Uniforms To You.

REVENUES

(05/31/99)	($000)	(%)
Rentals	1,297,248	74.0
Other Services	454,320	26.0
Total	1,751,568	100.0

ANNUAL FINANCIAL DATA

	5/31/99	5/31/98	5/31/97	5/31/96	5/31/95	5/31/94	5/31/93
Earnings Per Share	☐ 0.82	☐ 0.79	0.64	0.53	0.45	0.37	0.32
Cash Flow Per Share	1.35	1.16	0.97	0.84	0.71	0.62	0.55
Tang. Book Val. Per Share	5.24	4.17	2.83	2.29	1.84	2.21	1.90
Dividends Per Share	0.12	0.10	0.08	0.07	0.06	0.05	0.04
Dividend Payout %	14.6	12.6	13.1	12.5	12.7	12.5	11.3
INCOME STATEMENT (IN THOUSANDS):							
Total Revenues	1,751,568	1,198,307	839,949	730,130	615,098	523,216	452,722
Costs & Expenses	1,380,058	940,164	641,826	558,177	471,234	397,731	343,573
Depreciation & Amort.	90,228	57,237	47,748	43,104	37,706	35,060	32,224
Operating Income	281,282	200,906	150,375	128,849	106,158	90,425	76,925
Net Interest Inc./(Exp.)	d11,291	d4,356	d3,757	d6,619	d5,197	d4,974	d5,622
Income Before Income Taxes	223,994	179,434	146,618	122,230	100,961	85,451	71,303
Income Taxes	85,055	56,577	55,778	47,047	38,218	33,281	26,430
Net Income	☐ 138,939	☐ 122,857	90,840	75,183	62,743	52,170	44,873
Cash Flow	229,167	180,094	138,588	118,287	100,449	87,230	77,097
Average Shs. Outstg.	169,341	155,435	142,893	141,297	140,673	140,118	139,233
BALANCE SHEET (IN THOUSANDS):							
Cash & Cash Equivalents	88,118	100,871	102,876	82,543	45,482	60,782	54,969
Total Current Assets	634,485	508,601	355,975	297,502	241,422	221,453	187,133
Net Property	573,087	367,094	287,446	252,597	227,997	192,503	180,847
Total Assets	1,407,818	1,017,836	761,823	668,762	596,181	501,632	454,165
Total Current Liabilities	212,097	158,991	116,131	102,594	95,012	94,484	65,176
Long-Term Obligations	283,581	180,077	111,457	117,924	120,275	84,184	103,611
Net Stockholders' Equity	871,423	654,492	512,376	429,497	364,344	309,652	264,914
Net Working Capital	422,388	349,610	239,844	194,908	146,410	129,969	121,957
Year-end Shs. Outstg.	166,424	156,917	144,801	141,597	141,015	140,403	139,737
STATISTICAL RECORD:							
Operating Profit Margin %	16.1	16.8	17.9	17.6	17.3	17.3	17.0
Net Profit Margin %	7.9	10.3	10.8	10.3	10.2	10.0	9.9
Return on Equity %	15.9	18.8	17.7	17.5	17.2	16.8	16.9
Return on Assets %	9.9	12.1	11.9	11.2	10.5	10.4	9.9
Debt/Total Assets %	20.1	17.7	14.6	17.6	20.2	16.8	22.8
Price Range	47½-26	28⁵⁄₁₆-17	21³⁄₁₆-13¹⁵⁄₁₆	16-11³⁄₁₆	12¹⁄₁₆-9¹⁵⁄₁₆	11⁵⁄₁₆-8¹⁄₄	10¹¹⁄₁₆-7¹⁵⁄₁₆
P/E Ratio	57.9-31.7	35.7-21.4	33.2-21.8	30.0-20.9	27.0-22.2	30.4-22.1	33.1-24.5
Average Yield %	0.3	0.4	0.4	0.5	0.5	0.5	0.4

Statistics are as originally reported. Adj. for stk. splits: 3-for-2, 3/07/00; 2-for-1, 11/18/97
☐ Incl. non-recurr. chrg. $11.3 mill., 5/99; credit $17.1 mill., 5/98

OFFICERS:
R. T. Farmer, Chmn.
R. J. Kohlhepp, C.E.O.
S. D. Farmer, Pres., C.O.O.
W. C. Gale, V.P., C.F.O.

INVESTOR CONTACT: William C. Gale, V.P. & C.F.O., (513) 459-1200

PRINCIPAL OFFICE: 6800 Cintas Blvd., P.O. Box 625737 Cincinnati, OH 45262-5737

TELEPHONE NUMBER: (513) 459-1200
FAX: (513) 573-4030
WEB: www.cintas-corp.com
NO. OF EMPLOYEES: 22,000 (approx.)
SHAREHOLDERS: 2,250 (approx.)
ANNUAL MEETING: In Oct.
INCORPORATED: OH, 1968; reincorp., WA, Dec., 1986

INSTITUTIONAL HOLDINGS:
No. of Institutions: 267
Shares Held: 77,893,463 (Adj.)
% Held: 46.7

INDUSTRY: Men's and boys' work clothing (SIC: 2326)

TRANSFER AGENT(S): The Fifth Third Bank, Cincinnati, OH

CITIGROUP INC.

YIELD	1.0%
P/E RATIO	21.8

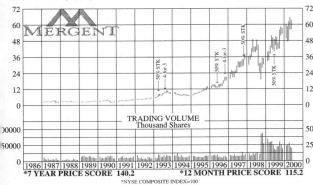

TRADING VOLUME
Thousand Shares

*7 YEAR PRICE SCORE 140.2   *12 MONTH PRICE SCORE 115.2
*NYSE COMPOSITE INDEX=100

INTERIM EARNINGS (Per Share):

Qtr.	Mar.	June	Sept.	Dec.
1995	0.22	0.27	0.33	0.41
1996	0.34	0.39	0.39	0.43
1997	0.43	0.45	0.55	0.20
1998	0.61	0.63	0.10	0.19
1999	0.69	0.71	0.70	0.75

INTERIM DIVIDENDS (Per Share):

Amt.	Decl.	Ex.	Rec.	Pay.
0.14Q	4/20/99	4/29/99	5/03/99	5/28/99
0.14Q	7/20/99	7/29/99	8/02/99	8/27/99
0.14Q	10/19/99	10/28/99	11/01/99	11/24/99
0.16Q	1/18/00	2/03/00	2/07/00	2/25/00
0.16Q	4/18/00	4/27/00	5/01/00	5/26/00

Indicated div.: $0.64 (Div. Reinv. Plan)

CAPITALIZATION (12/31/99):

	($000)	(%)
Long-Term Debt	47,092,000	46.3
Redeemable Pfd. Stock	4,920,000	4.8
Preferred Stock................	1,925,000	1.9
Common & Surplus	47,761,000	47.0
Total	101,698,000	100.0

DIVIDEND ACHIEVER STATUS:
Rank: 4   10-Year Growth Rate: 32.56%
Total Years of Dividend Growth: 13

RECENT DEVELOPMENTS: For the year ended 12/31/99, net income jumped 72.1% to $9.99 billion compared with $5.81 billion in the previous year. Results included a restructuring-related gain of $47.0 million and charges of $535.0 million in 1999 and 1998, respectively. Results for 1999 excluded an accounting charge of $127.0 million. Total revenue improved 7.3% to $82.00 billion from $76.43 billion in the prior year.

PROSPECTS: The Company's subsidiary, Salomon Smith Barney signed an agreement to acquire Schroders' investment banking business in a transaction valued at approximately $2.20 billion. The transaction is expected to be accretive to C's earnings per share mainly due to an increase in revenue and operating efficiencies. The transaction is subject to regulatory approvals and is expected close in the second quarter of 2000.

BUSINESS

CITIGROUP INC., (formerly Travelers Group Inc.) was formed on 10/8/98 by the merger of Travelers and Citicorp. The Company consists of businesses that produce a broad range of financial services -- asset management, banking and consumer finance, credit and charge cards, insurance, investments, investment banking and trading -- and use diverse channels to make them available to consumer and corporate customers around the world. Among its businesses are Citibank, Commercial Credit, Primerica Financial Services, Salomon Smith Barney, Salomon Smith Barney Asset Management, Travelers Life & Annuity, and Travelers Property Casualty. Citigroup is one of the largest asset gathering and asset management businesses in the world, with almost $300.0 billion under management.

BUSINESS LINE ANALYSIS

(12/31/99)	Rev(%)	Inc(%)
Global Consumer.......	45.9	43.0
Global Corp. & Invest Ban.............	47.8	51.4
Global Investment Mgmt &	4.7	6.1
Corporate/ Other........	(0.3)	(7.2)
Investment Activitiies	1.9	6.7
Total	100.0	100.0

ANNUAL FINANCIAL DATA

	12/31/99	⁶ 12/31/98	³ 12/31/97	12/31/96	12/31/95	⁶ 12/31/94	12/31/93
Earnings Per Share	² ⁴ 2.86	1.62	¹ 1.69	¹ ⁴ 1.53	¹ ⁴ 1.08	⁴ 0.86	² 0.86
Tang. Book Val. Per Share	14.18	7.95	7.68	4.82	4.79	2.55	2.97
Dividends Per Share	0.54	0.37	0.27	0.20	0.18	0.13	0.11
Dividend Payout %	18.9	22.8	15.8	13.0	16.5	14.9	12.6

INCOME STATEMENT (IN MILLIONS):

Total Premium Income	10,441.0	9,850.0	8,995.0	7,633.0	4,977.0	7,590.0	1,480.0
Net Investment Income	44,900.0	46,239.0	17,618.0	6,712.0	5,474.0	4,667.0	1,672.0
Other Income	26,664.0	20,342.0	10,996.0	7,000.0	6,132.0	6,208.0	3,481.0
Total Revenues	82,005.0	76,431.0	37,609.0	21,345.0	16,583.0	18,465.0	6,797.0
Policyholder Benefits	8,671.0	8,365.0	7,714.0	7,366.0	5,017.0	7,797.0	833.0
Income Before Income Taxes	15,948.0	9,269.0	5,012.0	3,398.0	2,521.0	2,149.0	1,523.0
Income Taxes	5,703.0	3,234.0	1,696.0	1,051.0	893.0	823.0	550.0
Equity Earnings/Minority Int.	d251.0	d228.0	d212.0	d47.0	. . .	. . .	142.0
Net Income	² ⁸ 9,994.0	5,807.0	⁴ 3,104.0	¹ ⁶ ⁴ 2,300.0	¹ ⁴ 1,628.0	⁴ 1,326.0	² 973.0
Average Shs. Outstg. (000)	3,443,500	3,472,800	1,769,850	1,437,300	1,428,300	1,428,300	1,071,000

BALANCE SHEET (IN MILLIONS):

Cash & Cash Equivalents	235,968.0	228,513.0	253,499.0	83,611.0	61,163.0	61,019.0	49,769.0
Premiums Due	32,677.0	30,905.0	30,939.0	22,408.0	16,584.0	17,282.0	15,476.0
Invst. Assets: Fixed-term	. . .	. . .	. . .	. . .	. . .	96.0	177.0
Invst. Assets: Equities	. . .	. . .	. . .	1,157.0	856.0	510.0	555.0
Invst. Assets: Loans	240,344.0	. . .	. . .	13,793.0	13,174.0	13,882.0	15,074.0
Invst. Assets: Total	462,625.0	223,517.0	201,566.0	77,281.0	57,187.0	52,950.0	53,486.0
Total Assets	716,937.0	668,641.0	386,555.0	151,067.0	114,475.0	115,297.0	101,360.0
Long-Term Obligations	47,092.0	48,671.0	28,352.0	11,327.0	9,190.0	7,075.0	6,991.0
Net Stockholders' Equity	49,686.0	42,708.0	20,893.0	13,085.0	11,710.0	8,640.0	9,326.0
Year-end Shs. Outstg. (000)	3,367,525	3,387,000	1,717,500	1,434,600	1,422,000	1,428,000	1,473,000

STATISTICAL RECORD:

Return on Revenues %	12.2	7.6	8.3	10.8	9.8	7.2	14.3
Return on Equity %	20.1	13.6	14.9	17.6	13.9	15.3	10.2
Return on Assets %	1.4	0.9	0.8	1.5	1.4	1.2	0.9
Price Range	58¼-32¹¹/₁₆	49-19	38¼-19⁷/₁₆	21⅛-12⁹/₁₆	14³/₁₆-7³/₁₆	9⁹/₁₆-6³/₄	11-5⅜
P/E Ratio	20.4-11.4	30.2-11.7	22.6-11.5	13.8-8.2	13.1-6.7	11.2-7.9	12.8-6.2
Average Yield %	1.2	1.1	0.9	1.2	1.7	1.6	1.3

Statistics are as originally reported. Adj. for stk. splits: 3-for-2, 5/99; 11/97; 4-for-3, 11/96; 3-for-2, 5/96. ¹ Bef. disc. oper. gain 1996, $31.0 mill.; 1995, $206.0 mill. ² Bef. acctg. change chrg. 1999, $127.0 mill.; 1993, $35.0 mill. ³ Results reflect the acquisition of Salomon Inc. in 11/97. ⁴ Incl. non-recurr. credit 1999, $47.0 mill.; 1998, $795.0 mill.; chrg. 1997, $255.4 mill.; credit 1996, $397.0 mill.; 1994, $117.0 mill.; 1994, $87.8 mill. ⁵ Results reflect merger of Primerica & Old Travelers in 12/93. ⁶ Results prior to fourth quarter of 1998 are for Travelers Group.

OFFICERS:
S. I. Weill, Co.-Chmn., Co-C.E.O.
J. S. Reed, Co.-Chmn., Co-C.E.O.
P. J. Collins, Vice-Chmn.

INVESTOR CONTACT: William F. Pike, (212) 559-1000

PRINCIPAL OFFICE: 153 East 53rd St., New York, NY 10043

TELEPHONE NUMBER: (212) 559-1000
FAX: (212) 816-8913
WEB: www.citigroupinfo.com
NO. OF EMPLOYEES: 108,800 full-time; 6,200 part-time
SHAREHOLDERS: 95,700 (approx.)
ANNUAL MEETING: In Apr.
INCORPORATED: DE, Dec., 1993

INSTITUTIONAL HOLDINGS:
No. of Institutions: 1,101
Shares Held: 2,087,107,100
% Held: 61.9

INDUSTRY: Fire, marine, and casualty insurance (SIC: 6331)

TRANSFER AGENT(S): Citibank Shareholder Services, Jersey City, NJ

CITIZENS BANKING CORPORATION

YIELD 5.7%
P/E RATIO 14.5

TRADING VOLUME
Thousand Shares

*7 YEAR PRICE SCORE 53.7   *12 MONTH PRICE SCORE 75.2
*NYSE COMPOSITE INDEX=100

INTERIM EARNINGS (Per Share):

Qtr.	Mar.	June	Sept.	Dec.
1996	0.45	0.43	0.42	0.40
1997	0.50	d0.18	0.40	0.39
1998	0.48	0.49	0.52	0.53
1999	0.47	0.50	0.49	d0.19

INTERIM DIVIDENDS (Per Share):

Amt.	Decl.	Ex.	Rec.	Pay.
0.235Q	4/20/99	4/23/99	4/27/99	5/05/99
0.235Q	7/16/99	7/21/99	7/23/99	8/04/99
0.235Q	10/22/99	10/28/99	11/01/99	11/10/99
0.235Q	1/21/00	1/26/00	1/28/00	2/09/00
0.26Q	4/18/00	4/20/00	4/25/00	5/10/00

Indicated div.: $1.04 (Div. Reinv. Plan)

CAPITALIZATION (12/31/99):

	($000)	(%)
Total Deposits	6,128,998	89.0
Long-Term Debt	127,104	1.8
Common & Surplus	633,669	9.2
Total	6,889,771	100.0

DIVIDEND ACHIEVER STATUS:

Rank: 167   10-Year Growth Rate: 9.48%
Total Years of Dividend Growth: 16

RECENT DEVELOPMENTS:

For the year ended 12/31/99, net income decreased 31.3% to $62.0 million compared with $90.3 million in the previous year. The 1999 results included an after-tax charge of $28.4 million for restructuring and merger-related items. Net interest income totaled $310.5 million, an increase of 6.0% from $293.0 million the year before. Total noninterest income climbed 13.9% to $81.1 million from $71.3 million a year earlier. Total non-interest expense grew 26.9% to $277.0 million from $218.2 million in the prior year. Return on average assets remained flat at 1.32%, while return on average shareholder's equity advanced to 14.45% from 13.62% a year ago. Recently, the Company and Mortgagebot.com, an on-line mortgage provider, announced that Mortgagebot.com would provide private-branded on-line mortgage services for CBCF.

BUSINESS

CITIZENS BANKING CORPORATION is a multibank holding company, which directly or indirectly owns two banking subsidiaries and four nonbanking subsidiaries, with total assets of $7.90 billion as of 12/31/99. The Corporation's subsidiary banks are full service commercial banks offering a variety of financial services to corporate, commercial, correspondent and individual bank customers. These services include commercial, agricultural, mortgage and consumer lending, demand and time deposits, trust services, investment services, safe deposit facilities, and other financial products and services. The bank subsidiaries are wholly owned by Citizens and operate through 226 banking offices located in the five midwestern states of Michigan, Wisconsin, Illinois, Iowa, and Minnesota.

LOAN DISTRIBUTION

(12/31/99)	($000)	(%)
Commercial	1,822,400	30.8
Commercial Real Estate	1,053,000	17.8
Real Estate Construction	185,400	3.2
Real Estate Mortgage	1,440,100	24.3
Consumer	1,415,600	23.9
Total	5,917,500	100.0

ANNUAL FINANCIAL DATA

	12/31/99	12/31/98	12/31/97	12/31/96	12/31/95	12/31/94	12/31/93
Earnings Per Share	② 1.28	1.98	① 1.11	1.28	1.16	1.02	0.94
Tang. Book Val. Per Share	11.28	13.76	12.47	8.73	7.91	8.60	9.04
Dividends Per Share	0.92	0.82	0.74	0.67	0.60	0.55	0.50
Dividend Payout %	71.5	41.4	67.0	52.8	51.9	53.9	52.8
INCOME STATEMENT (IN MILLIONS):							
Total Interest Income	542.4	339.9	335.9	255.9	240.6	180.0	166.5
Total Interest Expense	231.9	142.0	144.0	109.8	103.1	61.6	62.1
Net Interest Income	310.5	197.8	191.8	146.1	137.5	118.4	104.3
Provision for Loan Losses	24.7	14.1	15.3	8.3	6.4	5.3	5.6
Non-Interest Income	79.8	56.3	46.7	40.5	36.4	33.9	31.2
Non-Interest Expense	236.8	158.3	153.4	126.0	121.1	107.2	97.3
Income Before Taxes	90.0	81.7	46.0	52.3	46.4	39.7	32.7
Net Income	② 62.0	56.8	① 31.5	37.4	33.6	29.4	25.8
Average Shs. Outstg. (000)	48,617	28,743	28,420	29,332	29,150	28,926	27,448
BALANCE SHEET (IN MILLIONS):							
Cash & Due from Banks	250.7	140.5	168.4	137.9	172.8	132.1	113.3
Total Loans & Leases	5,917.5	3,584.5	3,541.6	2,620.7	2,428.5	1,816.2	1,780.2
Allowance for Credit Losses	76.4	46.4	45.9	36.0	34.8	24.7	22.5
Net Loans & Leases	5,841.1	3,538.1	3,495.7	2,584.7	2,393.7	1,791.5	1,757.6
Total Assets	7,899.4	4,501.4	4,439.3	3,483.9	3,463.9	2,703.8	2,714.1
Total Deposits	6,129.0	3,764.4	3,694.3	2,864.8	2,864.7	2,252.3	2,246.8
Long-Term Obligations	127.1	130.9	108.2	84.1	105.4	5.2	10.9
Total Liabilities	7,265.7	4,060.3	4,029.4	3,168.6	3,166.7	2,445.1	2,458.9
Net Stockholders' Equity	633.7	441.1	409.8	315.2	297.2	258.7	255.2
Year-end Shs. Outstg. (000)	47,568	28,100	28,048	28,680	28,668	28,256	28,230
STATISTICAL RECORD:							
Return on Equity %	9.8	12.9	7.7	11.9	11.3	11.4	10.1
Return on Assets %	0.8	1.3	0.7	1.1	1.0	1.1	0.9
Equity/Assets %	8.0	9.8	9.2	9.0	8.6	9.6	9.4
Non-Int. Exp./Tot. Inc. %	60.7	62.3	64.3	67.5	69.6	70.4	71.8
Price Range	42¼-21¼	37⅛-26¾	48½-28¾	32¼-27¼	33¼-24¹⁵⁄₁₆	29-22	28½-18½
P/E Ratio	33.0-16.6	18.7-13.5	43.7-25.9	25.3-21.4	28.8-21.6	28.6-21.7	30.3-19.7
Average Yield %	2.9	2.6	1.9	2.3	2.2	2.1	2.1

Statistics are as originally reported. Adj. for stk. splits: 50% div., 11/18/97; 2-for-1, 5/12/93. ① Incl. non-recurr. chrg. $23.7 mill. ($0.84/sh.) ② Incl. after-tax chrg. $28.4 mill.

OFFICERS:
C. Weeks, Chmn.
R. J. Vitito, Pres., C.E.O.
J. W. Ennest, Vice-Chmn., C.F.O., Treas.
T. W. Gallagher, Sr. V.P., Sec., Gen. Couns.

INVESTOR CONTACT: James M. Polehna,
V.P. & Inv. Rel. Mgr., (810) 257-2593

PRINCIPAL OFFICE: 1 Citizens Banking Ctr.,
328 S. Saginaw St., Flint, MI 48502

TELEPHONE NUMBER: (810) 766-7500
FAX: (810) 766-7503
WEB: www.cbclientsfirst.com

NO. OF EMPLOYEES: 3,220

SHAREHOLDERS: 15,000 (approx.)

ANNUAL MEETING: In Apr.

INCORPORATED: MI, Jan., 1982

INSTITUTIONAL HOLDINGS:
No. of Institutions: 80
Shares Held: 7,498,480
% Held: 15.7

INDUSTRY: National commercial banks
(SIC: 6021)

TRANSFER AGENT(S): Harris Trust and
Savings Bank, Chicago, IL

NASDAQ SYMBOL CHCO
Rec. Pr. 10 (5/31/00)

CITY HOLDING COMPANY

YIELD 3.2%
P/E RATIO 26.3

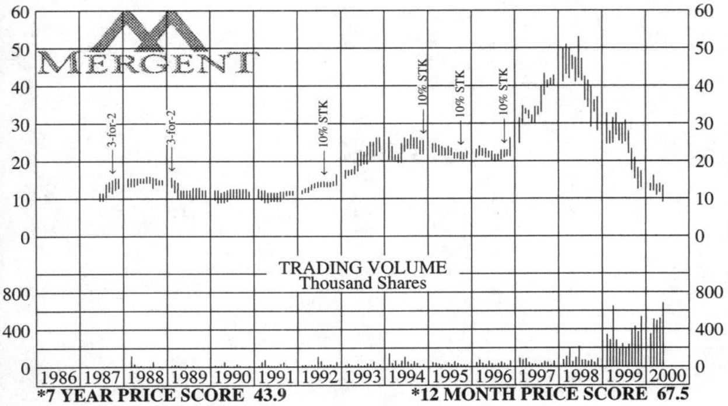

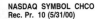

***7 YEAR PRICE SCORE 43.9** ***12 MONTH PRICE SCORE 67.5**

*NYSE COMPOSITE INDEX=100

INTERIM EARNINGS (Per Share):

Qtr.	Mar.	June	Sep.	Dec.
1996	0.44	0.46	0.45	0.46
1997	0.47	0.52	0.57	0.47
1998	0.40	0.41	0.39	d0.89
1999	0.31	0.42	0.14	d0.49

INTERIM DIVIDENDS (Per Share):

Amt.	Decl.	Ex.	Rec.	Pay.
0.20Q	5/14/99	5/27/99	6/01/99	6/15/99
0.20Q	8/09/99	8/30/99	9/01/99	9/15/99
0.20Q	11/08/99	11/29/99	12/01/99	12/15/99
0.20Q	2/29/00	3/08/00	3/10/00	3/15/00
0.08Q	5/15/00	5/30/00	6/01/00	6/15/00

Indicated div.: $0.32

CAPITALIZATION (12/31/99):

	($000)	(%)
Total Deposits	1,955,770	82.9
Long-Term Debt	116,000	4.9
Redeemable Pfd. Stock	87,500	3.7
Common & Surplus	198,542	8.4
Total	2,357,812	100.0

DIVIDEND ACHIEVER STATUS:

Rank: 130 10-Year Growth Rate: 11.34%
Total Years of Dividend Growth: 12

RECENT DEVELOPMENTS: For the year ended 12/31/99, net income improved 18.7% to $6.2 million compared with $5.2 million in the previous year. The 1998 results included a non-recurring pre-tax charge of $13.6 million. Net interest income totaled $98.4 million, a decline of 4.8% to $98.4 million from $103.3 million the year before. Provision for loan losses more than doubled to $19.3 million from $8.5 million in 1998. Total interest income fell slightly to $195.6 million from $196.7 million in the prior year. Total interest expense grew 4.1% to $97.1 million from $93.3 million a year ago. Return on average assets climbed to 0.23% from 0.20%, while return on average equity advanced to 2.83% from 2.22% a year earlier. On 4/16/00, the Company and Summit State Bank of California, announced that the two institutions have by mutual agreement terminated the merger agreement pursuant to which CHCO would have acquired Summit.

BUSINESS

CITY HODING COMPANY, is a multi-bank holding company that provides diversified financial products and services to consumers and local businesses. Through its network of 62 banking offices in West Virginia (56 offices), Ohio (2 offices) and California (4 offices), the Company provides credit, deposit, investment advisory, insurance, and technology products and services to its customers. In addition to its branch network, the Company's delivery channels include ATMs, check cards, telemarketing, direct mail solicitation, interactive voice response systems, and Internet technology. As of 12/31/00, CHCO had $2.71 billion in total assets. On 12/31/98, the Company aquired Horizon Bancorp., Inc.

LOAN DISTRIBUTION

(12/31/99)	($000)	(%)
Commercial	589,116	32.0
Real Estate-Mortgage	949,830	50.0
Installment loans	347,168	18.0
Total	1,886,114	100.0

ANNUAL FINANCIAL DATA

	12/31/99	12/31/98	12/31/97	12/31/96	12/31/95	12/31/94	12/31/93
Earnings Per Share	**0.37**	**[1] 0.31**	**2.02**	**1.81**	**1.55**	**1.68**	**1.40**
Tang. Book Val. Per Share	**11.76**	**13.09**	**16.56**	**14.21**	**13.06**	**13.68**	**11.88**
Dividends Per Share	**0.80**	**0.77**	**0.73**	**0.63**	**0.56**	**0.49**	**0.47**
Dividend Payout %	**216.2**	**248.3**	**36.1**	**35.0**	**36.1**	**29.0**	**33.3**
INCOME STATEMENT (IN MILLIONS):							
Total Interest Income	195.6	196.7	96.8	86.1	75.1	55.1	43.4
Total Interest Expense	97.1	93.3	44.7	39.1	33.6	22.2	17.6
Net Interest Income	98.4	103.3	52.1	47.0	41.5	32.9	25.8
Provision for Loan Losses	19.3	8.5	1.7	1.7	1.1	1.0	1.3
Non-Interest Income	59.5	72.4	26.7	11.1	6.3	4.6	2.8
Non-Interest Expense	130.6	155.6	57.7	41.0	33.9	26.4	19.3
Income Before Taxes	8.1	11.7	19.5	15.5	12.9	10.2	8.1
Net Income	6.2	[1] 5.2	12.5	10.1	8.7	7.0	5.5
Average Shs. Outstg. (000)	16,841	16,885	6,166	5,586	5,642	4,150	4,049
BALANCE SHEET (IN MILLIONS):							
Cash & Due from Banks	120.1	87.9	47.2	47.4	28.5	27.6	23.0
Securities Avail. for Sale	381.1	356.7	162.9	122.9	143.6	67.9	75.5
Total Loans & Leases	1,886.1	1,715.9	787.7	704.8	664.9	505.0	390.1
Allowance for Credit Losses	27.1	17.6	15.0	14.1	14.7	15.6	14.0
Net Loans & Leases	1,859.0	1,698.3	772.7	690.7	650.2	489.4	376.1
Total Assets	2,792.5	2,706.0	1,266.1	1,048.8	1,041.0	780.5	641.2
Total Deposits	1,955.8	2,064.4	938.5	828.7	797.4	651.3	560.7
Long-Term Obligations	116.0	102.7	68.4	34.3	20.0	6.9	5.9
Total Liabilities	2,593.9	2,485.9	1,159.9	969.4	967.8	723.7	594.3
Net Stockholders' Equity	198.5	220.1	106.3	79.4	73.1	56.9	46.9
Year-end Shs. Outstg. (000)	16,879	16,810	6,416	5,586	5,601	4,158	3,951
STATISTICAL RECORD:							
Return on Equity %	3.1	2.4	11.7	12.8	11.9	12.2	11.7
Return on Assets %	0.2	0.2	1.0	1.0	0.8	0.9	0.9
Equity/Assets %	7.1	8.1	8.4	7.6	7.0	7.3	7.3
Non-Int. Exp./Tot. Inc. %	82.7	88.5	73.2	70.5	70.8	70.4	67.2
Price Range	32¾-12½	53-28	43¼-24¾	26¼-19¾	24 13/16-20 7/16	27 1/16-19 9/16	26 5/16-15⅜
P/E Ratio	88.5-33.8	170.9-90.3	21.4-12.3	14.5-10.9	16.0-13.2	16.1-11.6	18.8-11.0
Average Yield %	3.5	1.9	2.1	2.8	2.5	2.1	2.2

Statistics are as originally reported. Adj. for 10% stk. splits: 11/30/96, 11/30/95, 1/15/95

[1] Incl. non-recurr. pre-tax chrg. $13.6 mill.

OFFICERS:
P. McLaughlin, Pres., C.E.O.
R. A. Henson, C.F.O.

PRINCIPAL OFFICE: 25 Gatewater Road, Charleston, WV 25313

TELEPHONE NUMBER: (304) 769-1100
FAX: (304) 925-5942
WEB: www.cityholding.com

NO. OF EMPLOYEES: 1,560

SHAREHOLDERS: 4,208

ANNUAL MEETING: In May

INCORPORATED: WV, Mar., 1982

INSTITUTIONAL HOLDINGS:
No. of Institutions: 22
Shares Held: 1,150,072
% Held: 6.8

INDUSTRY: National commercial banks (SIC: 6021)

TRANSFER AGENT(S): SunTrust Bank, Atlanta, GA

CLARCOR INC.

YIELD 2.6%
P/E RATIO 12.1

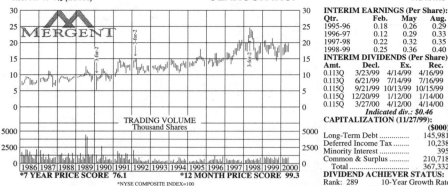

*7 YEAR PRICE SCORE 76.1   ***12 MONTH PRICE SCORE 99.3**

*NYSE COMPOSITE INDEX=100

INTERIM EARNINGS (Per Share):

Qtr.	Feb.	May	Aug.	Nov.
1995-96	0.18	0.26	0.29	0.39
1996-97	0.12	0.29	0.33	0.36
1997-98	0.22	0.32	0.35	0.41
1998-99	0.25	0.36	0.40	0.45

INTERIM DIVIDENDS (Per Share):

Amt.	Decl.	Ex.	Rec.	Pay.
0.113Q	3/23/99	4/14/99	4/16/99	4/30/99
0.113Q	6/21/99	7/14/99	7/16/99	7/30/99
0.115Q	9/21/99	10/13/99	10/15/99	10/29/99
0.115Q	12/20/99	1/12/00	1/14/00	1/28/00
0.115Q	3/27/00	4/12/00	4/14/00	4/28/00

Indicated div.: $0.46

CAPITALIZATION (11/27/99):

	($000)	(%)
Long-Term Debt	145,981	39.7
Deferred Income Tax	10,238	2.8
Minority Interest	395	0.1
Common & Surplus	210,718	57.4
Total	367,332	100.0

DIVIDEND ACHIEVER STATUS:

Rank: 289   10-Year Growth Rate: 3.53%
Total Years of Dividend Growth: 19

RECENT DEVELOPMENTS: For the year ended 11/30/99, net earnings increased 10.4% to $35.4 million from $32.1 million a year earlier. Results included gains of $1.7 million and $1.3 million in 1999 and 1998, respectively, from the sale of plant assets. Net sales improved 12.0% to $477.9 million from $426.8 million. Engine/Mobile Filtration segment sales increased 6.7% to $238.7 million due to new product introductions, additional OEM sales, and penetra-

tion into new distribution channels. Industrial/Environmental Filtration segment sales improved 28.8% to $174.9 million resulting from increased demand for air quality products and from acquisitions made in 1999. However, packaging segment sales declined 4.3% to $64.3 million due to lower promotional container sales. Gross profit amounted to $148.6 million compared with $135.2 million in 1998.

BUSINESS

CLARCOR INC. manufactures filtration products and consumer products. The Engine/Mobile Filtration segment markets a full line of oil, air, fuel, coolant and hydraulic fluid filters. The filters are used in a wide variety of applications and in processes where filter efficiency, reliability and durability are essential. The Industrial/Environmental Filtration segment includes products used primarily for commercial, residential and industrial applications. The segment markets commercial and industrial air filters and systems, electrostatic contamination control equipment and electrostatic high precision spraying equipment. The Packaging segment includes a variety of custom styled containers and packaging items used primarily by the food, confectionery, spice, drug, toiletries and chemical specialties industries.

BUSINESS LINE ANALYSIS

(11/27/1999)	Rev (%)	Inc (%)
Engine/Mobile		
Filtration	49.9	77.7
Industrial/Environmental	36.6	9.1
Packaging	13.5	13.2
Total	100.0	100.0

ANNUAL FINANCIAL DATA

	11/27/99	11/28/98	11/29/97	11/30/96	11/30/95	11/30/94	11/30/93
Earnings Per Share	1.46	1.30	①②1.11	1.12	0.99	0.93	0.77
Cash Flow Per Share	2.09	1.80	1.60	1.56	1.36	1.26	1.06
Tang. Book Val. Per Share	4.98	6.90	6.41	5.87	5.23	4.62	4.00
Dividends Per Share	0.453	0.443	0.435	0.428	0.422	0.415	0.406
Dividend Payout %	31.0	34.0	39.1	38.2	42.7	44.8	52.6
INCOME STATEMENT (IN THOUSANDS):							
Total Revenues	477,869	426,773	394,264	333,388	290,194	270,123	225,319
Costs & Expenses	406,420	362,730	335,268	283,073	246,585	230,465	189,957
Depreciation & Amort.	15,372	12,380	11,600	9,785	8,244	7,292	6,295
Operating Income	56,077	51,663	①②44,424	40,530	35,365	32,366	29,067
Net Interest Inc./(Exp.)	d2,282	d1,053	d2,759	d3,243	d1,863	d2,240	d2,650
Income Before Income Taxes	55,615	51,347	44,192	40,019	34,136	32,560	27,078
Income Taxes	20,137	19,262	17,164	14,896	12,182	11,935	9,827
Equity Earnings/Minority Int.	d66	d6	d110	d145	175	957	745
Net Income	35,412	32,079	①②26,918	24,978	21,954	20,625	17,251
Cash Flow	50,784	44,459	38,518	34,763	30,198	27,917	23,546
Average Shs. Outstg.	24,314	24,649	24,134	22,289	22,202	22,221	22,257
BALANCE SHEET (IN THOUSANDS):							
Cash & Cash Equivalents	14,745	33,321	30,324	17,372	18,769	19,567	13,838
Total Current Assets	227,670	168,173	160,527	124,379	117,570	98,450	86,161
Net Property	126,026	86,389	82,905	78,586	67,036	52,615	47,636
Total Assets	472,991	305,766	282,519	243,964	223,262	188,448	169,896
Total Current Liabilities	97,475	61,183	102,390	45,156	42,460	39,461	33,288
Long-Term Obligations	145,981	36,419	37,656	35,522	34,417	17,013	24,617
Net Stockholders' Equity	210,718	186,807	171,162	146,059	130,815	117,462	104,641
Net Working Capital	130,195	106,990	58,137	79,223	75,110	58,989	52,873
Year-end Shs. Outstg.	24,020	23,949	24,243	22,313	22,173	22,142	22,229
STATISTICAL RECORD:							
Operating Profit Margin %	11.7	12.1	11.3	12.2	12.2	12.0	12.9
Net Profit Margin %	7.4	7.5	6.8	7.5	7.6	7.6	7.7
Return on Equity %	16.8	17.2	15.7	17.1	16.8	17.6	16.5
Return on Assets %	7.5	10.5	9.5	10.2	9.8	10.9	10.2
Debt/Total Assets %	30.9	11.9	13.3	14.6	15.4	9.0	14.5
Price Range	21³/₈-14¼	24¹¹/₁₆-14¼	20¹³/₁₆-13⁵/₁₆	16³/₄-12⁷/₁₆	18-12⁷/₁₆	14¹⁵/₁₆-10⁹/₁₆	14¹/₁₆-10¹¹/₁₆
P/E Ratio	14.6-9.8	19.0-11.0	18.7-12.0	15.0-11.1	18.2-12.6	16.1-11.4	18.2-13.8
Average Yield %	2.5	2.3	2.5	2.9	2.8	3.3	3.3

Statistics are as originally reported. Adj. for stk. splits: 3-for-2, 4/98, 1/92 ① Incl. non-recurr. credit of $1.7 mill. ② Incl. non-recurr chrg. $3.0 mill.

OFFICERS:
L. E. Gloyd, Chmn. Emeritus
N. E. Johnson, Chmn., Pres., C.E.O.
B. A. Klein, C.F.O., V.P., Fin.

INVESTOR CONTACT: M. S. Blaylock, V.P., Corp. Sec., Contr., (815) 962-8867

PRINCIPAL OFFICE: 2323 Sixth St., P.O. Box 7007, Rockford, IL 61125

TELEPHONE NUMBER: (815) 962-8867
FAX: (815) 962-0417
WEB: www.clarcor.com
NO. OF EMPLOYEES: 4,278 (avg.)
SHAREHOLDERS: 1,650 (of record); 6,000 (beneficial)
ANNUAL MEETING: In Mar.
INCORPORATED: IL, 1904; reincorp., DE, 1969

INSTITUTIONAL HOLDINGS:
No. of Institutions: 97
Shares Held: 14,453,629
% Held: 60.3

INDUSTRY: Motor vehicle parts and accessories (SIC: 3714)

TRANSFER AGENT(S): First Chicago Trust Company of New York, Jersey City, NJ

CLECO CORPORATION

YIELD 5.0%
P/E RATIO 14.5

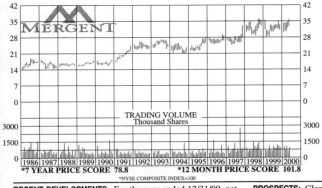

TRADING VOLUME
Thousand Shares

*7 YEAR PRICE SCORE 78.8   ***12 MONTH PRICE SCORE 101.8**
*NYSE COMPOSITE INDEX=100

INTERIM EARNINGS (Per Share):

Qtr.	Mar.	June	Sept.	Dec.
1996	0.42	0.63	0.91	0.27
1997	0.31	0.47	0.95	0.45
1998	0.29	0.63	0.95	0.37
1999	0.35	0.59	1.07	0.35

INTERIM DIVIDENDS (Per Share):

Amt.	Decl.	Ex.	Rec.	Pay.
0.415Q	7/23/99	7/29/99	8/02/99	8/15/99
0.415Q	10/29/99	11/02/99	11/04/99	11/15/99
0.415Q	1/28/00	2/02/00	2/04/00	2/15/00
0.425Q	4/28/00	5/02/00	5/04/00	5/15/00

Indicated div.: $1.70 (Div. Reinv. Plan)

CAPITALIZATION (12/31/99):

	($000)	(%)
Long-Term Debt..............	579,595	40.0
Deferred Income Tax........	418,351	28.8
Preferred Stock.................	13,889	1.0
Common & Surplus..........	438,656	30.2
Total............................	1,450,491	100.0

DIVIDEND ACHIEVER STATUS:
Rank: 297   10-Year Growth Rate: 3.19%
Total Years of Dividend Growth: 18

RECENT DEVELOPMENTS: For the year ended 12/31/99, net income grew 5.6% to $56.8 million from $53.8 million the year before. Operating revenues rose 48.9% to $767.0 million from $515.2 million. Total operating expenses soared 60.3% to $654.4 million. Earnings are being driven by increased demand of regulated utility operations, offset by higher interest costs, utility expenses and expansion expenses.

PROSPECTS: Cleco Midstream Resources LLC and International Energy Partners, L.P. entered into a joint venture to build a gas-fired power plant near Eunice, LA beginning midyear 2000. Separately, CNL signed a 20-year purchase agreement with Williams Companies, Inc. Williams will own and market the output of the Cleco Evangeline power plant starting in June 2000. The project is expected to add $.25 to earnings per share in the first year.

BUSINESS

CLECO CORPORATION is an energy services holding company. Under the holding company, CNL is the parent of three core businesses: Cleco Utility Group, Inc., Cleco Midstream Resources LLC and UtiliTech Solutions. Cleco Utility Group, Inc. contains the Company's generation, transmission and distribution electric utility operations. Cleco Midstream Resources LLC, operates the Company's competitive electric generation, oil and natural gas production, energy and generating fuel procurement and natural gas pipeline businesses. UtiliTech Solutions, sells utility support services to municipal governments, rural electric cooperatives and investor-owned electric companies.

ANNUAL FINANCIAL DATA

	12/31/99	12/31/98	12/31/97	12/31/96	12/31/95	12/31/94	12/31/93
Earnings Per Share	2.37	2.24	2.18	2.23	2.08	1.92	①1.78
Cash Flow Per Share	6.89	4.22	4.04	4.13	3.89	3.63	3.39
Tang. Book Val. Per Share	19.55	18.89	18.20	17.52	16.82	15.23	15.75
Dividends Per Share	1.65	1.61	1.57	1.53	1.49	1.45	1.41
Dividend Payout %	69.6	71.9	72.0	68.6	71.6	75.5	79.2
INCOME STATEMENT (IN MILLIONS):							
Total Revenues	767.0	515.2	456.2	435.4	394.4	379.6	382.4
Costs & Expenses	516.2	328.9	280.5	264.6	231.3	226.3	237.0
Depreciation & Amort.	49.5	49.1	45.9	42.7	40.6	38.3	36.1
Maintenance Exp.	29.9	30.3	23.3	23.5	22.6	24.7	25.0
Operating Income	112.5	80.3	78.8	78.4	74.7	70.4	64.7
Net Interest Inc./(Exp.)	d27.9	d27.0	d28.2	d27.8	d28.0	d26.1	d25.4
Income Taxes	27.2	26.7	27.7	26.2	25.2	19.9	19.6
Net Income	56.8	53.8	52.5	52.1	48.7	45.0	①41.8
Cash Flow	164.3	100.7	96.3	92.8	87.2	81.3	75.9
Average Shs. Outstg. (000)	23,849	23,867	23,864	22,453	22,431	22,415	22,389
BALANCE SHEET (IN MILLIONS):							
Gross Property	1,767.3	1,641.5	1,544.2	1,428.1	1,371.2	1,322.6	1,274.8
Accumulated Depreciation	555.7	551.7	518.7	475.2	441.7	410.5	379.8
Net Property	1,211.6	1,089.8	1,025.6	952.9	929.5	912.1	895.0
Total Assets	1,704.7	1,429.0	1,361.0	1,321.8	1,266.0	1,178.2	1,161.6
Long-Term Obligations	579.6	343.0	365.9	340.9	360.8	336.6	351.1
Net Stockholders' Equity	452.5	437.5	420.1	402.9	385.1	369.4	357.4
Year-end Shs. Outstg. (000)	22,442	22,481	22,463	22,453	22,427	23,842	22,382
STATISTICAL RECORD:							
Operating Profit Margin %	14.6	15.6	17.3	18.0	18.9	18.6	16.9
Net Profit Margin %	7.4	10.4	11.5	12.0	12.3	11.9	10.9
Net Inc./Net Property %	4.7	4.9	5.1	5.5	5.2	4.9	4.7
Net Inc./Tot. Capital %	3.9	4.6	4.5	4.7	4.3	4.7	4.3
Return on Equity %	12.6	11.8	12.0	12.3	11.9	11.4	10.9
Accum. Depr./Gross Prop. %	31.4	33.6	33.6	33.3	32.2	31.0	29.8
Price Range	35½-28¼	36⅛-28⅝	33⅛-24¾	29¼-25⅛	28⅛-22	25⅝-20⅞	27⅛-23
P/E Ratio	15.0-11.9	16.1-12.8	15.2-11.4	13.1-11.3	13.5-10.6	13.3-10.9	15.2-12.9
Average Yield %	5.2	5.0	5.4	5.6	5.9	6.2	5.6

Statistics are as originally reported. ① Incl. non-recurr. chrg. $6.9 mill. for restructuring

QUARTERLY DATA

(12/31/99)($000)	Rev	Inc
1st Quarter.................	121,719	19,481
2nd Quarter...............	222,474	29,519
3rd Quarter	285,032	47,291
4th Quarter................	138,975	16,250

OFFICERS:
G. L. Nesbitt, Chmn., C.E.O.
D. M. Eppler, Pres., C.O.O.
T. J. Howlin, C.F.O., Sr. V.P., Fin. Serv.

INVESTOR CONTACT: Rodney J. Hamilton, Dir. Inv. & Shareholder Rel., (318) 484-7400

PRINCIPAL OFFICE: 2030 Donahue Ferry Rd., Pineville, LA 71360-5226

TELEPHONE NUMBER: (318) 484-7400
FAX: (318) 484-7465
WEB: www.cleco.com

NO. OF EMPLOYEES: 1,416 (avg.)

SHAREHOLDERS: 9,984

ANNUAL MEETING: In Apr.

INCORPORATED: LA, Dec., 1932

INSTITUTIONAL HOLDINGS:
No. of Institutions: 108
Shares Held: 9,957,933
% Held: 44.2

INDUSTRY: Electric services (SIC: 4911)

TRANSFER AGENT(S): First Chicago Trust Company of New York, Jersey City, NJ

CLOROX COMPANY (THE)

YIELD 2.0%
P/E RATIO 40.4

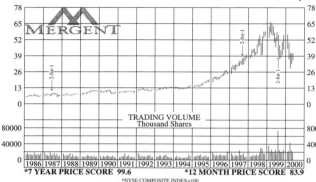

TRADING VOLUME
Thousand Shares

*7 YEAR PRICE SCORE 99.6   *12 MONTH PRICE SCORE 83.9
*NYSE COMPOSITE INDEX=100

INTERIM EARNINGS (Per Share):

Qtr.	Sept.	Dec.	Mar.	June
1995-96	0.28	0.19	0.29	0.32
1996-97	0.32	0.22	0.32	0.36
1997-98	0.36	0.24	0.36	0.47
1998-99	0.41	0.28	0.09	0.21
1999-00	0.36	0.32	...	...

INTERIM DIVIDENDS (Per Share):

Amt.	Decl.	Ex.	Rec.	Pay.
0.40Q	7/20/99	7/28/99	7/30/99	8/13/99
2-for-1	7/20/99	8/24/99	7/30/99	8/23/99
0.20Q	9/15/99	10/27/99	10/29/99	11/15/99
0.20Q	1/19/00	1/27/00	1/31/00	2/15/00
0.20Q	3/15/00	4/26/00	4/28/00	5/15/00

Indicated div.: $0.80 (Div. Reinv. Plan)

CAPITALIZATION (6/30/99):

	($000)	(%)
Long-Term Debt	702,000	28.0
Deferred Income Tax	237,000	9.4
Common & Surplus	1,570,000	62.6
Total	2,509,000	100.0

DIVIDEND ACHIEVER STATUS:
Rank: 157   10-Year Growth Rate: 9.83%
Total Years of Dividend Growth: 23

RECENT DEVELOPMENTS: For the quarter ended 12/31/99, net income improved 2.7% to $76.0 million compared with $74.0 million in the prior-year quarter. Results for the current quarter included merger, integration and restructuring charges of $6.0 million. Net sales increased slightly to $954.0 million from $947.0 million in the prior-year quarter. Comparisons were made with restated prior-year results.

PROSPECTS: Going forward, results should benefit from initiatives that have integrated First Brands' businesses to CLX. These initiatives include the consolidation of distribution networks and manufacturing and the elimination of unprofitable items in First Brands' businesses. In addition, CLX plans to introduce several new products, including five new GLAD items, improving packaging and targeting improved merchandising across its product portfolio.

BUSINESS

THE CLOROX COMPANY is a manufacturer and marketer of household products, both domestic and international, and products for institutional markets. CLX operates in four business segments: U.S. Home Care and Cleaning, U.S. Specialty Products, U.S. Food, Food Preparation and Storage, and International. The U.S. Home Care and Cleaning segment includes CLX's household cleaning, bleach and other home care products, as well as CLX's rofessional products business. The U.S. Specialty Products segment includes CLX's charcoal, automotive care, cat litter, insecticide and firelog categories. The U.S. Food, Food Preparation and Storage segment includes CLX's dressings, sauces, BRITA, GLAD, and GLADWARE businesses. The International segment focuses on the laundry, household cleaning and insecticide categories. On 1/29/99, the Company acquired First Brands Corp. for $2.00 billion.

QUARTERLY DATA

(6/30/99)($000,000)	Rev	Inc
1st Quarter	954	100
2nd Quarter	947	74
3rd Quarter	992	22
4th Quarter	1,100	50

ANNUAL FINANCIAL DATA

	[2] 6/30/99	6/30/98	6/30/97	6/30/96	6/30/95	6/30/94	6/30/93
Earnings Per Share	[3] 1.03	1.41	1.21	1.07	0.95	[1] 0.84	[1] 0.77
Cash Flow Per Share	1.87	2.06	1.82	1.63	1.43	1.27	1.15
Tang. Book Val. Per Share	0.31	...	...	1.11	1.68	1.82	1.89
Dividends Per Share	0.76	0.68	0.61	0.56	0.51	0.47	0.44
Dividend Payout %	73.8	48.2	50.6	51.9	53.4	55.5	57.7
INCOME STATEMENT (IN MILLIONS):							
Total Revenues	4,003.0	2,741.3	2,532.7	2,217.8	1,984.2	1,836.9	1,634.2
Costs & Expenses	3,250.0	2,065.6	1,939.9	1,686.3	1,521.2	1,416.9	1,254.2
Depreciation & Amort.	202.0	137.6	126.4	116.5	103.9	94.1	83.6
Operating Income	551.0	538.1	466.4	415.0	359.1	325.9	296.4
Net Interest Inc./(Exp.)	d97.0	d69.7	d55.6	d38.3	d25.1	d18.4	d18.9
Income Before Income Taxes	430.0	471.9	416.0	370.4	337.9	306.6	275.2
Income Taxes	184.0	174.0	166.6	148.3	137.1	126.6	107.3
Net Income	[3] 246.0	298.0	249.4	222.1	200.8	[1] 180.0	[1] 167.9
Cash Flow	448.0	435.5	375.8	338.6	304.7	274.1	251.5
Average Shs. Outstg. (000)	240,002	211,270	206,584	207,740	212,588	215,200	218,792
BALANCE SHEET (IN MILLIONS):							
Cash & Cash Equivalents	132.0	89.7	101.0	90.8	137.3	115.9	71.2
Total Current Assets	1,116.0	798.7	673.5	573.8	600.3	504.3	531.8
Net Property	1,054.0	596.3	570.6	551.4	525.0	532.6	538.1
Total Assets	4,132.0	3,030.0	2,778.0	2,178.9	1,906.7	1,697.6	1,649.2
Total Current Liabilities	1,368.0	1,225.1	892.7	623.9	479.3	375.8	371.6
Long-Term Obligations	702.0	316.3	565.9	356.3	253.1	216.1	204.0
Net Stockholders' Equity	1,570.0	1,085.2	1,036.0	932.8	943.9	909.4	879.3
Net Working Capital	d252.0	d426.4	d219.2	d50.0	121.0	128.4	160.2
Year-end Shs. Outstg. (000)	235,311	207,370	206,390	205,032	209,608	213,488	219,400
STATISTICAL RECORD:							
Operating Profit Margin %	13.8	19.6	18.4	18.7	18.1	17.7	18.1
Net Profit Margin %	6.1	10.9	9.8	10.0	10.1	9.8	10.3
Return on Equity %	15.7	27.5	24.1	23.8	21.3	19.8	19.1
Return on Assets %	6.0	9.8	9.0	10.2	10.5	10.6	10.2
Debt/Total Assets %	17.0	10.4	20.4	16.4	13.3	12.7	12.4
Price Range	66½-37½	58¾-37¾₁₆	40⅛-24⅜₁₆	27⅜₁₆-17½	19¹³₁₆-13¹³₁₆	14⅞₁₆-11¾	13⅞₁₆-11
P/E Ratio	64.5-36.4	41.7-26.4	33.3-20.2	25.8-16.4	21.0-14.6	17.7-14.0	18.0-14.3
Average Yield %	1.5	1.4	1.9	2.5	3.0	3.5	3.6

Statistics are as originally reported. Adj. for stk. splits: 2-for-1, 8/99 and 9/97. [1] Bef. disc. oper. gain 1994, $32.1 mill.; loss 1993, $867,000. [2] Incl. results of First Brands Corp. [3] Incl. one-time chrgs. totaling $180.0 mill.

OFFICERS:
G. C. Sullivan, Chmn., C.E.O.
G. E. Johnston, Pres., C.O.O.

INVESTOR CONTACT: William B. Osterland, Dir. Fin. Rel., (510) 271-7066

PRINCIPAL OFFICE: 1221 Broadway, Oakland, CA 94612

TELEPHONE NUMBER: (510) 271-7000
FAX: (510) 832-1463
WEB: www.clorox.com

NO. OF EMPLOYEES: 11,000 (approx.)

SHAREHOLDERS: 14,212 (approx.)

ANNUAL MEETING: In Nov.

INCORPORATED: DE, 1986

INSTITUTIONAL HOLDINGS:
No. of Institutions: 386
Shares Held: 251,425,660 (Adj.)
% Held: 53.2

INDUSTRY: Polishes and sanitation goods (SIC: 2842)

TRANSFER AGENT(S): EquiServe - First Chicago Trust Division, Jersey City, NJ

NYSE SYMBOL KO
Rec. Pr. 53⅜ (5/31/00)

COCA-COLA COMPANY (THE)

YIELD 1.3%
P/E RATIO 54.5

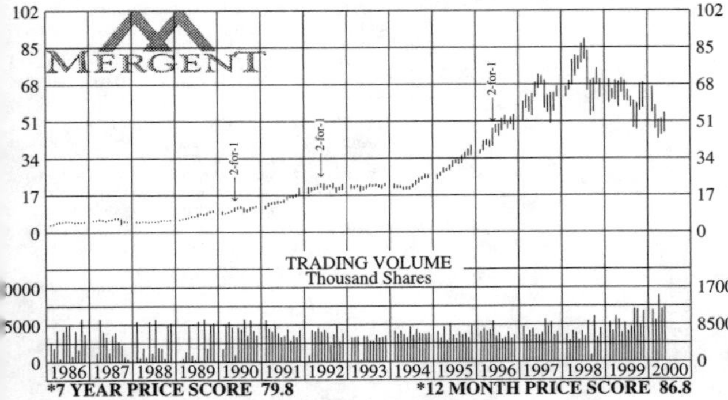

*7 YEAR PRICE SCORE 79.8 *12 MONTH PRICE SCORE 86.8

*NYSE COMPOSITE INDEX=100

INTERIM EARNINGS (Per Share):

Qtr.	Mar.	June	Sept.	Dec.
1997	0.40	0.53	0.41	0.33
1998	0.35	0.48	0.36	0.24
1999	0.30	0.38	0.32	d0.02

INTERIM DIVIDENDS (Per Share):

Amt.	Decl.	Ex.	Rec.	Pay.
0.16Q	4/21/99	6/11/99	6/15/99	7/01/99
0.16Q	7/15/99	9/13/99	9/15/99	10/01/99
0.16Q	10/21/99	11/29/99	12/01/99	12/15/99
0.17Q	2/17/00	3/13/00	3/15/00	4/01/00
0.17Q	4/19/00	6/13/00	6/15/00	7/01/00

Indicated div.: $0.68 (Div. Reinv. Plan)

CAPITALIZATION (12/31/99):

	($000)	(%)
Long-Term Debt	854,000	7.9
Deferred Income Tax	498,000	4.6
Common & Surplus	9,513,000	87.6
Total	10,865,000	100.0

DIVIDEND ACHIEVER STATUS:
Rank: 78 10-Year Growth Rate: 14.18%
Total Years of Dividend Growth: 37

RECENT DEVELOPMENTS: For the twelve months ended 12/31/99, net income was $2.43 billion, down 31.2% from $3.53 billion in the previous year. Results for 1999 included a charge of $813.0 million to reflect the impairment of certain bottling assets and the streamlining of manufacturing facilities in Russia, the Baltics, Japan and other countries. Net operating revenues increased 5.3% to $19.81 billion from $18.81 billion in the prior year. Revenues were enhanced by price increases and structural change in the bottling system.

PROSPECTS: The Company anticipates earnings for fiscal 2000 will be negatively affected by the financial effect of the organizational realignment and an intent to decrease concentrate inventory levels at selected bottlers. KO plans to reduce inventories carried by bottlers in Eastern Europe, Japan and Germany. This reduction is expected to decrease diluted earnings per share by $0.11-$0.13 after tax during the first half of fiscal 2000. This initiative is designed to strengthen the Company's bottling system.

BUSINESS

COCA-COLA COMPANY is the world's largest producer and distributor of soft drinks, soft drink concentrates and syrups. Principal soft drink products are: COCACOLA, COCACOLA CLASSIC, DIET COKE, FANTA, SPRITE plus other assorted diet and caffeine-free versions. The Minute Maid Company (formerly Coca-Cola Foods) markets and processes citrus and other fruit juices and fruit drink products, primarily orange juice. Popular brands include MINUTE MAID and HI-C. In 1999, Sales (operating income) were derived: North America, 38%, (32%); Europe, 23%, (23%); Middle and Far East, 26%, (23%); Latin America, 10%, (18%); and Africa, 3%, (4%). Coca-Cola holds an approximate 40% interest in Coca-Cola Enterprises, Inc., a soft drink bottling concern.

ANNUAL FINANCIAL DATA

	12/31/99	12/31/98	12/31/97	12/31/96	12/31/95	12/31/94	12/31/93
Earnings Per Share	**3 0.98**	**1.42**	**1 1.64**	**1.40**	**1.18**	**0.99**	**2 0.84**
Cash Flow Per Share	**1.30**	**1.67**	**1.89**	**1.59**	**1.36**	**1.15**	**0.98**
Tang. Book Val. Per Share	**3.06**	**3.19**	**2.66**	**2.18**	**1.78**	**1.79**	**1.55**
Dividends Per Share	**0.64**	**0.60**	**0.56**	**0.50**	**0.44**	**0.39**	**0.34**
Dividend Payout %	**65.3**	**42.3**	**34.1**	**35.7**	**37.3**	**39.4**	**40.5**
INCOME STATEMENT (IN MILLIONS):							
Total Revenues	19,805.0	18,813.0	18,868.0	18,546.0	18,018.0	16,172.0	13,957.0
Costs & Expenses	15,031.0	13,201.0	13,241.0	14,152.0	13,538.0	12,053.0	10,495.0
Depreciation & Amort.	792.0	645.0	626.0	479.0	454.0	411.0	360.0
Operating Income	3,982.0	4,967.0	1 5,001.0	3,915.0	4,026.0	3,708.0	3,102.0
Net Interest Inc./(Exp.)	d77.0	d58.0	d47.0	d48.0	d27.0	d18.0	d24.0
Income Before Income Taxes	3,819.0	5,198.0	6,055.0	4,596.0	4,328.0	3,728.0	3,185.0
Income Taxes	1,388.0	1,665.0	1,926.0	1,104.0	1,342.0	1,174.0	997.0
Equity Earnings/Minority Int.	d184.0	32.0	155.0	211.0	169.0	134.0	91.0
Net Income	3 2,431.0	3,533.0	1 4,129.0	3,492.0	2,986.0	2,554.0	2 2,188.0
Cash Flow	3,223.0	4,178.0	4,755.0	3,971.0	3,440.0	2,965.0	2,548.0
Average Shs. Outstg. (000)	2,487,000	2,496,000	2,515,000	2,494,000	2,524,000	2,580,000	2,604,000
BALANCE SHEET (IN MILLIONS):							
Cash & Cash Equivalents	1,812.0	1,807.0	1,843.0	1,658.0	1,315.0	1,531.0	1,078.0
Total Current Assets	6,480.0	6,380.0	5,969.0	5,910.0	5,450.0	5,205.0	4,434.0
Net Property	4,267.0	3,669.0	3,743.0	3,550.0	4,336.0	4,080.0	3,729.0
Total Assets	21,623.0	19,145.0	16,940.0	16,161.0	15,041.0	13,873.0	12,021.0
Total Current Liabilities	9,856.0	8,640.0	7,379.0	7,406.0	7,348.0	6,177.0	5,171.0
Long-Term Obligations	854.0	687.0	801.0	1,116.0	1,141.0	1,426.0	1,428.0
Net Stockholders' Equity	9,513.0	8,403.0	7,311.0	6,156.0	5,392.0	5,235.0	4,584.0
Net Working Capital	d3,376.0	d2,260.0	d1,410.0	d1,496.0	d1,898.0	d972.0	d737.0
Year-end Shs. Outstg. (000)	2,471,575	2,466,000	2,471,000	2,481,000	2,504,598	2,551,866	2,594,906
STATISTICAL RECORD:							
Operating Profit Margin %	20.1	26.4	26.5	21.1	22.3	22.9	22.2
Net Profit Margin %	12.3	18.8	21.9	18.8	16.6	15.8	15.7
Return on Equity %	25.6	42.0	56.5	56.7	55.4	48.8	47.7
Return on Assets %	11.2	18.5	24.4	21.6	19.9	18.4	18.2
Debt/Total Assets %	3.9	3.6	4.7	6.9	7.6	10.3	11.9
Price Range	70 7/8-47 5/16	88 15/16-53 5/8	72 5/8-50	54 1/4-36 1/16	40 3/16-24 3/8	26 3/4-19 7/16	22 9/16-18 3/4
P/E Ratio	72.3-48.3	62.6-37.8	44.3-30.5	38.7-25.8	34.1-20.7	27.0-19.6	26.9-22.3
Average Yield %	1.1	0.8	0.9	1.1	1.4	1.7	1.6

Statistics are as originally reported. Adj. for stk. splits: 2-for-1, 5/96 1 Incls. non-recurr. pre-tax net gain $290.0 mill. 2 Bef. acctg. change chrg. $12.0 mill. 3 Incls. non-recurr. chrg. of $813.0 mill.

OFFICERS:
D. N. Daft, Chmn., C.E.O.
J. L. Stahl, Pres., C.O.O.
G. P. Fayard, Sr. V.P., C.F.O.

PRINCIPAL OFFICE: One Coca-Cola Plaza, Atlanta, GA 30313

TELEPHONE NUMBER: (404) 676-2121
FAX: (404) 676-6792
WEB: www.coca-cola.com
NO. OF EMPLOYEES: 37,400 (approx.)
SHAREHOLDERS: 394,603
ANNUAL MEETING: In April
INCORPORATED: DE, Sep., 1919

INSTITUTIONAL HOLDINGS:
No. of Institutions: 954
Shares Held: 1,207,557,286
% Held: 48.9
INDUSTRY: Bottled and canned soft drinks (SIC: 2086)
TRANSFER AGENT(S): First Chicago Trust Company of New York, Jersey City, NJ

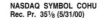

NASDAQ SYMBOL COHU
Rec. Pr. 35⅛ (5/31/00)

COHU, INC.

YIELD 0.6%
P/E RATIO 28.1

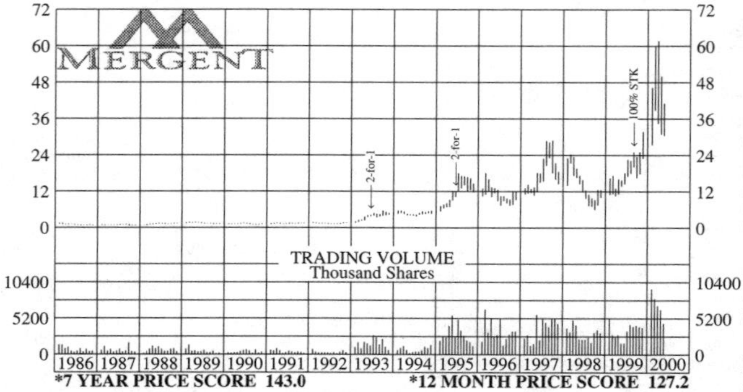

*7 YEAR PRICE SCORE 143.0   *12 MONTH PRICE SCORE 127.2
*NYSE COMPOSITE INDEX=100

TRADING VOLUME
Thousand Shares

INTERIM EARNINGS (Per Share):

Qtr.	Mar.	June	Sept.	Dec.
1996	0.41	0.39	0.42	0.45
1997	0.24	0.35	0.42	0.45
1998	0.41	0.27	0.03	d0.12
1999	0.07	0.24	0.36	0.58

INTERIM DIVIDENDS (Per Share):

Amt.	Decl.	Ex.	Rec.	Pay.
100% STK	8/19/99	9/27/99	9/03/99	9/24/99
0.045Q	7/15/99	9/01/99	9/03/99	10/22/99
0.045Q	10/14/99	11/29/99	12/01/99	1/14/00
0.05Q	1/27/00	3/16/00	3/20/00	4/26/00
0.05Q	5/17/00	6/21/00	6/23/00	8/04/00

Indicated div.: $0.20

CAPITALIZATION (12/31/99):

	($000)	(%)
Deferred Income Tax	674	0.4
Common & Surplus	162,356	99.6
Total	163,030	100.0

DIVIDEND ACHIEVER STATUS:

Rank: 35   10-Year Growth Rate: 17.87%
Total Years of Dividend Growth: 12

RECENT DEVELOPMENTS: For the year ended 12/31/99, net income advanced to $25.9 million compared with $11.6 million in the prior year. The 1998 results included a non-recurring charge of $1.0 million. Net sales were $208.8 million, an increase of 21.7% from $171.5 million the year before. Semiconductor equipment net sales improved 28.5% to $175.1 million, while television camera net sales climbed 1.6% to $21.3 million. Gross margin as a percentage of net sales grew to 39.3% versus 32.1% in 1998. New

orders for 1999 were $253.6 million versus $144.1 million a year earlier. Backlog at 12/31/99 was $72.9 million compared with $28.1 million at 12/31/98. On 1/10/00, COHU announced that it has united its semiconductor test handler companies, Delta Design and Daymarc, under the Delta Design name. By aligning the handler operations, COHU can more effectively leverage its capabilities and resources to meet the needs and expectations of its customers.

BUSINESS

COHU, INC. operates through two chief business segments. The semiconductor equipment segment, operated under the Company's wholly owned subsidiary Delta Design, Inc., designs, manufactures and sells semiconductor test handling equipment to semiconductor manufacturers throughout the world. The television camera segment (the Electronics Division) designs, manufactures and sells closed circuit television cameras and systems to original equipment manufacturers, contractors and government agencies. The Company's other operating segments include Fisher Research Laboratory, Inc., a metal detection business, and Broadcast Microwave Services, Inc., a microwave radio equipment company.

REVENUES

(12/31/99)	($000)	(%)
Semiconductor		
Equipment	115,671	87.1
Television Cameras	11,758	8.9
All Other	5,419	4.0
Total	132,848	100.0

ANNUAL FINANCIAL DATA

	12/31/99	12/31/98	12/31/97	12/31/96	12/31/95	12/31/94	12/31/93
Earnings Per Share	1.26	0.59	1.47	1.25	1.23	0.58	0.41
Cash Flow Per Share	1.43	0.72	1.57	1.34	1.33	0.64	0.46
Tang. Book Val. Per Share	8.10	6.97	6.49	5.02	3.82	2.50	2.05
Dividends Per Share	0.17	0.15	0.12	0.10	0.07	0.06	0.05
Dividend Payout %	13.9	25.6	7.8	7.6	5.9	10.0	12.0
INCOME STATEMENT (IN THOUSANDS):							
Total Revenues	208,780	171,511	187,756	159,353	178,759	102,726	75,278
Costs & Expenses	170,831	156,135	142,720	120,821	138,645	84,781	63,343
Depreciation & Amort.	3,294	2,799	2,148	1,653	1,884	1,181	952
Operating Income	34,655	12,577	42,888	36,879	38,230	16,764	10,983
Net Interest Inc./(Exp.)	4,271	3,469	2,999	1,960	692	d146	27
Income Before Income Taxes	38,926	16,046	45,887	38,839	38,922	16,618	11,010
Income Taxes	13,000	4,400	16,700	14,600	15,300	6,500	4,200
Net Income	25,926	11,646	29,187	24,239	23,622	10,118	6,810
Cash Flow	29,220	14,445	31,335	25,892	25,506	11,299	7,762
Average Shs. Outstg.	20,502	19,940	19,900	19,354	19,168	17,632	16,732
BALANCE SHEET (IN THOUSANDS):							
Cash & Cash Equivalents	81,600	86,703	53,550	52,986	28,874	3,096	3,911
Total Current Assets	202,769	143,398	141,530	98,585	88,076	55,912	33,737
Net Property	17,016	17,613	18,949	16,811	13,171	9,079	8,774
Total Assets	220,733	162,231	162,892	117,926	103,934	68,368	42,835
Total Current Liabilities	56,719	23,255	35,329	20,582	30,848	17,832	7,385
Long-Term Obligations	...	...	...	...	...	1,400	...
Net Stockholders' Equity	162,356	137,463	126,211	96,272	72,029	47,371	33,591
Net Working Capital	146,050	120,143	106,201	78,003	57,228	38,080	26,352
Year-end Shs. Outstg.	19,938	19,558	19,098	18,682	18,184	17,620	16,212
STATISTICAL RECORD:							
Operating Profit Margin %	16.6	7.3	22.8	23.1	21.4	16.3	14.6
Net Profit Margin %	12.4	6.8	15.5	15.2	13.2	9.8	9.0
Return on Equity %	16.0	8.5	23.1	25.2	32.8	21.4	20.3
Return on Assets %	11.7	7.2	17.9	20.6	22.7	14.8	15.9
Debt/Total Assets %	...	...	...	...	...	2.0	...
Price Range	31¾-10⁹/₁₆	24⁵/₁₆-8	28⅞-10¾	18⅛-7⅜	18-5⁷/₁₆	5¹¹/₁₆-3¹³/₁₆	5⅝-1⅝
P/E Ratio	25.2-8.4	41.6-10.3	19.7-7.3	14.5-5.9	14.6-4.4	9.9-6.6	13.8-4.0
Average Yield %	0.8	1.0	0.6	0.7	0.6	1.2	1.3

Statistics are as originally reported. Adj. for stk. splits: 2-for-1, 9/99; 6/95; 6/93.

OFFICERS:
C. A. Schwan, Chmn., C.E.O.
J. A. Donahue, Pres., C.O.O.
J. H. Allen, C.F.O., V.P., Sec.

INVESTOR CONTACT: John H. Allen, V.P.--Fin., C.F.O. and Sec., (858) 541-5194

PRINCIPAL OFFICE: 5755 Kearny Villa Road, San Diego, CA 92123

TELEPHONE NUMBER: (858) 277-6700
FAX: (858) 277-0221
WEB: www.cohu.com
NO. OF EMPLOYEES: 1,300 (approx.)
SHAREHOLDERS: 1,201 (of record); 10,000 (approx. total)
ANNUAL MEETING: In May
INCORPORATED: DE, Jan., 1957

INSTITUTIONAL HOLDINGS:
No. of Institutions: 76
Shares Held: 17,814,592 (Adj.)
% Held: 44.9
INDUSTRY: Instruments to measure electricity (SIC: 3825)
TRANSFER AGENT(S): ChaseMellon Shareholder Services, L.L.C., Ridgefield Park, NJ

NYSE SYMBOL CL
Rec. Pr. 52 5/8 (5/31/00)

COLGATE-PALMOLIVE COMPANY

YIELD 1.2%
P/E RATIO 35.6

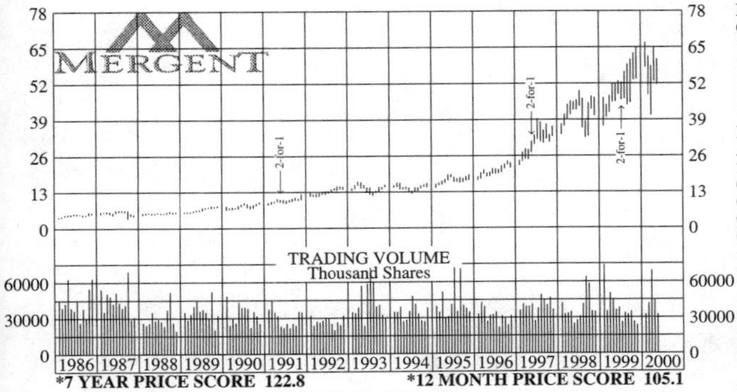

***7 YEAR PRICE SCORE 122.8** ***12 MONTH PRICE SCORE 105.1**

*NYSE COMPOSITE INDEX=100

INTERIM EARNINGS (Per Share):

Qtr.	Mar.	June	Sept.	Dec.
1995	0.27	0.24	d0.44	0.20
1996	0.24	0.25	0.27	0.30
1997	0.28	0.29	0.31	0.32
1998	0.30	0.31	0.33	0.37
1999	0.33	0.36	0.38	0.41

INTERIM DIVIDENDS (Per Share):

Amt.	Decl.	Ex.	Rec.	Pay.
2-for-1	5/05/99	7/01/99	5/19/99	6/30/99
0.158Q	7/08/99	7/22/99	7/26/99	8/16/99
0.158Q	10/14/99	10/22/99	10/26/99	11/15/99
0.158Q	1/13/00	1/24/00	1/26/00	2/15/00
0.158Q	3/09/00	4/24/00	4/26/00	5/15/00

Indicated div.: $0.63 (Div. Reinv. Plan)

CAPITALIZATION (12/31/99):

	($000)	(%)
Long-Term Debt	2,243,300	50.1
Deferred Income Tax	398,600	8.9
Preferred Stock	366,500	8.2
Common & Surplus	1,467,200	32.8
Total	4,475,600	100.0

DIVIDEND ACHIEVER STATUS:
Rank: 122 10-Year Growth Rate: 11.71%
Total Years of Dividend Growth: 37

RECENT DEVELOPMENTS: For the year ended 12/31/99, net income increased 10.5% to $937.3 million from $848.6 million in the previous year. Earnings benefited from new product initiatives and strong unit volume growth. Net sales were $9.12 billion, up slightly from $8.97 billion in the prior year. Gross profit as a percentage of sales was 53.7% compared with 52.2% in the preceding year.

PROSPECTS: Going forward, the Company will continue to focus on its global financial strategy which includes increasing gross margin, reducing overhead and increasing advertising. Meanwhile, the Company should continue to generate strong earnings and revenue growth due mainly to new product activity and improvements in operating efficiency.

BUSINESS

COLGATE-PALMOLIVE COMPANY is a consumer products company that markets its products in over 200 countries. The Company operates two segments. Oral, Personal and Household Care accounted for 88.0% of 1999 revenues and consists of toothpastes, toothbrushes, soaps, shampoos, baby products, deodorants, detergents, cleaners, shave products and other similar items under brand names including COLGATE, PALMOLIVE, MENNEN, PROTEX, AJAX, and FAB. Pet Nutrition, 12%, consists of pet food products manufactured and marketed by Hill's Pet Nutrition. Hill's markets pet foods primarily under SCIENCE DIET, which is sold by authorized pet supply retailers, breeders and veterinarians for every day nutritional needs, and PRESCRIPTION DIET for dogs and cats with disease conditions.

ANNUAL FINANCIAL DATA

	12/31/99	12/31/98	12/31/97	12/31/96	12/31/95	12/31/94	12/31/93
Earnings Per Share	**1.47**	**1.31**	**1.14**	**1.05**	[1] **0.26**	[1] **0.96**	[2] **0.85**
Cash Flow Per Share	**2.00**	**1.82**	**1.63**	**1.62**	**0.81**	**1.39**	**1.22**
Dividends Per Share	**0.59**	**0.55**	**0.53**	**0.47**	**0.44**	**0.39**	**0.34**
Dividend Payout %	**40.1**	**42.1**	**46.7**	**44.8**	**169.2**	**40.3**	**39.6**
INCOME STATEMENT (IN MILLIONS):							
Total Revenues	9,118.2	8,971.6	9,056.7	8,749.0	8,358.2	7,587.9	7,141.3
Costs & Expenses	7,138.2	7,157.1	7,378.6	7,186.9	7,392.9	6,303.4	5,977.4
Depreciation & Amort.	340.2	330.3	319.9	316.3	300.3	235.1	209.6
Operating Income	1,639.8	1,484.2	1,358.2	1,245.8	665.0	1,049.4	954.3
Net Interest Inc./(Exp.)	d171.6	d172.9	d183.5	d197.4	d205.4	d86.7	d46.8
Income Before Income Taxes	1,394.6	1,250.1	1,102.3	954.6	363.5	879.9	836.2
Income Taxes	457.3	401.5	361.9	319.6	191.5	299.7	288.1
Net Income	937.3	848.6	740.4	635.0	[1] 172.0	[1] 580.2	[2] 548.1
Cash Flow	1,256.5	1,158.0	1,039.2	929.9	450.7	793.7	736.1
Average Shs. Outstg. (000)	638,800	648,400	650,200	586,400	580,800	584,800	623,600
BALANCE SHEET (IN MILLIONS):							
Cash & Cash Equivalents	235.2	194.5	205.3	307.8	256.6	217.5	211.2
Total Current Assets	2,354.8	2,244.9	2,196.5	2,372.3	2,360.2	2,177.7	2,070.4
Net Property	2,551.1	2,589.2	2,441.0	2,428.9	2,155.2	1,988.1	1,766.3
Total Assets	7,423.1	7,685.2	7,538.7	7,901.5	7,642.3	6,142.4	5,761.2
Total Current Liabilities	2,273.5	2,114.4	1,959.5	1,904.3	1,753.1	1,529.2	1,394.0
Long-Term Obligations	2,243.3	2,300.6	2,340.3	2,786.8	2,992.0	1,751.5	1,532.4
Net Stockholders' Equity	1,833.7	2,085.6	2,178.6	2,034.1	1,679.8	1,822.9	1,875.0
Net Working Capital	81.3	130.5	237.0	468.0	607.1	648.5	676.4
Year-end Shs. Outstg. (000)	578,863	585,420	591,280	588,536	583,200	577,616	597,028
STATISTICAL RECORD:							
Operating Profit Margin %	18.0	16.5	15.0	13.2	6.9	13.1	13.4
Net Profit Margin %	10.3	9.5	8.2	7.3	2.1	7.6	7.7
Return on Equity %	51.1	40.7	34.0	31.2	10.2	31.8	29.2
Return on Assets %	12.6	11.0	9.8	8.0	2.3	9.4	9.5
Debt/Total Assets %	30.2	29.9	31.0	35.3	39.2	28.5	26.6
Price Range	65-36 9/16	49 7/16-32 9/16	39 3/8-22 1/2	24 1/8-17 1/4	19 3/8-14 1/2	16 3/8-12 3/8	16 13/16-11 11/16
P/E Ratio	44.2-24.9	37.9-24.9	34.7-19.8	23.0-16.4	74.4-55.7	17.1-13.0	19.9-13.8
Average Yield %	1.2	1.3	1.7	2.3	2.6	2.7	2.4

Statistics are as originally reported. Adj. for stk. splits: 2-for-1, 6/99, 5/97. [1] Incl. non-recurr. chrg. 1995, $369.2 mill.; 1994, $5.2 mill. [2] Bef. acctg. change chrg. $358.2 mill.

OFFICERS:
R. Mark, Chmn., C.E.O.
W. S. Shanahan, Pres., C.O.O.
S. C. Patrick, C.F.O.
A. D. Hendry, Sr. V.P., Couns., Sec.

INVESTOR CONTACT: Bina Thompson, Investor Relations, (212) 310-3072

PRINCIPAL OFFICE: 300 Park Ave., New York, NY 10022-7499

TELEPHONE NUMBER: (212) 310-2000
FAX: (212) 310-3284
WEB: www.colgate.com

NO. OF EMPLOYEES: 37,200 (approx.)

SHAREHOLDERS: 44,600 (com.); 275 (pfd.)

ANNUAL MEETING: In May

INCORPORATED: DE, Jul., 1923

INSTITUTIONAL HOLDINGS:
No. of Institutions: 688
Shares Held: 377,799,583
% Held: 64.8

INDUSTRY: Toilet preparations (SIC: 2844)

TRANSFER AGENT(S): First Chicago Trust Company of New York, Jersey City, NJ

COMERICA, INC.

YIELD	3.2%
P/E RATIO	12.2

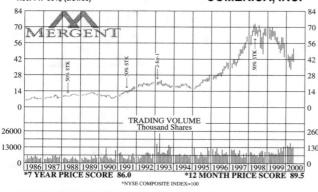

TRADING VOLUME
Thousand Shares

|1986|1987|1988|1989|1990|1991|1992|1993|1994|1995|1996|1997|1998|1999|2000|

*7 YEAR PRICE SCORE 86.0   ***12 MONTH PRICE SCORE 89.5**
*NYSE COMPOSITE INDEX=100

INTERIM EARNINGS (Per Share):

Qtr.	Mar.	June	Sept.	Dec.
1996	0.65	0.67	0.69	0.35
1997	0.73	0.77	0.82	0.85
1998	0.88	0.92	0.95	0.97
1999	0.98	1.03	1.05	1.08

INTERIM DIVIDENDS (Per Share):

Amt.	Decl.	Ex.	Rec.	Pay.
0.36Q	5/21/99	6/11/99	6/15/99	7/01/99
0.36Q	7/16/99	9/13/99	9/15/99	10/01/99
0.36Q	11/19/99	12/13/99	12/15/99	1/01/00
0.40Q	1/21/00	3/13/00	3/15/00	4/01/00
0.40Q	5/19/00	6/13/00	6/15/00	7/01/00

Indicated div.: $1.60 (Div. Reinv. Plan)

CAPITALIZATION (12/31/99):

	($000)	(%)
Total Deposits	23,291,403	65.9
Long-Term Debt	8,579,857	24.3
Preferred Stock	250,000	0.7
Common & Surplus	3,224,644	9.1
Total	35,345,904	100.0

DIVIDEND ACHIEVER STATUS:
Rank: 136   10-Year Growth Rate: 11.09%
Total Years of Dividend Growth: 16

RECENT DEVELOPMENTS: For the year ended 12/31/99, net income rose 10.8% to $672.6 million from $607.1 million in 1998. Net interest income grew 5.9% to $1.55 billion from $1.46 billion a year earlier. This improvement was principally due to an increase in average commercial loans compared with the year before. Net interest margin declined to 4.55% from 4.57% in the prior year. Non-interest income advanced 18.9% to $716.9 million.

PROSPECTS: Going forward, CMA expects to perform well due to continued strong commercial loan growth, as well as increased fee income and stabilized expenses. Separately, the Company and MBNA America Bank announced a strategic alliance to provide MBNA credit card and check-accessed line of credit services to CMA customers. Under the alliance, CMA will sell its $500.0 million credit card and Cash Reserve portfolio to MBNA.

BUSINESS

COMERICA, INC. is a bank holding company headquartered in Detroit, Michigan. The Company, as of 3/31/00, had assets of approximately $39.66 billion and total deposits of approximately $23.31 billion. The Company operates banking subsidiaries in Michigan, Texas and California, banking operations in Florida, and businesses in nine other states. CMA is a diversified financial services provider, offering a broad range of financial products and services for businesses and individuals. The Company also operates banking subsidiaries in Canada and Mexico.

LOAN DISTRIBUTION

(12/31/99)	($000)	(%)
Commercial	20,654,658	63.2
International	2,573,003	7.9
Real estate contruction	1,709,261	5.2
Commercial Mortgage	4,774,052	14.6
Residental Mortgage	870,029	2.7
Consumer	1,350,725	4.1
Lease financing	761,550	2.3
Total	32,693,278	100.0

ANNUAL FINANCIAL DATA

	12/31/99	12/31/98	12/31/97	12/31/96	12/31/95	12/31/94	12/31/93
Earnings Per Share	4.14	① 3.72	3.19	① 2.37	2.36	2.19	① 1.90
Tang. Book Val. Per Share	20.60	17.94	16.02	14.77	15.17	13.64	12.66
Dividends Per Share	1.40	1.25	1.12	0.99	0.89	0.80	0.70
Dividend Payout %	33.8	33.5	35.1	41.7	37.9	36.6	36.7
INCOME STATEMENT (IN MILLIONS):							
Total Interest Income	2,672.7	2,616.8	2,647.4	2,562.8	2,613.9	2,091.9	1,782.9
Total Interest Expense	1,125.6	1,155.5	1,204.6	1,150.5	1,314.0	861.8	649.3
Net Interest Income	1,547.1	1,461.3	1,442.8	1,412.3	1,299.9	1,230.1	1,133.5
Provision for Loan Losses	114.0	113.0	146.0	114.0	86.5	56.0	69.0
Non-Interest Income	716.9	603.1	528.0	507.0	498.7	450.2	449.7
Non-Interest Expense	1,117.0	1,020.0	1,008.0	1,159.0	1,086.4	1,042.2	1,025.6
Income Before Taxes	1,033.1	931.4	816.7	646.2	625.7	582.1	488.6
Net Income	672.6	① 607.1	530.5	① 417.2	413.4	387.2	① 340.6
Average Shs. Outstg. (000)	158,397	158,757	161,040	172,281	175,341	177,240	179,354
BALANCE SHEET (IN MILLIONS):							
Cash & Due from Banks	1,202.0	1,773.1	1,927.1	1,901.8	2,028.4	1,822.3	1,600.7
Securities Avail. for Sale	3,352.4	2,821.8	4,208.9	4,800.0	6,870.0	2,910.6	2,325.7
Total Loans & Leases	32,693.3	30,604.9	28,895.0	26,206.7	24,442.3	22,209.2	19,099.9
Allowance for Credit Losses	476.5	452.4	424.1	367.2	341.3	326.2	298.7
Net Loans & Leases	32,216.8	30,152.5	28,470.9	25,839.5	24,100.9	21,883.1	18,801.3
Total Assets	38,653.3	36,600.8	36,292.4	34,102.5	35,469.9	33,429.9	30,294.9
Total Deposits	23,291.4	24,313.1	22,586.3	22,367.2	23,167.2	22,432.3	20,949.9
Long-Term Obligations	8,579.9	5,282.3	7,286.4	4,241.8	4,644.4	4,097.9	1,460.6
Total Liabilities	35,178.7	33,554.2	33,530.6	31,590.5	32,862.1	31,038.1	28,113.2
Net Stockholders' Equity	3,474.6	3,046.6	2,761.8	2,615.6	2,607.7	2,391.8	2,181.7
Year-end Shs. Outstg. (000)	156,518	155,881	156,815	160,211	171,906	175,368	172,307
STATISTICAL RECORD:							
Return on Equity %	19.4	19.9	19.2	15.9	15.9	16.2	15.6
Return on Assets %	1.7	1.7	1.5	1.2	1.2	1.2	1.1
Equity/Assets %	9.0	8.3	7.6	7.7	7.4	7.2	7.2
Non-Int. Exp./Tot. Inc. %	49.3	49.4	51.1	60.4	60.4	62.0	64.8
Price Range	70-44	73-46½	61⅞-34¾₁₆	39⁹⁄₁₆-24¹⁵⁄₁₆	28½-16¹⁄₁₆	20¹³⁄₁₆-16¹⁄₁₆	23½-16¾₄
P/E Ratio	16.9-10.6	19.6-12.5	19.4-10.7	16.7-10.2	12.1-6.8	9.5-7.4	12.4-8.8
Average Yield %	2.5	2.1	2.3	3.1	4.0	4.3	3.5

Statistics are as originally reported. Adj. for 50% stk. div., 4/98; 2-for-1 split, 1/93. ① Incl. merger-related or restructuring charges: $6.8 mill., 1998; $90.0 mill., 1996; $22.0 mill., 1993.

OFFICERS:
E. A. Miller, Chmn., Pres., C.E.O.
R. W. Babb Jr., Vice-Chmn., C.F.O.

INVESTOR CONTACT: Allison McFerren Cicone, Investor Relations, (313) 222-6317

PRINCIPAL OFFICE: 500 Woodward Ave., Detroit, MI 48226

TELEPHONE NUMBER: (313) 222-3300
FAX: (313) 222-6091
WEB: www.comerica.com
NO. OF EMPLOYEES: 8,997 full-time; 1,845 part-time
SHAREHOLDERS: 17,511 (approx.)
ANNUAL MEETING: In May
INCORPORATED: DE, 1973

INSTITUTIONAL HOLDINGS:
No. of Institutions: 308
Shares Held: 89,568,399
% Held: 57.3

INDUSTRY: National commercial banks (SIC: 6021)

TRANSFER AGENT(S): Norwest Shareowner Services, South St. Paul, MN

COMMERCE BANCSHARES, INC.

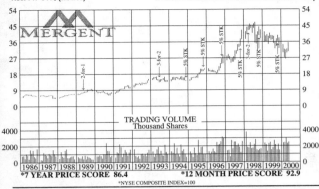

INTERIM EARNINGS (Per Share):

Qtr.	Mar.	June	Sept.	Dec.
1996	0.43	0.45	0.49	0.51
1997	0.47	0.52	0.55	0.59
1998	0.55	0.60	0.64	0.66
1999	0.62	0.68	0.68	0.70

INTERIM DIVIDENDS (Per Share):

Amt.	Decl.	Ex.	Rec.	Pay.
0.15Q	8/06/99	9/13/99	9/15/99	9/29/99
0.15Q	10/29/99	11/26/99	11/30/99	12/17/99
5% STK	10/29/99	11/26/99	11/30/99	12/17/99
0.155Q	2/04/00	3/07/00	3/09/00	3/30/00
0.155Q	4/19/00	6/07/00	6/09/00	6/29/00

Indicated div.: $0.62 (Div. Reinv. Plan)

CAPITALIZATION (12/31/99):

	($000)	(%)
Total Deposits	9,164,123	89.2
Long-Term Debt	25,735	0.3
Common & Surplus	1,079,832	10.5
Total	10,269,690	100.0

DIVIDEND ACHIEVER STATUS:
Rank: 145   10-Year Growth Rate: 10.59%
Total Years of Dividend Growth: 31

TRADING VOLUME
Thousand Shares

*7 YEAR PRICE SCORE 86.4   ***12 MONTH PRICE SCORE 92.9**

NYSE COMPOSITE INDEX=100

RECENT DEVELOPMENTS:

For the year ended 12/31/99, net income increased 10.7% to $166.2 million compared with $150.1 million in the prior year. Net interest income advanced 8.4% to $466.0 million from $427.7 million the year before. This increase was primarily attributed to average loan growth of 9.4% and lower deposit costs. Total interest income was $750.6 million, an improvement of 3.0% from $728.5 million in the previous year. Total non-interest income climbed 10.4% to $236.2 million from $214.0 million in 1998. Total non-interest expense improved 10.5% to $419.0 million from $379.3 million a year earlier. Provision for loan losses decreased 4.2% to $35.3 million from $36.9 million a year ago. The return on average assets was 1.50% compared to 1.43% in 1998, and the return on equity increased to 15.40% from 14.58% a year earlier. For the fourth quarter ended 12/31/99, net income increased 9.8% to $44.4 million versus $40.4 million in the 1998 quarter.

BUSINESS

COMMERCE BANCSHARES, INC., with assets of $11.40 billion as of 12/31/99, is a bank holding company that owns or controls substantially all of the outstanding capital stock of one national banking association located in Missouri, one national banking association located in Illinois, three national banking associations located in Kansas, and a credit card bank located in Nebraska. In addition, the Company owns directly several non-banking subsidiaries that are engaged in owning real estate. These real estate subsidiaries are engaged in leasing to the Company's banking subsidiaries, underwriting credit life and credit accident and health insurance, selling property and casualty insurance, providing venture capital through a small business investment corporation as well as a venture capital limited partnership, and mortgage banking.

LOAN DISTRIBUTION

(12/31/99)	($000)	(%)
Business	2,564,476	33.85
Real Estate-		
Construction	354,351	4.68
Real Estate-Business	1,247,956	16.47
Real Estate-Personal	1,377,903	18.19
Personal banking	1,510,380	19.93
Credit card	521,826	6.88
Total	7,576,892	100.0

ANNUAL FINANCIAL DATA

	12/31/99	12/31/98	12/31/97	12/31/96	12/31/95	12/31/94	12/31/93
Earnings Per Share	2.59	2.31	☐2.03	1.79	1.56	1.49	1.43
Tang. Book Val. Per Share	16.22	15.63	14.01	12.89	11.69	11.90	11.71
Dividends Per Share	0.57	0.53	0.47	0.42	0.38	0.33	0.29
Dividend Payout %	22.1	22.8	23.2	23.3	24.1	22.0	20.3
INCOME STATEMENT (IN MILLIONS):							
Total Interest Income	750.6	728.5	682.9	647.6	631.0	500.3	460.4
Total Interest Expense	284.6	300.7	285.1	281.9	275.3	185.7	175.9
Net Interest Income	466.0	427.7	397.8	365.7	355.7	314.6	284.5
Provision for Loan Losses	35.3	36.9	31.4	24.5	14.6	5.8	11.4
Non-Interest Income	236.2	214.0	180.1	159.2	133.2	121.0	121.4
Non-Interest Expense	419.0	379.3	344.4	318.0	305.5	282.1	257.3
Income Before Taxes	247.9	225.6	202.1	182.4	168.8	147.7	137.3
Net Income	166.2	150.1	☐132.7	119.5	107.6	96.1	86.9
Average Shs. Outstg. (000)	63,447	65,209	65,361	66,766	68,924	61,466	60,620
BALANCE SHEET (IN MILLIONS):							
Cash & Due from Banks	685.2	738.7	978.2	833.3	774.9	565.8	534.8
Securities Avail. for Sale	2,475.4	3,002.4	2,620.5	2,681.7	2,561.6	2,626.9	375.5
Total Loans & Leases	7,576.9	7,046.9	6,224.4	5,472.3	5,317.8	4,432.7	4,024.1
Allowance for Credit Losses	123.0	117.1	105.9	98.2	98.5	87.2	85.8
Net Loans & Leases	7,453.9	6,929.8	6,118.5	5,374.1	5,219.3	4,345.5	3,938.2
Total Assets	11,400.9	11,402.0	10,306.9	9,698.2	9,574.0	8,035.6	8,047.4
Total Deposits	9,164.1	9,530.2	8,700.6	8,166.4	8,193.1	6,990.4	6,839.5
Long-Term Obligations	25.7	27.1	7.2	14.1	14.6	6.5	6.9
Total Liabilities	10,321.1	10,321.2	9,326.2	8,773.9	8,690.2	7,307.4	7,334.8
Net Stockholders' Equity	1,079.8	1,080.8	980.8	924.3	883.8	728.2	712.6
Year-end Shs. Outstg. (000)	62,374	64,217	63,912	64,903	66,919	61,205	60,848
STATISTICAL RECORD:							
Return on Equity %	15.4	13.9	13.5	12.9	12.2	13.2	12.2
Return on Assets %	1.5	1.3	1.3	1.2	1.1	1.2	1.1
Equity/Assets %	9.5	9.5	9.5	9.5	9.2	9.1	8.9
Non-Int. Exp./Tot. Inc. %	59.7	59.1	59.6	60.6	62.5	64.7	63.4
Price Range	41⅔₁₆-32³₁₆	46¹³₁₆-30¹³₁₆	42½-24³₁₆	28½-18¼	20-14¹₁₆	16¹₁₆-13¹⁵₁₆	16⁹₁₆-13⁷₁₆
P/E Ratio	16.0-12.4	20.3-13.4	20.9-11.9	15.9-10.2	13.4-9.0	11.2-9.3	11.6-9.4
Average Yield %	1.5	1.4	1.4	1.8	2.1	2.1	1.9

Statistics are as originally reported. Adj. for stk. splits: 5% div., 12/18/98; 3-for-2, 3/30/98; 5% div., 12/12/97; 5% div., 12/13/96; 5% div., 12/15/95; 5% div., 12/29/94; 3-for-2, 6/93 ☐ Incl. non-recurr. credit $3.3 mill. ($0.08/sh.)

OFFICERS:
D. W. Kemper, Chmn., Pres., C.E.O.
J. M. Kemper, Vice-Chmn.
W. A. Sullins Jr., Vice-Chmn.
A. B. Clark, Exec. V.P., C.F.O., Treas.

INVESTOR CONTACT: Jeffery D. Aberdeen, Controller

PRINCIPAL OFFICE: 1000 Walnut, Kansas City, MO 64106

TELEPHONE NUMBER: (816) 234-2000
FAX: (816) 234-2369
WEB: www.commercebank.com

NO. OF EMPLOYEES: 4,586 full-time; 815 part-time

SHAREHOLDERS: 5,730

ANNUAL MEETING: In Apr.

INCORPORATED: MO, Aug., 1966

INSTITUTIONAL HOLDINGS:
No. of Institutions: 107
Shares Held: 22,903,745
% Held: 36.5

INDUSTRY: State commercial banks (SIC: 6022)

TRANSFER AGENT(S): First Chicago Trust Company of New York, Jersey City, NJ

COMMERCIAL NET LEASE REALTY, INC.

YIELD 11.5%
P/E RATIO 9.3

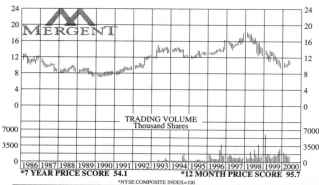

7 YEAR PRICE SCORE 54.1   **12 MONTH PRICE SCORE 95.7**
*NYSE COMPOSITE INDEX=100

INTERIM EARNINGS (Per Share):

Qtr.	Mar.	June	Sept.	Dec.
1996	0.28	0.29	0.31	0.30
1997	0.31	0.31	0.32	0.32
1998	0.15	0.32	0.34	0.29
1999	0.32	0.23	0.29	0.31

INTERIM DIVIDENDS (Per Share):

Amt.	Decl.	Ex.	Rec.	Pay.
0.31Q	4/16/99	4/28/99	4/30/99	5/14/99
0.31Q	7/14/99	7/28/99	7/30/99	8/13/99
0.31Q	10/13/99	10/27/99	10/29/99	11/15/99
0.31Q	1/14/00	1/27/00	1/31/00	2/15/00
0.31Q	4/14/00	4/26/00	4/28/00	5/15/00

Indicated div.: $1.24

CAPITALIZATION (12/31/99):

	($000)	(%)
Long-Term Debt	350,971	47.3
Common & Surplus	391,362	52.7
Total	742,333	100.0

DIVIDEND ACHIEVER STATUS:

Rank: 313   10-Year Growth Rate: 2.17%
Total Years of Dividend Growth: 10

RECENT DEVELOPMENTS: For the year ended 12/31/99, net income increased 8.8% to $35.3 million compared with $32.4 million in the previous year. Results included a gain on sale of real estate of $6.7 million and $1.4 million in 1999 and 1998, respectively. The Company sold 45 properties in fiscal 1999. Total revenues were $76.5 million, up 18.2% from $64.8 million the year before. Rental income from operating leases rose 19.5% to $57.5 million, while

earned income from direct financing leases grew 8.1% to $13.9 million. The Company's 99.0% occupancy rate and triple net leases provide a stable and predictable source of cash flow with limited growth opportunity. Therefore, NNN is pursuing opportunities in its service businesses. Meanwhile, the Company expects to report losses in the first half of the year with profits later in the year.

BUSINESS

COMMERCIAL NET LEASE REALTY, INC. is a fully integrated, self-administered real estate investment trust that acquires, owns, manages and indirectly develops a diversified portfolio of freestanding properties. The Company invests in single-tenant, freestanding retail properties that are located in intensive commercial corridors with purchase prices up to $7.5 million. As of 12/31/99, the Company owned 270 properties, of which 99.0% were leased, generally under full-credit and long-term commercial leases to major retail businesses. These businesses include Academy, Barnes & Noble, Bed Bath & Beyond, Best Buy, Borders, Eckerd, Food 4ᵉ Less, Good Guys, Heilig-Meyers, Hi-Lo Automotive, HomePlace/Waccamaw, Office Max, Sears Homelife Centers and the Sports Authority. In addition, the Company offers real estate services including acquisitions, build-to-suit development, geographic information systems, asset management and surplus property services to retailers.

ANNUAL FINANCIAL DATA

	12/31/99	12/31/98	12/31/97	12/31/96	12/31/95	12/31/94	12/31/93
Earnings Per Share	① 1.16	① 1.10	① 1.25	① 1.18	1.09	1.04	① 0.95
Tang. Book Val. Per Share	12.94	13.00	12.96	15.04	11.65	11.72	11.89
Dividends Per Share	1.24	1.23	1.20	1.18	1.16	1.14	1.10
Dividend Payout %	106.9	111.8	96.0	100.0	106.4	109.6	115.8
INCOME STATEMENT (IN THOUSANDS):							
Rental Income	58,417	48,935	38,143	25,140	15,200	8,945	4,396
Interest Income	16,243	13,476	11,992	8,229	5,380	3,344	673
Total Income	76,543	64,773	50,135	33,369	20,580	12,289	5,069
Costs & Expenses	16,436	13,835	3,723	2,844	1,981	1,545	896
Depreciation	8,634	6,759	5,302	3,553	2,058	1,331	645
Interest Expense	21,920	13,460	11,478	7,206	3,834	498	381
Income Before Income Taxes	36,277	32,074	30,283	19,839	12,707	8,915	3,522
Equity Earnings/Minority Int.	d966	367	102	...	...	...	...
Net Income	① 35,311	① 32,441	① 30,385	① 19,839	12,707	8,915	① 3,522
Average Shs. Outstg.	30,408	29,397	24,221	16,799	11,664	8,606	3,712
BALANCE SHEET (IN THOUSANDS):							
Cash & Cash Equivalents	3,329	1,442	2,160	1,410	301	1,070	19,847
Total Real Estate Investments	546,193	519,948	400,977	269,031	155,957	106,091	51,948
Total Assets	749,789	685,595	537,014	370,953	219,257	152,211	91,618
Long-Term Obligations	350,971	292,907	171,836	116,956	82,600	14,800	...
Total Liabilities	358,427	301,705	174,870	118,379	83,415	15,546	474
Net Stockholders' Equity	391,362	383,890	362,144	252,574	135,842	136,665	91,146
Year-end Shs. Outstg.	30,256	29,521	27,954	16,799	11,664	11,664	7,664
STATISTICAL RECORD:							
Net Inc.+Depr./Assets %	5.9	5.7	6.6	6.3	6.7	6.7	4.5
Return on Equity %	9.0	8.5	8.4	7.9	9.4	6.5	3.9
Return on Assets %	4.7	4.7	5.7	5.3	5.8	5.9	3.8
Price Range	13¹⁵/₁₆-9⁷/₁₆	18⁵/₁₆-12¹/₂	18¹/₈-13⁷/₈	16³/₈-12¾	13¾-11¾	14¹/₂-11⁷/₈	15-11¾
P/E Ratio	12.0-8.1	16.6-11.4	14.5-11.1	13.9-10.8	12.6-10.8	13.9-11.4	15.8-12.4
Average Yield %	10.6	8.0	7.5	8.1	9.1	8.6	8.2

Statistics are as originally reported. ① Incl. gain on sale of investment $6.7 mill., 1999; $1.4 mill., 1998; $651,000, 1997; $73,000, 1996; $374,000, 1993.

OFFICERS:
J. M. Seneff Jr., Chmn., C.E.O.
R. A. Bourne, Vice-Chmn.
G. M. Ralston, Pres., C.O.O.
K. B. Habicht, C.F.O., Sec., Treas., Exec. V.P.

INVESTOR CONTACT: Kevin B. Habicht, (407) 265-7348

PRINCIPAL OFFICE: 450 South Orange Avenue, Suite 900, Orlando, FL 32801

TELEPHONE NUMBER: (407) 265-7348
FAX: (407) 423-2894
WEB: www.cnlreit.com

NO. OF EMPLOYEES: 28

SHAREHOLDERS: 1,360 (approx.)

ANNUAL MEETING: In April

INCORPORATED: DE, June, 1984; reincorp., MD, June, 1994

INSTITUTIONAL HOLDINGS:
No. of Institutions: 64
Shares Held: 7,956,817
% Held: 26.2

INDUSTRY: Real estate investment trusts (SIC: 6798)

TRANSFER AGENT(S): First Union Bank of North Carolina, Charlotte, NC

COMMUNITY TRUST BANCORP, INC.

YIELD 5.2%
P/E RATIO 7.4

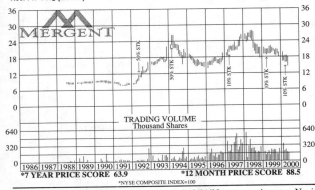

TRADING VOLUME
Thousand Shares

| 1986 | 1987 | 1988 | 1989 | 1990 | 1991 | 1992 | 1993 | 1994 | 1995 | 1996 | 1997 | 1998 | 1999 | 2000 |

*7 YEAR PRICE SCORE 63.9   ***12 MONTH PRICE SCORE 88.5**

*NYSE COMPOSITE INDEX=100

INTERIM EARNINGS (Per Share):

Qtr.	Mar.	June	Sept.	Dec.
1996	0.42	0.47	0.49	0.49
1997	0.44	0.45	0.44	0.25
1998	0.38	0.38	0.06	0.44
1999	0.46	0.49	0.50	0.51

INTERIM DIVIDENDS (Per Share):

Amt.	Decl.	Ex.	Rec.	Pay.
0.20Q	7/27/99	9/13/99	9/15/99	10/01/99
0.20Q	11/16/99	12/13/99	12/15/99	1/01/00
0.20Q	1/26/00	3/13/00	3/15/00	4/01/00
10% STK	1/26/00	3/16/00	3/20/00	4/15/00
0.19Q	4/25/00	6/13/00	6/15/00	7/01/00

Indicated div.: $0.76

CAPITALIZATION (12/31/99):

	($000)	(%)
Total Deposits	1,877,334	88.5
Long-Term Debt	70,598	3.3
Common & Surplus	172,419	8.1
Total	2,120,351	100.0

DIVIDEND ACHIEVER STATUS:

Rank: 185   10-Year Growth Rate: 8.75%
Total Years of Dividend Growth: 11

RECENT DEVELOPMENTS: For the year ended 12/31/99, net income soared 56.3% to $21.8 million compared with $14.0 million the previous year. Net interest income rose 9.4% to $83.8 million versus $76.6 million a year earlier. Total interest income advanced 1.8% to $163.5 million from $160.6 million the year before. Total interest expense declined 5.1% to $79.7 million from $84.0 million in the prior year. Noninterest income grew 8.0% to $21.0 million from $19.5 million the year before. Noninterest expense rose 3.6% to $64.4 million from $62.2 million a year ago. Provision for loan losses amounted to $9.1 million compared with $16.0 million in the prior year. Return on assets increased to 1.0% from 0.6% in the prior year, while return on equity improved to 12.7% versus 8.4% in the previous.

BUSINESS

COMMUNITY TRUST BANCORP, INC. is a bank holding company with assets of $2.18 billion as of 12/31/99 that currently owns all the capital stock of one commercial bank, one thrift and one trust company, serving small and mid-sized communities in eastern, central, south central Kentucky, and southern West Virginia. The commercial bank is Community Trust Bank, NA, Pikeville. The Company's thrift is Community Trust Bank, FSB, Campbellsville. The trust company, Trust Company of Kentucky, NA, Lexington, purchased the trust operations of its subsidiary banks and has additional offices in Pikeville, Ashland, Middlesboro and Louisville, Kentucky.

LOAN DISTRIBUTION

(12/31/99)	($000)	(%)
Comml-Secured by Real Est	406,330	25.1
Commercial-Other	293,659	18.1
Real Estate-Comml Constr	80,988	5.0
Real Estate-Resdtl Constr	18,002	1.1
Real Est-Consumer Mtge	397,168	24.5
Consumer	415,935	25.7
Equipment Lease Financing	7,398	0.5
Total	1,619,480	100.0

ANNUAL FINANCIAL DATA

	12/31/99	12/31/98	12/31/97	12/31/96	12/31/95	12/31/94	12/31/93
Earnings Per Share	1.97	1.25	① 1.44	1.55	0.91	0.67	1.28
Tang. Book Val. Per Share	10.23	9.24	11.52	10.28	9.36	8.47	8.31
Dividends Per Share	0.71	0.66	0.60	0.54	0.48	0.45	0.40
Dividend Payout %	36.1	52.9	41.6	34.9	52.7	67.4	31.4
INCOME STATEMENT (IN MILLIONS):							
Total Interest Income	163.5	160.6	150.6	144.4	131.0	98.9	97.1
Total Interest Expense	79.7	84.0	74.1	69.1	65.0	44.6	43.7
Net Interest Income	83.8	76.6	76.5	75.4	66.0	54.4	53.4
Provision for Loan Losses	9.1	16.0	11.2	7.3	5.9	4.9	3.6
Non-Interest Income	21.0	19.5	18.4	14.4	11.1	9.1	11.5
Non-Interest Expense	64.4	62.2	59.9	55.2	55.9	49.1	42.6
Income Before Taxes	31.3	17.9	23.9	27.3	15.4	9.5	18.7
Net Income	21.8	14.0	① 16.0	18.8	10.8	7.5	13.6
Average Shs. Outstg. (000)	11,089	11,069	11,132	12,163	11,926	11,177	10,657
BALANCE SHEET (IN MILLIONS):							
Cash & Due from Banks	99.8	98.1	61.4	63.9	67.5	60.5	56.1
Securities Avail. for Sale	270.3	301.1	165.6	230.0	279.7	82.4	...
Total Loans & Leases	1,619.5	1,502.4	1,428.4	1,309.6	1,115.1	850.6	792.0
Allowance for Credit Losses	25.1	26.1	20.5	18.8	16.1	11.0	12.0
Net Loans & Leases	1,594.4	1,476.3	1,408.0	1,290.8	1,099.0	839.6	780.1
Total Assets	2,176.1	2,248.0	1,852.7	1,840.0	1,730.2	1,397.8	1,352.9
Total Deposits	1,877.3	1,921.1	1,465.0	1,480.8	1,467.4	1,156.8	1,114.3
Long-Term Obligations	70.6	105.2	155.3	130.1	91.5	94.7	100.5
Total Liabilities	2,003.7	2,083.2	1,694.6	1,695.3	1,596.4	1,292.8	1,256.6
Net Stockholders' Equity	172.4	164.8	158.0	144.8	133.8	105.0	96.3
Year-end Shs. Outstg. (000)	11,043	11,072	12,176	12,151	12,144	11,164	10,278
STATISTICAL RECORD:							
Return on Equity %	12.7	8.5	10.1	13.0	8.1	7.1	14.2
Return on Assets %	1.0	0.6	0.9	1.0	0.6	0.5	1.0
Equity/Assets %	7.9	7.3	8.5	7.9	7.7	7.5	7.1
Non-Int. Exp./Tot. Inc. %	61.4	64.7	63.1	61.5	72.4	77.2	65.6
Price Range	22³⁄₁₆-17¹⁵⁄₁₆	27¹³⁄₁₆-17⁹⁄₁₆	26⁵⁄₁₆-18⁷⁄₁₆	19⁹⁄₁₆-13⁷⁄₈	19³⁄₄-14¹⁄₄	26⁵⁄₁₆-15⁷⁄₈	22¹⁄₄-15¹⁄₄
P/E Ratio	11.2-9.1	22.3-14.0	18.3-12.8	12.6-9.0	191.90⁄16-142.70⁄8	39.3-23.0	17.3-12.0
Average Yield %	3.5	2.9	2.7	3.2	3.2	2.2	2.1

Statistics are as originally reported. Adj. for 10% stk. splits, 4/15/00, 4/15/99, 4/15/97, 50% stk. split, 2/1/94. ① Bef. extraord. gain of $3.1 mill.

OFFICERS:
B. Coleman, Chmn.
J. R. Hale, Pres., C.E.O.
M. Gooch, Exec. V.P., Treas.
W. Hickman, Exec. V.P., Sec.

INVESTOR CONTACT: Jean Hale, (606) 437-3294

PRINCIPAL OFFICE: 346 North Mayo Trail, Pikeville, KY 41501

TELEPHONE NUMBER: (606) 432-1414
FAX: (606) 437-3345
WEB: www.ctbi.com

NO. OF EMPLOYEES: 830

SHAREHOLDERS: 3,600 (approx.)

ANNUAL MEETING: In Apr.

INCORPORATED: KY, Aug., 1980

INSTITUTIONAL HOLDINGS:
No. of Institutions: 37
Shares Held: 2,602,690
% Held: 21.4

INDUSTRY: National commercial banks (SIC: 6021)

TRANSFER AGENT(S): Community Trust Bank, NA, Versailles, KY

NASDAQ SYMBOL CBSS
Rec. Pr. 20¼ (5/31/00)

COMPASS BANCSHARES, INC.

YIELD 4.3%
P/E RATIO 10.8

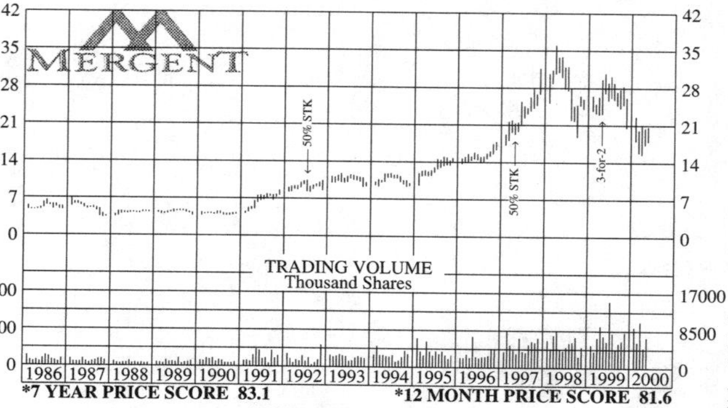

MERGENT
50% STK
50% STK
3-for-2
TRADING VOLUME
Thousand Shares
1986 1987 1988 1989 1990 1991 1992 1993 1994 1995 1996 1997 1998 1999 2000

*7 YEAR PRICE SCORE 83.1 *12 MONTH PRICE SCORE 81.6
*NYSE COMPOSITE INDEX=100

INTERIM EARNINGS (Per Share):

Qtr.	Mar.	June	Sept.	Dec.
1995	0.28	0.32	0.33	0.33
1996	0.41	0.35	0.29	0.37
1997	0.37	0.38	0.39	0.42
1998	0.41	0.42	0.43	0.34
1999	0.45	0.47	0.48	0.48

INTERIM DIVIDENDS (Per Share):

Amt.	Decl.	Ex.	Rec.	Pay.
0.20Q	5/17/99	6/11/99	6/15/99	7/01/99
0.20Q	8/17/99	9/13/99	9/15/99	10/01/99
0.20Q	11/15/99	12/13/99	12/15/99	1/03/00
0.22Q	2/22/00	3/13/00	3/15/00	4/03/00
0.22Q	5/15/00	6/13/00	6/15/00	7/03/00

Indicated div.: $0.88 (Div. Reinv. Plan)

CAPITALIZATION (12/31/99):

	($000)	(%)
Total Deposits	12,808,918	77.3
Long-Term Debt	2,564,328	15.5
Common & Surplus	1,196,204	7.2
Total	16,569,450	100.0

DIVIDEND ACHIEVER STATUS:
Rank: 90 10-Year Growth Rate: 13.27%
Total Years of Dividend Growth: 16

RECENT DEVELOPMENTS: For the year ended 12/31/99, net income improved 20.0% to $217.0 million compared with $180.9 million in the previous year. Earnigs for both periods included merger and integration expenses of $5.1 million and $21.7 million, respectively. Net interest income increased 10.8% to $639.2 million from $576.9 million in 1998. Provision for loan losses was $31.1 million versus $38.4 million in 1998. Recently, the Company completed the acquisition of MegaBank Financial Corporation, with more than $300.0 million in assets and nine full-service banking operations, for approximately 3.6 million shares of CBRS' common stock. On 4/18/00, the Company signed a definitive agreement to acquire Founders Bank of Arizona, and its 10 full-service banking offices. Founders possesses assets of $390.0 million.

BUSINESS

COMPASS BANCSHARES, INC. (formerly Central Bancshares of the South, Inc.) is a bank holding company headquartered in Birmingham, Alabama, with total assets of $18.15 billion as of 12/31/99. Principal subsidiaries include Compass Bank; Compass Banks of Texas, Inc., a Delaware bank holding company, which owns Compass Bank, a Texas state bank headquartered in Houston, Texas (''Compass Bank-Texas''); Central Bank of the South, an Alabama banking corporation headquartered in Anniston, Alabama; Arizona Bank; and Western Bancshares, Inc., in Albersuersue, New Mexico. Compass Bank conducts general commercial banking and trust services from 307 banking offices, including 122 in Texas, 88 in Alabama, 47 in Arizona, 41 in Florida and 9 in New Mexico.

LOAN DISTRIBUTION

(12/31/99)	($000)	(%)
Commercial, Fin & Agri	3,436	31.8
Real Estate-Construction	1,662	15.4
Real Estate-Residential	2,482	23.0
Real Estate-Commercial	1,595	14.8
Consumer Installment	1,613	15.0
Total	10,788	100.0

ANNUAL FINANCIAL DATA

	12/31/99	12/31/98	12/31/97	12/31/96	12/31/95	12/31/94	12/31/93
Earnings Per Share	**1.88**	**1.57**	**1.56**	**1.42**	**1.28**	**1.19**	**1.06**
Tang. Book Val. Per Share	**10.52**	**10.30**	**9.70**	**8.81**	**8.23**	**7.22**	**6.65**
Dividends Per Share	**0.78**	**0.68**	**0.62**	**0.55**	**0.48**	**0.39**	**0.33**
Dividend Payout %	**41.2**	**43.6**	**39.5**	**38.9**	**37.1**	**32.8**	**30.8**
INCOME STATEMENT (IN MILLIONS):							
Total Interest Income	1,247.6	1,134.5	949.0	820.4	726.9	577.7	522.6
Total Interest Expense	608.4	555.2	473.9	417.9	377.3	246.4	197.3
Net Interest Income	639.2	579.4	475.2	402.4	349.7	331.4	325.3
Provision for Loan Losses	31.1	38.4	22.4	17.6	10.2	3.4	36.0
Non-Interest Income	241.1	222.5	181.5	154.7	122.1	85.6	102.2
Non-Interest Expense	517.9	491.0	395.7	337.5	290.0	262.0	254.0
Income Before Taxes	331.2	272.4	238.5	202.1	171.5	151.6	137.5
Net Income	217.0	180.9	155.6	128.9	110.3	99.7	89.3
Average Shs. Outstg. (000)	114,441	113,745	99,771	90,835	86,265	83,693	82,622
BALANCE SHEET (IN MILLIONS):							
Cash & Due from Banks	684.5	831.6	693.7	670.4	530.9	483.3	279.6
Securities Avail. for Sale	4,243.8	3,773.4	2,422.2	2,132.6	2,119.7	760.0	879.3
Total Loans & Leases	10,789.5	10,103.2	8,677.0	7,459.8	6,361.4	5,762.7	5,150.4
Allowance for Credit Losses	143.6	138.6	127.4	121.2	108.6	108.4	111.9
Net Loans & Leases	10,645.8	9,964.6	8,549.5	7,338.7	6,252.7	5,654.3	5,038.5
Total Assets	18,150.8	17,288.9	13,459.6	11,814.2	10,262.2	9,123.3	7,252.3
Total Deposits	12,808.9	12,013.4	9,632.5	9,220.6	7,729.1	7,062.4	5,552.8
Long-Term Obligations	2,564.3	2,046.0	1,387.1	701.5	584.9	484.9	325.4
Total Liabilities	16,954.5	16,092.8	12,499.5	11,011.2	9,555.6	8,522.6	6,706.8
Net Stockholders' Equity	1,196.2	1,196.1	960.0	803.1	706.7	600.6	545.6
Year-end Shs. Outstg. (000)	113,709	113,351	98,987	91,181	85,842	83,187	82,040
STATISTICAL RECORD:							
Return on Equity %	18.1	15.1	16.2	16.1	15.6	16.6	16.4
Return on Assets %	1.2	1.0	1.2	1.1	1.1	1.1	1.2
Equity/Assets %	6.6	6.9	7.1	6.8	6.9	6.6	7.5
Non-Int. Exp./Tot. Inc. %	58.8	61.2	60.3	60.6	61.5	62.8	59.4
Price Range	30¾-20½	36-18¾	31 11/16-17¼	17 13/16-13 11/16	15-9 9/16	11⅞-9 5/16	11¾-9¼
P/E Ratio	16.4-10.9	23.0-12.0	20.3-11.0	12.6-9.6	11.7-7.5	10.0-7.8	11.1-8.7
Average Yield %	3.0	2.5	2.5	3.5	3.9	3.7	3.1

Statistics are as originally reported. Adj. for stk. splits: 3-for-2, 4/2/99 & 4/2/97

OFFICERS:
D. P. Jones Jr., Chmn., Pres., C.E.O.
G. R. Hegel, C.F.O.
J. W. Powell, Gen. Couns., Sec.

INVESTOR CONTACT: Ed Bilek, Dir., Investor Relations, (205) 933-3331

PRINCIPAL OFFICE: 15 South 20th St., Birmingham, AL 35233

TELEPHONE NUMBER: (205) 933-3000
FAX: (205) 933-3266
WEB: www.compassweb.com

NO. OF EMPLOYEES: 6,700 (approx.)

SHAREHOLDERS: 7,200 (approx.)

ANNUAL MEETING: In Apr.

INCORPORATED: DE, 1970

INSTITUTIONAL HOLDINGS:
No. of Institutions: 144
Shares Held: 32,020,603
% Held: 28.2

INDUSTRY: National commercial banks (SIC: 6021)

TRANSFER AGENT(S): Continental Stock Transfer & Trust Company, New York, NY

NYSE SYMBOL CAG
Rec. Pr. 23 1/16 (5/31/00)

CONAGRA, INC.

YIELD 3.5%
P/E RATIO 38.4

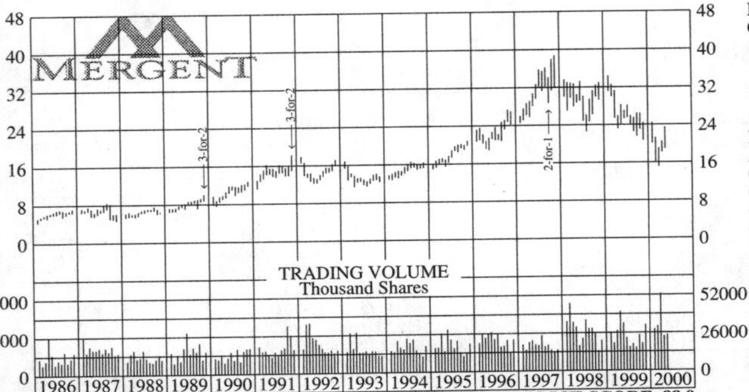

MERGENT
3-for-2
3-for-2
2-for-1
TRADING VOLUME
Thousand Shares
48
40
32
24
16
8
0
52000
26000
0
1986 1987 1988 1989 1990 1991 1992 1993 1994 1995 1996 1997 1998 1999 2000

***7 YEAR PRICE SCORE 66.6** ***12 MONTH PRICE SCORE 88.9**

*NYSE COMPOSITE INDEX=100

INTERIM EARNINGS (Per Share):

Qtr.	Aug.	Nov.	Feb.	May
1995-96	0.18	0.36	0.28	d0.42
1996-97	0.21	0.41	0.32	0.41
1997-98	0.48	0.46	0.30	0.36
1998-99	0.23	0.46	0.36	d0.30
1999-00	0.21	0.39	0.30	...

INTERIM DIVIDENDS (Per Share):

Amt.	Decl.	Ex.	Rec.	Pay.
0.178Q	4/12/99	4/28/99	4/30/99	6/01/99
0.178Q	7/09/99	7/28/99	7/30/99	9/01/99
0.203Q	9/23/99	11/03/99	11/05/99	12/01/99
0.203Q	12/02/99	1/26/00	1/28/00	3/01/00
0.203Q	4/10/00	4/26/00	4/28/00	6/01/00

Indicated div.: $0.81 (Div. Reinv. Plan)

CAPITALIZATION (5/30/99):

	($000)	(%)
Long-Term Debt	2,543,100	46.6
Common & Surplus	2,908,800	53.4
Total	5,451,900	100.0

DIVIDEND ACHIEVER STATUS:
Rank: 58 10-Year Growth Rate: 15.28%
Total Years of Dividend Growth: 22

RECENT DEVELOPMENTS: For the 13 weeks ended 2/27/00, net income slid 16.3% to $143.4 million from $171.4 million the year before. Earnings in the recent period included pre-tax restructuring charges totaling $84.6 million. Net sales rose 1.8% to $5.80 billion from $5.69 billion the previous year. Higher sales in the Refrigerated Foods and Packaged Foods segments were partially offset by lower sales in the Agricultural Products segment.

PROSPECTS: The Company is continuing to implement initiatives associated with its restructuring program. Pre-tax savings, stemming primarily from reducing duplicative efforts, lowering employee-related expenses, and reducing depreciation and amortization costs, are expected to total approximately $90.0 million in the current fiscal year, $150.0 million in fiscal 2001, and $200.0 million in fiscal 2002.

BUSINESS

CONAGRA, INC. is a diversified, international food company that operates in three industry segments: Refrigerated Foods (47.0% of fiscal 1999 sales) produces and markets branded processed meats, beef and pork products, and chicken and turkey products. Packaged Foods (30.4%) includes shelf-stable and frozen foods, dairy products, and products for foodservice markets. Major brands include: HEALTHY CHOICE, BANQUET, KID CUISINE, HUNT'S, WESSON, ORVILLE REDENBACHER'S, SLIM JIM, PETER PAN, PARKAY, BLUE BONNET, FLEISCHMANN'S, ARMOUR, and BUTTERBALL. Agricultural Products (22.6%) provides crop protection chemicals, fertilizers and seeds, and processes, distributes and trades ingredients for food products and meat and poultry production.

ANNUAL FINANCIAL DATA

	5/30/99	5/31/98	5/25/97	5/26/96	5/28/95	5/29/94	5/30/93
Earnings Per Share	**2 0.75**	**1 1.36**	**1.34**	**2 0.40**	**1.03**	**0.91**	**1 0.79**
Cash Flow Per Share	**1.80**	**2.33**	**2.24**	**1.28**	**1.85**	**1.71**	**1.54**
Tang. Book Val. Per Share	**1.02**	**0.85**	**0.08**	**...**	**0.15**	**...**	**...**
Dividends Per Share	**0.65**	**0.56**	**0.49**	**0.43**	**0.37**	**0.32**	**0.28**
Dividend Payout %	**86.3**	**41.5**	**36.8**	**108.8**	**36.3**	**35.6**	**35.4**
INCOME STATEMENT (IN MILLIONS):							
Total Revenues	24,594.3	23,840.5	24,002.1	24,821.6	24,108.9	23,512.2	21,519.1
Costs & Expenses	22,654.8	22,073.8	22,293.4	23,192.4	22,632.5	22,174.8	20,306.0
Depreciation & Amort.	499.8	446.3	413.8	407.9	375.8	368.4	348.7
Operating Income	1,439.7	1,320.4	1,294.9	1,221.3	1,100.6	969.0	864.4
Net Interest Inc./(Exp.)	d316.6	d299.3	d277.2	d304.9	d278.1	d254.2	d258.4
Income Before Income Taxes	682.3	1,021.1	1,017.7	408.6	825.9	720.0	631.4
Income Taxes	323.9	393.1	402.7	219.7	330.3	282.9	239.9
Equity Earnings/Minority Int.	...	...	...	...	3.4	5.2	25.4
Net Income	2 358.4	1 628.0	615.0	2 188.9	495.6	437.1	1 391.5
Cash Flow	858.2	1,074.3	1,028.8	588.2	847.4	781.5	716.2
Average Shs. Outstg. (000)	476,700	461,300	459,000	459,000	458,000	457,000	466,000
BALANCE SHEET (IN MILLIONS):							
Cash & Cash Equivalents	62.8	95.2	105.8	113.7	60.0	452.4	447.0
Total Current Assets	5,656.1	5,487.4	5,205.0	5,566.9	5,140.2	5,143.3	4,486.7
Net Property	3,614.2	3,395.8	3,242.5	2,820.5	2,796.0	2,586.3	2,388.2
Total Assets	12,146.1	11,702.8	11,277.1	11,196.6	10,801.0	10,721.8	9,988.7
Total Current Liabilities	5,386.4	5,070.2	4,989.6	5,193.7	3,964.9	4,752.8	4,272.6
Long-Term Obligations	2,543.1	2,487.4	2,355.7	2,262.9	2,520.0	2,206.8	2,159.2
Net Stockholders' Equity	2,908.8	2,778.9	2,471.7	2,255.5	2,495.4	2,226.9	2,054.5
Net Working Capital	269.7	417.2	215.4	373.2	1,175.3	390.5	214.1
Year-end Shs. Outstg. (000)	488,173	459,076	476,126	486,312	491,394	496,390	503,420
STATISTICAL RECORD:							
Operating Profit Margin %	5.9	5.5	5.4	4.9	4.6	4.1	4.0
Net Profit Margin %	1.5	2.6	2.6	0.8	2.1	1.9	1.8
Return on Equity %	12.3	22.6	24.9	8.4	19.9	19.6	19.1
Return on Assets %	3.0	5.4	5.5	1.7	4.6	4.1	3.9
Debt/Total Assets %	20.9	21.3	20.9	20.2	23.3	20.6	21.6
Price Range	33 5/8-22 9/16	38 3/4-24 1/2	27 3/8-18 13/16	20 7/8-14 7/8	16 9/16-12 3/4	16 13/16-11 3/8	17 7/8-12 1/4
P/E Ratio	44.8-30.1	28.5-18.0	20.4-14.0	52.8-37.6	16.1-12.4	18.6-12.6	22.6-15.5
Average Yield %	2.3	1.8	2.1	2.4	2.6	2.3	1.9

Statistics are as originally reported. Adj. for 2-for-1 stk. split, 10/97. 1 Bef. $14.8 mil ($0.03/sh) chg. for acctg. change, 1998; & $121.2 mil chg. for acctg. adj., 1993. 2 Incl. $337.9 mil ($0.71/sh) after-tax, non-recur chg., 1999; & $356.3 mil ($0.78/sh) after-tax, non-recur. chg., 1996.

OFFICERS:
B. C. Rohde, Vice-Chmn., Pres., C.E.O.
J. P. O'Donnell, Exec. V.P., C.F.O., Corp. Sec.
K. W. Gerhardt, Sr. V.P., Chief Info. Off.

INVESTOR CONTACT: Shareholder Services, (800) 840-3404

PRINCIPAL OFFICE: One ConAgra Drive, Omaha, NE 68102-5001

TELEPHONE NUMBER: (402) 595-4000
FAX: (402) 978-4447
WEB: www.conagra.com
NO. OF EMPLOYEES: 80,000 (approx.)
SHAREHOLDERS: 33,000 (approx.); 100,000 (approx. beneficial)
ANNUAL MEETING: In Sept.
INCORPORATED: NE, Sept., 1919; reincorp., DE, Feb., 1979

INSTITUTIONAL HOLDINGS:
No. of Institutions: 374
Shares Held: 266,788,609
% Held: 50.9

INDUSTRY: Meat packing plants (SIC: 2011)

TRANSFER AGENT(S): Norwest Shareowner Services, St.Paul, MN

CONNECTICUT WATER SERVICE, INC.

YIELD 4.4%
P/E RATIO 17.2

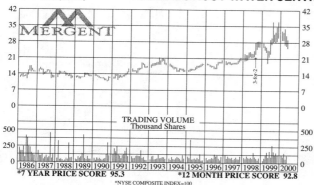

*7 YEAR PRICE SCORE 95.3   *12 MONTH PRICE SCORE 92.8
*NYSE COMPOSITE INDEX=100

INTERIM EARNINGS (Per Share):

Qtr.	Mar.	June	Sept.	Dec.
1996	0.27	0.27	0.56	0.36
1997	0.32	0.26	0.59	0.33
1998	0.31	0.32	0.57	0.33
1999	0.32	0.38	0.56	0.30

INTERIM DIVIDENDS (Per Share):

Amt.	Decl.	Ex.	Rec.	Pay.
0.293Q	5/12/99	5/27/99	6/01/99	6/15/99
0.297Q	8/11/99	8/30/99	9/01/99	9/15/99
0.297Q	11/17/99	11/29/99	12/01/99	12/15/99
0.297Q	1/12/00	2/28/00	3/01/00	3/15/00
0.297Q	5/11/00	5/30/00	6/01/00	6/15/00

Indicated div.: $1.19 (Div. Reinv. Plan)

CAPITALIZATION (12/31/99):

	($000)	(%)
Long-Term Debt	65,399	42.5
Deferred Income Tax	25,092	16.3
Preferred Stock	772	0.5
Common & Surplus	62,495	40.6
Total	153,758	100.0

DIVIDEND ACHIEVER STATUS:

Rank: 320   10-Year Growth Rate: 1.27%
Total Years of Dividend Growth: 24

RECENT DEVELOPMENTS:

For the year ended 12/31/99, income increased 4.5% to $7.5 million compared with income of $7.2 million in the prior year. Operating revenue grew 5.6% to $42.6 million from $40.3 million a year earlier. Metered revenues rose 6.6% to $35.5 million versus $33.3 million the year before, reflecting customer growth and higher-than-normal water consumption due to a hot and dry summer. Total operating expenses were $31.4 million, up 6.3% from $29.5 million the year before. Utility operating income grew 4.3% to $11.2 million compared with $10.8 million a year ago. During the year, the Company expanded into eastern Connecticut by acquiring Gallup Water and Crystal Water Companies, increasing CTWS's customer base by over 7.0% and the number of towns serviced to 39.

BUSINESS

CONNECTICUT WATER SERVICE, INC. is the parent company of The Connecticut Water Company, which supplies water to over 69,400 customers for residential, commercial, industrial and municipal purposes throughout 39 towns in the state of Connecticut. The Connecticut Water Company operates through three, non-contiguous operating regions. The Company represents the second largest investor-owned water system in the state of Connecticut in terms of operating revenues and utility plant investment. The area served has an estimated population of 243,000. Water supply sources vary among the regions, but from the systems as a whole, about 49% of the total dependable yield comes from reservoirs and 50% from wells. The remainder comes from interconnections with other systems.

REVENUES

(12/31/99)	($000)	(%)
Water activities	42,624	95.8
Real estate sales	447	1.0
Services/rentals	1,410	3.2
Total	44,481	100.0

ANNUAL FINANCIAL DATA

	12/31/99	12/31/98	12/31/97	12/31/96	12/31/95	12/31/94	12/31/93
Earnings Per Share	1.54	1.53	1.49	1.46	1.45	1.39	1.33
Cash Flow Per Share	2.47	2.41	2.30	2.22	2.19	2.15	2.10
Tang. Book Val. Per Share	12.92	12.77	12.39	12.04	11.64	22.28	21.58
Dividends Per Share	1.18	1.17	1.15	1.13	1.12	1.10	1.09
Dividend Payout %	76.6	76.2	77.2	77.6	77.4	79.3	82.0
INCOME STATEMENT (IN THOUSANDS):							
Total Revenues	42,624	37,924	38,501	38,592	39,350	38,129	38,131
Costs & Expenses	26,883	21,584	22,591	23,380	24,020	23,268	23,161
Depreciation & Amort.	4,514	3,981	3,624	3,420	3,282	3,236	3,194
Maintenance Exp.	...	2,055	1,952	1,664	2,026	1,970	1,793
Operating Income	11,227	10,304	10,334	10,128	10,022	9,655	9,983
Net Interest Inc./(Exp.)	d4,391	d4,177	d4,182	d3,788	d3,790	d3,840	d4,233
Income Taxes	57	262	215	21	33	cr26	cr65
Net Income	7,494	6,965	6,804	6,603	6,363	5,880	5,567
Cash Flow	11,970	10,908	10,390	9,985	9,607	9,078	8,723
Average Shs. Outstg.	4,848	4,535	4,524	4,496	4,377	4,218	4,154
BALANCE SHEET (IN THOUSANDS):							
Gross Property	244,653	223,661	216,103	202,957	192,100	183,242	177,698
Accumulated Depreciation	63,311	56,335	52,346	49,059	45,564	42,458	40,130
Net Property	181,342	167,326	163,757	153,898	146,536	140,784	137,568
Total Assets	210,885	194,586	189,277	184,640	176,459	171,241	163,080
Long-Term Obligations	65,399	62,501	54,532	54,430	54,460	54,600	51,600
Net Stockholders' Equity	63,267	58,717	56,841	55,167	52,560	96,738	91,092
Year-end Shs. Outstg.	4,839	4,536	4,527	4,518	4,451	4,307	4,185
STATISTICAL RECORD:							
Operating Profit Margin %	26.3	27.2	26.8	26.2	25.5	25.3	26.2
Net Profit Margin %	17.6	18.4	17.7	17.1	16.2	15.4	14.6
Net Inc./Net Property %	4.1	4.2	4.2	4.3	4.3	4.2	4.0
Net Inc./Tot. Capital %	4.9	4.8	5.1	5.0	5.0	3.4	3.4
Return on Equity %	11.8	11.9	12.0	12.0	12.1	6.1	6.1
Accum. Depr./Gross Prop. %	25.9	25.2	24.2	24.2	23.7	23.2	22.6
Price Range	37-19	28½-20	21½-18⁹/₁₆	20⁵/₁₆-16½	18¹³/₁₆-15³/₁₆	18¹¹/₁₆-15³/₁₆	21¼-16¹³/₁₆
P/E Ratio	24.0-12.3	18.6-13.1	14.4-12.3	13.9-11.3	13.0-10.5	13.5-10.9	15.9-12.6
Average Yield %	4.2	4.8	5.8	6.2	6.6	6.5	5.7

Statistics are as originally reported. Adj. for stk. split: 3-for-2, 9/15/98

OFFICERS:

M. T. Chiaraluce, Chmn., Pres., C.E.O.
D. C. Benoit, V.P., Fin., C.F.O. Treas.
P. J. Bancroft, Asst. Treas., Contr.
M. G. DiAcri, Corp. Sec.

INVESTOR CONTACT: Shareholder Relations, (800) 426-5523-305

PRINCIPAL OFFICE: 93 West Main Street, Clinton, CT 06413-1600

TELEPHONE NUMBER: (860) 669-8636
FAX: (860) 669-9326
WEB: www.ctwater.com

NO. OF EMPLOYEES: 168

SHAREHOLDERS: 5,200 (approx.)

ANNUAL MEETING: In Apr.

INCORPORATED: CT, Feb., 1956

INSTITUTIONAL HOLDINGS:
No. of Institutions: 24
Shares Held: 444,599
% Held: 9.2

INDUSTRY: Water supply (SIC: 4941)

TRANSFER AGENT(S): State Street Bank and Trust Company EquiServe, Boston, MA

NYSE SYMBOL ED
Rec. Pr. 32 5/8 (5/31/00)

CONSOLIDATED EDISON, INC.

YIELD	6.7%
P/E RATIO	10.4

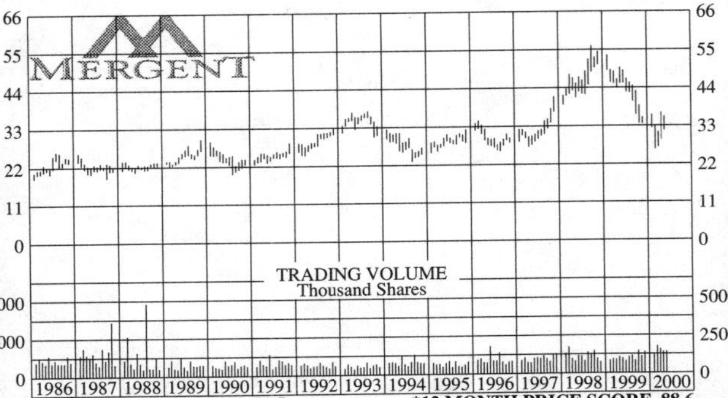

*7 YEAR PRICE SCORE 71.5 — *12 MONTH PRICE SCORE 88.6

*NYSE COMPOSITE INDEX=100

INTERIM EARNINGS (Per Share):

Qtr.	Mar.	June	Sept.	Dec.
1996	0.78	0.28	1.38	0.49
1997	0.69	0.18	1.49	0.59
1998	0.73	0.26	1.49	0.56
1999	0.76	0.30	1.50	0.57

INTERIM DIVIDENDS (Per Share):

Amt.	Decl.	Ex.	Rec.	Pay.
0.535Q	7/27/99	8/16/99	8/18/99	9/15/99
0.535Q	10/26/99	11/15/99	11/17/99	12/15/99
0.545Q	1/20/00	2/14/00	2/16/00	3/15/00
0.545Q	4/20/00	5/15/00	5/17/00	6/15/00

Indicated div.: $2.18 (Div. Reinv. Plan)

CAPITALIZATION (12/31/99):

	($000)	(%)
Long-Term Debt	4,524,604	36.2
Capital Lease Obligations	34,544	0.3
Deferred Income Tax	2,267,548	18.2
Redeemable Pfd. Stock	37,050	0.3
Preferred Stock	212,563	1.7
Common & Surplus	5,412,007	43.3
Total	12,488,316	100.0

DIVIDEND ACHIEVER STATUS:
Rank: 312 10-Year Growth Rate: 2.21%
Total Years of Dividend Growth: 25

RECENT DEVELOPMENTS: For the year ended 12/31/99, net income slipped 1.7% to $700.6 million versus $712.7 million in 1998. Total operating revenues were $7.49 billion, up 5.6% from $7.09 billion in the prior year. Operating income decreased 3.2% to $1.02 billion versus $1.05 billion in the previous year. Earnings per share improved due the positive effect of a strong local economy on ED's electric sales and revenues.

PROSPECTS: Results for 2000 will directly reflect the Company's ability to successfully complete its merger with Northeast Utilities as well as realize the expected synergies associated with the transaction. All of the necessary requests have been filed and are pending approval. The merger is expected to close by the end of the year. Separately, ED is investing $315.0 million on a five-year program to improve its electrical distribution system.

BUSINESS

CONSOLIDATED EDISON, INC. (formerly Consolidated Edison Company of New York) is a holding company. ED provides energy generation, transmission, and distribution services for electricity, natural gas, and steam. Con Edison provides electric service in all of New York City and most of Westchester County, gas service in Manhattan, The Bronx, Queens and Westchester, and steam service in part of Manhattan. Consolidated Edison Solutions, Inc. is a full-service energy company providing wholesale and retail electricity and natural gas sales, as well as energy-related products and services to business, governmental and residential customers throughout the Northeast. Consolidated Edison Development, Inc. invests in energy infrastructure development projects and markets technical services worldwide. Consolidated Edison Energy, Inc. markets specialized energy generation.

ANNUAL FINANCIAL DATA

	12/31/99	12/31/98	12/31/97	12/31/96	12/31/95	12/31/94	12/31/93
Earnings Per Share	**3.13**	**3.04**	**2.95**	**2.93**	**2.93**	**2.98**	**2.66**
Cash Flow Per Share	**5.49**	**5.25**	**5.09**	**5.04**	**4.87**	**4.78**	**4.39**
Tang. Book Val. Per Share	**25.90**	**25.88**	**25.18**	**24.37**	**23.51**	**22.62**	**21.63**
Dividends Per Share	**2.14**	**2.12**	**2.10**	**2.08**	**2.04**	**2.00**	**1.94**
Dividend Payout %	**68.4**	**69.7**	**71.2**	**71.0**	**69.6**	**67.1**	**72.9**
INCOME STATEMENT (IN MILLIONS):							
Total Revenues	7,491.3	7,093.0	7,121.3	6,959.7	6,536.9	6,373.1	6,265.4
Costs & Expenses	5,077.3	5,043.8	5,098.3	4,991.1	4,527.6	4,408.4	4,339.8
Depreciation & Amort.	526.2	518.5	502.8	496.4	455.8	422.4	403.7
Maintenance Exp.	438.0	477.4	474.8	458.6	512.1	506.2	570.8
Operating Income	1,019.8	1,053.3	1,045.4	1,013.6	1,041.4	1,036.2	951.1
Net Interest Inc./(Exp.)	d337.6	d325.8	d333.1	d323.5	d329.0	d305.2	d298.1
Income Taxes	cr26.9	cr2.2	cr3.2	cr1.0	1.1	0.4	cr1.0
Net Income	700.6	729.7	712.8	694.1	723.9	734.3	658.5
Cash Flow	1,226.8	1,231.3	1,197.3	1,184.6	1,144.1	1,121.0	1,026.6
Average Shs. Outstg. (000)	223,442	234,308	235,082	234,977	234,930	234,754	233,981
BALANCE SHEET (IN MILLIONS):							
Gross Property	16,002.8	16,033.9	15,557.2	15,251.6	14,766.1	14,297.4	13,680.5
Accumulated Depreciation	4,733.6	4,726.2	4,392.4	4,285.7	4,037.0	3,828.6	3,594.8
Net Property	11,353.8	11,406.5	11,267.1	11,067.3	10,814.4	10,561.2	10,156.2
Total Assets	15,531.5	14,381.4	14,722.5	14,057.2	13,949.9	13,728.4	13,483.5
Long-Term Obligations	4,559.1	4,087.4	4,228.8	4,281.3	3,962.5	4,078.3	3,694.2
Net Stockholders' Equity	5,624.6	6,238.2	6,163.5	5,965.7	6,062.7	5,853.3	5,609.3
Year-end Shs. Outstg. (000)	192,452	232,833	235,490	234,994	234,956	234,905	234,373
STATISTICAL RECORD:							
Operating Profit Margin %	13.6	14.9	14.7	14.6	15.9	16.3	15.2
Net Profit Margin %	9.4	10.3	10.0	10.0	11.1	11.5	10.5
Net Inc./Net Property %	6.2	6.4	6.3	6.3	6.7	7.0	6.5
Net Inc./Tot. Capital %	5.6	5.7	5.6	5.5	5.8	6.0	5.6
Return on Equity %	12.5	11.7	11.6	11.6	11.9	12.5	11.7
Accum. Depr./Gross Prop. %	29.6	29.5	28.2	28.1	27.3	26.8	26.3
Price Range	53 7/16-33 9/16	56 1/8-39 1/16	41 1/2-27	34 3/4-25 7/8	32 1/4-25 1/2	32 3/8-23	37 3/4-30 1/4
P/E Ratio	17.1-10.7	18.5-12.8	14.1-9.2	11.9-8.8	11.0-8.7	10.9-7.7	14.2-11.4
Average Yield %	4.9	4.5	6.1	6.9	7.1	7.2	5.7

Statistics are as originally reported.

OFFICERS:
E. R. McGrath, Chmn., Pres., C.E.O.
J. M. Evan, Pres., C.O.O.

INVESTOR CONTACT: Jan C. Childress, Dir. of Inv. Rel., (212) 460-6611

PRINCIPAL OFFICE: 4 Irving Place, New York, NY 10003

TELEPHONE NUMBER: (212) 460-4600
FAX: (212) 674-5470
WEB: www.conedison.com

NO. OF EMPLOYEES: 14,269 (avg.)

SHAREHOLDERS: 116,467

ANNUAL MEETING: In May

INCORPORATED: NY, Nov., 1884

INSTITUTIONAL HOLDINGS:
No. of Institutions: 283
Shares Held: 86,203,235
% Held: 39.7

INDUSTRY: Electric and other services combined (SIC: 4931)

TRANSFER AGENT(S): The Bank of New York, New York, NY.

NYSE SYMBOL CTB
Rec. Pr. 12 1/8 (5/31/00)

COOPER TIRE & RUBBER COMPANY

YIELD 3.5%
P/E RATIO 6.8

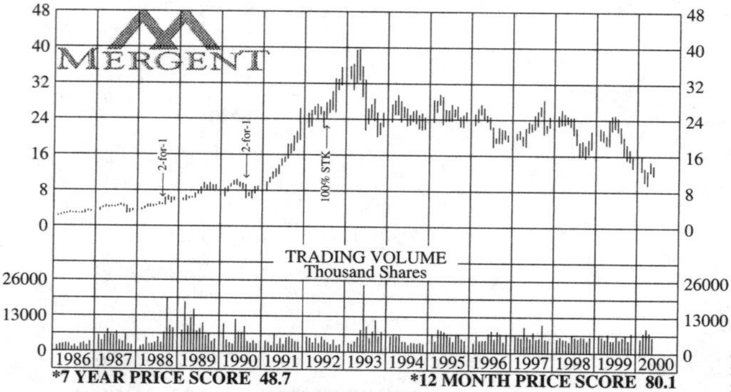

MERGENT
2-for-1
2-for-1
100% STK
TRADING VOLUME
Thousand Shares
1986 1987 1988 1989 1990 1991 1992 1993 1994 1995 1996 1997 1998 1999 2000

*7 YEAR PRICE SCORE 48.7 *12 MONTH PRICE SCORE 80.1

*NYSE COMPOSITE INDEX=100

INTERIM EARNINGS (Per Share):

Qtr.	Mar.	June	Sept.	Dec.
1996	0.28	0.30	0.32	0.40
1997	0.31	0.40	0.40	0.44
1998	0.34	0.41	0.39	0.50
1999	0.41	0.50	0.46	0.42

INTERIM DIVIDENDS (Per Share):

Amt.	Decl.	Ex.	Rec.	Pay.
0.105Q	5/04/99	5/28/99	6/02/99	6/30/99
0.105Q	7/20/99	9/07/99	9/09/99	9/30/99
0.105Q	11/19/99	11/26/99	11/30/99	12/24/99
0.105Q	2/08/00	3/02/00	3/06/00	3/31/00
0.105Q	5/03/00	5/31/00	6/02/00	6/30/00

Indicated div.: $0.42 (Div. Reinv. Plan)

CAPITALIZATION (12/31/99):

	($000)	(%)
Long-Term Debt	1,046,463	49.4
Deferred Income Tax	97,007	4.6
Common & Surplus	975,634	46.0
Total	2,119,104	100.0

DIVIDEND ACHIEVER STATUS:
Rank: 42 10-Year Growth Rate: 17.15%
Total Years of Dividend Growth: 20

RECENT DEVELOPMENTS: For the year ended 12/31/99, net income grew 6.7% to $135.5 million compared with net income of $127.0 million in the previous year. Net sales climbed 17.1% to $2.20 billion from $1.88 billion a year earlier. Tire sales rose 7.8% to $1.56 billion from $1.44 billion a year ago. Automotive group sales jumped 49.1% to $643.6 million from $431.8 million as a result of the integration of the Standard Products Company.

PROSPECTS: On 1/28/00, the Company completed the acquisition of Siebe Automotive group, an automotive fluid handling division of Invensys plc, for $244.5 million. The acquisition allows CTB to provide customers with complete fluid systems. Going forward, the Company expects to add new business to its automotive operations. The Company intends to focus on products and technologies that utilize its engineering, research and development strengths.

BUSINESS

COOPER TIRE & RUBBER COMPANY specializes in manufacturing and marketing rubber products for consumers and industrial users. Products include automobile and truck tires, inner tubes, vibration control products, hose and tubing, automotive body sealing products and specialty seating components. CTB markets its products nationally and internationally through well-established channels of distribution. Represented among its customers are automobile manufacturing companies, independent distributors and dealers, oil companies, large retail chains and industrial manufacturers. The Standard Products Company was acquired 10/27/99.

BUSINESS LINE ANALYSIS

(12/31/1999)	Rev(%)	Inc(%)
Tire	70.8	73.8
Automotive	29.2	26.2
Total	100.0	100.0

ANNUAL FINANCIAL DATA

	12/31/99	12/31/98	12/31/97	12/31/96	12/31/95	12/31/94	12/31/93
Earnings Per Share	**1.79**	**1.64**	**1.55**	**1.30**	**1.35**	**1.54**	**1.22**
Cash Flow Per Share	**3.44**	**2.95**	**2.74**	**2.22**	**2.11**	**2.20**	**1.78**
Tang. Book Val. Per Share	**7.15**	**11.45**	**10.58**	**9.67**	**8.95**	**7.92**	**6.58**
Dividends Per Share	**0.42**	**0.39**	**0.35**	**0.31**	**0.27**	**0.23**	**0.20**
Dividend Payout %	**23.5**	**23.8**	**22.6**	**23.8**	**20.0**	**14.9**	**16.4**
INCOME STATEMENT (IN MILLIONS):							
Total Revenues	2,196.3	1,879.8	1,814.4	1,620.2	1,497.5	1,405.5	1,194.2
Costs & Expenses	1,831.7	1,563.1	1,508.5	1,369.6	1,253.4	1,139.1	981.3
Depreciation & Amort.	125.6	103.2	95.5	76.8	63.3	55.6	46.4
Operating Income	239.1	213.4	210.4	173.7	180.8	210.8	166.6
Net Interest Inc./(Exp.)	d24.4	d15.2	d15.7	d1.7	d0.7	d2.7	d2.4
Income Before Income Taxes	215.5	198.2	194.8	172.1	180.1	208.1	164.3
Income Taxes	80.0	71.3	72.4	64.2	67.3	79.6	62.0
Net Income	135.5	127.0	122.4	107.9	112.8	128.5	102.2
Cash Flow	261.1	230.2	217.9	184.7	176.1	184.1	148.6
Average Shs. Outstg. (000)	75,837	77,598	79,128	83,214	83,646	83,623	83,350
BALANCE SHEET (IN MILLIONS):							
Cash & Cash Equivalents	71.1	42.0	52.9	19.5	23.2	103.3	25.8
Total Current Assets	945.4	569.5	554.6	443.6	430.6	454.7	332.0
Net Property	1,227.1	885.3	860.4	792.4	678.9	549.6	527.9
Total Assets	2,757.6	1,541.3	1,496.0	1,273.0	1,143.7	1,039.7	889.6
Total Current Liabilities	395.9	193.0	200.3	187.5	158.4	151.6	127.2
Long-Term Obligations	1,046.5	205.3	205.5	69.5	28.6	33.6	38.7
Net Stockholders' Equity	975.6	867.9	833.6	786.6	748.8	662.1	550.2
Net Working Capital	549.6	376.5	354.3	256.1	272.2	303.1	204.9
Year-end Shs. Outstg. (000)	75,810	75,791	78,760	81,367	83,662	83,634	83,582
STATISTICAL RECORD:							
Operating Profit Margin %	10.9	11.4	11.6	10.7	12.1	15.0	14.0
Net Profit Margin %	6.2	6.8	6.7	6.7	7.5	9.1	8.6
Return on Equity %	13.9	14.6	14.7	13.7	15.1	19.4	18.6
Return on Assets %	4.9	8.2	8.2	8.5	9.9	12.4	11.5
Debt/Total Assets %	37.9	13.3	13.7	5.5	2.5	3.2	4.4
Price Range	25-13 1/4	26 1/4-15 7/16	28 7/16-18	27 3/8-17 7/8	29 5/8-22 1/4	29 1/2-21 5/8	39 5/8-20
P/E Ratio	14.0-7.4	16.0-9.4	18.3-11.6	21.1-13.7	21.9-16.5	19.2-14.0	32.5-16.4
Average Yield %	2.2	1.9	1.5	1.4	1.0	0.9	0.7

Statistics are as originally reported.

OFFICERS:
T. A. Dattilo, Chmn.,Pres., C.E.O.
P. G. Weaver, C.F.O., V.P.
Richard D. Teeple, V.P., Gen. Coun.

INVESTOR CONTACT: Investor Relations, (419) 427-4768

PRINCIPAL OFFICE: 701 Lima & Western Avenues, Findlay, OH 45840

TELEPHONE NUMBER: (419) 423-1321
FAX: (419) 424-4305
WEB: www.coopertire.com

NO. OF EMPLOYEES: 21,586 (avg.)

SHAREHOLDERS: 4,801

ANNUAL MEETING: In May

INCORPORATED: DE, Mar., 1930

INSTITUTIONAL HOLDINGS:
No. of Institutions: 181
Shares Held: 47,659,514
% Held: 62.8

INDUSTRY: Tires and inner tubes (SIC: 3011)

TRANSFER AGENT(S): Fifth Third Bank, Cincinnati, OH

CORUS BANKSHARES, INC.

YIELD	2.4%
P/E RATIO	8.8

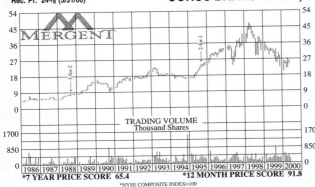

*7 YEAR PRICE SCORE 65.4   *12 MONTH PRICE SCORE 91.8
*NYSE COMPOSITE INDEX=100

INTERIM EARNINGS (Per Share):

Qtr.	Mar.	June	Sept.	Dec.
1994	0.35	0.39	0.42	0.41
1995	0.50	0.56	0.63	0.66
1996	0.77	0.71	0.73	0.72
1997	0.62	0.72	0.68	0.61
1998	0.67	0.69	0.69	0.70
1999	0.71	0.74	0.76	0.59

INTERIM DIVIDENDS (Per Share):

Amt.	Decl.	Ex.	Rec.	Pay.
0.14Q	2/18/99	3/25/99	3/29/99	4/09/99
0.145Q	4/28/99	6/23/99	6/27/99	7/09/99
0.145Q	8/11/99	9/23/99	9/27/99	10/08/99
0.145Q	11/17/99	12/22/99	12/27/99	1/10/00
0.145Q	2/16/00	3/23/00	3/27/00	4/10/00

Indicated div.: $0.58

CAPITALIZATION (12/31/99):

	($000)	(%)
Total Deposits	1,964,420	84.2
Long-Term Debt	40,000	1.7
Common & Surplus	327,825	14.1
Total	2,332,245	100.0

DIVIDEND ACHIEVER STATUS:
Rank: 27   10-Year Growth Rate: 19.01%
Total Years of Dividend Growth: 13

RECENT DEVELOPMENTS: For the year ended 12/31/99, net income increased slightly to $40.7 million compared with $40.6 million in 1998. Net interest income totaled $106.1 million, an improvement of 8.1% from $98.2 million the year before. Noninterest income declined 26.2% to $18.9 million from $25.7 million a year earlier. Noninterest expense grew 21.6% to $63.1 million from $51.9 million in the previous year. Provision for loan losses amounted to nil in 1999 compared with $10.0 million in 1998.. Return on average total assets declined to 1.60% from 1.70%, while return on average common shareholder's equity decreased to 12.46% from 13.70% a year ago. On 4/7/00, the Company settled a lawsuit filed by the Department of Justice in 1999. Under the terms of the settlement, CORS will pay $7.8 million for certain errors in its student loan department.

BUSINESS

CORUS BANKSHARES, INC. is a bank holding company with total assets of $2.39 billion as of 12/31/99. CORUS provides consumer and corporate banking products and services through its wholly-owned banking subsidiary, Corus Bank, N.A. The bank has eleven branches in the Chicago metropolitan area and offers general banking services such as checking, savings, money market and time deposit accounts; commercial, mortgage, home equity, student and personal loans; trust and management services; safe deposit boxes and a variety of additional services. The bank also provides clearing, depository and credit services to more than 525 currency exchanges in the Chicago area and an additional 20 in Milwaukee, Wisconsin. On 12/31/00, the Company's subsidiary, Bancorp operations Company merged with CORS.

ANNUAL FINANCIAL DATA

	12/31/99	12/31/98	12/31/97	12/31/96	12/31/95	12/31/94	12/31/93
Earnings Per Share	2.82	2.37	2.63	2.93	2.37	1.57	1.66
Tang. Book Val. Per Share	22.19	21.15	19.25	15.07	12.14	9.54	8.61
Dividends Per Share	0.57	0.55	0.52	0.45	0.34	0.29	0.27
Dividend Payout %	20.2	20.0	19.8	15.4	14.2	18.5	16.0
INCOME STATEMENT (IN MILLIONS):							
Total Interest Income	196.6	187.5	183.9	191.0	171.1	114.5	101.3
Total Interest Expense	90.4	89.3	82.7	79.6	72.6	45.7	35.6
Net Interest Income	106.1	98.2	101.3	111.3	98.5	68.8	65.8
Provision for Loan Losses	...	10.0	16.0	16.0	5.8	...	1.2
Non-Interest Income	18.9	25.7	26.9	22.8	14.1	13.2	12.5
Non-Interest Expense	63.1	51.9	51.7	50.2	51.6	45.2	38.6
Income Before Taxes	62.0	62.0	60.5	67.9	55.2	36.8	38.5
Net Income	40.7	40.6	39.4	43.9	35.8	24.0	25.3
Average Shs. Outstg. (000)	14,464	14,773	14,966	14,994	15,241	15,292	15,276
BALANCE SHEET (IN MILLIONS):							
Cash & Due from Banks	72.3	72.1	62.2	57.5	104.8	109.9	81.2
Securities Avail. for Sale	487.2	897.7	531.9	379.0	364.4	480.1	270.6
Total Loans & Leases	1,727.4	1,551.6	1,546.0	1,623.1	1,558.8	1,100.5	978.8
Allowance for Credit Losses	32.1	35.8	30.7	32.7	25.6	20.2	19.6
Net Loans & Leases	1,695.3	1,515.8	1,515.3	1,590.5	1,533.1	1,080.4	959.3
Total Assets	2,388.2	2,589.4	2,251.9	2,218.5	2,125.1	1,889.5	1,441.8
Total Deposits	1,964.4	2,154.7	1,863.1	1,900.7	1,898.5	1,698.5	1,267.8
Long-Term Obligations	40.0	40.0	40.0	40.0	...	...	1.2
Total Liabilities	2,060.4	2,271.3	1,960.3	1,982.9	1,930.4	1,732.6	1,298.4
Net Stockholders' Equity	327.8	318.1	291.6	235.6	194.7	156.9	143.4
Year-end Shs. Outstg. (000)	14,369	14,551	14,681	14,820	15,027	15,242	15,152
STATISTICAL RECORD:							
Return on Equity %	12.4	12.8	13.5	18.6	18.4	15.3	17.7
Return on Assets %	1.7	1.6	1.7	2.0	1.7	1.3	1.8
Equity/Assets %	13.7	12.3	13.0	10.6	9.2	8.3	9.9
Non-Int. Exp./Tot. Inc. %	49.9	43.7	42.0	38.4	45.3	55.6	49.1
Price Range	36⁷/₁₆-22½	47⅛-28⅝	41-23½	33-24¾	25½-16⅜	19¼-16⅛	22⅞-17¾
P/E Ratio	12.9-8.0	17.1-10.4	15.6-8.9	11.3-8.4	10.8-6.9	12.3-10.3	13.8-10.7
Average Yield %	1.9	1.5	1.6	1.6	1.6	1.6	1.3

Statistics are as originally reported. Adj. for stk. split: 2-for-1, 10/95

LOAN DISTRIBUTION

(12/31/1999)	($000)	(%)
Commercial Real Estate	916,512	53.0
Student	443,074	25.6
Residential First Mtg.	92,683	5.3
Commercial	117,021	6.7
Home Equity	135,603	7.8
Medical Finance	21,201	1.2
Consumer	1,263	0.4
Total	1,727,357	100.0

OFFICERS:
J. C. Glickman, Chmn.
R. J. Glickman, Pres., C.E.O.
T. H. Taylor, Exec. V.P., C.F.O.

PRINCIPAL OFFICE: 3959 N. Lincoln Ave., Chicago, IL 60613-2431

TELEPHONE NUMBER: (773) 832-3088
FAX: (773) 549-0734
WEB: www.corusbank.com
NO. OF EMPLOYEES: 630 full-time; 484 part-time
SHAREHOLDERS: 3,350
ANNUAL MEETING: In Apr.
INCORPORATED: MN, 1958

INSTITUTIONAL HOLDINGS:
No. of Institutions: 47
Shares Held: 4,263,123
% Held: 29.8

INDUSTRY: State commercial banks (SIC: 6022)

TRANSFER AGENT(S): ChaseMellon Shareholder Services, Ridgefield Park, NJ

NYSE SYMBOL CRDB
Rec. Pr. 11¾ (5/31/00)

CRAWFORD & COMPANY

YIELD 4.7%
P/E RATIO 15.1

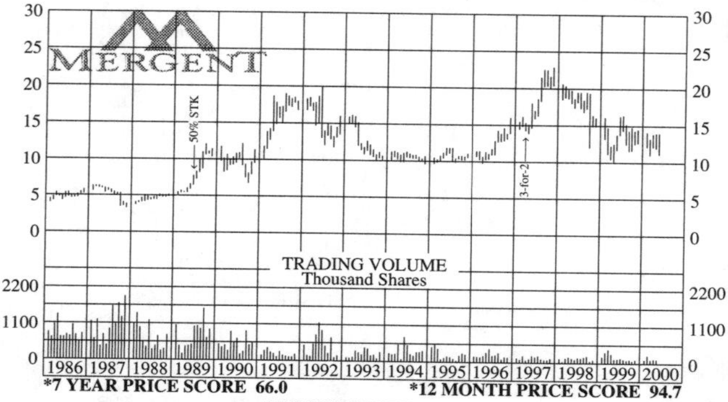

*7 YEAR PRICE SCORE 66.0 *12 MONTH PRICE SCORE 94.7

*NYSE COMPOSITE INDEX=100

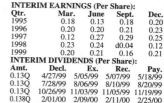

INTERIM EARNINGS (Per Share):

Qtr.	Mar.	June	Sept.	Dec.
1995	0.18	0.13	0.18	0.20
1996	0.20	0.20	0.21	0.23
1997	0.12	0.27	0.29	0.25
1998	0.23	0.24	d0.04	0.12
1999	0.20	0.21	0.16	0.21

INTERIM DIVIDENDS (Per Share):

Amt.	Decl.	Ex.	Rec.	Pay.
0.13Q	4/27/99	5/05/99	5/07/99	5/18/99
0.13Q	7/28/99	8/06/99	8/10/99	8/20/99
0.13Q	10/26/99	11/03/99	11/05/99	11/19/99
0.138Q	2/01/00	2/09/00	2/11/00	2/25/00
0.138Q	4/26/00	5/03/00	5/05/00	5/19/00

Indicated div.: $0.55

CAPITALIZATION (12/31/99):

	($000)	(%)
Long-Term Debt	16,053	5.9
Deferred Income Tax	6,571	2.4
Common & Surplus	250,279	91.7
Total	272,903	100.0

DIVIDEND ACHIEVER STATUS:
Rank: 273 10-Year Growth Rate: 4.34%
Total Years of Dividend Growth: 19

RECENT DEVELOPMENTS: For the year ended 12/31/99, net income improved 43.0% to $39.3 million compared with $27.5 million in the previous year. Results included year 2000 after-tax expenses of $3.2 million and $4.4 million in 1999 and 1998, respectively. Results for 1998 included an after-tax non-recurring charge of $9.7 million. Revenues were $701.9 million, up 5.2% from $667.3 million the year before.

PROSPECTS: Going forward, results should continue to benefit from the acquisition of The Garden City Group. The Company expects international revenue growth in 2000 and beyond due to the addition of two large accounts in U.K. The Company's outlook for claims referrals from its insurance company clients in the United States and Canada appear to be favorable as the outsourcing movement continues to gain momentum worldwide.

BUSINESS

CRAWFORD & COMPANY is a diversified services firm organized into three business units: Risk Management Services (RMS), Healthcare Management (HCM) and Claims Services. RMS primarily fulfills corporate market needs by providing risk management and claims adjusting services including risk management information systems and services through the subsidiary, Crawford Risk Sciences Group. HCM offers a full range of managed care services for both the corporate and insurance markets. Claims Service is responsible for handling claims support to the insurance industry through the complete investigation, evaluation, disposition and management of losses. In 1999, the Company acquired the Garden City Group, which manages class action litigation settlements.

ANNUAL FINANCIAL DATA

	12/31/99	12/31/98	12/31/97	12/31/96	12/31/95	12/31/94	12/31/93
Earnings Per Share	**0.78**	**[1] 0.54**	**[1] 0.93**	**0.84**	**0.69**	**0.76**	**0.71**
Cash Flow Per Share	**1.11**	**0.83**	**1.23**	**1.15**	**1.01**	**1.04**	**1.00**
Tang. Book Val. Per Share	**3.35**	**3.46**	**3.30**	**3.38**	**3.19**	**3.07**	**3.35**
Dividends Per Share	**0.52**	**0.50**	**0.44**	**0.39**	**0.36**	**0.33**	**0.29**
Dividend Payout %	**66.7**	**92.6**	**47.3**	**46.0**	**52.2**	**43.9**	**41.5**
INCOME STATEMENT (IN THOUSANDS):							
Total Revenues	701,926	667,271	692,322	633,625	607,577	587,781	576,298
Costs & Expenses	621,154	609,790	604,715	545,939	530,332	504,818	495,669
Depreciation & Amort.	17,028	14,798	15,423	15,716	16,865	14,912	15,779
Operating Income	63,744	42,683	72,184	71,970	60,380	68,051	64,850
Income Before Income Taxes	63,744	42,683	72,184	71,970	60,380	68,051	64,850
Income Taxes	24,480	16,395	27,697	29,160	24,360	27,450	26,800
Equity Earnings/Minority Int.	...	1,177	2,502	...	...	...	...
Net Income	39,264	[1] 27,465	[1] 46,989	42,810	36,020	40,601	38,050
Cash Flow	56,292	42,263	62,412	58,526	52,885	55,513	53,829
Average Shs. Outstg.	50,498	50,938	50,687	51,032	52,277	53,585	53,976
BALANCE SHEET (IN THOUSANDS):							
Cash & Cash Equivalents	17,716	8,423	55,380	55,485	46,398	57,734	69,291
Total Current Assets	267,836	251,146	278,814	246,896	234,380	243,639	248,739
Net Property	48,891	42,943	39,192	31,637	36,448	37,448	36,436
Total Assets	474,028	433,269	428,866	378,085	366,983	362,894	316,759
Total Current Liabilities	157,990	140,574	124,569	110,652	95,054	117,619	95,552
Long-Term Obligations	16,053	1,854	731	376	9,412	9,962	734
Net Stockholders' Equity	250,279	240,051	215,005	221,536	220,860	213,153	207,813
Net Working Capital	109,846	110,572	154,245	136,244	139,326	126,020	153,187
Year-end Shs. Outstg.	50,718	50,903	49,393	50,111	51,792	52,544	54,045
STATISTICAL RECORD:							
Operating Profit Margin %	9.1	6.4	10.4	11.4	9.9	11.6	11.3
Net Profit Margin %	5.6	4.1	6.8	6.8	5.9	6.9	6.6
Return on Equity %	15.7	11.4	21.9	19.3	16.3	19.0	18.3
Return on Assets %	8.3	6.3	11.0	11.3	9.8	11.2	12.0
Debt/Total Assets %	3.4	0.4	0.2	0.1	2.6	2.7	0.2
Price Range	16⅜-10⅛	20⅝-12	22⅞-13⅞	16-9¾	11 13/16-9 11/16	11 5/16-9 9/16	16 3/16-10
P/E Ratio	21.0-13.0	38.2-22.2	24.6-14.9	19.0-11.6	17.1-14.0	14.9-12.6	22.9-14.1
Average Yield %	3.9	3.1	2.4	3.0	3.3	3.2	2.2

Statistics are as originally reported. Adj. for stk. split: 3-for-2, 3/97 [1] Incl. non-recurr. chrg. 1998, $3.0 mill.; 1997, $13.0 mill.

OFFICERS:
A. L. Meyers Jr., Chmn., C.E.O.
G. L. Davis, Pres., C.O.O.
J. F. Osten, Exec. V.P., Gen. Couns., Corp. Sec.

INVESTOR CONTACT: Don R. Chapman, Executive Vice President

PRINCIPAL OFFICE: 5620 Glenridge Dr. N.E., Atlanta, GA 30342

TELEPHONE NUMBER: (404) 256-0830
FAX: (404) 847-4359
WEB: www.crawfordandcompany.com

NO. OF EMPLOYEES: 7,684

SHAREHOLDERS: 1,763 Cl. A; 914 (Cl. B).

ANNUAL MEETING: In Apr.

INCORPORATED: GA, May, 1943

INSTITUTIONAL HOLDINGS:
No. of Institutions: 35
Shares Held: 17,758,076
% Held: 71.5

INDUSTRY: Insurance agents, brokers, & service (SIC: 6411)

TRANSFER AGENT(S): SunTrust Bank, Atlanta, GA

NYSE SYMBOL DF
Rec. Pr. 30 3/8 (5/31/00)

DEAN FOODS COMPANY

YIELD 2.9%
P/E RATIO 11.8

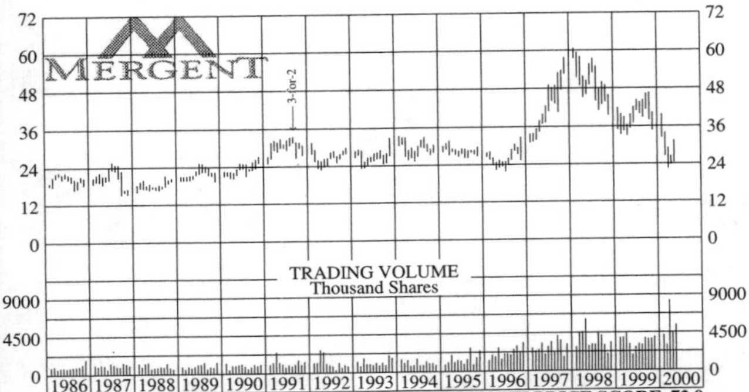

***7 YEAR PRICE SCORE 68.8** ***12 MONTH PRICE SCORE 72.9**

*NYSE COMPOSITE INDEX=100

INTERIM EARNINGS (Per Share):

Qtr.	Aug.	Nov.	Feb.	May
1995-96	0.34	0.40	0.17	d2.15
1996-97	0.45	0.47	0.51	0.73
1997-98	0.53	0.66	0.60	0.81
1998-99	0.56	0.58	0.08	0.52
1999-00	0.70	0.68	0.67	...

INTERIM DIVIDENDS (Per Share):

Amt.	Decl.	Ex.	Rec.	Pay.
0.22Q	7/23/99	8/18/99	8/20/99	9/15/99
0.22Q	9/29/99	11/17/99	11/19/99	12/15/99
0.22Q	1/28/00	2/23/00	2/25/00	3/15/00
0.22Q	3/24/00	5/24/00	5/26/00	6/15/00

Indicated div.: $0.88 (Div. Reinv. Plan)

CAPITALIZATION (5/30/99):

	($000)	(%)
Long-Term Debt	631,286	44.2
Deferred Income Tax	79,345	5.6
Common & Surplus	716,414	50.2
Total	1,427,045	100.0

DIVIDEND ACHIEVER STATUS:
Rank: 213 10-Year Growth Rate: 7.69%
Total Years of Dividend Growth: 27

RECENT DEVELOPMENTS: For the quarter ended 2/27/00, net income totaled $25.2 million versus $3.3 million the year before. Results in the prior-year period included a one-time after-tax charge of $4.7 million. Strong operating performance in DF's Dairy and Specialty segments were partially offset by lower earnings in the Pickles segment, reflecting increased pricing pressures. Net sales slipped 1.8% to $976.8 million from $995.2 million a year earlier, primarily due to lower raw milk costs.

PROSPECTS: On 4/13/00, DF announced that it will close its Sacramento, California milk plant in an effort to increase operational efficiencies. The closure is expected to result in an after-tax charge of about $3.0 million in the fourth quarter. Meanwhile, near-term results should benefit from increased distribution of the Company's Milk Chug product line, the national launch of Dips-For-One™, a single-serve refrigerated dip, and continued expansion of nutritional and functional products.

BUSINESS

DEAN FOODS COMPANY is a food processor and distributor engaged primarily in three business segments, Dairy Products, Pickles and Specialty Food Products. The Dairy Products segment includes fluid milk and cultured products, ice cream and frozen desserts, and extended shelf life products such as whipping creams and coffee creamers. The Pickle segment includes pickles, relishes, pickled peppers, and specialty sauces. The Specialty Food Products segment includes non-dairy creamers, ready-to-serve cheese sauces, puddings, and dips and salad dressings sold under the DEANS and MARIES brands. DF also operates a transportation business which provides less-than-truckload refrigerated and frozen cartage service. In the fiscal year ended 5/30/99, sales were derived: dairy, 79.5%; specialty foods, 10.8% and pickles, 9.7%.

ANNUAL FINANCIAL DATA

	5/30/99	5/31/98	5/25/97	5/26/96	5/28/95	5/29/94	5/30/93
Earnings Per Share	**[3] 1.74**	**2.13**	**2.16**	**[1] d1.24**	**2.01**	**[2] 1.78**	**1.73**
Cash Flow Per Share	**3.91**	**3.58**	**4.00**	**0.68**	**3.76**	**3.34**	**...**
Tang. Book Val. Per Share	**4.20**	**7.12**	**11.36**	**10.26**	**12.14**	**10.79**	**11.11**
Dividends Per Share	**0.82**	**0.78**	**0.74**	**0.70**	**0.66**	**0.62**	**0.57**
Dividend Payout %	**47.1**	**36.6**	**34.3**	**...**	**32.8**	**34.8**	**32.9**
INCOME STATEMENT (IN MILLIONS):							
Total Revenues	3,755.1	2,735.8	3,018.4	2,814.3	2,630.2	2,431.2	2,274.3
Costs & Expenses	3,513.9	2,512.9	2,774.2	2,629.7	2,403.1	2,236.3	2,094.4
Depreciation & Amort.	87.9	60.4	74.1	77.0	70.0	61.9	54.0
Operating Income	153.3	162.5	170.1	d42.4	157.1	133.1	126.0
Net Interest Inc./(Exp.)	d38.0	d18.8	d24.4	d27.0	d20.7	d14.7	d13.9
Income Before Income Taxes	115.3	143.7	145.7	d69.4	136.4	118.3	114.8
Income Taxes	45.0	55.8	59.0	cr19.7	56.3	47.6	46.4
Net Income	[3] 70.3	88.0	86.7	[1] d49.7	80.1	[2] 70.8	68.4
Cash Flow	158.3	148.4	160.8	27.4	150.1	132.6	122.4
Average Shs. Outstg. (000)	40,482	41,395	40,188	40,122	39,890	39,737	...
BALANCE SHEET (IN MILLIONS):							
Cash & Cash Equivalents	16.0	11.9	4.4	10.4	4.8	11.0	41.6
Total Current Assets	582.1	420.2	562.1	584.4	518.9	460.2	406.1
Net Property	764.9	551.1	527.2	525.7	570.1	543.2	443.8
Total Assets	1,911.9	1,607.2	1,217.4	1,222.2	1,202.4	1,109.2	892.8
Total Current Liabilities	439.5	352.9	354.1	398.5	303.9	367.3	207.7
Long-Term Obligations	631.3	558.2	211.9	221.7	224.7	136.2	151.1
Net Stockholders' Equity	716.4	619.3	567.7	507.7	584.5	524.8	476.3
Net Working Capital	142.7	67.3	208.0	185.9	215.0	92.9	198.4
Year-end Shs. Outstg. (000)	39,276	39,970	40,283	40,133	40,078	39,789	39,689
STATISTICAL RECORD:							
Operating Profit Margin %	4.1	5.9	5.6	...	6.0	5.5	5.5
Net Profit Margin %	1.9	3.2	2.9	...	3.0	2.9	3.0
Return on Equity %	9.8	14.2	15.3	...	13.7	13.5	14.4
Return on Assets %	3.7	5.5	7.1	...	6.7	6.4	7.7
Debt/Total Assets %	33.0	34.7	17.4	18.1	18.7	12.3	16.9
Price Range	60 11/16-39 1/2	57 3/4-31	32 3/4-21 3/4	31 3/4-26 1/4	33 1/2-25 1/4	32 7/8-23 1/8	31 1/2-22 3/4
P/E Ratio	34.9-22.7	27.1-14.6	15.2-10.1	...	16.7-12.6	18.5-13.0	18.2-13.1
Average Yield %	1.6	1.8	2.7	2.4	2.2	2.2	2.1

Statistics are as originally reported. [1] Incl. non-recur. chg. $97.7 mil. [2] Bef. $1.2 mil chg. for acctg. adj. [3] Bef. $80.9 mil ($2.03/sh) gain from discont. opers. & incl. $11.0 mil ($0.27/sh) net one-time plant closure costs.

OFFICERS:
H. M. Dean, Chmn., C.E.O.
R. E. Bailey, Pres., C.O.O.
W. M. Luegers, Jr., V.P., Treas., Contr.

INVESTOR CONTACT: LuAnn Lilja, Dir., Corporate Communications, (847) 233-5439

PRINCIPAL OFFICE: 3600 North River Road, Franklin Park, IL 60131

TELEPHONE NUMBER: (847) 678-1680
FAX: (847) 233-5501
WEB: www.deanfoods.com

NO. OF EMPLOYEES: 12,300 full-time; 1,300 part-time

SHAREHOLDERS: 8,622

ANNUAL MEETING: In Sept.

INCORPORATED: DE, May, 1968

INSTITUTIONAL HOLDINGS:
No. of Institutions: 169
Shares Held: 16,931,570
% Held: 43.3

INDUSTRY: Fluid milk (SIC: 2026)

TRANSFER AGENT(S): Harris Trust and Savings Bank, Chicago IL

DIEBOLD, INC.

YIELD 2.0%
P/E RATIO 16.4

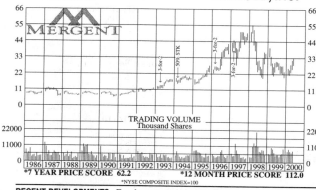

*7 YEAR PRICE SCORE 62.2   *12 MONTH PRICE SCORE 112.0
*NYSE COMPOSITE INDEX=100

TRADING VOLUME
Thousand Shares

INTERIM EARNINGS (Per Share):

Qtr.	Mar.	June	Sept.	Dec.
1996	0.26	0.35	0.39	0.41
1997	0.34	0.45	0.48	0.50
1998	0.39	d0.21	0.43	0.50
1999	0.42	0.46	0.47	0.50

INTERIM DIVIDENDS (Per Share):

Amt.	Decl.	Ex.	Rec.	Pay.
0.15Q	8/03/99	8/11/99	8/13/99	9/03/99
0.15Q	10/12/99	11/09/99	11/12/99	12/03/99
0.155Q	1/27/00	2/16/00	2/18/00	3/10/00
0.155Q	4/19/00	5/10/00	5/12/00	6/02/00

Indicated div.: $0.62 (Div. Reinv. Plan)

CAPITALIZATION (12/31/99):

	($000)	(%)
Long-Term Debt	20,800	2.4
Minority Interest	4,423	0.5
Common & Surplus	844,395	97.1
Total	869,618	100.0

DIVIDEND ACHIEVER STATUS:
Rank: 199   10-Year Growth Rate: 8.05%
Total Years of Dividend Growth: 46

RECENT DEVELOPMENTS: For the year ended 12/31/99, net income jumped 69.2% to $128.9 million from $76.1 million the year before. Results included a one-time pre-tax credit of $1.2 million in 1999 versus pre-tax non-recurring charges totaling $61.1 million in 1998. Total net sales rose 6.2% to $1.26 billion from $1.19 billion a year earlier. Product sales inched up to $757.2 million from $750.2 million the prior year, while service revenues grew 15.2% to $501.9 million from $435.5 million the previous year.

PROSPECTS: On 4/17/00, DBD acquired the financial self-service businesses of Amsterdam-based Getronics NV and France-based Groupe Bull, which have annual revenues totaling approximately $250.0 million, for approximately $160.0 million in cash. The acquisition will bolster the Company's product offering and custom maintenance capabilities in a number of European countries, as well as expand existing operations in Australia, Brazil, Canada and China.

BUSINESS

DIEBOLD, INC. provides card-based transaction systems, security products, and customer service solutions to the financial, education, and healthcare industries. The Company develops, manufactures, sells and services the following products: automated teller machines, electronic and physical security systems, bank facility equipment, software and integrated systems for global financial and commercial markets. The products segment accounted for 60% of revenues, while the services segment accounted for 40% for the year ended 12/31/99.

ANNUAL FINANCIAL DATA

	12/31/99	12/31/98	12/31/97	12/31/96	12/31/95	12/31/94	12/31/93
Earnings Per Share	☐ 1.85	☐ 1.10	1.76	1.42	1.11	0.93	0.71
Cash Flow Per Share	2.35	1.47	2.03	1.72	1.32	1.12	0.89
Tang. Book Val. Per Share	9.63	10.15	9.69	8.36	7.37	6.70	6.27
Dividends Per Share	0.60	0.56	0.50	0.45	0.43	0.39	0.36
Dividend Payout %	32.4	50.9	28.4	31.9	38.3	41.9	49.9
INCOME STATEMENT (IN MILLIONS):							
Total Revenues	1,259.2	1,185.7	1,226.9	1,030.2	863.4	760.2	623.3
Costs & Expenses	1,038.3	1,053.8	1,024.4	868.8	742.4	656.2	542.0
Depreciation & Amort.	34.7	25.6	18.7	21.0	14.2	13.2	12.2
Operating Income	186.1	106.2	183.9	140.4	106.8	90.8	69.1
Income Before Income Taxes	201.3	119.8	185.7	146.5	113.2	94.0	70.5
Income Taxes	72.5	43.7	63.1	49.1	37.0	30.5	22.1
Equity Earnings/Minority Int.	d1.2	d1.8	d5.1	d4.4	d0.2	d1.9	d4.2
Net Income	☐ 128.9	☐ 76.1	122.5	97.4	76.2	63.5	48.4
Cash Flow	163.6	101.8	141.2	118.4	90.4	76.8	60.6
Average Shs. Outstg. (000)	69,562	69,310	69,490	68,796	68,649	68,243	68,021
BALANCE SHEET (IN MILLIONS):							
Cash & Cash Equivalents	84.6	80.0	56.8	65.1	46.7	55.7	71.9
Total Current Assets	647.9	543.5	549.8	479.6	376.2	329.7	313.3
Net Property	160.7	147.1	143.9	95.9	84.1	64.7	60.7
Total Assets	1,298.8	1,004.2	991.1	859.1	745.2	666.2	609.0
Total Current Liabilities	382.4	235.5	242.1	228.2	186.0	159.8	138.6
Long-Term Obligations	20.8	20.8	20.8	...	...	...	...
Net Stockholders' Equity	844.4	699.1	668.6	575.6	506.2	459.2	427.0
Net Working Capital	265.5	308.0	307.8	251.4	190.2	169.9	174.8
Year-end Shs. Outstg. (000)	71,096	68,881	69,005	68,841	68,712	68,535	68,085
STATISTICAL RECORD:							
Operating Profit Margin %	14.8	9.0	15.0	13.6	12.4	11.9	11.1
Net Profit Margin %	10.2	6.4	10.0	9.5	8.8	8.4	7.8
Return on Equity %	15.3	10.9	18.3	16.9	15.1	13.8	11.3
Return on Assets %	9.9	7.6	12.4	11.3	10.2	9.5	7.9
Debt/Total Assets %	1.6	2.1	2.1	...	...	...	...
Price Range	39⁷/₈-19¹¹/₁₆	55⁵/₁₆-19³/₈	50⁵/₈-28	42⁵/₁₆-22⁷/₁₆	27⁵/₈-14¹¹/₁₆	20³/₄-15¹/₁₆	18¹/₄-11³/₈
P/E Ratio	21.6-10.6	50.3-17.4	28.8-15.9	29.8-15.8	24.8-13.2	22.3-16.2	25.6-16.2
Average Yield %	2.0	1.5	1.3	1.4	2.0	2.2	2.4

Statistics are as originally reported. Adj. for 3-for-2 stk. split, 2/96 & 3/94. ☐ Incl. one-time pre-tax $1.2 mil chg., 1999; $41.9 mil ($0.60/sh) after-tax chg. for realignment program, 1998.

OFFICERS:
W. W. O'Dell, Chmn., Pres., C.E.O.
G. T. Geswein, Sr. V.P., C.F.O.
R. J. Warren, V.P., Treas.

INVESTOR CONTACT: Sandy K. Upperman, Manager Investor Relations, (800) 766-5859

PRINCIPAL OFFICE: 5995 Mayfair Rd., North Canton, OH 44720-8077

TELEPHONE NUMBER: (330) 490-4000
FAX: (330) 588-3794
WEB: www.diebold.com

NO. OF EMPLOYEES: 9,935

SHAREHOLDERS: 98,462 (approx.)

ANNUAL MEETING: In Apr.

INCORPORATED: OH, Aug., 1876

INSTITUTIONAL HOLDINGS:
No. of Institutions: 215
Shares Held: 35,931,085
% Held: 50.7

INDUSTRY: Calculating and accounting equipment (SIC: 3578)

TRANSFER AGENT(S): The Bank of New York, New York, NY

DISNEY (WALT) COMPANY (THE)

YIELD 0.5%
P/E RATIO 73.6

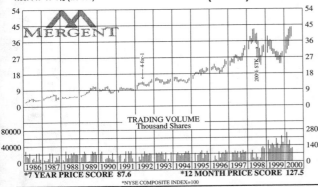

7 YEAR PRICE SCORE 87.6   **12 MONTH PRICE SCORE 127.5**

*NYSE COMPOSITE INDEX=100

INTERIM EARNINGS (Per Share):

Qtr.	Dec.	Mar.	June	Sept.
1997	0.36	0.16	0.23	0.20
1998	0.37	0.55	0.20	0.14
1999	0.30	0.11	0.18	0.03
2000	0.25	...	...	...

INTERIM DIVIDENDS (Per Share):

Amt.	Decl.	Ex.	Rec.	Pay.
0.158Q	1/30/98	4/07/98	4/10/98	5/22/98
200% STK	6/09/98	7/10/98	6/19/98	7/09/98
0.052Q	6/24/98	7/22/98	7/24/98	8/21/98
0.052A	9/29/98	10/07/98	10/09/98	11/20/98
0.21A	11/04/99	11/12/99	11/16/99	12/17/99

Indicated div.: $0.21

CAPITALIZATION (9/30/99):

	($000)	(%)
Long-Term Debt	9,278,000	28.2
Deferred Income Tax	2,660,000	8.1
Common & Surplus	20,975,000	63.7
Total	32,913,000	100.0

DIVIDEND ACHIEVER STATUS:
Rank: 29   10-Year Growth Rate: 18.55%
Total Years of Dividend Growth: 14

RECENT DEVELOPMENTS: For the quarter ended 12/31/99, net income advanced 7.0% to $515.0 milion. Revenues increased 5.0% to $6.80 billion. The improvement in results was attributed to the strength and popularity of DIS' broadcasting, cable and theme park assets and the programming-driven improved performance of the ABC-TV network. Comparisons were made with restated results.

PROSPECTS: More strategic investments in DIS's network television production and cable network businesses should result in higher costs in fiscal 2000. As a result, DIS believes that fiscal 2000 earnings per share should be about in line with fiscal 1999 results, excluding restructuring charges and Go.com. DIS remains committed to investing in core markets and pursuing international opportunities.

BUSINESS

THE WALT DISNEY COMPANY is a diversified international entertainment company with operations in five business segments. Media Networks, which accounted for 32.1% of revenues in 1999, includes Broadcasting, which operates the ABC Television Network and DIS's television stations and radio stations, and Cable Networks, which operates the ESPN-branded cable networks and start-up cable operations. Studio Entertainment, 28.0%, includes Theatrical Films and Home Video. Theme Parks and Resorts, 26.1%, includes Walt Disney World Resort, Disney Regional Entertainment, and Anaheim Sports, Inc. Consumer Products, 12.9%, includes Character Merchandise and Publications Licensing, The Disney Stores, and Books and Magazines. Internet and Direct Marketing, 0.9%, includes DIS's on-line services and the Walt Disney Catalog. On 2/29/96, DIS acquired Capital Cities/ABC, Inc. for $18.90 billion. In November 1999, DIS acquired the remaining 28% of Infoseek Corporation, an Internet search company, that it did not already own. Subsequently, DIS created and issued a new class of common stock, called GO.com, which comprises DIS's Internet business as well as its direct marketing operations.

ANNUAL FINANCIAL DATA

	② 9/30/99	9/30/98	9/30/97	9/30/96	9/30/95	9/30/94	9/30/93
Earnings Per Share	① 0.62	③ 0.89	④ 0.95	⑤ 0.65	0.87	0.68	⑥ 0.41
Cash Flow Per Share	2.44	2.70	3.36	2.78	2.03	1.66	1.04
Tang. Book Val. Per Share	2.55	1.34	0.63	...	4.23	3.50	3.13
Dividends Per Share	0.21	0.20	0.17	0.14	0.12	0.10	0.08
Dividend Payout %	33.9	22.7	17.7	21.4	13.3	14.1	19.5

INCOME STATEMENT (IN MILLIONS):

Total Revenues	23,402.0	22,976.0	22,473.0	18,739.0	12,112.1	10,055.1	8,529.2
Costs & Expenses	16,524.0	15,207.0	13,203.0	11,762.0	7,997.0	6,643.3	5,940.5
Depreciation & Amort.	3,779.0	3,754.0	4,958.0	3,944.0	1,853.0	1,608.3	1,028.4
Operating Income	3,099.0	4,015.0	4,312.0	3,033.0	2,262.1	1,803.5	1,560.3
Net Interest Inc./(Exp.)	d612.0	d622.0	d693.0	d479.0	d178.3	d119.9	d157.7
Income Before Income Taxes	2,314.0	3,157.0	3,387.0	2,061.0	2,116.7	1,703.1	1,074.0
Income Taxes	1,014.0	1,307.0	1,421.0	847.0	736.6	592.7	402.7
Equity Earnings/Minority Int.	...	...	...	...	d35.1	d110.4	d514.7
Net Income	① 1,300.0	③ 1,850.0	④ 1,966.0	⑤ 1,214.0	1,380.1	1,110.4	⑥ 671.3
Cash Flow	5,079.0	5,604.0	6,924.0	5,158.0	3,233.1	2,718.7	1,699.7
Average Shs. Outstg. (000)	2,083,000	2,079,000	2,061,000	1,857,000	1,591,200	1,635,600	1,633,500

BALANCE SHEET (IN MILLIONS):

Cash & Cash Equivalents	414.0	127.0	317.0	278.0	1,076.5	186.9	363.0
Total Current Assets	10,200.0	9,375.0	8,989.0	8,484.0	5,792.7	4,121.9	3,723.1
Net Property	11,346.0	10,346.0	8,951.0	8,031.0	6,190.3	5,814.5	5,228.2
Total Assets	43,679.0	41,378.0	37,379.0	37,306.0	14,605.8	12,826.3	11,751.1
Total Current Liabilities	7,707.0	7,525.0	12,149.0	13,330.0	5,885.2	5,217.0	2,821.1
Long-Term Obligations	9,278.0	9,562.0	11,068.0	12,342.0	2,984.3	2,936.9	2,385.8
Net Stockholders' Equity	20,975.0	19,388.0	17,285.0	16,086.0	6,650.8	5,508.3	5,030.5
Net Working Capital	2,493.0	1,850.0	d3,160.0	d4,846.0	d92.5	d1,095.1	902.0
Year-end Shs. Outstg. (000)	2,071,000	2,690,000	2,025,000	2,022,000	1,573,200	1,572,300	1,606,500

STATISTICAL RECORD:

Operating Profit Margin %	13.2	17.5	19.2	16.2	18.7	17.9	18.3
Net Profit Margin %	5.6	8.1	8.7	6.5	11.4	11.0	7.9
Return on Equity %	6.2	9.5	11.4	7.5	20.8	20.2	13.3
Return on Assets %	3.0	4.5	5.3	3.3	9.4	8.7	5.7
Debt/Total Assets %	21.2	23.1	29.6	33.1	20.4	22.9	20.3
Price Range	38¹¹/₁₆-23⅜	42¹³/₁₆-22½	33⁷/₁₆-22⅛	25¾-17¾	21⁷/₁₆-15	16³/₁₆-12⁹/₁₆	15¹⁵/₁₆-12
P/E Ratio	62.4-37.7	48.1-25.3	35.1-23.2	39.4-27.2	24.7-17.3	23.8-18.5	38.9-29.3
Average Yield %	0.7	0.6	0.6	0.6	0.6	0.6	0.7

Statistics are as originally reported. Adj. for stk. split: 200%, 7/98. Results from 1996 & forward incl. Capital Cities/ABC, Inc., acquired on 2/29/96 for $18.90 bill. ① 1Incl. restruct. chrg. of $132.0 mill. and gain on sale of Starwave of $345.0 mill. ② As of 11/98, DIS switched to an annual dividend payment method from a quarterly basis. ③ Incl. $24 mill. gain. Incl. chrg. of $64.0 mill. ④ Incl. $135 mill. gain. ⑤ Incl. acctg. chrg. of $300.0 mill. & acq. costs of $225 mill. ⑥ Bef. acctg. chrg. of $371.5 mill.

OFFICERS:
M. D. Eisner, Chmn., C.E.O.
R. E. Disney, Vice-Chmn.
S. M. Litvack, Vice-Chmn.
L. M. Meisinger, Exec. V.P., Gen. Couns.

PRINCIPAL OFFICE: 500 South Buena Vista Street, Burbank, CA 91521

TELEPHONE NUMBER: (818) 560-1000
FAX: (818) 560-1930
WEB: www.disney.com
NO. OF EMPLOYEES: 120,000 (avg.)
SHAREHOLDERS: 842,000 (approx.)
ANNUAL MEETING: In March
INCORPORATED: CA, Sept., 1938; reincorp., DE, Feb., 1987

INSTITUTIONAL HOLDINGS:
No. of Institutions: 871
Shares Held: 884,415,657
% Held: 42.9

INDUSTRY: Amusement parks (SIC: 7996)

TRANSFER AGENT(S): The Company

DONEGAL GROUP INC.

	YIELD	5.1%
	P/E RATIO	8.8

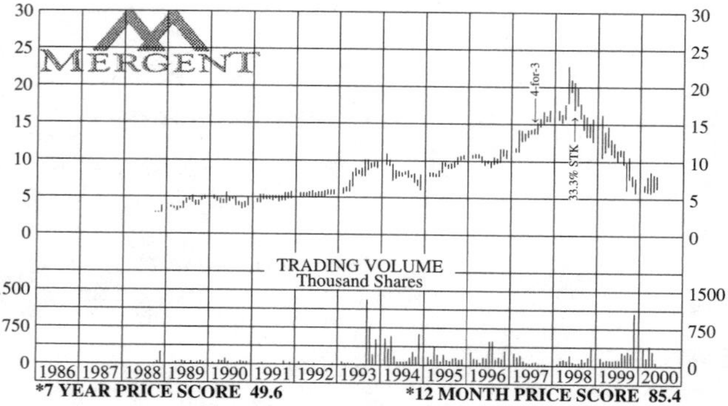

INTERIM EARNINGS (Per Share):

Qtr.	Mar.	June	Sept.	Dec.
1996	0.32	0.62	0.56	0.51
1997	0.43	0.40	0.48	0.45
1998	0.40	0.22	0.01	0.46
1999	0.26	0.16	d0.29	0.67

INTERIM DIVIDENDS (Per Share):

Amt.	Decl.	Ex.	Rec.	Pay.
0.09Q	4/15/99	4/29/99	5/03/99	5/17/99
0.09Q	7/16/99	7/29/99	8/02/99	8/16/99
0.09Q	10/22/99	10/28/99	11/01/99	11/15/99
0.09Q	12/16/99	1/28/00	2/01/00	2/15/00
0.09Q	4/20/00	4/27/00	5/01/00	5/15/00

Indicated div.: $0.36 (Div. Reinv. Plan)

CAPITALIZATION (12/31/99):

	($000)	(%)
Long-Term Debt	37,000	26.4
Common & Surplus	103,415	73.6
Total	140,415	100.0

TRADING VOLUME
Thousand Shares

| 1986 | 1987 | 1988 | 1989 | 1990 | 1991 | 1992 | 1993 | 1994 | 1995 | 1996 | 1997 | 1998 | 1999 | 2000 |

*7 YEAR PRICE SCORE 49.6

*NYSE COMPOSITE INDEX=100

*12 MONTH PRICE SCORE 85.4

DIVIDEND ACHIEVER STATUS:
Rank: 111   10-Year Growth Rate: 12.18%
Total Years of Dividend Growth: 10

RECENT DEVELOPMENTS: For the year ended 12/31/99, net income fell 26.1% to $6.7 million from $9.0 million the year before. The 1999 results include a pre-tax charge of $2.0 million for restructuring. Total revenues increased 22.3% to $159.7 million from $130.6 million in the prior year. The increase was fueled by growth in net premiums, which grew 23.8% to $143.9 million, as a result of the acquisition of Southern Heritage Insurance Company in 11/98. Total expenses as a percentage of total revenues rose 6.6% percentage points to 97.7% versus 91.1% in 1998 primarily due to the increase in losses and loss expenses, which jumped 31.7% to $145.5 million.

BUSINESS

DONEGAL GROUP INC. is an insurance holding company, which through its subsidiaries, engages in the property and casualty insurance business in 19 mid-Atlantic and southeastern states. DGI and its subsidiaries underwrite a line of personal and commercial coverages, consisting of private passenger and commercial automobile, homeowners, commercial multiperil, workers' compensation and other lines of insurance. The Company has three reportable segments, which consist of the investment function, the personal lines of insurance and the commercial lines of insurance. DGIC's subsidiaries include Atlantic States Insurance Company, Southern Insurance Company of Virginia, Pioneer Insurance Company, Delaware Atlantic Insurance Company, Southern Heritage Insurance Company and Atlantic Inspection Services, Inc.

REVENUES

(12/31/1999)	($000)	(%)
Net Premiums		
Earned	143,874	90.1
Investment Income	13,224	8.3
Installment Payment		
Fees	1,439	0.9
Lease Income	819	0.5
Service Fees	393	0.2
Realized Investment		
Loss	(39)	(0.0)
Total	159,710	100.0

ANNUAL FINANCIAL DATA

	12/31/99	12/31/98	12/31/97	12/31/96	12/31/95	12/31/94	12/31/93
Earnings Per Share	☐ 0.80	1.09	1.32	1.10	1.30	0.82	1.08
Cash Flow Per Share	0.91	1.16	1.37	1.17	1.35	0.86	1.12
Tang. Book Val. Per Share	12.24	12.27	15.19	13.64	9.54	8.38	7.89
Dividends Per Share	0.35	0.33	0.28	0.24	0.22	0.20	0.17
Dividend Payout %	44.4	30.0	21.2	22.0	16.9	24.0	16.1
INCOME STATEMENT (IN THOUSANDS):							
Total Revenues	159,711	130,586	121,328	112,519	97,885	81,742	77,699
Costs & Expenses	153,610	117,096	105,853	100,662	84,851	73,291	68,919
Depreciation & Amort.	936	521	391	236	380	290	223
Operating Income	5,164	12,970	15,084	11,622	12,653	8,161	8,557
Net Interest Inc./(Exp.)	d1,535	d1,293	d910	d375	d8	d9	d37
Income Before Income Taxes	3,629	11,677	14,174	11,246	12,646	8,151	8,520
Income Taxes	cr3,028	2,659	3,532	2,350	2,788	2,063	2,138
Net Income	☐ 6,657	9,018	10,641	8,896	9,858	6,089	6,382
Cash Flow	7,593	9,539	11,032	9,132	10,238	6,379	6,605
Average Shs. Outstg.	8,327	8,250	8,036	7,815	7,594	7,431	5,919
BALANCE SHEET (IN THOUSANDS):							
Cash & Cash Equivalents	119,961	129,275	83,857	73,708	67,893	67,275	54,981
Total Current Assets	195,423	200,831	138,853	123,860	110,829	99,365	81,932
Net Property	5,517	5,920	4,939	2,161	2,283	1,592	1,527
Total Assets	399,733	385,232	304,105	273,138	235,704	192,047	169,462
Total Current Liabilities	10,963	10,084	12,245	7,144	6,310	6,404	2,947
Long-Term Obligations	37,000	37,500	10,500	8,500	5,000	...	...
Net Stockholders' Equity	103,415	100,631	91,597	81,277	72,283	61,001	57,345
Net Working Capital	184,461	190,747	126,608	116,715	104,519	92,961	78,985
Year-end Shs. Outstg.	8,452	8,203	6,031	5,961	7,574	7,284	7,266
STATISTICAL RECORD:							
Operating Profit Margin %	3.2	9.9	12.4	10.3	12.9	10.0	11.0
Net Profit Margin %	4.2	6.9	8.8	7.9	10.1	7.4	8.2
Return on Equity %	6.4	9.0	11.6	10.9	13.6	10.0	11.1
Return on Assets %	1.7	2.3	3.5	3.3	4.2	3.2	3.8
Debt/Total Assets %	9.3	9.7	3.5	3.1	2.1	...	...
Price Range	16¼-5¾	22¹³⁄₁₆-12⅝	16⅞-11¼	11¹¹⁄₁₆-9⅛	10¹³⁄₁₆-7⅞	10-6¹⁄₁₆	10⅛-5½
P/E Ratio	20.3-7.2	20.9-11.6	12.8-8.5	10.6-8.3	8.3-6.0	13.3-7.4	9.4-5.1
Average Yield %	3.2	1.8	2.0	2.3	2.3	2.3	2.2

Statistics are as originally reported. Adj. for 33.3% stock split, 6/28/98 & 4-for-3 stock split, 1/15/97. ☐ Incl. a pre-tax charge of $2.0 million for restructuring.

OFFICERS:
C. E. Ireland, Chmn.
D. H. Nikolaus, Pres., C.E.O.
R. G. Spontak, Sr. V.P., C.F.O., Sec.
D. J. Wagner, Treas.

INVESTOR CONTACT: Ralph G. Spontak, Sr. V.P. & C.F.O., (717) 426-1931

PRINCIPAL OFFICE: 1195 River Road, P.O. Box 302, Marietta, PA 17547-0302

TELEPHONE NUMBER: (717) 426-1931
FAX: (717) 426-7030
WEB: www.donegalgroup.com

NO. OF EMPLOYEES: 403

SHAREHOLDERS: 622 (approx.)

ANNUAL MEETING: In Apr.

INCORPORATED: DE, Aug., 1986

INSTITUTIONAL HOLDINGS:
No. of Institutions: 14
Shares Held: 1,719,813
% Held: 20.5

INDUSTRY: Fire, marine, and casualty insurance (SIC: 6331)

TRANSFER AGENT(S): First Chicago Trust Company of New York, Jersey City, NJ

NYSE SYMBOL DNY
Rec. Pr. 24¾ (5/31/00)

DONNELLEY (R.R.) & SONS CO.

YIELD 3.6%
P/E RATIO 10.3

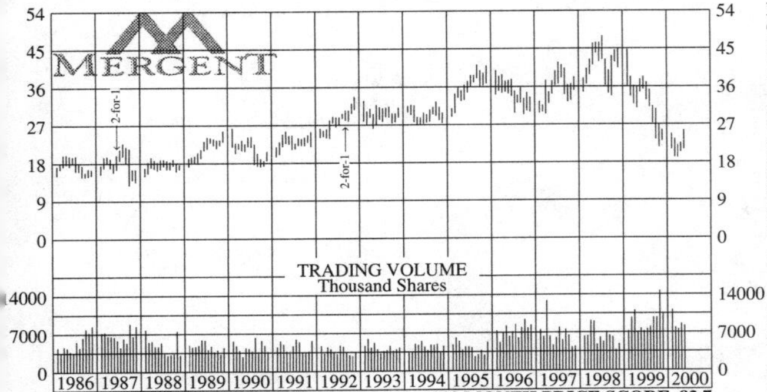
MERGENT
54
45
36
27
18
9
0
2-for-1
2-for-1
TRADING VOLUME
Thousand Shares
14000
7000
0
1986 1987 1988 1989 1990 1991 1992 1993 1994 1995 1996 1997 1998 1999 2000

*7 YEAR PRICE SCORE 52.5 *12 MONTH PRICE SCORE 83.7

*NYSE COMPOSITE INDEX=100

INTERIM EARNINGS (Per Share):

Qtr.	Mar.	June	Sept.	Dec.
1996	d2.45	0.35	0.45	0.66
1997	0.24	0.31	0.56	0.31
1998	0.30	0.61	0.71	0.67
1999	0.33	0.40	0.67	1.01

INTERIM DIVIDENDS (Per Share):

Amt.	Decl.	Ex.	Rec.	Pay.
0.21Q	3/25/99	5/06/99	5/10/99	6/01/99
0.22Q	7/22/99	8/05/99	8/09/99	9/01/99
0.22Q	9/23/99	11/04/99	11/08/99	12/01/99
0.22Q	1/31/00	2/04/00	2/08/00	3/01/00
0.22Q	3/22/00	5/10/00	5/12/00	6/01/00

Indicated div.: $0.88 (Div. Reinv. Plan)

CAPITALIZATION (12/31/99):

	($000)	(%)
Long-Term Debt	748,498	35.0
Deferred Income Tax	252,884	11.8
Common & Surplus	1,138,258	53.2
Total	2,139,640	100.0

DIVIDEND ACHIEVER STATUS:
Rank: 224 10-Year Growth Rate: 6.93%
Total Years of Dividend Growth: 30

RECENT DEVELOPMENTS: For the year ended 12/31/99, income from continuing operations fell 16.9% to $311.5 million versus $374.6 million in 1998. Results in 1999 included a $42.8 million gain from the sale of businesses and excluded a loss of $3.2 million from discontinued operations. Results in 1998 included gain of $168.9 million from the sale of businesses and excluded a loss of $80.1 million from discontinued operations. Net sales were $5.18 billion, up 3.3% from $5.02 billion in the prior year.

PROSPECTS: DNY announced the acquisition of EVACO, a financial printer with locations in Miami and St. Petersburg, FL. The acquisition was strategically in line with Donnelley Financial's expansion in the Southeast. Separately, DNY agreed to purchase Iridio, Inc., a full-service premedia provider of digital photography, digital print and on-line services. The acquisition strengthens DNY's presence in the Pacific Northwest and expands services for its catalog, corporate, agency, retail and magazine customers.

BUSINESS

DONNELLEY (R.R.) & SONS CO. is engaged in distributing, managing and reproducing print and digital information for the publishing, retailing, merchandising and information technology markets worldwide. Services provided to customers include presswork and binding, including on-demand customized publications; conventional and digital preproduction operations; software manufacturing, marketing and support services (through Stream International Holdings); design and related creative services (through Coris Inc.); electronic communication networks for simultaneous worldwide product releases; digital services to publishers; and the planning for and fulfillment of truck, rail, mail and air distribution for products of DNY and its customers. Revenues for 1999 were derived: merchandise media, 24%; magazine & book publishing, 38%; telecommunications, 17%; financial services, 12%; and other, 9%.

ANNUAL FINANCIAL DATA

	12/31/99	12/31/98	12/31/97	12/31/96	12/31/95	12/31/94	12/31/93
Earnings Per Share	**5 2.40**	**4 2.08**	**3 1.40**	**2 d1.04**	**1.95**	**1.75**	**1 1.16**
Cash Flow Per Share	**5.29**	**4.67**	**3.91**	**1.53**	**4.54**	**3.78**	**2.93**
Tang. Book Val. Per Share	**6.01**	**6.85**	**8.31**	**7.49**	**7.46**	**7.13**	**8.76**
Dividends Per Share	**0.86**	**0.82**	**0.78**	**0.74**	**0.68**	**0.60**	**0.54**
Dividend Payout %	**35.8**	**39.4**	**55.7**	**...**	**34.9**	**34.3**	**46.5**
INCOME STATEMENT (IN MILLIONS):							
Total Revenues	5,183.4	5,018.4	4,850.0	6,599.0	6,511.8	4,888.8	4,387.8
Costs & Expenses	4,278.6	4,242.3	4,110.8	6,345.8	5,554.2	4,115.9	3,787.4
Depreciation & Amort.	374.4	367.8	370.4	389.1	398.2	313.5	274.8
Operating Income	530.4	408.4	368.8	d136.0	559.4	459.4	325.6
Net Interest Inc./(Exp.)	d88.2	d78.2	d90.8	d95.5	d109.8	d53.5	d45.4
Income Before Income Taxes	506.5	509.3	303.8	d110.5	439.5	395.0	276.6
Income Taxes	195.0	214.7	97.2	47.1	140.7	126.4	97.6
Net Income	5 311.5	4 294.6	3 206.5	2 d157.6	298.8	268.6	1 178.9
Cash Flow	685.9	662.4	577.0	231.5	697.0	582.1	453.7
Average Shs. Outstg. (000)	129,566	141,865	147,508	151,800	153,500	153,900	154,600
BALANCE SHEET (IN MILLIONS):							
Cash & Cash Equivalents	41.9	66.2	47.8	31.1	33.1	20.6	10.7
Total Current Assets	1,229.9	1,145.0	1,146.6	1,752.9	1,908.0	1,353.3	1,109.9
Net Property	1,710.7	1,700.9	1,788.1	1,944.7	2,009.0	1,856.8	1,674.5
Total Assets	3,853.5	3,787.8	4,134.2	4,849.0	5,384.8	4,452.1	3,654.0
Total Current Liabilities	1,203.5	898.3	812.6	1,147.5	1,130.4	801.9	685.4
Long-Term Obligations	748.5	999.0	1,153.2	1,430.7	1,561.0	1,212.3	673.4
Net Stockholders' Equity	1,138.3	1,300.9	1,591.5	1,631.3	2,173.2	1,978.4	1,844.0
Net Working Capital	26.4	246.7	333.9	605.3	777.6	551.5	424.5
Year-end Shs. Outstg. (000)	123,237	134,322	145,118	145,554	153,953	153,085	154,158
STATISTICAL RECORD:							
Operating Profit Margin %	10.2	8.1	7.6	...	8.6	9.4	7.4
Net Profit Margin %	6.0	5.9	4.3	...	4.6	5.5	4.1
Return on Equity %	27.4	22.6	13.0	...	13.7	13.6	9.7
Return on Assets %	8.1	7.8	5.0	...	5.5	6.0	4.9
Debt/Total Assets %	19.4	26.4	27.9	29.5	29.0	27.2	18.4
Price Range	44¾-21½	48-33¾	41¾-29½	39⅞-29⅜	41¼-28⅞	32½-26⅞	32¾-26⅛
P/E Ratio	18.6-9.0	23.1-16.2	29.8-21.1	...	21.2-14.8	18.6-15.4	28.2-22.5
Average Yield %	2.6	2.0	2.2	2.1	1.9	2.0	1.8

Statistics are as originally reported. 1 Bef. $127.7 mill. acct. adj. & $60.8 mill. aft-tax restr. chg. 2 Incl. $560.6 mill. pre-tax restr. chg. & $80.0 mill. gains from IPO's. 3 Bef. loss fr. disc. ops. of $76.9 mill. ($0.51/sh) & incl. $70.7 mill. pre-tax restr. chg. 4 Incl. $168.9 mill. gain fr. sale of subsidiaries & $80.1 mill. loss fr. businesses held for sale. 5 Incl. $42.8 mill. gain fr. sale of bus. & excl. $3.2 mill. loss fr. disc. ops.

OFFICERS:
W. L. Davis, Chmn., C.E.O.
J. P. Ward, Pres., C.O.O.

INVESTOR CONTACT: Sara Gopal, Director, Investor Relations, (312) 326-7754

PRINCIPAL OFFICE: 77 West Wacker Drive, Chicago, IL 60601

TELEPHONE NUMBER: (312) 326-8000
FAX: (312) 326-8543
WEB: www.rrdonnelley.com

NO. OF EMPLOYEES: 34,000 (approx.)

SHAREHOLDERS: 10,155 (approx.)

ANNUAL MEETING: In Mar.

INCORPORATED: DE, May, 1956

INSTITUTIONAL HOLDINGS:
No. of Institutions: 238
Shares Held: 99,637,509
% Held: 78.1

INDUSTRY: Commercial printing, lithographic (SIC: 2752)

TRANSFER AGENT(S): First Chicago Trust Company of New York, Jersey City, NJ.

DOVER CORPORATION

YIELD 1.0%
P/E RATIO 24.2

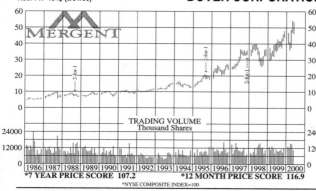

*7 YEAR PRICE SCORE 107.2   *12 MONTH PRICE SCORE 116.9
*NYSE COMPOSITE INDEX=100

INTERIM EARNINGS (Per Share):

Qtr.	Mar.	June	Sept.	Dec.
1996	0.34	0.39	0.64	0.36
1997	0.35	0.56	0.46	0.44
1998	0.40	0.45	0.42	0.36
1999	0.32	0.44	0.58	0.58

INTERIM DIVIDENDS (Per Share):

Amt.	Decl.	Ex.	Rec.	Pay.
0.105Q	5/06/99	5/26/99	5/28/99	6/14/99
0.115Q	8/06/99	8/27/99	8/31/99	9/15/99
0.115Q	11/04/99	11/26/99	11/30/99	12/15/99
0.115Q	2/10/00	2/25/00	2/29/00	3/15/00
0.115Q	5/04/00	5/24/00	5/29/00	6/15/00

Indicated div.: $0.46

CAPITALIZATION (12/31/99):

	($000)	(%)
Long-Term Debt	608,025	22.6
Deferred Income Tax	42,061	1.6
Common & Surplus	2,038,756	75.8
Total	2,688,842	100.0

DIVIDEND ACHIEVER STATUS:
Rank: 165   10-Year Growth Rate: 9.66%
Total Years of Dividend Growth: 44

RECENT DEVELOPMENTS: For the year ended 12/31/99, net earnings from continuing operations was $405.1 million versus net earnings from continuing operations of $326.4 million in 1998. Net sales rose 11.8% to $4.45 billion. Earnings from Dover Industries jumped 13.1% to $1.14 billion, while Dover Technologies' earnings rose 20.3% to $1.46 billion. Earnings from Dover Diversified increased 11.9% to $1.07 billion. Comparisons were made with restated prior-year figures.

PROSPECTS: The Company anticipates favorable earnings during the first part of fiscal 2000. DOV also expects earnings per share to increase by 20.0% compared with a year ago. The Company's earnings should continue to improve if the electronics industry remains strong throughout the year. Meanwhile, the 18 acquisitions completed during 1999 increased sales by $239.0 million and operating income by $44.0 million. The Company expects these numbers to double in 2000.

BUSINESS

DOVER CORPORATION groups its products and services into the following four segments: Dover Resources Inc. manufactures products for the automotive, fluid handling, petroleum and chemical industries. Dover Technologies builds automated assembly equipment for the electronics industry, industrial printers for coding and marking, and to a lesser degree, specialized electronic components. Dover Industries makes products used in waste handling, bulk transport, automotive service, commercial food service, commercial food service and machine tools industry. Dover Diversified, includes heat transfer equipment and specialized compressors, as well as products and control systems for use in defense, aerospace and commercial building industries. On 1/5/99, the Company sold Dover Elevator for $1.16 billion.

ANNUAL FINANCIAL DATA

	12/31/99	12/31/98	12/31/97	12/31/96	12/31/95	12/31/94	12/31/93
Earnings Per Share	③ 1.92	① 1.45	② 1.79	② 1.73	② 1.23	0.89	0.70
Cash Flow Per Share	2.79	2.20	2.54	2.27	1.70	1.30	1.03
Tang. Book Val. Per Share	1.07	2.11	2.66	2.29	1.79	1.86	1.42
Dividends Per Share	0.44	0.40	0.36	0.32	0.28	0.24	0.23
Dividend Payout %	22.9	27.6	20.1	18.5	22.9	27.7	32.4

INCOME STATEMENT (IN MILLIONS):

Total Revenues	4,446.4	3,977.7	4,547.7	4,076.3	3,745.9	3,085.3	2,483.9
Costs & Expenses	3,627.8	3,278.0	3,764.3	3,412.5	3,199.6	2,664.1	2,153.1
Depreciation & Amort.	183.2	167.7	170.7	125.1	107.8	95.8	77.0
Operating Income	635.4	532.0	② 612.7	② 538.7	② 438.4	325.4	253.9
Net Interest Inc./(Exp.)	d34.9	d46.4	d37.0	d23.5	d20.1	d17.8	d2.7
Income Before Income Taxes	615.0	488.6	616.8	588.7	417.1	306.9	245.5
Income Taxes	210.0	162.2	211.4	198.5	138.8	104.5	87.3
Net Income	③ 405.1	① 326.4	② 405.4	② 390.2	② 278.3	202.4	158.3
Cash Flow	588.3	494.1	576.1	515.3	386.1	298.2	235.2
Average Shs. Outstg. (000)	210,679	224,386	226,815	226,524	226,906	228,740	228,440

BALANCE SHEET (IN MILLIONS):

Cash & Cash Equivalents	138.0	96.8	146.7	217.8	148.8	144.9	96.3
Total Current Assets	1,611.6	1,304.5	1,591.3	1,489.8	1,384.4	1,133.1	903.6
Net Property	646.5	572.0	570.6	494.9	423.9	342.7	283.4
Total Assets	4,131.9	3,627.3	3,277.5	2,993.4	2,666.7	2,070.6	1,773.7
Total Current Liabilities	1,334.9	989.7	1,196.6	1,139.1	1,081.0	772.2	595.8
Long-Term Obligations	608.0	610.1	262.6	253.0	255.6	253.6	252.1
Net Stockholders' Equity	2,038.8	1,910.9	1,703.6	1,489.7	1,227.7	995.9	870.0
Net Working Capital	276.7	314.8	394.8	350.7	303.3	360.9	307.8
Year-end Shs. Outstg. (000)	204,629	220,407	234,507	225,060	227,340	226,920	228,652

STATISTICAL RECORD:

Operating Profit Margin %	14.3	13.4	13.5	13.2	11.7	10.5	10.2
Net Profit Margin %	9.1	8.2	8.9	9.6	7.4	6.6	6.4
Return on Equity %	19.9	17.1	23.8	26.2	22.7	20.3	18.2
Return on Assets %	9.8	9.0	12.4	13.0	10.4	9.8	8.9
Debt/Total Assets %	14.7	16.8	8.0	8.5	9.6	12.2	14.2
Price Range	47¹⁵/₁₆-29⁵/₁₆	39¹⁵/₁₆-25¹/₂	36¹¹/₁₆-24¹/₈	27⁹/₁₆-18⁵/₈	20⁵/₈-12¹⁵/₁₆	16³/₄-12⁷/₁₆	15¹/₂-11¹/₄
P/E Ratio	25.0-15.3	27.5-17.6	20.5-13.5	16.0-10.6	17.0-10.5	18.9-14.1	22.3-16.2
Average Yield %	1.1	1.2	1.2	1.4	1.7	1.7	1.7

Statistics are as originally reported. Adj. for stk. splits: 2-for-1, 12/97; 100%, 9/95. ① Bef. income from disc. ops. of $52.4 mill. ② Incls. pre-tax credit 12/31/97: $3.2 mill.; credit 12/31/96: $75.1 mill.; chrg. 12/31/95: $31.9 mill. ③ Bef. gain from disc. ops. of $523.9 mill. but incl. non-recurr. gain of $10.3 mill.

QUARTERLY DATA

(12/31/99)($000)	Rev	Inc
1st Quarter	969,755	69,220
2nd Quarter	1,077,850	93,310
3rd Quarter	1,150,531	121,535
4th Quarter	1,248,284	120,989

OFFICERS:
T. L. Reece, Chmn., Pres., C.E.O.
J. F. McNiff, V.P., Treas.
R. G. Kuhbach, V.P., Sec., Gen. Couns.

INVESTOR CONTACT: John F. McNiff, V.P., Fin., (212) 922-1640

PRINCIPAL OFFICE: 280 Park Avenue, New York, NY 10017-1292

TELEPHONE NUMBER: (212) 922-1640
FAX: (212) 922-1656
WEB: www.dovercorporation.com

NO. OF EMPLOYEES: 26,584 (approx.)

SHAREHOLDERS: 16,000 (approx.)

ANNUAL MEETING: In April

INCORPORATED: DE, 1947

INSTITUTIONAL HOLDINGS:
No. of Institutions: 378
Shares Held: 145,932,796
% Held: 71.7

INDUSTRY: Construction machinery (SIC: 3531)

TRANSFER AGENT(S): Harris Trust & Savings Bank, Chicago, Il

NYSE SYMBOL DQE
Rec. Pr. 42 1/4 (5/31/00)

DQE, INC.

YIELD 3.8%
P/E RATIO 16.2

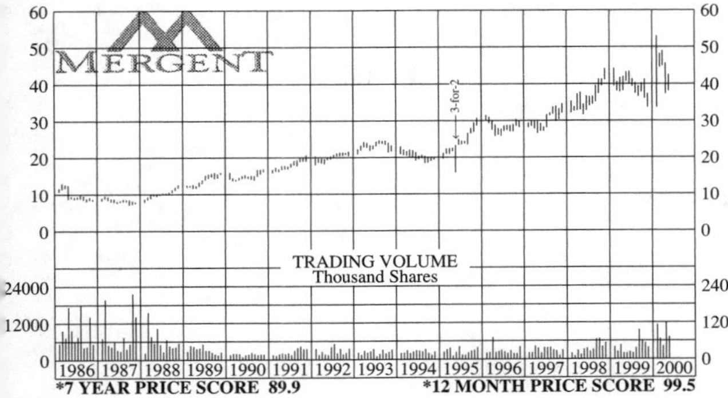

60
50
40
30
20
10
0
3-for-2
TRADING VOLUME
Thousand Shares
24000
12000
0
1986 1987 1988 1989 1990 1991 1992 1993 1994 1995 1996 1997 1998 1999 2000

***7 YEAR PRICE SCORE 89.9** ***12 MONTH PRICE SCORE 99.5**

*NYSE COMPOSITE INDEX=100

INTERIM EARNINGS (Per Share):

Qtr.	Mar.	June	Sept.	Dec.
1996	0.55	0.50	0.74	0.50
1997	0.58	0.61	0.75	0.55
1998	0.58	0.51	0.78	0.62
1999	0.61	0.53	0.63	0.84

INTERIM DIVIDENDS (Per Share):

Amt.	Decl.	Ex.	Rec.	Pay.
0.38Q	8/31/99	9/08/99	9/10/99	10/01/99
0.40Q	11/30/99	12/08/99	12/10/99	1/01/00
0.40Q	1/27/00	3/08/00	3/10/00	4/01/00
0.40Q	5/25/00	6/07/00	6/09/00	7/01/00

Indicated div.: $1.60 (Div. Reinv. Plan)

CAPITALIZATION (12/31/99):

	($000)	(%)
Long-Term Debt	1,633,077	38.0
Capital Lease Obligations	16,863	0.4
Deferred Income Tax	1,020,103	23.7
Preferred Stock	283,057	6.6
Common & Surplus	1,347,865	31.3
Total	4,300,965	100.0

DIVIDEND ACHIEVER STATUS:
Rank: 17 10-Year Growth Rate: 21.70%
Total Years of Dividend Growth: 10

RECENT DEVELOPMENTS: For the year ended 12/31/99, net income rose 2.4% to $201.4 million versus income of $196.7 million, before an extraordinary charge of $82.5 million, a year earlier. Total operating revenues climbed 6.8% to $1.34 billion from $1.25 billion in 1998. Electricity revenues decreased 3.0% to $1.09 billion from $1.13 billion in 1998. Meanwhile, water revenues more than tripled to $122.4 million from $96.8 million the year before.

PROSPECTS: Duquesne Enterprises, a subsidiary of DQE, will focus on utilizing technology to make electricity, gas, water, communications and information, more valuable for customers. Accordingly, DQE has outlined six E-commerce strategies designed to offer the maximum market potential and growth, as well as an opportunity to improve operating efficiencies. On 4/28/00, DQE's subsidiary sold its power generation facilities to Orion Power Holdings, Inc.

BUSINESS

DQE, INC. is a multi-utility delivery and services company. The Company's utility services operations include an electric utility engaged in the generation, transmission, distribution, and sale of electric energy and a water resource management company that acquires, develops and manages water and wastewater utilities. DQE's expanded business lines offer a range of energy-related technologies, industrial and commercial energy services, telecommunications and other complementary services. DQE's subsidiaries are Duquesne Light Company, AquaSource, Inc., DQE Capital Corp., DQE Energy Services, Inc., DQE Energy Partners, Inc, Duquesne Enterprises, Inc., and Montauk, Inc.

ANNUAL FINANCIAL DATA

	12/31/99	12/31/98	12/31/97	12/31/96	12/31/95	12/31/94	12/31/93
Earnings Per Share	**2.62**	**[1] 2.48**	**2.54**	**2.32**	**2.20**	**1.98**	**1.78**
Cash Flow Per Share	**5.10**	**5.32**	**5.70**	**5.20**	**4.80**	**4.08**	**3.57**
Tang. Book Val. Per Share	**18.78**	**19.18**	**19.30**	**18.01**	**17.13**	**16.27**	**15.48**
Dividends Per Share	**1.54**	**1.44**	**1.36**	**1.28**	**1.19**	**1.12**	**1.07**
Dividend Payout %	**58.0**	**58.1**	**53.5**	**55.2**	**53.9**	**56.6**	**59.9**
INCOME STATEMENT (IN MILLIONS):							
Total Revenues	1,341.2	1,269.6	1,230.2	1,225.2	1,220.2	1,223.9	1,195.6
Costs & Expenses	750.6	705.7	623.7	621.9	613.6	661.6	613.1
Depreciation & Amort.	196.3	217.2	242.8	222.9	202.6	165.9	142.7
Maintenance Exp.	75.4	74.9	82.9	78.4	81.5	79.5	80.3
Operating Income	318.8	271.9	280.7	302.0	322.5	316.9	253.2
Net Interest Inc./(Exp.)	d158.7	d110.2	d115.6	d110.3	d107.6	d110.0	d111.3
Income Taxes	110.7	101.0	95.8	87.4	96.7	93.0	87.3
Net Income	201.4	[1] 196.7	199.1	179.1	170.6	156.8	141.4
Cash Flow	396.2	413.0	441.9	402.1	373.1	322.7	284.1
Average Shs. Outstg. (000)	77,676	77,683	77,492	77,349	77,674	79,046	79,469
BALANCE SHEET (IN MILLIONS):							
Gross Property	4,369.3	4,884.1	4,625.1	4,787.5	4,746.1	4,709.5	4,554.5
Accumulated Depreciation	2,541.2	3,167.3	1,962.8	1,969.9	1,685.9	1,570.0	1,435.7
Net Property	1,828.1	1,716.8	2,662.3	2,817.5	3,060.2	3,139.5	3,118.8
Total Assets	5,609.0	5,247.6	4,694.4	4,639.0	4,458.8	4,427.0	4,574.0
Long-Term Obligations	1,649.9	1,401.5	1,413.7	1,468.2	1,435.5	1,418.7	1,472.7
Net Stockholders' Equity	1,630.9	1,761.8	1,743.6	1,634.5	1,422.0	1,396.9	1,352.5
Year-end Shs. Outstg. (000)	71,766	77,373	77,680	77,273	77,556	78,459	79,518
STATISTICAL RECORD:							
Operating Profit Margin %	23.8	21.4	22.8	24.6	26.4	25.9	21.2
Net Profit Margin %	15.0	15.5	16.2	14.6	14.0	12.8	11.8
Net Inc./Net Property %	11.0	11.5	7.5	6.4	5.6	5.0	4.5
Net Inc./Tot. Capital %	4.7	5.0	5.2	4.6	4.7	4.1	3.5
Return on Equity %	12.3	11.2	11.4	11.0	12.0	11.2	10.5
Accum. Depr./Gross Prop. %	58.2	64.8	42.4	41.1	35.5	33.3	31.5
Price Range	44 1/4-33 5/8	44 1/8-31 9/16	34 5/8-26 1/2	31 1/2-25 3/4	30 3/4-15 13/16	23-18 7/16	24 11/16-20 15/16
P/E Ratio	16.9-12.8	17.8-12.7	13.6-10.4	13.6-11.1	14.0-7.2	11.6-9.3	13.9-11.7
Average Yield %	3.9	3.8	4.4	4.5	5.1	5.4	4.7

Statistics are as originally reported. Adj. for stk. splits: 3-for-2, 5/95 [1] Bef. extraordinary item of $82.5 mill.

OFFICERS:
D. D. Marshall, Chmn., Pres., C.E.O.
G. L. Schwass, Exec. V.P., C.F.O.
V. A. Roque, Exec. V.P., Gen. Couns.

INVESTOR CONTACT: Shareholder Services, (412) 393-6167

PRINCIPAL OFFICE: Cherrington Corporate Center, 400 Fairway Drive, Suite 300, Moon Township, PA 15108-3184

TELEPHONE NUMBER: (412) 262-4700
FAX: (412) 393-6087
WEB: www.dqe.com

NO. OF EMPLOYEES: 3,578

SHAREHOLDERS: 61,000 (approx.)

ANNUAL MEETING: In May

INCORPORATED: PA, 1989

INSTITUTIONAL HOLDINGS:
No. of Institutions: 164
Shares Held: 29,905,326
% Held: 39.7

INDUSTRY: Electric services (SIC: 4911)

TRANSFER AGENT(S): BankBoston, N.A., c/o Boston EquiServe, Boston, MA

E.I. DU PONT DE NEMOURS AND COMPANY

YIELD 2.9%
P/E RATIO 612.5

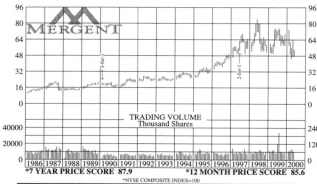

*7 YEAR PRICE SCORE 87.9   *12 MONTH PRICE SCORE 85.6

*NYSE COMPOSITE INDEX=100

INTERIM EARNINGS (Per Share):

Qtr.	Mar.	June	Sept.	Dec.
1996	0.79	0.89	0.80	0.76
1997	0.90	1.01	d0.02	0.23
1998	0.79	0.83	d0.50	0.68
1999	0.55	0.74	0.17	d1.38

INTERIM DIVIDENDS (Per Share):

Amt.	Decl.	Ex.	Rec.	Pay.
0.35Q	7/28/99	8/11/99	8/13/99	9/11/99
0.35Q	10/27/99	11/10/99	11/15/99	12/14/99
0.35Q	1/26/00	2/11/00	2/15/00	3/14/00
0.35Q	4/26/00	5/11/00	5/15/00	6/12/00

Indicated div.: $1.40 (Div. Reinv. Plan)

CAPITALIZATION (12/31/99):

	($000)	(%)
Long-Term Debt	6,625,000	30.6
Def. Inc. Tax & Minor. Int...	2,177,000	10.1
Preferred Stock	237,000	1.1
Common & Surplus	12,638,000	58.3
Total	21,677,000	100.0

DIVIDEND ACHIEVER STATUS:

Rank: 226   10-Year Growth Rate: 6.80%
Total Years of Dividend Growth: 17

RECENT DEVELOPMENTS: For the year ended 12/31/99, income from continuing operations was $219.0 million versus $1.65 billion in 1998. Results in 1999 included a $2.25 billion R&D charge and a $524.0 million employee separation charge, and excluded a $7.47 billion gain from discontinued operations. Results in 1998 included charges totaling $2.08 billion and excluded gains of $3.03 billion from discontinued operations and an extraordinary charge of $201.0 million. Total revenues rose 8.3% to $27.89 billion.

PROSPECTS: DD expects to report double-digit earnings growth in 2000. In order to achieve this goal, DD plans to improve prices, strengthen business conditions and develop its e-commerce business. Separately, DD sold its Fortress® soil insecticide business to AMVAC Chemical Corporation, a manufacturer of crop protection and specialty products. DD also formed a joint venture, CapScan, with Internet Capital Group to increase e-commerce development in key market places.

BUSINESS

E.I. DU PONT DE NEMOURS AND COMPANY is the largest chemical company in the U.S. and a leading chemical producer worldwide. Major products include: specialty chemicals, white pigment and mineral products, fluorochemicals, nylon intermediates, textiles, flooring systems, nonwovens, industrial nylon, automotive finishes, elastomers, fluoropolymers, packaging, industrial, engineering polymers, agricultural products, electronic material, medical and printing products and films. Revenues in 1999 were derived: agricultural & nutrition, 8.7%; nylon enterprises, 15.1%; performance coatings & polymers, 20.5%; pharmaceuticals, 5.5%; pigments & chemicals, 12.3%; pioneer, 1.4%; polyester enterprises, 9.0%; specialty fibers, 11.6%; specialty polymers, 14.3%; and other, 1.6%.

ANNUAL FINANCIAL DATA

	12/31/99	12/31/98	12/31/97	12/31/96	12/31/95	12/31/94	12/31/93
Earnings Per Share	④ 0.19	①② 1.43	① 2.08	3.24	① 2.81	① 2.00	①③ 0.42
Cash Flow Per Share	1.74	2.71	4.76	6.17	5.61	4.46	2.51
Tang. Book Val. Per Share	12.09	12.18	9.76	12.12	9.46	9.07	8.11
Dividends Per Share	1.40	1.37	1.23	1.11	1.01	0.91	0.88
Dividend Payout %	736.8	97.9	25.8	18.0	18.0	20.4	212.0

INCOME STATEMENT (IN MILLIONS):

Total Revenues	27,892.0	25,748.0	45,971.0	44,481.0	42,717.0	39,898.0	37,841.0
Costs & Expenses	23,977.0	21,163.0	38,946.0	35,835.0	34,392.0	32,342.0	33,456.0
Depreciation & Amort.	1,690.0	1,452.0	2,385.0	2,621.0	2,722.0	2,976.0	2,833.0
Operating Income	2,225.0	3,133.0	5,322.0	6,694.0	6,148.0	4,941.0	1,552.0
Net Interest Inc./(Exp.)	d535.0	d520.0	d642.0	d713.0	d758.0	d559.0	d594.0
Income Before Income Taxes	1,690.0	2,613.0	4,680.0	5,981.0	5,390.0	4,382.0	958.0
Income Taxes	1,410.0	941.0	2,275.0	2,345.0	2,097.0	1,655.0	392.0
Equity Earnings/Minority Int.	d61.0	d24.0	682.0	669.0	545.0	361.0	...
Net Income	④ 219.0	①② 1,648.0	① 3,087.0	4,305.0	① 3,293.0	① 3,088.0	①③ 566.0
Cash Flow	1,909.0	3,090.0	5,462.0	6,916.0	6,550.0	6,054.0	3,389.0
Average Shs. Outstg. (000)	1,097,970	1,145,000	1,150,000	1,122,000	1,170,000	1,360,000	1,354,000

BALANCE SHEET (IN MILLIONS):

Cash & Cash Equivalents	1,582.0	1,069.0	1,146.0	1,319.0	1,455.0	1,109.0	1,194.0
Total Current Assets	12,653.0	9,236.0	11,874.0	11,103.0	10,955.0	11,108.0	10,899.0
Net Property	14,871.0	14,131.0	23,583.0	21,213.0	21,341.0	21,120.0	21,423.0
Total Assets	40,777.0	38,536.0	42,942.0	37,987.0	37,312.0	36,892.0	37,053.0
Total Current Liabilities	11,228.0	11,610.0	14,070.0	10,987.0	12,731.0	7,565.0	9,439.0
Long-Term Obligations	6,625.0	4,495.0	5,929.0	5,087.0	5,678.0	6,376.0	6,531.0
Net Stockholders' Equity	12,875.0	13,954.0	11,270.0	10,709.0	8,436.0	12,822.0	11,230.0
Net Working Capital	1,425.0	d2,374.0	d2,196.0	116.0	d1,776.0	3,543.0	1,460.0
Year-end Shs. Outstg. (000)	1,045,130	1,126,000	1,130,000	846,000	846,000	1,362,000	1,356,000

STATISTICAL RECORD:

Operating Profit Margin %	8.0	12.2	11.4	14.8	14.2	12.3	4.1
Net Profit Margin %	0.8	6.4	6.6	9.5	8.9	7.7	1.5
Return on Equity %	1.7	11.8	27.4	40.2	45.5	24.1	5.0
Return on Assets %	0.5	4.3	7.2	11.3	10.3	8.4	1.5
Debt/Total Assets %	16.2	11.7	13.8	13.4	15.2	17.3	17.6
Price Range	75³/₁₆-50¹/₁₆	84⁷/₁₆-51¹¹/₁₆	69³/₄-46³/₈	49¹¹/₁₆-34¹³/₁₆	36¹/₂-26⁵/₁₆	31³/₁₆-24¹/₈	26¹⁵/₁₆-22¹/₄
P/E Ratio	395.5-263.4	59.0-36.1	33.5-22.3	15.4-10.8	13.0-9.4	15.6-12.1	64.9-53.6
Average Yield %	2.2	2.1	2.1	2.6	3.2	3.3	3.6

Statistics are as originally reported. Adj. for 2-for-1 split, 6/97. ① Incl. non-recur. chgs. $2.07 bill., 1998; $1.99 bill., 1997; $96.0 mill., 1995; cr$142.0 mill., 1994; $1.62 bill., 1993. ② Bef. disc. ops. inc. $3.03 bill. & extraord. chg. $201.0 mill. ③ Bef. extraord. chg. $11.00 mill. ④ Incl. $2.25 bill. R&D chg., $524.0 mill. sep. costs & excl. $7.47 bill. gain fr. disc. ops.

OFFICERS:
C. O. Holliday Jr., Chmn., C.E.O.
G. M. Pfeiffer, Sr. V.P., C.F.O.

INVESTOR CONTACT: Investor Relations, (302) 774-0195

PRINCIPAL OFFICE: 1007 Market St., Wilmington, DE 19898

TELEPHONE NUMBER: (302) 774-1000
FAX: (302) 774-0748
WEB: www.dupont.com

NO. OF EMPLOYEES: 94,000 (avg.)

SHAREHOLDERS: 139,835

ANNUAL MEETING: In Apr.

INCORPORATED: DE, Sep., 1915

EATON VANCE CORPORATION

YIELD 0.9%
P/E RATIO 17.8

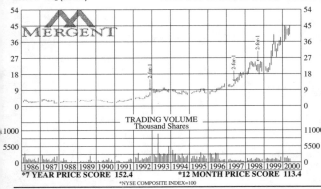

TRADING VOLUME Thousand Shares		

*7 YEAR PRICE SCORE 152.4   ***12 MONTH PRICE SCORE 113.4**
*NYSE COMPOSITE INDEX=100

INTERIM EARNINGS (Per Share):

Qtr.	Jan.	Apr.	July	Oct.
1996-97	0.25	0.24	0.27	0.26
1997-98	0.28	0.30	0.36	d0.15
1998-99	d0.27	0.27	0.70	0.70
1999-00	0.77	...	...	...

INTERIM DIVIDENDS (Per Share):

Amt.	Decl.	Ex.	Rec.	Pay.
0.075Q	4/21/99	4/29/99	5/03/99	5/10/99
0.075Q	7/14/99	7/28/99	7/30/99	8/09/99
0.095Q	10/13/99	10/27/99	10/29/99	11/08/99
0.095Q	1/12/00	1/27/00	1/31/00	2/14/00
0.095Q	4/12/00	4/26/00	4/28/00	5/08/00

Indicated div.: $0.38

CAPITALIZATION (10/31/99):

	($000)	(%)
Long-Term Debt	28,571	9.2
Deferred Income Tax	86,500	28.0
Common & Surplus	194,268	62.8
Total	309,339	100.0

DIVIDEND ACHIEVER STATUS:
Rank: 24   10-Year Growth Rate: 20.40%
Total Years of Dividend Growth: 18

RECENT DEVELOPMENTS: For the quarter ended 1/31/00, EV reported net income of $28.3 million compared with a loss of $9.8 million, before an accounting charge of $36.6 million, in the corresponding period of the previous year. Earnings for the 1998 quarter included a sales commission expense of $47.5 million. Total revenues advanced 35.5% to $102.2 million from $75.5 million in the prior year.

PROSPECTS: Going forward, the Company expects to continue to produce strong revenues as a result of further growth in average assets under management. Operating expenses should continue to decrease since the Company is no longer expensing sales commissions for its bank loan interval funds. In addition, lower sales and marketing costs are associated with the lower fund sales volume.

BUSINESS

EATON VANCE CORPORATION creates, markets and manages mutual funds and provides management and counseling services to institutions and individuals. The Company conducts its investment management and counseling business through two wholly-owned subsidiaries, Eaton Vance Management and Boston Management and Research. The Company provides investment advice and administration services to over 70 funds and to over 800 separately managed individual and institutional accounts. EV's funds consist of money markets, equities, bank loans, and taxable and non-taxable fixed income. As of 1/31/00, assets under management totaled $41.80 billion.

ANNUAL FINANCIAL DATA

	10/31/99	10/31/98	10/31/97	10/31/96	10/31/95	10/31/94	10/31/93
Earnings Per Share	③⑤ 1.41	④ 0.81	1.04	① 0.94	② 0.73	②③ 0.68	② 0.72
Cash Flow Per Share	3.17	2.58	2.51	2.37	2.14	2.14	1.94
Tang. Book Val. Per Share	5.46	5.89	6.06	5.54	5.18	4.50	3.92
Dividends Per Share	0.32	0.26	0.21	0.18	0.16	0.15	0.12
Dividend Payout %	22.7	31.5	20.2	19.0	22.4	22.1	17.0
INCOME STATEMENT (IN THOUSANDS):							
Total Revenues	348,950	249,987	200,910	181,361	167,922	171,216	152,276
Costs & Expenses	205,380	134,591	79,941	67,335	68,175	68,220	64,910
Depreciation & Amort.	65,666	66,744	57,064	55,005	52,563	55,130	43,226
Operating Income	77,904	48,652	63,905	59,021	47,184	47,866	44,140
Net Interest Inc./(Exp.)	671	1,791	d380	d7	d2,061	d4,374	d4,058
Income Before Income Taxes	85,910	50,038	67,470	59,922	43,741	43,203	43,976
Income Taxes	33,505	19,515	27,236	24,088	16,773	17,393	18,459
Equity Earnings/Minority Int.	10	105	384	1,639	...	...	...
Net Income	③⑤ 52,405	④ 30,523	40,234	① 35,834	② 26,968	②③ 25,810	② 25,517
Cash Flow	118,071	97,267	97,298	90,839	79,531	80,940	68,743
Average Shs. Outstg.	37,247	37,757	38,698	38,308	37,116	37,892	35,392
BALANCE SHEET (IN THOUSANDS):							
Cash & Cash Equivalents	77,395	96,435	140,520	116,375	79,121	34,025	28,655
Total Current Assets	90,488	130,433	164,168	130,072	98,602	38,963	35,975
Net Property	12,459	2,696	2,537	2,828	2,855	6,728	6,339
Total Assets	358,229	380,260	387,375	360,262	357,586	455,506	425,547
Total Current Liabilities	48,890	48,957	39,968	24,081	24,727	131,720	123,927
Long-Term Obligations	28,571	35,714	50,964	54,549	56,102	60,311	73,228
Net Stockholders' Equity	194,268	211,809	226,280	210,780	194,520	165,608	145,300
Net Working Capital	41,598	81,476	124,200	105,991	73,875	d92,757	d87,952
Year-end Shs. Outstg.	35,260	35,666	36,938	37,536	37,264	36,360	36,536
STATISTICAL RECORD:							
Operating Profit Margin %	22.3	19.5	31.8	32.5	28.1	28.0	29.0
Net Profit Margin %	15.0	12.2	20.0	19.8	16.1	15.1	16.8
Return on Equity %	27.0	14.4	17.8	17.0	13.9	15.6	17.6
Return on Assets %	14.6	8.0	10.4	9.9	7.5	5.7	6.0
Debt/Total Assets %	8.0	9.4	13.2	15.1	15.7	13.2	17.2
Price Range	40-18¹¹⁄₁₆	25⅛-17⁷⁄₁₆	19-10⁷⁄₁₆	12⁷⁄₁₆-6½	9¹³⁄₁₆-6¹³⁄₁₆	9³⁄₈-6¹⁄₈	10⁵⁄₁₆-7¼
P/E Ratio	28.4-13.3	31.0-21.5	18.3-10.0	13.3-7.0	13.5-9.4	13.8-9.0	14.3-10.1
Average Yield %	1.1	1.2	1.4	1.9	2.0	1.9	1.4

Statistics are as originally reported. Adj. for 2-for-1 stk. split, 8/98 & 5/97. ① Bef. extraord. credit $1.6 mill. ② Bef. disc. oper. gain 10/31/95: $3.4 mill.; 10/31/94: $2.7 mill.; 10/31/93: $1.8 mill. ③ Bef. acct. chrg. of $36.6 mill., 10/31/99; $1.3 mill., 10/31/94. ④ Incl. an impairment loss on real estate of $2.6 mill. & a gain of $2.1 mill. from the sale of an investment. ⑤ Incl. a gain on the sale of investments of $7.3 mill.

OFFICERS:
J. B. Hawkes, Chmn., Pres., C.E.O.
W. M. Steul, V.P., C.F.O., Treas.
T. Otis, V.P., Sec.

INVESTOR CONTACT: William M. Steul, VP & C.F.O., (617) 482-8260

PRINCIPAL OFFICE: 255 State Street, Boston, MA 02109

TELEPHONE NUMBER: (617) 482-8260
FAX: (617) 695-0907
WEB: www.eatonvance.com
NO. OF EMPLOYEES: 395
SHAREHOLDERS: 950 (approx. non-voting); 11 (voting)
ANNUAL MEETING: In January
INCORPORATED: MD, May, 1959; reincorp., MD, Feb., 1981

INSTITUTIONAL HOLDINGS:
No. of Institutions: 103
Shares Held: 10,972,728
% Held: 30.7

INDUSTRY: Investment advice (SIC: 6282)

TRANSFER AGENT(S): EquiServe, L.P., Boston, MA

NYSE SYMBOL EMR
Rec. Pr. 59 (5/31/00)

EMERSON ELECTRIC COMPANY

YIELD 2.4%
P/E RATIO 19.3

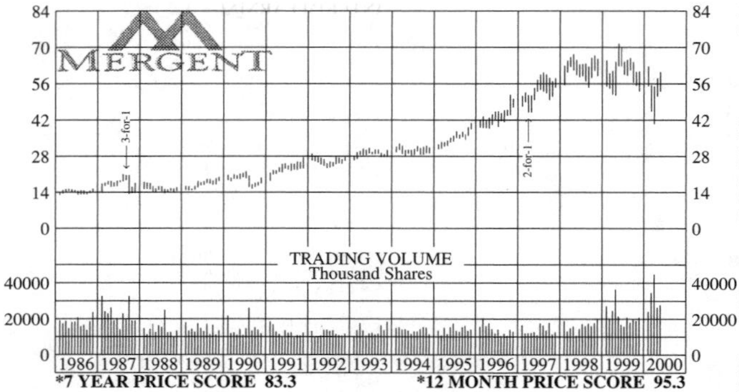

***7 YEAR PRICE SCORE 83.3** ***12 MONTH PRICE SCORE 95.3**

*NYSE COMPOSITE INDEX=100

INTERIM EARNINGS (Per Share):

Qtr.	Dec.	Mar.	June	Sept
1996-97	0.57	0.63	0.67	0.65
1997-98	0.64	0.69	0.73	0.71
1998-99	0.69	0.74	0.79	0.78
1999-00	0.75	...	...	...

INTERIM DIVIDENDS (Per Share):

Amt.	Decl.	Ex.	Rec.	Pay.
0.325Q	8/03/99	8/11/99	8/13/99	9/10/99
0.357Q	11/02/99	11/17/99	11/19/99	12/10/99
0.357Q	2/01/00	2/16/00	2/18/00	3/10/00
0.357Q	5/02/00	5/10/00	5/12/00	6/09/00

Indicated div.: $1.43 (Div. Reinv. Plan)

CAPITALIZATION (9/30/99):

	($000)	(%)
Long-Term Debt	1,317,100	17.6
Common & Surplus	6,180,500	82.4
Total	7,497,600	100.0

DIVIDEND ACHIEVER STATUS:
Rank: 187 10-Year Growth Rate: 8.72%
Total Years of Dividend Growth: 43

RECENT DEVELOPMENTS: For the quarter ended 12/31/99, net income improved 7.4% to $324.9 million from $302.4 million 1998. Net sales rose 3.4% to $3.54 billion versus $3.43 billion in the prior-year quarter. The top line included sales of $24.5 million in 1999 and $151.3 million in 1998 from businesses that have since been divested. Sales in the appliance and tools segment climbed 4.1% to $910.5 million, while sales in the industrial automation segment increased 1.3% to $858.9 million.

PROSPECTS: On 4/3/00, the Company completed its aquisition of Ericsson Energy Systems. The transaction should increase EMR's presence in the Internet and telecommunications equipment industries. In addition, the Company recently completed the acquisition of the telecommunications products business of Jordon Industries Inc., which was renamed Emerson Telecommunication Products. These transactions are part of EMR's strategy to reposition itself toward high-growth markets.

BUSINESS

EMERSON ELECTRIC COMPANY is a global manufacturer of a range of electrical-electronic products and systems sold through independent distributors and to OEMs. EMR produces instruments related to control systems and processing measurements. Commercial and industrial components and systems products include various motor-driven systems such as solid-, air- and gas-control devices. Consumer products offer a variety of tools and accessories primarily for the residential markets, including console humidifiers, electric waste disposers, hot water dispensers, automatic dishwashers and ventilating equipment.

ANNUAL FINANCIAL DATA

	9/30/99	9/30/98	9/30/97	9/30/96	9/30/95	9/30/94	9/30/93
Earnings Per Share	**3.00**	**2.77**	**2.52**	**2.27**	**2.03**	[1] **1.76**	**1.58**
Cash Flow Per Share	**4.45**	**4.03**	**3.67**	**3.31**	**2.99**	**2.83**	**2.33**
Tang. Book Val. Per Share	**4.43**	**4.79**	**5.23**	**5.75**	**5.55**	**5.54**	**4.63**
Dividends Per Share	**1.33**	**1.21**	**1.10**	**1.00**	**0.92**	**0.80**	**0.73**
Dividend Payout %	**44.4**	**43.7**	**43.8**	**44.3**	**45.3**	**45.5**	**46.7**
INCOME STATEMENT (IN MILLIONS):							
Total Revenues	14,269.5	13,447.2	12,298.6	11,149.9	10,012.9	8,607.2	8,173.8
Costs & Expenses	11,326.5	10,709.8	9,804.9	8,892.4	8,004.7	6,868.1	6,555.7
Depreciation & Amort.	637.5	562.5	511.6	464.6	408.9	364.5	340.7
Operating Income	2,305.5	2,174.9	1,982.1	1,792.9	1,599.3	1,374.6	1,277.4
Net Interest Inc./(Exp.)	d189.7	d151.7	d120.9	d126.9	d110.6	d88.5	d119.2
Income Before Income Taxes	2,020.9	1,923.5	1,783.6	1,609.0	1,459.9	1,427.8	1,112.0
Income Taxes	707.3	694.9	661.7	590.5	530.9	523.4	403.9
Net Income	1,313.6	1,228.6	1,121.9	1,018.5	929.0	[1] 904.4	708.1
Cash Flow	1,951.1	1,791.1	1,633.5	1,483.1	1,337.9	1,268.9	1,048.8
Average Shs. Outstg. (000)	438,400	444,100	445,000	448,096	447,506	448,464	450,166
BALANCE SHEET (IN MILLIONS):							
Cash & Cash Equivalents	266.1	209.7	221.1	149.0	117.3	113.3	101.9
Total Current Assets	5,124.4	5,001.3	4,716.8	4,187.2	3,784.1	3,338.2	3,074.3
Net Property	3,154.4	3,011.6	2,735.4	2,450.8	2,134.9	1,947.3	1,880.1
Total Assets	13,623.5	12,659.8	11,463.3	10,481.0	9,399.0	8,215.0	7,814.5
Total Current Liabilities	4,590.4	4,021.7	3,842.4	3,021.1	3,280.7	2,617.3	2,692.6
Long-Term Obligations	1,317.1	1,056.6	570.7	772.6	208.6	279.9	438.0
Net Stockholders' Equity	6,180.5	5,803.3	5,420.7	5,353.4	4,870.8	4,341.8	3,915.1
Net Working Capital	534.0	979.6	874.4	1,166.1	503.4	720.9	381.7
Year-end Shs. Outstg. (000)	433,044	438,224	440,804	447,440	447,898	447,172	449,526
STATISTICAL RECORD:							
Operating Profit Margin %	16.2	16.2	16.1	16.1	16.0	16.0	15.6
Net Profit Margin %	9.2	9.1	9.1	9.1	9.3	10.5	8.7
Return on Equity %	21.3	21.2	20.7	19.0	19.1	20.8	18.1
Return on Assets %	9.6	9.7	9.8	9.7	9.9	11.0	9.1
Debt/Total Assets %	9.7	8.3	5.0	7.4	2.2	3.4	5.6
Price Range	71 7/16-51 7/16	67 7/16-54 1/2	60 3/8-45	51 3/4-38 3/4	40 7/8-30 3/4	32 15/16-28 1/16	31 3/16-26 3/8
P/E Ratio	23.8-17.1	24.3-19.7	24.0-17.9	22.8-17.1	20.1-15.1	18.7-15.9	19.8-16.7
Average Yield %	2.2	2.0	2.1	2.2	2.6	2.6	2.6

Statistics are as originally reported. Adjusted for 2-for-1 stock split 11/96. [1] Bef. charge for cum. eff. of change in acctg. principle of $115.9 mill.

OFFICERS:
C. F. Knight, Chmn., C.E.O.
G. W. Tamke, Vice-Chmn., Co-C.E.O.
J. G. Berges, Pres.
W. J. Galvin, Sr. V.P., Fin., C.F.O.

INVESTOR CONTACT: Nancy Wulf, Dir. Inv. Rel., Asst. Treas. (314) 553-2197

PRINCIPAL OFFICE: 8000 W. Florissant Ave., P.O. Box 4100, St. Louis, MO 63136

TELEPHONE NUMBER: (314) 553-2000
FAX: (314) 553-3527
WEB: www.emersonelectric.com

NO. OF EMPLOYEES: 116,900 (avg.)

SHAREHOLDERS: 36,300 (approx.)

ANNUAL MEETING: In Feb.

INCORPORATED: MO, Sep., 1890

INSTITUTIONAL HOLDINGS:
No. of Institutions: 727
Shares Held: 312,226,102
% Held: 72.2

INDUSTRY: Process control instruments (SIC: 3823)

TRANSFER AGENT(S): ChaseMellon Shareholder Services, South Hackensack, NJ

NYSE SYMBOL EGN
Rec. Pr. 22⅛ (5/31/00)

ENERGEN CORPORATION

YIELD 3.0%
P/E RATIO 14.2

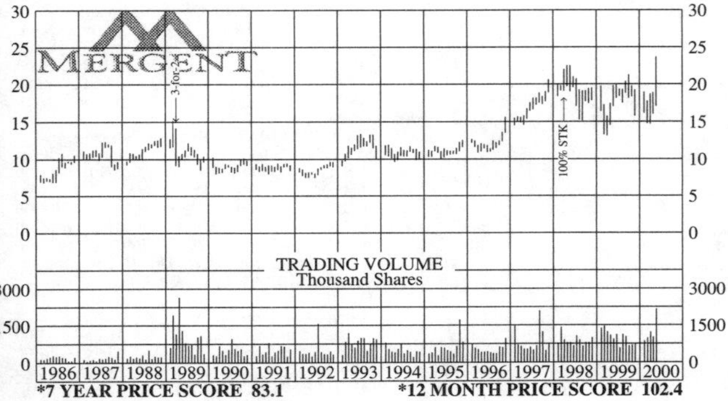
MERGENT
3-for-2
100% STK
TRADING VOLUME
Thousand Shares
30
25
20
15
10
5
0
3000
1500
0
1986 1987 1988 1989 1990 1991 1992 1993 1994 1995 1996 1997 1998 1999 2000

***7 YEAR PRICE SCORE 83.1** ***12 MONTH PRICE SCORE 102.4**

*NYSE COMPOSITE INDEX=100

INTERIM EARNINGS (Per Share):

Qtr.	Dec.	Mar.	June	Sept.
1994-95	0.13	1.00	0.05	d0.29
1995-96	0.11	1.07	0.05	d0.24
1996-97	0.14	1.21	0.12	d0.29
1997-98	0.21	1.37	Nil	d0.34
1998-99	0.13	1.42	0.12	d0.28
1999-00	0.30	. . .	. . .	. . .

INTERIM DIVIDENDS (Per Share):

Amt.	Decl.	Ex.	Rec.	Pay.
0.16Q	4/28/99	5/12/99	5/14/99	6/01/99
0.165Q	7/28/99	8/11/99	8/13/99	9/01/99
0.165Q	10/27/99	11/10/99	11/15/99	12/01/99
0.165Q	1/26/00	2/11/00	2/15/00	3/01/00
0.165Q	4/26/00	5/11/00	5/15/00	6/01/00

Indicated div.: $0.66 (Div. Reinv. Plan)

CAPITALIZATION (9/30/99):

	($000)	(%)
Long-Term Debt	371,824	50.7
Common & Surplus	361,504	49.3
Total	733,328	100.0

DIVIDEND ACHIEVER STATUS:
Rank: 276 10-Year Growth Rate: 4.26%
Total Years of Dividend Growth: 17

RECENT DEVELOPMENTS: For the quarter ended 12/31/99, net income rocketed 137.8% to $9.1 million from $3.8 million in 1998. Total operating revenues grew 13.2% to $129.0 million from $114.0 million in the prior year. Natural gas distribution operating revenues improved 19.4% to $85.4 million, while oil and gas operating revenues rose 2.8% to $43.6 million. Earnings for Energen Resources surged to $4.6 million from $1.0 million in 1998. Earnings in Alagasco advanced 58.6% to $4.6 million.

PROSPECTS: Going forward, the Company will focus on growing its oil and gas business through the acquisition and exploitation of producing oil and gas properties, while strengthening its utility foundation. Separately, EGN previously announced that the fiscal year 2000 capital investment target at Energen Resources will be approximately $100.0 million in property acquisitions and $50.0 million for exploitation and development. Meanwhile, diluted earnings per share in fiscal 2000 is estimated to be $1.47.

BUSINESS

ENERGEN CORPORATION is a diversified energy holding company engaged in the business of natural gas distribution and oil and gas exploration and production. EGN provides natural gas to residential, commercial and industrial customers located in Alabama. Alagasco, EGN's principal subsidiary, is the largest natural gas distribution utility in the State of Alabama. EGN's utility operations are subject to regulation by the Alabama Public Service Commission. The oil and gas exploration and production arm of Energen is Energen Resources, which conducts its activities in the Gulf of Mexico. In 1999, revenues were derived: 65.4% natural gas distribution and 34.6% oil and gas production activities.

BUSINESS LINE ANALYSIS

(9/30/1999)	REV(%)	INC(%)
Natural Gas		
Distribution...........	65.4	60.0
Oil & Gas Operations	34.6	40.0
Total	100.0	100.0

ANNUAL FINANCIAL DATA

	9/30/99	9/30/98	9/30/97	9/30/96	9/30/95	9/30/94	9/30/93
Earnings Per Share	**① 1.38**	**1.23**	**1.16**	**0.98**	**0.89**	**1.10**	**0.89**
Cash Flow Per Share	**4.35**	**3.98**	**3.53**	**2.84**	**2.24**	**2.39**	**2.12**
Tang. Book Val. Per Share	**12.09**	**11.23**	**13.49**	**8.44**	**7.96**	**7.65**	**6.80**
Dividends Per Share	**0.65**	**0.63**	**0.61**	**0.59**	**0.57**	**0.55**	**0.53**
Dividend Payout %	**47.1**	**51.2**	**52.8**	**60.5**	**64.4**	**50.2**	**59.9**
INCOME STATEMENT (IN THOUSANDS):							
Total Revenues	497,517	502,627	448,230	399,442	321,204	377,073	357,116
Costs & Expenses	331,519	360,143	325,444	308,449	249,369	303,696	292,325
Depreciation & Amort.	88,615	80,999	59,688	41,118	29,577	28,000	25,289
Maintenance Exp.	. . .	. . .	11,112	11,078	9,849	9,469	9,235
Operating Income	77,383	61,485	51,986	38,797	32,409	35,908	30,267
Net Interest Inc./(Exp.)	d37,173	d30,001	d22,906	d13,920	d11,818	d11,345	d10,605
Income Taxes	135	cr2,221	3,097	5,048	3,681	6,611	3,408
Net Income	① 41,410	36,249	28,997	21,541	19,308	23,751	18,081
Cash Flow	130,025	117,248	88,685	62,659	48,885	51,751	43,370
Average Shs. Outstg.	29,921	29,438	25,126	22,046	21,812	21,668	20,474
BALANCE SHEET (IN THOUSANDS):							
Gross Property	1,315,581	1,148,205	1,037,840	769,112	621,710	556,948	515,192
Accumulated Depreciation	458,614	395,794	375,303	328,262	299,096	274,379	251,042
Net Property	861,107	756,344	667,003	444,916	327,264	287,182	273,097
Total Assets	1,184,895	993,455	919,797	570,971	459,084	411,314	370,685
Long-Term Obligations	371,824	372,782	279,602	195,545	131,600	118,302	85,852
Net Stockholders' Equity	361,504	329,249	301,143	188,405	173,924	167,026	140,313
Year-end Shs. Outstg.	29,904	29,327	22,326	22,326	21,844	21,836	20,640
STATISTICAL RECORD:							
Operating Profit Margin %	15.6	12.2	11.6	9.7	10.1	9.5	8.5
Net Profit Margin %	8.3	7.2	6.5	5.4	6.0	6.3	5.1
Net Inc./Net Property %	4.8	4.8	4.3	4.8	5.9	8.3	6.6
Net Inc./Tot. Capital %	5.6	5.2	5.0	5.6	6.3	8.3	8.0
Return on Equity %	11.5	11.0	9.6	11.4	11.1	14.2	12.9
Accum. Depr./Gross Prop. %	34.9	34.5	36.2	42.7	48.1	49.3	48.7
Price Range	21¼-13⅛	22½-15⅛	20⅝-14½	15⅝-10⅞	12⁹⁄₁₆-10¹⁄₁₆	11¹⁵⁄₁₆-9⅝	13⅜-9¹⁄₁₆
P/E Ratio	15.4-9.5	18.3-12.3	17.9-12.6	16.0-11.2	14.2-11.4	10.9-8.8	15.1-10.2
Average Yield %	3.8	3.3	3.5	4.5	5.0	5.1	4.7

Statistics are as originally reported. Adjusted for 2-for-1 stock split, 3/98. ① Incl. an after-tax gain of $1.9 mill. on the sale of offshore properties.

OFFICERS:
W. M. Warren Jr., Chmn., Pres., C.E.O.
G. C. Ketcham, Exec. V.P., C.F.O., Treas.
D. C. Reynolds, Gen. Couns., Sec.

INVESTOR CONTACT: Julie S. Ryland, Asst. V.P. Inv. Rel., (800) 654-3206

PRINCIPAL OFFICE: 605 21st St. North, Birmingham, AL 35203-2707

TELEPHONE NUMBER: (205) 326-2704
FAX: (205) 326-2704
WEB: www.energen.com

NO. OF EMPLOYEES: 1,399

SHAREHOLDERS: 9,000 (approx.)

ANNUAL MEETING: In Jan.

INCORPORATED: AL, Jan., 1978

INSTITUTIONAL HOLDINGS:
No. of Institutions: 108
Shares Held: 14,837,018
% Held: 49.3

INDUSTRY: Natural gas distribution (SIC: 4924)

TRANSFER AGENT(S): First Chicago Trust Company of New York, Jersey City, NJ

ENERGYNORTH, INC.

YIELD 2.4%
P/E RATIO 48.8

*7 YEAR PRICE SCORE 126.5   *12 MONTH PRICE SCORE 119.7

*NYSE COMPOSITE INDEX=100

INTERIM EARNINGS (Per Share):

Qtr.	Dec.	Mar.	June	Sept.
1995-96	1.17	2.07	d0.53	d0.82
1996-97	1.12	2.03	d0.49	d0.65
1997-98	1.28	1.80	d0.54	d0.86
1998-99	0.97	2.14	d0.55	d1.19
1999-00	0.81	...	...	...

INTERIM DIVIDENDS (Per Share):

Amt.	Decl.	Ex.	Rec.	Pay.
0.35Q	7/14/99	8/30/99	9/01/99	9/15/99
0.35Q	10/07/99	11/29/99	12/01/99	12/15/99
0.35Q	1/27/00	2/28/00	3/01/00	3/15/00
0.35Q	4/27/00	5/30/00	6/01/00	6/15/00
0.35Q	4/27/00	8/30/00	9/01/00	9/15/00

Indicated div.: $1.40 (Div. Reinv. Plan)

CAPITALIZATION (9/30/99):

	($000)	(%)
Long-Term Debt	45,679	38.8
Deferred Income Tax	21,254	18.0
Common & Surplus	50,943	43.2
Total	117,876	100.0

DIVIDEND ACHIEVER STATUS:
Rank: 270   10-Year Growth Rate: 4.39%
Total Years of Dividend Growth: 16

RECENT DEVELOPMENTS: On 4/27/00, shareholders of EI approved a proposed merger agreement with Eastern Enterprises and KeySpan Energy. Under the terms of the agreement EI will be acquired by Eastern Enterprises at the same time Eastern is acquired by KeySpan Energy. The transactions should be completed in the third quarter of this year. For the three months ended 12/31/99, net income decreased 15.8% to $2.7 million from $3.2 million in the previous

year. Results for 1999 included reorganization costs of $685,000 due to the pending merger with Eastern Enterprises, Inc. Total operating revenues increased 18.1% to $37.2 million from $31.5 million in the prior year. EI's mechanical contracting sales increased $2.3 million year-over-year as a result of increased construction activity. Operating income amounted to $4.9 million compared with $4.2 million in the prior-year period.

BUSINESS

ENERGYNORTH, INC. owns all of the outstanding common stock of EnergyNorth Natural Gas, Inc. (ENGI), EnergyNorth Propane, Inc. (ENPI), ENI Mechanicals, Inc.; and EnergyNorth Realty, Inc. ENGI is engaged in the purchase, transportation and sale of natural gas for residential, commercial and industrial use in New Hampshire. ENPI is a retailer of liquefied petroleum gas and serves customers in central and southern New Hampshire. The service territory of ENGI has a population of approximately 482,000 in 28 communities situated in southern and central New Hampshire, which includes the communities of Nashua, Manchester, Concord and Laconia. ENPI sells propane to more than 15,300 customers, of which approximately 90% are residential and 10% are commercial and industrial. ENPI's service territory includes more than 150 communities primarily located within a 50-mile radius of Concord.

ANNUAL FINANCIAL DATA

	9/30/99	9/30/98	9/30/97	9/30/96	9/30/95	9/30/94	9/30/93
Earnings Per Share	1.36	1.64	2.01	1.89	1.30	1.74	1.74
Cash Flow Per Share	3.83	3.83	4.13	3.94	3.14	3.53	3.38
Tang. Book Val. Per Share	15.35	15.34	14.71	13.94	13.18	12.98	12.26
Dividends Per Share	1.39	1.32	1.25	1.21	1.13	1.09	1.06
Dividend Payout %	101.8	80.8	62.2	63.8	86.9	62.6	61.2
INCOME STATEMENT (IN THOUSANDS):							
Total Revenues	119,172	109,926	105,871	88,954	78,806	97,050	86,424
Costs & Expenses	98,091	90,721	85,647	69,766	63,990	80,101	71,507
Depreciation & Amort.	8,238	7,152	6,869	6,606	5,841	5,594	5,054
Operating Income	9,621	8,951	9,547	8,947	7,003	8,739	7,634
Net Interest Inc./(Exp.)	d4,956	d4,746	d3,985	d3,776	d4,433	d3,965	d3,765
Income Taxes	3,222	3,102	3,808	3,635	1,972	2,616	2,229
Net Income	4,537	5,378	6,518	6,078	4,104	5,422	5,368
Cash Flow	12,775	12,530	13,387	12,684	9,945	11,016	10,422
Average Shs. Outstg.	3,333	3,273	3,243	3,216	3,166	3,120	3,082
BALANCE SHEET (IN THOUSANDS):							
Gross Property	169,856	158,595	146,830	136,229	129,895	124,617	119,192
Accumulated Depreciation	56,126	51,313	47,815	44,683	41,452	38,521	35,438
Net Property	121,779	115,053	106,445	99,294	96,432	94,003	91,581
Total Assets	168,325	155,150	138,527	132,003	121,337	121,019	113,569
Long-Term Obligations	45,679	44,390	45,242	29,571	30,103	33,501	35,588
Net Stockholders' Equity	50,943	50,890	47,722	45,167	42,114	40,778	38,054
Year-end Shs. Outstg.	3,320	3,317	3,244	3,239	3,196	3,142	3,104
STATISTICAL RECORD:							
Operating Profit Margin %	8.1	8.1	9.0	10.1	8.9	9.0	8.8
Net Profit Margin %	3.8	4.9	6.2	6.8	5.2	5.6	6.2
Net Inc./Net Property %	3.7	4.7	6.1	6.1	4.3	5.8	5.9
Net Inc./Tot. Capital %	3.8	4.7	5.9	6.7	4.7	6.2	6.3
Return on Equity %	8.9	10.6	13.7	13.5	9.7	13.3	14.1
Accum. Depr./Gross Prop. %	33.0	32.4	32.6	32.8	31.9	30.9	29.7
Price Range	55¼-26⅝	29¾-25¼	28⅝-20¾	22⅛-17	18⅜-15½	22¼-15¼	22¼-17½
P/E Ratio	40.6-19.6	18.1-15.4	14.2-10.3	11.7-9.0	14.1-11.9	12.8-8.8	12.8-10.1
Average Yield %	3.4	4.8	5.1	6.2	6.7	5.8	5.4

Statistics are as originally reported.

OFFICERS:
E. T. Borer, Chmn.
N. G. Mattaini, Vice-Chmn.
R. R. Giordano, Pres., C.E.O.
F. L. Childs, Sr. V.P., C.F.O.

INVESTOR CONTACT: Michael J. Netkovick, Mgr. Public & Investor Relations, (603) 625-4000, Ext. 4267

PRINCIPAL OFFICE: 1260 Elm St., P.O. Box 329 Manchester, NH 03105

TELEPHONE NUMBER: (603) 625-4000
FAX: (603) 624-6864
WEB: www.energynorth.com

NO. OF EMPLOYEES: 459

SHAREHOLDERS: 1,839

ANNUAL MEETING: In February

INCORPORATED: NH, May, 1982

INSTITUTIONAL HOLDINGS:
No. of Institutions: 25
Shares Held: 710,403
% Held: 22.0

INDUSTRY: Natural gas distribution (SIC: 4924)

TRANSFER AGENT(S): BankBoston, N.A., Boston, MA

NYSE SYMBOL XOM
Rec. Pr. 83 5/16 (5/31/00)

EXXON MOBIL CORPORATION

YIELD 2.1%
P/E RATIO 38.4

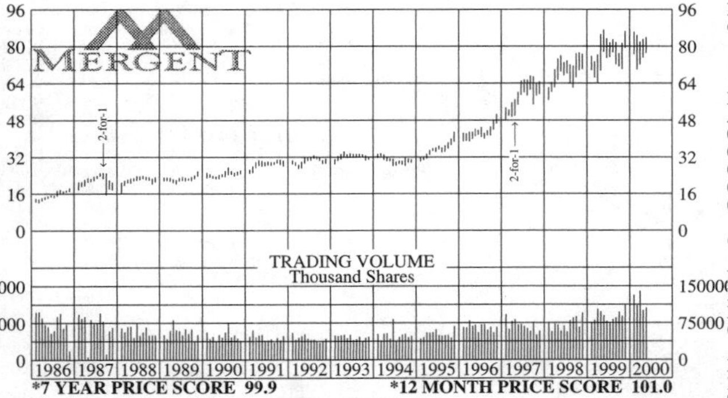

MERGENT
96
80
64
48
32
16
0
2-for-1
2-for-1
TRADING VOLUME
Thousand Shares
150000
75000
0
1986 1987 1988 1989 1990 1991 1992 1993 1994 1995 1996 1997 1998 1999 2000

***7 YEAR PRICE SCORE 99.9** ***12 MONTH PRICE SCORE 101.0**

*NYSE COMPOSITE INDEX=100

INTERIM EARNINGS (Per Share):

Qtr.	Mar.	June	Sept.	Dec.
1997	0.87	0.79	0.74	1.00
1998	0.76	0.65	0.58	0.62
1999	0.42	0.49	0.61	0.65

INTERIM DIVIDENDS (Per Share):

Amt.	Decl.	Ex.	Rec.	Pay.
0.41Q	4/28/99	5/10/99	5/12/99	6/10/99
0.41Q	7/28/99	8/11/99	8/13/99	9/10/99
0.44Q	10/27/99	11/09/99	11/12/99	12/10/99
0.44Q	1/26/00	2/09/00	2/11/00	3/10/00
0.44Q	4/26/00	5/11/00	5/15/00	6/10/00

Indicated div.: $1.76 (Div. Reinv. Plan)

CAPITALIZATION (12/31/99):

	($000)	(%)
Long-Term Debt	8,402,000	9.2
Deferred Income Tax	16,251,000	17.7
Minority Interest	3,688,000	4.0
Common & Surplus	63,466,000	69.1
Total	91,807,000	100.0

DIVIDEND ACHIEVER STATUS:
Rank: 286 10-Year Growth Rate: 3.80%
Total Years of Dividend Growth: 17

RECENT DEVELOPMENTS: For the twelve months ended 12/31/99, net income declined 2.9% to $7.91 billion from income of $8.14 billion, before accounting charges, in the previous year. Results for 1999 included merger expenses totaling $469.0 million. Total revenue increased 10.2% to $185.53 billion from $169.64 billion in the prior year. Worldwide capital and exploration expenditures fell 14.8% to $13.25 billion. Comparisons were made with restated 1998 results.

PROSPECTS: As a result of the merger with Mobil, the Company expects net income to increase by $1.00 billion in 2000, and rise to approximately $2.50 billion by 2003. The Company also expects asset sales to add $3.00 billion to cash flow. By year three, the merger should provide recurring positive cash flow of about $4.00 billion per year. Meanwhile, staffing requirements are expected to decrease by almost 16,000 people by the end of 2002.

BUSINESS

EXXON MOBIL CORPORATION's principal business is energy, involving exploration for and production of crude oil and natural gas, manufacturing of petroleum products, transportation and sale of crude oil, natural gas and petroleum products. ExxonMobil is a major manufacturer and marketer of basic petrochemicals, including olefins, aromatics, polyethylene and polypropylene plastics and a wide variety of specialty products. ExxonMobil is engaged in exploration for, and mining and sale of coal, copper and other minerals. ExxonMobil also has interests in electric power generation facilities. Exxon owns 69.6% of Imperial Oil Limited. In 1999, worldwide proved reserves were: crude oil and natural gas liquids, 11,260 million barrels; and natural gas, 56,796 billion cubic feet. On 11/30/99, Exxon Corp. and Mobil Corporation completed their $81.00 billion merger through the acquisition of Mobil by Exxon.

QUARTERLY DATA

(12/31/99)($Mill.)	REV	INC
First quarter	37,982	1,484
Second quarter	42,458	1,954
Third quarter	48,415	2,188
Fourth quarter	53,674	2,284

ANNUAL FINANCIAL DATA

	12/31/99	12/31/98	12/31/97	12/31/96	12/31/95	12/31/94	12/31/93
Earnings Per Share	**[3] 2.25**	**[1] 2.61**	**[2] 3.37**	**[2] 3.01**	**2.59**	**2.04**	**2.11**
Cash Flow Per Share	**4.70**	**4.77**	**5.56**	**5.17**	**4.77**	**4.07**	**4.09**
Tang. Book Val. Per Share	**18.24**	**17.98**	**17.69**	**17.41**	**16.10**	**14.84**	**13.74**
Dividends Per Share	**1.67**	**1.64**	**1.63**	**1.56**	**1.50**	**1.46**	**1.44**
Dividend Payout %	**74.2**	**62.8**	**48.2**	**51.8**	**57.9**	**71.5**	**68.4**
INCOME STATEMENT (IN MILLIONS):							
Total Revenues	185,527.0	117,772.0	137,242.0	134,249.0	123,920.0	113,904.0	111,211.0
Costs & Expenses	165,233.0	103,091.0	118,149.0	116,156.0	107,306.0	100,127.0	97,344.0
Depreciation & Amort.	8,304.0	5,340.0	5,474.0	5,329.0	5,386.0	5,015.0	4,884.0
Operating Income	11,990.0	9,341.0	13,619.0	12,764.0	11,228.0	8,762.0	8,983.0
Net Interest Inc./(Exp.)	d695.0	d100.0	d415.0	d464.0	d485.0	d725.0	d681.0
Income Before Income Taxes	11,150.0	9,056.0	12,798.0	11,916.0	10,442.0	7,804.0	8,052.0
Income Taxes	3,240.0	2,616.0	4,338.0	4,406.0	3,972.0	2,704.0	2,772.0
Equity Earnings/Minority Int.	d145.0	d185.0	d406.0	d384.0	d301.0	d233.0	d250.0
Net Income	[3] 7,910.0	[1] 6,440.0	[2] 8,460.0	[2] 7,510.0	6,470.0	5,100.0	5,280.0
Cash Flow	16,214.0	11,780.0	13,934.0	12,839.0	11,856.0	10,115.0	10,164.0
Average Shs. Outstg. (000)	3,453,000	2,428,000	2,505,000	2,484,000	2,484,000	2,484,000	2,484,000
BALANCE SHEET (IN MILLIONS):							
Cash & Cash Equivalents	1,761.0	1,461.0	4,062.0	2,969.0	1,789.0	1,775.0	1,652.0
Total Current Assets	31,141.0	17,593.0	21,192.0	19,910.0	17,318.0	16,460.0	14,859.0
Net Property	94,043.0	65,199.0	66,414.0	66,607.0	65,446.0	63,425.0	61,962.0
Total Assets	144,521.0	92,630.0	96,064.0	95,527.0	91,296.0	87,862.0	84,145.0
Total Current Liabilities	38,733.0	19,412.0	19,654.0	19,505.0	18,736.0	19,493.0	18,590.0
Long-Term Obligations	8,402.0	4,530.0	7,050.0	7,236.0	7,778.0	8,831.0	8,506.0
Net Stockholders' Equity	63,466.0	43,750.0	43,660.0	43,542.0	40,436.0	37,415.0	34,792.0
Net Working Capital	d7,592.0	d1,819.0	1,538.0	405.0	d1,418.0	d3,033.0	d3,731.0
Year-end Shs. Outstg. (000)	3,479,892	2,428,000	2,457,000	2,484,000	2,484,000	2,484,000	2,484,000
STATISTICAL RECORD:							
Operating Profit Margin %	6.5	7.9	9.9	9.5	9.1	7.7	8.1
Net Profit Margin %	4.3	5.5	6.2	5.6	5.2	4.5	4.7
Return on Equity %	12.5	14.7	19.4	17.2	16.0	13.6	15.2
Return on Assets %	5.5	7.0	8.8	7.9	7.1	5.8	6.3
Debt/Total Assets %	5.8	4.9	7.3	7.6	8.5	10.1	10.1
Price Range	87 1/4-64 5/16	77 5/16-56 5/8	67 1/4-48 1/4	50 5/8-38 13/16	43-30 1/16	33 11/16-28 1/16	34 1/2-28 7/8
P/E Ratio	38.8-28.6	29.6-21.7	20.0-14.3	16.8-12.9	16.6-11.6	16.6-13.8	16.4-13.7
Average Yield %	2.2	2.4	2.8	3.5	4.1	4.7	4.5

Statistics are as originally reported. Adj. for stk. splits: 2-for-1, 4/97 [1] Bef. acctg. chrg. of $70.0 mill. [2] Incls. non-recurr. credit 12/31/97; $305.0 mill.; credit 12/31/96: $90.0 mill. [3] Incls. non-recurr. chrg. of $469.0 mill.

OFFICERS:
L. R. Raymond, Chmn., C.E.O.
L. A. Notto, Vice-Chmn.
F. A. Risch, V.P., Treas.

INVESTOR CONTACT: T.P. Townsend, V.P., Investor Relations, (972) 444-1900

PRINCIPAL OFFICE: 5959 Las Colinas Blvd., Irving, TX 75039-2298

TELEPHONE NUMBER: (972) 444-1000
FAX: (972) 444-1348
WEB: www.exxonmobil.com

NO. OF EMPLOYEES: 123,000

SHAREHOLDERS: 633,151

ANNUAL MEETING: In May

INCORPORATED: NJ, Aug., 1882

INSTITUTIONAL HOLDINGS:
No. of Institutions: 1,166
Shares Held: 1,646,483,293
% Held: 47.6

INDUSTRY: Petroleum refining (SIC: 2911)

TRANSFER AGENT(S): Exxon Shareholder Services, Boston, MA

NYSE SYMBOL FMN
Rec. Pr. $23\frac{11}{16}$ (5/31/00)

F&M NATIONAL CORPORATION

YIELD 4.2%
P/E RATIO 13.4

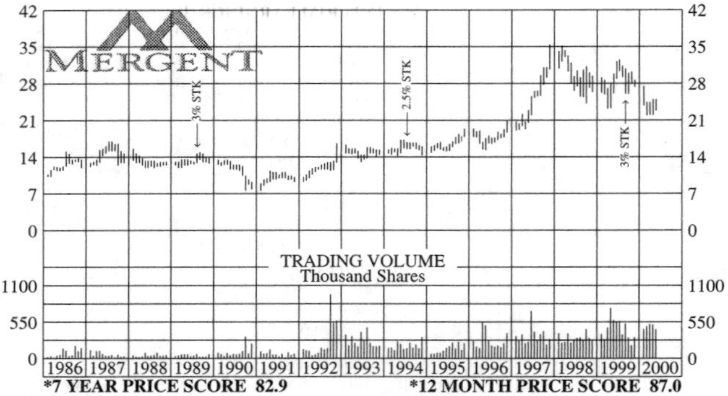

***7 YEAR PRICE SCORE 82.9** ***12 MONTH PRICE SCORE 87.0**

*NYSE COMPOSITE INDEX=100

INTERIM EARNINGS (Per Share):

Qtr.	Mar.	June	Sept.	Dec.
1995	0.35	0.33	0.36	0.34
1996	0.33	0.36	0.34	0.37
1997	0.37	0.37	0.38	0.37
1998	0.40	0.40	0.38	0.38
1999	0.47	0.41	0.45	0.44

INTERIM DIVIDENDS (Per Share):

Amt.	Decl.	Ex.	Rec.	Pay.
0.235Q	9/08/99	9/22/99	9/24/99	10/26/99
3% STK	8/11/99	9/22/99	9/24/99	10/26/99
0.235Q	11/10/99	12/21/99	12/24/99	1/25/00
0.235Q	3/08/00	3/22/00	3/24/00	4/25/00
0.25Q	5/10/00	6/21/00	6/23/00	7/25/00

Indicated div.: $1.00

CAPITALIZATION (12/31/99):

	($000)	(%)
Total Deposits	2,482,205	88.7
Long-Term Debt	25,443	0.9
Common & Surplus	291,565	10.4
Total	2,799,213	100.0

DIVIDEND ACHIEVER STATUS:
Rank: 241 10-Year Growth Rate: 6.07%
Total Years of Dividend Growth: 17

RECENT DEVELOPMENTS: For the year ended 12/31/99, net income advanced 13.2% to $41.3 million from $36.5 million in the previous year. Net interest income climbed 5.3% to $125.9 million from $119.5 million the year before primarily due to a 31.7% jump in taxable interest income to $22.8 million from $17.3 million in 1998. Total interest income totaled $204.2 million compared with $203.0 million in the previous year. Total interest expense fell 6.2% to $78.3 million, while non-interest expense rose 9.6% to $106.9 million. On 5/4/00, the Company announced that it has agreed to acquire 15 banking offices with approximately $310.0 million in deposits from Wachovia Bank, N.A. The transfer is scheduled for August 2000 and should be accretive to the Company in the first twelve months.

BUSINESS

F&M NATIONAL CORPORATION is a multi-bank holding company headquartered in Winchester, Virginia. FMN provides financial, insurance, and trust services to individuals and commercial customers through 17 subsidiary corporations including 125 banking locations, 13 mortgage banking offices, three trust offices and six insurance offices in Virginia, West Virginia and Maryland. FMN offers a full range of banking services principally to individuals and small and middle-market businesses in north, central and south Virginia including the Shenandoah Valley, and the eastern panhandle of West Virginia, along with the counties of Montgomery and Prince George in Maryland. At December 31, 1999, FMN had assets of $2.95 billion. On 4/1/98, the Company completed the acquisition of Peoples Bank of Virginia. On 3/22/99, the Company completed the merger of Security Bank into F & M Bank-Northern Virginia.

ANNUAL FINANCIAL DATA

	12/31/99	12/31/98	12/31/97	12/31/96	12/31/95
Earnings Per Share	**1.78**	**1.56**	**1.45**	**1.35**	**1.18**
Tang. Book Val. Per Share	**12.69**	**12.37**	**11.46**	**10.67**	**11.02**
Dividends Per Share	**0.83**	**0.73**	**[1] 0.75**	**0.64**	**0.59**
Dividend Payout %	**46.6**	**46.8**	**51.7**	**47.4**	**50.0**
INCOME STATEMENT (IN MILLIONS):					
Total Interest Income	204.2	198.8	178.6	168.0	133.3
Total Interest Expense	78.3	81.8	75.2	71.2	57.3
Net Interest Income	125.9	117.0	103.4	96.8	76.0
Provision for Loan Losses	3.6	5.0	5.7	2.0	1.1
Non-Interest Income	47.6	38.6	27.0	20.7	16.2
Non-Interest Expense	106.9	95.1	78.2	71.1	56.0
Income Before Taxes	63.0	55.5	46.5	44.4	35.1
Net Income	41.3	36.5	31.1	29.3	23.4
Average Shs. Outstg. (000)	23,233	23,417	23,194	23,284	23,122
BALANCE SHEET (IN MILLIONS):					
Cash & Due from Banks	122.8	160.8	125.2	112.9	81.6
Securities Avail. for Sale	...	...	...	...	...
Total Loans & Leases	1,763.4	1,695.8	1,547.3	1,444.8	1,060.2
Allowance for Credit Losses	23.8	24.7	24.3	23.7	21.4
Net Loans & Leases	1,739.6	1,671.1	1,523.0	1,421.2	1,038.8
Total Assets	2,945.9	2,888.7	2,520.3	2,303.8	1,833.8
Total Deposits	2,482.2	2,436.0	2,137.8	1,966.9	1,583.5
Long-Term Obligations	25.4	21.1	17.1	19.8	8.0
Total Liabilities	2,654.4	2,601.6	2,272.5	2,073.0	1,640.3
Net Stockholders' Equity	291.6	287.1	247.8	230.7	193.5
Year-end Shs. Outstg. (000)	22,985	22,511	24,427	24,423	24,210
STATISTICAL RECORD:					
Return on Equity %	14.2	12.7	12.6	12.7	12.1
Return on Assets %	1.4	1.3	1.2	1.3	1.3
Equity/Assets %	9.9	9.9	9.8	10.0	10.6
Non-Int. Exp./Tot. Inc. %	61.6	61.1	60.0	60.5	60.7
Price Range	$32\frac{1}{2}$-$23\frac{3}{16}$	$35\frac{3}{16}$-$24\frac{1}{8}$	$35\frac{3}{8}$-$19\frac{1}{16}$	$20\frac{7}{8}$-$15\frac{5}{16}$	$19\frac{7}{16}$-$14\frac{13}{16}$
P/E Ratio	18.3-13.0	22.6-15.5	24.5-13.2	15.4-11.3	16.5-12.6
Average Yield %	3.0	2.5	2.8	3.5	3.5

Statistics are as originally reported. Adj. for stk. split: 3.0% div., 8/99; 2.5% div., 9/1/94
[1] Includes $0.05 special div.

OFFICERS:
W. M. Feltner, Chmn., C.E.O.
A. B. Whitt, Pres., Vice-Chmn., C.F.O.
C. E. Curtis, Vice-Chmn., C.A.O.
B. H. Ward, Sr. V.P., Treas.

INVESTOR CONTACT: A. B. Whitt, (540) 665-4282

PRINCIPAL OFFICE: 9 Court Square, Winchester, VA 22601

TELEPHONE NUMBER: (540) 665-4200
FAX: (540) 665-4210
WEB: www.fmnatl.com

NO. OF EMPLOYEES: 1,446 full-time; 259 part-time

SHAREHOLDERS: 8,466

ANNUAL MEETING: In April

INCORPORATED: VA, Nov., 1968

INSTITUTIONAL HOLDINGS:
No. of Institutions: 51
Shares Held: 2,633,628
% Held: 11.4

INDUSTRY: National commercial banks (SIC: 6021)

TRANSFER AGENT(S): American Stock Transfer and Trust Company, New York, NY

NYSE SYMBOL FDO
Rec. Pr. 19¾ (5/31/00)

FAMILY DOLLAR STORES, INC.

YIELD	1.1%
P/E RATIO	21.2

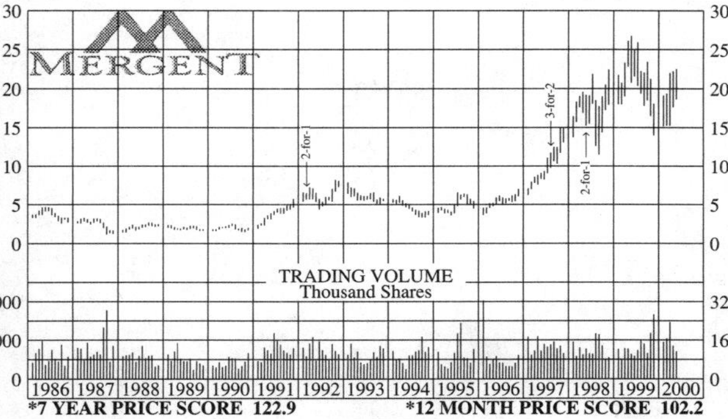

30
25
20
15
10
5
0
2-for-1
3-for-2
2-for-1
TRADING VOLUME
Thousand Shares
32000
16000
0
1986
1987
1988
1989
1990
1991
1992
1993
1994
1995
1996
1997
1998
1999
2000

*7 YEAR PRICE SCORE 122.9 *12 MONTH PRICE SCORE 102.2

*NYSE COMPOSITE INDEX=100

INTERIM EARNINGS (Per Share):

Qtr.	Nov.	Feb.	May	Aug.
1995-96	0.09	0.10	0.11	0.07
1996-97	0.11	0.12	0.14	0.09
1997-98	0.14	0.16	0.18	0.12
1998-99	0.17	0.24	0.24	0.16
1999-00	0.21	0.32	...	...

INTERIM DIVIDENDS (Per Share):

Amt.	Decl.	Ex.	Rec.	Pay.
0.05Q	8/24/99	9/13/99	9/15/99	10/15/99
0.05Q	11/11/99	12/13/99	12/15/99	1/14/00
0.055Q	1/20/00	3/13/00	3/15/00	4/14/00
0.055Q	5/15/00	6/13/00	6/15/00	7/14/00

Indicated div.: $0.22

CAPITALIZATION (8/28/99):

	($000)	(%)
Deferred Income Tax	26,054	3.6
Common & Surplus	690,651	96.4
Total	716,705	100.0

DIVIDEND ACHIEVER STATUS:
Rank: 98 10-Year Growth Rate: 12.83%
Total Years of Dividend Growth: 23

RECENT DEVELOPMENTS: For the quarter ended 2/26/00, net income advanced 31.9% to $55.0 million from $41.7 million a year earlier. Net sales climbed 14.1% to $858.5 million from $752.2 million the year before. The increase in sales was attributed to an approximate 5.6% increase in existing-store sales and from sales recorded in new stores opened under FDO's store-expansion program. Gross profit was $284.1 million, or 33.1% of net sales, versus $242.5 million, or 32.2% of net sales, in the prior year.

PROSPECTS: Results are benefiting from increased sales of higher-margin merchandise coupled with fewer clearance markdowns, reflecting improved inventory management. Going forward, revenue and earnings growth should continue to be driven by the Company's aggressive store expansion program. During the current fiscal year, FDO plans to open about 400 new stores and close 50 stores. In addition, FDO expects to expand or relocate approximately 150 stores and renovate about 300 locations.

BUSINESS

FAMILY DOLLAR STORES, INC. operated 3,505 discount stores as of 5/1/00. The stores are located in a contiguous 39-state area ranging as far northwest as South Dakota, northeast to Maine, southeast to Florida and southwest to Arizona. The stores' relatively small size, generally 6,000 to 8,000 square feet, gives FDO flexibility to open them in various markets from small rural towns to large urban centers. The stores are located in strip shopping centers or as freestanding buildings convenient to FDO's low- and middle-income customer base. The merchandise, which is generally priced under $10.00, is sold in a no-frills, low overhead, self-service environment.

ANNUAL FINANCIAL DATA

	8/28/99	8/29/98	8/31/97	8/31/96	8/31/95	8/31/94	8/31/93
Earnings Per Share	**0.81**	**0.60**	**0.44**	**0.35**	**0.34**	[1] **0.37**	**0.38**
Cash Flow Per Share	**1.07**	**0.80**	**0.61**	**0.50**	**0.47**	**0.48**	**0.48**
Tang. Book Val. Per Share	**4.00**	**3.36**	**2.75**	**2.61**	**2.40**	**2.06**	**1.91**
Dividends Per Share	**0.20**	**0.17**	**0.16**	**0.14**	**0.13**	**0.11**	**0.10**
Dividend Payout %	**24.1**	**29.2**	**36.0**	**40.9**	**37.4**	**30.0**	**25.2**
INCOME STATEMENT (IN MILLIONS):							
Total Revenues	2,751.2	2,361.9	1,995.0	1,714.6	1,546.9	1,428.4	1,297.4
Costs & Expenses	2,484.7	2,161.1	1,844.4	1,591.2	1,430.3	1,308.9	1,177.3
Depreciation & Amort.	43.8	34.8	29.1	24.6	22.2	19.5	17.2
Operating Income	222.7	166.0	121.5	98.8	94.4	100.1	102.9
Income Before Income Taxes	222.7	166.0	121.5	98.8	94.4	100.1	102.9
Income Taxes	82.6	62.7	46.8	38.2	36.3	38.2	38.5
Net Income	140.1	103.3	74.7	60.6	58.1	[1] 62.0	64.4
Cash Flow	183.9	138.1	103.8	85.2	80.3	81.4	81.6
Average Shs. Outstg. (000)	172,511	173,224	171,187	170,441	170,055	169,489	168,749
BALANCE SHEET (IN MILLIONS):							
Cash & Cash Equivalents	95.3	134.2	42.5	18.8	8.9	9.9	5.7
Total Current Assets	720.0	646.6	544.7	507.9	475.0	431.3	402.5
Net Property	371.1	291.8	231.2	184.6	156.6	151.9	130.1
Total Assets	1,095.3	942.2	780.3	696.8	636.2	588.3	537.4
Total Current Liabilities	378.5	343.3	261.2	234.2	210.4	205.6	196.6
Net Stockholders' Equity	690.7	578.2	500.2	445.0	407.8	370.2	323.3
Net Working Capital	341.4	303.4	283.5	273.7	264.7	225.7	205.9
Year-end Shs. Outstg. (000)	172,751	172,204	182,063	170,606	170,232	180,117	169,055
STATISTICAL RECORD:							
Operating Profit Margin %	8.1	7.0	6.1	5.8	6.1	7.0	7.9
Net Profit Margin %	5.1	4.4	3.7	3.5	3.8	4.3	5.0
Return on Equity %	20.3	17.9	14.9	13.6	14.3	16.7	19.9
Return on Assets %	12.8	11.0	9.6	8.7	9.1	10.5	12.0
Price Range	26¾-14	22 7/16-11½	15 1/16-6¼	7-3 11/16	6 9/16-3⅝	6⅛-3 5/16	7⅞-5 1/16
P/E Ratio	33.0-17.3	37.4-19.2	34.6-14.4	20.0-10.5	19.2-10.6	16.7-9.1	20.6-13.2
Average Yield %	1.0	1.0	1.5	2.7	2.5	2.3	1.5

Statistics are as originally reported. Adj. for 2-for-1 stk. split, 4/98 & 3-for-2 stk. split, 7/97. [1] Bef. $1.1 mil ($0.01/sh) cr. for acctg. adj.

OFFICERS:
L. Levine, Chmn.
R. J. Kelly, Vice-Chmn., C.F.O.
H. R. Levine, Pres., C.E.O.
G. R. Mahoney, Jr., Exec. V.P., Sec.

INVESTOR CONTACT: Janis Burris, Assistant Secretary, (704) 847-6961

PRINCIPAL OFFICE: 10401 Old Monroe Rd., Charlotte, NC 28201

TELEPHONE NUMBER: (704) 847-6961
FAX: (704) 847-5534
WEB: www.familydollar.com

NO. OF EMPLOYEES: 14,900 full-time (approx.); 13,400 part-time (approx.)

SHAREHOLDERS: 2,210 (approx.)

ANNUAL MEETING: In Jan.

INCORPORATED: DE, Nov., 1969

INSTITUTIONAL HOLDINGS:
No. of Institutions: 191
Shares Held: 116,591,084
% Held: 67.4

INDUSTRY: Variety stores (SIC: 5331)

TRANSFER AGENT(S): ChaseMellon Shareholder Services, LLC, Ridgefield Park, NJ

NYSE SYMBOL FNM
Rec. Pr. 60⅛ (5/31/00)

FANNIE MAE

YIELD 1.9%
P/E RATIO 16.2

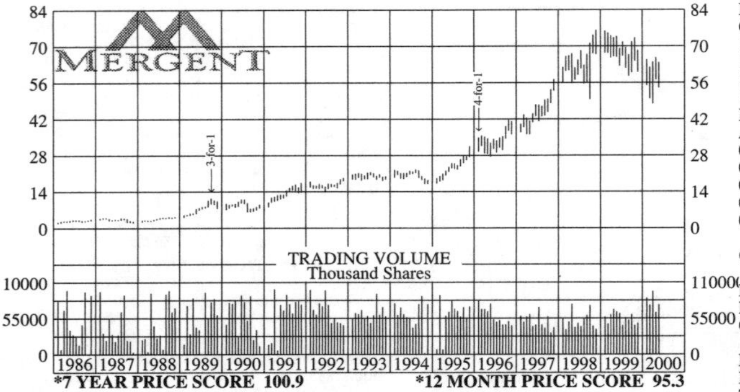

*7 YEAR PRICE SCORE 100.9 *12 MONTH PRICE SCORE 95.3

*NYSE COMPOSITE INDEX=100

INTERIM EARNINGS (Per Share):

Qtr.	Mar.	June	Sept.	Dec.
1996	0.61	0.61	0.63	0.65
1997	0.67	0.69	0.72	0.75
1998	0.78	0.80	0.82	0.85
1999	0.88	0.91	0.94	0.99

INTERIM DIVIDENDS (Per Share):

Amt.	Decl.	Ex.	Rec.	Pay.
0.27Q	4/20/99	4/28/99	4/30/99	5/25/99
0.27Q	7/20/99	7/28/99	7/30/99	8/25/99
0.27Q	10/19/99	10/27/99	10/29/99	11/25/99
0.28Q	1/18/00	1/27/00	1/31/00	2/25/00
0.28Q	4/18/00	4/26/00	4/30/00	5/25/00

Indicated div.: $1.12 (Div. Reinv. Plan)

CAPITALIZATION (12/31/99):

	($000)	(%)
Long-Term Debt	321,037,000	94.8
Preferred Stock	1,300,000	0.4
Common & Surplus	16,329,000	4.8
Total	338,666,000	100.0

DIVIDEND ACHIEVER STATUS:
Rank: 7 10-Year Growth Rate: 25.86%
Total Years of Dividend Growth: 14

RECENT DEVELOPMENTS: For the year ended 12/31/99, income from continuing operations totaled $3.92 billion compared with $3.44 billion the year before. Results excluded $9.2 million and $26.3 million in extraordinary losses resulting from the early extinguishment of debt in 1999 and 1998, respectively. Net interest income rose 19.0% to $4.89 billion from $4.11 billion in the prior year. At 12/31/99, FNM's net mortgage portfolio stood at $522.78 billion versus $415.22 billion in 1998.

PROSPECTS: Going forward, the Company expects to double FNM's earnings per share by the end of 2003. Meanwhile, FNM is on track to achieve its target earnings per share growth for fiscal 2000 and beyond. The Company will look to build on record mortgage purchase volumes despite a decline in mortgage originations. FNM should continue to experience growth due to new credit guaranty and portfolio purchase initiatives to broaden its range of mortgage products.

BUSINESS

FANNIE MAE (formerly Federal National Mortgage Association) is the largest investor in home mortgage loans in the U.S. The Company was established in 1938 as a U.S. government agency to provide supplemental liquidity to the mortgage market and was transformed into a stockholder-owned and privately-managed company by legislation enacted in 1968. FNM provides funds to the mortgage market by purchasing mortgage loans from lenders, thereby replenishing their funds for additional lending. FNM also issues mortgage-backed securities (MBS), primarily in exchange for pools of mortgage loans from lenders, which also increases the liquidity of residential mortgage loans. Fannie Mae receives guaranty fees for its guaranty of timely payment of principal of and interest on MBS certificates.

ANNUAL FINANCIAL DATA

	12/31/99	12/31/98	12/31/97	12/31/96	12/31/95	12/31/94	12/31/93
Earnings Per Share	[1] **3.73**	**3.26**	[1] **2.84**	[1] **2.50**	[1] **1.96**	[1] **1.95**	[1] **1.86**
Cash Flow Per Share	**10.45**	**8.88**	**7.59**	**6.51**	**6.56**	**4.65**	**3.08**
Tang. Book Val. Per Share	**16.02**	**13.95**	**12.34**	**11.10**	**10.04**	**8.75**	**7.40**
Dividends Per Share	**1.08**	**0.96**	**0.84**	**0.76**	**0.68**	**0.60**	**0.46**
Dividend Payout %	**29.0**	**29.4**	**29.6**	**30.4**	**34.7**	**30.8**	**24.7**
INCOME STATEMENT (IN MILLIONS):							
Total Revenues	36,968.0	31,499.0	27,777.0	25,054.0	22,250.0	18,573.0	16,053.0
Costs & Expenses	24,599.0	21,026.0	18,428.0	16,811.0	14,185.0	12,462.0	11,710.0
Depreciation & Amort.	6,929.0	5,828.0	5,012.0	4,338.0	5,070.0	2,965.0	1,338.0
Operating Income	5,440.0	4,645.0	4,337.0	3,905.0	2,995.0	3,146.0	3,005.0
Income Before Income Taxes	5,440.0	4,645.0	4,337.0	3,905.0	2,995.0	3,146.0	3,005.0
Income Taxes	1,519.0	1,201.0	1,269.0	1,151.0	840.0	1,005.0	963.0
Net Income	[1] 3,921.0	3,444.0	[1] 3,068.0	[1] 2,754.0	[1] 2,155.0	[1] 2,141.0	[1] 2,042.0
Cash Flow	10,772.0	9,206.0	8,015.0	7,050.0	7,225.0	5,106.0	3,380.0
Average Shs. Outstg. (000)	1,031,000	1,037,000	1,056,000	1,083,000	1,102,000	1,098,000	1,098,000
BALANCE SHEET (IN MILLIONS):							
Cash & Cash Equivalents	20,190.0	16,959.0	8,111.0	4,350.0	57,591.0	46,566.0	22,373.0
Total Current Assets	23,720.0	20,412.0	10,975.0	6,769.0	59,838.0	48,254.0	23,630.0
Total Assets	575,167.0	485,014.0	391,673.0	351,041.0	316,550.0	272,508.0	216,979.0
Total Current Liabilities	233,366.0	210,675.0	180,011.0	164,136.0	149,970.0	115,740.0	74,871.0
Long-Term Obligations	321,037.0	254,878.0	194,374.0	171,370.0	153,021.0	144,628.0	129,162.0
Net Stockholders' Equity	17,629.0	15,453.0	13,793.0	12,773.0	10,959.0	9,541.0	8,052.0
Net Working Capital	d209,646.0	d190,263.0	d169,036.0	d157,367.0	d90,132.0	d67,486.0	d51,241.0
Year-end Shs. Outstg. (000)	1,019,000	1,025,000	1,037,000	1,061,000	1,092,000	1,091,000	1,088,000
STATISTICAL RECORD:							
Operating Profit Margin %	14.7	14.7	15.6	15.6	13.5	16.9	18.7
Net Profit Margin %	10.6	10.9	11.0	11.0	9.7	11.5	12.7
Return on Equity %	22.2	22.3	22.2	21.6	19.7	22.4	25.4
Return on Assets %	0.7	0.7	0.8	0.8	0.7	0.8	0.9
Debt/Total Assets %	55.8	52.6	49.6	48.8	48.3	53.1	59.5
Price Range	75⅞-58 9/16	76 3/16-49 9/16	57 5/16-36⅛	41⅝-27½	31½-17 3/16	22⅝-17	21½-18¼
P/E Ratio	20.3-15.7	23.4-15.2	20.2-12.7	16.6-11.0	16.1-8.8	11.6-8.7	11.6-9.8
Average Yield %	1.6	1.5	1.8	2.2	2.8	3.0	2.3

Statistics are as originally reported. Adj. for stk. splits: 4-for-1, 1/96. [1] Bef. extraord. chrg. 1999, $9.2 mill.; 1998, $10.7 mill.; 1997, $12.8 mill.; 1996, $29.0 mill.; 1995, $11.4 mill.; 1994, $9.0 mill.; 1993, $169.3 mill.

OFFICERS:
F. D. Raines, Chmn., C.E.O.
D. H. Mudd, Vice-Chmn., C.O.O.
J. T. Howard, Exec. V.P., C.F.O.

INVESTOR CONTACT: Jayne Shontell, Sr. V.P., Inv. Rel., (202) 752-7115

PRINCIPAL OFFICE: 3900 Wisconsin Avenue, NW, Washington, DC 20016-2892

TELEPHONE NUMBER: (202) 752-7000
FAX: (202) 752-4934
WEB: www.fanniemae.com

NO. OF EMPLOYEES: 3,800

SHAREHOLDERS: 28,000 (approx.)

ANNUAL MEETING: In May

INCORPORATED: 1938

INSTITUTIONAL HOLDINGS:
No. of Institutions: 955
Shares Held: 836,815,029
% Held: 81.6

INDUSTRY: Federal & fed.-sponsored credit (SIC: 6111)

TRANSFER AGENT(S): First Chicago Trust Company of New York, Jersey City, NJ

NYSE SYMBOL FRT
Rec. Pr. 21¹⁵/₁₆ (5/31/00)

FEDERAL REALTY INVESTMENT TRUST

YIELD	8.0%
P/E RATIO	21.7

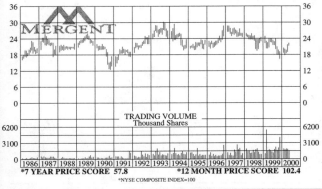

7 YEAR PRICE SCORE 57.8   **12 MONTH PRICE SCORE 102.4**
NYSE COMPOSITE INDEX=100

INTERIM EARNINGS (Per Share):

Qtr.	Mar.	June	Sept.	Dec.
1997	0.24	0.44	0.24	0.22
1998	0.27	0.26	0.14	0.27
1999	0.29	0.12	0.30	0.30

INTERIM DIVIDENDS (Per Share):

Amt.	Decl.	Ex.	Rec.	Pay.
0.43Q	5/06/98	6/23/98	6/25/98	7/15/98
0.44Q	9/02/98	9/23/98	9/25/98	10/15/98
0.44Q	12/11/98	12/30/98	1/04/99	1/15/99
0.44Q	2/22/99	3/23/99	3/25/99	4/15/99
0.44Q	5/05/99	6/23/99	6/25/99	7/15/99

Indicated div.: $1.76 (Div. Reinv. Plan)

CAPITALIZATION (12/31/99):

	($000)	(%)
Long-Term Debt	635,836	48.7
Capital Lease Obligations..	122,026	9.4
Minority Interest	45,330	3.5
Preferred Stock	100,000	7.7
Common & Surplus	401,827	30.8
Total	1,305,019	100.0

DIVIDEND ACHIEVER STATUS:

Rank: 307   10-Year Growth Rate: 2.67%
Total Years of Dividend Growth: 32

RECENT DEVELOPMENTS: For the year ended 12/31/99, net income increased 7.7% to $48.4 million compared with $45.0 million a year earlier. Results for the current year included a loss of 7.1 million on the sale of real estate. Total revenues were $264.7 million, up 11.0% from $238.5 million in the prior year. Rental income jumped 10.6% to $245.8 million from $222.2 million in the preceding year.

Interest and other income rose 28.7% to $7.6 million compared with $5.9 million a year earlier. Other property income improved 8.5% to $11.2 million from $10.3 million a year ago. Total expenses rose 7.8% to $205.3 million from $190.4 million in the previous year. Operating income before investors' share of operations totaled $59.4 million, an increase of 23.5% from $48.1 million in the prior year.

BUSINESS

FEDERAL REALTY INVESTMENT TRUST is an equity real estate investment trust specializing in the ownership, management and redevelopment of prime retail properties. The Company's real estate portfolio contains 123 retail properties, consisting of neighborhood and community shopping centers and main street retail properties. The properties are located in 15 different states and the District of Columbia.

ANNUAL FINANCIAL DATA

	12/31/99	12/31/98	12/31/97	12/31/96	12/31/95	12/31/94	12/31/93
Earnings Per Share	1.02	0.94	1.14	0.86	0.72	0.67	☐ 0.60
Tang. Book Val. Per Share	10.00	10.73	11.59	10.84	10.18	10.92	10.14
Dividends Per Share	1.77	1.73	1.69	1.65	1.59	1.56	1.54
Dividend Payout %	173.5	184.0	148.2	191.8	221.5	233.5	257.5
INCOME STATEMENT (IN MILLIONS):							
Rental Income	245.8	222.2	188.5	164.9	142.8	128.1	105.9
Interest Income	7.6	5.9	6.0	4.4	4.1	3.9	3.9
Total Income	264.7	238.5	204.3	179.1	154.4	137.8	115.3
Costs & Expenses	93.8	84.6	72.2	66.2	56.9	54.6	41.5
Depreciation	50.0	46.0	41.4	38.2	34.9	29.8	25.4
Interest Expense	61.5	55.1	47.3	45.6	39.3	31.5	31.6
Income Before Income Taxes	52.3	48.1	47.8	29.1	22.8	20.9	16.9
Equity Earnings/Minority Int.	d3.9	d3.1	d1.3	d0.4	0.3	d0.4	d0.8
Net Income	48.4	45.0	46.5	28.7	23.1	20.5	☐ 16.1
Average Shs. Outstg. (000)	40,638	40,080	38,988	33,573	31,860	30,679	27,009
BALANCE SHEET (IN MILLIONS):							
Cash & Cash Equivalents	11.7	17.2	17.0	11.0	10.5	4.0	9.6
Total Real Estate Investments	1,403.5	1,356.1	1,206.1	924.3	818.9	692.1	623.0
Total Assets	1,534.0	1,484.3	1,316.6	1,035.3	886.2	753.7	690.9
Long-Term Obligations	757.9	583.8	551.9	519.5	462.6	311.0	333.7
Total Liabilities	1,032.2	954.4	762.8	646.4	558.7	408.6	406.7
Net Stockholders' Equity	501.8	529.9	553.8	388.9	327.5	345.2	284.2
Year-end Shs. Outstg. (000)	40,201	40,080	39,148	35,886	32,160	31,609	28,018
STATISTICAL RECORD:							
Net Inc.+Depr./Assets %	6.4	6.1	7.0	6.5	6.5	6.7	6.0
Return on Equity %	9.7	8.5	9.1	7.4	7.1	5.9	5.7
Return on Assets %	3.2	3.0	3.8	2.8	2.6	2.7	2.3
Price Range	24⅞-16⅜	25¹⁵/₁₆-19⅜	28¾-24½	28¾-20¼	23⅝-19¾	29½-19⅝	30¼-23⅞
P/E Ratio	24.4-16.1	27.6-20.6	25.2-21.5	33.4-23.5	32.8-27.4	44.0-29.3	50.4-39.8
Average Yield %	8.6	7.6	6.3	6.7	7.4	6.4	5.7

Statistics are as originally reported. ☐ Bef. extraord. credit $2.0 mill., 1993.

NYSE SYMBOL FSS
Rec. Pr. 19 5/16 (5/31/00)

FEDERAL SIGNAL CORP.

YIELD 3.9%
P/E RATIO 15.3

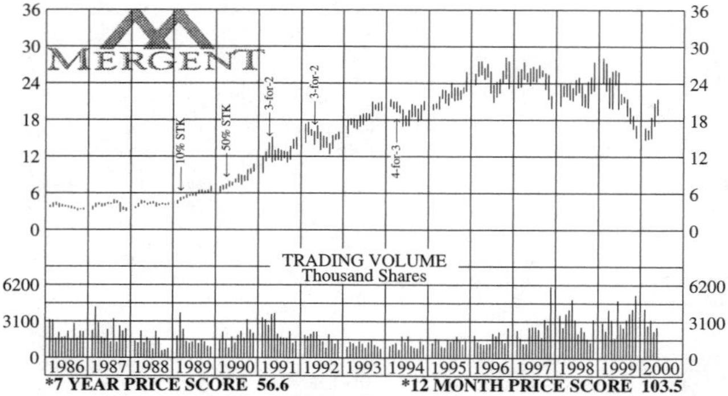

MERGENT
10% STK
50% STK
3-for-2
3-for-2
4-for-3
TRADING VOLUME
Thousand Shares
1986 1987 1988 1989 1990 1991 1992 1993 1994 1995 1996 1997 1998 1999 2000

*7 YEAR PRICE SCORE 56.6 *12 MONTH PRICE SCORE 103.5

*NYSE COMPOSITE INDEX=100

INTERIM EARNINGS (Per Share):

Qtr.	Mar.	June	Sept.	Dec.
1996	0.26	0.35	0.35	0.40
1997	0.30	0.35	0.35	0.29
1998	0.24	0.35	0.36	0.36
1999	0.29	0.30	0.30	0.37

INTERIM DIVIDENDS (Per Share):

Amt.	Decl.	Ex.	Rec.	Pay.
0.185Q	4/16/99	5/11/99	5/13/99	6/01/99
0.185Q	7/08/99	8/16/99	8/18/99	9/01/99
0.185Q	10/22/99	12/10/99	12/14/99	1/04/00
0.19Q	2/03/00	2/16/00	2/18/00	3/01/00
0.19Q	4/20/00	5/09/00	5/11/00	6/01/00

Indicated div.: $0.76 (Div. Reinv. Plan)

CAPITALIZATION (12/31/99):

	($000)	(%)
Long-Term Debt	307,020	44.4
Deferred Income Tax	30,445	4.4
Common & Surplus	354,033	51.2
Total	691,498	100.0

DIVIDEND ACHIEVER STATUS:
Rank: 57 10-Year Growth Rate: 15.32%
Total Years of Dividend Growth: 12

RECENT DEVELOPMENTS: For the year ended 12/31/99, net income fell 3.2% to $57.5 million compared with $59.4 million in 1998. Revenues grew 5.8% to $1.06 billion from $1.00 billion a year ago. Vehicle revenues rose 3.5% to $557.1 million, as environmental revenues increased 12.4% to $247.1 million. Fire rescue revenues fell 2.6% to $310.0 million. Safety products revenues advanced 3.5% to $261.9 million. Sign revenues improved 28.4% to $84.7 million, while tool revenues jumped 8.3% to $158.2 million.

PROSPECTS: The Company completed the acquisition of P.C.S. Company, a manufacturer and marketer of precision tooling and components to the plastic injection molding industry. The addition of P.C.S. should complement the metal stamping market of the Company's Tool Group. Going forward, FSS plans to increase performance in all market segments by targeting operating margins and reducing high inventories. Separately, the Company is seeking offers for the Sign Group. Proceeds from the sale will be used for improvements in the remaining groups.

BUSINESS

FEDERAL SIGNAL CORP. is a manufacturer and worldwide supplier of public safety, signaling and communications equipment, fire trucks, emergency and street sweeping vehicles, parking control equipment, custom on-premise signage, carbide cutting tools, precision punches and related die components. The Safety Products Group provides warning, signal and communication products while the Sign Group produces identification signs and communication displays. Standard and special die components and precision parts are manufactured by the Tool Group. The Vehicle Group makes commercial fire apparatus and rescue vehicles.

ANNUAL FINANCIAL DATA

	12/31/99	12/31/98	12/31/97	12/31/96	12/31/95	12/31/94	12/31/93
Earnings Per Share	**1.25**	**1.30**	**1.29**	**2 1.35**	**1 1.13**	**1.02**	**0.86**
Cash Flow Per Share	**1.84**	**1.81**	**1.73**	**1.75**	**1.47**	**1.33**	**1.06**
Tang. Book Val. Per Share	**1.67**	**1.98**	**2.45**	**2.36**	**2.24**	**2.31**	**2.92**
Dividends Per Share	**0.74**	**0.70**	**0.65**	**0.56**	**0.48**	**0.41**	**0.35**
Dividend Payout %	**59.2**	**53.8**	**50.2**	**41.5**	**42.5**	**39.7**	**40.5**
INCOME STATEMENT (IN MILLIONS):							
Total Revenues	1,061.9	1,002.8	924.9	896.4	816.1	677.6	566.2
Costs & Expenses	928.2	877.5	804.7	775.1	704.3	584.7	492.1
Depreciation & Amort.	27.2	23.6	20.5	18.4	15.9	14.3	9.2
Operating Income	106.5	101.8	99.7	102.9	95.9	78.7	64.9
Net Interest Inc./(Exp.)	d23.3	d19.3	d17.2	d15.4	d13.4	d8.5	d6.1
Income Before Income Taxes	84.4	86.2	84.8	93.4	77.3	70.2	58.8
Income Taxes	26.9	26.8	25.9	31.4	25.7	23.4	19.0
Net Income	57.5	59.4	59.0	2 62.0	1 51.6	46.8	39.8
Cash Flow	84.8	83.0	79.5	80.4	67.5	61.0	49.0
Average Shs. Outstg. (000)	45,958	45,846	45,840	45,952	45,859	45,957	46,293
BALANCE SHEET (IN MILLIONS):							
Cash & Cash Equivalents	8.8	15.3	10.7	12.4	9.4	4.6	2.6
Total Current Assets	346.1	311.2	268.6	267.0	235.5	196.3	151.8
Net Property	115.4	97.4	84.7	82.8	78.5	72.8	62.2
Total Assets	961.0	836.0	727.9	703.9	620.0	521.6	405.7
Total Current Liabilities	269.5	195.2	227.0	374.6	314.4	252.6	174.5
Long-Term Obligations	307.0	288.8	177.5	34.3	39.7	34.9	21.1
Net Stockholders' Equity	354.0	321.8	299.8	272.8	248.1	220.3	199.2
Net Working Capital	76.7	116.0	41.6	d107.6	d78.9	d56.3	d22.7
Year-end Shs. Outstg. (000)	46,114	45,329	45,606	45,318	45,290	45,372	45,738
STATISTICAL RECORD:							
Operating Profit Margin %	10.0	10.1	10.8	11.5	11.8	11.6	11.5
Net Profit Margin %	5.4	5.9	6.4	6.9	6.3	6.9	7.0
Return on Equity %	16.3	18.5	19.7	22.7	20.8	21.2	20.0
Return on Assets %	6.0	7.1	8.1	8.8	8.3	9.0	9.8
Debt/Total Assets %	31.9	34.5	24.4	4.9	6.4	6.7	5.2
Price Range	28 1/8-15 15/16	27 1/2-20	27 1/2-19 7/8	28 1/4-20 7/8	25 7/8-19 5/8	21 3/8-16 15/16	21-15 11/16
P/E Ratio	22.5-12.1	21.2-15.4	21.3-15.4	20.9-15.5	22.9-17.4	21.0-16.6	24.4-18.2
Average Yield %	3.5	2.9	2.7	2.3	2.1	2.1	1.9

Statistics are as originally reported. Adj for 4-for-3 split, 3/94. 1 Incl. $4.2 mill. ($0.09/sh) chg. for litigation. 2 Incl. $2.8 mill. after-tax gain on sale of assets.

OFFICERS:
J. J. Ross, Chmn., Pres., C.E.O.
H. L. Dykema, V.P., C.F.O.
R. W. Racic, V.P., Treas.

INVESTOR CONTACT: Henry L. Dykema, V.P. & C.F.O., (630) 954-2020

PRINCIPAL OFFICE: 1415 W. 22nd St., Oak Brook, IL 60523-9945

TELEPHONE NUMBER: (630) 954-2000
FAX: (630) 954-2030
WEB: www.federalsignal.com
NO. OF EMPLOYEES: 7,226 (avg.)
SHAREHOLDERS: 4,489
ANNUAL MEETING: In Apr.
INCORPORATED: IL, Mar., 1901; reincorp., DE, Mar., 1969

INSTITUTIONAL HOLDINGS:
No. of Institutions: 133
Shares Held: 24,364,202
% Held: 52.9

INDUSTRY: Motor vehicles and car bodies (SIC: 3711)

TRANSFER AGENT(S): Harris Trust and Savings Bank, Chicago, IL.

FIDELITY NATIONAL FINANCIAL, INC.

YIELD 2.6%
P/E RATIO 6.9

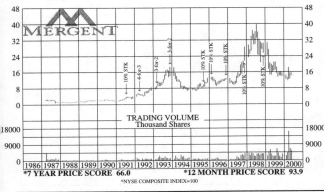

TRADING VOLUME
Thousand Shares

*7 YEAR PRICE SCORE 66.0   *12 MONTH PRICE SCORE 93.9
*NYSE COMPOSITE INDEX=100

INTERIM EARNINGS (Per Share):

Qtr.	Mar.	June	Sept.	Dec.
1995	d0.14	0.05	0.35	0.18
1996	0.30	0.41	0.36	0.34
1997	0.16	0.44	0.71	0.56
1998	0.56	0.98	0.82	0.87
1999	0.60	0.75	0.60	0.30

INTERIM DIVIDENDS (Per Share):

Amt.	Decl.	Ex.	Rec.	Pay.
0.07Q	3/17/99	4/07/99	4/09/99	5/28/99
0.07Q	6/14/99	7/07/99	7/09/99	7/22/99
0.07Q	9/30/99	10/08/99	10/13/99	10/27/99
0.10Q	12/23/99	12/30/99	1/03/00	1/18/00
0.10Q	3/17/00	4/06/00	4/10/00	5/30/00

Indicated div.: $0.40 (Div. Reinv. Plan)

CAPITALIZATION (12/31/99):

	($000)	(%)
Long-Term Debt	226,359	34.1
Minority Interest	4,613	0.7
Common & Surplus	432,494	65.2
Total	663,466	100.0

DIVIDEND ACHIEVER STATUS:
Rank: 37   10-Year Growth Rate: 17.36%
Total Years of Dividend Growth: 12

RECENT DEVELOPMENTS: For the year ended 12/31/99, net earnings dropped 33.0% to $70.9 million compared with $105.7 million in the previous year. The 1998 results included a non-recurring investment gain of $6.0 million. Earnings were hindered by a 4.9 percentage point increase in total expenses as a percentage of total revenues to 91.3% from 86.4% in 1998. Total revenue advanced 4.9% to $1.35 billion from $1.29 billion in the prior year.

PROSPECTS: On 3/20/00, the Company announced that it had acquired Chicago Title Corporation. The combined entity had total assets of approximately $3.00 billion and net worth of approximately $1.00 billion as of 12/31/99. Going forward, results should benefit from a strong resale and new purchase real estate market. In addition, the Company will continue to focus on maintaining a cost structure consistent with revenue levels.

BUSINESS

FIDELITY NATIONAL FINAN-CIAL, INC., through its principal subsidiaries, is one of the largest national underwriters engaged in the business of issuing title insurance policies and performing other title-related services such as escrow, collection and trust activities, real estate information and technology services, trustee's credit reporting, attorney services, flood certification, real estate tax services, reconveyances, recording, sale guarantees, foreclosure publishing and posting services, and exchange intermediary services in connection with real estate transactions. Title insurance services are provided through the Company's direct operations and otherwise through independent title insurance agents who issue title policies on behalf of the underwriting subsidiaries.

REVENUES

(12/31/1999)	($000)	(%)
Title Insurance Premiums	939,452	69.5
Escrow Fees	123,734	9.2
Other Fees & Revenue	260,623	19.2
Interest & Invest Income	28,395	2.1
Total	1,352,204	100.0

ANNUAL FINANCIAL DATA

	12/31/99	12/31/98	12/31/97	12/31/96	12/31/95	12/31/94	12/31/93
Earnings Per Share	2.27	③ 2.94	① 1.72	1.28	② 0.40	② 0.41	1.48
Tang. Book Val. Per Share	14.46	12.48	9.01	5.95	4.34	5.07	4.67
Dividends Per Share	0.28	0.25	0.23	0.21	0.18	0.17	0.14
Dividend Payout %	13.6	8.7	13.5	16.4	44.7	42.9	9.5
INCOME STATEMENT (IN THOUSANDS):							
Total Premium Income	939,452	910,278	533,220	475,961	285,552	369,275	429,772
Other Income	412,752	378,187	213,492	160,952	124,293	123,529	145,611
Total Revenues	1,352,204	1,288,465	746,712	636,913	409,845	492,804	575,383
Policyholder Benefits	52,713	59,294	38,661	33,302	19,031	27,838	39,220
Income Before Income Taxes	117,828	175,134	73,430	40,553	9,460	12,339	52,554
Income Taxes	46,975	69,442	31,959	16,216	1,828	2,594	16,259
Equity Earnings/Minority Int.	...	...	...	...	...	...	d1,200
Net Income	70,853	③ 105,692	① 41,471	24,337	② 7,632	② 9,745	36,295
Average Shs. Outstg.	34,470	36,821	25,994	18,987	18,989	24,123	24,642
BALANCE SHEET (IN THOUSANDS):							
Cash & Cash Equivalents	38,569	51,309	54,005	63,971	47,431	34,689	42,731
Premiums Due	79,088	86,701	61,548	73,261	58,177	48,622	31,965
Invst. Assets: Fixed-term	347,051	330,068	217,001	166,329	129,236	149,111	200,206
Invst. Assets: Total	506,916	510,515	326,277	227,674	180,082	217,648	236,533
Total Assets	1,029,173	969,470	600,559	509,296	405,063	418,119	396,279
Long-Term Obligations	226,359	214,624	123,023	148,922	136,047	142,129	52,769
Net Stockholders' Equity	432,494	396,740	196,319	110,251	77,947	73,954	114,926
Year-end Shs. Outstg.	29,907	31,785	21,797	18,529	17,965	14,584	24,624
STATISTICAL RECORD:							
Return on Revenues %	5.2	8.2	5.6	3.8	1.9	2.0	6.3
Return on Equity %	16.4	26.6	21.1	22.1	9.8	13.2	31.6
Return on Assets %	6.9	10.9	6.9	4.8	1.9	2.3	9.2
Price Range	30¾-13⁷⁄₁₆	36¹⁄₁₆-18¹⁵⁄₁₆	25-8⁵⁄₈	12⁵⁄₁₆-8³⁄₁₆	11¹³⁄₁₆-6¹⁄₈	16¹¹⁄₁₆-6¹⁄₁₆	16¹⁵⁄₁₆-6⁷⁄₈
P/E Ratio	13.5-5.9	12.3-6.5	15.1-5.0	9.6-6.4	29.6-15.4	41.1-14.9	11.5-4.7
Average Yield %	1.3	0.9	1.3	2.1	2.0	1.5	1.2

Statistics are as originally reported. Adjusted for 3-for-2 stock split, 12/93; 10.0% stk. div., 12/98; 12/97, 12/96, 1/96, 9/95. ① Excl. net extraord. loss of $1.7 mill. ② Excl. extraord. gain of $813,000, 1995; $2.4 mill., 1994. ③ Incl. $7.3 mil in pre-tax merger-related expenses.

OFFICERS:
W. P. Foley II, Chmn., C.E.O.
F. P. Willey, Vice-Chmn., Pres.
A. D. Meadows, Exec. V.P., C.F.O., Treas.

INVESTOR CONTACT: Investor Relations, (949) 622-4333

PRINCIPAL OFFICE: 17911 Von Karman Avenue, Suite 300, Irvine, CA 92614

TELEPHONE NUMBER: (949) 622-4333
FAX: (949) 622-4153
WEB: www.fnf.com

NO. OF EMPLOYEES: 6,000 (approx.)

SHAREHOLDERS: 900 (approx.)

ANNUAL MEETING: In Jan.

INCORPORATED: DE, Nov., 1984

INSTITUTIONAL HOLDINGS:
No. of Institutions: 86
Shares Held: 12,466,590
% Held: 43.8

INDUSTRY: Title insurance (SIC: 6361)

TRANSFER AGENT(S): Continental Stock Transfer and Trust Company, New York, NY

FIFTH THIRD BANCORP

YIELD 1.4%
P/E RATIO 31.9

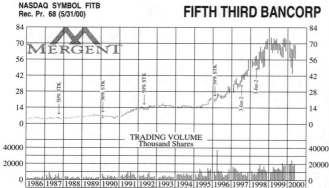

7 YEAR PRICE SCORE 116.3 **12 MONTH PRICE SCORE 97.9**

*NYSE COMPOSITE INDEX=100

INTERIM EARNINGS (Per Share):

Qtr.	Mar.	June	Sept.	Dec.
1996	0.35	0.35	0.33	0.39
1997	0.41	0.41	0.45	0.45
1998	0.46	0.22	0.53	0.55
1999	0.55	0.59	0.62	0.37

INTERIM DIVIDENDS (Per Share):

Amt.	Decl.	Ex.	Rec.	Pay.
0.20Q	3/16/99	3/29/99	3/31/99	4/15/99
0.20Q	6/15/99	6/28/99	6/30/99	7/15/99
0.24Q	9/21/99	9/28/99	9/30/99	10/15/99
0.24Q	12/21/99	12/29/99	12/31/99	1/14/00
0.24Q	3/21/00	3/29/00	3/31/00	4/14/00

Indicated div.: $0.96 (Div. Reinv. Plan)

CAPITALIZATION (12/31/99):

	($000)	(%)
Total Deposits	26,083,000	81.2
Long-Term Debt	1,977,000	6.2
Common & Surplus	4,077,000	12.7
Total	32,137,000	100.0

DIVIDEND ACHIEVER STATUS:

Rank: 39   10-Year Growth Rate: 17.32%
Total Years of Dividend Growth: 27

RECENT DEVELOPMENTS: For the year ended 12/31/99, net income climbed 22.1% to $668.0 million from $547.0 million in the prior year. Earnings for 1999 and 1998 included merger-related charges of $82.0 million and $121.0 million, respectively. Net interest income rose 10.7% to $1.41 billion from $1.27 billion the year before. The improvement in net interest income was attributed to a higher level of average interest-earning assets, improvement in the deposit mix, and the favorable repricing of interest-bearing liabili-

ties. Interest and fees grew 3.0% to $1.91 billion from $1.86 billion in the previous year. Interest on securities increased 13.2% to $814.0 million. Net interest margin improved to 3.99% versus 3.93% a year earlier. Total other operating income advanced 16.3% to $877.0 million from $754.0 million in 1998. Total operating expenses totaled $1.12 billion, up 5.3% to $1.07 billion in the prior-year period. Comparisons were made with restated 1998 figures.

BUSINESS

FIFTH THIRD BANCORP is a $44.39 billion bank holding company with its primary subsidiary, the Fifth Third Bank, headquartered in Cincinnati, Ohio. FITB provides full-service banking to individuals as well as to industry and government subdivisions located throughout Ohio, Indiana, Kentucky, Michigan, Florida and Arizona. As of 3/31/00, Fifth Third had 644 full-service Banking Centers, including 114 Bank-Mart® locations open seven days a week inside select grocery stores and 1,400 Jeanie® ATMs. The Company offers the retail banking market a variety of services, including the Jeanie® electronic funds transfer system which consists of automated teller machines and telephone banking and features a bill payment service. This service is used by banks and savings and loans in Ohio, Kentucky, Indiana, Arizona and Florida. FITB is engaged in commercial, retail and trust banking, investment services and leasing activities, credit life, accident and health insurance, discount brokerage services and property management for its properties. On 6/11/99, FITB completed the acquisition of South Florida Bank Holding Corporation, and its subsidiary South Florida Bank.

ANNUAL FINANCIAL DATA

	12/31/99	12/31/98	12/31/97	12/31/96	12/31/95	12/31/94	12/31/93
Earnings Per Share	☐ 2.15	☐ 1.76	1.69	☐ 1.43	1.29	1.13	0.97
Tang. Book Val. Per Share	13.20	11.91	9.78	9.00	7.63	6.40	5.78
Dividends Per Share	0.84	0.66	0.55	0.48	0.40	0.34	0.29
Dividend Payout %	39.1	37.3	32.6	33.2	31.2	30.5	30.2
INCOME STATEMENT (IN MILLIONS):							
Total Interest Income	2,738.0	2,018.7	1,478.4	1,385.1	1,173.2	922.3	727.3
Total Interest Expense	1,333.0	1,015.9	733.4	695.9	609.7	405.5	291.0
Net Interest Income	1,405.0	1,002.8	745.0	689.2	563.4	516.8	436.4
Provision for Loan Losses	134.0	109.2	80.3	64.0	43.0	35.8	44.5
Non-Interest Income	877.0	636.2	445.5	368.4	305.7	255.9	226.6
Non-Interest Expense	1,122.0	803.6	506.2	493.3	395.6	371.5	323.4
Income Before Taxes	1,026.0	726.3	603.9	500.3	430.6	365.3	295.1
Net Income	☐ 668.0	☐ 476.1	401.2	☐ 335.1	287.7	244.5	196.4
Average Shs. Outstg. (000)	314,570	265,338	236,526	233,987	222,478	217,305	202,338
BALANCE SHEET (IN MILLIONS):							
Cash & Due from Banks	1,213.0	819.9	720.1	808.9	628.5	695.0	580.9
Securities Avail. for Sale	13,043.0	8,453.2	6,426.5	6,268.5	4,158.0	1,153.3	816.0
Total Loans & Leases	25,887.0	18,468.2	13,985.8	12,963.0	12,016.7	10,518.6	8,965.7
Allowance for Credit Losses	1,290.0	956.1	748.1	635.4	503.4	388.1	289.7
Net Loans & Leases	24,597.0	17,512.2	13,237.8	12,327.5	11,513.3	10,130.5	8,675.9
Total Assets	41,589.0	28,921.8	21,375.1	20,549.0	17,052.9	14,957.0	11,966.0
Total Deposits	26,083.0	18,780.4	14,914.1	14,374.7	12,485.8	10,630.9	8,628.5
Long-Term Obligations	1,977.0	2,288.2	457.9	277.7	425.4	178.7	282.9
Total Liabilities	37,512.0	25,743.3	19,097.6	18,404.9	15,328.3	13,558.2	10,768.4
Net Stockholders' Equity	4,077.0	3,178.5	2,277.4	2,144.1	1,724.6	1,398.8	1,197.6
Year-end Shs. Outstg. (000)	308,887	266,918	232,838	238,259	225,952	218,394	207,232
STATISTICAL RECORD:							
Return on Equity %	16.4	15.0	17.6	15.6	16.7	17.5	16.4
Return on Assets %	1.6	1.6	1.9	1.6	1.7	1.6	1.6
Equity/Assets %	9.8	11.0	10.7	10.4	10.1	9.4	10.0
Non-Int. Exp./Tot. Inc. %	49.2	49.0	42.5	46.6	45.5	48.1	48.8
Price Range	75⁷/₁₆-57⁷/₈	74¹/₈-47¹/₂	55¹¹/₁₆-27	33-19⁵/₁₆	22¹¹/₁₆-13¹³/₁₆	16⁵/₁₆-13³/₁₆	17¹/₂-14¹¹/₁₆
P/E Ratio	35.1-26.9	42.1-27.0	32.9-15.9	23.1-13.5	17.5-10.8	14.5-11.9	18.0-15.1
Average Yield %	1.3	1.1	1.3	1.8	2.3	2.3	1.8

Statistics are as originally reported. Adj. for stk. splits: 3-for-2, 4/15/98; 3-for-2, 7/15/97; 3-for-2, 1/12/96 ☐ Incl. non-recurr. chrg. $82.0 mill., 12/99; $89.7 mill., 12/98; $16.6 mill., 12/96

OFFICERS:
G. A. Schaefer Jr., Pres., C.E.O.
N. E. Arnold, Exec. V.P., C.F.O., Treas.
M. K. Keating, Exec. V.P., Gen. Couns.
P. L. Reynolds, Sr. V.P., Asst. Sec.

INVESTOR CONTACT: Neal E.Arnold, Exec. V.P. & C.F.O., (513) 579-4356

PRINCIPAL OFFICE: 38 Fountain Sq. Plz., Fifth Third Center, Cincinnati, OH 45263

TELEPHONE NUMBER: (513) 579-5300
FAX: (513) 579-6246
WEB: www.53.com

NO. OF EMPLOYEES: 12,240 (avg.)

SHAREHOLDERS: 35,277

ANNUAL MEETING: In March

INCORPORATED: OH, 1974

NYSE SYMBOL FCF
Rec. Pr. 9 3/4 (5/31/00)

FIRST COMMONWEALTH FINANCIAL CORPORATION

YIELD 5.7%
P/E RATIO 11.2

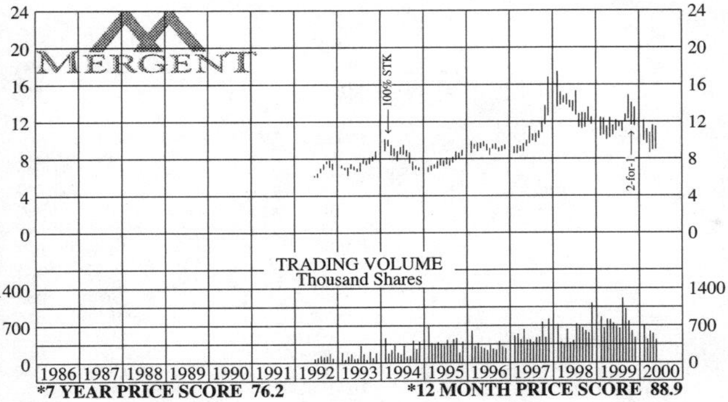

*7 YEAR PRICE SCORE 76.2 *12 MONTH PRICE SCORE 88.9

*NYSE COMPOSITE INDEX=100

INTERIM EARNINGS (Per Share):

Qtr.	3/31	6/30	9/30	12/31
1996	0.16	0.16	0.14	0.18
1997	0.18	0.17	0.20	0.16
1998	0.16	0.17	0.19	0.03
1999	0.20	0.24	0.22	0.21

INTERIM DIVIDENDS (Per Share):

Amt.	Decl.	Ex.	Rec.	Pay.
0.26Q	6/15/99	6/28/99	6/30/99	7/15/99
0.26Q	9/14/99	10/04/99	10/06/99	10/15/99
2-for-1	10/20/99	11/19/99	11/04/99	11/18/99
0.14Q	12/14/99	12/28/99	12/30/99	1/14/00
0.14Q	3/14/00	3/29/00	3/31/00	4/14/00

Indicated div.: $0.56

CAPITALIZATION (12/31/99):

	($000)	(%)
Total Deposits	2,948,829	76.1
Long-Term Debt	603,355	15.6
Redeemable Pfd. Stock	35,000	0.9
Common & Surplus	286,683	7.4
Total	3,873,867	100.0

DIVIDEND ACHIEVER STATUS:
Rank: 119 10-Year Growth Rate: 11.84%
Total Years of Dividend Growth: 12

RECENT DEVELOPMENTS: For the year ended 12/31/99, net income totaled $53.0 million, up 56.0%, compared with income before extraordinary items of $34.0 million in the previous year. Results for 1998 included merger and related charges of $7.9 million related to the acquisition of Southwest National Corporation, early retirement and postretirement benefit accruals and premises and equipment expenses to standardize depreciation methods. Net interest income grew 7.2% to $144.9 million versus $135.1 million a year earlier. Total other income was $30.9 million compared with $26.3 million the year before. Total other expense increased 6.6% to $93.6 million from $100.2 million in the prior year. Return on average assets was 1.25% compared with 0.85% a year ago. Return on average equity increased to 15.44% from 9.13% the year before. Net loans to deposit ratio was 83.6% versus 79.9% in 1998. Deposits totaled $2.95 billion, while net loans rose 5.3% to $2.50 billion.

BUSINESS

FIRST COMMONWEALTH FINANCIAL CORPORATION is a financial services holding company with $4.34 billion in assets. The Company operates two banks: First Commonwealth Bank, headquartered in Indiana, Pennsylvania; and Southwest Bank, headquartered in Greensburg, Pennsylvania. First Commonwealth Bank operates through divisions doing business under the following names: NBOC Bank; Deposit Bank; Cenwest Bank; First Bank of Leechburg; Peoples Bank; Central Bank; Peoples Bank of Western Pennsylvania; Unitas Bank; and Reliable Bank. Southwest Bank was obtained through the Company's 12/31/98 merger with Southwest National Corp. In addition to its bank operations, FCF provides financial services and insurance products through First Commonwealth Trust Company and First Commonwealth Insurance Agency. Also, the Company operates Commonwealth Systems Corporation, a data processing subsidiary, and First Commonwealth Professional Resources, Inc., a subsidiary providing professional affiliated organizations.

ANNUAL FINANCIAL DATA

	12/31/99	12/31/98	12/31/97	12/31/96	12/31/95	12/31/94	12/31/93
Earnings Per Share	**0.88**	**[1] 0.55**	**0.70**	**0.63**	**0.58**	**0.64**	**[2] 0.61**
Tang. Book Val. Per Share	**4.93**	**5.74**	**6.17**	**5.89**	**5.64**	**5.02**	**5.00**
Dividends Per Share	**0.49**	**0.44**	**0.40**	**0.36**	**0.32**	**0.28**	**0.25**
Dividend Payout %	**55.7**	**80.0**	**57.5**	**57.1**	**55.2**	**43.4**	**41.0**
INCOME STATEMENT (IN MILLIONS):							
Total Interest Income	297.5	283.4	199.8	182.3	175.7	159.6	131.7
Total Interest Expense	152.7	148.3	102.8	88.3	82.4	69.1	58.0
Net Interest Income	144.9	135.1	97.1	94.0	93.3	90.5	73.7
Provision for Loan Losses	9.5	15.0	6.9	4.5	4.1	2.9	2.2
Non-Interest Income	25.9	26.3	19.8	13.7	10.4	16.2	12.1
Non-Interest Expense	93.6	100.2	65.9	63.6	62.1	60.9	51.2
Income Before Taxes	72.6	46.2	44.1	39.7	37.5	43.0	32.4
Net Income	53.0	[1] 34.0	30.5	27.6	25.5	28.7	[2] 22.7
Average Shs. Outstg. (000)	60,569	61,666	43,932	43,908	44,010	44,864	37,284
BALANCE SHEET (IN MILLIONS):							
Cash & Due from Banks	92.7	96.6	60.1	69.4	62.4	66.1	51.0
Securities Avail. for Sale	1,144.0	1,042.6	396.6	244.4	244.2	443.2	465.2
Total Loans & Leases	2,503.7	2,382.2	1,937.7	1,778.1	1,531.2	1,422.3	1,037.7
Allowance for Credit Losses	37.2	39.7	36.6	50.1	61.8	61.9	46.0
Net Loans & Leases	2,466.5	2,342.5	1,901.1	1,728.0	1,469.4	1,360.5	991.6
Total Assets	4,340.8	4,096.8	2,929.3	2,584.6	2,364.3	2,334.9	1,955.3
Total Deposits	2,948.8	2,931.1	2,242.5	2,104.8	1,962.8	1,881.1	1,575.6
Long-Term Obligations	603.4	630.9	193.1	40.9	5.3	7.6	7.4
Total Liabilities	4,054.2	3,741.4	2,657.5	2,323.3	2,112.0	2,109.8	1,768.8
Net Stockholders' Equity	286.7	355.4	271.8	261.4	252.3	225.1	186.5
Year-end Shs. Outstg. (000)	58,143	61,876	44,092	44,388	44,744	44,862	37,284
STATISTICAL RECORD:							
Return on Equity %	18.5	9.6	11.2	10.6	10.1	12.8	12.2
Return on Assets %	1.2	0.8	1.0	1.1	1.1	1.2	1.2
Equity/Assets %	6.6	8.7	9.3	10.1	10.7	9.6	9.5
Non-Int. Exp./Tot. Inc. %	55.0	62.6	59.8	59.8	59.5	60.1	61.4
Price Range	14 7/8-10 1/16	17 7/16-11 1/4	16 13/16-8 9/16	9 7/8-8 3/8	8 15/16-6 9/16	10 1/8-6 3/4	8 13/16-6 3/16
P/E Ratio	16.9-11.4	31.6-20.5	24.2-12.3	15.7-13.3	15.4-11.3	15.8-10.5	14.4-10.1
Average Yield %	3.9	3.1	3.2	3.9	4.1	3.3	3.3

Statistics are as originally reported. Adj. for 100% stk. div., 10/99; 2/94

OFFICERS:
E. J. Trimarchi, Chmn.
D. S. Dahlman, Vice-Chmn.
J. E. O'Dell, Pres., C.E.O.
J. J. Dolan, Exec. V.P., C.F.O.

PRINCIPAL OFFICE: 22 North Sixth Street, Indiana, PA 15701

TELEPHONE NUMBER: (724) 349-7220
FAX: (724) 349-6427
WEB: www.fcfbank.com

NO. OF EMPLOYEES: 1,450 (approx.)

SHAREHOLDERS: 12,500 (approx.)

ANNUAL MEETING: In April

INCORPORATED: PA, Nov., 1983

INSTITUTIONAL HOLDINGS:
No. of Institutions: 54
Shares Held: 8,049,867
% Held: 13.8

INDUSTRY: National commercial banks (SIC: 6021)

TRANSFER AGENT(S): The Bank of New York, New York, NY

FIRST FINANCIAL BANCORP

YIELD 3.4%
P/E RATIO 16.4

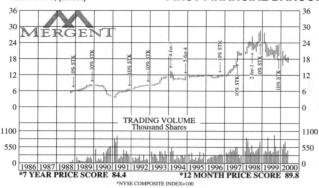

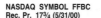

TRADING VOLUME
Thousand Shares

| | 1986 | 1987 | 1988 | 1989 | 1990 | 1991 | 1992 | 1993 | 1994 | 1995 | 1996 | 1997 | 1998 | 1999 | 2000 |

*7 YEAR PRICE SCORE 84.4   *12 MONTH PRICE SCORE 89.8

*NYSE COMPOSITE INDEX=100

INTERIM EARNINGS (Per Share):

Qtr.	Mar.	June	Sept.	Dec.
1995	0.25	0.27	0.27	0.26
1996	0.21	0.23	0.20	0.25
1997	0.24	0.25	0.25	0.26
1998	0.25	0.27	0.28	0.29
1999	0.28	0.19	0.31	0.30

INTERIM DIVIDENDS (Per Share):

Amt.	Decl.	Ex.	Rec.	Pay.
0.15Q	5/25/99	6/02/99	6/04/99	7/01/99
0.15Q	8/24/99	9/01/99	9/03/99	10/01/99
10% STK	11/24/99	12/03/99	12/03/99	1/03/00
0.15Q	11/24/99	12/01/99	12/03/99	1/03/00
0.15Q	2/22/00	3/01/00	3/03/00	4/03/00

Indicated div.: $0.60 (Div. Reinv. Plan)

CAPITALIZATION (12/31/99):

	($000)	(%)
Total Deposits	2,991,213	84.8
Long-Term Debt	161,799	4.6
Common & Surplus	372,539	10.6
Total	3,525,551	100.0

DIVIDEND ACHIEVER STATUS:

Rank: 123	10-Year Growth Rate: 11.69%
Total Years of Dividend Growth:	16

RECENT DEVELOPMENTS:

For the year ended 12/31/99, net earnings totaled $50.3 million compared with $51.0 million in the prior year. Results for 1999 included a restructuring charge of $6.9 million. Net interest income climbed 8.5% to $165.2 million from $152.2 million in the previous year. Noninterest income advanced 4.6% to $41.3 million from $39.5 million the year before. Noninterest expenses were up 11.9% to $120.7 million from $107.8 million a year ago.

Return on assets decreased to 1.37% from 1.53% in the prior year, while return on equity improved to 13.75% versus 14.59% in the previous year. Total interest income increased 7.5% to $282.4 million from $262.7 million in the previous year. Total interest expense advanced 6.1% from $110.4 million in the prior year. Comparisons were made with restated 1998 figures.

BUSINESS

FIRST FINANCIAL BANCORP is a bank and savings and loan holding company that engages in the business of commercial banking, and other permissible activities closely related to banking, through seventeen wholly-owned subsidiaries. The range of banking services provided by the Company's subsidiaries to their customers include commercial lending, real estate lending, consumer credit, credit card, and other personal loan financing. In addition, the institutions offer deposit services that include interest-bearing and noninterest-bearing deposit accounts and time deposits. Most subsidiaries provide safe deposit facilities. Trust and asset management services are provided by the Company's subsidiaries, excluding the savings banks.

LOAN DISTRIBUTION

(12/31/99)	($000)	(%)
Commercial	769,454	25.3
Real Estate-		
Construction	111,458	3.7
Real Estate-Mortgage	1,467,591	48.3
Installment	623,091	20.5
Credit Card	22,408	.7
Lease Financing	46,508	1.5
Total	3,040,510	100.0

ANNUAL FINANCIAL DATA

	12/31/99	12/31/98	12/31/97	12/31/96	12/31/95	12/31/94	12/31/93
Earnings Per Share	① 1.07	1.10	1.00	0.96	0.96	0.87	0.79
Tang. Book Val. Per Share	7.08	6.51	7.14	7.27	7.44	5.99	5.48
Dividends Per Share	0.55	0.50	0.45	0.41	0.38	0.30	0.27
Dividend Payout %	51.0	45.1	44.9	42.7	39.3	34.0	34.4
INCOME STATEMENT (IN MILLIONS):							
Total Interest Income	282.4	219.5	192.2	171.3	153.9	133.5	123.3
Total Interest Expense	117.2	88.4	76.8	69.7	63.5	49.6	47.6
Net Interest Income	165.2	131.1	115.4	101.6	90.3	83.9	75.7
Provision for Loan Losses	9.2	6.1	4.7	3.4	2.1	1.3	3.7
Non-Interest Income	41.3	34.3	27.0	22.1	20.6	17.5	17.8
Non-Interest Expense	120.7	92.7	77.7	71.3	63.3	62.1	58.5
Income Before Taxes	76.6	66.6	59.9	49.0	45.4	38.0	31.4
Net Income	① 50.3	44.1	40.3	33.9	31.8	28.2	24.3
Average Shs. Outstg. (000)	46,986	40,014	40,187	35,359	33,243	32,506	30,890
BALANCE SHEET (IN MILLIONS):							
Cash & Due from Banks	225.8	136.5	142.3	110.8	108.7	103.8	86.0
Securities Avail. for Sale	490.1	313.2	332.6	290.7	294.1	242.4	...
Total Loans & Leases	3,040.5	2,269.5	1,978.6	1,701.7	1,532.6	1,379.2	1,104.7
Allowance for Credit Losses	43.5	32.3	29.1	24.1	21.0	18.9	18.1
Net Loans & Leases	2,997.0	2,237.2	1,949.5	1,677.6	1,511.6	1,360.3	1,086.7
Total Assets	3,940.7	2,871.2	2,636.1	2,261.7	2,103.4	1,922.6	1,689.4
Total Deposits	2,991.2	2,326.6	2,230.2	1,880.0	1,785.6	1,587.3	1,476.2
Long-Term Obligations	161.8	105.3	41.1	6.5	2.8	...	...
Total Liabilities	3,568.2	2,569.2	2,349.9	2,003.2	1,869.2	1,728.0	1,520.3
Net Stockholders' Equity	372.5	301.9	286.3	258.5	234.2	194.7	169.2
Year-end Shs. Outstg. (000)	46,869	39,822	40,068	35,579	31,491	32,490	30,879
STATISTICAL RECORD:							
Return on Equity %	13.5	14.6	14.1	13.1	13.6	14.5	14.4
Return on Assets %	1.3	1.6	1.6	1.6	1.6	1.6	1.9
Equity/Assets %	9.5	10.6	11.1	11.8	11.7	10.9	13.2
Non-Int. Exp./Tot. Inc. %	38.4	36.1	34.6	54.6	57.6	57.1	62.5
Price Range	27¾-18¹⁵⁄₁₆	28½-19¹³⁄₁₆	20-11⁷⁄₁₆	12³⁄₁₆-10¾	12⅛-11⅛	13⁹⁄₁₆-9	11⁷⁄₁₆-7
P/E Ratio	25.9-17.0	25.9-18.0	20.9-11.4	12.7-11.2	12.7-11.6	15.7-11.5	14.5-10.2
Average Yield %	2.4	2.1	2.8	3.6	3.2	2.5	2.8

Statistics are as originally reported. Adj. for stk. splits: 6/1/98, 2-for-1; 10% div., 1/3/00; 10% div., 10/1/97; 10% div., 11/1/96; 5-for-4, 12/1/94; 4-for-3, 1/3/94; 10% div., 1/2/93. ① Incls. restr. chrg. of $6.9 mill.

OFFICERS:

S. N. Pontius, Pres., C.E.O.
M. R. O'Dell, Sr. V.P., C.F.O., Sec.

INVESTOR CONTACT: Richard E. Weinman, Sr. Vice Pres., (513) 425-7548

PRINCIPAL OFFICE: 300 High Street, Hamilton, OH 45011

TELEPHONE NUMBER: (513) 867-4700
FAX: (513) 425-7654
WEB: www.ffbc-oh.com

NO. OF EMPLOYEES: 1,871

SHAREHOLDERS: 4,747

ANNUAL MEETING: In March

INCORPORATED: OH, Aug., 1982

FIRST SECURITY CORPORATION

YIELD	3.6%
P/E RATIO	11.2

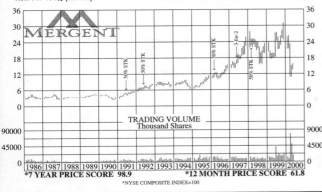

*7 YEAR PRICE SCORE 98.9   *12 MONTH PRICE SCORE 61.8
*NYSE COMPOSITE INDEX=100

INTERIM EARNINGS (Per Share):

Qtr.	Mar.	June	Sept.	Dec.
1996	0.21	0.25	0.27	0.29
1997	0.27	0.28	0.30	0.31
1998	0.32	0.29	0.33	0.35
1999	0.34	0.35	0.37	0.33

INTERIM DIVIDENDS (Per Share):

Amt.	Decl.	Ex.	Rec.	Pay.
0.14Q	4/26/99	5/12/99	5/14/99	6/07/99
0.14Q	7/27/99	8/11/99	8/13/99	9/07/99
0.14Q	10/25/99	11/09/99	11/12/99	12/06/99
0.14Q	1/31/00	2/02/00	2/04/00	2/28/00
0.14Q	4/18/00	5/17/00	5/19/00	6/05/00

Indicated div.: $0.56 (Div. Reinv. Plan)

CAPITALIZATION (12/31/99):

	($000)	(%)
Total Deposits	13,210,416	75.2
Long-Term Debt	2,585,755	14.7
Preferred Stock	451	0.0
Common & Surplus	1,769,449	10.1
Total	17,566,071	100.0

DIVIDEND ACHIEVER STATUS:
Rank: 91   10-Year Growth Rate: 13.11%
Total Years of Dividend Growth: 12

RECENT DEVELOPMENTS: On 4/10/00, the Company signed a definitive agreement to be acquired by Wells Fargo & Company. Under the agreement, shareholders will receive 0.355 shares of Wells Fargo common stock for each share of FSCO owned. For the year ended 12/31/99, net income increased 10.4% to $273.3 million from $247.7 million in the prior year. Net interest income rose 11.8% to $786.4 million from $703.7 million in the previous year. Results benefited from a strong demand for loans, growth in the securities portfolios, and the positive impact of acquisitions. Interest and fees on loans grew 7.3% to $1.19 billion from $1.11 billion in 1998. Net interest margin totaled 4.03% versus 4.15% the year before. Total noninterest income advanced 12.3% to $533.0 million from $474.4 million, reflecting growth in commissions and fees from securities and insurance transactions, partially offset by a decrease in bankcard fees. Total noninterest increased 16.8% to $844.4 million versus $723.1 million in 1998.

BUSINESS

FIRST SECURITY CORPORATION, headquartered in Salt Lake City, Utah, is a major financial services organization, with assets of $22.99 billion as of 12/31/99. Through its bank subsidiaries, First Security operates 333 full-service banking offices in seven states—Utah, Idaho, New Mexico, Oregon, Nevada, Wyoming and California. The Company's nonbank subsidiaries include a residential mortgage company; a leasing company; two insurance companies; an investment management firm; a full-service broker/dealer operation; a bankcard transaction processing company; an information technology subsidiary; and a small-business investment corporation.

ANNUAL FINANCIAL DATA

	12/31/99	12/31/98	12/31/97	12/31/96	12/31/95	12/31/94	12/31/93
Earnings Per Share	1.38	① 1.28	1.16	1.02	① 0.70	① 0.83	0.71
Tang. Book Val. Per Share	6.17	6.35	6.04	6.69	6.09	5.31	5.11
Dividends Per Share	0.56	0.52	0.44	0.38	0.33	0.31	0.26
Dividend Payout %	40.6	40.6	38.1	37.4	47.5	37.0	37.0
INCOME STATEMENT (IN MILLIONS):							
Total Interest Income	1,585.2	1,420.7	1,153.8	987.8	934.9	773.5	644.7
Total Interest Expense	798.8	717.0	571.3	471.2	459.9	315.4	240.8
Net Interest Income	786.4	703.7	582.5	516.6	475.0	458.1	403.9
Provision for Loan Losses	59.4	71.9	62.7	40.3	21.1	0.8	11.7
Non-Interest Income	584.9	512.5	341.2	285.9	266.5	206.6	167.2
Non-Interest Expense	896.4	764.6	554.1	497.4	530.2	442.7	386.1
Income Before Taxes	415.5	383.1	315.3	277.6	190.2	221.2	173.3
Net Income	273.3	① 247.7	205.9	177.8	① 120.0	① 140.1	114.1
Average Shs. Outstg. (000)	198,034	193,840	176,955	174,098	171,718	168,505	161,501
BALANCE SHEET (IN MILLIONS):							
Cash & Due from Banks	926.1	1,026.3	1,180.9	937.1	818.7	678.4	673.9
Securities Avail. for Sale	5,550.9	5,093.2	4,313.2	3,597.8	3,262.0	2,547.6	607.9
Total Loans & Leases	13,805.8	11,621.9	9,672.4	8,932.5	8,315.1	8,173.7	6,561.0
Allowance for Credit Losses	174.4	173.4	149.1	134.4	130.0	133.9	134.8
Net Loans & Leases	13,631.4	11,448.6	9,523.2	8,798.0	8,185.1	8,039.8	6,426.2
Total Assets	22,992.9	21,689.1	17,307.4	14,708.0	13,034.6	12,149.0	10,211.7
Total Deposits	13,210.4	12,658.6	10,716.3	9,439.3	8,773.6	8,053.3	7,503.7
Long-Term Obligations	2,585.8	2,609.6	1,304.5	944.1	720.5	685.4	224.8
Total Liabilities	21,223.0	20,093.6	15,990.0	13,567.4	12,004.3	11,259.5	9,376.0
Net Stockholders' Equity	1,769.9	1,595.5	1,317.4	1,140.6	1,030.3	889.5	835.7
Year-end Shs. Outstg. (000)	195,971	186,712	173,509	170,339	169,049	167,384	163,476
STATISTICAL RECORD:							
Return on Equity %	15.4	15.5	15.6	15.6	11.6	15.8	13.6
Return on Assets %	1.2	1.1	1.2	1.2	0.9	1.2	1.1
Equity/Assets %	7.7	7.4	7.6	7.8	7.9	7.3	8.2
Non-Int. Exp./Tot. Inc. %	65.4	62.9	60.0	62.0	71.5	68.8	67.6
Price Range	31-17½	27¹⁵/₁₆-15½	25¹³/₁₆-14⅛	15⅜-9⅞	11⁷/₁₆-6⁷/₁₆	9¹¹/₁₆-6⅜	9⅛-7¹/₁₆
P/E Ratio	22.5-12.7	21.8-12.1	22.2-12.2	15.1-9.7	16.3-9.2	11.6-7.6	12.9-10.0
Average Yield %	2.3	2.4	2.2	3.0	3.7	3.8	3.2

Statistics are as originally reported. Adj. for stk. splits: 3-for-2, 2/24/98; 3-for-2, 5/15/97; 3-for-2, 2/15/96 ① Incl. non-recurr. chrg. 12/31/98: 8.9 mill.; 12/31/95: $44.0 mill.; credit 12/31/94: $20.9 mill.

OFFICERS:
S. F. Eccles, Chmn., C.E.O.
M. J. Evans, Pres., C.O.O.
B. D. Hardy, Exec. V.P., C.F.O.

INVESTOR CONTACT: Leslie R. Nelson, Sr. V.P., (800) 574-6695

PRINCIPAL OFFICE: 79 South Main, Salt Lake City, UT 84130-0006

TELEPHONE NUMBER: (801) 246-5976
FAX: (801) 359-6928
WEB: www.firstsecuritybank.com
NO. OF EMPLOYEES: 9,602
SHAREHOLDERS: 12,253 (common); 449 (series A preferred)
ANNUAL MEETING: In March
INCORPORATED: DE, June, 1928

INSTITUTIONAL HOLDINGS:
No. of Institutions: 191
Shares Held: 74,622,054
% Held: 38.1

INDUSTRY: State commercial banks (SIC: 6022)

TRANSFER AGENT(S): First Chicago Trust Company of New York, Jersey City, NJ

NASDAQ SYMBOL SRCE
Rec. Pr. 17¾ (5/31/00)

1ST SOURCE CORPORATION

YIELD 2.0%
P/E RATIO 9.5

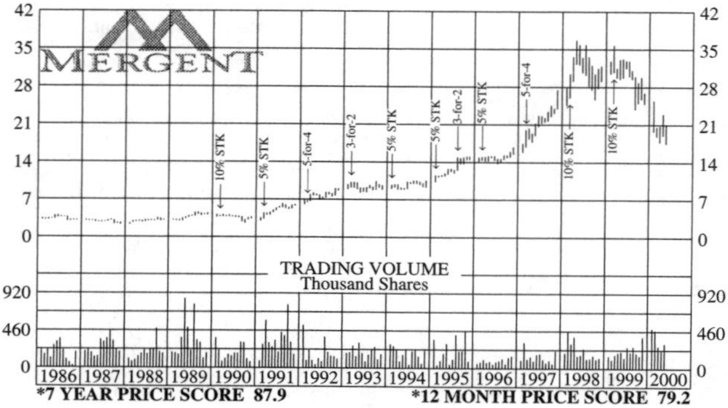

42
35
28
21
14
7
0
10% STK
5% STK
5-for-4
3-for-2
5% STK
5% STK
3-for-2
5% STK
5-for-4
10% STK
10% STK
TRADING VOLUME
Thousand Shares
920
460
0
1986 1987 1988 1989 1990 1991 1992 1993 1994 1995 1996 1997 1998 1999 2000

*7 YEAR PRICE SCORE 87.9 *12 MONTH PRICE SCORE 79.2

*NYSE COMPOSITE INDEX=100

INTERIM EARNINGS (Per Share):

Qtr.	Mar.	June	Sept.	Dec.
1995	0.29	0.21	0.22	0.47
1996	0.28	0.34	0.31	0.39
1997	0.31	0.33	0.34	0.38
1998	0.36	0.38	0.41	0.45
1999	0.44	0.41	0.45	0.56

INTERIM DIVIDENDS (Per Share):

Amt.	Decl.	Ex.	Rec.	Pay.
0.08Q	4/15/99	4/30/99	5/04/99	5/14/99
0.08Q	7/20/99	8/03/99	8/05/99	8/13/99
0.08Q	10/19/99	11/03/99	11/05/99	11/15/99
0.09Q	2/04/00	2/10/00	2/14/00	2/16/00
0.09Q	4/18/00	5/03/00	5/05/00	5/15/00

Indicated div.: $0.36

CAPITALIZATION (12/31/99):

	($000)	(%)
Total Deposits	2,127,452	89.4
Long-Term Debt	12,174	0.5
Common & Surplus	238,820	10.0
Total	2,378,446	100.0

DIVIDEND ACHIEVER STATUS:
Rank: 67 10-Year Growth Rate: 14.73%
Total Years of Dividend Growth: 11

RECENT DEVELOPMENTS: For the year ended 12/31/99, net income increased 13.7% to $35.8 million from $31.5 million in the previous year. Net interest income climbed 6.2% to $99.7 million from $93.9 million the year before. Total interest income inched up 2.2% to $200.4 million from $196.1 million in the prior year. Total interest expense declined 1.5% to $100.7 million from $102.2 million in the previous year. Total noninterest income rose 21.1% to $63.3 million from $52.3 million a year earlier. Noninterest income was positively affected by increased aircraft and auto loan securitization and servicing income and revenues generated from operating leases. Total noninterest expense increased 11.9% to $99.0 million from $85.5 million the year before. Provision for loan losses amounted to $7.4 million in 1999 compared with $9.2 million in 1998.

BUSINESS

1ST SOURCE CORPORATION is a registered bank holding company, and through its subsidiary, 1st Source Bank, provides consumer and commercial banking services to individual and business customers through 50 banking locations in northern Indiana and southwestern Michigan. 1st Source Bank's principal market area consists of nine counties in northern Indiana and three counties in lower Michigan. As of 12/31/99, the Company had assets of $2.87 billion. 1st Source Bank also competes for business nationwide by offering specialized financing services for used private aircraft, automobiles for leasing and rental agencies, heavy duty trucks and construction equipment.

LOAN DISTRIBUTION

(12/31/1999)	($000)	(%)
Commercial & Agricutural	440,909	21.4
Comm Loans Secur By Transportation	896,848	43.5
Loans Secur By Real Estate	591,401	28.6
Consumer Loans	134,031	6.5
Total	2,063,189	100.0

ANNUAL FINANCIAL DATA

	12/31/99	12/31/98	12/31/97	12/31/96	12/31/95	12/31/94	12/31/93
Earnings Per Share	**1.86**	**1.60**	**1.36**	**1.32**	**1.19**	**1.05**	**0.96**
Tang. Book Val. Per Share	**12.54**	**12.48**	**11.18**	**12.41**	**11.59**	**7.46**	**6.44**
Dividends Per Share	**0.31**	**0.28**	**0.25**	**0.22**	**0.19**	**0.17**	**0.14**
Dividend Payout %	**16.8**	**17.4**	**18.4**	**16.6**	**15.8**	**16.0**	**15.1**
INCOME STATEMENT (IN MILLIONS):							
Total Interest Income	200.4	196.1	173.3	148.8	135.1	112.9	104.1
Total Interest Expense	100.7	102.2	87.3	73.4	64.9	47.7	44.6
Net Interest Income	99.7	93.9	86.0	75.4	70.2	65.2	59.5
Provision for Loan Losses	7.4	9.2	6.1	4.6	2.8	4.2	3.5
Non-Interest Income	63.3	51.5	35.7	25.5	19.5	14.9	14.3
Non-Interest Expense	99.0	85.5	73.0	60.6	54.9	49.6	46.4
Income Before Taxes	56.5	50.8	42.6	35.6	32.0	26.3	23.9
Net Income	35.8	31.0	26.5	23.2	21.0	18.5	16.7
Average Shs. Outstg. (000)	19,239	19,371	19,543	17,598	17,637	17,575	17,520
BALANCE SHEET (IN MILLIONS):							
Cash & Due from Banks	101.9	132.5	90.9	137.6	94.5	79.2	77.4
Securities Avail. for Sale	470.0	443.7	299.9	302.6	270.3	245.8	266.8
Total Loans & Leases	2,063.2	1,881.7	1,796.8	1,455.6	1,259.4	1,100.7	1,019.8
Allowance for Credit Losses	40.2	40.9	35.4	29.5	27.5	23.9	22.4
Net Loans & Leases	2,023.0	1,840.8	1,761.4	1,426.0	1,231.9	1,076.8	997.5
Total Assets	2,872.9	2,732.0	2,418.2	2,079.8	1,799.3	1,583.0	1,488.1
Total Deposits	2,127.5	2,177.1	1,891.8	1,634.0	1,441.7	1,301.3	1,179.4
Long-Term Obligations	12.2	13.2	16.7	18.6	21.8	28.1	25.5
Total Liabilities	2,634.1	2,516.2	2,223.2	1,907.9	1,646.7	1,453.9	1,362.6
Net Stockholders' Equity	238.8	215.9	195.0	171.8	152.6	129.1	125.5
Year-end Shs. Outstg. (000)	19,039	17,291	17,444	13,849	13,170	17,313	19,485
STATISTICAL RECORD:							
Return on Equity %	15.0	14.4	13.6	13.5	13.8	14.3	13.3
Return on Assets %	1.2	1.1	1.1	1.1	1.2	1.2	1.1
Equity/Assets %	8.3	7.9	8.1	8.3	8.5	8.2	8.4
Non-Int. Exp./Tot. Inc. %	60.8	58.5	59.8	60.2	61.3	61.6	63.3
Price Range	35¾-23⅞	36 11/16-24 9/16	27½-15⅞	16⅞-13¾	15⅛-10 5/16	10⅝-8⅞	10½-8 5/16
P/E Ratio	19.2-12.8	22.9-15.4	20.2-11.7	12.8-10.4	12.7-8.6	10.1-8.5	11.0-8.7
Average Yield %	1.0	0.9	1.2	1.4	1.5	1.7	1.5

Statistics are as originally reported. Adj. for stk. splits: 10% div., 2/12/99 & 2/13/98; 5-for-4, 2/14/97; 5% div., 2/15/96, 2/15/95 & 2/15/94; 3-for-2, 8/18/95 & 2/15/93.

OFFICERS:
C. J. Murphy III, Chmn., Pres., C.E.O.
L. E. Lentych, C.F.O., Treas.
V. A. Tamburo, Sec., Gen. Counsel.

INVESTOR CONTACT: Larry E. Lentych, C.F.O., (219) 235-2702

PRINCIPAL OFFICE: 100 N. Michigan St., South Bend, IN 46601

TELEPHONE NUMBER: (219) 235-2702
FAX: (219) 235-2912
WEB: www.1stsource.com

NO. OF EMPLOYEES: 1,083 (approx.)

SHAREHOLDERS: 1,146

ANNUAL MEETING: In April

INCORPORATED: IN, Jan., 1922

INSTITUTIONAL HOLDINGS:
No. of Institutions: 39
Shares Held: 11,028,399
% Held: 58.4

INDUSTRY: State commercial banks (SIC: 6022)

TRANSFER AGENT(S): 1st Source Bank, South Bend, IN

NYSE SYMBOL FTN
Rec. Pr. 20½ (5/31/00)

FIRST TENNESSEE NATIONAL CORPORATION

YIELD 4.3%
P/E RATIO 11.1

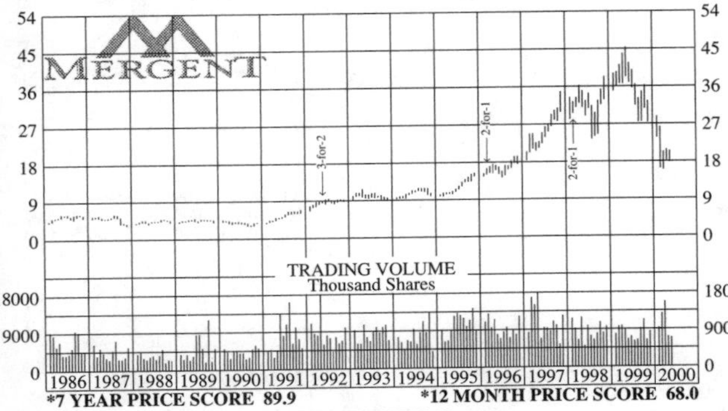

***7 YEAR PRICE SCORE 89.9** ***12 MONTH PRICE SCORE 68.0**

*NYSE COMPOSITE INDEX=100

INTERIM EARNINGS (Per Share):

Qtr.	Mar.	June	Sept.	Dec.
1996	0.28	0.32	0.35	0.40
1997	0.30	0.36	0.43	0.44
1998	0.35	0.40	0.47	0.50
1999	0.40	0.45	0.52	0.48

INTERIM DIVIDENDS (Per Share):

Amt.	Decl.	Ex.	Rec.	Pay.
0.19Q	4/20/99	6/09/99	6/11/99	7/01/99
0.19Q	7/20/99	9/08/99	9/10/99	10/01/99
0.22Q	10/20/99	12/08/99	12/10/99	1/01/00
0.22Q	1/18/00	3/08/00	3/10/00	4/01/00
0.22Q	4/18/00	6/07/00	6/09/00	7/01/00

Indicated div.: $0.88 (Div. Reinv. Plan)

CAPITALIZATION (12/31/99):

	($000)	(%)
Total Deposits	11,358,701	87.7
Long-Term Debt	358,663	2.8
Common & Surplus	1,241,467	9.6
Total	12,958,831	100.0

DIVIDEND ACHIEVER STATUS:
Rank: 105 10-Year Growth Rate: 12.54%
Total Years of Dividend Growth: 22

RECENT DEVELOPMENTS: For the twelve months ended 12/31/99, net income increased 9.3% to $247.5 million from $226.4 million in the previous year. Net interest income climbed 9.1% to $589.5 million compared with $540.5 million in the prior year. The increase was mainly due to strong loan growth, improvement in the regional banking group's net interest margin and increased net interest income from mortgage banking. Total non-interest income was $1.12 billion, up 14.0% from $985.5 million in the previous year. Total non-interest expense grew 13.7% to $1.28 billion from $1.12 billion the year before. Return on average assets slipped to 1.33% from 1.35% a year ago, while net interest margin remained flat at 3.80%. Total loans increased 9.4% to $9.36 billion.

BUSINESS

FIRST TENNESSEE NATIONAL CORPORATION is one of the nation's 50 largest bank holding companies with total assets of $18.40 billion as of 12/31/99. In terms of assets, FTEN is the second largest Tennessee-headquartered bank holding company. The Company provides banking and other financial services through its regional banking group and three national lines of business: FT Mortgage Companies, First Tennessee Capital Markets and transaction processing. Transaction processing includes credit card merchant processing, automated teller machine network, nationwide check clearing operation, and remittance processing. Through its principal subsidiary, First Tennessee Bank National Association, and other banking and bank-related subsidiaries, FTEN operates banking locations in Tennessee, Mississippi and Arkansas.

LOAN DISTRIBUTION

(12/31/99)	($000)	(%)
Commercial	4,430,516	47.3
Consumer	3,281,832	35.1
Permanent Mortgage	528,907	5.6
Credit Card Receivables	607,205	6.5
Real Estate Construction	485,580	5.2
Nonaccrual	29,118	0.3
Total	9,363,158	100.0

ANNUAL FINANCIAL DATA

	12/31/99	12/31/98	12/31/97	12/31/96	12/31/95	12/31/94	12/31/93
Earnings Per Share	**1.85**	**1.72**	**1.50**	**1.34**	**1.21**	**1.14**	**1.07**
Tang. Book Val. Per Share	**2.17**	**2.34**	**3.38**	**4.26**	**4.43**	**1.83**	**1.87**
Dividends Per Share	**0.76**	**0.66**	**0.60**	**0.53**	**0.47**	**0.42**	**0.36**
Dividend Payout %	**41.1**	**38.4**	**40.0**	**39.5**	**38.8**	**36.8**	**33.8**
INCOME STATEMENT (IN MILLIONS):							
Total Interest Income	1,207.2	1,133.8	941.3	896.5	822.5	668.7	586.5
Total Interest Expense	617.7	593.2	458.2	445.3	431.9	288.1	239.9
Net Interest Income	589.5	540.5	483.1	451.2	390.7	380.6	346.6
Provision for Loan Losses	57.9	51.4	51.1	35.7	20.6	16.7	34.5
Non-Interest Income	1,123.1	985.5	668.1	571.1	496.6	389.2	270.5
Non-Interest Expense	1,275.3	1,121.8	785.0	704.5	613.7	545.7	398.4
Income Before Taxes	379.4	352.9	315.1	282.2	253.0	207.3	184.1
Net Income	247.5	226.4	197.5	179.9	164.9	146.3	120.7
Average Shs. Outstg. (000)	133,979	131,862	131,987	134,394	136,050	128,456	113,300
BALANCE SHEET (IN MILLIONS):							
Cash & Due from Banks	956.1	811.9	775.8	959.6	710.9	691.1	602.4
Securities Avail. for Sale	2,479.4	2,174.8	2,386.5	2,324.0	2,219.3	1,321.3	517.1
Total Loans & Leases	9,363.2	8,557.1	8,311.4	7,728.2	8,122.5	6,347.5	5,279.1
Allowance for Credit Losses	139.6	136.0	125.9	117.7	112.6	107.0	114.8
Net Loans & Leases	9,223.6	8,421.1	8,185.5	7,610.5	8,009.9	6,240.5	5,164.3
Total Assets	18,373.4	18,734.0	14,387.9	13,058.9	12,076.9	10,522.4	9,608.8
Total Deposits	11,358.7	11,723.0	9,671.8	9,033.1	8,582.2	7,688.4	7,146.8
Long-Term Obligations	358.7	414.5	168.9	234.6	260.0	93.8	90.0
Total Liabilities	17,131.9	17,634.4	13,433.8	12,104.4	11,203.7	9,773.6	8,929.9
Net Stockholders' Equity	1,241.5	1,099.5	954.1	954.5	873.2	748.8	679.0
Year-end Shs. Outstg. (000)	129,878	128,974	128,209	133,716	134,356	127,412	113,304
STATISTICAL RECORD:							
Return on Equity %	19.9	20.6	20.7	18.8	18.9	19.5	17.8
Return on Assets %	1.3	1.2	1.4	1.4	1.4	1.4	1.3
Equity/Assets %	6.8	5.9	6.6	7.3	7.2	7.1	7.1
Non-Int. Exp./Tot. Inc. %	74.5	73.5	68.2	68.9	69.2	70.9	64.6
Price Range	45 3/8-27 3/8	38 3/8-23 3/8	34 13/16-18 3/8	19 7/16-14 1/4	15 7/16-9 13/16	11 15/16-9 1/4	11 13/16-8 15/16
P/E Ratio	24.5-14.8	22.3-13.6	23.2-12.2	14.5-10.6	12.8-8.1	10.5-8.1	11.1-8.4
Average Yield %	2.1	2.1	2.3	3.1	3.7	4.0	3.5

Statistics are as originally reported. Adj. for stk. splits: 2-for-1, 2/20/98; 2-for-1, 2/16/96.

OFFICERS:
R. Horn, Chmn., Pres., C.E.O.
E. L. Thomas Jr., Exec. V.P., C.F.O.
H. A. Johnson III, Exec. V.P., Gen. Couns.

INVESTOR CONTACT: Marty Mosby, (901) 523-5620

PRINCIPAL OFFICE: 165 Madison Avenue, Memphis, TN 38103

TELEPHONE NUMBER: (901) 523-5630
FAX: (901) 523-4945
WEB: www.ftb.com

NO. OF EMPLOYEES: 10,657

SHAREHOLDERS: 9,893

ANNUAL MEETING: In April

INCORPORATED: TN, 1968

INSTITUTIONAL HOLDINGS:
No. of Institutions: 212
Shares Held: 45,807,202
% Held: 35.1

INDUSTRY: National commercial banks (SIC: 6021)

TRANSFER AGENT(S): Norwest Bank Minnesota, N.A. South St. Paul, MN.

NYSE SYMBOL FTU
Rec. Pr. 35 3/16 (5/31/00)

FIRST UNION CORPORATION

YIELD 5.5%
P/E RATIO 10.6

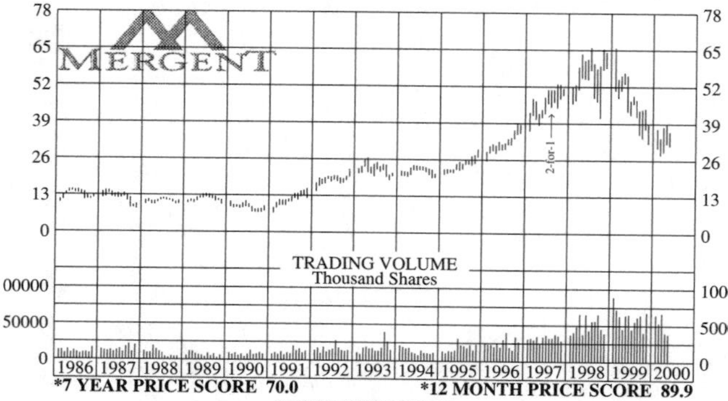

MERGENT
78
65
52
39
26
13
0
TRADING VOLUME
Thousand Shares
100000
50000
2-for-1
1986 1987 1988 1989 1990 1991 1992 1993 1994 1995 1996 1997 1998 1999 2000

*7 YEAR PRICE SCORE 70.0 *12 MONTH PRICE SCORE 89.9

*NYSE COMPOSITE INDEX=100

INTERIM EARNINGS (Per Share):

Qtr.	Mar.	June	Sept.	Dec.
1996	0.42	0.78	0.64	0.83
1997	0.84	0.87	0.90	0.56
1998	0.90	0.26	1.01	0.81
1999	0.73	0.90	0.84	0.86

INTERIM DIVIDENDS (Per Share):

Amt.	Decl.	Ex.	Rec.	Pay.
0.47Q	4/20/99	5/26/99	5/28/99	6/15/99
0.47Q	8/17/99	8/27/99	8/31/99	9/15/99
0.47Q	10/19/99	11/26/99	11/30/99	12/15/99
0.48Q	2/15/00	2/25/00	2/29/00	3/15/00
0.48Q	4/18/00	5/26/00	5/31/00	6/15/00

Indicated div.: $1.92 (Div. Reinv. Plan)

CAPITALIZATION (12/31/99):

	($000)	(%)
Total Deposits	141,047,000	74.3
Long-Term Debt	31,975,000	16.9
Common & Surplus	16,709,000	8.8
Total	189,731,000	100.0

DIVIDEND ACHIEVER STATUS:
Rank: 79 10-Year Growth Rate: 14.16%
Total Years of Dividend Growth: 22

RECENT DEVELOPMENTS: For the year ended 12/31/99, net income advanced 11.5% to $3.22 billion from $2.89 billion in the previous year. Results for 1999 and 1998 included pre-tax merger-related and restructuring charges of $404.0 million and $1.21 billion, respectively. Net interest income rose 2.4% to $7.45 billion from $7.28 billion in the prior year. Fee and other income grew 7.7% to $6.93 billion. Comparisons were made with restated 1998 figures.

PROSPECTS: On 5/9/00, the Company announced that its First Union Securities unit entered into an agreement with First Albany Companies, Inc. to acquire the firm's retail brokerage assets. The transaction, which is expected to be completed in August 2000, will add 200 brokers and 20 additional branch locations, primarily in the Northeastern U.S., as well as approximately 90,000 accounts and $11.40 billion in assets to FTU's retail brokerage unit.

BUSINESS

FIRST UNION CORPORATION, with assets of $253.65 billion as of 3/31/00, provides a wide range of commercial and retail banking and trust services through full-service banking offices in Connecticut, Delaware, Florida, Georgia, Maryland, New Jersey, New York, North Carolina, Pennsylvania, South Carolina, Tennessee, Virginia and Washington, D.C. The Company also provides mortgage banking, credit card, investment banking, investment advisory, home equity lending, asset-based lending, leasing, insurance, international and securities brokerage services through other subsidiaries. During 1998, FTU acquired Wheat First Butcher Singer, Inc., CoreStates Financial Corp., and The Money Store, Inc. On 10/1/99, FTU acquired EVEREN Capital Corporation.

LOAN DISTRIBUTION

(12/31/99)	($000)	(%)
Commercial, Finl & Agric	51,683,000	36.6
Real Est-Constr & Other	2,435,000	1.7
Real Estate-Mortgage	8,768,000	6.2
Lease Financing	12,742,000	9.0
Foreign	4,991,000	3.6
Retail	60,472,000	42.9
Total	141,091,000	100.0

ANNUAL FINANCIAL DATA

	12/31/99	12/31/98	12/31/97	12/31/96	12/31/95	12/31/94	12/31/93
Earnings Per Share	**3.33**	**[3] 2.95**	**[3] 2.99**	**[2] 2.68**	**[1] 2.52**	**2.49**	**2.37**
Tang. Book Val. Per Share	**11.22**	**12.36**	**14.71**	**12.46**	**11.30**	**11.68**	**12.07**
Dividends Per Share	**1.88**	**1.58**	**1.22**	**1.10**	**0.98**	**0.86**	**0.75**
Dividend Payout %	**56.5**	**53.6**	**40.8**	**41.1**	**38.9**	**34.5**	**31.7**
INCOME STATEMENT (IN MILLIONS):							
Total Interest Income	15,151.0	14,988.0	10,933.0	9,628.0	8,686.4	5,094.7	4,556.3
Total Interest Expense	7,699.0	7,711.0	5,190.0	4,632.0	4,051.8	2,060.9	1,790.4
Net Interest Income	7,452.0	7,277.0	5,743.0	4,996.0	4,634.6	3,033.7	2,765.9
Provision for Loan Losses	692.0	691.0	840.0	375.0	220.0	100.0	221.8
Non-Interest Income	6,933.0	6,555.0	3,396.0	2,357.0	1,896.5	1,159.0	1,198.3
Non-Interest Expense	8,862.0	9,176.0	5,692.0	4,668.0	4,092.5	2,677.2	2,521.6
Income Before Taxes	4,831.0	3,965.0	2,710.0	2,310.0	2,218.6	1,415.5	1,220.8
Net Income	3,223.0	[3] 2,891.0	[3] 1,793.0	[2] 1,499.0	[1] 1,430.2	925.4	817.5
Average Shs. Outstg. (000)	966,863	980,000	634,000	557,624	557,354	345,086	335,384
BALANCE SHEET (IN MILLIONS):							
Cash & Due from Banks	10,081.0	11,192.0	6,445.0	6,509.0	6,312.1	3,740.7	3,352.0
Securities Avail. for Sale	66,223.0	47,193.0	26,872.0	18,116.0	20,074.8	8,959.2	12,397.4
Total Loans & Leases	142,829.0	139,409.0	100,259.0	98,064.0	92,108.8	54,702.1	47,210.2
Allowance for Credit Losses	7,282.0	5,852.0	4,598.0	3,571.0	3,053.8	1,651.1	1,354.3
Net Loans & Leases	135,547.0	133,557.0	95,661.0	94,493.0	89,055.1	53,051.0	45,856.0
Total Assets	254,762.0	237,363.0	157,274.0	140,127.0	131,879.9	77,313.5	70,787.0
Total Deposits	141,047.0	142,467.0	102,889.0	94,815.0	92,555.2	58,958.3	53,742.4
Long-Term Obligations	31,975.0	22,949.0	9,033.0	8,155.0	7,120.9	3,428.5	3,061.9
Total Liabilities	236,315.0	220,190.0	145,242.0	130,119.0	122,836.7	71,916.0	65,579.3
Net Stockholders' Equity	16,709.0	17,173.0	12,032.0	10,008.0	9,043.1	5,397.5	5,207.6
Year-end Shs. Outstg. (000)	988,000	982,000	636,000	574,696	555,692	352,068	340,676
STATISTICAL RECORD:							
Return on Equity %	19.3	16.8	14.9	15.0	15.8	17.1	15.7
Return on Assets %	1.3	1.2	1.1	1.1	1.1	1.2	1.2
Equity/Assets %	6.6	7.2	7.7	7.1	6.9	7.0	7.4
Non-Int. Exp./Tot. Inc. %	61.6	66.3	62.3	63.5	62.7	63.9	63.6
Price Range	65 3/4-32	65 15/16-40 15/16	53-36 5/16	38 7/8-25 9/16	29 3/4-20 11/16	24-19 1/2	26 9/16-18 5/8
P/E Ratio	19.7-9.6	22.4-13.9	17.7-12.1	14.5-9.6	11.8-8.2	9.6-7.8	11.2-7.9
Average Yield %	3.8	3.0	2.7	3.4	3.9	4.0	3.3

Statistics are as originally reported. Adj. for 2-for-1 stk. split, 7/97. [1] Incl. merger with First Fidelity and after-tax merger-related charges of $72.8 mill. [2] Incl. pre-tax SAIF chrg. of $133.0 mill. and merger-related chrgs. of $281.0 mill. [3] Incl. pre-tax restruct. chrgs. of $404.0 mill., 1999; $1.21 bill., 1998; $269.0 mill., 1997.

OFFICERS:
E. E. Crutchfield, Chmn.
G. K. Thompson, Pres., C.E.O.
R. T. Atwood, Exec. V.P., C.F.O.

INVESTOR CONTACT: Alice Lehman, Managing Dir. of Corp. Relations, (704) 374-2137

PRINCIPAL OFFICE: One First Union Center, Charlotte, NC 28288-0570

TELEPHONE NUMBER: (704) 374-6565
FAX: (704) 374-4609
WEB: www.firstunion.com

NO. OF EMPLOYEES: 71,659 (avg.)

SHAREHOLDERS: 168,989

ANNUAL MEETING: In Apr.

INCORPORATED: NC, Dec., 1967

INSTITUTIONAL HOLDINGS:
No. of Institutions: 619
Shares Held: 483,738,650
% Held: 49.0

INDUSTRY: National commercial banks (SIC: 6021)

TRANSFER AGENT(S): First Union National Bank, Charlotte, NC

NYSE SYMBOL FVB
Rec. Pr. 39 11/16 (5/31/00)

FIRST VIRGINIA BANKS, INC.

YIELD 3.7%
P/E RATIO 13.2

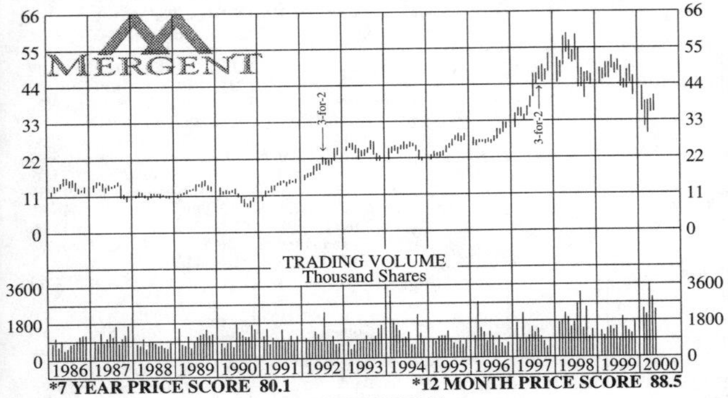

MERGENT
66
55
44
33
22
11
0
3-for-2
3-for-2
TRADING VOLUME
Thousand Shares
3600
1800
0
1986 1987 1988 1989 1990 1991 1992 1993 1994 1995 1996 1997 1998 1999 2000

***7 YEAR PRICE SCORE 80.1** ***12 MONTH PRICE SCORE 88.5**

*NYSE COMPOSITE INDEX=100

INTERIM EARNINGS (Per Share):

Qtr.	Mar.	June	Sept.	Dec.
1996	0.56	0.57	0.58	0.63
1997	0.61	0.63	0.67	0.56
1998	0.61	0.62	0.62	0.68
1999	0.88	0.68	0.75	0.70

INTERIM DIVIDENDS (Per Share):

Amt.	Decl.	Ex.	Rec.	Pay.
0.34Q	5/26/99	6/28/99	6/30/99	7/19/99
0.34Q	8/25/99	9/28/99	9/30/99	10/18/99
0.36Q	11/17/99	12/29/99	12/31/99	1/10/00
0.36Q	2/23/00	3/29/00	3/31/00	4/17/00
0.37Q	5/24/00	6/28/00	6/30/00	7/17/00

Indicated div.: $1.48 (Div. Reinv. Plan)

CAPITALIZATION (12/31/99):

	($000)	(%)
Total Deposits	7,863,948	88.4
Long-Term Debt	2,205	0.0
Preferred Stock	485	0.0
Common & Surplus	1,030,002	11.6
Total	8,896,640	100.0

DIVIDEND ACHIEVER STATUS:
Rank: 164 10-Year Growth Rate: 9.67%
Total Years of Dividend Growth: 22

RECENT DEVELOPMENTS: For the year ended 12/31/99, net income advanced 15.9% to $150.9 million from $130.2 million in the prior year. Earnings for 1999 included a pre-tax gain of $17.9 million from the sale of the Company's credit card portfolio. Net interest income rose 1.0% to $433.7 million from $429.3 million a year earlier. Non-interest income, including the above gain, grew 17.0% to $136.6 million.

PROSPECTS: Looking ahead, the Company expects to continue to perform well due to the significant growth in FVB's automobile financing activities, which reflects the Company's new system of processing loans on-line. In addition, the Company continues to experience increases in commercial lending to businesses in its markets, as well as in non-lending activities, including cash management, item processing, insurance and asset management services.

BUSINESS

FIRST VIRGINIA BANKS, INC., with assets of approximately $9.52 billion as of 3/31/00, provides retail, commercial, international, and mortgage banking; insurance; trust and asset management services; and personal investment services through its subsidiaries. There are 10 banks in the First Virginia group, including six banks with 309 offices in Virginia, two banks with 58 offices in Maryland and two banks with 27 offices in East Tennessee. FVB also operates two mortgage subsidiaries, First Virginia Mortgage Company and First General Mortgage Company, with 10 offices in the Mid-Atlantic and Southeastern states. In addition, FVB operates a full-service insurance agency, First Virginia Insurance Services, Inc.

LOAN DISTRIBUTION

(12/31/99)	($000)	(%)
Consumer	4,317,239	67.6
Real Estate	1,463,850	22.9
Commercial	604,311	9.5
Total	6,385,400	100.0

ANNUAL FINANCIAL DATA

	12/31/99	12/31/98	12/31/97	12/31/96	12/31/95	12/31/94	12/31/93
Earnings Per Share	**③ 3.00**	**2.53**	**② 2.45**	**① 2.33**	**2.19**	**2.34**	**2.38**
Tang. Book Val. Per Share	**17.49**	**16.07**	**16.13**	**15.98**	**15.19**	**14.11**	**13.85**
Dividends Per Share	**1.32**	**1.16**	**1.02**	**0.95**	**0.89**	**0.84**	**0.72**
Dividend Payout %	**44.0**	**45.8**	**41.6**	**40.6**	**40.8**	**35.9**	**30.3**
INCOME STATEMENT (IN MILLIONS):							
Total Interest Income	640.6	663.6	631.1	587.2	573.6	503.6	504.8
Total Interest Expense	206.9	234.3	222.9	212.3	215.5	161.6	165.0
Net Interest Income	433.7	429.3	408.2	374.9	358.1	342.0	339.8
Provision for Loan Losses	14.2	20.8	17.2	17.7	8.3	6.5	6.5
Non-Interest Income	136.6	116.8	103.6	98.5	89.9	84.7	82.5
Non-Interest Expense	327.3	325.7	303.2	279.3	271.4	252.5	245.8
Income Before Taxes	228.8	199.6	191.3	176.3	168.3	167.8	170.1
Net Income	③ 150.9	130.2	② 124.8	① 116.3	111.6	113.2	116.0
Average Shs. Outstg. (000)	50,238	51,529	50,880	49,905	51,084	48,422	48,768
BALANCE SHEET (IN MILLIONS):							
Cash & Due from Banks	441.8	377.4	385.8	378.2	397.9	420.7	326.1
Securities Avail. for Sale	227.0	286.1	243.2	323.6	299.5	30.0	235.0
Total Loans & Leases	6,385.4	6,093.2	5,938.0	5,364.8	5,038.1	5,352.5	4,345.8
Allowance for Credit Losses	70.1	70.3	68.1	62.8	57.9	414.2	378.6
Net Loans & Leases	6,315.3	6,022.9	5,869.9	5,302.0	4,980.2	4,938.3	3,967.2
Total Assets	9,451.8	9,564.7	9,011.6	8,236.1	8,221.5	7,865.4	7,036.9
Total Deposits	7,863.9	8,055.1	7,619.8	7,042.7	7,056.1	6,815.8	6,136.4
Long-Term Obligations	2.2	3.2	2.8	3.9	2.7	3.8	1.0
Total Liabilities	8,421.3	8,574.4	8,000.5	7,364.8	7,351.9	7,058.5	6,345.4
Net Stockholders' Equity	1,030.5	990.3	1,011.2	871.3	869.6	806.9	691.5
Year-end Shs. Outstg. (000)	49,162	50,094	51,817	48,612	50,927	51,075	48,666
STATISTICAL RECORD:							
Return on Equity %	14.6	13.1	12.3	13.4	12.8	14.0	16.8
Return on Assets %	1.6	1.4	1.4	1.4	1.4	1.4	1.6
Equity/Assets %	10.9	10.4	11.2	10.6	10.6	10.3	9.8
Non-Int. Exp./Tot. Inc. %	57.5	59.8	59.3	59.2	60.6	59.3	58.3
Price Range	52 5/8-40 1/2	59 7/16-39 11/16	53 3/8-30 13/16	32 11/16-25 1/2	29 5/16-21 5/16	26 15/16-21 1/16	27 5/16-21 3/16
P/E Ratio	17.5-13.5	23.5-15.7	21.8-12.6	14.0-10.9	13.4-9.8	11.5-9.0	11.5-8.9
Average Yield %	2.8	2.3	2.4	3.3	3.5	3.5	3.0

Statistics are as originally reported. Adj. for 3-for-2 split, 9/97 ① Incl. one-time pre-tax SAIF chg. of $1.1 mill. ② Incl. $2.1 mill. gain from the sale of seven offices. ③ Incl. a pre-tax gain of $17.9 million from the sale of the Company's credit card portfolio.

OFFICERS:
B. J. Fitzpatrick, Chmn., Pres., C.E.O.
R. F. Bowman, Exec. V.P., C.F.O., Treas.
T. P. Jennings, Sr. V.P., Gen. Couns.

INVESTOR CONTACT: Thomas P. Jennings, Sr. V.P., Gen. Couns. & Sec., (800) 995-9416

PRINCIPAL OFFICE: 6400 Arlington Blvd., Falls Church, VA 22042-2336

TELEPHONE NUMBER: (703) 241-4000
FAX: (703) 241-3360
WEB: www.firstvirginia.com

NO. OF EMPLOYEES: 5,117 full-time; 563 part-time

SHAREHOLDERS: 19,825

ANNUAL MEETING: In Apr.

INCORPORATED: VA, Oct., 1949

INSTITUTIONAL HOLDINGS:
No. of Institutions: 141
Shares Held: 13,460,156
% Held: 27.1

INDUSTRY: State commercial banks (SIC: 6022)

TRANSFER AGENT(S): Registrar and Transfer Company, Cranford, NJ

FIRSTAR CORPORATION

YIELD 2.5%
P/E RATIO 32.0

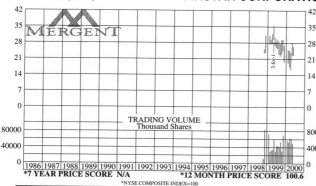

TRADING VOLUME
Thousand Shares

| | 1986 | 1987 | 1988 | 1989 | 1990 | 1991 | 1992 | 1993 | 1994 | 1995 | 1996 | 1997 | 1998 | 1999 | 2000 |

*7 YEAR PRICE SCORE N/A   *12 MONTH PRICE SCORE 100.6

*NYSE COMPOSITE INDEX=100

INTERIM EARNINGS (Per Share):

Qtr.	Mar.	June	Sept.	Dec.
1996	----	----	0.65	----
1997	0.19	0.20	0.21	0.22
1998	0.21	0.22	0.19	0.02
1999	0.25	0.25	0.03	0.27

INTERIM DIVIDENDS (Per Share):

Amt.	Decl.	Ex.	Rec.	Pay.
3-for-1	3/09/99	4/16/99	3/31/99	4/15/99
0.10Q	6/08/99	6/28/99	6/30/99	7/15/99
0.10Q	9/14/99	9/15/99	9/17/99	10/15/99
0.163Q	12/14/99	12/29/99	12/31/99	1/15/00
0.163Q	3/14/00	3/29/00	3/31/00	4/14/00

Indicated div.: $0.65 (Div. Reinv. Plan)

CAPITALIZATION (12/31/99):

	($000)	(%)
Total Deposits	51,886,411	82.1
Long-Term Debt	5,038,383	8.0
Common & Surplus	6,308,636	10.0
Total	63,233,430	100.0

DIVIDEND ACHIEVER STATUS:

Rank: 52   10-Year Growth Rate: 15.98%
Total Years of Dividend Growth: 21

RECENT DEVELOPMENTS:

For the year ended 12/31/99, net income rose 8.7% to $875.3 million compared with $805.5 million in the previous year. Earnings for 1999 and 1998 included pre-tax merger-related charges of $470.5 million and $377.3 million, respectively. Net interest income rose 4.2% to $2.64 billion from $2.54 billion a year earlier. Total non-interest income increased 2.7% to $1.40 billion. Net interest margin grew to 4.17% from 4.07% in the prior year. Comparisons were made with restated 1998 figures.

PROSPECTS:

FSR remains on schedule with the integration of Mercantile Bancorporation Inc., and has successfully completed a number of systems conversions. In connection with the merger, the Company anticipates a total of $560.0 million of restructuring and merger-related charges. In the first quarter of 2000, FSR outsourced the brokerage business of Mercantile Bancorporation and expects an incremental annual reduction in expenses of $6.0 million, as well a $4.5 million decrease in non-interest income.

BUSINESS

FIRSTAR CORPORATION, with $73.06 billion in assets as of 3/31/00, is a regional, multi-state bank holding company headquartered in Milwaukee, Wisconsin. The Company owns approximately 1,200 full-service banking offices and more than 2,200 ATM locations in Wisconsin, Ohio, Iowa, Minnesota, Illinois, Indiana, Iowa, Kentucky, Tennessee, Arizona, Florida, Missouri, Arkansas, and Kansas. The Company offers banking, trust, investment, insurance, securities brokerage and other financial services. On 11/20/98, Firstar completed the merger with Star Bancorp. On 9/20/99, Firstar completed the merger with Mercantile Bancorporation, Inc.

LOAN DISTRIBUTION

(12/31/99)	($000)	(%)
Commercial	17,346,596	34.3
Real Estate	19,815,017	39.1
Retail	13,464,395	26.6
Total	50,626,008	100.0

ANNUAL FINANCIAL DATA

	[4] 12/31/99	[3] 12/31/98	[3] 12/31/97	[3] 12/31/96
Earnings Per Share	[1] 0.87	[1] 0.65	[2] 0.81	[1] 0.65
Tang. Book Val. Per Share	6.47	5.38	4.45	...
Dividends Per Share	0.40	0.30	0.27	0.25
Dividend Payout %	46.0	46.2	33.3	38.5
INCOME STATEMENT (IN MILLIONS):				
Total Interest Income	5,021.7	2,641.5	2,377.1	2,275.7
Total Interest Expense	2,378.6	1,228.7	1,074.9	1,023.4
Net Interest Income	2,643.1	1,412.8	1,302.2	1,252.3
Provision for Loan Losses	187.3	113.6	117.8	97.3
Non-Interest Income	1,402.6	860.1	712.0	621.4
Non-Interest Expense	2,445.8	1,521.2	1,126.5	1,152.3
Income Before Taxes	1,412.6	638.1	769.9	624.1
Net Income	[1] 875.3	[1] 430.1	[2] 513.9	[1] 415.4
Average Shs. Outstg. (000)	1,002,754	663,054	634,149	633,858
BALANCE SHEET (IN MILLIONS):				
Cash & Due from Banks	3,288.3	2,349.5	1,902.5	...
Securities Avail. for Sale	13,816.3	6,299.2	3,322.0	...
Total Loans & Leases	50,626.0	25,868.1	23,216.0	...
Allowance for Credit Losses	714.9	396.0	372.9	...
Net Loans & Leases	49,911.1	25,472.1	22,843.1	...
Total Assets	72,787.8	38,475.8	32,860.4	...
Total Deposits	51,886.4	28,850.8	24,486.1	...
Long-Term Obligations	5,038.4	1,708.9	1,744.8	...
Total Liabilities	66,479.2	34,945.9	30,110.6	...
Net Stockholders' Equity	6,308.6	3,529.9	2,749.9	...
Year-end Shs. Outstg. (000)	975,546	656,241	617,070	633,756
STATISTICAL RECORD:				
Return on Equity %	13.9	12.2	18.7	...
Return on Assets %	1.2	1.1	1.6	...
Equity/Assets %	8.7	9.2	8.4	...
Non-Int. Exp./Tot. Inc. %	60.5	66.9	55.9	61.5
Price Range	35 5/16-19 9/16	31 5/16-23 1/2	...	...
P/E Ratio	40.6-22.5	48.2-36.1	...	...
Average Yield %	1.5	...	...	...

Statistics are as originally reported. Adj. for stk. split: 3-for-1, 4/99. [1] Incl. pre-tax merger & restruct. chrgs.: $470.5 mill., 1999; $243.0 mill., 1998; $53.3 mill., 1996. [2] Incl. a gain of $22.8 mill. from the sale of merchant processing. [3] Results have been restated to reflect the 11/20/98 merger of Star Banc and Firstar Corporation (Old); Dividend Achiever Status reflects Firstar Corporation (Old). [4] Refl. merger with Mercantile Bancorporation, Inc.

OFFICERS:

T. H. Jacobsen, Chmn.
D. M. Moffett, Vice-Chmn., C.F.O.
J. A. Grundhofer, Pres., C.E.O.

INVESTOR CONTACT: Joseph D. Messinger, Sr. Vice Pres.-Inv. Rel., (414) 765-5235

PRINCIPAL OFFICE: 777 East Wisconsin Avenue, Milwaukee, WI 53202

TELEPHONE NUMBER: (414) 765-4321
FAX: (414) 765-4349
WEB: www.firstar.com

NO. OF EMPLOYEES: 24,000

SHAREHOLDERS: 46,000

ANNUAL MEETING: In Apr.

INCORPORATED: WI, Sep., 1999

INSTITUTIONAL HOLDINGS:
No. of Institutions: 423
Shares Held: 453,073,524
% Held: 46.2

INDUSTRY: Commercial banks, nec (SIC: 6029)

TRANSFER AGENT(S): Firstar Bank Milwaukee, NA, Milwaukee, WI

NASDAQ SYMBOL FMER
Rec. Pr. 18 15/16 (5/31/00)

FIRSTMERIT CORPORATION

YIELD 4.6%
P/E RATIO 14.5

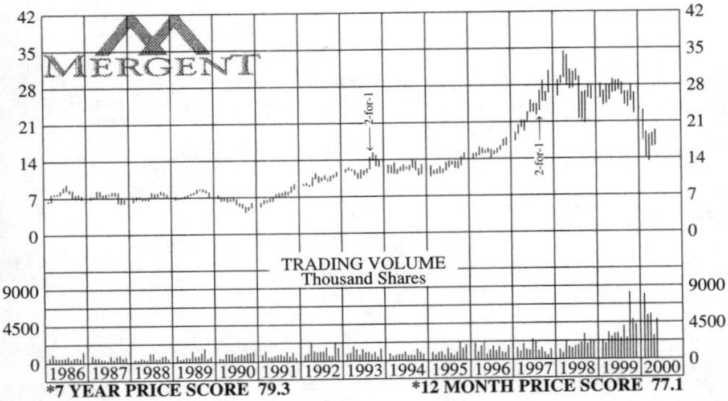

*7 YEAR PRICE SCORE 79.3 *12 MONTH PRICE SCORE 77.1

*NYSE COMPOSITE INDEX=100

INTERIM EARNINGS (Per Share):

Qtr.	Mar.	June	Sept.	Dec
1996	0.29	0.30	0.21	0.30
1997	0.32	0.34	0.35	0.36
1998	0.35	0.38	0.38	0.23
1999	Nil	0.41	0.44	0.46

INTERIM DIVIDENDS (Per Share):

Amt.	Decl.	Ex.	Rec.	Pay.
0.18Q	5/20/99	5/27/99	6/01/99	6/21/99
0.20Q	8/19/99	8/26/99	8/30/99	9/20/99
0.20Q	11/18/99	11/24/99	11/29/99	12/20/99
0.20Q	2/17/00	2/24/00	2/28/00	3/20/00
0.22Q	5/18/00	5/25/00	5/30/00	6/19/00

Indicated div.: $0.88 (Div. Reinv. Plan)

CAPITALIZATION (12/31/99):

	($000)	(%)
Total Deposits	6,860,147	88.9
Redeemable Pfd. Stock	21,450	0.3
Preferred Stock	3,878	0.1
Common & Surplus	829,697	10.8
Total	7,715,172	100.0

DIVIDEND ACHIEVER STATUS:
Rank: 214 10-Year Growth Rate: 7.59%
Total Years of Dividend Growth: 17

RECENT DEVELOPMENTS: For the year ended 12/31/99, net income before an extraordinary item totaled $125.7 million compared with $72.5 million in 1998. Results for 1999 and 1998 included merger-related charges of $33.6 million and $17.2 million, respectively. In addition, results for 1998 included a loss on the sale of a subsidiary of $8.4 million. Net interest income rose 7.8% to $384.0 million. The increase was attributed to volume gains, as average earning assets increased 11.4%, partially offset by increases in funding rates. Total interest income increased 6.6% to $684.9 million from $642.6 million in the previous year. Total interest expense increased 5.1% to $300.9 million from $286.4 million in 1998. Total other income rose 10.4% to $154.7 million from $140.1 million a year earlier. Comparisons were made with restated prior-year figures.

BUSINESS

FIRSTMERIT CORPORATION is a multi-bank holding company with approximately $10.10 billion in assets as of 12/31/99. The Company, through its affiliates, operates principally as a regional banking organization, providing banking, fiduciary, financial, insurance and investment services to corporate, institutional and individual customers throughout northeastern and Central Ohio. At 12/31/99, FirstMerit Bank, N.A., one of the Company's subsidiaries, operated 170 full-service banking offices and 184 automated teller machines. FMER acquired Signal Corp. on 2/12/99.

LOAN DISTRIBUTION

(12/31/99)	($000)	(%)
Commercial, Fin. & Agriculture	1,563,142	22.3
Loans to Individuals	1,506,334	21.5
Loans Secured by Real Estate	3,672,275	52.4
Lease Financing	272,430	3.8
Total	7,014,181	100.0

ANNUAL FINANCIAL DATA

	12/31/99	12/31/98	12/31/97	12/31/96	12/31/95	12/31/94	12/31/93
Earnings Per Share	**2 1.31**	**1.34**	**1.36**	**1.09**	**1 0.39**	**1.11**	**1.10**
Tang. Book Val. Per Share	**9.39**	**10.39**	**8.56**	**8.19**	**8.10**	**7.94**	**7.76**
Dividends Per Share	**0.76**	**0.66**	**0.61**	**0.55**	**0.51**	**0.49**	**0.45**
Dividend Payout %	**58.0**	**49.3**	**44.8**	**50.5**	**132.4**	**44.4**	**41.1**
INCOME STATEMENT (IN MILLIONS):							
Total Interest Income	684.9	503.1	407.8	411.7	416.6	316.8	277.7
Total Interest Expense	300.9	197.7	152.4	160.8	180.9	115.9	93.2
Net Interest Income	384.0	305.4	255.5	251.0	235.7	200.9	184.5
Provision for Loan Losses	37.4	28.4	21.6	17.8	19.8	4.5	6.6
Non-Interest Income	154.7	110.5	83.6	82.5	68.5	56.9	54.3
Non-Interest Expense	316.5	242.7	191.1	209.7	227.8	167.0	151.5
Income Before Taxes	184.8	144.8	126.4	106.0	56.7	86.4	80.7
Net Income	2 125.7	97.5	86.4	70.9	1 25.7	60.3	55.2
Average Shs. Outstg. (000)	91,523	72,703	63,537	65,216	66,908	54,304	50,438
BALANCE SHEET (IN MILLIONS):							
Cash & Due from Banks	215.1	246.0	166.7	222.2	287.7	222.5	222.3
Total Loans & Leases	7,014.2	4,997.4	3,834.9	3,656.0	3,770.4	3,179.9	2,396.5
Allowance for Credit Losses	104.9	78.9	53.8	49.3	46.8	33.1	31.2
Net Loans & Leases	6,909.3	4,918.4	3,781.1	3,606.7	3,723.5	3,146.8	2,365.2
Total Assets	10,115.5	7,127.4	5,307.5	5,228.0	5,596.5	4,924.2	3,996.7
Total Deposits	6,860.1	5,461.6	4,255.2	4,204.9	4,501.9	3,862.8	3,427.2
Total Liabilities	9,281.9	6,358.7	4,777.1	4,704.3	5,053.6	4,492.6	3,605.1
Net Stockholders' Equity	833.6	768.6	530.3	523.7	542.9	431.5	391.6
Year-end Shs. Outstg. (000)	88,375	74,009	61,967	63,912	66,996	54,332	50,498
STATISTICAL RECORD:							
Return on Equity %	15.1	12.7	16.3	13.5	4.7	14.0	14.1
Return on Assets %	1.2	1.4	1.6	1.4	0.5	1.2	1.4
Equity/Assets %	8.2	10.8	10.0	10.0	9.7	8.8	9.8
Non-Int. Exp./Tot. Inc. %	58.8	58.4	56.4	62.9	74.9	64.8	63.4
Price Range	29 1/8-22 9/16	34 3/8-20 3/4	30 3/4-17 3/8	18-13 7/8	15 1/4-10 3/4	13 7/8-10 7/8	15 3/8-10 3/8
P/E Ratio	22.2-17.2	25.7-15.5	22.6-12.8	16.5-12.7	39.6-27.8	12.5-9.8	14.0-9.5
Average Yield %	2.9	2.4	2.5	3.5	3.9	4.0	3.5

Statistics are as originally reported. Adj. for stk. splits: 2-for-1, 9/29/97; 2-for-1, 9/27/93
1 Bef. extraord. credit $5.6 mill. ($0.09/sh.) 2 Bef. extraord. chrg. of $5.8 mill.

OFFICERS:
J. R. Cochran, Chmn., C.E.O.
S. A. Bostic, Pres., C.O.O.
T. Bichsel, Exec. V.P., C.F.O.
T. E. Patton, Exec. V.P., Couns., Sec.

INVESTOR CONTACT: Terry E. Patton, Secretary, (330) 996-6300

PRINCIPAL OFFICE: III Cascade Plaza, 7th Floor, Akron, OH 44308-1103

TELEPHONE NUMBER: (330) 996-6300
FAX: (330) 253-1849
WEB: www.fmer.com

NO. OF EMPLOYEES: 2,300 (approx.)

SHAREHOLDERS: 11,350 (approx.)

ANNUAL MEETING: In Apr.

INCORPORATED: OH, Nov., 1981

INSTITUTIONAL HOLDINGS:
No. of Institutions: 113
Shares Held: 22,888,673
% Held: 25.5

INDUSTRY: National commercial banks (SIC: 6021)

TRANSFER AGENT(S): FirstMerit Bank, N.A., Akron, Ohio.

FLEETWOOD ENTERPRISES, INC.

YIELD 5.3%
P/E RATIO 5.3

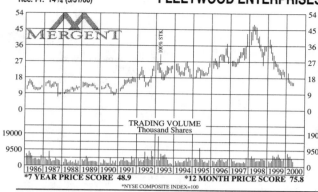

*7 YEAR PRICE SCORE 48.9   *12 MONTH PRICE SCORE 75.8
*NYSE COMPOSITE INDEX=100

TRADING VOLUME Thousand Shares

INTERIM EARNINGS (Per Share):

Qtr.	July	Oct.	Jan.	Apr.
1996-97	0.64	0.68	0.38	0.60
1997-98	0.84	0.77	0.57	0.81
1998-99	0.86	0.84	0.59	0.66
1999-00	0.72	0.84	0.48	...

INTERIM DIVIDENDS (Per Share):

Amt.	Decl.	Ex.	Rec.	Pay.
0.19Q	6/08/99	6/30/99	7/02/99	8/11/99
0.19Q	9/14/99	9/29/99	10/01/99	11/10/99
0.19Q	12/14/99	1/05/00	1/07/00	2/09/00
0.19Q	3/14/00	4/05/00	4/07/00	5/10/00

Indicated div.: $0.76

CAPITALIZATION (4/25/99):

	($000)	(%)
Long-Term Debt	55,000	5.6
Deferred Income Tax	60,832	6.1
Redeemable Pfd. Stock	287,500	29.0
Common & Surplus	586,703	59.3
Total	990,035	100.0

DIVIDEND ACHIEVER STATUS:
Rank: 207   10-Year Growth Rate: 7.77%
Total Years of Dividend Growth: 17

RECENT DEVELOPMENTS: For the quarter ended 1/30/00, net income declined 25.2% to $15.9 million compared with $21.3 million in the equivalent 1999 quarter. Manufactured housing operating income, before elimination of intercompany profits, declined 25.0% to $20.4 million from $27.2 million in 1998. Net sales were $852.3 million, up 5.9% from $804.4 million a year earlier driven by growth in sales of recreational vehicles.

PROSPECTS: Industry wholesale shipments to manufactured housing retailers continue to decline due to overcapacity and excess inventories in the retail sector. As a result, lenders have increased credit standards and down payment requirements for retail buyers. These actions combined with higher interest rates have eliminated many potential buyers of manufactured homes.

BUSINESS

FLEETWOOD ENTERPRISES, INC. is a producer of recreational vehicles and manufactured homes. FLE's motor homes, travel trailers, folding trailers and slide-in truck campers are used for leisure-time activities, including vacation, sightseeing and fishing trips. FLE operates manufacturing plants in 18 U.S. states and in Canada. Products are marketed through independent dealers. For the fiscal year ended 4/25/99, sales were derived: manufactured housing, 49.2%; RVs, 49.6%; and supply operations, 1.2%. In May 1996, the Company sold its RV finance subsidiary, Fleetwood Credit Corp.

ANNUAL FINANCIAL DATA

	4/25/99	4/26/98	4/27/97	4/28/96	4/30/95	4/24/94	4/25/93
Earnings Per Share	2.94	④ 3.01	③ 2.30	② 1.50	1.82	① 1.43	1.23
Cash Flow Per Share	3.46	3.69	3.00	2.09	2.34	1.90	1.61
Tang. Book Val. Per Share	9.63	11.96	12.40	14.22	13.20	11.88	11.01
Dividends Per Share	0.70	0.66	0.62	0.58	0.53	0.49	0.45
Dividend Payout %	23.8	21.9	27.0	38.7	29.1	34.3	36.6
INCOME STATEMENT (IN MILLIONS):							
Total Revenues	3,490.2	3,050.6	2,874.4	2,809.3	2,855.7	2,369.4	1,941.9
Costs & Expenses	3,268.0	2,852.6	2,707.3	2,650.7	2,694.6	2,244.6	1,841.1
Depreciation & Amort.	31.8	27.8	27.6	27.1	24.1	20.4	17.3
Operating Income	190.3	170.2	139.6	131.5	136.9	104.4	83.5
Net Interest Inc./(Exp.)	d9.8	d3.6	d4.0	d1.4	d4.0	d2.5	d2.0
Income Before Income Taxes	178.9	174.9	147.1	111.0	142.1	112.0	91.3
Income Taxes	71.8	66.4	57.0	41.5	58.3	45.9	34.8
Equity Earnings/Minority Int.	...	...	...	0.5	0.8	1.3	0.1
Net Income	107.1	④ 108.5	③ 90.1	② 69.9	84.6	① 67.4	56.6
Cash Flow	139.0	136.3	117.6	97.0	108.8	87.8	73.9
Average Shs. Outstg. (000)	40,171	36,933	39,162	46,469	46,531	46,207	45,961
BALANCE SHEET (IN MILLIONS):							
Cash & Cash Equivalents	257.3	284.1	110.4	287.9	198.2	158.5	158.5
Total Current Assets	820.2	682.9	437.0	696.7	950.8	886.4	786.1
Net Property	303.9	277.2	278.3	266.6	263.1	220.8	172.4
Total Assets	1,531.2	1,129.5	871.5	1,108.9	1,345.1	1,224.1	1,061.9
Total Current Liabilities	514.7	325.8	225.8	197.6	574.8	534.9	438.7
Long-Term Obligations	55.0	55.0	55.0	80.0	...	...	...
Net Stockholders' Equity	586.7	376.0	443.1	649.1	608.1	546.5	502.6
Net Working Capital	305.5	357.0	211.3	499.1	376.0	351.5	347.4
Year-end Shs. Outstg. (000)	35,198	31,451	35,747	45,640	46,062	45,996	45,667
STATISTICAL RECORD:							
Operating Profit Margin %	5.5	5.6	4.9	4.7	4.8	4.4	4.3
Net Profit Margin %	3.1	3.6	3.1	2.5	3.0	2.8	2.9
Return on Equity %	18.3	28.9	20.3	10.8	13.9	12.3	11.3
Return on Assets %	7.0	9.6	10.3	6.3	6.3	5.5	5.3
Debt/Total Assets %	3.6	4.9	6.3	7.2	...	...	...
Price Range	48-25	42¹³⁄₁₆-24⅜	37¼-23⅛	26⅜-17¾	27¼-17⅞	26⁷⁄₈-16½	24⁹⁄₁₆-12¹¹⁄₁₆
P/E Ratio	16.3-8.5	14.2-8.1	16.2-10.1	17.6-11.8	15.0-9.8	18.8-11.5	20.0-10.3
Average Yield %	1.9	2.0	2.1	2.6	2.3	2.3	2.4

Statistics are as originally reported. Adj. for stk. split: 2-for-1, 3/93. ① Bef. acctg. chrg. of $1.5 mill. ② Bef. discont. oper. gain $9.7 mill. and incl. non-recurring chrg. of $16.4 mill. ③ Bef. discont. oper. gain of $34.8 mill. ④ Incl. non-recurring pre-tax gain $16.2 mill.

OFFICERS:
G. F. Kummer, Chmn., C.E.O.
N. W. Potter, Pres., C.O.O.
P. M. Bingham, Sr. V.P., C.F.O.
L. N. Larkin, V.P., Treas., Asst. Sec.

INVESTOR CONTACT: Paul Bingham, Sr. V.P., C.F.O., (909) 351-3504

PRINCIPAL OFFICE: 3125 Myers Street, P.O. Box 7638, Riverside, CA 92503-5527

TELEPHONE NUMBER: (909) 351-3500
FAX: (909) 351-3690
WEB: www.fleetwood.com

NO. OF EMPLOYEES: 21,000 (approx.)

SHAREHOLDERS: 1,500 (approx.)

ANNUAL MEETING: In Sept.

INCORPORATED: CA, 1957; reincorp., DE, Sep., 1977

INSTITUTIONAL HOLDINGS:
No. of Institutions: 149
Shares Held: 25,633,683
% Held: 78.5

INDUSTRY: Motor homes (SIC: 3716)

TRANSFER AGENT(S): BankBoston, N.A., Boston, MA

NYSE SYMBOL FPC
Rec. Pr. 49 5/8 (5/31/00)

FLORIDA PROGRESS CORPORATION

YIELD 4.5%
P/E RATIO 15.5

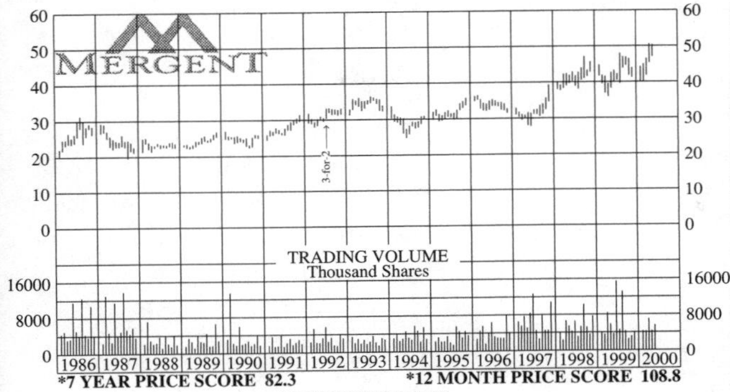

MERGENT
60
50
40
30
20
10
0
3-for-2
TRADING VOLUME
Thousand Shares
16000
8000
0
1986 1987 1988 1989 1990 1991 1992 1993 1994 1995 1996 1997 1998 1999 2000

*7 YEAR PRICE SCORE 82.3 *12 MONTH PRICE SCORE 108.8

*NYSE COMPOSITE INDEX=100

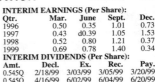

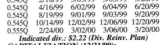

INTERIM EARNINGS (Per Share):

Qtr.	Mar.	June	Sept.	Dec.
1996	0.50	0.35	1.01	0.73
1997	0.43	d0.39	1.05	1.53
1998	0.52	0.80	1.21	0.37
1999	0.69	0.78	1.40	0.34

INTERIM DIVIDENDS (Per Share):

Amt.	Decl.	Ex.	Rec.	Pay.
0.545Q	2/18/99	3/03/99	3/05/99	3/20/99
0.545Q	4/16/99	6/02/99	6/04/99	6/20/99
0.545Q	8/19/99	9/01/99	9/03/99	9/20/99
0.545Q	10/14/99	12/02/99	12/06/99	12/20/99
0.555Q	2/24/00	3/02/00	3/06/00	3/20/00

Indicated div.: $2.22 (Div. Reinv. Plan)

CAPITALIZATION (12/31/99):

	($000)	(%)
Long-Term Debt	2,154,100	42.6
Deferred Income Tax	565,300	11.2
Preferred Stock	333,500	6.6
Common & Surplus	2,008,700	39.7
Total	5,061,600	100.0

DIVIDEND ACHIEVER STATUS:

Rank: 309 10-Year Growth Rate: 2.40%
Total Years of Dividend Growth: 47

RECENT DEVELOPMENTS: For the year ended 12/31/99, net income advanced 11.8% to $314.9 million compared with $281.7 million the year before. Total revenues grew 6.2% to $3.85 billion from $3.62 billion a year earlier. Electric utility revenues were $2.63 billion versus $2.65 billion in 1998. The decline reflected the deferral of $44.4 million in revenues by Florida Power Corp. as authorized by the Florida Public Service Commission. Revenues from diversified operations jumped 24.7% to $1.21 billion mainly due to the sale of a new coal-based synthetic fuel. Upon completion of Carolina Power & Light's acquisition of FPC, the combined company will be one of the 10 largest energy companies in the U.S. based on generating capacity with more than 19,000 megawatts. The Company will be organized into five business units including energy supply, energy delivery, Florida Power, energy ventures and gas & energy services. The transaction is expected to close in Fall of 2000.

BUSINESS

FLORIDA PROGRESS CORPORATION is a diversified electric utility holding company and defines its principal business segments as utility and diversified operations. Florida Power Corporation, FPC's largest subsidiary, is the Company's utility segment and is engaged the generation, purchase, transmission, distribution and sale of electricity. In 1999, Florida Power provided electric service to 1.4 million customers in west central Florida. Progress Capital Holdings, Inc. is the downstream holding company for FPC's diversified subsidiaries, and provides financing for non-utility operations. Also, the Company's diversified operations segment includes Electric Fuels Corporation, an energy and transportation company with services in energy and related services, rail services and inland marine transportation. In addition to its subsidiaries, FPC has interest in life insurance, real estate, and commercial lending and leasing. On 8/23/99, the Company agreed to be acquired by North Carolina-based Carolina Power & Light Company in a cash and stock transaction valued at nearly $5.30 billion.

ANNUAL FINANCIAL DATA

	12/31/99	12/31/98	12/31/97	12/31/96	12/31/95	12/31/94	12/31/93
Earnings Per Share	**3.21**	**2.90**	**1 0.56**	**2 2.59**	**2.50**	**2.28**	**2.22**
Cash Flow Per Share	**7.76**	**7.27**	**4.31**	**6.38**	**6.25**	**5.74**	**5.61**
Tang. Book Val. Per Share	**18.66**	**17.75**	**18.30**	**19.84**	**21.55**	**20.85**	**20.40**
Dividends Per Share	**2.18**	**2.14**	**2.10**	**2.06**	**2.02**	**1.99**	**1.95**
Dividend Payout %	**67.9**	**73.8**	**374.9**	**79.5**	**80.8**	**87.3**	**87.8**
INCOME STATEMENT (IN MILLIONS):							
Total Revenues	3,845.1	3,620.3	3,315.6	3,157.9	3,055.6	2,771.5	2,449.0
Costs & Expenses	2,228.0	1,999.7	2,220.7	1,899.1	1,626.8	1,420.5	1,120.7
Depreciation & Amort.	446.2	424.6	364.2	366.7	359.1	321.7	299.9
Maintenance Exp.	...	...	...	...	114.1	122.9	136.8
Operating Income	574.9	600.3	1 272.6	482.4	523.6	476.0	442.6
Net Interest Inc./(Exp.)	d173.6	d187.1	d158.7	d135.9	d142.0	d144.8	d141.1
Income Taxes	91.7	148.6	66.4	145.9	136.4	109.7	110.4
Net Income	314.9	281.7	1 54.3	2 250.7	238.9	212.0	195.8
Cash Flow	761.1	706.3	418.5	617.4	598.0	533.7	495.7
Average Shs. Outstg. (000)	98,100	97,100	97,100	96,800	95,700	93,000	88,300
BALANCE SHEET (IN MILLIONS):							
Gross Property	6,924.5	6,686.1	6,446.2	6,105.9	5,999.3	5,825.5	5,606.0
Accumulated Depreciation	3,341.3	3,101.5	2,863.2	2,648.7	2,449.3	2,209.2	2,033.0
Net Property	4,355.3	4,190.6	4,087.2	3,826.4	4,064.3	4,090.1	4,033.0
Total Assets	6,528.2	6,160.8	5,760.0	5,348.4	5,791.1	5,718.7	5,638.8
Long-Term Obligations	2,154.1	2,250.4	2,377.8	1,776.9	1,685.2	1,859.6	1,866.6
Net Stockholders' Equity	2,342.2	1,895.5	1,809.5	1,957.7	2,191.6	2,097.9	1,934.0
Year-end Shs. Outstg. (000)	98,454	97,000	97,063	97,007	96,421	95,175	89,260
STATISTICAL RECORD:							
Operating Profit Margin %	15.0	16.6	8.2	15.3	17.1	17.2	18.1
Net Profit Margin %	8.2	7.8	1.6	7.9	7.8	7.6	8.0
Net Inc./Net Property %	7.2	6.7	1.3	6.6	5.9	5.2	4.9
Net Inc./Tot. Capital %	6.2	5.9	1.2	6.0	5.2	4.5	4.3
Return on Equity %	13.4	14.9	3.0	12.8	10.9	10.1	10.1
Accum. Depr./Gross Prop. %	48.3	46.4	44.4	43.4	40.8	37.9	36.3
Price Range	48-35 7/8	47 1/8-37 11/16	39 1/4-27 3/4	36 1/2-31 1/2	35 3/4-29 3/8	33 5/8-24 3/4	36 3/8-31 1/4
P/E Ratio	15.0-11.2	16.2-13.0	70.1-49.5	14.1-12.2	14.3-11.7	14.7-10.9	16.4-14.1
Average Yield %	5.2	5.0	6.3	6.1	6.2	6.8	5.8

Statistics are as originally reported. 1 Incl. non-recurr. chg. of $173.3 mill. 2 Bef. disc. oper loss $26.3 mill.

OFFICERS:
R. Korpan, Chmn., Pres., C.E.O.
E. W. Moneypenny, Sr. V.P., C.F.O.
K. E. Armstrong, V.P., Gen. Couns.

INVESTOR CONTACT: Mark A. Myers, Manage, Investor Relations, (800) 937-2640

PRINCIPAL OFFICE: One Progress Plaza, Suite 2600, St. Petersburg, FL 33701

TELEPHONE NUMBER: (727) 824-6400
FAX: (727) 824-6527
WEB: www.fpc.com

NO. OF EMPLOYEES: 9,329

SHAREHOLDERS: 41,113 (approx.)

ANNUAL MEETING: In June

INCORPORATED: FL, Jan., 1982

INSTITUTIONAL HOLDINGS:
No. of Institutions: 250
Shares Held: 50,615,451
% Held: 51.4

INDUSTRY: Electric services (SIC: 4911)

TRANSFER AGENT(S): BankBoston, N.A., Boston, MA

ASE SYMBOL FPU
Rec. Pr. 14 5/8 (5/31/00)

FLORIDA PUBLIC UTILITIES COMPANY

YIELD 4.6%
P/E RATIO 12.5

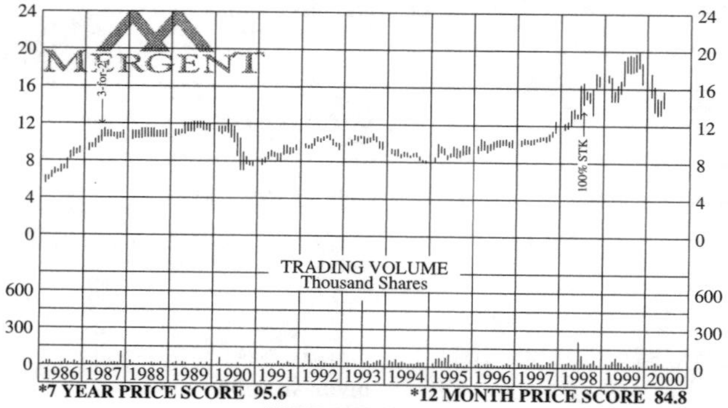

*7 YEAR PRICE SCORE 95.6 *12 MONTH PRICE SCORE 84.8

*NYSE COMPOSITE INDEX=100

INTERIM EARNINGS (Per Share):

Qtr.	Mar.	June	Sept.	Dec.
1995	0.38	0.15	0.12	0.19
1996	0.53	0.15	0.12	0.13
1997	0.35	0.18	0.31	0.24
1998	0.47	0.19	0.15	0.21
1999	0.48	0.24	0.18	0.27

INTERIM DIVIDENDS (Per Share):

Amt.	Decl.	Ex.	Rec.	Pay.
0.16Q	3/02/99	3/10/99	3/12/99	4/01/99
0.17Q	6/01/99	6/16/99	6/18/99	7/01/99
0.17Q	8/31/99	9/08/99	9/10/99	10/01/99
0.17Q	11/30/99	12/08/99	12/10/99	1/03/00
0.17Q	3/07/00	3/15/00	3/17/00	4/03/00

Indicated div.: $0.68 (Div. Reinv. Plan)

CAPITALIZATION (12/31/99):

	($000)	(%)
Long-Term Debt	23,500	41.3
Deferred Income Tax	6,900	12.1
Redeemable Pfd. Stock	600	1.1
Common & Surplus	25,866	45.5
Total	56,866	100.0

DIVIDEND ACHIEVER STATUS:
Rank: 294 10-Year Growth Rate: 3.34%
Total Years of Dividend Growth: 31

RECENT DEVELOPMENTS: For the year ended 12/31/99, net income increased 15.0% to $3.5 million from $3.1 million in the previous year. Results for 1999 benefited from an after-tax gain of $134,000 from the sale of a non-utility property. Total revenues fell 2.7% to $74.1 million from $76.2 million in the previous year. Electric revenues declined 6.7% to $37.5 million from $40.3 million the year before. Natural gas revenues increased 1.9% to $30.3 million from $29.7 million a year ago. Propane gas revenues decreased 4.4% to $3.9 million from $4.0 million in the previous year. Water revenues increased 11.1% to $2.4 million from $2.2 million in the prior year. Operating margin increased 3.0% to $29.3 million from $28.5 million the year before. Operating income was up 4.6% to $6.2 million from $5.9 million in the prior year.

BUSINESS

FLORIDA PUBLIC UTILITIES COMPANY is a public utility regulated by the Florida Public Service Commission (except for propane gas service) and provides natural and propane gas service, electric service and water service to consumers in Florida. The Company is comprised of the following four divisions as of 12/31/99: West Palm Beach, located in southeast Florida, provides natural gas to 28,784 customers and propane gas to 5,405 customers; Mid-Florida, consisting of the Sanford and DeLand districts, serves 9,622 natural gas customers and 2,856 propane customers; Marianna, located in the Florida panhandle, provides electricity to 11,934 customers; and Fernandina Beach, located in extreme northeast Florida, serves 12,956 electric customers and 6,665 water customers.

REVENUES

(12/31/99)	($000)	(%)
Electric	37,544	50.7
Natural Gas	30,287	40.9
Propane Gas	3,866	5.2
Water	2,401	3.2
Total	74,098	100.0

ANNUAL FINANCIAL DATA

	12/31/99	12/31/98	12/31/97	12/31/96	12/31/95	12/31/94	12/31/93
Earnings Per Share	[2] **1.17**	**1.02**	[1] **1.07**	**0.93**	**0.83**	**0.59**	**0.61**
Cash Flow Per Share	**2.90**	**2.44**	**2.42**	**2.25**	**2.10**	**1.87**	**1.86**
Tang. Book Val. Per Share	**9.23**	**9.21**	**8.79**	**8.31**	**7.98**	**7.84**	**7.71**
Dividends Per Share	**0.66**	**0.62**	**0.60**	**0.59**	**0.58**	**0.57**	**0.56**
Dividend Payout %	**56.4**	**60.8**	**56.3**	**64.3**	**69.9**	**97.4**	**91.0**
INCOME STATEMENT (IN THOUSANDS):							
Total Revenues	74,098	76,192	78,134	78,810	72,027	62,400	66,584
Costs & Expenses	60,608	63,220	66,075	66,780	60,760	52,187	56,467
Depreciation & Amort.	4,557	4,269	4,029	3,876	3,694	3,673	3,533
Maintenance Exp.	2,763	2,807	2,512	2,526	2,409	2,193	2,104
Operating Income	6,170	5,896	[1] 5,518	5,628	5,164	4,347	4,480
Net Interest Inc./(Exp.)	d2,968	d2,840	d2,895	d2,858	d2,767	d2,669	d2,688
Net Income	[2] 3,529	3,068	[1] 3,191	2,751	2,438	1,717	1,751
Cash Flow	8,057	7,308	7,191	6,598	6,103	5,361	5,255
Average Shs. Outstg.	2,776	2,993	2,968	2,938	2,908	2,870	2,832
BALANCE SHEET (IN THOUSANDS):							
Gross Property	123,898	117,656	112,356	106,684	100,658	95,400	90,962
Accumulated Depreciation	45,626	42,429	39,632	36,808	34,380	31,687	29,395
Net Property	78,272	75,227	72,724	69,876	66,278	63,713	61,567
Total Assets	96,807	92,406	88,622	90,994	85,240	82,281	78,035
Long-Term Obligations	23,500	23,500	23,500	23,500	23,500	23,500	24,173
Net Stockholders' Equity	25,866	27,622	26,189	24,511	23,302	22,334	21,961
Year-end Shs. Outstg.	2,802	3,000	2,978	2,948	2,920	2,850	2,850
STATISTICAL RECORD:							
Operating Profit Margin %	8.3	7.7	7.1	7.1	7.2	7.0	6.7
Net Profit Margin %	4.8	4.0	4.1	3.5	3.4	2.8	2.6
Net Inc./Net Property %	4.5	4.1	4.4	3.9	3.7	2.7	2.8
Net Inc./Tot. Capital %	6.2	5.3	5.7	5.4	4.8	3.5	3.7
Return on Equity %	13.6	11.1	12.2	11.2	10.5	7.7	8.0
Accum. Depr./Gross Prop. %	36.8	36.1	35.3	34.5	34.2	33.2	32.3
Price Range	20-14 5/8	17 5/8-11 9/16	12 1/2-9 13/16	10 9/16-9	10-8	9 7/16-7 7/8	11 1/16-9 5/16
P/E Ratio	17.1-12.5	17.3-11.3	11.7-9.2	11.4-9.7	12.0-9.6	16.0-13.3	18.1-15.3
Average Yield %	3.8	4.2	5.4	6.1	6.4	6.6	5.4

Statistics are as originally reported. Adj. for stk. splits: 2-for-1, 7/98 [1] Incl. non-recurr. credit $837,000 [2] Incl. non-recurr. credit of $134,000

OFFICERS:
J. T. English, Pres., C.E.O., C.O.O.
C. L. Stein, Sr. V.P.
J. R. Brown, Treas., Corp. Sec.

INVESTOR CONTACT: Jack Brown, Treasurer, (561) 838-1729

PRINCIPAL OFFICE: 401 South Dixie Hwy., West Palm Beach, FL 33401

TELEPHONE NUMBER: (561) 832-2461
FAX: (561) 833-0151
WEB: www.fpuc.com

NO. OF EMPLOYEES: 301 (avg.)

SHAREHOLDERS: 1,024

ANNUAL MEETING: In April

INCORPORATED: FL, Mar., 1924

INSTITUTIONAL HOLDINGS:
No. of Institutions: 11
Shares Held: 725,913
% Held: 24.0

INDUSTRY: Electric and other services combined (SIC: 4931)

TRANSFER AGENT(S): The Bank of New York, New York, NY

NYSE SYMBOL FLO
Rec. Pr. 18 1/16 (5/31/00)

FLOWERS INDUSTRIES, INC.

YIELD 2.9%
P/E RATIO 258.0

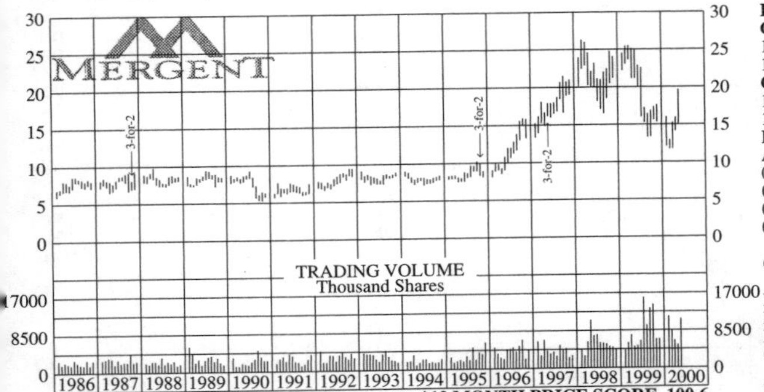
MERGENT
3-for-2
3-for-2
3-for-2
TRADING VOLUME
Thousand Shares
1986 1987 1988 1989 1990 1991 1992 1993 1994 1995 1996 1997 1998 1999 2000

*7 YEAR PRICE SCORE 76.1 *12 MONTH PRICE SCORE 100.6

*NYSE COMPOSITE INDEX=100

INTERIM EARNINGS (Per Share):

Qtr.	Sept.	Dec.	Mar.	June
1996-97	0.23	0.14	0.14	0.21
1997-98	0.17	0.15	...	...
Qtr.	**Apr.**	**July**	**Oct.**	**Jan.**
1998-99	0.17	0.19	0.26	d0.13
1999-00	0.25	d0.28	d0.09	0.19

INTERIM DIVIDENDS (Per Share):

Amt.	Decl.	Ex.	Rec.	Pay.
0.128Q	5/28/99	6/09/99	6/11/99	6/25/99
0.13Q	9/10/99	9/22/99	9/24/99	10/08/99
0.133Q	11/19/99	12/01/99	12/03/99	12/17/99
0.133Q	2/25/00	3/08/00	3/10/00	3/24/00

Indicated div.: $0.53 (Div. Reinv. Plan)

CAPITALIZATION (1/1/00):

	($000)	(%)
Long-Term Debt	1,208,630	57.7
Deferred Income Tax	162,470	7.8
Minority Interest	183,578	8.8
Common & Surplus	538,754	25.7
Total	2,093,432	100.0

DIVIDEND ACHIEVER STATUS:
Rank: 208 10-Year Growth Rate: 7.74%
Total Years of Dividend Growth: 27

RECENT DEVELOPMENTS: For the year ended 1/1/00, net income was $7.3 million versus income of $46.0 million, before an extraordinary charge and an accounting change, the year before. Results included pre-tax, one-time charges of $60.4 million and $68.3 million in 1999 and 1998, respectively. Earnings were hurt by production problems at FLO's Mrs. Smith's Bakeries business unit. Sales rose 12.5% to $4.24 billion from $3.77 billion a year earlier.

PROSPECTS: The Company is beginning to realize productivity improvements in its Mrs. Smith's Bakeries division. In December 1999, FLO signed a letter of intent for AmeriCold to manage Mrs. Smith's nationwide warehousing network for its frozen baked foods. The agreement, which is expected to be finalized in early 2000, should improve the cost efficiency and cycle times of Mrs. Smith's service to retail, foodservice and deli/bakery customers.

BUSINESS

FLOWERS INDUSTRIES, INC. operates in the packaged foods industry, serving primarily the grocery, food service, restaurant and fast-food markets. FLO produces a variety of branded food products, including: fresh and frozen breads, buns, specialty rolls, cakes and snacks, frozen specialty vegetables, batter-dipped and breaded vegetables, and fruits and desserts. Products are distributed primarily in the Southeast, Central and Western U.S., and are sold chiefly to restaurants, fast-food chains, wholesalers, institutions, supermarkets and vending companies. Major brands include KEEBLER, CHEEZ-IT, FAMOUS AMOS, MRS SMITH'S, NATURE'S OWN, COBBLESTONE MILL, BLUE BIRD, and SUNBEAM. FLO acquired Mrs. Smith's Pies in May 1996, Allied Bakery Products in September 1997, President Baking Company, Inc. in September 1998, and has a controlling interest in the Keebler Co.

BUSINESS LINE ANALYSIS

(1/1/2000)	Rev(%)	Inc(%)
Flowers Bakeries	22.4	24.1
Mrs. Smith's Bakeries	15.6	(19.2)
Keebler	62.0	95.1
Total	100.0	100.0

ANNUAL FINANCIAL DATA

	1/1/00	1/2/99	[4] 1/3/98	6/28/97	6/29/96	7/1/95	7/2/94
Earnings Per Share	[2] 0.07	[1][2][3] 0.47	[3] 0.38	[2] 0.71	0.36	0.50	0.36
Cash Flow Per Share	1.51	1.81	0.68	1.23	0.83	0.93	0.76
Tang. Book Val. Per Share	...	...	3.09	3.08	2.97	3.41	3.15
Dividends Per Share	0.52	0.47	...	0.43	0.40	0.37	0.35
Dividend Payout %	734.7	101.0	...	61.0	110.2	74.6	99.5
INCOME STATEMENT (IN MILLIONS):							
Total Revenues	4,236.0	3,776.5	786.5	1,484.5	1,250.6	1,140.0	999.7
Costs & Expenses	3,907.4	3,415.3	722.8	1,325.6	1,143.5	1,028.2	914.1
Depreciation & Amort.	144.6	128.8	26.9	46.0	40.8	36.6	34.1
Operating Income	184.0	232.4	36.8	112.9	66.3	75.1	51.6
Net Interest Inc./(Exp.)	d80.9	d68.7	d11.8	d25.1	d13.0	d7.1	d4.3
Income Before Income Taxes	103.1	163.7	25.0	87.8	48.3	68.0	47.2
Income Taxes	56.3	74.4	9.6	33.2	18.2	25.7	17.7
Equity Earnings/Minority Int.	d39.6	d43.3	18.1	7.7	0.6	...	...
Net Income	[2] 7.3	[1][2][3] 46.0	[3] 33.4	[2] 62.3	30.8	42.3	29.5
Cash Flow	151.9	174.7	60.4	108.3	71.6	78.9	63.6
Average Shs. Outstg. (000)	100,420	96,801	88,773	88,000	86,174	85,302	83,417
BALANCE SHEET (IN MILLIONS):							
Cash & Cash Equivalents	39.4	57.0	3.9	31.1	25.0	31.8	19.8
Total Current Assets	690.5	783.2	252.9	271.5	230.2	189.0	176.1
Net Property	1,149.6	987.7	438.3	448.0	420.5	374.5	320.3
Total Assets	2,900.5	2,860.9	899.4	898.2	849.4	655.9	560.9
Total Current Liabilities	655.8	761.0	232.6	242.5	181.7	146.7	121.5
Long-Term Obligations	1,208.6	1,039.0	276.2	275.2	274.7	120.9	92.9
Net Stockholders' Equity	538.8	573.0	348.6	340.0	305.3	304.0	275.7
Net Working Capital	34.7	22.2	20.3	29.1	48.5	42.4	54.6
Year-end Shs. Outstg. (000)	100,297	99,821	88,428	88,073	87,876	86,418	84,380
STATISTICAL RECORD:							
Operating Profit Margin %	4.3	6.2	4.7	7.6	5.3	6.6	5.2
Net Profit Margin %	0.2	1.2	4.3	4.2	2.5	3.7	3.0
Return on Equity %	1.4	8.0	9.6	18.3	10.1	13.9	10.7
Return on Assets %	0.3	1.6	3.7	6.9	3.6	6.4	5.3
Debt/Total Assets %	41.7	36.3	30.7	30.6	32.3	18.4	16.6
Price Range	25 1/2-13 5/16	26 5/16-16 1/2	21 1/2-13 5/16	21 1/2-13 5/16	15 15/16-8 1/16	10 1/4-7 1/2	9-7 1/8
P/E Ratio	363.8-189.9	56.0-35.1	56.6-35.1	30.3-18.8	44.2-22.4	20.5-15.1	25.3-20.0
Average Yield %	2.7	2.2	2.5	2.5	3.3	4.2	4.4

Statistics are as originally reported. Adj. for 3-for-2 stk. split, 5/97 & 10/95. [1] Bef. $938,000 ($0.01/sh) extraord. chg. [2] Incl. $60.4 mil pre-tax, non-recur. chg., 1/1/00; $68.3 mil pre-tax, non-recur. chg., 1/2/99; & $43 mil pre-tax, non-recur. gain., 6/28/97. [3] Bef. $3.1 mil ($0.03/sh) acctg. chg., 1/2/99; & $8.8 mil acctg. chg., 1/3/98. [4] For six months ended 1/3/98 due to fiscal year-end change.

OFFICERS:
A. R. McMullian, Chmn., C.E.O.
R. P. Crozer, Vice-Chmn.
J. M. Woodward, V.P., C.F.O.
T. B. Jones, Jr., Treas.

PRINCIPAL OFFICE: 1919 Flowers Circle, Thomasville, GA 31757

TELEPHONE NUMBER: (912) 226-9110
FAX: (912) 226-9231
WEB: www.flowersindustries.com
NO. OF EMPLOYEES: 6,300 (avg.)
SHAREHOLDERS: 8,205
ANNUAL MEETING: In May
INCORPORATED: DE, May, 1968; reincorp., GA, Dec., 1987

INSTITUTIONAL HOLDINGS:
No. of Institutions: 161
Shares Held: 43,771,264
% Held: 43.6

INDUSTRY: Bread, cake, and related products (SIC: 2051)

TRANSFER AGENT(S): First Union National Bank, Charlotte, NC

F.N.B. CORPORATION

YIELD 3.7%
P/E RATIO 10.7

*7 YEAR PRICE SCORE 76.2   *12 MONTH PRICE SCORE 83.4

*NYSE COMPOSITE INDEX=100

TRADING VOLUME
Thousand Shares

INTERIM EARNINGS (Per Share,):

Qtr.	Mar.	June	Sept.	Dec.
1996	0.42	0.44	0.30	0.44
1997	0.39	0.47	0.46	0.57
1998	0.37	0.35	0.36	0.35
1999	0.39	0.43	0.45	0.45

INTERIM DIVIDENDS (Per Share):

Amt.	Decl.	Ex.	Rec.	Pay.
0.18Q	8/23/99	9/01/99	9/03/99	9/15/99
0.18Q	11/30/99	12/07/99	12/09/99	12/15/99
0.18Q	2/24/00	3/02/00	3/06/00	3/15/00
5% STK	4/17/00	4/26/00	4/28/00	5/31/00
0.18Q	5/23/00	5/31/00	6/02/00	6/15/00

Indicated div.: $0.69 (Adj.)(Div. Reinv. Plan)

CAPITALIZATION (12/31/99):

	($000)	(%)
Total Deposits	2,909,434	87.7
Long-Term Debt	117,634	3.5
Preferred Stock	2,075	0.1
Common & Surplus	288,240	8.7
Total	3,317,383	100.0

DIVIDEND ACHIEVER STATUS:
Rank: 40   10-Year Growth Rate: 17.19%
Total Years of Dividend Growth: 15

RECENT DEVELOPMENTS: For the year ended 12/31/99, net income was $39.3 million, up 19.0% from $33.0 million the year before. Results included merger-related and other nonrecurring charges of $1.8 million and $5.5 million, respectively, in 1999 and 1998. Net interest income improved 7.7% to $148.4 million from $137.9 million a year earlier. Total interest income improved 3.6% to $254.9 million compared with $246.0 million in the previous year. Total non-interest income advanced 19.4% to $46.9 million versus $39.3 million in 1998. For the year, total assets rose 6.0% to $3.70 billion, reflecting the Company's efforts to expand in southwestern Florida, Pennsylvania and Ohio. In February 2000, the Company acquired L.J. Kuder, Inc., an independent insurance agency in Greenville, PA.

BUSINESS

F.N.B. CORPORATION is a bank holding company that provides, through its subsidiaries, a full range of financial services to consumers and small- to medium-size businesses in its market areas. The bank subsidiaries offer traditional full-service commercial banking services, including commercial and individual demand and time deposit accounts and commercial, mortgage and individual installment loans. In addition, the bank subsidiaries offer various alternative investment products, including mutual funds and annuities. The consumer finance subsidiary offers personal installment loans to individuals and purchase installment sales finance contracts from retail merchants. As of 12/31/99, the Company owned and operated nine community banks and one consumer finance company in Pennsylvania, southwestern Florida, northern and central Tennessee, eastern Ohio, southwestern Kentucky and western New York. FBAN also owns two insurance agencies in northwestern Pennsylvania and southwestern Florida.

ANNUAL FINANCIAL DATA

	12/31/99	12/31/98	12/31/97	12/31/96	12/31/95	12/31/94	12/31/93
Earnings Per Share	1.70	① 1.45	① 1.88	① 1.59	1.65	1.22	0.97
Tang. Book Val. Per Share	12.52	12.97	13.44	13.52	13.35	12.27	11.72
Dividends Per Share	0.68	0.65	0.55	0.52	0.29	0.21	0.20
Dividend Payout %	39.9	44.5	29.0	32.8	17.5	17.0	20.3
INCOME STATEMENT (IN MILLIONS):							
Total Interest Income	254.9	236.0	195.5	139.0	135.4	124.9	125.5
Total Interest Expense	106.5	103.4	84.5	58.2	58.1	50.2	55.3
Net Interest Income	148.4	132.6	111.0	80.7	77.3	74.7	70.2
Provision for Loan Losses	9.2	7.3	10.6	6.1	5.7	8.5	9.5
Non-Interest Income	46.9	31.7	23.1	15.3	15.0	14.4	16.0
Non-Interest Expense	129.7	109.2	88.2	62.8	60.0	60.3	61.7
Income Before Taxes	56.5	47.9	35.4	27.1	26.7	20.3	15.0
Net Income	39.3	① 31.9	① 24.3	① 18.4	18.1	13.5	10.5
Average Shs. Outstg. (000)	24,007	22,010	17,555	11,047	10,448	10,416	9,923
BALANCE SHEET (IN MILLIONS):							
Cash & Due from Banks	171.2	128.9	87.9	70.3	59.8	60.5	60.0
Securities Avail. for Sale	486.1	536.6	555.3	152.8	223.5	120.1	127.4
Total Loans & Leases	2,803.8	4,690.5	3,791.3	2,630.9	2,452.1	2,398.8	2,074.9
Allowance for Credit Losses	36.3	61.9	47.6	45.7	48.2	42.3	38.6
Net Loans & Leases	2,767.5	4,628.7	3,743.7	2,585.2	2,403.9	2,356.5	2,036.2
Total Assets	3,706.2	5,580.5	4,535.0	3,030.6	2,919.7	2,874.9	2,716.5
Total Deposits	2,909.4	2,708.6	2,192.7	1,429.7	1,442.1	1,425.4	1,458.7
Long-Term Obligations	117.6	69.5	67.2	34.2	39.8	39.0	31.3
Total Liabilities	3,415.9	2,978.5	2,418.9	1,572.0	1,563.1	1,560.5	1,575.1
Net Stockholders' Equity	290.3	272.2	230.6	154.8	143.9	126.1	115.1
Year-end Shs. Outstg. (000)	23,025	20,797	16,942	11,184	10,440	9,899	9,430
STATISTICAL RECORD:							
Return on Equity %	13.5	11.7	10.5	11.9	12.6	10.7	9.1
Return on Assets %	1.1	0.6	0.5	0.6	0.6	0.5	0.4
Equity/Assets %	7.8	4.9	5.1	5.1	4.9	4.4	4.2
Non-Int. Exp./Tot. Inc. %	66.4	66.4	65.8	65.4	64.9	67.7	71.6
Price Range	25⅜-19	33¹/₁₆-20¾	31-18	19¹³/₁₆-14¹⁵/₁₆	16¼-10½	12¹³/₁₆-8¹³/₁₆	11¼-6⅝
P/E Ratio	15.0-11.2	22.8-14.3	17.0-9.6	12.5-9.4	9.9-6.4	10.5-7.2	11.6-6.8
Average Yield %	3.1	2.4	2.2	3.0	2.2	1.9	2.2

Statistics are as originally reported. Adj. for stk. splits: 5% div., 5/93, 5/94, 5/95, 5/96, 5/97, 5/98, 5/99, 5/00. ① Incl. non-recurr. chg. $1.8 mill., 1999; $5.5 mill., 1998; $13.4 mill., 1997, $1.9 mill., 1996.

OFFICERS:
P. Mortensen, Chmn., C.E.O.
S. J. Gurgovits, Vice-Chmn.
G. L. Tice, Pres., C.O.O.
J. D. Waters, V.P., C.F.O.

INVESTOR CONTACT: John D. Waters, (724) 983-3440

PRINCIPAL OFFICE: One F.N.B. Boulevard, Hermitage, PA 16148

TELEPHONE NUMBER: (724) 981-6000
FAX: (724) 983-4194
WEB: www.fnbcorporation.com

NO. OF EMPLOYEES: 1,514 full-time; 407 part-time

SHAREHOLDERS: 6,764

ANNUAL MEETING: In April

INCORPORATED: PA, June, 1974

INSTITUTIONAL HOLDINGS:
No. of Institutions: 49
Shares Held: 2,789,491 (Adj.)
% Held: 13.2

INDUSTRY: National commercial banks (SIC: 6021)

TRANSFER AGENT(S): F.N.B. Shareholder Services, Naples, FL

FRANKLIN RESOURCES, INC.

YIELD	0.8%
P/E RATIO	15.2

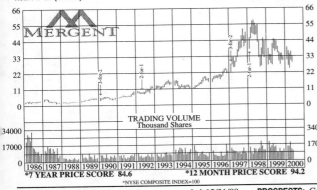

TRADING VOLUME
Thousand Shares

*7 YEAR PRICE SCORE 84.6   *12 MONTH PRICE SCORE 94.2

*NYSE COMPOSITE INDEX=100

INTERIM EARNINGS (Per Share):

Qtr.	Dec.	Mar.	June	Sept.
1995-96	0.30	0.31	0.33	0.34
1996-97	0.38	0.40	0.44	0.50
1997-98	0.52	0.50	0.52	0.44
1998-99	0.27	0.41	0.49	0.52
1999-00	0.55	...	...	...

INTERIM DIVIDENDS (Per Share):

Amt.	Decl.	Ex.	Rec.	Pay.
0.055Q	3/17/99	3/29/99	3/31/99	4/15/99
0.055Q	6/22/99	6/28/99	6/30/99	7/15/99
0.055Q	9/16/99	9/28/99	9/30/99	10/15/99
0.06Q	12/10/99	12/29/99	12/31/99	1/14/00
0.06Q	3/22/00	3/31/00	3/31/00	4/14/00

Indicated div.: $0.24 (Div. Reinv. Plan)

CAPITALIZATION (9/30/99):

	($000)	(%)
Long-Term Debt	294,260	10.0
Common & Surplus	2,656,994	90.0
Total	2,951,254	100.0

DIVIDEND ACHIEVER STATUS:
Rank: 19   10-Year Growth Rate: 21.61%
Total Years of Dividend Growth: 10

RECENT DEVELOPMENTS: For the quarter ended 12/31/99, net income more than doubled to $137.5 million from $68.5 million in the prior-year quarter. Results for 1998 included restructuring charges of $46.1 million. Total revenues declined slightly to $565.7 million versus $567.7 million in the prior-year quarter. Investment management fees improved 4.1% to $344.0 million compared with $330.4 million in the year-earlier quarter.

PROSPECTS: Going forward, the Company will focus on investing in technology, international development and its institutional investment advisory business. Internationally, the Company will place emphasis on building a global brand. Also, the Company plans to expand its institutional capabilities through enhancements in client services and marketing support and expansion of its product offerings.

BUSINESS

FRANKLIN RESOURCES, INC., is engaged in providing investment management, marketing, distribution, transfer agency and other administrative services to the open-end investment companies of the Franklin Templeton Group and to U.S. and international managed and institutional accounts. The Company also provides investment management and related services to a number of closed-end investment companies. In addition, the Company provides investment management, marketing and distribution services to certain sponsored investment companies organized in the Grand Duchy of Luxembourg. The Franklin Templeton Group of Funds consists of 42 open-end investment companies with multiple portfolios. In addition, the Company also provides advisory services, variable annuity products, and sponsors and manages public and private real estate programs

BUSINESS LINE ANALYSIS

(09/30/99)	REV (%)	INC (%)
Investment Management	99.3	99.3
Banking / Finance	0.7	0.7
Company Totals	100.0	100.0

ANNUAL FINANCIAL DATA

	9/30/99	9/30/98	9/30/97	9/30/96	9/30/95	9/30/94	9/30/93
Earnings Per Share	[1] 1.69	1.98	1.72	1.26	1.08	1.00	0.71
Cash Flow Per Share	2.48	2.74	2.20	1.42	1.27	1.17	0.82
Tang. Book Val. Per Share	5.79	4.08	2.50	3.15	2.06	1.03	0.16
Dividends Per Share	0.22	0.20	0.17	0.15	0.13	0.11	0.09
Dividend Payout %	13.0	10.1	9.9	11.6	12.3	10.7	13.2
INCOME STATEMENT (IN MILLIONS):							
Total Revenues	2,262.5	2,577.3	2,163.3	1,522.6	845.8	826.9	640.7
Costs & Expenses	1,445.2	1,653.3	1,361.3	1,065.0	436.7	411.2	322.2
Depreciation & Amort.	200.0	191.4	123.9	40.5	40.9	36.7	24.3
Operating Income	617.3	732.6	678.1	417.1	368.1	378.9	294.2
Net Interest Inc./(Exp.)	d21.0	d22.5	d25.3	d11.3	d11.2	d39.1	d34.6
Income Before Income Taxes	574.1	676.3	615.7	456.2	386.7	362.5	274.4
Income Taxes	147.4	175.8	181.7	141.5	117.7	111.2	98.9
Net Income	[1] 426.7	500.5	434.1	314.7	268.9	251.3	175.5
Cash Flow	626.7	691.8	558.0	355.2	309.9	288.0	199.8
Average Shs. Outstg. (000)	252,757	252,941	253,430	249,939	243,729	245,796	244,785
BALANCE SHEET (IN MILLIONS):							
Cash & Cash Equivalents	819.2	556.0	442.7	502.2	261.7	210.4	303.0
Total Current Assets	1,395.1	1,061.1	1,196.6	1,282.3	1,170.5	966.2	563.0
Net Property	416.4	349.2	...	...	...	...	0.2
Total Assets	3,666.8	3,480.0	3,095.2	2,374.2	2,244.7	1,738.0	1,581.5
Total Current Liabilities	651.9	652.5	707.7	550.0	684.7	408.7	382.7
Long-Term Obligations	294.3	494.5	493.2	399.5	382.4	383.7	454.8
Net Stockholders' Equity	2,657.0	2,280.8	1,854.2	1,400.6	1,161.0	930.8	737.0
Net Working Capital	743.3	408.7	488.9	732.3	485.8	557.4	180.3
Year-end Shs. Outstg. (000)	251,007	251,742	252,064	240,816	242,820	244,791	246,297
STATISTICAL RECORD:							
Operating Profit Margin %	27.3	24.9	27.3	27.4	43.5	44.7	44.5
Net Profit Margin %	18.9	19.4	20.1	20.7	31.8	30.4	27.4
Return on Equity %	16.1	21.9	23.4	22.5	23.2	27.0	24.4
Return on Assets %	11.6	14.4	14.0	13.3	12.0	14.5	11.1
Debt/Total Assets %	8.0	14.2	17.1	18.1	18.0	20.5	30.0
Price Range	45-27	57⅞-25¾	51¹⁵/₁₆-22¹¹/₁₆	24¹⁵/₁₆-15⁷/₁₆	19⁵/₁₆-11	17-11³/₁₆	17⁵/₁₆-10¹¹/₁₆
P/E Ratio	26.6-16.0	29.2-13.0	30.3-12.9	19.8-12.3	17.9-10.2	17.0-11.2	24.5-15.1
Average Yield %	0.6	0.5	0.5	0.7	0.9	0.8	0.7

Statistics are as originally reported. Adj. for stk. splits: 3-for-2, 12/96; 2-for-1, 12/97. [1] Incl. restr. chrg. $58.5 mill.

OFFICERS:
C. B. Johnson, Chmn., C.E.O.
H. E. Burns, Vice-Chmn.
R. H. Johnson Jr., Vice-Chmn.
M. L. Flanagan, Pres., C.F.O.

INVESTOR CONTACT: Alan Weinfeld, Investor Relations, (800) 632-2350 ext. 28900

PRINCIPAL OFFICE: 777 Mariners Island Blvd., San Mateo, CA 94404

TELEPHONE NUMBER: (650) 312-2000
FAX: (650) 312-3655
WEB: www.frk.com

NO. OF EMPLOYEES: 6,700 (approx.)

SHAREHOLDERS: 5,100 (approx.); 31,400 (approx. beneficial)

ANNUAL MEETING: In Jan.

INCORPORATED: DE, Nov., 1969

INSTITUTIONAL HOLDINGS:
No. of Institutions: 247
Shares Held: 92,441,762
% Held: 36.9

INDUSTRY: Investment advice (SIC: 6282)

TRANSFER AGENT(S): Bank of New York, New York, NY

FRISCH'S RESTAURANTS, INC.

YIELD	3.3%
P/E RATIO	9.8

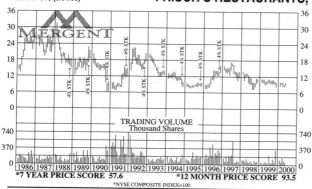

7 YEAR PRICE SCORE 57.6   **12 MONTH PRICE SCORE 93.5**
*NYSE COMPOSITE INDEX=100

INTERIM EARNINGS (Per Share):

Qtr.	Sept.	Dec.	Feb.	May
1996-97	0.20	0.13	0.03	d0.19
1997-98	0.28	0.23	0.12	0.12
1998-99	0.23	0.12	0.16	0.23
1999-00	0.30	0.25	0.22	...

INTERIM DIVIDENDS (Per Share):

Amt.	Decl.	Ex.	Rec.	Pay.
0.07Q	3/17/99	3/26/99	3/30/99	4/09/99
0.07Q	6/08/99	6/23/99	6/25/99	7/09/99
0.08Q	9/01/99	9/24/99	9/28/99	10/08/99
0.08Q	11/23/99	12/28/99	12/30/99	1/10/00
0.08Q	3/14/00	3/29/00	3/31/00	4/10/00

Indicated div.: $0.32

CAPITALIZATION (5/30/99):

	($000)	(%)
Long-Term Debt	24,268	28.7
Capital Lease Obligations..	5,146	6.1
Common & Surplus	55,288	65.3
Total	84,702	100.0

DIVIDEND ACHIEVER STATUS:

Rank: 262	10-Year Growth Rate: 5.16%	
Total Years of Dividend Growth:		16

RECENT DEVELOPMENTS:

For the twelve weeks ended 3/5/00, earnings from continuing operations remained essentially flat at $1.2 million versus the prior year. Total revenues were $37.5 million, up 13.1% from $33.2 million in the prior year. Revenues benefited from an increase in same-store Big Boy sales, which were up more than 4.0% for the quarter. This increase marks the tenth consecutive quarter that Big Boy same-store sales gains have been achieved. Also, improved dining room sales increases complemented the continuing strong sales from carryout and drive-thru trade. For the forty weeks ended 3/5/00, earnings from continuing operations totaled $4.3 million compared with $3.3 million a year ago. Total revenues rose 12.1% to $126.1 million from $112.4 million the year before. On 3/14/00, FRS announced that its Board of Directors has authorized management to develop a plan to divest its Clarion Riverview Hotel and the Quality Central Hotel.

BUSINESS

FRISCH'S RESTAURANTS, INC. operates 88 family restaurants with drive-through service under the name Frisch's Big Boy, and licenses another 37 restaurants to other Big Boy operators. These restaurants are located in various regions of Ohio, Indiana and Kentucky. Additionally, the Company operates five Golden Corral grill buffet restaurants and two hotels with banquet facilities and dining rooms in metropolitan Cincinnati, where it is headquartered. Trademarks which the Company has the right to use include "Frisch's," "Big Boy," "Quality Hotel," and "Golden Corral."

ANNUAL FINANCIAL DATA

	5/30/99	5/31/98	6/1/97	6/2/96	5/28/95	5/29/94	5/30/93
Earnings Per Share	① 0.74	0.73	0.17	0.32	0.33	0.74	0.78
Cash Flow Per Share	2.41	2.21	1.63	1.77	1.70	2.09	2.00
Tang. Book Val. Per Share	9.24	6.68	8.94	9.02	8.92	9.53	8.82
Dividends Per Share	0.28	0.24	0.23	0.22	0.213	0.205	0.20
Dividend Payout %	37.8	32.9	135.7	69.3	64.6	27.7	25.3
INCOME STATEMENT (IN THOUSANDS):							
Total Revenues	159,551	152,222	165,931	166,945	163,059	160,065	148,987
Costs & Expenses	140,221	133,077	151,344	150,766	148,184	141,304	130,844
Depreciation & Amort.	9,937	9,256	10,486	10,350	9,821	9,289	8,362
Operating Income	9,394	9,889	4,101	5,829	5,054	9,472	9,781
Net Interest Inc./(Exp.)	d2,437	d3,076	d2,373	d2,411	d1,961	d1,554	d1,341
Income Before Income Taxes	6,957	6,813	1,728	3,417	3,093	7,918	8,440
Income Taxes	2,539	2,268	541	1,108	735	2,842	3,048
Net Income	① 4,418	4,545	1,187	2,310	2,358	5,076	5,392
Cash Flow	14,355	13,801	11,673	12,660	12,179	14,365	13,754
Average Shs. Outstg.	5,967	6,238	7,151	7,157	7,157	6,887	6,885
BALANCE SHEET (IN THOUSANDS):							
Cash & Cash Equivalents	200	84	231	135	220	201	547
Total Current Assets	6,924	6,508	6,882	8,564	8,141	8,797	7,859
Net Property	84,369	82,196	80,764	99,240	98,058	86,249	78,511
Total Assets	103,426	106,724	111,260	118,396	115,548	104,349	97,731
Total Current Liabilities	16,534	14,958	15,699	18,458	18,224	16,200	19,095
Long-Term Obligations	29,415	39,135	28,082	30,489	22,286	15,882
Net Stockholders' Equity	55,288	49,910	64,684	65,307	64,627	63,830	60,059
Net Working Capital	d9,610	d8,450	d8,816	d9,894	d10,084	d7,404	d11,236
Year-end Shs. Outstg.	5,901	7,362	7,148	7,158	7,158	6,620	6,623
STATISTICAL RECORD:							
Operating Profit Margin %	5.9	6.5	2.5	3.5	3.1	5.9	6.6
Net Profit Margin %	2.8	3.0	0.7	1.4	1.4	3.2	3.6
Return on Equity %	8.0	9.1	1.8	3.5	3.6	8.0	9.0
Return on Assets %	4.3	4.3	1.1	2.0	2.0	4.9	5.5
Debt/Total Assets %	28.4	36.7	25.2	27.2	26.4	21.4	16.3
Price Range	13⁷⁄₈-7¹⁄₈	17³⁄₈-10¹⁄₂	16-7³⁄₈	9¹⁵⁄₁₆-7⁵⁄₈	13¹¹⁄₁₆-8¹⁄₁₆	20⁵⁄₁₆-11⁵⁄₈	22⁵⁄₈-14³⁄₁₆
P/E Ratio	...	23.8-14.4	94.1-43.5	31.0-23.8	41.4-24.5	27.4-15.7	29.0-18.2
Average Yield %	2.7	1.7	2.0	2.5	2.0	1.3	1.1

Statistics are as originally reported. Adj. for stk. splits: 4% div., 12/27/96; 4% div., 12/27/95; 4% div., 12/27/94; 4% div., 12/28/93. ① Bef. extraord. gain of $3.7 mill.

OFFICERS:
J. C. Maier, Chmn.
C. F. Maier, Pres., C.E.O.
D. H. Walker, V.P., C.F.O., Treas.
W. G. King, Sec., Couns.

INVESTOR CONTACT: Donald H. Walker, V.P., C.F.O. & Treas., (513) 961-2660

PRINCIPAL OFFICE: 2800 Gilbert Avenue, Cincinnati, OH 45206

TELEPHONE NUMBER: (513) 961-2660
FAX: (513) 559-5160
WEB: www.frischs.com

NO. OF EMPLOYEES: 3,200 full-time (approx.); 2,300 part-time (approx.)

SHAREHOLDERS: 2,800 (approx.)

ANNUAL MEETING: In Oct.

INCORPORATED: OH, Oct., 1947

INSTITUTIONAL HOLDINGS:
No. of Institutions: 23
Shares Held: 1,810,554
% Held: 31.1

INDUSTRY: Eating places (SIC: 5812)

TRANSFER AGENT(S): Continental Stock Transfer & Trust Company, New York, NY.

FULLER (H.B.) COMPANY

YIELD 2.2%
P/E RATIO 11.8

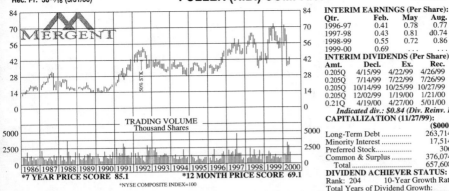

TRADING VOLUME
Thousand Shares

| | 1986 | 1987 | 1988 | 1989 | 1990 | 1991 | 1992 | 1993 | 1994 | 1995 | 1996 | 1997 | 1998 | 1999 | 2000 |

*7 YEAR PRICE SCORE 85.1   ***12 MONTH PRICE SCORE 69.1**

*NYSE COMPOSITE INDEX=100

INTERIM EARNINGS (Per Share):

Qtr.	Feb.	May	Aug.	Nov.
1996-97	0.41	0.78	0.77	0.90
1997-98	0.43	0.81	d0.74	0.65
1998-99	0.55	0.72	0.86	1.02
1999-00	0.69	...	...	...

INTERIM DIVIDENDS (Per Share):

Amt.	Decl.	Ex.	Rec.	Pay.
0.205Q	4/15/99	4/22/99	4/26/99	5/10/99
0.205Q	7/14/99	7/22/99	7/26/99	8/10/99
0.205Q	10/14/99	10/25/99	10/27/99	11/10/99
0.205Q	12/02/99	1/19/00	1/21/00	2/10/00
0.21Q	4/19/00	4/27/00	5/01/00	5/12/00

Indicated div.: $0.84 (Div. Reinv. Plan)

CAPITALIZATION (11/27/99):

	($000)	(%)
Long-Term Debt	263,714	40.1
Minority Interest	17,514	2.7
Preferred Stock	306	0.0
Common & Surplus	376,074	57.2
Total	657,608	100.0

DIVIDEND ACHIEVER STATUS:

Rank: 204   10-Year Growth Rate: 7.84%
Total Years of Dividend Growth: 32

RECENT DEVELOPMENTS:

For the quarter ended 2/26/00, net income amounted to $9.7 million, an increase of 28.0% compared with $7.6 million in the corresponding quarter the year before. Results for the 2000 quarter included a $300,000 non-recurring pre-tax gain, while the 1999 quarter included a $2.1 million non-recurring pre-tax charge. Net sales decreased 1.8% to $321.2 million from $327.2 million in the comparable quarter a year earlier. Net sales decreased primarily due to a 1.2% decline in pricing and foreign currency fluctuations, which reflected the weakening of the Euro against the U.S. dollar, partially offset by a 1.0% increase in volume and a change in the pruct mix. Sales in North America increased 1.3%, while sales from Europe and Asia declined 7.2% and 8.9%, respectively.

BUSINESS

H.B. FULLER COMPANY and its subsidiaries are principally engaged in the manufacture and distribution of industrial adhesives, coatings, sealants, paints and other specialty chemical products in the United States and Canada. The Company's subsidiary, Kativo Chemical Industries, S.A. and its subsidiaries manufacture and distribute paints, adhesives, plastics, printing inks and related chemical products in Central America, Panama, Mexico and South America.

ANNUAL FINANCIAL DATA

	11/27/99	11/28/98	11/29/97	11/30/96	11/30/95	11/30/94	11/30/93
Earnings Per Share	② 3.15	② 1.15	① 2.86	3.22	① 2.22	2.20	① ② 1.55
Cash Flow Per Share	6.79	4.73	6.18	6.55	5.15	4.58	3.67
Tang. Book Val. Per Share	19.76	17.02	21.03	20.12	17.42	15.50	16.44
Dividends Per Share	0.81	0.79	0.72	0.66	0.63	0.57	0.54
Dividend Payout %	25.9	68.3	25.2	20.3	28.2	26.1	34.8
INCOME STATEMENT (IN MILLIONS):							
Total Revenues	1,364.5	1,347.2	1,306.8	1,275.7	1,243.8	1,097.4	975.3
Costs & Expenses	1,209.9	1,236.5	1,172.8	1,148.0	1,132.9	998.0	892.1
Depreciation & Amort.	50.8	49.5	46.8	47.0	41.2	33.4	29.7
Operating Income	103.7	61.2	87.3	80.8	69.8	66.0	53.5
Net Interest Inc./(Exp.)	d26.8	d27.0	d19.8	d18.9	d18.1	d11.7	d10.5
Income Before Income Taxes	74.4	32.8	65.3	76.6	50.4	51.0	40.9
Income Taxes	31.8	18.8	26.7	31.2	19.1	19.8	19.2
Equity Earnings/Minority Int.	1.5	2.0	1.6	0.1	d0.1	d0.4	...
Net Income	② 44.1	② 16.0	① 40.3	45.4	① 31.2	30.9	① ② 21.7
Cash Flow	94.9	65.5	87.1	92.4	72.4	64.2	51.4
Average Shs. Outstg. (000)	13,978	13,844	14,100	14,114	14,059	14,036	14,018
BALANCE SHEET (IN MILLIONS):							
Cash & Cash Equivalents	5.8	4.6	2.7	3.5	9.1	9.8	17.4
Total Current Assets	440.1	457.9	409.2	388.2	387.6	361.4	295.9
Net Property	412.5	414.5	398.6	391.2	355.1	295.1	232.5
Total Assets	1,025.6	1,046.2	917.6	869.3	828.9	742.6	564.5
Total Current Liabilities	265.9	285.2	237.5	246.6	245.6	231.7	175.9
Long-Term Obligations	263.7	300.1	230.0	172.8	166.5	130.0	60.3
Net Stockholders' Equity	376.4	341.4	339.1	334.7	299.4	274.8	249.4
Net Working Capital	174.2	172.7	171.6	141.6	142.1	129.7	119.9
Year-end Shs. Outstg. (000)	14,040	13,983	13,841	14,066	14,007	13,935	13,898
STATISTICAL RECORD:							
Operating Profit Margin %	7.6	4.5	6.7	6.3	5.6	6.0	5.5
Net Profit Margin %	3.2	1.2	3.1	3.6	2.5	2.8	2.2
Return on Equity %	11.7	4.7	11.9	13.6	10.4	11.2	8.7
Return on Assets %	4.3	1.5	4.4	5.2	3.8	4.2	3.8
Debt/Total Assets %	25.7	28.7	25.1	19.9	20.1	17.5	10.7
Price Range	72⁷⁄₈-38¹⁄₈	65-34	60¹⁄₄-45	49⅝-29½	39¾-29¾	42¼-27¾	42¾-31¼
P/E Ratio	23.1-12.1	56.5-29.6	21.1-15.7	15.4-9.2	17.9-13.4	19.2-12.6	27.6-20.2
Average Yield %	1.5	1.6	1.4	1.7	1.8	1.6	1.6

Statistics are as originally reported. ① Bef. acctg. chrg. 11/29/97: $3.4 mill. ($0.24/sh.); 11/30/95: $2.5 mill. ($0.18/sh.); 11/30/93: $11.7 mill. ($0.84/sh.) ② Incl. non-recurr. chrg. 11/27/99: $17.2 mill.; 11/28/98: $26.7 mill.; 11/30/93: $6.0 mill.

OFFICERS:
A. P. Stroucken, Chmn., Pres., C.E.O.
R. A. Tucker, Sr. V.P., C.F.O.
W. L. Gacki, V.P., Treas.
R. C. Baker, V.P., Gen. Couns., Sec.

INVESTOR CONTACT: Richard Edwards, Director of Investor Relations, (651) 236-5150

PRINCIPAL OFFICE: 1200 Willow Lake Boulevard, St. Paul, MN 55110-5101

TELEPHONE NUMBER: (651) 236-5900
FAX: (651) 236-5898
WEB: www.hbfuller.com

NO. OF EMPLOYEES: 5,400 (approx.)

SHAREHOLDERS: 4,125 (approx.)

ANNUAL MEETING: In April

INCORPORATED: MN, Dec., 1915

INSTITUTIONAL HOLDINGS:
No. of Institutions: 111
Shares Held: 8,577,846
% Held: 61.1

INDUSTRY: Adhesives and sealants (SIC: 2891)

TRANSFER AGENT(S): Norwest Bank Minnesota, NA, St. Paul, MN

FULTON FINANCIAL CORPORATION

YIELD 3.1%
P/E RATIO 15.4

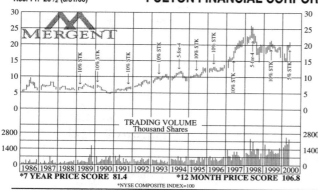

*7 YEAR PRICE SCORE 81.4   *12 MONTH PRICE SCORE 106.8
*NYSE COMPOSITE INDEX=100

INTERIM EARNINGS (Per Share):

Qtr.	Mar.	June	Sept.	Dec.
1996	0.28	0.28	0.27	0.29
1997	0.27	0.27	0.29	0.29
1998	0.29	0.30	0.30	0.32
1999	0.32	0.33	0.33	0.35

INTERIM DIVIDENDS (Per Share):

Amt.	Decl.	Ex.	Rec.	Pay.
0.15Q	7/20/99	9/17/99	9/21/99	10/15/99
0.15Q	10/19/99	12/21/99	12/23/99	1/15/00
0.15Q	1/18/00	3/15/00	3/17/00	4/15/00
5% STK	4/18/00	5/04/00	5/08/00	5/31/00
0.16Q	4/18/00	6/14/00	6/16/00	7/15/00

Indicated div.: $0.64 (Div. Reinv. Plan)

CAPITALIZATION (12/31/99):

	($000)	(%)
Total Deposits	4,546,813	82.8
Long-Term Debt	328,250	6.0
Common & Surplus	614,294	11.2
Total	5,489,357	100.0

DIVIDEND ACHIEVER STATUS:
Rank: 192   10-Year Growth Rate: 8.35%
Total Years of Dividend Growth: 26

RECENT DEVELOPMENTS: For the year ended 12/31/99, net income advanced 9.8% to $97.2 million from $88.5 million in the prior year. Net interest income totaled $244.1 million, up 5.4% versus $231.7 million in the previous year. Total other income climbed 4.8% to $62.8 million from $59.9 million a year ago. Total other expenses rose 2.1% to $161.0 million from $157.7 million the year before. Return on average shareholders' equity increased to 15.79% from 15.06% in the prior year. Return on average total assets advanced to 1.65% from 1.60% a year ago. On 2/23/00, FULT signed a definitive agreement to acquire New Jersey-based Skylands Financial Corporation in a stock transaction. On 4/13/00, FULT announced that it will consolidate all of the trust and related financial services performed by its subsidiary banks into a single company, Fulton Financial Advisors, N.A.

BUSINESS

FULTON FINANCIAL CORPORATION is a $6.07 billion bank holding company that provides retail and commercial banking and investment management and trust services to customers located primarily in central and eastern Pennsylvania, southern New Jersey, northern Maryland and southern Delaware through its eleven wholly-owned banking subsidiaries: Fulton Bank, Lebanon Valley Farmers Bank, Swineford National Bank, Lafayette Ambassador Bank, FNB Bank, N.A., Great Valley Bank, Hagerstown Trust Company, Delaware National Bank, The Bank of Gloucester County, The Woodstown National Bank & Trust Company, and The Peoples Bank of Elkton.

LOAN DISTRIBUTION

(12/31/1999)	($000)	(%)
Comm, Finl & Agri	668,069	15.1
Real Estate-		
Construction	166,291	3.7
Real Estate-		
Mortgages	2,819,261	63.6
Consumer	700,049	15.8
Leasing & other	78,360	1.8
Total	4,432,030	100.0

ANNUAL FINANCIAL DATA

	12/31/99	12/31/98	12/31/97	12/31/96	12/31/95
Earnings Per Share	1.33	1.21	1.05	0.96	0.84
Tang. Book Val. Per Share	8.55	9.20	8.10	8.09	8.31
Dividends Per Share	0.56	0.50	0.45	0.41	0.37
Dividend Payout %	40.9	40.9	42.9	42.7	44.0
INCOME STATEMENT (IN MILLIONS):					
Total Interest Income	418.9	409.3	319.6	268.7	235.9
Total Interest Expense	174.8	177.8	137.0	113.8	102.1
Net Interest Income	244.1	231.5	182.6	154.9	133.8
Provision for Loan Losses	8.2	5.6	7.7	4.2	2.0
Non-Interest Income	62.8	60.6	41.1	32.8	29.0
Non-Interest Expense	161.0	158.2	122.3	110.2	100.0
Income Before Taxes	137.7	128.3	93.6	73.3	60.7
Net Income	97.2	88.5	65.2	52.0	45.6
Average Shs. Outstg. (000)	72,829	* 73,170	73,179	72,850	72,532
BALANCE SHEET (IN MILLIONS):					
Cash & Due from Banks	245.6	247.6	172.4	165.0	140.1
Securities Avail. for Sale	1,137.8	1,206.1	597.4	317.1	222.3
Total Loans & Leases	4,432.0	4,040.5	3,317.2	2,783.6	2,364.8
Allowance for Credit Losses	67.3	67.5	56.6	48.2	44.0
Net Loans & Leases	4,364.8	3,973.0	3,260.6	2,735.4	2,320.8
Total Assets	6,070.0	5,838.7	4,460.8	3,769.4	3,334.7
Total Deposits	4,546.8	4,593.0	3,621.6	3,054.2	2,730.4
Long-Term Obligations	328.3	296.0	47.7	49.2	34.7
Total Liabilities	5,455.7	5,230.3	3,985.5	3,383.7	2,994.8
Net Stockholders' Equity	614.3	608.3	475.3	385.7	339.9
Year-end Shs. Outstg. (000)	71,872	72,749	58,619	47,677	40,900
STATISTICAL RECORD:					
Return on Equity %	15.8	14.5	13.7	13.5	13.4
Return on Assets %	1.6	1.5	1.5	1.4	1.4
Equity/Assets %	10.1	10.4	10.7	10.2	10.2
Non-Int. Exp./Tot. Inc. %	53.9	56.3	56.1	59.7	62.7
Price Range	21⁷/₁₆-16³/₁₆	26¹/₁₆-14³/₄	22¹/₂-12¹⁵/₁₆	13¹³/₁₆-11⁷/₁₆	13-9⅝
P/E Ratio	16.1-12.1	21.5-12.1	21.4-11.7	14.4-11.9	15.5-11.5
Average Yield %	2.9	2.4	2.5	3.2	3.3

Statistics are as originally reported. Adj. for stk. split: 5%, 5/00; 10% div., 6/1/99; 5-for-4, 5/27/98; 10% div., 6/13/97; 10% div., 5/31/96; 10% div., 6/9/95; 5-for-4, 5/31/94; 10% div., 6/9/93

OFFICERS:
R. A. Fulton Jr., Chmn., Pres., C.E.O.
C. J. Nugent, Exec. V.P., C.F.O.

INVESTOR CONTACT: Kenneth E. Shenenberger, Secretary, (717) 291-2411

PRINCIPAL OFFICE: One Penn Square, P.O. Box 4887, Lancaster, PA 17604-4887

TELEPHONE NUMBER: (717) 291-2411
FAX: (717) 295-5312
WEB: www.fult.com

NO. OF EMPLOYEES: 2,083 full-time; 609 part-time

SHAREHOLDERS: 15,696 (of record)

ANNUAL MEETING: In April

INCORPORATED: PA, 1982

INSTITUTIONAL HOLDINGS:
No. of Institutions: 62
Shares Held: 8,964,590
% Held: 13.1

INDUSTRY: National commercial banks (SIC: 6021)

TRANSFER AGENT(S): Stock Transfer Agent, Lancaster, PA.

GALLAGHER (ARTHUR J.) & COMPANY

YIELD 2.4%
P/E RATIO 22.1

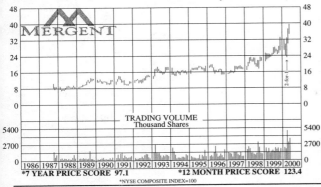

TRADING VOLUME
Thousand Shares

| 1986 | 1987 | 1988 | 1989 | 1990 | 1991 | 1992 | 1993 | 1994 | 1995 | 1996 | 1997 | 1998 | 1999 | 2000 |

*7 YEAR PRICE SCORE 97.1   ***12 MONTH PRICE SCORE 123.4**
*NYSE COMPOSITE INDEX=100

INTERIM EARNINGS (Per Share):

Qtr.	Mar.	June	Sept.	Dec.
1994	0.17	0.15	0.41	0.37
1995	0.21	0.18	0.47	0.42
1996	0.26	0.22	0.52	0.33
1997	0.27	0.37	0.53	0.37
1998	0.32	0.26	0.54	0.42
1999	0.35	0.33	0.60	0.47

INTERIM DIVIDENDS (Per Share):

Amt.	Decl.	Ex.	Rec.	Pay.
0.40Q	9/17/99	9/28/99	9/30/99	10/15/99
0.40Q	11/18/99	12/29/99	12/31/99	1/14/00
2-for-1	1/24/00	3/16/00	3/01/00	3/15/00
0.23Q	1/24/00	3/29/00	3/31/00	4/14/00
0.23Q	5/16/00	6/28/00	6/30/00	7/14/00

Indicated div.: $0.92

CAPITALIZATION (12/31/99):

	($000)	(%)
Common & Surplus	242,467	100.0
Total	242,467	100.0

DIVIDEND ACHIEVER STATUS:

Rank: 120   10-Year Growth Rate: 11.76%
Total Years of Dividend Growth: 15

RECENT DEVELOPMENTS: For the year ended 12/31/99, net income jumped 16.5% to $67.8 million compared with $58.1 million in the previous year. Total revenue grew 8.3% to $605.8 million from $559.6 million in the prior year. Commission revenues advanced 4.3% to $342.9 million compared with $328.6 million in the comparable year. Fee revenues improved 10.7% to $234.6 million from $212.0 million in the previous year.

PROSPECTS: Going forward, the Company expects intense pricing pressure in the insurance market to continue for fiscal 2000. However, strong new business sales coupled with strict cost controls should help to offset the pressure. On 1/3/00, the Company entered into an agreement to sell its investments in landfill gas collection partnerships for approximately $50.0 million. The transaction is subject to regulatory approvals.

BUSINESS

ARTHUR J. GALLAGHER & COMPANY is engaged in providing insurance brokerage, risk management, employee benefit and other related services to clients in the United States and abroad. The Company's principal activity is the negotiation and placement of insurance for its clients. In addition, AJG also specializes in furnishing risk management services that include assisting clients in analyzing risks and determining whether proper protection is best obtained through the purchase of insurance or through retention of those risks and the adoption of corporate risk management policies and cost-effective loss control and prevention programs. Risk management also includes claims management, loss control consulting and property appraisals. The Company operates through a network of approximately 200 offices in seven countries.

BUSINESS LINE ANALYSIS

(12/31/99)	REV (000s)	%
Insurance brokerage servs	397,691	65.6
Risk management servs	188,363	32.1
Financial services	19,782	2.3
Total	605,836	100.0

ANNUAL FINANCIAL DATA

	12/31/99	12/31/98	12/31/97	12/31/96	12/31/95	12/31/94	12/31/93
Earnings Per Share	1.76	1.55	1.57	1.32	1.27	1.09	1.01
Tang. Book Val. Per Share	6.29	5.38	4.63	3.79	3.58	3.00	3.83
Dividends Per Share	0.78	0.68	0.61	0.56	0.48	0.42	0.35
Dividend Payout %	44.0	43.9	39.0	42.6	38.2	38.7	34.7
INCOME STATEMENT (IN MILLIONS):							
Total Revenues	605.8	540.7	488.0	456.7	412.0	356.4	317.7
Income Before Income Taxes	104.2	84.5	80.8	69.4	62.9	53.2	51.2
Income Taxes	36.5	28.0	27.5	23.6	21.4	18.7	19.0
Net Income	67.8	56.5	53.3	45.8	41.5	34.5	32.3
Average Shs. Outstg. (000)	38,566	36,412	34,076	35,550	32,630	31,804	31,978
BALANCE SHEET (IN MILLIONS):							
Cash & Cash Equivalents	170.0	148.1	148.3	144.2	121.3	108.8	129.6
Premiums Due	364.9	288.3	217.6	237.6	193.7	179.8	152.5
Invst. Assets: Total	20.3	20.1	39.2	36.9	41.7	37.8	48.2
Total Assets	884.1	746.0	641.8	590.4	495.8	451.1	463.5
Long-Term Obligations	...	...	...	...	...	3.4	24.5
Net Stockholders' Equity	242.5	202.5	163.9	134.5	118.1	96.7	124.0
Year-end Shs. Outstg. (000)	36,840	35,290	33,182	32,586	30,852	29,568	30,372
STATISTICAL RECORD:							
Return on Revenues %	11.2	10.5	10.9	10.0	10.1	9.7	10.2
Return on Equity %	27.9	27.9	32.5	34.0	35.1	35.7	26.0
Return on Assets %	7.7	7.6	8.3	7.8	8.4	7.7	7.0
Price Range	33⅛-21⅛	23⅜-16¹³/₁₆	19⅛-14⅞	19¾-14⁹/₁₆	19-15¹/₁₆	18³/₁₆-14¹/₁₆	18¹¹/₁₆-12¾
P/E Ratio	18.8-12.0	15.1-10.8	12.2-9.5	15.0-11.1	15.0-11.9	16.8-13.0	18.5-12.6
Average Yield %	2.9	3.4	3.6	3.3	2.8	2.6	2.2

Statistics are as originally reported. Adjusted for 2-for-1 stock split, 3/00

OFFICERS:
R. E. Gallagher, Chmn.
J. P. Gallagher Jr., Pres., C.E.O.
M. J. Cloherty, Exec. V.P., C.F.O.

INVESTOR CONTACT: Marsha J. Akin, Investor Relations, (630) 773-3800

PRINCIPAL OFFICE: Two Pierce Place, Itasca, IL 60143-3141

TELEPHONE NUMBER: (630) 773-3800
FAX: (630) 285-4000
WEB: www.ajg.com

NO. OF EMPLOYEES: 4,600 (approx.)

SHAREHOLDERS: 650 (approx.)

ANNUAL MEETING: In May

INCORPORATED: IL, 1960

INSTITUTIONAL HOLDINGS:
No. of Institutions: 128
Shares Held: 10,579,073
% Held: 28.8

INDUSTRY: Insurance agents, brokers, & service (SIC: 6411)

TRANSFER AGENT(S): Harris Trust and Savings Bank, Chicago, IL

NYSE SYMBOL GCI
Rec. Pr. 64 3/4 (5/31/00)

GANNETT CO., INC.

YIELD 1.3%
P/E RATIO 19.2

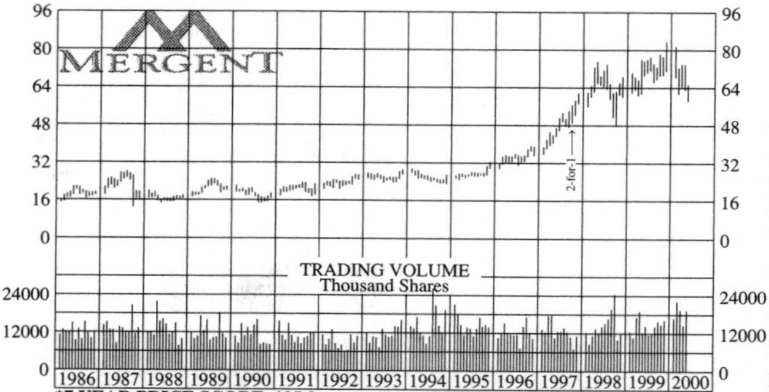

MERGENT
96
80
64
48
32
16
0
2-for-1
TRADING VOLUME
Thousand Shares
24000
12000
0
1986 1987 1988 1989 1990 1991 1992 1993 1994 1995 1996 1997 1998 1999 2000

*7 YEAR PRICE SCORE 105.3 *12 MONTH PRICE SCORE 91.2
*NYSE COMPOSITE INDEX=100

INTERIM EARNINGS (Per Share):

Qtr.	Mar.	June	Sept.	Dec.
1996		2.22		
1997	0.48	0.69	0.27	0.80
1998	1.20	0.78	0.62	0.92
1999	0.64	0.98	0.74	1.01

INTERIM DIVIDENDS (Per Share):

Amt.	Decl.	Ex.	Rec.	Pay.
0.20Q	5/04/99	6/02/99	6/04/99	7/01/99
0.21Q	8/30/99	9/08/99	9/10/99	10/01/99
0.21Q	10/19/99	12/15/99	12/17/99	1/03/00
0.21Q	2/23/00	3/01/00	3/03/00	4/03/00
0.21Q	5/02/00	6/07/00	6/09/00	7/03/00

Indicated div.: $0.84 (Div. Reinv. Plan)

CAPITALIZATION (12/26/99):

	($000)	(%)
Long-Term Debt	2,463,250	32.5
Deferred Income Tax	479,547	6.3
Common & Surplus	4,629,646	61.1
Total	7,572,443	100.0

DIVIDEND ACHIEVER STATUS:
Rank: 279 10-Year Growth Rate: 4.14%
Total Years of Dividend Growth: 28

RECENT DEVELOPMENTS: For the year ended 12/26/99, income from continuing operations slipped 4.9% to $919.4 million versus $966.4 million in 1998. Results for 1999 included a net gain of $33.0 million from the exchange of television stations and excluded a gain of $38.5 million from discontinued operations. Results for 1998 included a net non-recurring gain of $184.0 million and excluded a gain from discontinued operations of $33.5 million. Total operating revenues were $5.26 billion, up 7.8% from $4.88 billion in the prior year.

PROSPECTS: Gannett U.K. Limited agreed to acquire News Communications & Media PLC for $702.0 million. The acquisition includes four daily newspapers, paid and free weeklies, niche publications, a printing company and an interest in magazine and electronic publishing. The transaction strengthens GCI's presence in the U.K. Separately, GCI along with 11 other television broadcast groups formed iBlast™, a U.S. network that will use a portion of the digital spectrum assigned to local television stations to deliver a range of broadband digital content to consumers.

BUSINESS

GANNETT CO., INC. is a diversified news and information company that publishes newspapers and operates broadcasting stations, cable television systems, and a television entertainment programming unit. GCI is also engaged in marketing, commercial printing, a newswire data service, data services, news programming and alarm services. GCI has operations in 45 states, the District of Columbia, Canada, Guam, and the U.S. Virgin Islands. GCI is the largest U.S. newspaper group in terms of circulation, with 74 daily newspapers, including USA TODAY, a variety of non-daily publications and USA WEEKEND, a weekly newspaper magazine. GCI owns and operates 21 television stations in major markets. Gannett acquired WLTX-TV on 4/30/98 and sold its Multimedia Security Service Inc. in 3/98.

REVENUES

(12/26/99)	($000)	(%)
Newspaper advertising	3,292,894	62.6
Newspaper circulation	1,022,520	19.4
Broadcasting	728,642	13.9
All other	216,134	4.1
Total	5,260,190	100.0

ANNUAL FINANCIAL DATA

	12/26/99	12/27/98	12/28/97	[2] 12/31/96	12/31/95	12/25/94	12/26/93
Earnings Per Share	[4] 3.26	[3] 3.50	2.50	[1] 2.22	1.71	1.62	1.36
Cash Flow Per Share	4.26	4.59	3.55	3.23	2.45	2.34	2.07
Tang. Book Val. Per Share	...	0.66	...	...	...	1.25	1.38
Dividends Per Share	0.84	0.80	0.73	0.70	0.69	0.67	0.65
Dividend Payout %	25.8	22.9	29.2	31.8	40.2	41.2	47.4
INCOME STATEMENT (IN MILLIONS):							
Total Revenues	5,260.2	5,121.3	4,729.5	4,421.1	4,006.7	3,824.5	3,641.6
Costs & Expenses	3,417.0	3,367.6	3,112.2	3,067.3	2,944.9	2,802.9	2,717.6
Depreciation & Amort.	280.1	310.2	301.1	287.4	210.0	208.8	209.6
Operating Income	1,563.1	1,443.5	1,316.3	1,066.4	851.9	812.8	714.4
Net Interest Inc./(Exp.)	d88.9	d60.1	d91.7	d128.8	d44.7	d42.4	d46.8
Income Before Income Taxes	1,527.2	1,669.4	1,209.0	1,086.7	803.5	782.1	668.5
Income Taxes	607.8	669.5	496.3	462.7	326.2	316.7	270.7
Net Income	[4] 919.4	[3] 999.9	712.7	[1] 624.0	477.3	465.4	397.8
Cash Flow	1,199.5	1,310.1	1,013.8	911.3	687.2	674.2	607.4
Average Shs. Outstg. (000)	281,608	285,711	285,610	281,782	280,312	288,552	292,948
BALANCE SHEET (IN MILLIONS):							
Cash & Cash Equivalents	46.2	66.2	52.8	31.2	47.0	44.3	75.5
Total Current Assets	1,075.2	906.4	884.6	766.6	854.1	650.8	758.0
Net Property	2,223.9	2,063.8	2,192.0	1,994.1	2,070.7	1,428.1	1,478.3
Total Assets	9,006.4	6,979.5	6,890.4	6,349.6	6,503.8	3,707.1	3,823.8
Total Current Liabilities	883.8	728.0	767.5	719.0	812.8	527.1	455.1
Long-Term Obligations	2,463.3	1,306.9	1,740.5	1,880.3	2,767.9	767.3	850.7
Net Stockholders' Equity	4,629.6	3,979.8	3,479.7	2,930.8	2,145.6	1,822.2	1,907.9
Net Working Capital	191.4	178.4	117.1	47.6	41.3	123.8	302.8
Year-end Shs. Outstg. (000)	277,926	279,001	283,874	282,636	281,130	279,534	293,934
STATISTICAL RECORD:							
Operating Profit Margin %	29.7	28.2	27.8	24.1	21.3	21.3	19.6
Net Profit Margin %	17.5	19.5	15.1	14.1	11.9	12.2	10.9
Return on Equity %	19.9	25.1	20.5	21.3	22.2	25.5	20.8
Return on Assets %	10.2	14.3	10.3	9.8	7.3	12.6	10.4
Debt/Total Assets %	27.3	18.7	25.3	29.6	42.6	20.7	22.2
Price Range	83 5/8-60 5/8	75 1/8-47 5/8	61 11/16-35 11/16	39 3/8-29 1/2	32 7/16-24 3/4	29 1/2-23 1/16	29 1/8-23 3/8
P/E Ratio	25.7-18.6	21.5-13.6	24.7-14.3	17.8-13.3	19.0-14.5	18.3-14.3	21.4-17.2
Average Yield %	1.1	1.3	1.5	2.0	2.4	2.5	2.5

Statistics are as originally reported. Adj. for 2-for-1 spl., 10/97. [1] Excl. $294.6 mill. aft-tx gain & $24.5 mill. inco. fr. disc. ops; incl. $93.0 mill. aft-tx gain. [2] Incl. ops. of Multimedia Inc., acq. on 12/9/95. [3] Incl. $184.0 mill. aft-tax gain fr. disp. of bus. [4] Incl. $33.0 mill. net gain fr. exchange of TV stations & excl. $38.5 mill. gain fr. disc. ops.

OFFICERS:
J. J. Curley, Chmn.
D. H. McCorkindale, Pres., C.E.O.
L. F. Miller, Exec. V.P., C.F.O.
INVESTOR CONTACT: Garcia Martore, Investor Relations, (703) 284-6922
PRINCIPAL OFFICE: 1100 Wilson Blvd., Arlington, VA 22234

TELEPHONE NUMBER: (703) 284-6000
FAX: (703) 364-0855
WEB: www.gannett.com
NO. OF EMPLOYEES: 45,800 (approx.)
SHAREHOLDERS: 14,000 (approx.)
ANNUAL MEETING: In May
INCORPORATED: NY, Dec., 1923; reincorp., DE, May, 1972

INSTITUTIONAL HOLDINGS:
No. of Institutions: 587
Shares Held: 207,610,868
% Held: 74.5

INDUSTRY: Newspapers (SIC: 2711)

TRANSFER AGENT(S): Norwest Bank Minnesota, St. Paul, MN.

GATX CORPORATION

	YIELD	3.6%
	P/E RATIO	11.2

TRADING VOLUME
Thousand Shares

*7 YEAR PRICE SCORE 81.8   ***12 MONTH PRICE SCORE 103.8**
*NYSE COMPOSITE INDEX=100

INTERIM EARNINGS (Per Share):

Qtr.	Mar.	June	Sept.	Dec.
1997	0.68	0.62	0.56	d2.87
1998	0.74	0.61	0.76	0.51
1999	0.78	0.75	0.93	0.64

INTERIM DIVIDENDS (Per Share):

Amt.	Decl.	Ex.	Rec.	Pay.
0.275Q	7/23/99	9/13/99	9/15/99	9/30/99
0.275Q	10/22/99	12/13/99	12/15/99	12/31/99
0.30Q	1/28/00	3/08/00	3/10/00	3/31/00
0.30Q	4/28/00	6/13/00	6/15/00	6/30/00

Indicated div.: $1.20 (Div. Reinv. Plan)

CAPITALIZATION (12/31/99):

	($000)	(%)
Long-Term Debt	3,249,500	68.8
Capital Lease Obligations..	183,100	3.9
Deferred Income Tax	457,200	9.7
Common & Surplus	836,000	17.7
Total	4,725,800	100.0

DIVIDEND ACHIEVER STATUS:
Rank: 197   10-Year Growth Rate: 8.20%
Total Years of Dividend Growth: 14

RECENT DEVELOPMENTS: For the twelve months ended 12/31/99, net income was $151.3 million, up 14.7% from $131.9 million in the previous year. Revenues totaled $1.86 billion compared with $1.85 billion a year earlier. Revenues from GATX Rail increased 6.7% to $570.9 million, while revenues from Integrated Solutions rose 2.2% to $599.4 million. However, Financial Services income declined 5.0% to $693.6 million.

PROSPECTS: GATX Rail expects to achieve its long-term target of 8.0% to 10.0% earnings growth as a result of new product introductions, enhanced services, fleet acquisitions and international expansion. GATX Capital plans to continue to expand its asset pool and diversify its income sources via direct ownership of assets or third-party asset management. As a result, GMT expects GATX Capital to report a 15.0% year-over-year increase in earnings.

BUSINESS

GATX CORPORATION, through its subsidiaries, engages in the leasing and management of railroad tank cars and other specialized railcars; arranges and services the financing of equipment and other capital assets; and provides logisitics and supply chain services related to chemicals, petroleum, and dry goods. GATX Rail leases specialized railcars, primarily tank cars, under full service leases. GATX Capital arranges and services the financing of equipment and other capital assets on a worldwide basis. American Steamship Company operatesself-unloading vessels on the Great Lakes. GATX Integrated Solutions Group provides logistics and supply chain services related to chemicals, petroleum, and dry goods.

ANNUAL FINANCIAL DATA

	12/31/99	12/31/98	12/31/97	12/31/96	12/31/95	12/31/94	12/31/93
Earnings Per Share	3.01	2.62	① d1.27	2.19	2.15	1.94	① 1.50
Cash Flow Per Share	9.14	7.92	4.32	7.13	6.37	6.04	5.61
Tang. Book Val. Per Share	17.20	14.87	13.39	16.73	15.60	14.52	14.89
Dividends Per Share	1.10	1.00	0.92	0.86	0.80	0.76	0.70
Dividend Payout %	36.5	38.2	...	39.4	37.2	39.3	46.8
INCOME STATEMENT (IN MILLIONS):							
Total Revenues	1,858.9	1,763.1	1,701.9	1,414.4	1,246.4	1,155.0	1,086.9
Costs & Expenses	1,053.3	1,083.4	1,078.6	868.0	769.3	704.7	650.4
Depreciation & Amort.	308.2	267.5	252.3	202.4	171.6	165.1	150.7
Operating Income	497.4	412.2	① 371.0	344.0	305.5	285.2	① 285.8
Net Interest Inc./(Exp.)	d232.2	d234.9	d222.4	d202.8	d170.1	d148.2	d151.8
Income Before Income Taxes	253.9	162.6	d87.3	128.7	117.0	117.8	104.4
Income Taxes	102.6	74.3	cr5.5	54.4	47.6	48.8	51.4
Equity Earnings/Minority Int.	...	43.6	30.9	28.4	31.4	22.5	19.7
Net Income	151.3	131.9	① d50.9	102.7	100.8	91.5	① 72.7
Cash Flow	459.5	399.3	194.7	291.9	259.2	243.3	223.4
Average Shs. Outstg. (000)	50,301	50,426	45,084	40,966	40,718	40,306	39,788
BALANCE SHEET (IN MILLIONS):							
Cash & Cash Equivalents	102.5	94.5	77.8	46.2	34.8	27.3	26.2
Total Current Assets	1,144.1	1,032.4	1,168.5	1,039.1	963.9	803.9	781.3
Net Property	3,282.0	2,790.1	2,710.5	2,846.4	2,369.1	2,192.3	1,962.3
Total Assets	5,866.8	4,939.3	4,947.8	4,750.2	4,042.9	3,650.7	3,392.1
Total Current Liabilities	815.5	707.0	805.2	608.1	611.7	587.3	469.7
Long-Term Obligations	3,432.6	2,821.7	2,819.4	2,664.1	2,092.5	1,805.1	1,713.8
Net Stockholders' Equity	836.0	732.9	655.4	774.9	717.8	662.4	589.9
Net Working Capital	328.6	325.4	363.3	431.0	352.2	216.6	311.6
Year-end Shs. Outstg. (000)	48,599	49,284	48,942	46,128	45,792	45,372	39,400
STATISTICAL RECORD:							
Operating Profit Margin %	26.8	22.5	8.0	23.4	23.0	23.0	23.5
Net Profit Margin %	8.1	7.5	...	7.3	8.1	7.9	6.7
Return on Equity %	18.1	18.0	...	13.3	14.0	13.8	12.3
Return on Assets %	2.6	2.7	...	2.2	2.5	2.5	2.1
Debt/Total Assets %	58.5	57.1	57.0	56.1	51.8	49.4	50.5
Price Range	40⁷/₈-28¹/₁₆	47⁹/₁₆-26¹/₄	36-23³/₄	25⁵/₈-21¹/₂	27¹/₈-20³/₁₆	22⁵/₁₆-19¹/₈	21¹/₈-15¹¹/₁₆
P/E Ratio	13.6-9.3	18.2-10.0	...	11.7-9.8	12.6-9.4	11.5-9.9	14.1-10.5
Average Yield %	3.2	2.7	3.1	3.6	3.4	3.7	3.8

Statistics are as originally reported. Adj. for 2-for-1 stk. split, 6/98 ① Incls. non-recurr. chrg. 12/31/97: $163.0 mill.; chrg. 12/31/93: $8.5 mill.

OFFICERS:
R. H. Zech, Chmn., Pres., C.E.O.
B. A. Kenney, V.P., C.F.O.
D. B. Anderson, V.P., Gen. Couns., Sec.
W. J. Hasek, Treas.

INVESTOR CONTACT: R. C. Lyons, Dir. of Inv. Rel., (312) 621-6633

PRINCIPAL OFFICE: 500 W. Monroe Street, Chicago, IL 60661-3676

TELEPHONE NUMBER: (312) 621-6200
FAX: (312) 621-6665
WEB: www.gatx.com

NO. OF EMPLOYEES: 6,300 (approx.)

SHAREHOLDERS: 3,652

ANNUAL MEETING: In Apr.

INCORPORATED: NY, July, 1916

INSTITUTIONAL HOLDINGS:
No. of Institutions: 172
Shares Held: 38,936,018
% Held: 79.2

INDUSTRY: Rental of railroad cars (SIC: 4741)

TRANSFER AGENT(S): ChaseMellon Shareholder Services, Ridgefield Park, NJ

GENERAL ELECTRIC COMPANY

YIELD 1.0%
P/E RATIO 48.3

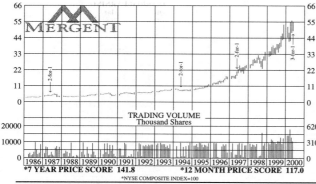

TRADING VOLUME
Thousand Shares

*7 YEAR PRICE SCORE 141.8 *12 MONTH PRICE SCORE 117.0
*NYSE COMPOSITE INDEX=100

INTERIM EARNINGS (Per Share):

Qtr.	Mar.	June	Sept.	Dec.
1996	0.15	0.19	0.18	0.21
1997	0.17	0.22	0.21	0.23
1998	0.19	0.25	0.23	0.27
1999	0.22	0.29	0.27	0.31

INTERIM DIVIDENDS (Per Share):

Amt.	Decl.	Ex.	Rec.	Pay.
0.35Q	9/10/99	9/28/99	9/30/99	10/25/99
0.41Q	12/17/99	12/22/99	12/27/99	1/25/00
0.41Q	2/11/00	3/06/00	3/08/00	4/25/00
3-for-1	2/11/00	5/08/00	4/27/00	5/05/00

Indicated div.: $0.55 (Adj.; Div. Reinv. Plan)

CAPITALIZATION (12/31/99):

	($000)	(%)
Long-Term Debt	71,427,000	55.6
Deferred Income Tax	9,238,000	7.2
Minority Interest	5,214,000	4.1
Common & Surplus	42,557,000	33.1
Total	128,436,000	100.0

DIVIDEND ACHIEVER STATUS:
Rank: 103   10-Year Growth Rate: 12.57%
Total Years of Dividend Growth: 24

RECENT DEVELOPMENTS: For the year ended 12/31/99, net income increased 15.2% to $10.72 billion compared with $9.30 billion in the previous year. Revenues were up 11.1% to $111.63 billion. Revenues in the Aircraft Engines business segment grew 2.5% to $10.56 billion, while Power Systems segment revenues advanced 18.7% to $10.05 billion. Industrial Products and Systems segment revenues rose 2.9% to $11.56 billion, while GE Capital Services segment revenues improved 14.4% to $55.75 billion.

PROSPECTS: The Company and Toshiba Corporation announced an intent to create an international joint venture named Toshiba GE Automation Systems International LLC. The new company is expected to start operations in October 2000. GE will own 49.0% and Toshiba will own 51.0% of the new company. Separately, GE Energy Services, Inc. has completed a cash tender offer for shares of Showpower, Inc. As a result of the offer, GE Energy Services has acquired more than 90.0% of Sharepower's shares.

BUSINESS

GENERAL ELECTRIC COMPANY'S businesses and their contributions to 1999 revenues are as follows: Aircraft Engines (9.4%) develops and manufactures engines for commercial aircraft. Appliances (5.0%) is a supplier of kitchen appliances. The Industrial Products and Systems segment (10.3%) includes lighting, transportation systems, industrial systems, and GE Supply. Broadcasting (5.1%) operations are conducted through NBC. Financial Services (49.9%) are provided by GE Capital Services. The Plastics, Power Systems, Technical Products and Services, and All Other (21.3%) sectors are providers of medical systems, power generation, motors and transportation systems.

REVENUES

(12/31/1999)	($000)	(%)
Sales of goods	47,785,000	42.8
Sales of services	16,283,000	14.6
Other income	798,000	0.7
GECS rev from services	46,764,000	41.9
Total	111,630,000	100.0

ANNUAL FINANCIAL DATA

	12/31/99	12/31/98	12/31/97	12/31/96	12/31/95	12/31/94	12/31/93
Earnings Per Share	1.07	0.93	③0.82	0.73	0.65	②0.58	①0.43
Cash Flow Per Share	1.77	1.52	1.34	1.11	1.01	0.89	0.75
Tang. Book Val. Per Share	1.68	1.55	1.56	1.53	1.80	1.47	1.51
Dividends Per Share	0.47	0.40	0.35	0.31	0.27	0.24	0.21
Dividend Payout %	43.9	42.9	42.3	41.8	42.0	41.6	48.6
INCOME STATEMENT (IN MILLIONS):							
Total Revenues	111,630.0	100,469.0	90,840.0	79,179.0	70,028.0	60,109.0	60,562.0
Costs & Expenses	50,295.0	46,028.0	43,097.0	37,484.0	33,076.0	34,473.0	28,825.0
Depreciation & Amort.	6,691.0	5,860.0	5,269.0	3,785.0	3,594.0	3,207.0	3,261.0
Operating Income	54,644.0	48,581.0	42,474.0	37,281.0	32,605.0	21,646.0	28,476.0
Net Interest Inc./(Exp.)	d10,013.0	d9,753.0	d8,384.0	d7,904.0	d7,286.0	d4,949.0	d6,989.0
Income Before Income Taxes	15,942.0	13,742.0	11,419.0	10,446.0	9,188.0	8,048.0	6,726.0
Income Taxes	4,860.0	4,181.0	2,976.0	3,526.0	3,164.0	2,746.0	2,151.0
Equity Earnings/Minority Int.	d365.0	d265.0	d240.0	d269.0	d204.0	d170.0	d151.0
Net Income	10,717.0	9,296.0	③8,203.0	7,280.0	6,573.0	②5,915.0	①4,424.0
Cash Flow	17,408.0	15,156.0	13,472.0	11,065.0	10,167.0	9,122.0	7,685.0
Average Shs. Outstg. (000)	9,834,000	9,990,000	10,035,000	9,924,000	10,104,000	10,254,000	10,248,000
BALANCE SHEET (IN MILLIONS):							
Cash & Cash Equivalents	90,312.0	83,034.0	76,482.0	64,080.0	43,890.0	33,556.0	103,657.0
Total Current Assets	105,850.0	97,307.0	91,301.0	77,633.0	57,020.0	44,963.0	115,676.0
Net Property	41,022.0	35,730.0	32,316.0	28,795.0	25,679.0	23,465.0	21,228.0
Total Assets	405,200.0	355,935.0	304,012.0	237,567.0	200,042.0	170,534.0	251,506.0
Total Current Liabilities	161,216.0	141,579.0	120,668.0	20,307.0	17,538.0	72,854.0	93,594.0
Long-Term Obligations	71,427.0	59,663.0	46,603.0	49,246.0	51,027.0	36,979.0	28,270.0
Net Stockholders' Equity	42,557.0	38,880.0	34,438.0	31,125.0	29,609.0	26,387.0	25,824.0
Net Working Capital	d55,366.0	d44,272.0	d29,367.0	57,326.0	39,482.0	d27,891.0	22,082.0
Year-end Shs. Outstg. (000)	9,854,529	9,813,000	9,795,000	9,870,000	10,002,000	10,236,000	10,248,000
STATISTICAL RECORD:							
Operating Profit Margin %	49.0	48.4	46.8	47.9	47.6	37.3	47.0
Net Profit Margin %	9.6	9.3	9.0	9.2	9.4	9.8	7.3
Return on Equity %	25.2	23.9	23.8	23.4	22.2	22.4	17.1
Return on Assets %	2.6	2.6	2.7	2.7	2.9	3.0	1.8
Debt/Total Assets %	17.6	16.8	15.3	20.7	25.5	21.7	11.2
Price Range	53³⁄₁₆-31³⁄₈	34⁵⁄₈-23	25¹⁄₂-15	17¹¹⁄₁₆-11¹¹⁄₁₆	12³⁄₁₆-8⁵⁄₁₆	9¹⁄₈-7¹⁄₂	8¹⁵⁄₁₆-6³⁄₄
P/E Ratio	16.3-9.6	37.1-24.7	31.1-19.5	24.1-15.8	18.7-12.8	15.8-13.0	20.6-15.6
Average Yield %	1.1	1.4	1.7	2.1	2.7	2.9	2.7

Statistics are as originally reported. Adj. for 3-for-1 stk. split, 5/00, 2-for-1 stk. split, 5/97 & 5/94. ① Excl. an acctg. change of $862.0 mill. ② Bef. disc. opers. of d$1.19 bill. ③ Incl. an after-tax gain of $1.50 bill. from the exchange of Lockheed Martin pfd. stk. & after-tax charges of $1.50 bill. for restruct. & oth. spec. matters.

OFFICERS:
J. F. Welch Jr., Chmn., C.E.O.
D. D. Dammerman, Vice-Chmn., Exec. Off.
J. D. Opie, Vice-Chmn., Exec. Off.

INVESTOR CONTACT: Pauline Telep, Shareholder Relations, (203) 373-2816

PRINCIPAL OFFICE: 3135 Easton Turnpike, Fairfield, CT 06431

TELEPHONE NUMBER: (203) 373-2211
FAX: (203) 373-3131
WEB: www.ge.com
NO. OF EMPLOYEES: 340,000 (avg.)
SHAREHOLDERS: 577,000
ANNUAL MEETING: In Apr.
INCORPORATED: NY, Apr., 1892

INSTITUTIONAL HOLDINGS:
No. of Institutions: 1,231
Shares Held: 4,946,168,784 (Adj.)
% Held: 50.3

INDUSTRY: Electric lamps (SIC: 3641)

TRANSFER AGENT(S): GE Share Owner Services,c/o The Bank of New York, New York, NY

NYSE SYMBOL GPC
Rec. Pr. 23 7/8 (5/31/00)

GENUINE PARTS COMPANY

YIELD 4.6%
P/E RATIO 11.3

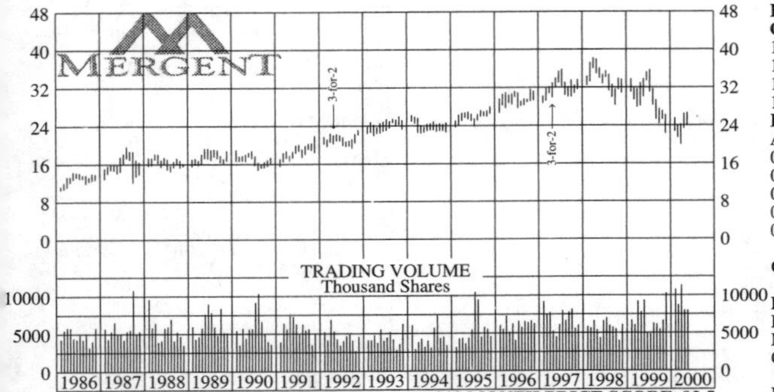

MERGENT
3-for-2
3-for-2
TRADING VOLUME
Thousand Shares
48
40
32
24
16
8
0
10000
5000
0
1986 1987 1988 1989 1990 1991 1992 1993 1994 1995 1996 1997 1998 1999 2000

*7 YEAR PRICE SCORE 62.2 *12 MONTH PRICE SCORE 93.5

*NYSE COMPOSITE INDEX=100

INTERIM EARNINGS (Per Share):

Qtr.	Mar.	June	Sept.	Dec.
1996	0.41	0.45	0.45	0.52
1997	0.43	0.47	0.47	0.55
1998	0.45	0.48	0.48	0.58
1999	0.48	0.52	0.51	0.61

INTERIM DIVIDENDS (Per Share):

Amt.	Decl.	Ex.	Rec.	Pay.
0.26Q	4/19/99	6/02/99	6/04/99	7/01/99
0.26Q	8/16/99	9/01/99	9/03/99	10/01/99
0.26Q	11/15/99	12/01/99	12/03/99	1/03/00
0.275Q	2/22/00	3/01/00	3/03/00	4/03/00
0.275Q	4/18/00	6/07/00	6/09/00	7/03/00

Indicated div.: $1.10 (Div. Reinv. Plan)

CAPITALIZATION (12/31/99):

	($000)	(%)
Long-Term Debt	702,417	23.3
Deferred Income Tax	87,446	2.9
Minority Interest	46,260	1.5
Common & Surplus	2,177,517	72.3
Total	3,013,640	100.0

DIVIDEND ACHIEVER STATUS:
Rank: 221 10-Year Growth Rate: 7.17%
Total Years of Dividend Growth: 43

RECENT DEVELOPMENTS: For the year ended 12/31/99, net income rose 6.1% to $377.6 million from $355.8 million in the previous year. Net sales advanced 20.7% to $7.98 billion from $6.61 billion a year ago. The Automotive Parts group sales increased 25.2% to $4.08 billion, while Industrial Parts sales climbed 7.3% to $2.16 billion. Office Products sales advanced 8.5% to $1.22 billion. Electrical and Electronic Materials sales more than doubled to $522.4 million.

PROSPECTS: The Automotive Parts group's NAPA Auto Parts and Mitchell Repair Information Company, introduced an application that enables automotive service professionals to efficiently quote repair estimates, procure necessary parts and access technical information needed for repairs. The application should reduce bay turnover and increase effectiveness of NAPA's service writers and technicians. On 4/21/00, GPC launched www.napaonline.com, an on-line NAPA parts store.

BUSINESS

GENUINE PARTS COMPANY is a service organization engaged in the distribution of automotive replacement parts, industrial replacement parts, office products and electrical and electronic materials. GPC's largest division is its NAPA Automotive Parts Group, which serves 5,000 auto parts jobbing stores. The Industrial Parts Group distributes replacement parts, equipment and related supplies from approximately 499 operations in 47 states, Canada and Mexico. The Office Products Group distributes products including information processing, supplies, furniture and machines. The Electrical/Electronic Materials Group distributes materials for the manufacture and repair of electrical and electronic apparatus. GPC owns a 15% interest in Mitchell Repair Information Company, LLC.

BUSINESS LINE ANALYSIS

(12/31/99)	Rev(%)	Inc(%)
Automotive	51.2	54.8
Industrial	27	25.7
Office Products	15.3	16.3
Electrical/Electronic Mat	6.5	3.2
Total	100.0	100.0

ANNUAL FINANCIAL DATA

	12/31/99	12/31/98	12/31/97	12/31/96	12/31/95	12/31/94	12/31/93
Earnings Per Share	**2.11**	**1.98**	**1.90**	**1.82**	**1.68**	**1.55**	**[1] 1.39**
Cash Flow Per Share	**2.61**	**2.36**	**2.23**	**2.10**	**1.92**	**1.75**	**1.57**
Tang. Book Val. Per Share	**9.80**	**9.52**	**10.39**	**9.62**	**9.03**	**8.30**	**7.75**
Dividends Per Share	**1.03**	**0.99**	**0.94**	**0.88**	**0.82**	**0.75**	**0.70**
Dividend Payout %	**48.8**	**50.0**	**49.6**	**48.3**	**48.9**	**48.4**	**50.2**
INCOME STATEMENT (IN MILLIONS):							
Total Revenues	7,981.7	6,614.0	6,005.2	5,720.5	5,261.9	4,858.4	4,384.3
Costs & Expenses	7,263.7	5,955.6	5,380.8	5,124.8	4,707.9	4,346.2	3,924.0
Depreciation & Amort.	90.0	69.3	58.9	50.4	43.2	37.4	34.4
Operating Income	628.1	589.1	565.6	545.2	510.8	474.9	425.8
Income Before Income Taxes	628.1	589.1	565.6	545.2	510.8	474.9	425.8
Income Taxes	250.4	233.3	223.2	215.2	201.6	186.3	167.0
Net Income	377.6	355.8	342.4	330.1	309.2	288.5	[1] 258.9
Cash Flow	467.6	425.1	401.3	380.5	352.4	325.9	293.3
Average Shs. Outstg. (000)	179,238	180,081	180,165	181,568	183,923	186,062	186,326
BALANCE SHEET (IN MILLIONS):							
Cash & Cash Equivalents	45.7	85.0	72.8	67.4	44.3	82.4	187.8
Total Current Assets	2,895.2	2,683.4	2,093.6	1,937.6	1,764.0	1,595.8	1,506.2
Net Property	413.5	404.0	372.5	346.0	303.2	258.0	231.2
Total Assets	3,929.7	3,600.4	2,754.4	2,521.6	2,274.1	2,029.5	1,870.8
Total Current Liabilities	916.0	818.4	556.9	568.4	475.5	422.4	353.5
Long-Term Obligations	702.4	588.6	209.5	110.2	60.6	11.4	12.3
Net Stockholders' Equity	2,177.5	2,053.3	1,859.5	1,732.1	1,650.9	1,526.2	1,445.3
Net Working Capital	1,979.2	1,864.9	1,536.6	1,369.3	1,288.4	1,173.4	1,152.7
Year-end Shs. Outstg. (000)	177,276	179,505	178,948	180,048	182,870	183,941	186,423
STATISTICAL RECORD:							
Operating Profit Margin %	7.9	8.9	9.4	9.5	9.7	9.8	9.7
Net Profit Margin %	4.7	5.4	5.7	5.8	5.9	5.9	5.9
Return on Equity %	17.3	17.3	18.4	19.1	18.7	18.9	17.9
Return on Assets %	9.6	9.9	12.4	13.1	13.6	14.2	13.8
Debt/Total Assets %	17.9	16.3	7.6	4.4	2.7	0.6	0.7
Price Range	35 3/4-22 1/4	38 1/4-28 1/4	35 7/8-28 11/16	31 11/16-26 11/16	28-23 11/16	26 1/4-22 7/16	26-21 15/16
P/E Ratio	16.9-10.5	19.3-14.3	18.9-15.1	17.4-14.7	16.7-14.1	16.9-14.4	18.7-15.8
Average Yield %	3.6	3.0	2.9	3.0	3.2	3.1	2.9

Statistics are as originally reported. Adj. for stk. splits: 3-for-2, 4/97. [1] Bef. acctg change chrg. $1.1 mill.

OFFICERS:
L. L. Prince, Chmn., C.E.O.
T. C. Gallagher, Pres., C.O.O.
J. W. Nix, Exec. V.P., Fin., C.F.O.

INVESTOR CONTACT: Jerry Nix, Exec. V.P.-Fin., (770) 953-1700

PRINCIPAL OFFICE: 2999 Circle 75 Parkway, Atlanta, GA 30339

TELEPHONE NUMBER: (770) 953-1700
FAX: (770) 956-2211
WEB: www.genpt.com

NO. OF EMPLOYEES: 33,000 (avg.)

SHAREHOLDERS: 7,332

ANNUAL MEETING: In Apr.

INCORPORATED: GA, May, 1928

INSTITUTIONAL HOLDINGS:
No. of Institutions: 269
Shares Held: 123,197,911
% Held: 69.3

INDUSTRY: Motor vehicle supplies and new parts (SIC: 5013)

TRANSFER AGENT(S): Sun Trust Bank, Atlanta, GA

NYSE SYMBOL G
Rec. Pr. 33 3/8 (5/31/00)

GILLETTE COMPANY (THE)

YIELD 1.9%
P/E RATIO 29.3

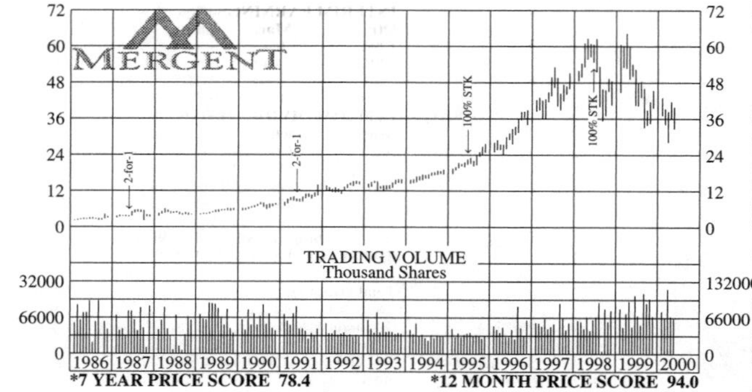

MERGENT
72 60 48 36 24 12 0
2-for-1
2-for-1
100% STK
100% STK
TRADING VOLUME
Thousand Shares
32000 66000 0
132000 66000 0
1986 1987 1988 1989 1990 1991 1992 1993 1994 1995 1996 1997 1998 1999 2000

***7 YEAR PRICE SCORE 78.4** ***12 MONTH PRICE SCORE 94.0**

*NYSE COMPOSITE INDEX=100

INTERIM EARNINGS (Per Share):

Qtr.	Mar.	June	Sept.	Dec.
1996	0.23	0.25	0.28	0.11
1997	0.26	0.29	0.32	0.41
1998	0.23	0.33	Nil	0.39
1999	0.24	0.26	0.32	0.32

INTERIM DIVIDENDS (Per Share):

Amt.	Decl.	Ex.	Rec.	Pay.
0.147Q	4/15/99	4/29/99	5/03/99	6/04/99
0.147Q	12/30/99	7/29/99	8/02/99	9/03/99
0.147Q	10/21/99	10/28/99	11/01/99	12/03/99
0.147Q	12/16/99	1/28/00	2/01/00	3/03/00
0.163Q	3/16/00	4/27/00	5/01/00	6/05/00

Indicated div.: $0.65 (Div. Reinv. Plan)

CAPITALIZATION (12/31/99):

	($000)	(%)
Long-Term Debt	2,931,000	45.4
Deferred Income Tax	423,000	6.6
Minority Interest	38,000	0.6
Preferred Stock	85,000	1.3
Common & Surplus	2,975,000	46.1
Total	6,452,000	100.0

DIVIDEND ACHIEVER STATUS:
Rank: 41 10-Year Growth Rate: 17.17%
Total Years of Dividend Growth: 22

RECENT DEVELOPMENTS: For the year ended 12/31/99, net income improved 16.6% to $1.26 billion from $1.08 billion a year earlier. Results for 1998 included a one-time pre-tax realignment charge of $535.0 million. Net sales decreased slightly to $9.90 billion compared with $10.06 billion in the previous year. Profit from operations rose 17.7% to $2.11 billion from $1.79 billion in the prior year.

PROSPECTS: Near-term results should continue to benefit from strong performance within G's core businesses, the reorganization and optimization of trade inventories, and an improvement in international economies. Meanwhile, G has retained J.P. Morgan & Co. to assist in the assessment of strategic alternatives for its Braun household, hair care and personal diagnostics products.

BUSINESS

THE GILLETTE COMPANY is a consumer products firm engaged in the development, manufacture and sale of a wide range of products for personal care. Major lines include blades and razors, toiletries and cosmetics, stationery products, Braun electric shavers and small appliances, Duracell battery products, and Oral-B oral care products. Gillette is the market leader of blades and razors in North America and most other areas of the world. The Company holds a major position in North America in sales of toiletries and writing instruments. Braun markets electric shavers in Germany, Europe, North America and Japan. Blades & Razors represented 32% of 1999 revenues; Braun Products, 16%; Toiletries & Cosmetics, 11%; Stationery Products, 7%; Oral-B products, 6%; and Duracell products, 28%.

ANNUAL FINANCIAL DATA

	12/31/99	12/31/98	12/31/97	12/31/96	12/31/95	12/31/94	12/31/93
Earnings Per Share	**1.14**	[2] **0.95**	**1.25**	[2] **0.86**	**0.93**	**0.79**	[1] [2] **0.48**
Cash Flow Per Share	**1.58**	**1.35**	**1.61**	**1.20**	**1.20**	**1.03**	**0.73**
Tang. Book Val. Per Share	**0.58**	**1.81**	**2.07**	**1.56**	**1.34**	**1.16**	**0.52**
Dividends Per Share	**0.57**	**0.49**	**0.41**	**0.34**	**0.29**	**0.24**	**0.20**
Dividend Payout %	**50.0**	**51.3**	**33.1**	**40.3**	**31.1**	**30.6**	**42.2**
INCOME STATEMENT (IN MILLIONS):							
Total Revenues	9,897.0	10,056.0	10,062.0	9,697.7	6,794.7	6,070.2	5,410.8
Costs & Expenses	7,292.0	7,808.0	7,316.0	7,680.3	5,175.0	4,628.1	4,367.6
Depreciation & Amort.	500.0	459.0	422.0	381.1	248.4	215.4	218.5
Operating Income	2,105.0	1,789.0	2,324.0	[2] 1,636.3	1,371.3	1,226.7	[2] 824.7
Net Interest Inc./(Exp.)	d129.0	d86.0	d69.0	d66.9	d49.1	d42.1	d32.5
Income Before Income Taxes	1,930.0	1,669.0	2,221.0	1,525.0	1,296.9	1,104.1	682.7
Income Taxes	670.0	588.0	794.0	576.3	473.4	405.8	255.8
Net Income	1,260.0	[2] 1,081.0	1,427.0	[2] 948.7	823.5	698.3	[1] [2] 426.9
Cash Flow	1,760.0	1,540.0	1,849.0	1,325.2	1,067.2	909.0	640.7
Average Shs. Outstg. (000)	1,111,000	1,144,000	1,148,000	1,107,000	887,000	884,800	881,600
BALANCE SHEET (IN MILLIONS):							
Cash & Cash Equivalents	80.0	102.0	105.0	83.9	49.5	46.1	38.6
Total Current Assets	5,132.0	5,440.0	4,690.0	4,753.2	3,104.5	2,747.4	2,528.0
Net Property	3,667.0	3,472.0	3,104.0	2,565.8	1,636.9	1,411.0	1,214.5
Total Assets	11,786.0	11,902.0	10,864.0	10,435.3	6,340.3	5,494.0	5,102.3
Total Current Liabilities	4,180.0	3,478.0	2,641.0	2,934.7	2,124.0	1,783.2	1,760.3
Long-Term Obligations	2,931.0	2,256.0	1,476.0	1,490.4	691.1	715.1	840.1
Net Stockholders' Equity	3,060.0	4,543.0	4,841.0	4,490.9	2,513.3	2,017.3	1,479.0
Net Working Capital	952.0	1,962.0	2,049.0	1,818.5	980.5	964.2	767.7
Year-end Shs. Outstg. (000)	1,065,000	1,105,000	1,120,938	1,132,156	888,928	885,800	883,560
STATISTICAL RECORD:							
Operating Profit Margin %	21.3	17.8	23.1	16.9	20.2	20.2	15.2
Net Profit Margin %	12.7	10.7	14.2	9.8	12.1	11.5	7.9
Return on Equity %	41.2	23.8	29.5	21.1	32.8	34.6	28.9
Return on Assets %	10.7	9.1	13.1	9.1	13.0	12.7	8.4
Debt/Total Assets %	24.9	19.0	13.6	14.3	10.9	13.0	16.5
Price Range	64 3/8-33 1/16	62 11/16-35 5/16	53 3/16-36	38 7/8-24 1/8	27 11/16-17 11/16	19 1/8-14 7/16	15 15/16-11 7/8
P/E Ratio	56.5-29.0	65.9-37.2	42.7-28.9	45.5-28.2	29.9-19.1	24.4-18.4	33.2-24.7
Average Yield %	1.2	1.0	0.9	1.1	1.3	1.4	1.5

Statistics are as originally reported. Adj. for stk. splits: 2-for-1, 6/98, 6/95. [1] Bef. acctg. change chrg. $138.6 mill. [2] Incl. non-recurr. chrg. 1998, $535.0 mill.; 1996, $413.0 mill.; 1993, $164.1 mill.

OFFICERS:
M. C. Hawley, Chmn., C.E.O.
A. Livis, Exec. V.P.
C. W. Cramb Jr., Sr. V.P., Fin., C.F.O.

INVESTOR CONTACT: Investor Relations, (617) 421-7000

PRINCIPAL OFFICE: Prudential Tower Building, Boston, MA 02199

TELEPHONE NUMBER: (617) 421-7000
FAX: (617) 421-7123
WEB: www.gillette.com

NO. OF EMPLOYEES: 39,800 (approx.)

SHAREHOLDERS: 57,340

ANNUAL MEETING: In Feb.

INCORPORATED: DE, Sep., 1917

INSTITUTIONAL HOLDINGS:
No. of Institutions: 815
Shares Held: 615,330,346
% Held: 57.4

INDUSTRY: Hand and edge tools, nec (SIC: 3423)

TRANSFER AGENT(S): BankBoston, N.A., Boston, MA

GOLDEN WEST FINANCIAL CORPORATION

YIELD 0.5%
P/E RATIO 14.5

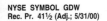
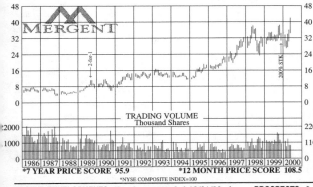

*7 YEAR PRICE SCORE 95.9   *12 MONTH PRICE SCORE 108.5
*NYSE COMPOSITE INDEX=100

INTERIM EARNINGS (Per Share):

Qtr.	Mar.	June	Sept.	Dec.
1996	0.42	0.44	0.78	0.44
1997	0.48	0.50	0.52	0.54
1998	0.64	0.68	0.62	0.66
1999	0.70	0.72	0.72	0.73

INTERIM DIVIDENDS (Per Share):

Amt.	Decl.	Ex.	Rec.	Pay.
0.14Q	7/28/99	8/12/99	8/16/99	9/10/99
200% STK	11/02/99	12/13/99	11/15/99	12/10/99
0.052Q	11/02/99	11/10/99	11/15/99	12/10/99
0.052Q	2/09/00	2/11/00	2/15/00	3/10/00
0.052Q	5/5/00	5/11/00	5/15/00	6/12/00

Indicated div.: $0.21 (Adj.)

CAPITALIZATION (12/31/99):

	($000)	(%)
Total Deposits	27,714,910	87.4
Long-Term Debt	812,950	2.6
Common & Surplus	3,194,854	10.1
Total	31,722,714	100.0

DIVIDEND ACHIEVER STATUS:

Rank: 74   10-Year Growth Rate: 14.43%
Total Years of Dividend Growth: 16

RECENT DEVELOPMENTS: For the year ended 12/31/99, the Company reported net income of $480.0 million compared with income of $447.1 million, before an extraordinary loss of $12.5 million, in the previous year. Results for 1999 and 1998 included gains of $22.8 million and $38.8 million, respectively, on the sale of securities, mortgage-backed securities, and loans. Net interest income grew 3.7% to $1.00 billion from $967.3 million a year earlier.

PROSPECTS: Looking ahead, the Company should continue to benefit from significant growth in loan originations, as well as from the strong national economy. In addition, GDW expects the high demand for adjustable rate mortgages, which is the Company's primary product, to be advantageous to its growth. Customers favor adjustable rate mortgages over fixed rate mortgages due to recently increased fixed rates.

BUSINESS

GOLDEN WEST FINANCIAL CORPORATION, with assets of $45.64 billion as of 3/31/00, is a savings and loan holding company. The Company's principal subsidiaries are World Savings Bank, FSB and World Savings & Loan Association. WFSB and WSL had $37.80 billion and $5.10 billion, respectively, in assets as of 12/31/99. GDW has a network of 119 savings branch offices in California, 38 in Colorado, 33 in Florida, 21 in Texas, eight in Kansas, 15 in Arizona, 11 in New Jersey, and four in Illinois. GDW operates 269 offices in 29 states as a financial intermediary attracting deposits (primarily in the form of savings accounts) and investing funds in loans and securities backed by residential real estate.

LOAN DISTRIBUTION

(12/31/99)	($000)	(%)
1-to-4 Family Dwelling	26,041,066	92.7
Over 4-Family Dwelling	1,979,199	7.0
Commercial Property	49,149	0.2
Land	612	0.0
Loans on Savings Accounts	20,107	0.1
Total	28,090,133	100.0

ANNUAL FINANCIAL DATA

	12/31/99	12/31/98	12/31/97	12/31/96	12/31/95	12/31/94	12/31/93
Earnings Per Share	2.87	② 2.58	2.04	① 2.11	1.33	1.24	1.43
Tang. Book Val. Per Share	19.80	18.32	15.76	13.66	12.12	10.60	10.06
Dividends Per Share	0.19	0.17	0.15	0.13	0.12	0.10	0.09
Dividend Payout %	6.7	6.7	7.4	6.2	8.8	8.1	6.3
INCOME STATEMENT (IN MILLIONS):							
Total Interest Income	2,825.8	2,962.6	2,832.5	2,581.6	2,427.4	1,876.5	1,870.2
Total Interest Expense	1,822.4	1,995.2	1,942.0	1,750.6	1,704.6	1,155.1	1,137.4
Net Interest Income	1,003.5	967.3	890.5	831.0	722.8	721.4	732.8
Provision for Loan Losses	cr2.1	11.3	57.6	84.3	61.2	63.0	65.8
Non-Interest Income	143.3	137.6	81.3	74.9	42.5	37.5	62.0
Non-Interest Expense	386.1	354.5	327.0	453.4	319.0	305.5	271.6
Income Before Taxes	762.7	739.2	587.2	368.2	385.2	390.4	457.4
Net Income	480.0	② 447.1	354.1	① 369.2	234.5	230.4	273.9
Average Shs. Outstg. (000)	166,951	173,462	173,319	173,967	175,971	186,387	191,934
BALANCE SHEET (IN MILLIONS):							
Securities Avail. for Sale	79.0	113.6	157.3	227.5	282.9	323.3	1,114.1
Total Loans & Leases	28,090.1	25,991.6	33,553.5	30,397.2	28,435.1	27,330.5	24,171.7
Allowance for Credit Losses	170.3	270.3	292.8	283.8	253.8	259.2	259.1
Net Loans & Leases	27,919.8	25,721.3	33,260.7	30,113.4	28,181.4	27,071.3	23,912.6
Total Assets	42,142.2	38,468.7	39,421.3	37,730.6	35,118.2	31,683.7	28,829.3
Total Deposits	27,714.9	26,219.1	24,109.7	22,099.9	20,847.9	19,219.4	17,422.5
Long-Term Obligations	813.0	911.8	1,110.5	1,324.0	1,324.4	1,221.6	1,220.1
Total Liabilities	38,947.4	35,344.4	36,892.2	35,380.1	32,839.8	29,683.5	26,763.7
Net Stockholders' Equity	3,194.9	3,124.3	2,698.0	2,350.5	2,278.4	2,000.3	2,065.6
Year-end Shs. Outstg. (000)	161,358	170,583	171,207	172,026	176,613	175,770	191,787
STATISTICAL RECORD:							
Return on Equity %	15.0	14.3	13.1	15.7	10.3	11.5	13.3
Return on Assets %	1.1	1.2	0.9	1.0	0.7	0.7	0.9
Equity/Assets %	7.6	8.1	6.8	6.2	6.5	6.3	7.2
Non-Int. Exp./Tot. Inc. %	33.7	32.1	35.8	50.1	41.7	40.3	34.2
Price Range	38⁷/₁₆-28¹⁵/₁₆	38³/₁₆-23¹/₄	32⁵/₁₆-19⅝	22¹⁵/₁₆-16⁵/₁₆	19³/₁₆-11⁹/₁₆	15⁵/₁₆-11⁷/₁₆	16¹³/₁₆-12⅜
P/E Ratio	13.4-10.1	14.8-9.0	15.8-9.6	10.9-7.7	14.4-8.7	12.4-9.2	11.8-8.7
Average Yield %	0.6	0.6	0.6	0.7	0.8	0.7	0.6

Statistics are as originally reported. Adj. for stk. split: 3-for-1, 12/10/99. ① Bef. acct. chg. of $205.2 mill. & incl. one-time SAIF chg. of $133.0 mill. & a tax benefit of $139.5 mill. ② Bef. extraord. loss of $12.5 mill.

OFFICERS:
H. M. Sandler, Co-Chmn., Co-C.E.O.
M. O. Sandler, Co-Chmn., Co-C.E.O.
R. W. Kettell, Pres., Treas.
M. Roster, Exec. V.P., Gen. Couns., Sec.

INVESTOR CONTACT: William C. Nunan, Sr. Vice-Pres., (510) 446-3614

PRINCIPAL OFFICE: 1901 Harrison Street, Oakland, CA 94612

TELEPHONE NUMBER: (510) 466-3420
FAX: (510) 446-3072

NO. OF EMPLOYEES: 4,737 full-time; 913 part-time

SHAREHOLDERS: 1,358 (of record)

ANNUAL MEETING: In May

INCORPORATED: DE, May, 1959

INSTITUTIONAL HOLDINGS:
No. of Institutions: 231
Shares Held: 111,712,792 (Adj.)
% Held: 69.1

INDUSTRY: Federal savings institutions (SIC: 6035)

TRANSFER AGENT(S): ChaseMellon Shareholder Services, L.C., San Francisco, CA

GORMAN-RUPP COMPANY

YIELD	3.4%
P/E RATIO	11.5

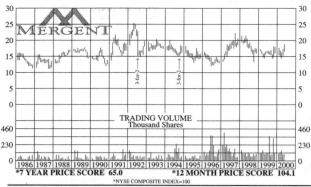

7 YEAR PRICE SCORE 65.0   **12 MONTH PRICE SCORE 104.1**

*NYSE COMPOSITE INDEX=100

INTERIM EARNINGS (Per Share):

Qtr.	Mar.	June	Sept.	Dec.
1996	0.23	0.21	0.34	0.37
1997	0.32	0.32	0.35	0.24
1998	0.38	0.35	0.39	0.25
1999	0.33	0.40	0.45	0.34

INTERIM DIVIDENDS (Per Share):

Amt.	Decl.	Ex.	Rec.	Pay.
0.15Q	7/22/99	8/11/99	8/13/99	9/10/99
0.15Q	10/28/99	11/09/99	11/12/99	12/10/99
0.15Q	1/27/00	2/11/00	2/15/00	3/10/00
0.15Q	4/27/00	5/11/00	5/15/00	6/09/00

Indicated div.: $0.60 (Div. Reinv. Plan)

CAPITALIZATION (12/31/99):

	($000)	(%)
Long-Term Debt	3,107	3.3
Common & Surplus	92,295	96.7
Total	95,402	100.0

DIVIDEND ACHIEVER STATUS:

Rank: 292   10-Year Growth Rate: 3.47%
Total Years of Dividend Growth: 27

RECENT DEVELOPMENTS: For the year ended 12/31/99, net income increased 11.3% to $13.1 million from $11.8 million in the prior year. Net sales grew 4.7% to $179.3 million from $171.2 million a year ago. The increase in sales was attributed to increased shipments of pumps and fabricated products due to growth in the wastewater, fire protection and original equipment markets. This growth was partially offset by a decline in demand from the construction market. Export shipments represented 17.0% of total sales versus 16.0% of total sales in 1998. Gross profit increased 8.9% to $46.3 million versus $43.7 million a year ago, reflecting improved product mix, cost control, and increased operating efficiency. Selling, general and administrative expenses remained essentially flat at $25.7 million. On 2/16/00, GRC's Industries division acquired selected assets of the fluid products division of the Xolox Corporation. The acquisition of the pump and flowmeter line will expand the GRC's presence in the fluid handling market.

BUSINESS

THE GORMAN-RUPP COMPANY designs, manufactures and sells pumps and related equipment, such as pump and motor controls. The Company's larger pumps are sold principally for use in the water, wastewater, construction, industrial, petroleum, original equipment, agricultural, fire, military and other liquid-handling applications.

QUARTERLY DATA

(12/31/1999)($000)	REV	INC
1st Quarter	43,184	2,861
2nd Quarter	45,118	3,381
3rd Quarter	46,898	3,903
4th Quarter	44,084	2,936

ANNUAL FINANCIAL DATA

	12/31/99	12/31/98	12/31/97	12/31/96	12/31/95	12/31/94	12/31/93
Earnings Per Share	1.52	1.37	1.23	1.15	1.10	1.09	1.03
Cash Flow Per Share	2.28	2.10	1.92	1.81	1.70	1.62	1.52
Tang. Book Val. Per Share	10.74	9.75	9.07	8.44	7.81	7.18	6.63
Dividends Per Share	0.60	0.58	0.56	0.53	0.52	0.49	0.48
Dividend Payout %	39.5	42.3	45.5	46.1	47.3	45.0	46.7
INCOME STATEMENT (IN THOUSANDS):							
Total Revenues	180,165	172,246	165,568	155,678	150,793	138,019	132,124
Costs & Expenses	152,135	146,764	142,657	134,340	130,569	118,533	113,992
Depreciation & Amort.	6,489	6,330	5,959	5,675	5,173	4,534	4,274
Operating Income	21,541	19,152	16,952	15,663	15,051	14,952	13,858
Income Before Income Taxes	21,541	19,152	16,952	15,663	15,051	14,952	13,858
Income Taxes	8,460	7,400	6,340	5,735	5,590	5,625	5,063
Net Income	13,081	11,752	10,612	9,928	9,461	9,327	8,795
Cash Flow	19,570	18,082	16,571	15,603	14,634	13,861	13,069
Average Shs. Outstg.	8,586	8,600	8,609	8,617	8,587	8,580	8,589
BALANCE SHEET (IN THOUSANDS):							
Cash & Cash Equivalents	7,339	8,665	7,737	4,284	3,250	3,062	2,782
Total Current Assets	78,185	78,556	81,695	71,926	71,401	60,070	55,746
Net Property	53,609	43,916	40,919	40,549	42,163	40,879	36,835
Total Assets	136,875	127,477	127,865	117,650	119,816	107,100	98,706
Total Current Liabilities	16,410	17,431	17,036	15,199	19,727	16,391	14,382
Long-Term Obligations	3,107	783	6,689	3,796	7,188	4,715	4,274
Net Stockholders' Equity	92,295	83,706	78,060	72,737	67,240	61,608	56,911
Net Working Capital	61,775	61,125	64,659	56,727	51,674	43,679	41,364
Year-end Shs. Outstg.	8,592	8,581	8,609	8,618	8,607	8,580	8,580
STATISTICAL RECORD:							
Operating Profit Margin %	12.0	11.1	10.2	10.1	10.0	10.8	10.5
Net Profit Margin %	7.3	6.8	6.4	6.4	6.3	6.8	6.7
Return on Equity %	14.2	14.0	13.6	13.6	14.1	15.1	15.5
Return on Assets %	9.6	9.2	8.3	8.4	7.9	8.7	8.9
Debt/Total Assets %	2.3	0.6	5.2	3.2	6.0	4.4	4.3
Price Range	18⅛-14¼	21½-13¼	22¼-13⅜	16⅜-12	16⅜-12	20-15³/₁₆	20⁵/₁₆-16⁹/₁₆
P/E Ratio	11.9-9.4	15.7-9.7	18.1-10.9	14.2-10.4	16.6-11.8	18.3-13.9	19.8-16.1
Average Yield %	3.7	3.3	3.1	3.7	3.3	2.8	2.6

Statistics are as originally reported. Adj. for stk. splits: 3-for-2, 10/27/94

OFFICERS:
J. C. Gorman, Chmn.
J. S. Gorman, Pres. & C.E.O.
K. E. Dudley, Treas.
R. E. Kirkendall, Corp. Sec.& Asst. Treas.

INVESTOR CONTACT: Robert Kirkendall, Corp. Sec. & Asst. Treas., (419)755-1294

PRINCIPAL OFFICE: 305 Bowman St., Mansfield, OH 44903

TELEPHONE NUMBER: (419) 755-1011
FAX: (419) 755-1233
WEB: www.gormanrupp.com

NO. OF EMPLOYEES: 1,015 (approx.)

SHAREHOLDERS: 1,462

ANNUAL MEETING: In April

INCORPORATED: OH, April, 1934

INSTITUTIONAL HOLDINGS:
No. of Institutions: 29
Shares Held: 3,819,065
% Held: 44.4

INDUSTRY: Pumps and pumping equipment (SIC: 3561)

TRANSFER AGENT(S): National City Bank, Cleveland, OH

GPU, INC.

YIELD 7.7%
P/E RATIO 7.7

TRADING VOLUME
Thousand Shares

*7 YEAR PRICE SCORE 63.9   *12 MONTH PRICE SCORE 86.8

*NYSE COMPOSITE INDEX=100

INTERIM EARNINGS (Per Share):

Qtr.	Mar.	June	Sept.	Dec.
1996	0.90	0.61	0.29	0.67
1997	1.28	0.58	0.14	0.77
1998	1.07	d1.54	2.65	0.65
1999	1.49	0.38	1.18	0.60

INTERIM DIVIDENDS (Per Share):

Amt.	Decl.	Ex.	Rec.	Pay.
0.53Q	6/03/99	7/28/99	7/30/99	8/25/99
0.53Q	10/07/99	10/27/99	10/29/99	11/24/99
0.53Q	12/02/99	1/26/00	1/28/00	2/23/00
0.545Q	4/06/00	4/26/00	4/28/00	5/31/00

Indicated div.: $2.18 (Div. Reinv. Plan)

CAPITALIZATION (12/31/99):

	($000)	(%)
Long-Term Debt	5,850,596	44.0
Deferred Income Tax	3,563,078	26.8
Redeemable Pfd. Stock	73,167	0.6
Preferred Stock	337,649	2.5
Common & Surplus	3,464,953	26.1
Total	13,289,443	100.0

DIVIDEND ACHIEVER STATUS:
Rank: 210   10-Year Growth Rate: 7.73%
Total Years of Dividend Growth: 12

RECENT DEVELOPMENTS: For the year ended 12/31/99, net income rose 27.5% to $459.0 million versus $360.1 million in 1998. Results for 1999 included an after-tax gain of $36.1 million from the sale of GPU Energy's electric generating stations, an after-tax gain of $6.8 million from the sale of the Midlands supply business, and an after-tax charge of $68.0 million from a restructuring order. Results for 1998 included an after-tax charge of $65.8 million. Total operating revenues rose 12.0% to $4.76 billion.

PROSPECTS: On 4/27/00, the Company announced that it has completed the acquisition of MYR Group, Inc., an infrastructure construction company, for $215.0 million in cash. The acquisition is strategically in line with GPU's needs for outsourcing construction for its utility operations and expanding its telecommunications business. Meanwhile, GPU announced that its energy unit did not receive bids in its offer to provide competitive default energy supply service for 20.0% of its customers in 2000.

BUSINESS

GPU, INC. (formerly General Public Utilities) is a holding company that owns all the outstanding common stock of three electric utilities - Jersey Central Power & Light Company (JCP&L), Metropolitan Edison Company (Met-Ed) and Pennsylvania Electric Company (Penelec). Collectively, these three companies do business as GPU Energy. The subsidiaries serve areas of NJ and PA with a population of about five million. GPU owns all the common stock of GPU Service Inc., a services company; GPU Nuclear Inc., which operates and maintains the nuclear units of the subsidiaries; and GPU International, Inc., GPU Electric, Inc. and GPU Power, Inc., which develop, own, and operate generation, transmission, and distribution facilities in the U.S. and in foreign countries.

ANNUAL FINANCIAL DATA

	12/31/99	12/31/98	12/31/97	12/31/96	12/31/95	12/31/94	12/31/93
Earnings Per Share	④ 3.66	③ 3.03	① 2.77	① 2.47	② 3.79	① 1.42	2.65
Cash Flow Per Share	8.56	7.77	6.72	6.43	9.13	3.91	6.40
Tang. Book Val. Per Share	6.98	22.81	20.84	25.27	24.70	22.33	22.71
Dividends Per Share	2.12	2.04	1.99	1.93	1.86	1.77	1.65
Dividend Payout %	57.9	67.5	71.7	77.9	49.1	125.0	62.3

INCOME STATEMENT (IN MILLIONS):

Total Revenues	4,757.1	4,248.8	4,143.4	3,918.1	3,804.7	3,649.5	3,596.1
Costs & Expenses	1,636.5	1,881.3	1,964.5	1,840.8	1,841.6	1,664.2	1,733.2
Depreciation & Amort.	616.4	602.7	538.1	478.1	438.9	419.9	425.4
Maintenance Exp.	1,495.4	1,106.9	993.7	1,090.9	963.6	1,076.9	909.8
Operating Income	1,008.8	657.8	647.1	508.3	560.6	488.5	527.8
Net Interest Inc./(Exp.)	d438.5	d349.1	d277.9	d205.1	d209.1	d215.3	d203.4
Income Taxes	239.6	240.1	...	...	...	...	...
Equity Earnings/Minority Int.	d3.5	d2.2	d1.3	...	...	...	...
Net Income	④ 459.0	③ 385.9	① 335.1	① 298.6	② 440.1	① 163.7	295.7
Cash Flow	1,075.4	988.6	813.0	776.8	1,060.6	450.8	715.5
Average Shs. Outstg. (000)	125,570	127,312	121,002	120,743	116,214	115,160	111,779

BALANCE SHEET (IN MILLIONS):

Gross Property	11,954.9	11,265.2	409.1	445.5	506.8	535.6	481.6
Accumulated Depreciation	3,930.0	4,460.3	4,050.2	3,704.0	3,433.2	3,148.7	2,929.3
Net Property	8,024.9	6,804.9	d3,641.1	d3,258.6	d2,926.4	d2,613.0	d2,447.7
Total Assets	21,718.1	16,288.1	12,924.7	10,941.2	9,849.5	9,209.8	8,868.7
Long-Term Obligations	5,850.6	3,825.6	4,326.0	3,177.0	2,567.9	2,345.4	2,320.4
Net Stockholders' Equity	3,802.6	3,861.1	3,496.4	3,444.1	3,402.8	2,875.7	2,768.6
Year-end Shs. Outstg. (000)	121,806	127,996	120,839	120,611	120,423	115,208	114,967

STATISTICAL RECORD:

Operating Profit Margin %	21.2	15.5	15.6	13.0	14.7	13.4	14.7
Net Profit Margin %	9.6	9.1	8.1	7.6	11.6	4.5	8.2
Net Inc./Net Property %	5.7	5.7	4.5	4.7	6.9	2.6	4.9
Net Inc./Tot. Capital %	3.5	3.6	3.5	3.6	5.8	2.4	4.5
Return on Equity %	12.1	10.0	9.6	8.7	12.9	5.7	10.7
Accum. Depr./Gross Prop. %	32.9	39.6	35.0	36.7	35.0	33.4	32.8
Price Range	45-28¾	47³⁄₁₆-35⁵⁄₁₆	42¾-30¾	35¼-30⅛	34-26¼	31⅝-23¾	34¾-25¾
P/E Ratio	12.3-7.9	15.6-11.6	15.4-11.1	14.3-12.2	9.0-6.9	22.3-16.7	13.1-9.7
Average Yield %	5.7	5.0	5.4	6.0	6.2	6.4	5.5

Statistics are as originally reported. ① Incl. $109.3 mill. non-recur. net chg., 1997; $74.5 mil., 1996; $191.6 mill., 1994. ② Incl. $104.9 mill. net credit & $8.4 mill. net chg. ③ Incl. $65.8 mill. net non-recur. chg. rel. to restr. orders; bef. $25.8 mill. extraord. loss. ④ Incl. $36.1 mill. net non-recur. gain fr. sale of generating station, $68.0 mill. net chg. fr. the restr. order on JCP&L, and $6.8 mill. net gain.

OFFICERS:
F. D. Hafer, Chmn., C.E.O., Pres.
B. L. Levy, C.F.O., Sr. V.P.

INVESTOR CONTACT: Ned Reynolds, (973) 455-8294

PRINCIPAL OFFICE: 300 Madison Ave., Morristown, NJ 07962-1911

TELEPHONE NUMBER: (973) 401-8200
FAX: (973) 263-6822
WEB: www.gpu.com
NO. OF EMPLOYEES: 10,800 (approx.)
SHAREHOLDERS: 34,986 (of record).
ANNUAL MEETING: In May
INCORPORATED: PA, Jul., 1969

INSTITUTIONAL HOLDINGS:
No. of Institutions: 251
Shares Held: 88,073,687
% Held: 71.4

INDUSTRY: Electric services (SIC: 4911)

TRANSFER AGENT(S): ChaseMellon Shareholder Services, Ridgefield Park, NJ.

NYSE SYMBOL GWW
Rec. Pr. 39 15/16 (5/31/00)

GRAINGER (W.W.), INC.

YIELD 1.7%
P/E RATIO 20.8

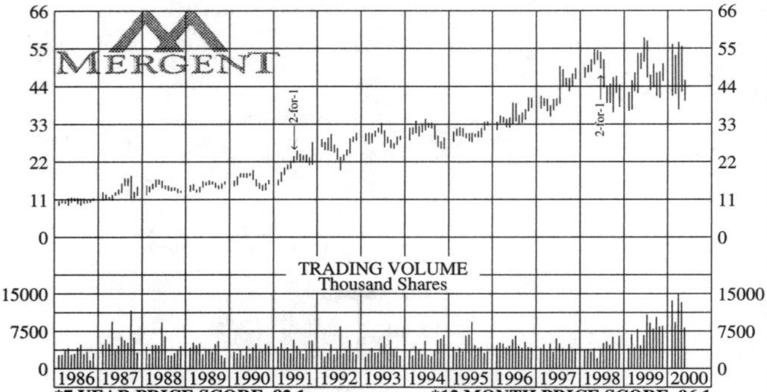

***7 YEAR PRICE SCORE 82.1** ***12 MONTH PRICE SCORE 96.1**

*NYSE COMPOSITE INDEX=100

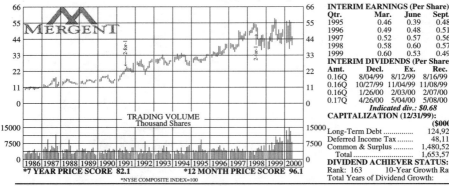

INTERIM EARNINGS (Per Share):

Qtr.	Mar.	June	Sept.	Dec.
1995	0.46	0.39	0.48	0.50
1996	0.49	0.48	0.51	0.54
1997	0.52	0.57	0.56	0.63
1998	0.58	0.60	0.57	0.69
1999	0.60	0.53	0.49	0.30

INTERIM DIVIDENDS (Per Share):

Amt.	Decl.	Ex.	Rec.	Pay.
0.16Q	8/04/99	8/12/99	8/16/99	9/01/99
0.16Q	10/27/99	11/04/99	11/08/99	12/01/99
0.16Q	1/26/00	2/03/00	2/07/00	3/01/00
0.17Q	4/26/00	5/04/00	5/08/00	6/01/00

Indicated div.: $0.68

CAPITALIZATION (12/31/99):

	($000)	(%)
Long-Term Debt	124,928	7.6
Deferred Income Tax	48,117	2.9
Common & Surplus	1,480,529	89.5
Total	1,653,574	100.0

DIVIDEND ACHIEVER STATUS:
Rank: 163 10-Year Growth Rate: 9.68%
Total Years of Dividend Growth: 28

RECENT DEVELOPMENTS: For the year ended 12/31/99, net earnings slid 24.2% to $180.7 million from $238.5 million the previous year. Earnings were hampered by an inventory adjustment during the fourth quarter related to GWW's installation of a new enterprise resource planning system. Net sales climbed 4.4% to $4.53 billion from $4.34 billion a year earlier. Operating earnings slid 22.2% to $317.2 million from $408.0 million in 1998.

PROSPECTS: Going forward, GWW will focus on aggressively investing in its Internet-related business. In 2000, the Company expects to spend between $110.0 million and $120.0 million on growing its Internet business, up from $44.4 million in 1999. On 4/10/00, GWW launched TotalMRO.com, an Internet-based marketplace that provides a platform for procurement of maintenance, repair, and operating products and services.

BUSINESS

W.W. GRAINGER, INC. is a nationwide distributor of equipment, components, and supplies to the commercial, industrial, contractor and institutional markets. Products include motors, fans, blowers, pumps, compressors, air and power tools, heating and air conditioning equipment, as well as other items offered in its Grainger Industrial Supply Catalog that features more than 81,000 products. GWW serves its more than one million customers from regional distribution facilities in Chicago, IL, Kansas City, MO, and Greenville County, SC through a nationwide network of 352 branches in 50 states, Puerto Rico, and Mexico. The Company also has Zone Distribution Centers in Atlanta, GA, Arlington, TX, Cranbury, NJ, Carol Stream, IL and Ontario, CA.

BUSINESS LINE ANALYSIS

(12/31/99)	REV (%)	INC (%)
Branch-based Distribution	90.8	98.3
Digital	0.1	(5.6)
Other	9.1	7.3
Total	100.0	100.0

ANNUAL FINANCIAL DATA

	12/31/99	12/31/98	12/31/97	12/31/96	12/31/95	12/31/94	12/31/93
Earnings Per Share	**1.92**	**2.44**	**2.27**	**2.02**	**1.82**	**[2] 1.25**	**[1] 1.44**
Cash Flow Per Share	**2.96**	**3.24**	**3.05**	**2.74**	**2.51**	**1.88**	**1.98**
Tang. Book Val. Per Share	**13.47**	**11.39**	**11.13**	**11.65**	**10.87**	**9.33**	**9.29**
Dividends Per Share	**0.63**	**0.58**	**0.53**	**0.49**	**0.45**	**0.39**	**0.35**
Dividend Payout %	**32.8**	**24.0**	**23.3**	**24.3**	**24.4**	**31.2**	**24.5**
INCOME STATEMENT (IN MILLIONS):							
Total Revenues	4,533.9	4,341.3	4,136.6	3,537.2	3,276.9	3,023.1	2,628.4
Costs & Expenses	4,118.4	3,854.4	3,663.8	3,117.4	2,889.8	2,727.2	2,320.3
Depreciation & Amort.	98.2	78.9	79.7	74.3	70.9	64.3	56.0
Operating Income	317.2	408.0	393.2	345.5	316.3	231.5	252.2
Net Interest Inc./(Exp.)	d14.0	d5.1	d2.6	3.3	d4.1	d1.9	d1.2
Income Before Income Taxes	303.8	400.8	389.6	348.9	312.1	228.8	250.0
Income Taxes	123.0	162.3	157.8	140.4	125.5	100.9	100.8
Net Income	180.7	238.5	231.8	208.5	186.7	[2] 127.9	[1] 149.3
Cash Flow	279.0	317.4	311.5	282.8	257.5	192.2	205.2
Average Shs. Outstg. (000)	94,315	97,847	102,178	103,272	102,482	102,454	103,822
BALANCE SHEET (IN MILLIONS):							
Cash & Cash Equivalents	62.7	43.1	46.9	126.9	11.5	15.3	2.6
Total Current Assets	1,471.1	1,206.4	1,183.0	1,320.2	1,062.7	963.6	823.9
Net Property	697.8	660.5	592.9	551.0	518.4	469.1	409.4
Total Assets	2,564.8	2,103.9	1,997.8	2,119.0	1,669.2	1,534.8	1,376.7
Total Current Liabilities	870.5	664.5	533.9	616.1	444.1	459.1	381.4
Long-Term Obligations	124.9	122.9	131.2	6.2	8.7	1.0	6.2
Net Stockholders' Equity	1,480.5	1,278.7	1,294.7	1,462.7	1,179.1	1,032.8	941.9
Net Working Capital	600.6	541.9	649.1	704.2	618.5	504.6	442.5
Year-end Shs. Outstg. (000)	93,382	93,505	97,722	105,856	101,790	101,500	101,370
STATISTICAL RECORD:							
Operating Profit Margin %	7.0	9.4	9.5	9.8	9.7	7.7	9.6
Net Profit Margin %	4.0	5.5	5.6	5.9	5.7	4.2	5.7
Return on Equity %	12.2	18.7	17.9	14.3	15.8	12.4	15.8
Return on Assets %	7.0	11.3	11.6	9.8	11.2	8.3	10.8
Debt/Total Assets %	4.9	5.8	6.6	0.3	0.5	0.1	0.5
Price Range	58 1/8-36 7/8	54 3/4-36 7/16	49 7/8-35 1/4	40 3/4-31 5/16	33 13/16-27 3/4	34 9/16-25 3/4	33 3/8-25 13/16
P/E Ratio	30.3-19.2	22.4-14.9	22.0-15.5	20.2-15.5	18.6-15.2	27.6-20.6	23.2-17.9
Average Yield %	1.3	1.3	1.2	1.4	1.4	1.3	1.2

Statistics are as originally reported. Adj. for 2-for-1 stk. split, 6/98. [1] Bef. $820,000 chg. for acctg. adj. [2] Incl. $49.8 mil ($0.97/sh) non-recur. chg.

OFFICERS:
D. W. Grainger, Sr. Chmn.
R. L. Keyser, Chmn., C.E.O.
J. D. Fluno, Vice-Chmn.
P. O. Loux, Sr. V.P., C.F.O.

INVESTOR CONTACT: Bill Chapman, Investor Relations Manager, (847) 535-0881

PRINCIPAL OFFICE: 100 Grainger Parkway, Lake Forest, IL 60045-5201

TELEPHONE NUMBER: (847) 535-1000
FAX: (847) 535-0878
WEB: www.grainger.com

NO. OF EMPLOYEES: 14,030 full-time; 2,700 part-time

SHAREHOLDERS: 1,700 (approx.)

ANNUAL MEETING: In Apr.

INCORPORATED: IL, Dec., 1928

INSTITUTIONAL HOLDINGS:
No. of Institutions: 299
Shares Held: 61,747,130
% Held: 66.1

INDUSTRY: Electrical apparatus and equipment (SIC: 5063)

TRANSFER AGENT(S): BankBoston, N.A., Boston, MA

NYSE SYMBOL MAH
Rec. Pr. 11 11/16 (5/31/00)

HANNA (M.A.) COMPANY

YIELD	4.3%
P/E RATIO	15.0

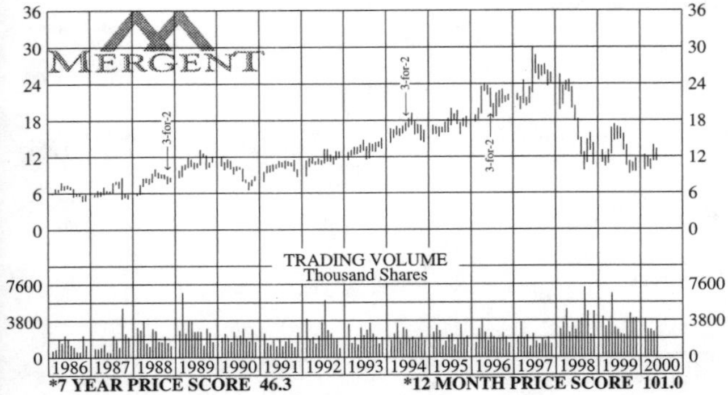

*7 YEAR PRICE SCORE 46.3 *12 MONTH PRICE SCORE 101.0

*NYSE COMPOSITE INDEX=100

INTERIM EARNINGS (Per Share):

Qtr.	Mar.	June	Sept.	Dec.
1996	0.29	0.34	0.34	0.32
1997	0.34	0.38	0.37	0.34
1998	0.34	0.29	Nil	0.05
1999	0.17	0.23	0.36	0.02

INTERIM DIVIDENDS (Per Share):

Amt.	Decl.	Ex.	Rec.	Pay.
0.12Q	5/05/99	5/19/99	5/21/99	6/11/99
0.12Q	8/04/99	8/16/99	8/18/99	9/13/99
0.125Q	11/03/99	11/22/99	11/24/99	12/13/99
0.125Q	2/02/00	2/16/00	2/18/00	3/13/00
0.125Q	5/03/00	5/18/00	5/22/00	6/12/00

Indicated div.: $0.50

CAPITALIZATION (12/31/99):

	($000)	(%)
Long-Term Debt	423,689	43.5
Common & Surplus	549,514	56.5
Total	973,203	100.0

DIVIDEND ACHIEVER STATUS:
Rank: 171 10-Year Growth Rate: 9.26%
Total Years of Dividend Growth: 12

RECENT DEVELOPMENTS: For the year ended 12/31/99, net income increased 16.8% to $35.4 million compared with income of $30.3 million, before an accounting charge of $2.1 million in 1998. Results for 1998 included a special pre-tax charge of $29.8 million. Net sales were $2.30 billion, up slightly from $2.29 billion a year earlier. Selling, general and administrative expenses were 13.3% of sales compared with 12.9% the year before.

PROSPECTS: In May, the Company and The Geon Company (GON) agreed to consolidate. Under the arrangement, MAH and GON will consolidate in a stock-for-stock, non-cash exchange to form a new corporation, which is subject to customary and regulatory approvals. The new company will have initial annual revenues of approximately $3.50 billion, with anticipated market capitalization well above $1.00 billion. Closing is anticipated in August 2000.

BUSINESS

M.A. HANNA COMPANY is an international specialty polymers company focused on the plastics and rubber industries through its operations in North America, Europe and Asia. MAH's primary businesses are plastic compounding and color additive systems, rubber compounding and additives, and distribution of plastic resins and engineered plastic shapes. The Company has operations in four business segments. Plastic processing accounted for 39.1% of sales in 1999, distribution, 38.0%, rubber processing, 22.2%, and other, 0.6%. In 1999, MAH sold its Hanna Resin Distribution thermoset resin business. On 4/10/00, the Company sold its Diversified Polymer Products business.

ANNUAL FINANCIAL DATA

	12/31/99	12/31/98	12/31/97	12/31/96	12/31/95	12/31/94	12/31/93
Earnings Per Share	**0.79**	[1] [2] **0.67**	**1.40**	[3] **1.29**	[4] **1.22**	[3] **0.80**	[4] **0.65**
Cash Flow Per Share	**2.23**	**2.00**	**2.53**	**2.39**	**2.23**	**1.70**	**1.48**
Tang. Book Val. Per Share	**2.39**	**1.43**	**2.35**	**3.00**	**3.14**	**1.57**	...
Dividends Per Share	**0.48**	**0.46**	**0.43**	**0.40**	**0.37**	**0.34**	**0.32**
Dividend Payout %	**61.4**	**68.3**	**30.5**	**31.1**	**30.1**	**42.5**	**48.8**
INCOME STATEMENT (IN MILLIONS):							
Total Revenues	2,304.6	2,285.9	2,200.3	2,066.2	1,902.0	1,719.4	1,519.7
Costs & Expenses	2,142.4	2,135.0	2,015.2	1,892.9	1,738.2	1,576.9	1,391.5
Depreciation & Amort.	64.2	59.7	52.6	50.1	47.2	41.9	38.2
Operating Income	97.9	91.1	132.5	123.3	116.5	100.5	90.1
Net Interest Inc./(Exp.)	d31.7	d33.9	d23.8	d20.0	d26.3	d28.5	d32.3
Income Before Income Taxes	68.6	35.0	110.4	102.9	98.8	66.2	53.4
Income Taxes	33.2	4.7	45.8	43.7	42.1	29.2	23.4
Net Income	35.4	[1] [2] 30.3	64.6	[3] 59.2	[4] 56.7	[3] 37.0	[4] 30.0
Cash Flow	99.6	90.1	117.2	109.3	103.9	78.9	68.2
Average Shs. Outstg. (000)	44,719	45,037	46,272	45,789	46,512	46,299	46,245
BALANCE SHEET (IN MILLIONS):							
Cash & Cash Equivalents	40.9	32.3	41.4	30.0	111.2	23.1	42.7
Total Current Assets	697.5	654.4	642.9	533.5	574.6	565.6	419.9
Net Property	333.9	339.6	288.3	254.4	227.0	204.1	212.6
Total Assets	1,590.6	1,593.9	1,469.0	1,250.8	1,231.6	1,215.2	1,141.3
Total Current Liabilities	412.3	364.1	399.0	351.9	335.3	337.5	273.8
Long-Term Obligations	423.7	480.9	325.2	207.7	232.0	288.9	322.1
Net Stockholders' Equity	549.5	538.5	539.3	508.3	484.8	414.9	365.5
Net Working Capital	285.2	290.4	243.9	181.6	239.4	228.1	146.1
Year-end Shs. Outstg. (000)	48,952	49,620	50,477	50,990	51,964	53,541	53,417
STATISTICAL RECORD:							
Operating Profit Margin %	4.2	4.0	6.0	6.0	6.1	5.8	5.9
Net Profit Margin %	1.5	1.3	2.9	2.9	3.0	2.2	2.0
Return on Equity %	6.4	5.6	12.0	11.6	11.7	8.9	8.2
Return on Assets %	2.2	1.9	4.4	4.7	4.6	3.0	2.6
Debt/Total Assets %	26.6	30.2	22.1	16.6	18.8	23.8	28.2
Price Range	17 3/8-9 1/8	25 9/16-9 3/4	30-19 3/4	24 1/16-17 3/4	20-15 5/16	19 1/4-14 1/4	15 1/8-11 7/16
P/E Ratio	22.0-11.5	38.1-14.6	21.4-14.1	18.7-13.8	16.4-12.6	24.1-17.8	23.3-17.6
Average Yield %	3.7	2.6	1.7	1.9	2.1	2.0	2.4

Statistics are as originally reported. Adj. for stk. splits: 3-for-2, 6/94 & 6/96. [1] Incl. special pre-tax chrg. $29.8 mill. [2] Bef. acctg. change chrg. 12/31/98: $2.1 mill. [3] Bef. extraord. chrg. 12/31/96: $5.4 mill.; 12/31/94: $3.7 mill. [4] Bef. disc. oper. gain 12/31/95: $45.3 mill.; loss 12/31/93: $28.0 mill.

OFFICERS:
P. D. Ashkettle, Chmn., Pres., C.E.O.
C. R. Sachs, Treas.
J. S. Pyke Jr., V.P., Gen. Couns., Sec.

INVESTOR CONTACT: Christopher M. Farage, Director, Investor Relations, (800) 688-4259

PRINCIPAL OFFICE: 200 Public Square, Suite 36-5000, Cleveland, OH 44114-2304

TELEPHONE NUMBER: (216) 589-4000
FAX: (216) 589-4200
WEB: www.mahanna.com

NO. OF EMPLOYEES: 7,149

SHAREHOLDERS: 4,452

ANNUAL MEETING: In May

INCORPORATED: DE, Mar., 1927

INSTITUTIONAL HOLDINGS:
No. of Institutions: 123
Shares Held: 34,796,292
% Held: 71.2

INDUSTRY: Plastics products, nec (SIC: 3089)

TRANSFER AGENT(S): First Chicago Trust Company of New York, Jersey City, NJ.

NYSE SYMBOL HRD
Rec. Pr. 72¼ (5/31/00)

HANNAFORD BROS. CO.

YIELD 0.9%
P/E RATIO 31.8

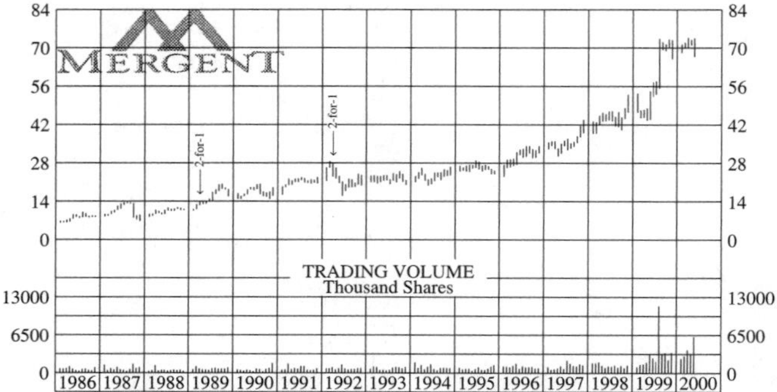

*7 YEAR PRICE SCORE 120.6 *12 MONTH PRICE SCORE 104.6

*NYSE COMPOSITE INDEX=100

INTERIM EARNINGS (Per Share):

Qtr.	Mar.	June	Sept.	Dec.
1996	0.35	0.46	0.47	0.50
1997	0.37	0.47	0.54	0.02
1998	0.42	0.54	0.60	0.65
1999	0.47	0.59	0.56	0.65

INTERIM DIVIDENDS (Per Share):

Amt.	Decl.	Ex.	Rec.	Pay.
0.165Q	5/19/99	6/09/99	6/11/99	6/24/99
0.165Q	8/12/99	9/08/99	9/10/99	9/23/99
0.165Q	10/05/99	12/08/99	12/10/99	12/23/99
0.165Q	2/10/00	3/08/00	3/10/00	3/23/00

Indicated div.: $0.66 (Div. Reinv. Plan)

CAPITALIZATION (1/1/00):

	($000)	(%)
Long-Term Debt	185,126	18.2
Capital Lease Obligations	71,464	7.0
Deferred Income Tax	32,676	3.2
Common & Surplus	727,188	71.5
Total	1,016,454	100.0

DIVIDEND ACHIEVER STATUS:
Rank: 82 10-Year Growth Rate: 13.87%
Total Years of Dividend Growth: 28

RECENT DEVELOPMENTS: For the year ended 1/1/00, net earnings grew 3.6% to $98.0 million from $94.6 million a year earlier. Earnings in the recent period included pre-tax merger-related costs of $9.5 million. Sales and other revenues climbed 4.2% to $3.46 billion from $3.32 billion the previous year. Identical-store sales rose 1.1%, while comparable-store sales, including expanded and relocated stores, were up 1.7%. Gross margin was $918.3 million, up 8.9% from $843.2 million the year before.

PROSPECTS: On 2/10/00, HRD shareholders approved the pending acquisition of the Company by Delhaize America, Inc., which is expected to be completed by the end of the second quarter of 2000, subject to shareholder and regulatory approval. In 2000, the Company plans to spend approximately $165.0 million for the construction of eight new stores and two major store expansions. This expansion is expected to boost selling square footage by about 4.8%.

BUSINESS

HANNAFORD BROS. CO. is involved in the retail food and drug business through supermarkets, drug stores and supermarket/drug combination stores. HRD operates 153 supermarkets throughout Maine, New Hampshire and Vermont, and in parts of New York, Massachusetts, Virginia, North Carolina and South Carolina primarily under the names SHOP 'N SAVE and HANNAFORD. In addition, the Company operates 112 pharmacies within its supermarkets or combination stores. In July 1994, the Company acquired 20 supermarkets in the Carolinas from Wilson's Supermarkets (based in Wilmington, NC). The Sobey Family of Nova Scotia owns 25.6% of HRD.

QUARTERLY DATA

(1/1/2000)($000)	Rev	Inc
1st Quarter	839,124	19,990
2nd Quarter	854,325	25,414
3rd Quarter	881,934	24,325
4th Quarter	887,559	28,289

ANNUAL FINANCIAL DATA

	1/1/00	1/2/99	1/3/98	12/31/96	12/31/95	12/31/94	1/1/94
Earnings Per Share	**[1] 2.28**	**2.21**	**[1] 1.40**	**1.78**	**1.67**	**1.50**	**[2] 1.33**
Cash Flow Per Share	**4.67**	**4.46**	**3.59**	**3.61**	**3.31**	**3.01**	**2.70**
Tang. Book Val. Per Share	**15.21**	**13.74**	**12.21**	**10.88**	**9.82**	**8.81**	**9.41**
Dividends Per Share	**0.66**	**0.60**	**0.54**	**0.48**	**0.42**	**0.38**	**0.34**
Dividend Payout %	**28.9**	**27.1**	**38.6**	**27.0**	**25.1**	**25.3**	**25.6**
INCOME STATEMENT (IN MILLIONS):							
Total Revenues	3,462.9	3,323.6	3,226.4	2,957.6	2,568.1	2,291.8	2,054.9
Costs & Expenses	3,176.7	3,048.0	3,008.6	2,733.4	2,363.2	2,103.3	1,887.0
Depreciation & Amort.	103.3	96.7	94.0	77.4	69.0	62.8	56.4
Operating Income	183.0	178.9	123.8	146.7	135.8	125.7	111.5
Net Interest Inc./(Exp.)	d23.5	d26.6	d26.4	d22.2	d19.4	d21.4	d19.3
Income Before Income Taxes	159.5	152.3	97.4	124.5	116.4	104.3	92.2
Income Taxes	61.5	57.7	37.8	49.3	46.2	42.1	37.6
Net Income	[1] 98.0	94.6	[1] 59.6	75.2	70.2	62.3	[2] 54.6
Cash Flow	201.3	191.4	153.6	152.6	139.2	125.0	110.7
Average Shs. Outstg. (000)	43,061	42,884	42,732	42,298	42,092	41,544	41,049
BALANCE SHEET (IN MILLIONS):							
Cash & Cash Equivalents	53.6	59.7	57.7	42.5	7.0	41.0	97.4
Total Current Assets	326.8	295.9	276.1	262.0	194.3	201.3	255.7
Net Property	892.9	878.3	836.4	783.1	633.8	562.8	487.7
Total Assets	1,330.0	1,284.5	1,227.2	1,183.7	961.8	877.6	795.4
Total Current Liabilities	273.3	259.6	255.2	240.2	170.8	158.6	136.8
Long-Term Obligations	256.6	294.0	311.5	302.7	220.4	223.2	215.6
Net Stockholders' Equity	727.2	663.4	601.0	569.2	518.7	454.5	396.7
Net Working Capital	53.6	36.3	20.9	21.8	23.5	42.7	118.8
Year-end Shs. Outstg. (000)	42,270	42,253	42,338	42,281	42,298	41,779	41,211
STATISTICAL RECORD:							
Operating Profit Margin %	5.3	5.4	3.8	5.0	5.3	5.5	5.4
Net Profit Margin %	2.8	2.8	1.8	2.5	2.7	2.7	2.7
Return on Equity %	13.5	14.3	9.9	13.2	13.5	13.7	13.8
Return on Assets %	7.4	7.4	4.9	6.4	7.3	7.1	6.9
Debt/Total Assets %	19.3	22.9	25.4	25.6	22.9	25.4	27.1
Price Range	73⅜-43⅝	53-38¾	43⅞-30½	34¼-23	29-23⅞	26⅝-19¾	25-20
P/E Ratio	32.2-19.1	24.0-17.5	31.3-21.8	19.2-12.9	17.4-14.3	17.7-13.2	18.8-15.0
Average Yield %	1.1	1.3	1.5	1.7	1.6	1.6	1.5

Statistics are as originally reported. [1] Incl. $9.5 mil pre-tax non-recur. chg., 1/1/00; & $40 mil pre-tax, non-recur. chg., 1/3/98. [2] Bef. $2.1 mil ($0.05/sh) cr. for acctg. adj.

OFFICERS:
W. J. Salmon, Chmn.
H. G. Farrington, Pres., C.E.O.
R. C. Hodge, Exec. V.P., C.O.O.
P. A. Fritzson, Exec. V.P., C.F.O.

INVESTOR CONTACT: Charles H. Crockett, Asst. Sec. & Dir., Inv. Rel., (207) 885-2349

PRINCIPAL OFFICE: 145 Pleasant Hill Rd., Scarborough, ME 04074

TELEPHONE NUMBER: (207) 883-2911
FAX: (207) 885-3121
WEB: www.hannaford.com

NO. OF EMPLOYEES: 9,200 full-time; 15,400 part-time

SHAREHOLDERS: 14,000

ANNUAL MEETING: In May

INCORPORATED: ME, Dec., 1902

INSTITUTIONAL HOLDINGS:
No. of Institutions: 155
Shares Held: 13,510,026
% Held: 32.0

INDUSTRY: Grocery stores (SIC: 5411)

TRANSFER AGENT(S): Continental Stock Transfer & Trust Company, New York, NY

HARCOURT GENERAL, INC.

YIELD	2.1%
P/E RATIO	18.6

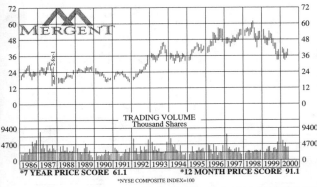

*7 YEAR PRICE SCORE 61.1 *NYSE COMPOSITE INDEX=100 ***12 MONTH PRICE SCORE 91.1**

INTERIM EARNINGS (Per Share):

Qtr.	Jan.	Apr.	July	Oct.
1996-97	0.20	0.04	d2.00	0.11
1997-98	d0.21	d0.25	1.54	0.87
1998-99	d0.28	d0.33	1.95	0.97
1999-00	d0.47	...	...	...

INTERIM DIVIDENDS (Per Share):

Amt.	Decl.	Ex.	Rec.	Pay.
0.20Q	6/18/99	7/12/99	7/14/99	8/02/99
0.21Q	10/01/99	10/07/99	10/12/99	11/01/99
0.21Q	12/14/99	1/12/00	1/14/00	1/31/00
0.21Q	3/10/00	4/06/00	4/10/00	5/01/00

Indicated div.: $0.84 (Div. Reinv. Plan)

CAPITALIZATION (10/31/99):

	($000)	(%)
Long-Term Debt	1,356,804	65.4
Deferred Income Tax	55,946	2.7
Minority Interest	19,093	0.9
Preferred Stock	863	0.0
Common & Surplus	641,000	30.9
Total	2,073,706	100.0

DIVIDEND ACHIEVER STATUS:
Rank: 222   10-Year Growth Rate: 7.05%
Total Years of Dividend Growth: 32

TRADING VOLUME Thousand Shares

RECENT DEVELOPMENTS: For the quarter ended 1/31/00, net loss was $33.4 million versus a loss from continuing operations of $32.3 million the year before. Earnings were hurt by seasonal losses in the K-12 Education and Corporate and Professional Groups. Results in the recent period included an after-tax gain of $4.8 million from the sale of securities. Total revenues rose 3.9% to $402.9 million. Comparisons were made with restated prior-year results.

PROSPECTS: Results in the K-12 Education Group are being hampered by higher-than-expected selling, marketing and sampling expenses by the Company's K-12 publishers in anticipation of strong demand for instructional programs later in the year. In addition, H is experiencing increased expenses associated with new programs being developed and introduced. The Company is rolling out these programs due to a large number of adoptions scheduled this year.

BUSINESS

HARCOURT GENERAL, INC. (formerly General Cinema) operates through Harcourt, Inc., a publisher of textbooks and other materials for educational institutions, as well as scientific, technical, medical and professional books and journals, fiction, non-fiction, and children's books; National Education Corp., a provider of distance education in vocational, academic and professional studies, a developer of interactive media-based learning products and a publisher of supplemental education materials that was acquired in 1997; and Drake Beam Morin, a provider of human resources management consulting services. On 10/22/99, the Company spun-off to shareholders its controlling interest in The Neiman Marcus Group, Inc.

REVENUES

(10/31/99)	($000)	(%)
Education Group	581,465	27.2
Higher Education Group	365,996	17.1
Corporate & Prof. Services	497,573	23.3
Worlwide STM Group	697,588	32.4
Total	2,142,622	100.0

ANNUAL FINANCIAL DATA

	10/31/99	10/31/98	10/31/97	10/31/96	10/31/95	10/31/94	10/31/93
Earnings Per Share	①② 1.67	1.96	① d1.64	2.62	② 2.31	①② 1.22	② 2.08
Cash Flow Per Share	5.21	6.21	3.22	5.10	4.60	3.27	4.21
Tang. Book Val. Per Share	...	...	...	8.10	6.84	8.00	8.40
Dividends Per Share	0.81	0.77	0.73	0.69	0.65	0.61	0.57
Dividend Payout %	48.5	39.3	...	26.3	28.1	50.0	27.4
INCOME STATEMENT (IN MILLIONS):							
Total Revenues	2,142.6	4,235.3	3,691.6	3,289.9	3,034.7	3,154.2	3,655.7
Costs & Expenses	1,607.5	3,518.1	3,354.1	2,764.8	2,541.1	2,766.8	3,172.2
Depreciation & Amort.	255.5	306.2	343.2	180.4	175.7	163.1	169.3
Operating Income	279.6	410.9	d5.7	344.7	317.9	224.4	314.3
Net Interest Inc./(Exp.)	d94.4	d103.4	d65.3	d55.6	d48.8	d72.0	d70.5
Income Before Income Taxes	185.2	307.5	d71.0	289.2	269.1	152.4	262.1
Income Taxes	68.5	116.8	38.2	98.3	91.5	54.9	96.6
Equity Earnings/Minority Int.	3.7	d49.0	d5.9	...	...	...	...
Net Income	①② 120.3	141.6	① d115.1	190.9	② 177.6	①② 97.5	② 165.5
Cash Flow	375.8	447.8	228.1	371.2	353.3	260.6	334.7
Average Shs. Outstg. (000)	72,168	72,141	70,812	72,770	76,764	79,809	79,600
BALANCE SHEET (IN MILLIONS):							
Cash & Cash Equivalents	24.1	115.2	82.6	774.9	606.8	819.7	466.9
Total Current Assets	830.8	1,649.0	1,484.9	1,933.3	1,609.8	2,021.0	1,503.9
Net Property	128.8	645.2	593.9	574.9	540.3	521.7	516.5
Total Assets	2,950.1	4,449.1	3,781.4	3,326.2	2,884.3	3,242.4	5,976.8
Total Current Liabilities	693.6	1,124.6	993.3	948.3	745.0	875.0	791.9
Long-Term Obligations	1,356.8	1,729.5	1,275.1	702.0	780.7	1,123.3	923.6
Net Stockholders' Equity	641.9	925.7	845.5	1,033.5	941.1	1,047.4	1,051.6
Net Working Capital	137.2	524.5	491.6	984.9	864.8	1,146.0	712.0
Year-end Shs. Outstg. (000)	71,167	71,029	70,755	71,119	72,699	77,887	77,307
STATISTICAL RECORD:							
Operating Profit Margin %	13.1	9.7	...	10.5	10.5	7.1	8.6
Net Profit Margin %	5.6	3.3	...	5.8	5.9	3.1	4.5
Return on Equity %	18.7	15.3	...	18.5	18.9	9.3	15.7
Return on Assets %	4.1	3.2	...	5.7	6.2	3.0	2.8
Debt/Total Assets %	46.0	38.9	33.7	21.1	27.1	34.6	15.5
Price Range	55½-32¹³⁄₁₆	61¹⁵⁄₁₆-41⅞	55¹¹⁄₁₆-42⅝	57-38	45¾-32⅜	39½-30¼	46⅛-31¼
P/E Ratio	33.2-19.6	31.6-21.4	...	21.8-14.5	19.8-14.0	32.4-24.8	22.2-15.0
Average Yield %	1.8	1.5	1.5	1.5	1.7	1.7	1.5

Statistics are as originally reported. ① Incl. $3.9 mil ($0.05/sh) after-tax gain, 1999; $314.1 mil non-recur. chg., 1997; & $28.1 mil chg., 1994. ② Bef. discont. opers. cr$63.5 mil ($0.88/sh), 1999; cr$11.7 mil, 1995; cr$80 mil, 1994; & cr$5.8 mil, 1993.

OFFICERS:
R. A. Smith, Chmn.
B. J. Knez, Pres., Co- C.E.O.
R. A. Smith, Pres., Co- C.E.O.
J. R. Cook, Sr. V.P., C.F.O.

INVESTOR CONTACT: Peter Farwell, V.P., Corp. Rel., (617) 232-8200

PRINCIPAL OFFICE: 27 Boylston Street, Chestnut Hill, MA 02467

TELEPHONE NUMBER: (617) 232-8200
FAX: (617) 739-0639
WEB: www.harcourtgeneral.com

NO. OF EMPLOYEES: 13,600 (approx.)

SHAREHOLDERS: 1,624 (Cl. B com.); 7,121 (com.)

ANNUAL MEETING: In Mar.
INCORPORATED: DE, 1950

INSTITUTIONAL HOLDINGS:
No. of Institutions: 204
Shares Held: 45,657,587
% Held: 89.3

INDUSTRY: Department stores (SIC: 5311)

TRANSFER AGENT(S): BankBoston, N.A., Boston, MA

NASDAQ SYMBOL HGIC
Rec. Pr. 16⅞ (5/31/00)

HARLEYSVILLE GROUP INC.

YIELD 3.2%
P/E RATIO 11.6

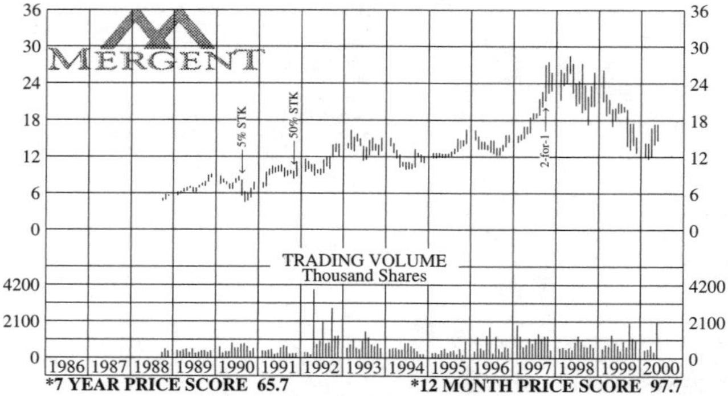

MERGENT
5% STK
50% STK
2-for-1
TRADING VOLUME
Thousand Shares
36
30
24
18
12
6
0
4200
2100
0
1986 1987 1988 1989 1990 1991 1992 1993 1994 1995 1996 1997 1998 1999 2000

*7 YEAR PRICE SCORE 65.7 *12 MONTH PRICE SCORE 97.7

*NYSE COMPOSITE INDEX=100

INTERIM EARNINGS (Per Share):

Qtr.	Mar.	June	Sept.	Dec.
1995	0.64	0.78	0.77	0.86
1996	0.06	0.85	0.25	0.50
1997	0.38	0.46	0.55	0.49
1998	0.47	0.56	0.48	0.64
1999	0.50	0.52	d0.01	0.44

INTERIM DIVIDENDS (Per Share):

Amt.	Decl.	Ex.	Rec.	Pay.
0.125Q	5/26/99	6/11/99	6/15/99	6/30/99
0.135Q	8/25/99	9/13/99	9/15/99	9/30/99
0.135Q	11/17/99	12/13/99	12/15/99	12/30/99
0.135Q	2/23/00	3/13/00	3/15/00	3/30/00
0.135Q	5/17/00	6/13/00	6/15/00	6/30/00

Indicated div.: $0.54

CAPITALIZATION (12/31/99):

	($000)	(%)
Long-Term Debt	96,810	15.5
Common & Surplus	526,894	84.5
Total	623,704	100.0

DIVIDEND ACHIEVER STATUS:
Rank: 121 10-Year Growth Rate: 11.73%
Total Years of Dividend Growth: 13

RECENT DEVELOPMENTS: For the year ended 12/31/99, net income fell 32.5% to $42.8 million from $63.4 million in the prior year. Earnings for 1999 included restructuring charges of $2.5 million, but excluded an accounting change charge of $2.9 million. Total revenues rose 5.8% to $824.8 million from $779.3 million a year ago. Premiums earned were $707.2 million, up 6.4% from $664.6 million in the previous year. Investment income, net of investment expenses, was $85.9 million versus $86.0 million in 1998. Realized investment gains increased slightly to $16.2 million from $16.1 million a year earlier. Total expenses climbed 11.2% to $777.0 million from $698.9 million in 1998. Results reflected losses from Hurricane Floyd and charges related to the consolidation of the Company's claims operation. For the quarter ended 12/31/99, net income declined 31.7% to $12.8 million from $18.1 million in the year-earlier quarter. Total revenues increased 7.0% to $216.3 million versus $202.1 million the year before.

BUSINESS

HARLEYSVILLE GROUP INC. is a regional insurance holding company headquartered in Pennsylvania which engages, through its subsidiaries, in the property and casualty insurance business. The Company is approximately 57% owned by Harleysville Mutual Insurance Company. HGIC and Harleysville Mutual Insurance Company operate together as a network of regional insurance companies that underwrite personal and commercial coverages. These insurance coverages are marketed primarily in the eastern and midwestern United States through approximately 19,800 independent insurance agents associated with approximately 3,000 insurance agencies. Regional offices are maintained in Georgia, Illinois, Indiana, Maryland, Massachusetts, Michigan, Minnesota, New Jersey, New York, North Carolina, Ohio, Pennsylvania, Tennessee and Virginia. The Company's property and casualty insurance subsidiaries are: Great Oaks Insurance Company, Harleysville-Atlantic Insurance Company, Harleysville Insurance Company of New Jersey, Huron Insurance Company, Lake States Insurance Company, Mid-America Insurance Company, Minnesota Fire and Casualty Company, New York Casualty Insurance Company, and Worcester Insurance Company.

ANNUAL FINANCIAL DATA

	12/31/99	12/31/98	12/31/97	12/31/96	12/31/95	12/31/94	12/31/93
Earnings Per Share	**[1] 1.45**	**2.15**	**1.86**	**1.03**	**1.53**	**0.70**	**[1] 1.25**
Tang. Book Val. Per Share	**18.29**	**18.17**	**15.49**	**13.09**	**12.58**	**10.36**	**10.25**
Dividends Per Share	**0.52**	**0.48**	**0.44**	**0.40**	**0.39**	**0.33**	**0.30**
Dividend Payout %	**35.9**	**22.3**	**23.7**	**38.8**	**25.2**	**47.1**	**24.0**
INCOME STATEMENT (IN MILLIONS):							
Total Premium Income	707.2	664.6	624.9	615.2	477.0	447.7	388.5
Net Investment Income	85.9	86.0	81.8	78.0	68.4	64.4	59.2
Other Income	31.7	28.7	17.5	14.2	13.1	13.4	8.7
Total Revenues	824.8	779.3	724.2	707.4	558.5	525.5	456.4
Policyholder Benefits	523.0	464.5	439.5	468.5	335.5	348.9	283.8
Income Before Income Taxes	47.8	80.4	67.3	31.4	52.6	16.8	38.6
Income Taxes	4.9	17.0	13.2	2.7	11.3	cr1.6	6.4
Net Income	[1] 42.8	63.4	54.1	28.7	41.3	18.5	[1] 32.2
Average Shs. Outstg. (000)	29,565	29,520	29,032	27,844	27,064	26,396	25,812
BALANCE SHEET (IN MILLIONS):							
Cash & Cash Equivalents	79.5	18.8	29.8	37.3	47.4	11.9	18.4
Premiums Due	194.3	179.0	181.6	185.1	155.7	158.8	141.1
Invst. Assets: Fixed-term	1,346.6	1,389.6	1,301.4	1,186.2	1,006.4	931.8	892.6
Invst. Assets: Equities	198.2	174.9	121.8	69.9	34.6	14.2	. . .
Invst. Assets: Total	1,604.0	1,579.6	1,451.6	1,291.3	1,085.2	956.3	908.4
Total Assets	2,020.1	1,934.5	1,801.2	1,622.6	1,378.3	1,241.1	1,180.4
Long-Term Obligations	96.8	97.1	97.4	97.7	98.0	100.2	100.4
Net Stockholders' Equity	526.9	529.7	446.5	370.2	345.0	276.9	267.7
Year-end Shs. Outstg. (000)	28,812	29,151	28,822	28,278	27,436	26,728	26,112
STATISTICAL RECORD:							
Return on Revenues %	5.2	8.1	7.5	4.1	7.4	3.5	7.1
Return on Equity %	8.1	12.0	12.1	7.7	12.0	6.7	12.0
Return on Assets %	2.1	3.3	3.0	1.8	3.0	1.5	2.7
Price Range	26⅛-12⅝	28½-17¼	27½-14⅜	16⅜-12¼	16½-11¾	15⅛-9⅞	16⅜-11$^{5}/_{16}$
P/E Ratio	18.0-8.7	13.3-8.0	14.8-7.7	15.9-11.9	10.8-7.7	21.6-14.1	13.1-9.0
Average Yield %	2.7	2.1	2.1	2.8	2.7	2.6	2.2

Statistics are as originally reported. Adj. for stk. splits: 2-for-1, 10/6/97 [1] Bef. acctg. change chrg. $2.9 mill.($0.10/sh.), 12/99; $281,000 ($0.01/sh.)

OFFICERS:
W. R. Bateman II, Chmn., Pres., C.E.O.
B. J. Magee, Sr. V.P., C.F.O.
M. R. Cummins, Exec. V.P., Treas.
R. A. Brown, Sr. V.P., Sec., Gen. Couns.

INVESTOR CONTACT: Carol D. Manning, V.P., Invest. Relations, (215) 256-5020

PRINCIPAL OFFICE: 355 Maple Avenue, Harleysville, PA 19438-2297

TELEPHONE NUMBER: (215) 256-5000
FAX: (215) 256-5340
WEB: www.harleysvillegroup.com

NO. OF EMPLOYEES: 2,804 (avg.)

SHAREHOLDERS: 2,247

ANNUAL MEETING: In April

INCORPORATED: DE, 1979

INSTITUTIONAL HOLDINGS:
No. of Institutions: 45
Shares Held: 8,431,591
% Held: 29.0

INDUSTRY: Fire, marine, and casualty insurance (SIC: 6331)

TRANSFER AGENT(S): ChaseMellon Shareholder Services, New York, NY

HASBRO, INC.

	YIELD	1.5%
	P/E RATIO	17.2

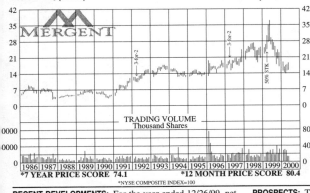

*7 YEAR PRICE SCORE 74.1   ***12 MONTH PRICE SCORE 80.4**
*NYSE COMPOSITE INDEX=100

TRADING VOLUME
Thousand Shares

INTERIM EARNINGS (Per Share):

Qtr.	Mar.	June	Sept.	Dec.
1995	0.11	d0.07	0.32	0.43
1996	0.12	0.03	0.36	0.50
1997	0.13	0.07	0.40	0.09
1998	0.04	0.03	0.30	0.65
1999	0.07	0.16	0.43	0.29

INTERIM DIVIDENDS (Per Share):

Amt.	Decl.	Ex.	Rec.	Pay.
0.06Q	5/13/99	7/29/99	8/02/99	8/16/99
0.06Q	7/23/99	10/28/99	11/01/99	11/15/99
0.06Q	12/06/99	1/28/00	2/01/00	2/15/00
0.06Q	2/17/00	4/27/00	5/01/00	5/15/00
0.06Q	5/17/00	7/28/00	8/01/00	8/15/00

Indicated div.: $0.24 (Div. Reinv. Plan)

CAPITALIZATION (12/26/99):

	($000)	(%)
Long-Term Debt	420,654	18.3
Common & Surplus	1,878,975	81.7
Total	2,299,629	100.0

DIVIDEND ACHIEVER STATUS:

Rank: 33   10-Year Growth Rate: 18.05%
Total Years of Dividend Growth: 18

RECENT DEVELOPMENTS: For the year ended 12/26/99, net income declined 8.5% to $189.0 million compared with $206.4 million the previous year. The 1999 and 1998 results included pre-tax non-recurring charges of $64.2 million and $20.0 million, respectively. Total revenues jumped 28.0% to $4.23 billion from $3.30 billion in 1998. Gross profit climbed 30.7% to $2.53 billion from $1.94 billion a year earlier.

PROSPECTS: The Company is performing well in its three major business segments and should continue to expand its operations with the launch of Games.com in the summer of 2000. The Company is focused on the video releases of STAR WARS and POKEMON movies, plus the second POKEMON movie for summer 2000. Looking ahead, the Company expects revenues to increase approximately 5.0% and earnings per share to grow up to 10.0% in fiscal 2000.

BUSINESS

HASBRO, INC. is a worldwide leader in toy manufacturing, offering a diverse line of toys, board and card games, dolls, preschool toys, boys' and girls' action toys as well as infant care products. In 1984, HAS acquired Milton Bradley Co. and Tonka Corp. in 1991, which also included Parker Bros. and Kenner. The Company's products now include MILTON BRADLEY games and puzzles, PARKER BROS. games, G.I. JOE, MR. POTATO HEAD, KOOSH, PLAYSKOOL, TONKA trucks and the Kenner products including EASY BAKE OVEN, GALOOB, TIGER, SUPER SOAKER and PLAYDOH. Hasbro Interactive publishes entertainment software including CD-ROM games based on the Company's traditional games and brands, including MONOPOLY, RISK, SORRY! and, for younger children, a series of TONKA titles.

ANNUAL FINANCIAL DATA

	12/26/99	12/27/98	12/28/97	12/31/96	12/31/95	12/31/94	12/26/93
Earnings Per Share	① 0.93	① 1.00	① 0.68	1.01	① 0.78	① ② 0.89	① 0.99
Cash Flow Per Share	2.38	1.83	1.46	1.71	1.44	1.50	1.48
Tang. Book Val. Per Share	0.64	1.92	4.36	4.28	3.61	3.15	3.11
Dividends Per Share	0.23	0.21	0.20	0.17	0.14	0.12	0.10
Dividend Payout %	25.1	21.3	30.1	16.7	17.6	13.4	10.4

INCOME STATEMENT (IN MILLIONS):

Total Revenues	4,232.3	3,304.5	3,188.6	3,002.4	2,858.2	2,670.3	2,747.2
Costs & Expenses	3,627.4	2,810.4	2,786.9	2,531.8	2,454.7	2,252.3	2,295.3
Depreciation & Amort.	277.3	169.2	166.6	138.3	129.9	122.3	100.6
Operating Income	327.6	324.9	235.1	332.3	273.6	295.7	351.2
Net Interest Inc./(Exp.)	d69.3	d36.1	d27.5	d31.5	d37.6	d30.8	d29.8
Income Before Income Taxes	273.8	303.5	204.5	306.9	252.6	291.6	325.2
Income Taxes	84.9	97.1	69.5	107.0	97.0	112.3	125.2
Net Income	① 189.0	① 206.4	① 135.0	199.9	① 155.6	① ② 179.3	① 200.0
Cash Flow	466.3	375.6	301.6	338.2	285.5	301.6	300.7
Average Shs. Outstg. (000)	196,175	205,420	206,354	197,784	198,569	200,995	202,570

BALANCE SHEET (IN MILLIONS):

Cash & Cash Equivalents	280.2	177.7	361.8	219.0	161.0	137.0	186.3
Total Current Assets	2,131.7	1,790.0	1,573.9	1,486.6	1,425.5	1,252.5	1,301.1
Net Property	318.8	330.4	280.6	313.5	313.2	308.9	279.8
Total Assets	4,463.3	3,793.8	2,899.7	2,701.5	2,616.4	2,378.4	2,293.0
Total Current Liabilities	2,071.3	1,366.3	1,003.5	830.8	869.9	763.7	748.3
Long-Term Obligations	420.7	407.2	. . .	149.4	150.0	150.0	200.5
Net Stockholders' Equity	1,879.0	1,944.8	1,838.1	1,652.0	1,525.6	1,395.4	1,276.7
Net Working Capital	60.3	423.7	570.3	655.8	555.6	488.7	552.8
Year-end Shs. Outstg. (000)	192,984	209,700	200,162	193,295	196,526	196,938	197,539

STATISTICAL RECORD:

Operating Profit Margin %	7.7	9.8	7.4	11.1	9.6	11.1	12.8
Net Profit Margin %	4.5	6.2	4.2	6.7	5.4	6.7	7.3
Return on Equity %	10.1	10.6	7.3	12.1	10.2	12.9	15.7
Return on Assets %	4.2	5.4	4.7	7.4	5.9	7.5	8.7
Debt/Total Assets %	9.4	10.7	. . .	5.5	5.7	6.3	8.7
Price Range	37-16⅞	27⁵⁄₁₆-18¹¹⁄₁₆	24⁵⁄₁₆-15¹⁄₄	19¹¹⁄₁₆-12³⁄₁₆	15¹¹⁄₁₆-12³⁄₈	16¹⁄₄-12⅜	17¹³⁄₁₆-12½
P/E Ratio	39.8-18.1	27.3-18.7	35.8-22.4	19.4-12.7	20.0-16.1	18.2-13.9	18.1-12.7
Average Yield %	0.9	0.9	1.0	1.0	1.0	0.8	0.7

Statistics are as originally reported. Adj. for stk. splits: 3-for-2, 3/1/99; 3-for-2, 3/97 ① Incl. non-recurr. chrg. 12/26/99: $64.2 mill.; 12/27/98: $20.0 mill.; 12/28/97: $125.0 mill.; 12/31/95: $31.1 mill.; 12/31/94: $12.5 mill.; 12/26/93: $15.5 mill. ② Bef. acctg. change chrg. $4.3 mill. ($0.03/sh.).

QUARTERLY DATA

(12/26/99)($000)	Rev	Inc
1st Quarter	668,398	13,795
2nd Quarter	874,574	32,289
3rd Quarter	1,098,179	85,170
4th Quarter	1,591,112	57,699

OFFICERS:

A. G. Hassenfeld, Chmn., C.E.O.
H. P. Gordon, Vice-Chmn.
H. M. Baum, Pres., C.O.O.
A. J. Verrecchia, Exec. V.P., C.F.O.

INVESTOR CONTACT: Renita E. O'Connell, (401) 727-5401

PRINCIPAL OFFICE: 1027 Newport Avenue, Pawtucket, RI 02861

TELEPHONE NUMBER: (401) 431-8697
FAX: (401) 727-5544
WEB: www.hasbro.com

NO. OF EMPLOYEES: 9,500 (approx.)

SHAREHOLDERS: 7,800 (approx.)

ANNUAL MEETING: In May

INCORPORATED: RI, Jan., 1926

INSTITUTIONAL HOLDINGS:
No. of Institutions: 243
Shares Held: 143,731,059
% Held: 74.2

INDUSTRY: Games, toys, and children's vehicles (SIC: 3944)

TRANSFER AGENT(S): BankBoston, NA, Boston, MA

HAVERTY FURNITURE COMPANIES, INC.

YIELD 1.8%
P/E RATIO 9.3

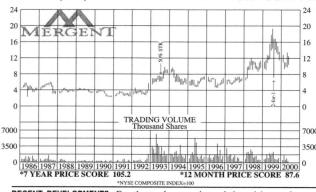

TRADING VOLUME
Thousand Shares

*7 YEAR PRICE SCORE 105.2   *12 MONTH PRICE SCORE 87.6
*NYSE COMPOSITE INDEX=100

INTERIM EARNINGS (Per Share):

Qtr.	Mar.	June	Sept.	Dec.
1996	0.11	0.04	0.16	0.22
1997	0.12	0.06	0.17	0.23
1998	0.14	0.09	0.21	0.30
1999	0.28	0.22	0.31	0.40

INTERIM DIVIDENDS (Per Share):

Amt.	Decl.	Ex.	Rec.	Pay.
0.10Q	7/30/99	8/09/99	8/11/99	8/25/99
2-for-1	7/30/99	8/26/99	8/11/99	8/25/99
0.05Q	10/29/99	11/08/99	11/10/99	11/24/99
0.05Q	2/04/00	2/11/00	2/15/00	2/25/00
0.05Q	5/04/00	5/11/00	5/15/00	5/26/00

Indicated div.: $0.20

CAPITALIZATION (12/31/99):

	($000)	(%)
Long-Term Debt	134,687	44.4
Common & Surplus	168,793	55.6
Total	303,480	100.0

DIVIDEND ACHIEVER STATUS:
Rank: 265   10-Year Growth Rate: 4.70%
Total Years of Dividend Growth: 29

RECENT DEVELOPMENTS:

For the twelve months ended 12/31/99, net income jumped 62.8% to $27.4 million from $16.8 million in the corresponding period a year earlier. Net sales climbed 14.5% to $618.8 million from $540.3 million the previous year. Comparable-store sales increased 12.1% over the prior-year period. Results benefited from favorable economic conditions along with effective adver-

tising and merchandising efforts. Gross profit totaled $293.0 million, or 47.4% of net sales, versus $254.5 million, or 47.1% of net sales, the year before. During 1999, the Company opened eight new stores, one store in each of three new markets, three additional store locations in existing markets, and two replacement stores. In 2000, HVT plans to open four new stores in existing markets.

BUSINESS

HAVERTY FURNITURE COMPANIES, INC. is a full-service home furnishings retailer with 103 showrooms in 14 states throughout the Southeast and Southwest. The Company targets middle and upper-middle income families as its chief market. The Company has maintained a continual program of store relocation, modernization of older units, and upgrading of its merchandising. The relocation program, principally a shift to suburban areas, has been completed. The Company has regional warehouses located in Charlotte, North Carolina, Jackson, Mississippi and Ocala, Florida serving all of the Company's local markets except for Dallas, Texas, and Atlanta, Georgia, which each have a metropolitan area warehouse.

ANNUAL FINANCIAL DATA

	12/31/99	12/31/98	12/31/97	12/31/96	12/31/95	12/31/94	12/31/93
Earnings Per Share	1.19	0.72	0.57	0.53	0.53	0.55	0.46
Cash Flow Per Share	1.84	1.36	1.16	1.06	0.99	0.93	0.77
Tang. Book Val. Per Share	7.81	7.08	6.79	6.42	6.06	5.70	5.29
Dividends Per Share	0.19	0.17	0.16	· 0.153	0.15	0.14	0.13
Dividend Payout %	16.0	22.9	28.1	29.0	28.6	25.0	29.1
INCOME STATEMENT (IN THOUSANDS):							
Total Revenues	618,796	540,298	490,007	456,860	395,470	370,132	322,859
Costs & Expenses	560,744	496,428	449,650	419,777	365,880	340,577	300,024
Depreciation & Amort.	14,844	14,272	13,792	12,644	10,634	8,602	6,875
Operating Income	58,133	46,558	42,676	37,829	31,332	32,617	26,460
Net Interest Inc./(Exp.)	d11,402	d13,183	d14,330	d14,463	d11,158	d8,470	d7,240
Income Before Income Taxes	42,870	26,295	20,787	19,132	19,444	20,279	15,650
Income Taxes	15,470	9,460	7,400	6,885	7,261	7,741	5,934
Net Income	27,400	16,835	13,387	12,247	12,183	12,538	9,716
Cash Flow	42,244	31,107	27,179	24,891	22,817	21,140	16,591
Average Shs. Outstg.	22,982	22,912	23,340	23,388	23,110	22,850	21,466
BALANCE SHEET (IN THOUSANDS):							
Cash & Cash Equivalents	1,762	1,874	390	414	2,146	1,925	614
Total Current Assets	271,678	278,177	289,629	283,130	257,410	232,994	195,174
Net Property	126,997	111,333	114,618	114,350	112,405	80,198	67,439
Total Assets	404,648	392,901	406,514	399,875	371,778	315,103	264,353
Total Current Liabilities	98,434	70,467	132,908	125,440	97,473	93,299	47,441
Long-Term Obligations	134,687	161,778	111,489	120,434	129,233	87,164	94,197
Net Stockholders' Equity	168,793	158,058	159,554	150,916	140,955	131,055	120,418
Net Working Capital	173,244	207,710	156,721	157,690	159,937	139,695	147,733
Year-end Shs. Outstg.	21,610	22,330	23,482	23,510	23,248	22,988	22,744
STATISTICAL RECORD:							
Operating Profit Margin %	9.4	8.6	8.7	8.3	7.9	8.8	8.2
Net Profit Margin %	4.4	3.1	2.7	2.7	3.1	3.4	3.0
Return on Equity %	16.2	10.7	8.4	8.1	8.6	9.6	8.1
Return on Assets %	6.8	4.3	3.3	3.1	3.3	4.0	3.7
Debt/Total Assets %	33.3	41.2	27.4	30.1	34.8	27.7	35.6
Price Range	19⁹⁄₁₆-7³⁄₁₆	12-6½	7³⁄₈-5⁷⁄₁₆	7⁵⁄₁₆-4⁵⁄₈	7½-4¹³⁄₁₆	9⁵⁄₈-5³⁄₈	9¹³⁄₁₆-5⁷⁄₁₆
P/E Ratio	16.2-6.0	16.7-9.0	12.9-9.5	13.9-8.8	14.3-9.2	17.5-9.8	21.6-11.9
Average Yield %	1.4	1.8	2.5	2.6	2.4	1.8	1.7

Statistics are as originally reported. Adj. for stk. split: 2-for-1, 8/25/99.

QUARTERLY DATA

(12/31/1999)($000)	Rev	Inc
1st Quarter	149,781	6,290
2nd Quarter	142,239	4,970
3rd Quarter	157,875	7,192
4th Quarter	168,901	8,948

OFFICERS:
R. Haverty, Chmn.
J. E. Slater, Jr., Pres., C.E.O.
D. L. Fink, Exec. V.P., C.F.O.
J. H. Parker, Treas., Corp. Sec.

INVESTOR CONTACT: Dennis L. Fink, Exec. V.P. & C.F.O., (404) 443-2900

PRINCIPAL OFFICE: 780 Johnson Ferry Road, Suite 800, Atlanta, GA 30342

TELEPHONE NUMBER: (404) 443-2900
FAX: (404) 443-4180
WEB: www.havertys.com

NO. OF EMPLOYEES: 3,636 (avg.)

SHAREHOLDERS: 3,400 (approx. com.); 200 (cl. A)

ANNUAL MEETING: In Mar.

INCORPORATED: MD, Sept., 1929

INSTITUTIONAL HOLDINGS:
No. of Institutions: 77
Shares Held: 11,078,037
% Held: 64.0

INDUSTRY: Furniture stores (SIC: 5712)

TRANSFER AGENT(S): SunTrust Bank, Atlanta, GA

HEALTH CARE PROPERTY INVESTORS, INC.

YIELD 10.9%
P/E RATIO 11.8

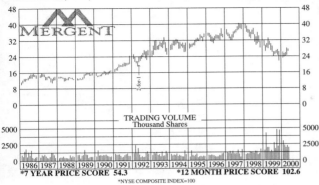

TRADING VOLUME
Thousand Shares

*7 YEAR PRICE SCORE 54.3   ***12 MONTH PRICE SCORE 102.6**

*NYSE COMPOSITE INDEX=100

INTERIM EARNINGS (Per Share):

Qtr.	Mar.	June	Sept.	Dec.
1995	0.50	1.33	0.51	0.49
1996	0.51	0.54	0.52	0.54
1997	0.60	0.54	0.54	0.53
1998	0.54	0.53	0.72	0.73
1999	0.49	0.49	0.80	0.49

INTERIM DIVIDENDS (Per Share):

Amt.	Decl.	Ex.	Rec.	Pay.
0.69Q	4/20/99	4/29/99	5/03/99	5/20/99
0.70Q	7/21/99	7/29/99	8/02/99	8/20/99
0.71Q	10/08/99	10/19/99	10/21/99	11/19/99
0.72Q	1/19/00	2/01/00	2/03/00	2/18/00
0.73Q	4/20/00	5/01/00	5/03/00	5/19/00

Indicated div.: $2.92

CAPITALIZATION (12/31/99):

	($000)	(%)
Long-Term Debt	1,179,507	48.7
Minority Interest	40,404	1.7
Preferred Stock	275,041	11.4
Common & Surplus	925,216	38.2
Total	2,420,168	100.0

DIVIDEND ACHIEVER STATUS:
Rank: 223   10-Year Growth Rate: 6.97%
Total Years of Dividend Growth: 14

RECENT DEVELOPMENTS: For the year ended 12/31/99, net income increased 10.4% to $96.2 million from $87.2 million in the previous year. Earnings in 1999 included a gain of $10.3 million from the sale of real estate properties. This compares with a similar gain of $14.1 million in 1998. Total revenue grew 39.1% to $224.8 million from $161.5 million the year before. Rental income advanced 41.5% to $189.8 million from $134.2 million in the prior year. Tenant reimbursements totaled $9.8 million compared with $2.8 million the year before. Interest and other income rose 2.6% to $25.2 million from $24.6 million in the prior year. Revenue and earnings growth was primarily due to the acquisition of American Health Properties, Inc. in 1999.

BUSINESS

HEALTH CARE PROPERTY INVESTORS, INC. is a real estate investment trust that invests in health-care-related facilities throughout the United States, including long-term care facilities, congregate care and assisted living facilities, acute care and rehabilitation hospitals, medical office buildings and physician group practice clinics. The Company's investment portfolio as of 12/31/99 included 428 facilities in 42 states. The Company's investments include 176 long-term care facilities, nine rehabilitation hospitals, 93 congregate care and assisted living centers, 22 acute care hospitals, 82 medical office buildings and 46 physician group practice clinics. On 11/4/99, HCP acquired American Health Properties, Inc., in a stock-for-stock transaction, and its 72 healthcare properties in 22 states.

REVENUES

(12/31/99)	($000)	(%)
Base Rental Income	189,800	84.4
Tenant Reimbursements	9,770	4.3
Interest & Other Income	25,223	11.3
Total	224,793	100.0

ANNUAL FINANCIAL DATA

	12/31/99	12/31/98	12/31/97	12/31/96	12/31/95	12/31/94	12/31/93
Earnings Per Share	☐ 2.25	☐ 2.54	☐ 2.19	2.12	☐ 2.83	1.87	1.66
Tang. Book Val. Per Share	17.99	13.15	12.72	11.74	11.88	10.08	10.13
Dividends Per Share	2.78	2.62	2.46	2.30	2.14	1.98	1.84
Dividend Payout %	123.6	103.1	117.1	108.5	75.6	105.9	111.1
INCOME STATEMENT (IN THOUSANDS):							
Rental Income	199,570	138,439	113,920	104,627	86,795	81,518	75,087
Total Income	224,793	161,549	128,503	120,393	105,696	98,996	92,549
Costs & Expenses	85,535	50,372	36,401	33,227	26,093	27,913	27,181
Depreciation	47,860	32,523	25,656	23,149	19,208	17,521	17,862
Income Before Income Taxes	101,701	92,707	68,493	64,017	83,945	53,562	47,506
Equity Earnings/Minority Int.	d5,476	d5,540	d3,704	d3,376	d3,679	d3,585	d3,419
Net Income	☐ 96,225	☐ 87,167	☐ 64,789	60,641	☐ 80,266	49,977	44,087
Average Shs. Outstg.	34,861	33,664	28,994	28,652	28,348	26,679	26,580
BALANCE SHEET (IN THOUSANDS):							
Cash & Cash Equivalents	7,696	4,504	4,084	2,811	2,000	2,928	27,210
Total Real Estate Investments	2,192,988	1,131,119	786,502	623,734	527,994	475,795	434,817
Total Assets	2,469,390	1,356,612	940,964	753,653	667,831	573,826	549,638
Long-Term Obligations	1,179,507	709,045	452,858	379,504	299,084	271,463	245,291
Total Liabilities	1,269,133	761,193	498,695	416,847	328,371	304,423	279,765
Net Stockholders' Equity	1,200,257	595,419	442,269	336,806	339,460	269,403	269,873
Year-end Shs. Outstg.	51,421	30,987	30,216	28,678	28,574	26,734	26,633
STATISTICAL RECORD:							
Net Inc.+Depr./Assets %	5.8	8.8	9.6	11.1	14.9	11.8	11.3
Return on Equity %	8.0	14.6	14.6	18.0	23.6	18.6	16.3
Return on Assets %	3.9	6.4	6.9	8.0	12.0	8.7	8.0
Price Range	33⅛-21¹¹/₁₆	40-28¼	40⅜-31⅞	37¾-30½	35¼-28	32⅝-26¼	33⅝-24
P/E Ratio	14.7-9.6	15.7-11.1	18.4-14.6	17.8-14.4	12.5-9.9	17.4-14.0	20.3-14.5
Average Yield %	10.1	7.7	6.8	6.7	6.8	6.7	6.4

Statistics are as originally reported. ☐ Incl non-recurr. credit 12/31/99: $10.3 mill.; 12/31/98: $14.1 mill.; 12/31/97: $2.0 mill.; 12/31/95: $23.6 mill.

OFFICERS:
K. B. Roath, Chmn., Pres., C.E.O.
J. G. Reynolds, Exec. V.P., C.F.O.
D. Ghose, Sr. V.P., Fin., Treas.
E. J. Henning, Sr. V.P., Gen. Couns., Corp. Sec.
INVESTOR CONTACT: Kenneth B. Roath, Chmn. & CEO, (949) 221-0600
PRINCIPAL OFFICE: 4675 Macarthur Court, Suite 900, Newport Beach, CA 92660

TELEPHONE NUMBER: (949) 221-0600
FAX: (949) 221-0607
WEB: www.hcpi.com
NO. OF EMPLOYEES: 36
SHAREHOLDERS: 3,668 (approx. of record); 64,000 (approx. beneficial)
ANNUAL MEETING: In May
INCORPORATED: MD, Mar., 1985

INSTITUTIONAL HOLDINGS:
No. of Institutions: 123
Shares Held: 20,839,533
% Held: 40.5

INDUSTRY: Real estate investment trusts (SIC: 6798)

TRANSFER AGENT(S): The Bank of New York, New York, N.Y.

HEALTH CARE REIT, INC.

YIELD 14.6%
P/E RATIO 7.3

*7 YEAR PRICE SCORE 52.8   *12 MONTH PRICE SCORE 86.3
*NYSE COMPOSITE INDEX=100

INTERIM EARNINGS (Per Share):

Qtr.	Mar.	June	Sept.	Dec.
1996	0.47	0.66	0.50	0.55
1997	0.51	0.55	0.54	0.54
1998	0.54	0.54	0.56	0.60
1999	0.57	0.56	0.57	0.51

INTERIM DIVIDENDS (Per Share):

Amt.	Decl.	Ex.	Rec.	Pay.
0.565Q	4/21/99	4/30/99	5/04/99	5/20/99
0.57Q	7/21/99	7/30/99	8/03/99	8/20/99
0.575Q	10/20/99	10/29/99	11/02/99	11/22/99
0.58Q	1/18/00	1/28/00	2/01/00	2/21/00
0.585Q	4/18/00	4/28/00	5/02/00	5/22/00

Indicated div.: $2.34

CAPITALIZATION (12/31/99):

	($000)	(%)
Long-Term Debt	538,842	43.3
Preferred Stock	150,000	12.0
Common & Surplus	556,996	44.7
Total	1,245,838	100.0

DIVIDEND ACHIEVER STATUS:

Rank: 293   10-Year Growth Rate: 3.43%
Total Years of Dividend Growth: 10

RECENT DEVELOPMENTS:

For the year ended 12/31/99, net income increased 21.4% to $75.6 million compared with $62.3 million in the previous year. Results for 1999 and 1998 included gains on the sale of properties of $103,000 and $1.0 million, respectively. Total revenues jumped 32.7% to $128.6 million from $96.9 million from a year earlier. Revenues from rental income soared 73.3% to $72.7 million from $42.0 million, while interest income fell 0.8% to $48.1 million from $48.5 million in the prior year. Commitment fees and other income advanced 5.9% to $6.3 million from $5.9 million, while revenues from prepayment fees more than doubled to $1.6 million from $588,000 the year before. For the quarter ended 12/31/99, net income was $14.6 million versus $16.5 million in 1998. Total revenues climbed 21.8% to $33.8 million compared with $27.8 million in the corresponding period of 1998.

BUSINESS

HEALTH CARE REIT, INC. is a self-administered real estate investment trust that invests in health care facilities, primarily nursing homes and assisted living facilities. The Company also invests in specialty care facilities. As of 3/31/00, the Company had $1.30 billion of real estate investments in 235 facilities located in 33 states and managed by 38 different operators. Long-term care facilities, which include nursing homes and assisted living facilities, comprised approximately 92% of the Company's investment portfolio.

REVENUES

(12/31/1999)	($000)	(%)
Rental income	72,700	56.5
Interest income	48,076	37.4
Commitment fees & other	6,263	4.9
Prepayment fees	1,565	1.2
Total	128,604	100.0

ANNUAL FINANCIAL DATA

	12/31/99	12/31/98	12/31/97	12/31/96	12/31/95	12/31/94	12/31/93
Earnings Per Share	2.21	2.24	2.12	2.18	1.16	2.17	2.15
Tang. Book Val. Per Share	19.52	19.79	19.31	17.77	15.59	16.32	16.09
Dividends Per Share	2.27	2.19	2.11	2.08	2.075	2.01	1.93
Dividend Payout %	102.7	97.8	99.5	95.4	178.9	92.6	89.8
INCOME STATEMENT (IN MILLIONS):							
Rental Income	72.7	42.0	22.2	10.0	6.4	5.6	2.8
Interest Income	48.1	47.5	46.0	36.7	30.8	26.0	21.6
Total Income	128.6	98.0	73.3	54.4	44.6	42.7	36.0
Costs & Expenses	8.0	6.7	5.5	5.9	10.1	6.1	4.0
Depreciation	17.9	10.3	5.3	2.4	1.6	1.4	0.8
Interest Expense	26.9	18.0	15.4	14.6	12.8	9.7	10.8
Income Before Income Taxes	75.6	62.3	46.5	30.7	13.6	25.0	20.1
Net Income	75.6	62.3	46.5	30.7	13.6	25.0	20.1
Average Shs. Outstg. (000)	28,384	25,954	21,929	14,093	11,710	11,519	9,339
BALANCE SHEET (IN MILLIONS):							
Cash & Cash Equivalents	28.4	31.6	11.0	1.3	1.7	0.9	4.9
Total Assets	1,271.2	1,073.4	734.3	519.8	358.1	324.1	285.0
Long-Term Obligations	538.8	419.0	249.1	184.4	162.8	128.3	96.3
Total Liabilities	564.2	439.7	264.4	194.3	170.5	134.9	100.9
Net Stockholders' Equity	707.0	633.8	469.9	325.5	187.6	189.2	184.1
Year-end Shs. Outstg. (000)	28,532	28,240	24,341	18,320	12,034	11,595	11,446
STATISTICAL RECORD:							
Net Inc.+Depr./Assets %	7.4	6.8	7.0	6.4	4.2	8.1	7.3
Return on Equity %	10.7	9.8	9.9	9.4	7.3	13.2	10.9
Return on Assets %	6.0	5.8	6.3	5.9	3.8	7.7	7.0
Price Range	26⅝-14¹¹/₁₆	29¼-20	28⅝-22¼	25¼-17⅞	23⅛-15½	25⅜-19¾	27-20½
P/E Ratio	12.0-6.6	13.1-8.9	13.5-10.5	11.6-8.2	19.9-13.4	11.7-9.1	12.6-9.5
Average Yield %	11.0	8.9	8.9	8.3	9.6	10.7	8.9	8.1

Statistics are as originally reported.

OFFICERS:
G. L. Chapman, Chmn., Pres., C.E.O.
E. F. Lange Jr., C.F.O.
E. C. Ibele, V.P., Sec.

INVESTOR CONTACT: Erin C. Ibele, Vice President & Corp. Sec., (419) 247-2800

PRINCIPAL OFFICE: One Seagate Suite 1500, Toledo, OH 43603-1475

TELEPHONE NUMBER: (419) 247-2800
FAX: (419) 247-2826
WEB: www.hcreit.com

NO. OF EMPLOYEES: 23

SHAREHOLDERS: 5,240

ANNUAL MEETING: In May

INCORPORATED: DE, Apr., 1985

INSTITUTIONAL HOLDINGS:
No. of Institutions: 81
Shares Held: 4,668,145
% Held: 16.4

INDUSTRY: Real estate investment trusts (SIC: 6798)

TRANSFER AGENT(S): ChaseMellon Shareholder Serices, LLC, Ridgefield Park, NJ

NYSE SYMBOL HNZ
Rec. Pr. 39½ (5/31/00)

HEINZ (H.J.) COMPANY

YIELD 3.7%
P/E RATIO 20.5

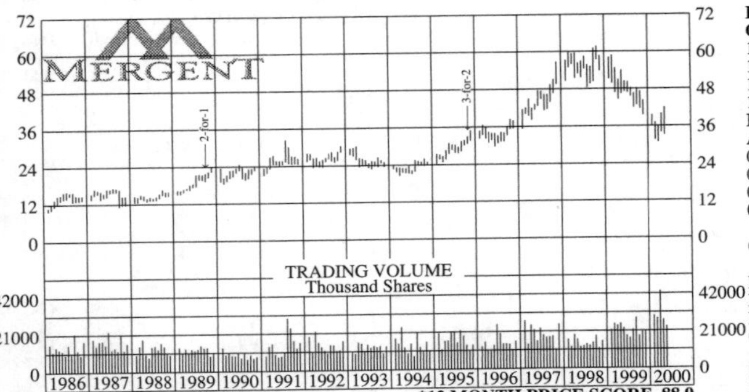

*7 YEAR PRICE SCORE 73.4 *12 MONTH PRICE SCORE 88.9

*NYSE COMPOSITE INDEX=100

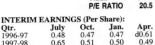

INTERIM EARNINGS (Per Share):

Qtr.	July	Oct.	Jan.	Apr.
1996-97	0.48	0.47	0.47	d0.61
1997-98	0.65	0.51	0.50	0.49
1998-99	0.58	0.63	0.33	d0.25
1999-00	0.57	1.14	0.47	...

INTERIM DIVIDENDS (Per Share):

Amt.	Decl.	Ex.	Rec.	Pay.
0.343Q	6/09/99	6/17/99	6/21/99	7/10/99
0.367Q	9/08/99	9/17/99	9/21/99	10/10/99
0.367Q	12/08/99	12/16/99	12/20/99	1/10/00
0.367Q	3/08/00	3/16/00	3/20/00	4/10/00

Indicated div.: $1.47 (Div. Reinv. Plan)

CAPITALIZATION (4/28/99):

	($000)	(%)
Long-Term Debt	2,472,206	53.9
Deferred Income Tax	310,799	6.8
Preferred Stock	173	0.0
Common & Surplus	1,802,831	39.3
Total	4,586,009	100.0

DIVIDEND ACHIEVER STATUS:
Rank: 138 10-Year Growth Rate: 10.81%
Total Years of Dividend Growth: 36

RECENT DEVELOPMENTS: For the quarter ended 1/26/00, net income rose 41.9% to $171.1 million from $120.6 million the previous year. Results in the recent period included after-tax restructuring charges of $56.0 million, while earnings in the prior-year period included after-tax restructuring charges of $98.9 million. Sales inched up to $2.29 billion from $2.28 billion the year before, due to higher volume and acquisitions, partially offset by divestitures, lower prices and unfavorable foreign currency exchange rates.

PROSPECTS: On 2/28/00, the Company signed an agreement to acquire Milnot Holding Corporation, a producer of branded and private-label food products with annual sales of approximately $226.0 million. Milnot's largest subsidiary, Beech-Nut Nutrition Corporation, is the maker of the Beech-Nut brand of prepared baby foods. Meanwhile, HNZ has created a new core category that will enable the Company to increase its focus on growing its global organic and nutritional foods businesses.

BUSINESS

H.J. HEINZ COMPANY manufactures and markets an extensive line of processed food products including ketchup and other sauces/condiments, pet food, tuna and other seafood products, baby food, frozen potato products, canned and frozen soups, beans, pasta, frozen dinners, frozen and canned vegatables and fruits, juices, pickles, and vinegar. Major U.S. brands include HEINZ, WEIGHT WATCHERS, ORE-IDA, THE BUDGET GOURMET, SMART ONES, STARKIST, 9-LIVES, KEN-L RATION, SKIPPY, and POUNCE. Overseas, well-known brands include PLASMON, PUDLISZKI, ABC, ORLANDO, WATTIE'S, OLIVINE, FARLEY'S, and GULOSO. Foreign operations produced 47% of net sales in the year ended 4/28/99.

ANNUAL FINANCIAL DATA

	4/28/99	4/29/98	4/30/97	5/1/96	5/3/95	4/27/94	4/28/93
Earnings Per Share	[1] **1.29**	[1] **2.15**	[1] **0.80**	**1.74**	**1.59**	[1] **1.57**	[2] **1.36**
Cash Flow Per Share	**2.11**	**2.99**	**1.72**	**2.66**	**2.43**	**2.24**	**1.96**
Tang. Book Val. Per Share	...	...	**0.03**	**0.87**	**0.34**	**2.67**	**2.49**
Dividends Per Share	**1.29**	**1.19**	**1.08**	**0.98**	**0.90**	**0.82**	**0.74**
Dividend Payout %	**99.8**	**55.1**	**135.6**	**56.6**	**56.6**	**52.3**	**54.4**
INCOME STATEMENT (IN MILLIONS):							
Total Revenues	9,299.6	9,209.3	9,357.0	9,112.3	8,086.8	7,046.7	7,103.4
Costs & Expenses	7,888.1	7,375.3	8,260.2	7,480.9	6,615.7	5,845.6	6,007.6
Depreciation & Amort.	302.2	313.6	340.5	343.8	315.3	259.8	234.9
Operating Income	1,109.3	1,520.3	756.3	1,287.6	1,155.8	1,068.3	860.9
Net Interest Inc./(Exp.)	d233.7	d226.0	d235.4	d232.6	d174.0	d112.5	d117.0
Income Before Income Taxes	835.1	1,255.0	479.1	1,023.7	938.0	922.4	715.8
Income Taxes	360.8	453.4	177.2	364.3	347.0	319.4	185.8
Net Income	[1] 474.3	[1] 801.6	[1] 301.9	659.3	591.0	[1] 602.9	[2] 529.9
Cash Flow	776.5	1,115.2	642.3	1,003.1	906.2	862.7	764.8
Average Shs. Outstg. (000)	367,830	372,953	373,703	377,156	372,807	385,218	389,682
BALANCE SHEET (IN MILLIONS):							
Cash & Cash Equivalents	123.1	99.4	188.4	108.4	207.0	142.4	224.3
Total Current Assets	2,886.8	2,686.5	3,013.1	3,046.7	2,823.0	2,291.5	2,623.4
Net Property	2,171.0	2,394.7	2,479.2	2,616.8	2,534.4	2,167.7	2,162.2
Total Assets	8,053.6	8,023.4	8,437.8	8,623.7	8,247.2	6,381.1	6,821.3
Total Current Liabilities	2,786.3	2,164.3	2,880.4	2,715.1	2,564.1	1,692.4	2,866.3
Long-Term Obligations	2,472.2	2,768.3	2,284.0	2,281.7	2,326.8	1,727.0	1,009.4
Net Stockholders' Equity	1,803.0	2,216.5	2,440.4	2,706.8	2,472.9	2,338.6	2,321.0
Net Working Capital	100.5	522.2	132.7	331.6	259.0	599.2	d242.9
Year-end Shs. Outstg. (000)	359,128	363,418	367,184	368,598	365,514	373,562	381,548
STATISTICAL RECORD:							
Operating Profit Margin %	11.9	16.5	8.1	14.1	14.3	15.2	12.1
Net Profit Margin %	5.1	8.7	3.2	7.2	7.3	8.6	7.5
Return on Equity %	26.3	36.2	12.4	24.4	23.9	25.8	22.8
Return on Assets %	5.9	10.0	3.6	7.6	7.2	9.4	7.8
Debt/Total Assets %	30.7	34.5	27.1	26.5	28.2	27.1	14.8
Price Range	61¾-48½	56¹¹⁄₁₆-35¼	38⅜-29¾	34⅞-24¼	26-20½	30³⁄₁₆-22¾	30⁵⁄₁₆-23⁷⁄₁₆
P/E Ratio	47.9-37.6	26.4-16.4	48.0-37.2	20.0-13.9	16.4-12.9	19.3-14.5	22.3-17.2
Average Yield %	2.3	2.6	3.2	3.3	3.9	3.1	2.8

Statistics are as originally reported. Adj. for 3-for-2 stk. split, 9/95. [1] Incl. $408.2 mil ($1.11/sh) net chg., 1999; $12.5 mil net gain, 1998; $664.6 mil net chg., 1996; & $127.0 mil gain, 1993. [2] Bef. $133.6 mil chg. for acctg. adj. & incl. $117.0 mil non-recur restr. chg.

OFFICERS:
A. J. O'Reilly, Chmn.
W. R. Johnson, Pres., C.E.O.
P. F. Renne, Exec. V.P., C.F.O.
L. J. McCabe, Sr. V.P., Gen. Couns., Sec.

INVESTOR CONTACT: Jack Runkel, V.P., Investor Relations, (412) 456-6034

PRINCIPAL OFFICE: 600 Grant Street, Pittsburgh, PA 15219

TELEPHONE NUMBER: (412) 456-5700
FAX: (412) 456-6128
WEB: www.heinz.com

NO. OF EMPLOYEES: 38,600 (approx.)

SHAREHOLDERS: 61,306 (approx.)

ANNUAL MEETING: In Sept.

INCORPORATED: PA, July, 1900

INSTITUTIONAL HOLDINGS:
No. of Institutions: 515
Shares Held: 203,735,083
% Held: 57.4

INDUSTRY: Food preparations, nec (SIC: 2099)

TRANSFER AGENT(S): ChaseMellon Shareholder Services, L.L.C., Ridgefield Park, NJ

NYSE SYMBOL HSY
Rec. Pr. 51 7/8 (5/31/00)

HERSHEY FOODS CORPORATION

YIELD 2.0%
P/E RATIO 16.0

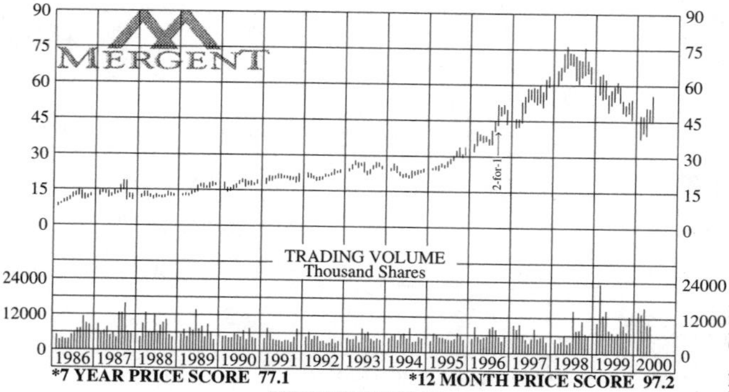

MERGENT
90
75
60
45
30
15
0
2-for-1
TRADING VOLUME
Thousand Shares
24000
12000
0
1986 1987 1988 1989 1990 1991 1992 1993 1994 1995 1996 1997 1998 1999 2000

*7 YEAR PRICE SCORE 77.1 *12 MONTH PRICE SCORE 97.2

*NYSE COMPOSITE INDEX=100

INTERIM EARNINGS (Per Share):

Qtr.	Mar.	June	Sept.	Dec.
1995		1.74		
1996	0.39	0.53	0.61	0.51
1997	0.45	0.33	0.68	0.80
1998	0.52	0.33	0.74	0.76
1999	1.57	0.35	0.62	0.70

INTERIM DIVIDENDS (Per Share):

Amt.	Decl.	Ex.	Rec.	Pay.
0.24Q	4/06/99	5/20/99	5/24/99	6/15/99
0.26Q	8/03/99	8/23/99	8/25/99	9/15/99
0.26Q	11/02/99	11/18/99	11/22/99	12/15/99
0.26Q	2/09/00	2/23/00	2/25/00	3/15/00
0.26Q	4/25/00	5/23/00	5/25/00	6/15/00

Indicated div.: $1.04 (Div. Reinv. Plan)

CAPITALIZATION (12/31/99):

	($000)	(%)
Long-Term Debt	878,213	38.1
Deferred Income Tax	326,045	14.2
Common & Surplus	1,098,627	47.7
Total	2,302,885	100.0

DIVIDEND ACHIEVER STATUS:
Rank: 149 10-Year Growth Rate: 10.45%
Total Years of Dividend Growth: 25

RECENT DEVELOPMENTS: For the twelve months ended 12/31/99, net income increased 35.0% to $460.3 million from $340.9 million in 1998. Results for 1999 included a net gain of $165.0 million from the sale of HSY's pasta business. The 1998 results included a non-recurring pre-tax gain of $13.0 million. Net sales fell 10.5% to $3.97 billion from $4.44 billion in 1998. Results were pressured by customer service and order fulfillment problems.

PROSPECTS: Customer service levels should continue to be enhanced with further improvement of the Company's new business systems and processes, and as the first phase of the new 1.2 million square-foot distribution center becomes operational in the Spring of 2000 with full utilization expected during the Fall shipping season. The new distribution center should improve the Company's logisitics efficiency and ultimately reduce HSY's logistics costs.

BUSINESS

HERSHEY FOODS CORPORATION and its subsidiaries are engaged in the manufacture, distribution and sale of consumer food products including: chocolate and non-chocolate confectionery products sold in the form of bar goods, bagged items and boxed items; and grocery products sold in the form of baking ingredients, chocolate drink mixes, peanut butter, dessert toppings and beverages. HSY's products are marketed in over 90 countries worldwide. Principal brands include: HERSHEY'S, REESE'S, MOUNDS, JOLLY RANCHER, KIT KAT, MILK DUDS and ALMOND JOY. In January 1999, the Company sold 94.0% majority interest in its former U.S. pasta business to New World, LLC.

QUARTERLY DATA

(12/31/99)($000)	Rev	Inc
1st Quarter	945,152	224,670
2nd Quarter	853,239	50,055
3rd Quarter	1,066,695	87,578
4th Quarter	1,105,838	98,007

ANNUAL FINANCIAL DATA

	12/31/99	12/31/98	12/31/97	12/31/96	12/31/95	12/31/94	12/31/93
Earnings Per Share	**[3] 3.26**	**2.34**	**2.23**	**1.77**	**1.70**	**[1] 1.06**	**[1] [2] 1.66**
Cash Flow Per Share	**4.41**	**3.43**	**3.24**	**2.64**	**2.50**	**1.80**	**2.29**
Tang. Book Val. Per Share	**4.68**	**3.58**	**2.11**	**3.89**	**4.23**	**5.69**	**5.36**
Dividends Per Share	**1.00**	**0.92**	**0.84**	**0.76**	**0.69**	**0.63**	**0.57**
Dividend Payout %	**30.7**	**39.3**	**37.7**	**42.9**	**40.3**	**59.0**	**34.4**
INCOME STATEMENT (IN MILLIONS):							
Total Revenues	3,970.9	4,435.6	4,302.2	3,989.3	3,690.7	3,606.3	3,488.2
Costs & Expenses	3,249.3	3,634.8	3,519.3	3,292.7	3,046.0	3,108.7	2,837.3
Depreciation & Amort.	163.3	158.2	152.8	133.5	133.9	129.0	113.1
Operating Income	558.4	642.7	630.2	563.1	510.8	368.5	537.9
Net Interest Inc./(Exp.)	d74.3	d85.7	d76.3	d48.0	d44.8	d35.4	d27.0
Income Before Income Taxes	727.9	557.0	554.0	479.7	466.0	333.1	510.9
Income Taxes	267.6	216.1	217.7	206.6	184.0	148.9	213.6
Net Income	[3] 460.3	340.9	336.3	273.2	281.9	[1] 184.2	[1] [2] 297.2
Cash Flow	623.6	499.0	489.0	406.7	415.8	313.3	410.3
Average Shs. Outstg. (000)	141,300	145,563	151,016	153,995	166,036	174,367	179,514
BALANCE SHEET (IN MILLIONS):							
Cash & Cash Equivalents	118.1	39.0	54.2	61.4	32.3	26.7	16.0
Total Current Assets	1,280.0	1,134.0	1,034.8	986.2	922.3	948.7	889.0
Net Property	1,510.5	1,648.1	1,648.2	1,601.9	1,436.0	1,468.4	1,460.9
Total Assets	3,346.7	3,404.1	3,291.2	3,184.8	2,830.6	2,891.0	2,855.1
Total Current Liabilities	712.8	814.8	795.7	817.3	864.4	796.2	813.8
Long-Term Obligations	878.2	879.1	1,029.1	655.3	357.0	157.2	165.8
Net Stockholders' Equity	1,098.6	1,042.3	852.8	1,161.0	1,083.0	1,441.1	1,412.3
Net Working Capital	567.2	319.1	239.1	169.0	58.0	152.4	75.2
Year-end Shs. Outstg. (000)	138,460	143,147	142,932	152,942	154,532	173,470	175,226
STATISTICAL RECORD:							
Operating Profit Margin %	14.1	14.5	14.6	14.1	13.8	10.2	15.4
Net Profit Margin %	11.6	7.7	7.8	6.8	7.6	5.1	8.5
Return on Equity %	41.9	32.7	39.4	23.5	26.0	12.8	21.0
Return on Assets %	13.8	10.0	10.2	8.6	10.0	6.4	10.4
Debt/Total Assets %	26.2	25.8	31.3	20.6	12.6	5.4	5.8
Price Range	64 7/8-45 3/4	76 3/8-59 11/16	63 7/8-42 1/8	51 3/4-31 15/16	33 15/16-24	26 3/4-20 9/16	27 15/16-21 3/4
P/E Ratio	19.9-14.0	32.6-25.5	28.6-18.9	29.2-18.0	20.0-14.1	25.2-19.4	16.9-13.1
Average Yield %	1.8	1.4	1.6	1.8	2.4	2.6	2.3

Statistics are as originally reported. Adj. for 2-for-1 stk. split, 9/96 [1] Incls. non-recurr. chrg. 12/31/94, $80.2 mill.; credit 12/31/93, $40.6 mill. [2] Bef. acctg. change chrg. $103.9 mill. [3] Incls. non-recurring credit of $165.0 mill.

OFFICERS:
K. L. Wolfe, Chmn., C.E.O.
J. P. Viviano, Pres.
W. F. Christ, Sr. V.P., C.F.O., Treas.

INVESTOR CONTACT: James A. Edris, Dir., Investor Relations, (717) 534-7556

PRINCIPAL OFFICE: 100 Crystal A Drive, Hershey, PA 17033

TELEPHONE NUMBER: (717) 534-4000
FAX: (717) 531-6161
WEB: www.hersheys.com

NO. OF EMPLOYEES: 13,900 full-time (approx.); 1,400 part-time (approx.)

SHAREHOLDERS: 43,265

ANNUAL MEETING: In Apr.

INCORPORATED: DE, Oct., 1927

INSTITUTIONAL HOLDINGS:
No. of Institutions: 323
Shares Held: 57,296,482
% Held: 53.1

INDUSTRY: Chocolate and cocoa products (SIC: 2066)

TRANSFER AGENT(S): ChaseMellon Shareholder Services, Ridgefield Park, NJ

NYSE SYMBOL HWP
Rec. Pr. 120 3/16 (5/31/00)

HEWLETT-PACKARD COMPANY

YIELD 0.5%
P/E RATIO 37.7

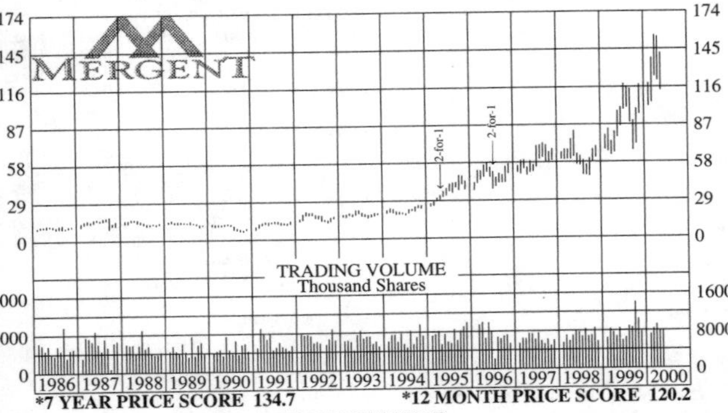

*7 YEAR PRICE SCORE 134.7 *12 MONTH PRICE SCORE 120.2

*NYSE COMPOSITE INDEX=100

INTERIM EARNINGS (Per Share):

Qtr.	Jan.	Apr.	July	Oct.
1996	0.75	0.69	0.40	0.62
1997	0.87	0.75	0.58	0.75
1998	0.86	0.65	0.58	0.68
1999	0.92	0.88	0.81	0.73
2000	0.77	...	...	...

INTERIM DIVIDENDS (Per Share):

Amt.	Decl.	Ex.	Rec.	Pay.
0.16Q	5/21/99	6/21/99	6/23/99	7/14/99
0.16Q	7/23/99	9/20/99	9/22/99	10/13/99
0.16Q	11/19/99	12/20/99	12/22/99	1/12/00
0.16Q	1/28/00	3/20/00	3/22/00	4/12/00
0.16Q	5/19/00	6/19/00	6/21/00	7/12/00

Indicated div.: $0.64 (Div. Reinv. Plan)

CAPITALIZATION (10/31/99):

	($000)	(%)
Long-Term Debt	1,764,000	8.8
Common & Surplus	18,295,000	91.2
Total	20,059,000	100.0

DIVIDEND ACHIEVER STATUS:
Rank: 18 10-Year Growth Rate: 21.67%
Total Years of Dividend Growth: 13

RECENT DEVELOPMENTS: For the quarter ended 1/31/00, net income was $794.0 million compared with income from continuing operations of $882.0 million in the corresponding quarter of 1999. Total net revenue rose 14.1% to $11.67 billion versus $10.24 billion in the year-earlier quarter. Imaging and printing systems net revenue grew 13.3% to $5.14 billion. Net revenue from computing systems jumped 14.8% to $5.13 billion. IT services segment net revenue climbed 14.2% to $1.62 billion.

PROSPECTS: On 5/20/00, HWP plans to spin off to shareholders its 84% stake in Agilent Technologies. As per the terms of the spin off, 0.37 shares of Agilent will be distributed for each HWP share. Separately, HWP recently released its HP JETDIRECT X home print server, which enables home- and small-business users to share printers. The home print server marks HP's entry into the home network printing market, which is expected to grow exponentially in coming years.

BUSINESS

HEWLETT-PACKARD COMPANY designs, manufactures and services electronic products and systems. The computer products, service and support develops hardware and software systems, networking products, printers, plotters, drives, calculators and offers support and maintenance services. The electronic test and measurement instrumentation unit provides maintenance and support for electronic equipment. The medical electronic equipment group performs monitoring, diagnostic, therapeutic and data-management applications for hospitals. The analytical and electronic components divisions offer gas and liquid chromatographs and microwave semiconductor and optoelectronic devices.

REVENUES

(10/31/1999)	($000)	(%)
Imaging and Printing	18,832	44.1
Computing Systems	17,877	42.0
IT Services	5,880	13.7
All Other Segments	79	0.2
Total	42,668	100.0

ANNUAL FINANCIAL DATA

	10/31/99	10/31/98	10/31/97	10/31/96	10/31/95	10/31/94	10/31/93
Earnings Per Share	**2 2.97**	**1 2.77**	**2.95**	**2.46**	**2.32**	**1.54**	**1.16**
Cash Flow Per Share	**4.20**	**4.49**	**4.42**	**3.69**	**3.40**	**2.53**	**2.00**
Tang. Book Val. Per Share	**18.21**	**16.67**	**15.52**	**13.25**	**11.61**	**9.73**	**8.44**
Dividends Per Share	**0.64**	**0.60**	**0.52**	**0.44**	**0.35**	**0.28**	**0.23**
Dividend Payout %	**21.5**	**21.7**	**17.6**	**17.9**	**15.1**	**17.9**	**19.3**
INCOME STATEMENT (IN MILLIONS):							
Total Revenues	42,370.0	47,061.0	42,895.0	38,420.0	31,519.0	24,991.0	20,317.0
Costs & Expenses	37,366.0	41,351.0	37,000.0	33,397.0	26,812.0	21,436.0	17,592.0
Depreciation & Amort.	1,316.0	1,869.0	1,556.0	1,297.0	1,139.0	1,006.0	846.0
Operating Income	3,688.0	3,841.0	4,339.0	3,726.0	3,568.0	2,549.0	1,879.0
Net Interest Inc./(Exp.)	d202.0	d235.0	d215.0	d327.0	d206.0	d155.0	d121.0
Income Before Income Taxes	4,194.0	4,091.0	4,455.0	3,694.0	3,632.0	2,423.0	1,783.0
Income Taxes	1,090.0	1,146.0	1,336.0	1,108.0	1,199.0	796.0	606.0
Net Income	2 3,104.0	1 2,945.0	3,119.0	2,586.0	2,433.0	1,627.0	1,177.0
Cash Flow	4,420.0	4,814.0	4,675.0	3,883.0	3,572.0	2,633.0	2,023.0
Average Shs. Outstg. (000)	1,052,000	1,072,000	1,057,000	1,052,000	1,052,000	1,040,000	1,012,000
BALANCE SHEET (IN MILLIONS):							
Cash & Cash Equivalents	5,590.0	4,067.0	4,569.0	3,327.0	2,616.0	2,478.0	1,644.0
Total Current Assets	21,642.0	21,584.0	20,947.0	17,991.0	16,239.0	12,509.0	10,236.0
Net Property	4,333.0	6,358.0	6,312.0	5,536.0	4,711.0	4,328.0	4,180.0
Total Assets	31,764.0	33,673.0	31,749.0	27,699.0	24,427.0	19,567.0	16,736.0
Total Current Liabilities	14,321.0	13,473.0	11,219.0	10,623.0	10,944.0	8,230.0	6,868.0
Long-Term Obligations	1,764.0	2,063.0	3,158.0	2,579.0	663.0	547.0	667.0
Net Stockholders' Equity	18,295.0	16,919.0	16,155.0	13,438.0	11,839.0	9,926.0	8,511.0
Net Working Capital	7,321.0	8,111.0	9,728.0	7,368.0	5,295.0	4,279.0	3,368.0
Year-end Shs. Outstg. (000)	1,004,596	1,015,000	1,041,000	1,014,000	1,020,000	1,020,000	1,008,000
STATISTICAL RECORD:							
Operating Profit Margin %	8.7	8.2	10.1	9.7	11.3	10.2	9.2
Net Profit Margin %	7.3	6.3	7.3	6.7	7.7	6.5	5.8
Return on Equity %	17.0	17.4	19.3	19.2	20.6	16.4	13.8
Return on Assets %	9.8	8.7	9.8	9.3	10.0	8.3	7.0
Debt/Total Assets %	4.9	6.1	9.9	9.3	2.7	2.8	4.0
Price Range	118 7/16-63 3/8	82 3/8-47 1/16	72 15/16-48 1/8	57 11/16-36 13/16	48 5/16-24 1/2	25 5/8-17	22 5/16-16 1/8
P/E Ratio	39.9-21.3	29.7-17.0	24.7-16.3	23.4-15.0	20.9-10.6	16.7-11.7	19.2-13.8
Average Yield %	0.7	0.9	0.9	0.9	1.0	1.3	1.2

Statistics are as originally reported. Adjusted for a 2-for-1 stock split 4/13/95 & 7/15/96. 1 Incl. spec. pre-tax chrgs. of approx. $170.0 mill. 2 Incl. pre-tax chrgs. of approx. $60.0 mill. assoc. with the Company's separation into two separate companies.

OFFICERS:
R. A. Hackborn, Chmn.
C. S. Fiorina, Pres., C.E.O.

INVESTOR CONTACT: Ann O. Baskins, V.P., Gen. Couns., Sec., (415) 857-3755

PRINCIPAL OFFICE: 3000 Hanover Street, Palo Alto, CA 94304

TELEPHONE NUMBER: (650) 857-1501
FAX: (650) 857-5518
WEB: www.hp.com

NO. OF EMPLOYEES: 84,400 (approx.)

SHAREHOLDERS: 127,900 (approx.)

ANNUAL MEETING: In Jan.

INCORPORATED: CA, Aug., 1947; reincorp., DE, May, 1998

INSTITUTIONAL HOLDINGS:
No. of Institutions: 1,009
Shares Held: 546,831,290
% Held: 53.7

INDUSTRY: Electronic computers (SIC: 3571)

TRANSFER AGENT(S): Harris Trust and Savings Bank, Chicago, IL

NYSE SYMBOL HRH
Rec. Pr. 31 5/16 (5/31/00)

HILB, ROGAL & HAMILTON COMPANY

YIELD 2.2%
P/E RATIO 21.2

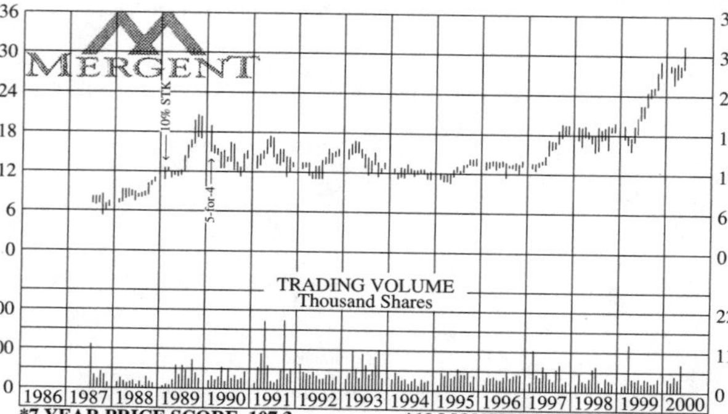

*7 YEAR PRICE SCORE 107.3 *12 MONTH PRICE SCORE 108.8

*NYSE COMPOSITE INDEX=100

INTERIM EARNINGS (Per Share):

Qtr.	Mar.	June	Sept.	Dec.
1996	0.38	0.20	0.17	0.10
1997	0.41	0.27	0.19	0.10
1998	0.46	0.35	0.25	0.12
1999	0.60	0.23	0.42	0.23

INTERIM DIVIDENDS (Per Share):

Amt.	Decl.	Ex.	Rec.	Pay.
0.165Q	6/08/99	6/14/99	6/16/99	6/30/99
0.165Q	8/03/99	9/14/99	9/16/99	9/30/99
0.165Q	11/09/99	12/14/99	12/16/99	12/31/99
0.165Q	2/10/00	3/15/00	3/17/00	3/31/00
0.17Q	5/02/00	6/14/00	6/16/00	6/30/00

Indicated div.: $0.68

CAPITALIZATION (12/31/99):

	($000)	(%)
Long-Term Debt	111,826	61.1
Common & Surplus	71,176	38.9
Total	183,002	100.0

DIVIDEND ACHIEVER STATUS:
Rank: 97 10-Year Growth Rate: 12.88%
Total Years of Dividend Growth: 13

RECENT DEVELOPMENTS: For the year ended 12/31/99, net income jumped 30.4% to $19.5 million versus $14.9 million in 1998. Results for 1999 included a charge of $1.9 million from integration costs and a non-recurring gain of $4.9 million from the sale of assets. Results for 1998 included a non-recurring gain of $2.6 million. Total revenues rose 29.6% to $227.2 million from $175.4 million in the previous year. Commission and fees increased 28.8% to $219.3 million versus $170.2 million the year before.

PROSPECTS: Going forward, the Company should continue to benefit from the addition of American Phoenix Corporation, which was acquired on 5/3/99, and the successful introduction of its new software program to all offices. The Company plans to expand its product line with more specialty, employee benefit and affinity group insurance programs and develop new distribution channels. HRH also plans to strengthen its presence in existing markets through strategic acquisitions.

BUSINESS

HILB, ROGAL & HAMILTON COMPANY places various types of insurance, including property, casualty marine, aviation and employee benefits, with insurance underwriters on behalf of its clients through the network of its wholly-owned subsidiary insurance agencies. The agencies operate 70 offices in 18 states. The client base consists mainly of middle market commercial and industrial accounts. The Company has acquired 175 independent agencies since 1984. HRH attributes its growth to the acquisitions of these independent agencies with local market shares in small to medium-size metropolitan areas. On 5/3/99, the Company acquired all of the outstanding common stock of American Phoenix Corporation.

ANNUAL FINANCIAL DATA

	12/31/99	12/31/98	12/31/97	12/31/96	12/31/95	12/31/94	12/31/93
Earnings Per Share	**[1] 1.44**	**1.18**	**0.97**	**0.85**	**0.82**	**0.77**	**0.61**
Cash Flow Per Share	**2.48**	**2.08**	**1.85**	**1.65**	**1.49**	**1.40**	**1.29**
Dividends Per Share	**0.66**	**0.64**	**0.62**	**0.60**	**0.57**	**0.50**	**0.45**
Dividend Payout %	**45.5**	**53.8**	**63.9**	**71.2**	**69.5**	**64.9**	**73.8**
INCOME STATEMENT (IN THOUSANDS):							
Total Revenues	227,226	175,364	173,709	158,243	148,147	140,810	134,954
Costs & Expenses	170,576	136,174	138,159	127,098	118,234	111,437	110,530
Depreciation & Amort.	15,191	11,509	11,667	10,856	9,757	9,286	9,494
Operating Income	41,458	27,681	23,882	20,290	20,156	20,087	14,930
Net Interest Inc./(Exp.)	d6,490	d2,317	d2,037	d1,245	d560	d812	d1,231
Income Before Income Taxes	33,069	25,364	21,845	19,045	19,597	18,787	13,196
Income Taxes	13,583	10,418	9,055	7,638	7,768	7,394	4,774
Net Income	[1] 19,486	14,945	12,790	11,406	11,829	11,392	8,422
Cash Flow	34,677	26,454	24,457	22,262	21,586	20,678	17,916
Average Shs. Outstg.	14,007	12,709	13,215	13,493	14,470	14,778	13,912
BALANCE SHEET (IN THOUSANDS):							
Cash & Cash Equivalents	25,276	22,779	26,207	24,862	28,175	35,747	30,740
Total Current Assets	111,201	78,202	76,833	76,256	78,615	84,907	81,095
Net Property	15,413	12,387	11,762	16,092	13,700	12,427	13,389
Total Assets	317,981	188,066	301,848	302,018	265,916	242,722	240,085
Total Current Liabilities	124,307	88,505	88,273	89,112	87,340	87,147	81,942
Long-Term Obligations	111,826	43,658	32,458	27,196	11,750	3,173	7,047
Net Stockholders' Equity	71,176	45,710	51,339	55,298	56,646	66,430	64,291
Net Working Capital	d13,106	d10,303	d11,440	d12,856	d8,724	d2,240	d847
Year-end Shs. Outstg.	13,059	12,117	12,813	13,321	14,679	14,679	12,699
STATISTICAL RECORD:							
Operating Profit Margin %	18.2	15.8	13.7	12.8	13.6	14.3	11.1
Net Profit Margin %	8.6	8.5	7.4	7.2	8.0	8.1	6.2
Return on Equity %	27.4	32.7	24.9	20.6	20.9	17.1	13.1
Return on Assets %	6.1	7.9	4.2	3.8	4.4	4.7	3.5
Debt/Total Assets %	35.2	23.2	10.8	9.0	4.4	1.3	2.9
Price Range	29 1/8-15 9/16	19 7/8-15 3/8	19 5/8-12 1/2	14-11 3/8	14 3/8-10 1/2	13 3/8-11	16 7/8-11 3/8
P/E Ratio	20.2-10.8	16.8-13.0	20.2-12.9	16.5-13.4	17.5-12.8	17.4-14.3	27.7-18.6
Average Yield %	2.9	3.6	3.9	4.8	4.6	4.1	3.2

Statistics are as originally reported. [1] Incl. $1.9 mill. integration chg. & $4.9 mill. non-recur. gain.

OFFICERS:
A. L. Rogal, Chmn., C.E.O.
M. H. Vaughan III, Pres., C.O.O.
C. Jones, Sr. V.P., C.F.O., Treas.
W. L. Smith, V.P., General Counsel, Sec.

INVESTOR CONTACT: Carolyn Jones, Sr. V.P. & C.F.O., (804) 747-3108

PRINCIPAL OFFICE: 4235 Innslake Drive, Glen Allen, VA 23060-1220

TELEPHONE NUMBER: (804) 747-6500
FAX: (804) 747-6046
WEB: www.hrh.com

NO. OF EMPLOYEES: 2,100 (approx.)

SHAREHOLDERS: 565 (of record)

ANNUAL MEETING: In May

INCORPORATED: VA, 1982

INSTITUTIONAL HOLDINGS:
No. of Institutions: 64
Shares Held: 9,093,881
% Held: 69.3

INDUSTRY: Insurance agents, brokers, & service (SIC: 6411)

TRANSFER AGENT(S): ChaseMellon Shareholder Services, Ridgefield Park, NJ.

HILLENBRAND INDUSTRIES, INC.

YIELD	2.6%
P/E RATIO	15.0

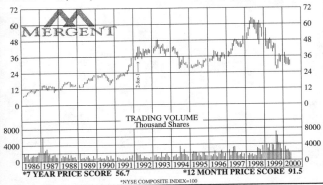

TRADING VOLUME
Thousand Shares

| 1986 | 1987 | 1988 | 1989 | 1990 | 1991 | 1992 | 1993 | 1994 | 1995 | 1996 | 1997 | 1998 | 1999 | 2000 |

*7 YEAR PRICE SCORE 56.7   ***12 MONTH PRICE SCORE 91.5**

*NYSE COMPOSITE INDEX=100

INTERIM EARNINGS (Per Share):

Qtr.	Feb.	May	Aug.	Nov.
1995-96	0.48	0.48	0.50	0.56
1996-97	0.56	0.54	0.51	0.67
1997-98	0.64	0.66	0.63	0.80
1998-99	0.67	0.53	0.35	0.58
1999-00	0.58	...	...	...

INTERIM DIVIDENDS (Per Share):

Amt.	Decl.	Ex.	Rec.	Pay.
0.195Q	7/13/99	7/21/99	7/23/99	8/27/99
0.195Q	10/05/99	10/20/99	10/22/99	11/26/99
0.20Q	1/18/00	2/09/00	2/11/00	2/25/00
0.20Q	4/11/00	4/18/00	4/21/00	5/26/00

Indicated div.: $0.80 (Div. Reinv. Plan)

CAPITALIZATION (11/27/99):

	($000)	(%)
Long-Term Debt	302,000	26.4
Deferred Income Tax	3,000	0.3
Common & Surplus	838,000	73.3
Total	1,143,000	100.0

DIVIDEND ACHIEVER STATUS:
Rank: 113   10-Year Growth Rate: 12.05%
Total Years of Dividend Growth: 29

RECENT DEVELOPMENTS: For the quarter ended 2/26/00, net income declined 20.0% to $36.0 million versus $45.0 million in the same period in 1999. Results for 1999 included a $2.0 million gain, while 1998 results included one-time charges of $1.0 million. Net revenues slipped to $514.0 million from $516.0 million. Sales of the funeral services group grew primarily from double-digit growth in cremation products. Health care group sales declined as a result of reduced shipments to nursing home customers.

PROSPECTS: The Company plans to capitalize on growth opportunities by introducing new and differentiated products and services as well as acquiring and developing related businesses. There has been a rise in demand for more personalized burial caskets, urns and funeral services. In the health care market, opportunities exist for improved patient care processes and outcomes, enhanced caregiver safety and productivity, and greater efficiencies for providers.

BUSINESS

HILLENBRAND INDUSTRIES, INC. is organized into two business segments. The Health Care Group consists of Hill-Rom, Inc., a manufacturer of equipment for the health care market and provider of wound care and pulmonary/trauma management services. Hill-Rom produces adjustable hospital beds, infant incubators, radiant warmers, hospital procedural stretchers, hospital patient room furniture, medical gas and vacuum systems and architectural systems designed to meet the needs of medical-surgical critical care, long-term care, home-care and perinatal providers. The Funeral Services Group consists of Batesville Casket Company, Inc., a manufacturer of caskets and other products for the funeral industry and Forethought Financial Services, Inc. a provider of funeral planning financial products.

ANNUAL FINANCIAL DATA

	11/27/99	11/28/98	11/29/97	11/30/96	12/2/95	12/3/94	11/27/93
Earnings Per Share	④ 1.87	① 2.73	2.28	2.02	1.27	1.26	② 1.86
Cash Flow Per Share	3.35	4.93	3.76	3.44	3.07	2.62	3.43
Tang. Book Val. Per Share	10.17	11.29	11.09	9.28	8.30	7.12	7.04
Dividends Per Share	0.78	0.72	0.66	0.62	0.60	0.57	0.45
Dividend Payout %	41.7	26.4	28.9	30.7	47.2	45.2	24.2
INCOME STATEMENT (IN MILLIONS):							
Total Revenues	2,047.0	2,001.0	1,776.0	1,684.0	1,624.9	1,577.0	1,447.9
Costs & Expenses	1,738.0	1,624.0	1,410.0	1,349.0	1,317.8	1,320.5	1,100.9
Depreciation & Amort.	98.0	149.0	102.0	99.0	127.6	97.5	112.7
Operating Income	211.0	228.0	264.0	236.0	179.5	159.0	234.3
Net Interest Inc./(Exp.)	d27.0	d27.0	d21.0	d22.0	d20.3	d23.5	d21.3
Income Before Income Taxes	195.0	293.0	259.0	233.0	169.8	144.8	221.5
Income Taxes	71.0	109.0	102.0	93.0	79.9	55.3	89.1
Net Income	④ 124.0	① 184.0	157.0	140.0	89.9	89.5	② 132.5
Cash Flow	222.0	333.0	259.0	239.0	217.5	187.0	245.2
Average Shs. Outstg. (000)	66,296	67,578	68,796	69,474	70,758	71,278	71,407
BALANCE SHEET (IN MILLIONS):							
Cash & Cash Equivalents	170.0	297.0	364.0	266.0	171.3	120.4	210.2
Total Current Assets	782.0	858.0	821.0	694.0	640.2	546.1	574.0
Net Property	267.0	302.0	329.0	346.0	367.1	358.6	326.8
Total Assets	4,433.0	4,280.0	3,828.0	3,396.0	3,070.3	2,693.8	2,270.7
Total Current Liabilities	371.0	375.0	359.0	320.0	300.7	238.9	290.0
Long-Term Obligations	302.0	303.0	203.0	204.0	206.8	208.7	107.9
Net Stockholders' Equity	838.0	952.0	886.0	787.0	745.8	693.5	639.9
Net Working Capital	411.0	483.0	462.0	374.0	339.4	307.3	284.0
Year-end Shs. Outstg. (000)	63,547	66,759	68,511	68,786	70,177	70,923	71,263
STATISTICAL RECORD:							
Operating Profit Margin %	10.3	11.4	14.9	14.0	11.0	10.1	16.2
Net Profit Margin %	6.1	9.2	8.8	8.3	5.5	5.7	9.2
Return on Equity %	14.8	19.3	17.7	17.8	12.0	12.9	20.7
Return on Assets %	2.8	4.3	4.1	4.1	2.9	3.3	5.8
Debt/Total Assets %	6.8	7.1	5.3	6.0	6.7	7.7	4.8
Price Range	56¹³/₁₆-26¹/₈	64¹¹/₁₆-44⅜	50⅞-35½	40¼-31⅞	34⅛-27	43⅝-26⅝	48⅝-36½
P/E Ratio	30.4-14.0	23.7-16.3	22.3-15.6	19.9-15.8	26.9-21.3	34.6-21.1	26.1-19.6
Average Yield %	1.9	1.3	1.5	1.7	2.0	1.6	1.1

Statistics are as originally reported. ① Incl. non-recurr. chrg. $66.0 mill. ② Bef. disc. oper. gain $13.3 mill. ③ Bef. acctg. change credit $10.7 mill. ④ Incl. unusual chrg. $38.0 mill.

OFFICERS:
D. A. Hillenbrand, Chmn.
W. A. Hillenbrand, C.E.O.
F. W. Rockwood, Pres.
D. G. Barger Jr., V.P., C.F.O.
INVESTOR CONTACT: Mark R. Lanning, V.P. & Treas., (812) 934-8400
PRINCIPAL OFFICE: 700 State Route 46 East, Batesville, IN 47006-8835

TELEPHONE NUMBER: (812) 934-7000
FAX: (812) 934-7364
WEB: www.hillenbrand.com
NO. OF EMPLOYEES: 10,800 (approx.)
SHAREHOLDERS: 22,900 (approx.)
ANNUAL MEETING: In April
INCORPORATED: IN, Aug., 1969

INSTITUTIONAL HOLDINGS:
No. of Institutions: 154
Shares Held: 19,796,136
% Held: 30.2
INDUSTRY: Burial caskets (SIC: 3995)
TRANSFER AGENT(S): Harris Trust & Savings Bank, Chicago, IL

HOME DEPOT (THE), INC.

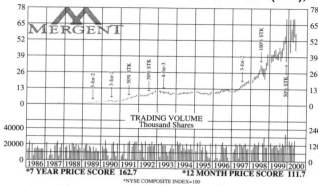

TRADING VOLUME
Thousand Shares

*7 YEAR PRICE SCORE 162.7   ***12 MONTH PRICE SCORE 111.7**

*NYSE COMPOSITE INDEX=100

INTERIM EARNINGS (Per Share):

Qtr.	Apr.	July	Oct.	Jan.
1996-97	0.09	0.13	0.11	0.12
1997-98	0.12	0.16	0.11	0.14
1998-99	0.15	0.21	0.17	0.18
1999-00	0.21	0.29	0.25	0.25

INTERIM DIVIDENDS (Per Share):

Amt.	Decl.	Ex.	Rec.	Pay.
0.04Q	5/26/99	6/08/99	6/10/99	6/24/99
0.04Q	8/19/99	8/31/99	9/02/99	9/16/99
0.06Q	11/18/99	11/30/99	12/02/99	12/16/99
50% STK	11/18/99	12/31/99	12/02/99	12/30/99
0.04Q	2/25/00	3/07/00	3/09/00	3/23/00

Indicated div.: $0.16 (Div. Reinv. Plan)

CAPITALIZATION (1/30/00):

	($000)	(%)
Long-Term Debt	750,000	5.7
Deferred Income Tax	87,000	0.7
Minority Interest	10,000	0.1
Common & Surplus	12,341,000	93.6
Total	13,188,000	100.0

DIVIDEND ACHIEVER STATUS:
Rank: 2   10-Year Growth Rate: 35.58%
Total Years of Dividend Growth: 12

RECENT DEVELOPMENTS: For the fiscal year ended 1/30/00, net earnings jumped 43.7% to $2.32 billion from $1.61 billion a year earlier. Net sales grew 27.2% to $38.43 billion from $30.22 billion the previous year, driven by a 19.8% jump in the number of customer transactions and a 6.3% increase in the average sale per transaction. Comparable-store sales were up 10.0%. Gross profit climbed 32.6% to $11.41 billion from $8.61 billion the year before.

PROSPECTS: Going forward, results should benefit from the Company's focus on improving its product selection, increasing sales to professional customers, and continuing to aggressively expand its store base. HD anticipates selling appliances in most of its stores by the end of the year. In an effort to draw more professional customers, the Company is adding more plumbing and janitorial supplies and hiring workers skilled in those areas.

BUSINESS

THE HOME DEPOT, INC. operates 960 retail warehouse stores in the United States, Canada, Chile, and Puerto Rico that offer a wide assortment of building materials and home improvement products primarily to the "do-it-yourself" and home remodeling markets. The average Home Depot store is approximately 108,000 square feet of interior floor space and is stocked with approximately 40,000 to 50,000 separate items. Most stores have an additional approximately 24,000 square feet of outdoor selling area for landscaping supplies. HD also operates 15 EXPO Design Center stores in California, Florida, Georgia, New York and Texas that sell products and services primarily for design and renovation projects, and two Villager's Hardware test stores in the U.S.

QUARTERLY DATA

(1/30/00)($000)	Rev	Inc
1st Quarter	8,952,000	489,000
2nd Quarter	10,431,000	679,000
3rd Quarter	9,877,000	573,000
4th Quarter	9,174,000	579,000

ANNUAL FINANCIAL DATA

	1/30/00	1/31/99	2/1/98	2/2/97	1/28/96	1/29/95	1/30/94
Earnings Per Share	1.00	0.71	☐ 0.52	0.43	0.34	0.29	0.22
Cash Flow Per Share	1.19	0.86	0.63	0.53	0.42	0.34	0.27
Tang. Book Val. Per Share	5.22	3.83	3.17	2.71	2.71	2.28	1.64	1.38
Dividends Per Share	0.113	0.077	0.063	0.051	0.042	0.033	0.025
Dividend Payout %	11.3	10.8	12.1	11.9	12.4	11.4	10.9
INCOME STATEMENT (IN MILLIONS):							
Total Revenues	38,434.0	30,219.0	24,156.0	19,535.5	15,470.4	12,476.7	9,238.8
Costs & Expenses	34,176.0	27,185.0	21,961.0	17,769.5	14,109.3	11,359.9	8,442.2
Depreciation & Amort.	463.0	373.0	283.0	232.3	181.2	129.6	89.8
Operating Income	3,795.0	2,661.0	1,912.0	1,533.7	1,179.8	987.2	706.7
Net Interest Inc./(Exp.)	9.0	d7.0	2.0	9.5	15.4	d7.4	30.2
Income Before Income Taxes	3,804.0	2,654.0	1,898.0	1,534.8	1,195.3	979.8	736.9
Income Taxes	1,484.0	1,040.0	738.0	597.0	463.8	375.3	279.5
Equity Earnings/Minority Int.	...	d16.0	d8.4	...	...	...	...
Net Income	2,320.0	1,614.0	☐ 1,160.0	937.7	731.5	604.5	457.4
Cash Flow	2,783.0	1,987.0	1,443.0	1,170.1	912.7	734.1	547.2
Average Shs. Outstg. (000)	2,342,000	2,320,000	2,286,000	2,194,884	2,150,897	2,141,762	2,038,667
BALANCE SHEET (IN MILLIONS):							
Cash & Cash Equivalents	170.0	62.0	174.0	558.4	108.0	57.9	431.0
Total Current Assets	6,390.0	4,933.0	4,460.0	3,709.4	2,672.0	2,133.0	1,966.6
Net Property	10,227.0	8,160.0	6,509.0	5,437.0	4,461.0	3,397.2	2,370.9
Total Assets	17,081.0	13,465.0	11,229.0	9,341.7	7,354.0	5,778.0	4,700.9
Total Current Liabilities	3,656.0	2,857.0	2,456.0	1,842.1	1,416.5	1,214.2	972.6
Long-Term Obligations	750.0	1,566.0	1,303.0	1,246.6	720.1	983.4	874.0
Net Stockholders' Equity	12,341.0	8,740.0	7,098.0	5,955.2	4,987.8	3,442.2	2,814.1
Net Working Capital	2,734.0	2,076.0	2,004.0	1,867.2	1,255.5	918.7	994.0
Year-end Shs. Outstg. (000)	2,304,317	2,213,178	2,196,324	2,162,318	2,146,977	2,040,143	2,022,138
STATISTICAL RECORD:							
Operating Profit Margin %	9.9	8.8	7.9	7.9	7.6	7.9	7.6
Net Profit Margin %	6.0	5.3	4.8	4.8	4.7	4.8	5.0
Return on Equity %	18.8	18.5	16.3	15.7	14.7	17.6	16.3
Return on Assets %	13.6	12.0	10.3	10.0	9.9	10.5	9.7
Debt/Total Assets %	4.4	11.6	11.6	13.3	9.8	17.0	18.6
Price Range	69¾-34⁹/₁₆	41⁵/₁₆-18⁷/₁₆	20³/₁₆-10⅝	13¼-9¼	11⅛-8⅛	10¾-8⅛	11⁵/₁₆-7¾
P/E Ratio	69.7-34.6	58.2-26.0	39.0-20.5	30.7-21.4	32.5-23.8	36.6-27.7	51.4-35.2
Average Yield %	0.2	0.3	0.4	0.5	0.4	0.4	0.3

Statistics are as originally reported. Adj. for 3-for-2 stk. split, 12/99; 100% stk. div., 7/98; & 3-for-2 stk. split, 7/97. ☐ Incl. $104 mil pre-tax, non-recur. chg.

OFFICERS:
B. Marcus, Chmn.
A. M. Blank, Pres., C.E.O.
M. Baker, Exec. V.P., C.O.O.
D. J. Carrey, Exec. V.P., C.F.O.

INVESTOR CONTACT: Investor Relations, (770) 384-4388

PRINCIPAL OFFICE: 2455 Paces Ferry Road, Atlanta, GA 30339-4024

TELEPHONE NUMBER: (770) 433-8211
FAX: (770) 431-2707
WEB: www.homedepot.com

NO. OF EMPLOYEES: 201,000 (approx.)

SHAREHOLDERS: 196,126

ANNUAL MEETING: In May

INCORPORATED: DE, June, 1978

INSTITUTIONAL HOLDINGS:
No. of Institutions: 961
Shares Held: 1,344,808,409
% Held: 58.4

INDUSTRY: Lumber and other building materials (SIC: 5211)

TRANSFER AGENT(S): Boston EquiServe, Boston, MA

NYSE SYMBOL HNI
Rec. Pr. 24$\frac{15}{16}$ (5/31/00)

HON INDUSTRIES INCORPORATED

YIELD 1.8%
P/E RATIO 17.3

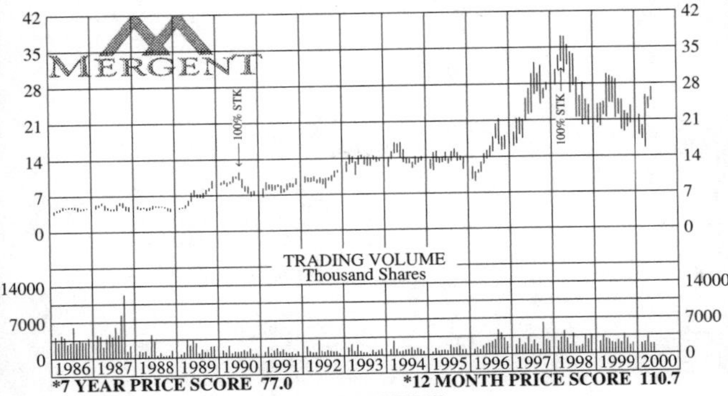

*7 YEAR PRICE SCORE 77.0 *12 MONTH PRICE SCORE 110.7

*NYSE COMPOSITE INDEX=100

INTERIM EARNINGS (Per Share):

Qtr.	Mar.	June	Sept.	Dec.
1996	0.28	0.20	0.30	0.35
1997	0.28	0.32	0.43	0.42
1998	0.36	0.38	0.50	0.48
1999	0.19	0.37	0.47	0.41

INTERIM DIVIDENDS (Per Share):

Amt.	Decl.	Ex.	Rec.	Pay.
0.095Q	5/10/99	5/18/99	5/20/99	6/01/99
0.095Q	8/09/99	8/17/99	8/19/99	9/01/99
0.095Q	11/08/99	11/16/99	11/18/99	12/01/99
0.11Q	2/16/00	2/18/00	2/23/00	3/01/00
0.11Q	5/02/00	5/10/00	5/12/00	6/01/00

Indicated div.: $0.44

CAPITALIZATION (1/1/00):

	($000)	(%)
Long-Term Debt	137,875	20.2
Capital Lease Obligations	4,313	0.6
Deferred Income Tax	38,141	5.6
Common & Surplus	501,271	73.5
Total	681,600	100.0

DIVIDEND ACHIEVER STATUS:
Rank: 110 10-Year Growth Rate: 12.22%
Total Years of Dividend Growth: 11

RECENT DEVELOPMENTS: For the year ended 1/1/00, net income declined 17.8% to $87.4 million compared with $106.3 million in 1999. Results for 1999 included an after-tax charge of $12.5 million to cover closing facilities and reorganization expenses. Earnings were pressured by increased freight costs. Net sales were $1.79 billion, up 5.5% from $1.70 billion a year earlier. The increase in revenues reflected sales growth of nearly 4.0% for offices furniture.

PROSPECTS: On 3/1/99, the Company's Hearth Technologies Inc. subsidiary acquired two hearth products distributors, American Fireplace Company (AFC) and the Allied Group (Allied). AFC and Allied, with combined 1999 sales of nearly $200.0 million, will be joined to form Hearth Services Inc., a subsidiary of Hearth Technologies Inc. Meanwhile, the Company announced that Allsteel Inc. is now an independent operating entity of HNI.

BUSINESS

HON INDUSTRIES INCORPORATED manufactures and markets office furniture and hearth products. Office products include filing cabinets, seating, including task chairs, executive desk chairs and side chairs, desks, tables, bookcases and credenzas. The office products are sold through mass merchandisers, warehouse clubs, a national system of dealers, retail superstores, end-user customers, and federal and state governments. The Hearth Technologies operating company products are comprised of wood-burning, pellet-burning, and gas-burning factory-built fireplaces, fireplace inserts, gas logs, and stoves. The hearth products are sold through wholesalers, a national system of dealers and large regional contractors. The Company has locations in the U.S. and Canada.

REVENUES

(01/01/2000)	($000)	(%)
Office Furniture	1,504,422	84.1
Hearth Products	284,859	15.9
Total	1,789,281	100.0

ANNUAL FINANCIAL DATA

	1/1/00	1/2/99	1/3/98	12/28/96	12/31/95	12/31/94	1/1/94
Earnings Per Share	**[1] 1.44**	**1.72**	**1.45**	**[1] 1.13**	**0.67**	**0.87**	**0.70**
Cash Flow Per Share	**2.51**	**2.58**	**2.05**	**1.44**	**1.02**	**1.18**	**0.95**
Tang. Book Val. Per Share	**6.45**	**5.77**	**4.59**	**3.39**	**3.54**	**3.17**	**2.59**
Dividends Per Share	**0.38**	**0.32**	**0.28**	**0.25**	**0.24**	**0.22**	**0.20**
Dividend Payout %	**26.4**	**18.6**	**19.3**	**22.1**	**35.8**	**25.3**	**28.8**
INCOME STATEMENT (IN MILLIONS):							
Total Revenues	1,789.3	1,696.4	1,362.7	998.1	893.1	846.0	780.3
Costs & Expenses	1,577.4	1,464.3	1,181.9	873.1	805.0	739.8	692.2
Depreciation & Amort.	65.5	53.0	35.6	25.3	21.4	19.0	16.6
Operating Income	146.4	179.2	145.2	106.2	66.7	87.1	71.5
Net Interest Inc./(Exp.)	d8.9	d9.1	d6.0	d0.9	d1.2	d0.8	d0.6
Income Before Income Taxes	137.6	170.1	139.1	105.3	65.5	86.3	70.9
Income Taxes	50.2	63.8	52.2	37.2	24.4	31.9	26.2
Net Income	[1] 87.4	106.3	87.0	[1] 61.7	41.1	54.4	44.6
Cash Flow	152.8	159.3	122.6	86.9	62.5	73.4	61.3
Average Shs. Outstg. (000)	60,855	61,650	59,780	60,228	60,992	62,436	64,182
BALANCE SHEET (IN MILLIONS):							
Cash & Cash Equivalents	22.2	17.7	46.3	32.7	46.9	30.7	44.4
Total Current Assets	316.6	290.3	295.2	205.5	194.2	188.8	188.4
Net Property	455.6	444.2	341.0	234.6	210.0	177.8	157.8
Total Assets	906.7	864.5	754.7	513.5	409.5	372.6	352.4
Total Current Liabilities	225.1	217.4	200.8	152.6	128.9	111.1	110.8
Long-Term Obligations	142.2	153.6	153.1	97.8	53.6	54.7	51.1
Net Stockholders' Equity	501.3	462.0	381.7	252.4	216.2	194.6	179.6
Net Working Capital	91.4	72.9	94.4	53.0	65.3	77.7	77.7
Year-end Shs. Outstg. (000)	60,172	61,290	61,659	59,426	60,788	61,350	69,352
STATISTICAL RECORD:							
Operating Profit Margin %	8.2	10.6	10.7	10.6	7.5	10.3	9.2
Net Profit Margin %	4.9	6.3	6.4	6.2	4.6	6.4	5.7
Return on Equity %	17.4	23.0	22.8	24.4	19.0	27.9	24.9
Return on Assets %	9.6	12.3	11.5	12.0	10.0	14.6	12.7
Debt/Total Assets %	15.7	17.8	20.3	19.0	13.1	14.7	14.5
Price Range	29$\frac{7}{8}$-18$\frac{3}{4}$	37$\frac{3}{16}$-20	32$\frac{1}{8}$-16	21$\frac{3}{8}$-9$\frac{1}{4}$	15$\frac{5}{8}$-11$\frac{1}{2}$	17-12	14$\frac{5}{8}$-10$\frac{3}{4}$
P/E Ratio	20.7-13.0	21.6-11.6	22.2-11.0	18.9-8.2	23.3-17.2	19.5-13.8	21.0-15.5
Average Yield %	1.6	1.1	1.2	1.6	1.8	1.5	1.6

Statistics are as originally reported. Adj. for stk. split: 2-for-1, 3/27/98. [1] Incl. non-recurr. credit $3.2 mill., 1996; net chrg. $12.5 mill., 1999.

OFFICERS:
J. D. Michaels, Chmn., Pres., C.E.O.
D. C. Stuebe, V.P., C.F.O.
J. I. Johnson, V.P., Gen. Couns., Sec.

INVESTOR CONTACT: Elizabeth P. Coronelli, Investor Relations Mgr., (319) 264-7992

PRINCIPAL OFFICE: 414 East Third Street, P.O. Box 1109, Muscatine, IA 52761

TELEPHONE NUMBER: (319) 264-7400
FAX: (319) 264-7217
WEB: www.honi.com

NO. OF EMPLOYEES: 10,100 (approx.)

SHAREHOLDERS: 6,737

ANNUAL MEETING: In May

INCORPORATED: IA, Jan., 1944

INSTITUTIONAL HOLDINGS:
No. of Institutions: 112
Shares Held: 25,108,862
% Held: 41.6

INDUSTRY: Office furniture, except wood (SIC: 2522)

TRANSFER AGENT(S): Harris Trust & Savings Bank, Chicago, IL

HORMEL FOODS CORPORATION

YIELD 2.0%
P/E RATIO 15.3

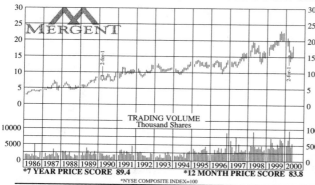

TRADING VOLUME
Thousand Shares

| | 1986 | 1987 | 1988 | 1989 | 1990 | 1991 | 1992 | 1993 | 1994 | 1995 | 1996 | 1997 | 1998 | 1999 | 2000 |

*7 YEAR PRICE SCORE 89.4   ***12 MONTH PRICE SCORE 83.8**
*NYSE COMPOSITE INDEX=100

INTERIM EARNINGS (Per Share):

Qtr.	Jan.	Apr.	July	Oct.
1995-96	0.14	0.16	0.03	0.20
1996-97	0.14	0.17	0.12	0.30
1997-98	0.31	0.17	0.14	0.31
1998-99	0.29	0.22	0.20	0.41
1999-00	0.30	...	...	...

INTERIM DIVIDENDS (Per Share):

Amt.	Decl.	Ex.	Rec.	Pay.
0.165Q	5/25/99	7/21/99	7/24/99	8/15/99
0.165Q	10/04/99	10/20/99	10/23/99	11/15/99
0.175Q	11/23/99	1/19/00	1/22/00	2/15/00
2-for-1	11/24/99	2/16/00	1/25/00	2/15/00
0.087Q	3/27/00	4/18/00	4/22/00	5/15/00

Indicated div.: $0.35 (Div. Reinv. Plan)

CAPITALIZATION (10/30/99):

	($000)	(%)
Long-Term Debt	184,723	18.0
Common & Surplus	841,142	82.0
Total	1,025,865	100.0

DIVIDEND ACHIEVER STATUS:

Rank: 124   10-Year Growth Rate: 11.61%
Total Years of Dividend Growth: 32

RECENT DEVELOPMENTS: For the quarter ended 1/29/00, net earnings rose 3.5% to $43.8 million from $42.4 million a year earlier. The prior-year results include a one-time gain of $3.8 million. Net sales grew 13.1% to $903.9 million from $799.0 million the previous year. Sales benefited from a 5.4% increase in tonnage volume, driven by strong gains in many of HRL's best-known brands, including SPAM luncheon meat, DINTY MOORE stew, and HORMEL chili, chunk chicken and chunk ham.

PROSPECTS: On 1/26/00, HRL announced the formation of a joint venture with Eridania Beghin-Say of Paris, France, to market the Carapelli brand of olive oil in the United States and Puerto Rico. The new joint venture is expected to stimulate sales of olive oil in the U.S. as consumers discover its many healthful benefits. Initial trade acceptance has exceeded expectations. Also, the joint venture is consistent with the Company's ongoing strategy to enhance its ethnic foods business.

BUSINESS

HORMEL FOODS CORPORATION (formerly Geo. A. Hormel & Co.) and its subsidiaries produce and market a variety of processed, packaged food products. The Company's main products include: meat and meat products, hams, sausages, wieners, sliced bacon, luncheon meats, stews, chilies, hash and meat spreads. The products are sold fresh, frozen, cured, smoked, cooked or canned. The majority of products are sold under the HORMEL name. Other tradenames include: SPAM, LIGHT & LEAN, FARM FRESH, DINTY MOORE, BLACK LABEL, TOP SHELF, MARY KITCHEN, KIDS KITCHEN and OLD SMOKEHOUSE. Through its wholly-owned subsidiary, Jennie-O Foods, Inc., the Company is a producer and marketer of whole and processed turkey products.

QUARTERLY DATA

(10/30/1999)($000)	Rev	Inc
1st Quarter	799,005	42,380
2nd Quarter	791,095	31,831
3rd Quarter	816,818	29,550
4th Quarter	950,839	59,674

ANNUAL FINANCIAL DATA

	10/30/99	10/31/98	10/25/97	10/26/96	10/28/95	10/29/94	10/30/93
Earnings Per Share	② 1.11	② 0.93	0.72	② 0.52	0.79	0.77	① 0.66
Cash Flow Per Share	1.55	1.33	1.06	0.80	1.03	1.00	0.87
Tang. Book Val. Per Share	5.20	4.82	4.55	4.27	4.24	3.79	3.25
Dividends Per Share	0.33	0.32	0.31	0.30	0.29	0.25	0.22
Dividend Payout %	29.7	34.6	43.4	57.7	36.9	32.5	33.6
INCOME STATEMENT (IN MILLIONS):							
Total Revenues	3,357.8	3,261.0	3,256.6	3,098.7	3,046.2	3,064.8	2,854.0
Costs & Expenses	3,052.2	2,988.9	3,030.3	2,943.0	2,825.5	2,841.1	2,666.5
Depreciation & Amort.	64.7	60.3	52.9	42.7	37.2	36.6	32.2
Operating Income	240.9	211.9	173.3	113.0	183.4	187.1	155.3
Net Interest Inc./(Exp.)	10.6	d9.4	d11.6	d1.6	d1.5	d2.5	d1.4
Income Before Income Taxes	251.5	217.3	170.9	125.5	194.7	191.1	161.1
Income Taxes	88.0	78.0	61.4	46.1	74.2	73.1	60.4
Net Income	② 163.4	② 139.3	109.5	② 79.4	120.4	118.0	① 100.8
Cash Flow	228.1	199.6	162.4	122.1	157.7	154.6	132.9
Average Shs. Outstg. (000)	147,010	150,406	152,990	153,018	153,378	...	...
BALANCE SHEET (IN MILLIONS):							
Cash & Cash Equivalents	248.6	238.0	152.4	203.1	198.0	260.0	172.4
Total Current Assets	800.1	717.4	671.4	723.3	659.3	708.2	619.9
Net Property	505.6	486.9	488.7	421.5	333.1	270.9	245.0
Total Assets	1,685.6	1,555.9	1,528.5	1,436.1	1,223.9	1,196.7	1,093.6
Total Current Liabilities	385.4	267.7	260.6	266.4	217.8	264.9	227.1
Long-Term Obligations	184.7	204.9	198.2	127.0	17.0	10.3	5.7
Net Stockholders' Equity	841.1	813.3	802.2	785.6	732.0	661.1	570.9
Net Working Capital	414.7	449.7	410.8	456.9	441.5	443.3	392.8
Year-end Shs. Outstg. (000)	142,725	146,992	151,552	155,020	153,404	153,704	153,344
STATISTICAL RECORD:							
Operating Profit Margin %	7.2	6.5	5.3	3.6	6.0	6.1	5.4
Net Profit Margin %	4.9	4.3	3.4	2.6	4.0	3.8	3.5
Return on Equity %	19.4	17.1	13.6	10.1	16.5	17.8	17.7
Return on Assets %	9.7	9.0	7.2	5.5	9.8	9.9	9.2
Debt/Total Assets %	11.0	13.2	13.0	8.8	1.4	0.9	0.5
Price Range	23⅛-15½	19¹¹⁄₁₆-12⅞	16⅜-11¾	14-9¹¹⁄₁₆	14-11⁷⁄₁₆	13⅜-9⅜	12¾-10⅛
P/E Ratio	20.8-14.0	21.3-13.9	22.9-16.4	26.9-18.6	17.8-14.6	17.4-12.2	19.5-15.5
Average Yield %	1.7	2.0	2.2	2.5	2.3	2.2	1.9

Statistics are as originally reported. Adj. for 2-for-1 stk. split, 2/15/00. ① ($0.83/sh) mil chg. for acctg. adj. ② Incl. $3.8 mil ($0.03/sh) gain, 1999; $17.4 mil ($0.12/sh) after-tax gain, 1998; $5.4 mil ($0.04/sh) non-recur. chg., 1996. ① Bef. $127.5

OFFICERS:
J. W. Johnson, Chmn., Pres., C.E.O.
M. J. McCoy, Sr. V.P., C.F.O.
G. J. Ray, Exec. V.P.
J. N. Sheehan, V.P., Contr.

INVESTOR CONTACT: Michael J. McCoy, Sr. V.P. & C.F.O., (507) 437-5663

PRINCIPAL OFFICE: 1 Hormel Place, Austin, MN 55912-3680

TELEPHONE NUMBER: (507) 437-5611
FAX: (507) 437-5489
WEB: www.hormel.com

NO. OF EMPLOYEES: 12,100

SHAREHOLDERS: 11,500 (approx.)

ANNUAL MEETING: In Jan.

INCORPORATED: DE, Sept., 1928

INDUSTRY: Meat packing plants (SIC: 2011)

TRANSFER AGENT(S): Norwest Bank Minesota, N.A., South St. Paul, MN

NYSE SYMBOL HTN
Rec. Pr. 40 (5/31/00)

HOUGHTON MIFFLIN COMPANY

YIELD 1.3%
P/E RATIO 26.3

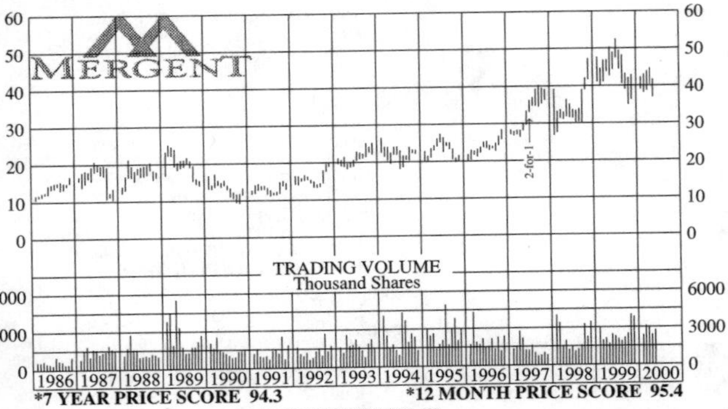

*7 YEAR PRICE SCORE 94.3 *12 MONTH PRICE SCORE 95.4

*NYSE COMPOSITE INDEX=100

INTERIM EARNINGS (Per Share):

Qtr.	Mar.	June	Sept.	Dec.
1996	d0.80	0.34	2.72	d0.71
1997	d0.94	0.39	2.91	d0.59
1998	d1.26	0.24	4.43	d0.71
1999	d1.29	0.29	3.07	d0.55

INTERIM DIVIDENDS (Per Share):

Amt.	Decl.	Ex.	Rec.	Pay.
0.125Q	4/28/99	5/10/99	5/12/99	5/26/99
0.13Q	7/28/99	8/09/99	8/11/99	8/25/99
0.13Q	10/27/99	11/08/99	11/10/99	11/24/99
0.13Q	1/26/00	2/07/00	2/09/00	2/23/00
0.13Q	4/26/00	5/08/00	5/10/00	5/24/00

Indicated div.: $0.52 (Div. Reinv. Plan)

CAPITALIZATION (12/31/99):

	($000)	(%)
Long-Term Debt	254,638	35.6
Deferred Income Tax	28,301	4.0
Common & Surplus	433,021	60.5
Total	715,960	100.0

DIVIDEND ACHIEVER STATUS:
Rank: 275 10-Year Growth Rate: 4.29%
Total Years of Dividend Growth: 17

RECENT DEVELOPMENTS: For the year ended 12/31/99, HTN reported income of $46.0 million, before an extraordinary net gain of $30.3 million, versus income of $45.6 million, before an extraordinary net gain of $18.0 million, in 1998. The 1999 results included a net loss of $3.0 million for the redemption of INSO Corp. common stock. Results for 1998 included a non-recurring net gain of $4.9 million. Net sales rose 6.8% to $920.1 million.

PROSPECTS: In 2000, HTN anticipates to achieve its goals of $1.00 billion in revenue, an operating margin of 17.0% and repayment of $200.0 million of debt before major acquisitions. HTN expects to achieve these goals by developing products and services that meet customer needs, selling those products effectively and increasing operational efficiency. HTN should continue to benefit from the acquisitions of Discovery Works and Sunburst Communications

BUSINESS

HOUGHTON MIFFLIN COMPANY is a publisher of textbooks, instructional technology for the elementary, secondary, and college markets, as well as supplementary materials. The Company operates in the K-12 publishing segment through Houghton's School Division and its three principal subsidiaries: McDougal Littell Inc., Great Source Education Group, Inc. and The Riverside Publishing Company. The Company also publishes reference works, fiction, and non-fiction for adults and young readers through its Trade & Reference Division, and educational software and video through Sunburst Technology. On 12/23/98, HTN acquired Discovery Works. In May 1999, HTN acquired Sunburst Communications.

BUSINESS LINE ANALYSIS

(12/31/1999)	REV(%)	INC(%)
K-12 Publishing	71.4	86.7
College Publishing	18.7	21.2
Other	9.9	(7.9)
Total	100.0	100.0

ANNUAL FINANCIAL DATA

	12/31/99	12/31/98	12/31/97	12/31/96	12/31/95	12/31/94	12/31/93
Earnings Per Share	[6] 1.57	[5] 1.57	[4] 1.73	[4] 1.57	[2] d0.26	[3] 1.90	[1][3] 1.14
Cash Flow Per Share	4.82	5.03	4.84	4.59	1.64	3.50	2.56
Tang. Book Val. Per Share	...	...	...	...	...	4.16	7.04
Dividends Per Share	0.51	0.50	0.49	0.48	0.47	0.43	0.41
Dividend Payout %	32.5	31.8	28.3	30.7	...	23.0	36.6
INCOME STATEMENT (IN MILLIONS):							
Total Revenues	920.1	861.7	797.3	717.9	529.0	483.1	463.0
Costs & Expenses	712.8	658.8	601.0	546.1	489.7	385.2	372.2
Depreciation & Amort.	95.3	100.9	89.7	84.3	52.4	44.4	39.4
Operating Income	112.0	102.0	106.6	87.4	d13.1	53.5	51.4
Net Interest Inc./(Exp.)	d29.8	d37.0	d38.9	d40.9	d13.0	d6.5	d2.3
Income Before Income Taxes	77.1	79.3	83.5	74.0	d11.4	85.1	49.0
Income Taxes	31.1	33.6	33.7	30.3	cr4.2	32.7	17.7
Equity Earnings/Minority Int.	...	...	1.0	d6.8	1.6	2.0	...
Net Income	[6] 46.0	[5] 45.6	[4] 49.8	[4] 43.6	[2] d7.2	[3] 52.4	[1][3] 31.4
Cash Flow	141.3	146.5	139.6	128.0	45.2	96.8	70.7
Average Shs. Outstg. (000)	29,308	29,111	28,826	27,866	27,624	27,644	27,646
BALANCE SHEET (IN MILLIONS):							
Cash & Cash Equivalents	12.7	53.2	6.2	12.1	17.3	47.2	85.3
Total Current Assets	365.1	349.8	324.7	338.0	371.2	250.1	267.8
Net Property	172.2	130.3	120.4	116.4	123.1	68.9	66.2
Total Assets	1,038.7	975.6	981.1	1,006.4	1,046.4	497.3	398.2
Total Current Liabilities	259.2	244.3	238.7	185.9	342.4	104.7	111.3
Long-Term Obligations	254.6	274.5	371.1	501.0	426.1	99.4	26.4
Net Stockholders' Equity	433.0	398.3	317.8	270.3	233.3	244.5	224.1
Net Working Capital	105.9	105.5	86.0	152.0	28.8	145.4	156.6
Year-end Shs. Outstg. (000)	29,504	30,176	29,937	29,332	28,970	28,860	29,052
STATISTICAL RECORD:							
Operating Profit Margin %	12.2	11.8	13.4	12.2	...	11.1	11.1
Net Profit Margin %	5.0	5.3	6.2	6.1	...	10.9	6.8
Return on Equity %	10.6	11.5	15.7	16.1	...	21.4	14.0
Return on Assets %	4.4	4.7	5.1	4.3	...	10.5	7.9
Debt/Total Assets %	24.5	28.1	37.8	49.8	40.7	20.0	6.6
Price Range	52½-34⅞	47¼-26¾	40¼-26$\frac{5}{16}$	28$\frac{7}{16}$-20$\frac{3}{16}$	27⅜-19$\frac{13}{16}$	26½-18$\frac{1}{16}$	25$\frac{3}{16}$-18$\frac{3}{16}$
P/E Ratio	33.4-22.2	30.1-17.0	23.3-15.2	18.2-12.9	...	14.0-9.5	22.2-16.0
Average Yield %	1.2	1.4	1.5	2.0	2.0	2.0	1.9

Statistics are as originally reported. Adj. for 100% stk. div., 7/97. [1] Incl. non-recurr. gain $22.8 mill., 1994. [2] Incl. net chrgs. $26.4 mill. [3] Bef. extraord. chrg. $1.2 mill., 1994; $1.0 mill., 1993. [4] Incl. aft.-tax gain of $19.9 mill. in 1996; $8.6 mill. gain & $1.5 mill. chrg. in 1997. [5] Bef. extraord. gain $18.0 mill. & incl. net pre-tax non-recurr. gain of $12.3 mill. [6] Bef. extraord. gain $30.3 mill. & incl. a non-recurr. loss of $3.0 mill.

OFFICERS:
N. F. Darehshori, Chmn., Pres., C.E.O.
G. Deegan, Exec. V.P., C.F.O.
P. D. Weaver, Sr. V.P., Sec., Gen. Counsel

INVESTOR CONTACT: Susan E. Hardy, V.P.-Inv. Rel., (617) 351-5114

PRINCIPAL OFFICE: 222 Berkeley Street, Boston, MA 02116-3764

TELEPHONE NUMBER: (617) 351-5000
FAX: (617) 351-1100
WEB: www.hmco.com

NO. OF EMPLOYEES: 3,300 (approx.)

SHAREHOLDERS: 5,940 (approx.)

ANNUAL MEETING: In Apr.

INCORPORATED: MS, 1908

INSTITUTIONAL HOLDINGS:
No. of Institutions: 148
Shares Held: 23,326,586
% Held: 75.0

INDUSTRY: Book publishing (SIC: 2731)

TRANSFER AGENT(S): BankBoston, N.A. c/o EquiServe, Boston, MA

HOUSEHOLD INTERNATIONAL INC.

YIELD 1.6%
P/E RATIO 15.3

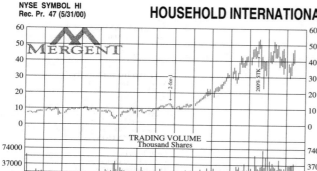

TRADING VOLUME
Thousand Shares

| 1986 | 1987 | 1988 | 1989 | 1990 | 1991 | 1992 | 1993 | 1994 | 1995 | 1996 | 1997 | 1998 | 1999 | 2000 |

*7 YEAR PRICE SCORE 94.2   ***12 MONTH PRICE SCORE 105.1**
*NYSE COMPOSITE INDEX=100

INTERIM EARNINGS (Per Share):

Qtr.	Mar.	June	Sept.	Dec.
1996	0.36	0.41	0.46	0.54
1997	0.43	0.49	0.57	0.66
1998	0.51	d1.03	0.63	0.71
1999	0.65	0.67	0.83	0.92

INTERIM DIVIDENDS (Per Share):

Amt.	Decl.	Ex.	Rec.	Pay.
0.17Q	5/13/99	6/28/99	6/30/99	7/15/99
0.17Q	9/15/99	9/28/99	9/30/99	10/15/99
0.17Q	11/09/99	12/29/99	12/31/99	1/15/00
0.17Q	3/14/00	3/29/00	3/31/00	4/15/00
0.19Q	5/10/00	6/28/00	6/30/00	7/15/00

Indicated div.: $0.76 (Div. Reinv. Plan)

CAPITALIZATION (12/31/99):

	($000)	(%)
Long-Term Debt	34,887,300	83.3
Preferred Stock	539,400	1.3
Common & Surplus	6,450,900	15.4
Total	41,877,600	100.0

DIVIDEND ACHIEVER STATUS:
Rank: 236   10-Year Growth Rate: 6.35%
Total Years of Dividend Growth: 47

RECENT DEVELOPMENTS: For the year ended 12/31/99, net income more than doubled to $1.49 billion compared with $524.1 million in the previous year. Results for 1998 included merger and integration related costs of $1.00 billion and a gain on sale of Beneficial Canada of $189.4 million. Net interest margin improved 8.7% to $5.54 billion compared with $5.09 billion in the prior year. Total other revenues declined 3.3% to $1.99 billion.

PROSPECTS: In February 2000, the Company acquired Renaissance Holdings, Inc., a privately held issuer of secured and unsecured credit cards, for approximately $300.0 million. Meanwhile, the Company signed a definitive agreement to purchase for cash a $2.15 billion real easte loan portfolio from Banc One Financial Services. The transaction also includes 97 Banc One Financial Services offices and most employees in 29 states.

BUSINESS

HOUSEHOLD INTERNATIONAL INC. is a major provider of consumer finance, credit card, auto finance and credit insurance products in the United States, United Kingdom and Canada. Its subsidiaries include: Household Finance Corp., a consumer finance company in the United States; Household Credit Services, an issuer of VISA and MasterCards; Household Retail Services, a private-label credit card issuer; HFC Bank Plc, a provider of secured and unsecured consumer loans, and Household Life Insurance, which offers credit life, accident, disability and unemployment insurance to its consumer finance and credit card customers. In June 1997, HI acquired the consumer finance subsidiary of Transamerica Corp. In June 1998, HI acquired Beneficial Corporation.

ANNUAL FINANCIAL DATA

	12/31/99	12/31/98	12/31/97	12/31/96	12/31/95	12/31/94	12/31/93
Earnings Per Share	① 3.07	1.03	2.17	1.77	1.44	1.17	0.97
Cash Flow Per Share	3.67	1.65	2.99	2.58	2.32	2.00	1.81
Tang. Book Val. Per Share	10.39	9.36	8.59	6.77	7.25	5.35	5.66
Dividends Per Share	0.66	0.59	0.53	0.47	0.43	0.41	0.39
Dividend Payout %	21.5	57.3	24.5	26.6	29.8	34.5	40.2
INCOME STATEMENT (IN MILLIONS)							
Total Revenues	9,499.1	8,897.0	5,503.1	5,058.8	5,144.4	4,603.3	4,454.5
Costs & Expenses	6,986.3	7,636.2	4,217.2	3,996.0	4,127.0	3,831.7	3,760.7
Depreciation & Amort.	292.1	308.1	256.7	240.5	263.7	243.3	243.1
Operating Income	2,220.7	952.7	1,029.2	822.3	753.7	528.3	450.7
Income Before Income Taxes	2,220.7	952.7	1,029.2	822.3	753.7	528.3	450.7
Income Taxes	734.3	428.6	342.6	283.7	300.5	160.7	152.0
Net Income	① 1,486.4	524.1	686.6	538.6	453.2	367.6	298.7
Cash Flow	1,769.3	817.2	931.5	762.4	690.5	583.3	513.6
Average Shs. Outstg. (000)	481,800	496,400	311,400	295,500	297,900	291,600	284,400
BALANCE SHEET (IN MILLIONS)							
Cash & Cash Equivalents	270.6	457.4	280.4	239.2	270.4	541.2	317.4
Total Current Assets	52,429.0	44,405.5	24,143.1	24,484.0	22,114.5	21,319.5	19,880.4
Net Property	476.4	472.1	309.4	353.1	391.7	512.0	434.3
Total Assets	60,749.4	52,892.7	30,302.6	29,594.5	29,218.8	34,338.4	32,961.5
Total Current Liabilities	15,757.8	12,022.9	7,869.9	8,793.2	11,368.2	12,811.1	13,158.2
Long-Term Obligations	34,887.3	30,438.6	14,849.0	14,802.0	11,227.9	10,274.1	9,113.8
Net Stockholders' Equity	6,990.3	6,760.8	4,841.2	3,321.2	2,970.9	2,523.0	2,417.6
Net Working Capital	36,671.2	32,382.6	16,273.2	15,690.8	10,746.3	8,508.4	6,722.2
Year-end Shs. Outstg. (000)	467,911	483,100	321,474	291,195	291,486	289,809	283,344
STATISTICAL RECORD:							
Operating Profit Margin %	23.4	10.7	18.7	16.3	14.7	11.5	10.1
Net Profit Margin %	15.6	5.9	12.5	10.6	8.8	8.0	6.7
Return on Equity %	21.3	7.8	14.2	16.2	15.3	14.6	12.4
Return on Assets %	2.4	1.0	2.3	1.8	1.6	1.1	0.9
Debt/Total Assets %	57.4	57.5	49.0	50.0	38.4	29.9	27.6
Price Range	52⁵/₁₆-32³/₁₆	53¹¹/₁₆-23	43⁵/₁₆-26³/₁₆	32¹¹/₁₆-17⁹/₁₆	22¹³/₁₆-11¹⁵/₁₆	13¹/₄-9¹/₂	13¹/₂-8
P/E Ratio	17.0-10.5	52.1-22.3	20.0-12.1	18.5-9.8	15.9-8.3	11.3-8.1	13.9-9.3
Average Yield %	1.6	1.5	1.5	1.9	2.5	3.6	3.5

Statistics are as originally reported. Adj. for stk. splits: 3-for-1, 6/98 ① Incl. chrg. of $1.00 bill. for merger costs & gain of $189.4 mill. for sale of Beneficial Canada.

OFFICERS:
W. F. Aldinger, Chmn., C.E.O.
L. N. Bangs, Vice-Chmn.
D. A. Schoenholz, Exec. V.P., C.F.O.
E. D. Ancona, Treas.

INVESTOR CONTACT: Craig A. Streen, V.P., Inv. Rel., (847) 564-7369

PRINCIPAL OFFICE: 2700 Sanders Road, Prospect Heights, IL 60070-2799

TELEPHONE NUMBER: (847) 564-5000
FAX: (847) 205-7401
WEB: www.household.com

NO. OF EMPLOYEES: 23,600 (approx.)

SHAREHOLDERS: 19,991 com.; 2,501 pfd.

ANNUAL MEETING: In May

INCORPORATED: DE, Feb., 1981

INSTITUTIONAL HOLDINGS:
No. of Institutions: 420
Shares Held: 380,655,968
% Held: 81.0

INDUSTRY: Personal credit institutions (SIC: 6141)

TRANSFER AGENT(S): Harris Trust & Savings Bank, Chicago, IL

NYSE SYMBOL HSB
Rec. Pr. 29 1/16 (5/31/00)

HSB GROUP, INC.

YIELD 6.1%
P/E RATIO 11.8

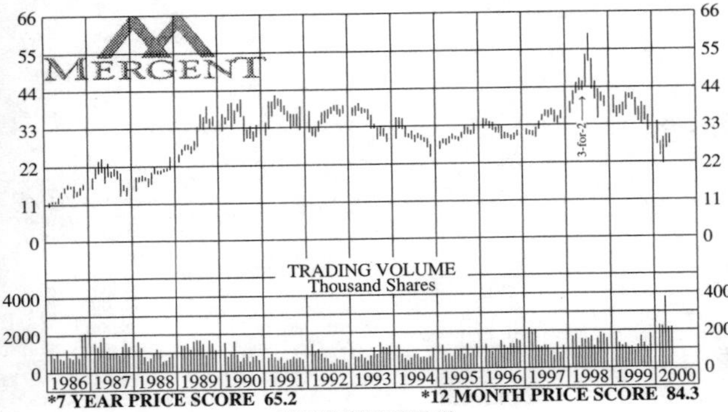

***7 YEAR PRICE SCORE 65.2** ***12 MONTH PRICE SCORE 84.3**

*NYSE COMPOSITE INDEX=100

INTERIM EARNINGS (Per Share):

Qtr.	Mar.	June	Sept.	Dec.
1996	0.56	0.44	0.39	0.38
1997	0.52	0.53	0.51	0.64
1998	1.31	0.68	0.72	0.63
1999	0.71	0.76	0.64	0.35

INTERIM DIVIDENDS (Per Share):

Amt.	Decl.	Ex.	Rec.	Pay.
0.42Q	4/20/99	7/07/99	7/09/99	7/29/99
0.44Q	7/26/99	10/06/99	10/11/99	10/28/99
0.44Q	11/29/99	1/06/00	1/10/00	1/27/00
0.44Q	1/24/00	4/06/00	4/10/00	4/27/00
0.44Q	4/18/00	7/06/00	7/10/00	7/27/00

Indicated div.: $1.76 (Div. Reinv. Plan)

CAPITALIZATION (12/31/99):

	($000)	(%)
Long-Term Debt	25,100	3.0
Capital Lease Obligations	27,800	3.3
Deferred Income Tax	2,800	0.3
Redeemable Pfd. Stock	409,000	48.6
Common & Surplus	376,500	44.8
Total	841,200	100.0

DIVIDEND ACHIEVER STATUS:
Rank: 260 10-Year Growth Rate: 5.45%
Total Years of Dividend Growth: 34

RECENT DEVELOPMENTS: For the year ended 12/31/99, net income was $72.8 million versus income from continuing operations of $104.1 million in 1998. Results included realized investment gains of $40.6 million and $25.4 million in 1999 and 1998, respectively. Results for 1998 included a gain on the sale of Industrial Risk Insurers of $36.6 million. Total revenues rose 4.7% to $606.2 million.

PROSPECTS: The Company entered into an agreement to provide engineering services, project management and other technical assistance to Enron Energy Services. Going forward, long-term results should be favorably affected by the rapid growth of the engineering services business, though near-term results have suffered from the consolidation of certain domestic engineering operations.

BUSINESS

HSB GROUP, INC. (formerly Hartford Steam Boiler Inspection and Insurance Company) is the holding company for The Hartford Steam Boiler Inspection and Insurance Company. The Company is a global provider of loss prevention and engineering services, equipment breakdown insurance and other specialty insurance services. The core business is boiler and machinery and all-risk property insurance for commercial and industrial facilities. Other areas include environmental services, property insurance and products and services for the international market. Subsidiaries include The Boiler Inspection and Insurance Co. of Canada, and Engineering Insurance Group. In 1999, revenues were derived as follows: insurance premiums, 63%; engineering services, 20%; and other, 17%.

ANNUAL FINANCIAL DATA

	12/31/99	12/31/98	12/31/97	12/31/96	12/31/95	12/31/94	12/31/93
Earnings Per Share	**2.50**	**③ 3.35**	**2.19**	**1.77**	**2.05**	**① 1.69**	**①② 0.42**
Tang. Book Val. Per Share	**12.94**	**14.51**	**11.74**	**11.52**	**11.20**	**9.79**	**10.56**
Dividends Per Share	**1.70**	**1.62**	**1.54**	**1.52**	**1.48**	**1.43**	**1.41**
Dividend Payout %	**68.0**	**48.4**	**70.3**	**85.9**	**72.2**	**84.6**	**335.7**
INCOME STATEMENT (IN MILLIONS):							
Total Premium Income	381.9	396.1	491.2	448.6	389.1	336.6	349.2
Other Income	224.3	183.1	112.2	100.2	283.1	267.0	286.9
Total Revenues	606.2	579.2	603.4	548.8	672.2	603.6	636.1
Policyholder Benefits	165.8	174.9	217.9	204.4	154.9	143.2	199.1
Income Before Income Taxes	126.7	173.9	93.7	71.3	86.3	73.6	16.9
Income Taxes	35.7	51.4	25.1	17.9	23.7	21.7	3.8
Equity Earnings/Minority Int.	d18.2	d18.4	d2.3	d1.2	...	1.4	d2.1
Net Income	72.8	③ 104.1	66.3	53.4	62.6	① 51.9	①② 13.1
Average Shs. Outstg. (000)	34,600	35,200	30,150	30,300	30,600	30,750	31,050
BALANCE SHEET (IN MILLIONS):							
Cash & Cash Equivalents	998.1	1,094.8	996.7	600.9	553.8	489.7	506.0
Premiums Due	993.8	803.2	274.7	281.0	215.5	200.1	192.0
Invst. Assets: Total	925.1	1,076.5	1,034.8	676.1	544.5	477.6	498.7
Total Assets	2,263.2	2,144.0	1,533.2	1,116.3	971.5	905.7	877.9
Long-Term Obligations	52.9	53.0	53.0	53.0	53.4	28.4	28.4
Net Stockholders' Equity	376.5	419.3	345.3	365.6	341.1	299.5	324.7
Year-end Shs. Outstg. (000)	29,100	28,900	29,400	30,000	30,450	30,600	30,750
STATISTICAL RECORD:							
Return on Revenues %	12.0	18.0	11.0	9.7	9.3	8.6	2.1
Return on Equity %	19.3	24.8	19.2	14.6	18.4	17.3	4.0
Return on Assets %	3.2	4.9	4.3	4.8	6.4	5.7	1.5
Price Range	42¼-30⅞	59 9/16-34¾	37 13/16-29 5/16	35-28½	33 9/16-26 3/16	35 9/16-23 15/16	39 15/16-28 7/16
P/E Ratio	16.9-12.3	17.8-10.4	17.2-13.4	19.8-16.1	16.4-12.8	21.0-14.1	95.0-67.6
Average Yield %	4.6	3.4	4.6	4.8	5.0	4.8	4.1

Statistics are as originally reported. Adj. for stk. split: 3-for-2, 5/98 ① Bef. non-recurr. chrg. 1994, $2.9 mill., 1993, $20.0 mill. ② Bef. acctg. change chrg. $3.6 mill. ③ Bef. disc. oper. gain $30.3 mill., but incl. $36.6 mill. gain on sale of Industrial Risk Insurers.

OFFICERS:
R. H. Booth, Chmn., Pres., C.E.O.
S. L. Basch, Sr. V.P., C.F.O., Treas.
R. K. Price, Sr. V.P., Corp. Sec.

INVESTOR CONTACT: James C. Rowan, Jr., Chief Invest. Off., (860) 722-5180

PRINCIPAL OFFICE: One State Street, P.O. Box 5024, Hartford, CT 06102-5024

TELEPHONE NUMBER: (860) 722-1866
FAX: (860) 722-5106
WEB: www.hsb.com

NO. OF EMPLOYEES: 2,471 (avg.)

SHAREHOLDERS: 4,826

ANNUAL MEETING: In Apr.

INCORPORATED: CT, 1866

INSTITUTIONAL HOLDINGS:
No. of Institutions: 138
Shares Held: 13,174,011
% Held: 45.2

INDUSTRY: Fire, marine, and casualty insurance (SIC: 6331)

TRANSFER AGENT(S): EquiServe, L.P., Boston, MA

NYSE SYMBOL HUBB
Rec. Pr. 26⅜ (5/31/00)

HUBBELL, INC.

YIELD 4.9%
P/E RATIO 11.9

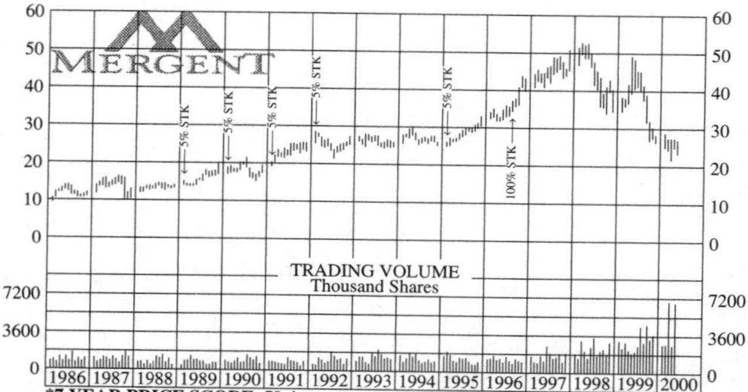

MERGENT
60
50
40
30
20
10
0
5% STK
5% STK
5% STK
5% STK
5% STK
100% STK
TRADING VOLUME
Thousand Shares
7200
3600
0
1986
1987
1988
1989
1990
1991
1992
1993
1994
1995
1996
1997
1998
1999
2000

***7 YEAR PRICE SCORE 59.4** ***12 MONTH PRICE SCORE 81.7**

*NYSE COMPOSITE INDEX=100

INTERIM EARNINGS (Per Share):

Qtr.	Mar.	June	Sept.	Dec.
1996	0.24	0.27	0.55	0.55
1997	0.53	0.60	0.60	0.16
1998	0.58	0.67	0.64	0.63
1999	0.60	0.65	0.54	0.42

INTERIM DIVIDENDS (Per Share):

Amt.	Decl.	Ex.	Rec.	Pay.
0.31Q	3/08/99	3/18/99	3/22/99	4/12/99
0.32Q	6/10/99	6/17/99	6/21/99	7/12/99
0.32Q	9/09/99	9/16/99	9/20/99	10/11/99
0.32Q	12/08/99	12/16/99	12/20/99	1/11/00
0.32Q	3/06/00	3/16/00	3/20/00	4/11/00

Indicated div.: $1.28 (Div. Reinv. Plan)

CAPITALIZATION (12/31/99):

	($000)	(%)
Long-Term Debt	99,600	10.3
Deferred Income Tax	9,900	1.0
Common & Surplus	855,800	88.7
Total	965,300	100.0

DIVIDEND ACHIEVER STATUS:
Rank: 166 10-Year Growth Rate: 9.58%
Total Years of Dividend Growth: 39

RECENT DEVELOPMENTS: For the year ended 12/31/99, net income fell 13.9% to $145.8 million versus $169.4 million in 1998. Results for 1999 included a gain of $8.8 million from the sale of The Kerite Company subsidiary in September 1999. Net sales were $1.45 billion, up 1.9% from $1.42 billion a year earlier. Results were negatively affected by poor performances in the power and telecommunications divisions. Operating income slipped 17.9% to $185.6 million from $226.1 million the year before.

PROSPECTS: HUBB expects the factors that hampered earnings in 1999 will be resolved by mid-2000. These issues included additional costs related to streamlining operations, lower sales and unexpected delays. Results for 2000 should benefit from the inclusion of acquisitions completed in 1999. Separately, HUBB sold its WavePacer Digital Subscriber Line assets to ECI Telecom Ltd. of Petah Tikva, Israel for approximately $61.0 million.

BUSINESS

HUBBELL, INC. specializes in the engineering, manufacture, and sale of electrical and electronic products for the commercial, industrial, utility, and telecommunications markets. These products may be classified into four segments: Electrical, Power, Telecommunications and Other. The Company operates manufacturing facilities in North America, Switzerland, Puerto Rico, Mexico, and the United Kingdom and maintains sales offices in Mexico, Hong Kong, the People's Republic of China, southeast Asia, South Korea, and the Middle East. Hubbell participates in joint ventures with partners in South America, Germany and Taiwan.

BUSINESS LINE ANALYSIS

(12/31/99)	REV (000)	REV(%)
Electrical	863,000	59.4
Power	399,500	27.5
Telecommunications	102,400	7.1
Other	86,900	6.0
Total	1451,800	100.0

ANNUAL FINANCIAL DATA

	12/31/99	12/31/98	12/31/97	12/31/96	12/31/95	12/31/94	12/31/93
Earnings Per Share	**② 2.21**	**2.50**	**① 1.89**	**2.10**	**1.83**	**1.60**	**1.00**
Cash Flow Per Share	**3.01**	**3.21**	**2.52**	**2.74**	**2.37**	**2.11**	**1.45**
Tang. Book Val. Per Share	**9.56**	**9.27**	**9.54**	**8.79**	**8.04**	**7.09**	**7.48**
Dividends Per Share	**1.26**	**1.20**	**1.10**	**0.99**	**0.89**	**0.80**	**0.77**
Dividend Payout %	**57.0**	**48.0**	**58.2**	**47.1**	**48.8**	**50.0**	**77.1**
INCOME STATEMENT (IN MILLIONS):							
Total Revenues	1,451.8	1,424.6	1,378.8	1,297.4	1,143.1	1,013.7	832.4
Costs & Expenses	1,204.6	1,150.4	1,164.0	1,060.6	941.9	839.1	732.1
Depreciation & Amort.	52.8	48.1	43.2	39.3	36.2	34.0	30.1
Operating Income	194.4	226.1	171.6	197.5	165.0	140.6	70.2
Net Interest Inc./(Exp.)	d15.9	d9.9	d7.3	d8.4	d8.5	d6.1	d3.4
Income Before Income Taxes	197.0	230.5	180.2	199.3	167.0	145.9	81.5
Income Taxes	51.2	61.1	49.9	57.8	45.1	39.4	15.2
Net Income	② 145.8	169.4	① 130.3	141.5	121.9	106.5	66.3
Cash Flow	198.6	217.5	173.5	180.8	158.2	140.5	96.4
Average Shs. Outstg. (000)	65,900	67,700	68,843	65,938	66,744	66,582	66,402
BALANCE SHEET (IN MILLIONS):							
Cash & Cash Equivalents	24.0	30.1	75.2	134.4	87.0	38.9	44.2
Total Current Assets	552.8	564.8	596.2	591.2	500.1	444.9	362.1
Net Property	308.9	310.1	251.9	217.9	204.2	202.0	154.6
Total Assets	1,399.2	1,390.4	1,284.8	1,185.4	1,057.2	1,041.6	874.3
Total Current Liabilities	343.4	345.0	256.3	255.4	194.9	332.1	230.2
Long-Term Obligations	99.6	99.6	99.5	99.5	102.1	2.7	2.7
Net Stockholders' Equity	855.8	840.6	830.3	743.1	667.3	609.0	557.7
Net Working Capital	209.4	219.8	339.9	335.8	305.2	112.8	131.9
Year-end Shs. Outstg. (000)	64,272	65,600	67,027	66,059	65,852	65,904	65,644
STATISTICAL RECORD:							
Operating Profit Margin %	13.4	15.9	12.4	15.2	14.4	13.9	8.4
Net Profit Margin %	10.0	11.9	9.5	10.9	10.7	10.5	8.0
Return on Equity %	17.0	20.2	15.7	19.0	18.3	17.5	11.9
Return on Assets %	10.4	12.2	10.1	11.9	11.5	10.2	7.6
Debt/Total Assets %	7.1	7.2	7.7	8.4	9.7	0.3	0.3
Price Range	49 3/16-26 1/4	52 3/4-33 7/8	50 15/16-40 3/4	43 7/8-31 3/4	33 1/16-24 13/16	29 15/16-25	28 1/16-24 3/16
P/E Ratio	22.3-11.9	21.1-13.5	26.9-21.6	20.9-15.1	18.1-13.6	18.7-15.6	28.0-24.2
Average Yield %	3.3	2.8	2.4	2.6	3.1	2.9	3.0

Statistics are as originally reported. Adj. for 5% stock dividend, 2/95; 2-for-1 stock split, 8/96. ① Incl. after-tax chrg. of $32.2 mill. for consolidation & reorganization. ② Incl. a one-time gain of $8.8 mill. from the sale of The Kerite Company.

OFFICERS:
G. J. Ratcliffe, Chmn., Pres., C.E.O.
T. H. Powers, Sr. V.P., C.F.O.
J. H. Biggart Jr., V.P., Treas.
R. W. Davies, V.P., Sec., Gen. Couns.

INVESTOR CONTACT: Thomas R. Conlin, Dir. Pub. Affairs, (203) 799-4293

PRINCIPAL OFFICE: 584 Derby Milford Rd., Orange, CT 06477-4024

TELEPHONE NUMBER: (203) 799-4100
FAX: (203) 799-4333
WEB: www.hubbell.com

NO. OF EMPLOYEES: 10,190

SHAREHOLDERS: 1,090 (Cl. A); 4,805 (Cl. B)

ANNUAL MEETING: In Mar.

INCORPORATED: CT, 1905

INSTITUTIONAL HOLDINGS:
No. of Institutions: 203
Shares Held: 37,334,398
% Held: 68.6

INDUSTRY: Commercial lighting fixtures (SIC: 3646)

TRANSFER AGENT(S): ChaseMellon Shareholder Services LLC, Ridgefield Park, NJ

NASDAQ SYMBOL HBAN
Rec. Pr. 19⅜ (Adj.; 5/31/00)

HUNTINGTON BANCSHARES, INC.

YIELD 4.5%
P/E RATIO 10.6

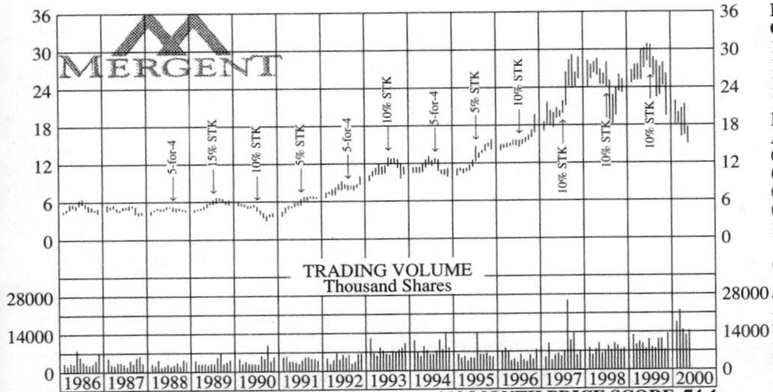

*7 YEAR PRICE SCORE 84.9 *12 MONTH PRICE SCORE 74.4

*NYSE COMPOSITE INDEX=100

INTERIM EARNINGS (Per Share):

Qtr.	Mar.	June	Sept.	Dec.
1996	0.32	0.34	0.35	0.35
1997	0.31	0.32	0.16	0.35
1998	0.35	0.35	0.35	0.13
1999	0.38	0.41	0.42	0.45

INTERIM DIVIDENDS (Per Share):

Amt.	Decl.	Ex.	Rec.	Pay.
0.20Q	8/18/99	9/14/99	9/16/99	10/01/99
0.20Q	11/17/99	12/14/99	12/16/99	1/03/00
0.20Q	2/16/00	3/14/00	3/16/00	4/03/00
0.20Q	5/17/00	6/14/00	6/16/00	7/03/00
10% STK	5/17/00	7/12/00	7/14/00	7/31/00

Indicated div.: $0.80 (Div. Reinv. Plan)

CAPITALIZATION (12/31/99):

	($000)	(%)
Total Deposits	19,792,603	75.5
Long-Term Debt	3,951,827	15.1
Redeemable Pfd. Stock	300,000	1.1
Common & Surplus	2,182,356	8.3
Total	26,226,786	100.0

DIVIDEND ACHIEVER STATUS:
Rank: 94 10-Year Growth Rate: 13.04%
Total Years of Dividend Growth: 33

RECENT DEVELOPMENTS: For the year ended 12/31/99, net income climbed 39.9% to $422.1 million. Earnings for 1999 included non-recurring charges of $96.8 million and a gain of $108.5 million related to the sale of credit card portfolios. Earnings for 1998 included special charges of $90.0 million. Net interest income increased 2.0% to $1.04 billion from $1.02 billion in the prior year. Total non-interest income climbed 30.9% to $573.6 million. On 2/7/00, the Company entered into a merger agreement with Empire Banc Corporation, a $506 million one-bank holding company headquartered in Traverse City, Michigan. The Company will issue its common stock at a ratio of 2.0355 shares for each outstanding share of Empire Banc common stock in a transaction that will be accounted for as a purchase. HBAN plans to purchase on the open market and then reissue approximately 6.5 million shares in connection with the transaction. The merger is expected to be completed by the second quarter of 2000.

BUSINESS

HUNTINGTON BANCSHARES, INC. was incorporated in Maryland in 1966. The Company is a multi-state bank holding company, headquartered in Columbus, Ohio, with assets, as of 12/31/99, of $29.03 billion. Huntington's subsidiaries conduct a full-service commercial and consumer banking business, engage in mortgage banking, lease financing, trust services, discount brokerage services, underwriting credit life and disability insurance, selling other insurance products and issuing commercial paper. The Company's subsidiaries operate 515 offices domestically in Florida, Georgia, Indiana, Kentucky, Maryland, Michigan, New Jersey, North Carolina, Ohio, South Carolina and West Virginia. International offices are located in the Cayman Islands and Hong Kong. The Company has more than 1,400 ATMs. HBAN also owns The Huntington Mortgage Company.

ANNUAL FINANCIAL DATA

	12/31/99	12/31/98	12/31/97	12/31/96	12/31/95	12/31/94	12/31/93
Earnings Per Share	**[2] 1.65**	**[1] 1.28**	**[1] 1.26**	**1.49**	**1.34**	**1.34**	**1.32**
Tang. Book Val. Per Share	**8.90**	**9.21**	**8.73**	**8.76**	**8.58**	**8.15**	**7.67**
Dividends Per Share	**0.68**	**0.62**	**0.56**	**0.51**	**0.48**	**0.40**	**0.34**
Dividend Payout %	**41.2**	**48.4**	**44.4**	**34.2**	**35.8**	**29.9**	**25.8**
INCOME STATEMENT (IN MILLIONS):							
Total Interest Income	2,026.0	1,999.4	1,981.5	1,510.5	1,461.9	1,219.7	1,236.3
Total Interest Expense	984.2	978.3	954.2	751.6	737.3	463.7	440.1
Net Interest Income	1,041.8	1,021.1	1,027.2	758.8	724.6	756.0	796.2
Provision for Loan Losses	88.4	105.2	107.8	65.1	28.7	15.3	79.3
Non-Interest Income	573.6	438.2	342.8	273.0	243.0	213.9	247.1
Non-Interest Expense	912.1	913.9	803.1	567.9	560.4	588.2	600.2
Income Before Taxes	614.8	440.1	459.2	398.8	378.4	366.5	363.8
Net Income	[2] 422.1	[1] 301.8	[1] 292.7	262.1	244.5	242.6	236.9
Average Shs. Outstg. (000)	255,647	234,799	233,692	176,608	183,176	181,296	179,324
BALANCE SHEET (IN MILLIONS):							
Cash & Due from Banks	1,208.0	1,215.8	1,142.5	915.6	861.0	885.3	704.0
Securities Avail. for Sale	26.7	28.8	40.1	62.3	80.5	485.1	381.3
Total Loans & Leases	20,668.4	19,454.6	17,738.2	14,260.7	13,261.7	12,264.4	10,953.9
Allowance for Credit Losses	299.3	290.9	258.2	199.1	194.5	200.5	211.8
Net Loans & Leases	20,369.1	19,163.6	17,480.1	14,061.7	13,067.2	12,063.9	10,742.1
Total Assets	29,037.0	28,296.3	26,730.5	20,851.5	20,254.6	17,770.6	17,618.7
Total Deposits	19,792.6	19,722.8	17,983.7	13,385.9	12,636.6	11,965.1	12,044.7
Long-Term Obligations	3,951.8	3,247.3	2,686.0	1,556.3	2,103.0	1,214.1	762.3
Total Liabilities	26,854.6	26,147.5	24,705.1	19,340.0	18,735.7	16,358.8	16,294.1
Net Stockholders' Equity	2,182.4	2,134.6	2,025.4	1,511.5	1,518.9	1,411.8	1,324.6
Year-end Shs. Outstg. (000)	223,932	231,821	232,001	172,545	177,091	173,316	172,712
STATISTICAL RECORD:							
Return on Equity %	19.3	14.1	14.4	17.3	16.1	17.2	17.9
Return on Assets %	1.5	1.1	1.1	1.3	1.2	1.4	1.3
Equity/Assets %	7.5	7.5	7.6	7.2	7.5	7.9	7.5
Non-Int. Exp./Tot. Inc. %	61.1	64.4	59.8	56.7	59.0	61.2	59.6
Price Range	30⅞-19½	28 9/16-18 3/16	29 3/16-17 1/16	19¾-13	15¾-9	13⅛-9 13/16	13-9¼
P/E Ratio	18.1-11.8	22.3-14.2	23.2-13.6	13.3-9.4	11.8-7.5	9.8-7.3	9.8-7.0
Average Yield %	2.7	2.6	2.4	3.0	3.7	3.5	3.0

Statistics are as originally reported. Adj. for 10% stock div., 7/00, 7/99, 7/98, 7/97, 7/96 & 7/93; 5% stock div., 7/95 & 7/93; 5-for-4 split, 7/94 [1] Incl. special chrg. of $90.0 mill., 1998; $47.2 mill., 1997. [2] Incl. non-recurr. chrg. $96.8 mill.

OFFICERS:
F. Wobst, Chmn., C.E.O.
R. J. Seiffert, Vice Chmn.
P. E. Geier, Pres., C.O.O.

INVESTOR CONTACT: Laurie Counsel, Investor Relations Director, (614) 480-3878

PRINCIPAL OFFICE: Huntington Ctr., 41 South High St., Columbus, OH 43287

TELEPHONE NUMBER: (614) 480-8300
WEB: www.Huntington.com

NO. OF EMPLOYEES: 9,516

SHAREHOLDERS: 35,182

ANNUAL MEETING: In April

INCORPORATED: MD, April, 1966

INSTITUTIONAL HOLDINGS:
No. of Institutions: 220
Shares Held: 65,383,940 (Adj.)
% Held: 25.9

INDUSTRY: National commercial banks (SIC: 6021)

TRANSFER AGENT(S): Harris Trust and Savings Bank, Chicago, IL

NYSE SYMBOL ITW
Rec. Pr. 58 1/16 (5/31/00)

ILLINOIS TOOL WORKS, INCORPORATED

YIELD 1.2%
P/E RATIO 21.0

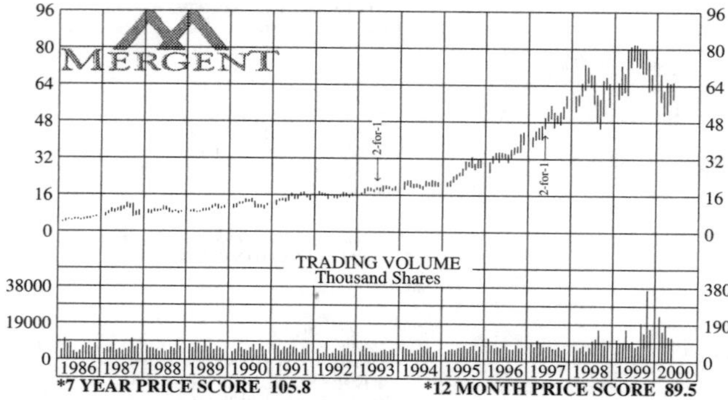

***7 YEAR PRICE SCORE 105.8** ***12 MONTH PRICE SCORE 89.5**

*NYSE COMPOSITE INDEX=100

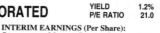

INTERIM EARNINGS (Per Share):

Qtr.	Mar.	June	Sept.	Dec.
1996	0.41	0.53	0.50	0.54
1997	0.49	0.61	0.59	0.64
1998	0.59	0.70	0.65	0.73
1999	0.65	0.79	0.74	0.59

INTERIM DIVIDENDS (Per Share):

Amt.	Decl.	Ex.	Rec.	Pay.
0.15Q	5/14/99	6/28/99	6/30/99	7/22/99
0.18Q	8/06/99	9/28/99	9/30/99	10/23/99
0.18Q	10/29/99	12/29/99	12/31/99	1/28/00
0.18Q	2/18/00	3/29/00	3/31/00	4/20/00
0.18Q	5/12/00	6/28/00	6/30/00	7/21/00

Indicated div.: $0.72 (Div. Reinv. Plan)

CAPITALIZATION (12/31/99):

	($000)	(%)
Long-Term Debt	1,360,746	22.0
Common & Surplus	4,815,423	78.0
Total	6,176,169	100.0

DIVIDEND ACHIEVER STATUS:
Rank: 44 10-Year Growth Rate: 16.65%
Total Years of Dividend Growth: 37

RECENT DEVELOPMENTS: For the year ended 12/31/99, net income increased 3.9% to $841.1 million compared with $809.7 million in 1998. Operating revenues were $9.33 billion, up 11.3% from $8.39 billion a year earlier. Results for 1999 included Premark merger-related costs of $81.0 million. North American Engineered Products revenues increased 16.0%, while International Engineered Products revenues advanced 28.0%.

PROSPECTS: Acquisitions and strong base business growth should benefit North American Engineered Products revenues. International Engineered Products should continue to enjoy strong growth due to acquisitions as well as contributions from base automotive and polymers businesses. North American Specialty Systems revenues should continue to benefit from contributions from base businesses and acquisitions.

BUSINESS

ILLINOIS TOOL WORKS, INCORPORATED manufactures and markets a variety of products and systems. ITW has more than 500 operations in 40 countries. Businesses in the Engineered Products-North America segment and businesses in the Engineered Products-International segment manufacture short lead-time components and fasteners, and specialty products. Businesses in the Specialty Systems-North America segment produce longer lead-time machinery and related consumables, and specialty equipment for applications. Businesses in the Specialty Systems-International segment manufacture longer lead-time machinery and related consumables, and specialty equipment for industrial spray coating and other applications. The Leasing and Investment segment makes opportunistic investments in mortgage-related assets, leveraged and direct financing leases of equipment, properties and property developments, and affordable housing. ITW acquired Premark International, Inc. in November 1999 for $3.40 billion.

ANNUAL FINANCIAL DATA

	12/31/99	12/31/98	12/31/97	12/31/96	12/31/95	12/31/94	12/31/93
Earnings Per Share	**1 2.76**	**2.67**	**2.33**	**1.97**	**1.65**	**1.23**	**0.92**
Cash Flow Per Share	**3.89**	**3.50**	**3.07**	**2.68**	**2.29**	**1.81**	**1.50**
Tang. Book Val. Per Share	**9.27**	**8.59**	**8.14**	**6.80**	**5.94**	**5.03**	**3.95**
Dividends Per Share	**0.63**	**0.51**	**0.43**	**0.35**	**0.31**	**0.27**	**0.24**
Dividend Payout %	**22.8**	**19.1**	**18.5**	**17.8**	**18.8**	**22.0**	**26.8**
INCOME STATEMENT (IN MILLIONS):							
Total Revenues	9,333.2	5,647.9	5,220.4	4,996.7	4,152.2	3,461.3	3,159.2
Costs & Expenses	7,584.5	4,356.8	4,107.8	4,017.9	3,373.7	2,853.9	2,658.0
Depreciation & Amort.	343.3	211.8	185.4	178.2	151.9	132.1	131.7
Operating Income	1,405.4	1,079.3	927.2	800.6	626.5	475.3	369.5
Net Interest Inc./(Exp.)	d67.5	d14.2	d19.4	d27.8	d31.6	d26.9	d35.0
Income Before Income Taxes	1,352.7	1,059.6	924.4	770.3	623.7	450.3	335.9
Income Taxes	511.6	386.8	337.4	284.0	236.1	172.5	129.3
Net Income	1 841.1	672.8	587.0	486.3	387.6	277.8	206.6
Cash Flow	1,184.4	884.6	772.3	664.5	539.5	409.9	338.3
Average Shs. Outstg. (000)	304,649	252,443	251,760	247,556	235,978	226,774	225,958
BALANCE SHEET (IN MILLIONS):							
Cash & Cash Equivalents	233.0	93.5	185.9	137.7	116.6	76.9	70.8
Total Current Assets	3,272.9	1,834.5	1,858.6	1,701.1	1,532.5	1,262.9	1,129.0
Net Property	1,633.9	987.5	884.1	808.3	694.9	641.2	583.8
Total Assets	9,060.3	6,118.2	5,394.8	4,806.2	3,613.1	2,580.5	2,372.3
Total Current Liabilities	2,045.4	1,222.0	1,157.9	1,219.3	850.9	628.4	546.1
Long-Term Obligations	1,360.7	947.0	854.3	818.9	615.6	273.0	375.6
Net Stockholders' Equity	4,815.4	3,338.0	2,806.5	2,396.0	1,924.2	1,541.5	1,258.7
Net Working Capital	1,227.6	612.5	700.8	481.8	681.6	634.5	582.9
Year-end Shs. Outstg. (000)	300,569	250,128	249,598	247,772	236,466	227,916	226,300
STATISTICAL RECORD:							
Operating Profit Margin %	15.1	19.1	17.8	16.0	15.1	13.7	11.7
Net Profit Margin %	9.0	11.9	11.2	9.7	9.3	8.0	6.5
Return on Equity %	17.5	20.2	20.9	20.3	20.1	18.0	16.4
Return on Assets %	9.3	11.0	10.9	10.1	10.7	10.8	8.7
Debt/Total Assets %	15.0	15.5	15.8	17.0	17.0	10.6	15.8
Price Range	82-58 1/8	73 3/16-45 3/16	59 1/2-37 3/8	43 5/8-25 15/16	32 3/4-19 7/8	22 3/4-18 1/2	20 1/4-16 1/4
P/E Ratio	29.7-21.1	27.4-16.9	25.5-16.0	22.2-13.2	19.9-12.1	18.6-15.1	22.1-17.8
Average Yield %	0.9	0.9	0.9	1.0	1.2	1.3	1.3

Statistics are as originally reported. Adj. for stk. splits: 2-for-1, 6/93 & 5/97. 1 Incl. Premark International, Inc. merger-related costs of $81.0 mill.

OFFICERS:
W. J. Farrell, Chmn., C.E.O.
F. S. Ptak, Vice-Chmn.
J. C. Kinney, Sr. V.P., C.F.O.
S. S. Hudnut, Sr. V.P., Sec., Gen. Couns.

INVESTOR CONTACT: John L. Brooklier, Investor Relations, (847) 724-7500

PRINCIPAL OFFICE: 3600 W. Lake Ave., Glenview, IL 60025-5811

TELEPHONE NUMBER: (847) 724-7500
FAX: (847) 657-4261
WEB: www.itwinc.com

NO. OF EMPLOYEES: 52,800 (approx.)

SHAREHOLDERS: 5,764

ANNUAL MEETING: In May

INCORPORATED: DE, June, 1961

INSTITUTIONAL HOLDINGS:
No. of Institutions: 536
Shares Held: 220,683,801
% Held: 73.5

INDUSTRY: Plastics products, nec (SIC: 3089)

TRANSFER AGENT(S): Harris Trust and Savings Bank, Chicago, IL

NYSE SYMBOL IEI
Rec. Pr. 19½ (3/31/00)

INDIANA ENERGY, INC.

YIELD 5.0%
P/E RATIO 15.0

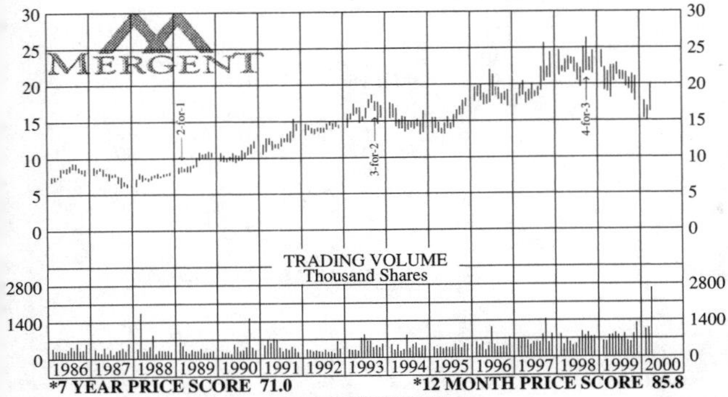

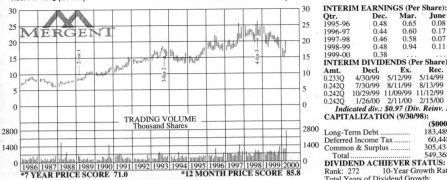

MERGENT
2-for-1
3-for-2
4-for-3
TRADING VOLUME
Thousand Shares
1986 1987 1988 1989 1990 1991 1992 1993 1994 1995 1996 1997 1998 1999 2000

***7 YEAR PRICE SCORE 71.0** ***12 MONTH PRICE SCORE 85.8**

*NYSE COMPOSITE INDEX=100

INTERIM EARNINGS (Per Share):

Qtr.	Dec.	Mar.	June	Sept.
1995-96	0.48	0.65	0.08	d0.15
1996-97	0.44	0.60	0.17	d0.69
1997-98	0.46	0.58	0.07	d0.11
1998-99	0.48	0.94	0.11	d0.13
1999-00	0.38	...	...	...

INTERIM DIVIDENDS (Per Share):

Amt.	Decl.	Ex.	Rec.	Pay.
0.233Q	4/30/99	5/12/99	5/14/99	6/01/99
0.242Q	7/30/99	8/11/99	8/13/99	9/01/99
0.242Q	10/29/99	11/09/99	11/12/99	12/01/99
0.242Q	1/26/00	2/11/00	2/15/00	3/01/00

Indicated div.: $0.97 (Div. Reinv. Plan)

CAPITALIZATION (9/30/98):

	($000)	(%)
Long-Term Debt	183,489	33.4
Deferred Income Tax	60,448	11.0
Common & Surplus	305,431	55.6
Total	549,368	100.0

DIVIDEND ACHIEVER STATUS:
Rank: 272 10-Year Growth Rate: 4.36%
Total Years of Dividend Growth: 24

RECENT DEVELOPMENTS: For the quarter ended 12/31/99, net income rose 2.8% to $38.7 million from $36.1 million in 1998. Operating revenues grew 7.1% to $433.3 million versus $421.3 million in 1998. Earnings were pressured by higher depreciation and interest expense, as well as the recognition of certain hedging losses by IEI's marketing affiliate, ProLiance Energy. However, the rise in earnings was due to margin growth from customer additions and weather that was 8.0% colder than the prior year.

PROSPECTS: IEI and Sigcorp, Inc. completed their merger on 3/31/00. The resulting company, Vectren Corporation, began trading on the NYSE on 4/3/00 under the ticker symbol VVC. On 12/15/99, IEI's board of directors approved an agreement to acquire DPL Inc.'s natural gas distribution business for $425.0 million in cash. The acquisition should add approximately 305,000 customers to IEI's existing customer base of nearly 510,000 customers, and 5,000 miles to its existing 11,000 miles of pipeline.

BUSINESS

INDIANA ENERGY, INC. is an investor-owned holding company of Indiana Gas Company, Inc., IEI Services, LLC and IEI Investments, Inc. IEI's principal subsidiary, Indiana Gas Company, provides gas utility service to approximately 510,000 customers in central and southern Indiana. Terre Haute Gas Corp. and Richmond Gas Corp. were acquired in July 1990. Both companies are public utilities providing local distribution of natural gas in the state of Indiana. While the companies technically still exist as separate corporate entities, their business operations were merged with those of Indiana Gas in 1991. IEI Investments is a wholly-owned subsidiary formed to group the operations and financing of non-regulated businesses.

ANNUAL FINANCIAL DATA

	9/30/99	9/30/98	9/30/97	9/30/96	9/30/95	9/30/94	9/30/93
Earnings Per Share	1.40	1.33	[2] 0.68	1.40	1.10	1.15	[1] 1.22
Cash Flow Per Share	...	2.59	1.85	2.52	2.14	2.12	2.17
Tang. Book Val. Per Share	10.46	10.16	9.72	9.89	9.33	9.02	8.64
Dividends Per Share	0.97	0.91	0.87	0.84	0.81	0.78	0.75
Dividend Payout %	69.3	68.2	127.5	59.9	74.0	68.0	61.9
INCOME STATEMENT (IN THOUSANDS):							
Total Revenues	420,463	466,434	530,407	530,594	403,810	475,297	713,049
Costs & Expenses	...	359,624	458,303	420,426	306,921	378,583	627,397
Depreciation & Amort.	...	37,842	35,241	33,441	31,485	29,404	27,386
Operating Income	...	68,968	36,863	76,727	65,404	67,310	58,266
Net Interest Inc./(Exp.)	...	d16,640	d16,774	d15,907	d15,530	d16,037	d16,820
Income Taxes	...	21,849	7,852	23,174	19,216	19,467	15,765
Equity Earnings/Minority Int.	...	7,226	...	...	...	...	137
Net Income	41,751	40,204	[2] 20,503	42,201	32,956	34,441	[1] 34,578
Cash Flow	...	78,046	55,744	75,642	64,441	63,845	61,964
Average Shs. Outstg.	...	30,116	30,107	30,017	30,080	30,072	28,501
BALANCE SHEET (IN THOUSANDS):							
Gross Property	...	993,202	951,617	931,092	872,287	824,839	773,174
Accumulated Depreciation	...	383,485	361,936	344,268	316,991	291,823	267,629
Net Property	...	609,717	589,681	586,824	555,296	533,016	505,545
Total Assets	777,378	712,350	690,845	682,463	663,397	656,645	631,280
Long-Term Obligations	...	183,489	157,791	178,063	176,296	158,766	164,901
Net Stockholders' Equity	...	305,431	292,597	296,322	280,715	271,245	258,647
Year-end Shs. Outstg.	...	30,064	30,108	29,965	30,083	30,076	29,947
STATISTICAL RECORD:							
Operating Profit Margin %	16.5	14.8	6.9	14.5	16.2	14.2	8.2
Net Profit Margin %	9.9	8.6	3.9	8.0	8.2	7.2	4.8
Net Inc./Net Property %	6.5	6.6	3.5	7.2	5.9	6.5	6.8
Net Inc./Tot. Capital %	8.4	7.3	4.1	7.8	6.3	7.0	7.2
Return on Equity %	13.4	13.2	7.0	14.2	11.7	12.7	13.4
Accum. Depr./Gross Prop. %	39.6	38.6	38.0	37.0	36.3	35.4	34.6
Price Range	16½-165/16	263/8-195/8	2511/16-173/16	221/16-16	181/8-131/4	179/16-131/8	185/8-141/8
P/E Ratio	11.8-11.7	19.8-14.7	37.7-25.2	15.7-12.1	16.5-12.1	15.3-11.4	15.3-11.6
Average Yield %	2.9	3.9	4.1	4.3	5.2	5.1	4.6

Statistics are as originally reported. Adjusted for 3-for-2 stock split, 10/93 & 4-for-3 stock split 4-for-3, 10/98. [1] Incl. a gain of $7.1 mill. from the sale of a former affiliate. [2] Incl. an after-tax restruct. chg. of $24.5 mill.

OFFICERS:
L. A. Ferger, Chmn.
N. C. Ellerbrook, Pres., C.E.O., C.O.O.
C. L. Chapman, Sr. V.P., C.F.O.

INVESTOR CONTACT: Mary Kay Lindop, (800) 777-3389

PRINCIPAL OFFICE: 1630 North Meridian Street, Indianapolis, IN 46202

TELEPHONE NUMBER: (317) 926-3351
FAX: (317) 321-0498
WEB: www.indiana-energy.com

NO. OF EMPLOYEES: 890 full-time; 39 part-time

SHAREHOLDERS: 8,818

ANNUAL MEETING: N/A

INCORPORATED: IN, Oct., 1985

INSTITUTIONAL HOLDINGS:
No. of Institutions: 97
Shares Held: 8,609,931
% Held: 28.9

INDUSTRY: Natural gas distribution (SIC: 4924)

TRANSFER AGENT(S): EquiServe Trust Company, N.A., Jersey City, NJ

INGERSOLL-RAND COMPANY

YIELD	1.5%
P/E RATIO	13.5

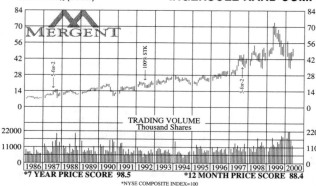

TRADING VOLUME
Thousand Shares

*7 YEAR PRICE SCORE 98.5   ***12 MONTH PRICE SCORE 88.4**

*NYSE COMPOSITE INDEX=100

INTERIM EARNINGS (Per Share):

Qtr.	Mar.	June	Sept.	Dec.
1995	0.29	0.42	0.39	0.60
1996	0.47	0.57	0.51	0.67
1997	0.17	0.69	0.60	0.57
1998	0.60	0.85	0.72	0.91
1999	0.73	0.99	0.80	0.86

INTERIM DIVIDENDS (Per Share):

Amt.	Decl.	Ex.	Rec.	Pay.
0.15Q	5/05/99	5/13/99	5/17/99	6/01/99
0.17Q	8/04/99	8/13/99	8/17/99	9/01/99
0.17Q	11/01/99	11/12/99	11/16/99	12/01/99
0.17Q	2/02/00	2/11/00	2/15/00	3/01/00
0.17Q	5/03/00	5/12/00	5/16/00	6/01/00

Indicated div.: $0.68 (Div. Reinv. Plan)

CAPITALIZATION (12/31/99):

	($000)	(%)
Long-Term Debt	2,113,300	37.1
Minority Interest	95,700	1.7
Redeemable Pfd. Stock	402,500	7.1
Common & Surplus	3,083,000	54.1
Total	5,694,500	100.0

DIVIDEND ACHIEVER STATUS:
Rank: 261   10-Year Growth Rate: 5.17%
Total Years of Dividend Growth: 12

RECENT DEVELOPMENTS: For the twelve months ended 12/31/99, net earnings from continuing operations totaled $544.9 million versus net earnings from continuing operations of $455.5 million in 1998. Net sales rose 3.8% to $7.67 billion from $7.38 billion in 1998. Specialty Vehicle sales rose to $2.35 billion. Sales from the Air & Temperature Control unit fell 1.1% to $2.21 billion. Hardware & Tools segment sales grew 8.7% to $1.87 billion.

PROSPECTS: IR has signed a definitive agreement to expand its global climate control business by acquiring Hussmann International, Inc., a major manufacturer of food-store equipment and commercial refrigeration products. The transaction is valued at about $1.83 billion, including the assumption of about $275.0 million of debt. IR expects the acquisition to be immediately accretive to earnings by $0.02 to $0.05 for the year ended 12/31/00.

BUSINESS

INGERSOLL-RAND COMPANY'S operations consist of the following worldwide business segments: The Specialty Vehicles segment, 31% of sales (35% of operating income) in 1999; the Engineered Products segment, 16% (13%); Hardware & Tools segment, 24% (28%); and Air & Temperature Control, 29% (25%). The Specialty Vehicles segment includes skid-steer loaders and compact hydraulic excavators, golf cars, pavers, compactors, drilling equipment and rough-terrain material handlers. The Engineered Products segment includes Torrington® and Fafnir® bearings and components. The Hardware & Tools segment includes architectural hardware products such as Schlage® locks. The Air & Temperature Control Segment segment includes Thermo King® transport temperature-control equipment and Ingersoll-Rand air compressors.

ANNUAL FINANCIAL DATA

	12/31/99	12/31/98	12/31/97	12/31/96	12/31/95	12/31/94	12/31/93
Earnings Per Share	③ 3.29	3.08	2.31	2.22	1.70	1.33	①② 1.04
Cash Flow Per Share	4.93	4.78	3.60	3.48	2.83	2.17	1.82
Tang. Book Val. Per Share	...	...	...	5.56	3.29	8.89	7.88
Dividends Per Share	0.64	0.60	0.57	0.52	0.49	0.48	0.47
Dividend Payout %	19.5	19.5	24.8	23.4	29.0	36.0	44.9
INCOME STATEMENT (IN MILLIONS):							
Total Revenues	7,666.7	8,291.5	7,103.3	6,702.9	5,729.0	4,507.5	4,021.1
Costs & Expenses	6,295.0	6,964.5	6,130.7	5,816.6	5,052.6	3,997.9	3,606.0
Depreciation & Amort.	272.4	282.6	212.3	202.6	179.4	132.5	123.5
Operating Income	1,099.3	1,044.4	760.3	683.5	497.0	377.0	291.5
Net Interest Inc./(Exp.)	d203.1	d225.8	d136.6	d119.9	d86.6	d43.8	d52.0
Income Before Income Taxes	844.8	789.2	613.7	568.3	429.1	329.9	253.5
Income Taxes	299.9	280.1	233.2	210.3	158.8	118.8	90.0
Equity Earnings/Minority Int.	d29.1	d7.4	11.5	4.1	9.3	11.4	21.5
Net Income	③ 544.9	509.1	380.5	358.0	270.3	211.1	①② 163.5
Cash Flow	817.3	791.7	592.8	560.6	449.7	343.7	287.0
Average Shs. Outstg. (000)	165,753	165,482	164,825	161,238	159,150	158,187	157,488
BALANCE SHEET (IN MILLIONS):							
Cash & Cash Equivalents	223.4	77.6	111.8	192.1	146.6	211.3	234.2
Total Current Assets	2,868.3	2,427.6	2,544.9	2,535.6	2,345.6	2,002.9	1,902.2
Net Property	1,240.2	1,347.6	1,283.2	1,145.4	1,278.4	959.3	875.1
Total Assets	8,400.2	8,309.5	8,415.6	5,621.6	5,563.3	3,596.9	3,375.3
Total Current Liabilities	1,738.9	1,848.8	2,327.8	1,290.2	1,329.2	1,040.1	1,024.3
Long-Term Obligations	2,113.3	2,166.0	2,528.0	1,163.8	1,304.4	315.9	314.1
Net Stockholders' Equity	3,083.0	2,707.5	2,341.4	2,090.8	1,795.5	1,531.3	1,349.8
Net Working Capital	1,129.4	578.8	217.1	1,245.4	1,016.4	962.8	877.8
Year-end Shs. Outstg. (000)	163,129	164,389	164,825	164,223	164,558	158,244	157,901
STATISTICAL RECORD:							
Operating Profit Margin %	14.3	12.6	10.7	10.2	8.7	8.4	7.2
Net Profit Margin %	7.1	6.1	5.4	5.3	4.7	4.7	4.1
Return on Equity %	17.7	18.8	16.3	17.1	15.1	13.8	12.1
Return on Assets %	6.5	6.1	4.5	6.4	4.9	5.9	4.8
Debt/Total Assets %	25.2	26.1	30.0	20.7	23.4	8.8	9.3
Price Range	73¹³⁄₁₆-44⁵⁄₈	54-34	46¹⁄₄-27¹³⁄₁₆	31³⁄₄-23⁷⁄₁₆	28¹⁄₄-18¹⁵⁄₁₆	27³⁄₄-19¹¹⁄₁₆	26⁹⁄₁₆-19³⁄₁₆
P/E Ratio	22.4-13.6	17.5-11.0	20.0-12.0	14.3-10.5	16.6-11.1	20.8-14.8	25.6-18.4
Average Yield %	1.1	1.4	1.5	1.9	2.1	2.0	2.0

Statistics are as originally reported. Adj. for 3-for-2 stk. split, 9/97. ① Incl. non-recurr. net chrg. $31.0 mill. ② Bef. acctg. adj. chrg. $21.0 mill. ③ Bef. inc. from disc. oper. $46.2 mill.

OFFICERS:
H. L. Henkel, Chmn., Pres., C.E.O.
D. W. Devonshire, Exec. V.P., C.F.O.
P. Nachtigal, V.P., Gen. Couns.
INVESTOR CONTACT: Joseph Fimbianti, (201) 573-3113
PRINCIPAL OFFICE: 200 Chestnut Ridge Rd., P.O. Box 8738, Woodcliff Lake, NJ 07675

TELEPHONE NUMBER: (201) 573-0123
FAX: (201) 573-3168
WEB: www.ingersoll-rand.com
NO. OF EMPLOYEES: 46,500 (approx.)
SHAREHOLDERS: 11,190 (approx.)
ANNUAL MEETING: In May
INCORPORATED: NJ, 1905

INSTITUTIONAL HOLDINGS:
No. of Institutions: 411
Shares Held: 124,532,433
% Held: 76.1
INDUSTRY: General industrial machinery, nec (SIC: 3569)
TRANSFER AGENT(S): The Bank of New York, New York, NY

NYSE SYMBOL IFF
Rec. Pr. 34 (5/31/00)

INTERNATIONAL FLAVORS & FRAGRANCES, INC.

YIELD 4.5%
P/E RATIO 22.2

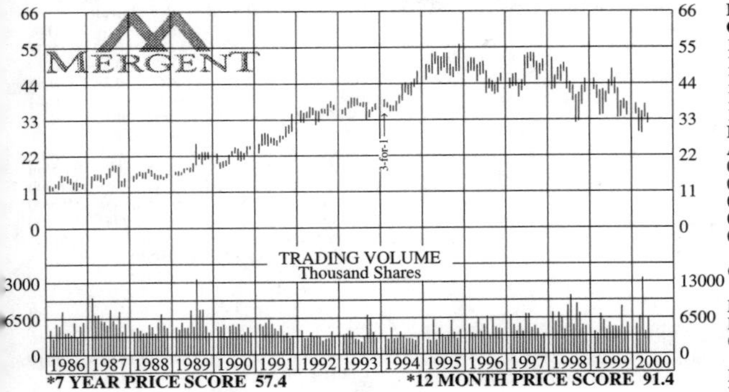

MERGENT
3-for-1
TRADING VOLUME
Thousand Shares
1986 1987 1988 1989 1990 1991 1992 1993 1994 1995 1996 1997 1998 1999 2000

*7 YEAR PRICE SCORE 57.4 *12 MONTH PRICE SCORE 91.4

*NYSE COMPOSITE INDEX=100

INTERIM EARNINGS (Per Share):

Qtr.	Mar.	June	Sept.	Dec.
1995	0.63	0.68	0.57	0.36
1996	0.60	0.26	0.48	0.37
1997	0.58	0.58	0.52	0.32
1998	0.58	0.52	0.47	0.33
1999	0.46	0.26	0.46	0.35

INTERIM DIVIDENDS (Per Share):

Amt.	Decl.	Ex.	Rec.	Pay.
0.38Q	2/09/99	3/23/99	3/25/99	4/09/99
0.38Q	5/20/99	6/23/99	6/25/99	7/09/99
0.38Q	9/14/99	9/22/99	9/24/99	10/08/99
0.38Q	12/14/99	12/20/99	12/22/99	1/11/00
0.38Q	2/08/00	3/22/00	3/24/00	4/10/00

Indicated div.: $1.52 (Div. Reinv. Plan)

CAPITALIZATION (12/31/99):

	($000)	(%)
Long-Term Debt	3,832	0.4
Deferred Income Tax	32,785	3.7
Common & Surplus	858,497	95.9
Total	895,114	100.0

DIVIDEND ACHIEVER STATUS:
Rank: 177 10-Year Growth Rate: 9.04%
Total Years of Dividend Growth: 38

RECENT DEVELOPMENTS: For the year ended 12/31/99, net income dropped 20.5% to $162.0 million compared with $203.8 million in the previous year. Results for 1999 included a one-time nonrecurring charge of $32.9 million. Net sales were $1.44 billion, an increase of 2.3% from $1.41 billion in the comparable year. The increase in sales was primarily due to strong flavor and fragrance sales in the Asia-Pacific region.

PROSPECTS: The Company has announced a program to streamline its operations worldwide. The program will include the closure of certain manufacturing, distribution and sales facilities, the consolidation of remaining manufacturing locations, and the reduction of its workforce by 5.0%. The program is expected to increase pre-tax earnings by $15.0 million annually, beginning in 2000.

BUSINESS

INTERNATIONAL FLAVORS & FRAGRANCES, INC. supplies compounds that enhance the aroma or taste of other manufacturers' products. It is one of the largest companies in its field producing and marketing on an international basis. Fragrance products (accounting for approximately 57% of 1999 total sales) are sold principally to makers of perfumes, cosmetics, soaps and detergents, pharmaceuticals and confectionery products. Flavor products (accounting for approximately 43% of 1999 total sales) are sold principally to the food and beverage industries for use in such consumer products as soft drinks, candies, baked goods, desserts, prepared foods, dietary foods, dairy products, drink powders pharmaceuticals and alcoholic beverages. The United States accounted for 31% of 1999 sales.

GEOGRAPHIC DATA

(12/31/1999)	REV (%)	INC (%)
North America	33.1	21.7
EAME	39.9	55.5
Latin America	14.8	12.9
Asia-Pacific	12.2	9.9
Total	100.0	100.0

ANNUAL FINANCIAL DATA

	12/31/99	12/31/98	12/31/97	12/31/96	12/31/95	12/31/94	12/31/93
Earnings Per Share	**[1] 1.53**	**1.90**	**1.99**	**[1] 1.71**	**2.24**	**2.03**	**1.78**
Cash Flow Per Share	**2.06**	**2.35**	**2.45**	**2.15**	**2.60**	**2.35**	**2.09**
Tang. Book Val. Per Share	**8.19**	**8.91**	**9.17**	**9.79**	**10.06**	**9.04**	**7.96**
Dividends Per Share	**1.52**	**1.48**	**1.44**	**1.36**	**1.24**	**1.08**	**1.00**
Dividend Payout %	**99.3**	**77.9**	**72.4**	**79.5**	**55.4**	**53.2**	**56.2**
INCOME STATEMENT (IN MILLIONS):							
Total Revenues	1,439.5	1,407.3	1,426.8	1,436.1	1,439.5	1,315.2	1,188.6
Costs & Expenses	1,101.9	1,051.6	1,044.3	1,048.1	1,014.8	930.3	847.6
Depreciation & Amort.	56.4	49.0	50.3	47.8	40.7	36.4	35.1
Operating Income	281.3	306.8	332.2	340.1	384.0	348.6	306.0
Net Interest Inc./(Exp.)	d5.2	d2.0	d2.4	d2.7	d3.2	d13.5	d17.4
Income Before Income Taxes	243.5	311.1	340.2	299.1	393.7	360.4	323.8
Income Taxes	81.5	107.3	122.0	109.2	144.9	134.3	121.3
Net Income	[1] 162.0	203.8	218.2	[1] 189.9	248.8	226.0	202.5
Cash Flow	218.4	252.8	268.5	237.7	289.5	262.4	237.5
Average Shs. Outstg. (000)	105,943	107,430	109,625	110,773	111,262	111,527	113,925
BALANCE SHEET (IN MILLIONS):							
Cash & Cash Equivalents	63.0	116.0	260.4	318.0	296.9	301.8	311.3
Total Current Assets	835.4	848.0	935.5	1,006.4	1,036.0	964.5	879.0
Net Property	523.9	498.8	446.5	467.8	468.6	405.7	323.4
Total Assets	1,401.5	1,388.1	1,422.3	1,506.9	1,534.3	1,399.7	1,225.3
Total Current Liabilities	369.7	272.9	264.9	280.5	276.4	259.7	226.6
Long-Term Obligations	3.8	4.3	5.1	8.3	11.6	14.3	...
Net Stockholders' Equity	858.5	945.1	1,000.5	1,076.5	1,116.6	1,008.1	891.9
Net Working Capital	465.7	575.1	670.6	725.9	759.6	704.8	652.4
Year-end Shs. Outstg. (000)	104,822	106,046	109,131	109,972	110,954	111,464	112,060
STATISTICAL RECORD:							
Operating Profit Margin %	19.5	21.8	23.3	23.7	26.7	26.5	25.7
Net Profit Margin %	11.3	14.5	15.3	13.2	17.3	17.2	17.0
Return on Equity %	18.9	21.6	21.8	17.6	22.3	22.4	22.7
Return on Assets %	11.6	14.7	15.3	12.6	16.2	16.1	16.5
Debt/Total Assets %	0.3	0.3	0.4	0.6	0.8	1.0	...
Price Range	48½-33⅝	51⅞-32 1/16	53 7/16-39⅞	51⅞-40¾	55⅞-45⅛	47⅞-35⅝	39 13/16-33
P/E Ratio	31.7-22.0	27.3-16.9	26.9-20.0	30.3-23.8	24.9-20.1	23.6-17.5	22.4-18.5
Average Yield %	3.7	3.5	3.1	2.9	2.5	2.6	2.7

Statistics are as originally reported. Adj. for stk. split: 3-for-1, 1/94. [1] Incl. non-recurr. chrg. $49.7 mill., 1996; $32.9 mill., 1999.

OFFICERS:
E. P. Grisanti, Chmn., Pres.
D. J. Wetmore, V.P., C.F.O.
S. A. Block, Sr. V.P., Gen. Couns., Sec.

PRINCIPAL OFFICE: 521 West 57th Street, New York, NY 10019-2960

TELEPHONE NUMBER: (212) 765-5500
FAX: (212) 708-7132
WEB: www.iff.com

NO. OF EMPLOYEES: 4,680 (approx.)

SHAREHOLDERS: 4,209 (approx.)

ANNUAL MEETING: In May

INCORPORATED: NY, Dec., 1909

INSTITUTIONAL HOLDINGS:
No. of Institutions: 266
Shares Held: 70,380,244
% Held: 67.0

INDUSTRY: Industrial organic chemicals, nec (SIC: 2869)

TRANSFER AGENT(S): Bank of New York, New York, NY

INTERPUBLIC GROUP OF COMPANIES, INC.

YIELD 0.9%
P/E RATIO 38.0

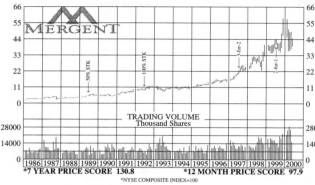

TRADING VOLUME
Thousand Shares

| 1986 | 1987 | 1988 | 1989 | 1990 | 1991 | 1992 | 1993 | 1994 | 1995 | 1996 | 1997 | 1998 | 1999 | 2000 |

*7 YEAR PRICE SCORE 130.8   *12 MONTH PRICE SCORE 97.9

*NYSE COMPOSITE INDEX=100

INTERIM EARNINGS (Per Share):

Qtr.	Mar.	June	Sept.	Dec.
1996	0.08	0.35	0.12	0.32
1997	0.09	0.37	0.14	0.36
1998	0.11	0.42	0.17	0.38
1999	0.16	0.49	0.21	0.27

INTERIM DIVIDENDS (Per Share):

Amt.	Decl.	Ex.	Rec.	Pay.
2-for-1	5/17/99	7/16/99	6/29/99	7/15/99
0.085Q	7/29/99	8/26/99	8/30/99	9/15/99
0.085Q	10/26/99	11/24/99	11/29/99	12/15/99
0.085Q	12/16/99	2/24/00	2/28/00	3/15/00
0.095Q	5/15/00	5/25/00	5/30/00	6/15/00

Indicated div.: $0.38 (Div. Reinv. Plan)

CAPITALIZATION (12/31/99):

	($000)	(%)
Long-Term Debt	867,262	33.2
Deferred Income Tax	41,429	1.6
Minority Interest	78,643	3.0
Common & Surplus	1,628,071	62.2
Total	2,615,405	100.0

DIVIDEND ACHIEVER STATUS:
Rank: 117   10-Year Growth Rate: 11.90%
Total Years of Dividend Growth: 18

RECENT DEVELOPMENTS: For the year ended 12/31/99, net income advanced 3.9% to $321.9 million from $309.9 million in the prior year. Earnings for 1999 included pre-tax restructuring and other merger-related costs of $84.2 million. Total gross income increased 14.9% to $4.56 billion from $3.97 billion a year earlier. Domestic gross income advanced 18.6% to $2.35 billion, while foreign gross income improved 11.3% to $2.21 billion.

PROSPECTS: On 4/20/00, the Company acquired NFO Worldwide, Inc., a provider of research-based marketing information and counsel to the worldwide business community. Separately, IPG announced the merger of its two units, Lowe & Partners Worldwide and Ammirati Puris Lintas. The new agency network, Lowe Lintas & Partners Worldwide, will have billings of more than $11.00 billion and offices in over 80 countries.

BUSINESS

INTERPUBLIC GROUP OF COMPANIES, INC. is a large organization of advertising agencies. The agencies owned include McCann-Erickson WorldGroup, the Lowe Group, DraftWorldwide, Initiative Media Worldwide, International Public Relations, NFO Worldwide, Octagon, Zentropy Partners, Allied Communications Group and other related companies. IPG also offers advertising agency services through association arrangements with local agencies in various parts of the world. Other activities conducted by the Company within the area of marketing communications include public relations, graphic design and market research. The Company also conducts business in sales promotion, interactive services, sports and event marketing, consulting and other related services.

ANNUAL FINANCIAL DATA

	12/31/99	12/31/98	12/31/97	12/31/96	12/31/95	12/31/94	12/31/93
Earnings Per Share	⑤ 1.11	1.11	0.95	④ 0.85	③ 0.55	② 0.51	① 0.56
Cash Flow Per Share	1.86	1.74	1.43	1.28	0.94	0.84	0.87
Tang. Book Val. Per Share	...	...	0.32	0.50	0.47	0.21	0.32
Dividends Per Share	0.33	0.29	0.25	0.22	0.20	0.18	0.16
Dividend Payout %	29.7	26.2	26.5	26.0	36.5	35.6	29.3
INCOME STATEMENT (IN MILLIONS):							
Total Revenues	4,561.5	3,968.7	3,125.8	2,537.5	2,179.7	1,984.3	1,793.9
Costs & Expenses	3,694.1	3,168.0	2,504.3	2,036.2	1,796.4	1,674.9	1,465.5
Depreciation & Amort.	215.9	179.1	130.8	103.4	91.2	75.6	70.1
Operating Income	651.5	621.6	490.7	397.9	292.2	233.7	258.2
Net Interest Inc./(Exp.)	d66.4	d58.7	d49.4	d40.8	d38.0	d32.9	d26.4
Income Before Income Taxes	585.1	562.9	441.3	357.1	254.2	200.8	231.8
Income Taxes	236.3	232.0	184.9	150.0	122.7	86.3	99.8
Equity Earnings/Minority Int.	d26.8	d21.0	d17.2	d1.9	d1.6	0.8	d6.7
Net Income	⑤ 321.9	309.9	239.1	④ 205.2	③ 129.8	② 115.2	① 125.3
Cash Flow	537.9	489.0	370.0	308.6	221.0	190.8	195.4
Average Shs. Outstg. (000)	289,548	281,050	259,088	240,879	234,540	226,710	225,648
BALANCE SHEET (IN MILLIONS):							
Cash & Cash Equivalents	1,018.2	840.5	745.9	503.9	457.4	441.6	322.4
Total Current Assets	5,767.8	4,776.9	4,025.7	3,353.5	2,974.4	2,675.3	2,003.2
Net Property	534.3	439.6	348.8	307.0	279.3	248.1	216.7
Total Assets	8,727.3	6,942.8	5,702.5	4,765.1	4,259.8	3,793.4	2,869.8
Total Current Liabilities	5,636.9	4,658.4	3,751.6	3,199.0	2,826.7	2,595.2	1,836.0
Long-Term Obligations	867.3	506.6	452.7	347.0	283.5	241.8	226.1
Net Stockholders' Equity	1,628.1	1,265.1	1,107.2	872.0	749.7	649.4	564.0
Net Working Capital	130.9	118.6	274.0	154.4	147.7	80.1	167.2
Year-end Shs. Outstg. (000)	287,658	279,070	261,638	243,396	238,884	233,112	224,403
STATISTICAL RECORD:							
Operating Profit Margin %	14.3	15.7	15.7	15.7	13.4	11.8	14.4
Net Profit Margin %	7.1	7.8	7.7	8.1	6.0	5.8	7.0
Return on Equity %	19.8	24.5	21.6	23.5	17.3	17.7	22.2
Return on Assets %	3.7	4.5	4.2	4.3	3.0	3.0	4.4
Debt/Total Assets %	9.9	7.3	7.9	7.3	6.7	6.4	7.9
Price Range	58⅜-34⁷/₁₆	40⁵/₁₆-22¹¹/₁₆	26½-15¹¹/₁₆	16¾-13³/₁₆	14⁷/₁₆-10⁹/₁₆	11¹⁵/₁₆-9³/₁₆	11⁷/₈-7¹⁵/₁₆
P/E Ratio	52.6-31.0	36.5-20.4	27.9-16.5	19.6-15.5	26.1-19.1	23.4-18.0	21.3-14.3
Average Yield %	0.7	0.9	1.2	1.5	1.5	1.6	1.7	1.6

Statistics are as originally reported. Adj. for stk splits: 2-for-1, 7/99; and 3-for-2, 7/97. ① Bef. acct. change of $512,000. ② Incl. acctg. chrg. of $21.8 mill. & restruct. chrg. of $25.7 mill. ③ Incl. aft.-tax chg. of $38.2 mill. for write-down of assets. ④ Incl. $8.1 mill. gain from sale of a portion of IPG's interest in CKS Group, Inc. ⑤ Incl. pre-tax restruct. & other merger-rel. chrgs. of $84.2 mill.

QUARTERLY DATA

(12/31/1999)($000)	REV	INC
1st Quarter	925,080	44,785
2nd Quarter	1,134,433	139,409
3rd Quarter	1,044,003	59,044
4th Quarter	1,458,002	78,683

OFFICERS:
P. H. Geier Jr., Chmn., C.E.O.
J. J. Dooner Jr., Pres., C.O.O.
S. F. Orr, Exec. V.P., C.F.O.
INVESTOR CONTACT: Thomas Volpe, Sr. V.P., Fin. Oper., (212) 399-8078
PRINCIPAL OFFICE: 1271 Avenue of the Americas, New York, NY 10020

TELEPHONE NUMBER: (212) 399-8000
FAX: (212) 399-8130
WEB: www.interpublic.com
NO. OF EMPLOYEES: 38,600 (approx.)
SHAREHOLDERS: 10,965
ANNUAL MEETING: In May
INCORPORATED: DE, Sep., 1930

INSTITUTIONAL HOLDINGS:
No. of Institutions: 450
Shares Held: 217,649,508
% Held: 77.6
INDUSTRY: Advertising agencies (SIC: 7311)
TRANSFER AGENT(S): First Chicago Trust Company of New York, Jersey City, NJ

JEFFERSON-PILOT CORP.

YIELD	2.2%
P/E RATIO	15.5

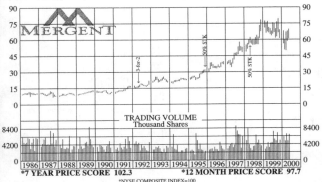

TRADING VOLUME
Thousand Shares

*7 YEAR PRICE SCORE 102.3   ***12 MONTH PRICE SCORE 97.7**

*NYSE COMPOSITE INDEX=100

INTERIM EARNINGS (Per Share):

Qtr.	Mar.	June	Sept.	Dec.
1995	0.53	0.47	0.61	0.81
1996	0.65	0.68	0.69	0.70
1997	1.03	0.96	0.75	0.75
1998	1.04	0.94	1.02	0.90
1999	1.19	1.10	1.09	1.04

INTERIM DIVIDENDS (Per Share):

Amt.	Decl.	Ex.	Rec.	Pay.
0.33Q	5/03/99	8/11/99	8/13/99	9/05/99
0.33Q	8/02/99	11/09/99	11/12/99	12/05/99
0.33Q	11/01/99	2/09/00	2/11/00	3/05/00
0.37Q	2/14/00	5/10/00	5/12/00	6/05/00
0.37Q	5/01/00	8/09/00	8/11/00	9/05/00

Indicated div.: $1.48 (Div. Reinv. Plan)

CAPITALIZATION (12/31/99):

	($000)	(%)
Long-Term Debt	290,000	9.3
Deferred Income Tax	87,000	2.8
Common & Surplus	2,753,000	88.0
Total	3,130,000	100.0

DIVIDEND ACHIEVER STATUS:

Rank: 106	10-Year Growth Rate: 12.46%
Total Years of Dividend Growth:	32

RECENT DEVELOPMENTS: For the year ended 12/31/99, net income increased 11.5% to $495.0 million from $444.0 million in the previous year. Results included realized investment gains of $100.6 million and $92.8 million in 1999 and 1998, respectively. Total revenues were $2.56 billion versus $2.61 billion the year before, a decrease of 1.9%.

PROSPECTS: Going forward, results should continue to benefit from strong growth in the core individual life insurance segment, in annuity sales and at the Company's radio operations. In addition, the Company expects new product introductions will bode well for future life insurance growth. Also, the Company anticipates a strong contribution from the acquisition of Guarantee Life.

BUSINESS

JEFFERSON-PILOT CORP. is a holding company that conducts insurance, investment, broadcasting and other business through its subsidiaries. Jefferson-Pilot Life Insurance Company offers both group and individual life insurance, health insurance, annuity and pension products. Other subsidiaries provide fire and casualty insurance, title insurance and mutual fund sales and management services. Jefferson-Pilot Communications Company provides information and entertainment services through three network television and 17 radio stations, and produces and syndicates sports programming. On 12/30/99, JP acquired The Guarantee Life Companies Inc. Contributions to revenues in 1999 were as follows: Premiums & other, 35.2%; Net investment income, 49.7%; Realized investment gains, 3.9%; Communications sales, 8.0%; and Other, 3.2%.

ANNUAL FINANCIAL DATA

	12/31/99	12/31/98	12/31/97	12/31/96	12/31/95	12/31/94	12/31/93
Earnings Per Share	4.42	3.91	3.47	2.73	② 2.37	② 2.10	① 1.94
Tang. Book Val. Per Share	23.71	26.66	23.59	20.84	19.54	15.40	15.22
Dividends Per Share	1.28	1.15	1.04	0.93	0.83	0.75	0.67
Dividend Payout %	29.1	29.5	30.0	34.2	35.1	35.6	34.6
INCOME STATEMENT (IN MILLIONS)							
Total Premium Income	903.0	1,049.0	1,135.0	994.0	810.0	655.3	669.8
Net Investment Income	1,272.0	1,202.0	1,103.0	893.0	540.8	375.2	369.6
Other Income	1,289.0	1,408.0	1,475.0	1,232.0	617.5	494.5	447.4
Total Revenues	2,561.0	2,610.0	2,578.0	2,125.0	1,569.4	1,268.8	1,246.6
Policyholder Benefits	1,208.0	1,307.0	1,399.0	1,211.0	842.3	627.9	629.8
Income Before Income Taxes	751.0	670.0	591.0	443.0	380.8	347.6	322.0
Income Taxes	256.0	226.0	195.0	149.0	125.4	117.7	102.8
Net Income	495.0	444.0	396.0	294.0	② 255.3	② 229.9	① 219.3
Average Shs. Outstg. (000)	106,232	107,052	106,793	106,611	107,541	109,040	113,067
BALANCE SHEET (IN MILLIONS)							
Cash & Cash Equivalents	97.0	53.0	52.0	159.0	164.2	60.6	64.0
Premiums Due	1,576.0	1,342.0	1,526.0	1,260.0	1,583.7	94.2	86.3
Invst. Assets: Fixed-term	15,182.0	14,503.0	13,945.0	10,550.0	9,985.6	3,546.9	3,221.9
Invst. Assets: Equities	737.0	949.0	893.0	929.0	862.8	718.0	833.4
Invst. Assets: Loans	3,449.0	3,408.0	3,138.0	2,535.0	2,201.4	887.0	798.2
Invst. Assets: Total	19,536.0	18,978.0	18,094.0	14,143.0	13,168.1	5,220.7	4,916.9
Total Assets	26,446.0	24,338.0	23,131.0	17,562.0	16,478.0	6,140.3	5,640.6
Long-Term Obligations	290.0	327.0	331.0	148.0	137.1	. . .	. . .
Net Stockholders' Equity	2,753.0	3,052.0	2,732.0	2,297.0	2,156.1	1,732.5	1,733.1
Year-end Shs. Outstg. (000)	103,344	105,896	106,278	106,119	106,820	109,016	111,294
STATISTICAL RECORD:							
Return on Revenues %	19.3	17.0	15.4	13.8	16.3	18.1	17.6
Return on Equity %	18.0	14.5	14.5	12.8	11.8	13.3	12.7
Return on Assets %	1.9	1.8	1.7	1.7	1.5	3.7	3.9
Price Range	79⅝-61³/₁₆	78⅜-48¹¹/₁₆	57¹³/₁₆-34⁵/₁₆	39¾-30¹/₁₆	32³/₁₆-22⁷/₁₆	24½-19¼	25¾-20¼
P/E Ratio	18.0-13.8	20.0-12.4	16.7-9.9	14.6-11.0	13.6-9.5	11.7-9.2	13.3-10.4
Average Yield %	1.8	1.8	2.3	2.7	3.0	3.4	2.9

Statistics are as originally reported. Adj. for stk. splits: 3-for-2, 4/98; 12/95 ① Bef. acctg. change chrg. $24.1 mill. ② Bef. disc. oper gain 1995, $18.5 mill.; 1994, $9.3 mill.

NYSE SYMBOL JNJ
Rec. Pr. 89½ (5/31/00)

JOHNSON & JOHNSON

YIELD 1.4%
P/E RATIO 29.9

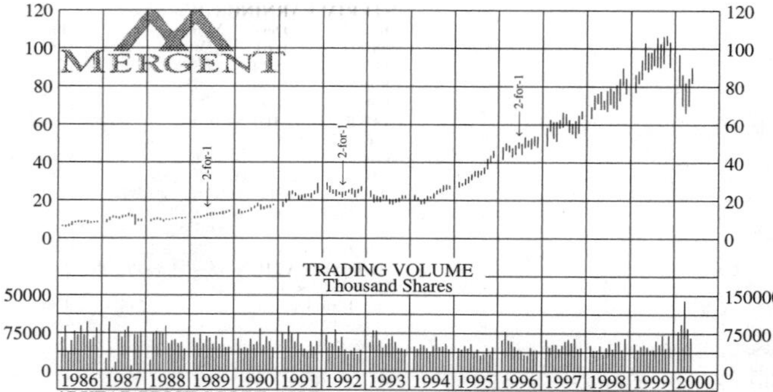

***7 YEAR PRICE SCORE 110.7** ***12 MONTH PRICE SCORE 89.5**

*NYSE COMPOSITE INDEX=100

INTERIM EARNINGS (Per Share):

Qtr.	Mar.	June	Sept.	Dec.
1996	0.60	0.60	0.56	0.42
1997	0.68	0.68	0.64	0.47
1998	0.73	0.74	0.70	0.50
1999	0.82	0.84	0.80	0.53

INTERIM DIVIDENDS (Per Share):

Amt.	Decl.	Ex.	Rec.	Pay.
0.28Q	4/22/99	5/14/99	5/18/99	6/08/99
0.28Q	7/19/99	8/13/99	8/17/99	9/07/99
0.28Q	10/18/99	11/12/99	11/16/99	12/07/99
0.28Q	1/03/00	2/11/00	2/15/00	3/07/00
0.32Q	4/19/00	5/19/00	5/23/00	6/13/00

Indicated div.: $1.28 (Div. Reinv. Plan)

CAPITALIZATION (1/2/00):

	($000)	(%)
Long-Term Debt	2,450,000	12.9
Deferred Income Tax	287,000	1.5
Common & Surplus	16,213,000	85.6
Total	18,950,000	100.0

DIVIDEND ACHIEVER STATUS:
Rank: 72 10-Year Growth Rate: 14.56%
Total Years of Dividend Growth: 37

RECENT DEVELOPMENTS: For the year ended 1/2/00, net earnings advanced 38.8% to $4.17 billion compared with $3.00 billion in the corresponding 1998 period. Results for 1999 included special after-tax charges of $42.0 million associated with the Centocor merger in 1999, the reconfiguration of the worldwide manufacturing network and acquired in-process research and development. The 1998 results included nonrecurring charges totaling $851.0 million. Worldwide sales climbed 14.5% to $27.72 billion.

PROSPECTS: The pharmaceuticals segment should continue to enjoy strong demand for PROCRIT, for the treatment of anemia, RISPERDAL, an antipsychotic medication, and DURAGESIC, a transdermal patch for chronic pain. The consumer segment is likely to continue to experience solid demand for its skin care products. On 2/11/00, JNJ completed the acquisition of Innovasive Devices, Inc., a manufacturer of surgical devices and instrumentation, for approximately $85.0 million.

BUSINESS

JOHNSON & JOHNSON is engaged in the manufacture and sale of a broad range of products in health care and other fields. The consumer segment, 25% of 1999 sales (12% of operating profit), consists of toiletries and hygienic products. The professional segment, 36% (27%), includes ligatures and sutures, mechanical wound closure products, diagnostic products, dental products, medical equipment and devices, surgical dressings, surgical apparel and accessories, surgical instruments and related items. The pharmaceutical segment, 39% (61%), consists of prescription drugs, including contraceptives and therapeutics, antifungal, and dermatological products.

ANNUAL FINANCIAL DATA

	1/2/00	1/3/99	12/28/97	12/29/96	12/31/95	1/1/95	1/2/94
Earnings Per Share	**3 2.94**	**2 2.23**	**2.41**	**2.17**	**1.86**	**1.56**	**1.37**
Cash Flow Per Share	**3.96**	**3.14**	**3.19**	**3.36**	**2.52**	**2.12**	**1.84**
Tang. Book Val. Per Share	**6.22**	**4.75**	**6.76**	**5.80**	**4.71**	**3.67**	**3.61**
Dividends Per Share	**1.16**	**0.97**	**0.85**	**0.73**	**0.64**	**0.56**	**0.51**
Dividend Payout %	**37.1**	**43.5**	**35.3**	**33.9**	**34.4**	**36.2**	**36.9**
INCOME STATEMENT (IN MILLIONS):							
Total Revenues	27,717.0	23,493.0	22,629.0	21,620.0	18,842.0	15,734.0	14,138.0
Costs & Expenses	20,101.0	17,979.0	16,940.0	16,308.0	14,474.0	12,203.0	11,127.0
Depreciation & Amort.	1,444.0	1,246.0	1,067.0	1,009.0	857.0	724.0	617.0
Operating Income	6,172.0	4,268.0	4,622.0	4,303.0	3,511.0	2,807.0	2,394.0
Net Interest Inc./(Exp.)	d197.0	152.0	83.0	14.0	d28.0	d82.0	d46.0
Income Before Income Taxes	5,753.0	4,269.0	4,576.0	4,033.0	3,317.0	2,681.0	2,332.0
Income Taxes	1,586.0	1,210.0	1,273.0	569.0	914.0	675.0	545.0
Net Income	3 4,167.0	2 3,059.0	3,303.0	3,464.0	2,403.0	2,006.0	1,787.0
Cash Flow	5,611.0	4,305.0	4,370.0	4,473.0	3,260.0	2,730.0	2,404.0
Average Shs. Outstg. (000)	1,418,200	1,371,600	1,369,900	1,333,000	1,292,000	1,286,000	1,304,000
BALANCE SHEET (IN MILLIONS):							
Cash & Cash Equivalents	3,879.0	2,578.0	2,899.0	2,136.0	1,364.0	704.0	476.0
Total Current Assets	13,200.0	11,132.0	10,563.0	9,370.0	7,938.0	6,680.0	5,217.0
Net Property	6,719.0	6,240.0	5,810.0	5,651.0	5,196.0	4,910.0	4,406.0
Total Assets	29,163.0	26,211.0	21,453.0	20,010.0	17,873.0	15,668.0	12,242.0
Total Current Liabilities	7,454.0	8,162.0	5,283.0	5,184.0	4,388.0	4,266.0	3,212.0
Long-Term Obligations	2,450.0	1,269.0	1,126.0	1,410.0	2,107.0	2,199.0	1,493.0
Net Stockholders' Equity	16,213.0	13,590.0	12,359.0	10,836.0	9,045.0	7,122.0	5,568.0
Net Working Capital	5,746.0	2,970.0	5,280.0	4,186.0	3,550.0	2,414.0	2,005.0
Year-end Shs. Outstg. (000)	1,389,683	1,344,000	1,345,000	1,332,000	1,294,000	1,286,000	1,286,000
STATISTICAL RECORD:							
Operating Profit Margin %	22.3	18.2	20.4	19.9	18.6	17.8	16.9
Net Profit Margin %	15.0	13.0	14.6	16.0	12.8	12.7	12.6
Return on Equity %	25.7	22.5	26.7	32.0	26.6	28.2	32.1
Return on Assets %	14.3	11.7	15.4	17.3	13.4	12.8	14.6
Debt/Total Assets %	8.4	4.8	5.2	7.0	11.8	14.0	12.2
Price Range	106 7/8-77	89 3/4-63 3/8	67 5/16-48 5/8	54-41 9/16	46 3/16-26 13/16	28 1/4-18	25 3/16-17 13/16
P/E Ratio	36.4-26.2	40.2-28.4	27.9-20.2	24.9-19.2	24.8-14.4	18.1-11.5	18.4-13.0
Average Yield %	1.2	1.3	1.5	1.5	1.8	2.4	2.3

Statistics are as originally reported. Adjusted for 2-for-1 stock split, 6/96. 1 Bef. loss from acctg. adj. of $595.0 mill. 2 Incl. a pre-tax in-process R&D chrg. $164.0 mill. and a pre-tax restruct. chrg. $613.0 mill. 3 Incl. nonrecurr. after-tax chrg. of $42.0 mill.

OFFICERS:
R. S. Larsen, Chmn., C.E.O.
R. N. Wilson, Vice-Chmn.
J. A. Papa, Treas.
M. U. Ullmann, Sec., Asst. Gen. Couns.

INVESTOR CONTACT: Helen E. Short, Vice President, (800) 950-5089

PRINCIPAL OFFICE: One Johnson & Johnson Plaza, New Brunswick, NJ 08933

TELEPHONE NUMBER: (732) 524-0400
FAX: (732) 214-0332
WEB: www.jnj.com

NO. OF EMPLOYEES: 97,800 (approx.)

SHAREHOLDERS: 169,384 (approx.)

ANNUAL MEETING: In Apr.

INCORPORATED: NJ, Nov., 1887

INSTITUTIONAL HOLDINGS:
No. of Institutions: 1,148
Shares Held: 782,733,543
% Held: 56.3

INDUSTRY: Pharmaceutical preparations (SIC: 2834)

TRANSFER AGENT(S): First Chicago Trust Company a Division of EquiServe, Jersey City, NJ

JOHNSON CONTROLS, INC.

YIELD	2.0%
P/E RATIO	12.2

INTERIM EARNINGS (Per Share):

Qtr.	Dec.	Mar.	June	Sept.
1996-97	0.61	0.46	0.85	1.06
1997-98	0.70	0.56	0.90	1.47
1998-99	0.86	1.05	1.19	1.38
1999-00	1.06	...	...	...

INTERIM DIVIDENDS (Per Share):

Amt.	Decl.	Ex.	Rec.	Pay.
0.25Q	5/19/99	6/09/99	6/11/99	6/30/99
0.25Q	7/28/99	9/08/99	9/10/99	9/30/99
0.28Q	11/17/99	12/13/99	12/15/99	1/05/00
0.28Q	1/26/00	3/08/00	3/10/00	3/31/00
0.28Q	5/17/00	6/07/00	6/09/00	6/30/00

Indicated div.: $1.12 (Div. Reinv. Plan)

CAPITALIZATION (9/30/99):

	($000)	(%)
Long-Term Debt	1,283,300	36.1
Preferred Stock	134,700	3.8
Common & Surplus	2,135,300	60.1
Total	3,553,300	100.0

TRADING VOLUME
Thousand Shares

DIVIDEND ACHIEVER STATUS:
Rank: 252   10-Year Growth Rate: 5.60%
Total Years of Dividend Growth: 24

*7 YEAR PRICE SCORE 97.8   ***12 MONTH PRICE SCORE 97.6**
*NYSE COMPOSITE INDEX=100

RECENT DEVELOPMENTS: For the quarter ended 12/31/99, net income rose 24.2% to $99.0 million compared with $79.7 million in the corresponding quarter of 1998. Net sales were $4.32 billion, up 11.5% from $3.87 billion in the prior-year period. Sales in the Automotive Group, which rose 11.3% to $3.34 billion, benefited from solid demand in the North American market for the Company's seating systems, interior systems and batteries. Operating income increased 17.4% to $215.0 million.

PROSPECTS: The Company introduced the Cardkey PEGASYS 2000 security management system for Microsoft Windows NT®. The system allows users to manage all the electronic security devices for an organization from one location. Separately, the Company's majority-owned joint venture, Brookfield LePage Johnson Controls, entered into a $1.36 billion agreement to manage the Canadian Real Estate operations of Royal Bank of Canada. The five-year contract will be effective 7/1/00.

BUSINESS

JOHNSON CONTROLS, INC. operates in two business segments. The Automotive segment is engaged in the design and manufacture of complete seat systems, seating components and interior trim systems for North American and European manufacturers of cars, vans and light trucks. The Controls segment is a worldwide supplier of control systems, services and products providing energy management, temperature and ventilation control, security and fire safety for non-residential buildings. On 7/1/98, JCI acquired Becker Group, Inc., a supplier of automotive interior systems, which include door systems and instrument panels. Also, JCI completed the sale of its plastics machinery division to Milacron, Inc. for about $190.0 million on 9/30/98.

ANNUAL FINANCIAL DATA

	9/30/99	9/30/98	9/30/97	9/30/96	9/30/95	9/30/94	9/30/93
Earnings Per Share	⑤ 4.48	④ 3.63	③ 2.48	② 2.55	2.27	1.90	① 0.09
Cash Flow Per Share	5.36	7.78	6.67	6.49	5.76	5.05	4.50
Tang. Book Val. Per Share	...	...	...	9.70	8.04	6.69	7.60
Dividends Per Share	1.00	0.92	0.86	0.82	0.78	0.72	0.68
Dividend Payout %	22.3	25.3	34.7	32.2	34.4	37.9	799.1
INCOME STATEMENT (IN MILLIONS):							
Total Revenues	16,139.4	12,586.8	11,145.4	9,210.0	8,330.3	6,870.5	6,181.7
Costs & Expenses	14,838.9	11,538.6	10,263.4	8,401.4	7,593.0	6,247.0	5,645.1
Depreciation & Amort.	445.6	384.2	354.9	329.7	288.5	258.3	238.3
Operating Income	854.9	664.0	527.1	478.9	448.8	365.2	298.3
Net Interest Inc./(Exp.)	d136.0	d118.7	d112.8	d65.5	d97.6	d82.9	d41.9
Income Before Income Taxes	769.9	616.8	425.6	421.5	387.9	326.4	250.7
Income Taxes	311.7	256.0	180.9	171.8	162.9	140.3	112.8
Equity Earnings/Minority Int.	d38.6	d23.1	d24.1	d27.0	d29.2	d20.9	...
Net Income	⑤ 419.6	④ 337.7	③ 220.6	② 222.7	195.8	165.2	① 137.9
Cash Flow	852.2	712.4	565.9	542.9	474.9	414.2	367.1
Average Shs. Outstg. (000)	92,100	91,600	84,800	83,600	82,400	82,000	81,600
BALANCE SHEET (IN MILLIONS):							
Cash & Cash Equivalents	276.2	134.0	111.8	165.2	103.8	132.6	87.7
Total Current Assets	3,848.5	3,404.2	2,529.3	2,849.1	2,063.9	1,778.5	1,532.0
Net Property	1,996.0	1,882.9	1,533.0	1,320.2	1,518.8	1,333.4	1,213.6
Total Assets	8,614.2	7,942.1	6,048.6	4,991.2	4,320.9	3,806.9	3,230.8
Total Current Liabilities	4,266.6	4,288.4	2,972.7	2,182.6	1,909.5	1,516.4	1,284.9
Long-Term Obligations	1,283.3	997.5	706.4	752.2	630.0	670.3	500.4
Net Stockholders' Equity	2,270.0	1,941.4	1,687.9	1,507.8	1,340.2	1,202.8	1,079.0
Net Working Capital	d418.1	d884.2	d443.4	666.5	154.4	262.1	247.1
Year-end Shs. Outstg. (000)	85,395	84,700	84,100	83,000	82,200	81,400	77,600
STATISTICAL RECORD:							
Operating Profit Margin %	5.3	5.3	4.7	5.2	5.4	5.3	4.8
Net Profit Margin %	2.6	2.7	2.0	2.4	2.4	2.4	2.2
Return on Equity %	18.5	17.4	13.1	14.8	14.6	13.7	12.8
Return on Assets %	4.9	4.3	3.6	4.5	4.5	4.3	4.3
Debt/Total Assets %	14.9	12.6	11.7	15.1	14.6	17.6	15.5
Price Range	76¹¹/₁₆-49	61⁷/₈-40¹/₂	51-35³/₈	42¹¹/₁₆-27¹/₄	34⁷/₈-22⁷/₈	30⁷/₈-22⁷/₁₆	29³/₁₆-21¹/₂
P/E Ratio	17.1-10.9	17.0-11.2	20.6-14.3	16.7-12.3	15.4-10.1	16.2-11.8	347.4-252.6
Average Yield %	1.6	1.8	2.0	2.4	2.7	2.7	2.7

Statistics are as originally reported. Adj. for 100% stk. div., 3/97. ① Bef. $122.0 mill. ($2.99/sh) acct. chg. ② Bef. $12.0 mill. chg. fr. disc. ops. ③ Bef. $67.9 mill. disc. ops. ④ Incl. $35.0 mill. after-tax gain fr. sale of bus. ⑤ Incl. $32.5 mill. net one-time gain on sale of bus.

OFFICERS:
J. H. Keyes, Chmn., C.E.O.
J. M. Barth, Pres., C.O.O.
S. A. Roell, Sr. V.P., C.F.O.
B. C. Bastianen, Treas.

INVESTOR CONTACT: Arlene Gumm,
Investor Relations, (414) 228-1200

PRINCIPAL OFFICE: 5757 North Green Bay
Avenue, Milwaukee, WI 53201

TELEPHONE NUMBER: (414) 228-1200
FAX: (414) 228-2646
WEB: www.johnsoncontrols.com

NO. OF EMPLOYEES: 95,000

SHAREHOLDERS: 61,225

ANNUAL MEETING: In Jan.

INCORPORATED: WI, Jul., 1900

INSTITUTIONAL HOLDINGS:
No. of Institutions: 300
Shares Held: 53,097,080
% Held: 62.2

INDUSTRY: Building maintenance services,
nec (SIC: 7349)

TRANSFER AGENT(S): Firstar Trust
Company, Milwaukee, WI.

NASDAQ SYMBOL JMED
Rec. Pr. 36 7/16 (5/31/00)

JONES PHARMA INCORPORATED

YIELD 0.2%
P/E RATIO 49.2

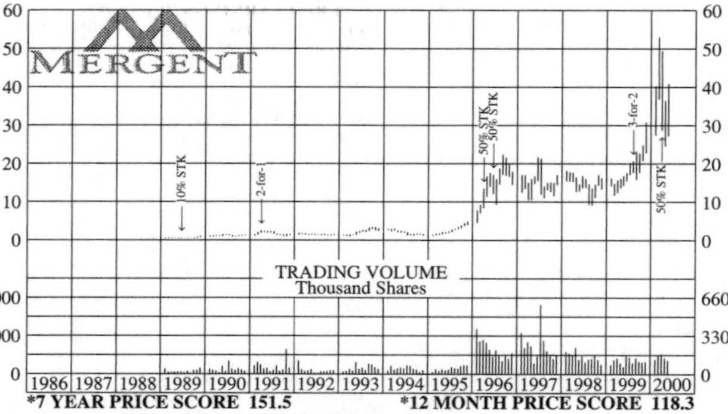

*7 YEAR PRICE SCORE 151.5 *12 MONTH PRICE SCORE 118.3

*NYSE COMPOSITE INDEX=100

INTERIM EARNINGS (Per Share):

Qtr.	Mar.	June	Sept.	Dec.
1996	0.10	0.13	0.04	0.16
1997	0.19	0.15	0.19	0.21
1998	0.17	d0.05	0.20	0.22
1999	0.22	0.26	0.28	0.34

INTERIM DIVIDENDS (Per Share):

Amt.	Decl.	Ex.	Rec.	Pay.
3-for-2	7/14/99	8/09/99	7/26/99	8/06/99
0.025Q	7/14/99	9/13/99	9/15/99	10/01/99
0.025Q	10/19/99	12/13/99	12/15/99	1/03/00
50% STK	2/03/00	3/02/00	2/15/00	3/01/00
0.02Q	2/03/00	3/22/00	3/24/00	4/03/00

Indicated div.: $0.08

CAPITALIZATION (12/31/99):

	($000)	(%)
Deferred Income Tax	5,135	1.8
Common & Surplus	279,604	98.2
Total	284,739	100.0

DIVIDEND ACHIEVER STATUS:
Rank: 11 10-Year Growth Rate: 23.16%
Total Years of Dividend Growth: 10

RECENT DEVELOPMENTS: For the year ended 12/31/99, the Company reported net income of $48.9 million compared with income of $23.6 million, from continuing operations, in the previous year. Sales from continuing operations increased 28.2% to $132.5 million from $103.4 million the year before. This increase was primarily due to increases in net pricing arising in part from renegotiation of contract pricing for THROMBINJMI and other key products throughout 1999. Endocrine product sales improved 23.0% to $71.3 million from $57.9 million in 1998 primarily due to a 31.0% increase in LEVOXYL sales. Critical Care product sales advanced 44.0% to $52.4 million primarily due to thrombin product sales increases. Gross profit grew 35.1% to $107.5 million, or 81.1% of sales, versus $103.4 million, or 76.9% of sales a year earlier as a result of more favorable contract pricing, increased sales of higher-margin products, and control of product costs. Operating income from continuing operations totaled $73.1 million, up 83.1% from $39.6 million a year ago.

BUSINESS

JONES PHARMA INCORPORATED (formerly Jones Medical Industries, Inc.) manufactures, markets and distributes critical care pharmaceutical products. These products are marketed under JMED's trademarks and trade names. JMED's strategy is to generate growth through its portfolio of pharmaceutical products and to acquire additional specialty pharmaceutical product lines or operations that complement or expand the marketing or distribution of its existing product line. JMED's principal products serve the endocrine treatment and the critical care segments of the health care industry as well as the companion animal segment of the veterinary industry. JMED's principal products include TAPAZOLE, LEVOXYL, TRIOSTAT, CYTOMEL, THROMBINJMI, BREVITAL SODIUM, SOLOXINE, TUSSIGON, LIQUICHAR, THEREVAC, DERMASCRUB and PAN CREZYME. On 4/30/98, JMED sold its nutritional supplement business for $55.0 million.

ANNUAL FINANCIAL DATA

	12/31/99	12/31/98	12/31/97	12/31/96	12/31/95	12/31/94	12/31/93
Earnings Per Share	**0.73**	**[1] 0.36**	**[2] 0.38**	**[1] 0.29**	**0.19**	**0.12**	**0.13**
Cash Flow Per Share	**0.83**	**0.47**	**0.47**	**0.35**	**0.24**	**0.16**	**0.17**
Tang. Book Val. Per Share	**3.33**	**2.57**	**1.59**	**1.44**	**0.35**	**0.45**	**0.31**
Dividends Per Share	**0.06**	**0.05**	**0.04**	**0.03**	**0.02**	**0.019**	**0.016**
Dividend Payout %	**8.1**	**13.8**	**10.6**	**10.8**	**10.9**	**16.7**	**12.9**
INCOME STATEMENT (IN THOUSANDS):							
Total Revenues	132,544	103,414	88,781	100,153	56,397	47,549	43,215
Costs & Expenses	53,238	47,377	44,590	61,743	38,674	36,023	31,443
Depreciation & Amort.	6,204	5,603	6,111	3,992	2,397	2,161	1,781
Operating Income	73,102	39,934	38,080	28,674	15,326	9,365	9,992
Net Interest Inc./(Exp.)	7,193	4,871	2,324	1,723	d279	d415	d165
Income Before Income Taxes	80,108	44,817	40,395	30,429	14,925	9,039	9,948
Income Taxes	31,164	21,250	15,351	12,290	5,597	3,299	3,744
Net Income	48,944	[1] 23,567	[2] 25,044	[1] 18,139	9,328	5,740	6,204
Cash Flow	55,148	29,170	31,155	22,131	11,721	7,875	7,947
Average Shs. Outstg.	66,671	62,522	65,804	63,109	49,238	48,570	48,116
BALANCE SHEET (IN THOUSANDS):							
Cash & Cash Equivalents	174,231	122,745	49,877	52,172	5,411	7,032	2,320
Total Current Assets	206,810	153,977	85,113	80,551	25,012	20,793	18,326
Net Property	24,509	23,692	27,543	24,170	15,443	12,603	10,460
Total Assets	300,465	248,778	204,228	177,233	74,697	54,927	51,824
Total Current Liabilities	15,726	11,722	6,580	10,031	11,563	5,779	6,330
Long-Term Obligations	...	...	...	...	9,125	3,800	5,400
Net Stockholders' Equity	279,604	232,670	191,726	161,920	49,890	41,490	36,236
Net Working Capital	191,084	142,255	78,533	70,519	13,449	15,015	11,995
Year-end Shs. Outstg.	65,156	64,798	64,456	63,980	47,851	46,732	45,320
STATISTICAL RECORD:							
Operating Profit Margin %	55.2	38.6	42.9	28.6	27.2	19.7	23.1
Net Profit Margin %	36.9	22.8	28.2	18.1	16.5	12.1	14.4
Return on Equity %	17.5	10.1	13.1	11.2	18.7	13.8	17.1
Return on Assets %	16.3	9.5	12.3	10.2	12.5	10.4	12.0
Debt/Total Assets %	...	...	...	...	12.2	6.9	10.4
Price Range	30 13/16-11 3/4	18 3/16-9 1/8	21 11/16-10 1/2	22 7/16-4 5/8	4 7/8-1 1/4	3 1/16-1 1/4	3 7/16-1
P/E Ratio	42.2-16.1	51.2-25.7	57.3-27.8	77.6-16.0	25.6-6.5	25.9-10.7	26.6-7.8
Average Yield %	0.3	0.4	0.2	0.2	0.7	0.9	0.8

Statistics are as originally reported. Adj. for stk. splits: 3-for-2, 3/2/00; 8/6/99; 6/10/96; 3/1/96 [1] Incl. non-recurr. chrg. 12/31/98: $10.5 mill.; 12/31/96: $5.7 mill. [2] Bef. disc. oper. gain $6.9 mill. ($0.24/sh.)

OFFICERS:
D. M. Jones, Chmn., Pres., C.E.O.
J. A. Jones, Exec. V.P., Sec., Treas.
G. A. Franz, Exec. V.P., Oper., C.O.O.

PRINCIPAL OFFICE: 1945 Craig Road, St. Louis, MO 63146

TELEPHONE NUMBER: (314) 576-6100
FAX: (314) 469-5749
WEB: www.jmedpharma.com
NO. OF EMPLOYEES: 381
SHAREHOLDERS: 865
ANNUAL MEETING: In May
INCORPORATED: DE, Mar., 1981

INSTITUTIONAL HOLDINGS:
No. of Institutions: 165
Shares Held: 28,278,129
% Held: 43.5
INDUSTRY: Pharmaceutical preparations (SIC: 2834)
TRANSFER AGENT(S): United Missouri Bank, Kansas City, MO

NYSE SYMBOL KLT
Rec. Pr. 23 11/16 (5/31/00)

KANSAS CITY POWER & LIGHT COMPANY

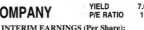

YIELD 7.0%
P/E RATIO 18.7

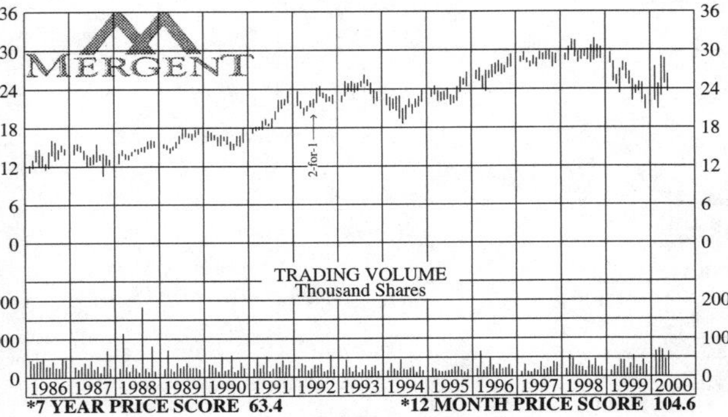

*7 YEAR PRICE SCORE 63.4 *12 MONTH PRICE SCORE 104.6

*NYSE COMPOSITE INDEX=100

INTERIM EARNINGS (Per Share):

Qtr.	Mar.	June	Sept.	Dec.
1996	0.38	0.43	0.57	0.31
1997	0.26	0.37	0.92	0.37
1998	0.22	0.60	0.94	0.13
1999	0.18	0.39	0.59	0.11

INTERIM DIVIDENDS (Per Share):

Amt.	Decl.	Ex.	Rec.	Pay.
0.415Q	8/03/99	8/25/99	8/27/99	9/20/99
0.415Q	11/02/99	11/24/99	11/29/99	12/20/99
0.415Q	2/01/00	2/24/00	2/28/00	3/20/00
0.415Q	5/02/00	5/25/00	5/30/00	6/20/00

Indicated div.: $1.66 (Div. Reinv. Plan)

CAPITALIZATION (12/31/99):

	($000)	(%)
Long-Term Debt	685,884	29.4
Deferred Income Tax	592,227	25.4
Redeemable Pfd. Stock	150,062	6.4
Preferred Stock	39,000	1.7
Common & Surplus	864,644	37.1
Total	2,331,817	100.0

DIVIDEND ACHIEVER STATUS:
Rank: 301 10-Year Growth Rate: 2.88%
Total Years of Dividend Growth: 14

RECENT DEVELOPMENTS: For the year ended 12/31/99, net income fell 32.1% to $81.9 million from $120.7 million in 1998. Results for 1999 included a net gain of $1.7 million and a net loss of $15.0 million related to a proposed merger. Earnings fell due to unfavorable weather conditions, higher purchased power expenses, increased operating expenses, a rate reduction and losses at Home Services Solutions. Operating revenues fell 4.4% to $897.4 million.

PROSPECTS: On 2/1/00, KLT changed its method of amortizing unrecognized net gains and losses and the determination of expected return related to its accounting for pension expenses. The accounting change should reduce pension costs by $10.0 million and increase earnings by $0.10 per share in 2000. In addition, KLT estimates expenses related to the Hawthorn #5 power plant explosion of $31.0 million and $3.0 million in 2000 and 2001, respectively.

BUSINESS

KANSAS CITY POWER & LIGHT COMPANY is engaged in the generation, transmission, distribution and sale of electricity to approximately 463,000 customers located in all or portions of 31 counties in western Missouri and eastern Kansas. The Company customers include approximately 407,000 residences, 53,000 commercial firms, and 3,000 industrials, municipalities and other electric utilities. Retail electric revenues in Missouri and Kansas accounted for approximately 93% of KCPL's total electric revenues in 1999. KLT Inc. and Home Service Solutions, Inc., wholly-owned subsidiaries of KLT, pursue unregulated business ventures nationally, seeking growth opportunities in markets outside the regulated utility business.

ANNUAL FINANCIAL DATA

	12/31/99	12/31/98	12/31/97	12/31/96	12/31/95	12/31/94	12/31/93
Earnings Per Share	**[2] 1.26**	**1.89**	**[1] 1.18**	**1.69**	**1.92**	**1.64**	**1.66**
Cash Flow Per Share	**3.63**	**4.21**	**3.34**	**3.90**	**4.06**	**3.69**	**3.61**
Tang. Book Val. Per Share	**13.97**	**14.41**	**14.19**	**14.71**	**14.51**	**14.13**	**13.99**
Dividends Per Share	**1.66**	**1.64**	**1.62**	**1.59**	**1.54**	**1.50**	**1.46**
Dividend Payout %	**131.7**	**86.8**	**137.3**	**94.1**	**80.2**	**91.5**	**87.9**
INCOME STATEMENT (IN MILLIONS):							
Total Revenues	897.4	938.9	895.9	903.9	886.0	868.3	857.5
Costs & Expenses	485.8	461.3	453.9	449.3	430.7	448.0	431.9
Depreciation & Amort.	146.5	143.7	137.3	137.1	132.7	127.2	121.2
Maintenance Exp.	62.6	71.0	70.9	71.5	78.4	72.5	78.6
Operating Income	143.9	184.2	[1] 162.7	177.8	167.0	149.7	156.3
Net Interest Inc./(Exp.)	d68.3	d71.7	d72.2	d58.1	d54.5	d47.4	d52.4
Income Taxes	3.2	32.8	8.1	31.8	66.8	66.4	68.0
Net Income	[2] 81.9	120.7	[1] 76.6	108.2	122.6	104.8	105.8
Cash Flow	224.7	260.5	210.1	241.5	251.2	228.5	223.8
Average Shs. Outstg. (000)	61,898	61,884	62,895	61,902	61,902	61,903	61,909
BALANCE SHEET (IN MILLIONS):							
Gross Property	3,815.2	3,727.2	3,637.7	3,581.7	3,515.6	3,428.6	3,338.0
Accumulated Depreciation	1,516.3	1,410.8	1,314.2	1,238.2	1,156.1	1,092.4	1,019.7
Net Property	2,298.9	2,316.4	2,323.6	2,343.5	2,359.5	2,336.1	2,318.3
Total Assets	2,990.1	3,012.4	3,058.0	2,914.5	2,882.5	2,770.4	2,755.1
Long-Term Obligations	685.9	749.3	934.0	944.1	835.7	798.5	733.7
Net Stockholders' Equity	903.6	980.8	967.4	999.5	988.4	965.3	956.9
Year-end Shs. Outstg. (000)	61,909	61,909	61,909	61,902	61,902	61,909	61,909
STATISTICAL RECORD:							
Operating Profit Margin %	16.0	19.6	18.2	19.7	18.9	17.2	18.2
Net Profit Margin %	9.1	12.9	8.5	12.0	13.8	12.1	12.3
Net Inc./Net Property %	3.6	5.2	3.3	4.6	5.2	4.5	4.6
Net Inc./Tot. Capital %	3.5	5.1	2.8	4.2	5.0	4.4	4.6
Return on Equity %	9.1	12.3	7.9	10.8	12.4	10.9	11.1
Accum. Depr./Gross Prop. %	39.7	38.3	36.5	35.0	33.4	32.2	30.8
Price Range	29 5/8-20 13/16	31 13/16-28	29 15/16-27 3/8	29 3/8-23 5/8	26 5/8-21 1/2	23 7/8-18 5/8	26 1/4-21 3/4
P/E Ratio	23.5-16.5	16.8-14.8	25.4-23.2	17.4-14.0	13.9-11.2	14.6-11.4	15.8-13.1
Average Yield %	6.6	5.5	5.7	6.0	6.4	7.1	6.1

Statistics are as originally reported. [1] Incl. non-recurr. chrg. $60.0 mill. [2] Incl. net gain of $1.7 mill. and net loss of $15.0 mill.

OFFICERS:
D. Jennings, Chmn., C.E.O.
B. J. Beaudoin, Pres.
M. Jackson, Exec. V.P., C.F.O.
A. F. Bielsker, V.P., Fin., Treas.

INVESTOR CONTACT: Susan M. Johnson, (816) 556-2312

PRINCIPAL OFFICE: 1201 Walnut Ave., Kansas City, MO 64106-2124

TELEPHONE NUMBER: (816) 556-2200
FAX: (816) 556-2924
WEB: www.kcpl.com

NO. OF EMPLOYEES: 2,222 (avg.)

SHAREHOLDERS: 20,661

ANNUAL MEETING: In May

INCORPORATED: MO, July, 1922

INSTITUTIONAL HOLDINGS:
No. of Institutions: 142
Shares Held: 18,141,857
% Held: 29.3

INDUSTRY: Power transmission equipment, nec (SIC: 3568)

TRANSFER AGENT(S): UMB Bank, N.A., Kansas City, MO

KAYDON CORPORATION

	YIELD	1.9%
	P/E RATIO	12.6

INTERIM EARNINGS (Per Share):

Qtr.	Mar.	June	Sept.	Dec.
1996	0.37	0.40	0.37	0.39
1997	0.42	0.48	0.47	0.49
1998	0.55	0.57	0.54	0.51
1999	0.50	0.50	0.41	0.44

INTERIM DIVIDENDS (Per Share):

Amt.	Decl.	Ex.	Rec.	Pay.
0.10Q	4/30/99	6/10/99	6/14/99	7/05/99
0.10Q	7/30/99	9/09/99	9/13/99	10/04/99
0.11Q	11/01/99	12/10/99	12/14/99	1/03/00
0.11Q	2/22/00	3/09/00	3/13/00	4/03/00
0.11Q	5/04/00	6/08/00	6/12/00	7/03/00
	Indicated div.: $0.44			

TRADING VOLUME
Thousand Shares

CAPITALIZATION (12/31/99):

	($000)	(%)
Common & Surplus	316,950	100.0
Total	316,950	100.0

*7 YEAR PRICE SCORE 81.5   *12 MONTH PRICE SCORE 88.0
*NYSE COMPOSITE INDEX=100

DIVIDEND ACHIEVER STATUS:
Rank: 32   10-Year Growth Rate: 18.22%
Total Years of Dividend Growth: 12

RECENT DEVELOPMENTS: For the year ended 12/31/99, net income declined 17.4% to $58.8 million compared with $71.2 million in 1998. Net sales were $325.7 million, down 13.4% from $376.2 million a year earlier. Gross profit was 38.6% of net sales compared with gross profit of 40.5% of net sales in 1998. The Company had a challenging and disappointing year as many of its major markets did not have the anticipated second-half recovery.

PROSPECTS: During the quarter, KDN's completed two strategic acquisitions, with combined annual sales of approximately $12.0 million. Filterdyne Filtration Systems, Inc. is a manufacturer of custom-designed filtration and vacuum distillation systems. Filterdyne's product lines will strengthen and complement KDN's Filtration Division. Focal Technologies, Inc. designs and manufactures fiber optic, electronic data and fluid transmission devices.

BUSINESS

KAYDON CORPORATION designs, manufactures and sells custom-engineered products for a broad and diverse customer base primarily in domestic markets. The Company's principal products include antifriction bearings, bearing systems and components, filters and filter housings, specialty retraining rings, specialty balls, custom rings, shaft seals, hydraulic cylinders, metal castings and various types of slip-rings. These products are used by customers in a wide variety of medical, instrumentation, material handling, machine tool positioning, aerospace, defense, construction and other industrial applications. The Company aims to provide cost-effective solutions for its customers through close engineering relationships with manufacturers throughout the world.

ANNUAL FINANCIAL DATA

	12/31/99	12/31/98	12/31/97	12/31/96	12/31/95	12/31/94	12/31/93
Earnings Per Share	1.85	2.17	1.86	1.53	1.14	☐ 0.94	0.80
Cash Flow Per Share	2.34	2.59	2.24	1.88	1.47	1.25	1.10
Tang. Book Val. Per Share	7.78	7.68	6.57	5.42	3.91	3.69	3.00
Dividends Per Share	0.40	0.36	0.28	0.24	0.22	0.20	0.18
Dividend Payout %	21.6	16.6	15.1	15.7	19.3	21.4	22.5
INCOME STATEMENT (IN THOUSANDS):							
Total Revenues	325,696	376,172	329,036	290,670	229,924	204,695	184,060
Costs & Expenses	220,894	251,748	220,599	199,967	159,462	144,295	129,482
Depreciation & Amort.	15,634	14,044	12,756	11,749	11,176	10,641	10,264
Operating Income	89,168	110,380	95,681	78,954	59,286	49,759	44,314
Net Interest Inc./(Exp.)	4,877	4,434	3,780	2,662	2,505	609	142
Income Before Income Taxes	94,045	114,814	99,461	81,616	61,791	50,368	44,456
Income Taxes	35,266	43,630	37,795	31,095	23,588	19,142	16,761
Net Income	58,779	71,184	61,666	50,521	38,203	☐ 31,226	27,695
Cash Flow	74,413	85,228	74,422	62,270	49,379	41,867	37,959
Average Shs. Outstg.	31,775	32,871	33,163	33,098	33,482	33,452	34,626
BALANCE SHEET (IN THOUSANDS):							
Cash & Cash Equivalents	89,749	96,203	96,802	83,267	47,159	39,667	24,528
Total Current Assets	211,553	229,800	214,778	186,056	135,454	126,788	106,520
Net Property	98,844	99,259	85,510	76,176	72,345	61,247	60,077
Total Assets	406,749	413,808	383,985	331,538	267,675	243,584	217,422
Total Current Liabilities	54,183	71,200	71,015	66,824	44,047	40,902	34,710
Long-Term Obligations	...	...	...	4,000	8,000	8,000	13,688
Net Stockholders' Equity	316,950	311,656	283,596	232,056	187,905	166,570	143,840
Net Working Capital	157,370	158,600	143,763	119,232	91,407	85,886	71,810
Year-end Shs. Outstg.	31,097	32,150	32,992	32,934	35,266	33,296	33,380
STATISTICAL RECORD:							
Operating Profit Margin %	27.4	29.3	29.1	27.2	25.8	24.3	24.1
Net Profit Margin %	18.0	18.9	18.7	17.4	16.6	15.3	15.0
Return on Equity %	18.5	22.8	21.7	21.8	20.3	18.7	19.3
Return on Assets %	14.5	17.2	16.1	15.2	14.3	12.8	12.7
Debt/Total Assets %	...	...	...	1.2	3.0	3.3	6.3
Price Range	41 1/16-23	45 15/16-22 13/16	34 15/16-20 7/8	24 3/4-14 7/16	15 13/16-11 3/8	12 5/8-9 7/8	16-8 3/4
P/E Ratio	22.2-12.4	21.2-10.5	18.8-11.2	16.2-9.5	13.9-10.0	13.5-10.6	20.0-10.9
Average Yield %	1.2	1.0	1.0	1.2	1.6	1.8	1.5

Statistics are as originally reported. Adj. for stk. splits: 2-for-1, 10/97. ☐ Bef. acctg. change chrg. of $2.0 mill. ($0.06/sh.).

OFFICERS:
L. J. Cawley, Chmn.
B. P. Campbell, Pres., C.E.O., C.F.O.
J. F. Brocci, V.P., Admin., Sec.

INVESTOR CONTACT: Brian P. Campbell, (734) 747-7025-131

PRINCIPAL OFFICE: 315 East Eisenhower Parkway, Suite 300, Ann Arbor, MI 48108

TELEPHONE NUMBER: (734) 747-7025
FAX: (734) 747-6565
WEB: www.kaydon.com

NO. OF EMPLOYEES: 2,362

SHAREHOLDERS: 1,224

ANNUAL MEETING: In Apr.

INCORPORATED: DE, Oct., 1983

INSTITUTIONAL HOLDINGS:
No. of Institutions: 130
Shares Held: 24,797,460
% Held: 80.5

INDUSTRY: Ball and roller bearings (SIC: 3562)

TRANSFER AGENT(S): Continental Stock Transfer & Trust Company, New York, NY.

NYSE SYMBOL K
Rec. Pr. 30⅜ (5/31/00)

KELLOGG COMPANY

YIELD 3.2%
P/E RATIO 36.2

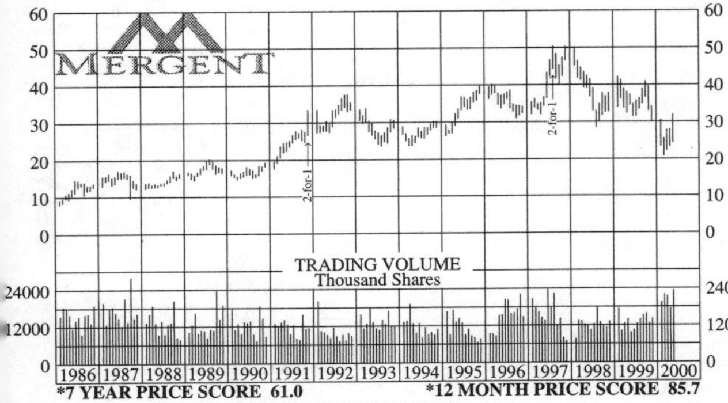

*7 YEAR PRICE SCORE 61.0 *12 MONTH PRICE SCORE 85.7

*NYSE COMPOSITE INDEX=100

INTERIM EARNINGS (Per Share):

Qtr.	Mar.	June	Sept.	Dec.
1995	0.45	0.31	0.53	d0.17
1996	0.48	0.19	0.38	0.21
1997	0.39	0.40	0.50	0.08
1998	0.42	0.35	0.35	0.11
1999	0.29	0.38	d0.08	0.25

INTERIM DIVIDENDS (Per Share):

Amt.	Decl.	Ex.	Rec.	Pay.
0.245Q	7/30/99	8/27/99	8/31/99	9/15/99
0.245Q	10/29/99	11/26/99	11/30/99	12/15/99
0.245Q	2/18/00	2/25/00	2/29/00	3/15/00
0.245Q	4/28/00	5/26/00	5/31/00	6/15/00

Indicated div.: $0.98 (Div. Reinv. Plan)

CAPITALIZATION (12/31/99):

	($000)	(%)
Long-Term Debt	1,612,800	66.5
Common & Surplus	813,200	33.5
Total	2,426,000	100.0

DIVIDEND ACHIEVER STATUS:
Rank: 191 10-Year Growth Rate: 8.36%
Total Years of Dividend Growth: 43

RECENT DEVELOPMENTS: For the year ended 12/31/99, net earnings slid 32.7% to $338.3 million from $502.6 million the previous year. Results in the recent period were hampered by pre-tax restructuring charges totaling $244.6 million and pre-tax disposition-related charges of $168.5 million. Earnings in the prior-year included a pre-tax restructuring charge of $70.5 million. Net sales rose 3.3% to $6.98 billion from $6.76 billion a year earlier.

PROSPECTS: Long-term revenue growth is expected to be driven by the roll out of new cereal brands and convenience foods that cater to consumers looking for healthier alternatives. The Company plans to launch an aggressive advertising and promotional campaign during 2000 aimed at accelerating growth of its vegetarian and other healthful foods. Advertising spending for the campaign is expected to more than double the amount spent in 1999.

BUSINESS

KELLOGG COMPANY is a major producer of ready-to-eat cereal products and convenience foods such as frozen pies, toaster pastries, frozen waffles, cereal bars, and other snack items. Brand names include KELLOGG'S, SPECIAL K, RICE KRISPIES, EGGO, POP-TARTS, NUTRI-GRAIN, and MORNINGSTAR FARMS. Products are manufactured in 20 countries and distributed in 160 countries, including many in Asia, Australia, Europe, Africa and Latin America. Contributions to sales (and operating profit) in 1999 were: North America, 62% (67%); Europe, 23% (18%); Latin America, 8% (11%); and Asia-Pacific, 7% (4%).

ANNUAL FINANCIAL DATA

	12/31/99	12/31/98	12/31/97	12/31/96	12/31/95	12/31/94	12/31/93
Earnings Per Share	[2] **0.83**	[2] **1.23**	[2][3] **1.36**	[1] **1.25**	[1] **1.12**	[2] **1.58**	[2] **1.47**
Cash Flow Per Share	**1.54**	**1.91**	**2.06**	**1.84**	**1.71**	**2.14**	**2.04**
Tang. Book Val. Per Share	**2.01**	**2.20**	**2.43**	**3.06**	**3.67**	**4.08**	**3.63**
Dividends Per Share	**0.96**	**0.92**	**0.87**	**0.81**	**0.75**	**0.70**	**0.66**
Dividend Payout %	**115.6**	**74.8**	**64.0**	**64.8**	**67.0**	**44.4**	**44.9**
INCOME STATEMENT (IN MILLIONS):							
Total Revenues	6,984.2	6,762.1	6,830.1	6,676.6	7,003.7	6,562.0	6,295.4
Costs & Expenses	5,867.4	5,588.8	5,533.7	5,466.2	5,907.4	5,143.3	4,961.3
Depreciation & Amort.	288.0	278.1	287.3	251.5	258.8	256.1	265.2
Operating Income	828.8	895.1	1,009.1	958.9	837.5	1,162.6	1,068.9
Net Interest Inc./(Exp.)	d118.8	d119.5	d108.3	d65.6	d62.6	d45.4	d33.3
Income Before Income Taxes	536.7	782.5	904.5	859.9	796.0	1,130.0	1,034.1
Income Taxes	198.4	279.9	340.5	328.9	305.7	424.6	353.4
Net Income	[2] 338.3	[2] 502.6	[2][3] 564.0	[1] 531.0	[1] 490.3	[2] 705.4	[2] 680.7
Cash Flow	626.3	780.9	851.3	782.5	749.1	961.5	945.9
Average Shs. Outstg. (000)	405,700	408,600	414,100	424,900	438,300	448,400	463,000
BALANCE SHEET (IN MILLIONS):							
Cash & Cash Equivalents	150.6	136.4	173.2	243.8	221.9	266.3	98.1
Total Current Assets	1,569.2	1,496.5	1,467.7	1,528.6	1,428.8	1,433.5	1,245.1
Net Property	2,640.9	2,888.8	2,773.3	2,932.9	2,784.8	2,892.8	2,768.4
Total Assets	4,808.7	5,051.5	4,877.6	5,050.0	4,414.6	4,467.3	4,237.1
Total Current Liabilities	1,587.8	1,718.5	1,657.3	2,199.0	1,265.4	1,185.2	1,214.6
Long-Term Obligations	1,612.8	1,614.5	1,415.4	726.7	717.8	719.2	521.6
Net Stockholders' Equity	813.2	889.8	997.5	1,282.4	1,590.9	1,807.5	1,713.4
Net Working Capital	d18.6	d222.0	d189.6	d670.4	163.4	248.3	30.5
Year-end Shs. Outstg. (000)	405,500	405,000	410,800	419,296	433,410	443,402	455,840
STATISTICAL RECORD:							
Operating Profit Margin %	11.9	13.2	14.8	14.4	12.0	17.7	17.0
Net Profit Margin %	4.8	7.4	8.3	8.0	7.0	10.7	10.8
Return on Equity %	41.6	56.5	56.5	41.4	30.8	39.0	39.7
Return on Assets %	7.0	9.9	11.6	10.5	11.1	15.8	16.1
Debt/Total Assets %	33.5	32.0	29.0	14.4	16.3	16.1	12.3
Price Range	42¼-30	50³⁄₁₆-28½	50½-32	40⁵⁄₁₆-31	39¾-26¼	30⅜-23¹¹⁄₁₆	33¹⁵⁄₁₆-23⅝
P/E Ratio	50.9-36.1	40.8-23.2	37.1-23.5	32.2-24.8	35.5-23.4	19.3-15.0	23.1-16.1
Average Yield %	2.7	2.3	2.1	2.3	2.3	2.6	2.3

Statistics are as originally reported. Adj. for 2-for-1 stk. split, 8/97. [1] Incl. discont. opers. loss $120.1 mil, 1996; & loss $271.3 mil, 1995. [2] Incl. pre-tax non-recur. chg. $244.6 mil & $168.5 mil pre-tax disposition-related chgs., 1999; $46.3 mil ($0.12/sh) after-tax, 1998; $140.5 mil ($0.34/sh) chg., 1997; net gain $200,000, 1994; & net gain $5.3 mil, 1993. [3] Bef. $18.0 mil ($0.04/sh) chg. for acctg. change.

OFFICERS:
C. M. Gutierrez, Chmn., Pres., C.E.O.
T. J. Webb, Exec. V.P., C.F.O.
W. S. Perry, V.P., Treas.

INVESTOR CONTACT: Investor Relations, (616) 961-2767

PRINCIPAL OFFICE: One Kellogg Square, P.O. Box 3599, Battle Creek, MI 49016

TELEPHONE NUMBER: (616) 961-2000
FAX: (616) 961-2871
WEB: www.kelloggs.com

NO. OF EMPLOYEES: 15,501

SHAREHOLDERS: 47,511

ANNUAL MEETING: In Apr.

INCORPORATED: DE, Dec., 1922

INSTITUTIONAL HOLDINGS:
No. of Institutions: 313
Shares Held: 314,631,536
% Held: 77.6

INDUSTRY: Cereal breakfast foods (SIC: 2043)

TRANSFER AGENT(S): Harris Trust and Savings Bank, Chicago, IL

NASDAQ SYMBOL KELYA
Rec. Pr. 23 (5/31/00)

KELLY SERVICES, INC.

YIELD 4.3%
P/E RATIO 9.7

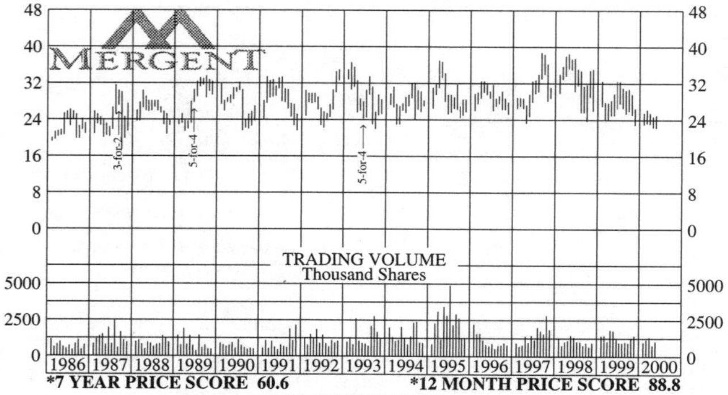

MERGENT
TRADING VOLUME
Thousand Shares
3-for-2
5-for-4
5-for-4
1986 1987 1988 1989 1990 1991 1992 1993 1994 1995 1996 1997 1998 1999 2000

***7 YEAR PRICE SCORE 60.6** ***12 MONTH PRICE SCORE 88.8**

*NYSE COMPOSITE INDEX=100

INTERIM EARNINGS (Per Share):

Qtr.	Mar.	June	Sept.	Dec.
1996	0.34	0.46	0.56	0.56
1997	0.37	0.51	0.62	0.61
1998	0.39	0.54	0.65	0.66
1999	0.42	0.58	0.69	0.67

INTERIM DIVIDENDS (Per Share):

Amt.	Decl.	Ex.	Rec.	Pay.
0.24Q	5/10/99	5/27/99	6/01/99	6/11/99
0.24Q	8/16/99	8/26/99	8/30/99	9/10/99
0.24Q	11/16/99	11/24/99	11/29/99	12/10/99
0.24Q	2/09/00	2/24/00	2/28/00	3/10/00
0.25Q	5/15/00	5/25/00	5/30/00	6/09/00

Indicated div.: $1.00 (Div. Reinv. Plan)

CAPITALIZATION (1/2/00):

	($000)	(%)
Common & Surplus	582,373	100.0
Total	582,373	100.0

DIVIDEND ACHIEVER STATUS:
Rank: 217 10-Year Growth Rate: 7.37%
Total Years of Dividend Growth: 28

RECENT DEVELOPMENTS: For the 52 weeks ended 1/2/00, net income increased slightly to $85.1 million from $84.7 million in the prior year. Sales of services grew 4.3% to $4.27 billion from $4.09 billion in the previous year. U. S. Commercial Staffing sales decreased to $2.24 billion versus $2.26 billion, reflecting continued tight U.S. labor market conditions. Sales in the Professional, Technical and Staffing Alternatives segment advanced 8.4% to $937.1 million. International sales climbed 12.4% to $1.08 billion primarily due to the October 1999 acquisitions of the HTM Group in Mexico and Interim Job SARL in Luxembourg. Gross margin remained flat at 17.9% compared with the year before. Interest expense totaled $241,000 versus interest income of $3.0 million a year earlier. In March 2000, KELY launched an updated version of its Internet recruiting service, which includes an improved search engine as well as automated systems for interfacing with other job-posting sites.

BUSINESS

KELLY SERVICES, INC. is a service organization that provides staffing services to a diversified group of customers. The Company divides its operations into three segments: U.S. Commercial Staffing, Professional, Technical and Staffing Alternatives (PTSA), and International. U.S. Commercial Staffing includes office clerical, marketing and semi-skilled light industrial. PTSA includes technical skills related to engineering, information technology, scientific, accounting and finance, and management services. Staff leasing services are provided under the name of Kelly Staff Leasing, Inc. Home care services to those who need help with their daily living needs and personal care are furnished under the name Kelly Assisted Living Services, Inc. Engineering Staffing Services are provided under the name Kelly Engineering Resources. Kelly owns and operates more than 1,800 offices in 19 countries.

ANNUAL FINANCIAL DATA

	1/2/00	1/3/99	12/28/97	12/29/96	12/31/95	1/1/95	1/2/94
Earnings Per Share	**2.36**	**2.23**	**2.12**	**1.92**	**1.83**	**1.61**	**1.18**
Cash Flow Per Share	**3.37**	**2.99**	**2.86**	**2.61**	**2.43**	**2.06**	**1.62**
Tang. Book Val. Per Share	**13.15**	**12.28**	**12.48**	**11.41**	**10.53**	**10.17**	**9.52**
Dividends Per Share	**0.95**	**0.91**	**0.87**	**0.83**	**0.78**	**0.70**	**0.63**
Dividend Payout %	**40.3**	**40.8**	**41.0**	**43.2**	**42.6**	**43.5**	**53.6**
INCOME STATEMENT (IN MILLIONS):							
Total Revenues	4,269.1	4,092.3	3,852.9	3,302.3	2,689.8	2,362.6	1,954.5
Costs & Expenses	4,088.9	3,922.8	3,688.8	3,155.2	2,560.8	2,253.5	1,874.0
Depreciation & Amort.	36.2	28.9	28.3	26.1	22.7	17.3	16.6
Operating Income	144.0	140.6	135.8	121.0	106.3	91.7	63.9
Net Interest Inc./(Exp.)	d0.2	3.0	1.2	2.0	7.0	6.7	7.0
Income Before Income Taxes	143.7	143.6	137.0	122.9	113.3	98.5	70.9
Income Taxes	58.6	58.9	56.2	49.9	43.8	37.4	26.3
Net Income	85.1	84.7	80.8	73.0	69.5	61.1	44.6
Cash Flow	121.3	113.6	109.1	99.1	92.2	78.4	61.2
Average Shs. Outstg. (000)	36,030	37,945	38,191	38,043	37,993	37,956	37,728
BALANCE SHEET (IN MILLIONS):							
Cash & Cash Equivalents	60.1	71.9	144.0	61.4	127.5	191.9	181.0
Total Current Assets	736.2	719.9	771.0	658.6	558.6	526.4	447.1
Net Property	187.0	146.4	112.7	97.7	84.4	70.2	68.3
Total Assets	1,033.7	964.2	967.2	838.9	718.7	642.1	542.1
Total Current Liabilities	451.3	426.5	407.4	322.0	242.6	210.6	155.9
Net Stockholders' Equity	582.4	537.8	559.8	516.9	476.1	431.5	386.2
Net Working Capital	284.9	293.4	363.6	336.6	316.0	315.8	291.2
Year-end Shs. Outstg. (000)	35,874	35,807	38,163	38,059	38,015	37,963	37,755
STATISTICAL RECORD:							
Operating Profit Margin %	3.4	3.4	3.5	3.7	4.0	3.9	3.3
Net Profit Margin %	2.0	2.1	2.1	2.2	2.6	2.6	2.3
Return on Equity %	14.6	15.8	14.4	14.1	14.6	14.1	11.5
Return on Assets %	8.2	8.8	8.4	8.7	9.7	9.5	8.2
Price Range	32½-22⅞	38½-23¾	38¾-23¼	32½-25¼	37-24½	32-23	36⅝-22
P/E Ratio	13.8-9.7	17.3-10.6	18.3-11.0	16.9-13.2	20.2-13.4	19.9-14.3	31.0-18.6
Average Yield %	3.4	2.9	2.8	2.9	2.5	2.5	2.2

Statistics are as originally reported. Adj. for stk. split: 5-for-4, 6/11/93

OFFICERS:
T. E. Adderley, Chmn., Pres., C.E.O.
W. K. Gerber, Exec. V.P., C.F.O.
G. M. Reardon, Sr. V.P., Gen. Couns., Sec.

INVESTOR CONTACT: William K. Gerber, Exec. V.P., C.F.O., (248) 244-5271

PRINCIPAL OFFICE: 999 West Big Beaver Road, Troy, MI 48084

TELEPHONE NUMBER: (248) 362-4444
FAX: (248) 362-2258
WEB: www.kellyservices.com

NO. OF EMPLOYEES: 7,400 (approx.)

SHAREHOLDERS: 947 (Cl. A.); 210 (Cl. B.)

ANNUAL MEETING: In May

INCORPORATED: DE, Aug., 1952

INSTITUTIONAL HOLDINGS:
No. of Institutions: 89
Shares Held: 26,424,316
% Held: 81.6

INDUSTRY: Help supply services (SIC: 7363)

TRANSFER AGENT(S): State Street Bank and Trust Company, Boston, MA

KENAN TRANSPORT COMPANY

YIELD	1.6%
P/E RATIO	9.7

*7 YEAR PRICE SCORE 79.3   *12 MONTH PRICE SCORE 68.1
*NYSE COMPOSITE INDEX=100

INTERIM EARNINGS (Per Share):

Qtr.	Mar.	June	Sept.	Dec.
1996	0.44	0.32	0.30	0.54
1997	0.41	0.34	0.35	0.61
1998	0.49	0.48	0.51	0.66
1999	0.54	0.44	0.51	0.44

INTERIM DIVIDENDS (Per Share):

Amt.	Decl.	Ex.	Rec.	Pay.
0.072Q	3/15/99	3/29/99	3/31/99	4/15/99
0.075Q	6/15/99	6/28/99	6/30/99	7/15/99
0.075Q	9/15/99	9/28/99	9/30/99	10/15/99
0.075Q	12/15/99	12/29/99	12/31/99	1/14/00
0.075Q	3/23/00	3/30/00	4/03/00	4/17/00

Indicated div.: $0.30

CAPITALIZATION (12/31/99):

	($000)	(%)
Long-Term Debt	6,000	7.5
Capital Lease Obligations..	3,261	4.1
Deferred Income Tax	12,434	15.5
Common & Surplus	58,351	72.9
Total	80,046	100.0

DIVIDEND ACHIEVER STATUS:
Rank: 267   10-Year Growth Rate: 4.50%
Total Years of Dividend Growth: 16

RECENT DEVELOPMENTS: For the year ended 12/31/99, net income decreased 9.6% to $4.7 million compared with $5.2 million in the previous year. Operating revenue improved 8.9% to $141.6 million versus $130.0 million in 1998 primarily due to the inclusion of Petro-Chemical Transport, Inc. (PCT) for a full year in 1999 compared to ten months in 1998, and volume growth with new and existing customers. Total operating expenses grew 10.8% to $133.9 million, or 94.6% of operating revenues, from $120.9 million,

or 93.0% of revenues, a year earlier due to to the inclusion of PCT for a full year, and the significant increases in driver wages and benefits and diesel fuel prices. In response to the higher operating costs, KTCO began implementing price increases to its customers in December. Fuel surcharges as a result of high fuel costs are in place with the Company's contract and non-contract customers. The pricing actions are expected to have a positive effect on KTCO's future financial performance.

BUSINESS

KENAN TRANSPORT COMPANY business involves transportation of petroleum, propane gas and chemical products throughout the United States. Petroleum and propane gas products are typically transported from bulk storage facilities to local retail outlets. Chemical products are generally transported longer distances to manufacturing locations. In February 1998, the Company acquired from Citgo Petroleum Corporation, 100% of the outstanding stock of Petro-Chemical Transport, Inc. (PCT) which significantly expanded KTCO's national presence and geographic service area. PCT operates a nationwide inventory control and logistics management system. The Company considers its business to be somewhat seasonal, with the winter heating season providing the highest demand level. At 12/31/99, the Company operated a network of terminals and a fleet of 785 tractors and 1.031 specialized trailers.

ANNUAL FINANCIAL DATA

	12/31/99	12/31/98	12/31/97	12/31/96	12/31/95	12/31/94	12/31/93
Earnings Per Share	1.93	2.14	1.71	1.59	1.39	① 1.55	1.45
Cash Flow Per Share	6.50	6.51	4.61	4.35	3.73	3.78	3.53
Tang. Book Val. Per Share	19.81	17.85	17.46	19.19	17.86	16.72	15.76
Dividends Per Share	0.29	0.285	0.275	0.27	0.26	0.24	0.23
Dividend Payout %	15.3	13.3	16.1	16.7	18.3	15.8	16.2
INCOME STATEMENT (IN THOUSANDS):							
Total Revenues	141,552	130,046	73,308	68,795	61,717	59,100	57,063
Costs & Expenses	122,855	110,363	59,884	55,953	51,015	48,000	46,710
Depreciation & Amort.	11,070	10,553	6,962	6,598	5,578	5,313	4,932
Operating Income	7,627	9,130	6,462	6,244	5,124	5,787	5,421
Net Interest Inc./(Exp.)	d852	d762	d40	d20	d28	...	...
Income Before Income Taxes	7,600	8,669	6,596	6,254	5,539	6,121	5,778
Income Taxes	2,938	3,510	2,506	2,449	2,216	2,439	2,343
Net Income	4,662	5,159	4,090	3,805	3,323	① 3,682	3,435
Cash Flow	15,732	15,712	11,052	10,403	8,901	8,995	8,367
Average Shs. Outstg.	2,422	2,415	2,396	2,389	2,387	2,377	2,368
BALANCE SHEET (IN THOUSANDS):							
Cash & Cash Equivalents	7,466	8,023	3,422	11,181	10,106	13,759	11,996
Total Current Assets	24,710	24,404	16,067	20,054	19,312	22,139	20,831
Net Property	61,082	57,625	52,239	44,133	41,265	35,015	32,747
Total Assets	98,291	94,644	77,115	65,044	61,188	57,625	54,727
Total Current Liabilities	18,245	17,165	14,314	10,020	9,744	9,879	10,065
Long-Term Obligations	9,261	12,056	4,075	...	...	...	...
Net Stockholders' Equity	58,351	54,180	49,368	45,843	42,677	39,771	37,363
Net Working Capital	6,465	7,239	1,753	10,034	9,568	12,260	10,766
Year-end Shs. Outstg.	2,422	2,422	2,395	2,389	2,389	2,378	2,370
STATISTICAL RECORD:							
Operating Profit Margin %	5.4	7.0	8.8	9.1	8.3	9.8	9.5
Net Profit Margin %	3.3	4.0	5.6	5.5	5.4	6.2	6.0
Return on Equity %	8.0	9.5	8.3	8.3	7.8	9.3	9.2
Return on Assets %	4.7	5.5	5.3	5.8	5.4	6.4	6.3
Debt/Total Assets %	9.4	12.7	5.3	...	...	...	...
Price Range	35¼-30	39¾-28	41-18½	22¼-18¾	22½-17½	20½-16½	17¾-13
P/E Ratio	18.3-15.5	18.6-13.1	24.0-10.8	14.0-11.8	16.2-12.6	13.2-10.6	12.2-9.0
Average Yield %	0.9	0.8	0.9	1.3	1.3	1.3	1.5

Statistics are as originally reported. ① Bef. extraord. chrg. $823,000 ($0.35/sh.)

OFFICERS:
T. S. Kenan III, Chmn.
O. G. Kenan, Vice-Chmn.
L. P. Shaffer, Pres., C.E.O.
W. L. Boone, V.P., Sec., C.F.O.

PRINCIPAL OFFICE: University Square - West, 143 W. Franklin St., P.O. Box 2729 Chapel Hill, NC 27516-2729

TELEPHONE NUMBER: (919) 967-8221
FAX: (919) 929-5295
NO. OF EMPLOYEES: 1,674 (avg.)
SHAREHOLDERS: 632 (approx.)
ANNUAL MEETING: In May
INCORPORATED: NC, Apr., 1949

INSTITUTIONAL HOLDINGS:
No. of Institutions: 12
Shares Held: 884,286
% Held: 36.5
INDUSTRY: Trucking, except local (SIC: 4213)
TRANSFER AGENT(S): First Union National Bank of North Carolina, Charlotte, NC

KEYCORP

YIELD	5.3%
P/E RATIO	8.5

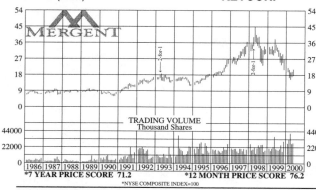

TRADING VOLUME
Thousand Shares

| 1986|1987|1988|1989|1990|1991|1992|1993|1994|1995|1996|1997|1998|1999|2000 |

*7 YEAR PRICE SCORE 71.2   *12 MONTH PRICE SCORE 76.2
*NYSE COMPOSITE INDEX=100

INTERIM EARNINGS (Per Share):

Qtr.	Mar.	June	Sept.	Dec.
1996	0.44	0.46	0.45	0.34
1997	0.48	0.51	0.54	0.56
1998	0.53	0.56	0.57	0.57
1999	0.65	0.62	0.60	0.59

INTERIM DIVIDENDS (Per Share):

Amt.	Decl.	Ex.	Rec.	Pay.
0.26Q	5/20/99	5/27/99	6/01/99	6/15/99
0.26Q	7/22/99	8/27/99	8/31/99	9/15/99
0.26Q	11/22/99	12/01/99	12/03/99	12/15/99
0.28Q	1/19/00	2/25/00	2/29/00	3/15/00
0.28Q	5/19/00	5/25/00	5/30/00	6/15/00

Indicated div.: $1.12 (Div. Reinv. Plan)

CAPITALIZATION (12/31/99):

	($000)	(%)
Total Deposits	43,233,000	66.0
Long-Term Debt	15,881,000	24.2
Common & Surplus	6,389,000	9.8
Total	65,503,000	100.0

DIVIDEND ACHIEVER STATUS:
Rank: 153   10-Year Growth Rate: 10.03%
Total Years of Dividend Growth: 20

RECENT DEVELOPMENTS: For the year ended 12/31/99, net income rose 11.1% to $1.11 billion from $996.0 million in the previous year. Earnings for 1999 and 1998 included various net gains of $448.0 million and $102.0 million, respectively. Earnings for 1999 also included restructuring charges of $98.0 million. Net interest income advanced 3.8% to $2.79 billion from $2.68 billion the year before. Non-interest income, including the above gains, increased 45.7% to $2.29 billion.

PROSPECTS: Going forward, the Company intends to expand and diversify its principal investing capabilities. As a part of this strategy, KEY announced that it will spin off Key Equity Capital, an investment group that focuses on larger equity investments in middle market companies. The spin-off will enable the Company to continue to participate in the group's healthy returns and provide funding to accommodate future growth of the group. In January 2000, KEY sold its credit card business.

BUSINESS

KEYCORP (formerly Society Corporation) is a multi-line financial services company, with assets of $83.50 billion as of 3/31/00. The Company provides investment management, retail and commercial banking, consumer finance, and investment banking products and services to individuals and companies throughout the U.S. and, for certain businesses, internationally. The Company operates in 46 states with a network of more than 2,500 ATMs, a Web site named Key.com, and telephone banking centers. In October 1998, the Company acquired McDonald & Company Investments, Inc.

LOAN DISTRIBUTION

(12/31/99)	($000)	(%)
Commercial Loans	36,526,000	56.9
Consumer Loans	24,093,000	37.5
Loans Held for Sale	3,603,000	5.6
Total	64,222,000	100.0

ANNUAL FINANCIAL DATA

	12/31/99	12/31/98	12/31/97	12/31/96	12/31/95	12/31/94	12/31/93
Earnings Per Share	⑤ 2.45	④ 2.23	④ 2.07	① 1.69	1.65	1.73	1.47
Tang. Book Val. Per Share	11.14	10.31	9.14	7.97	8.77	8.20	7.77
Dividends Per Share	1.04	0.94	0.84	0.76	0.72	0.64	0.56
Dividend Payout %	42.4	42.2	40.6	45.1	43.6	37.1	38.2
INCOME STATEMENT (IN MILLIONS):							
Total Interest Income	5,695.0	5,525.0	5,262.0	4,951.0	5,121.0	4,490.1	1,871.3
Total Interest Expense	2,908.0	2,841.0	2,468.0	2,234.0	2,484.3	1,796.8	672.3
Net Interest Income	2,787.0	2,749.0	2,794.0	2,717.0	2,636.7	2,693.2	1,199.0
Provision for Loan Losses	348.0	297.0	320.0	197.0	100.5	125.2	72.2
Non-Interest Income	2,294.0	1,575.0	1,306.0	1,087.0	933.0	882.6	509.8
Non-Interest Expense	3,049.0	2,483.0	2,435.0	2,464.0	2,311.6	2,167.2	1,101.9
Income Before Taxes	1,684.0	1,479.0	1,345.0	1,157.0	1,157.7	1,283.5	534.6
Net Income	⑤ 1,107.0	④ 996.0	④ 919.0	① 783.0	789.2	853.5	347.2
Average Shs. Outstg. (000)	452,363	447,437	444,544	459,810	469,574	486,134	236,646
BALANCE SHEET (IN MILLIONS):							
Cash & Due from Banks	2,816.0	3,296.0	3,651.0	3,444.0	3,443.8	3,511.4	1,375.6
Securities Avail. for Sale	8,525.0	7,252.0	9,636.0	8,424.0	8,742.3	3,191.1	806.0
Total Loans & Leases	64,222.0	62,012.0	53,380.0	49,235.0	47,691.7	46,224.6	17,897.6
Allowance for Credit Losses	930.0	900.0	900.0	870.0	876.0	830.3	480.6
Net Loans & Leases	63,292.0	61,112.0	52,480.0	48,365.0	46,815.7	45,394.3	17,417.0
Total Assets	83,395.0	80,020.0	73,699.0	67,621.0	66,339.1	66,798.1	27,007.3
Total Deposits	43,233.0	42,583.0	45,073.0	45,317.0	47,281.9	48,564.2	19,880.7
Long-Term Obligations	15,881.0	12,967.0	7,446.0	4,213.0	4,003.6	3,569.8	952.7
Total Liabilities	77,006.0	73,853.0	68,518.0	62,740.0	61,186.5	62,099.7	24,968.7
Net Stockholders' Equity	6,389.0	6,167.0	5,181.0	4,881.0	5,152.5	4,698.5	2,038.6
Year-end Shs. Outstg. (000)	443,427	452,452	438,064	491,888	447,406	480,724	234,754
STATISTICAL RECORD:							
Return on Equity %	17.3	16.2	17.7	16.0	15.3	18.2	17.0
Return on Assets %	1.3	1.2	1.2	1.2	1.2	1.3	1.3
Equity/Assets %	7.7	7.7	7.0	7.2	7.8	7.0	7.5
Non-Int. Exp./Tot. Inc. %	60.0	58.3	59.4	64.8	64.8	60.6	64.5
Price Range	38⅛-21	44⅞-23⅜	36⅝-23¹⁵/₁₆	27⅛-16¹¹/₁₆	18⅝-12⅜	16⅞-11¹³/₁₆	18⅝-13⅝
P/E Ratio	15.6-8.6	20.1-10.5	17.7-11.6	16.1-9.9	11.3-7.5	9.8-6.8	12.7-9.3
Average Yield %	3.5	2.8	2.8	3.5	4.6	4.5	3.5

Statistics are as originally reported. Adj. for 2-for-1 splits 3/98 & 3/93. ① Incl. pre-tax SAIF chg. & restruct. chgs. totaling $17.0 mill. ② Reflects pooling of interests for merger of KeyCorp (old) into and with Society Corp., 3/1/94. ③ Reflects sale of 140 KeyCenters. ④ Incl. pre-tax gain fr. sale of branch: $89.0 mill., 1998; $151.0 mill., 1997. ⑤ Incl. various pre-tax net gains of $448.0 mill. & restruct. chrgs. of $98.0 mill.

OFFICERS:
R. W. Gillespie, Chmn., C.E.O.
H. L. Meyer III, Pres, C.O.O.

INVESTOR CONTACT: Jay S. Gould, Investor Relations, (216) 689-4721

PRINCIPAL OFFICE: 127 Public Square, Cleveland, OH 44114-1306

TELEPHONE NUMBER: (216) 689-6300
FAX: (216) 689-3595
WEB: www.key.com

NO. OF EMPLOYEES: 24,568

SHAREHOLDERS: 58,600

ANNUAL MEETING: In May

INCORPORATED: OH, Dec., 1958

INSTITUTIONAL HOLDINGS:
No. of Institutions: 361
Shares Held: 210,841,427
% Held: 47.1

INDUSTRY: National commercial banks (SIC: 6021)

TRANSFER AGENT(S): Harris Trust and Savings Bank, Chicago, IL

KEYSPAN CORP.

YIELD 5.8%
P/E RATIO 19.2

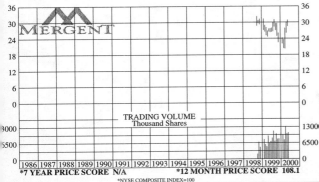

INTERIM EARNINGS (Per Share):

Qtr.	June	Sept.	Dec.	Mar.
1997-98	---------------- 2.56 ----------------			

Qtr.	Mar.	June	Sept.	Dec.
1998	------------------d1.34------------------			
1999	0.94	0.10	Nil	0.56

INTERIM DIVIDENDS (Per Share):

Amt.	Decl.	Ex.	Rec.	Pay.
0.445Q	9/30/99	10/12/99	10/14/99	11/01/99
0.445Q	12/21/99	1/10/00	1/12/00	2/01/00
0.445Q	2/28/00	4/11/00	4/13/00	5/01/00

Indicated div.: $1.78 (Div. Reinv. Plan)

CAPITALIZATION (12/31/99):

	($000)	(%)
Long-Term Debt	1,682,702	18.2
Deferred Income Tax	186,230	2.0
Minority Interest	79,722	0.9
Preferred Stock	84,339	0.9
Common & Surplus	7,197,091	78.0
Total	9,230,084	100.0

DIVIDEND ACHIEVER STATUS:
Rank: 279   10-Year Growth Rate: 4.14%
Total Years of Dividend Growth: 23

TRADING VOLUME
Thousand Shares

| 1986 | 1987 | 1988 | 1989 | 1990 | 1991 | 1992 | 1993 | 1994 | 1995 | 1996 | 1997 | 1998 | 1999 | 2000 |

*7 YEAR PRICE SCORE N/A   ***12 MONTH PRICE SCORE 108.1**

NYSE COMPOSITE INDEX=100

RECENT DEVELOPMENTS: For the year ended 12/31/99, KSE reported net income of $258.6 million. Operating revenues were recorded at $2.95 billion. For the quarter ended 12/31/99, net income rose 55.3% to $83.4 million versus a net loss of $186.5 million in 1998. Operating revenues grew 26.1% to $911.5 million. The increase in resulted reflected sales growth in KSE's core gas distribution business, the acquisition of the Ravenswood generating station, and an ongoing program of cost reduction.

PROSPECTS: KSE's immediate objectives include the acquisition and integration of the business units of Eastern Enterprises. The merger is awaiting approval from the New Hampshire Public Utility Commission. In its expanded service territory, KSE estimates it has 1.0 million potential new gas customers. In addition, KSE will focus on accelerating its marketing and expansion efforts following the pattern of de-regulation, and developing a strategic partnership for maximum realization of its fiber-optic capability.

BUSINESS

KEYSPAN CORP. (formerly KeySpan Energy Corporation) is a holding company for Brooklyn Union Gas (BU), a natural gas distribution company with diversified businesses in gas exploration and production, propane distribution and gas-cogeneration projects. BU distributes natural gas to 1.6 million customers in New York City's boroughs of Brooklyn, Staten Island, two-thirds of Queens and on Long Island in Nassau and Suffolk counties. KSE owns the common plant, non-nuclear electric-generation assets and operations, and the regulated natural gas businesses of Long Island Lighting Company (LILCO). Also, KSE owns the unregulated subsidiaries and its investments in gas exploration, production and transportation, including a 64.0% ownership in the Houston Exploration Company. KSE operated under the name MarketSpan Corporation for a three-month period ending 10/20/98. KSE merged with LILCO on 5/29/98. KSE acquired the Ravenswood electric generating facility in 6/99.

ANNUAL FINANCIAL DATA

	12/31/99	[2] 12/31/98	3/31/98	[1] 3/31/97	[4] 12/31/96
Earnings Per Share	[5] 1.62	[2] d1.34	2.56	0.62	2.20
Cash Flow Per Share	3.45	0.41	3.87	1.06	4.22
Tang. Book Val. Per Share	51.85	21.63	21.88	...	...
Dividends Per Share	1.78	1.49	1.46	1.42	1.39
Dividend Payout %	109.9	...	57.0	229.0	63.1
INCOME STATEMENT (IN MILLIONS):					
Total Revenues	2,954.6	1,721.9	3,124.1	851.2	3,150.7
Costs & Expenses	2,219.0	1,340.0	2,085.2	607.3	2,170.0
Depreciation & Amort.	253.4	254.9	159.5	53.9	244.1
Operating Income	482.2	13.2	768.3	190.0	736.6
Net Interest Inc./(Exp.)	d76.1	d138.7	d404.5	d105.9	d447.6
Income Before Income Taxes	406.1	d196.1	362.2	87.7	316.5
Income Taxes	136.4	...	...	...	...
Equity Earnings/Minority Int.	d11.1	29.1	...	...	...
Net Income	[5] 258.6	[2] d166.9	362.2	87.7	316.5
Cash Flow	477.3	59.3	469.9	128.6	508.4
Average Shs. Outstg. (000)	138,526	145,767	121,415	120,995	120,360
BALANCE SHEET (IN MILLIONS):					
Cash & Cash Equivalents	128.6	942.8	180.9	...	...
Total Current Assets	1,158.0	1,912.0	858.3	...	...
Net Property	4,240.0	3,778.3	3,814.1	...	...
Total Assets	6,730.7	6,895.1	11,900.7	11,849.6	12,209.7
Total Current Liabilities	1,388.3	1,103.0	827.8	...	...
Long-Term Obligations	1,682.7	1,619.1	4,381.9	4,457.0	4,456.8
Net Stockholders' Equity	7,281.4	3,470.9	3,225.0	...	...
Net Working Capital	d230.3	809.0	30.5	...	...
Year-end Shs. Outstg. (000)	133,866	130,420	121,681	...	...
STATISTICAL RECORD:					
Operating Profit Margin %	16.3	0.8	24.6	22.3	23.4
Net Profit Margin %	8.8	...	11.6	10.3	10.0
Return on Equity %	3.6	...	11.2	...	...
Return on Assets %	3.8	...	3.0	0.7	2.6
Debt/Total Assets %	25.0	23.5	36.8	37.6	36.5
Price Range	31 5/16-20 1/2	32 1/4-28 11/16	...	...	...
P/E Ratio	19.3-13.9	...	...	...	...
Average Yield %	6.9	4.9	...	...	...

Statistics are as originally reported. [1] For 3 mos. due to fiscal year-end change. [2] Incl. a net chg. of $108.0 mill. rel. to the LIPA transaction, a net chg. of $83.0 mill. assoc./with the merger with LILCO, & a non-cash net impair. chg. [3] For nine months due to fiscal year end change. [4] As reported from the 12/31/98 10K. [5] Reflects full-year results of LILCO.

OFFICERS:
R. B. Catell, Chmn., C.E.O.
C. Matthews, Pres., C.O.O.
G. Luterman, Sr. V.P., C.F.O.

INVESTOR CONTACT: KeySpan Investor Services, (718) 403-3196

PRINCIPAL OFFICE: One MetroTech Center, Brooklyn, NY 11201

TELEPHONE NUMBER: (718) 403-1000
FAX: (718) 545-2293
WEB: www.keyspanenergy.com

NO. OF EMPLOYEES: 7,723

SHAREHOLDERS: 90,500 (approx.)

ANNUAL MEETING: In May

INCORPORATED: NY, Apr., 1998

INSTITUTIONAL HOLDINGS:
No. of Institutions: 180
Shares Held: 55,435,262
% Held: 41.4

INDUSTRY: Natural gas distribution (SIC: 4924)

TRANSFER AGENT(S): The Bank of New York, New York, NY.

NASDAQ SYMBOL KSTN
Rec. Pr. 21 15/16 (5/31/00)

KEYSTONE FINANCIAL, INC.

YIELD 5.4%
P/E RATIO 28.4

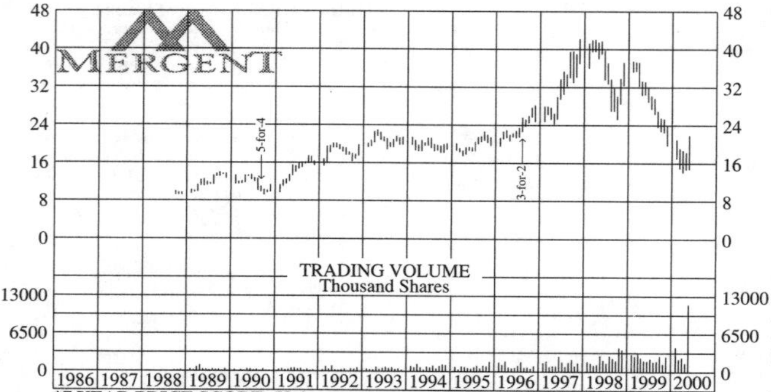

MERGENT
5-for-4
3-for-2
TRADING VOLUME
Thousand Shares

*7 YEAR PRICE SCORE 58.4 *12 MONTH PRICE SCORE 77.0
*NYSE COMPOSITE INDEX=100

INTERIM EARNINGS (Per Share):

Qtr.	Mar.	June	Sept.	Dec.
1995		1.73		
1996	0.45	0.47	0.45	0.44
1997	0.46	0.29	0.48	0.49
1998	0.46	0.48	0.50	0.48
1999	0.17	0.49	0.46	d0.37

INTERIM DIVIDENDS (Per Share):

Amt.	Decl.	Ex.	Rec.	Pay.
0.29Q	3/29/99	4/07/99	4/09/99	4/20/99
0.29Q	5/20/99	7/07/99	7/09/99	7/20/99
0.29Q	7/22/99	10/06/99	10/09/99	10/20/99
0.29Q	11/22/99	1/05/00	1/09/00	1/20/00
0.29Q	3/23/00	4/06/00	4/10/00	4/20/00

Indicated div.: $1.16 (Div. Reinv. Plan)

CAPITALIZATION (12/31/99):

	($000)	(%)
Total Deposits	4,960,334	77.9
Long-Term Debt	858,696	13.5
Common & Surplus	550,025	8.6
Total	6,369,055	100.0

DIVIDEND ACHIEVER STATUS:
Rank: 178 10-Year Growth Rate: 9.02%
Total Years of Dividend Growth: 13

RECENT DEVELOPMENTS: For the year ended 12/31/99, net income fell 62.8% to $37.1 million compared with $99.7 million in 1998. Results for 1999 included a $43.7 million pre-tax settlement charge and a $26.9 million pre-tax special charge. Since the second half of 1999, the Federal Reserve has continued to increase interest rates. These upward rate changes have increased funding costs and compressed net interest margin. Net interest income fell 7.1% to $257.4 million from $277.0 million a year ago. Interest income declined 6.1% to $486.0 versus $517.6 million in 1998, while interest expense decreased 5.0% to $228.7 million from $240.7 million in 1998. Non-interest income slid 4.1% to $104.3 million from $108.8 million the year before. Non-interest expense jumped 29.8% to $289.7 million from $223.2 million.

BUSINESS

KEYSTONE FINANCIAL, INC. is a bank holding company with assets totaling $6.89 billion as of 12/31/99. Keystone is the parent of seven community banks including American Trust Bank, N.A., Financial Trust Company, Keystone Bank, N.A., Keystone National Bank, Mid-State Bank and Trust Company, Northern Central Bank, and Pennsylvania National Bank and Trust Company. These subsidiary banks operate in thirty-one Pennsylvania counties, three Maryland counties and one county in West Virginia. KSTN also has numerous nonbank subsidiaries that offer a variety of financial services including discount brokerage services, sales of mutual funds and annuities, asset management and investment advisory services, reinsurance, mortgage banking, and community development.

LOAN DISTRIBUTION

(12/31/1999)	($000)	(%)
Consumer Financings	1,224,809	27.5
Secured by Real Estate	2,379,499	53.3
Commercial	671,881	15.1
Floor Plan Financing	183,357	4.1
Total	4,459,546	100.0

ANNUAL FINANCIAL DATA

	12/31/99	12/31/98	12/31/97	12/31/96	12/31/95	12/31/94	12/31/93
Earnings Per Share	**① ② 0.75**	**1.92**	**① 1.68**	**1.83**	**1.73**	**1.46**	**1.66**
Tang. Book Val. Per Share	**11.53**	**13.12**	**13.26**	**13.38**	**12.69**	**11.64**	**12.53**
Dividends Per Share	**1.16**	**1.12**	**1.04**	**0.96**	**0.91**	**0.85**	**0.77**
Dividend Payout %	**154.6**	**58.3**	**61.9**	**52.5**	**52.4**	**58.4**	**46.6**
INCOME STATEMENT (IN MILLIONS):							
Total Interest Income	486.0	517.6	510.7	384.5	363.9	313.2	220.2
Total Interest Expense	228.7	240.7	232.5	174.8	166.6	124.8	91.8
Net Interest Income	257.4	277.0	278.2	209.8	197.4	188.4	128.4
Provision for Loan Losses	23.4	17.2	15.3	9.9	7.9	9.5	5.6
Non-Interest Income	104.3	108.8	89.9	62.7	50.3	44.6	36.0
Non-Interest Expense	219.1	223.2	214.6	162.6	150.6	151.7	104.1
Income Before Taxes	48.7	145.4	126.9	100.0	89.2	71.8	54.6
Net Income	① ② 37.1	99.7	① 87.9	69.5	61.3	51.4	39.4
Average Shs. Outstg. (000)	49,186	52,042	52,320	38,046	35,463	35,093	23,697
BALANCE SHEET (IN MILLIONS):							
Cash & Due from Banks	334.3	190.6	206.2	167.4	182.5	182.0	104.0
Securities Avail. for Sale	1,073.3	1,129.8	1,091.4	856.4	837.9	755.8	443.2
Total Loans & Leases	4,459.5	4,459.8	4,712.6	3,553.7	3,365.7	3,193.4	2,105.6
Allowance for Credit Losses	60.0	60.3	65.1	45.0	44.4	42.4	25.4
Net Loans & Leases	4,399.6	4,399.5	4,647.5	3,508.6	3,321.3	3,151.0	2,080.2
Total Assets	6,887.5	6,968.2	6,841.3	5,231.3	5,074.8	4,706.0	3,151.4
Total Deposits	4,960.3	5,231.7	5,233.2	4,097.1	4,061.9	3,828.0	2,481.0
Long-Term Obligations	858.7	557.3	349.9	208.1	167.8	154.9	118.8
Total Liabilities	6,337.5	6,306.6	6,155.9	4,724.0	4,594.1	4,298.2	2,853.9
Net Stockholders' Equity	550.0	661.7	685.5	507.3	480.7	407.8	297.4
Year-end Shs. Outstg. (000)	47,717	50,435	51,693	37,908	37,884	35,042	23,729
STATISTICAL RECORD:							
Return on Equity %	6.7	15.1	12.8	13.7	12.8	12.6	13.2
Return on Assets %	0.5	1.4	1.3	1.3	1.2	1.1	1.2
Equity/Assets %	8.0	9.5	10.0	9.7	9.5	8.7	9.4
Non-Int. Exp./Tot. Inc. %	60.5	59.6	59.3	59.8	61.1	65.3	63.8
Price Range	37½-19¾	42⅛-25¼	42¼-24¼	28¼-19½	22 11/16-17½	21½-18 3/16	23-18 13/16
P/E Ratio	50.0-26.3	21.9-13.2	25.1-14.4	15.4-10.7	13.1-10.1	14.7-12.4	13.9-11.3
Average Yield %	4.1	3.3	3.1	4.0	4.5	4.3	3.7

Statistics are as originally reported. Adj. for 3-for-2 stk. split, 8/96. ① Incl. merger-related special chrgs. $26.9 mill., 12/31/99; $11.4 mill., 12/31/97 ② Incl. school district settlement chrg. $43.7 mill.

OFFICERS:
C. L. Campbell, Chmn. & C.E.O.
B. G. Rooke, Vice-Chmn., Exec. V.P., Gen. Couns. & Sec.
D. F. Holt, Exec. V.P. & C.F.O.

PRINCIPAL OFFICE: One Keystone Plaza, Front and Market Streets, Harrisburg, PA 17105-3660

TELEPHONE NUMBER: (717) 233-1555
FAX: (717) 231-5759
WEB: www.keyfin.com

NO. OF EMPLOYEES: 2,553

SHAREHOLDERS: 15,027 (approx.)

ANNUAL MEETING: In May

INCORPORATED: PA, Dec., 1984

INSTITUTIONAL HOLDINGS:
No. of Institutions: 92
Shares Held: 12,974,523
% Held: 26.6

INDUSTRY: National commercial banks (SIC: 6021)

TRANSFER AGENT(S): American Stock Transfer & Trust Company, New York, NY

NASDAQ SYMBOL KBALB
Rec. Pr. 16⅛ (5/31/00)

KIMBALL INTERNATIONAL, INC.

YIELD 4.0%
P/E RATIO 11.7

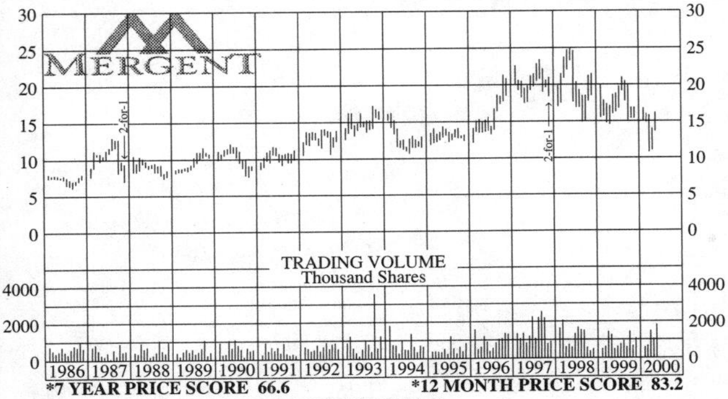

MERGENT
2-for-1
2-for-1
TRADING VOLUME
Thousand Shares
1986 1987 1988 1989 1990 1991 1992 1993 1994 1995 1996 1997 1998 1999 2000

*7 YEAR PRICE SCORE 66.6 *12 MONTH PRICE SCORE 83.2

*NYSE COMPOSITE INDEX=100

INTERIM EARNINGS (Per Share):

Qtr.	Sept.	Dec.	Mar.	June
1996-97	0.33	0.36	0.35	0.37
1997-98	0.31	0.37	0.33	0.31
1998-99	0.31	0.37	0.38	0.42
1999-00	0.28	0.30	...	...

INTERIM DIVIDENDS (Per Share):

Amt.	Decl.	Ex.	Rec.	Pay.
0.16Q	6/08/99	6/23/99	6/25/99	7/15/99
0.16Q	8/10/99	9/22/99	9/24/99	10/15/99
0.16Q	12/07/99	12/21/99	12/24/99	1/14/00
0.16Q	2/08/00	3/22/00	3/25/00	4/15/00

Indicated div.: $0.64

CAPITALIZATION (6/30/99):

	($000)	(%)
Long-Term Debt	1,730	0.4
Common & Surplus	464,277	99.6
Total	466,007	100.0

DIVIDEND ACHIEVER STATUS:
Rank: 168 10-Year Growth Rate: 9.43%
Total Years of Dividend Growth: 16

RECENT DEVELOPMENTS: For the second quarter ended 12/31/99, net income decreased 18.1% to $12.2 million compared with $14.9 million in the corresponding prior-year quarter. Results were negatively affected by a decline in profits for the Electronic Contract Assemblies segment due to high start-up costs for new product line introductions and continued competitive pricing pressure. Net sales increased 5.1% to $294.3 million from $280.1 million the year before. Furniture and Cabinet segment sales grew 6.7% to $208.7 million from $195.7 million in the year-earlier period. Results benefited from continued strength in sales of office furniture, OEM furniture and cabinets, home furniture and furniture component product lines, partially offset by a decline in lodging and healthcare product sales. Sales in the Electronic Contract Assembly segment rose 1.4% to $85.5 million. Income from operations totaled $16.5 million versus $18.3 million in the comparable 1998 quarter.

BUSINESS

KIMBALL INTERNATIONAL, INC. has three business segments: (1) Furniture and Cabinet sales include office, lodging and home furniture; television and stereo cabinets; and other miscellaneous products; (2) Electronic Contract Assemblies includes the sale of electronic and electromechanical products (electronic assemblies) manufactured on a contract basis to customers specifications; (3) Processed Wood Products and Other includes the sale of lumber, lumber banded particleboard, dimension lumber, plywood, veneer and other sales. Other sales include plastic components, carbide cutting tools and related services on cutting tools, fleet and automotive services and other miscellaneous products and services. On 5/24/99, the Company sold Kimball Furniture Reproductions in Montgomery, AL and on 6/30/99, KBAL sold Tool Pro in Jasper, IN.

ANNUAL FINANCIAL DATA

	6/30/99	6/30/98	6/30/97	6/30/96	6/30/95	6/30/94	6/30/93
Earnings Per Share	**1.45**	**1.31**	**2.79**	**2.16**	**1.97**	**0.86**	**0.72**
Cash Flow Per Share	**2.43**	**2.12**	**2.20**	**1.94**	**1.70**	**...**	**...**
Tang. Book Val. Per Share	**11.51**	**10.89**	**10.21**	**9.39**	**8.84**	**8.29**	**7.87**
Dividends Per Share	**0.64**	**0.62**	**0.55**	**0.49**	**0.44**	**0.42**	**0.40**
Dividend Payout %	**44.1**	**47.3**	**19.7**	**22.7**	**22.4**	**49.1**	**55.5**
INCOME STATEMENT (IN MILLIONS):							
Total Revenues	1,107.0	1,032.3	992.0	923.6	895.9	822.5	722.4
Costs & Expenses	989.7	926.0	877.7	825.0	804.0	736.6	648.5
Depreciation & Amort.	39.7	33.8	33.4	36.1	30.1	28.7	27.3
Operating Income	77.6	72.5	81.0	62.5	61.8	57.2	46.6
Net Interest Inc./(Exp.)	6.1	9.0	7.9	7.0	5.5	2.0	3.0
Income Before Income Taxes	92.4	87.4	88.6	74.3	70.8	59.4	53.3
Income Taxes	32.6	32.4	30.8	29.2	29.4	23.3	22.7
Net Income	59.7	55.0	57.7	45.1	41.4	36.2	30.6
Cash Flow	99.4	88.8	91.1	81.2	71.5	64.9	57.9
Average Shs. Outstg. (000)	40,839	41,814	41,450	41,810	42,142	...	...
BALANCE SHEET (IN MILLIONS):							
Cash & Cash Equivalents	131.8	172.8	168.5	114.1	112.8	91.9	107.2
Total Current Assets	386.3	412.9	376.8	342.3	306.8	288.2	295.5
Net Property	221.5	182.8	174.0	174.0	177.1	171.2	152.4
Total Assets	661.4	629.6	581.6	538.2	497.1	471.4	452.7
Total Current Liabilities	168.6	153.2	133.3	122.0	105.0	102.2	100.1
Long-Term Obligations	1.7	1.9	2.3	3.0	0.9	0.8	2.0
Net Stockholders' Equity	464.3	448.6	422.8	391.0	371.3	351.0	333.3
Net Working Capital	217.8	259.7	243.5	220.2	201.8	186.1	195.4
Year-end Shs. Outstg. (000)	40,326	41,212	41,430	41,622	41,996	42,324	42,348
STATISTICAL RECORD:							
Operating Profit Margin %	7.0	7.0	8.2	6.8	6.9	7.0	6.4
Net Profit Margin %	5.4	5.3	5.8	4.9	4.6	4.4	4.2
Return on Equity %	12.9	12.3	13.7	11.5	11.2	10.3	9.2
Return on Assets %	9.0	8.7	9.9	8.4	8.3	7.7	6.8
Debt/Total Assets %	0.3	0.3	0.4	0.6	0.2	0.2	0.4
Price Range	21-14 9/16	24 15/16-14 7/8	23 7/16-17 1/2	21 3/8-12 1/8	14 3/8-11 7/8	16 1/4-10 11/16	17 1/4-12 5/8
P/E Ratio	14.5-10.0	19.0-11.4	8.4-6.3	9.9-5.6	7.3-6.0	19.0-12.5	24.0-17.5
Average Yield %	3.6	3.1	2.7	2.9	3.4	3.1	2.7

Statistics are as originally reported. Adj. for stk. split: 2-for-1, 12/8/97

OFFICERS:
D. A. Habig, Chmn., C.E.O.
T. L. Habig, Vice-Chmn.
J. C. Thyen, Pres.
R. F. Schneider, Exec. V.P., C.F.O.

INVESTOR CONTACT: Gregory J. Shields, Dir. Inv. Relations, (800) 482-1616

PRINCIPAL OFFICE: 1600 Royal St., Jasper, IN 47549-1001

TELEPHONE NUMBER: (812) 482-1600
FAX: (812) 482-8060
WEB: www.kimball.com

NO. OF EMPLOYEES: 9,903

SHAREHOLDERS: 650 (approx. Cl. A com.); 2,470 (approx. Cl. B com.)

ANNUAL MEETING: In Oct.

INCORPORATED: IN, 1939

INSTITUTIONAL HOLDINGS:
No. of Institutions: 60
Shares Held: 9,935,345
% Held: 38.1

INDUSTRY: Wood office furniture (SIC: 2521)

TRANSFER AGENT(S): ChaseMellon Shareholder Services, L.L.C., Ridgefield Park, NJ

KIMBERLY-CLARK CORPORATION

YIELD 1.8%
P/E RATIO 19.3

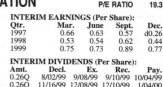

78 **65** **52** **39** **26** **13** **0**

TRADING VOLUME
Thousand Shares

62000
31000
0

1986|1987|1988|1989|1990|1991|1992|1993|1994|1995|1996|1997|1998|1999|2000

*7 YEAR PRICE SCORE 93.1   ***12 MONTH PRICE SCORE 99.2**
*NYSE COMPOSITE INDEX=100

INTERIM EARNINGS (Per Share):

Qtr.	Mar.	June	Sept.	Dec.
1997	0.66	0.63	0.57	d0.26
1998	0.53	0.54	0.62	0.44
1999	0.75	0.73	0.89	0.77

INTERIM DIVIDENDS (Per Share):

Amt.	Decl.	Ex.	Rec.	Pay.
0.26Q	8/02/99	9/08/99	9/10/99	10/04/99
0.26Q	11/16/99	12/08/99	12/10/99	1/04/00
0.27Q	2/22/00	3/08/00	3/10/00	4/04/00
0.27Q	5/09/00	6/07/00	6/09/00	7/06/00

Indicated div.: $1.08 (Div. Reinv. Plan)

CAPITALIZATION (12/31/99):

	($000)	(%)
Long-Term Debt	1,926,600	26.5
Minority Interest	244,600	3.4
Common & Surplus	5,093,100	70.1
Total	7,264,300	100.0

DIVIDEND ACHIEVER STATUS:

Rank: 250   10-Year Growth Rate: 5.77%
Total Years of Dividend Growth: 25

RECENT DEVELOPMENTS: For the year ended 12/31/99, net income increased 49.7% to $1.67 billion compared with income of $1.11 billion, before the cumulative effect of an accounting change, in 1998. Net sales were $13.00 billion, up 5.8% from $12.30 billion a year earlier. Results for 1999 and 1998 included a credit of $27.0 million and a charge of $111.8 million, respectively.

PROSPECTS: KMB completed the acquisition of Safeskin Corporation, a maker of high-quality, disposable gloves, in a transaction valued at about $800.0 million. KMB's combined professional health care operation should post sales of nearly $1.00 billion in 2000. Separately, KMB will add state-of-the-art tissue machines to existing facilities at Jenks, OK and Loudon, TN for nearly $300.0 million.

BUSINESS

KIMBERLY-CLARK CORPORATION is a global manufacturer of tissue, personal care and health care products. The Company's global brands include HUGGIES, PULLUPS, KOTEX DEPEND, KLEENEX, SCOTT, KIMBERLY-CLARK, KIMWIPES, WYPALL and TECNOL. Other brands well known outside the U.S. include ANDREX, SCOTTEX, PAGE, POPEE and KIMBIES. Kimberly-Clark also is a major producer of premium business, correspondence and technical papers. The Company has manufacturing operations in 40 countries and sells its products in more than 150 countries.

Net sales (and operating profit) for 1999 were derived from the following: tissue, 53.4% (47.2%); personal care, 39.4% (46.3%); and health care and other, 7.2% (6.5%).

ANNUAL FINANCIAL DATA

	12/31/99	12/31/98	12/31/97	12/31/96	12/31/95	12/31/94	12/31/93
Earnings Per Share	[7]3.09	[6]2.13	[5]1.58	[2]2.49	[4]0.06	[1]1.67	[1]1.59
Cash Flow Per Share	4.25	3.11	2.49	3.48	1.10	2.69	2.51
Tang. Book Val. Per Share	7.12	6.13	6.36	7.96	6.11	8.10	7.64
Dividends Per Share	1.03	0.99	0.95	0.92	0.90	0.88	0.85
Dividend Payout %	33.3	46.5	60.1	36.7	1,489.2	52.5	53.5
INCOME STATEMENT (IN MILLIONS):							
Total Revenues	13,006.8	12,297.8	12,546.6	13,149.1	13,373.0	7,364.2	6,972.9
Costs & Expenses	9,943.4	10,079.2	10,735.7	10,534.4	12,578.3	6,215.5	5,883.5
Depreciation & Amort.	628.0	542.5	507.7	561.0	581.7	329.6	295.9
Operating Income	2,435.4	1,676.1	1,303.2	2,053.7	213.0	819.1	793.5
Net Interest Inc./(Exp.)	d183.7	d174.4	d133.4	d158.6	d212.2	d129.4	d112.6
Income Before Income Taxes	2,251.7	1,626.1	1,187.5	2,002.3	104.4	740.6	713.0
Income Taxes	730.2	561.9	433.1	700.8	153.5	276.4	284.4
Equity Earnings/Minority Int.	146.6	112.8	129.6	102.3	82.3	70.9	82.3
Net Income	[7]1,668.1	[6]1,177.0	[5]884.0	[2]1,403.8	[4]33.2	[1]535.1	[1]510.9
Cash Flow	2,296.1	1,719.5	1,391.7	1,964.8	614.6	864.7	806.8
Average Shs. Outstg. (000)	540,100	553,100	559,300	564,000	559,000	321,800	321,800
BALANCE SHEET (IN MILLIONS):							
Cash & Cash Equivalents	322.8	144.0	90.8	83.2	221.6	23.8	34.8
Total Current Assets	3,561.8	3,366.9	3,489.0	3,539.2	3,813.8	1,809.9	1,675.2
Net Property	6,222.0	5,845.0	5,600.6	6,813.3	6,053.3	4,199.4	4,042.8
Total Assets	12,815.5	11,510.3	11,266.0	11,845.7	11,439.2	6,715.7	6,380.7
Total Current Liabilities	3,845.8	3,790.7	3,698.3	5,723.5	6,242.7	3,464.5	3,187.9
Long-Term Obligations	1,926.6	2,068.2	1,803.9	1,738.6	1,984.7	929.5	933.1
Net Stockholders' Equity	5,093.1	3,887.2	4,133.3	4,483.1	3,650.4	2,595.8	2,457.2
Net Working Capital	d284.0	d423.8	d209.3	d2,184.3	d2,428.9	d1,654.6	d1,512.7
Year-end Shs. Outstg. (000)	540,600	538,300	556,300	563,400	597,000	320,400	321,800
STATISTICAL RECORD:							
Operating Profit Margin %	18.7	13.6	10.4	15.6	1.6	11.1	11.4
Net Profit Margin %	12.8	9.6	7.0	10.7	0.2	7.3	7.3
Return on Equity %	32.8	30.3	21.4	31.3	0.9	20.6	20.8
Return on Assets %	13.0	10.2	7.8	11.9	0.3	8.0	8.0
Debt/Total Assets %	15.0	18.0	16.0	14.7	17.3	13.8	14.6
Price Range	69⁹/₁₆-44	59⁷/₁₆-35⁷/₈	56⁷/₈-43¹/₄	49¹³/₁₆-34⁷/₁₆	41¹/₂-23⁵/₈	30-23¹/₂	31-22⁵/₁₆
P/E Ratio	22.5-14.5	27.9-16.8	36.0-27.4	20.0-13.8	690.5-393.1	18.0-14.1	19.5-14.0
Average Yield %	1.8	2.1	1.9	2.2	2.7	3.3	3.2

Statistics are as originally reported. Adj. for stk. split: 2-for-1, 4/97. [1] Incl. gain of $9.4 mill., 1993; $62.5 mill., 1994; $72.6 mill., 1996. [2] Incl. restruct. chrg. $250.0 mill.; bef. acctg. chrg. $210.0 mill. [3] Refl. acq. of Scott Paper Co. on 12/15/95. [4] Incl. $1.44 bill. chrg. for merger & incl. $40.0 mill. gain. [5] Bef. extraord. cr. $17.5 mill. & incl. restruct. chrg. $481.1 mill. [6] Bef. acctg. chrg. of $11.2 mill. [7] Incl. restruct. cr. $27.0 mill.

OFFICERS:
W. R. Sanders, Chmn., C.E.O.
T. J. Falk, Pres., C.O.O.
J. W. Donehower, Sr. V.P., C.F.O.
D. M. Crook, V.P., Sec.

INVESTOR CONTACT: Michael D. Masseth, V.P.-Investor Relations, (800) 639-1352

PRINCIPAL OFFICE: P.O. Box 619100, Dallas, TX 75261-9100

TELEPHONE NUMBER: (972) 281-1200
FAX: (972) 281-1435
WEB: www.kimberly-clark.com

NO. OF EMPLOYEES: 54,800 (avg.)

SHAREHOLDERS: 52,331

ANNUAL MEETING: In Apr.

INCORPORATED: DE, June, 1928

INSTITUTIONAL HOLDINGS:
No. of Institutions: 736
Shares Held: 387,850,466
% Held: 71.3

INDUSTRY: Paper mills (SIC: 2621)

TRANSFER AGENT(S): Boston Equiserve, Boston, MA

LA-Z-BOY INCORPORATED

YIELD 2.0%
P/E RATIO 10.5

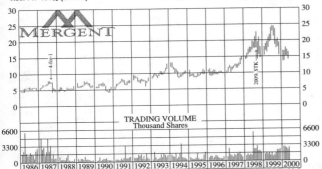

*7 YEAR PRICE SCORE 94.0   *12 MONTH PRICE SCORE 83.8
*NYSE COMPOSITE INDEX=100

INTERIM EARNINGS (Per Share):

Qtr.	July	Oct.	Jan.	Apr.
1996-97	0.08	0.28	0.18	0.29
1997-98	0.03	0.31	0.21	0.37
1998-99	0.13	0.35	0.33	0.43
1999-00	0.25	0.44	0.41	...

INTERIM DIVIDENDS (Per Share):

Amt.	Decl.	Ex.	Rec.	Pay.
0.08Q	5/04/99	5/19/99	5/21/99	6/10/99
0.08Q	7/27/99	8/25/99	8/27/99	9/10/99
0.08Q	11/09/99	11/17/99	11/19/99	12/10/99
0.08Q	2/15/00	2/23/00	2/25/00	3/10/00
0.08Q	5/09/00	5/24/00	5/26/00	6/09/00

Indicated div.: $0.32 (Div. Reinv. Plan)

CAPITALIZATION (4/24/99):

	($000)	(%)
Long-Term Debt	62,469	12.9
Capital Lease Obligations..	219	0.0
Deferred Income Tax	—	—
Common & Surplus	5,697	1.2
	414,915	85.9
Total	483,300	100.0

DIVIDEND ACHIEVER STATUS:
Rank: 237   10-Year Growth Rate: 6.32%
Total Years of Dividend Growth: 18

RECENT DEVELOPMENTS: For the quarter ended 1/22/00, net income increased 20.4% to $21.3 million compared with $17.7 million in the equivalent 1999 quarter. Sales were $376.9 million, up 18.5% from $318.1 million a year earlier. Kincaid, LZB's solid wood casegoods division, had strong sales growth in its dedicated store programs. Sam Moore, a LZB upholstery division also reported strong sales across most of its distribution channels.

PROSPECTS: On 1/29/00, the Company completed the acquisition of LADD Furniture, Inc. Following the reported combination with LADD, LZB will have annual sales in excess of $2.00 billion and market capitalization of more than $900.0 million. Separately, the Company completed the acquisition of Alexvale Furniture, Inc., based in Taylorsville, NC. Alexvale reported annual sales of $60.0 million in fiscal 1999.

BUSINESS

LA-Z-BOY INCORPORATED (formerly La-Z-Boy Chair Company) is one of the world's largest furniture producers. La-Z-Boy controls a majority share of the marketplace for upholstered recliners. La-Z-Boy sells a wide variety of upholstered furniture and casegoods consisting of bedroom, dining room and occasional furniture. LZB operates 57 manufacturing facilities in the United States, Canada, England, Mexico and Thailand. In addition to La-Z-Boy, the Company's major brand names include AMERICAN DREW, AMERICAN OF MARTINSVILLE, BARCLAY, BAUHAUS, CENTURION, CLAYTON MARCUS, ENGLAND/CORSAIR, HAMMARY, HICKORYMARK, KINCAID LEA, PENNSYLVANIA HOUSE, PILLIOD and SAM MOORE. The Company acquired Bauhaus USA, Inc. in June 1999, Alexvale Furniture, Inc. in December 1999, and LADD Furniture, Inc. in January 2000.

ANNUAL FINANCIAL DATA

	4/24/99	4/25/98	4/26/97	4/27/96	4/29/95	4/30/94	4/24/93
Earnings Per Share	1.24	0.93	0.83	0.71	0.67	① 0.63	0.50
Cash Flow Per Share	1.66	1.32	1.21	1.07	0.95	0.89	0.76
Tang. Book Val. Per Share	7.03	6.33	5.97	5.49	5.06	4.92	4.43
Dividends Per Share	0.30	0.28	0.25	0.24	0.23	0.21	0.20
Dividend Payout %	24.2	30.1	30.4	33.9	33.8	32.6	40.0
INCOME STATEMENT (IN MILLIONS):							
Total Revenues	1,287.6	1,108.0	1,005.8	947.3	850.3	804.9	684.1
Costs & Expenses	1,158.7	1,009.8	911.5	859.6	772.6	730.6	623.2
Depreciation & Amort.	22.1	21.0	20.4	20.1	15.2	14.0	14.1
Operating Income	106.8	77.2	73.9	67.5	62.5	60.3	46.8
Net Interest Inc./(Exp.)	d2.3	d2.1	d2.6	d3.3	d1.7	d1.7	d1.8
Income Before Income Taxes	107.2	79.3	73.8	66.2	62.0	58.2	45.3
Income Taxes	41.1	29.4	28.5	26.9	25.7	23.4	18.0
Net Income	66.1	49.9	45.3	39.3	36.3	① 34.7	27.3
Cash Flow	88.2	70.9	65.7	59.4	51.5	48.7	41.3
Average Shs. Outstg. (000)	53,148	53,821	54,324	55,494	54,132	54,804	54,516
BALANCE SHEET (IN MILLIONS):							
Cash & Cash Equivalents	33.6	28.7	25.4	27.1	27.0	25.9	28.8
Total Current Assets	425.6	383.0	342.8	337.1	325.4	295.6	279.0
Net Property	126.0	121.8	114.7	116.2	117.2	94.3	90.4
Total Assets	629.8	580.4	528.4	517.5	503.8	430.3	401.1
Total Current Liabilities	132.4	108.3	97.7	96.5	88.1	71.5	77.5
Long-Term Obligations	62.7	67.3	54.7	61.3	76.4	52.5	55.4
Net Stockholders' Equity	414.9	388.2	359.3	343.4	323.6	290.9	263.4
Net Working Capital	293.2	274.7	245.1	240.6	237.3	224.1	201.5
Year-end Shs. Outstg. (000)	52,340	53,551	53,724	55,155	55,686	54,861	54,585
STATISTICAL RECORD:							
Operating Profit Margin %	8.3	7.0	7.4	7.1	7.4	7.5	6.8
Net Profit Margin %	5.1	4.5	4.5	4.1	4.3	4.3	4.0
Return on Equity %	15.9	12.9	12.6	11.4	11.2	11.9	10.4
Return on Assets %	10.5	8.6	8.6	7.6	7.2	8.1	6.8
Debt/Total Assets %	10.0	11.6	10.3	11.8	15.2	12.2	13.8
Price Range	22⅝-14¹¹⁄₁₆	14¹⁵⁄₁₆-9⅞	11⁵⁄₁₆-8¹⁵⁄₁₆	11³⁄₁₆-8⁹⁄₁₆	13⁵⁄₁₆-8⁷⁄₁₆	12¹⁵⁄₁₆-8⅜	9⁹⁄₁₆-5¹⁵⁄₁₆
P/E Ratio	18.2-11.4	16.1-10.6	13.6-10.8	15.8-12.1	19.9-12.6	20.5-13.2	19.2-11.8
Average Yield %	1.6	2.3	2.5	2.4	2.1	1.9	2.6

Statistics are as originally reported. Adj. for stk split: 200%, 9/98. ① Bef. acctg. change credit $3.4 mill. ($0.18/sh.).

OFFICERS:
P. H. Norton, Chmn.
G. L. Kiser, Pres., C.O.O.
F. H. Jackson, Exec. V.P., C.F.O.

INVESTOR CONTACT: Gene M. Hardy, Sec. & Treas., (734) 241-4414

PRINCIPAL OFFICE: 1284 N. Telegraph Rd., Monroe, MI 48162-3390

TELEPHONE NUMBER: (734) 242-4414
FAX: (734) 241-4422
WEB: www.lazyboy.com

NO. OF EMPLOYEES: 12,796 (avg.)

SHAREHOLDERS: 16,329

ANNUAL MEETING: In July

INCORPORATED: MI, May, 1941

INSTITUTIONAL HOLDINGS:
No. of Institutions: 104
Shares Held: 26,342,670
% Held: 50.5

INDUSTRY: Wood household furniture (SIC: 2511)

TRANSFER AGENT(S): American Stock Transfer & Trust Company, New York, NY

LANCASTER COLONY CORPORATION

YIELD 2.7%
P/E RATIO 9.4

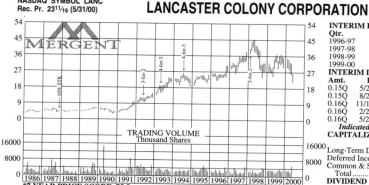

INTERIM EARNINGS (Per Share):

Qtr.	Sept.	Dec.	Mar.	June
1996-97	0.41	0.57	0.47	0.55
1997-98	0.48	0.67	0.52	0.55
1998-99	0.48	0.67	0.53	0.61
1999-00	0.56	0.83	...	...

INTERIM DIVIDENDS (Per Share):

Amt.	Decl.	Ex.	Rec.	Pay.
0.15Q	5/26/99	6/08/99	6/10/99	6/30/99
0.15Q	8/25/99	9/08/99	9/10/99	9/30/99
0.16Q	11/15/99	12/08/99	12/10/99	12/31/99
0.16Q	2/23/00	3/08/00	3/10/00	3/31/00
0.16Q	5/24/00	6/07/00	6/09/00	6/30/00

Indicated div.: $0.64 (Div. Reinv. Plan)

CAPITALIZATION (6/30/99):

	($000)	(%)
Long-Term Debt	3,575	0.8
Deferred Income Tax	8,286	1.9
Common & Surplus	414,855	97.2
Total	426,716	100.0

DIVIDEND ACHIEVER STATUS:
Rank: 98   10-Year Growth Rate: 12.83%
Total Years of Dividend Growth: 30

TRADING VOLUME
Thousand Shares

1986|1987|1988|1989|1990|1991|1992|1993|1994|1995|1996|1997|1998|1999|2000

*7 YEAR PRICE SCORE 75.5   *12 MONTH PRICE SCORE 82.9
*NYSE COMPOSITE INDEX=100

RECENT DEVELOPMENTS: For the quarter ended 12/31/99, net income increased 17.4% to $33.1 million compared with $28.2 million in the corresponding quarter the year before. Net sales increased 7.9% to $324.4 million from $300.6 million in the comparable quarter a year earlier. Specialty food net sales rose 9.1% to $129.4 million reflecting increased sales of both retail and foodservice products. Retail growth was achieved through increased sales of frozen bread items, produce dips and dressings.

Glassware and candles net sales, which grew 5.9% to $131.0 million, benefited from higher sales of both consumer glassware and candles. New glass drinkware and increased candle sales to private-label customers led to this growth. Automotive segment net sales rose 9.9% to $64.0 million due to increased demand from original equipment manufacturers for floor mats and aluminum accessories. Gross margin as a percentage of sales grew to 31.3% from 30.7% a year earlier.

BUSINESS

LANCASTER COLONY CORPORATION operates in three business segments--Specialty Foods, Glassware and Candles, and Automotive. The Specialty Foods segment manufactures and sells salad dressings and sauces, frozen unbaked pies, frozen breads, refrigerated chip and produce dips, dairy snacks and desserts, premium dry egg noodles, frozen noodles, pastas and specialty items, croutons, and caviar. The Glassware and Candles segment produces a broad range of machine-pressed and machine-blown consumer glassware, technical glass products, and candles and other home fragrances of all sizes, forms and fragrance. The Automotive segment manufactures and sells rubber, vinyl and carpeted car mats, pickup truck bed liners, tool boxes, and other accessories. The Specialty Foods, Glassware and Candles, and Automotive business segments accounted for 42.2%, 34.8%, and 23.0%, respectively, of consolidated net sales for the fiscal year ended 6/30/99.

ANNUAL FINANCIAL DATA

	6/30/99	6/30/98	6/30/97	6/30/96	6/30/95	6/30/94	6/30/93
Earnings Per Share	2.28	2.22	2.01	1.71	1.57	1.31	1.01
Cash Flow Per Share	3.13	2.97	2.62	2.25	2.07	1.81	1.49
Tang. Book Val. Per Share	9.35	8.74	8.00	6.83	5.86	6.94	5.60
Dividends Per Share	0.61	0.57	0.51	0.46	0.41	0.33	0.27
Dividend Payout %	26.8	25.7	25.2	26.9	26.0	25.0	26.5
INCOME STATEMENT (IN MILLIONS):							
Total Revenues	1,045.7	1,008.8	922.8	855.9	795.1	721.7	630.6
Costs & Expenses	854.4	820.3	751.5	705.8	655.9	598.7	530.8
Depreciation & Amort.	35.6	32.6	27.0	24.4	22.7	22.4	21.8
Operating Income	155.7	155.9	144.4	125.7	116.5	100.7	78.0
Net Interest Inc./(Exp.)	d2.7	d2.6	d2.6	d2.9	d2.7	d2.8	d3.6
Income Before Income Taxes	153.5	155.4	142.5	123.2	114.8	98.1	74.3
Income Taxes	58.3	59.2	53.8	47.1	44.3	38.2	28.1
Net Income	95.1	96.1	88.7	76.1	70.5	59.9	46.2
Cash Flow	130.7	128.7	115.7	100.5	93.2	82.3	68.1
Average Shs. Outstg. (000)	41,799	43,364	44,108	44,624	45,057	45,476	45,725
BALANCE SHEET (IN MILLIONS):							
Cash & Cash Equivalents	18.9	23.2	32.1	4.7	8.2	30.4	16.5
Total Current Assets	328.4	311.5	308.8	273.3	249.8	237.8	188.2
Net Property	175.6	170.8	151.3	139.1	113.2	101.6	98.6
Total Assets	550.0	529.4	484.4	435.4	379.9	355.4	302.1
Total Current Liabilities	116.2	76.5	73.7	69.4	60.5	74.3	61.5
Long-Term Obligations	3.6	29.1	30.7	31.2	31.8	32.9	34.6
Net Stockholders' Equity	414.9	410.6	367.9	323.4	276.1	236.0	190.8
Net Working Capital	212.2	235.0	235.1	204.0	189.3	163.5	126.6
Year-end Shs. Outstg. (000)	40,548	42,753	43,526	44,345	44,744	34,011	34,076
STATISTICAL RECORD:							
Operating Profit Margin %	14.9	15.5	15.6	14.7	14.7	13.9	12.4
Net Profit Margin %	9.1	9.5	9.6	8.9	8.9	8.3	7.3
Return on Equity %	22.9	23.4	24.1	23.5	25.5	25.4	24.2
Return on Assets %	17.3	18.2	18.3	17.5	18.6	16.8	15.3
Debt/Total Assets %	0.6	5.5	6.3	7.2	8.4	9.3	11.5
Price Range	37-24¹¹/₁₆	45⅜-24¹/₁₆	38½-26³/₁₆	30¹¹/₁₆-24	25⁵/₁₆-19³/₁₆	26³/₁₆-18¹³/₁₆	23¾-13¹³/₁₆
P/E Ratio	16.2-10.8	20.4-10.8	19.1-13.0	18.0-12.9	16.2-12.2	19.9-14.3	23.4-13.6
Average Yield %	2.0	1.6	1.6	1.7	1.8	1.5	1.4

Statistics are as originally reported. Adj. for stk. splits: 3-for-2, 1/27/98; 4-for-3, 7/20/94; 33.3% div., 4/16/93

OFFICERS:
J. B. Gerlach Jr., Chmn., Pres., C.E.O.
J. L. Boylan, V.P., C.F.O., Treas., Asst. Sec.

INVESTOR CONTACT: Investor Relations, (727) 781-5574

PRINCIPAL OFFICE: 37 West Broad Street, Columbus, OH 43215

TELEPHONE NUMBER: (614) 224-7141
FAX: (614) 469-8219
WEB: www.lancastercolony.com
NO. OF EMPLOYEES: 6,700 (approx.)
SHAREHOLDERS: 8,700 (approx.)
ANNUAL MEETING: In Nov.
INCORPORATED: DE, 1961; reincorp., OH, Jan., 1992

INSTITUTIONAL HOLDINGS:
No. of Institutions: 134
Shares Held: 17,496,188
% Held: 43.7

INDUSTRY: Frozen specialties, nec (SIC: 2038)

TRANSFER AGENT(S): American Stock Transfer and Trust Company, Brooklyn, NY

NYSE SYMBOL LEE
Rec. Pr. 21 7/8 (5/31/00)

LEE ENTERPRISES, INC.

YIELD 2.9%
P/E RATIO 12.4

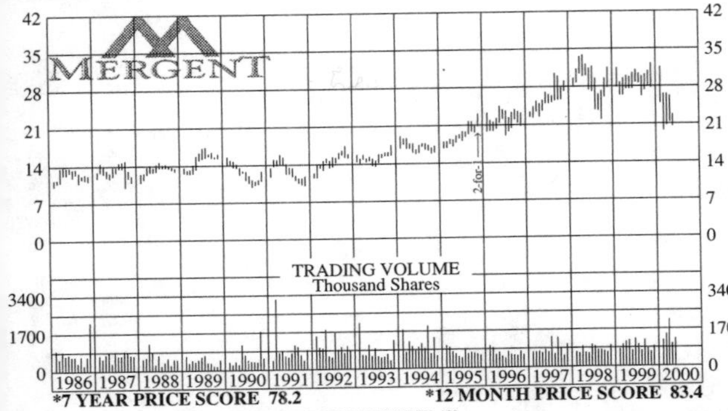

*7 YEAR PRICE SCORE 78.2 | *12 MONTH PRICE SCORE 83.4

*NYSE COMPOSITE INDEX=100

INTERIM EARNINGS (Per Share):

Qtr.	Dec.	Mar.	June	Sept.
1996-97	0.40	0.24	0.38	0.31
1997-98	0.36	0.28	0.40	0.33
1998-99	0.44	0.27	0.43	0.38
1999-00	0.68	...	...	...

INTERIM DIVIDENDS (Per Share):

Amt.	Decl.	Ex.	Rec.	Pay.
0.15Q	5/20/99	5/27/99	6/01/99	7/01/99
0.15Q	7/14/99	8/30/99	9/01/99	9/30/99
0.16Q	11/16/99	11/29/99	12/01/99	1/03/00
0.16Q	12/30/99	2/28/00	3/01/00	4/03/00
0.16Q	5/17/00	5/30/00	6/01/00	7/03/00

Indicated div.: $0.64

CAPITALIZATION (9/30/99):

	($000)	(%)
Long-Term Debt	187,005	31.9
Deferred Income Tax	44,950	7.7
Common & Surplus	354,329	60.4
Total	586,284	100.0

DIVIDEND ACHIEVER STATUS:
Rank: 248 10-Year Growth Rate: 5.84%
Total Years of Dividend Growth: 39

RECENT DEVELOPMENTS: For the quarter ended 12/31/99, net income soared 55.5% to $30.5 million versus $19.6 million in 1998. Operating revenues were $142.7 million, up from $142.1 million the year before. Revenues from the publishing segment rose 2.0% to $108.7 million, while revenues from the broadcasting segment declined 4.6% to $34.0 million. Revenues included $1.7 million from a local marketing agreement contract termination. Newsprint costs fell 19.4% due to reduced prices and consumption.

PROSPECTS: LEE agreed to sell eight network-affiliated and seven satellite television stations to EMMIS Communications Corporation for $562.5 million. The transaction is expected to close either late this summer or early fall. Meanwhile, LEE will purchase three daily newspapers and 15 other publications in Nebraska and Wisconsin from Independent Media Group, Inc. Madison Newspapers, Inc., which is 50.0% owned by LEE, will purchase Independent's 11 remaining publications in Wisconsin.

BUSINESS

LEE ENTERPRISES, INC. is a diversified media company operating primarily in the Midwest, West, Pacific Northwest and Southwestern United States. LEE has two principal businesses, newspaper publishing and broadcasting. As of 1/20/00, LEE owned and operated nine full-service network affiliated television stations and seven satellite television stations and published 21 daily and more than 75 other weekly, classified, shopper or specialty publications. In fiscal 1999, revenues (and operating income) were as follows: publications, 77.2% (85.4%); and broadcasting, 22.8% (14.6%). LEE acquired five classified or specialty publications and one commercial printer in 1998. Also, LEE owns a 50% interest in Madison Newspapers, Inc.

ANNUAL FINANCIAL DATA

	9/30/99	9/30/98	9/30/97	9/30/96	9/30/95	9/30/94	9/30/93
Earnings Per Share	**1.52**	**1.37**	**[2] 1.33**	**[1] 1.12**	**1.24**	**1.09**	**0.88**
Cash Flow Per Share	**2.40**	**2.19**	**1.95**	**1.79**	**1.80**	**1.59**	**1.41**
Tang. Book Val. Per Share	**4.14**	**...**	**...**	**1.68**	**...**	**0.36**	**...**
Dividends Per Share	**0.60**	**0.56**	**0.52**	**0.48**	**0.44**	**0.42**	**0.40**
Dividend Payout %	**39.5**	**40.9**	**39.1**	**42.9**	**35.5**	**38.5**	**45.4**
INCOME STATEMENT (IN MILLIONS):							
Total Revenues	536.3	517.3	446.7	427.4	443.2	402.6	372.9
Costs & Expenses	379.8	366.9	313.0	300.5	313.8	283.6	267.0
Depreciation & Amort.	39.7	37.6	29.6	32.2	26.0	23.5	24.8
Operating Income	116.7	112.8	104.2	94.7	103.4	95.5	81.1
Net Interest Inc./(Exp.)	d10.9	d12.7	d2.9	d7.0	d8.2	d10.6	d13.2
Income Before Income Taxes	106.5	100.1	101.2	87.7	95.2	84.9	67.9
Income Taxes	38.6	37.9	38.5	34.0	36.8	34.0	26.7
Net Income	68.0	62.2	[2] 62.7	[1] 53.7	58.5	50.9	41.2
Cash Flow	107.7	99.8	92.3	85.8	84.4	74.4	66.0
Average Shs. Outstg. (000)	44,861	45,557	47,312	47,991	46,962	46,850	46,920
BALANCE SHEET (IN MILLIONS):							
Cash & Cash Equivalents	10.5	16.9	14.2	19.3	10.9	57.6	62.6
Total Current Assets	102.5	99.6	94.0	146.7	104.5	135.7	135.1
Net Property	139.2	128.4	120.0	104.7	108.2	82.2	75.4
Total Assets	679.5	660.6	651.0	527.4	559.9	474.7	482.3
Total Current Liabilities	79.4	98.1	248.9	97.8	116.5	99.7	91.7
Long-Term Obligations	187.0	186.0	26.2	52.3	75.5	98.6	127.5
Net Stockholders' Equity	354.3	319.8	319.4	325.0	311.0	241.9	223.5
Net Working Capital	23.1	1.5	d154.9	48.9	d12.0	36.0	43.4
Year-end Shs. Outstg. (000)	44,259	44,350	45,508	47,022	47,366	45,520	46,200
STATISTICAL RECORD:							
Operating Profit Margin %	21.8	21.8	23.3	22.2	23.3	23.7	21.8
Net Profit Margin %	12.7	12.0	14.0	12.6	13.2	12.6	11.1
Return on Equity %	19.2	19.5	19.6	16.5	18.8	21.0	18.5
Return on Assets %	10.0	9.4	9.6	10.2	10.4	10.7	8.5
Debt/Total Assets %	27.5	28.2	4.0	9.9	13.5	20.8	26.4
Price Range	32 1/4-26 1/8	33 7/8-21 13/16	30 1/2-22 1/4	24 1/2-19	23 1/8-16 3/4	19 1/8-15 3/4	17 1/2-13 1/2
P/E Ratio	21.2-17.2	24.7-15.9	22.9-16.7	21.9-17.0	18.6-13.5	17.5-14.4	19.9-15.3
Average Yield %	2.1	2.0	2.0	2.2	2.2	2.4	2.6

Statistics are as originally reported. Adj. for 2-for-1 stock split, 12/95. [1] Excl. $7.7 mill. ($0.16/sh) income fr. disc. ops. [2] Excl. $1.0 mill. ($0.02/sh) income fr. disc. ops.

OFFICERS:
R. D. Gottlieb, Chmn., C.E.O.
M. E. Junck, Pres., C.O.O.

INVESTOR CONTACT: Dan Hayes, Dir. of Comm., (319) 383-2163

PRINCIPAL OFFICE: 400 Putnam Bldg., 215 N. Main St., Davenport, IA 52801-1924

TELEPHONE NUMBER: (319) 383-2100
FAX: (319) 323-9608
WEB: www.lee.net
NO. OF EMPLOYEES: 4,600 full-time; 1,500 part-time
SHAREHOLDERS: 3,424 (com.); 2,159 (class B com.).
ANNUAL MEETING: In Jan.
INCORPORATED: DE, Sep., 1950

INSTITUTIONAL HOLDINGS:
No. of Institutions: 121
Shares Held: 22,488,259
% Held: 68.2

INDUSTRY: Newspapers (SIC: 2711)

TRANSFER AGENT(S): EquiServe First Chicago Trust Divison, Jersey City, NJ.

NYSE SYMBOL LM
Rec. Pr. 44⅛ (5/31/00)

LEGG MASON, INC.

YIELD 0.7%
P/E RATIO 22.2

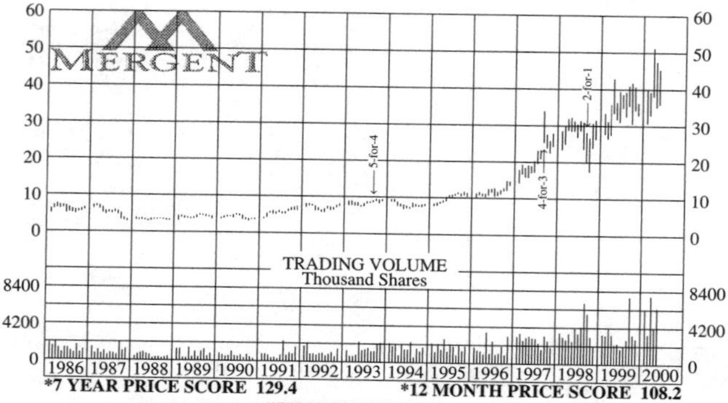

60
50
40
30
20
10
0
5-for-4
4-for-3
2-for-1
TRADING VOLUME
Thousand Shares
8400
4200
0
1986 1987 1988 1989 1990 1991 1992 1993 1994 1995 1996 1997 1998 1999 2000

*7 YEAR PRICE SCORE 129.4 *12 MONTH PRICE SCORE 108.2

*NYSE COMPOSITE INDEX=100

INTERIM EARNINGS (Per Share):

Qtr.	June	Sept.	Dec.	Mar.
1996-97	0.30	0.30	0.31	0.28
1997-98	0.31	0.36	0.39	0.40
1998-99	0.42	0.37	0.39	0.43
1999-00	0.54	0.47	0.55	...

INTERIM DIVIDENDS (Per Share):

Amt.	Decl.	Ex.	Rec.	Pay.
0.065Q	4/27/99	6/11/99	6/15/99	7/12/99
0.08Q	7/27/99	10/05/99	10/07/99	10/25/99
0.08Q	10/26/99	12/13/99	12/15/99	1/10/00
0.08Q	1/25/00	3/07/00	3/09/00	4/10/00
0.08Q	4/25/00	6/09/00	6/13/00	7/10/00

Indicated div.: $0.32

CAPITALIZATION (3/31/99):

	($000)	(%)
Long-Term Debt	99,676	15.2
Common & Surplus	554,177	84.8
Total	653,853	100.0

DIVIDEND ACHIEVER STATUS:
Rank: 82 10-Year Growth Rate: 13.87%
Total Years of Dividend Growth: 16

RECENT DEVELOPMENTS: For the quarter ended 12/31/99, net income increased 81.8% to $33.3 million from $18.3 million in the corresponding period of the previous year. Earnings for 1998 included an expense of $7.5 million for non-cash deferred compensation. Revenues grew 31.6% to $342.7 million from $260.5 million in the prior year. Investment advisory and related fees revenues increased 43.1% to a record $136.5 million.

PROSPECTS: On 3/10/00, the Company announced that it has entered into a definitive merger agreement, under which LM will acquire Perigee Inc. of Canada, an investment management firm with approximately $14.00 billion of assets under management. Separately, LM acquired U.K.-based Johnson Fry Holdings PLC, a retail fund management company with approximately $2.00 billion in assets under management.

BUSINESS

LEGG MASON, INC. is a holding company that provides securities brokerage, investment advisory, corporate and public finance, and mortgage banking services to individuals, institutions, corporations and municipalities. The Company serves brokerage clients through 120 offices. As investment advisors, the Company manages approximately $112.00 billion in assets as of 3/31/00. Its mortgage-banking subsidiaries have direct and master servicing responsibility for commercial mortgages.

REVENUES

(03/31/99)	($000)	(%)
Invest Advis & Rltd Fees	390,216	37.3
Principal Transactions	279,136	26.7
Commissions	94,105	9.0
Investment Banking	76,118	7.3
Interest	160,292	15.3
Other	46,139	4.4
Total	1,046,006	100.0

ANNUAL FINANCIAL DATA

	3/31/99	3/31/98	3/31/97	3/31/96	3/31/95	3/31/94	3/31/93
Earnings Per Share	**1.55**	**1.32**	**1.17**	**0.93**	**[1] 0.49**	**1.12**	**0.98**
Cash Flow Per Share	**1.92**	**1.69**	**1.53**	**1.28**	**0.80**	**1.37**	**1.25**
Tang. Book Val. Per Share	**8.83**	**7.97**	**7.33**	**5.64**	**4.71**	**6.01**	**6.30**
Dividends Per Share	**0.23**	**0.20**	**0.18**	**0.17**	**0.15**	**0.13**	**0.11**
Dividend Payout %	**14.8**	**15.3**	**15.7**	**18.1**	**31.6**	**11.4**	**11.3**
INCOME STATEMENT (IN MILLIONS):							
Total Revenues	1,046.0	889.1	639.7	516.0	371.6	397.5	336.3
Costs & Expenses	682.2	594.4	425.1	354.9	267.3	276.3	234.7
Depreciation & Amort.	21.6	22.0	17.2	14.2	10.5	8.3	8.4
Operating Income	342.2	272.7	197.3	146.9	93.8	112.9	93.3
Net Interest Inc./(Exp.)	d94.9	d73.7	d43.4	d26.2	d17.1	d15.4	d11.6
Income Before Income Taxes	148.8	128.4	95.2	63.9	27.7	59.2	49.0
Income Taxes	59.4	52.3	38.6	26.0	11.4	23.2	18.8
Net Income	89.3	76.1	56.6	37.9	[1] 16.3	36.0	30.2
Cash Flow	110.9	98.1	73.8	52.1	26.7	44.4	38.6
Average Shs. Outstg. (000)	57,657	58,006	48,157	40,728	33,411	32,293	30,864
BALANCE SHEET (IN MILLIONS):							
Cash & Cash Equivalents	1,740.6	1,334.3	793.1	450.1	173.9	294.9	209.3
Total Current Assets	2,805.9	2,129.2	1,399.4	932.7	532.7	607.8	535.0
Net Property	55.8	52.0	35.8	33.3	25.9	15.7	11.1
Total Assets	3,473.7	2,832.3	1,879.0	1,314.5	816.7	811.5	640.5
Total Current Liabilities	2,718.4	2,147.2	1,303.4	798.0	451.3	457.3	394.5
Long-Term Obligations	99.7	99.6	99.6	167.5	102.5	102.5	34.6
Net Stockholders' Equity	554.2	500.1	418.6	298.9	226.5	211.7	176.9
Net Working Capital	87.5	d18.1	96.0	134.7	81.4	150.5	140.5
Year-end Shs. Outstg. (000)	56,376	55,050	48,723	41,021	32,667	31,293	23,997
STATISTICAL RECORD:							
Operating Profit Margin %	32.7	30.7	30.8	28.5	25.2	28.4	27.7
Net Profit Margin %	8.5	8.6	8.8	7.3	4.4	9.1	9.0
Return on Equity %	16.1	15.2	13.5	12.7	7.2	17.0	17.1
Return on Assets %	2.6	2.7	3.0	2.9	2.0	4.4	4.7
Debt/Total Assets %	2.9	3.5	5.3	12.7	12.5	12.6	5.4
Price Range	32 5/16-17 5/16	33-14⅛	14¾-9 15/16	11¾-7 11/16	9½-6 13/16	9½-7¼	8⅛-5 11/16
P/E Ratio	20.8-11.2	25.8-10.8	12.6-8.5	12.7-8.3	19.4-14.0	8.5-6.5	8.3-5.8
Average Yield %	0.9	0.8	1.5	1.7	1.9	1.5	1.6

Statistics are as originally reported. Adj. for 2-for-1 split, 9/98; 4-for-3 split, 9/97; 5-for-4 splits, 9/93. [1] Incl. $2.0 mill. ($0.06 sh.) pre-tax chg. for litigation.

OFFICERS:
R. A. Mason, Chmn., Pres., C.E.O.
C. J. Daley Jr., C.F.O.
T. L. Souders, Sr. V.P., Treas.
R. F. Price, Sr. V.P., Gen. Couns.

INVESTOR CONTACT: F. Barry Bilson, Inv. Rel., (410) 539-0000

PRINCIPAL OFFICE: 100 Light Street, Baltimore, MD 21202

TELEPHONE NUMBER: (410) 539-0000
FAX: (410) 539-8010
WEB: www.leggmason.com

NO. OF EMPLOYEES: 4,350 (approx.)

SHAREHOLDERS: 2,151

ANNUAL MEETING: In July

INCORPORATED: MD, 1981

INSTITUTIONAL HOLDINGS:
No. of Institutions: 131
Shares Held: 32,812,729
% Held: 57.4

INDUSTRY: Security brokers and dealers (SIC: 6211)

TRANSFER AGENT(S): First Union National Bank, Charlotte, NC

NYSE SYMBOL LEG
Rec. Pr. 20 (5/31/00)

LEGGETT & PLATT, INCORPORATED

YIELD 2.0%
P/E RATIO 13.8

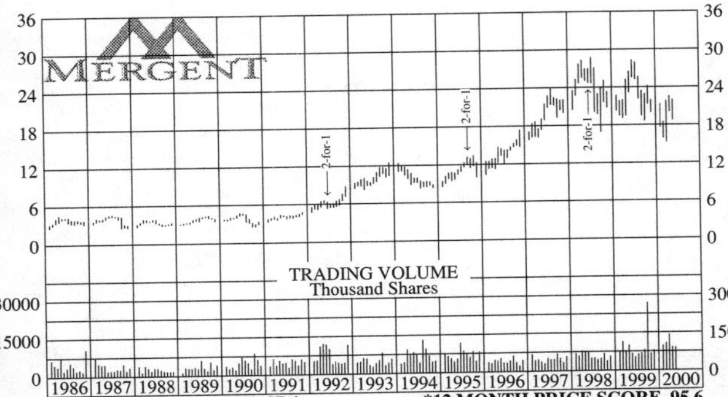

*7 YEAR PRICE SCORE 87.4   *12 MONTH PRICE SCORE 95.6

*NYSE COMPOSITE INDEX=100

INTERIM EARNINGS (Per Share):

Qtr.	Mar.	June	Sept.	Dec.
1997	0.26	0.28	0.27	0.28
1998	0.29	0.32	0.32	0.31
1999	0.33	0.36	0.39	0.37

INTERIM DIVIDENDS (Per Share):

Amt.	Decl.	Ex.	Rec.	Pay.
0.09Q	5/12/99	5/26/99	5/28/99	6/15/99
0.09Q	8/11/99	8/25/99	8/27/99	9/15/99
0.09Q	11/10/99	11/23/99	11/26/99	1/03/00
0.10Q	2/09/00	2/23/00	2/25/00	3/15/00
0.10Q	5/03/00	5/17/00	5/19/00	6/15/00

Indicated div.: $0.40

CAPITALIZATION (12/31/99):

	($000)	(%)
Long-Term Debt	787,400	31.5
Deferred Income Tax	68,500	2.7
Common & Surplus	1,646,200	65.8
Total	2,502,100	100.0

DIVIDEND ACHIEVER STATUS:
Rank: 68   10-Year Growth Rate: 14.69%
Total Years of Dividend Growth: 30

RECENT DEVELOPMENTS: For the year ended 12/31/99, net income advanced 17.1% to $290.5 million compared with $248.0 million in 1998. Net sales were $3.78 billion, up 12.1% from $3.37 billion a year earlier. The improvement in earnings and revenues was primarily attributed to benefits from the Company's continuous improvement programs, acquisitions, and other initiatives which have strengthened LEG's potential in the markets it serves.

PROSPECTS: The Company is benefiting from the addition of approximately $480.0 million in annualized revenues from acquisitions. LEG has added facilities in Brazil, China, Italy, Mexico, Spain and the U.K. Growth through acquisitions coupled with the Company's commitment to the Internet and other information technology, should help facilitate business relationships with the Company's customers and vendors, as well as its employee-partners.

BUSINESS

LEGGETT & PLATT, INCORPORATED is engaged primarily in the manufacture and distribution of components used by companies that manufacture furniture and bedding for homes, offices and institutions. Also in the furnishings area, the Company produces and sells some finished products for the furnishings industry. These finished products include sleep-related finished furniture and carpet cushioning materials. In addition, a group of diversified products made principally from steel, steel wire, aluminum, plastics, textile fibers and woven and non-woven fabrics is sold in many different markets unrelated to the home furnishings industry. LEG's international division is involved primarily in the sale of machinery and equipment designed to manufacture the Company's MIRACOIL innersprings.

ANNUAL FINANCIAL DATA

	12/31/99	12/31/98	12/31/97	12/31/96	12/31/95	12/31/94	12/31/93
Earnings Per Share	**1.45**	**1.24**	**1.08**	**[1] 0.84**	**0.80**	**0.70**	**0.52**
Cash Flow Per Share	**2.19**	**1.87**	**1.62**	**1.34**	**1.19**	**1.04**	**0.80**
Tang. Book Val. Per Share	**4.50**	**4.59**	**3.88**	**3.37**	**3.45**	**2.90**	**2.46**
Dividends Per Share	**0.35**	**0.30**	**0.26**	**0.22**	**0.18**	**0.16**	**0.14**
Dividend Payout %	**24.1**	**24.6**	**24.1**	**26.3**	**22.6**	**22.9**	**26.0**
INCOME STATEMENT (IN MILLIONS):							
Total Revenues	3,779.0	3,370.4	2,909.2	2,466.2	2,059.3	1,858.1	1,526.7
Costs & Expenses	3,129.4	2,815.6	2,441.9	2,070.4	1,756.0	1,599.2	1,324.8
Depreciation & Amort.	149.3	127.9	105.6	92.2	67.1	56.9	45.3
Operating Income	500.3	426.9	361.7	303.6	236.2	202.0	156.6
Net Interest Inc./(Exp.)	d39.9	d33.5	d31.8	d30.0	d11.5	d9.8	d10.2
Income Before Income Taxes	462.6	395.6	333.3	249.7	220.7	189.5	141.0
Income Taxes	172.1	147.6	125.0	96.7	85.8	74.1	55.1
Net Income	290.5	248.0	208.3	[1] 153.0	134.9	115.4	85.9
Cash Flow	439.8	375.9	313.9	245.2	202.0	172.3	131.2
Average Shs. Outstg. (000)	200,938	200,670	193,190	183,600	170,000	166,200	164,600
BALANCE SHEET (IN MILLIONS):							
Cash & Cash Equivalents	20.6	83.5	7.7	3.7	6.7	2.7	0.4
Total Current Assets	1,256.2	1,137.1	944.6	763.3	571.9	544.7	435.6
Net Property	915.0	820.4	693.2	582.9	451.8	396.0	313.1
Total Assets	2,977.5	2,535.3	2,106.3	1,712.9	1,218.3	1,119.9	901.9
Total Current Liabilities	431.5	401.4	372.5	292.8	226.8	232.9	166.2
Long-Term Obligations	787.4	574.1	466.2	388.5	191.9	204.9	165.8
Net Stockholders' Equity	1,646.2	1,436.8	1,174.0	941.1	734.1	625.2	515.6
Net Working Capital	824.7	735.7	572.1	470.5	345.1	311.8	269.4
Year-end Shs. Outstg. (000)	196,880	197,684	192,754	184,216	167,520	166,388	161,272
STATISTICAL RECORD:							
Operating Profit Margin %	13.2	12.7	12.4	12.3	11.5	10.9	10.3
Net Profit Margin %	7.7	7.4	7.2	6.2	6.6	6.2	5.6
Return on Equity %	17.6	17.3	17.7	16.3	18.4	18.5	16.7
Return on Assets %	9.8	9.8	9.9	8.9	11.1	10.3	9.5
Debt/Total Assets %	26.4	22.6	22.1	22.7	15.8	18.3	18.4
Price Range	28 5/16-18 5/8	28 3/4-16 7/8	23 7/8-15 3/4	17 3/8-10 5/16	13 7/16-8 1/2	12 3/8-8 5/16	12 9/16-8 3/16
P/E Ratio	19.5-12.8	23.2-13.6	22.1-14.6	20.8-12.3	16.9-10.7	17.8-12.0	24.1-15.7
Average Yield %	1.5	1.3	1.3	1.6	1.6	1.5	1.3

Statistics are as originally reported. Adj. for stk. split: 2-for-1, 9/95 and 6/98. [1] Bef. extraord. chrg. $12.5 mill. ($0.14/sh.).

OFFICERS:
H. M. Cornell Jr., Chmn.
F. E. Wright, Vice-Chmn., Pres., C.E.O.

INVESTOR CONTACT: J. Richard Calhoun, V.P., Inv. Rel., (417) 358-8131

PRINCIPAL OFFICE: No. 1 Leggett Rd., Carthage, MO 64836

TELEPHONE NUMBER: (417) 358-8131
FAX: (417) 358-8449
WEB: www.leggett.com

NO. OF EMPLOYEES: 31,000 (approx.)

SHAREHOLDERS: 15,426

ANNUAL MEETING: In May

INCORPORATED: MO, 1901

INSTITUTIONAL HOLDINGS:
No. of Institutions: 238
Shares Held: 109,813,267
% Held: 55.9

INDUSTRY: Mattresses and bedsprings (SIC: 2515)

TRANSFER AGENT(S): ChaseMellon Sharehholdler Services, LLC, Ridgefield Park, NJ

LESCO, INC.

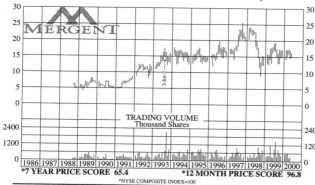

7 YEAR PRICE SCORE 65.4   *NYSE COMPOSITE INDEX=100   **12 MONTH PRICE SCORE 96.8**

INTERIM EARNINGS (Per Share):

Qtr.	Mar.	June	Sept.	Dec.
1996	d0.21	0.58	0.44	d1.12
1997	d0.12	0.75	0.52	d0.14
1998	d0.18	0.85	0.30	d0.29
1999	d0.21	1.04	0.68	d0.16

INTERIM DIVIDENDS (Per Share):

Amt.	Decl.	Ex.	Rec.	Pay.
0.13A	5/07/98	6/02/98	6/04/98	6/12/98
0.14A	5/20/99	6/01/99	6/03/99	6/11/99
0.15A	5/25/00	6/21/00	6/23/00	7/03/00

Indicated div.: $0.15 (Div. Reinv. Plan)

CAPITALIZATION (12/31/99):

	($000)	(%)
Long-Term Debt	95,199	50.5
Deferred Income Tax	2,750	1.5
Common & Surplus	90,542	48.0
Total	188,491	100.0

DIVIDEND ACHIEVER STATUS:
Rank: 55   10-Year Growth Rate: 15.44%
Total Years of Dividend Growth: 14

RECENT DEVELOPMENTS: For the year ended 12/31/99, net income almost doubled to $11.6 million compared with $5.9 million in the previous year. Net sales increased 10.5% to $460.4 million from $416.7 million the year before. Each of the Company's key sales groups contributed to the overall sales growth, with Service Centers and Golf Course sales contributing the largest increase. During 1999, the Company did not open any new stores, instead management focused on increasing sales and profitability through LSCO's existing network. Comparable-store sales increased 7.9% year over year. Gross profit as a percentage of net sales improved to 33.7% compared with 31.9% in 1998 primarily due to a decrease in the Company's cost of major raw materials and a more favorable product mix.

BUSINESS

LESCO, INC. is a fully-integrated manufacturer and marketer of a broad range of turf maintenance products and equipment. The Company serves more than 100,000 customers internationally and distributes through 234 LESCO Service Centers®, LESCO Stores-on-Wheels™, lawn care service representatives and other direct sales efforts. These facilities sell LESCO fertilizer, turf protection products, seed, equipment and replacement parts. Golf courses are served by a fleet of 71 tractor-trailer LESCO Stores-on-Wheels, calling directly on golf course superintendents and greenskeepers, serving more than 40% of the nation's golf courses. LSCO has expanded distribution through Home Depot stores as well as its presence in Europe through its agreement with WOLF-Gerate, a manufacturer and marketer of professional turf care and consumer lawn and garden products in Europe.

ANNUAL FINANCIAL DATA

	12/31/99	12/31/98	12/31/97	12/31/96	12/31/95	12/31/94	12/31/93
Earnings Per Share	1.36	0.69	1.02	d0.29	0.59	①0.72	0.68
Cash Flow Per Share	2.16	1.35	1.52	0.17	0.99	1.11	1.11
Tang. Book Val. Per Share	10.65	9.37	8.76	7.65	8.04	7.46	6.60
Dividends Per Share	0.14	0.13	0.12	0.11	0.10	0.09	0.08
Dividend Payout %	10.3	18.8	11.8	...	16.9	12.5	11.8
INCOME STATEMENT (IN THOUSANDS):							
Total Revenues	460,354	416,738	356,841	312,031	241,667	204,523	166,203
Costs & Expenses	430,949	398,430	336,483	310,678	230,012	191,953	155,553
Depreciation & Amort.	6,920	5,658	4,275	3,728	3,234	3,119	2,936
Operating Income	22,485	12,650	16,083	d2,375	8,421	9,451	7,714
Net Interest Inc./(Exp.)	d6,251	d5,635	d4,749	d4,214	d2,831	d1,931	d2,195
Income Before Income Taxes	18,902	9,453	14,140	d3,552	7,836	9,380	7,525
Income Taxes	7,256	3,561	5,515	cr1,203	3,009	3,608	2,765
Net Income	11,646	5,892	8,625	d2,349	4,827	①5,772	4,760
Cash Flow	18,566	11,550	12,900	1,379	8,061	8,891	7,696
Average Shs. Outstg.	8,579	8,575	8,496	8,007	8,117	8,034	6,964
BALANCE SHEET (IN THOUSANDS):							
Cash & Cash Equivalents	2,110	1,841	3,403	1,900	2,620	3,337	2,456
Total Current Assets	177,124	159,027	160,115	136,546	115,503	96,603	84,874
Net Property	46,161	39,078	35,977	23,293	21,441	17,066	17,858
Total Assets	232,783	207,748	200,318	164,673	137,821	114,612	104,471
Total Current Liabilities	44,292	42,926	42,404	36,642	29,553	25,763	19,460
Long-Term Obligations	95,199	83,698	83,353	64,704	43,258	29,542	33,122
Net Stockholders' Equity	90,542	78,697	72,293	61,699	63,878	58,175	50,883
Net Working Capital	132,882	116,101	117,711	99,904	85,950	70,839	65,414
Year-end Shs. Outstg.	8,499	8,401	8,250	8,064	7,950	7,799	7,710
STATISTICAL RECORD:							
Operating Profit Margin %	4.9	3.0	4.5	...	3.5	4.6	4.6
Net Profit Margin %	2.5	1.4	2.4	...	2.0	2.8	2.9
Return on Equity %	12.9	7.5	11.9	...	7.6	9.9	9.4
Return on Assets %	5.0	2.8	4.3	...	3.5	5.0	4.6
Debt/Total Assets %	40.9	40.3	41.6	39.3	31.4	25.8	31.7
Price Range	19½-12½	24¼-9	25½-14	19¾-12	17¾-12¾	17¾-12½	17½-11
P/E Ratio	14.3-9.2	35.1-13.0	25.0-13.7		...	30.1-21.6	24.6-17.4	25.7-16.2
Average Yield %	0.9	0.8	0.6	0.7	0.7	0.6	0.6

Statistics are as originally reported. Adj. for stk. splits: 3-for-2, 8/2/93 ① Bef. acctg. change credit $1.1 mill. ($0.14/sh.)

OFFICERS:
W. A. Foley, Chmn., Pres., C.E.O.
R. B. Denny, V.P., C.F.O.
C. J. Mc Gonigle, V.P., Operations

PRINCIPAL OFFICE: 20005 Lake Rd., Rocky River, OH 44116

TELEPHONE NUMBER: (440) 333-9250
FAX: (440) 356-3588
WEB: www.lesco.com

NO. OF EMPLOYEES: 1,363

SHAREHOLDERS: 1,343

ANNUAL MEETING: In May

INCORPORATED: OH, 1962

INSTITUTIONAL HOLDINGS:
No. of Institutions: 21
Shares Held: 2,570,651
% Held: 30.4

INDUSTRY: Fertilizers, mixing only (SIC: 2875)

TRANSFER AGENT(S): National City Bank, Cleveland, OH

LG&E ENERGY CORP.

YIELD 5.4%
P/E RATIO 12.9

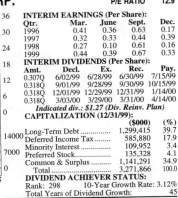

INTERIM EARNINGS (Per Share):

Qtr.	Mar.	June	Sept.	Dec.
1996	0.41	0.36	0.63	0.17
1997	0.32	0.33	0.44	0.39
1998	0.27	0.10	0.61	0.16
1999	0.44	0.39	0.67	0.33

INTERIM DIVIDENDS (Per Share):

Amt.	Decl.	Ex.	Rec.	Pay.
0.307Q	6/02/99	6/28/99	6/30/99	7/15/99
0.318Q	9/01/99	9/28/99	9/30/99	10/15/99
0.318Q	12/01/99	12/29/99	12/31/99	1/14/00
0.318Q	3/03/00	3/29/00	3/31/00	4/14/00

Indicated div.: $1.27 (Div. Reinv. Plan)

CAPITALIZATION (12/31/99):

	($000)	(%)
Long-Term Debt	1,299,415	39.7
Deferred Income Tax	585,880	17.9
Minority Interest	109,952	3.4
Preferred Stock	135,328	4.1
Common & Surplus	1,141,291	34.9
Total	3,271,866	100.0

DIVIDEND ACHIEVER STATUS:
Rank: 298   10-Year Growth Rate: 3.12%
Total Years of Dividend Growth: 45

*7 YEAR PRICE SCORE 64.3   *12 MONTH PRICE SCORE 108.5
*NYSE COMPOSITE INDEX=100

RECENT DEVELOPMENTS: For the year ended 12/31/99, income from continuing operations was $236.3 million versus income from continuing operations of $158.7 million in 1998. Results for 1999 excluded a net loss from discontinued operations of $174.2 million. The 1998 results excluded a net loss from discontinued operations of $247.0 million and a net accounting charge of $7.2 million. Total revenues rose 28.5% to $2.71 billion from $2.11 billion.

PROSPECTS: On 2/28/00, the Company entered into a definitive merger agreement with PowerGen plc, under which PowerGen will acquire all of the outstanding shares of the Company in an all-cash transaction valued at approximately $3.20 billion. The merger is on schedule to close in late 2000. The combined company will have assets of nearly $12.00 billion and total revenues of $8.70 billion.

BUSINESS

LG&E ENERGY CORP. is a diversified energy-services holding corporation. LG&E Energy Services, a wholly-owned subsidiary, oversees non-utility electric power project development domestically and internationally. LG&E Power Inc., LGE's independent power subsidiary, develops, designs, engineers, builds, finances, operates and maintains power plants. Louisville Gas and Electric Company supplies electricity and natural gas to an estimated 640,000 people in Louisville and surrounding territory in Kentucky. The Company acquired KU Energy in mid-1998, and CRC-Evans International and Gas Natural BAN in the first quarter and third quarter of 1999, respectively.

REVENUES

(12/31/1999)	($000)	(%)
Electric utility	1,693,033	62.5
Gas utility	177,579	6.6
Internatnl & non-utility	844,299	31.2
Provision for rate refund	(7,635)	(0.3)
Total	2,707,276	100.0

ANNUAL FINANCIAL DATA

	12/31/99	12/31/98	12/31/97	12/31/96	12/31/95	12/31/94	12/31/93
Earnings Per Share	[6] 1.82	[4] 1.23	1.47	[3] 1.57	1.26	[2] 0.86	[1] 1.24
Cash Flow Per Share	3.51	2.76	3.21	3.13	2.68	2.14	2.50
Tang. Book Val. Per Share	8.23	9.47	11.88	11.50	11.07	11.55	11.07
Dividends Per Share	1.24	1.20	1.16	1.12	1.08	1.05	1.01
Dividend Payout %	68.1	97.6	78.9	71.3	86.3	121.9	82.1
INCOME STATEMENT (IN MILLIONS):							
Total Revenues	2,707.3	1,976.4	4,263.8	3,589.5	1,374.7	829.7	900.0
Costs & Expenses	2,043.1	1,403.5	3,959.9	3,267.0	1,132.9	569.3	504.2
Depreciation & Amort.	219.3	197.4	115.7	103.6	94.4	84.2	82.7
Operating Income	494.6	384.0	210.5	211.4	175.6	140.3	193.0
Net Interest Inc./(Exp.)	...	...	...	...	d47.5	d58.0	d48.2
Income Taxes	133.5	111.8	55.3	57.4	44.3	33.4	52.4
Equity Earnings/Minority Int.	37.7	63.3	12.0	18.8	28.2	12.9	8.5
Net Income	[6] 236.3	[4] 160.3	97.8	[3] 104.0	82.8	[2] 56.8	[1] 80.8
Cash Flow	455.6	357.7	213.6	207.6	177.2	141.0	163.5
Average Shs. Outstg. (000)	129,677	129,679	66,471	66,294	66,106	65,982	65,378
BALANCE SHEET (IN MILLIONS):							
Gross Property	5,916.9	5,581.7	2,779.2	2,685.2	2,598.9	2,502.9	2,412.3
Accumulated Depreciation	2,503.9	2,352.3	1,072.8	1,000.0	934.9	881.9	823.1
Net Property	3,413.1	3,229.4	1,706.4	1,685.2	1,663.9	1,656.0	1,641.0
Total Assets	5,133.8	4,773.3	3,366.4	3,011.9	2,628.9	2,217.5	2,284.8
Long-Term Obligations	1,299.4	1,510.8	664.3	646.8	646.8	662.9	662.9
Net Stockholders' Equity	1,276.6	1,377.8	933.4	906.5	874.5	879.2	846.4
Year-end Shs. Outstg. (000)	129,677	129,677	66,528	66,431	66,194	66,032	65,912
STATISTICAL RECORD:							
Operating Profit Margin %	18.3	19.4	4.9	5.9	12.8	16.9	21.4
Net Profit Margin %	8.7	8.1	2.3	2.9	6.0	6.8	9.0
Net Inc./Net Property %	6.9	5.0	5.7	6.2	5.0	3.4	4.9
Net Inc./Tot. Capital %	7.2	4.6	4.8	5.6	4.7	3.1	4.4
Return on Equity %	18.5	11.6	10.5	11.5	9.5	6.5	9.5
Accum. Depr./Gross Prop. %	42.3	42.1	38.6	37.2	36.0	35.2	34.1
Price Range	28 3/4-17 3/8	29 5/16-22 1/2	25 7/8-21 1/4	24 7/8-20 9/16	21 3/4-18 3/16	20 1/2-16 13/16	21 11/16-16 7/8
P/E Ratio	15.8-9.5	23.8-18.3	17.6-14.5	15.8-13.1	17.3-14.5	23.8-19.5	17.6-13.7
Average Yield %	5.4	4.6	4.9	4.9	5.5	5.6	5.3

Statistics are as originally reported. Adj. for stk. splits: 2-for-1, 4/96. [1] Incl. non-recurr. chrg. $128.7 mill.; bef. disc. oper. gain $7.4 mill. [2] Incl. non-recurr. chrg. $48.7 mill.; bef. disc. oper. gain $51.8 mill. & acctg. chg. $3.4 mill. [3] Incl. non-recurr. chrg. $26.3 mill. [4] Bef. disc. oper. loss $248.6 mill. & acctg. chg. chrg. $7.2 mill. [5] Refl. exit of merchant trading and sales business. [6] Bef. disc. oper. loss of $174.2 mill.

OFFICERS:
R. W. Hale, Chmn., C.E.O.
V. A. Staffieri, Pres., C.O.O.
R. F. Duncan, C.F.O., Exec. V.P.
J. R. McCall, Exec. V.P., Gen. Couns. & Sec.

INVESTOR CONTACT: Steve Cave, Inv. Relations Mgr., (502) 627-3867

PRINCIPAL OFFICE: 220 W. Main St., P.O. Box 32030, Louisville, KY 40232-2030

TELEPHONE NUMBER: (502) 627-2000
FAX: (502) 627-2584
WEB: www.lgeenergy.com

NO. OF EMPLOYEES: 5,836

SHAREHOLDERS: 48,296

ANNUAL MEETING: In June

INCORPORATED: KY, Nov., 1989

INSTITUTIONAL HOLDINGS:
No. of Institutions: 193
Shares Held: 32,167,009
% Held: 24.8

INDUSTRY: Electric and other services combined (SIC: 4931)

TRANSFER AGENT(S): Harris Trust & Savings Bank, Louisville, KY 40202-2030

LIBERTY CORPORATION (THE)

YIELD	2.5%
P/E RATIO	15.8

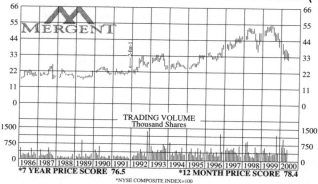

TRADING VOLUME
Thousand Shares

| 1986 | 1987 | 1988 | 1989 | 1990 | 1991 | 1992 | 1993 | 1994 | 1995 | 1996 | 1997 | 1998 | 1999 | 2000 |

*7 YEAR PRICE SCORE 76.5   ***12 MONTH PRICE SCORE 78.4**

*NYSE COMPOSITE INDEX=100

INTERIM EARNINGS (Per Share):

Qtr.	Mar.	June	Sept.	Dec.
1996	0.64	0.75	d0.55	0.82
1997	0.72	0.94	0.92	0.81
1998	d0.15	0.82	0.55	d0.42
1999	0.11	0.66	0.87	0.59

INTERIM DIVIDENDS (Per Share):

Amt.	Decl.	Ex.	Rec.	Pay.
0.22Q	5/04/99	6/11/99	6/15/99	7/02/99
0.22Q	8/03/99	9/13/99	9/15/99	10/02/99
0.22Q	11/02/99	12/13/99	12/15/99	1/04/00
0.22Q	2/01/00	3/13/00	3/15/00	4/04/00
0.22Q	5/02/00	6/13/00	6/15/00	7/05/00

Indicated div.: $0.88

CAPITALIZATION (12/31/99):

	($000)	(%)
Long-Term Debt	235,300	26.2
Deferred Income Tax	107,304	12.0
Preferred Stock	15,031	1.7
Common & Surplus	539,193	60.1
Total	896,828	100.0

DIVIDEND ACHIEVER STATUS:

Rank: 197   10-Year Growth Rate: 8.20%
Total Years of Dividend Growth: 10

RECENT DEVELOPMENTS:

For the year ended 12/31/99, net income more than doubled to $44.6 million compared with $17.8 million in the previous year. Results included realized investment losses of $8.2 million in 1999 versus realized investments gains of $861,000 in 1998. Results for 1998 included a loss on the sale of a subsidiary of $18.9 million and special charges of $17.5 million. Total revenues were $556.0 million, a decrease of 4.8% from $584.3 million in the prior year.

PROSPECTS:

Going forward, the Company will continue to focus on developing and growing its broadcasting and insurance businesses through acquisitions and improved internal efficiencies. Meanwhile, results should continue to benefit from the Company's strategic initiatives to improve agencies' processes and build a stronger, more competitive market presence. In addition, LC's investment in Liberty Insurance Services should begin to have a favorable effect on earnings in the near future.

BUSINESS

THE LIBERTY CORPORATION is a holding company with subsidiaries operating in the life insurance and television broadcasting industries. Primary subsidiaries are Liberty Life Insurance Company and Cosmos Broadcasting Corporation. Liberty Life markets a broad range of traditional and interest-sensitive life insurance products to individuals in 49 states and the District of Columbia. Cosmos Broadcasting operates twelve television stations and a cable advertising sales company. The Company also owns Liberty Capital Advisors, Inc., a registered investment advisory firm, and Liberty Properties Group, Inc., which develops real estate. In 1999, contributions to revenues (and operating income) were Insurance, 68% (69%) and Broadcasting, 32% (31%).

REVENUES

(12/31/1999)	($000)	(%)
Insurance Premiums & Policies	252,401	45.4
Broadcasting	178,144	32.0
Net Investment Income	98,444	17.7
Service Contract Revenue	22,905	4.1
Other Income	18,052	3.1
Real Invest (Loss) Gain	(13,906)	(2.5)
Total	556,040	100.0

ANNUAL FINANCIAL DATA

	12/31/99	12/31/98	12/31/97	12/31/96	12/31/95	12/31/94	12/31/93
Earnings Per Share	2.24	① 0.80	3.34	① 1.66	2.76	① 1.22	② 2.62
Tang. Book Val. Per Share	13.58	12.70	22.56	17.78	16.53	10.60	18.35
Dividends Per Share	0.88	0.84	0.77	0.71	0.65	0.60	0.56
Dividend Payout %	39.3	105.0	23.1	42.8	23.5	49.6	21.4
INCOME STATEMENT (IN MILLIONS):							
Total Premium Income	252.4	284.9	350.7	321.4	331.4	315.8	250.9
Other Income	303.6	299.3	309.6	297.7	274.3	225.5	222.0
Total Revenues	556.0	584.3	660.3	619.1	605.7	541.2	472.9
Policyholder Benefits	131.7	154.7	227.9	218.8	236.8	225.7	159.5
Income Before Income Taxes	66.8	49.1	111.6	56.5	88.8	38.9	77.3
Income Taxes	22.3	31.3	36.6	19.2	29.4	12.7	26.2
Net Income	44.6	① 17.8	75.0	① 37.3	59.4	① 26.4	② 51.1
Average Shs. Outstg. (000)	19,896	18,955	22,434	20,903	20,572	19,808	19,496
BALANCE SHEET (IN MILLIONS):							
Cash & Cash Equivalents	874.3	952.1	1,735.9	1,554.6	1,510.8	941.7	42.8
Premiums Due	336.3	345.1	347.6	351.8	332.0	296.8	291.9
Invst. Assets: Fixed-term	...	...	...	...	...	299.1	857.7
Invst. Assets: Equities	81.3	63.7	74.6	75.6	82.5	78.2	20.3
Invst. Assets: Loans	322.5	306.2	345.1	329.7	311.6	299.5	252.7
Invst. Assets: Total	1,311.3	1,361.3	2,161.5	2,078.3	2,024.0	1,734.3	1,359.5
Total Assets	2,352.9	2,410.7	3,184.8	3,060.8	3,034.3	2,667.3	2,187.0
Long-Term Obligations	235.3	285.0	191.9	247.9	258.4	231.6	149.5
Net Stockholders' Equity	554.2	529.5	674.4	580.9	575.8	395.6	433.8
Year-end Shs. Outstg. (000)	19,508	18,684	20,713	20,215	20,060	19,841	19,498
STATISTICAL RECORD:							
Return on Revenues %	8.0	3.0	11.4	6.0	9.8	4.8	10.8
Return on Equity %	8.0	3.4	11.1	6.4	10.3	6.6	11.8
Return on Assets %	1.9	0.7	2.4	1.2	2.0	1.0	2.3
Price Range	54⁹/₁₆-39¹³/₁₆	52¹⁵/₁₆-36¼	47⁵/₁₆-37⅜	41¼-30⅛	34¼-24⅜	29⅞-23⅞	34¾-23¾
P/E Ratio	24.4-17.8	66.2-45.3	14.2-11.2	24.8-18.1	12.4-8.8	24.5-19.6	13.3-9.1
Average Yield %	1.9	1.9	1.8	2.0	2.2	2.3	1.9

Statistics are as originally reported. ① Incl. non-recurr. chrg. 1998, $13.8 mill.; 1996, $26.9 mill.; 1994, $20.3 mill. ② Bef. acctg. change chrg. $11.9 mill.

OFFICERS:

H. Hipp, Chmn., Pres. , C.E.O.
M. G. Williams, V.P., Sec., Gen. Couns.

PRINCIPAL OFFICE: P.O. Box 789, Wade Hampton Blvd., Greenville, SC 29602

TELEPHONE NUMBER: (864) 609-8256
FAX: (864) 609-4390
WEB: www.libertycorp.com
NO. OF EMPLOYEES: 1,500 (avg.)
SHAREHOLDERS: 1,124
ANNUAL MEETING: In May
INCORPORATED: SC, Nov., 1967

INSTITUTIONAL HOLDINGS:
No. of Institutions: 59
Shares Held: 8,480,990
% Held: 43.6

INDUSTRY: Life insurance (SIC: 6311)

TRANSFER AGENT(S): Wachovia Bank, NA, Winston-Salem, NC

LILLY (ELI) & COMPANY

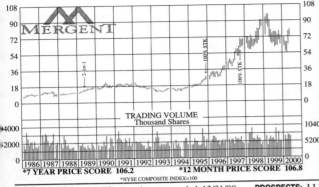

INTERIM EARNINGS (Per Share):

Qtr.	Mar.	June	Sept.	Dec.
1996	0.36	0.32	0.38	0.34
1997	0.40	d1.57	0.41	0.40
1998	0.48	0.44	0.46	0.51
1999	0.40	0.52	0.67	0.73

INTERIM DIVIDENDS (Per Share):

Amt.	Decl.	Ex.	Rec.	Pay.
0.23Q	4/19/99	5/12/99	5/14/99	6/10/99
0.23Q	7/19/99	8/11/99	8/13/99	9/10/99
0.23Q	10/18/99	11/10/99	11/15/99	12/10/99
0.26Q	12/20/99	2/11/00	2/15/00	3/10/00
0.26Q	4/17/00	5/11/00	5/15/00	6/09/00

Indicated div.: $1.04 (Div. Reinv. Plan)

CAPITALIZATION (12/31/99):

	($000)	(%)
Long-Term Debt	2,811,900	35.3
Deferred Income Tax	137,000	1.7
Common & Surplus	5,013,000	63.0
Total	7,961,900	100.0

DIVIDEND ACHIEVER STATUS:

Rank: 146   10-Year Growth Rate: 10.55%
Total Years of Dividend Growth: 32

*7 YEAR PRICE SCORE 106.2   *12 MONTH PRICE SCORE 106.8
*NYSE COMPOSITE INDEX=100

RECENT DEVELOPMENTS: For the year ended 12/31/99, income from continuing operations, before a gain from discontinued operations, rose 21.5% to $2.55 billion versus earnings, before an extraordinary loss and income from discontinued operations, of $2.10 billion in 1998. Earnings included nonrecurring items that resulted in a gain of $30.4 million. The 1998 results included nonrecurring charges of 127.5 million. Net sales rose 8.3% to $10.00 billion.

PROSPECTS: LLY should benefit from the introduction of new products generated through LLY's pipeline as well as its partnerships. LLY should also benefit from the continuing strong sales growth from products introduced in 1999. For the year 2000, LLY expects that both marketing and administrative expenses and research and development expenses will return to historical growth rates of the low double-digit to mid-teen increases.

BUSINESS

LILLY (ELI) & COMPANY discovers, develops, manufactures and markets pharmaceuticals and animal health products. Neuroscience products, 47% of 1999 sales, include PROZAC®, ZYPREXA®, DARVON®, and PERMAX®. Endocrine products, 21%, include HUMULIN®, HUMALOG®, ILETIN®, ACTOS®, EVISTA® and HUMATROPE®. Anti-infective products, 10%, include CECLOR®, KEFLEX®, KEFTAB®, LORABID®, DYNABAC®, NEBCIN®, TAZIDIME®, KEFUROX®, KEFZOL®, and VANCOCIN®. Animal Health products, 6%, include TYLAN®, MICOTIL®, cattle feed additives, and antibodies for poultry. Cardiovascular products, 6%, consist primarily of REOPRO® and DOBUTREX®. Oncology products, 5%, include GEMZAR® and ONCOVIN®. Gastrointestinal products, 4%, are entirely comprised of the ulcer treatment AXID® and other pharmaceutical products, 1%.

QUARTERLY DATA

(12/31/99)	Rev	Inc
1st quarter	2,820,500	786,300
2nd quarter	2,585,200	732,600
3rd quarter	2,341,600	576,400
4th quarter	2,255,600	625,700

ANNUAL FINANCIAL DATA

	12/31/99	12/31/98	12/31/97	12/31/96	12/31/95	12/31/94	12/31/93
Earnings Per Share	[7] 2.30	[6] 1.87	[5] d0.35	1.39	[2] 1.15	[3][4] 1.03	[1] 0.42
Cash Flow Per Share	2.70	2.31	0.11	1.89	1.63	1.40	0.76
Tang. Book Val. Per Share	4.49	2.86	2.79	1.87	1.21	0.81	3.56
Dividends Per Share	0.92	0.80	0.74	0.69	0.66	0.63	0.60
Dividend Payout %	40.0	42.8	...	49.3	57.0	61.0	145.0
INCOME STATEMENT (IN MILLIONS):							
Total Revenues	10,002.9	9,236.8	8,517.6	7,346.6	6,763.8	5,711.6	6,452.4
Costs & Expenses	6,199.5	6,049.4	5,549.5	4,756.3	4,228.3	3,608.9	5,401.5
Depreciation & Amort.	439.7	490.4	509.8	543.5	553.7	432.2	398.3
Operating Income	3,363.7	2,697.0	2,458.3	2,046.8	1,981.8	1,670.5	652.6
Net Interest Inc./(Exp.)	d183.8	d181.3	d234.1	d288.8	d286.3	d103.8	...
Income Before Income Taxes	3,245.4	2,665.0	5,396.2	2,031.3	1,765.6	1,698.6	701.9
Income Taxes	698.7	568.7	895.3	507.8	459.0	513.5	210.8
Net Income	[7] 2,546.7	[6] 2,096.3	[5] d385.1	1,523.5	[2] 1,306.6	1,185.1	[1] 491.1
Cash Flow	2,986.4	2,586.7	124.7	2,067.0	1,860.3	1,617.3	889.4
Average Shs. Outstg. (000)	1,106,055	1,121,486	1,101,099	1,093,654	1,138,052	1,156,756	1,177,156
BALANCE SHEET (IN MILLIONS):							
Cash & Cash Equivalents	3,836.0	1,597.1	2,024.6	955.1	1,084.1	746.7	987.1
Total Current Assets	7,055.5	5,406.8	5,320.7	3,891.3	4,138.6	3,962.3	3,697.1
Net Property	3,981.5	4,096.3	4,101.7	4,307.0	4,239.3	4,411.5	4,200.2
Total Assets	12,825.2	12,595.5	12,577.4	14,307.2	14,412.5	14,507.4	9,623.6
Total Current Liabilities	3,935.4	4,607.2	4,191.6	4,222.2	4,967.0	5,669.5	2,928.0
Long-Term Obligations	2,811.9	2,185.5	2,326.1	2,516.5	2,592.9	2,125.8	835.2
Net Stockholders' Equity	5,013.0	4,429.6	4,645.6	6,100.1	5,432.6	5,355.6	4,568.8
Net Working Capital	3,120.1	799.6	1,129.1	d330.9	d828.4	d1,707.2	769.1
Year-end Shs. Outstg. (000)	1,090,238	1,019,090	1,110,522	1,105,646	1,101,506	1,167,744	1,170,992
STATISTICAL RECORD:							
Operating Profit Margin %	33.6	29.2	28.9	27.9	29.3	29.2	10.1
Net Profit Margin %	25.5	22.7	...	20.7	19.3	20.7	7.6
Return on Equity %	50.8	47.3	...	25.0	24.1	22.1	10.7
Return on Assets %	19.9	16.6	...	10.6	9.1	8.2	5.1
Debt/Total Assets %	21.9	17.4	18.5	17.6	18.0	14.7	8.7
Price Range	97¾-60³⁄₁₆	91⁵⁄₁₆-57¹¹⁄₁₆	70⁵⁄₁₆-35⁹⁄₁₆	40³⁄₁₆-24¹¹⁄₁₆	28½-15⅝	16⁹⁄₁₆-11¹³⁄₁₆	15½-10¹⁵⁄₁₆
P/E Ratio	42.5-26.3	48.8-30.8	...	28.9-17.8	24.8-13.6	16.2-11.5	37.2-26.1
Average Yield %	1.2	1.1	1.4	2.1	3.0	4.4	4.6

Statistics are as originally reported. Adj. for 2-for-1 stock split, 10/97 & 12/95. [1] Bef. acctg. chg. of $10.9 mill. [2] Bef. inc. fr. disc. ops. of $984.3 mill., 1995; $1.19 bill., 1994. [3] Incl. nonrecurr. chgs. of $66.0 mill., 1994; $856.0 mill., 1993. [4] Ref. divest. of bus. [5] Incl. a net gain of $631.8 mill. & non-cash chg. of approx. $2.40 bill. [6] Excl. an extra. chg. of $7.2 mill. & a gain of $8.8 mill. fr. disc. opers.; incl. a pre-tax chg. of $127.5 mill. [7] Incl. a pre-tax chgs. of $237.4 mill., & a pre-tax gain of $267.8 mill.; excl. a net gain of $174.3 mill. fr. disc. opers.

OFFICERS:
S. Taurel, Chmn., Pres., C.E.O.
C. E. Golden, Exec. V.P., C.F.O.
R. O. Kendall, Sr. V.P., Gen. Couns.

INVESTOR CONTACT: R.B. Graper, Dir. of Investor Relations, (317) 276-2506

PRINCIPAL OFFICE: Lilly Corporate Center, Indianapolis, IN 46285

TELEPHONE NUMBER: (317) 276-2000
FAX: (317) 276-6331
WEB: www.lilly.com
NO. OF EMPLOYEES: 31,300 (approx.)
SHAREHOLDERS: 62,300
ANNUAL MEETING: In July
INCORPORATED: IN, Jan., 1901; reincorp., IN, Jan., 1936

INSTITUTIONAL HOLDINGS:
No. of Institutions: 793
Shares Held: 668,066,642
% Held: 61.3

INDUSTRY: Pharmaceutical preparations (SIC: 2834)

TRANSFER AGENT(S): First Chicago Trust Company of New York, Jersey City, NJ.

NYSE SYMBOL LNC
Rec. Pr. 38¾ (5/31/00)

LINCOLN NATIONAL CORPORATION

YIELD 3.0%
P/E RATIO 17.0

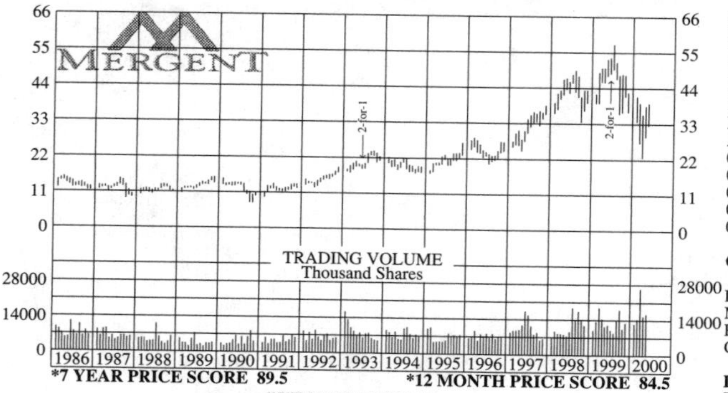

MERGENT
2-for-1
2-for-1
TRADING VOLUME
Thousand Shares
1986 1987 1988 1989 1990 1991 1992 1993 1994 1995 1996 1997 1998 1999 2000

*7 YEAR PRICE SCORE 89.5 *12 MONTH PRICE SCORE 84.5

*NYSE COMPOSITE INDEX=100

INTERIM EARNINGS (Per Share):

Qtr.	Mar.	June	Sept.	Dec.
1996	0.67	0.54	0.57	0.69
1997	0.64	d0.23	0.61	d0.67
1998	0.60	0.73	0.56	0.62
1999	0.71	0.73	0.66	0.18

INTERIM DIVIDENDS (Per Share):

Amt.	Decl.	Ex.	Rec.	Pay.
0.275Q	5/13/99	7/07/99	7/09/99	8/01/99
0.275Q	8/12/99	10/06/99	10/08/99	11/01/99
0.29Q	11/11/99	1/06/00	1/10/00	2/01/00
0.29Q	3/10/00	4/06/00	4/10/00	5/01/00
0.29Q	5/11/00	7/06/00	7/10/00	8/01/00

Indicated div.: $1.16 (Div. Reinv. Plan)

CAPITALIZATION (12/31/99):

	($000)	(%)
Long-Term Debt	711,963	12.4
Minority Interest	745,000	13.0
Preferred Stock	948	0.0
Common & Surplus	4,262,920	74.5
Total	5,720,831	100.0

DIVIDEND ACHIEVER STATUS:
Rank: 243 10-Year Growth Rate: 5.90%
Total Years of Dividend Growth: 16

RECENT DEVELOPMENTS: For the year ended 12/31/99, net income declined 9.7% to $460.4 million compared with $509.8 million in the previous year. Results included restructuring charges of $18.9 million and $34.3 million in 1999 and 1998, respectively. Results also included after-tax realized gains on investments of $3.8 million and $13.7 million in 1999 and 1998, respectively. Revenue totaled $6.80 billion, up 11.7% from $6.09 billion in the prior year. Life insurance and annuities revenue jumped 13.7% to $4.14 billion

PROSPECTS: The Company is benefiting from an increase in business volume from the Life Insurance & Annuities and Reinsurance businesses, primarily due to the acquisition of the block of business from Aetna in 1998 and elevated business levels in the Individual markets line of business. Going forward, the Company will continue to devote substantial resources to achieving significant scale and profitability in its life insurance and annuities businesses.

BUSINESS

LINCOLN NATIONAL CORPORATION, a multi-line holding company, is one of the nation's largest diversified financial services companies. Through its subsidiaries, the Company operates multiple insurance and investment management businesses. The Company's operations are divided into four business segments: Life Insurance and Annuities, Lincoln UK, Reinsurance and Investment Management. In January 1998, the Company acquired the individual life insurance and annuities business of CIGNA Corporation for $1.40 billion. In 1997, the Company sold its property-casualty operations. In 1994, the Company sold its employee life health benefit operations.

ANNUAL FINANCIAL DATA

	12/31/99	12/31/98	12/31/97	12/31/96	12/31/95	12/31/94	12/31/93
Earnings Per Share	[1] 2.30	2.51	[3] 0.11	2.46	[1] 2.32	[1] 1.69	[1][2] 2.03
Tang. Book Val. Per Share	5.59	10.16	19.38	15.97	16.20	13.68	18.75
Dividends Per Share	1.10	1.04	0.98	0.92	0.86	0.82	0.76
Dividend Payout %	47.8	41.4	932.4	37.5	37.1	48.7	37.4
INCOME STATEMENT (IN MILLIONS):							
Total Premium Income	1,881.5	1,620.6	1,328.7	3,182.0	3,253.8	4,444.1	5,356.8
Other Income	4,916.4	4,463.1	3,569.7	3,537.8	3,367.1	2,525.6	2,933.0
Total Revenues	6,797.9	6,083.7	4,898.5	6,719.8	6,620.9	6,969.7	8,289.8
Policyholder Benefits	3,805.0	3,328.9	3,191.7	3,921.3	4,113.1	4,849.2	5,628.3
Income Before Income Taxes	570.0	697.4	34.9	712.3	626.6	376.3	587.8
Income Taxes	109.6	187.6	12.7	179.2	144.4	26.4	172.5
Equity Earnings/Minority Int.	5.8	3.3	...	d18.1	12.4	14.7	...
Net Income	[1] 460.4	509.8	[3] 22.2	513.6	[1] 482.2	[1] 349.9	[1][2] 415.3
Average Shs. Outstg. (000)	200,418	203,262	207,992	209,122	208,232	207,726	204,614
BALANCE SHEET (IN MILLIONS):							
Cash & Cash Equivalents	1,895.9	2,433.4	3,794.7	1,231.7	1,572.9	1,041.6	709.7
Premiums Due	4,559.0	3,577.4	2,548.3	3,195.0	3,033.2	3,169.4	2,061.9
Invst. Assets: Fixed-term	27,688.6	30,232.9	24,066.4	27,906.4	25,834.5	21,644.2	23,964.3
Invst. Assets: Equities	604.0	542.8	660.4	992.7	1,164.8	1,038.6	1,080.3
Invst. Assets: Loans	6,627.8	6,233.1	4,051.3	4,031.1	3,789.4	3,406.4	3,896.0
Invst. Assets: Total	35,604.2	37,948.3	29,839.8	34,066.2	31,942.0	27,068.2	29,731.9
Total Assets	103,095.7	93,836.3	77,174.7	71,713.4	63,257.7	49,330.1	48,380.4
Long-Term Obligations	712.0	712.2	511.0	626.3	659.3	419.6	335.1
Net Stockholders' Equity	4,263.9	5,387.9	4,982.9	4,470.0	4,378.1	3,042.1	4,072.3
Year-end Shs. Outstg. (000)	195,495	202,112	201,718	207,318	208,370	188,956	188,366
STATISTICAL RECORD:							
Return on Revenues %	6.8	8.4	0.5	7.6	7.3	5.0	5.0
Return on Equity %	10.8	9.5	0.4	11.5	11.0	11.5	10.2
Return on Assets %	0.4	0.5	...	0.7	0.8	0.7	0.9
Price Range	57½-36	49 7/16-33½	38 9/16-24½	28½-20⅜	26⅞-17 5/16	22 3/16-17 5/16	24⅛-17⅜
P/E Ratio	25.0-15.7	19.7-13.3	366.9-233.1	11.6-8.3	11.6-7.5	13.2-10.3	11.9-8.5
Average Yield %	2.4	2.5	3.1	3.8	3.9	4.2	3.7

Statistics are as originally reported. Adj. for stk. split: 2-for-1, 6/99. [1] Incl. non-recurr. chrg. 1999, $18.9 mill.; credit 1995, $54.2 mill.; credit 1994, $48.8 mill.; chrg. 1993, $98.5 mill. [2] Bef. acctg. change chrg. $96.4 mill. [3] Bef. disc. oper. gain $911.8 mill.

OFFICERS:
J. A. Boscia, Chmn., Pres., C.E.O.
R. C. Vaughan, Exec. V.P., C.F.O.

INVESTOR CONTACT: V.P., Investor Relations, (215) 448-1422

PRINCIPAL OFFICE: 1500 Market Street, Suite 3900, Philadelphia, PA 19102-2112

TELEPHONE NUMBER: (215) 448-1400
FAX: (215) 448-3962
WEB: www.lnc.com
NO. OF EMPLOYEES: 6,630 (approx.)
SHAREHOLDERS: 11,646
ANNUAL MEETING: In May
INCORPORATED: IN, Jan., 1968

INSTITUTIONAL HOLDINGS:
No. of Institutions: 319
Shares Held: 143,874,124
% Held: 73.6

INDUSTRY: Life insurance (SIC: 6311)

TRANSFER AGENT(S): First Chicago Trust Company of New York, Jersey City, NJ

LIQUI-BOX CORPORATION

YIELD 1.6%
P/E RATIO 12.6

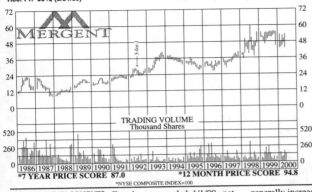

*7 YEAR PRICE SCORE 87.0   *12 MONTH PRICE SCORE 94.8
*NYSE COMPOSITE INDEX=100

INTERIM EARNINGS (Per Share):

Qtr.	Mar.	June	Sept.	Dec.
1996	0.50	0.74	0.78	0.35
1997	0.53	0.80	0.87	0.48
1998	0.74	1.10	1.08	0.55
1999	0.91	1.24	1.23	0.62

INTERIM DIVIDENDS (Per Share):

Amt.	Decl.	Ex.	Rec.	Pay.
0.18Q	3/22/99	3/30/99	4/01/99	4/12/99
0.18Q	6/22/99	6/30/99	7/02/99	7/12/99
0.20Q	9/20/99	9/29/99	10/01/99	10/11/99
0.20Q	12/23/99	12/31/99	1/04/00	1/12/00
0.20Q	3/21/00	3/29/00	3/31/00	4/10/00

Indicated div.: $0.80 (Div. Reinv. Plan)

CAPITALIZATION (1/1/00):

	($000)	(%)
Deferred Income Tax	1,468	2.0
Common & Surplus	73,544	98.0
Total	75,012	100.0

DIVIDEND ACHIEVER STATUS:
Rank: 140   10-Year Growth Rate: 10.74%
Total Years of Dividend Growth: 21

RECENT DEVELOPMENTS: For the year ended 1/1/00, net income increased 12.3% to $19.1 million compared with $17.0 million in the previous year. The increase in net income reflected an increase in gross profit, which was partially offset by the increase in selling, administrative and development expenses. Net sales increased 6.8% to $165.2 million from $154.6 million the year before. The increase in net sales was primarily attributed to comparable increases in unit sales. Selling prices on most products generally increased as did the cost of the Company's prime raw material, plastic resin. Gross margin as a percentage of net sales, which improved to 37.2% compared with 35.4% a year earlier, was primarily the result of improvements in plant efficiencies and mix of product sales. Selling, administrative and development expenses jumped 16.9% to $29.0 million from $25.6 million a year ago. Operating income amounted to $31.6 million compared with $29.2 million in 1998.

BUSINESS

LIQUI-BOX CORPORATION and its subsidiaries specialize in the research, development and manufacture of bag-in-box flexible liquid packaging systems. The Company is a major producer of bag-in-box flexible packaging and related filling equipment systems for the beverage, processed foods, dairy, wine and other specialty products industries. The Company is also a major supplier of containers and dispensing systems to the bottled water industry. The Company and its subsidiaries operate 11 manufacturing plants in the United States and Europe.

GEOGRAPHIC DATA

(01/01/2000)	Rev (%)	Inc (%)
United States	87.0	97.7
Europe	13.0	2.3
Total	100.0	100.0

ANNUAL FINANCIAL DATA

	1/1/00	1/2/99	1/3/98	12/28/96	12/30/95	12/31/94	1/1/94
Earnings Per Share	4.00	3.45	2.72	2.37	1.89	2.06	2.00
Cash Flow Per Share	5.91	5.26	4.14	3.64	3.04	3.22	3.03
Tang. Book Val. Per Share	14.56	12.31	12.29	12.78	11.36	10.04	8.54
Dividends Per Share	0.74	0.61	0.52	0.46	0.41	0.40	0.38
Dividend Payout %	18.5	17.7	19.1	19.4	21.7	19.4	19.0
INCOME STATEMENT (IN THOUSANDS):							
Total Revenues	165,227	154,656	154,145	152,368	156,373	147,772	130,081
Costs & Expenses	124,460	116,488	120,941	120,505	129,069	117,919	101,411
Depreciation & Amort.	9,141	8,950	8,194	7,790	7,366	7,494	6,722
Operating Income	31,626	29,218	25,010	24,073	19,938	22,359	21,948
Net Interest Inc./(Exp.)	66	d205	864	536	d1	d26	7
Income Before Income Taxes	31,649	28,838	26,115	24,109	20,038	22,246	21,594
Income Taxes	12,515	11,795	10,469	9,590	7,953	8,919	8,657
Net Income	19,134	17,043	15,646	14,519	12,085	13,327	12,937
Cash Flow	28,275	25,993	23,840	22,309	19,451	20,821	19,659
Average Shs. Outstg.	4,786	4,944	5,760	6,128	6,397	6,475	6,484
BALANCE SHEET (IN THOUSANDS):							
Cash & Cash Equivalents	11,635	8,685	17,425	15,248	9,424	4,341	6,376
Total Current Assets	49,120	41,284	47,380	51,725	48,699	47,848	44,341
Net Property	33,229	36,595	37,554	35,029	28,439	27,216	27,510
Total Assets	94,890	92,074	97,442	100,016	90,796	89,185	86,072
Total Current Liabilities	19,878	25,037	23,859	14,257	9,775	14,672	19,452
Long-Term Obligations	...	...	...	...	...	...	55
Net Stockholders' Equity	73,544	65,766	72,514	84,380	79,655	73,683	65,210
Net Working Capital	29,242	16,247	23,521	37,468	38,924	33,176	24,889
Year-end Shs. Outstg.	4,511	4,651	5,157	5,830	6,118	6,268	6,360
STATISTICAL RECORD:							
Operating Profit Margin %	19.1	18.9	16.2	15.8	12.8	15.1	16.9
Net Profit Margin %	11.6	11.0	10.2	9.5	7.7	9.0	9.9
Return on Equity %	26.0	25.9	21.6	17.2	15.2	18.1	19.8
Return on Assets %	20.2	18.5	16.1	14.5	13.3	14.9	15.0
Debt/Total Assets %	...	...	...	...	...	...	0.1
Price Range	55½-44¹⁵⁄₁₆	60-35¼	40½-28¾	34-26½	36¾-27¼	38½-31¼	40½-25½
P/E Ratio	13.9-11.2	17.4-10.2	14.9-10.6	14.3-11.2	19.4-14.4	18.7-15.2	20.2-12.7
Average Yield %	1.5	1.3	1.5	1.5	1.3	1.1	1.2

Statistics are as originally reported.

OFFICERS:
S. B. Davis, Chmn., C.E.O., Treas.
R. S. Hamilton, Vice-Chmn.
C. W. McBee, Pres., C.O.O., Sec.

PRINCIPAL OFFICE: 6950 Worthington-Galena Road, Worthington, OH 43085

TELEPHONE NUMBER: (614) 888-9280
FAX: (614) 888-0982
WEB: www.liquibox.com

NO. OF EMPLOYEES: 729

SHAREHOLDERS: 653

ANNUAL MEETING: In Apr.

INCORPORATED: OH, Jan., 1962

INSTITUTIONAL HOLDINGS:
No. of Institutions: 34
Shares Held: 1,077,959
% Held: 23.9

INDUSTRY: Plastics products, nec (SIC: 3089)

TRANSFER AGENT(S): National City Bank, Cleveland, OH

LOCKHEED MARTIN CORPORATION

YIELD 1.8%
P/E RATIO 12.9

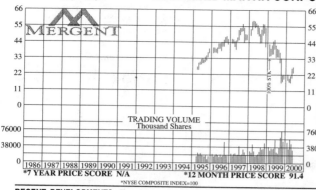

	66	66
	55	55
	44	44
	33	33
	22	22
	11	11
	0	0

TRADING VOLUME
Thousand Shares

76000	76000
38000	38000
0	0

1986|1987|1988|1989|1990|1991|1992|1993|1994|1995|1996|1997|1998|1999|2000

*7 YEAR PRICE SCORE N/A   *12 MONTH PRICE SCORE 91.4
*NYSE COMPOSITE INDEX=100

INTERIM EARNINGS (Per Share):

Qtr.	Mar.	June	Sept.	Dec.
1996	0.68	0.76	0.78	1.20
1997	0.68	0.72	0.76	0.92
1998	0.72	0.76	0.84	0.34
1999	0.70	d0.11	0.57	0.76

INTERIM DIVIDENDS (Per Share):

Amt.	Decl.	Ex.	Rec.	Pay.
0.22Q	5/13/99	5/27/99	6/01/99	6/30/99
0.22Q	7/22/99	8/30/99	9/01/99	9/30/99
0.22Q	10/28/99	11/29/99	12/01/99	12/31/99
0.11Q	1/27/00	3/02/00	3/06/00	3/31/00
0.11Q	4/27/00	5/30/00	6/01/00	6/30/00

Indicated div.: $0.44 (Div. Reinv. Plan)

CAPITALIZATION (12/31/99):

	($000)	(%)
Long-Term Debt	11,427,000	64.2
Common & Surplus	6,361,000	35.8
Total	17,788,000	100.0

DIVIDEND ACHIEVER STATUS:

Rank: 135   10-Year Growth Rate: 11.14%
Total Years of Dividend Growth: 15

RECENT DEVELOPMENTS: For the year ended 12/31/99, LMT reported income of $737.0 million, before an accounting charge of $355.0 million, versus net income of $1.00 billion in 1998. Earnings for 1999 included various gains of $249.0 million. Net sales declined 2.8% to $25.53 billion. Sales for the Systems Integration segment rose to $10.95 billion from $10.90 billion the year before. Sales for the Space Systems segment fell 17.2% to $5.83 billion.

PROSPECTS: Going forward, LMT intends to reduce general and administrative costs, shorten decision-making processes and focus resources on program execution. As a result, the Company estimates annual savings of $200.0 million, as well as earnings per share of $1.00, before one-time items, for 2000. LMT expects to increase earnings per share at 15% to 25% annually, with 2001 falling at the lower end of that range.

BUSINESS

LOCKHEED MARTIN CORPORATION was created on 3/15/95 through a merger of equals between Lockheed Corporation and Martin Marietta Corporation, both Dividend Achiever companies. LMT designs, develops, manufactures and integrates advanced technology systems, products, and services for government and commercial customers worldwide. Business areas include aeronautics, space, systems integration, and technology services. The Company is the world's largest defense, Department of Energy, and NASA contractor. In April 1996, LMT purchased all issued and outstanding shares of Loral Corp., presently Lockheed Martin Tactical Systems, Inc.

BUSINESS LINE ANALYSIS

(12/31/99) (%)	REV	INC
Systems Integration ...	42.9	48.1
Space Systems	22.8	23.5
Aeronautical Systems	21.5	12.2
Technology Services .	8.8	6.8
Corporate & Other.....	0.4	9.4
Total	100.0	100.0

ANNUAL FINANCIAL DATA

	12/31/99	12/31/98	12/31/97	12/31/96	12/31/95	12/31/94	12/31/93
Earnings Per Share	④ 1.92	2.63	③ 3.05	② 3.40	① 1.64	2.66	2.13
Cash Flow Per Share	4.44	5.26	5.51	6.73	4.24	5.33	4.66
Tang. Book Val. Per Share	...	...	...	...	2.03	0.71	...
Dividends Per Share	0.88	0.82	0.80	0.78	0.53	0.47	0.44
Dividend Payout %	45.8	31.2	26.3	23.5	32.0	17.7	20.7
INCOME STATEMENT (IN MILLIONS):							
Total Revenues	25,530.0	26,266.0	28,069.0	26,875.0	22,853.0	22,906.0	9,436.0
Costs & Expenses	22,896.0	22,909.0	24,720.0	23,397.0	20,650.0	20,190.0	8,212.0
Depreciation & Amort.	969.0	1,005.0	1,052.0	1,197.0	921.0	937.0	436.0
Operating Income	1,665.0	2,352.0	2,297.0	2,281.0	1,282.0	1,779.0	788.0
Net Interest Inc./(Exp.)	d809.0	d861.0	d842.0	d640.0	d288.0	d270.0	d110.0
Income Before Income Taxes	1,200.0	1,661.0	1,937.0	2,033.0	1,089.0	1,675.0	725.0
Income Taxes	463.0	660.0	637.0	686.0	407.0	620.0	275.0
Net Income	④ 737.0	1,001.0	③ 1,300.0	② 1,347.0	① 682.0	1,055.0	450.0
Cash Flow	1,706.0	1,696.0	2,299.0	2,484.0	1,543.0	1,932.0	841.0
Average Shs. Outstg. (000)	384,100	381,100	427,000	378,200	378,000	374,000	190,000
BALANCE SHEET (IN MILLIONS):							
Cash & Cash Equivalents	455.0	285.0	...	...	653.0	639.0	373.0
Total Current Assets	10,696.0	10,611.0	10,105.0	9,940.0	8,177.0	8,143.0	2,448.0
Net Property	3,634.0	3,513.0	3,669.0	3,721.0	3,165.0	3,455.0	1,693.0
Total Assets	30,012.0	28,744.0	28,361.0	29,257.0	17,648.0	18,049.0	7,745.0
Total Current Liabilities	8,812.0	10,267.0	9,189.0	8,704.0	5,291.0	5,635.0	1,810.0
Long-Term Obligations	11,427.0	8,957.0	10,528.0	10,188.0	3,010.0	3,594.0	1,479.0
Net Stockholders' Equity	6,361.0	6,137.0	5,176.0	6,856.0	6,433.0	6,086.0	2,877.0
Net Working Capital	1,884.0	344.0	916.0	1,236.0	2,886.0	2,508.0	638.0
Year-end Shs. Outstg. (000)	398,164	393,000	388,000	394,400	398,000	398,000	192,000
STATISTICAL RECORD:							
Operating Profit Margin %	6.5	9.0	8.2	8.5	5.6	7.8	8.4
Net Profit Margin %	2.9	3.8	4.6	5.0	3.0	4.6	4.8
Return on Equity %	11.6	16.3	25.1	19.6	10.6	17.3	15.6
Return on Assets %	2.5	3.5	4.6	4.6	3.9	5.8	5.8
Debt/Total Assets %	38.1	31.2	37.1	34.8	17.1	19.9	19.1
Price Range	46-16³⁄₈	58¹⁵⁄₁₆-41	56³⁄₄-39¹⁄₈	48⁵⁄₁₆-36½	39¾-25	39¼-29³⁄₈	23³⁄₈-16
P/E Ratio	24.0-8.5	22.4-15.6	18.6-12.8	14.2-10.7	24.2-15.2	14.9-11.0	11.0-7.5
Average Yield %	2.8	1.6	1.7	1.9	1.6	1.4	2.2

Statistics are as originally reported. All financial information for 1994 is unaudited and pro forma using the pooling of interests accounting method. Financial data for 12/31/93 and earlier are for Martin Marietta Corp. Adj. for 2-for-1 split, 12/98. ① Incl. aft.-tax merg.-rel. & consol. chgs. of $436.0 mill. ② Incl. a $365.0 mill. pre-tax gain result. from divest. & $25.0 mill. pre-tax chg. rel. to restruct. & other initiative. ③ Incl. tax-free gn. of $311.0 mill. & af.-tax chgs. of $303.0 mill. ④ Bef. acctg. change chrg. $355.0 mill. & incl. various gains of $249.0 mill.

OFFICERS:
V. D. Coffman, Chmn., C.E.O.
L. R. Hughes, Pres., C.O.O.
R. J. Stevens, Exec. V.P., C.F.O.

INVESTOR CONTACT: Lilliam M. Trippett, Investor Relations, (301) 897-6167

PRINCIPAL OFFICE: 6801 Rockledge Drive, Bethesda, MD 20817-1877

TELEPHONE NUMBER: (301) 897-6000
FAX: (301) 897-6083
WEB: www.lockheedmartin.com
NO. OF EMPLOYEES: 147,000 (approx.)
SHAREHOLDERS: 398,164,999 (approx.)
ANNUAL MEETING: In May
INCORPORATED: MD, Oct., 1961; reincorp., MD, Aug., 1994

INSTITUTIONAL HOLDINGS:
No. of Institutions: 312
Shares Held: 369,771,440
% Held: 93.4

INDUSTRY: Guided missiles and space vehicles (SIC: 3761)

TRANSFER AGENT(S): First Chicago Trust Company of New York, Jersey City, NJ

LOWE'S COMPANIES, INC.

YIELD 0.3%
P/E RATIO 26.5

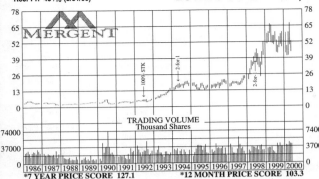

*7 YEAR PRICE SCORE 127.1   *12 MONTH PRICE SCORE 103.3
*NYSE COMPOSITE INDEX=100

INTERIM EARNINGS (Per Share):

Qtr.	Apr.	July	Oct.	Jan.
1996-97	0.15	0.35	0.22	0.16
1997-98	0.21	0.37	0.25	0.21
1998-99	0.27	0.47	0.33	0.30
1999-00	0.33	0.60	0.44	0.39

INTERIM DIVIDENDS (Per Share):

Amt.	Decl.	Ex.	Rec.	Pay.
0.03Q	6/01/99	7/14/99	7/16/99	7/30/99
0.03Q	9/21/99	10/13/99	10/15/99	10/29/99
0.035Q	12/07/99	1/12/00	1/14/00	1/28/00
0.035Q	4/06/00	4/12/00	4/14/00	4/28/00

Indicated div.: $0.14 (Div. Reinv. Plan)

CAPITALIZATION (1/28/00):

	($000)	(%)
Long-Term Debt	1,726,579	26.1
Deferred Income Tax	199,824	3.0
Common & Surplus	4,695,471	70.9
Total	6,621,874	100.0

DIVIDEND ACHIEVER STATUS:

Rank: 220   10-Year Growth Rate: 7.18%
Total Years of Dividend Growth: 22

RECENT DEVELOPMENTS: For the year ended 1/28/00, net earnings jumped 34.5% to $672.8 million from $500.4 million the previous year. Results in the recent period included a non-recurring pre-tax charge of $24.4 million. Net sales rose 19.3% to $15.91 billion from $13.33 billion the year before. Comparable-store sales were up 6.2% versus the prior year. Gross margin climbed 22.6% to $4.38 billion from $3.57 billion a year earlier. Comparisons were made with restated prior-year results.

PROSPECTS: Going forward, results should continue to benefit from the Company's expansion program. LOW anticipates opening 95 during the current year, including relocating 25 existing stores, and opening approximately 125 new stores next year. On 2/10/00, LOW began construction on a new $80.0 million regional distribution center located in Perris, California, which is expected to open on 3/1/01 and will support LOW's aggressive expansion into California, Nevada and Arizona.

BUSINESS

LOWE'S COMPANIES, INC. is a specialty retailer that combines the merchandise, sales and service of a home improvement center, a building materials supplier and a consumer-durables retailer to serve the do-it-yourself home improvement and construction markets. As of 4/28/00, 589 retail stores were in operation in 39 states. The sales mix for 1999: Fashion Plumbing & Electrical, 11%; Tools, 10%; Building Materials, 8%; Hardware, 8%; Outdoor Hardlines, 8%; Appliances, 7%; Lumber, 7%; Nursery & Gardening Products, 7%; Floors, Windows & Walls, 7%; Millwork, 6%; Paint & Sundries, 6%; Rough Plumbing & Electrical, 6%; Cabinets & Furniture, 4%; and Other, 5%. On 4/2/99, LOW acquired Eagle Hardware & Garden, Inc.

QUARTERLY DATA

(1/28/00)($000)	Rev	Inc
1st Quarter	3,771,919	124,958
2nd Quarter	4,435,219	230,217
3rd Quarter	3,909,188	168,688
4th Quarter	3,789,269	148,932

ANNUAL FINANCIAL DATA

	1/28/00	1/29/99	1/30/98	1/31/97	1/31/96	1/31/95	1/31/94
Earnings Per Share	①1.75	1.36	1.03	0.87	0.71	0.72	0.45
Cash Flow Per Share	2.63	2.13	1.72	1.47	1.18	1.09	0.73
Tang. Book Val. Per Share	12.28	8.89	7.42	6.39	5.15	4.45	2.95
Dividends Per Share	0.12	0.115	0.11	0.10	0.093	0.085	0.08
Dividend Payout %	6.9	8.5	10.7	11.5	13.1	11.8	17.8
INCOME STATEMENT (IN MILLIONS):							
Total Revenues	15,905.6	12,244.9	10,136.9	8,600.2	7,075.4	6,110.5	4,538.0
Costs & Expenses	14,419.8	11,139.5	9,271.7	7,897.8	6,531.7	5,626.3	4,239.3
Depreciation & Amort.	337.8	272.2	241.1	199.8	153.6	112.9	82.1
Operating Income	1,148.0	833.2	624.1	502.7	390.1	371.4	216.6
Net Interest Inc./(Exp.)	d84.9	d74.7	d65.6	d49.1	d38.0	d27.9	d18.3
Income Before Income Taxes	1,063.1	758.4	558.5	453.6	352.1	343.5	198.3
Income Taxes	390.3	276.0	201.1	161.5	126.1	120.0	66.5
Net Income	①672.8	482.4	357.5	292.1	226.0	223.6	131.8
Cash Flow	1,010.6	754.6	598.6	491.9	379.6	336.4	213.9
Average Shs. Outstg. (000)	383,854	353,795	348,759	335,356	320,906	309,852	294,796
BALANCE SHEET (IN MILLIONS):							
Cash & Cash Equivalents	568.8	243.1	211.3	70.5	171.3	268.5	108.5
Total Current Assets	3,709.5	2,585.7	2,109.6	1,851.5	1,603.7	1,557.2	1,083.9
Net Property	5,177.2	3,636.9	3,005.2	2,494.4	1,858.3	1,397.7	1,020.2
Total Assets	9,012.3	6,344.7	5,219.3	4,435.0	3,556.4	3,106.0	2,201.6
Total Current Liabilities	2,386.0	1,765.3	1,449.3	1,348.5	949.9	945.9	681.2
Long-Term Obligations	1,726.6	1,283.1	1,045.6	767.3	866.2	681.2	592.3
Net Stockholders' Equity	4,695.5	3,136.0	2,600.6	2,217.5	1,656.7	1,419.9	873.7
Net Working Capital	1,323.6	820.3	660.3	502.9	653.8	611.3	402.7
Year-end Shs. Outstg. (000)	382,359	352,643	350,632	346,808	321,836	319,054	295,774
STATISTICAL RECORD:							
Operating Profit Margin %	7.2	6.8	6.2	5.8	5.5	6.1	4.8
Net Profit Margin %	4.2	3.9	3.5	3.4	3.2	3.7	2.9
Return on Equity %	14.3	15.4	13.7	13.2	13.6	15.7	15.1
Return on Assets %	7.5	7.6	6.8	6.6	6.4	7.2	6.0
Debt/Total Assets %	19.2	20.2	20.0	17.3	24.4	21.9	26.9
Price Range	66⁷/₁₆-43	52³/₁₆-21⁵/₈	24⁹/₁₆-15¹³/₁₆	21³/₄-15¹¹/₁₆	19⁷/₁₆-13³³/₁₆	20¹¹/₁₆-13³/₁₆	14-6¹/₁₆
P/E Ratio	38.0-24.6	38.4-15.9	23.8-15.4	25.0-16.4	27.6-18.4	28.7-18.4	33.6-13.6
Average Yield %	0.2	0.3	0.5	0.5	0.6	0.5	0.8

Statistics are as originally reported. Adj. for 2-for-1 stk. split, 6/98 & 3/94. ① Incl. $24.4 mil pre-tax, non-recur. chg.

OFFICERS:

R. L. Tillman, Chmn., Pres., C.E.O.
T. E. Whiddon, Exec. V.P., C.F.O
L. D. Stone, Exec. V.P., C.O.O.

INVESTOR CONTACT: Carson Anderson, Asst. Treas., (336) 658-4385

PRINCIPAL OFFICE: 1605 Curtis Bridge Road, Wilkesboro, NC 28697

TELEPHONE NUMBER: (336) 658-4000
FAX: (336) 658-4766
WEB: www.lowes.com
NO. OF EMPLOYEES: 70,000 full-time (approx.); 16,000 part-time (approx.)
SHAREHOLDERS: 15,446
ANNUAL MEETING: In May
INCORPORATED: NC, Aug., 1952

INSTITUTIONAL HOLDINGS:
No. of Institutions: 462
Shares Held: 261,059,505
% Held: 68.3

INDUSTRY: Lumber and other building materials (SIC: 5211)

TRANSFER AGENT(S): EquiServe Trust Company, NA, Boston, MA

M & T BANK CORPORATION

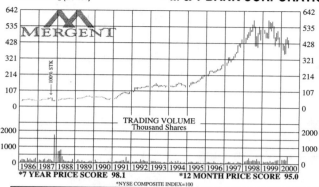

7 YEAR PRICE SCORE 98.1　　**12 MONTH PRICE SCORE 95.0**

*NYSE COMPOSITE INDEX=100

INTERIM EARNINGS (Per Share):

Qtr.	Mar.	June	Sept.	Dec.
1996	5.20	5.36	5.05	5.70
1997	6.17	6.46	6.96	6.66
1998	7.01	5.32	6.81	7.14
1999	8.34	8.00	8.29	8.20

INTERIM DIVIDENDS (Per Share):

Amt.	Decl.	Ex.	Rec.	Pay.
1.00Q	4/21/99	5/27/99	6/01/99	6/30/99
1.25Q	7/21/99	8/30/99	9/01/99	9/30/99
1.25Q	10/20/99	11/29/99	12/01/99	12/30/99
1.25Q	2/16/00	2/28/00	3/01/00	3/31/00
1.25Q	4/19/00	5/30/00	6/01/00	6/30/00

Indicated div.: $5.00 (Div. Reinv. Plan)

CAPITALIZATION (12/31/99):

	($000)	(%)
Total Deposits	15,373,620	81.1
Long-Term Debt	1,775,133	9.4
Common & Surplus	1,797,046	9.5
Total	18,945,799	100.0

DIVIDEND ACHIEVER STATUS:

Rank: 62　　10-Year Growth Rate: 15.13%
Total Years of Dividend Growth: 19

RECENT DEVELOPMENTS:

For the year ended 12/31/99, net income rose 27.7% to $265.6 million versus $208.0 million in 1998. Results for 1999 and 1998 included non-recurring merger and acquisition charges of $3.0 million and $14.0 million, respectively. Total interest income increased 8.8% to $1.48 billion versus $1.36 billion a year earlier. Total interest expense increased 4.6% to $719.2 million from $687.5 million the year before. Net interest income climbed 13.0% to $759.4 million from $671.9 million in 1998. The increase was mainly attributed to growth in average loans and leases. Total other income grew 7.4% to $282.4 million from $262.9 million in the prior year. Total other expense increased 2.3% to $579.0 million from $566.1 million in 1998. On 3/1/00, the Company completed the acquisition of Matthews, Bartlett & Decker, Inc., a property and casualty insurace agency based in Buffalo, NY.

BUSINESS

M&T BANK CORPORATION (formerly First Empire State Corporation) is a $22.40 billion bank holding company. The Company has two wholly-owned bank subsidiaries, Manufacturers and Traders Trust Company (M&T Bank) and M&T Bank, National Association (M&T Bank, N.A.), that offer commercial banking, trust and investment services to their customers. At 12/31/99, M&T Bank represented 96.0% of consolidated assets of the Company and operated 261 banking offices located throughout New York State, 19 banking offices in northeastern Pennsylvania, plus a branch in Nassau, The Bahamas. On 5/24/97, The East New York Savings Bank, formerly a wholly-owned savings bank subsidiary of the Company, was merged with and into M&T Bank. On 4/1/98, MTB acquired ONBANCorp, Inc. of Syracuse, NY. On 6/1/99, MTB acquired the bank holding company FNB Rochester Corp. On 9/24/99, MTB acquired 29 upstate New York branch offices from The Chase Manhattan Bank.

ANNUAL FINANCIAL DATA

	12/31/99	12/31/98	12/31/97	12/31/96	12/31/95	12/31/94	12/31/93
Earnings Per Share	[1] 32.83	[1] 26.16	25.26	21.31	18.79	16.90	14.32
Tang. Book Val. Per Share	148.76	137.22	155.86	135.46	125.33	103.01	99.43
Dividends Per Share	4.50	3.80	3.20	2.80	2.50	2.20	1.90
Dividend Payout %	13.7	14.5	12.7	13.1	13.3	13.0	13.3
INCOME STATEMENT (IN MILLIONS):							
Total Interest Income	1,478.6	1,351.8	1,065.0	997.4	928.2	747.3	740.6
Total Interest Expense	719.2	687.5	508.1	466.4	441.7	279.2	269.9
Net Interest Income	759.4	664.3	556.9	531.0	486.4	468.1	470.8
Provision for Loan Losses	44.5	43.2	46.0	43.3	40.4	60.5	80.0
Non-Interest Income	282.4	270.6	193.1	170.2	149.5	123.7	110.5
Non-Interest Expense	579.0	566.1	421.8	409.0	374.4	336.9	327.8
Income Before Taxes	418.3	325.6	282.2	249.0	221.2	194.5	173.5
Net Income	[1] 265.6	[1] 208.0	176.2	151.1	131.0	117.3	102.0
Average Shs. Outstg. (000)	8,090	7,950	6,977	7,048	6,781	6,952	7,091
BALANCE SHEET (IN MILLIONS):							
Cash & Due from Banks	592.8	493.8	333.8	324.7	363.1	377.8	195.8
Securities Avail. for Sale	2,321.9	2,756.9	1,640.6	1,434.0	1,541.6	1,519.8	2,183.9
Total Loans & Leases	17,572.9	16,005.7	11,765.5	11,120.2	9,873.7	8,447.1	7,439.1
Allowance for Credit Losses	482.3	520.5	543.6	668.6	580.2	473.2	373.8
Net Loans & Leases	17,090.6	15,485.2	11,221.9	10,451.7	9,293.5	7,974.0	7,065.2
Total Assets	22,409.1	20,583.9	14,002.9	12,943.9	11,955.9	10,528.6	10,365.0
Total Deposits	15,373.6	14,737.2	11,163.2	10,514.5	9,469.6	8,243.1	7,353.3
Long-Term Obligations	1,775.1	1,567.5	427.8	178.0	192.8	96.2	75.6
Total Liabilities	20,612.1	18,981.5	12,972.7	12,038.3	11,109.6	9,807.6	9,641.0
Net Stockholders' Equity	1,797.0	1,602.4	1,030.3	905.7	846.3	721.0	724.0
Year-end Shs. Outstg. (000)	7,724	7,698	6,610	6,686	6,433	6,611	6,879
STATISTICAL RECORD:							
Return on Equity %	14.8	13.0	17.1	16.7	15.5	16.3	14.1
Return on Assets %	1.2	1.0	1.3	1.2	1.1	1.1	1.0
Equity/Assets %	8.0	7.8	7.4	7.0	7.1	6.8	7.0
Non-Int. Exp./Tot. Inc. %	55.6	60.6	56.2	58.3	58.9	56.9	56.4
Price Range	582½-406	582-400	455-281	289⅝-209	218-136	165-134½	159-130¼
P/E Ratio	17.7-12.4	22.2-15.3	18.0-11.1	13.6-9.8	11.6-7.2	9.8-8.0	11.1-9.1
Average Yield %	0.9	0.8	0.9	1.1	1.4	1.5	1.3

Statistics are as originally reported. [1] Incl. non-recurr. merger & acquistion chrgs.: $3.0 mill., 12/31/99; $14.0 mill., 12/31/98.

OFFICERS:
R. J. Bennett, Chmn.
R. G. Wilmers, Pres. & C.E.O.
M. P. Pinto, Exec. V.P. & C.F.O.
A. C. Kugler, Exec. V.P. & Treas.

PRINCIPAL OFFICE: One M&T Plaza, Buffalo, NY 14203

TELEPHONE NUMBER: (716) 842-5445
FAX: (716) 842-5177
WEB: www.mandtbank.com

NO. OF EMPLOYEES: 5,604 full-time; 965 part-time

SHAREHOLDERS: 5,991

ANNUAL MEETING: In Apr.

INCORPORATED: NY, Nov., 1969

INSTITUTIONAL HOLDINGS:
No. of Institutions: 127
Shares Held: 4,400,214
% Held: 55.9

INDUSTRY: State commercial banks (SIC: 6022)

TRANSFER AGENT(S): BankBoston, N.A., c/o Equiserve, Boston, MA

MADISON GAS & ELECTRIC COMPANY

YIELD	7.0%
P/E RATIO	12.6

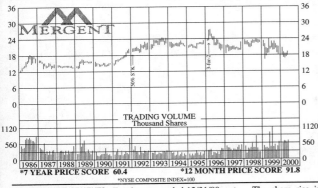

*7 YEAR PRICE SCORE 60.4   ***12 MONTH PRICE SCORE 91.8**

*NYSE COMPOSITE INDEX=100

INTERIM EARNINGS (Per Share):

Qtr.	Mar.	June	Sept.	Dec.
1996	0.46	0.19	0.34	d0.59
1997	0.50	0.16	0.35	0.39
1998	0.53	0.15	0.36	0.34
1999	0.56	0.15	0.38	0.39

INTERIM DIVIDENDS (Per Share):

Amt.	Decl.	Ex.	Rec.	Pay.
0.326Q	5/04/99	5/27/99	6/01/99	6/15/99
0.328Q	8/20/99	8/30/99	9/01/99	9/15/99
0.328Q	11/22/99	11/29/99	12/01/99	12/15/99
0.328Q	2/18/00	2/28/00	3/01/00	3/15/00
0.328Q	5/10/00	5/30/00	6/01/00	6/15/00

Indicated div.: $1.31 (Div. Reinv. Plan)

CAPITALIZATION (12/31/99):

	($000)	(%)
Long-Term Debt	148,599	39.4
Deferred Income Tax	42,981	11.4
Common & Surplus	185,686	49.2
Total	377,266	100.0

DIVIDEND ACHIEVER STATUS:
Rank: 319   10-Year Growth Rate: 1.56%
Total Years of Dividend Growth: 24

RECENT DEVELOPMENTS: For the year ended 12/31/99, net income amounted to $23.7 million, up 6.8% compared with $22.2 million the previous year. Total operating revenues rose 9.7% to $274.0 million from $249.8 million the year before. Electric operating revenues grew 9.7% to $186.0 million from $169.6 million primarily due to growth in retail sales, a 5.1% electric rate increase effective in January 1999, a 3.6% interim rate increase during the fourth quarter of 1999, and a 306.9% increase in sales for resale.

The sharp rise in sales for resale occurred after MDSN agreed to sell 30 megawatts of firm capacity to Wisconsin Public Power, Inc. Gas operating revenues rose 9.8% to $88.1 million from $80.2 million as a result of increased deliveries and higher gas costs that were passed on to customers through the Purchased Gas Adjustment Clause. Net operating income amounted to $32.6 million compared with $29.8 million a year earlier.

BUSINESS

MADISON GAS & ELECTRIC COMPANY is a public utility that generates, transmits and distributes electricity in Dane County, Wisconsin (250 sq. miles). MDSN also purchases, transports and distributes natural gas in six Wisconsin counties: Columbia, Crawford, Dane Iowa, Juneau, Monroe and Vernon (1,325 sq. miles). At 12/31/99, MDSN supplied electric service to approximately 125,000 customers. Of the total number of customers, approximately 108,000 were residential and 17,000 were commercial and industrial.

REVENUES

(12/31/99)	($000)	(%)
Electric	185,955	67.8
Gas	88,079	32.2
Total	274,034	100.0

ANNUAL FINANCIAL DATA

	12/31/99	12/31/98	12/31/97	12/31/96	12/31/95	12/31/94	12/31/93
Earnings Per Share	1.48	1.38	1.40	0.40	1.49	1.53	1.51
Cash Flow Per Share	3.66	3.54	3.21	2.07	3.15	3.05	2.97
Tang. Book Val. Per Share	11.49	11.34	11.25	11.14	12.01	11.78	11.50
Dividends Per Share	1.31	1.30	1.29	1.27	1.26	1.25	1.23
Dividend Payout %	88.4	94.1	91.9	318.2	84.6	81.5	81.2
INCOME STATEMENT (IN THOUSANDS):							
Total Revenues	274,034	249,752	264,648	253,291	248,590	244,972	244,133
Costs & Expenses	146,471	159,291	179,902	169,992	161,789	159,269	159,436
Depreciation & Amort.	37,053	34,759	29,081	26,816	26,787	24,403	23,474
Maintenance Exp.	13,304	15,167	12,735	12,414	11,858	12,416	13,029
Operating Income	32,550	29,812	30,990	31,516	33,871	34,062	34,230
Net Interest Inc./(Exp.)	d12,039	d10,855	d10,724	d10,891	d11,507	d11,122	d11,624
Income Taxes	12,268	10,723	11,940	12,553	14,285	14,822	13,964
Net Income	23,746	22,230	22,523	6,427	23,970	25,011	24,675
Cash Flow	58,900	56,989	51,604	33,243	50,693	48,493	47,660
Average Shs. Outstg.	16,084	16,080	16,080	16,080	16,080	16,055	16,056
BALANCE SHEET (IN THOUSANDS):							
Gross Property	879,253	814,286	770,695	739,514	715,487	695,177	671,497
Accumulated Depreciation	484,428	446,984	407,602	374,315	348,254	323,511	302,904
Net Property	394,825	367,302	363,093	365,199	367,233	371,666	368,593
Total Assets	495,510	466,265	471,790	484,169	493,876	487,759	465,364
Long-Term Obligations	148,599	159,761	129,923	128,886	129,048	130,800	120,396
Net Stockholders' Equity	185,686	182,275	180,923	179,089	193,137	189,489	184,995
Year-end Shs. Outstg.	16,161	16,080	16,080	16,080	16,080	16,080	16,080
STATISTICAL RECORD:							
Operating Profit Margin %	11.9	11.9	11.7	12.4	13.6	13.9	14.0
Net Profit Margin %	20.5	8.9	8.5	2.5	9.6	10.2	10.1
Net Inc./Net Property %	14.2	6.1	6.2	1.8	6.5	6.7	6.7
Net Inc./Tot. Capital %	14.9	5.8	6.3	1.8	6.4	6.5	6.8
Return on Equity %	30.2	12.2	12.4	3.6	12.4	13.2	13.3
Accum. Depr./Gross Prop. %	55.1	54.9	52.9	50.6	48.7	46.5	45.1
Price Range	23⁷⁄₈-16³⁄₈	23³⁄₄-20⁵⁄₈	22³⁄₄-18¹⁄₂	27¹⁄₂-19⁵⁄₈	23⁵⁄₁₆-20⁵⁄₁₆	23⁵⁄₁₆-20¹¹⁄₁₆	24¹⁄₂-20³⁄₁₆
P/E Ratio	16.1-11.1	17.2-14.9	16.2-13.2	68.7-49.1	15.7-13.6	15.2-13.5	16.2-13.4
Average Yield %	6.5	5.9	6.2	5.4	5.8	5.7	5.5

Statistics are as originally reported. Adj. for stk. split: 3-for-2, 2/20/96.

OFFICERS:
D. C. Mebane, Chmn.
G. J. Wolter, Pres., C.E.O.
T. A. Hanson, V.P.-Fin.

INVESTOR CONTACT: Steve Kraus, (608) 252-7907

PRINCIPAL OFFICE: 133 South Blair St., P.O. Box 1231, Madison, WI 53701

TELEPHONE NUMBER: (608) 252-7000
FAX: (608) 252-7098
WEB: www.mge.com

NO. OF EMPLOYEES: 692

SHAREHOLDERS: 18,405 (approx.)

ANNUAL MEETING: In Mar.

INCORPORATED: WI, Apr., 1896

INSTITUTIONAL HOLDINGS:
No. of Institutions: 52
Shares Held: 2,619,733
% Held: 16.3

INDUSTRY: Electric and other services combined (SIC: 4931)

TRANSFER AGENT(S): Harris Trust and Savings Bank, Chicago, IL

NYSE SYMBOL MMC
Rec. Pr. 110 1/16 (5/31/00)

MARSH & MCLENNAN COMPANIES, INC.

YIELD 1.8%
P/E RATIO 41.8

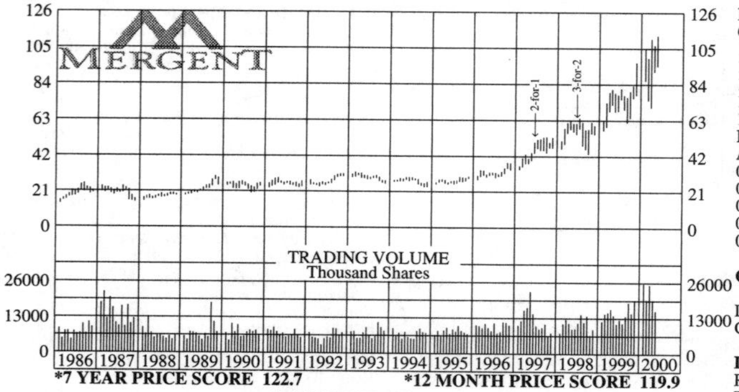

MERGENT
126
105
84
63
42
21
0
2-for-1
3-for-2
TRADING VOLUME
Thousand Shares
26000
13000
0
1986 1987 1988 1989 1990 1991 1992 1993 1994 1995 1996 1997 1998 1999 2000

***7 YEAR PRICE SCORE 122.7** ***12 MONTH PRICE SCORE 119.9**

*NYSE COMPOSITE INDEX=100

INTERIM EARNINGS (Per Share):

Qtr.	Mar.	June	Sept.	Dec.
1995	0.57	0.47	0.42	0.39
1996	0.65	0.53	0.48	0.46
1997	0.75	0.58	0.55	d0.19
1998	0.87	0.72	0.69	0.70
1999	1.03	0.63	0.81	0.16

INTERIM DIVIDENDS (Per Share):

Amt.	Decl.	Ex.	Rec.	Pay.
0.45Q	5/20/99	7/08/99	7/12/99	8/13/99
0.45Q	9/16/99	10/07/99	10/12/99	11/15/99
0.45Q	11/18/99	1/06/00	1/10/00	2/14/00
0.45Q	3/16/00	4/06/00	4/10/00	5/15/00
0.50Q	5/18/00	7/06/00	7/10/00	8/15/00

Indicated div.: $2.00 (Div. Reinv. Plan)

CAPITALIZATION (12/31/99):

	($000)	(%)
Long-Term Debt	2,357,000	36.1
Common & Surplus	4,170,000	63.9
Total	6,527,000	100.0

DIVIDEND ACHIEVER STATUS:
Rank: 216 10-Year Growth Rate: 7.39%
Total Years of Dividend Growth: 38

RECENT DEVELOPMENTS: For the year ended 12/31/99, net income declined 8.8% to $726.0 million compared with $796.0 million the year before. Results included special charges of $337.0 million and a credit of $4.0 million in 1999 and 1998, respectively. Total revenue was $9.16 billion, up 27.4% from $7.19 billion in the previous year. Revenues from risk and insurance services rose 35.0% to $4.52 billion, while investment management revenues increased 16.9% to $2.68 billion.

PROSPECTS: Going forward, results should benefit from the acquisition of Sedgwick Group plc. Accordingly, MMC expects net consolidation savings of approximately $160.0 million over three years mainly due to improvements in operating efficiency. Meanwhile, the Company announced the creation of MMC Enterprise Risk, a new operating entity that offers companies an integrated approach to risk and helps clarify decisions, stabilize earnings and cash flow and improve communications about risk.

BUSINESS

MARSH & MCLENNAN COMPANIES, INC. is engaged in the worldwide business of providing retail and wholesale insurance services, principally as a broker or consultant for insurers, insurance underwriters and other brokers. MMC subsidiaries include Marsh, a major risk and insurance services firm; Putman Investments, one of the largest investment management companies in the United States; and Mercer Consulting Group, a major global provider of consulting services. Other subsidiaries render advisory services in the area of employee benefits and compensation consulting, management consulting, economic consulting and environmental consulting. Contributions to revenues by type of service in 1999 were as follows: insurance services, 49.4%; consulting, 21.3%; and investment management, 29.3%.

ANNUAL FINANCIAL DATA

	12/31/99	12/31/98	12/31/97	12/31/96	12/31/95	12/31/94	12/31/93
Earnings Per Share	[3] **2.62**	**2.98**	[1] **1.59**	**2.11**	**1.84**	[2] **1.73**	**1.51**
Tang. Book Val. Per Share	...	...	**3.07**	**6.19**	**4.29**	**3.46**	**3.18**
Dividends Per Share	**1.70**	**1.47**	**1.27**	**1.10**	**0.99**	**0.93**	**0.90**
Dividend Payout %	**64.9**	**49.2**	**79.5**	**52.1**	**53.8**	**53.9**	**59.7**
INCOME STATEMENT (IN MILLIONS):							
Total Revenues	9,157.0	7,190.0	6,008.6	4,149.0	3,770.3	3,435.0	3,163.4
Income Before Income Taxes	1,247.0	1,305.0	662.4	668.0	649.8	631.5	558.6
Income Taxes	521.0	509.0	263.0	208.7	246.9	249.5	226.2
Net Income	[3] 726.0	796.0	[1] 399.4	459.3	402.9	[2] 382.0	332.4
Average Shs. Outstg. (000)	272,000	264,000	250,800	217,200	218,700	220,800	220,500
BALANCE SHEET (IN MILLIONS):							
Cash & Cash Equivalents	428.0	610.0	424.3	299.6	328.1	294.9	332.0
Premiums Due	2,323.0	1,909.0	1,498.2	1,085.8	1,132.5	955.0	853.0
Invst. Assets: Total	687.0	828.0	720.2	573.3	411.8	282.8	363.6
Total Assets	13,021.0	11,871.0	7,914.2	4,545.2	4,329.5	3,830.6	3,546.6
Long-Term Obligations	2,357.0	1,590.0	1,239.8	458.2	410.6	409.4	409.8
Net Stockholders' Equity	4,170.0	3,659.0	3,198.8	1,888.6	1,665.5	1,460.6	1,365.3
Year-end Shs. Outstg. (000)	267,026	257,000	254,925	216,957	218,322	219,600	221,796
STATISTICAL RECORD:							
Return on Revenues %	7.9	11.1	6.6	11.1	10.7	11.1	10.5
Return on Equity %	17.4	21.8	12.5	24.3	24.2	26.2	24.3
Return on Assets %	5.6	6.7	5.0	10.1	9.3	10.0	9.4
Price Range	96 3/4-57 1/8	64 5/16-43 3/8	53 5/16-34 3/16	38 5/16-28 1/16	30 1/16-25 3/8	29 9/16-23 3/4	32 9/16-25 11/16
P/E Ratio	36.9-21.8	21.6-14.6	33.5-21.5	18.1-13.3	16.3-13.8	17.1-13.7	21.6-17.0
Average Yield %	2.2	2.7	2.9	3.3	3.6	3.5	3.1

Statistics are as originally reported. Adj. for stk. split: 3-for-2, 6/98; 2-for-1, 6/97 [1] Incl. non-recurr. chrg. 1997, $296.8 mill. [2] Bef. acctg. change chrg. 1994, $10.5 mill. [3] Incl. special chrg. $337.0 mill.

OFFICERS:
A. J. Smith, Chmn.
M. Cabiallavetta, Vice-Chmn.
C. A. Davis, Vice-Chmn.
J. W. Greenberg, Pres., C.E.O.

INVESTOR CONTACT: J. Michael Bischoff, V.P. Corp. Development, (212) 345-5475

PRINCIPAL OFFICE: 1166 Avenue Of The Americas, New York, NY 10036-2774

TELEPHONE NUMBER: (212) 345-5000
FAX: (212) 345-4809
WEB: www.mmc.com

NO. OF EMPLOYEES: 52,900 (approx.)

SHAREHOLDERS: 29,100

ANNUAL MEETING: In May

INCORPORATED: DE, Mar., 1969

INSTITUTIONAL HOLDINGS:
No. of Institutions: 512
Shares Held: 184,650,346
% Held: 69.2

INDUSTRY: Insurance agents, brokers, & service (SIC: 6411)

TRANSFER AGENT(S): The Bank of New York, New York, NY

NYSE SYMBOL MI
Rec. Pr. 48½ (5/31/00)

MARSHALL & ILSLEY CORP.

YIELD 2.2%
P/E RATIO 15.4

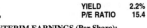

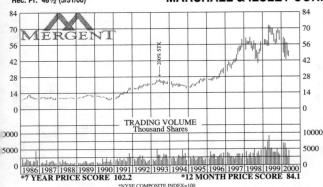

84
70
56
42
28
14
0
84
70
56
42
28
14
0
MERGENT
200% STK
TRADING VOLUME
Thousand Shares
10000
5000
0
1986
1987
1988
1989
1990
1991
1992
1993
1994
1995
1996
1997
1998
1999
2000

*7 YEAR PRICE SCORE 102.2 *12 MONTH PRICE SCORE 84.1

*NYSE COMPOSITE INDEX=100

INTERIM EARNINGS (Per Share):

Qtr.	Mar.	June	Sept.	Dec.
1996	0.47	0.51	0.46	0.63
1997	0.57	0.58	0.63	0.65
1998	0.66	0.54	0.70	0.72
1999	0.75	0.77	0.81	0.81

INTERIM DIVIDENDS (Per Share):

Amt.	Decl.	Ex.	Rec.	Pay.
0.24Q	4/27/99	5/26/99	5/28/99	6/14/99
0.24Q	8/12/99	8/27/99	8/31/99	9/14/99
0.24Q	10/14/99	11/26/99	11/30/99	12/14/99
0.24Q	2/25/00	2/25/00	2/29/00	3/14/00
0.265Q	4/25/00	5/26/00	5/31/00	6/14/00

Indicated div.: $1.06 (Div. Reinv. Plan)

CAPITALIZATION (12/31/99):

	($000)	(%)
Total Deposits	16,435,182	85.5
Long-Term Debt	665,024	3.5
Preferred Stock	336	0.0
Common & Surplus	2,116,590	11.0
Total	19,217,132	100.0

DIVIDEND ACHIEVER STATUS:
Rank: 150 10-Year Growth Rate: 10.38%
Total Years of Dividend Growth: 26

RECENT DEVELOPMENTS: For the year ended 12/31/99, net income amounted to $354.5 million, up 17.7% compared with $301.3 million in the previous year. Results for 1998 included a non-recurring merger and restructuring charge of $23.4 million. Total interest income increased 4.4% to $1.50 billion from $1.43 billion in 1998. The increase in total interest income was primarily the result of increased loans and leases income. Total interest expense increased 4.4% to $791.3 million from $758.0 million the year before. Net interest income rose 4.3% to $705.3 million from $676.1 million a year earlier. Total other income rose 11.8% to $845.8 million from $756.3 million, fueled by revenue increases for data processing services, trust services, and contributions from Internet banking, which was launched in the fourth quarter of 1998. Total other expense increased 6.1% to $997.7 million from $940.0 million in the prior year.

BUSINESS

MARSHALL & ILSLEY CORP., a $24.40 billion multibank holding company as of 12/31/99, is headquartered in Milwaukee, Wisconsin. M&I Marshall and Ilsley Bank is the Corporation's lead bank. The Corporation has 27 affiliate banks serving the state from more than 230 banking offices in Wisconsin. The Corporation also has a bank in Phoenix, Arizona with 13 offices, a bank in Nevada with 4 offices located in Illinois, one office in Nevada and one office in Florida and trust companies in Wisconsin, Florida, and Arizona. In addition, the holding company owns and operates 49 offices throughout the country that provide trust and investment management, equipment leasing, mortgage banking, and data processing. On 10/1/97, MI acquired Security Capital Corp. On 6/1/99, MI launched its on-line brokerage service, MiBroker Online.

LOAN DISTRIBUTION

(12/31/1999)	($000)	(%)
Comm, Finl & Agricultural	4,754,857	29.0
Construction	494,558	3.0
Residential Mortgage	4,941,450	30.0
Commericial Mortgage	4,034,771	25.0
Personal	1,299,416	8.0
Lease Financing	810,009	5.0
Total	16,335,061	100.0

ANNUAL FINANCIAL DATA

	12/31/99	12/31/98	12/31/97	12/31/96	12/31/95	12/31/94	12/31/93
Earnings Per Share	**3.14**	[3] **2.61**	**2.42**	**2.07**	**1.96**	[1][3] **0.95**	**1.87**
Tang. Book Val. Per Share	**16.54**	**17.98**	**18.90**	**14.23**	**13.44**	**11.47**	**11.29**
Dividends Per Share	**0.94**	**0.86**	**0.79**	**0.72**	**0.65**	**0.59**	**0.54**
Dividend Payout %	**29.9**	**32.9**	**32.4**	**34.8**	**32.9**	**62.1**	**29.1**
INCOME STATEMENT (IN MILLIONS):							
Total Interest Income	1,496.6	1,434.0	1,143.7	971.4	924.7	817.3	487.5
Total Interest Expense	791.3	758.0	579.6	465.7	433.2	326.1	178.4
Net Interest Income	705.3	676.1	564.0	505.7	491.5	491.2	309.2
Provision for Loan Losses	25.4	27.1	17.3	15.2	16.2	24.9	9.1
Non-Interest Income	845.8	1,424.2	598.9	503.3	424.2	361.5	299.9
Non-Interest Expense	997.7	944.9	775.4	680.7	599.6	660.0	403.4
Income Before Taxes	527.9	465.3	370.3	313.1	299.9	167.8	196.6
Net Income	354.5	[3] 964.3	245.1	203.4	193.3	[1][3] 94.4	125.5
Average Shs. Outstg. (000)	113,005	115,240	101,510	98,482	98,757	99,420	67,047
BALANCE SHEET (IN MILLIONS):							
Cash & Due from Banks	705.3	760.4	800.1	780.6	745.9	685.9	479.5
Securities Avail. for Sale	4,477.0	4,247.2	4,182.2	3,213.9	2,677.8	2,005.8	1,591.7
Total Loans & Leases	16,335.1	13,996.2	12,542.3	9,301.9	8,868.9	8,792.5	5,371.1
Allowance for Credit Losses	225.9	226.1	202.8	155.9	161.4	154.0	93.2
Net Loans & Leases	16,109.2	13,770.1	12,339.5	9,146.0	8,707.5	8,638.5	5,277.9
Total Assets	24,369.7	21,566.3	19,477.5	14,763.3	13,343.1	12,612.9	7,970.2
Total Deposits	16,435.2	15,919.9	14,356.0	10,952.4	10,280.8	9,499.1	6,195.9
Long-Term Obligations	665.0	794.5	791.2	336.1	422.6	653.8	202.8
Total Liabilities	22,252.8	19,322.5	17,557.4	13,502.1	12,085.5	11,551.7	7,219.9
Net Stockholders' Equity	2,116.9	2,243.8	1,920.1	1,261.2	1,257.6	1,061.3	750.4
Year-end Shs. Outstg. (000)	105,816	106,103	101,537	88,584	93,526	92,529	66,425
STATISTICAL RECORD:							
Return on Equity %	16.7	43.0	12.8	16.1	15.4	8.9	16.7
Return on Assets %	1.5	4.5	1.3	1.4	1.4	0.7	1.6
Equity/Assets %	8.7	10.4	9.9	8.5	9.4	8.4	9.4
Non-Int. Exp./Tot. Inc. %	64.3	45.0	66.7	67.5	65.5	77.4	66.2
Price Range	72¾-54⅜	62¼-39⅜	60½-32⅜	35⅝-24⅜	26½-18	24-17¾	26-20 15/16
P/E Ratio	23.2-17.3	23.8-15.1	25.0-13.4	17.2-11.8	13.5-9.2	25.3-18.7	13.9-11.2
Average Yield %	1.5	1.7	1.7	2.4	2.9	2.8	2.3

Statistics are as originally reported. Adj. for stk. splits: 3-for-1, 6/1/93 [1] Bef. extraord. credit $11.5 mill. ($0.12/sh.) [2] Bef. acctg. change chrg. $7.4 mill. ($0.11/sh.) [3] Incl. non-recurr. chrg. $23.4 mill., 12/31/98; $75.2 mill.; 12/31/94

OFFICERS:
J. B. Wigdale, Chmn., C.E.O.
D. J. Kuester, Pres.
J. L. Delgadillo, Sr. V.P.
G. H. Gunnlaugsson, Exec. V.P., C.F.O.

PRINCIPAL OFFICE: 770 North Water St., Milwaukee, WI 53202

TELEPHONE NUMBER: (414) 765-7801
FAX: (414) 765-8026
WEB: www.micorp.com

NO. OF EMPLOYEES: 11,433 (approx.)

SHAREHOLDERS: 20,549 (approx.)

ANNUAL MEETING: In Apr.

INCORPORATED: WI, Feb., 1959

INSTITUTIONAL HOLDINGS:
No. of Institutions: 197
Shares Held: 35,523,812
% Held: 33.4

INDUSTRY: National commercial banks (SIC: 6021)

TRANSFER AGENT(S): BankBoston, N.A., c/o EquiServe, Boston, MA

MASCO CORPORATION

YIELD 2.4%
P/E RATIO 14.9

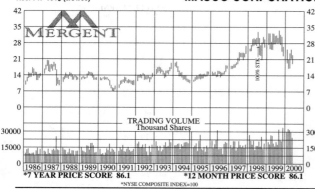

INTERIM EARNINGS (Per Share):

Qtr.	Mar.	June	Sept.	Dec.
1996	0.20	0.21	0.26	0.26
1997	0.26	0.29	0.30	0.30
1998	0.33	0.34	0.37	0.36
1999	0.36	0.41	0.15	0.40

INTERIM DIVIDENDS (Per Share):

Amt.	Decl.	Ex.	Rec.	Pay.
0.11Q	3/19/99	3/30/99	4/02/99	5/03/99
0.11Q	6/30/99	7/14/99	7/16/99	8/09/99
0.12Q	9/23/99	10/27/99	10/29/99	11/12/99
0.12Q	12/09/99	1/05/00	1/07/00	2/07/00
0.12Q	3/17/00	4/05/00	4/07/00	5/08/00

Indicated div.: $0.48 (Div. Reinv. Plan)

CAPITALIZATION (12/31/99):

	($000)	(%)
Long-Term Debt	2,431,270	43.7
Common & Surplus	3,136,500	56.3
Total	5,567,770	100.0

TRADING VOLUME
Thousand Shares

7 YEAR PRICE SCORE 86.1   **12 MONTH PRICE SCORE 86.1**
NYSE COMPOSITE INDEX=100

DIVIDEND ACHIEVER STATUS:
Rank: 242   10-Year Growth Rate: 6.05%
Total Years of Dividend Growth: 41

RECENT DEVELOPMENTS: For the year ended 12/31/99, net income advanced slightly to $569.6 million compared with $565.1 million in 1998. Net sales were $6.31 billion, up 19.5% from $5.28 billion a year earlier. The improvement in results was primarily attributed to internal growth and acquisitions. Comparisons were made with restated 1998 results. For the quarter ended 12/31/99, net income rose 29.7% to $178.7 million.

PROSPECTS: The Company reached an agreement to acquire Tvilum-Scanbirk A/S, a European manufacturer of ready-to-assemble products, including cabinetry, shelving, storage units, workstations, and furniture. Headquartered in Faarvang, Denmark, Tvilum-Scanbirk had sales in 1999 in excess of $200.0 million. The Tvilum-Scanbirk acquisition offers opportunities for both MAS and Tvilum-Scanbirk to expand their customer bases.

BUSINESS

MASCO CORPORATION manufactures building, home improvement and home furnishings products. Masco's kitchen and bath products segment includes faucets, plumbing fittings, kitchen and bathroom cabinets, bathtubs and whirlpools, builders' hardware, venting and ventilating equipment, insulation products and water pumps. Other specialty products include high-quality furniture and other home furnishings products, giftware, and recreational accessories. Brand-names include DELTA DELEX PEERLESS ARTISTIC and EPIC faucets; MERILLAT kitchen and bathroom cabinets; WEISER and BALDWIN locks, BRASSCRAFT and PLUMB SHOP plumbing fittings; THERMADOR and WASTE KING appliances.

ANNUAL FINANCIAL DATA

	12/31/99	12/31/98	12/31/97	12/31/96 ③	12/31/95	12/31/94	12/31/93
Earnings Per Share	④ 1.28	1.39	1.15	0.92	② 0.63	① 0.61	0.73
Cash Flow Per Share	1.68	1.78	1.48	1.23	0.91	0.99	1.10
Tang. Book Val. Per Share	3.14	4.99	4.53	4.30	4.09	4.48	4.56
Dividends Per Share	0.45	0.43	0.41	0.39	0.36	0.34	0.33
Dividend Payout %	35.2	30.9	35.2	41.8	58.4	56.5	44.8
INCOME STATEMENT (IN MILLIONS):							
Total Revenues	6,307.0	4,345.0	3,760.0	3,237.0	2,927.0	4,468.0	3,886.0
Costs & Expenses	5,213.8	3,528.2	3,056.9	2,656.8	2,434.6	3,837.8	3,362.2
Depreciation & Amort.	181.8	136.3	116.1	99.7	90.1	120.6	116.0
Operating Income	911.4	680.5	587.1	480.5	402.3	509.6	403.8
Net Interest Inc./(Exp.)	d120.4	d85.3	d79.8	d74.7	d73.8	d104.7	d89.6
Income Before Income Taxes	904.1	755.0	630.9	502.7	351.8	322.6	362.6
Income Taxes	334.5	279.0	248.5	207.5	151.7	128.9	141.5
Equity Earnings/Minority Int.	23.9	29.2	24.1	20.1	26.2	d101.3	18.7
Net Income	④ 569.6	476.0	382.4	295.2	② 200.1	① 193.7	221.1
Cash Flow	751.4	612.3	498.5	394.9	290.1	314.3	337.1
Average Shs. Outstg. (000)	446,200	343,700	337,600	321,200	319,200	317,600	305,400
BALANCE SHEET (IN MILLIONS):							
Cash & Cash Equivalents	230.8	541.7	441.3	473.7	60.5	71.1	124.9
Total Current Assets	2,109.8	1,862.6	1,626.7	1,429.8	964.5	1,891.4	1,643.8
Net Property	1,624.4	1,164.3	1,037.3	940.6	856.7	1,231.8	1,095.2
Total Assets	6,634.9	5,167.4	4,333.8	3,701.7	3,778.6	4,390.0	4,021.1
Total Current Liabilities	846.4	846.6	620.0	518.4	445.9	601.3	490.4
Long-Term Obligations	2,431.3	1,391.4	1,321.5	1,236.3	1,577.1	1,592.6	1,418.3
Net Stockholders' Equity	3,136.5	2,728.6	2,229.0	1,839.8	1,655.4	2,112.7	1,998.4
Net Working Capital	1,263.3	1,016.0	1,006.7	911.3	518.6	1,290.2	1,153.4
Year-end Shs. Outstg. (000)	443,510	339,330	331,140	321,740	320,760	313,980	305,700
STATISTICAL RECORD:							
Operating Profit Margin %	14.5	15.7	15.6	14.8	13.7	11.4	10.4
Net Profit Margin %	9.0	11.0	10.2	9.1	6.8	4.3	5.7
Return on Equity %	18.2	17.4	17.2	16.0	12.1	9.2	11.1
Return on Assets %	8.6	9.2	8.8	8.0	5.3	4.4	5.5
Debt/Total Assets %	36.6	26.9	30.5	33.4	41.7	36.3	35.3
Price Range	33¹¹/₁₆-22½	33-20¾	26¹⁵/₁₆-16⅞	18⁷/₁₆-13¼	15³/₄-11¼	19¹⁵/₁₆-10⅝	19⁷/₁₆-12¾
P/E Ratio	26.3-17.6	23.7-14.9	23.4-14.7	20.0-14.4	25.2-18.0	32.7-17.4	26.8-17.6
Average Yield %	1.6	1.6	1.9	2.4	2.7	2.3	2.0

Statistics are as originally reported. Adj. for stk. split: 2-for-1, 7/98. ① Incl. non-recurr. chrg. $79.3 mill. ($0.50/sh.). ② Incl. non-recurr. chrg. $47.9 mill. Bef. discont. oper. loss $641.7 mill. ③ Reflects the planned sale of the Masco Home Furnishings Group businesses. ④ Incl. aftertax non-recurr. chrg. of approx. $126.0 mill. ($0.28/sh.).

OFFICERS:
R. A. Manoogian, Chmn., C.E.O.
R. F. Kennedy, Pres., C.O.O.
R. B. Rosowski, V.P., Treas., Contr.
E. A. Gargaro Jr., V.P., Sec.

INVESTOR CONTACT: Samual A. Cypert, Investor Contact, (313) 274-7400

PRINCIPAL OFFICE: 21001 Van Born Rd., Taylor, MI 48180

TELEPHONE NUMBER: (313) 274-7400
FAX: (313) 792-6135
WEB: www.masco.com
NO. OF EMPLOYEES: 42,500 (approx.)
SHAREHOLDERS: 6,445 (approx.)
ANNUAL MEETING: In May
INCORPORATED: MI, Dec., 1929; reincorp., DE, 1968

INSTITUTIONAL HOLDINGS:
No. of Institutions: 339
Shares Held: 272,219,127
% Held: 61.4

INDUSTRY: Wood household furniture (SIC 2511)

TRANSFER AGENT(S): Bank of New York, New York, NY

MAY DEPARTMENT STORES COMPANY (THE)

YIELD	3.1%
P/E RATIO	11.6

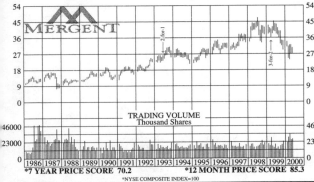

INTERIM EARNINGS (Per Share):

Qtr.	Apr.	July	Oct.	Jan.
1996-97	0.27	0.27	0.29	1.13
1997-98	0.26	0.32	0.33	1.19
1998-99	0.29	0.35	0.35	1.31
1999-00	0.34	0.43	0.38	1.45

INTERIM DIVIDENDS (Per Share):

Amt.	Decl.	Ex.	Rec.	Pay.
0.223Q	8/20/99	8/30/99	9/01/99	9/15/99
0.223Q	11/12/99	11/29/99	12/01/99	12/15/99
0.233Q	2/10/00	2/28/00	3/01/00	3/15/00
0.233Q	3/10/00	5/30/00	6/01/00	6/15/00

Indicated div.: $0.93 (Div. Reinv. Plan)

CAPITALIZATION (1/29/00):

	($000)	(%)
Long-Term Debt	3,560,000	43.5
Deferred Income Tax	540,000	6.6
Common & Surplus	4,077,000	49.9
Total	8,177,000	100.0

TRADING VOLUME
Thousand Shares

1986 1987 1988 1989 1990 1991 1992 1993 1994 1995 1996 1997 1998 1999 2000

*7 YEAR PRICE SCORE 70.2   ***12 MONTH PRICE SCORE 85.3**

*NYSE COMPOSITE INDEX=100

DIVIDEND ACHIEVER STATUS:
Rank: 228   10-Year Growth Rate: 6.78%
Total Years of Dividend Growth: 24

RECENT DEVELOPMENTS: For the 52 weeks ended 1/29/00, net earnings totaled $927.0 million, up 9.2% versus $849.0 million in the previous year. Revenues grew 6.0% to $14.22 billion from $13.41 billion a year earlier. Net retail sales rose 6.3% to $13.87 billion. Comparable-store sales rose 2.6%. Sales were slightly hampered by the discontinuation of the consumer electronics business in early 1999. Operating earnings advanced 8.2% to $1.81 billion from $1.67 billion in the prior year.

PROSPECTS: Going forward, the Company will focus on becoming a more merchandise-driven, sales-driven company. Separately, the Company completed its acquisition of Zions Co-operative Mercantile Institution (ZCMI). MAY's Meier & Frank division opened 13 ZCMI stores on 1/31/00. In addition to the ZCMI stores, MAY anticipates opening ten new stores by the end of 2000, including four Lord & Taylor stores, four Foley's stores, a Kaufmann's store and a Famous-Barr store.

BUSINESS

THE MAY DEPARTMENT STORES COMPANY operates eight regional department store companies through 422 stores in 36 states and the District of Columbia. The department store companies include: Lord & Taylor, Hecht's, Strawbridge's, Foley's, Robinsons-May, Filene's, Kaufmann's, Famous-Barr, L.S. Ayers, The Jones Store and Meier & Frank. Thalhimers was acquired for $317 million in 1990, and was consolidated with the Hecht's division in January 1992. On 5/4/96, the Company completed its spin-off of Payless ShoeSource, Inc. through the distribution of 16 shares of common stock of Payless ShoeSource, Inc. for every one share of May common stock held.

ANNUAL FINANCIAL DATA

	1/29/00	1/30/99	1/31/98	2/1/97 [3]	2/3/96	1/28/95	1/29/94
Earnings Per Share	2.60	2.30	[1] 2.07	[1] 1.96	[2] 1.82	2.04	1.85
Cash Flow Per Share	3.93	3.51	3.19	3.01	2.75	3.10	2.82
Tang. Book Val. Per Share	9.51	8.67	8.82	8.09	10.48	9.50	8.12
Dividends Per Share	0.89	0.85	0.80	0.77	0.74	0.67	0.60
Dividend Payout %	34.2	36.8	38.6	39.3	40.8	33.0	32.4
INCOME STATEMENT (IN MILLIONS):							
Total Revenues	14,224.0	13,413.0	12,685.0	12,000.0	10,952.0	12,223.0	11,529.0
Costs & Expenses	11,945.0	11,301.0	10,400.0	10,118.0	9,209.0	10,319.0	9,758.0
Depreciation & Amort.	469.0	439.0	412.0	373.0	333.0	374.0	348.0
Operating Income	1,810.0	1,673.0	1,578.0	1,509.0	1,410.0	1,530.0	1,423.0
Net Interest Inc./(Exp.)	d287.0	d278.0	d299.0	d277.0	d250.0	d234.0	d245.0
Income Before Income Taxes	1,523.0	1,395.0	1,279.0	1,232.0	1,160.0	1,296.0	1,178.0
Income Taxes	596.0	546.0	500.0	483.0	460.0	514.0	467.0
Net Income	927.0	849.0	[1] 779.0	[1] 749.0	[2] 700.0	782.0	711.0
Cash Flow	1,377.0	1,270.0	1,173.0	1,104.0	1,014.0	1,137.0	1,042.0
Average Shs. Outstg. (000)	355,600	367,400	373,600	373,050	375,000	373,500	375,000
BALANCE SHEET (IN MILLIONS):							
Cash & Cash Equivalents	41.0	112.0	199.0	102.0	159.0	55.0	46.0
Total Current Assets	5,115.0	4,987.0	4,878.0	5,035.0	5,097.0	4,910.0	4,679.0
Net Property	4,769.0	4,513.0	4,224.0	4,159.0	3,744.0	3,866.0	3,411.0
Total Assets	10,935.0	10,533.0	9,930.0	10,059.0	10,122.0	9,472.0	8,800.0
Total Current Liabilities	2,415.0	2,059.0	1,866.0	1,923.0	1,602.0	1,895.0	1,771.0
Long-Term Obligations	3,560.0	3,825.0	3,512.0	3,849.0	3,333.0	2,875.0	2,822.0
Net Stockholders' Equity	4,077.0	3,836.0	3,809.0	3,650.0	4,585.0	4,135.0	3,639.0
Net Working Capital	2,700.0	2,928.0	3,012.0	3,112.0	3,495.0	3,015.0	2,908.0
Year-end Shs. Outstg. (000)	325,500	334,700	346,500	355,350	373,500	372,000	372,000
STATISTICAL RECORD:							
Operating Profit Margin %	12.7	12.5	12.4	12.6	12.9	12.5	12.3
Net Profit Margin %	6.5	6.3	6.1	6.2	6.4	6.4	6.2
Return on Equity %	22.7	22.1	20.5	20.5	15.3	18.9	19.5
Return on Assets %	8.5	8.1	7.8	7.4	6.9	8.3	8.1
Debt/Total Assets %	32.6	36.3	35.4	38.3	32.9	30.4	32.1
Price Range	45⅜-29³⁄₁₆	47¼-33³⁄₁₆	38¹⁄₁₆-29¹⁄₁₆	34¹³⁄₁₆-26¹¹⁄₁₆	30¼-21¹⁵⁄₁₆	30¹⁄₁₆-21½	31-22⁵⁄₁₆
P/E Ratio	17.5-11.2	20.5-14.4	18.4-14.0	17.8-13.6	16.6-12.0	14.7-10.5	16.8-12.1
Average Yield %	2.4	2.1	2.4	2.5	2.8	2.6	2.2

Statistics are as originally reported. Adj. for 3-for-2 stk. split, 3/99. [1] Bef. $4 mil extraord. loss, 1997; & bef. $5 mil extraord. loss & cr$11 mil from discont. opers., 1996. [2] Bef. discont. opers. cr$55 mil; bef. $3 mil extraord. loss; & incl. $44 mil non-recur. chg. [3] Excl. results of spun-off PayLess ShoeSource, Inc.

OFFICERS:
J. T. Loeb, Chmn.
E. S. Kahn, Pres., C.E.O.
J. L. Dunham, Vice-Chmn., C.F.O.
A. J. Torcasio, Vice-Chmn.

INVESTOR CONTACT: Jan R. Kniffen, Sr.
V.P. & Treas., (314) 342-6413

PRINCIPAL OFFICE: 611 Olive Street, St. Louis, MO 63101-1799

TELEPHONE NUMBER: (314) 342-6300
FAX: (314) 342-6497
WEB: www.maycompany.com
NO. OF EMPLOYEES: 62,000 full-time (approx.); 72,000 part-time (approx.)
SHAREHOLDERS: 45,000 (approx.)
ANNUAL MEETING: In May
INCORPORATED: NY, June, 1910; reincorp., DE, May, 1996

INSTITUTIONAL HOLDINGS:
No. of Institutions: 424
Shares Held: 256,773,797
% Held: 77.6

INDUSTRY: Department stores (SIC: 5311)

TRANSFER AGENT(S): The Bank of New York, New York, NY

NYSE SYMBOL MBI
Rec. Pr. 57 13/16 (5/31/00)

MBIA INC.

YIELD 1.4%
P/E RATIO 18.1

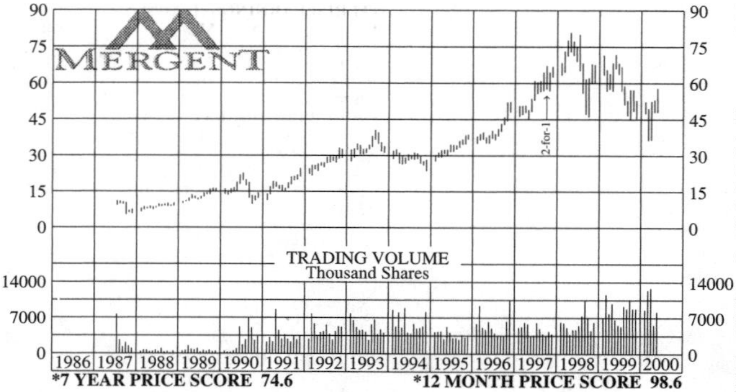

MERGENT
2-for-1
TRADING VOLUME
Thousand Shares
1986 1987 1988 1989 1990 1991 1992 1993 1994 1995 1996 1997 1998 1999 2000

*7 YEAR PRICE SCORE 74.6 *12 MONTH PRICE SCORE 98.6

*NYSE COMPOSITE INDEX=100

INTERIM EARNINGS (Per Share):

Qtr.	Mar.	June	Sept.	Dec.
1996	0.91	0.92	0.96	0.94
1997	1.04	1.02	1.08	1.08
1998	1.01	1.17	1.08	1.03
1999	0.09	0.56	1.27	1.27

INTERIM DIVIDENDS (Per Share):

Amt.	Decl.	Ex.	Rec.	Pay.
0.20Q	3/18/99	3/25/99	3/29/99	4/15/99
0.20Q	6/14/99	6/23/99	6/25/99	7/15/99
0.20Q	9/17/99	9/23/99	9/27/99	10/15/99
0.205Q	12/09/99	12/16/99	12/20/99	1/14/00
0.205Q	3/16/00	3/23/00	3/27/00	4/15/00

Indicated div.: $0.82

CAPITALIZATION (12/31/99):

	($000)	(%)
Long-Term Debt	689,204	16.3
Deferred Income Tax	32,805	0.8
Common & Surplus	3,513,101	83.0
Total	4,235,110	100.0

DIVIDEND ACHIEVER STATUS:
Rank: 36 10-Year Growth Rate: 17.84%
Total Years of Dividend Growth: 12

RECENT DEVELOPMENTS: For the year ended 12/31/99, net income decreased 25.9% to $320.5 million compared with $432.7 million in the previous year. Results included net realized gains of $25.2 million and $35.0 million in 1999 and 1998, respectively. Results also included one-time charges of $105.0 million and $75.2 million in 1999 and 1998, respectively. Total revenues rose 4.7% to $964.4 million versus $921.0 million in 1998.

PROSPECTS: MBI and Ambac Financial Group, Inc. restructured their international joint marketing and reinsurance arrangements. As per the agreement, the companies will market and originate international financial guarantee insurance independently. Going forward, MBI is positioned to achieve long-term growth due to its disciplined approach to pricing and risk selection, strengthened balance sheet and more effectively managed capital position.

BUSINESS

MBIA INC. is the holding company of MBIA Insurance Corporation, a major company in the municipal bond and structured finance insurance business. MBIA's principal business guarantees timely payment of principal and interest for new municipal bond issues, asset-backed securities, bonds traded in the secondary market and those held in unit investment trusts and mutual funds. In addition, it guarantees high quality obligations offered by financial institutions and provides investment management and other financial services for school districts and municipalities. MBIA serves state and local governments and other agencies, issuers of asset-backed securities, financial advisors, investment banking firms, bond traders, sponsors of unit investment trusts and mutual funds and the investing public. MBI's operations take place in North America, Europe, Asia and Australia. MBI acquired CapMAC Holdings, Inc. on 2/17/98 and 1838 Investment Advisors on 7/31/98.

QUARTERLY DATA

	Rev	Inc
1st Quarter	11,954	9,420
2nd Quarter	53,358	56,793
3rd Quarter	160,178	127,410
4th Quater	162,393	126,907

ANNUAL FINANCIAL DATA

	12/31/99	12/31/98	12/31/97	12/31/96	12/31/95	12/31/94	12/31/93
Earnings Per Share	**3 3.19**	**2 4.32**	**4.22**	**3.72**	**3.22**	**3.09**	**1 2.90**
Tang. Book Val. Per Share	**34.18**	**36.88**	**32.73**	**27.42**	**25.33**	**19.14**	**17.70**
Dividends Per Share	**0.80**	**0.79**	**0.77**	**0.71**	**0.64**	**0.55**	**0.45**
Dividend Payout %	**25.1**	**18.2**	**18.1**	**19.0**	**19.8**	**17.6**	**15.3**
INCOME STATEMENT (IN MILLIONS):							
Total Premium Income	442.8	424.6	297.4	251.7	215.1	218.3	231.3
Net Investment Income	359.5	331.8	281.5	247.6	219.9	193.9	178.9
Other Income	162.2	164.7	75.1	46.3	27.3	27.4	18.8
Total Revenues	964.4	921.0	654.0	545.5	462.2	439.5	429.0
Income Before Income Taxes	387.9	565.0	479.6	408.1	345.0	329.4	324.0
Income Taxes	67.4	132.3	105.4	86.0	345.0	69.2	77.9
Net Income	3 320.5	2 432.7	374.2	322.2	271.4	260.2	1 246.1
Average Shs. Outstg. (000)	100,402	100,163	88,747	86,696	84,480	84,172	84,932
BALANCE SHEET (IN MILLIONS):							
Cash & Cash Equivalents	5,264.3	4,755.4	4,099.4	3,722.8	2,978.0	1,822.8	750.1
Premiums Due	459.0	402.2	266.3	217.8	207.0	187.4	202.5
Invst. Assets: Fixed-term	5,784.0	5,884.1	4,867.3	4,149.7	3,652.6	3,051.9	2,796.7
Invst. Assets: Total	10,954.8	10,618.7	8,943.4	7,865.2	6,607.3	4,866.8	3,544.3
Total Assets	12,263.9	11,796.6	9,810.8	8,562.0	7,267.5	5,456.4	4,106.3
Long-Term Obligations	689.2	689.0	473.9	374.0	373.9	298.8	298.7
Net Stockholders' Equity	3,513.1	3,792.2	3,048.3	2,479.7	2,234.3	1,704.7	1,596.4
Year-end Shs. Outstg. (000)	99,552	99,548	89,461	86,588	84,008	83,232	83,628
STATISTICAL RECORD:							
Return on Revenues %	33.2	47.0	57.2	59.1	58.7	59.2	57.4
Return on Equity %	9.1	11.4	12.3	13.0	12.1	15.3	15.4
Return on Assets %	2.6	3.7	3.8	3.8	3.7	4.8	6.0
Price Range	71 7/8-45 1/8	80 15/16-46 1/16	67 1/4-45 7/16	52 5/16-35	38 3/4-27 11/16	32 5/8-23 5/8	40 5/8-27 5/8
P/E Ratio	22.5-14.1	18.7-10.7	15.9-10.8	14.1-9.4	12.1-8.6	10.6-7.6	14.0-9.5
Average Yield %	1.4	1.2	1.4	1.6	1.9	1.9	1.3

Statistics are as originally reported. Adj. for stk. splits: 2-for-1, 10/97 1 Bef. acctg. change credit $12.9 mill. 2 Incl. non-recurr. chrg. of $36.1 mill. 3 Incl. non-recurr. chrg. of $105.0 mill.

OFFICERS:
J. W. Brown Jr., Chmn., C.E.O.
G. C. Dunton, Pres.
N. G. Budnick, C.F.O., Treas.
R. D. Wertheim, General Couns.

INVESTOR CONTACT: Judith C. Radasch, Director Investor Relations, (914) 765-3014

PRINCIPAL OFFICE: 113 King Street, Armonk, NY 10504

TELEPHONE NUMBER: (914) 273-4545
FAX: (914) 765-3163
WEB: www.mbia.com

NO. OF EMPLOYEES: 775

SHAREHOLDERS: 955

ANNUAL MEETING: In May

INCORPORATED: CT, Nov., 1986

INSTITUTIONAL HOLDINGS:
No. of Institutions: 340
Shares Held: 88,506,386
% Held: 88.9

INDUSTRY: Surety insurance (SIC: 6351)

TRANSFER AGENT(S): ChaseMellon Shareholder Services L.L.C., Ridgefield Park, NJ

NYSE SYMBOL MKC
Rec. Pr. 32½ (5/31/00)

MCCORMICK & COMPANY, INC.

YIELD 2.3%
P/E RATIO 22.6

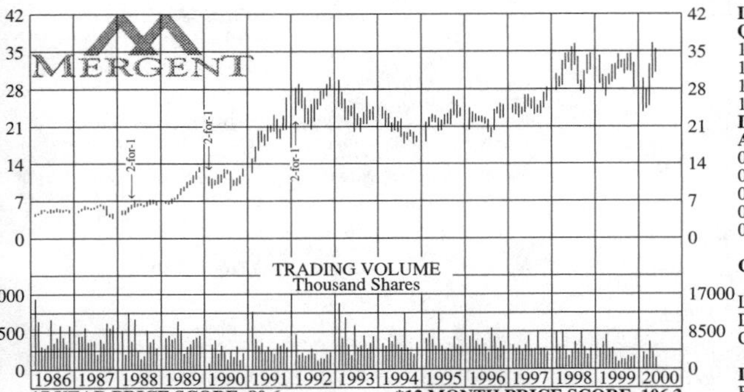

MERGENT
2-for-1
2-for-1
2-for-1
TRADING VOLUME
Thousand Shares
1986 1987 1988 1989 1990 1991 1992 1993 1994 1995 1996 1997 1998 1999 2000

***7 YEAR PRICE SCORE 80.6** ***12 MONTH PRICE SCORE 106.3**

*NYSE COMPOSITE INDEX=100

INTERIM EARNINGS (Per Share):

Qtr.	Feb.	May	Aug.	Nov.
1995-96	0.12	0.12	d0.26	0.58
1996-97	0.20	0.20	0.27	0.65
1997-98	0.22	0.22	0.29	0.68
1998-99	0.25	0.08	0.35	0.76

INTERIM DIVIDENDS (Per Share):

Amt.	Decl.	Ex.	Rec.	Pay.
0.17Q	3/18/99	3/29/99	3/31/99	4/13/99
0.17Q	6/21/99	6/30/99	7/02/99	7/15/99
0.17Q	9/20/99	9/29/99	10/01/99	10/13/99
0.19Q	12/20/99	12/29/99	12/31/99	1/24/00
0.19Q	3/15/00	3/29/00	3/31/00	4/13/00

Indicated div.: $0.76 (Div. Reinv. Plan)

CAPITALIZATION (11/30/99):

	($000)	(%)
Long-Term Debt	241,400	38.5
Deferred Income Tax	3,800	0.6
Common & Surplus	382,400	60.9
Total	627,600	100.0

DIVIDEND ACHIEVER STATUS:
Rank: 64 10-Year Growth Rate: 14.87%
Total Years of Dividend Growth: 13

RECENT DEVELOPMENTS: For the fiscal year ended 11/30/99, net income fell slightly to $103.3 million from $103.8 million a year earlier. Results included one-time after-tax special charges of $18.4 million and $2.3 million in 1999 and 1998, respectively. Net sales increased 6.7% to $2.01 billion from $1.88 billion in the prior year. Gross profit climbed 10.5% to $717.2 million from $648.9 million the previous year. Operating income slipped 3.3% to $176.9 million from $182.8 million in 1998.

PROSPECTS: Sales growth is being fueled by increased volume stemming from new distribution agreements with warehouse clubs, new product introductions and extensive promotional and marketing programs. Going forward, results in the consumer segment should benefit from MKC's continued focus on launching new products and expanding distribution. In the industrial segment, the Company is seeking to increase operating performance through ongoing cost-control efforts and improved global sourcing.

BUSINESS

MCCORMICK & COMPANY, INC. is a diversified specialty food company primarily engaged in the manufacture of spices, seasonings, flavors and other specialty food products. MKC operates in three business segments: consumer, industrial, and packaging. The consumer segment sells spices, herbs, extracts, proprietary seasoning blends, sauces and marinades to the consumer food market under a variety of brands, including the McCORMICK brand, the CLUB HOUSE brand in Canada, and the SCHWARTZ brand in the U.K. The industrial segment sells spices, herbs, extracts, proprietary seasonings, condiments, coatings and compound flavors to food processors, restaurant chains, distributors, warehouse clubs and institutional operations. The packaging segment sells plastic packaging products to the food, personal care and other industries, primarily in the U.S.

ANNUAL FINANCIAL DATA

	11/30/99	11/30/98	11/30/97	11/30/96	11/30/95	11/30/94	11/30/93
Earnings Per Share	**[1] 1.43**	**[1] 1.41**	**[1][2] 1.29**	**[3] 0.54**	**[1] 1.07**	**[1] 0.75**	**[4] 1.22**
Cash Flow Per Share	**2.23**	**2.15**	**1.94**	**1.33**	**1.99**	**1.52**	**1.86**
Tang. Book Val. Per Share	**3.40**	**3.13**	**3.18**	**3.64**	**4.17**	**3.62**	**4.15**
Dividends Per Share	**0.68**	**0.64**	**0.60**	**0.56**	**0.52**	**0.48**	**0.44**
Dividend Payout %	**47.5**	**45.4**	**46.5**	**103.7**	**48.6**	**64.0**	**36.1**
INCOME STATEMENT (IN MILLIONS):							
Total Revenues	2,006.9	1,881.1	1,801.0	1,732.5	1,858.7	1,694.8	1,556.6
Costs & Expenses	1,772.6	1,643.5	1,580.8	1,575.4	1,590.0	1,504.0	1,325.6
Depreciation & Amort.	57.4	54.8	49.3	63.8	63.7	62.5	50.5
Operating Income	176.9	182.8	170.8	93.3	205.0	128.2	180.5
Net Interest Inc./(Exp.)	d32.4	d36.9	d36.3	d33.8	d55.3	d38.7	d31.1
Income Before Income Taxes	150.0	152.5	142.3	61.7	149.2	87.0	149.9
Income Taxes	60.1	54.9	52.7	23.9	53.7	33.8	60.5
Equity Earnings/Minority Int.	13.4	6.2	7.8	5.6	2.1	7.9	10.3
Net Income	[1] 103.3	[1] 103.8	[1][2] 97.4	[3] 43.5	[1] 97.5	[1] 61.2	[4] 99.7
Cash Flow	160.7	158.6	146.8	107.3	161.2	123.7	150.2
Average Shs. Outstg. (000)	72,000	73,800	75,658	80,641	81,181	81,240	80,799
BALANCE SHEET (IN MILLIONS):							
Cash & Cash Equivalents	12.0	17.7	13.5	22.4	12.5	15.6	12.8
Total Current Assets	490.6	503.8	506.5	534.4	670.7	657.7	540.2
Net Property	363.3	377.0	380.0	400.4	524.8	504.6	465.6
Total Assets	1,188.8	1,259.1	1,256.2	1,326.6	1,614.3	1,568.7	1,313.2
Total Current Liabilities	470.6	518.0	498.2	499.3	646.9	600.8	392.9
Long-Term Obligations	241.4	250.4	276.5	291.2	349.1	374.3	346.4
Net Stockholders' Equity	382.4	388.1	393.1	450.0	519.3	490.0	466.8
Net Working Capital	20.0	d14.2	8.3	35.1	23.9	56.8	147.3
Year-end Shs. Outstg. (000)	70,400	72,500	74,024	78,205	81,218	81,206	80,999
STATISTICAL RECORD:							
Operating Profit Margin %	8.8	9.7	9.5	5.4	11.0	7.6	11.6
Net Profit Margin %	5.1	5.5	5.4	2.5	5.2	3.6	6.4
Return on Equity %	27.0	26.7	24.8	9.7	18.8	12.5	21.4
Return on Assets %	8.7	8.2	7.8	3.3	6.0	3.9	7.6
Debt/Total Assets %	20.3	19.9	22.0	22.0	21.6	23.9	26.4
Price Range	34⅝-26⅝	36 7/16-27 1/16	28⅜-22⅝	25⅜-18⅞	26⅝-18⅛	24¾-17¾	29¾-20
P/E Ratio	24.2-18.6	25.8-19.2	22.0-17.5	47.0-34.9	24.9-16.9	33.0-23.7	24.4-16.4
Average Yield %	2.2	2.0	2.4	2.5	2.3	2.3	1.8

Statistics are as originally reported. [1] Incl. $18.4 mill. after-tax chrg., 1999; $2.3 mill. pre-tax chrg., 1998; $3.2 mill. pre-tax credit, 1997; $3.9 mill. pre-tax credit, 1995; $70.4 mil pre-tax chrg., 1994 [2] Bef. $1.0 mill. disc. oper. gain [3] Bef. $7.8 mill. extraord. chrg., $6.2 mill. disc. oper. gain & incl. $58.1 mill. pre-tax chrg. [4] Bef. $26.6 mill. acctg. change chrg.

OFFICERS:
R. J. Lawless, Chmn., Pres., C.E.O.
F. A. Contino, Exec. V.P., C.F.O.
J. A. Anderson, Sr. V.P.

INVESTOR CONTACT: Chris Kurtzman, (410) 771-7244

PRINCIPAL OFFICE: 18 Loveton Circle, Sparks, MD 21152-6000

TELEPHONE NUMBER: (410) 771-7301
FAX: (410) 771-7462
WEB: www.mccormick.com
NO. OF EMPLOYEES: 7,300 (avg.)
SHAREHOLDERS: 2,000 (voting); 9,000 (non-voting)
ANNUAL MEETING: In Mar.
INCORPORATED: MD, Nov., 1915

INSTITUTIONAL HOLDINGS:
No. of Institutions: 170
Shares Held: 40,644,146
% Held: 65.8

INDUSTRY: Food preparations, nec (SIC: 2099)

TRANSFER AGENT(S): Shareholder Relations Office, Sparks, MD

MCDONALD'S CORPORATION

YIELD	0.5%
P/E RATIO	25.6

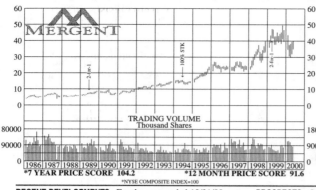

INTERIM EARNINGS (Per Share):

Qtr.	Mar.	June	Sept.	Dec.
1996	0.21	0.30	0.31	0.29
1997	0.25	0.32	0.32	0.29
1998	0.26	0.25	0.35	0.25
1999	0.29	0.37	0.39	0.35

INTERIM DIVIDENDS (Per Share):

Amt.	Decl.	Ex.	Rec.	Pay.
2-for-1	1/26/99	3/08/99	2/12/99	3/05/99
0.049Q	1/26/99	3/11/99	3/15/99	3/31/99
0.049Q	5/20/99	5/27/99	6/01/99	6/15/99
0.049Q	7/13/99	8/30/99	9/01/99	9/15/99
0.049Q	11/17/99	11/29/99	12/01/99	12/15/99

Indicated div.: $0.20 (Div. Reinv. Plan)

CAPITALIZATION (12/31/99):

	($mill.)	(%)
Long-Term Debt	5,632.4	34.2
Deferred Income Tax	1,173.6	7.1
Common & Surplus	9,639.1	58.6
Total	16,445.1	100.0

DIVIDEND ACHIEVER STATUS:
Rank: 156   10-Year Growth Rate: 9.94%
Total Years of Dividend Growth: 23

TRADING VOLUME
Thousand Shares

| 1986 | 1987 | 1988 | 1989 | 1990 | 1991 | 1992 | 1993 | 1994 | 1995 | 1996 | 1997 | 1998 | 1999 | 2000 |

*7 YEAR PRICE SCORE 104.2   *12 MONTH PRICE SCORE 91.6
*NYSE COMPOSITE INDEX=100

RECENT DEVELOPMENTS: For the year ended 12/31/99, net income jumped 25.7% to $1.95 billion versus $1.55 billion the year before. Results for 1999 included non-recurring charges of $18.9 million related to the installation of the Made For You food preparation system, while 1998 results included non-recurring charges of $321.6 million. Total revenues improved 6.7% to $13.26 billion from $12.42 billion a year earlier. Sales from Company-operated restaurants increased 6.9% to $9.51 billion.

PROSPECTS: On 2/22/00, the Company announced the opening of its first restaurant in French Guiana, bringing MCD's global presence to 119 countries. During 2000, the Company plans to open between 1,800 to 1,900 McDonald's restaurants, with 90.0% of the expansion taking place outside of the US. In addition, MCD expects to open 160 to 180 non-hamburger restaurants. Going forward, earnings per share are expected to grow at annual rate of 10.0% to 15.0% through 2002.

BUSINESS

MCDONALD'S CORPORATION develops, licenses, leases and services a worldwide system of restaurants. Units serve a standardized menu of moderately priced food consisting of hamburgers, cheeseburgers, chicken sandwiches, salads, desserts and beverages. As of 12/31/99, there were 16,265 units operated by franchisees, 6,213 units operated by the Company, and 4,328 units operated by affiliates. In addition to its McDonald's units, MCD also operates 147 Donatos Pizzas, 37 Chipotle Mexican Grills, and 30 Aroma Cafes. Revenues in 1999 were derived from: Company-owned units' sales, 71.7%; franchised restaurants, 28.3%. Independent operators normally lease on a 20-year basis with rental derived as a percentage of sales.

ANNUAL FINANCIAL DATA

	12/31/99	12/31/98	12/31/97	12/31/96	12/31/95	12/31/94	12/31/93
Earnings Per Share	☐ 1.39	☐ 1.10	1.15	1.11	0.99	0.84	0.73
Cash Flow Per Share	2.07	1.73	1.73	1.66	1.52	1.32	1.16
Tang. Book Val. Per Share	7.14	6.98	5.33	5.48	4.98	4.13	3.66
Dividends Per Share	0.20	0.18	0.16	0.15	0.13	0.12	0.11
Dividend Payout %	14.0	16.0	14.1	13.2	13.3	13.9	14.6
INCOME STATEMENT (IN MILLIONS):							
Total Revenues	13,259.3	12,421.4	11,408.8	10,686.5	9,794.5	8,320.8	7,408.1
Costs & Expenses	8,983.4	8,618.4	7,806.7	7,359.9	6,595.4	5,545.1	4,923.0
Depreciation & Amort.	956.3	881.1	793.8	742.9	709.0	628.6	568.4
Operating Income	3,319.6	2,761.9	2,808.3	2,632.6	2,601.3	2,241.2	1,984.0
Net Interest Inc./(Exp.)	d396.3	d413.8	d364.4	d342.5	d340.2	d305.7	d316.1
Income Before Income Taxes	2,884.1	2,307.4	2,407.3	2,251.0	2,169.1	1,886.6	1,675.7
Income Taxes	936.2	757.3	764.8	678.4	741.8	662.2	593.2
Equity Earnings/Minority Int.	…	…	…	76.8	96.5	47.0	34.6
Net Income	☐ 1,947.9	☐ 1,550.1	1,642.5	1,572.6	1,427.3	1,224.4	1,082.5
Cash Flow	2,904.2	2,431.2	2,411.0	2,287.9	2,095.8	1,805.8	1,604.0
Average Shs. Outstg. (000)	1,404,200	1,405,700	1,410,200	1,396,400	1,403,000	1,403,600	1,423,600
BALANCE SHEET (IN MILLIONS):							
Cash & Cash Equivalents	419.5	299.2	341.4	329.9	334.8	179.9	185.8
Total Current Assets	1,572.3	1,309.4	1,142.3	1,102.5	955.8	740.7	662.8
Net Property	16,324.5	16,041.6	14,961.4	14,352.1	12,811.3	11,328.4	10,081.4
Total Assets	20,983.2	19,784.4	18,241.5	17,386.0	15,414.6	13,591.9	12,035.2
Total Current Liabilities	3,274.3	2,497.1	2,984.5	2,135.3	1,794.9	2,451.3	1,102.0
Long-Term Obligations	5,632.4	6,188.6	4,834.1	4,830.1	4,257.8	2,935.4	3,489.4
Net Stockholders' Equity	9,639.1	9,464.7	8,851.6	8,718.2	7,861.3	6,885.4	6,274.1
Net Working Capital	d1,702.0	d1,187.7	d1,842.2	d1,032.8	d839.1	d1,710.6	d439.2
Year-end Shs. Outstg. (000)	1,350,800	1,356,200	1,660,600	1,389,200	1,399,400	1,387,400	1,414,800
STATISTICAL RECORD:							
Operating Profit Margin %	25.0	22.2	24.6	24.6	26.6	26.9	26.8
Net Profit Margin %	14.7	12.5	14.4	14.7	14.6	14.7	14.6
Return on Equity %	20.2	16.4	18.6	18.0	18.2	17.8	17.3
Return on Assets %	9.3	7.8	9.0	9.0	9.3	9.0	9.0
Debt/Total Assets %	26.8	31.3	26.5	27.8	27.6	21.6	29.0
Price Range	49⁹/₁₆-35¹⁵/₁₆	39³/₄-22³/₁₆	27¹¹/₁₆-21¹/₁₆	27¹/₈-20¹/₂	24-14⁵/₁₆	15¹¹/₁₆-12¹³/₁₆	14¹³/₁₆-11³/₈
P/E Ratio	35.7-25.9	36.1-20.3	24.0-18.4	24.5-18.6	24.4-14.5	18.7-15.2	20.4-15.7
Average Yield %	0.5	0.6	0.7	0.6	0.7	0.8	0.8

Statistics are as originally reported. Adj. for stk. splits: 2-for-1, 3/99, 5/94. ☐ Incl. non-recurr. chrg. of $18.9 mill., 1999; $321.6 mill., 1998.

OFFICERS:
F. L. Turner, Sr. Chmn.
J. M. Greenberg, Chmn., C.E.O.
J. R. Cantalupo, Vice-Chmn., Pres.

INVESTOR CONTACT: Sharon Vuinovich,
V.P. Fin. & Inv. Rel., (708) 575-3395

PRINCIPAL OFFICE: McDonald's Plaza, Oak Brook, IL 60523

TELEPHONE NUMBER: (630) 623-3000
FAX: (630) 623-5027
WEB: www.mcdonalds.com

NO. OF EMPLOYEES: 314,000 (avg.)

SHAREHOLDERS: 899,100 (approx.)

ANNUAL MEETING: In May

INCORPORATED: DE, March, 1965

INSTITUTIONAL HOLDINGS:
No. of Institutions: 836
Shares Held: 846,680,402
% Held: 62.5

INDUSTRY: Eating places (SIC: 5812)

TRANSFER AGENT(S): First Chicago Trust Company of New York, Jersey City, NJ

NYSE SYMBOL MHP
Rec. Pr. 51 7/16 (5/31/00)

MCGRAW-HILL COMPANIES, INC. (THE)

YIELD 1.8%
P/E RATIO 24.0

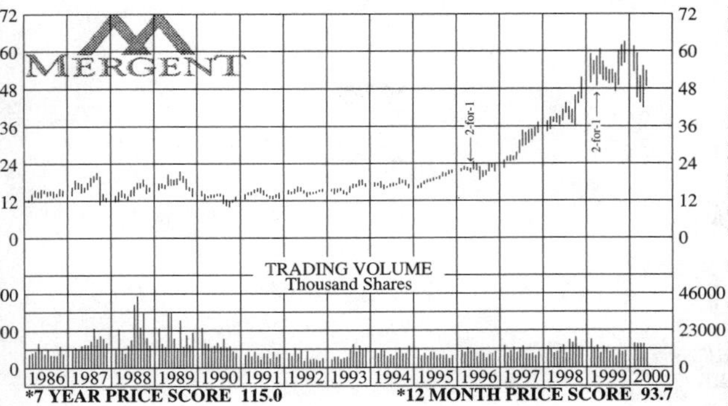

*7 YEAR PRICE SCORE 115.0 *12 MONTH PRICE SCORE 93.7

*NYSE COMPOSITE INDEX=100

INTERIM EARNINGS (Per Share):

Qtr.	Mar.	June	Sept.	Dec.
1996	0.08	0.29	0.58	1.54
1997	0.08	0.33	0.72	0.34
1998	0.10	0.39	0.86	0.38
1999	0.12	0.45	0.96	0.61

INTERIM DIVIDENDS (Per Share):

Amt.	Decl.	Ex.	Rec.	Pay.
0.215Q	4/28/99	5/24/99	5/26/99	6/10/99
0.215Q	7/28/99	8/24/99	8/26/99	9/10/99
0.215Q	10/27/99	11/23/99	11/26/99	12/10/99
0.235Q	1/26/00	2/23/00	2/25/00	3/10/00
0.235Q	4/26/00	5/24/00	5/26/00	6/12/00

Indicated div.: $0.94 (Div. Reinv. Plan)

CAPITALIZATION (12/31/99):

	($000)	(%)
Long-Term Debt	354,775	16.3
Deferred Income Tax	135,426	6.2
Preferred Stock	14	0.0
Common & Surplus	1,691,479	77.5
Total	2,181,694	100.0

DIVIDEND ACHIEVER STATUS:
Rank: 254 10-Year Growth Rate: 5.57%
Total Years of Dividend Growth: 26

RECENT DEVELOPMENTS: For the year ended 12/31/99, MHP reported net income of $425.8 million versus income of $341.9 million, before an extraordinary loss of $8.7 million, in 1998. Results for 1999 included an after-tax gain of $24.2 million on the sale of MHP's petrochemical publications. Results for 1998 included a one-time net after-tax gain of $6.5 million. Operating revenue rose 7.0% to $4.00 billion from $3.73 billion the year before.

PROSPECTS: Looking ahead, the Company expects Standard & Poor's to continue to produce international double-digit revenue growth throughout 2000 due to the healthy market environment in Europe. MHP also intends to expand its global publishing operations with increased global circulation of Business Week and continued investment in MHP's Spanish-language publishing program.

BUSINESS

THE MCGRAW-HILL COMPANIES, INC., a multimedia publishing and information services company, serves worldwide markets in education, business, industry, professions and government. The Company has more than 400 offices in 32 countries. It provides information in print through books, newsletters, and magazines, including Business Week; on-line over electronic networks; over the air by television, satellite and FM sideband; and on software, videotape, facsimile and compact disks. Among the Company's business units are Standard & Poor's Financial Information Services and Standard & Poor's Ratings Services divisions.

ANNUAL FINANCIAL DATA

	12/31/99	12/31/98	12/31/97	12/31/96	12/31/95	12/31/94	12/31/93
Earnings Per Share	**[5] 2.14**	**[4] 1.71**	**[3] 1.46**	**[2] 2.48**	**1.14**	**1.03**	**[1] 0.06**
Cash Flow Per Share	**3.70**	**3.22**	**2.93**	**3.67**	**2.30**	**2.19**	**0.77**
Tang. Book Val. Per Share	**2.24**	**1.48**	**0.64**	**0.28**	**0.38**	...	...
Dividends Per Share	**0.86**	**0.78**	**0.72**	**0.66**	**0.60**	**0.58**	**0.57**
Dividend Payout %	**40.2**	**45.8**	**49.5**	**26.6**	**52.6**	**56.6**	**981.1**
INCOME STATEMENT (IN MILLIONS):							
Total Revenues	3,992.0	3,729.1	3,534.1	3,074.7	2,935.3	2,760.9	2,195.5
Costs & Expenses	2,943.7	2,821.5	2,716.8	1,973.7	2,258.8	2,133.7	1,723.4
Depreciation & Amort.	308.3	299.2	293.5	238.6	231.4	230.0	139.6
Operating Income	740.0	608.4	523.8	862.5	445.0	397.2	102.6
Net Interest Inc./(Exp.)	d42.0	d48.0	d52.5	d47.7	d58.8	d51.7	d36.3
Income Before Income Taxes	698.0	560.4	471.3	814.8	386.3	345.4	66.3
Income Taxes	272.2	218.6	180.6	319.1	159.1	142.3	54.8
Net Income	[5] 425.8	[4] 341.9	[3] 290.7	[2] 495.7	227.2	203.1	[1] 11.4
Cash Flow	734.1	641.1	584.2	734.3	458.6	433.1	151.1
Average Shs. Outstg. (000)	198,557	199,104	199,504	199,994	199,504	197,996	196,756
BALANCE SHEET (IN MILLIONS):							
Cash & Cash Equivalents	6.5	10.5	4.8	3.4	10.3	8.1	48.0
Total Current Assets	1,553.7	1,428.8	1,464.4	1,349.6	1,239.8	1,124.1	1,131.8
Net Property	430.4	364.0	273.6	311.5	336.1	345.8	345.3
Total Assets	4,088.8	3,788.1	3,724.5	3,642.2	3,104.4	3,008.5	3,084.2
Total Current Liabilities	1,525.5	1,291.5	1,206.2	1,218.7	1,046.5	1,008.0	1,068.9
Long-Term Obligations	354.8	452.1	607.0	556.9	557.4	657.5	757.6
Net Stockholders' Equity	1,691.5	1,551.8	1,434.7	1,361.1	1,035.1	913.1	823.0
Net Working Capital	28.3	137.3	258.2	130.9	193.3	116.1	62.9
Year-end Shs. Outstg. (000)	195,709	197,111	198,204	199,062	200,286	198,688	197,656
STATISTICAL RECORD:							
Operating Profit Margin %	18.5	16.3	14.8	28.1	15.2	14.4	4.7
Net Profit Margin %	10.7	9.2	8.2	16.1	7.7	7.4	0.5
Return on Equity %	25.2	22.0	20.3	36.4	21.9	22.2	1.4
Return on Assets %	10.4	9.0	7.8	13.6	7.3	6.8	0.4
Debt/Total Assets %	8.7	11.9	16.3	15.3	18.0	21.9	24.6
Price Range	63 1/8-47 1/8	51 11/16-34 1/4	37 3/8-22 7/16	24 5/8-18 5/8	21 15/16-15 15/16	19 5/16-15 5/8	18 13/16-13 13/16
P/E Ratio	29.5-22.0	30.2-20.0	25.7-15.4	9.9-7.5	19.2-14.0	18.8-15.2	323.8-237.7
Average Yield %	1.6	1.8	2.4	3.1	3.2	3.3	3.5

Statistics are as originally reported. Adj. for 2-for-1 splits 3/8/99 & 4/96. [1] Incl. non-recurring net chgs. of $160.8 mill. ($1.63 sh.). [2] Incl. $260.5 mill. net gain from the exchange of its legal publishing unit for Times Mirror Higher Education Group. [3] Incl. provision of $19.9 mill. for consolidation of office space & $20.2 mill. gain from sale of Datapro. [4] Bef. extraord. chrg. of $8.7 mill. [5] Incl. after-tax gain of $24.2 mill. fr. the sale of the Co.'s Petrochemical publications.

OFFICERS:
H. McGraw III, Chmn., Pres., C.E.O.
R. J. Bahash, Exec. V.P., C.F.O.

INVESTOR CONTACT: Steven H. Weiss, V.P., Corp. Comm., (212) 512-2247

PRINCIPAL OFFICE: 1221 Avenue Of The Americas, New York, NY 10020-1095

TELEPHONE NUMBER: (212) 512-2000
FAX: (212) 512-2305
WEB: www.mcgraw-hill.com
NO. OF EMPLOYEES: 16,376
SHAREHOLDERS: 5,397 (approx.)
ANNUAL MEETING: In Mar.
INCORPORATED: NY, Dec., 1925

INSTITUTIONAL HOLDINGS:
No. of Institutions: 382
Shares Held: 146,911,111
% Held: 74.9

INDUSTRY: Book publishing (SIC: 2731)

TRANSFER AGENT(S): ChaseMellon Shareholder Services, New York, NY

NYSE SYMBOL MDT
Rec. Pr. 51⅝ (5/31/00)

MEDTRONIC, INC.

YIELD	0.3%
P/E RATIO	66.2

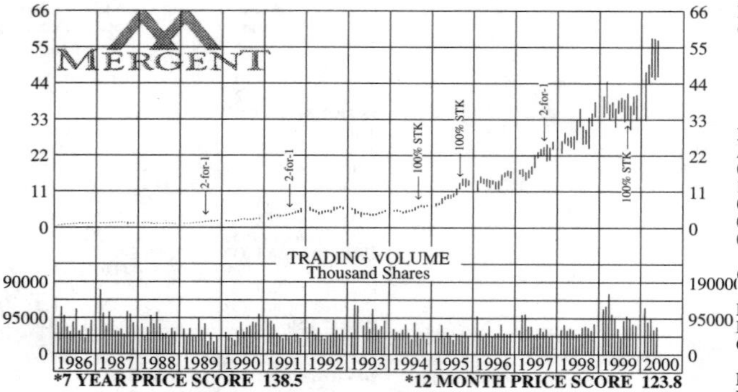

*7 YEAR PRICE SCORE 138.5   *12 MONTH PRICE SCORE 123.8

*NYSE COMPOSITE INDEX=100

INTERIM EARNINGS (Per Share):

Qtr.	July	Oct.	Jan.	Apr.
1995-96	0.11	0.12	0.12	0.14
1996-97	0.21	0.14	0.14	0.16
1997-98	0.32	0.16	0.01	0.17
1998-99	0.16	0.15	d0.03	0.13
1999-00	0.21	0.22	0.22	...

INTERIM DIVIDENDS (Per Share):

Amt.	Decl.	Ex.	Rec.	Pay.
0.08Q	6/24/99	6/30/99	7/02/99	7/30/99
100% STK	8/25/99	9/27/99	9/10/99	9/24/99
0.04Q	8/25/99	10/06/99	10/08/99	10/29/99
0.04Q	10/28/99	1/05/00	1/07/00	1/28/00
0.04Q	3/06/00	4/05/00	4/07/00	4/28/00

Indicated div.: $0.16 (Div. Reinv. Plan)

CAPITALIZATION (4/30/99):

	($000)	(%)
Long-Term Debt	17,600	0.5
Deferred Income Tax	30,800	0.8
Common & Surplus	3,654,600	98.7
Total	3,703,000	100.0

DIVIDEND ACHIEVER STATUS:
Rank: 16   10-Year Growth Rate: 21.73%
Total Years of Dividend Growth: 22

RECENT DEVELOPMENTS: For the quarter ended 1/28/00, MDT reported net income of $263.2 million versus a net loss of $34.1 million in the prior-year period. Results included nonrecurring pre-tax charges of $14.7 million in 1999 and $287.3 million in 1998. Net sales jumped 18.2% to $1.26 billion from $1.06 billion a year earlier. Comparisons were made with restated prior-year results to account for the acquisition of Xomed Surgical Products, Inc.

PROSPECTS: On 2/16/00, MDT completed the acquisition of XRT Corporation, a developer of minimally invasive, intravascular radiation therapies. The acquisition should further strengthen the Company's position in the emerging market of radiation therapies to prevent restenosis. Separately, the Company announced plans to expand its European headquarters and production facilities located in Switzerland. Medtronic Europe S.A. will invest $31.0 million.

BUSINESS

MEDTRONIC, INC. is a leading medical technology company specializing in implantable and interventional therapies. Primary products include those for bradycardia pacing, tachyarrhythmia management, atrial fibrillation management, heart failure management, coronary and peripheral vascular disease, heart valve replacement, extracorporeal cardiac support, minimally invasive cardiac surgery, malignant and non-malignant pain, movement disorders, neurosurgery and neurodegenerative disorders. MDT does business in more than 120 countries and reports on four primary product line platforms, Cardiac Rhythm Management, Cardiac Surgery, Neurological and Vascular.

ANNUAL FINANCIAL DATA

	4/30/99	4/30/98	4/30/97	4/30/96	4/30/95	4/30/94	4/30/93
Earnings Per Share	**③ 0.79**	**② 0.48**	**0.56**	**0.47**	**0.32**	**① 0.25**	**0.22**
Cash Flow Per Share	**1.15**	**0.63**	**0.68**	**0.59**	**0.43**	**0.34**	**0.30**
Tang. Book Val. Per Share	**3.98**	**1.68**	**1.34**	**1.41**	**1.05**	**0.74**	**0.76**
Dividends Per Share	**0.12**	**0.10**	**0.08**	**0.06**	**0.05**	**0.04**	**0.03**
Dividend Payout %	**15.2**	**21.3**	**14.4**	**12.4**	**14.7**	**15.3**	**14.6**
INCOME STATEMENT (IN MILLIONS):							
Total Revenues	4,134.1	2,604.8	2,438.2	2,169.1	1,742.4	1,390.9	1,328.2
Costs & Expenses	3,121.2	1,744.0	1,536.9	1,410.2	1,199.6	979.7	981.5
Depreciation & Amort.	213.1	137.6	116.9	111.8	106.5	78.6	69.6
Operating Income	799.8	723.2	784.5	647.2	436.3	332.7	277.1
Net Interest Inc./(Exp.)	22.2	14.8	24.7	21.2	5.8	0.2	d1.7
Income Before Income Taxes	822.0	702.0	809.1	668.4	442.1	346.8	313.5
Income Taxes	353.6	244.6	279.2	230.6	148.1	114.4	101.9
Net Income	③ 468.4	② 457.4	530.0	437.8	294.0	① 232.4	211.6
Cash Flow	681.5	594.9	646.9	549.6	400.5	310.9	281.2
Average Shs. Outstg. (000)	592,900	951,168	954,772	932,628	921,920	918,464	950,656
BALANCE SHEET (IN MILLIONS):							
Cash & Cash Equivalents	375.9	425.9	250.6	460.8	323.6	181.4	156.0
Total Current Assets	2,395.2	1,551.6	1,237.9	1,343.2	1,103.9	845.9	774.7
Net Property	748.8	508.8	487.2	415.3	331.1	301.8	282.8
Total Assets	4,870.3	2,774.7	2,409.2	2,503.3	1,946.7	1,623.3	1,286.5
Total Current Liabilities	990.3	572.0	518.7	525.0	456.1	439.4	348.1
Long-Term Obligations	17.6	16.2	14.0	15.3	14.2	20.2	10.9
Net Stockholders' Equity	3,654.6	2,044.2	1,746.2	1,789.3	1,335.0	1,053.5	841.5
Net Working Capital	1,404.9	979.6	719.2	818.2	647.8	406.4	426.6
Year-end Shs. Outstg. (000)	585,226	938,090	935,256	937,272	924,072	930,064	925,120
STATISTICAL RECORD:							
Operating Profit Margin %	19.3	27.8	32.2	29.8	25.0	23.9	20.9
Net Profit Margin %	11.3	17.6	21.7	20.2	16.9	16.7	15.9
Return on Equity %	12.8	22.4	30.4	24.5	22.0	22.1	25.1
Return on Assets %	9.6	16.5	22.0	17.5	15.1	14.3	16.4
Debt/Total Assets %	0.4	0.6	0.6	0.6	0.7	1.2	0.8
Price Range	38⅜-22¾	26⅜-14 7/16	17½-11⅛	15-6 9/16	6-4 5/16	5-3¼	6 9/16-3 15/16
P/E Ratio	48.6-28.8	54.9-30.0	31.5-20.0	31.9-13.9	21.9-13.5	23.6-12.7	29.3-17.7
Average Yield %	0.4	0.5	0.6	0.5	0.8	0.8	0.6

Statistics are as originally reported. Adj. for 2-for-1 stk split, 9/99, 9/97, 9/95, 9/94. ① Incl. pre-tax gain of $14.0 mill. ② Incl. a pre-tax chrg. of $12.9 mill. & a nonrecur. pre-tax chrg. of $156.4 mill. ③ Incl. a pre-tax nonrecur. chg. of $371.3 mill. & a pre-tax chg. of $150.9 mill. for pchsd. in-process R&D.

OFFICERS:
W. W. George, Chmn., C.E.O.
G. D. Nelson M.D., Vice-Chmn.
A. D. Collins Jr., Pres., C.O.O.
R. L. Ryan, Sr. V.P., C.F.O.

INVESTOR CONTACT: Rachel Scherer, Investor Relations, (612) 574-4971

PRINCIPAL OFFICE: 7000 Central Avenue N.E., Minneapolis, MN 55432

TELEPHONE NUMBER: (612) 574-4000
FAX: (612) 514-4879
WEB: www.medtronic.com

NO. OF EMPLOYEES: 19,334 full-time; 2,460 part-time (approx.)

SHAREHOLDERS: 25,939

ANNUAL MEETING: In Aug.

INCORPORATED: MN, 1957

INSTITUTIONAL HOLDINGS:
No. of Institutions: 716
Shares Held: 756,703,041
% Held: 63.4

INDUSTRY: Electromedical equipment (SIC: 3845)

TRANSFER AGENT(S): Norwest Bank Minnesota, N.A., St. Paul, MN

MERCANTILE BANKSHARES CORPORATION

YIELD	2.9%
P/E RATIO	14.7

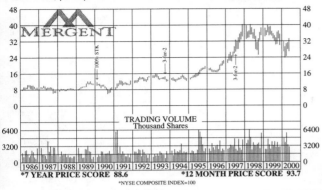

TRADING VOLUME
Thousand Shares

1986|1987|1988|1989|1990|1991|1992|1993|1994|1995|1996|1997|1998|1999|2000

*7 YEAR PRICE SCORE 88.6   *12 MONTH PRICE SCORE 93.7

*NYSE COMPOSITE INDEX=100

INTERIM EARNINGS (Per Share):

Qtr.	Mar.	June	Sept.	Dec.
1995	0.50	0.55	0.58	0.56
1996	0.58	0.61	0.63	0.64
1997	0.45	0.46	0.48	0.45
1998	0.49	0.50	0.52	0.53
1999	0.53	0.55	0.59	0.59

INTERIM DIVIDENDS (Per Share):

Amt.	Decl.	Ex.	Rec.	Pay.
0.22Q	3/09/99	3/19/99	3/23/99	3/31/99
0.24Q	6/08/99	6/16/99	6/18/99	6/30/99
0.24Q	9/14/99	9/22/99	9/24/99	9/30/99
0.24Q	12/14/99	12/21/99	12/24/99	12/31/99
0.24Q	3/14/00	3/22/00	3/24/00	3/31/00

Indicated div.: $0.96 (Div. Reinv. Plan)

CAPITALIZATION (12/31/99):

	($000)	(%)
Total Deposits	5,925,083	84.9
Long-Term Debt	82,683	1.2
Common & Surplus	974,040	14.0
Total	6,981,806	100.0

DIVIDEND ACHIEVER STATUS:

Rank: 131   10-Year Growth Rate: 11.30%
Total Years of Dividend Growth: 23

RECENT DEVELOPMENTS: For the year ended 12/31/99, net income increased 7.2% to $157.7 million compared with $147.1 million in the previous year. Net interest income advanced 4.4% to $369.1 million from $353.4 million the year before. Total interest income was $559.2 million, up 0.7% from $554.4 million the year before. Total interest expense decreased 5.9% to $190.1 million from $202.0 million a year earlier. The decline in interest expense was primarily due to a decrease in the rate paid on interest-bearing deposits. Noninterest income was $122.0 million versus $108.7 million in 1998. Noninterest expense increased 5.2% to $230.4 million from $219.0 million a year earlier. Return on average assets was 2.07% compared with 2.03% in 1998.

BUSINESS

MERCANTILE BANKSHARES CORPORATION is a bank holding company that owns substantially all of the outstanding shares of capital stock of twenty-one banks, the Affiliated Banks. The Affiliated Banks are engaged in a general commercial and retail banking business with normal banking services, including acceptance of demand, savings and time deposits and the making of various types of loans. Mercantile-Safe Deposit and Trust Company offers a full range of personal trust services, investment management services and (for corporate and institutional customers) investment advisory, financial and pension and profit sharing services. The Company also owns all of the outstanding shares of Mercantile Mortgage Corporation, a mortgage banking company, MBC Agency, Inc., an insurance agency, Hopkins Plaza Agency, Inc., an agent in the sale of fixed rate annuities, MBC Leasing, Inc., a leasing company, and MBC Realty, Inc., which owns and operates various properties used by Mercantile Safe Deposit and Trust Company.

ANNUAL FINANCIAL DATA

	12/31/99	12/31/98	12/31/97	12/31/96	12/31/95	12/31/94	12/31/93
Earnings Per Share	2.25	2.04	1.64	1.44	1.25	1.20	
Tang. Book Val. Per Share	13.51	13.36	12.50	11.35	10.55	9.77	9.20
Dividends Per Share	0.94	0.86	0.77	0.65	0.57	0.49	0.43
Dividend Payout %	41.8	42.2	42.0	39.8	39.3	39.4	35.6
INCOME STATEMENT (IN MILLIONS):							
Total Interest Income	559.2	555.4	534.0	498.1	467.3	403.4	370.8
Total Interest Expense	190.1	202.0	197.9	187.6	180.5	140.4	133.2
Net Interest Income	369.1	353.4	336.0	310.6	286.8	263.0	237.6
Provision for Loan Losses	12.1	11.5	13.7	14.7	8.0	7.1	12.6
Non-Interest Income	122.0	108.7	98.7	89.4	80.9	84.8	84.1
Non-Interest Expense	230.4	219.0	213.4	198.4	193.7	193.8	174.5
Income Before Taxes	248.6	231.6	207.6	186.9	166.0	146.9	134.6
Net Income	157.7	147.1	132.0	117.4	104.4	90.4	82.4
Average Shs. Outstg. (000)	70,020	72,237	71,904	71,477	71,652	72,249	68,852
BALANCE SHEET (IN MILLIONS):							
Cash & Due from Banks	219.4	255.0	337.2	257.3	247.3	257.0	161.5
Securities Avail. for Sale	1,743.9	1,880.5	1,607.3	1,596.7	1,551.7	333.0	...
Total Loans & Leases	5,718.9	5,220.9	4,978.5	4,582.7	4,301.3	3,938.1	3,577.4
Allowance for Credit Losses	118.0	112.4	106.1	97.7	91.4	91.3	89.8
Net Loans & Leases	5,600.9	5,108.5	4,872.4	4,485.0	4,209.9	3,846.8	3,487.6
Total Assets	7,895.0	7,609.6	7,170.7	6,642.7	6,349.1	5,938.2	5,554.0
Total Deposits	5,925.1	5,958.3	5,693.9	5,339.7	5,169.4	4,765.4	4,524.0
Long-Term Obligations	82.7	40.9	50.0	49.4	25.6	31.5	32.4
Total Liabilities	6,921.0	6,610.2	6,235.7	5,806.6	5,555.3	5,214.3	4,899.1
Net Stockholders' Equity	974.0	999.4	935.0	836.0	793.8	723.9	654.9
Year-end Shs. Outstg. (000)	68,646	71,027	71,874	71,153	72,408	72,171	68,996
STATISTICAL RECORD:							
Return on Equity %	16.2	14.7	14.1	14.0	13.2	12.5	12.6
Return on Assets %	2.0	1.9	1.8	1.8	1.6	1.5	1.5
Equity/Assets %	12.3	13.1	13.0	12.6	12.5	12.2	11.8
Non-Int. Exp./Tot. Inc. %	46.9	47.4	49.1	49.6	52.7	55.7	54.2
Price Range	39¹⁵/₁₆-30	40¼-25¼	40¼-21³/₁₆	22½-16½	19¹¹/₁₆-13	15³/₁₆-11¹³/₁₆	15⁷/₈-12
P/E Ratio	17.7-13.3	19.7-12.4	21.9-11.5	13.7-10.1	13.5-8.9	12.3-9.4	13.2-10.0
Average Yield %	2.7	2.6	2.5	3.4	3.5	3.6	3.1

Statistics are as originally reported. Adjusted for 3-for-2 stock split, 7/97 & 10/93.

OFFICERS:
H. F. Baldwin, Chmn., Pres., C.E.O.
T. L. Troupe, C.F.O., Treas.
A. D. Yarbro, Sec., Gen. Couns.

PRINCIPAL OFFICE: Two Hopkins Plaza, P. O. Box 1477, Baltimore, MD 21203

TELEPHONE NUMBER: (410) 237-5900
FAX: (410) 347-8493
WEB: www.mercantile.net

NO. OF EMPLOYEES: 2,796 (approx.)

SHAREHOLDERS: 9,138

ANNUAL MEETING: In Apr.

INCORPORATED: MD, May, 1969

INSTITUTIONAL HOLDINGS:
No. of Institutions: 161
Shares Held: 26,419,310
% Held: 38.3

INDUSTRY: State commercial banks (SIC: 6022)

TRANSFER AGENT(S): The Bank of New York, New York, NY.

MERCK & CO., INC.

YIELD 1.6%
P/E RATIO 31.5

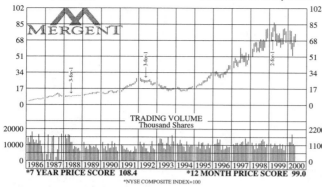

*7 YEAR PRICE SCORE 108.4   *12 MONTH PRICE SCORE 99.0
*NYSE COMPOSITE INDEX=100

TRADING VOLUME
Thousand Shares

INTERIM EARNINGS (Per Share):

Qtr.	Mar.	June	Sept.	Dec.
1995	0.31	0.35	0.35	0.35
1996	0.35	0.40	0.42	0.44
1997	0.42	0.48	0.50	0.51
1998	0.48	0.54	0.56	0.58
1999	0.54	0.61	0.64	0.66

INTERIM DIVIDENDS (Per Share):

Amt.	Decl.	Ex.	Rec.	Pay.
0.27Q	5/25/99	6/02/99	6/04/99	7/01/99
0.29Q	7/27/99	9/01/99	9/03/99	10/01/99
0.29Q	11/23/99	12/01/99	12/03/99	1/03/00
0.29Q	2/22/00	3/01/00	3/03/00	4/03/00
0.29Q	5/22/00	5/31/00	6/02/00	7/03/00

Indicated div.: $1.16 (Div. Reinv. Plan)

CAPITALIZATION (12/31/99):

	($000)	(%)
Long-Term Debt	3,143,900	15.8
Minority Interest	3,460,500	17.4
Common & Surplus	13,241,600	66.7
Total	19,846,000	100.0

DIVIDEND ACHIEVER STATUS:

Rank: 63   10-Year Growth Rate: 14.94%
Total Years of Dividend Growth: 16

RECENT DEVELOPMENTS: For the year ended 12/31/99, net income rose 12.2% to $5.89 billion versus $5.25 billion in 1998. Results included a pre-tax charge of $51.1 million in 1999 for acquired research. The 1998 results also included a nonrecurring gain of $2.15 billion. Sales jumped 21.6% to $32.71 billion from $26.90 billion a year earlier. Sales growth was fueled by established major products, the introduction of VIOXX, a treatment for arthritis, and a strong performance from Merck-Medco Managed care business.

PROSPECTS: The Company expects to experience a significant decline in sales in PEPCID, a treatment for ulcers, and MEVACOR, a cholesterol-lowering medicine and PRINIVIL/PRINZIDE, VASERETIC, and VASOTEC, treatments for heart failure and hypertension, in the years 2000 through 2005 as the patents for these products expire in the U.S. and abroad. Separately, MRK expects earnings per share for 2000 to be in the range of $2.73 to $2.81.

BUSINESS

MERCK & CO., INC. is research-driven pharmaceutical company that discovers, develops, manufactures and markets human and animal health products, directly through its joint ventures, and provides pharmaceutical benefit services through Merck-Medco Managed Care LLC. The Merck Pharmaceuticals segment consists of therapeutic and preventive agents, generally sold by prescription, for the treatment of human disorders. Human health products include ZOCOR, a cholesterol-lowering medicine, FOSAMAX, a treatment for osteoporosis in men and women, and PROPECIA, a treatment for male pattern hair loss. Animal health products include medicines used to control and alleviate disease in livestock, small animals, and poultry. The Merck-Medco segment primarily includes sales of non-Merck products and Merck-Medco pharmaceutical benefit services, principally sales of prescription drugs through managed prescription drug programs as well as services provided through programs to help manage patient health.

ANNUAL FINANCIAL DATA

	12/31/99	12/31/98	12/31/97	12/31/96	12/31/95	12/31/94	12/31/93
Earnings Per Share	④ 2.45	③ 2.15	② 1.87	1.60	① 1.35	1.19	① 0.94
Cash Flow Per Share	2.93	2.57	2.21	2.00	1.74	1.56	1.12
Tang. Book Val. Per Share	2.43	1.91	2.44	2.17	2.00	1.57	1.35
Dividends Per Share	1.10	0.94	0.84	0.71	0.62	0.57	0.52
Dividend Payout %	44.9	44.0	45.2	44.4	45.9	47.9	55.1

INCOME STATEMENT (IN MILLIONS):

Total Revenues	32,714.0	26,898.2	23,636.9	19,828.7	16,681.1	14,969.8	10,498.2
Costs & Expenses	23,708.7	20,282.3	16,936.1	13,916.9	11,593.3	9,689.2	6,972.8
Depreciation & Amort.	1,144.8	1,015.1	837.1	730.9	667.2	681.6	386.5
Operating Income	7,860.5	5,600.8	5,863.7	5,180.9	4,420.6	4,599.0	3,138.9
Income Before Income Taxes	8,619.5	8,133.1	6,462.3	5,540.8	4,797.2	4,415.2	3,102.7
Income Taxes	2,729.0	2,884.9	1,848.2	1,659.5	1,462.0	1,418.2	936.5
Equity Earnings/Minority Int.	762.0	884.3	727.9	600.7	...	56.6	...
Net Income	④ 5,890.5	③ 5,248.2	② 4,614.1	4,122.1	① 3,641.5	3,229.8	① 2,202.4
Cash Flow	7,035.3	6,263.3	5,451.2	4,853.0	4,308.7	3,911.4	2,588.9
Average Shs. Outstg. (000)	2,404,600	2,441,100	2,469,400	2,427,300	2,472,200	2,514,400	2,313,000

BALANCE SHEET (IN MILLIONS):

Cash & Cash Equivalents	3,202.4	3,355.7	2,309.3	2,181.6	3,349.8	2,269.7	1,542.3
Total Current Assets	11,259.2	10,228.5	8,213.0	7,726.6	8,617.5	6,921.7	5,734.6
Net Property	9,676.7	7,843.8	6,609.4	5,926.7	5,269.1	5,296.3	4,894.6
Total Assets	35,634.9	31,853.4	25,735.9	24,293.1	23,831.8	21,856.6	19,927.5
Total Current Liabilities	8,758.8	6,068.8	5,568.6	4,829.2	5,689.5	5,448.6	5,895.7
Long-Term Obligations	3,143.9	3,220.8	1,346.5	1,155.9	1,372.8	1,145.9	1,120.8
Net Stockholders' Equity	13,241.6	12,801.8	12,594.6	11,970.5	11,735.7	11,139.0	10,021.7
Net Working Capital	2,500.4	4,159.7	2,644.4	2,897.4	2,928.0	1,473.1	d161.1
Year-end Shs. Outstg. (000)	2,329,078	2,360,453	2,387,296	2,413,204	2,457,698	2,495,652	2,507,870

STATISTICAL RECORD:

Operating Profit Margin %	24.0	20.8	24.8	26.1	26.5	30.7	29.9
Net Profit Margin %	18.0	19.5	19.5	20.8	21.8	21.6	21.0
Return on Equity %	44.5	41.0	36.6	34.4	31.0	29.0	22.0
Return on Assets %	16.5	16.5	17.9	17.0	15.3	14.8	11.1
Debt/Total Assets %	8.8	10.1	5.2	4.8	5.8	5.2	5.6
Price Range	87⅜-60¹⁵⁄₁₆	80⅞-50¹¹⁄₁₆	60⁵⁄₁₆-39	42¹⁄₈-28¹⁄₄	33⅝-18³⁄₁₆	19¾-14¹⁄₁₆	22¹⁄₁₆-14¹⁵⁄₁₆
P/E Ratio	35.7-24.9	37.6-23.6	32.3-20.9	26.3-17.7	24.9-13.5	16.6-11.8	23.6-15.3
Average Yield %	1.5	1.4	1.7	2.0	2.4	3.4	2.8

Statistics are as originally reported. Adj. for 2-for-1 stock split, 2/99. ① Inc. a net pre-tax gain of $169.4 mill., 1995; & a chg. of $775.0 mill., 1993. ② Inc. a nonrecurr. pre-tax gain of $213.0 mill. & non-recurr. pre-tax chgs. totaling $207.0 mill. ③ Incl. a pre-tax gain of $2.15 bill. from the sale of businesses, and a pre-tax charge of $1.04 bill. for acq. R&D. ④ Incl. a pre-tax chg. of $51.1 mill. for acq. research.

OFFICERS:
R. V. Gilmartin, Chmn., Pres., C.E.O.
J. C. Lewent, Sr. V.P., C.F.O.
C. A. Colbert, V.P., Sec., Asst. Gen. Couns.
INVESTOR CONTACT: Laura Jordan, Investor Relations, (908) 423-5185
PRINCIPAL OFFICE: One Merck Dr, P.O. Box 100, Whitehouse Station, NJ 08889

TELEPHONE NUMBER: (908) 423-1000
FAX: (908) 735-1500
WEB: www.merck.com
NO. OF EMPLOYEES: 62,300
SHAREHOLDERS: 280,500
ANNUAL MEETING: In Apr.
INCORPORATED: NJ, Jun., 1927

INSTITUTIONAL HOLDINGS:
No. of Institutions: 1,167
Shares Held: 1,218,792,193
% Held: 52.1
INDUSTRY: Pharmaceutical preparations (SIC: 2834)
TRANSFER AGENT(S): Norwest Bank Minnesota, NA, South St. Paul, MN

MERCURY GENERAL CORPORATION

YIELD 3.8%
P/E RATIO 10.5

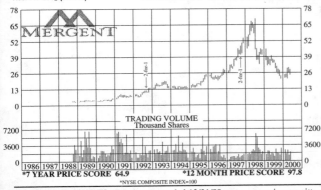

| 1986 | 1987 | 1988 | 1989 | 1990 | 1991 | 1992 | 1993 | 1994 | 1995 | 1996 | 1997 | 1998 | 1999 | 2000 |

*7 YEAR PRICE SCORE 64.9   ***12 MONTH PRICE SCORE 97.8**

*NYSE COMPOSITE INDEX=100

INTERIM EARNINGS (Per Share):

Qtr.	Mar.	June	Sept.	Dec.
1996	0.40	0.48	0.53	0.51
1997	0.56	0.65	0.74	0.88
1998	0.93	0.90	0.75	0.63
1999	0.73	0.60	0.51	0.60

INTERIM DIVIDENDS (Per Share):

Amt.	Decl.	Ex.	Rec.	Pay.
0.21Q	4/30/99	6/14/99	6/16/99	6/30/99
0.21Q	8/02/99	9/14/99	9/16/99	9/30/99
0.21Q	10/29/99	12/13/99	12/15/99	12/30/99
0.24Q	1/28/00	3/13/00	3/15/00	3/30/00
0.24Q	4/28/00	6/13/00	6/15/00	6/29/00

Indicated div.: $0.96

CAPITALIZATION (12/31/99):

	($000)	(%)
Long-Term Debt	92,000	9.2
Common & Surplus	909,591	90.8
Total	1,001,591	100.0

DIVIDEND ACHIEVER STATUS:

Rank: 12   10-Year Growth Rate: 22.96%
Total Years of Dividend Growth: 13

RECENT DEVELOPMENTS: For the year ended 12/31/99, net income fell 24.7% to $133.7 million compared with $177.5 million in the previous year. Results for 1999 included a net realized investment loss of $11.9 million. The 1998 results included a net realized investment loss of $3.9 million and a net realized gain from the sale of a subsidiary of $2.6 million. Total revenues climbed 4.8% to $1.28 billion from $1.22 billion in the previous year. Company-wide premiums written increased 5.9% to $1.19 billion, primarily due to higher volume of private passenger insurance policies issued in Florida and homeowners insurance in California and the introduction of a non-standard automobile policy in California. The California private passenger automobile insurance rates continue to be pressured by the expansion of competitors.

BUSINESS

MERCURY GENERAL CORPORATION, through its subsidiaries, engages primarily in writing all risk classifications of automobile insurance in a number of states, principally in California. The Company also writes homeowners insurance, mechanical breakdown insurance, commercial and dwelling fire insurance and commercial property insurance. The Company sells its policies through more than 1,800 independent agents, of which approximately 900 are located in California, 300 in Florida and 590 in Oklahoma and Texas.

REVENUES

(12/31/1999)	($000)	(%)
Earned Premiums	1,188,307	92.79
Net Investment Income	99,374	7.76
Net Real Investment Gains	(11,929)	(0.93)
Other	4,924	0.38
Total	1,280,676	100.00

ANNUAL FINANCIAL DATA

	12/31/99	12/31/98	12/31/97	12/31/96	12/31/95	12/31/94	12/31/93
Earnings Per Share	2.44	3.21	2.82	1.93	1.66	1.22	1.76
Tang. Book Val. Per Share	16.71	16.78	14.51	11.66	10.30	8.34	8.22
Dividends Per Share	0.84	0.70	0.58	0.48	0.40	0.35	0.30
Dividend Payout %	34.4	21.8	20.6	24.9	24.2	28.8	17.0
INCOME STATEMENT (IN MILLIONS):							
Total Premium Income	1,188.3	1,121.6	1,031.3	754.7	616.3	529.4	474.1
Net Investment Income	99.4	96.2	86.8	70.2	63.0	54.6	54.1
Other Income	d7.0	4.4	9.9	0.1	4.4	d6.7	5.5
Total Revenues	1,280.7	1,222.1	1,127.9	825.0	683.7	577.2	533.8
Income Before Income Taxes	168.5	235.3	209.8	136.6	114.3	82.4	125.5
Income Taxes	34.8	57.8	53.5	30.8	24.0	16.1	29.3
Net Income	133.7	177.5	156.3	105.8	90.3	66.3	96.2
Average Shs. Outstg. (000)	54,815	55,354	55,383	54,794	54,624	54,546	54,724
BALANCE SHEET (IN MILLIONS):							
Cash & Cash Equivalents	51.6	47.9	62.8	69.7	31.4	26.0	31.8
Premiums Due	178.6	152.5	144.3	125.8	76.7	83.0	51.2
Invst. Assets: Fixed-term	1,322.1	1,324.9	1,215.0	954.1	779.8	644.3	625.1
Invst. Assets: Equities	209.8	219.7	173.5	148.1	114.9	84.6	85.6
Invst. Assets: Total	1,575.5	1,590.6	1,448.2	1,168.3	923.2	751.6	740.5
Total Assets	1,906.4	1,877.0	1,725.5	1,419.9	1,081.7	911.7	864.0
Long-Term Obligations	92.0	78.0	75.0	75.0	25.0	25.0	15.0
Net Stockholders' Equity	909.6	917.4	799.6	641.2	565.2	457.2	450.3
Year-end Shs. Outstg. (000)	54,425	54,684	55,125	55,014	54,886	54,830	54,774
STATISTICAL RECORD:							
Return on Revenues %	10.4	14.5	13.9	12.8	13.2	11.5	18.0
Return on Equity %	14.7	19.4	19.5	16.5	16.0	14.5	21.4
Return on Assets %	7.0	9.5	9.1	7.4	8.3	7.3	11.1
Price Range	45½-20¹⁵⁄₁₆	70-33	54⁷⁄₁₆-26⅛	29⅛-19⅞	24⅞-14⅛	15¾-12¾	19¾-13¹⁄₁₆
P/E Ratio	18.6-8.6	21.8-10.3	19.3-9.3	15.1-10.3	15.0-8.5	13.0-10.5	11.2-7.4
Average Yield %	2.5	1.4	1.4	2.0	2.1	2.5	1.8

Statistics are as originally reported. Adj. for 2-for-1 stk. split, 10/97.

OFFICERS:

G. Joseph, Chmn., C.E.O.
M. D. Curtius, Pres., C.O.O.
G. Tirador, V.P., C.F.O.
J. A. Walters, V.P., Corp. Affairs, Sec.

INVESTOR CONTACT: Investor Relations, (800) 900-6729

PRINCIPAL OFFICE: 4484 Wilshire Boulevard, Los Angeles, CA 90010

TELEPHONE NUMBER: (323) 937-1060
FAX: (323) 857-7116
WEB: www.mercuryinsurance.com

NO. OF EMPLOYEES: 2,500 (approx.)

SHAREHOLDERS: 287 (approx.); 9224 (approx. beneficial)

ANNUAL MEETING: In May

INCORPORATED: CA, Jan. 1961

INSTITUTIONAL HOLDINGS:
No. of Institutions: 79
Shares Held: 19,073,716
% Held: 34.9

INDUSTRY: Fire, marine, and casualty insurance (SIC: 6331)

TRANSFER AGENT(S): The Bank of New York, New York, NY

MIDDLESEX WATER COMPANY

YIELD 4.2%
P/E RATIO 19.1

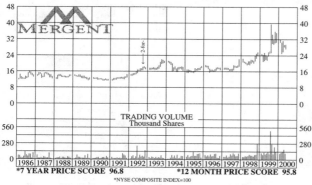

TRADING VOLUME
Thousand Shares

1986 1987 1988 1989 1990 1991 1992 1993 1994 1995 1996 1997 1998 1999 2000

*7 YEAR PRICE SCORE 96.8   ***12 MONTH PRICE SCORE 95.8**
*NYSE COMPOSITE INDEX=100

INTERIM EARNINGS (Per Share):

Qtr.	Mar.	June	Sept.	Dec.
1996	0.27	0.30	0.35	0.28
1997	0.30	0.30	0.43	0.30
1998	0.28	0.34	0.51	0.28
1999	0.29	0.50	0.54	0.19

INTERIM DIVIDENDS (Per Share):

Amt.	Decl.	Ex.	Rec.	Pay.
0.295Q	4/22/99	5/12/99	5/14/99	6/01/99
0.295Q	7/22/99	8/12/99	8/16/99	9/01/99
0.305Q	11/01/99	11/10/99	11/15/99	12/01/99
0.305Q	1/31/00	2/11/00	2/15/00	3/01/00
0.305Q	4/20/00	5/11/00	5/15/00	6/01/00

Indicated div.: $1.22 (Div. Reinv. Plan)

CAPITALIZATION (12/31/99):

	($000)	(%)
Long-Term Debt	82,330	48.7
Deferred Income Tax	12,113	7.2
Preferred Stock	4,063	2.4
Common & Surplus	70,489	41.7
Total	168,995	100.0

DIVIDEND ACHIEVER STATUS:

Rank: 303   10-Year Growth Rate: 2.86%
Total Years of Dividend Growth: 27

RECENT DEVELOPMENTS: For the year ended 12/31/99, net income increased 20.9% to $7.9 million compared with $6.5 million in the previous year. Operating revenues grew 24.2% to $53.5 million from $43.1 million the year before. The increase in operating revenues was attributed to contract service revenues from the operations of the City of Perth Amboy's water and wastewater systems, rate increases at all of the Company's regulated companies, and customer growth in the Company's Delaware service territory. Record water usage in New Jersey during July and early August was completely offset by the statewide drought restrictions set on 8/6/99. Operating income as a percentage of revenues improved to 19.9% versus 15.1% the year before.

BUSINESS

MIDDLESEX WATER COMPANY is engaged in the business of collecting, treating and distributing water for domestic, commercial, industrial and fire protection purposes in New Jersey and, through its wholly-owned subsidiary Tidewater Utilities, Inc., Delaware. The Company operates Public Water Supply Company, Inc., a 2,500 customer system in Southern Delaware and a subsidiary of Tidewater; Pinelands Water Company and Pinelands Wastewater Company in New Jersey; and Utility Service Affiliates, Inc., which provides contract operations and maintenance services for non-affiliated water and wastewater systems. On 1/1/99, the Company launched water and waste water operations in Perth Amboy, New Jersey.

ANNUAL FINANCIAL DATA

	12/31/99	12/31/98	12/31/97	12/31/96	12/31/95	12/31/94	12/31/93
Earnings Per Share	1.52	1.41	1.33	1.20	1.36	1.33	1.33
Cash Flow Per Share	2.31	2.18	2.00	1.92	2.08	2.07	2.04
Tang. Book Val. Per Share	14.10	13.63	12.00	11.70	11.52	11.13	10.77
Dividends Per Share	1.19	1.15	1.13	1.10	1.08	1.06	1.01
Dividend Payout %	78.3	81.6	84.6	92.1	79.8	79.5	76.1
INCOME STATEMENT (IN THOUSANDS):							
Total Revenues	53,497	43,058	40,294	38,025	37,847	36,122	35,479
Costs & Expenses	35,910	28,397	26,614	25,263	24,323	23,046	23,004
Depreciation & Amort.	4,303	3,797	3,145	3,011	2,926	2,962	2,790
Maintenance Exp.	2,619	1,715	1,741	1,528	1,686	1,550	1,460
Operating Income	10,665	9,149	8,793	8,222	8,912	8,565	8,225
Net Interest Inc./(Exp.)	d4,695	d4,424	d3,337	d3,280	d3,115	d3,044	d3,014
Net Income	7,881	6,521	5,861	5,167	5,704	5,495	5,480
Cash Flow	11,883	9,999	8,780	8,020	8,471	8,269	8,014
Average Shs. Outstg.	5,148	4,580	4,382	4,169	4,079	4,003	3,924
BALANCE SHEET (IN THOUSANDS):							
Gross Property	214,896	191,484	165,323	149,707	144,335	130,412	125,069
Accumulated Depreciation	35,175	32,368	30,252	28,463	26,402	21,669	19,677
Net Property	181,809	162,827	137,109	123,019	119,668	109,143	105,547
Total Assets	215,036	203,501	159,761	148,660	144,822	132,413	125,676
Long-Term Obligations	82,330	78,032	52,918	52,961	52,960	49,500	24,500
Net Stockholders' Equity	74,552	71,725	56,221	51,882	50,310	47,641	46,790
Year-end Shs. Outstg.	5,001	4,897	4,269	4,205	4,137	4,031	3,979
STATISTICAL RECORD:							
Operating Profit Margin %	19.9	21.2	21.8	21.6	23.5	23.7	23.2
Net Profit Margin %	14.7	15.1	14.5	13.6	15.1	15.2	15.4
Net Inc./Net Property %	4.3	4.0	4.3	4.2	4.8	5.0	5.2
Net Inc./Tot. Capital %	4.7	4.0	4.8	4.4	5.0	5.1	6.8
Return on Equity %	10.6	9.1	10.4	10.0	11.3	11.5	11.7
Accum. Depr./Gross Prop. %	16.4	16.9	18.3	19.0	18.3	16.6	15.7
Price Range	39½-21	25¾-19¼	22¼-16⅜	19¼-15½	18¾-15¼	21¼-15¾	22-16¾
P/E Ratio	26.0-13.8	18.3-13.7	16.7-12.3	16.0-12.9	13.8-11.2	16.0-11.8	16.5-12.6
Average Yield %	3.9	5.1	5.8	6.4	6.4	5.7	5.2

Statistics are as originally reported.

OFFICERS:
J. R. Tompkins, Chmn., Pres.
M. F. Reynolds, V.P., Treas., Sec.
D. G. Sullivan, V.P., Asst. Treas., Asst. Sec., Gen. Couns.

INVESTOR CONTACT: Marion F. Reynolds, (908) 634-1500

PRINCIPAL OFFICE: 1500 Ronson Rd., Iselin, NJ 08830-3020

TELEPHONE NUMBER: (732) 634-1500
FAX: (732) 750-5981
WEB: www.middlesexwater.com

NO. OF EMPLOYEES: 180 (avg.)

SHAREHOLDERS: 2,211 (common); 22 (preferred)

ANNUAL MEETING: In May

INCORPORATED: usa, 1897

INSTITUTIONAL HOLDINGS:
No. of Institutions: 19
Shares Held: 441,268
% Held: 8.9

INDUSTRY: Water supply (SIC: 4941)

TRANSFER AGENT(S): Registrar and Transfer Company, Cranford, NJ

MIDLAND CO.

YIELD 1.2%
P/E RATIO 7.6

TRADING VOLUME
Thousand Shares

| 1986 | 1987 | 1988 | 1989 | 1990 | 1991 | 1992 | 1993 | 1994 | 1995 | 1996 | 1997 | 1998 | 1999 | 2000 |

*7 YEAR PRICE SCORE 83.9   ***12 MONTH PRICE SCORE 106.9**
*NYSE COMPOSITE INDEX=100

INTERIM EARNINGS (Per Share):

Qtr.	Mar.	Jun.	Sep.	Dec.
1995	0.41	0.10	0.24	0.28
1996	0.57	0.07	0.04	0.66
1997	0.46	0.55	0.66	0.96
1998	0.64	0.39	0.77	1.06
1999	0.83	0.55	0.77	1.15

INTERIM DIVIDENDS (Per Share):

Amt.	Decl.	Ex.	Rec.	Pay.
0.068Q	4/29/99	6/16/99	6/18/99	7/06/99
0.068Q	7/29/99	9/21/99	9/23/99	10/06/99
0.068Q	10/28/99	12/20/99	12/22/99	1/06/00
0.075Q	1/27/00	3/08/00	3/10/00	4/05/00
0.075Q	4/27/00	6/21/00	6/23/00	7/07/00

Indicated div.: $0.30

CAPITALIZATION (12/31/99):

	($000)	(%)
Long-Term Debt	44,288	13.4
Deferred Income Tax	28,171	8.5
Common & Surplus	258,002	78.1
Total	330,461	100.0

DIVIDEND ACHIEVER STATUS:
Rank: 196   10-Year Growth Rate: 8.24%
Total Years of Dividend Growth: 13

RECENT DEVELOPMENTS: For the year ended 12/31/99, net income rose 15.8% to $31.2 million compared with $26.9 million in the previous year. Total revenues were $469.1 million, up 6.1% from $442.4 million a year earlier. Direct and assumed written premiums generated from AMIG's property and casualty and life insurance subsidiaries grew 7.8% to $493.2 million from $457.6 million in 1998. This growth is primarily the result of volume increases in manufactured home and related coverages premium. Revenues from premiums earned rose 6.8% to $401.0 million from $375.5 million in 1998. Net investment income improved 5.8% to $25.3 million from $23.9 million due to the investment of positive cash flow generated from underwriting operations and to the increase of the Company's investment portfolio. Transportation revenues fell 5.2% to $31.3 million from $33.1 million due to reduced demand for petroleum coke and barite products, negatively affected shipping patterns.

BUSINESS

MIDLAND CO. is a holding company primarily engaged in insurance and river transportation services through its two primary subsidiaries. American Modern Insurance Group, Inc., (AMIG) an insurance holding company licensed in all 50 states through its six property and casualty companies and two credit life companies. AMIG specializes in writing physical damage insurance and related coverages on manufactured housing. Also, AMIG has expanded to other areas of insurance including Homeowners, Lower Valued Homes, Dwelling Fire, Mortgage Fire, Collateral Protection, Watercraft, Long-Haul Truck, Commercial and Excess and Surplus Lines. The Company's other subsidiary, M/G Transport, currently charters barges and brokers freight for the movement of commodities on the inland waterways.

REVENUES

(12/31/99)	($000)	(%)
Premiums Earned	400,991	85.4
Net Investment Income	25,292	5.4
Net Realized Invest Gains	3,486	0.7
Other Insurance Income	6,793	1.5
Transportation	31,327	6.7
Other	1,237	0.3
Total	469,126	100.0

ANNUAL FINANCIAL DATA

	12/31/99	12/31/98	12/31/97	12/31/96	12/31/95	12/31/94	12/31/93
Earnings Per Share	3.30	2.86	[1] 2.63	0.12	1.04	1.03	1.42
Cash Flow Per Share	4.38	3.80	3.73	1.09	2.04	2.23	2.60
Tang. Book Val. Per Share	27.11	26.61	21.11	17.50	17.28	14.73	14.79
Dividends Per Share	0.27	0.25	0.23	0.21	0.20	0.19	0.18
Dividend Payout %	8.0	8.6	8.8	182.2	19.6	18.4	12.4

INCOME STATEMENT (IN THOUSANDS):

Total Revenues	469,126	442,362	375,430	370,492	350,960	315,915	267,667
Costs & Expenses	411,059	391,046	325,475	356,525	325,050	288,554	234,979
Depreciation & Amort.	10,287	8,798	10,269	8,863	8,960	10,609	10,291
Operating Income	47,780	42,518	39,686	5,104	16,950	16,752	22,397
Net Interest Inc./(Exp.)	d4,067	d4,991	d4,983	d5,873	d4,434	d4,865	d4,144
Income Before Income Taxes	43,713	37,527	34,703	d769	12,516	11,887	18,253
Income Taxes	12,534	10,595	10,336	cr1,837	2,964	2,468	5,148
Net Income	31,179	26,932	[1] 24,367	1,068	9,552	9,419	13,105
Cash Flow	41,466	35,730	34,636	9,931	18,512	20,028	23,396
Average Shs. Outstg.	9,463	9,412	9,291	...	...	...	...

BALANCE SHEET (IN THOUSANDS):

Cash & Cash Equivalents	620,957	593,857	504,106	404,079	373,439	282,124	228,549
Total Current Assets	724,534	687,153	671,353	587,412	568,385	464,531	341,836
Net Property	62,585	67,837	71,623	81,675	85,849	66,042	107,892
Total Assets	888,057	837,220	819,955	718,789	699,380	568,959	484,816
Total Current Liabilities	111,045	113,909	114,265	116,289	112,100	82,684	88,369
Long-Term Obligations	44,288	54,563	62,518	62,470	62,470	44,640	47,110
Net Stockholders' Equity	258,002	248,832	197,026	159,868	156,595	132,437	133,110
Net Working Capital	613,489	573,244	557,088	471,123	456,285	381,847	253,467
Year-end Shs. Outstg.	9,516	9,352	9,333	9,126	9,060	8,991	8,997

STATISTICAL RECORD:

Operating Profit Margin %	10.2	9.6	10.6	1.4	4.8	5.3	8.4
Net Profit Margin %	6.6	6.1	6.5	0.3	2.7	3.0	4.9
Return on Equity %	12.1	10.8	12.4	0.7	6.1	7.1	9.8
Return on Assets %	3.5	3.2	3.0	0.1	1.4	1.7	2.7
Debt/Total Assets %	5.0	6.5	7.6	8.7	8.9	7.8	9.7
Price Range	29⁹⁄₁₆-19¼	32¹³⁄₁₆-19³⁄₁₆	21¹¹⁄₁₆-12⁵⁄₁₆	16¹⁵⁄₁₆-11¼	17-14⁵⁄₁₆	15¹⁄₁₆-11⁵⁄₁₆	16⁷⁄₁₆-13³⁄₁₆
P/E Ratio	8.9-5.8	11.5-6.7	8.3-4.7	144.5-96.1	16.4-13.8	14.6-11.0	11.9-9.3
Average Yield %	1.1	0.9	1.4	1.4	1.3	1.4	1.2

Statistics are as originally reported. Adj. for 3-for-1 stk. split, 5/98 [1] Bef. loss from disc. ops. of $6.8 mill. ($2.21/sh.)

OFFICERS:
J. P. Hayden III, Chmn., C.O.O.
M. J. Conaton, Vice-Chmn.
J. W. Hayden, Pres., C.E.O.
J. I. Von Lehman, Exec. V.P., C.F.O., Sec.

PRINCIPAL OFFICE: 7000 Midland Blvd., P.O. Box 125, Amelia, OH 45102-2607

TELEPHONE NUMBER: (513) 943-7100
FAX: (513) 943-7111
WEB: www.midlandcompany.com
NO. OF EMPLOYEES: 980 (approx.)
SHAREHOLDERS: 1,530 approx.
ANNUAL MEETING: In Apr.
INCORPORATED: OH, 1938

INSTITUTIONAL HOLDINGS:
No. of Institutions: 25
Shares Held: 1,653,817
% Held: 17.4

INDUSTRY: Fire, marine, and casualty insurance (SIC: 6331)

TRANSFER AGENT(S): Fifth Third Bank, Cincinnati, OH

MILLIPORE CORPORATION

YIELD	0.6%
P/E RATIO	51.3

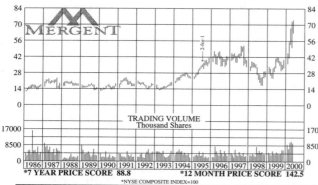

1986	1987	1988	1989	1990	1991	1992	1993	1994	1995	1996	1997	1998	1999	2000

TRADING VOLUME Thousand Shares

*7 YEAR PRICE SCORE 88.8   ***12 MONTH PRICE SCORE 142.5**
NYSE COMPOSITE INDEX=100

INTERIM EARNINGS (Per Share):

Qtr.	Mar.	June	Sept.	Dec.
1996	0.57	0.57	0.51	d0.66
1997	d2.25	0.38	0.49	0.48
1998	0.71	0.15	d0.83	0.18
1999	0.25	0.32	0.37	0.47

INTERIM DIVIDENDS (Per Share):

Amt.	Decl.	Ex.	Rec.	Pay.
0.11Q	2/11/99	3/10/99	3/12/99	4/27/99
0.11Q	6/17/99	6/28/99	6/30/99	7/27/99
0.11Q	9/23/99	10/06/99	10/08/99	10/26/99
0.11Q	12/09/99	12/22/99	12/27/99	1/25/00
0.11Q	2/17/00	3/01/00	3/03/00	4/25/00

Indicated div.: $0.44 (Div. Reinv. Plan)

CAPITALIZATION (12/31/99):

	($000)	(%)
Long-Term Debt	313,107	63.9
Common & Surplus	176,851	36.1
Total	489,958	100.0

DIVIDEND ACHIEVER STATUS:
Rank: 184   10-Year Growth Rate: 8.76%
Total Years of Dividend Growth: 29

RECENT DEVELOPMENTS: For the year ended 12/31/99, net income soared to $64.3 million versus $9.9 million in 1998. Results for 1999 included a credit of $5.2 million from restructuring items. Results in 1998 included a restructuring charge of $33.6 million and a gain of $35.6 million from the sale of equity securities. Net sales rose 10.3% to $771.2 million from $699.3 million the year before. Sales reflected strong performances in the microelectronics division and high demand for biotechnology manufacturing products.

PROSPECTS: MIL's restructuring program, which was implemented in 1998, has contributed to an upturn in the semiconductor industry. In addition, MIL's asset management program has reflected an improved cash flow position. Going forward, MIL expects to realize efficiency gains from its new European shared service center, supply chain management organization and global data center. New products generated by MIL's research and development should contribute to future growth.

BUSINESS

MILLIPORE CORPORATION develops, manufactures and sells products that are used primarily for the analysis and purification of fluids. MIL's products are based on a variety of membranes and certain other technologies that affect separations, principally through physical and chemical methods. The principal separation technologies utilized by the Company are based on membrane filters, and certain chemistries, resins and enzyme immunoassays. Membranes are used to filter either the wanted or the unwanted particulate, bacterial, molecular or viral entities from fluids, or to concentrate and retain such entities (in the fluid) for further processing. In 1999, revenues (and operating income) were derived: biopharmaceutical and research, 73.4% (86.9%); and microelectronics, 26.6% (13.1%).

ANNUAL FINANCIAL DATA

	12/31/99	12/31/98	12/31/97	12/31/96	12/31/95	12/31/94	⑥ 12/31/93
Earnings Per Share	⑧ 1.42	⑤ 0.22	d0.89	⑪ 1.00	1.90	1.09	③ 0.88
Cash Flow Per Share	2.40	1.23	0.04	1.70	2.51	1.59	1.30
Tang. Book Val. Per Share	2.36	1.37	1.64	3.66	4.95	4.67	8.18
Dividends Per Share	0.44	0.42	0.38	0.34	0.31	0.29	0.27
Dividend Payout %	31.0	190.8	...	34.0	16.3	26.6	30.9
INCOME STATEMENT (IN THOUSANDS):							
Total Revenues	771,188	699,307	758,919	618,735	594,466	497,252	445,366
Costs & Expenses	617,416	655,564	717,151	527,736	447,912	378,989	350,399
Depreciation & Amort.	44,291	44,409	40,661	30,587	27,478	27,604	23,775
Operating Income	109,481	d666	1,107	60,412	119,076	90,659	71,192
Net Interest Inc./(Exp.)	d27,130	d26,384	d27,547	d8,718	d8,941	d2,944	d7,969
Income Before Income Taxes	82,351	8,544	d18,110	57,023	110,135	76,915	63,223
Income Taxes	18,023	cr1,320	20,674	13,401	24,781	17,306	14,225
Net Income	⑥ 64,328	⑤ 9,864	d38,784	⑪ 43,622	85,354	59,609	③ 48,998
Cash Flow	108,619	54,273	1,877	74,209	112,832	87,213	72,773
Average Shs. Outstg.	45,274	44,289	43,527	43,602	44,985	54,726	55,902
BALANCE SHEET (IN THOUSANDS):							
Cash & Cash Equivalents	51,060	36,022	20,269	46,870	23,758	30,236	40,642
Total Current Assets	358,947	304,752	352,408	311,912	261,759	258,804	356,961
Net Property	226,477	237,414	220,094	203,017	191,250	187,525	194,895
Total Assets	792,733	762,440	766,244	682,892	530,945	527,653	702,604
Total Current Liabilities	269,783	298,681	304,873	216,400	171,422	158,155	120,287
Long-Term Obligations	313,107	299,110	286,844	224,359	105,272	100,231	102,047
Net Stockholders' Equity	176,851	136,908	148,994	217,605	226,475	221,277	461,154
Net Working Capital	89,164	6,071	47,535	95,512	90,337	100,649	236,674
Year-end Shs. Outstg.	45,194	44,067	43,707	43,322	44,261	46,226	56,006
STATISTICAL RECORD:							
Operating Profit Margin %	14.2	...	0.1	9.8	20.0	18.2	16.0
Net Profit Margin %	8.3	1.4	...	7.1	14.4	12.0	11.0
Return on Equity %	36.4	7.2	...	20.0	37.7	26.9	10.6
Return on Assets %	8.1	1.3	...	6.4	16.1	11.3	7.0
Debt/Total Assets %	39.5	39.2	37.4	32.9	19.8	19.0	14.5
Price Range	42⅛-23⁷/₁₆	38⁷/₁₆-17¼	52-33½	47⅛-33⅝	41½-22⅞	38½-19³/₁₆	20⅛-12¹⁵/₁₆
P/E Ratio	29.7-16.5	174.6-78.4	...	47.1-33.6	21.8-12.0	26.1-17.6	23.0-14.8
Average Yield %	1.3	1.5	0.9	0.8	1.0	1.2	1.6

Statistics are as originally reported. Adj. for 2-for-1 split, 7/95. ⑪ Incl. $68.3 mill. ($1.21/sh. net) pre-tax chg. to purch. R&D & $5.3 mill. gains fr. sale of eq. sec. ③ Incl. $13.0 mill. restr. chg. & excl. $3.5 mill. extrord. item & $10.9 mill. disc. ops. ④ Refl. effect of divest. of chromo. bus. & instrum. div. ⑤ Incl. $33.6 mill. pre-tax restr. chg., $35.6 mill. gain fr. sale of equity secs. & excl. $5.8 mill. loss on the disp. of disc. ops. ⑥ Incl. cr$5.2 mill. restr. chgs.

OFFICERS:
C. W. Zadel, Chmn., Pres., C.E.O.
K. B. Allen, V.P., Treas., C.F.O.

INVESTOR CONTACT: Geoffrey E. Helliwell, Dir. Treas. Operations, (781) 533-2032

PRINCIPAL OFFICE: 80 Ashby Road, Bedford, MA 01730-2271

TELEPHONE NUMBER: (781) 533-6000
FAX: (781) 533-3110
WEB: www.millipore.com

NO. OF EMPLOYEES: 1,300 (approx.)

SHAREHOLDERS: 2,962 (approx.)

ANNUAL MEETING: In Apr.

INCORPORATED: MA, May, 1954

INSTITUTIONAL HOLDINGS:
No. of Institutions: 208
Shares Held: 37,678,647
% Held: 83.7

INDUSTRY: Analytical instruments (SIC: 3826)

TRANSFER AGENT(S): BankBoston, N.A., Boston, MA.

MINE SAFETY APPLIANCES COMPANY

YIELD 2.1%
P/E RATIO 18.6

INTERIM EARNINGS (Per Share):

Qtr.	Mar.	June	Sept.	Dec.
1996	0.20	0.25	0.42	0.70
1997	0.26	0.37	0.43	0.55
1998	0.41	0.36	0.23	0.37
1999	0.20	0.05	0.33	0.67

INTERIM DIVIDENDS (Per Share):

Amt.	Decl.	Ex.	Rec.	Pay.
0.34Q	6/23/99	8/11/99	8/13/99	9/10/99
0.34Q	10/27/99	11/17/99	11/19/99	12/10/99
0.34Q	1/18/00	2/23/00	2/25/00	3/10/00
3-for-1	3/16/00	5/25/00	5/12/00	5/24/00
0.12Q	5/10/00	5/24/00	5/26/00	6/10/00

Indicated div.: $0.48 (Div. Reinv. Plan)

CAPITALIZATION (12/31/99):

	($000)	(%)
Long-Term Debt	36,550	11.6
Deferred Income Tax	35,961	11.4
Preferred Stock...............	3,569	1.1
Common & Surplus	238,888	75.8
Total	314,968	100.0

DIVIDEND ACHIEVER STATUS:

Rank: 234   10-Year Growth Rate: 6.42%
Total Years of Dividend Growth: 29

TRADING VOLUME Thousand Shares

```
1986 1987 1988 1989 1990 1991 1992 1993 1994 1995 1996 1997 1998 1999 2000
```

*7 YEAR PRICE SCORE 77.5   *12 MONTH PRICE SCORE 104.1
*NYSE COMPOSITE INDEX=100

RECENT DEVELOPMENTS: For the year ended 12/31/99, income was $16.3 million before an accounting charge, compared with net income of $18.3 million in the previous year. Results for 1999 and 1998 included pre-tax restructuring charges of $4.0 million and $1.0 million, respectively. Net sales slipped $494.2 million from $496.1 million in 1998. Net sales for 1998 included a $13.6 million sales contribution from the Hazco and Baseline business units until they were divested at the end of the 1998 second quarter. The decline in sales was due to weakness in the U.S. and European markets. European sales were adversely affected by pricing pressures and unfavorable currency exchange rates. Operations outside the U.S. and Europe experienced sales growth, particularly in South Africa, Australia, Canada, China, Brazil and Mexico. On 2/22/00, MSA acquired ISI Group, Inc., a developer of infrared thermal imaging cameras used for firefighting and in industrial maintenance markets.

BUSINESS

MINE SAFETY APPLIANCES COMPANY's primary business is the manufacture and sale of products designed to guard the safety and health of workers throughout the world. Principal products include respiratory protective equipment that is air-purifying, air-supplied and self-contained in design. MNES also produces instruments that monitor and analyze workplace environments and control industrial processes. Personal protective products include head, eye and face, body and hearing protectors. For the mining industry, MNES provides mine lighting, rockdusting equipment, fire-fighting foam and foam application equipment. MNES health-related products include emergency care items, hospital filters and instruments and heart pacemaker power cells. MNES also manufactures specialized high-efficiency space filters with applications ranging from safeguarding clean rooms to the protection of sophisticated electronic equipment. Many of these products have wide application for workers in industries that include manufacturing, public utilities, chemicals, petroleum, construction, transportation, municipal fire departments, the military and hazardous materials clean-up.

ANNUAL FINANCIAL DATA

	12/31/99	12/31/98	12/31/97	12/31/96	12/31/95	12/31/94	12/31/93
Earnings Per Share	①②1.25	①1.37	①1.60	①1.58	①1.11	①0.86	①0.58
Cash Flow Per Share	3.07	3.05	3.18	3.12	2.28	1.91	1.53
Tang. Book Val. Per Share	18.55	18.21	17.79	17.20	16.08	15.04	14.20
Dividends Per Share	0.45	0.44	0.41	0.37	0.35	0.313	0.307
Dividend Payout %	36.3	32.4	25.8	23.2	31.9	36.4	53.2

INCOME STATEMENT (IN THOUSANDS):

Total Revenues	498,051	497,207	499,409	506,855	491,859	465,070	435,105
Costs & Expenses	447,662	443,028	438,833	445,485	435,762	414,525	394,656
Depreciation & Amort.	23,625	22,398	21,516	22,373	20,002	18,527	17,294
Operating Income	26,764	31,781	39,060	38,997	36,095	32,018	23,155
Net Interest Inc./(Exp.)	d4,273	d3,258	d2,781	d1,595	d1,730	d2,224	d1,713
Income Before Income Taxes	23,185	28,208	36,239	36,667	33,132	25,826	18,241
Income Taxes	6,859	9,933	14,385	13,606	14,220	10,497	7,686
Net Income	①②16,326	①18,275	①21,854	①23,061	①18,912	①15,329	①10,555
Cash Flow	39,901	40,624	43,333	45,370	38,861	33,803	27,793
Average Shs. Outstg.	13,005	13,341	13,647	14,556	17,043	17,763	18,207

BALANCE SHEET (IN THOUSANDS):

Cash & Cash Equivalents	17,108	24,020	19,921	25,096	31,950	54,420	46,434
Total Current Assets	203,090	229,209	219,613	228,407	228,625	237,316	224,609
Net Property	163,509	164,561	155,184	147,058	151,106	151,956	153,529
Total Assets	451,741	456,716	406,404	407,682	406,600	417,051	407,884
Total Current Liabilities	80,005	110,006	103,240	91,814	71,984	70,822	60,410
Long-Term Obligations	36,550	11,919	12,270	13,278	14,746	16,564	27,476
Net Stockholders' Equity	242,457	242,846	241,449	241,432	253,540	265,975	259,744
Net Working Capital	123,085	119,203	116,373	136,593	156,641	166,494	164,199
Year-end Shs. Outstg.	12,875	13,137	13,368	13,833	15,549	17,448	18,036

STATISTICAL RECORD:

Operating Profit Margin %	5.4	6.4	7.8	7.7	7.3	6.9	5.3
Net Profit Margin %	3.3	3.7	4.4	4.5	3.8	3.3	2.4
Return on Equity %	6.7	7.5	9.1	9.6	7.5	5.8	4.1
Return on Assets %	3.6	4.0	5.4	5.7	4.7	3.7	2.6
Debt/Total Assets %	8.1	2.6	3.0	3.3	3.6	4.0	6.7
Price Range	27-16¹³⁄₁₆	29-19¹⁄₁₆	24⁹⁄₁₆-17¹³⁄₁₆	18½-13¹¹⁄₁₆	18³⁄₁₆-13¹¹⁄₁₆	15½-13⁵⁄₁₆	16⁵⁄₁₆-13¼
P/E Ratio	21.6-13.5	21.2-14.0	15.4-11.1	11.7-8.6	16.6-12.3	18.0-15.3	28.3-23.0
Average Yield %	2.1	1.8	1.9	2.3	2.2	2.2	2.1

Statistics are as originally reported. Adj. for stk. split: 3-for-1, 5/24/00. ① Incl. restr. chrgs.: $2.0 mill., 12/31/99; $552,000, 12/31/98; $2.2 mill., 12/31/97; $7.8 mill., 12/31/96; $730,000, 12/31/95; $3.1 mill., 12/31/94; credit $223,000, 12/31/93. ② Bef. acctg. chrg. of $1.2 mill.

OFFICERS:
J. T. Ryan III, Chmn., C.E.O.
T. B. Hotopp, Pres.
J. E. Herald, V.P., Fin., C.F.O.

PRINCIPAL OFFICE: 121 Gamma Dr., RIDC Industrial Park, O'Hara Township, Pittsburgh, PA 15238

TELEPHONE NUMBER: (412) 967-3000
FAX: (412) 967-3451
WEB: www.msanet.com
NO. OF EMPLOYEES: 4,100 (avg.)
SHAREHOLDERS: 875 (approx.)
ANNUAL MEETING: In May
INCORPORATED: PA, Jan., 1917

INSTITUTIONAL HOLDINGS:
No. of Institutions: 33
Shares Held: 4,357,917 (Adj.)
% Held: 29.8
INDUSTRY: Men's and boys' work clothing (SIC: 2326)
TRANSFER AGENT(S): Wells Fargo, St.Paul, MN

NYSE SYMBOL MMM
Rec. Pr. 85 3/4 (5/31/00)

MINNESOTA MINING & MANUFACTURING COMPANY

YIELD 2.7%
P/E RATIO 19.7

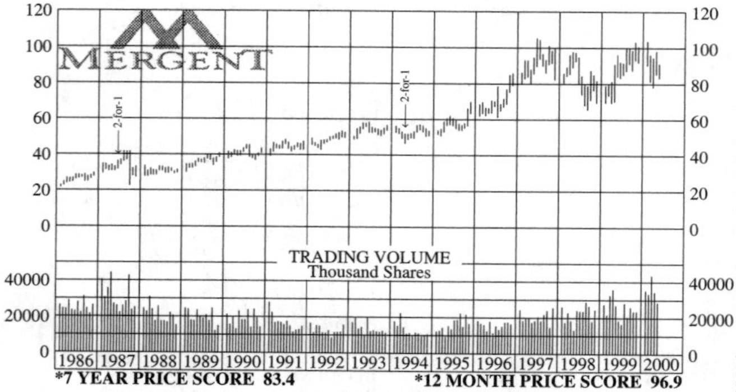

*7 YEAR PRICE SCORE 83.4 *12 MONTH PRICE SCORE 96.9

*NYSE COMPOSITE INDEX=100

INTERIM EARNINGS (Per Share):

Qtr.	Mar.	June	Sept.	Dec.
1996	0.87	0.91	0.95	0.90
1997	0.99	1.01	2.25	0.89
1998	0.98	0.94	0.44	0.61
1999	0.95	1.17	1.13	1.10

INTERIM DIVIDENDS (Per Share):

Amt.	Decl.	Ex.	Rec.	Pay.
0.56Q	5/11/99	5/19/99	5/21/99	6/12/99
0.56Q	8/09/99	8/18/99	8/20/99	9/12/99
0.56Q	11/08/99	11/17/99	11/19/99	12/12/99
0.58Q	2/14/00	2/23/00	2/25/00	3/12/00
0.58Q	5/04/00	5/17/00	5/19/00	6/12/00

Indicated div.: $2.32 (Div. Reinv. Plan)

CAPITALIZATION (12/31/99):

	($000)	(%)
Long-Term Debt	1,480,000	19.1
Common & Surplus	6,289,000	80.9
Total	7,769,000	100.0

DIVIDEND ACHIEVER STATUS:
Rank: 253 10-Year Growth Rate: 5.59%
Total Years of Dividend Growth: 41

RECENT DEVELOPMENTS: For the year ended 12/31/99, the Company reported net income of $1.76 billion compared with income of $1.21 billion, before an extraordinary loss of $38.0 million, in the previous year. The 1999 results included nonrecurring net gains of $100.0 million. Results for 1998 included nonrecurring net charges of $351.0 million. Net sales grew 4.2% to $15.66 billion from $15.02 billion the year before.

PROSPECTS: In 2000, MMM expects domestic sales to grow nearly 6% and international sales to increase 7% to 8% in local currencies. In addition, MMM expects capital spending to total $1.00 billion to $1.10 billion in 2000. MMM also expects to realize savings of approximately $60.0 million related to its restructuring plan. The restructuring plan is expected to generate approximately $250.0 million in annual pre-tax savings.

BUSINESS

MINNESOTA, MINING & MANUFACTURING CO. (3M) is a worldwide producer of a diverse variety of industrial and consumer products. 3M operates in six business sectors: Industrial provides telecommunications products, industrial tapes, and industrial abrasives; Electro and Communications provides electronic and electrical products; Consumer and Office provides consumer and office products; Transportation, Graphics and Safety provides reflective sheeting, high-performance graphics, respirators, automotive components, and optical films; Specialty Material provides specialty materials; and Health Care provides skin health products, medical/surgical supplies and devices, infection control, cardiovascular systems, health care information systems, pharmaceuticals, and dental products.

BUSINESS LINE ANALYSIS

(12/31/99)	REV (%)	INC (%)
Industrial	21.7	20.7
Transportation, Graphics	20.6	23
Health Care	19.9	23.2
Consumer and Office	17.2	13.8
Electro and Communication	12.9	13.7
Specialty Material	7.4	6.4
Corporate and Unallocated	.3	-.8
Total	100.0	100.0

ANNUAL FINANCIAL DATA

	12/31/99	12/31/98	12/31/97	12/31/96	12/31/95	12/31/94	12/31/93
Earnings Per Share	**[5] 4.34**	**[4] 2.97**	**[3] 5.06**	**3.63**	**[2] 3.11**	**[1] 3.13**	**2.91**
Cash Flow Per Share	**6.55**	**5.10**	**7.14**	**5.74**	**5.15**	**5.73**	**5.39**
Tang. Book Val. Per Share	**15.77**	**14.80**	**14.63**	**15.07**	**16.43**	**16.03**	**15.14**
Dividends Per Share	**2.24**	**2.20**	**2.12**	**1.92**	**1.88**	**1.76**	**1.66**
Dividend Payout %	**51.6**	**74.1**	**41.9**	**52.9**	**60.4**	**56.2**	**57.0**
INCOME STATEMENT (IN MILLIONS):							
Total Revenues	15,659.0	15,021.0	15,070.0	14,236.0	13,460.0	15,079.0	14,020.0
Costs & Expenses	11,803.0	12,116.0	11,525.0	10,862.0	10,380.0	11,727.0	10,988.0
Depreciation & Amort.	900.0	866.0	870.0	883.0	859.0	1,101.0	1,076.0
Operating Income	2,956.0	2,039.0	2,675.0	2,491.0	2,221.0	2,251.0	1,956.0
Net Interest Inc./(Exp.)	d109.0	d139.0	d94.0	d79.0	d102.0	d87.0	d50.0
Income Before Income Taxes	2,880.0	1,952.0	3,440.0	2,479.0	2,168.0	2,154.0	2,002.0
Income Taxes	1,032.0	685.0	1,241.0	886.0	785.0	771.0	707.0
Equity Earnings/Minority Int.	d85.0	d54.0	d78.0	d77.0	d77.0	d61.0	d32.0
Net Income	[5] 1,763.0	[4] 1,213.0	[3] 2,121.0	1,516.0	[2] 1,306.0	[1] 1,322.0	1,263.0
Cash Flow	2,663.0	2,079.0	2,991.0	2,399.0	2,165.0	2,423.0	2,339.0
Average Shs. Outstg. (000)	406,500	408,000	419,000	418,000	420,000	423,000	434,000
BALANCE SHEET (IN MILLIONS):							
Cash & Cash Equivalents	441.0	448.0	477.0	744.0	772.0	491.0	656.0
Total Current Assets	6,066.0	6,318.0	6,168.0	6,486.0	6,395.0	6,928.0	6,363.0
Net Property	5,656.0	5,566.0	5,034.0	4,844.0	4,638.0	5,054.0	4,830.0
Total Assets	13,896.0	14,153.0	13,238.0	13,364.0	14,183.0	13,496.0	12,197.0
Total Current Liabilities	3,819.0	4,386.0	3,983.0	3,606.0	6,096.0	3,605.0	3,282.0
Long-Term Obligations	1,480.0	1,614.0	1,015.0	851.0	1,203.0	1,031.0	796.0
Net Stockholders' Equity	6,289.0	5,936.0	5,926.0	6,284.0	6,884.0	6,734.0	6,512.0
Net Working Capital	2,247.0	1,932.0	2,185.0	2,880.0	299.0	3,323.0	3,081.0
Year-end Shs. Outstg. (000)	398,700	401,000	405,000	417,000	419,000	420,000	430,000
STATISTICAL RECORD:							
Operating Profit Margin %	18.9	13.6	17.8	17.5	16.5	14.9	14.0
Net Profit Margin %	11.3	8.1	14.1	10.6	9.7	8.8	9.0
Return on Equity %	28.0	20.4	35.8	24.1	19.0	19.6	19.4
Return on Assets %	12.7	8.6	16.0	11.3	9.2	9.8	10.4
Debt/Total Assets %	10.7	11.4	7.7	6.4	8.5	7.6	6.5
Price Range	103 3/8-69 5/16	97 7/8-65 5/8	105 1/2-80	85 7/8-61 1/4	69 7/8-50 3/4	57 1/8-46 3/8	58 1/2-48 5/8
P/E Ratio	23.8-16.0	33.0-22.1	20.8-15.8	23.7-16.9	22.5-16.3	18.3-14.8	20.1-16.7
Average Yield %	2.6	2.7	2.3	2.6	3.1	3.4	3.1

Statistics are as originally reported. Adj. for 2-for-1 split, 4/94. [1] Incl. pre-tax chg. of $35.0 mill. rel. to mammary-implant litigation. [2] Bef. disc. ops. loss of $330.0 mill. [3] Incl. $803.0 mill. gain from sale of outdoor adver. bus. [4] Bef. extraord. chrg. of $38.0 mill.; incl. pre-tax restruct. chrg. of $493.0 mill. & a gain on divestiture of $10.0 mill. [5] Incl. pre-tax chrg. of $73.0 mill. rel. to litigation, a gain on divestitures of $147.0 mill., & a $26.0 mill. gain rel. to a change in estimate of the restruct. liability.

OFFICERS:
L. D. DeSimone, Chmn., C.E.O.
G. Agostini, Sr. V.P., C.F.O.

INVESTOR CONTACT: Jon Greer, Director, Investor Relations, (651) 736-1915

PRINCIPAL OFFICE: 3M Center, St. Paul, MN 55144-1000

TELEPHONE NUMBER: (651) 733-1110
FAX: (651) 733-9973
WEB: www.mmm.com
NO. OF EMPLOYEES: 70,549 (avg.)
SHAREHOLDERS: 132,877
ANNUAL MEETING: In May
INCORPORATED: MN, July, 1902; reincorp., DE, Jun., 1929

INSTITUTIONAL HOLDINGS:
No. of Institutions: 765
Shares Held: 275,303,519
% Held: 68.6

INDUSTRY: Adhesives and sealants (SIC: 2891)

TRANSFER AGENT(S): Norwest Bank Minnesota, N.A. St. Paul, MN

MODINE MANUFACTURING COMPANY

YIELD 5.0%
P/E RATIO 8.8

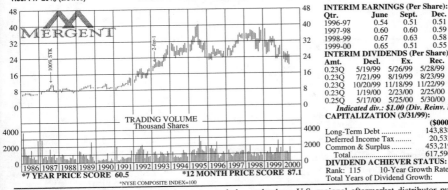

TRADING VOLUME
Thousand Shares

1986|1987|1988|1989|1990|1991|1992|1993|1994|1995|1996|1997|1998|1999|2000
*7 YEAR PRICE SCORE 60.5   *12 MONTH PRICE SCORE 87.1
*NYSE COMPOSITE INDEX=100

INTERIM EARNINGS (Per Share):

Qtr.	June	Sept.	Dec.	Mar.
1996-97	0.54	0.51	0.51	0.54
1997-98	0.60	0.60	0.59	0.60
1998-99	0.67	0.63	0.58	0.58
1999-00	0.65	0.51	0.55	...

INTERIM DIVIDENDS (Per Share):

Amt.	Decl.	Ex.	Rec.	Pay.
0.23Q	5/19/99	5/26/99	5/28/99	6/07/99
0.23Q	7/21/99	8/19/99	8/23/99	9/02/99
0.23Q	10/20/99	11/18/99	11/22/99	12/02/99
0.23Q	1/19/00	2/23/00	2/25/00	3/09/00
0.25Q	5/17/00	5/25/00	5/30/00	6/08/00

Indicated div.: $1.00 (Div. Reinv. Plan)

CAPITALIZATION (3/31/99):

	($000)	(%)
Long-Term Debt	143,838	23.3
Deferred Income Tax	20,533	3.3
Common & Surplus	453,219	73.4
Total	617,590	100.0

DIVIDEND ACHIEVER STATUS:
Rank: 115   10-Year Growth Rate: 11.99%
Total Years of Dividend Growth: 13

RECENT DEVELOPMENTS: For the third quarter ended 12/26/99, net earnings fell 6.6% to $16.2 million compared with $17.3 million in the corresponding 1998 quarter. Net sales declined slightly to $283.5 million from $284.4 million the year before. Overall, sales to the original equipment segment grew 2.0%. Strong sales growth to OEM customers in the truck market was offset by lower sales to the OEMs of agricultural and earthmoving equipment. Sales to the distributed products segment registered a 3.0% increase for the quarter. Higher revenues resulting from

sales by a U.S. regional aftermarket distributor purchased in October 1999 were virtually offset by lower-than-planned demand from the automotive aftermarket and building-HVAC market. Revenues for the European segment declined approximately 3.0% primarily due to negative currency translation. Gross margin as a percentage of sales improved to 27.6% from 27.1% due to improvements in the truck and HVAC markets, partially offset by reductions in other markets.

BUSINESS

MODINE MANUFACTURING COMPANY is engaged in heat-transfer technology serving vehicular, industrial, and building HVAC (heating, ventilating, air conditioning) markets. The Company develops, manufactures, and markets heat exchangers for use in various OEM (original equipment manufacturer) applications and for sale to the automotive aftermarket as replacement parts and to a wide array of building markets. On 1/16/2000, the Company announced the formation of an Engine Products Group for North America. The new business group will focus on the design and development of components, systems, and services in support of OEM engine manufacturers' needs.

ANNUAL FINANCIAL DATA

	3/31/99	3/31/98	3/31/97	3/31/96	3/31/95	3/31/94	3/31/93
Earnings Per Share	2.46	2.39	2.10	2.02	2.24	Ⓐ 1.41	Ⓑ 1.12
Cash Flow Per Share	3.94	3.77	3.46	3.32	3.37	2.34	1.96
Tang. Book Val. Per Share	12.63	12.24	11.02	9.14	8.88	7.41	7.21
Dividends Per Share	0.82	0.74	0.66	0.58	0.51	0.45	0.41
Dividend Payout %	33.3	31.0	31.4	28.7	22.5	31.9	36.6
INCOME STATEMENT (IN MILLIONS):							
Total Revenues	1,111.4	1,040.4	999.0	990.5	913.0	669.6	570.8
Costs & Expenses	954.0	881.2	856.7	856.6	766.5	565.2	487.8
Depreciation & Amort.	44.2	41.8	41.5	39.6	34.5	28.1	25.5
Operating Income	113.3	117.5	100.9	94.3	112.1	76.2	57.5
Net Interest Inc./(Exp.)	d5.7	d4.0	d5.0	d6.8	d6.4	d6.0	d6.0
Income Before Income Taxes	118.1	116.0	97.8	99.1	108.8	73.0	54.1
Income Taxes	44.1	43.5	34.0	37.8	40.4	29.9	20.4
Net Income	73.9	72.5	63.8	61.4	68.4	Ⓐ 43.1	Ⓑ 33.7
Cash Flow	118.1	114.2	105.3	101.0	102.9	71.2	59.2
Average Shs. Outstg. (000)	30,015	30,289	30,420	30,416	30,534	30,471	30,164
BALANCE SHEET (IN MILLIONS):							
Cash & Cash Equivalents	49.2	36.4	34.8	18.0	32.7	38.5	33.6
Total Current Assets	453.1	393.2	366.1	351.3	340.4	271.7	221.5
Net Property	303.8	248.3	210.1	201.3	170.9	164.0	135.6
Total Assets	915.7	759.0	695.0	671.8	590.2	510.0	405.2
Total Current Liabilities	256.6	192.7	170.0	181.0	169.6	139.9	94.7
Long-Term Obligations	143.8	89.6	85.2	87.8	62.2	77.6	52.4
Net Stockholders' Equity	453.2	422.5	391.7	342.6	298.0	251.4	220.4
Net Working Capital	196.5	200.5	196.1	170.3	170.7	131.9	126.8
Year-end Shs. Outstg. (000)	29,525	29,664	29,833	29,759	29,700	29,624	29,539
STATISTICAL RECORD:							
Operating Profit Margin %	10.2	11.3	10.1	9.5	12.3	11.4	10.1
Net Profit Margin %	6.7	7.0	6.4	6.2	7.5	6.4	5.9
Return on Equity %	16.3	17.2	16.3	17.9	23.0	17.1	15.3
Return on Assets %	8.1	9.5	9.2	9.1	11.6	8.4	8.3
Debt/Total Assets %	15.7	11.8	12.3	13.1	10.5	15.2	12.9
Price Range	38⅝-26⅝	36-24½	29¾-22½	40½-23¾	31¼-23¾	30¼-17½	18⅞-11¾
P/E Ratio	15.7-10.8	15.1-10.3	14.2-10.7	20.0-11.8	14.0-10.6	21.5-12.4	16.9-10.5
Average Yield %	2.5	2.4	2.5	1.8	1.8	1.9	2.7

Statistics are as originally reported. Adj. for stk. splits: 2-for-1, 2/19/93 Ⓐ Bef. acctg. change credit 3/31/94: $899,000 ($0.03/sh.); chrg. 3/31/93: $13.7 mill. ($0.46/sh.)

QUARTERLY DATA

(03/31/99)($000)	Rev	Inc
1st Quarter	273,104	20,080
2nd Quarter	272,961	19,081
3rd Quarter	284,355	17,341
4th Quarter	281,027	17,441

OFFICERS:
R. T. Savage, Chmn.
D. R. Johnson, Pres., C.E.O.
A. D. Reid, V.P., C.F.O.
INVESTOR CONTACT: Gerald J. Sweda, (414) 636-1361
PRINCIPAL OFFICE: 1500 DeKoven Ave., Racine, WI 53403-2552

TELEPHONE NUMBER: (414) 636-1200
FAX: (414) 636-1424
WEB: www.modine.com
NO. OF EMPLOYEES: 8,700 (approx.)
SHAREHOLDERS: 6,528 (approx.); 13,500 (approx. bene)
ANNUAL MEETING: In July
INCORPORATED: WI, Jun., 1916

INSTITUTIONAL HOLDINGS:
No. of Institutions: 79
Shares Held: 13,120,927
% Held: 44.5
INDUSTRY: Motor vehicle parts and accessories (SIC: 3714)
TRANSFER AGENT(S): Norwest Bank Minnesota, N.A., St. Paul, MN

NYSE SYMBOL JPM
Rec. Pr. 128 3/4 (5/31/00)

MORGAN (J.P.) & COMPANY INC.

YIELD 3.1%
P/E RATIO 12.4

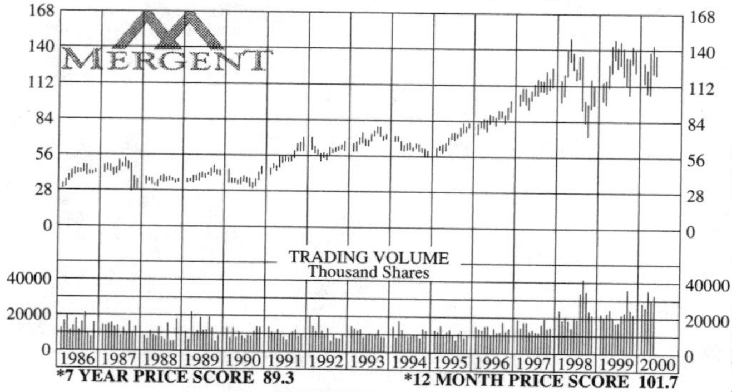

***7 YEAR PRICE SCORE 89.3** ***12 MONTH PRICE SCORE 101.7**

*NYSE COMPOSITE INDEX=100

INTERIM EARNINGS (Per Share):

Qtr.	Mar.	June	Sept.	Dec.
1996	2.13	2.14	1.32	2.04
1997	2.04	1.85	1.96	1.33
1998	1.15	2.36	0.75	0.42
1999	3.01	2.52	2.22	2.63

INTERIM DIVIDENDS (Per Share):

Amt.	Decl.	Ex.	Rec.	Pay.
0.99Q	3/10/99	3/18/99	3/22/99	4/15/99
0.99Q	6/09/99	6/17/99	6/21/99	7/15/99
0.99Q	9/08/99	9/16/99	9/20/99	10/15/99
1.00Q	12/08/99	12/16/99	12/20/99	1/14/00
1.00Q	3/08/00	3/16/00	3/20/00	4/14/00

Indicated div.: $4.00 (Div. Reinv. Plan)

CAPITALIZATION (12/31/99):

	($000)	(%)
Total Deposits	45,319,000	55.2
Long-Term Debt	24,250,000	29.5
Redeemable Pfd. Stock	1,150,000	1.4
Preferred Stock	694,000	0.8
Common & Surplus	10,745,000	13.1
Total	82,158,000	100.0

DIVIDEND ACHIEVER STATUS:
Rank: 176 10-Year Growth Rate: 9.08%
Total Years of Dividend Growth: 23

RECENT DEVELOPMENTS: For the year ended 12/31/99, net income jumped to $2.06 billion from $963.0 million in 1998. Results for 1999 included a reversal of provision for loan losses of $175.0 million. Results for 1998 included nonrecurring items that resulted in a net charge of $102.0 million. Net interest revenue rose 20.3% to $1.54 billion, reflecting higher net interest revenue in JPM's equities and credit markets segments.

PROSPECTS: JPM expects to continue to perform well due to strong markets and fees from advising on mergers. Results should continue to reflect strength in stocks, fixed income, investment banking and money management, which is being driven by investment banking and underwriting and the trading business. In addition, JPM intends to spend up to $1.00 billion on electronic business initiatives in 2000.

BUSINESS

J.P. MORGAN & COMPANY INC. provides a wide range of financial services to corporations, governments, financial institutions, institutional investors, financially sophisticated individuals, private firms, and non-profit organizations. Activities include providing corporate finance advice and executing financing transactions; underwriting, trading, and investing in securities; providing trust, agency, and operational services; and serving as an investment advisor and manager. JPM's principal subsidiary is Morgan Guaranty Trust Company of New York.

LOAN DISTRIBUTION

(12/31/99)	($000)	(%)
Commercial & Industrial	16,711,000	62.2
Financial Institution	4,448,000	16.6
Real Estate	2,900,000	10.8
Foreign Governments	396,000	1.5
Other, primarily	2,394,000	8.9
Total	26,849,000	100.0

ANNUAL FINANCIAL DATA

	12/31/99	12/31/98	12/31/97	12/31/96	12/31/95	12/31/94	12/31/93
Earnings Per Share	[6] **10.39**	[5] **4.71**	[4] **7.17**	[3] **7.63**	[2] **6.42**	**6.02**	[1] **8.48**
Tang. Book Val. Per Share	**65.12**	**60.38**	**60.85**	**58.04**	**53.25**	**48.27**	**48.52**
Dividends Per Share	**3.96**	**3.80**	**3.52**	**3.24**	**3.00**	**2.72**	**2.40**
Dividend Payout %	**38.1**	**80.7**	**49.1**	**42.5**	**46.7**	**45.2**	**28.3**
INCOME STATEMENT (IN MILLIONS):							
Total Interest Income	10,970.0	12,641.0	12,353.0	10,713.0	9,937.0	8,379.0	7,442.0
Total Interest Expense	9,429.0	11,360.0	10,481.0	9,011.0	7,934.0	6,398.0	5,670.0
Net Interest Income	1,541.0	1,281.0	1,872.0	1,702.0	2,003.0	1,981.0	1,772.0
Provision for Loan Losses	cr175.0	110.0	...	...	...	...	...
Non-Interest Income	7,140.0	5,784.0	5,348.0	5,153.0	3,901.0	3,536.0	4,499.0
Non-Interest Expense	5,742.0	5,538.0	5,066.0	4,523.0	3,998.0	3,692.0	3,580.0
Income Before Taxes	3,114.0	1,417.0	2,154.0	2,332.0	1,906.0	1,825.0	2,691.0
Net Income	[6] 2,055.0	[5] 963.0	[4] 1,465.0	[3] 1,574.0	[2] 1,296.0	1,215.0	[1] 1,723.0
Average Shs. Outstg. (000)	194,000	197,000	199,000	202,000	199,000	199,000	201,000
BALANCE SHEET (IN MILLIONS):							
Cash & Due from Banks	2,463.0	1,203.0	1,758.0	906.0	1,535.0	2,210.0	1,008.0
Securities Avail. for Sale	166,594.0	180,918.0	172,997.0	143,776.0	113,876.0	91,849.0	71,714.0
Total Loans & Leases	31,578.0	25,495.0	31,578.0	28,120.0	23,453.0	22,080.0	24,380.0
Allowance for Credit Losses	281.0	470.0	546.0	566.0	1,130.0	1,131.0	1,157.0
Net Loans & Leases	31,297.0	25,025.0	31,032.0	27,554.0	22,323.0	20,949.0	23,223.0
Total Assets	265,627.0	261,067.0	262,159.0	222,026.0	184,879.0	154,917.0	133,888.0
Total Deposits	45,319.0	55,028.0	58,879.0	52,724.0	46,438.0	43,085.0	40,402.0
Long-Term Obligations	24,250.0	27,607.0	22,989.0	13,103.0	9,327.0	6,802.0	5,276.0
Total Liabilities	249,459.0	179,163.0	179,614.0	159,675.0	129,139.0	108,942.0	105,813.0
Net Stockholders' Equity	11,439.0	11,261.0	11,404.0	11,432.0	10,451.0	9,568.0	9,859.0
Year-end Shs. Outstg. (000)	165,000	175,000	176,000	185,000	187,000	188,000	193,000
STATISTICAL RECORD:							
Return on Equity %	18.0	8.6	12.8	13.8	12.4	12.7	17.5
Return on Assets %	0.8	0.4	0.6	0.7	0.7	0.8	1.3
Equity/Assets %	4.3	4.3	4.4	5.1	5.7	6.2	7.4
Non-Int. Exp./Tot. Inc. %	66.1	78.4	70.2	66.0	67.7	66.9	57.1
Price Range	147 13/16-97 1/4	148 3/4-72 1/8	125 3/4-93 1/8	100 1/8-73 1/2	82 1/2-56 1/8	72-55 1/8	79 3/8-59 3/8
P/E Ratio	14.2-9.4	31.6-15.3	17.5-13.0	13.1-9.6	12.9-8.7	12.0-9.2	9.4-7.0
Average Yield %	3.2	3.4	3.2	3.7	4.3	4.3	3.5

Statistics are as originally reported. [1] Bef. acctg. chrge. $137.0 mill. [2] Incl. after-tax chrge. of $33.0 mill. for severance & after-tax gain of $19.0 mill. from sale of securities custody business. [3] Incl. pre-tax chrg. of $71.0 mill. for formation of strategic alliance. [4] Incl. gain of $79.0 mill. from sale of global trust & agency svcs. business. [5] Incl. after-tax non-recurr. chrgs. of $102.0 mill. [6] Incl. a reversal of prov. for loan losses of $175.0 mill.

OFFICERS:
D. A. Warner III, Chmn., C.E.O.
W. A. Gubert, Vice-Chmn.

INVESTOR CONTACT: Investor Relations, (212) 648-9446

PRINCIPAL OFFICE: 60 Wall St., New York, NY 10260-0060

TELEPHONE NUMBER: (212) 483-2323
FAX: (212) 648-5210
WEB: www.jpmorgan.com

NO. OF EMPLOYEES: 15,512

SHAREHOLDERS: 26,395

ANNUAL MEETING: In Apr.

INCORPORATED: DE, Dec., 1968

INSTITUTIONAL HOLDINGS:
No. of Institutions: 704
Shares Held: 103,325,275
% Held: 59.7

INDUSTRY: State commercial banks (SIC: 6022)

TRANSFER AGENT(S): First Chicago Trust Company of New York, Jersey City, NJ

ASE SYMBOL MYE
Rec. Pr. 13⅝ (5/31/00)

MYERS INDUSTRIES, INC.

YIELD 1.8%
P/E RATIO 9.0

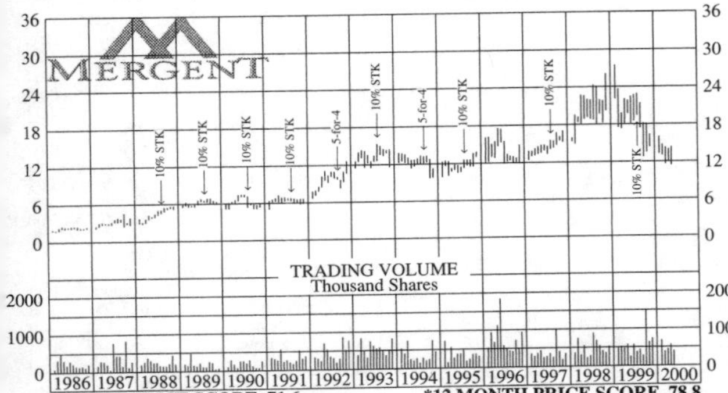

*7 YEAR PRICE SCORE 71.6 *12 MONTH PRICE SCORE 78.8
*NYSE COMPOSITE INDEX=100

INTERIM EARNINGS (Per Share):

Qtr.	Mar.	June	Sept.	Dec.
1997	0.24	0.25	0.19	0.41
1998	0.35	0.38	0.25	0.45
1999	0.41	0.45	0.20	0.49
2000	0.42	...	...	...

INTERIM DIVIDENDS (Per Share):

Amt.	Decl.	Ex.	Rec.	Pay.
10% STK	7/29/99	8/11/99	8/13/99	8/31/99
0.06Q	7/29/99	9/08/99	9/10/99	10/01/99
0.06Q	10/28/99	12/08/99	12/10/99	1/03/00
0.06Q	2/24/00	3/08/00	3/10/00	4/03/00
0.06Q	4/18/00	6/14/00	6/16/00	7/03/00

Indicated div.: $0.24 (Div. Reinv. Plan)

CAPITALIZATION (12/31/99):

	($000)	(%)
Long-Term Debt	280,104	56.2
Deferred Income Tax	10,314	2.1
Common & Surplus	207,747	41.7
Total	498,165	100.0

DIVIDEND ACHIEVER STATUS:
Rank: 101 10-Year Growth Rate: 12.76%
Total Years of Dividend Growth: 23

RECENT DEVELOPMENTS: For the first quarter ended 3/31/00, net income remained flat at $8.3 million. Earnings growth was constrained by the escalating prices for raw materials used in MYE's plastic products. MYE is continuing to focus on reducing costs, using volume purchasing power for raw material, and balancing product pricing with raw material costs to improve the Company's long-term performance. Net sales were $161.6 million, an increase of 27.5% from $126.7 million in the prior year. Gross profit as a percentage of net sales declined to 35.2% versus 37.3% a year earlier. Operating income grew 17.2% to $20.0 million from $17.0 million in 1999. The continued escalation of raw material costs may affect the Company's ability to grow earnings in 2000. Prices for the Company's primary raw materials, High Density Polyethylene and Polypropylene, increased substantially throughout last year. Additional increases are expected to continue through the first half of 2000.

BUSINESS

MYERS INDUSTRIES, INC. is comprised of two distinct segments: the manufacturing business and the distribution business. The manufacturing business designs, manufactures and markets reusable plastic storage systems for use in distribution and material handling, and other plastic and metal products for storage, assembly and material handling application. The Company markets reusable plastics under the brand names NesTier, Akro-Bins and Buckhorn. MYE also manufactures and sells molded rubber products and other materials used primarily in the tire and tire repair industries and for various other uses. The distribution business, primarily conducted by the Myers Tire Supply division, is engaged in the nationwide distribution of equipment, tools and supplies used for tire servicing and automotive underbody repair.

ANNUAL FINANCIAL DATA

	12/31/99	12/31/98	12/31/97	12/31/96	12/31/95	12/31/94	12/31/93
Earnings Per Share	**1.55**	**1.43**	**1.10**	**1.03**	**0.79**	**0.88**	**0.79**
Cash Flow Per Share	**3.41**	**2.29**	**1.75**	**1.58**	**1.29**	**1.34**	**1.18**
Tang. Book Val. Per Share	**0.42**	**8.09**	**7.65**	**7.13**	**6.12**	**5.81**	**5.03**
Dividends Per Share	**0.22**	**0.19**	**0.17**	**0.14**	**0.12**	**0.11**	**0.10**
Dividend Payout %	**14.4**	**13.4**	**15.4**	**13.7**	**15.7**	**12.6**	**12.8**
INCOME STATEMENT (IN THOUSANDS):							
Total Revenues	580,761	392,020	339,626	320,944	300,699	274,054	245,136
Costs & Expenses	473,711	325,129	288,098	273,733	262,408	233,907	210,906
Depreciation & Amort.	37,542	17,518	13,214	11,311	10,450	9,480	7,690
Operating Income	69,507	49,373	38,313	35,901	27,840	30,666	26,540
Net Interest Inc./(Exp.)	d15,206	d888	d248	d285	d784	d620	d1,092
Income Before Income Taxes	54,301	48,485	38,066	35,615	27,056	30,046	25,449
Income Taxes	23,125	19,806	15,727	14,612	11,087	12,215	10,054
Net Income	31,176	28,679	22,339	21,003	15,969	17,831	15,395
Cash Flow	68,719	46,197	35,553	32,314	26,419	27,312	23,085
Average Shs. Outstg.	20,167	20,135	20,318	20,481	20,414	20,365	19,598
BALANCE SHEET (IN THOUSANDS):							
Cash & Cash Equivalents	1,094	34,832	6,298	5,600	3,388	1,795	1,662
Total Current Assets	206,991	153,650	107,427	106,310	101,087	94,725	78,922
Net Property	189,496	109,443	90,551	80,660	69,430	61,378	57,694
Total Assets	600,410	306,708	224,078	207,122	193,604	172,027	152,386
Total Current Liabilities	102,244	51,234	39,644	36,853	32,372	34,094	24,381
Long-Term Obligations	280,104	48,832	4,261	4,569	13,335	4,155	10,655
Net Stockholders' Equity	207,747	202,689	176,677	162,445	145,184	130,909	115,287
Net Working Capital	104,747	102,417	67,783	69,457	68,715	60,631	54,542
Year-end Shs. Outstg.	19,987	20,172	20,107	20,394	20,456	20,364	20,336
STATISTICAL RECORD:							
Operating Profit Margin %	12.0	12.6	11.3	11.2	9.3	11.2	10.8
Net Profit Margin %	5.4	7.3	6.6	6.5	5.3	6.5	6.3
Return on Equity %	15.0	14.1	12.6	12.9	11.0	13.6	13.4
Return on Assets %	5.2	9.4	10.0	10.1	8.2	10.4	10.1
Debt/Total Assets %	46.7	15.9	1.9	2.2	6.9	2.4	7.0
Price Range	27½-12¾	26¹⁄₁₆-14⅞	17¹⁄₁₆-12⅜	17⁹⁄₁₆-11⅞	13¹³⁄₁₆-9⅞	13¹³⁄₁₆-9¹¹⁄₁₆	15⁵⁄₁₆-11½
P/E Ratio	17.7-8.2	18.3-10.4	15.5-11.3	17.1-11.6	17.6-12.6	15.7-11.0	19.4-14.6
Average Yield %	1.1	0.9	1.2	1.0	1.0	0.9	0.8

Statistics are as originally reported. Adj. for stk. splits: 10% div., 8/99, 8/97, 8/95 & 8/93; 5-for-4, 8/94.

OFFICERS:
S. E. Myers, Pres., C.E.O.
G. J. Stodnick, V.P.-Fin.
M. I. Wiskind, Sr. V.P., Sec.

INVESTOR CONTACT: Gregory J. Stodnick, V.P., Finance, (330) 761-6156

PRINCIPAL OFFICE: 1293 South Main Street, Akron, OH 44301

TELEPHONE NUMBER: (330) 253-5592
FAX: (330) 253-6568
WEB: www.myersind.com

NO. OF EMPLOYEES: 4,152

SHAREHOLDERS: 2,100 (approx.)

ANNUAL MEETING: In Apr.

INCORPORATED: OH, Jan., 1955

INSTITUTIONAL HOLDINGS:
No. of Institutions: 67
Shares Held: 8,830,236
% Held: 44.2

INDUSTRY: Plastics products, nec (SIC: 3089)

TRANSFER AGENT(S): First Chicago Trust Company of New York, Jersey City, NJ

NACCO INDUSTRIES INC.

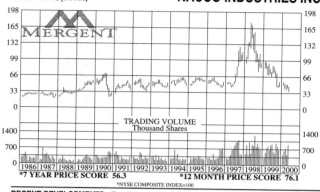

TRADING VOLUME
Thousand Shares

*7 YEAR PRICE SCORE 56.3   *12 MONTH PRICE SCORE 76.1
*NYSE COMPOSITE INDEX=100

INTERIM EARNINGS (Per Share):

Qtr.	Mar.	June	Sept.	Dec.
1996	1.44	1.56	0.85	1.83
1997	0.35	1.82	1.78	3.62
1998	2.95	3.21	2.50	3.87
1999	1.59	2.00	0.86	2.22

INTERIM DIVIDENDS (Per Share):

Amt.	Decl.	Ex.	Rec.	Pay.
0.215Q	5/12/99	5/27/99	6/01/99	6/15/99
0.215Q	8/11/99	8/30/99	9/01/99	9/15/99
0.215Q	11/09/99	11/29/99	12/01/99	12/15/99
0.215Q	2/09/00	2/28/00	3/01/00	3/15/00
0.225Q	5/10/00	5/30/00	6/01/00	6/15/00

Indicated div.: $0.90

CAPITALIZATION (12/31/99):

	($000)	(%)
Long-Term Debt	615,500	51.8
Minority Interest	11,500	1.0
Common & Surplus	562,200	47.3
Total	1,189,200	100.0

DIVIDEND ACHIEVER STATUS:
Rank: 283   10-Year Growth Rate: 3.99%
Total Years of Dividend Growth: 16

RECENT DEVELOPMENTS: For the year ended 12/31/99, NC reported net income of $54.3 million, before an accounting charge of $1.2 million, compared with $102.3 million in the previous year. This decline primarily reflected a decrease in the Materials Handling Group (NMHG) due to a reduction in average sales prices, adverse currency movements and an unfavorable sales mix. Revenues rose 2.6% to $2.60 billion from $2.54 billion in the prior year.

PROSPECTS: Going forward, NACCO Materials Handling Group may continue to incur losses related to certain existing and newly acquired dealerships and the elimination of intercompany profits. However, NMHG expects continued benefits from cost reduction programs and increased efficiency at its new Mexican manufacturing facility. NMHG also expects to continue to expand its retail distribution network in 2000.

BUSINESS

NACCO INDUSTRIES, INC., with assets of $2.01 billion as of 12/31/99, is a holding company with three operating subsidiaries: NACCO Materials Handling Group (NMHG), The North American Coal Corp., and the Housewares Group, comprised of Hamilton Beach/Proctor-Silex, Inc. (HB/PS) and the Kitchen Collection, Inc. NMHG designs and manufactures forklift trucks, marketed under the HYSTER and YALE brand names. North American Coal mines and markets lignite coal, primarily as fuel for power generation by electric utilities. HB/PS is a leading manufacturer of small electric appliances, and the Kitchen Collection, Inc. is a national specialty retailer of kitchenware and small electric appliances.

ANNUAL FINANCIAL DATA

	12/31/99	12/31/98	12/31/97	12/31/96	12/31/95	12/31/94	12/31/93
Earnings Per Share	③ 6.66	② 12.53	② 7.55	5.67	① 7.31	① 5.06	① 1.30
Cash Flow Per Share	19.41	23.43	18.37	15.22	16.13	14.02	10.03
Tang. Book Val. Per Share	11.51	9.52	...	...	...	...	...
Dividends Per Share	0.85	0.81	0.77	0.74	0.71	0.68	0.66
Dividend Payout %	12.8	6.5	10.2	13.1	9.7	13.3	50.4
INCOME STATEMENT (IN MILLIONS):							
Total Revenues	2,602.8	2,536.2	2,246.9	2,273.2	2,204.5	1,864.9	1,549.4
Costs & Expenses	2,367.5	2,249.1	2,026.3	2,056.7	1,974.2	1,649.6	1,377.9
Depreciation & Amort.	104.0	89.0	88.6	85.3	79.3	80.2	78.1
Operating Income	131.3	198.1	132.0	131.2	151.1	135.1	93.4
Net Interest Inc./(Exp.)	d43.3	d34.6	d36.6	d45.9	d50.0	d58.8	d64.0
Income Before Income Taxes	86.6	166.0	89.1	86.3	103.5	78.5	24.7
Income Taxes	31.7	60.7	26.4	34.3	34.7	30.7	13.5
Equity Earnings/Minority Int.	d0.6	d3.0	d0.9	d1.4	d3.3	d2.5	0.4
Net Income	③ 54.3	② 102.3	② 61.8	50.6	① 65.5	① 45.3	① 11.6
Cash Flow	158.3	191.3	150.4	135.9	144.8	125.4	89.7
Average Shs. Outstg. (000)	8,154	8,166	8,189	8,931	8,975	8,948	8,938
BALANCE SHEET (IN MILLIONS):							
Cash & Cash Equivalents	36.2	34.7	24.1	47.8	30.9	19.5	29.1
Total Current Assets	772.2	703.2	599.6	591.8	722.0	586.6	504.8
Net Property	625.4	593.4	541.7	550.3	534.4	485.3	496.2
Total Assets	2,013.0	1,898.3	1,729.1	1,708.1	1,833.7	1,694.3	1,642.5
Total Current Liabilities	583.1	548.6	506.5	416.0	523.7	481.4	397.5
Long-Term Obligations	615.5	569.6	558.2	674.8	666.7	618.6	855.6
Net Stockholders' Equity	562.2	518.3	425.1	379.3	370.1	279.4	235.6
Net Working Capital	189.1	154.6	93.1	175.8	198.3	105.2	107.3
Year-end Shs. Outstg. (000)	9,804	8,120	8,154	8,186	8,952	8,952	8,036
STATISTICAL RECORD:							
Operating Profit Margin %	5.0	7.8	5.9	5.8	6.9	7.2	6.0
Net Profit Margin %	2.1	4.0	2.8	2.2	3.0	2.4	0.7
Return on Equity %	9.7	19.7	14.5	13.3	17.7	16.2	4.9
Return on Assets %	2.7	5.4	3.6	3.0	3.6	2.7	0.7
Debt/Total Assets %	30.6	30.0	32.3	39.5	36.4	36.5	52.1
Price Range	97-44½	177-76¼	127-44⅜	64-43⅛	64-46⅞	64-45¾	58¼-42
P/E Ratio	14.6-6.7	14.1-6.1	16.8-5.9	11.3-7.6	8.8-6.4	12.6-9.0	44.8-32.3
Average Yield %	1.2	0.6	0.9	1.4	1.3	1.2	1.3

Statistics are as originally reported. ① Bef. extra. net gain $28.9 mill., 1995; chrg. $3.2 mill., 1994; chrg. $3.3 mill., 1993. ② Incl. restruct. chrgs. $1.6 mill., 1998; $8.0 mill., 1997. ③ Bef. acctg. chrg. of $1.2 mill. & incl. chrg. of $1.9 mill. rel. to the proposed acq. of Nissan Motor Co., Ltd.'s global lift truck business.

OFFICERS:
A. M. Rankin, Jr., Chmn., Pres., C.E.O.
J. C. Butler, Jr., V.P., Corp. Devel., Treas.
C. A. Bittenbender, V.P., Gen. Couns., Sec.

INVESTOR CONTACT: Ira Gamm, Manager of Investor Relations, (440) 449-9676

PRINCIPAL OFFICE: 5875 Landerbrook Drive, Mayfield Heights, OH 44124-4017

TELEPHONE NUMBER: (440) 449-9600
FAX: (440) 449-9607
WEB: www.naccoind.com

NO. OF EMPLOYEES: 15,120

SHAREHOLDERS: 500 (approx. Cl. A com,); 300 (approx. Cl. B com.)

ANNUAL MEETING: In May

INCORPORATED: DE, 1986

INSTITUTIONAL HOLDINGS:
No. of Institutions: 118
Shares Held: 3,502,354
% Held: 53.8

INDUSTRY: Industrial trucks and tractors (SIC: 3537)

TRANSFER AGENT(S): First Chicago Trust Company of New York, Jersey City, NJ

NYSE SYMBOL NFG
Rec. Pr. 51 13/16 (5/31/00)

NATIONAL FUEL GAS COMPANY

YIELD 3.6%
P/E RATIO 16.6

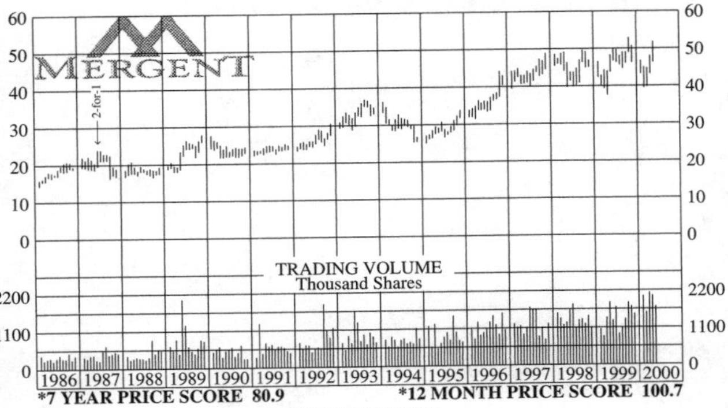
MERGENT
2-for-1
60
50
40
30
20
10
0
TRADING VOLUME
Thousand Shares
2200
1100
0
1986 1987 1988 1989 1990 1991 1992 1993 1994 1995 1996 1997 1998 1999 2000

*7 YEAR PRICE SCORE 80.9 *12 MONTH PRICE SCORE 100.7

*NYSE COMPOSITE INDEX=100

INTERIM EARNINGS (Per Share):

Qtr.	Dec.	Mar.	June	Sept.
1995-96	0.87	1.48	0.46	d0.02
1996-97	1.02	1.50	0.50	Nil
1997-98	0.95	d0.56	0.49	d0.04
1998-99	0.97	1.57	0.30	0.11
1999-00	1.14	...	...	...

INTERIM DIVIDENDS (Per Share):

Amt.	Decl.	Ex.	Rec.	Pay.
0.45Q	2/18/99	3/29/99	3/31/99	4/15/99
0.465Q	6/17/99	6/28/99	6/30/99	7/15/99
0.465Q	9/16/99	9/28/99	9/30/99	10/15/99
0.465Q	12/09/99	12/29/99	12/31/99	1/14/00
0.465Q	2/17/00	3/29/00	3/31/00	4/15/00

Indicated div.: $1.86 (Div. Reinv. Plan)

CAPITALIZATION (9/30/99):

	($000)	(%)
Long-Term Debt	822,743	39.8
Deferred Income Tax	275,008	13.3
Minority Interest	27,589	1.3
Common & Surplus	939,293	45.5
Total	2,064,633	100.0

DIVIDEND ACHIEVER STATUS:
Rank: 290 10-Year Growth Rate: 3.48%
Total Years of Dividend Growth: 28

RECENT DEVELOPMENTS: For the three months ended 12/31/99, net income increased 19.3% to $44.9 million from $37.6 million in the corresponding period of the previous year. Results reflected higher earnings in the Utility, Exploration and Production and International segments. Total revenues were $1.26 billion versus $1.25 billion a year earlier. Operating revenues advanced 10.8% to $377.0 million from $340.4 million in the prior-year quarter.

PROSPECTS: Results should continue to benefit from strong earnings growth in the Exploration and Production, Utility and International segments. Meanwhile, the National Fuel Gas Distribution Corporation requested a decrease in overall gas costs of $5.4 million for its customers in northwestern Pennsylvania for the period of 8/1/00 through 7/31/01. The decrease has been requested to reflect anticipated gas costs for the period 8/1/00 through 7/31/01.

BUSINESS

NATIONIONAL FUEL GAS COMPANY is the public utility holding company of National Fuel Gas Distribution Corporation, National Fuel Gas Supply Corporation, Seneca Resources Corporation, Horizon Energy Development, Inc., National Fuel Resources, Inc. and Highland Land & Minerals, Inc. These operations are involved in all phases of the natural gas industry; utility, pipeline and storage, exploration, production, international, energy marketing and timber. Other subsidiaries included Upstate Energy Inc., Niagara Independence Marketing Company, Leidy Hub, Inc., Data Track Account Services, Inc. and NFR Power, Inc.

BUSINESS LINE ANALYSIS

(9/30/99)	Rev(%)	Inc(000)
Utility Operation	63.5	56,875
Pipeline & Storage	6.58	39,765
Exploration & Production	11.11	7,127
International	8.49	2,276
Energy Martketing	7.85	2,054
Timber	2.47	4,769
Total	100.0	112,866

ANNUAL FINANCIAL DATA

	9/30/99	9/30/98	9/30/97	9/30/96	9/30/95	9/30/94	9/30/93
Earnings Per Share	**2.95**	**0.84**	**3.01**	**2.78**	**2.03**	[1] **2.23**	**2.15**
Cash Flow Per Share	**6.27**	**3.91**	**5.94**	**5.39**	**3.95**	**4.24**	**4.14**
Tang. Book Val. Per Share	**24.19**	**23.14**	**23.94**	**22.61**	**21.39**	**20.93**	**20.08**
Dividends Per Share	**1.83**	**1.77**	**1.71**	**1.65**	**1.60**	**1.56**	**1.52**
Dividend Payout %	**62.0**	**210.7**	**56.8**	**59.4**	**78.8**	**70.0**	**70.7**
INCOME STATEMENT (IN MILLIONS):							
Total Revenues	1,263.3	1,248.0	1,265.8	1,208.0	975.5	1,141.3	1,020.4
Costs & Expenses	917.7	1,021.1	891.5	859.6	709.7	861.9	763.3
Depreciation & Amort.	129.7	118.9	111.7	98.2	71.8	74.8	69.4
Maintenance Exp.	23.9	25.8	25.7	26.4	25.7	31.0	24.3
Operating Income	192.0	83.9	168.3	157.4	124.4	125.9	122.3
Net Interest Inc./(Exp.)	d87.7	d85.3	d56.8	d56.6	d53.9	d47.1	d51.9
Equity Earnings/Minority Int.	d1.6	d2.2	...	...	...	...	...
Net Income	115.0	32.3	114.7	104.7	75.9	[1] 82.4	75.2
Cash Flow	244.7	151.2	226.3	202.9	147.7	157.2	144.6
Average Shs. Outstg. (000)	39,042	38,703	38,084	37,613	37,397	37,046	34,939
BALANCE SHEET (IN MILLIONS):							
Gross Property	3,383.5	3,186.9	2,668.5	2,471.1	2,322.3	2,169.1	2,039.4
Accumulated Depreciation	1,029.6	938.7	849.1	761.5	673.2	623.5	561.4
Net Property	2,353.9	2,248.1	1,819.4	1,709.6	1,649.2	1,545.6	1,478.0
Total Assets	2,842.6	2,684.5	2,267.3	2,149.8	2,038.3	1,981.7	1,801.5
Long-Term Obligations	822.7	692.7	581.6	574.0	474.0	462.5	478.4
Net Stockholders' Equity	939.3	890.1	913.7	856.0	800.6	780.3	736.2
Year-end Shs. Outstg. (000)	38,837	38,469	38,166	37,852	37,434	37,278	36,661
STATISTICAL RECORD:							
Operating Profit Margin %	15.2	6.7	13.3	13.0	12.8	11.0	12.0
Net Profit Margin %	9.1	2.6	9.1	8.7	7.8	7.2	7.4
Net Inc./Net Property %	4.9	1.4	6.3	6.1	4.6	5.3	5.1
Net Inc./Tot. Capital %	5.6	1.7	6.4	6.1	4.9	5.4	5.4
Return on Equity %	12.2	3.6	12.6	12.2	9.5	10.6	10.2
Accum. Depr./Gross Prop. %	30.4	29.5	31.8	30.8	29.0	28.7	27.5
Price Range	52 15/16-37 1/2	49 5/8-39 5/8	48 7/8-39 3/8	44 1/8-31 3/8	33 7/8-25	36 1/4-25 1/4	36 7/8-28 3/4
P/E Ratio	17.9-12.7	59.1-47.2	16.2-13.1	15.9-11.3	16.7-12.3	16.3-11.3	17.2-13.4
Average Yield %	4.0	4.0	3.9	4.4	5.4	5.1	4.6

Statistics are as originally reported. [1] Bef. acctg. change credit $3.2 mill.

OFFICERS:
B. J. Kennedy, Chmn., C.E.O.
P. C. Ackerman, Pres.
J. P. Pawlowski, Treas.

INVESTOR CONTACT: Margaret M. Suto, Director, Investor Relations, (716) 857-6987

PRINCIPAL OFFICE: 10 Lafayette Square, Buffalo, NY 14203

TELEPHONE NUMBER: (716) 857-7000
FAX: (716) 541-7841
WEB: www.nationalfuelgas.com

NO. OF EMPLOYEES: 3,807

SHAREHOLDERS: 22,336

ANNUAL MEETING: In Feb.

INCORPORATED: NJ, Dec., 1902

INSTITUTIONAL HOLDINGS:
No. of Institutions: 170
Shares Held: 16,133,427
% Held: 41.6

INDUSTRY: Natural gas distribution (SIC: 4924)

TRANSFER AGENT(S): ChaseMellon Shareholder Services, South Hackensack, NJ

NATIONAL SERVICE INDUSTRIES, INC.

YIELD 6.1%
P/E RATIO 7.2

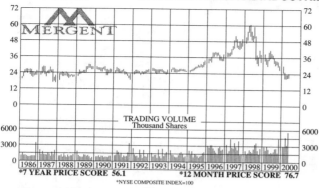

7 YEAR PRICE SCORE 56.1
NYSE COMPOSITE INDEX=100
12 MONTH PRICE SCORE 76.7

INTERIM EARNINGS (Per Share):

Qtr.	Nov.	Feb.	May	Aug.
1995-96	0.48	0.40	0.58	0.66
1996-97	0.54	0.45	0.65	0.71
1997-98	0.61	0.54	0.66	0.72
1998-99	0.62	0.60	0.75	1.07
1999-00	0.60	0.50	...	...

INTERIM DIVIDENDS (Per Share):

Amt.	Decl.	Ex.	Rec.	Pay.
0.32Q	4/07/99	4/14/99	4/16/99	5/03/99
0.32Q	7/07/99	7/15/99	7/19/99	8/02/99
0.32Q	10/13/99	10/20/99	10/22/99	11/01/99
0.33Q	1/05/00	1/12/00	1/17/00	2/01/00
0.33Q	4/05/00	4/13/00	4/17/00	5/01/00

Indicated div.: $1.32 (Div. Reinv. Plan)

CAPITALIZATION (8/31/99):

	($000)	(%)
Long-Term Debt	435,199	38.0
Deferred Income Tax	95,557	8.3
Common & Surplus	615,874	53.7
Total	1,146,630	100.0

DIVIDEND ACHIEVER STATUS:
Rank: 274   10-Year Growth Rate: 4.30%
Total Years of Dividend Growth: 38

RECENT DEVELOPMENTS: For the quarter ended 2/29/00, net income fell 18.2% to $20.3 million from $24.8 million in the same quarter in 1999. Total revenues rose 18.6% to $605.4 million from $510.4 million the year before. Revenue from lighting equipment jumped 29.9% to $354.1 million. Chemical revenues grew 2.4% to $119.6 million, while Textile rental revenues climbed 4.9% to $77.4 million. Envelope revenues increased 14.8% to $54.3 million.

PROSPECTS: NSI will continue to focus its efforts on the integration of Holophane into the lighting equipment segment. NSI remains on target to deliver its total year performance expectation of 8%-10% core operating profit growth. Also, NSI will look to overcome industry challenges with increased productivity, new product development, technological advances, and cost synergies. Going forward, NSI will continue to focus on strategic acquisitions to complement its operating initiatives.

BUSINESS

NATIONAL SERVICE INDUSTRIES, INC., is a diversified manufacturing and service company with operations in four separate divisions. The lighting equipment division manufactures a wide variety of lighting equipment for commercial, industrial, institutional, and residential use. The textile rental division rents textile items to restaurants and lodging, hospitals, clinics, nursing homes and industrial concerns. The chemical division manufactures a broad line of specialty chemicals for industrial and commercial maintenance, sanitation and housekeeping. The Company also provides envelope services. Sales (and operating profit) in fiscal 1999 were derived as follows: 55% (54%), lighting equipment; 14% (19%), textile rental; 22% (20%), chemical; 9% (8%), envelopes.

ANNUAL FINANCIAL DATA

	8/31/99	8/31/98	8/31/97	8/31/96	8/31/95	8/31/94	8/31/93
Earnings Per Share	② 3.03	① 2.53	① 2.37	2.11	1.93	1.67	1.52
Cash Flow Per Share	4.38	3.66	3.66	3.33	3.11	2.89	2.77
Tang. Book Val. Per Share	0.62	11.83	14.06	13.53	13.31	12.49	11.63
Dividends Per Share	1.28	1.24	1.20	1.16	1.12	1.08	1.04
Dividend Payout %	42.2	49.0	50.6	55.0	58.0	64.7	68.4
INCOME STATEMENT (IN MILLIONS)							
Total Revenues	2,219.2	2,031.3	2,036.2	2,013.6	1,970.6	1,881.9	1,804.8
Costs & Expenses	1,959.9	1,812.9	1,867.7	1,795.9	1,753.2	1,678.3	1,608.7
Depreciation & Amort.	55.8	48.8	58.0	58.4	57.1	60.5	62.1
Operating Income	203.5	169.6	① 110.5	159.3	160.3	143.0	134.0
Net Interest Inc./(Exp.)	d14.1	d0.7	d1.6	d1.6	d3.8	d3.7	d5.0
Income Before Income Taxes	198.3	173.1	179.1	161.8	150.5	132.2	119.5
Income Taxes	74.0	64.4	71.8	60.7	56.4	49.5	44.4
Net Income	② 124.3	① 108.7	① 107.3	101.1	94.1	82.7	75.1
Cash Flow	180.2	157.6	165.3	159.6	151.2	143.2	137.2
Average Shs. Outstg. (000)	41,093	43,022	45,191	47,941	48,696	49,547	49,556
BALANCE SHEET (IN MILLIONS)							
Cash & Cash Equivalents	2.3	19.1	262.4	59.2	83.0	61.2	20.6
Total Current Assets	680.4	607.1	780.8	606.4	640.4	608.3	556.9
Net Property	382.3	271.9	236.7	357.4	349.9	348.3	365.2
Total Assets	1,695.8	1,010.7	1,106.4	1,094.6	1,131.3	1,106.4	1,087.5
Total Current Liabilities	423.9	222.0	282.0	197.4	202.6	250.8	243.7
Long-Term Obligations	435.2	78.1	26.2	24.9	26.8	26.9	28.4
Net Stockholders' Equity	615.9	578.9	671.8	718.0	744.4	727.4	704.0
Net Working Capital	256.5	385.1	498.8	409.0	437.8	357.5	313.2
Year-end Shs. Outstg. (000)	102,550	41,462	44,199	46,472	48,308	49,240	49,561
STATISTICAL RECORD:							
Operating Profit Margin %	9.2	8.3	5.4	7.9	8.1	7.6	7.4
Net Profit Margin %	5.6	5.4	5.3	5.0	4.8	4.4	4.2
Return on Equity %	20.2	18.8	16.0	14.1	12.6	11.4	10.7
Return on Assets %	7.3	10.8	9.7	9.2	8.3	7.5	6.9
Debt/Total Assets %	25.7	7.7	2.4	2.3	2.4	2.4	2.6
Price Range	41⁷⁄₁₆-26⁷⁄₈	60¾-30⅛	52¼-36¾	40¼-31⅞	33⅞-24⅞	28⅜-24¾	27⅞-23⅛
P/E Ratio	13.7-8.9	24.0-11.9	22.0-15.5	19.1-15.1	17.6-12.9	17.0-14.8	18.3-15.2
Average Yield %	3.7	2.7	2.7	3.2	3.8	4.1	4.1

Statistics are as originally reported. ① Incl. non-recurr. credit 1998, $1.8 mill.; 1997, $12.1 mill. ② Incl. $11.2 mill. gain on sale of bus. & $9.3 mill. non-recurr. chrg.

OFFICERS:
J. S. Balloun, Chmn., Pres., C.E.O.
B. A. Hattox, Exec. V.P., C.F.O.
C. J. Popkowski, V.P., Treas.

INVESTOR CONTACT: David Levy, Exec. V.P., (404) 853-1000

PRINCIPAL OFFICE: 1420 Peachtree Street, N.E., Atlanta, GA 30309-3002

TELEPHONE NUMBER: (404) 853-1000
FAX: (404) 853-1300
WEB: www.nationalservice.com
NO. OF EMPLOYEES: 19,700 (approx.)
SHAREHOLDERS: 6,292
ANNUAL MEETING: In Jan.
INCORPORATED: DE, Aug., 1928

NICOR INC.

YIELD **4.5%**
P/E RATIO **13.9**

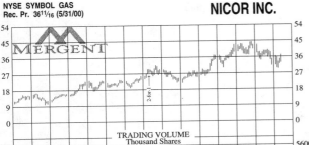

54 45 36 27 18 9 0

TRADING VOLUME
Thousand Shares

5600 2800 0

| 1986 | 1987 | 1988 | 1989 | 1990 | 1991 | 1992 | 1993 | 1994 | 1995 | 1996 | 1997 | 1998 | 1999 | 2000 |

*7 YEAR PRICE SCORE 72.9   *12 MONTH PRICE SCORE 95.8

*NYSE COMPOSITE INDEX=100

INTERIM EARNINGS (Per Share):

Qtr.	Mar.	June	Sept.	Dec.
1995	0.80	0.34	0.12	0.71
1996	0.90	0.50	0.30	0.70
1997	0.82	0.58	0.40	0.81
1998	0.75	0.59	0.43	0.65
1999	0.82	0.56	0.42	0.83

INTERIM DIVIDENDS (Per Share):

Amt.	Decl.	Ex.	Rec.	Pay.
0.39Q	6/08/99	6/28/99	6/30/99	8/01/99
0.39Q	9/08/99	9/28/99	9/30/99	11/01/99
0.39Q	12/07/99	12/28/99	12/30/99	2/01/00
0.415Q	3/16/00	3/29/00	3/31/00	5/01/00
0.415Q	4/20/00	6/28/00	6/30/00	8/01/00

Indicated div.: $1.66 (Div. Reinv. Plan)

CAPITALIZATION (12/31/99):

	($000)	(%)
Long-Term Debt	436,100	27.8
Deferred Income Tax	341,400	21.7
Redeemable Pfd. Stock	6,300	0.4
Common & Surplus	787,700	50.1
Total	1,571,500	100.0

DIVIDEND ACHIEVER STATUS:

Rank: 266   10-Year Growth Rate: 4.57%
Total Years of Dividend Growth: 12

RECENT DEVELOPMENTS: For the year ended 12/31/99, net income increased 6.9% to $124.4 million versus $116.4 million in 1998. Operating revenues climbed 10.2% to $1.62 billion from $1.47 billion the year before. The growth in revenues reflected a 7.9% advancement to $1.33 billion in operating revenues in the gas distribution segment and a 2.4% increase to $229.9 million in operating revenues in the shipping segment.

PROSPECTS: The Company agreed to become an equal partner in the planned Horizon Pipeline with Natural Gas Pipeline Company of America, a subsidiary of Kinder Morgan, Inc. Under the agreement, the Horizon Pipeline will originate in Joliet, Illinois and connect NICOR Gas' distribution system and NGPL pipeline. Construction of the pipeline will begin in Spring of 2001, and completion is estimated for Spring of 2002.

BUSINESS

NICOR INC. is engaged in the purchase, storage, distribution, transportation, sale, and gathering of natural gas. The Company's natural gas unit, Northern Illinois Gas, is the largest gas distribution company in Illinois and one of the biggest in the nation. Northern Illinois serves 1.9 million customers in the northern third of the state, generally outside Chicago. NICOR also owns Tropical Shipping Co., a containerized shipping business serving 26 Caribbean ports from the Port of Palm Beach in Florida.

BUSINESS LINE ANALYSIS

(12/31/1999)	Rev(%)	Inc(%)
Gas Distribution	82.1	90.4
Shipping	14.2	10.6
Other	3.8	0.6
Corporate & eliminations	(0.1)	(1.6)
Total	100.0	100.0

ANNUAL FINANCIAL DATA

	12/31/99	12/31/98	12/31/97	12/31/96	12/31/95	12/31/94	12/31/93
Earnings Per Share	② 2.62	2.42	2.61	① 2.42	1.96	2.07	1.97
Cash Flow Per Share	5.58	5.25	5.29	4.92	4.17	4.03	3.72
Tang. Book Val. Per Share	16.80	15.97	15.43	14.74	13.67	13.26	13.05
Dividends Per Share	1.54	1.46	1.37	1.31	1.27	1.25	1.21
Dividend Payout %	58.8	60.3	52.5	54.1	65.0	60.4	61.4
INCOME STATEMENT (IN MILLIONS):							
Total Revenues	1,615.2	1,465.1	1,992.6	1,850.7	1,480.1	1,609.4	1,673.9
Costs & Expenses	1,262.9	1,120.0	1,631.6	1,492.3	1,178.5	1,316.8	1,379.3
Depreciation & Amort.	140.3	136.5	131.2	125.3	111.8	103.1	96.5
Operating Income	212.0	208.6	229.8	233.1	189.8	189.5	198.1
Net Interest Inc./(Exp.)	d45.1	d46.6	d46.2	d46.2	d38.7	d37.8	d39.5
Income Taxes	65.7	61.1	69.0	67.7	54.4	51.1	54.2
Net Income	② 124.4	116.4	127.9	① 121.2	99.8	109.5	109.4
Cash Flow	264.4	252.6	258.7	246.1	211.2	212.0	204.9
Average Shs. Outstg. (000)	47,400	48,100	48,900	50,000	50,700	52,600	55,100
BALANCE SHEET (IN MILLIONS):							
Gross Property	3,483.1	3,379.8	3,267.7	3,192.7	3,110.4	2,951.5	2,884.1
Accumulated Depreciation	1,747.9	1,648.0	1,531.9	1,420.8	1,331.1	1,234.5	1,227.9
Net Property	1,735.2	1,731.8	1,735.8	1,771.9	1,779.3	1,717.0	1,656.2
Total Assets	2,451.8	2,364.6	2,394.6	2,438.6	2,259.1	2,209.9	2,222.1
Long-Term Obligations	436.1	557.3	550.2	518.0	468.7	458.9	458.9
Net Stockholders' Equity	787.7	759.0	744.1	729.7	687.7	683.5	704.0
Year-end Shs. Outstg. (000)	46,890	47,514	48,217	49,492	50,302	51,540	53,959
STATISTICAL RECORD:							
Operating Profit Margin %	13.1	14.2	11.5	12.6	12.8	11.8	11.8
Net Profit Margin %	7.7	7.9	6.4	6.5	6.7	6.8	6.5
Net Inc./Net Property %	7.2	6.7	7.4	6.8	5.6	6.4	6.6
Net Inc./Tot. Capital %	7.9	7.1	8.0	7.8	6.8	7.8	7.6
Return on Equity %	15.8	8.3	17.2	16.6	14.5	16.0	15.5
Accum. Depr./Gross Prop. %	50.2	48.8	46.9	44.5	42.8	41.8	42.6
Price Range	42¹⁵/₁₆-31³/₁₆	44⁷/₁₆-37¹/₈	42¹⁵/₁₆-30	37¹/₈-25³/₈	28¹/₂-21³/₄	29¹/₄-21⁷/₈	31⁵/₈-24¹/₈
	16.4-11.9	18.4-15.3	16.5-11.5	15.3-10.5	14.5-11.1	14.1-10.6	16.1-12.2
P/E Ratio							
Average Yield %	4.2	3.6	3.8	4.2	5.1	4.9	4.3

Statistics are as originally reported. Adjusted for 2-for-1 stock split, 4/93. ① Bef. inc. fr. dis. ops. of $150.0 mill. ② Incl. a pre-tax gain of $3.8 million on the sale of the Company's interest in QuickTrade.

OFFICERS:
T. L. Fisher, Chmn., Pres., C.E.O.
D. L. Cyranoski, Sr. V.P., Sec., Contr., Treas.

INVESTOR CONTACT: Mark Knox, Asst. Sec. Dir. Inv. Rel., (630) 305-9500-2529

PRINCIPAL OFFICE: 1844 Ferry Road, Naperville, IL 60563-9600

TELEPHONE NUMBER: (630) 305-9500
FAX: (630) 983-9328
WEB: www.nicorinc.com

NO. OF EMPLOYEES: 3,400 (approx.)

SHAREHOLDERS: 31,500 (approx.)

ANNUAL MEETING: In Apr.

INCORPORATED: IL, 1976

INSTITUTIONAL HOLDINGS:
No. of Institutions: 189
Shares Held: 23,956,248
% Held: 50.9

INDUSTRY: Natural gas distribution (SIC: 4924)

TRANSFER AGENT(S): Harris Trust & Savings Bank, Chicago, IL.

NISOURCE, INC.

YIELD 6.0%
P/E RATIO 14.2

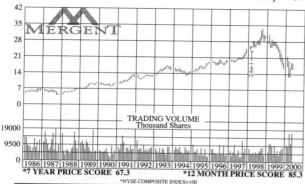

*7 YEAR PRICE SCORE 67.3   *12 MONTH PRICE SCORE 85.3
*NYSE COMPOSITE INDEX=100

TRADING VOLUME
Thousand Shares

INTERIM EARNINGS (Per Share):

Qtr.	Mar.	June	Sept.	Dec.
1996	0.54	0.19	0.28	0.43
1997	0.59	0.22	0.29	0.22
1998	0.48	0.24	0.35	0.51
1999	0.62	0.18	0.22	0.25

INTERIM DIVIDENDS (Per Share):

Amt.	Decl.	Ex.	Rec.	Pay.
0.255Q	8/24/99	10/27/99	10/29/99	11/19/99
0.27Q	12/17/99	1/27/00	1/31/00	2/18/00
0.27Q	3/28/00	4/26/00	4/28/00	5/19/00
0.27Q	5/24/00	7/27/00	7/31/00	8/18/00

Indicated div.: $1.08 (Div. Reinv. Plan)

CAPITALIZATION (12/31/99):

	($000)	(%)
Long-Term Debt	1,975,184	57.2
Deferred Income Tax	996,193	28.8
Redeemable Pfd. Stock	399,030	11.5
Preferred Stock	85,611	2.5
Total	3,456,018	100.0

DIVIDEND ACHIEVER STATUS:

Rank: 170   10-Year Growth Rate: 9.28%
Total Years of Dividend Growth: 11

RECENT DEVELOPMENTS: For the year ended 12/31/99, net income declined 17.3% to $160.4 million versus $193.9 million in 1998. The decline in earnings was attributable to the acquisitions of Bay State Gas Company and Energy USA-TPC. Total operating revenues rose 7.2% to $3.14 billion from $2.93 billion in the prior year. Gas revenues soared 36.7% to $1.65 billion. Electric revenues decreased 21.5% to $1.12 billion, while water revenues climbed 17.2% to $98.4 million.

PROSPECTS: The Company and Columbia Energy Group have agreed to merger terms, under which NI will acquire all of the outstanding shares of Columbia's common equity, valued at approximately $6.00 billion. The Company will also assume $2.50 billion of Columbia's long-term debt. The combined company is expected to have an enterprise value of $13.70 billion. The transaction is expected to be dilutive to NI's earnings per share in the first year after the close of the merger.

BUSINESS

NISOURCE, INC. (formerly NIPSCO Industries, Inc.) is an energy-based holding company that provides electric energy, natural gas and water to the public through its six wholly-owned regulated subsidiaries: Northern Indiana Public Service Co., Kokomo Gas and Fuel Co., Northern Indiana Fuel and Light Co., Inc., Crossroads Pipeline Company, Indianapolis Water Company, and Harbour Water Corp. The Company provides non-regulated energy/utility-related services including energy marketing and trading, power generation, gas transmission, supply and storage, installation, repair and maintenance of underground pipelines, utility line locating and marking and related products targeted at customer services through the following subsidiaries: NIPSCO Energy Services, Inc., Primary Energy, Inc. and NIPSCO Capital Markets, Inc. On 3/25/97, NI acquired IWC Resources Corp.

ANNUAL FINANCIAL DATA

	12/31/99	12/31/98	12/31/97	12/31/96	12/31/95	12/31/94	12/31/93
Earnings Per Share	1.27	1.59	1.53	1.44	1.36	1.24	1.16
Cash Flow Per Share	3.76	3.71	3.56	3.20	2.95	2.74	2.57
Tang. Book Val. Per Share	...	9.22	8.10	9.20	8.99	7.50	8.33
Dividends Per Share	1.02	0.96	0.90	0.84	0.78	0.72	0.66
Dividend Payout %	80.3	60.4	58.8	58.3	57.3	58.1	57.1
INCOME STATEMENT (IN MILLIONS):							
Total Revenues	3,144.6	2,932.8	2,586.5	1,821.6	1,722.3	1,676.4	1,677.9
Costs & Expenses	2,289.4	2,180.2	1,849.6	1,139.3	1,049.5	1,043.1	1,048.4
Depreciation & Amort.	311.4	256.5	249.8	215.0	201.1	194.3	187.0
Maintenance Exp.	82.2	74.6	76.6	70.0	78.3	80.2	83.5
Operating Income	461.5	421.5	410.6	286.3	284.9	261.1	262.0
Net Interest Inc./(Exp.)	d166.6	d128.8	d120.6	d106.5	d96.2	d89.5	d93.5
Income Taxes	90.4	100.9	105.0	111.0	108.4	97.7	96.8
Net Income	160.4	193.9	190.8	176.7	175.5	164.0	156.1
Cash Flow	471.8	450.4	440.7	391.6	376.5	355.2	340.1
Average Shs. Outstg. (000)	125,339	121,335	123,849	122,382	126,562	129,640	132,272
BALANCE SHEET (IN MILLIONS):							
Gross Property	8,241.1	6,630.2	6,416.1	5,741.0	5,587.0	5,433.0	5,283.4
Accumulated Depreciation	3,444.3	2,968.1	2,759.9	2,546.2	2,373.7	2,202.1	2,052.2
Net Property	5,230.4	3,748.7	3,752.9	3,342.2	3,349.3	3,357.6	3,355.4
Total Assets	6,835.2	4,986.5	4,937.0	4,274.3	3,999.5	3,944.5	3,912.3
Long-Term Obligations	1,975.2	1,668.0	1,667.9	1,127.1	1,175.7	1,180.3	1,192.5
Net Stockholders' Equity	85.6	1,234.8	1,350.4	1,181.6	1,203.5	1,195.2	1,194.1
Year-end Shs. Outstg. (000)	124,139	117,531	147,784	119,612	124,760	147,784	131,658
STATISTICAL RECORD:							
Operating Profit Margin %	14.7	14.4	15.9	15.7	16.5	15.6	15.6
Net Profit Margin %	5.1	6.6	7.4	9.7	10.2	9.8	9.3
Net Inc./Net Property %	3.1	5.2	5.1	5.3	5.2	4.9	4.7
Net Inc./Tot. Capital %	4.6	5.3	5.1	5.9	5.7	5.4	5.1
Return on Equity %	187.4	15.7	14.1	15.0	14.6	13.7	13.1
Accum. Depr./Gross Prop. %	41.8	44.8	43.0	44.4	42.5	40.5	38.8
Price Range	30 15/16-16 3/8	33 3/4-24 11/16	24 15/16-19	20 3/8-17 5/8	19 1/4-14 5/8	16 1/2-13 1/16	17 7/16-13 1/16
P/E Ratio	24.4-12.9	21.2-15.5	16.3-12.4	14.0-12.2	14.2-10.8	13.3-10.5	15.1-11.3
Average Yield %	4.3	3.3	4.1	4.5	4.6	4.9	4.3

Statistics are as originally reported. Adj. for stk. split 2-for-1: 2/98

OFFICERS:

G. L. Neale, Chmn., Pres., C.E.O.
S. P. Adik, Sr. Exec. V.P., C.F.O., Treas.
M. D. Wyckoff, V.P., Hum. Res., Asst. Treas.

INVESTOR CONTACT: Francis P. Girot, Jr., Treas., (219) 853-6970

PRINCIPAL OFFICE: 801 East 86th Ave., Merrillville, IN 46410

TELEPHONE NUMBER: (219) 853-5200
FAX: (219) 647-6061
WEB: www.nipsco.com

NO. OF EMPLOYEES: 7,399 (avg.)

SHAREHOLDERS: 40,463

ANNUAL MEETING: In April

INCORPORATED: IN, Sept., 1987

INSTITUTIONAL HOLDINGS:
No. of Institutions: 207
Shares Held: 55,663,524
% Held: 44.5

INDUSTRY: Electric and other services combined (SIC: 4931)

TRANSFER AGENT(S): Harris Trust and Savings Bank, Chicago, IL

NORDSON CORPORATION

YIELD	2.1%
P/E RATIO	17.9

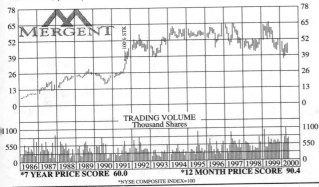

*7 YEAR PRICE SCORE 60.0   *12 MONTH PRICE SCORE 90.4

*NYSE COMPOSITE INDEX=100

INTERIM EARNINGS (Per Share):

Qtr.	Jan.	Apr.	July	Oct.
1996-97	0.52	0.50	0.70	1.14
1997-98	0.30	0.03	0.84	0.09
1998-99	0.42	0.77	0.80	0.85
1999-00	0.29	...	...	...

INTERIM DIVIDENDS (Per Share):

Amt.	Decl.	Ex.	Rec.	Pay.
0.24Q	5/19/99	6/02/99	6/04/99	6/22/99
0.24Q	8/18/99	9/01/99	9/03/99	9/21/99
0.26Q	11/29/99	12/15/99	12/17/99	1/04/00
0.26Q	2/16/00	3/01/00	3/03/00	3/21/00
0.26Q	5/17/00	5/31/00	6/02/00	6/20/00

Indicated div.: $1.04 (Div. Reinv. Plan)

CAPITALIZATION (10/31/99):

	($000)	(%)
Long-Term Debt	61,762	21.5
Capital Lease Obligations..	4,213	1.5
Common & Surplus	221,398	77.0
Total	287,373	100.0

DIVIDEND ACHIEVER STATUS:
Rank: 124   10-Year Growth Rate: 11.61%
Total Years of Dividend Growth: 18

RECENT DEVELOPMENTS: For the first quarter ended 1/30/00, net income decreased 31.7% to $4.8 million from $7.0 million in the corresponding quarter of the prior year. Earnings for 2000 included severance and restructuring costs of $2.8 million. Net sales fell 2.7% to $152.9 million from $157.1 million a year earlier due to a decrease in sales volume and unfavorable currency effects. Sales volume in North America decreased 6.0%, while sales volume declined 1.0%. in Europe. However, sales volume in the Pacific South region increased 28.0% as a result of growth in the Company's electronic business. Gross margins as a percentage of net sales grew to 56.4% from 53.8% the year before. This increase was primarily due to a sales mix skewed to the Company's standard products. Year-to-date orders through the middle of February are up nearly 20.0% and the Company's backlog is at a record level, up more than $50.0 million since the beginning of fiscal 2000.

BUSINESS

NORDSON CORPORATION designs, manufactures and markets systems that apply adhesives, sealants and coatings to a broad range of consumer and industrial products during manufacturing operations. The Company's high value-added product line includes customized electronic controls for the precise application and curing of materials to meet customers' productivity, quality and environmental targets. NDSN's production operations include machining and assembly. The Company finishes specially designed parts and assembles components into finished equipment. Many components are made in standard modules that can be used in more than one product or in combination with other components for a variety of models. NDSN products are used around the world in the appliance, automotive, bookbinding, construction, container, converting, electronics, food and beverage, furniture, metal finishing, nonwovens, packaging and other diverse industries. NDSN has principal manufacturing facilities in Ohio, Georgia, Alabama, California, Connecticut, New Jersey, Florida, Germany, The Netherlands, and the United Kingdom.

ANNUAL FINANCIAL DATA

	10/31/99	11/1/98	11/2/97	11/3/96	10/29/95	10/30/94	10/31/93
Earnings Per Share	2.84	[2] 1.25	2.89	2.97	2.84	2.45	[1] 2.13
Cash Flow Per Share	4.83	4.73	4.36	4.28	3.95	3.41	3.02
Tang. Book Val. Per Share	4.90	7.79	9.51	10.21	11.08	9.92	9.03
Dividends Per Share	0.96	0.88	0.80	0.72	0.64	0.56	0.48
Dividend Payout %	33.8	70.4	27.7	24.2	22.5	22.9	22.5
INCOME STATEMENT (IN THOUSANDS):							
Total Revenues	700,465	660,900	636,710	609,444	581,444	506,692	461,557
Costs & Expenses	591,180	557,866	537,344	501,661	476,886	413,870	377,076
Depreciation & Amort.	32,300	57,963	25,307	23,522	20,614	18,418	17,107
Operating Income	76,985	45,071	74,059	84,261	83,944	74,404	67,374
Net Interest Inc./(Exp.)	d10,244	d9,647	d7,763	d5,955	d4,553	d4,392	d6,426
Income Before Income Taxes	71,438	38,927	71,745	81,061	80,642	70,858	62,248
Income Taxes	23,932	18,102	21,778	27,990	27,966	24,204	21,473
Net Income	47,506	[2] 20,825	49,967	53,071	52,676	46,654	[1] 40,775
Cash Flow	79,806	78,788	75,274	76,593	73,290	65,072	57,882
Average Shs. Outstg.	16,524	16,661	17,276	17,896	18,577	19,067	19,184
BALANCE SHEET (IN THOUSANDS):							
Cash & Cash Equivalents	16,060	6,850	1,717	9,531	1,584	11,064	23,363
Total Current Assets	341,316	328,476	318,815	317,702	285,941	250,307	241,672
Net Property	128,639	101,183	101,667	107,018	99,499	88,655	78,689
Total Assets	591,790	538,944	502,996	510,493	434,710	380,944	357,970
Total Current Liabilities	251,940	207,082	179,663	207,216	155,379	123,311	116,281
Long-Term Obligations	65,975	70,444	66,502	20,562	17,134	19,254	22,089
Net Stockholders' Equity	221,398	214,775	220,545	245,297	231,330	212,424	196,405
Net Working Capital	89,376	121,394	139,152	110,486	130,562	126,996	125,391
Year-end Shs. Outstg.	24,506	16,740	16,839	17,634	18,006	18,399	18,726
STATISTICAL RECORD:							
Operating Profit Margin %	11.0	6.8	11.6	13.8	14.4	14.7	14.6
Net Profit Margin %	6.8	3.2	7.8	8.7	9.1	9.2	8.8
Return on Equity %	21.5	9.7	22.7	21.6	22.8	22.0	20.8
Return on Assets %	8.0	3.9	9.9	10.4	12.1	12.2	11.4
Debt/Total Assets %	11.1	13.1	13.2	4.0	3.9	5.1	6.2
Price Range	65¹⁵/₁₆-43	52⅜-42¼	65-44⅜	65-45½	61-53¾	63-52	54¾-38¼
P/E Ratio	23.2-15.1	41.9-33.8	22.5-15.4	21.9-15.3	21.5-18.9	25.7-21.2	25.7-18.0
Average Yield %	1.8	1.9	1.5	1.3	1.1	1.0	1.0

Statistics are as originally reported. [1] Bef. acctg. change chrg. $4.8 mill. ($0.27/sh.) [2] Incl. chrg. $26.0 mill.

OFFICERS:
W. P. Madar, Chmn.
E. P. Campbell, Pres., C.E.O.
R. L. Cushing, Treas.

INVESTOR CONTACT: Barbara T. Price, Manager, Shareholder Services, (440) 414-5344

PRINCIPAL OFFICE: 28601 Clemens Rd. Westlake, OH 44145

TELEPHONE NUMBER: (440) 892-1580
FAX: (440) 892-9507
WEB: www.nordson.com

NO. OF EMPLOYEES: 4,154 (avg.)

SHAREHOLDERS: 2,675 (approx.)

ANNUAL MEETING: In Mar.

INCORPORATED: OH, 1954

INSTITUTIONAL HOLDINGS:
No. of Institutions: 82
Shares Held: 4,315,862
% Held: 26.2

INDUSTRY: Adhesives and sealants (SIC: 2891)

TRANSFER AGENT(S): National City Bank, Cleveland, OH

NORTH PITTSBURGH SYSTEMS, INC.

YIELD 5.4%
P/E RATIO 14.7

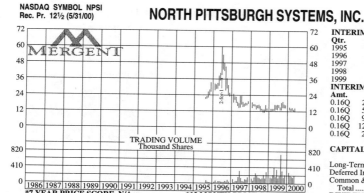

TRADING VOLUME
Thousand Shares

*7 YEAR PRICE SCORE N/A   *12 MONTH PRICE SCORE 87.9

*NYSE COMPOSITE INDEX=100

INTERIM EARNINGS (Per Share):

Qtr.	Mar.	June	Sept.	Dec.
1995	0.18	0.19	0.17	0.17
1996	0.20	0.17	0.19	0.21
1997	0.21	0.25	0.23	0.79
1998	0.28	0.27	0.21	0.21
1999	0.23	0.18	0.22	0.22

INTERIM DIVIDENDS (Per Share):

Amt.	Decl.	Ex.	Rec.	Pay.
0.16Q	2/26/99	3/30/99	4/01/99	4/15/99
0.16Q	5/21/99	6/29/99	7/01/99	7/15/99
0.16Q	9/01/99	9/29/99	10/01/99	10/15/99
0.16Q	12/15/99	12/30/99	1/03/00	1/14/00
0.16Q	2/24/00	3/30/00	4/03/00	4/14/00

Indicated div.: $0.64

CAPITALIZATION (12/31/99):

	($000)	(%)
Long-Term Debt	38,940	31.0
Deferred Income Tax	9,526	7.6
Common & Surplus	77,247	61.4
Total	125,713	100.0

DIVIDEND ACHIEVER STATUS:
Rank: 212   10-Year Growth Rate: 7.70%
Total Years of Dividend Growth: 37

RECENT DEVELOPMENTS: For the year ended 12/31/99, net income decreased 12.7% to $12.7 million compared with $14.5 million in 1998. Total operating revenues grew 6.7% to $70.9 million from $66.4 million the previous year. This was attributable to customer growth, growth in second lines and expanded penetration of enhanced services. Local network services operating revenues increased 10.9% to $13.8 million, while long distance and access services operating revenues advanced 5.1% to $47.2 million the year before. Directory advertising, billing and other services operating revenues rose 7.8% to $2.7 million, while telecommunication equipment sales climbed 2.7% to $3.0 million a year earlier. Other operating revenues jumped 14.8% to $4.3 million from $3.7 million a year ago. Net operating revenues declined 11.2% to $19.5 million versus $22.0 million the previous year.

BUSINESS

NORTH PITTSBURGH SYSTEMS, INC. is a holding company. Its predecessor, North Pittsburgh Telephone Company (North Pittsburgh), a telephone public utility engaged in providing telecommunication services and equipment to customers generally located in Western Pennsylvania. North Pittsburgh is a wholly-owned subsidiary of the Company. Penn Telecom, Inc. is also a wholly-owned subsidiary of the Company. The principal business activities of Penn Telecom consist of the sale, rental and servicing of telecommunication equipment to end users, the resale of bulk billed message toll services and high capacity intercity facilities. Penn Telecom is also certified as a Competitive Access Provider and a Competitive Local Exchange Carrier and has entered into these businesses. Pinnatech, Inc., a wholly-owned subsidiary of the Company formed in 1995, provides Internet related services.

ANNUAL FINANCIAL DATA

	12/31/99	12/31/98	12/31/97	12/31/96	12/31/95	12/31/94	12/31/93
Earnings Per Share	0.85	0.97	①1.48	0.78	0.71	0.66	②0.58
Cash Flow Per Share	1.75	1.76	2.18	1.41	1.26	1.15	1.08
Tang. Book Val. Per Share	5.16	4.93	4.57	3.68	3.43	3.19	2.97
Dividends Per Share	0.63	③0.64	0.55	0.51	0.47	0.43	0.39
Dividend Payout %	74.1	66.0	37.2	65.4	66.2	65.1	67.2
INCOME STATEMENT (IN THOUSANDS):							
Total Revenues	70,888	66,788	66,207	59,933	52,757	49,188	44,241
Costs & Expenses	37,722	32,513	33,511	31,072	25,554	24,374	20,908
Depreciation & Amort.	13,622	11,864	10,579	9,407	8,194	7,353	7,459
Operating Income	19,544	22,411	22,117	19,454	19,009	17,460	15,874
Net Interest Inc./(Exp.)	d1,287	d576	d1,102	d444	d530	d873	d695
Income Taxes	8,833	9,264	14,186	7,909	7,054	6,885	5,906
Net Income	12,685	14,518	①22,185	11,730	10,687	9,904	②8,715
Cash Flow	26,307	26,382	32,764	21,137	18,881	17,258	16,174
Average Shs. Outstg.	15,005	15,005	15,019	15,040	15,040	15,040	15,040
BALANCE SHEET (IN THOUSANDS):							
Gross Property	174,437	155,184	140,500	125,927	111,291	98,590	93,192
Accumulated Depreciation	86,688	78,854	69,303	60,333	52,675	47,596	45,546
Net Property	87,749	76,330	71,197	65,594	58,616	50,994	47,646
Total Assets	147,792	135,315	127,833	99,523	96,156	91,578	88,771
Long-Term Obligations	38,940	32,196	27,037	21,311	21,694	22,396	23,058
Net Stockholders' Equity	77,247	73,806	68,560	55,306	51,527	47,911	44,624
Year-end Shs. Outstg.	14,970	14,970	15,005	15,040	15,040	15,040	15,040
STATISTICAL RECORD:							
Operating Profit Margin %	27.6	33.6	33.4	32.5	36.0	35.5	35.9
Net Profit Margin %	17.9	21.7	33.5	19.6	20.3	20.1	19.7
Net Inc./Net Property %	14.5	19.0	31.2	17.9	18.2	19.4	18.3
Net Inc./Tot. Capital %	10.1	12.7	21.7	14.2	13.5	13.0	11.9
Return on Equity %	16.4	19.7	32.4	21.2	20.7	20.7	19.5
Accum. Depr./Gross Prop. %	49.7	50.8	49.3	47.9	47.3	48.3	48.9
Price Range	19¼-12¹¹/₁₆	18³/₄-11	25-14³/₈	60-23	33½-20½	...	...
P/E Ratio	22.6-14.2	19.3-11.3	16.9-9.7	76.9-29.5	47.2-28.9	...	...
Average Yield %	4.0	4.3	2.8	1.2	1.7	...	...

Statistics are as originally reported. Adjusted for 2-for-1 stock split, 5/96. ① Includes net gain of $14.5 million on the sale of investment. ② Excl. a gain of $450,000 fr. the cum. effect. of a change in acctg. ③ Incl. special dividend of $0.05.

OFFICERS:
C. E. Thomas Jr., Chmn.
H. R. Brown, Pres.
A. P. Kimble, V.P., Treas.
N. W. Barthlow, V.P., Sec.

PRINCIPAL OFFICE: 4008 Gibsonia Road, Gibsonia, PA 15044-9311

TELEPHONE NUMBER: (724) 443-9600
FAX: (412) 443-9431
WEB: www.penntele.com

NO. OF EMPLOYEES: 342

SHAREHOLDERS: 2,871 (approx.)

ANNUAL MEETING: In May

INCORPORATED: PA, May, 1985

INSTITUTIONAL HOLDINGS:
No. of Institutions: 24
Shares Held: 1,292,343
% Held: 8.6

INDUSTRY: Telephone communications, exc. radio (SIC: 4813)

TRANSFER AGENT(S): North Pittsburgh Systems, Inc., Gibsonia, PA

NORTHERN STATES POWER COMPANY

YIELD 6.6%
P/E RATIO 15.4

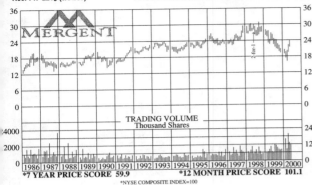

TRADING VOLUME
Thousand Shares

| 1986 | 1987 | 1988 | 1989 | 1990 | 1991 | 1992 | 1993 | 1994 | 1995 | 1996 | 1997 | 1998 | 1999 | 2000 |

*7 YEAR PRICE SCORE 59.9   *12 MONTH PRICE SCORE 101.1

*NYSE COMPOSITE INDEX=100

INTERIM EARNINGS (Per Share):

Qtr.	Mar.	June	Sept.	Dec.
1996	0.47	0.30	0.59	0.56
1997	0.45	0.12	0.62	0.43
1998	0.37	0.23	0.67	0.58
1999	0.34	0.06	0.72	0.32

INTERIM DIVIDENDS (Per Share):

Amt.	Decl.	Ex.	Rec.	Pay.
0.357Q	3/24/99	4/05/99	4/07/99	4/20/99
0.362Q	6/23/99	7/06/99	7/08/99	7/20/99
0.362Q	8/25/99	9/29/99	10/01/99	10/20/99
0.362Q	12/15/99	12/31/99	1/04/00	1/20/00
0.362Q	3/29/00	4/11/00	4/13/00	4/20/00

Indicated div.: **$1.45** (Div. Reinv. Plan)

CAPITALIZATION (12/31/99):

	($000)	(%)
Long-Term Debt	3,453,364	48.4
Deferred Income Tax	811,638	11.4
Redeemable Pfd. Stock	200,000	2.8
Preferred Stock	105,340	1.5
Common & Surplus	2,557,530	35.9
Total	7,127,872	100.0

DIVIDEND ACHIEVER STATUS:

Rank: 302   10-Year Growth Rate: 2.87%
Total Years of Dividend Growth: 24

RECENT DEVELOPMENTS: For the year ended 12/31/99, net income decreased 20.6% to $224.3 million versus $282.4 million in 1998. Earnings for 1999 reflected unfavorable regulatory treatment for conservation incentive recovery, write-downs of nonregulated investments and adverse weather conditions. Total revenue improved 1.8% to $2.87 billion from $2.82 billion. Electric revenues rose 1.5% to $2.40 billion. Gas revenues grew 3.3% to $471.9 million.

PROSPECTS: The Company plans to grow NRG Energy and Seren Industries, Inc., position its generation business for long-term value, create an independent nuclear company, expand energy marketing, expand its co-electric and gas distribution business, and provide for independent transmission operations. NSP expects to achieve earnings per share of $1.95 in 2000. Meanwhile, NSP's merger with New Century Energies Inc. is progressing on schedule.

BUSINESS

NORTHERN STATES POWER COMPANY, an operating holding company, is engaged in the generation, transmission and distribution of electricity and the transportation, storage and distribution of natural gas. NSP-Minnesota serves retail customers in Minnesota, North Dakota, South Dakota and Arizona. NSP-Wisconsin serves retail customers in Wisconsin and Michigan. Through its wholly-owned subsidiary NRG Energy, Inc., the Company operates several nonregulated energy businesses and is an equity investor in many nonregulated energy affiliates throughout the world. About 84% of 1999 revenues were derived from electric operations, and 16% from gas operations.

ANNUAL FINANCIAL DATA

	12/31/99	12/31/98	12/31/97	12/31/96	12/31/95	12/31/94	12/31/93
Earnings Per Share	1.43	1.84	① 1.61	1.91	1.96	1.73	1.51
Cash Flow Per Share	4.52	4.64	4.44	4.69	4.71	4.35	4.04
Tang. Book Val. Per Share	15.97	15.62	15.27	14.71	14.24	13.57	13.13
Dividends Per Share	1.44	1.42	1.40	1.36	1.33	1.30	1.27
Dividend Payout %	100.7	77.2	86.6	71.5	68.3	75.4	84.4

INCOME STATEMENT (IN MILLIONS):

	12/31/99	12/31/98	12/31/97	12/31/96	12/31/95	12/31/94	12/31/93
Total Revenues	2,869.0	2,819.2	2,733.7	2,654.2	2,568.6	2,486.5	2,404.0
Costs & Expenses	1,873.1	1,850.6	1,808.5	1,751.0	1,692.4	1,657.9	1,608.7
Depreciation & Amort.	473.9	423.2	398.9	381.4	372.1	350.1	330.0
Maintenance Exp.	178.6	181.1	164.5	155.8	158.2	170.1	161.4
Operating Income	343.5	364.3	361.8	366.0	345.9	308.3	303.9
Net Interest Inc./(Exp.)	d220.5	d162.7	d144.7	d130.7	d122.9	d107.2	d108.1
Income Taxes	cr61.0	cr40.6	cr48.1	cr14.6	5.1	...	...
Equity Earnings/Minority Int.	...	...	...	31.0	29.2	35.9	3.0
Net Income	224.3	282.4	① 237.3	274.5	216.1	243.5	211.7
Cash Flow	692.9	700.0	625.2	643.7	635.4	581.2	527.1
Average Shs. Outstg. (000)	153,443	150,743	140,870	137,358	134,832	133,690	130,422

BALANCE SHEET (IN MILLIONS):

	12/31/99	12/31/98	12/31/97	12/31/96	12/31/95	12/31/94	12/31/93
Gross Property	9,783.9	9,424.2	9,062.3	8,741.3	8,406.9	8,109.2	7,775.9
Accumulated Depreciation	5,332.5	5,028.9	4,701.0	4,403.4	4,096.6	3,835.5	3,561.8
Net Property	4,451.5	4,395.2	4,361.3	4,337.9	4,310.3	4,273.7	4,214.1
Total Assets	9,767.7	7,396.3	7,144.1	6,636.9	6,228.6	5,953.6	5,587.7
Long-Term Obligations	3,453.4	1,851.1	1,878.9	1,592.6	1,542.3	1,463.4	1,291.9
Net Stockholders' Equity	2,662.9	2,586.6	2,572.1	2,376.3	2,267.9	2,137.4	2,067.9
Year-end Shs. Outstg. (000)	153,041	152,697	149,236	138,126	136,352	133,844	133,760

STATISTICAL RECORD:

	12/31/99	12/31/98	12/31/97	12/31/96	12/31/95	12/31/94	12/31/93
Operating Profit Margin %	12.0	12.9	8.5	13.8	13.5	12.4	12.6
Net Profit Margin %	7.8	10.0	8.7	10.3	8.4	9.8	8.8
Net Inc./Net Property %	5.0	6.4	5.4	6.3	5.0	5.7	5.0
Net Inc./Tot. Capital %	3.1	5.2	4.4	5.8	4.6	5.5	5.1
Return on Equity %	8.4	10.9	9.2	11.6	9.5	11.4	10.2
Accum. Depr./Gross Prop. %	54.5	53.4	51.9	50.4	48.7	47.3	45.8
Price Range	27¹⁵/₁₆-19⁵/₁₆	30¹/₁₆-25¹¹/₁₆	29⁷/₁₆-22¹/₄	26¹¹/₁₆-22¹/₄	24³/₄-21¹/₄	23¹/₂-19³/₈	23¹⁵/₁₆-20¹/₁₆
P/E Ratio	19.5-13.5	16.7-14.0	18.3-13.8	14.0-11.6	12.7-10.9	13.6-11.2	15.9-13.3
Average Yield %	6.1	5.0	5.4	5.6	5.8	6.1	5.8

Statistics are as originally reported. Adj. for stk. splits: 2-for-1, 6/1/98 ① Incl. non-recurr chrg. $29.0 mill. fr. termination of merger.

OFFICERS:
J. J. Howard, Chmn., Pres., C.E.O.
E. J. McIntyre, V.P., C.F.O.
P. E. Pender, V.P., Fin., Treas.

INVESTOR CONTACT: Richard J. Kolkmann, (612) 330-6622

PRINCIPAL OFFICE: 414 Nicollet Mall, 4th Floor, Minneapolis, MN 55401

TELEPHONE NUMBER: (612) 330-5500
FAX: (612) 330-5688
WEB: www.nspco.com

NO. OF EMPLOYEES: 17,278 (avg.)

SHAREHOLDERS: 82,135

ANNUAL MEETING: In April

INCORPORATED: MN, June, 1909

INSTITUTIONAL HOLDINGS:
No. of Institutions: 216
Shares Held: 56,886,208
% Held: 36.9

INDUSTRY: Electric and other services combined (SIC: 4931)

TRANSFER AGENT(S): The Company

NORTHERN TRUST CORPORATION

YIELD 0.8%
P/E RATIO 37.6

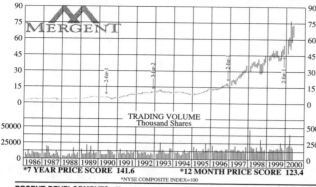

*7 YEAR PRICE SCORE 141.6   ***12 MONTH PRICE SCORE 123.4**

INTERIM EARNINGS (Per Share):

Qtr.	Mar.	June	Sept.	Dec.
1997	0.31	0.33	0.35	0.35
1998	0.37	0.38	0.39	0.40
1999	0.41	0.43	0.45	0.46

INTERIM DIVIDENDS (Per Share):

Amt.	Decl.	Ex.	Rec.	Pay.
0.24Q	7/20/99	9/08/99	9/10/99	10/01/99
2-for-1	11/16/99	12/10/99	11/29/99	12/09/99
0.135Q	11/16/99	12/08/99	12/10/99	1/03/00
0.135Q	2/15/00	3/08/00	3/10/00	4/03/00
0.135Q	5/16/00	6/07/00	6/09/00	6/30/00

Indicated div.: $0.54

CAPITALIZATION (12/31/99):

	($000)	(%)
Total Deposits	21,371,000	85.6
Long-Term Debt	1,426,900	5.7
Preferred Stock	120,000	0.5
Common & Surplus	2,054,700	8.2
Total	24,972,600	100.0

DIVIDEND ACHIEVER STATUS:

Rank: 45   10-Year Growth Rate: 16.60%
Total Years of Dividend Growth: 14

RECENT DEVELOPMENTS:

For the year ended 12/31/99, net income increased 14.4% to $405.0 million compared with $353.9 million in 1998. The increase in earnings reflected trust fees, which grew 19.3% to $974.2 million from $816.3 million a year earlier. Net interest income climbed 8.7% to $518.8 million from $477.2 million in 1998. Total non-interest income was $1.24 billion, an increase of 15.3% from $1.07 billion the year before. Provision for credit losses amounted to $12.5 million versus $9.0 million in 1998. Return on average assets increased to 1.34% from 1.30%, while return on average equity advanced to 20.67% from 20.47% in the previous year. On 3/17/00, the Company announced that it entered into a definitive agreement to acquire Carl Domino Associates, L.P., a registered investment adviser in West Palm Beach, Florida, that provides equity and balanced portfolio management services, providing NSTR with a value equity investment management capability.

BUSINESS

NORTHERN TRUST CORPORATION is a Chicago-based multibank holding company with subsidiaries in Illinois, Colorado, Connecticut, Florida, New York, Arizona, California and Texas. Its principal subsidiary is The Northern Trust Company. With total assets of $28.71 billion, NTRS offers financial services including fiduciary, banking, investment and financial consulting services for individuals as well as credit operating, trust and investment management services for corporations, institutions and organizations. The Company is a leading provider of personal fiduciary, master trust/custody and global custody, and treasury management services. NTRS and its subsidiaries also provide corporate banking, automated clearing house and leasing services. On 6/30/98, the Company exited the futures brokerage business.

LOAN DISTRIBUTION

(12/31/99)	($000)	(%)
Residential Real		
Estate	6,257,700	42.4
Commercial	4,704,100	31.9
Broker	88,800	0.6
Comerical Real		
Estate	780,400	5.3
Personal	1,659,900	11.3
Other & Lease		
Financing	566,500	3.8
International	691,500	4.7
Total	14,748,900	100.00

ANNUAL FINANCIAL DATA

	12/31/99	12/31/98	12/31/97	12/31/96	12/31/95	12/31/94	12/31/93
Earnings Per Share	1.74	1.52	1.33	1.11	0.94	0.79	0.74
Tang. Book Val. Per Share	9.25	8.18	7.27	6.40	5.76	5.13	4.61
Dividends Per Share	0.48	0.42	0.36	0.31	0.26	0.22	0.18
Dividend Payout %	27.6	27.6	27.1	27.9	27.7	27.8	24.3
INCOME STATEMENT (IN MILLIONS):							
Total Interest Income	1,568.6	1,503.1	1,332.8	1,151.5	1,104.0	848.7	706.4
Total Interest Expense	1,049.8	1,025.9	894.6	763.2	746.4	510.5	377.1
Net Interest Income	518.8	477.2	438.2	388.3	357.6	338.2	329.3
Provision for Loan Losses	12.5	9.0	9.0	12.0	6.0	6.0	19.5
Non-Interest Income	1,235.2	1,071.6	934.5	777.9	678.1	629.8	552.4
Non-Interest Expense	1,125.0	997.1	891.8	766.8	709.2	700.5	628.2
Income Before Taxes	616.5	542.7	471.9	387.4	320.5	261.5	234.0
Net Income	405.0	353.9	309.4	258.8	220.0	182.2	167.9
Average Shs. Outstg. (000)	229,874	229,794	229,322	229,296	225,352	220,576	218,360
BALANCE SHEET (IN MILLIONS):							
Cash & Due from Banks	1,977.9	2,366.0	1,738.9	1,292.5	1,308.9	1,192.5	1,519.7
Securities Avail. for Sale	5,491.0	5,384.3	3,741.8	4,316.5	5,225.2	4,411.8	247.9
Total Loans & Leases	15,374.5	13,646.9	12,588.2	10,937.4	9,906.0	8,590.6	7,623.0
Allowance for Credit Losses	150.8	146.8	147.6	148.3	147.1	144.8	145.5
Net Loans & Leases	15,223.6	13,500.1	12,440.6	10,789.1	9,758.9	8,445.8	7,477.5
Total Assets	28,708.2	27,870.0	25,315.1	21,608.3	19,933.5	18,561.6	16,902.6
Total Deposits	21,371.0	18,202.7	16,360.0	13,796.2	12,488.2	11,734.4	10,333.4
Long-Term Obligations	1,426.9	1,425.6	1,491.9	732.8	351.6	791.8	1,143.8
Total Liabilities	26,533.5	25,929.7	23,576.4	20,064.2	18,480.9	17,280.9	15,750.9
Net Stockholders' Equity	2,174.7	1,940.3	1,739.0	1,544.1	1,452.6	1,280.7	1,151.7
Year-end Shs. Outstg. (000)	222,162	222,430	222,734	222,496	222,656	216,356	213,172
STATISTICAL RECORD:							
Return on Equity %	18.6	18.2	17.8	16.8	15.1	14.2	14.6
Return on Assets %	1.4	1.3	1.2	1.2	1.1	1.0	1.0
Equity/Assets %	7.6	7.0	6.9	7.1	7.3	6.9	6.8
Non-Int. Exp./Tot. Inc. %	64.1	64.4	65.0	65.8	68.5	72.4	71.2
Price Range	54⅝-40³/₁₆	44¹⁵/₁₆-27⅞	35¾-17	18⁷/₈-12⁵/₁₆	14-7¹⁵/₁₆	10¹³/₁₆-8¹/₁₆	12⅝-9¼
P/E Ratio	31.4-23.1	29.6-18.3	26.9-12.8	17.1-11.1	14.9-8.5	13.7-10.2	17.1-12.5
Average Yield %	1.0	1.2	1.4	2.0	2.4	2.3	1.7

Statistics are as originally reported. Adj. for stk. splits: 2-for-1, 12/9/96; 2-for-1, 12/11/99

OFFICERS:

W. A. Osborn, Chmn., C.E.O.
P. R. Pero, Vice-Chmn., C.F.O.
B. G. Hastings, Pres., C.O.O.
D. L. Eddy, Sr. V.P., Treas.

INVESTOR CONTACT: Laurie K. McMahon, Dir. of Invest. Rel., (312) 444-7811

PRINCIPAL OFFICE: 50 South La Salle St., Chicago, IL 60675

TELEPHONE NUMBER: (312) 630-6000
FAX: (312) 444-7843
WEB: www.northerntrust.com

NO. OF EMPLOYEES: 8,583

SHAREHOLDERS: 3,251

ANNUAL MEETING: In Apr.

INCORPORATED: DE, Aug., 1971

INSTITUTIONAL HOLDINGS:
No. of Institutions: 349
Shares Held: 136,562,150
% Held: 61.4

INDUSTRY: State commercial banks (SIC: 6022)

TRANSFER AGENT(S): Norwest Bank Minnesota, N.A., Minnesota, MN

NYSE SYMBOL NOR
Rec. Pr. 23¼ (5/31/00)

NORTHWESTERN CORPORATION

YIELD 4.8%
P/E RATIO 14.4

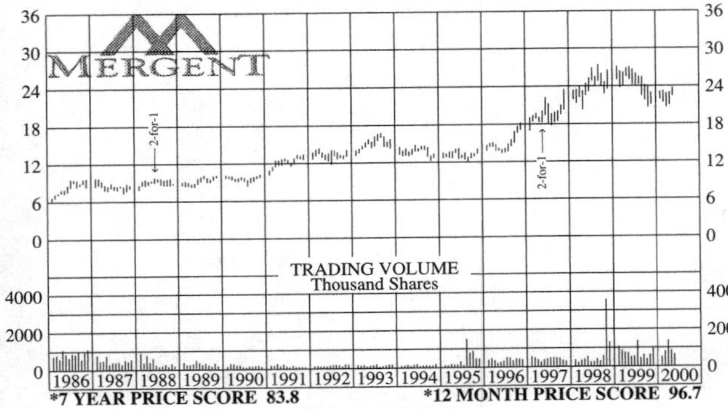

*7 YEAR PRICE SCORE 83.8 *12 MONTH PRICE SCORE 96.7

*NYSE COMPOSITE INDEX=100

INTERIM EARNINGS (Per Share):

Qtr.	Mar.	June	Sept.	Dec.
1997	0.55	0.14	0.17	0.45
1998	0.58	0.15	0.20	0.48
1999	0.56	0.22	0.31	0.53

INTERIM DIVIDENDS (Per Share):

Amt.	Decl.	Ex.	Rec.	Pay.
0.258Q	5/05/99	5/12/99	5/15/99	6/01/99
0.258Q	8/06/99	8/11/99	8/15/99	9/01/99
0.278Q	11/03/99	11/10/99	11/15/99	12/01/99
0.278Q	2/03/00	2/11/00	2/15/00	3/01/00
0.278Q	5/03/00	5/11/00	5/15/00	6/01/00

Indicated div.: $1.11 (Div. Reinv. Plan)

CAPITALIZATION (12/31/99):

	($000)	(%)
Long-Term Debt	783,107	48.9
Deferred Income Tax	64,855	4.1
Minority Interest	361,549	22.6
Redeemable Pfd. Stock	88,650	5.5
Preferred Stock..................	2,600	0.2
Common & Surplus	300,156	18.7
Total..............................	1,600,917	100.0

DIVIDEND ACHIEVER STATUS:
Rank: 282 10-Year Growth Rate: 4.03%
Total Years of Dividend Growth: 16

RECENT DEVELOPMENTS: For the year ended 12/31/99, net income soared 46.9% to $44.7 million compared with $30.4 million in the previous year. Total operating revenues more than doubled to $3.00 billion from $1.19 billion the year before. This reflected a 7.0% increase in electric operating revenues to $83.9 million, a 95.3% leap in propane operating revenues to $1.50 billion, and a 2.0% increase in natural gas revenues from 1998. Gross margins surged 54.4% to $536.6 million from $347.4 million in the prior year. Operating income increased 17.7% to $79.6 million from $67.5 million. Revenue growth at the Company's subsidiary, CornerStone Propane Partners, L.P., was primarily due to expansion of the wholesale business. Revenues in the Company's NorthWestern Public Service subsidiary was a result of slight increases in power costs and a customer base increase of 2.0% in 1999.

BUSINESS

NORTHWESTERN CORPORATION (formerly Public Service Company) is a service company that provides integrated energy, communications, air conditioning, heating, ventilating, plumbing and related services to residential and business customers throughout North America. NOR generates and distributes energy in the upper midwest, where it furnishes electric service to approximately 125,000 customers. NOR also purchases, distributes, sells, and transports natural gas to approximately 80,000 customers in Nebraska and South Dakota. NOR's propane operations are conducted through Cornerstone Propane Partners, L.P., a publicly traded limited partnership, created through the combined and newly acquired propane businesses of NOR. Cornerstone serves more than 460,000 customers from 298 service centers in 34 states.

ANNUAL FINANCIAL DATA

	12/31/99	12/31/98	12/31/97	12/31/96	12/31/95	12/31/94	12/31/93
Earnings Per Share	**1.62**	**1.44**	**1.31**	**[1] 1.28**	**1.10**	**1.00**	**0.98**
Cash Flow Per Share	**4.60**	**3.70**	**3.06**	**2.37**	**2.01**	**2.68**	**1.73**
Tang. Book Val. Per Share	...	...	**9.48**	**9.32**	**8.70**	**7.27**	**7.31**
Dividends Per Share	**1.05**	**0.98**	**0.93**	**0.89**	**0.86**	**0.83**	**0.81**
Dividend Payout %	**64.8**	**68.4**	**71.2**	**69.5**	**78.2**	**85.3**	**83.2**
INCOME STATEMENT (IN THOUSANDS):							
Total Revenues	3,004,340	1,187,187	918,070	344,009	204,970	157,266	153,257
Costs & Expenses	2,856,482	1,070,620	827,838	268,258	146,220	94,890	108,085
Depreciation & Amort.	68,302	42,626	31,235	19,414	14,633	12,439	11,559
Maintenance Exp.	...	...	5,881	5,919	6,020	6,170	6,368
Operating Income	79,556	73,941	58,997	50,418	38,097	30,369	20,306
Net Interest Inc./(Exp.)	d53,154	d35,732	d31,476	d18,668	d11,694	d9,670	d8,945
Income Taxes	14,466	13,196	11,111	15,415	10,126	7,869	6,940
Equity Earnings/Minority Int.	22,927	d767	d1,710	...	...	...	...
Net Income	44,663	30,391	26,264	[1] 26,054	19,306	28,839	15,190
Cash Flow	106,173	69,712	54,646	42,277	32,624	41,158	26,628
Average Shs. Outstg.	23,094	18,816	17,843	17,840	16,261	15,354	15,354
BALANCE SHEET (IN THOUSANDS):							
Gross Property	918,111	825,866	720,892	682,022	487,372	389,926	369,106
Accumulated Depreciation	236,448	196,588	175,270	162,909	150,469	139,381	130,610
Net Property	681,663	629,278	545,622	519,113	336,902	250,545	238,495
Total Assets	1,956,761	1,736,216	1,106,123	1,113,716	558,721	359,066	342,357
Long-Term Obligations	783,107	588,875	457,781	456,913	245,340	127,053	126,600
Net Stockholders' Equity	302,756	284,701	169,196	166,405	155,278	117,305	112,267
Year-end Shs. Outstg.	23,109	23,017	17,843	17,840	17,840	15,334	15,354
STATISTICAL RECORD:							
Operating Profit Margin %	2.6	6.2	6.4	14.7	18.6	19.3	13.2
Net Profit Margin %	1.5	2.6	2.9	7.6	9.4	9.8	9.9
Net Inc./Net Property %	6.6	4.8	4.8	5.0	5.7	6.2	6.4
Net Inc./Tot. Capital %	2.8	2.3	2.9	2.9	4.3	5.5	5.5
Return on Equity %	14.8	10.7	15.5	15.7	12.4	13.0	13.5
Accum. Depr./Gross Prop. %	25.8	23.8	24.3	23.9	30.9	35.7	35.4
Price Range	27 1/8-20 5/8	27 3/8-20 1/4	23 1/2-16 15/16	18 1/4-13 3/8	14 3/16-12 1/8	14 13/16-12 1/4	16 3/4-13 1/8
P/E Ratio	16.7-12.7	19.0-14.1	17.9-12.9	14.3-10.4	12.8-10.9	14.8-12.2	17.1-13.4
Average Yield %	4.4	4.1	4.6	5.6	6.5	6.2	5.5

Statistics are as originally reported. Adjusted for 2-for-1 stock split 5/97. [1] Incl. a nonrecurring, one-time gain of $0.09 a share.

OFFICERS:
M. D. Lewis, Chmn., C.E.O.
R. R. Hylland, Pres., C.O.O.

INVESTOR CONTACT: Investor Relations, (605) 978-2904

PRINCIPAL OFFICE: 125 S. Dakota Ave., Sioux Falls, SD 57104

TELEPHONE NUMBER: (605) 978-2908
FAX: (605) 353-7631
WEB: www.northwestern.com
NO. OF EMPLOYEES: 8,314 full-time; 23 part-time
SHAREHOLDERS: 10,475
ANNUAL MEETING: In May
INCORPORATED: DE, Nov., 1923

INSTITUTIONAL HOLDINGS:
No. of Institutions: 94
Shares Held: 8,059,715
% Held: 34.9

INDUSTRY: Electric and other services combined (SIC: 4931)

TRANSFER AGENT(S): Norwest Bank Minnesota, N.A., South St. Paul, MN

NUCOR CORPORATION

YIELD 1.5%
P/E RATIO 14.0

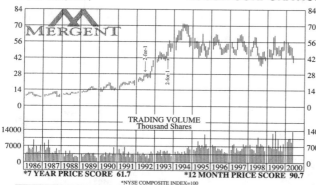

7 YEAR PRICE SCORE 61.7 *NYSE COMPOSITE INDEX=100* **12 MONTH PRICE SCORE 90.7**

TRADING VOLUME Thousand Shares

INTERIM EARNINGS (Per Share):

Qtr.	Mar.	June	Sept.	Dec.
1997	0.74	0.83	0.91	0.87
1998	0.74	0.82	0.74	0.70
1999	0.32	0.58	0.78	1.12

INTERIM DIVIDENDS (Per Share):

Amt.	Decl.	Ex.	Rec.	Pay.
0.13Q	3/04/99	3/29/99	3/31/99	5/12/99
0.13Q	6/02/99	6/28/99	6/30/99	8/11/99
0.13Q	9/03/99	9/28/99	9/30/99	11/11/99
0.13Q	11/30/99	12/29/99	12/31/99	2/11/00
0.15Q	3/08/00	3/29/00	3/31/00	5/12/00

Indicated div.: $0.60 (Div. Reinv. Plan)

CAPITALIZATION (12/31/99):

	($000)	(%)
Long-Term Debt	390,450	13.3
Minority Interest	280,871	9.6
Common & Surplus	2,262,248	77.1
Total	2,933,569	100.0

DIVIDEND ACHIEVER STATUS:
Rank: 43   10-Year Growth Rate: 16.85%
Total Years of Dividend Growth: 27

RECENT DEVELOPMENTS: For the year ended 12/31/99, net income declined 7.3% to $244.6 million compared with $263.7 million in 1998. Net sales were $4.01 billion, down 3.4% from $4.15 billion a year earlier. Total steel shipments were up 7.2% to 10.1 million tons. Pre-operating and start-up costs of new facilities decreased 40.9% to $42.8 million in 1999. For the quarter ended 12/31/99, net income increased 59.5% to $97.6 million and sales jumped 25.1% to $1.09 million.

PROSPECTS: NUE has signed a letter of intent with The Broken Hill Proprietary Corporation (BHP) of Melbourne, Australia and Ishikawajima-Harima Heavy Industries of Tokyo, Japan for the establishment of a joint venture for the worldwide licensing of patents and technology, and sale of key equipment required for strip casting. The joint venture will focus on the final stage of strip casting development.

BUSINESS

NUCOR CORPORATION is engaged in the manufacture and sale of steel and steel products. The Company's principal steel products are hot-rolled steel, cold-rolled steel, cold-finished steel, steel joists and joist girders, steel deck and steel-grinding balls. Hot-rolled steel products include angles, rounds, flats, channels, sheet, wide-flange beams, pilings, billets, blooms and beam blanks. The primary raw material is ferrous scrap, which is acquired from numerous sources throughout the U.S. Hot-rolled steel, cold-rolled steel, cold-finished steel and steel-grinding balls are manufactured in standard sizes and inventories are maintained. Steel joists, joist girders and steel deck are sold to general contractors and fabricators throughout the U.S.

ANNUAL FINANCIAL DATA

	12/31/99	12/31/98	12/31/97	12/31/96	12/31/95	12/31/94	12/31/93
Earnings Per Share	2.80	3.00	3.34	2.83	3.14	2.60	1.42
Cash Flow Per Share	5.74	5.88	5.84	4.91	5.13	4.41	2.83
Tang. Book Val. Per Share	25.93	23.73	21.32	18.33	15.78	12.85	10.36
Dividends Per Share	0.51	0.46	0.38	0.31	0.26	0.17	0.15
Dividend Payout %	18.2	15.3	11.4	11.0	8.1	6.7	10.9
INCOME STATEMENT (IN MILLIONS):							
Total Revenues	4,009.3	4,151.2	4,184.5	3,647.0	3,462.0	2,975.6	2,253.7
Costs & Expenses	3,378.6	3,486.6	3,505.6	3,077.3	2,857.0	2,447.5	1,931.2
Depreciation & Amort.	256.6	253.1	218.8	182.2	173.9	157.7	122.3
Operating Income	374.1	411.5	460.1	387.5	431.2	370.4	200.3
Net Interest Inc./(Exp.)	5.1	3.8	...	0.3	1.1	d13.5	d13.2
Income Before Income Taxes	379.2	415.3	460.2	387.8	432.3	356.9	187.1
Income Taxes	134.6	151.6	165.7	139.6	157.8	130.3	63.6
Net Income	244.6	263.7	294.5	248.2	274.5	226.6	123.5
Cash Flow	501.2	516.8	513.2	430.4	448.4	384.3	245.8
Average Shs. Outstg. (000)	87,287	87,878	87,922	87,686	87,430	87,166	86,909
BALANCE SHEET (IN MILLIONS):							
Cash & Cash Equivalents	572.2	308.7	283.4	104.4	201.8	101.9	27.3
Total Current Assets	1,538.5	1,129.5	1,125.5	828.4	830.7	638.7	468.2
Net Property	2,191.3	2,097.1	1,858.9	1,791.2	1,465.4	1,363.2	1,361.0
Total Assets	3,729.8	3,226.5	2,984.4	2,619.5	2,296.1	2,001.9	1,829.3
Total Current Liabilities	531.0	486.9	524.5	465.7	447.1	382.5	350.5
Long-Term Obligations	390.5	215.5	168.0	152.6	106.9	173.0	352.3
Net Stockholders' Equity	2,262.2	2,072.6	1,876.4	1,609.3	1,382.1	1,122.6	902.2
Net Working Capital	1,007.5	642.6	601.1	362.7	383.6	256.2	117.7
Year-end Shs. Outstg. (000)	87,247	87,353	87,997	87,796	87,599	87,333	87,073
STATISTICAL RECORD:							
Operating Profit Margin %	9.3	9.9	11.0	10.6	12.5	12.4	8.9
Net Profit Margin %	6.1	6.4	7.0	6.8	7.9	7.6	5.5
Return on Equity %	10.8	12.7	15.7	15.4	19.9	20.2	13.7
Return on Assets %	6.6	8.2	9.9	9.5	12.0	11.3	6.8
Debt/Total Assets %	10.5	6.7	5.6	5.8	4.7	8.6	19.3
Price Range	61¹³⁄₁₆-41⅝	60⅝-35¼	62¹⁵⁄₁₆-44¾	63-45⅛	63¼-42	72-48¾	57¼-38
P/E Ratio	22.1-14.9	20.2-11.7	18.8-13.4	22.3-15.9	20.1-13.4	27.7-18.7	40.3-26.8
Average Yield %	1.0	1.0	0.7	0.6	0.5	0.3	0.3

Statistics are as originally reported.

OFFICERS:
H. D. Aycock, Chmn., Pres., C.E.O.
T. S. Lisenby, Exec. V.P., C.F.O., Treas.

INVESTOR CONTACT: Terry S. Lisenby, V.P.
C.F.O., (704) 366-7000

PRINCIPAL OFFICE: 28211 Rexford Road,
Charlotte, NC 28211

TELEPHONE NUMBER: (704) 366-7000
FAX: (704) 362-4208
WEB: www.nucor.com

NO. OF EMPLOYEES: 7,500

SHAREHOLDERS: 55,000

ANNUAL MEETING: In May

INCORPORATED: MI, Jan., 1940; reincorp.,
DE, Mar., 1958

INSTITUTIONAL HOLDINGS:
No. of Institutions: 292
Shares Held: 57,510,008
% Held: 65.9

INDUSTRY: Blast furnaces and steel mills
(SIC: 3312)

TRANSFER AGENT(S): American Stock
Transfer & Trust Company, New York, NY

NASDAQ SYMBOL OCAS
Rec. Pr. 11 15/16 (5/31/00)

OHIO CASUALTY CORPORATION

YIELD 4.0%
P/E RATIO 6.6

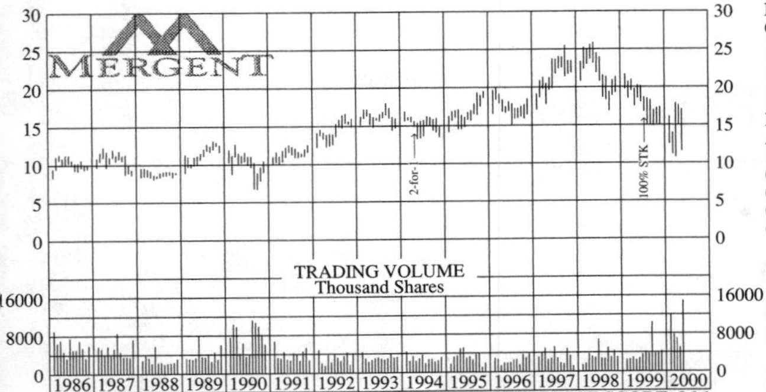

MERGENT
TRADING VOLUME
Thousand Shares
2-for-1
100% STK
1986 1987 1988 1989 1990 1991 1992 1993 1994 1995 1996 1997 1998 1999 2000

*7 YEAR PRICE SCORE 58.3 *12 MONTH PRICE SCORE 96.1

*NYSE COMPOSITE INDEX=100

INTERIM EARNINGS (Per Share):

Qtr.	Mar.	June	Sept.	Dec.
1996	0.05	0.19	0.41	0.79
1997	0.46	0.47	0.36	0.69
1998	0.46	0.15	0.35	0.32
1999	0.19	1.58	d0.11	0.14

INTERIM DIVIDENDS (Per Share):

Amt.	Decl.	Ex.	Rec.	Pay.
100% STK	5/27/99	7/23/99	7/01/99	7/22/99
0.23Q	8/19/99	8/30/99	9/01/99	9/10/99
0.23Q	11/18/99	11/29/99	12/01/99	12/10/99
0.23Q	2/17/00	2/28/00	3/01/00	3/10/00
0.12Q	5/18/00	5/30/00	6/01/00	6/10/00

Indicated div.: $0.48

CAPITALIZATION (12/31/99):

	($000)	(%)
Long-Term Debt	241,446	16.6
Deferred Income Tax	62,843	4.3
Common & Surplus	1,150,987	79.1
Total	1,455,276	100.0

DIVIDEND ACHIEVER STATUS:
Rank: 246 10-Year Growth Rate: 5.87%
Total Years of Dividend Growth: 54

RECENT DEVELOPMENTS: For the year ended 12/31/99, the Company reported income from continuing operations of $105.9 million, before a gain of $10.5 million from discontinued operations and an accounting charge of $2.3 million, compared with income of $83.0 million, before a gain of $1.9 million from discontinued operations, in the previous year. Earnings for 1999 and 1998 included amortization of deferred policy acquisition costs of $402.0 million and $316.5 million, respectively. Earnings for 1999 also included a restructuring credit of $2.4 million, while earnings for 1998 included a restructuring charge of $10.0 million. Total revenue increased 30.8% to $1.90 billion from $1.45 billion the year before. Premiums and finance charges earned improved 22.6% to $1.55 billion. Property and casualty premiums written climbed 10.4% to $1.59 billion from $1.44 billion in the previous year. The combined ratio climbed to 112.8% from 107.2% in 1998.

BUSINESS

OHIO CASUALTY CORPORATION operates primarily as a holding company and is principally engaged, through its direct and indirect subsidiaries, in the business of property and casualty insurance and insurance premium finance. The Corporation conducts its property and casualty insurance business through The Ohio Casualty Insurance Company and its five property and casualty insurance subsidiaries: West American Insurance Company, Ohio Security Insurance Company, American Fire and Casualty Company, Avomark Insurance Company and Ohio Casualty of New Jersey, Inc. This group of companies presently underwrites most forms of property and casualty insurance. The Corporation conducts its insurance premium finance business through Ocasco Budget, Inc. Ocasco is a direct subsidiary of Ohio Casualty Insurance Company. On 12/1/98, Ohio Casualty Insurance Company acquired the Commercial Lines Division of Great American Insurance Company for $300.0 million in cash, plus warrants to purchase 3.0 million shares of Ohio Casualty common stock.

ANNUAL FINANCIAL DATA

	12/31/99	12/31/98	12/31/97	12/31/96	12/31/95	12/31/94	12/31/93
Earnings Per Share	**[4] 1.73**	**1.26**	**[1][2] 1.43**	**[2] 1.38**	**[2] 1.34**	**[3] 1.35**	**1.21**
Tang. Book Val. Per Share	**14.27**	**16.19**	**19.55**	**16.72**	**15.69**	**11.82**	**11.97**
Dividends Per Share	**0.92**	**0.88**	**0.84**	**0.80**	**0.76**	**0.73**	**0.71**
Dividend Payout %	**53.2**	**69.8**	**58.9**	**58.0**	**56.9**	**54.1**	**58.8**
INCOME STATEMENT (IN MILLIONS):							
Total Premium Income	1,555.0	1,268.8	1,209.0	1,226.7	1,268.3	1,321.6	1,400.6
Net Investment Income	184.3	169.0	177.7	183.3	188.1	213.8	219.4
Other Income	160.8	14.4	50.7	49.7	6.1	23.2	49.8
Total Revenues	1,900.1	1,452.3	1,437.4	1,459.6	1,462.5	1,558.7	1,669.8
Policyholder Benefits	1,008.7	805.0	751.2	812.2	774.3	828.8	919.8
Income Before Income Taxes	136.9	103.0	173.5	115.0	120.2	116.9	96.2
Income Taxes	31.0	20.0	43.1	17.8	24.8	19.6	9.2
Net Income	[4] 105.9	83.0	[1][2] 130.4	[2] 97.2	[2] 95.4	[3] 97.2	87.0
Average Shs. Outstg. (000)	61,139	65,870	68,456	70,494	71,500	72,066	72,032
BALANCE SHEET (IN MILLIONS):							
Cash & Cash Equivalents	150.0	305.0	120.1	61.6	38.3	28.7	30.4
Premiums Due	366.2	301.9	193.6	186.7	196.2	199.2	200.7
Invst. Assets: Fixed-term	2,377.0	2,415.9	2,226.0	2,310.9	2,407.9	2,510.0	2,629.2
Invst. Assets: Equities	698.1	924.9	859.5	721.2	661.2	520.0	492.2
Invst. Assets: Total	3,179.5	3,603.7	3,151.4	3,073.6	3,083.4	3,043.5	3,137.6
Total Assets	4,476.4	4,802.3	3,778.8	3,890.0	3,980.1	3,739.0	3,816.8
Long-Term Obligations	241.4	265.0	40.0	50.0	60.0	70.0	103.0
Net Stockholders' Equity	1,151.0	1,321.0	1,314.8	1,175.1	1,111.0	850.8	862.3
Year-end Shs. Outstg. (000)	60,083	62,538	67,244	70,282	70,792	71,998	72,060
STATISTICAL RECORD:							
Return on Revenues %	5.6	5.7	9.1	6.7	6.5	6.2	5.2
Return on Equity %	9.2	6.3	9.9	8.3	8.6	11.4	10.1
Return on Assets %	2.4	1.7	3.5	2.5	2.4	2.6	2.3
Price Range	21 11/16-14 7/8	25 7/8-16 7/8	25 1/2-17	20-15	19 1/2-14 1/8	16 7/8-13 1/4	18-14 7/16
P/E Ratio	12.5-8.6	20.5-13.4	17.9-11.9	14.5-10.9	14.6-10.6	12.5-9.8	14.9-11.9
Average Yield %	5.0	4.1	4.0	4.6	4.5	4.8	4.4

Statistics are as originally reported. Adj. for stk. splits: 2-for-1, 7/99; 2-for-1, 4/94 [1] Incl. non-recurr. credit $50.7 mill. ($1.48/sh.) [2] Bef. disc. opers. gain: 12/31/98, $1.9 mill. ($0.06/sh.); 12/31/97, $8.7 mill. ($0.25/sh.); 12/31/96, $5.2 mill. ($0.15/sh.); 12/31/95, $4.4 mill. ($0.12/sh.) [3] Bef. acctg. change chrg. 12/31/94: $319,000 ($0.01/sh.); credit 12/31/92: $1.5 mill. ($0.08/sh.) [4] Incl. restruc. credit of $2.3 mill.; excl. gain from disc. opers. of $10.5 mill. & acctg. chrg. of $2.3 mill.

OFFICERS:
J. L. Marcum, Chmn.
W. L. Woodall, Vice-Chmn., Pres., C.E.O.

INVESTOR CONTACT: Barry Porter, Treas., (513) 867-3904

PRINCIPAL OFFICE: 136 North Third Street, Hamilton, OH 45025

TELEPHONE NUMBER: (513) 867-3000
FAX: (513) 867-3215
WEB: www.ocas.com

NO. OF EMPLOYEES: 3,900 (avg.)

SHAREHOLDERS: 6,200

ANNUAL MEETING: In Apr.

INCORPORATED: OH, Aug., 1969

INSTITUTIONAL HOLDINGS:
No. of Institutions: 118
Shares Held: 38,617,852
% Held: 64.3

INDUSTRY: Fire, marine, and casualty insurance (SIC: 6331)

TRANSFER AGENT(S): First Chicago Trust Company of New York, Jersey City, NJ

NYSE SYMBOL OK
Rec. Pr. $33\frac{1}{4}$ (5/31/00)

OLD KENT FINANCIAL CORPORATION

YIELD 2.6%
P/E RATIO 15.5

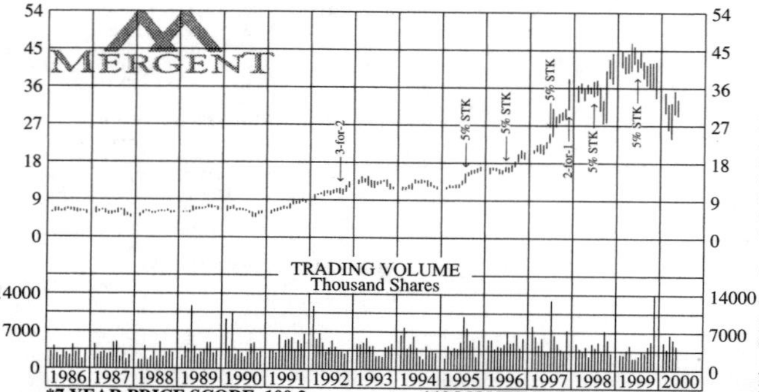

MERGENT
3-for-2
5% STK
5% STK
5% STK
2-for-1
5% STK
5% STK
TRADING VOLUME
Thousand Shares
1986 1987 1988 1989 1990 1991 1992 1993 1994 1995 1996 1997 1998 1999 2000

*7 YEAR PRICE SCORE 100.2 *12 MONTH PRICE SCORE 87.9

*NYSE COMPOSITE INDEX=100

INTERIM EARNINGS (Per Share):

Qtr.	Mar.	June	Sept.	Dec.
1996	0.35	0.34	0.38	0.40
1997	0.39	0.50	0.42	0.42
1998	0.46	0.50	0.50	0.34
1999	0.53	0.57	0.44	0.60

INTERIM DIVIDENDS (Per Share):

Amt.	Decl.	Ex.	Rec.	Pay.
5% STK	6/21/99	6/25/99	6/29/99	7/19/99
0.20Q	8/16/99	8/27/99	8/31/99	9/15/99
0.22Q	10/18/99	11/08/99	11/11/99	12/15/99
0.22Q	1/17/00	2/08/00	2/10/00	3/15/00
0.22Q	4/17/00	5/09/00	5/11/00	6/15/00

Indicated div.: $0.88 (Div. Reinv. Plan)

CAPITALIZATION (12/31/99):

	($000)	(%)
Total Deposits	13,695,012	90.6
Long-Term Debt	200,000	1.3
Common & Surplus	1,226,873	8.1
Total	15,121,885	100.0

DIVIDEND ACHIEVER STATUS:
Rank: 108 10-Year Growth Rate: 12.38%
Total Years of Dividend Growth: 19

RECENT DEVELOPMENTS: For the year ended 12/31/99, net income advanced 12.1% to $252.5 million compared with $225.3 million in the previous year. Earnings for 1999 and 1998 included after-tax merger charges of $17.6 million and $19.7 million, respectively. Net interest income grew 4.8% to $677.2 million from $646.4 million in the prior year. The 1998 results were restated to reflect the acquisitions of CFSB Bancorp, Inc. and Pinnacle Banc Group, Inc.

PROSPECTS: Going forward, OK expects to benefit from the acquisition of Grand Premier Financial, Inc. on 4/3/00, which had assets of $1.70 billion, deposits of $1.80 billion, and 23 banking locations. On 2/11/00, OK acquired Merchants Bancorp, Inc., which had assets of $979.0 million and deposits of $721.0 million. As a result of the transaction, OK operates 16 banking centers in Kane county and has expanded its presence in Chicago.

BUSINESS

OLD KENT FINANCIAL CORPORATION, with assets of approximately $19.00 billion as of 2/15/00, is a bank holding company. The Company's principal subsidiary, Old Kent Bank, serves communities in Michigan, Illinois and Indiana with nearly 300 banking offices. Old Kent mortgage companies operate 147 offices located in 32 states. Old Kent Bank engages in commercial and retail banking and provides trust and other financial services. These include commercial, mortgage, and retail loans, business and personal checking accounts, savings and retirement accounts, time deposit instruments, ATMs, electronic banking services, money transfer services, safe deposit facilities, cash management, real estate and lease financing, international banking services, investment management and trust services, brokerage and investment advisory services, and access to insurance products.

ANNUAL FINANCIAL DATA

	12/31/99	12/31/98	12/31/97	12/31/96	12/31/95	12/31/94	12/31/93
Earnings Per Share	**[2] 2.11**	**[1] [2] 1.75**	**[1] 1.71**	**1.46**	**1.29**	**1.25**	**1.17**
Tang. Book Val. Per Share	**10.43**	**10.35**	**10.04**	**9.55**	**9.67**	**7.91**	**7.48**
Dividends Per Share	**0.80**	**0.69**	**0.61**	**0.55**	**0.50**	**0.46**	**0.42**
Dividend Payout %	**38.0**	**39.3**	**35.8**	**37.5**	**39.0**	**37.0**	**35.8**
INCOME STATEMENT (IN MILLIONS):							
Total Interest Income	1,282.3	1,155.6	1,020.4	946.8	907.0	722.3	656.1
Total Interest Expense	605.1	569.4	496.2	453.5	436.0	291.8	257.2
Net Interest Income	677.2	586.3	524.3	493.3	471.0	430.5	398.8
Provision for Loan Losses	26.2	46.8	45.7	35.2	21.7	21.2	34.0
Non-Interest Income	424.8	347.9	284.4	212.2	161.7	151.5	146.8
Non-Interest Expense	686.5	584.2	490.8	432.5	402.1	357.9	326.0
Income Before Taxes	389.3	304.7	273.9	238.7	214.6	204.9	193.6
Net Income	[2] 252.5	[1] [2] 197.2	[1] 178.7	157.7	136.1	134.1	120.0
Average Shs. Outstg. (000)	119,715	113,483	105,542	108,416	110,137	108,892	109,211
BALANCE SHEET (IN MILLIONS):							
Cash & Due from Banks	589.4	615.8	501.9	530.4	527.6	461.1	371.8
Securities Avail. for Sale	3,514.2	5,378.5	3,309.6	2,503.5	2,527.5	3,612.9	4,080.8
Total Loans & Leases	12,067.1	8,883.7	8,469.5	8,097.1	7,430.6	6,498.0	5,016.7
Allowance for Credit Losses	184.3	167.7	157.4	165.9	174.2	161.9	140.7
Net Loans & Leases	11,882.8	8,716.1	8,312.1	7,931.1	7,256.3	6,336.1	4,876.0
Total Assets	17,969.8	16,588.9	13,773.5	12,646.8	12,003.1	10,946.4	9,855.7
Total Deposits	13,695.0	12,939.4	10,228.3	10,080.1	9,357.4	8,957.6	7,971.2
Long-Term Obligations	200.0	200.0	100.0	100.0	100.0	1.1	1.2
Total Liabilities	16,743.0	15,453.7	12,746.1	11,653.1	10,987.1	10,087.0	9,042.9
Net Stockholders' Equity	1,226.9	1,135.1	1,027.5	993.8	1,015.9	859.5	812.8
Year-end Shs. Outstg. (000)	117,610	109,724	102,290	104,057	105,073	108,658	108,652
STATISTICAL RECORD:							
Return on Equity %	20.6	17.4	17.4	15.9	13.4	15.6	14.8
Return on Assets %	1.4	1.2	1.3	1.2	1.1	1.2	1.2
Equity/Assets %	6.8	6.8	7.5	7.9	8.5	7.9	8.2
Non-Int. Exp./Tot. Inc. %	62.3	62.8	60.7	61.3	63.6	61.6	59.9
Price Range	$46\frac{7}{8}$-$33\frac{9}{16}$	$44\frac{5}{16}$-$27\frac{1}{2}$	$38\frac{3}{16}$-$20\frac{1}{16}$	$21\frac{1}{8}$-$15\frac{3}{8}$	$17\frac{1}{8}$-$11\frac{3}{4}$	14-$11\frac{7}{16}$	$14\frac{11}{16}$-$11\frac{5}{8}$
P/E Ratio	22.2-15.9	25.3-15.7	22.4-11.8	14.4-10.5	13.3-9.1	11.2-9.1	12.5-10.0
Average Yield %	2.0	1.9	2.1	3.0	3.5	3.6	3.2

Statistics are as originally reported. Adj. for stk. splits: 5% div., 7/99; 5% div., 7/98; 5% div., 7/97; 2-for-1, 12/97; 5% div., 7/96; 5% div., 8/95. [1] Incl. pre-tax non-recurr. credit $5.0 mill., 1998; credit $16.3 mill., 1997. [2] Incl. merger-related net chrgs. of $17.6 mill., 1999; $19.7 mill., 1998.

OFFICERS:
D. J. Wagner, Chmn., Pres., C.E.O.
R. H. Warrington, Vice-Chmn.
K. T. Kabat, Vice-Chmn.
M. F. Furlong, Exec. V.P., C.F.O.

INVESTOR CONTACT: Investor Relations, (616) 771-1034

PRINCIPAL OFFICE: 111 Lyon St. N.W., Grand Rapids, MI 49503

TELEPHONE NUMBER: (616) 771-5000
FAX: (616) 940-2763
WEB: www.oldkent.com

NO. OF EMPLOYEES: 8,018

SHAREHOLDERS: 19,221 (approx.)

ANNUAL MEETING: In Apr.

INCORPORATED: DE, Oct., 1971

INSTITUTIONAL HOLDINGS:
No. of Institutions: 197
Shares Held: 33,118,590
% Held: 28.1

INDUSTRY: State commercial banks (SIC: 6022)

TRANSFER AGENT(S): Old Kent Bank Shareholders Services, Grand Rapids, MI

NASDAQ SYMBOL OLDB
Rec. Pr. 29 7/16 (5/31/00)

OLD NATIONAL BANCORP

YIELD 2.3%
P/E RATIO 17.6

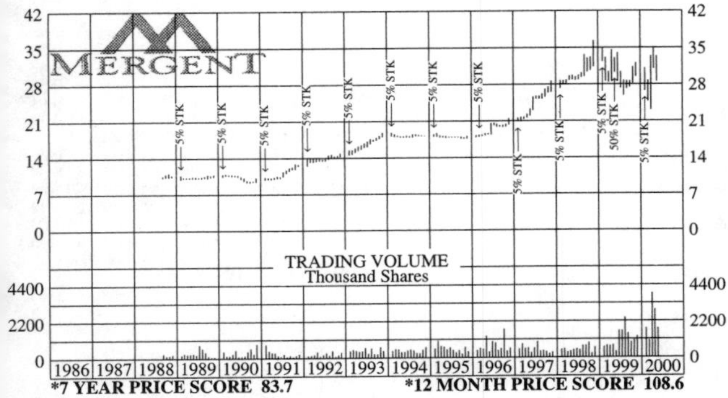

MERGENT
TRADING VOLUME
Thousand Shares

*7 YEAR PRICE SCORE 83.7 *12 MONTH PRICE SCORE 108.6

*NYSE COMPOSITE INDEX=100

INTERIM EARNINGS (Per Share):

Qtr.	Mar.	June	Sept.	Dec.
1995	0.27	0.29	0.30	0.27
1996	0.30	0.31	0.31	0.32
1997	0.33	0.34	0.35	0.25
1998	0.36	0.37	0.41	0.39
1999	0.40	0.43	0.43	0.41

INTERIM DIVIDENDS (Per Share):

Amt.	Decl.	Ex.	Rec.	Pay.
0.17Q	7/22/99	8/30/99	9/01/99	9/15/99
0.17Q	10/28/99	11/29/99	12/01/99	12/15/99
5% STK	12/09/99	1/05/00	1/07/00	1/28/00
0.17Q	1/27/00	2/28/00	3/01/00	3/15/00
0.17Q	4/27/00	5/30/00	6/01/00	6/15/00

Indicated div.: $0.68

CAPITALIZATION (12/31/99):

	($000)	(%)
Total Deposits	5,071,298	81.4
Long-Term Debt	662,973	10.6
Common & Surplus	492,744	7.9
Total	6,227,015	100.0

DIVIDEND ACHIEVER STATUS:
Rank: 227 10-Year Growth Rate: 6.79%
Total Years of Dividend Growth: 16

RECENT DEVELOPMENTS: For the year ended 12/31/99, the Company reported income of $82.7 million, from continuing operations, compared with income of $74.1 million, from continuing operations, in the previous year. The increase in income was the result of strong revenue growth. Net interest income improved 6.0% to $238.4 million from $224.9 million the year before. Net interest margin fell to 4.00% from 4.17% due to a decline in the earning asset yield, the cost of interest-bearing liabilities, and growth in higher-rate certificate of deposits and borrowings. The provision for loan losses decreased 4.7% to $11.4 million from $12.2 million in 1998. Total noninterest income advanced 15.5% to $67.5 million from $58.4 million. Noninterest expense grew 10.8% to $185.6 million from $167.5 million a year earlier. Recently, the Company received approval from the Federal Reserve Board for the acquisitions of Heritage Financial Services, Inc. in Clarksville, Tennessee, and ANB Corporation in Muncie, Indiana.

BUSINESS

OLD NATIONAL BANCORP is a multibank holding company headquartered in Evansville, Indiana, with total assets of $6.98 billion as of 12/31/99. As a bank holding company, the Corporation engages in banking and related activities through seventeen banks and two thrifts located in Indiana; six banks located in Kentucky; and eleven banks and one thrift located in Illinois. Through its nonbank affiliates, the Corporation provides services incidental to the business of banking. As of December 31, 1999, the Registrant's affiliate banks operated 119 banking offices throughout Indiana, Illinois, and Kentucky.

LOAN DISTRIBUTION

(12/31/99)	($000)	(%)
Commercial	1,174,698	24.28
Commercial real estate	1,096,850	22.67
Residential real estate	1,811,768	37.45
Consumer credit, net	754,618	15.60
Total loans	4,837,934	100.0

ANNUAL FINANCIAL DATA

	12/31/99	12/31/98	12/31/97	12/31/96	12/31/95	12/31/94	12/31/93
Earnings Per Share	**1.67**	**1.53**	**1.28**	**1.27**	**1.10**	**1.09**	**1.05**
Tang. Book Val. Per Share	**10.42**	**10.95**	**11.03**	**9.86**	**9.41**	**8.73**	**7.74**
Dividends Per Share	**0.63**	**0.56**	**0.53**	**0.50**	**0.48**	**0.46**	**0.40**
Dividend Payout %	**37.8**	**36.4**	**41.3**	**39.8**	**43.7**	**42.1**	**37.9**
INCOME STATEMENT (IN MILLIONS):							
Total Interest Income	488.9	437.9	429.4	394.4	355.3	277.9	254.2
Total Interest Expense	250.5	223.1	210.2	190.6	174.1	118.5	110.1
Net Interest Income	238.4	214.8	219.2	203.8	181.2	159.4	144.1
Provision for Loan Losses	11.5	11.4	27.0	11.0	6.7	5.0	6.2
Non-Interest Income	67.5	54.6	47.1	44.8	39.2	32.7	29.7
Non-Interest Expense	185.6	158.1	154.4	152.3	142.8	127.2	109.6
Income Before Taxes	108.8	99.9	85.0	85.3	70.9	59.9	58.0
Net Income	82.7	71.7	60.7	60.2	51.7	46.0	42.5
Average Shs. Outstg. (000)	49,875	47,584	48,440	47,604	49,146	42,396	40,573
BALANCE SHEET (IN MILLIONS):							
Cash & Due from Banks	169.2	150.9	147.3	180.4	175.1	178.3	149.8
Securities Avail. for Sale	1,678.7	1,596.9	1,567.0	1,514.6	1,390.2	378.1	1,212.0
Total Loans & Leases	4,837.9	4,162.2	3,730.2	3,523.3	3,037.7	2,561.1	2,172.8
Allowance for Credit Losses	57.0	49.4	46.2	44.1	39.8	37.9	36.1
Net Loans & Leases	4,780.9	4,112.8	3,684.0	3,479.2	2,997.9	2,523.2	2,136.8
Total Assets	6,982.9	6,166.0	5,688.2	5,366.6	4,822.6	4,152.1	3,714.5
Total Deposits	5,071.3	4,443.5	4,298.7	4,268.0	3,973.7	3,268.9	3,045.5
Long-Term Obligations	663.0	629.9	388.8	74.6	81.5	70.0	76.6
Total Liabilities	6,490.2	5,671.4	5,211.0	4,908.1	4,394.6	3,786.2	3,398.9
Net Stockholders' Equity	492.7	494.6	477.2	458.5	428.1	365.9	315.6
Year-end Shs. Outstg. (000)	47,289	45,180	43,245	46,498	45,498	41,920	40,777
STATISTICAL RECORD:							
Return on Equity %	16.8	14.5	12.7	13.1	12.1	12.6	13.5
Return on Assets %	1.2	1.2	1.1	1.1	1.1	1.1	1.1
Equity/Assets %	7.1	8.0	8.4	8.5	8.9	8.8	8.5
Non-Int. Exp./Tot. Inc. %	60.7	58.7	58.0	61.3	64.8	66.2	63.1
Price Range	35 1/16-25 13/16	36 3/8-27 3/16	28 5/8-20 7/8	21 1/2-17 7/8	18 3/4-17 5/8	18 13/16-17 15/16	18 13/16-14 9/16
P/E Ratio	21.0-15.5	23.8-17.8	22.3-16.3	17.0-14.1	17.0-16.0	17.3-16.5	17.9-13.9
Average Yield %	2.1	1.8	2.1	2.6	2.6	2.5	2.4

Statistics are as originally reported. Adj. for stk. splits: 5% div., 1/00; 50% div., 5/24/99; 5% div., 1/29/98; 5% div., 1/97; 5% div., 2/96, 5% div., 1/95; 5% div., 1/94; 5% div., 1/93.

OFFICERS:
J. A. Risinger, Chmn., C.E.O.
R. B. Lankford, Pres., C.O.O.
J. S. Poelker, Exec. V.P., C.F.O.

INVESTOR CONTACT: John C. Claybon, Inv. Rel. Off. & Asst. V.P., (812) 464-1442

PRINCIPAL OFFICE: 420 Main St., Evansville, IN 47708

TELEPHONE NUMBER: (812) 464-1434
FAX: (812) 464-1567
WEB: www.oldnational.com

NO. OF EMPLOYEES: 2,451

SHAREHOLDERS: 14,478

ANNUAL MEETING: In Apr.

INCORPORATED: IN, Jun., 1982

INSTITUTIONAL HOLDINGS:
No. of Institutions: 47
Shares Held: 8,187,459 (Adj.)
% Held: 17.1

INDUSTRY: National commercial banks (SIC: 6021)

TRANSFER AGENT(S): Old National Bancorp, Evansville, IN

OLD REPUBLIC INTERNATIONAL CORPORATION

YIELD 3.2%
P/E RATIO 10.2

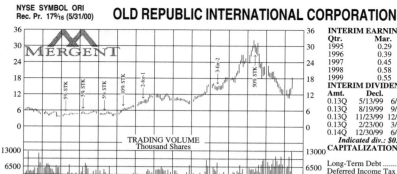

7 YEAR PRICE SCORE 59.2   **12 MONTH PRICE SCORE 102.5**
*NYSE COMPOSITE INDEX=100

INTERIM EARNINGS (Per Share):

Qtr.	Mar.	June	Sept.	Dec.
1995	0.29	0.32	0.47	0.53
1996	0.39	0.39	0.43	0.43
1997	0.45	0.63	0.49	0.53
1998	0.58	0.57	0.54	0.64
1999	0.55	0.48	0.31	0.39

INTERIM DIVIDENDS (Per Share):

Amt.	Decl.	Ex.	Rec.	Pay.
0.13Q	5/13/99	6/02/99	6/04/99	6/15/99
0.13Q	8/19/99	9/01/99	9/03/99	9/15/99
0.13Q	11/23/99	12/01/99	12/03/99	12/15/99
0.13Q	2/23/00	3/01/00	3/03/00	3/15/00
0.14Q	12/30/99	6/01/00	6/05/00	6/15/00

Indicated div.: $0.56 (Div. Reinv. Plan)

CAPITALIZATION (12/31/99):

	($000)	(%)
Long-Term Debt	208,300	6.0
Deferred Income Tax	203,000	5.8
Preferred Stock	700	0.0
Common & Surplus	3,078,000	88.2
Total	3,490,000	100.0

DIVIDEND ACHIEVER STATUS:

Rank: 88   10-Year Growth Rate: 13.29%
Total Years of Dividend Growth: 18

RECENT DEVELOPMENTS: For the year ended 12/31/99, net income decreased 29.9% to $226.8 million compared with $323.7 million a year earlier. Results included realized investment gains of $29.5 milion in 1999 and $53.0 million in 1998. Total revenues declined 3.2% to $2.10 billion from $2.17 billion in the prior year. Title insurance revenues rose 3.2% to $597.1 million, while mortgage guaranty revenues increased 2.2% to $355.9 million.

PROSPECTS: Earnings may continue to be negatively affected by major portions of the ORI's General Insurance segment that are being repriced and re-underwritten at renewal dates. In addition, the Title Insurance segment is being hampered by much lower mortgage refinancing volume and a cyclical downtrend in mortgage lending activity. Meanwhile, ORI's Mortgage Guaranty operations should continue to experience solid revenue and earnings growth.

BUSINESS

OLD REPUBLIC INTERNA-TIONAL CORPORATION is a multiple line insurance holding company. The Company's subsidiaries market, underwrite, and manage a wide range of specialty and general insurance programs in the property & liability, title, mortgage guaranty insurance and life & disability businesses. The Company primarily serves the insurance and related needs of major financial services and industrial corporations, with an emphasis on energy services, construction and forest products, transportation and housing industries. In 1999, revenues were derived as follows: general insurance, 50%; title insurance, 28%; mortgage guaranty, 17%; life insurance, 3% and other, 2%.

ANNUAL FINANCIAL DATA

	12/31/99	12/31/98	12/31/97	12/31/96	12/31/95	12/31/94	12/31/93
Earnings Per Share	1.75	2.33	2.10	② 1.64	1.61	1.13	① 1.26
Tang. Book Val. Per Share	19.65	17.27	15.59	14.57	13.58	11.46	10.77
Dividends Per Share	0.49	0.39	0.33	0.28	0.23	0.21	0.19
Dividend Payout %	28.0	16.6	15.9	16.9	14.1	18.4	15.2
INCOME STATEMENT (IN MILLIONS):							
Total Premium Income	1,567.2	1,568.1	1,464.6	1,360.4	1,251.7	1,282.9	1,246.0
Net Investment Income	263.2	273.1	270.8	260.5	251.9	227.5	220.7
Other Income	271.5	330.3	227.2	182.7	192.1	168.4	269.4
Total Revenues	2,101.9	2,171.5	1,962.8	1,803.7	1,695.9	1,679.0	1,736.3
Income Before Income Taxes	317.0	466.7	426.7	342.4	316.0	225.9	243.3
Income Taxes	92.9	145.7	129.1	108.5	103.5	73.3	77.9
Equity Earnings/Minority Int.	2.7	2.7	0.6	0.9	0.2	d1.4	1.1
Net Income	226.8	323.7	298.1	② 234.8	212.7	151.0	① 166.4
Average Shs. Outstg. (000)	129,787	139,150	141,768	140,438	128,867	128,718	128,426
BALANCE SHEET (IN MILLIONS):							
Cash & Cash Equivalents	294.0	400.5	354.9	301.0	332.1	203.2	298.2
Premiums Due	1,626.3	1,572.2	1,634.3	1,677.9	1,714.4	1,873.1	1,863.6
Invst. Assets: Fixed-term	4,261.1	4,286.7	4,259.6	4,007.1	3,860.1	3,347.5	3,152.2
Invst. Assets: Equities	160.1	164.8	117.1	116.1	126.1	263.8	191.9
Invst. Assets: Total	4,739.4	4,854.2	4,720.1	4,414.0	4,325.8	3,810.7	3,618.2
Total Assets	6,937.7	7,019.7	6,923.4	6,656.2	6,593.5	6,262.9	6,098.3
Long-Term Obligations	208.3	145.1	142.9	154.0	320.5	314.7	282.7
Net Stockholders' Equity	3,078.7	2,305.4	2,153.0	1,901.1	1,667.8	1,387.9	1,318.2
Year-end Shs. Outstg. (000)	156,679	133,403	138,070	130,408	118,716	115,957	116,649
STATISTICAL RECORD:							
Return on Revenues %	10.8	14.9	15.2	13.0	12.8	9.0	9.6
Return on Equity %	7.4	14.0	13.8	12.4	12.8	10.9	13.2
Return on Assets %	3.3	4.6	4.3	3.5	3.2	2.4	2.7
Price Range	22¾-12¹/₁₆	32¼-17¹⁵/₁₆	26¹³/₁₆-16⁷/₁₆	18½-13¹/₁₆	15³/₄-9⁵/₁₆	10⁷/₈-8³/₈	12¼-9⁹/₁₆
P/E Ratio	13.0-6.9	13.8-7.7	12.8-7.8	11.3-8.2	9.8-5.8	9.6-7.4	9.8-7.6
Average Yield %	2.8	1.5	1.5	1.7	1.8	2.2	1.8

Statistics are as originally reported. Adj. for stk. splits: 50% div., 5/98; 3-for-2, 5/96. ① Bef. acctg. change credit $8.6 mill. ② Bef. extraord. chrg. $4.4 mill.

NYSE SYMBOL OCR
Rec. Pr. 16½ (5/31/00)

OMNICARE, INC.

YIELD 0.5%
P/E RATIO 26.2

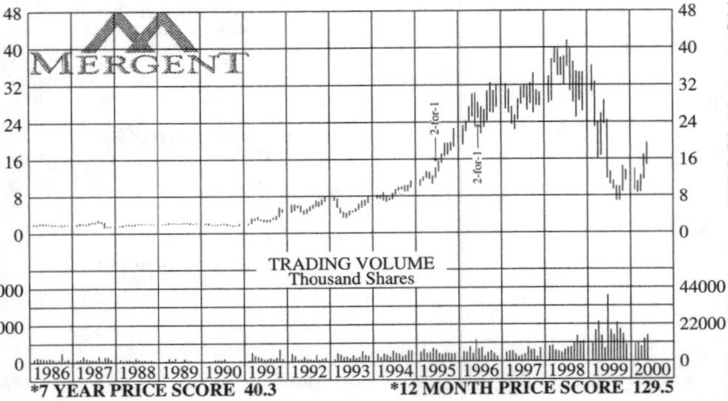

*7 YEAR PRICE SCORE 40.3 *12 MONTH PRICE SCORE 129.5

*NYSE COMPOSITE INDEX=100

INTERIM EARNINGS (Per Share):

Qtr.	Mar.	June	Sept.	Dec.
1997	0.18	0.19	0.13	0.20
1998	0.24	0.09	0.29	0.29
1999	0.31	0.05	0.15	0.12

INTERIM DIVIDENDS (Per Share):

Amt.	Decl.	Ex.	Rec.	Pay.
0.022Q	8/04/99	8/25/99	8/27/99	9/10/99
0.022Q	11/03/99	11/22/99	11/24/99	12/10/99
0.022Q	2/02/00	2/24/00	2/28/00	3/13/00
0.022Q	5/15/00	5/30/00	6/01/00	6/12/00

Indicated div.: $0.09 (Div. Reinv. Plan)

CAPITALIZATION (12/31/99):

	($000)	(%)
Long-Term Debt	736,944	40.9
Deferred Income Tax	37,360	2.1
Common & Surplus	1,028,380	57.0
Total	1,802,684	100.0

DIVIDEND ACHIEVER STATUS:
Rank: 48 10-Year Growth Rate: 16.23%
Total Years of Dividend Growth: 10

RECENT DEVELOPMENTS: For the year ended 12/31/99, net income dropped 28.2% to $57.7 million versus $80.4 million the year before. Results for 1999 included after-tax charges totaling $23.1 million. The decrease in earnings reflected declines in occupancy rates of OCR's skilled nursing facility clients. Sales climbed 22.7% to $1.86 billion from $1.52 billion in the previous year.

PROSPECTS: The Company expects that the impact of the Prospective Payment System, which pays facilities a federal per diem rate for all covered services, on the long-term care industry will continue to affect it in 2000. Meanwhile, earnings should benefit from the contribution of productivity and consolidation initiatives. Going forward, OCR will look to build upon its pharmaceutical distribution and clinical services to meet the need of lower health care costs.

BUSINESS

OMNICARE, INC. is a provider of pharmacy services to long-term care institutions such as skilled nursing facilities, assisted living communities and other institutional health care facilities. OCR purchases, repackages and dispenses pharmaceuticals, both prescription and non-prescription, and provides computerized medical record-keeping and third-party billing for residents in such facilities. OCR also provides consultant pharmacist services, including evaluating residents' drug therapy, monitoring the control, distribution and administration of drugs and assisting in compliance with state and federal regulations. Additionally, OCR provides ancillary services, such as infusion therapy, distributes medical supplies and offers clinical and financial software information systems to its client nursing facilities.

ANNUAL FINANCIAL DATA

	12/31/99	[7] 12/31/98	12/31/97	12/31/96	12/31/95	12/31/94	12/31/93
Earnings Per Share	[6] 0.63	[5] 0.90	[3] [6] 0.69	[3] 0.64	[3] 0.47	[2] 0.30	[1] 0.24
Cash Flow Per Share	1.39	1.43	1.01	0.87	0.68	0.47	0.35
Tang. Book Val. Per Share	...	...	0.99	4.87	1.08	1.21	0.18
Dividends Per Share	0.09	0.08	0.07	0.06	0.05	0.045	0.04
Dividend Payout %	14.3	8.9	10.1	9.4	10.6	14.9	17.0
INCOME STATEMENT (IN MILLIONS):							
Total Revenues	1,861.9	1,517.4	895.7	536.6	399.6	275.7	159.6
Costs & Expenses	1,656.3	1,313.6	772.7	456.7	344.9	241.5	139.8
Depreciation & Amort.	69.4	47.6	25.7	15.4	11.1	7.4	4.4
Operating Income	136.3	156.1	97.3	64.5	43.7	26.7	15.4
Net Interest Inc./(Exp.)	d46.2	d23.6	d5.6	d3.7	d6.0	d5.8	d2.1
Income Before Income Taxes	91.7	135.9	96.8	72.1	41.2	22.5	13.9
Income Taxes	34.0	55.5	41.1	28.7	16.4	9.1	5.2
Net Income	[6] 57.7	[5] 80.4	[3] [6] 55.7	[3] 43.5	[3] 24.8	[2] 13.4	[1] 8.7
Cash Flow	127.1	128.0	81.4	58.9	35.9	20.8	13.1
Average Shs. Outstg. (000)	91,238	89,786	80,303	67,388	52,396	44,152	37,256
BALANCE SHEET (IN MILLIONS):							
Cash & Cash Equivalents	97.3	54.3	131.0	216.5	40.1	79.6	63.3
Total Current Assets	752.3	603.3	472.0	390.7	161.1	162.2	111.2
Net Property	162.1	136.4	84.1	56.1	32.5	20.5	12.3
Total Assets	2,168.0	1,903.8	1,289.6	721.7	360.8	305.8	218.8
Total Current Liabilities	322.2	233.5	128.1	61.7	54.7	37.2	34.2
Long-Term Obligations	736.9	651.6	352.6	2.0	82.7	83.0	83.5
Net Stockholders' Equity	1,028.4	963.5	774.2	634.4	214.8	178.9	96.6
Net Working Capital	430.1	369.7	343.9	329.0	106.4	125.1	77.1
Year-end Shs. Outstg. (000)	91,286	90,265	82,153	77,026	52,640	50,584	37,268
STATISTICAL RECORD:							
Operating Profit Margin %	7.3	10.3	10.9	12.0	10.9	9.7	9.6
Net Profit Margin %	3.1	5.3	6.2	8.1	6.2	4.9	5.5
Return on Equity %	5.6	8.3	7.2	6.8	11.5	7.5	9.0
Return on Assets %	2.7	4.2	4.3	6.0	6.9	4.4	4.0
Debt/Total Assets %	34.0	34.2	27.3	0.3	22.9	27.1	38.2
Price Range	36 3/16-6 7/8	41 9/16-25	34 9/16-22 3/8	32½-19⅛	22 11/16-10¼	11 5/16-6¾	8 1/16-3 5/16
P/E Ratio	57.4-10.9	46.2-27.8	50.1-32.4	50.8-29.9	48.3-21.7	37.4-22.2	34.2-14.1
Average Yield %	0.4	0.2	0.2	0.2	0.3	0.5	0.7

Statistics are as originally reported. Adj. for 2-for-1 stk. split 6/95 & 6/96. [1] Bef. cr$280,000 fr. an acc. adj. [2] Incl. nonrecur. chg. of $1.9 mil. [3] Incl. a net chg. of $989,000, 1995; $534,000, 1996; $3.1 mil., 1997. [4] Incl. a net chg. of $6.0 mil. [5] Incl. a net chg. of $13.9 mil. for trans-rel. exps. in CompScript and IBAH acqs. & a nonrecur. net restr. chg. of $2.7 mil. [6] Incl. a net restr. chg. of $23.1 mil. [7] Incl. the results of CompScript, Inc. and IBAH, Inc.

OFFICERS:
E. L. Hutton, Chmn.
J. F. Gemunder, Pres.
D. W. Froesel Jr., Sr. V.P., C.F.O.
C. D. Hodges, Sr. V.P., Sec.

INVESTOR CONTACT: Investor Relations Dept., (606) 392-3331

PRINCIPAL OFFICE: 100 East RiverCenter Boulevard, Covington, KY 41011

TELEPHONE NUMBER: (606) 392-3300
FAX: (606) 392-3333
WEB: www.omnicare.com

NO. OF EMPLOYEES: 6,805 full-time (approx.); 4,201 part-time (approx.)

SHAREHOLDERS: 2,822

ANNUAL MEETING: In May

INCORPORATED: DE, May, 1981

INSTITUTIONAL HOLDINGS:
No. of Institutions: 153
Shares Held: 71,477,400
% Held: 78.3

INDUSTRY: Drug stores and proprietary stores (SIC: 5912)

TRANSFER AGENT(S): First Chicago Trust Company of New York, Jersey City, NJ

NYSE SYMBOL OV
Rec. Pr. 37⅛ (5/31/00)

ONE VALLEY BANCORP, INC.

YIELD 2.8%
P/E RATIO 15.7

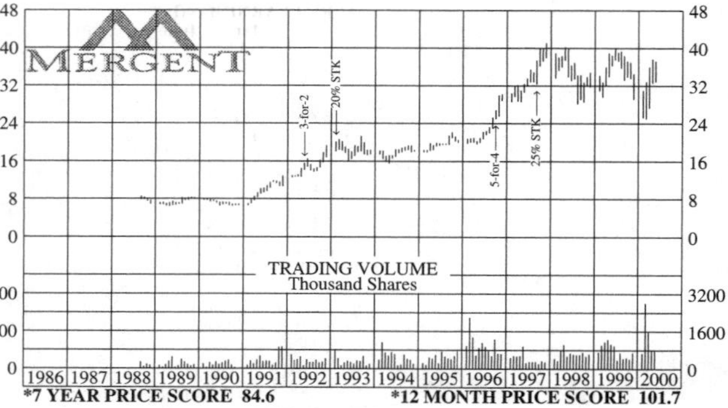

MERGENT
3-for-2
20% STK
5-for-4
25% STK
TRADING VOLUME
Thousand Shares
1986 1987 1988 1989 1990 1991 1992 1993 1994 1995 1996 1997 1998 1999 2000

*7 YEAR PRICE SCORE 84.6 *12 MONTH PRICE SCORE 101.7

*NYSE COMPOSITE INDEX=100

INTERIM EARNINGS (Per Share):

Qtr.	Mar.	June	Sept.	Dec.
1995	0.43	0.46	0.46	0.50
1996	0.48	0.51	0.43	0.52
1997	0.52	0.53	0.53	0.49
1998	0.51	0.55	0.56	0.56
1999	0.57	0.60	0.61	0.59

INTERIM DIVIDENDS (Per Share):

Amt.	Decl.	Ex.	Rec.	Pay.
0.24Q	3/15/99	3/29/99	3/31/99	4/15/99
0.24Q	6/15/99	6/28/99	6/30/99	7/15/99
0.26Q	9/21/99	9/28/99	9/30/99	10/15/99
0.26Q	12/07/99	12/28/99	12/31/99	1/14/00
0.26Q	3/21/00	3/29/00	3/31/00	4/14/00

Indicated div.: $1.04

CAPITALIZATION (12/31/99):

	($000)	(%)
Total Deposits	4,573,435	80.6
Long-Term Debt	541,824	9.5
Common & Surplus	558,729	9.8
Total	5,673,988	100.0

DIVIDEND ACHIEVER STATUS:

Rank: 142 10-Year Growth Rate: 10.67%

Total Years of Dividend Growth: 18

RECENT DEVELOPMENTS: For the year ended 12/31/99, net income totaled $80.8 million, an increase of 10.7% compared with $73.0 million in the previous year. The increase in net income was primarily attributed to increased net interest income and non-interest income. Net interest income improved 6.6% to $235.2 million from $220.7 million a year earlier. Provision for loan losses declined 9.4% to $9.1 million from $10.1 million the year before. Non-interest income grew 15.2% to $68.1 million from $59.1 million in the prior year, reflecting growth in trust income, credit/debt card fees, service charges on deposit accounts, investment and insurance fees, and miscellaneous income. Return on average assets grew to 1.30% from 1.29% and return on average equity climbed to 14.15% from 13.08% in the prior-year period. On 2/7/00, the Company and BB&T Corporation announced an agreement whereby BB&T will acquire One Valley in a $1.20 billion stock swap.

BUSINESS

ONE VALLEY BANCORP is the largest bank holding company based in West Virginia, with total assets of $6.23 billion as of 12/31/99. The Corporation currently owns 9 affiliate banks, which include One Valley Bank, N.A., One Valley Bank of Huntington, Inc., One Valley Bank of Mercer County, Inc., One Valley Bank-South, N.A., One Valley Bank-East, N.A., One Valley Bank, Inc., One Valley Bank-North, Inc., One Valley Bank-Shenandoah, N.A., and One Valley Bank-Central Virginia, N.A., and 123 locations.

LOAN DISTRIBUTION

(12/31/99)	($000)	(%)
Commercial, financial & agriculture	528,013	12.0
Real estate	3,158,999	71.9
Installment loans to individuals	658,783	15.0
Other loans	45,831	1.1
Total	4,391,626	100.0

ANNUAL FINANCIAL DATA

	12/31/99	12/31/98	12/31/97	12/31/96	12/31/95	12/31/94	12/31/93
Earnings Per Share	**2.37**	**2.15**	**2.07**	**2.43**	**2.29**	**2.16**	**2.02**
Tang. Book Val. Per Share	**16.72**	**17.14**	**15.61**	**18.46**	**17.18**	**15.14**	**15.05**
Dividends Per Share	**0.98**	**0.87**	**0.79**	**0.71**	**0.65**	**0.58**	**0.51**
Dividend Payout %	**41.3**	**40.5**	**38.0**	**29.2**	**28.5**	**27.0**	**25.2**
INCOME STATEMENT (IN MILLIONS):							
Total Interest Income	445.4	420.0	332.9	312.2	282.4	251.4	195.1
Total Interest Expense	210.1	199.3	153.8	139.3	121.1	94.9	78.1
Net Interest Income	235.2	220.7	179.2	172.9	161.3	156.5	116.9
Provision for Loan Losses	9.1	10.1	7.4	5.2	5.6	4.8	4.8
Non-Interest Income	68.2	60.2	47.2	40.8	37.6	37.8	36.2
Non-Interest Expense	174.0	161.9	132.3	128.4	119.6	121.4	99.4
Income Before Taxes	120.2	109.0	86.6	80.0	73.6	68.1	49.0
Net Income	80.8	73.0	57.4	53.2	49.1	46.2	32.5
Average Shs. Outstg. (000)	34,164	33,940	27,760	21,896	21,468	21,415	16,105
BALANCE SHEET (IN MILLIONS):							
Cash & Due from Banks	214.5	155.2	122.6	146.2	140.6	178.9	141.1
Securities Avail. for Sale	1,288.9	1,307.8	1,102.0	952.9	871.7	541.2	720.7
Total Loans & Leases	4,391.6	3,991.1	2,968.7	2,810.2	2,512.0	2,373.0	1,830.9
Allowance for Credit Losses	54.2	52.3	41.7	41.7	39.5	37.4	29.2
Net Loans & Leases	4,337.5	3,938.8	2,927.0	2,768.5	2,472.4	2,335.5	1,801.8
Total Assets	6,583.1	5,963.6	4,582.3	4,267.3	3,858.3	3,673.2	2,805.1
Total Deposits	4,573.4	4,552.9	3,517.6	3,406.0	3,048.3	2,926.5	2,328.6
Long-Term Obligations	541.8	35.5	21.9	28.9	13.4	19.5	0.1
Total Liabilities	6,024.3	5,368.0	4,158.0	3,858.7	3,492.0	3,351.4	2,531.8
Net Stockholders' Equity	558.7	595.5	424.3	408.6	366.3	321.9	242.6
Year-end Shs. Outstg. (000)	33,426	34,743	27,174	22,131	21,328	21,256	16,118
STATISTICAL RECORD:							
Return on Equity %	14.5	12.3	13.5	13.0	13.4	14.4	13.4
Return on Assets %	1.2	1.2	1.3	1.2	1.3	1.3	1.2
Equity/Assets %	8.5	10.0	9.3	9.6	9.5	8.8	8.6
Non-Int. Exp./Tot. Inc. %	57.4	57.6	58.5	60.1	60.1	62.5	64.9
Price Range	40⅛-29⅛	40¼-28⅛	41⅛-28⅝	30 3/16-19⅝	22 3/16-17 15/16	19⅜-15½	21¼-16 3/16
P/E Ratio	16.9-12.3	18.7-13.1	19.9-13.8	12.4-8.1	9.7-7.8	9.0-7.2	10.6-8.0
Average Yield %	2.8	2.5	2.3	2.9	3.3	3.3	2.7

Statistics are as originally reported.

OFFICERS:
J. H. Morrison, Chmn., Pres., C.E.O.
L. G. Jones, Exec. V.P., Treas.
J. A. Winter, Sr. V.P., C.A.O.

INVESTOR CONTACT: Linda S. Dugan, Shareholder Relations, (304) 348-7023

PRINCIPAL OFFICE: One Valley Sq., P.O. Box 1793, Charleston, WV 25326

TELEPHONE NUMBER: (304) 348-7000
FAX: (304) 348-7250
WEB: www.onevalley.com

NO. OF EMPLOYEES: 2,375 (approx.)

SHAREHOLDERS: 19,000 (approx.)

ANNUAL MEETING: In Apr.

INCORPORATED: WV, Sep., 1981

INSTITUTIONAL HOLDINGS:
No. of Institutions: 72
Shares Held: 9,630,458
% Held: 28.8

INDUSTRY: State commercial banks (SIC: 6022)

TRANSFER AGENT(S): Harris Trust & Savings Bank, Chicago, IL

OTTER TAIL POWER COMPANY

YIELD	4.9%
P/E RATIO	11.6

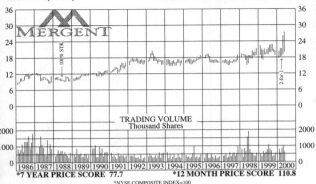

*7 YEAR PRICE SCORE 77.7   *12 MONTH PRICE SCORE 110.8
*NYSE COMPOSITE INDEX=100

TRADING VOLUME
Thousand Shares

INTERIM EARNINGS (Per Share):

Qtr.	Mar.	June	Sept.	Dec.
1996	0.42	0.24	0.25	0.32
1997	0.43	0.21	0.31	0.34
1998	0.06	0.32	0.40	0.44
1999	0.37	0.28	0.41	0.75

INTERIM DIVIDENDS (Per Share):

Amt.	Decl.	Ex.	Rec.	Pay.
0.495Q	7/29/99	8/11/99	8/13/99	9/10/99
0.495Q	10/26/99	11/10/99	11/15/99	12/10/99
0.51Q	1/31/00	2/11/00	2/15/00	3/10/00
2-for-1	1/31/00	3/16/00	2/15/00	3/15/00
0.255Q	4/11/00	5/11/00	5/15/00	6/10/00

Indicated div.: $1.02 (Div. Reinv. Plan)

CAPITALIZATION (12/31/99):

	($000)	(%)
Long-Term Debt	176,437	32.5
Deferred Income Tax	87,972	16.2
Preferred Stock	33,500	6.2
Common & Surplus	245,693	45.2
Total	543,602	100.0

DIVIDEND ACHIEVER STATUS:
Rank: 306   10-Year Growth Rate: 2.68%
Total Years of Dividend Growth: 24

RECENT DEVELOPMENTS: For the year ended 12/31/99, the Company reported net income of $45.0 million compared with income of $30.7 million, before a cumulative effect of a change in accounting principle, in the previous year. Earnings for 1999 included a net gain from the sale of radio station assets of $8.1 million. Earnings for 1998 included nonrecurring charges of $9.5 million. Total operating revenues were $464.6 million, an increase of 7.3% from $433.1 million in 1998. Electric operating revenues improved

2.7% to $233.5 million from $227.5 million the year before due to an increase in power pool revenues, partially offset by a decrease in retail revenue and other electric revenue. Manufacturing revenues advanced 6.8% to $93.4 million from $87.4 million a year earlier. Meanwhile, health services revenue decreased slightly to $69.3 million from $69.4 million in 1998, while other business operations revenues climbed 39.9% to $68.3 million.

BUSINESS

OTTER TAIL POWER COMPANY is an operating electric utility engaged in the production, transmission and distribution and sale of electric energy in western Minnesota, eastern North Dakota and northeastern South Dakota. OTTR, through its subsidiaries, is also engaged in manufacturing, health services, and other business operations, which include electrical and telephone construction contracting, transportation, telecommunications, entertainment, energy services and natural gas marketing. The aggregate population of OTTR's retail electric service area is approximately 230,000. The territory served by OTTR is predominately agricultural, including part of the Red River Valley. The Company's subsidiary Varistar Corp. owns nonutility businesses.

BUSINESS LINE ANALYSIS

(12/31/1999)	REV (%)	INC (%)
Electric	50.3	70.1
Manufacturing	20.1	10.7
Health Services	14.9	7.9
Other Business Operations	14.7	11.3
Total	100.0	100.0

ANNUAL FINANCIAL DATA

	12/31/99	12/31/98	12/31/97	12/31/96	12/31/95	12/31/94	12/31/93
Earnings Per Share	② 1.79	① 1.21	1.29	1.24	1.19	1.17	1.12
Cash Flow Per Share	3.25	2.68	2.98	2.79	2.47	2.33	2.25
Tang. Book Val. Per Share	9.32	8.58	8.07	7.64	7.39	7.21	7.62
Dividends Per Share	0.99	0.96	0.93	0.90	0.88	0.86	0.84
Dividend Payout %	55.3	79.7	72.1	72.9	73.9	73.5	75.3
INCOME STATEMENT (IN THOUSANDS):							
Total Revenues	464,577	431,078	394,279	361,739	326,329	286,726	265,227
Costs & Expenses	362,415	338,883	295,944	268,725	239,429	204,648	172,979
Depreciation & Amort.	34,796	34,965	39,302	34,788	28,602	25,899	25,348
Maintenance Exp.	...	...	...	...	...	...	12,914
Operating Income	67,366	57,230	59,033	58,226	58,298	56,179	39,655
Net Interest Inc./(Exp.)	d14,771	d15,566	d18,519	d16,601	d15,075	d13,687	d13,825
Income Taxes	23,915	15,140	14,308	14,308	16,159	15,881	14,331
Net Income	② 44,977	① 30,701	32,346	29,955	28,945	28,475	27,369
Cash Flow	77,545	63,308	69,290	62,385	55,189	52,016	50,240
Average Shs. Outstg.	23,831	23,596	23,278	22,364	22,360	22,360	22,360
BALANCE SHEET (IN THOUSANDS):							
Gross Property	889,574	870,476	860,413	847,510	785,856	745,143	722,249
Accumulated Depreciation	386,618	370,290	350,647	327,672	308,174	287,902	270,385
Net Property	502,956	500,186	509,766	519,838	477,682	457,241	451,864
Total Assets	680,788	655,612	655,441	662,287	609,196	578,972	563,905
Long-Term Obligations	176,437	181,046	189,973	160,492	168,261	162,196	166,563
Net Stockholders' Equity	279,193	245,907	230,987	214,057	205,073	197,479	191,277
Year-end Shs. Outstg.	23,850	23,760	23,462	22,430	22,360	22,360	22,360
STATISTICAL RECORD:							
Operating Profit Margin %	14.5	13.3	15.0	16.1	17.9	19.6	15.0
Net Profit Margin %	9.7	7.1	8.2	8.3	8.9	9.9	10.3
Net Inc./Net Property %	8.9	6.1	6.3	5.8	6.1	6.2	6.1
Net Inc./Tot. Capital %	8.3	5.7	6.0	6.1	5.9	6.0	5.8
Return on Equity %	16.1	12.5	14.0	14.0	14.1	14.4	14.3
Accum. Depr./Gross Prop. %	43.5	42.5	40.8	38.7	39.2	38.6	37.4
Price Range	22¹³⁄₁₆-17	21³⁄₈-15¹¹⁄₁₆	19-15	19⁵⁄₁₆-15⁷⁄₈	18⁷⁄₈-15³⁄₈	17³⁄₈-14³⁄₄	20⅝-15¹¹⁄₁₆
P/E Ratio	12.7-9.5	17.7-12.5	14.7-11.6	15.6-12.9	15.9-12.9	14.8-12.6	18.5-13.7
Average Yield %	5.0	5.3	5.5	5.1	5.1	5.4	4.7

Statistics are as originally reported. Adj. for stk. split: 2-for-1, 3/15/00 ① Incl. special chrg. $9.5 mill. & bef. acctg. change credit $3.8 mill. ② Incl. nonrecurring net gain of $8.1 mill. for the sale of radio station assets.

OFFICERS:
J. C. MacFarlane, Chmn., Pres., C.E.O.
J. D. Erickson, V.P., C.F.O.
J. D. Myster, Sec.

INVESTOR CONTACT: Shareholder Services, (218) 739-8479

PRINCIPAL OFFICE: 215 S. Cascade St., P.O. Box 496, Fergus Falls, MN 56538-0496

TELEPHONE NUMBER: (218) 739-8479
FAX: (218) 739-8218
WEB: www.otpco.com

NO. OF EMPLOYEES: 1,973 (approx.)

SHAREHOLDERS: 13,438

ANNUAL MEETING: In Jan.

INCORPORATED: MN, Jul., 1907

INSTITUTIONAL HOLDINGS:
No. of Institutions: 65
Shares Held: 2,220,667
% Held: 9.3

INDUSTRY: Electric services (SIC: 4911)

TRANSFER AGENT(S): Otter Tail Power Company, Fergus Falls, MN

PACIFIC CAPITAL BANCORP

INTERIM EARNINGS (Per Share):

Qtr.	Mar.	June	Sept.	Dec.
1996	0.26	0.25	0.24	0.57
1997	0.44	0.29	0.28	0.62
1998	0.52	0.40	0.34	0.06
1999	0.59	0.37	0.40	0.43

INTERIM DIVIDENDS (Per Share):

Amt.	Decl.	Ex.	Rec.	Pay.
0.18Q	3/29/99	4/16/99	4/20/99	5/11/99
0.18Q	6/24/99	7/16/99	7/20/99	8/10/99
0.18Q	9/22/99	10/22/99	10/26/99	11/16/99
0.18Q	12/16/99	1/21/00	1/25/00	2/15/00
0.20Q	3/20/00	4/20/00	4/25/00	5/16/00

Indicated div.: $0.80

CAPITALIZATION (12/31/99):

	($000)	(%)
Total Deposits	2,440,181	88.0
Long-Term Debt	98,801	3.6
Common & Surplus	234,573	8.5
Total	2,773,555	100.0

TRADING VOLUME
Thousand Shares

| 1986 | 1987 | 1988 | 1989 | 1990 | 1991 | 1992 | 1993 | 1994 | 1995 | 1996 | 1997 | 1998 | 1999 | 2000 |

*7 YEAR PRICE SCORE N/A   ***12 MONTH PRICE SCORE 87.6**

*NYSE COMPOSITE INDEX=100

DIVIDEND ACHIEVER STATUS:
Rank: 8   10-Year Growth Rate: 25.15%
Total Years of Dividend Growth: 30

RECENT DEVELOPMENTS:

For the year ended 12/31/99, net income jumped 49.7% to $44.3 million from $29.6 million in 1998. Net income growth was due to the following factors: the integration of 8 new branch offices through the acquisitions of First Valley Bank and Citizens State Bank, growth in the tax refund anticipation loan and refund transfer programs, strong loan demand over the last two years, continued growth in trust and investment service fees due to the strong stock market performance, and new custom-

ers. In addition, during 1999, the Company began to experience some of the expected cost savings from the merger with Pacific Capital Bancorp. However, these savings were more than offset in the first year by the expenses incurred to complete the integration of the two computer systems. Total interest income grew 9.3% to $211.6 million from $193.6 million in 1998. Total interest expense fell to $67.9 million from $68.1 million a year ago. Net interest income rose 14.5% to $143.8 million from $125.5 million in 1998.

BUSINESS

PACIFIC CAPITAL BANCORP (formerly Santa Barbara Bancorp) is a bank holding company with two banking subsidiaries and two-nonbank subsidiaries. In 1998, Santa Barbara Bancorp merged with Pacific Capital Bancorp, where Santa Barbara Bancorp was the surviving company, but took the name of Pacific Capital Bancorp. The Company's two banking subsidiaries are: Santa Barbara Bank and Trust (SBB&T) and First National Bank of Central California (FNB). SBB&T has grown to 27 banking offices with loan, trust and escrow offices. FNB has 10 banking offices in Monterey, Santa Cruz, Santa Clara and San Benito counties. The Company provides the following support services to its banks: executive management, personnel and benefits, risk management, data processing, strategic planning, legal, accounting and treasury services. The third subsidiary is Pacific Capital Commercial Mortgage Company, which is primarily involved in mortgage brokering services and the servicing of brokered loans. The fourth subsidiary is Pacific Capital Services Corporation, which is currently inactive.

ANNUAL FINANCIAL DATA

	12/31/99	12/31/98	12/31/97	12/31/96	12/31/95	12/31/94	12/31/93
Earnings Per Share	1.79	1.21	1.29	1.03	0.68	0.85	0.79
Tang. Book Val. Per Share	9.55	8.84	7.75	7.09	6.58	6.11	5.66
Dividends Per Share	0.72	0.61	0.46	0.33	0.27	0.25	0.23
Dividend Payout %	40.2	50.4	35.7	32.0	39.2	29.9	28.7
INCOME STATEMENT (IN MILLIONS):							
Total Interest Income	211.6	193.5	114.9	89.6	82.2	74.9	68.4
Total Interest Expense	67.9	68.1	43.2	35.0	33.6	25.0	22.4
Net Interest Income	143.8	125.4	71.7	54.5	48.6	49.9	46.1
Provision for Loan Losses	6.4	9.1	7.0	4.3	9.9	6.3	6.2
Non-Interest Income	41.6	36.0	25.1	18.9	17.7	13.1	14.1
Non-Interest Expense	110.4	103.7	60.1	46.6	42.0	39.3	37.3
Income Before Taxes	68.6	48.5	29.8	22.6	14.4	17.5	16.7
Net Income	44.3	29.6	20.1	15.7	10.4	13.0	12.3
Average Shs. Outstg. (000)	24,790	24,447	15,584	15,270	15,354	15,294	15,568
BALANCE SHEET (IN MILLIONS):							
Cash & Due from Banks	121.5	114.2	67.8	51.2	74.7	69.6	50.9
Securities Avail. for Sale	153.3	194.8	222.4	276.4	0.5	. . .	. . .
Total Loans & Leases	1,981.9	1,582.8	881.5	684.2	558.8	499.4	464.2
Allowance for Credit Losses	28.7	29.3	21.1	16.6	12.3	12.9	10.1
Net Loans & Leases	1,953.2	1,553.5	860.4	667.6	546.5	486.5	454.2
Total Assets	2,879.3	2,649.4	1,592.4	1,301.3	1,212.4	1,067.6	979.1
Total Deposits	2,440.2	2,329.7	1,404.2	1,113.1	1,054.0	956.7	866.3
Long-Term Obligations	98.8	45.0	39.0	39.0	1.2	1.0	1.2
Total Liabilities	2,644.7	2,435.4	1,474.2	1,193.7	1,111.4	973.7	893.2
Net Stockholders' Equity	234.6	214.0	118.2	107.6	101.0	94.0	86.0
Year-end Shs. Outstg. (000)	24,554	24,209	15,242	15,176	15,358	15,378	15,196
STATISTICAL RECORD:							
Return on Equity %	18.9	13.8	17.0	14.6	10.3	13.8	14.3
Return on Assets %	1.5	1.1	1.3	1.2	0.9	1.2	1.3
Equity/Assets %	8.1	8.1	7.4	8.3	8.3	8.8	8.8
Non-Int. Exp./Tot. Inc. %	59.5	64.3	62.0	63.4	63.3	62.3	62.0
Price Range	38-20⅛	25¾-24¾	. . .	. . .	. . .	. . .	. . .
P/E Ratio	21.2-11.2	21.3-20.5	. . .	. . .	. . .	. . .	. . .
Average Yield %	2.5	2.4	. . .	. . .	. . .	. . .	. . .

Statistics are as originally reported.

OFFICERS:
D. M. Anderson, Chmn.
D. W. Spainhour, Pres.
W. S. Thomas Jr., Vice-Chmn., C.O.O.
D. Lafler, Exec. V.P., C.F.O.

INVESTOR CONTACT: Carol Kelleher, (805) 564-6298

PRINCIPAL OFFICE: 200 E. Carrillo St., Suite 300, Santa Barbara, CA 93101

TELEPHONE NUMBER: (805) 564-6298
FAX: (805) 564-6293
WEB: www.pcbancorp.com

NO. OF EMPLOYEES: 1,100 (approx.)

SHAREHOLDERS: 10,500 (approx.)

ANNUAL MEETING: In Apr.

INCORPORATED: CA, July, 1982

INSTITUTIONAL HOLDINGS:
No. of Institutions: 45
Shares Held: 4,767,355
% Held: 19.4

INDUSTRY: State commercial banks (SIC: 6022)

TRANSFER AGENT(S): Norwest Shareowner Services, South St. Paul, MN

PACIFIC CENTURY FINANCIAL CORPORATION

YIELD	3.2%
P/E RATIO	13.6

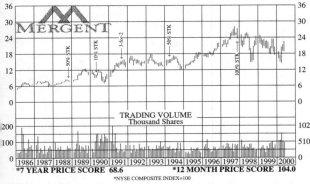

TRADING VOLUME
Thousand Shares

| 1986 | 1987 | 1988 | 1989 | 1990 | 1991 | 1992 | 1993 | 1994 | 1995 | 1996 | 1997 | 1998 | 1999 | 2000 |

*7 YEAR PRICE SCORE 68.6　　　　***12 MONTH PRICE SCORE 104.0**

*NYSE COMPOSITE INDEX=100

INTERIM EARNINGS (Per Share):

Qtr.	Mar.	June	Sept.	Dec.
1996	0.40	0.42	0.38	0.42
1997	0.44	0.44	0.43	0.41
1998	0.42	0.04	0.43	0.43
1999	0.44	0.47	0.27	0.47

INTERIM DIVIDENDS (Per Share):

Amt.	Decl.	Ex.	Rec.	Pay.
0.17Q	4/26/99	5/26/99	5/28/99	6/14/99
0.17Q	7/23/99	8/20/99	8/24/99	9/15/99
0.17Q	10/22/99	11/16/99	11/18/99	12/14/99
0.17Q	1/31/00	2/24/00	2/28/00	3/14/00
0.18Q	4/28/00	5/24/00	5/26/00	6/14/00

Indicated div.: $0.72 (Div. Reinv. Plan)

CAPITALIZATION (12/31/99):

	($000)	(%)
Total Deposits	9,394,218	82.9
Long-Term Debt	727,657	6.4
Minority Interest	4,435	0.0
Common & Surplus	1,212,330	10.7
Total	11,338,640	100.0

DIVIDEND ACHIEVER STATUS:
Rank: 188　　10-Year Growth Rate: 8.71%
Total Years of Dividend Growth: 22

RECENT DEVELOPMENTS: For the year ended 12/31/99, net income advanced 24.3% to $133.0 million from $107.0 million in 1998. Earnings for 1999 and 1998 included restructuring charges of $22.5 million and $19.4 million, respectively, related to BOH's New Era Redesign program. Net interest income fell to $574.7 million from $576.6 million due to a decrease in average earning assets. Total non-interest income grew 25.4% to $265.6 million.

PROSPECTS: Going forward, BOH expects to benefit from its New Era Redesign program, which was announced in September 1999 and is aimed at improving the delivery of financial services in Hawaii and the Pacific. Upon completion of the new program's implemention in the fourth quarter of 2000, the Company estimates total annualized benefits of $43.0 million in cost savings and $21.0 million in revenue enhancements.

BUSINESS

PACIFIC CENTURY FINANCIAL CORPORATION (formerly Bancorp Hawaii, Inc.), with assets of $14.25 billion as of 3/31/00, is a bank holding company that provides a broad range of products and services to customers in Hawaii, the West and South Pacific, Asia, and the U.S. mainland. BOH's principal subsidiaries are the Bank of Hawaii and Pacific Century Bank, N.A.

LOAN DISTRIBUTION

(12/31/99)	($000)	(%)
Commercial & Industrial	2,493,000	25.65
Construction loans	328,900	3.38
Mortgage loans	3,890,200	40.03
Installment	756,100	7.78
Foreign loans	1,621,800	16.69
Lease financing	627,600	6.47
Total	9,717,600	100.0

ANNUAL FINANCIAL DATA

	12/31/99	12/31/98	12/31/97	12/31/96	12/31/95	12/31/94	12/31/93
Earnings Per Share	① 1.64	① 1.32	1.72	1.63	1.45	1.38	1.55
Tang. Book Val. Per Share	12.57	12.07	11.47	12.13	11.69	10.42	9.79
Dividends Per Share	0.68	0.66	0.63	0.58	0.54	0.52	0.45
Dividend Payout %	41.5	49.8	36.3	35.6	37.4	37.8	29.3
INCOME STATEMENT (IN MILLIONS):							
Total Interest Income	1,026.5	1,099.8	1,062.6	982.1	896.7	813.0	808.8
Total Interest Expense	451.8	523.2	526.3	499.8	468.2	363.7	335.4
Net Interest Income	574.7	576.6	536.3	482.3	428.5	449.3	473.4
Provision for Loan Losses	60.9	84.0	30.3	22.2	17.0	21.9	54.2
Non-Interest Income	265.6	211.8	187.8	164.5	146.4	128.4	129.3
Non-Interest Expense	553.2	540.3	474.3	419.8	363.0	359.9	336.1
Income Before Taxes	225.7	163.6	218.0	203.3	193.8	195.4	212.4
Equity Earnings/Minority Int.	d0.5	d0.4	d1.5	d1.4	d1.1	d0.5	. . .
Net Income	① 133.0	① 107.0	135.8	133.1	121.8	117.7	132.6
Average Shs. Outstg. (000)	80,045	81,142	80,946	81,596	84,054	85,650	85,936
BALANCE SHEET (IN MILLIONS):							
Cash & Due from Banks	639.9	564.2	795.3	581.2	469.0	508.8	395.3
Securities Avail. for Sale	2,542.2	3,018.4	2,651.3	2,306.6	2,194.0	1,378.6	967.8
Total Loans & Leases	9,717.6	9,854.0	9,498.4	8,699.3	8,152.4	7,892.0	7,258.4
Allowance for Credit Losses	436.7	437.2	384.1	351.4	299.4	292.5	275.2
Net Loans & Leases	9,280.8	9,416.8	9,114.3	8,347.9	7,853.0	7,599.5	6,983.1
Total Assets	14,440.3	15,016.6	14,995.5	14,009.2	13,206.8	12,586.4	12,462.1
Total Deposits	9,394.2	9,576.3	9,621.3	8,684.1	7,576.8	7,115.1	7,005.0
Long-Term Obligations	727.7	585.6	705.8	932.1	1,063.4	861.6	378.2
Total Liabilities	13,228.0	13,831.0	13,878.3	12,943.0	12,152.3	11,619.6	11,524.0
Net Stockholders' Equity	1,212.3	1,185.6	1,117.2	1,066.1	1,054.4	966.8	938.1
Year-end Shs. Outstg. (000)	80,036	80,326	79,685	79,918	82,682	83,702	85,276
STATISTICAL RECORD:							
Return on Equity %	11.0	9.0	12.5	12.5	11.6	12.2	14.1
Return on Assets %	0.9	0.7	0.9	1.0	0.9	0.9	1.1
Equity/Assets %	8.4	7.9	7.5	7.6	8.0	7.7	7.5
Non-Int. Exp./Tot. Inc. %	67.0	68.9	65.8	65.0	63.4	60.4	56.7
Price Range	24¹⁵/₁₆-17⅜	25⁷/₁₆-14³/₄	28¹/₁₆-20⁵/₁₆	22-16⁹/₁₆	18⁹/₁₆-12⁷/₁₆	17⅜-12¹/₁₆	17¹⁵/₁₆-13⁹/₁₆
P/E Ratio	15.2-10.6	19.6-11.2	16.3-11.8	13.5-10.2	12.8-8.6	12.6-8.8	11.6-8.6
Average Yield %	3.2	3.2	2.6	3.0	3.5	3.5	2.9

Statistics are as originally reported. Adj. for stk. split: 100% div., 12/97; 50% div., 3/94.
① Incl. a restructuring charge of $22.5 mill., 1999; $19.4 mill., 1998.

OFFICERS:
L. M. Johnson, Chmn., C.E.O.
M. P. Carryer, Vice-Chmn.
R. J. Dahl, Pres., C.O.O.
D. A. Houle, Exec. V.P., C.F.O., Treas.

INVESTOR CONTACT: David A. Houle, Exec. V.P., C.F.O. & Treas., (808) 537-8288

PRINCIPAL OFFICE: 130 Merchant St., Honolulu, HI 96813

TELEPHONE NUMBER: (808) 643-3888
FAX: (808) 521-7602
WEB: www.boh.com

NO. OF EMPLOYEES: 4,700 (avg.)

SHAREHOLDERS: 10,396

ANNUAL MEETING: In Apr.

INCORPORATED: HI, Aug., 1971; reincorp., DE, Apr., 1998

INSTITUTIONAL HOLDINGS:
No. of Institutions: 154
Shares Held: 51,881,247
% Held: 64.7

INDUSTRY: State commercial banks (SIC: 6022)

TRANSFER AGENT(S): Continental Stock Transfer & Trust Company, New York, NY

NYSE SYMBOL PLL
Rec. Pr. 21 (5/31/00)

PALL CORPORATION

YIELD 3.1%
P/E RATIO 32.8

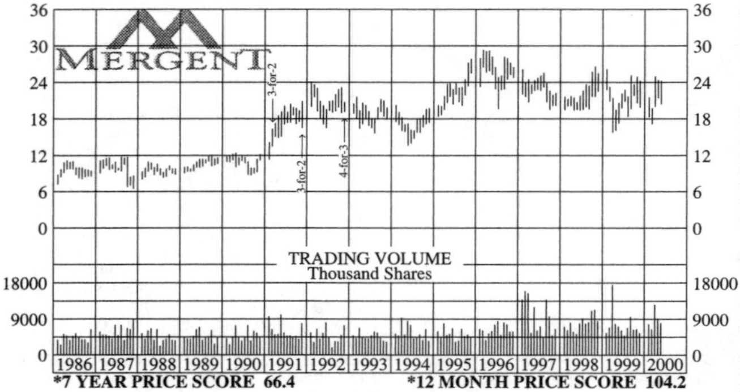

MERGENT
36
30
24
18
12
6
0
3-for-2
3-for-2
4-for-3
TRADING VOLUME
Thousand Shares
18000
9000
0
1986 1987 1988 1989 1990 1991 1992 1993 1994 1995 1996 1997 1998 1999 2000

***7 YEAR PRICE SCORE 66.4** ***12 MONTH PRICE SCORE 104.2**

*NYSE COMPOSITE INDEX=100

INTERIM EARNINGS (Per Share):

Qtr.	Oct.	Jan.	Apr.	July
1996-97	0.14	0.23	d0.18	0.34
1997-98	0.15	0.22	0.06	0.32
1998-99	0.12	0.15	d0.23	0.40
1999-00	0.20	0.27	...	...

INTERIM DIVIDENDS (Per Share):

Amt.	Decl.	Ex.	Rec.	Pay.
0.16Q	4/20/99	4/29/99	5/03/99	5/17/99
0.16Q	6/29/99	7/08/99	7/12/99	8/03/99
0.16Q	10/05/99	10/25/99	10/27/99	11/15/99
0.165Q	1/19/00	1/28/00	2/01/00	2/15/00
0.165Q	4/19/00	5/02/00	5/04/00	5/19/00

Indicated div.: $0.66 (Div. Reinv. Plan)

CAPITALIZATION (7/31/99):

	($000)	(%)
Long-Term Debt	116,815	13.4
Deferred Income Tax	21,232	2.4
Common & Surplus	730,664	84.1
Total	868,711	100.0

DIVIDEND ACHIEVER STATUS:

Rank: 64 10-Year Growth Rate: 14.87%
Total Years of Dividend Growth: 19

RECENT DEVELOPMENTS: For the quarter ended 1/29/00, net income more than doubled to $33.8 million compared with $16.0 million in the equivalent 1999 quarter. The 1999 results included a non-recurring charge of $4.2 million. Net sales were $294.7 million, up 5.9% from $278.3 million a year earlier. Medical segment sales increased 15.3% to $76.1 million, while BioPharmaceuticals segment sales decreased 3.9% to $79.1 million.

PROSPECTS: PLL added filtration manufacturing capacity in Europe through the purchase of a manufacturing plant in Italy, from Instrumentation Laboratory SpA. Demand for filtration to remove leukocytes from blood products is rapidly increasing. The acquisition along with the Company's alliance with the manufacturing arm of the Austrian Red Cross enhances PLL's position in the European market.

BUSINESS

PALL CORPORATION is a supplier of fine filters mainly made by the Company using its proprietary filter media, and other fluid clarification and separations equipment for the removal of solid, liquid and gaseous contaminants from a wide variety of liquids and gases. The Health Care segment consists of two sub-segments: BioPharmaceuticals and Medical. The BioPharmaceuticals sub-segment serves biopharmaceuticals, specialty materials, and food markets, while sales in the Medical sub-segment are primarily to hospitals and blood centers. The Aeropower segment serves aerospace and industrial hydraulics markets. The Fluid Processing segment encompasses the microelectronics and industrial process markets.

ANNUAL FINANCIAL DATA

	7/31/99	8/1/98	8/2/97	8/3/96	7/29/95	7/30/94	7/31/93
Earnings Per Share	**[1] 0.41**	**[2] 0.75**	**[3] 0.53**	**1.21**	**[4] 1.04**	**[1] 0.86**	**[1] 0.68**
Cash Flow Per Share	**1.01**	**1.33**	**1.03**	**1.67**	**1.43**	**1.20**	**1.00**
Tang. Book Val. Per Share	**5.88**	**6.18**	**6.48**	**6.37**	**5.70**	**5.09**	**4.68**
Dividends Per Share	**0.64**	**0.62**	**0.56**	**0.49**	**0.42**	**0.37**	**0.32**
Dividend Payout %	**156.1**	**82.7**	**105.6**	**40.5**	**40.4**	**43.0**	**47.1**
INCOME STATEMENT (IN MILLIONS):							
Total Revenues	1,147.1	1,087.3	1,062.0	967.4	829.3	706.1	691.9
Costs & Expenses	1,000.4	871.4	910.2	706.0	606.1	524.4	542.0
Depreciation & Amort.	74.8	73.1	62.8	53.1	46.1	39.5	37.0
Operating Income	71.9	142.9	89.0	208.3	177.2	142.2	113.0
Net Interest Inc./(Exp.)	d13.0	d7.9	d2.8	d10.4	d9.5	d7.1	d8.7
Income Before Income Taxes	58.9	135.0	86.1	197.9	167.7	135.1	104.3
Income Taxes	7.4	41.4	18.8	59.4	48.5	36.2	26.0
Net Income	[1] 51.5	[2] 93.6	[3] 67.3	138.5	[4] 119.2	[1] 98.9	[1] 78.3
Cash Flow	126.3	166.7	130.1	191.6	165.3	138.5	115.3
Average Shs. Outstg. (000)	124,800	125,681	126,319	114,839	115,184	115,678	115,856
BALANCE SHEET (IN MILLIONS):							
Cash & Cash Equivalents	137.2	28.9	55.5	106.0	110.8	89.0	107.1
Total Current Assets	744.2	602.5	606.6	581.2	524.8	470.4	470.3
Net Property	507.0	520.6	504.0	463.9	427.9	397.6	357.6
Total Assets	1,488.3	1,346.9	1,265.6	1,185.0	1,074.9	959.6	902.3
Total Current Liabilities	558.3	394.1	301.0	330.2	287.7	256.8	277.8
Long-Term Obligations	116.8	111.5	62.1	46.7	68.8	54.1	24.5
Net Stockholders' Equity	730.7	765.6	824.8	732.3	651.8	587.2	542.9
Net Working Capital	185.9	208.4	305.6	251.0	237.0	213.6	192.5
Year-end Shs. Outstg. (000)	124,210	123,919	127,362	114,976	114,431	115,319	116,063
STATISTICAL RECORD:							
Operating Profit Margin %	6.3	13.1	8.4	21.5	21.4	20.1	16.3
Net Profit Margin %	4.5	8.6	6.3	14.3	14.4	14.0	11.3
Return on Equity %	7.0	12.2	8.2	18.9	18.3	16.8	14.4
Return on Assets %	3.5	7.0	5.3	11.7	11.1	10.3	8.7
Debt/Total Assets %	7.8	8.3	4.9	3.9	6.4	5.6	2.7
Price Range	26³⁄₁₆-15³⁄₄	26⁵⁄₈-19³⁄₈	26¹⁄₈-19¹⁄₂	29³⁄₈-19⁵⁄₈	27⁷⁄₈-18³⁄₈	20¹⁄₄-13⁵⁄₈	21⁵⁄₈-15⁵⁄₈
P/E Ratio	63.9-38.4	35.5-25.8	49.3-36.8	24.3-16.2	26.8-17.7	23.5-15.8	31.8-23.0
Average Yield %	3.1	2.7	2.5	2.0	1.8	2.2	1.7

Statistics are as originally reported. [1] Incl. restruct. chrg. $17.3 mill. (d$0.15/sh.), 1993; $2.3 mill., 1994; $89.4 mill., 1999. [2] Incl. non-recurr. income of $5.0 mill. from litigation settlement & a chrg. of $27.0 mill. acq. related Rochem chrg. [3] Incl. merger (Gelman Sciences) restruct. chrgs. & other one-time chrgs. of $95.9 mill. [4] Bef. acctg. chrg. $780,000, 1995.

OFFICERS:
E. Krasnoff, Chmn., C.E.O.
J. Hayward-Surry, Pres.
J. Adamovich, Jr., C.F.O., Treas.
M. Bartlett, Sec.

INVESTOR CONTACT: Diane Foster, Investor Relations, (516) 484-3600

PRINCIPAL OFFICE: 2200 Northern Blvd., East Hills, NY 11548

TELEPHONE NUMBER: (516) 484-5400
FAX: (516) 484-3529
WEB: www.pall.com

NO. OF EMPLOYEES: 8,600

SHAREHOLDERS: 6,900 (approx.)

ANNUAL MEETING: In Nov.

INCORPORATED: NY, July, 1946

INSTITUTIONAL HOLDINGS:
No. of Institutions: 265
Shares Held: 95,412,209
% Held: 76.9

INDUSTRY: General industrial machinery, nec (SIC: 3569)

TRANSFER AGENT(S): Equiserve Trust Co., N.A., Boston, MA

ASE SYMBOL PRK
Rec. Pr. 91¼ (4/30/00)

PARK NATIONAL CORPORATION

YIELD 2.8%
P/E RATIO 18.8

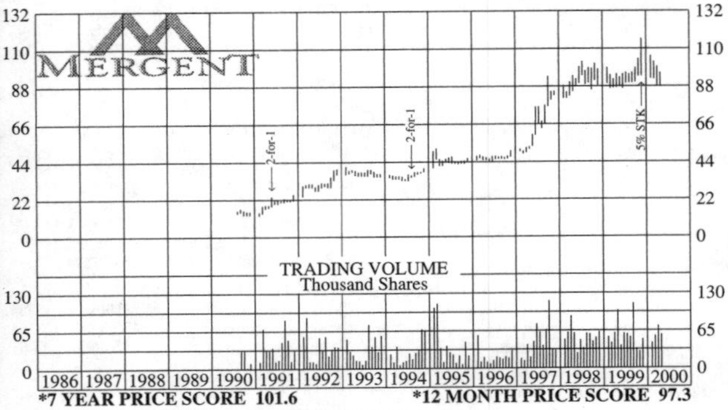

132
110
88
66
44
22
0
MERGENT
2-for-1
2-for-1
5% STK
TRADING VOLUME
Thousand Shares
130
65
0
1986 1987 1988 1989 1990 1991 1992 1993 1994 1995 1996 1997 1998 1999 2000

*7 YEAR PRICE SCORE 101.6 *12 MONTH PRICE SCORE 97.3

*NYSE COMPOSITE INDEX=100

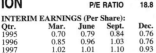

INTERIM EARNINGS (Per Share):

Qtr.	Mar.	June	Sept.	Dec.
1995	0.70	0.79	0.84	0.76
1996	0.85	0.96	1.03	0.76
1997	1.02	1.01	1.10	0.93
1998	1.12	1.17	1.15	0.99
1999	1.24	1.29	1.27	1.06

INTERIM DIVIDENDS (Per Share):

Amt.	Decl.	Ex.	Rec.	Pay.
0.60Q	7/19/99	8/25/99	8/27/99	9/10/99
5% STK	11/15/99	12/01/99	12/03/99	12/15/99
0.65Q	11/15/99	12/21/99	12/23/99	1/03/00
0.65Q	1/18/00	2/16/00	2/18/00	3/10/00
0.65Q	4/17/00	5/24/00	5/26/00	6/09/00

Indicated div.: $2.60 (Div. Reinv. Plan)

CAPITALIZATION (12/31/99):

	($000)	(%)
Total Deposits	2,015,147	89.4
Long-Term Debt	76	0.0
Common & Surplus	239,580	10.6
Total	2,254,803	100.0

DIVIDEND ACHIEVER STATUS:
Rank: 49 10-Year Growth Rate: 16.14%
Total Years of Dividend Growth: 12

RECENT DEVELOPMENTS: For the year ended 12/31/99, net income increased 10.0% to $45.7 million compared with $41.6 million in the previous year. Total interest income increased 3.2% to $191.9 million from $185.9 million in 1998. Total interest expense decreased 2.9% to $76.1 million from $78.3 million the year before. Net interest income increased 7.6% to $115.9 million versus $107.7 million the year before. Interest and fees on loans revenues amounted to $150.9 million, up 2.2% to $147.6 million in 1998. Interest expense on demand and savings deposits declined 19.5% to $12.9 million from $16.0 million, while interest expense on time deposits fell 5.4% to $49.5 million from $52.3 million in 1998. On 4/28/00, the Company announced the acquisitions of U.B. Bancshares, Inc., of Bucyrus, OH and SNB Corp., Greenville, OH. Both banks were merged into PRK as of 4/30/00.

BUSINESS

PARK NATIONAL CORPORATION is a bank holding company with more than $2.60 billion in total assets. Through its subsidiaries, The Park National Bank, The Richland Trust Company, Century National Bank, and The First-Knox National Bank, the Company is engaged in a general commercial banking and trust business. The Company's subsidiaries provide the following principle services: the acceptance of deposits for demand, savings and time accounts and the servicing of these accounts; comercial, industrial, consumer and real estate lending, including installment loans, credit cards, home equity lines of credit and commercial and auto leasing; safe deposit operations; trust services; cash management; electronic funds transfers; and a variety of additional banking-related services tailored to the needs of individual customers. As of 12/31/99, the Company had fifty-nine full service banking offices and a network of sixty-five automatic teller machines in fifteen central and southern Ohio counties.

ANNUAL FINANCIAL DATA

	12/31/99	12/31/98	12/31/97	12/31/96	12/31/95	12/31/94	12/31/93
Earnings Per Share	**4.67**	**4.22**	**3.81**	**3.43**	**2.94**	**2.67**	**1 2.36**
Tang. Book Val. Per Share	**24.60**	**23.50**	**22.52**	**19.89**	**18.21**	**14.86**	**14.30**
Dividends Per Share	**2.29**	**1.83**	**1.52**	**1.33**	**1.14**	**1.08**	**0.90**
Dividend Payout %	**48.9**	**43.3**	**40.0**	**38.9**	**38.8**	**40.4**	**38.3**
INCOME STATEMENT (IN MILLIONS):							
Total Interest Income	191.9	185.9	180.5	122.3	113.2	94.8	90.4
Total Interest Expense	76.1	78.3	77.0	49.3	46.8	35.2	33.8
Net Interest Income	115.9	107.7	103.5	73.0	66.4	59.7	56.6
Provision for Loan Losses	7.0	6.8	7.0	4.5	4.7	1.8	2.8
Non-Interest Income	23.1	24.0	20.5	13.1	12.9	9.0	10.9
Non-Interest Expense	67.5	64.3	62.4	43.2	41.6	37.9	39.1
Income Before Taxes	64.4	60.5	54.6	38.3	33.0	29.0	25.5
Net Income	45.7	41.6	37.7	25.7	22.1	20.0	1 17.5
Average Shs. Outstg. (000)	9,811	9,856	9,908	7,494	7,524	7,513	7,440
BALANCE SHEET (IN MILLIONS):							
Cash & Due from Banks	104.2	100.3	93.6	61.5	92.8	64.1	49.6
Securities Avail. for Sale	619.0	646.4	532.9	386.2	317.4	250.0	304.8
Total Loans & Leases	1,850.7	1,654.0	1,603.6	1,123.6	1,036.3	993.6	882.8
Allowance for Credit Losses	58.0	50.5	47.3	38.8	36.6	34.0	30.6
Net Loans & Leases	1,792.7	1,603.5	1,556.3	1,084.8	999.7	959.6	852.2
Total Assets	2,634.3	2,460.8	2,288.4	1,614.8	1,476.2	1,362.2	1,285.3
Total Deposits	2,015.1	1,939.8	1,855.0	1,336.6	1,206.5	1,078.3	1,058.4
Long-Term Obligations	0.1	8.4	30.9	...	...	...	...
Total Liabilities	2,394.8	2,225.1	2,066.3	1,465.8	1,339.8	1,248.1	1,176.4
Net Stockholders' Equity	239.6	235.7	222.1	149.0	136.4	114.2	108.9
Year-end Shs. Outstg. (000)	9,740	10,031	9,862	7,490	7,492	7,550	7,440
STATISTICAL RECORD:							
Return on Equity %	19.1	17.6	17.0	17.2	16.2	17.5	16.1
Return on Assets %	1.7	1.7	1.6	1.6	1.5	1.5	1.4
Equity/Assets %	9.1	9.6	9.7	9.2	9.2	8.4	8.5
Non-Int. Exp./Tot. Inc. %	48.6	48.9	50.3	50.2	52.5	55.1	58.0
Price Range	116-86 11/16	102 5/8-80 15/16	93 7/8-48 11/16	50 5/8-44 3/16	51 7/8-40 3/8	40 1/2-32 7/8	41 7/16-35 1/4
P/E Ratio	24.8-18.6	24.3-19.2	24.6-12.8	14.8-12.9	17.6-13.7	15.2-12.3	17.5-14.9
Average Yield %	2.3	2.0	2.1	2.8	2.5	2.9	2.4

Statistics are as originally reported. 1 Bef. acctg. change credit $1.5 mill.

OFFICERS:
W. T. McConnell, Chmn.
C. D. DeLawder, Pres., C.E.O.
J. W. Kozak, C.F.O., C.A.O.

PRINCIPAL OFFICE: 50 N. Third St., PO Box 3500, Newark, OH 43058-3500

TELEPHONE NUMBER: (740) 349-8451
FAX: (740) 349-3765
WEB: www.parknationalbank.com

NO. OF EMPLOYEES: 1,023

SHAREHOLDERS: 2,780

ANNUAL MEETING: In Apr.

INCORPORATED: DE, July, 1986; reincorp., OH,

INSTITUTIONAL HOLDINGS:
No. of Institutions: 35
Shares Held: 2,136,841
% Held: 22.0

INDUSTRY: National commercial banks (SIC: 6021)

TRANSFER AGENT(S): First-Knox National Bank, Mount Vernon, OH

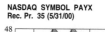

PAYCHEX, INC.

		YIELD	0.7%
		P/E RATIO	76.1

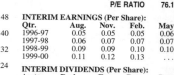

INTERIM EARNINGS (Per Share):

Qtr.	Aug.	Nov.	Feb.	May
1996-97	0.05	0.05	0.05	0.06
1997-98	0.06	0.07	0.07	0.07
1998-99	0.09	0.09	0.10	0.10
1999-00	0.11	0.12	0.13	...

INTERIM DIVIDENDS (Per Share):

Amt.	Decl.	Ex.	Rec.	Pay.
0.06Q	7/08/99	7/29/99	8/02/99	8/16/99
0.09Q	10/07/99	10/28/99	11/01/99	11/15/99
0.09Q	1/13/00	1/28/00	2/01/00	2/15/00
0.09Q	4/13/00	4/27/00	5/01/00	5/15/00
3-for-2	4/13/00	5/23/00	5/12/00	5/22/00

Indicated div.: $0.24 (Adj.)

TRADING VOLUME
Thousand Shares

7 YEAR PRICE SCORE 148.5 *12 MONTH PRICE SCORE 127.0*

*NYSE COMPOSITE INDEX=100

CAPITALIZATION (5/31/99):

	($000)	(%)
Common & Surplus	435,800	100.0
Total	435,800	100.0

DIVIDEND ACHIEVER STATUS:

Rank: 1 10-Year Growth Rate: 42.91%
Total Years of Dividend Growth: 11

RECENT DEVELOPMENTS: For the quarter ended 2/29/00, net income rose 37.1% to $49.6 million versus $36.2 million in the prior-year period. Results benefited from an expanded client base, an increase in client utilization of ancillary services, development of new services, implementation of price increases and a decrease in operating expenses as a percent of service revenues. Total service revenues were $192.2 million, an increase of 21.3% from

$158.4 million the year before. Payroll service revenues climbed 19.1% to $171.8 million, while HRS-PEO service revenues improved 43.7% to $20.4 million. Operating income was $67.9 million from $48.5 million in 1999. Recently, the Company announced that PAYX will expand its mid-sized payroll processing capabilities to serve companies in Atlanta, Baltimore, Boston, Cleveland, Houston, Long Island, Minneapolis, Orlando and Philadelphia.

BUSINESS

PAYCHEX, INC. operates in two business segments: Payroll and Human Resource Services-Professional Employer Organization ("HRS-PEO"). The Payroll segment is engaged in the preparation of payroll checks, internal accounting records, all federal, state and local payroll tax returns, and collection and remittance of payroll obligations for small- to medium-sized businesses. The HRS-PEO segment specializes in providing small- and medium-sized businesses with outsourcing services for their employee benefits. HRS-PEO products include 401(k) plan recordkeeping services, group benefits and workers' compensation insurance services, section 125 plans, employee handbooks and management services.

REVENUES

(05/31/99)	($000)	(%)
Payroll	545,249	91.3
HRS-PEO	52,047	8.7
Total	597,296	100.0

ANNUAL FINANCIAL DATA

	5/31/99	5/31/98	5/31/97	5/31/96	5/31/95	5/31/94	5/31/93
Earnings Per Share	0.37	0.28	0.21	0.15	0.11	0.08	0.06
Cash Flow Per Share	0.46	0.35	0.27	0.19	0.15	0.12	0.09
Tang. Book Val. Per Share	1.18	0.90	0.69	0.55	0.41	0.32	0.25
Dividends Per Share	0.12	0.08	0.05	0.04	0.03	0.02	0.01
Dividend Payout %	32.1	29.0	25.7	23.4	20.7	19.1	17.9
INCOME STATEMENT (IN MILLIONS):							
Total Revenues	1,175.4	993.4	734.7	325.3	267.2	224.1	190.0
Costs & Expenses	955.0	831.5	616.6	243.8	205.1	176.1	152.7
Depreciation & Amort.	32.9	27.3	21.4	13.9	11.0	11.2	10.7
Operating Income	187.6	134.7	96.6	67.5	51.0	36.8	26.7
Net Interest Inc./(Exp.)	12.6	9.5	7.0	5.2	3.4	2.2	1.4
Income Before Income Taxes	200.1	144.2	103.7	72.7	54.4	39.0	28.0
Income Taxes	61.0	42.0	28.5	20.4	15.3	10.9	8.1
Net Income	139.1	102.2	75.2	52.3	39.0	28.1	20.0
Cash Flow	172.0	129.5	96.6	66.3	50.1	39.3	30.7
Average Shs. Outstg. (000)	373,182	370,829	364,503	346,032	341,157	340,124	338,643
BALANCE SHEET (IN MILLIONS):							
Cash & Cash Equivalents	1,704.8	1,405.0	1,079.6	117.2	83.7	55.6	38.1
Total Current Assets	1,793.1	1,478.8	1,140.7	165.3	124.2	87.0	64.2
Net Property	65.9	64.7	54.2	50.0	43.7	42.4	42.1
Total Assets	1,873.1	1,549.8	1,201.3	220.2	168.4	128.9	106.9
Total Current Liabilities	1,432.3	1,215.7	946.0	28.1	26.7	19.0	17.8
Long-Term Obligations	...	...	...	...	0.5	0.7	1.2
Net Stockholders' Equity	435.8	329.6	251.5	190.8	139.9	108.5	85.2
Net Working Capital	360.8	263.1	194.6	137.2	97.6	68.0	46.4
Year-end Shs. Outstg. (000)	369,489	367,173	366,252	347,784	341,962	340,663	339,479
STATISTICAL RECORD:							
Operating Profit Margin %	16.0	13.6	13.2	20.8	19.1	16.4	14.0
Net Profit Margin %	11.8	10.3	10.2	16.1	14.6	12.5	10.5
Return on Equity %	31.9	31.0	29.9	27.4	27.9	25.9	23.4
Return on Assets %	7.4	6.6	6.3	23.8	23.2	21.6	18.7
Debt/Total Assets %	...	...	...	...	0.3	0.6	1.2
Price Range	24½-13⅜	15⁵⁄₁₆-7⁷⁄₁₆	12⁹⁄₁₆-6	6⁹⁄₁₆-3⅜	3⁹⁄₁₆-2½	3⁵⁄₁₆-1	2⁵⁄₁₆-1¼
P/E Ratio	65.5-35.8	55.7-27.4	60.6-29.0	43.2-22.3	31.2-21.8	40.1-23.9	39.9-21.6
Average Yield %	0.6	0.7	0.6	0.7	0.8	0.6	0.6

Statistics are as originally reported. Adj. for stk. splits: 3-for-2, 5/15/00; 5/21/99; 5/22/98; 5/29/97; 5/23/96; 5/25/95; 8/27/93

OFFICERS:
B. T. Golisano, Chmn., Pres. & C.E.O.
J. M. Morphy, V.P., C.F.O. & Sec.

INVESTOR CONTACT: John M. Morphy,
V.P., C.F.O. & Sec., (716) 385-6666

PRINCIPAL OFFICE: 911 Panorama Trail
South, Rochester, NY 14625-0397

TELEPHONE NUMBER: (716) 385-6666
FAX: (716) 383-3428
WEB: www.paychex.com

NO. OF EMPLOYEES: 5,200 full-time; 300 part-time

SHAREHOLDERS: 6,805

ANNUAL MEETING: In Oct.

INCORPORATED: DE, Jun., 1979

INSTITUTIONAL HOLDINGS:
No. of Institutions: 318
Shares Held: 213,406,929 (Adj.)
% Held: 57.7

INDUSTRY: Accounting, auditing, & bookkeeping (SIC: 8721)

TRANSFER AGENT(S): American Stock
Transfer & Trust Company, New York, NY

PENTAIR, INC.

	YIELD	1.6%
	P/E RATIO	17.1

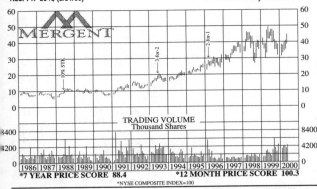

*7 YEAR PRICE SCORE 88.4   *12 MONTH PRICE SCORE 100.3
*NYSE COMPOSITE INDEX=100

INTERIM EARNINGS (Per Share):

Qtr.	Mar.	June	Sept.	Dec.
1996	0.40	0.42	0.46	0.55
1997	0.48	0.50	0.54	0.68
1998	0.54	0.56	0.64	0.76
1999	0.05	0.66	0.69	0.90

INTERIM DIVIDENDS (Per Share):

Amt.	Decl.	Ex.	Rec.	Pay.
0.16Q	4/16/99	4/28/99	4/30/99	5/14/99
0.16Q	7/15/99	7/28/99	7/30/99	8/13/99
0.16Q	10/15/99	10/27/99	10/29/99	11/12/99
0.16Q	1/13/00	1/26/00	1/28/00	2/11/00
0.16Q	4/13/00	4/26/00	4/28/00	5/12/00

Indicated div.: $0.64 (Div. Reinv. Plan)

CAPITALIZATION (12/31/99):

	($000)	(%)
Long-Term Debt	857,296	46.3
Common & Surplus	993,205	53.7
Total	1,850,501	100.0

DIVIDEND ACHIEVER STATUS:
Rank: 175   10-Year Growth Rate: 9.15%
Total Years of Dividend Growth: 23

RECENT DEVELOPMENTS: For the year ended 12/31/99, net income declined 3.3% to $103.3 million from $106.8 million in 1998. Net sales advanced 22.2% to $2.37 billion. On a segment basis, sales from the Professional Tools and Equipment group jumped 26.4% to $1.07 billion, while Water and Fluid Technologies group sales advanced 24.5% to $669.6 million. Sales from the Electrical and Electronic Enclosures group rose 12.4% to $633.7 million.

PROSPECTS: Going forward, the Company plans to grow its business through strategic acquisitions, increased market penetration and by taking full advantage of the positive trend in business activity in Europe and Asia. Near-term prospects remain promising as the demand for power tools and service equipment, clean water and sensitivity electronics increases. The Company expects to meet earnings estimates of $3.64 in fiscal 2000.

BUSINESS

PENTAIR, INC. is a diversified manufacturer operating in three principal markets: professional tools and equipment, water and fluid technologies and electrical and electronic enclosures. The Professional Tools and Equipment segment (45.2% of 1999 sales) is made up of Delta International, Porter-Cable, Century Manufacturing and DeVilbiss Air Power Company, which markets products to professional users and specialized individuals. The Water and Fluid Technologies segment (28.2%), consists of the Pentair pump businesses, Essef businesses, Fleck Controls and Lincoln Industrial. Pentair's Hoffman and Schroff enclosures businesses comprise the Electrical and Electronic Enclosures segment (26.7%). On 10/31/97, the Company sold its sporting ammunitions business.

ANNUAL FINANCIAL DATA

	12/31/99	12/31/98	12/31/97	12/31/96	12/31/95	12/31/94	12/31/93
Earnings Per Share	2.33	2.46	☐ 2.11	☐ 1.83	☐ 1.48	1.31	1.13
Cash Flow Per Share	4.33	3.96	3.59	3.40	2.79	3.05	2.53
Tang. Book Val. Per Share	...	4.71	3.71	5.39	4.18	5.28	5.86
Dividends Per Share	0.64	0.60	0.54	0.50	0.40	0.36	0.34
Dividend Payout %	27.5	24.4	25.6	27.3	27.0	27.5	30.1
INCOME STATEMENT (IN MILLIONS):							
Total Revenues	2,367.8	1,937.6	1,839.1	1,567.1	1,402.9	1,649.2	1,328.2
Costs & Expenses	2,064.8	1,676.0	1,601.4	1,364.6	1,237.7	1,467.6	1,177.9
Depreciation & Amort.	88.6	68.4	67.8	59.5	48.9	64.1	50.1
Operating Income	214.3	193.2	169.8	142.9	116.2	119.2	98.2
Net Interest Inc./(Exp.)	d47.8	d22.2	d21.7	d18.3	d14.6	d30.1	d20.8
Income Before Income Taxes	166.5	170.9	158.4	124.6	101.7	89.1	77.4
Income Taxes	63.2	64.1	66.8	50.1	41.2	35.5	30.8
Equity Earnings/Minority Int.	...	...	...	...	...	1.8	d1.9
Net Income	103.3	106.8	☐ 91.6	☐ 74.5	☐ 60.5	53.6	46.6
Cash Flow	192.0	171.0	154.6	129.1	104.2	112.3	90.6
Average Shs. Outstg. (000)	44,287	43,149	43,067	37,949	37,300	36,844	35,782
BALANCE SHEET (IN MILLIONS):							
Cash & Cash Equivalents	66.2	32.0	34.3	23.0	36.6	32.7	10.3
Total Current Assets	1,150.5	748.6	705.4	614.3	647.2	569.2	438.8
Net Property	403.8	308.3	293.6	298.8	266.7	411.0	315.9
Total Assets	2,803.0	1,554.7	1,472.9	1,289.0	1,252.5	1,281.5	958.8
Total Current Liabilities	760.9	394.8	392.2	301.6	396.8	285.7	218.5
Long-Term Obligations	857.3	288.0	294.5	279.9	219.9	408.5	238.9
Net Stockholders' Equity	993.2	709.4	630.6	563.9	502.9	432.0	370.8
Net Working Capital	389.5	353.8	313.2	312.6	250.4	283.5	220.3
Year-end Shs. Outstg. (000)	48,317	38,504	38,185	37,717	37,035	36,496	36,270
STATISTICAL RECORD:							
Operating Profit Margin %	9.1	10.0	9.2	9.1	8.3	7.2	7.4
Net Profit Margin %	4.4	5.5	5.0	4.8	4.3	3.3	3.5
Return on Equity %	10.4	15.1	14.5	13.2	12.0	12.4	12.6
Return on Assets %	3.7	6.9	6.2	5.8	4.8	4.2	4.9
Debt/Total Assets %	30.6	18.5	20.0	21.7	17.6	31.9	24.9
Price Range	49⁷/₁₆-29⁷/₈	46¼-26¾	39⁷/₈-27¼	32¼-22⅞	26½-19⅞	22⅜-16⅛	20⅝-13
P/E Ratio	21.2-12.8	18.8-10.9	18.9-12.9	17.6-12.5	17.9-13.4	17.1-12.3	18.3-11.5
Average Yield %	1.6	1.6	1.6	1.8	1.7	1.9	2.0

Statistics are as originally reported. Adj. for stk. splits: 2-for-1, 2/96; 3-for-2, 6/93 ☐ Incls. non-recurr. credit 12/31/97: $10.3 mill.; credit 12/31/96: $12.1 mill. ☐ Bef. disc. oper. gain $4.7 mill.

OFFICERS:
W. H. Buxton, Chmn., C.E.O.
J. R. Collins, Vice-Chmn.
R. J. Hogan, Pres., C.O.O.
D. D. Harrison, Exec. V.P., C.F.O.

INVESTOR CONTACT: Mark Cain, (651) 639-5278

PRINCIPAL OFFICE: Waters Edge Plaza, 1500 County Rd. - B2 West, Suite 400, St. Paul, MN 55113-3105

TELEPHONE NUMBER: (651) 636-7920
FAX: (651) 639-5203
WEB: www.pentair.com

NO. OF EMPLOYEES: 13,900 (avg.)

SHAREHOLDERS: 4,395

ANNUAL MEETING: In April

INCORPORATED: MN, Aug., 1966

INSTITUTIONAL HOLDINGS:
No. of Institutions: 169
Shares Held: 31,904,859
% Held: 66.2

INDUSTRY: Woodworking machinery (SIC: 3553)

TRANSFER AGENT(S): Norwest Bank Minnesota, N.A., South St. Paul, MN

NYSE SYMBOL PGL
Rec. Pr. 33 15/16 (5/31/00)

PEOPLES ENERGY CORPORATION

YIELD 5.9%
P/E RATIO 12.2

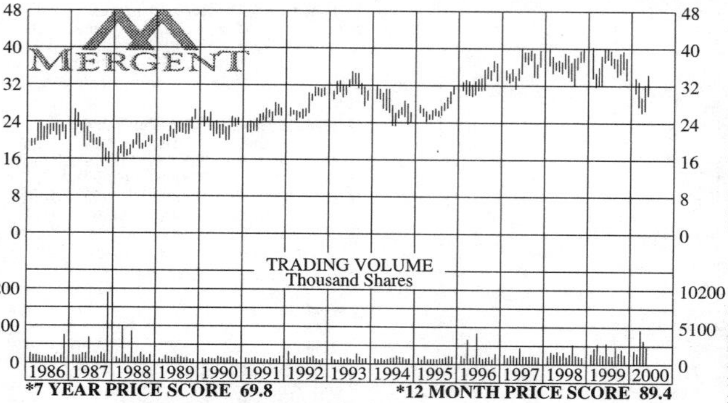

***7 YEAR PRICE SCORE 69.8** ***12 MONTH PRICE SCORE 89.4**

*NYSE COMPOSITE INDEX=100

INTERIM EARNINGS (Per Share):

Qtr.	Dec.	Mar.	June	Sept.
1996-97	1.07	1.81	0.34	d0.40
1997-98	1.01	1.34	0.23	d0.32
1998-99	0.66	1.86	0.20	d0.11
1999-00	0.83	...	...	...

INTERIM DIVIDENDS (Per Share):

Amt.	Decl.	Ex.	Rec.	Pay.
0.49Q	5/05/99	6/18/99	6/22/99	7/15/99
0.49Q	8/03/99	9/20/99	9/22/99	10/15/99
0.49Q	12/01/99	12/20/99	12/22/99	1/14/00
0.50Q	2/02/00	3/20/00	3/22/00	4/14/00
0.50Q	5/18/00	6/20/00	6/22/00	7/14/00

Indicated div.: $2.00 (Div. Reinv. Plan)

CAPITALIZATION (9/30/99):

	($000)	(%)
Long-Term Debt	521,734	32.8
Deferred Income Tax	299,524	18.8
Common & Surplus	768,730	48.3
Total	1,589,988	100.0

DIVIDEND ACHIEVER STATUS:
Rank: 316 10-Year Growth Rate: 2.13%
Total Years of Dividend Growth: 16

RECENT DEVELOPMENTS: For the three months ended 12/31/99, net income increased 26.5% to $29.6 million from $23.4 million in the corresponding period of the previous year. Revenues increased 33.0% to $412.5 million from $310.2 million a year earlier. Gas distribution revenues increased 23.7% to $334.7 million, while Midstream services revenues amounted to $39.8 million. Retail energy services revenues surged 53.8% to $34.7 million from $22.6 million in the prior year.

PROSPECTS: Results should continue to benefit from earnings growth in PGL's diversified energy businesses. The Company anticipates that it will achieve its goal of deriving 25.0% of earnings from these businesses by 2002. Meanwhile, PGL and Dominion Resources Inc. announced the expansion of Elwood Energy LLC's peaking plant in Elwood, IL, by an additional 600 megawatts, which should make a major contribution towards PGL's goal of achieving 25.0% of earnings from diversified businesses.

BUSINESS

PEOPLES ENERGY CORPORATION is a holding company of two natural gas utilites: Peoples Gas Light and Coke Company and North Shore Gas Company. These utilities distribute natural and synthetic gas to 983,000 customers in Chicago and northeastern Illinois. Other operations are conducted through PGL's subsidiaries engaged in non-regulated diversified energy operations. These subsidiaries consists of: Peoples District Energy Corp., a provider of district energy services; Peoples Energy Services, a provider of nonregulated retail energy sales; Peoples Energy Resources, a provider of gas-fired electric generation; Peoples NGV, a fueling station for natural gas fueled vehicles; and Peoples Energy Ventures, which acquires investments in oil and gas production properties.

ANNUAL FINANCIAL DATA

	9/30/99	9/30/98	9/30/97	9/30/96	9/30/95	9/30/94	9/30/93
Earnings Per Share	**2.61**	**2.25**	**2.81**	**2.96**	**1.78**	**2.13**	**2.11**
Cash Flow Per Share	**4.96**	**4.44**	**4.93**	**4.98**	**3.68**	**3.99**	**3.86**
Tang. Book Val. Per Share	**21.66**	**20.94**	**20.43**	**19.48**	**18.38**	**18.39**	**18.05**
Dividends Per Share	**1.95**	**1.91**	**1.87**	**1.83**	**1.80**	**1.79**	**1.77**
Dividend Payout %	**74.7**	**84.9**	**66.5**	**61.8**	**101.1**	**84.3**	**84.1**
INCOME STATEMENT (IN MILLIONS):							
Total Revenues	1,194.4	1,138.1	1,274.4	1,198.7	1,033.4	1,279.5	1,258.9
Costs & Expenses	954.8	858.4	964.5	893.4	788.0	1,042.9	1,011.8
Depreciation & Amort.	83.5	77.2	74.1	70.6	66.4	64.7	60.9
Maintenance Exp.	...	44.0	47.6	45.6	41.7	37.9	35.7
Operating Income	156.0	113.8	133.5	132.4	108.6	101.8	113.0
Net Interest Inc./(Exp.)	d39.5	d35.5	d33.1	d37.5	d43.8	d41.9	d42.2
Income Taxes	52.6	45.1	56.4	62.5	32.6	32.1	37.6
Net Income	92.6	79.4	98.4	103.4	62.2	74.4	73.4
Cash Flow	176.2	156.6	172.5	174.1	128.6	139.1	134.2
Average Shs. Outstg. (000)	35,490	35,276	35,000	34,942	34,901	34,854	34,809
BALANCE SHEET (IN MILLIONS):							
Gross Property	2,330.9	2,210.0	2,117.5	2,046.2	2,088.3	2,019.4	1,951.0
Accumulated Depreciation	811.1	763.3	715.3	665.1	715.2	677.4	633.0
Net Property	1,519.8	1,446.7	1,402.2	1,381.1	1,373.1	1,341.9	1,318.0
Total Assets	2,100.2	1,904.5	1,820.8	1,783.8	1,822.5	1,809.3	1,765.9
Long-Term Obligations	521.7	516.6	527.0	527.1	621.9	626.1	528.1
Net Stockholders' Equity	768.7	741.4	716.5	681.2	641.7	641.4	628.5
Year-end Shs. Outstg. (000)	35,489	35,402	35,070	34,960	34,913	34,868	34,823
STATISTICAL RECORD:							
Operating Profit Margin %	13.1	10.0	10.5	11.0	10.5	8.0	9.1
Net Profit Margin %	7.8	7.0	7.7	8.6	6.0	5.8	5.8
Net Inc./Net Property %	6.1	5.5	7.0	7.5	4.5	5.5	5.6
Net Inc./Tot. Capital %	5.8	5.2	6.6	7.2	4.2	5.1	5.4
Return on Equity %	12.1	10.7	13.7	15.2	9.7	11.6	11.7
Accum. Depr./Gross Prop. %	34.8	34.5	33.8	32.5	34.2	33.5	32.4
Price Range	40¼-31¾	40⅛-32⅛	39⅞-31¼	37⅜-29⅝	32-24¼	32⅛-23 5/16	35-27½
P/E Ratio	15.4-12.2	17.8-14.3	14.2-11.1	12.6-10.0	18.0-13.6	15.1-10.9	16.6-13.0
Average Yield %	5.4	5.3	5.3	5.5	6.4	6.5	5.7

Statistics are as originally reported.

OFFICERS:
R. E. Terry, Chmn., C.E.O.
T. M. Patrick, Pres., C.O.O.
J. M. Luebbers, C.F.O., Contr.

INVESTOR CONTACT: Mary Ann Wall, Manager - Inv. Rel., (312) 240-7534

PRINCIPAL OFFICE: 130 East Randolph Drive, 24th Floor, Chicago, IL 60601-6207

TELEPHONE NUMBER: (312) 240-4000
FAX: (312) 240-4220
WEB: www.pecorp.com

NO. OF EMPLOYEES: 2,810

SHAREHOLDERS: 24,753

ANNUAL MEETING: In Feb.

INCORPORATED: IL, 1967

INSTITUTIONAL HOLDINGS:
No. of Institutions: 169
Shares Held: 16,664,677
% Held: 47.0

INDUSTRY: Natural gas distribution (SIC: 4924)

TRANSFER AGENT(S): Harris Trust and Savings Bank, Chicago, IL.

NYSE SYMBOL PBY
Rec. Pr. 8 (5/31/00)

PEP BOYS-MANNY, MOE & JACK

YIELD 3.4%
P/E RATIO 13.8

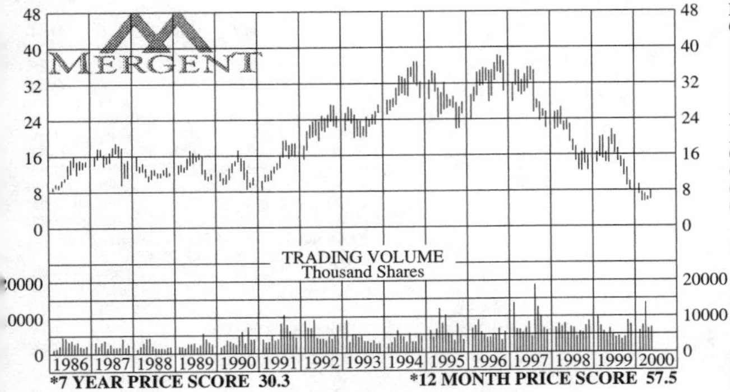

*7 YEAR PRICE SCORE 30.3 *12 MONTH PRICE SCORE 57.5

*NYSE COMPOSITE INDEX=100

INTERIM EARNINGS (Per Share):

Qtr.	Apr.	July	Oct.	Jan.
1996-97	0.33	0.49	0.44	0.36
1997-98	0.37	0.47	0.38	d0.45
1998-99	0.16	0.29	d0.06	d0.31
1999-00	0.20	0.39	0.20	d0.21

INTERIM DIVIDENDS (Per Share):

Amt.	Decl.	Ex.	Rec.	Pay.
0.068Q	6/02/99	7/08/99	7/12/99	7/26/99
0.068Q	8/31/99	10/06/99	10/11/99	10/25/99
0.068Q	12/07/99	1/06/00	1/10/00	1/24/00
0.068Q	3/28/00	4/06/00	4/10/00	4/24/00

Indicated div.: $0.27 (Div. Reinv. Plan)

CAPITALIZATION (1/29/00):

	($000)	(%)
Long-Term Debt	784,024	51.4
Deferred Income Tax	81,964	5.4
Common & Surplus	658,284	43.2
Total	1,524,272	100.0

DIVIDEND ACHIEVER STATUS:
Rank: 159 10-Year Growth Rate: 9.80%
Total Years of Dividend Growth: 22

RECENT DEVELOPMENTS: For the 52 weeks ended 1/29/00, net earnings totaled $29.3 million compared with $5.0 million the year before. The prior-year results included after-tax charges totaling $20.1 million related to the sale and closure of 109 Express stores. Total revenues inched down to $2.39 billion from $2.40 billion a year earlier. Comparable-store sales increased 1.5% during the fiscal year.

PROSPECTS: Going forward, results should benefit from the Company's aggressive efforts to improve profitability. In February, PBY began implementing initiatives that are focused on streamlining and standardizing inventory processes, and are expected to result in increased productivity and higher earnings. The Company anticipates completing the implementation by the end of 2000.

BUSINESS

PEP BOYS-MANNY, MOE & JACK operate a chain of 662 specialty retail stores that sell a full range of brand name and private label automotive parts and accessories at discount prices and offer automotive maintenance and service and the installation of parts. PBY's stores are located in 37 states, mainly in the middle Atlantic, Southwest and Southeast regions of the United States, the District of Columbia, and Puerto Rico. The Supercenter stores contain automotive merchandise along with a full-service maintenance center. The PartsUSA stores do not provide service bays, nor do they stock tires.

REVENUES

(1/29/00)	($000)	(%)
Merchandise Sales	1,954,010	81.6
Service Revenue	440,523	18.4
Total	2,394,533	100.0

ANNUAL FINANCIAL DATA

	1/29/00	1/30/99	1/31/98	2/1/97	2/3/96	1/28/95	1/29/94
Earnings Per Share	**0.58**	**[2] 0.08**	**[2] 0.80**	**1.62**	**1.34**	**[1] 1.32**	**1.06**
Cash Flow Per Share	**2.48**	**1.65**	**2.15**	**2.58**	**2.16**	**2.05**	**1.78**
Tang. Book Val. Per Share	**12.38**	**12.71**	**12.92**	**12.33**	**10.72**	**9.53**	**9.11**
Dividends Per Share	**0.27**	**0.26**	**0.23**	**0.20**	**0.18**	**0.17**	**0.15**
Dividend Payout %	**46.1**	**318.4**	**29.1**	**12.7**	**13.8**	**12.5**	**13.9**
INCOME STATEMENT (IN MILLIONS):							
Total Revenues	2,394.5	2,398.7	2,056.5	1,828.5	1,594.3	1,407.0	1,241.1
Costs & Expenses	2,203.3	2,247.8	1,862.9	1,575.7	1,381.5	1,213.7	1,076.1
Depreciation & Amort.	97.0	96.9	82.9	65.8	53.5	44.4	44.4
Operating Income	94.2	54.1	110.8	187.1	159.4	148.9	120.6
Net Interest Inc./(Exp.)	d51.6	d48.9	d39.7	d30.3	d32.1	d25.9	d19.7
Income Before Income Taxes	45.0	7.3	75.5	159.2	129.5	126.5	104.5
Income Taxes	15.7	2.3	25.8	58.4	48.0	46.5	39.0
Net Income	29.3	[2] 5.0	[2] 49.6	100.8	81.5	[1] 80.0	65.5
Cash Flow	126.3	101.8	132.5	166.6	135.0	124.4	109.9
Average Shs. Outstg. (000)	50,840	61,740	61,657	64,605	62,588	60,565	61,891
BALANCE SHEET (IN MILLIONS):							
Cash & Cash Equivalents	18.5	114.5	10.8	2.6	11.5	11.7	12.1
Total Current Assets	720.7	754.1	770.2	604.9	466.5	411.3	341.7
Net Property	1,335.7	1,330.3	1,377.7	1,189.7	1,014.1	861.9	723.5
Total Assets	2,072.7	2,096.1	2,161.4	1,818.4	1,500.0	1,291.0	1,078.5
Total Current Liabilities	548.4	512.4	618.9	534.2	426.6	289.5	249.2
Long-Term Obligations	784.0	691.7	646.6	455.7	367.0	380.8	253.0
Net Stockholders' Equity	658.3	811.8	822.6	778.1	665.5	586.3	547.8
Net Working Capital	172.3	241.7	151.3	70.7	39.9	121.9	92.5
Year-end Shs. Outstg. (000)	53,189	63,848	63,658	63,119	62,084	61,502	60,112
STATISTICAL RECORD:							
Operating Profit Margin %	3.9	2.3	5.4	10.2	10.0	10.6	9.7
Net Profit Margin %	1.2	0.2	2.4	5.5	5.1	5.7	5.3
Return on Equity %	4.5	0.6	6.0	13.0	12.2	13.6	12.0
Return on Assets %	1.4	0.2	2.3	5.5	5.4	6.2	6.1
Debt/Total Assets %	37.8	33.0	29.9	25.1	24.5	29.5	23.5
Price Range	21⅝-8 1/16	26 11/16-12⅜	35⅝-22	38¼-23⅞	34¾-21⅞	36⅞-25⅛	27⅜-19⅞
P/E Ratio	37.3-13.9	333.2-154.5	44.5-27.5	23.6-14.7	25.9-16.3	27.9-19.0	25.8-18.7
Average Yield %	1.8	1.3	0.8	0.7	0.7	0.5	0.6

Statistics are as originally reported. [1] Bef. $4.3 mil ($0.07/sh) chg. for acctg. adj. [2] Incl. $20.1 mil ($0.33/sh) net non-recur. chg., 1999; $18.4 mil ($0.30/sh) net non-recur. chg., 1998.

OFFICERS:
M. G. Leibovitz, Chmn., Pres., C.E.O.
M. J. Holden, Exec. V.P., C.F.O.
F. A. Stampone, Sr. V.P., C.A.O., Sec.

INVESTOR CONTACT: Nancy R. Kyle, Dir., Investor Relations, (215) 430-9720

PRINCIPAL OFFICE: 3111 West Allegheny Avenue, Philadelphia, PA 19132

TELEPHONE NUMBER: (215) 430-9000
FAX: (215) 227-4067
WEB: www.pepboys.com

NO. OF EMPLOYEES: 20,544 full-time; 7,443 part-time

SHAREHOLDERS: 6,357

ANNUAL MEETING: In May

INCORPORATED: PA, Jan., 1925

INSTITUTIONAL HOLDINGS:
No. of Institutions: 122
Shares Held: 30,482,173
% Held: 57.3

INDUSTRY: Auto and home supply stores (SIC: 5531)

TRANSFER AGENT(S): American Stock & Transfer Company, New York, NY

PEPSICO INC.

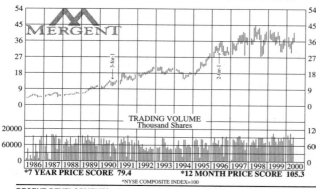

INTERIM EARNINGS (Per Share):

Qtr.	Mar.	June	Sept.	Dec.
1996	0.25	0.36	0.09	0.03
1997	0.27	0.42	0.35	0.29
1998	0.24	0.33	0.50	0.24
1999	0.22	0.49	0.32	0.33

INTERIM DIVIDENDS (Per Share):

Amt.	Decl.	Ex.	Rec.	Pay.
0.135Q	5/05/99	6/09/99	6/11/99	6/30/99
0.135Q	7/22/99	9/08/99	9/10/99	9/30/99
0.135Q	11/18/99	12/08/99	12/10/99	1/03/00
0.135Q	1/27/00	3/08/00	3/10/00	3/31/00
0.14Q	5/03/00	6/07/00	6/09/00	6/30/00

Indicated div.: $0.56 (Div. Reinv. Plan)

CAPITALIZATION (12/25/99):

	($000)	(%)
Long-Term Debt	2,812,000	25.8
Deferred Income Tax	1,209,000	11.1
Common & Surplus	6,881,000	63.1
Total	10,902,000	100.0

TRADING VOLUME
Thousand Shares

*7 YEAR PRICE SCORE 79.4   ***12 MONTH PRICE SCORE 105.3**
*NYSE COMPOSITE INDEX=100

DIVIDEND ACHIEVER STATUS:
Rank: 89   10-Year Growth Rate: 13.28%
Total Years of Dividend Growth: 28

RECENT DEVELOPMENTS: For the year ended 12/25/99, net income rose 2.9% to $2.05 billion from $1.99 billion in the previous year. Total net sales decreased 8.9% to $20.37 billion from $22.35 billion the year before. Net sales from Pepsi-Cola increased 46.4% to $4.38 billion, while Frito-Lay group sales climbed 5.8% to $11.62 billion. Tropicana sales amounted to $2.25 billion. Operating profit amounted to $2.81 billion compared to $2.58 billion a year earlier.

PROSPECTS: Results are benefiting from PEP's strategy of focusing on high-margin, high-return businesses that generate strong cash flow. PEP will be focusing more on its international snack segment going forward. As part of this intiative, PEP plans to expand the Frito-Lay structure from its current two divisions, Frito-Lay North America and Frito-Lay International, by establishing two new companies: Frito-Lay Europe/Middle East/Africa and Frito-Lay Latin America/Asia Pacific/Australia.

BUSINESS

PEPSICO INC. operates on a worldwide basis within the soft drinks, juice and snack-foods businesses. The beverages segment, which accounted for 21% of sales in 1999 (30% of operating profit), manufactures concentrates, and markets PEPSI, PEPSI-COLA, DIET PEPSI, PEPSI ONE, PEPSI MAX, MOUNTAIN DEW, MUG, ALL SPORT, AQUAFINA, MIRINDA, SLICE and allied brands worldwide, and 7-UP internationally. This segment also operates soft drink bottling businesses principally in the United States. The juice segment, 11% (6%), includes Tropicana Products, Inc., which manufactures and sells its products under trademarks such as TROPICANA PURE PREMIUM, and TROPICANA SEASONS BEST. Snack Foods, 57% (70%), manufactures and markets snack chips through Frito-Lay Inc. Well-known brands include: DORITOS, RUFFLES and LAYS. On 10/6/97, the Company spun off its Restaurant unit, TRICON Global Restaurants.

ANNUAL FINANCIAL DATA

	12/25/99	12/26/98	12/27/97	12/28/96	12/30/95	12/31/94	12/25/93
Earnings Per Share	⑤ 1.37	④ 1.31	① 0.95	② 0.72	② 1.00	③ 1.11	0.98
Cash Flow Per Share	2.06	2.12	1.65	1.79	2.08	2.09	1.97
Tang. Book Val. Per Share	1.47	...	0.72	...	...	...	...
Dividends Per Share	0.53	0.51	0.48	0.43	0.38	0.34	0.29
Dividend Payout %	38.7	38.9	50.5	59.7	38.0	30.6	29.6
INCOME STATEMENT (IN MILLIONS):							
Total Revenues	20,367.0	22,348.0	20,917.0	31,645.0	30,421.0	28,472.4	25,020.7
Costs & Expenses	16,452.0	18,530.0	17,149.0	27,380.0	25,694.0	23,694.2	20,670.0
Depreciation & Amort.	1,032.0	1,234.0	1,106.0	1,719.0	1,740.0	1,577.0	1,444.2
Operating Income	2,818.0	2,584.0	2,662.0	2,546.0	2,987.0	3,201.2	2,906.5
Net Interest Inc./(Exp.)	d245.0	d321.0	d353.0	d499.0	d555.0	d554.6	d484.0
Income Before Income Taxes	3,656.0	2,263.0	2,309.0	2,047.0	2,432.0	2,664.4	2,422.5
Income Taxes	1,606.0	270.0	818.0	898.0	826.0	880.4	668.0
Equity Earnings/Minority Int.	83.0	...	...	...	...	...	...
Net Income	⑤ 2,050.0	④ 1,993.0	① 1,491.0	② 1,149.0	② 1,606.0	③ 1,784.0	1,754.5
Cash Flow	3,082.0	3,227.0	2,597.0	2,868.0	3,346.0	3,361.0	3,198.7
Average Shs. Outstg. (000)	1,496,000	1,519,000	1,570,000	1,606,000	1,608,000	1,607,200	1,620,200
BALANCE SHEET (IN MILLIONS):							
Cash & Cash Equivalents	1,056.0	394.0	2,883.0	786.0	1,498.0	1,488.1	1,856.2
Total Current Assets	4,173.0	4,362.0	6,251.0	5,139.0	5,546.0	5,072.2	5,164.1
Net Property	5,266.0	7,318.0	6,261.0	10,191.0	9,870.0	9,882.8	8,855.6
Total Assets	17,551.0	22,660.0	20,101.0	24,512.0	25,432.0	24,792.0	23,705.8
Total Current Liabilities	3,788.0	7,914.0	4,257.0	5,139.0	5,230.0	5,270.4	6,574.9
Long-Term Obligations	2,812.0	4,028.0	4,946.0	8,439.0	8,509.0	8,840.5	7,442.6
Net Stockholders' Equity	6,881.0	6,401.0	6,936.0	6,623.0	7,313.0	6,856.1	6,338.7
Net Working Capital	385.0	d3,552.0	1,994.0	...	316.0	d198.2	d1,410.8
Year-end Shs. Outstg. (000)	1,455,000	1,471,000	1,502,000	1,545,000	1,576,000	1,579,800	1,597,600
STATISTICAL RECORD:							
Operating Profit Margin %	13.8	11.6	12.7	8.0	9.8	11.2	11.6
Net Profit Margin %	10.1	8.9	7.1	3.6	5.3	6.3	7.0
Return on Equity %	29.8	31.1	21.5	17.3	22.0	26.0	27.7
Return on Assets %	11.7	8.8	7.4	4.7	6.3	7.2	7.4
Debt/Total Assets %	16.0	17.8	24.6	34.4	33.5	35.7	31.4
Price Range	42⁹⁄₁₆-30⅛	44¹³⁄₁₆-27⁹⁄₁₆	41⁵⁄₁₆-28¹⁄₄	35⁷⁄₈-27¹⁄₄	29³⁄₈-16¹⁵⁄₁₆	20⁹⁄₁₆-14⅝	21¹³⁄₁₆-17¼
P/E Ratio	31.1-22.0	34.2-21.0	43.5-29.7	49.8-37.8	29.4-16.9	18.5-13.2	22.3-17.6
Average Yield %	1.5	1.4	1.4	1.4	1.6	1.9	1.5

Statistics are as originally reported. Adj. for 2-for-1 stk. split, 5/96 ① Incls. non-recurr. chrgs. $290.0 million; bef. disc. oper. gain $651.0 mill. ② Incls. non-recurr. chrgs. 1/31/96, $716.0 mill.; non-cash chrg. 12/31/95, $520.0 mill. ③ Bef. acctg. change chrg. 12/31/94: $32.0 mill. ④ Incl. one-time chrg. of $288.0 mill. ⑤ Incls. one-time chrg of $65.0 mill.

OFFICERS:
R. A. Enrico, Chmn., C.E.O.
K. M. von der Heyden, Vice-Chmn.
S. S. Reinemund, Pres., C.O.O.

INVESTOR CONTACT: M. D. Moore, (914) 253-3035

PRINCIPAL OFFICE: 700 Anderson Hill Rd., Purchase, NY 10577-1444

TELEPHONE NUMBER: (914) 253-2000
FAX: (914) 253-2070
WEB: www.pepsico.com
NO. OF EMPLOYEES: 118,000 (approx.)
SHAREHOLDERS: 220,000 (approx.)
ANNUAL MEETING: In May
INCORPORATED: DE, Sep., 1919; reincorp., NC, Dec., 1986

INSTITUTIONAL HOLDINGS:
No. of Institutions: 903
Shares Held: 859,297,794
% Held: 59.0

INDUSTRY: Bottled and canned soft drinks (SIC: 2086)

TRANSFER AGENT(S): BankBoston, N.A., Boston, MA

PFIZER INC.

YIELD		0.8%
P/E RATIO		57.1

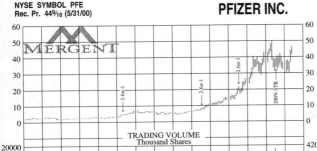

TRADING VOLUME
Thousand Shares

| 1986 | 1987 | 1988 | 1989 | 1990 | 1991 | 1992 | 1993 | 1994 | 1995 | 1996 | 1997 | 1998 | 1999 | 2000 |

*7 YEAR PRICE SCORE 125.7   *12 MONTH PRICE SCORE 114.2
*NYSE COMPOSITE INDEX=100

INTERIM EARNINGS (Per Share):

Qtr.	Mar.	June	Sept.	Dec.
1995	0.11	0.08	0.11	0.11
1996	0.14	0.10	0.13	0.13
1997	0.16	0.12	0.15	0.14
1998	0.18	0.16	0.13	0.08
1999	0.16	0.19	0.18	0.25

INTERIM DIVIDENDS (Per Share):

Amt.	Decl.	Ex.	Rec.	Pay.
200% STK	4/22/99	7/01/99	6/02/99	6/30/99
0.08Q	6/24/99	8/04/99	8/06/99	9/09/99
0.08Q	10/28/99	11/09/99	11/12/99	12/09/99
0.09Q	12/13/99	2/16/00	2/18/00	3/09/00
0.09Q	4/27/00	5/09/00	5/11/00	6/08/00

Indicated div.: $0.36 (Div. Reinv. Plan)

CAPITALIZATION (12/31/99):

	($000)	(%)
Long-Term Debt	525,000	5.4
Deferred Income Tax	301,000	3.1
Common & Surplus	8,887,000	91.5
Total	9,713,000	100.0

DIVIDEND ACHIEVER STATUS:
Rank: 98   10-Year Growth Rate: 12.83%
Total Years of Dividend Growth: 32

RECENT DEVELOPMENTS: For the year ended 12/31/99, income from continuing operations soared 64.1% to $3.20 billion compared with $1.95 billion in 1998. The 1999 results included a charge of $310.0 million to write off TROVAN inventories. Results for 1998 included non-recurring charges of $909.0 million. Total revenues increased 19.6% to $16.20 billion from $13.54 billion a year earlier. Worldwide revenues of pharmaceutical advanced 21.4% to $14.86 billion due the strength of in-line products.

PROSPECTS: The Company entered into a definitive agreement to acquire all outstanding shares of Warner-Lambert Company for $98.31 per share or $90.00 billion. The combined company will have annual revenues of approximately $28.00 billion, including $21.00 billion in prescription pharmaceutical sales and a market capitalization of over $230.00 billion. The transaction should be accretive to earnings in the first full year of operations.

BUSINESS

PFIZER INC. is a research-based, global pharmaceutical company that discovers, develops, manufactures and markets innovative medicines for humans and animals. The Company operates in two business segments. The pharmaceutical segment includes prescription pharmaceuticals for treating cardiovascular diseases, infectious diseases, central nervous system disorders, diabetes, erectile dysfunction, allergies, arthritis and other disorders, as well as non-prescription self-medications. The animal health segment includes anti-parasitic, anti-infective and anti-inflammatory medicines, and vaccines for livestock, poultry and companion animals. Revenues for 1999 were derived as follows: 91.6% from the pharmaceutical segment and 8.4% from the animal health segment.

ANNUAL FINANCIAL DATA

	12/31/99	12/31/98	12/31/97	12/31/96	12/31/95	12/31/94	12/31/93
Earnings Per Share	[4] 0.82	[3] 0.49	0.57	0.50	[2] 0.41	0.35	[1] 0.17
Cash Flow Per Share	0.96	0.62	0.69	0.61	0.51	0.43	0.24
Tang. Book Val. Per Share	2.11	2.06	1.75	1.35	1.03	0.96	0.93
Dividends Per Share	0.31	0.25	0.23	0.20	0.17	0.16	0.14
Dividend Payout %	37.4	51.7	40.0	40.2	42.1	44.9	81.8
INCOME STATEMENT (IN MILLIONS):							
Total Revenues	16,204.0	13,544.0	12,504.0	11,306.0	10,021.4	8,281.3	7,477.7
Costs & Expenses	11,113.0	9,452.0	8,656.0	7,796.0	7,087.2	6,016.8	6,306.2
Depreciation & Amort.	542.0	489.0	502.0	430.0	374.0	292.0	258.2
Operating Income	4,549.0	3,603.0	3,346.0	3,080.0	2,560.2	1,972.5	913.3
Income Before Income Taxes	4,448.0	2,594.0	3,088.0	2,804.0	2,299.2	1,861.5	851.4
Income Taxes	1,244.0	642.0	865.0	869.0	738.0	558.5	191.3
Equity Earnings/Minority Int.	d5.0	d2.0	d10.0	d6.0	d7.0	d4.6	d2.6
Net Income	[4] 3,199.0	[3] 1,950.0	2,213.0	1,929.0	[2] 1,554.2	1,298.4	[1] 657.5
Cash Flow	3,741.0	2,439.0	2,715.0	2,359.0	1,928.2	1,590.4	915.7
Average Shs. Outstg. (000)	3,884,000	3,945,000	3,909,000	3,864,000	3,777,000	3,722,580	3,844,800
BALANCE SHEET (IN MILLIONS):							
Cash & Cash Equivalents	4,442.0	3,929.0	1,589.0	1,637.0	1,512.0	2,018.6	1,176.5
Total Current Assets	11,191.0	9,931.0	6,820.0	6,468.0	6,154.4	5,788.4	4,733.2
Net Property	5,343.0	4,415.0	4,137.0	3,850.0	3,472.6	3,073.2	2,632.5
Total Assets	20,574.0	18,302.0	15,336.0	14,667.0	12,729.3	11,098.5	9,330.9
Total Current Liabilities	9,185.0	7,192.0	5,305.0	5,640.0	5,187.2	4,825.9	3,443.6
Long-Term Obligations	525.0	527.0	729.0	687.0	833.0	604.2	570.5
Net Stockholders' Equity	8,887.0	8,810.0	8,103.0	6,664.0	5,179.8	3,931.9	3,802.1
Net Working Capital	2,006.0	2,739.0	1,515.0	828.0	965.2	962.5	1,289.6
Year-end Shs. Outstg. (000)	3,847,000	3,883,000	3,882,000	3,870,000	3,823,602	3,770,712	3,851,064
STATISTICAL RECORD:							
Operating Profit Margin %	28.1	26.6	26.8	27.2	25.5	23.8	12.2
Net Profit Margin %	19.7	14.4	17.7	17.1	15.5	15.7	8.8
Return on Equity %	36.0	22.1	27.3	28.9	30.0	33.0	17.3
Return on Assets %	15.5	10.7	14.4	13.2	12.2	11.7	7.0
Debt/Total Assets %	2.6	2.9	4.8	4.7	6.5	5.4	6.1
Price Range	50¹/₁₆-31½	42-23¹¹/₁₆	26¹¹/₁₆-13⁷/₁₆	15³/₁₆-13⁷/₁₆	11⅛-6³/₁₆	6⁵/₈-4⁷/₁₆	6⁵/₁₆-4³/₈
P/E Ratio	61.0-38.5	87.7-48.3	47.0-23.7	30.5-20.2	27.0-15.1	18.9-12.7	36.8-25.6
Average Yield %	0.8	0.8	1.1	1.6	2.0	2.8	2.6

Statistics are as originally reported. Adj. for stock splits: 200% div., 6/30/99; 2-for-1, 9/97 & 6/95. [1] Incl. chg. for restruct. & unusual items of $750.0 mill. [2] Excl. gain of $18.8 mill. for dis. ops. [3] Incl. unusual & nonrecurr. pre-tax chgs. total. $1.37 bill. for TROVAN inventories; excl. a $1.40 bill. gain from disc. opers. [4] Incl. after-tax charge of $310.0 mill.

OFFICERS:
W. C. Steere Jr., Chmn., C.E.O.
J. F. Niblack Ph.D., Vice-Chmn.
H. A. McKinnell, Pres., C.O.O.
D. Shedlarz, Exec. V.P., C.F.O.

PRINCIPAL OFFICE: 235 East 42nd St., New York, NY 10017-5755

TELEPHONE NUMBER: (212) 573-2323
FAX: (212) 573-2641
WEB: www.pfizer.com
NO. OF EMPLOYEES: 50,900 (approx.)
SHAREHOLDERS: 149,747
ANNUAL MEETING: In Apr.
INCORPORATED: DE, 1942

INSTITUTIONAL HOLDINGS:
No. of Institutions: 1,029
Shares Held: 1,874,006,572
% Held: 48.4

INDUSTRY: Pharmaceutical preparations (SIC: 2834)

TRANSFER AGENT(S): First Chicago Trust Company of New York, Jersey City, NJ

NYSE SYMBOL MO
Rec. Pr. 26⅛ (5/31/00)

PHILIP MORRIS COMPANIES, INC.

YIELD 7.3%
P/E RATIO 8.2

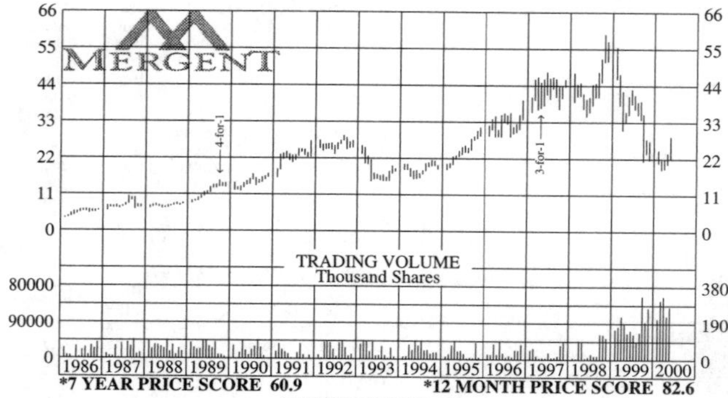

*7 YEAR PRICE SCORE 60.9 *12 MONTH PRICE SCORE 82.6
*NYSE COMPOSITE INDEX=100

INTERIM EARNINGS (Per Share):

Qtr.	Mar.	June	Sept.	Dec.
1996	0.63	0.66	0.67	0.60
1997	0.73	0.76	0.58	0.53
1998	0.57	0.74	0.81	0.11
1999	0.73	0.84	0.84	0.79

INTERIM DIVIDENDS (Per Share):

Amt.	Decl.	Ex.	Rec.	Pay.
0.44Q	2/24/99	3/11/99	3/15/99	4/12/99
0.44Q	5/26/99	6/11/99	6/15/99	7/12/99
0.48Q	8/25/99	9/13/99	9/15/99	10/12/99
0.48Q	11/24/99	12/13/99	12/15/99	1/10/00
0.48Q	3/10/00	3/16/00	3/20/00	4/10/00

Indicated div.: $1.92 (Div. Reinv. Plan)

CAPITALIZATION (12/31/99):

	($000)	(%)
Long-Term Debt	12,226,000	36.8
Deferred Income Tax	5,680,000	17.1
Common & Surplus	15,305,000	46.1
Total	33,211,000	100.0

DIVIDEND ACHIEVER STATUS:
Rank: 47 10-Year Growth Rate: 16.35%
Total Years of Dividend Growth: 31

RECENT DEVELOPMENTS: For the year ended 12/31/99, net earnings increased 42.9% to $7.68 billion from $5.37 billion in the previous year. Results for 1999 included pre-tax charges of $136.0 million related to the International tobacco Brazil capacity reduction and separation program and pre-tax charges of $340.0 million related to separation programs. Results for 1998 included pre-tax charges of $319.0 million related to other separation programs and pre-tax non-recurring settlement charges totaling $3.38 billion. Operating revenues increased 5.7% to $78.60 billion.

PROSPECTS: The Company announced plans to phase out cigarette production capacity at its manufacturing facility in Louisville, KY, by August 2000. The Company predicts that its domestic tobacco shipments may continue to be materially adversely affected by price increases related to tobacco litigation settlements and, if enacted, by increased excise taxes or other tobacco legislation. Meanwhile, MO's international tobacco business is benefiting from solid volume and share gains in most of its profitable markets.

BUSINESS

PHILIP MORRIS COMPANIES, INC. is one of the world's largest consumer products company with major operations in tobacco, food, and beer. Tobacco (66% of 1999 operating profit) is manufactured and sold through Philip Morris U.S.A. and Philip Morris International Inc. Retail packaged foods (29%) are processed and marketed through Kraft Foods Inc. in the U.S. and Canada and Kraft Foods International in Europe and the Asia/Pacific region. Miller Brewing Co. (3%) produces MILLER/Miller Lite, LOWENBRAU and MILLER GENUINE DRAFT beers. Philip Morris Capital Corporation (2%) engages in financing and investment activities. In May 1993, Kraft General Foods acquired Freia Marabou A.S., a Norwegian confectionary and snack food company.

ANNUAL FINANCIAL DATA

	12/31/99	12/31/98	12/31/97	12/31/96	12/31/95	12/31/94	12/31/93
Earnings Per Share	[3] **3.19**	[1] **2.20**	[1] **2.58**	**2.56**	[2] **2.17**	**1.82**	[2] **1.35**
Cash Flow Per Share	**3.90**	**2.89**	**3.25**	**3.25**	**2.83**	**2.48**	**1.97**
Dividends Per Share	**1.80**	**1.64**	**1.60**	**1.40**	**1.16**	**0.95**	**0.87**
Dividend Payout %	**56.4**	**74.5**	**62.0**	**54.7**	**53.5**	**52.4**	**64.1**
INCOME STATEMENT (IN MILLIONS):							
Total Revenues	78,596.0	74,391.0	72,055.0	69,204.0	66,071.0	65,125.0	60,901.0
Costs & Expenses	63,404.0	62,724.0	58,763.0	55,744.0	53,874.0	53,954.0	51,695.0
Depreciation & Amort.	1,702.0	1,690.0	1,629.0	1,691.0	1,671.0	1,722.0	1,619.0
Operating Income	13,490.0	9,977.0	11,663.0	11,769.0	10,526.0	9,449.0	7,587.0
Net Interest Inc./(Exp.)	d795.0	d890.0	d1,052.0	d1,086.0	d1,179.0	d1,233.0	d1,391.0
Income Before Income Taxes	12,695.0	9,087.0	10,611.0	10,683.0	9,347.0	8,216.0	6,196.0
Income Taxes	5,020.0	3,715.0	4,301.0	4,380.0	3,869.0	3,491.0	2,628.0
Net Income	[3] 7,675.0	[1] 5,372.0	[1] 6,310.0	6,303.0	[2] 5,478.0	4,725.0	[2] 3,568.0
Cash Flow	9,377.0	7,062.0	7,939.0	7,994.0	7,149.0	6,447.0	5,187.0
Average Shs. Outstg. (000)	2,403,000	2,446,000	2,442,000	2,463,327	2,524,674	2,601,867	2,634,363
BALANCE SHEET (IN MILLIONS):							
Cash & Cash Equivalents	5,100.0	4,081.0	2,282.0	240.0	1,138.0	184.0	182.0
Total Current Assets	20,895.0	20,230.0	17,440.0	15,190.0	14,879.0	13,908.0	12,808.0
Net Property	12,271.0	12,335.0	11,621.0	11,751.0	11,116.0	11,171.0	10,463.0
Total Assets	61,381.0	59,920.0	55,947.0	54,871.0	53,811.0	52,649.0	51,205.0
Total Current Liabilities	18,017.0	16,379.0	15,071.0	15,040.0	14,944.0	13,569.0	14,468.0
Long-Term Obligations	12,226.0	12,615.0	12,430.0	12,961.0	13,107.0	14,975.0	15,221.0
Net Stockholders' Equity	15,305.0	16,197.0	14,920.0	13,834.0	13,051.0	12,880.0	13,049.0
Net Working Capital	2,878.0	3,851.0	2,369.0	150.0	d65.0	339.0	d1,660.0
Year-end Shs. Outstg. (000)	2,338,520	2,431,000	2,425,487	2,431,347	2,493,510	2,558,577	2,631,273
STATISTICAL RECORD:							
Operating Profit Margin %	17.2	13.4	16.2	17.0	15.9	14.5	12.5
Net Profit Margin %	9.8	7.2	8.8	9.1	8.3	7.3	5.9
Return on Equity %	50.1	33.2	42.3	45.6	42.0	36.7	27.3
Return on Assets %	12.5	9.0	11.3	11.5	10.2	9.0	7.0
Debt/Total Assets %	19.9	21.1	22.2	23.6	24.4	28.4	29.7
Price Range	55 9/16-21 1/4	59 1/2-34 3/4	48 1/8-36	39 11/16-28 9/16	31 7/16-18 9/16	21 1/2-15 3/4	25 7/8-15
P/E Ratio	17.4-6.7	27.0-15.8	18.7-14.0	15.5-11.1	14.5-8.6	11.8-8.7	19.1-11.1
Average Yield %	4.7	3.5	3.8	4.1	4.6	5.1	4.2

Statistics are as originally reported. Adj. for 3-for-1 stk. split, 4/97 [1] Incls. pre-tax non-recurr. chrg. 12/31/98, $3.38 bill.; 12/31/97, $1.46 bill. [2] Bef. acctg. change chrg. 12/31/95, $28.0 mill.; 12/31/93, $477.0 mill. [3] Incls. one-time chrgs. of $476.0 mill. for separation programs.

OFFICERS:
G. C. Bible, Chmn., C.E.O.
M. H. Bring, Vice-Chmn., Couns.
L. C. Camilleri, Sr. V.P., C.F.O.

INVESTOR CONTACT: Nicholas M. Rolli, (917) 663-3460

PRINCIPAL OFFICE: 120 Park Ave., New York, NY 10017

TELEPHONE NUMBER: (917) 663-5000
FAX: (917) 878-2167
WEB: www.pmdocs.com

NO. OF EMPLOYEES: 137,000 (approx.)

SHAREHOLDERS: 139,700 (approx.)

ANNUAL MEETING: In April

INCORPORATED: VA, Mar., 1985

INSTITUTIONAL HOLDINGS:
No. of Institutions: 756
Shares Held: 1,358,020,102
% Held: 57.4

INDUSTRY: Cigarettes (SIC: 2111)

TRANSFER AGENT(S): First Chicago Trust Company of New York, Jersey City, NJ

NYSE SYMBOL PNY
Rec. Pr. 29 3/4 (5/31/00)

PIEDMONT NATURAL GAS COMPANY, INC.

YIELD 4.9%
P/E RATIO 15.0

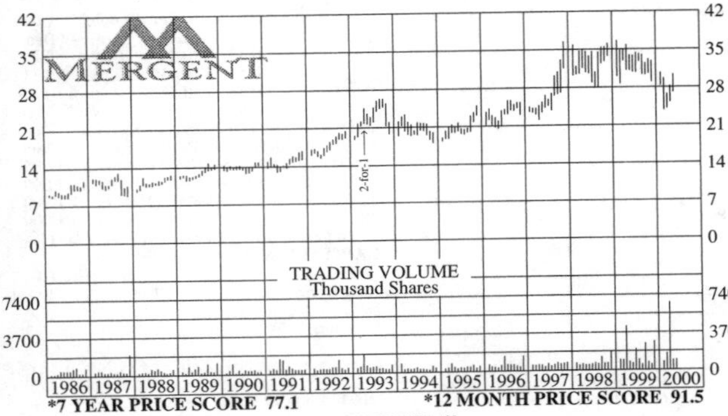

*7 YEAR PRICE SCORE 77.1 *12 MONTH PRICE SCORE 91.5

*NYSE COMPOSITE INDEX=100

INTERIM EARNINGS (Per Share):

Qtr.	Jan.	Apr.	July	Oct.
1995-96	1.18	1.12	d0.28	d0.33
1996-97	1.26	1.08	d0.19	d0.32
1997-98	1.36	1.17	d0.20	d0.35
1998-99	1.32	1.12	d0.26	d0.28
1999-00	1.40	...	...	...

INTERIM DIVIDENDS (Per Share):

Amt.	Decl.	Ex.	Rec.	Pay.
0.345Q	2/26/99	3/23/99	3/25/99	4/15/99
0.345Q	6/04/99	6/22/99	6/24/99	7/15/99
0.345Q	8/27/99	9/22/99	9/24/99	10/15/99
0.345Q	12/03/99	12/21/99	12/23/99	1/14/00
0.365Q	2/25/00	3/22/00	3/24/00	4/14/00

Indicated div.: $1.46 (Div. Reinv. Plan)

CAPITALIZATION (10/31/99):

	($000)	(%)
Long-Term Debt	423,000	41.0
Deferred Income Tax	116,134	11.3
Common & Surplus	491,747	47.7
Total	1,030,881	100.0

DIVIDEND ACHIEVER STATUS:
Rank: 251 10-Year Growth Rate: 5.65%
Total Years of Dividend Growth: 20

RECENT DEVELOPMENTS: For the quarter ended 1/31/00, net income rose 8.7% to $44.1 million compared with $40.6 million in the corresponding quarter of 1999. Operating revenues grew 5.0% to $268.6 million from $255.7 million in the previous year. Results were positively affected by the SouthStar Energy Services joint venture and the Pine Needle LNG joint venture storage facility. System throughput rose 2.5% to 44.3 million dekatherms.

PROSPECTS: The Company agreed to form a joint venture that combines its propane operations with the operations of AGL Resources, Atmos Energy Corporation and TECO Energy. The combined entity, called U.S. Propane L.P., will be among the ten largest propane retailers, with close to 200,000 customers. The transaction is subject to regulatory and customary approval and is expected to be completed by 5/1/00.

BUSINESS

PIEDMONT NATURAL GAS COMPANY, INC. is engaged in the purchase, distribution and sale of natural gas to 710,000 residential, commercial and industrial customers in North Carolina, South Carolina and Tennessee. Non-utility subsidiaries and divisions are involved in the exploration, development, marketing and transportation of natural gas, oil, and propane. PNY's utility operations are subject to regulation by the North Carolina Utilities Commission, the Tennessee Public Service Commission and the Public Service Commission of South Carolina. PNY also owns Tennessee Natural Resources, Inc., and its subsidiaries. In 1999, revenues were derived as follows: 43.0% residential, 24.0% commercial, 21.0% industrial, 11.0% secondary market sales, and 1.0% other. PNY serves nearly 48,000 propane customers in a three-state area.

ANNUAL FINANCIAL DATA

	10/31/99	10/31/98	10/31/97	10/31/96	10/31/95	10/31/94	10/31/93
Earnings Per Share	**1.86**	**1.96**	**[1] 1.81**	**1.67**	**1.45**	**1.35**	**1.45**
Cash Flow Per Share	**3.40**	**3.46**	**3.26**	**3.04**	**2.73**	**2.42**	**2.42**
Tang. Book Val. Per Share	**15.71**	**14.91**	**13.90**	**13.07**	**12.31**	**11.36**	**10.90**
Dividends Per Share	**1.36**	**1.28**	**1.21**	**1.15**	**1.08**	**1.02**	**0.96**
Dividend Payout %	**73.1**	**65.3**	**66.6**	**68.6**	**74.8**	**75.9**	**66.5**
INCOME STATEMENT (IN THOUSANDS):							
Total Revenues	686,470	765,277	775,517	685,055	505,223	575,354	552,760
Costs & Expenses	492,904	576,050	599,982	526,934	365,279	456,031	434,331
Depreciation & Amort.	47,917	46,113	43,441	40,107	35,712	28,366	25,313
Maintenance Exp.	15,562	14,708	16,160	15,776	16,409	15,526	14,969
Operating Income	91,722	91,157	83,986	74,629	65,312	55,870	56,575
Net Interest Inc./(Exp.)	d32,371	d33,187	d33,996	d31,067	d29,478	d24,541	d21,907
Income Taxes	38,365	37,249	31,948	27,609	22,511	19,561	21,572
Net Income	58,207	60,313	[1] 54,074	48,562	40,310	35,506	37,534
Cash Flow	106,124	106,426	97,515	88,669	76,022	63,872	62,847
Average Shs. Outstg.	31,242	30,717	29,883	29,161	27,890	26,346	25,960
BALANCE SHEET (IN THOUSANDS):							
Gross Property	1,441,322	1,345,925	1,256,772	1,168,448	1,074,666	978,218	876,927
Accumulated Depreciation	420,140	381,585	342,418	306,419	273,350	243,325	222,423
Net Property	1,046,975	990,640	941,736	889,101	827,615	760,081	677,910
Total Assets	1,288,657	1,162,844	1,098,156	1,064,916	964,895	887,770	796,453
Long-Term Obligations	423,000	371,000	381,000	391,000	361,000	313,000	278,000
Net Stockholders' Equity	491,747	458,268	419,826	386,091	354,979	301,992	285,020
Year-end Shs. Outstg.	31,295	30,738	30,193	29,549	28,835	26,577	26,152
STATISTICAL RECORD:							
Operating Profit Margin %	13.4	11.9	10.8	10.9	12.9	9.7	10.2
Net Profit Margin %	8.5	7.9	7.0	7.1	8.0	6.2	6.8
Net Inc./Net Property %	5.6	6.1	5.7	5.5	4.9	4.7	5.5
Net Inc./Tot. Capital %	5.6	6.4	6.0	5.6	5.0	5.2	5.8
Return on Equity %	11.8	13.2	12.9	12.6	11.4	11.8	13.2
Accum. Depr./Gross Prop. %	29.1	28.4	27.2	26.2	25.4	24.9	25.4
Price Range	36 5/8-28 5/8	36 1/8-27 7/8	36 7/16-22	25 3/4-20 1/2	24 7/8-18 1/4	23 3/8-18	26 3/8-18 13/16
P/E Ratio	19.7-15.4	18.4-14.2	20.1-12.2	15.4-12.3	17.2-12.6	17.3-13.3	18.2-13.0
Average Yield %	4.2	4.0	4.1	5.0	5.0	5.0	4.3

Statistics are as originally reported. Adjusted for 2-for-1 stock split 3/93. [1] Incl. pre-tax restruct. chg. of $1.8 mill.

OFFICERS:
J. H. Maxhiem, Chmn.
W. F. Schiefer, Pres., C.E.O.
T. C. Coble, Treas., V.P., Asst. Sec.
M. C. Ruegsegger, V.P., Corp. Couns., Sec.

INVESTOR CONTACT: Headen B. Thomas, Dir. Inv. Rel. (704 364-3120 ext.6438

PRINCIPAL OFFICE: 1915 Rexford Road, Charlotte, NC 28211

TELEPHONE NUMBER: (704) 364-3120
FAX: (704) 365-8515
WEB: www.piedmontng.com

NO. OF EMPLOYEES: 1,821

SHAREHOLDERS: 18,302

ANNUAL MEETING: In Feb.

INCORPORATED: NY, May, 1950; reincorp., NC, Mar., 1994

INSTITUTIONAL HOLDINGS:
No. of Institutions: 129
Shares Held: 8,255,217
% Held: 26.5

INDUSTRY: Natural gas distribution (SIC: 4924)

TRANSFER AGENT(S): American Stock Transfer & Trust Company, New York, NY

PITNEY BOWES INC.

YIELD 2.6%
P/E RATIO 17.8

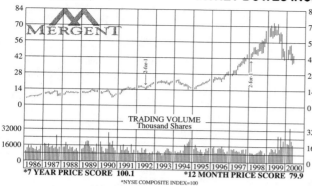

INTERIM EARNINGS (Per Share):

Qtr.	Mar.	June	Sept.	Dec.
1996	0.35	0.40	0.39	0.43
1997	0.41	0.45	0.44	0.51
1998	0.46	0.51	0.50	0.59
1999	0.52	0.58	0.69	0.66

INTERIM DIVIDENDS (Per Share):

Amt.	Decl.	Ex.	Rec.	Pay.
0.255Q	7/12/99	8/25/99	8/27/99	9/12/99
0.255Q	10/11/99	11/23/99	11/26/99	12/12/99
0.285Q	2/08/00	2/23/00	2/25/00	3/12/00
0.285Q	4/10/00	5/24/00	5/26/00	6/12/00

Indicated div.: $1.14 (Div. Reinv. Plan)

CAPITALIZATION (12/31/99):

	($000)	(%)
Long-Term Debt	1,997,856	39.8
Deferred Income Tax	1,082,019	21.6
Redeemable Pfd. Stock	310,000	6.2
Preferred Stock	1,870	0.0
Common & Surplus	1,623,740	32.4
Total	5,015,485	100.0

DIVIDEND ACHIEVER STATUS:
Rank: 69   10-Year Growth Rate: 14.65%
Total Years of Dividend Growth: 16

*7 YEAR PRICE SCORE 100.1   *12 MONTH PRICE SCORE 79.9
NYSE COMPOSITE INDEX=100

TRADING VOLUME
Thousand Shares

RECENT DEVELOPMENTS: For the year ended 12/31/99, income from continuing operations was $659.2 million, up 21.5% versus income from continuing operations of $542.5 million the year before. Total revenue rose 8.4% to $4.43 billion from $4.09 billion a year earlier. Operating profit climbed 15.2% to $1.09 billion, fueled by a 20.8% jump to $798.4 million in operating profit from the Mailing and Integrated Logistics segment. Results were restated to reflect the sale of Atlantic Mortgage & Investment Corp.

PROSPECTS: Going forward, PBI plans to spur revenue and earnings growth through the introduction of new e-commerce services. On 3/29/00, the Company received approval from the U.S. Postal Service to commercially launch ClickStamp™ Online, an Internet-based postage product targeting customers in the small business and small office/home office segments. Meanwhile, PBI has formed docSense.com, a new stand-alone business offering Internet billing, payment and statement application services.

BUSINESS

PITNEY BOWES INC. and its subsidiaries operate within three industry segments: Mailing and Integrated Logistics, Office Solutions, and Capital Services. Mailing and Integrated Logistics includes rental, sale and financing of mailing and shipping equipment, related supplies and service, and software. Office Solutions includes facilities management, through Pitney Bowes Management Services, Inc. and Pitney Bowes Office Systems. Capital Services includes large ticket financing programs, covering a broad range of products, and other financial services to the commercial and industrial markets in the U.S.

BUSINESS LINE ANALYSIS

(12/31/99)	Rev(%)	Inc(%)
Mail & Integrated Logistics	67.5	73.1
Office Solutions	28.6	22.2
Capital Services	3.9	4.7
Total	100.0	100.0

ANNUAL FINANCIAL DATA

	12/31/99	12/31/98	12/31/97	12/31/96	12/31/95	12/31/94	12/31/93
Earnings Per Share	[1] 2.42	[1] 2.03	1.80	[4] 1.56	[2] 1.34	[1][3] 1.11	1.11
Cash Flow Per Share	3.94	3.32	2.82	2.51	2.25	1.97	1.89
Tang. Book Val. Per Share	5.28	5.26	5.96	6.86	6.20	5.02	5.18
Dividends Per Share	1.02	0.90	0.80	0.69	0.60	0.52	0.45
Dividend Payout %	42.1	46.4	44.4	44.2	44.8	47.1	40.5
INCOME STATEMENT (IN MILLIONS):							
Total Revenues	4,432.6	4,220.5	4,100.5	3,858.6	3,554.8	3,270.6	3,542.9
Costs & Expenses	2,906.2	2,845.8	2,796.5	2,698.8	2,445.5	2,272.0	2,544.2
Depreciation & Amort.	412.1	361.3	300.1	278.2	271.6	268.3	247.9
Operating Income	1,114.3	1,013.4	1,003.8	881.6	837.6	730.3	750.8
Net Interest Inc./(Exp.)	d179.3	d149.2	d200.7	d197.2	d218.6	d189.1	d176.0
Income Before Income Taxes	984.6	864.2	803.1	684.4	618.9	566.5	574.8
Income Taxes	325.4	296.2	277.1	215.0	211.2	218.1	221.6
Net Income	[1] 659.2	[1] 567.9	526.0	[4] 469.4	[2] 407.7	[1][3] 348.4	353.2
Cash Flow	1,071.1	929.1	825.9	747.4	679.1	616.5	600.8
Average Shs. Outstg. (000)	272,006	279,657	292,517	298,234	302,280	312,918	318,738
BALANCE SHEET (IN MILLIONS):							
Cash & Cash Equivalents	256.7	129.0	138.8	136.8	88.6	75.7	55.8
Total Current Assets	3,342.6	2,509.0	2,463.5	2,222.1	2,101.1	2,083.7	1,936.7
Net Property	1,306.1	1,287.8	1,289.7	1,307.2	1,276.2	1,286.6	1,212.1
Total Assets	8,222.7	7,661.0	7,893.4	8,155.7	7,844.6	7,399.7	6,793.8
Total Current Liabilities	2,872.8	2,721.8	3,373.2	3,305.3	3,501.6	3,978.5	3,273.4
Long-Term Obligations	1,997.9	1,712.9	1,068.4	1,300.4	1,048.5	779.2	847.3
Net Stockholders' Equity	1,625.6	1,648.0	1,872.6	2,239.0	2,071.1	1,745.1	1,871.6
Net Working Capital	469.8	d212.8	d909.7	d1,083.2	d1,400.5	d1,894.7	d1,336.6
Year-end Shs. Outstg. (000)	264,695	270,378	279,674	295,960	299,892	302,552	316,348
STATISTICAL RECORD:							
Operating Profit Margin %	25.1	24.0	24.5	22.8	23.6	22.3	21.2
Net Profit Margin %	14.9	13.5	12.8	12.2	11.5	10.7	10.0
Return on Equity %	40.5	34.5	28.1	21.0	19.7	20.0	18.9
Return on Assets %	8.0	7.4	6.7	5.8	5.2	4.7	5.2
Debt/Total Assets %	24.3	22.4	13.5	15.9	13.4	10.5	12.5
Price Range	73⁵⁄₁₆-40⁷⁄₈	66³⁄₈-42¼	45¼-26¹³⁄₁₆	30¹¹⁄₁₆-20⁵⁄₁₆	24¹⁄₈-15	23³⁄₁₆-14⅝	22¼-18¹⁄₈
P/E Ratio	30.3-16.9	32.7-20.8	25.4-14.9	19.7-13.4	18.0-11.2	21.0-13.2	20.0-16.3
Average Yield %	1.8	1.7	2.2	2.7	3.1	2.8	2.2

Statistics are as originally reported. Adj. for 2-for-1 stk. split, 1/98. [1] Bef. discont. opers. chg. $22.9 mil ($0.08/sh), 1999; $8.5 mil ($0.03/sh), 1998; & cr.$32.5 mil, 1994. [2] Bef. discont. opers. cr$175.4 mil & incl. $155 mil non-recur. gain. [3] Bef. $119.5 mil chg. for acctg. adj. [4] Incl. $30 mil restr. chg.

NYSE SYMBOL PPG
Rec. Pr. 49 9/16 (5/31/00)

PPG INDUSTRIES, INC.

YIELD 3.2%
P/E RATIO 15.3

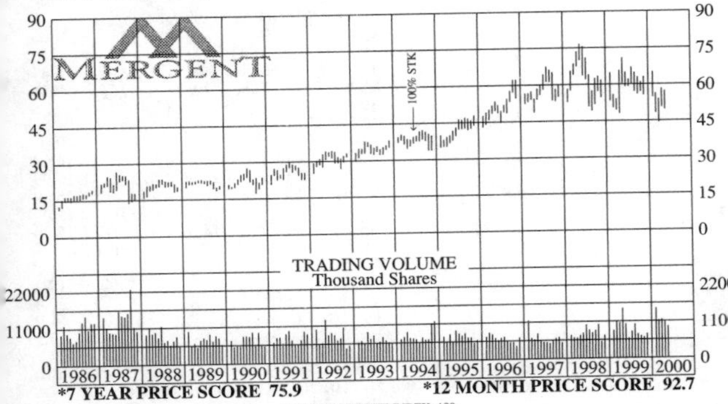

MERGENT
100% STK
TRADING VOLUME
Thousand Shares
90
75
60
45
30
15
0
22000
11000
0
1986 1987 1988 1989 1990 1991 1992 1993 1994 1995 1996 1997 1998 1999 2000

*7 YEAR PRICE SCORE 75.9   *12 MONTH PRICE SCORE 92.7

*NYSE COMPOSITE INDEX=100

INTERIM EARNINGS (Per Share):

Qtr.	Mar.	June	Sept.	Dec.
1997	0.91	1.21	0.96	0.89
1998	1.08	1.11	1.39	0.91
1999	0.70	1.05	0.56	0.92

INTERIM DIVIDENDS (Per Share):

Amt.	Decl.	Ex.	Rec.	Pay.
0.38Q	7/15/99	8/06/99	8/10/99	9/10/99
0.38Q	10/21/99	11/08/99	11/10/99	12/10/99
0.40Q	1/20/00	2/17/00	2/22/00	3/10/00
0.40Q	4/20/00	5/08/00	5/10/00	6/12/00

Indicated div.: $1.60 (Div. Reinv. Plan)

CAPITALIZATION (12/31/99):

	($000)	(%)
Long-Term Debt	1,836,000	33.0
Deferred Income Tax	520,000	9.4
Minority Interest	98,000	1.8
Common & Surplus	3,106,000	55.9
Total	5,560,000	100.0

DIVIDEND ACHIEVER STATUS:
Rank: 215   10-Year Growth Rate: 7.46%
Total Years of Dividend Growth: 28

RECENT DEVELOPMENTS: For the year ended 12/31/99, net income fell 29.1% to $568.0 million. Results for 1999 included pre-tax charges of $40.0 million for R&D, $42.0 million for the disposal of a plant, $23.0 million for the adjustment to market value of acquired inventories, $6.0 million from the bankruptcy of a chain, $1.0 million for cost reduction efforts, and $1.0 million reversal of restructuring reserves. Net sales climbed 3.3% to $7.76 billion.

PROSPECTS: PPG plans to report an after-tax charge of about $35.0 million in the first quarter of 2000 from a write-off of the Company's investment in Pittsburgh Corning Corp., a producer of glass block and specialty glass products. The one-time charge does not involve a cash payment and should not have an adverse effect on PPG's sales. Separately, PPG divested its minority interest in three Chinese glass businesses to Asahi Glass Co. of Tokyo.

BUSINESS

PPG INDUSTRIES, INC. is a leading supplier of products for manufacturing, construction, automotive, chemical processing and numerous other world industries. The diversified global manufacturer makes protective and decorative coatings, flat glass, fabricated glass products, continuous-strand fiberglass, and industrial and specialty chemicals. PPG operates 70 major manufacturing facilities in countries including Canada, China, England, France, Germany, Ireland, Italy, Mexico, the Netherlands, Portugal, Spain, Taiwan, and the U.S. In 1999, revenues (and operating income) were derived: coatings, 52.6% (48.1%); glass, 29.1% (35.6%); and chemicals, 18.3% (16.3%).

ANNUAL FINANCIAL DATA

	12/31/99	12/31/98	12/31/97	12/31/96	12/31/95	12/31/94	12/31/93
Earnings Per Share	**[6] 3.23**	**[5] 4.48**	**[4] 3.94**	**3.96**	**[3] 3.80**	**[2] 2.43**	**[1] 1.39**
Cash Flow Per Share	**5.62**	**6.63**	**5.99**	**5.89**	**5.54**	**4.81**	**4.22**
Tang. Book Val. Per Share	**8.30**	**13.17**	**21.29**	**13.55**	**13.21**	**14.12**	**11.57**
Dividends Per Share	**1.52**	**1.42**	**1.33**	**1.26**	**1.18**	**1.12**	**1.04**
Dividend Payout %	**47.1**	**31.7**	**33.8**	**31.8**	**31.1**	**46.1**	**74.8**
INCOME STATEMENT (IN MILLIONS):							
Total Revenues	7,757.0	7,510.0	7,379.0	7,218.1	7,057.7	6,331.2	5,753.9
Costs & Expenses	6,180.0	5,851.0	5,690.0	5,561.3	5,405.5	4,984.9	4,687.1
Depreciation & Amort.	419.0	383.0	373.0	362.6	351.6	335.2	350.2
Operating Income	1,158.0	1,276.0	1,316.0	1,294.2	1,300.6	1,011.1	716.6
Net Interest Inc./(Exp.)	d182.0	d110.0	d105.0	d85.0	d74.0	d76.8	d87.9
Income Before Income Taxes	973.0	1,294.0	1,175.0	1,239.6	1,262.3	855.7	544.1
Income Taxes	377.0	466.0	435.0	471.0	479.7	325.2	236.2
Equity Earnings/Minority Int.	d28.0	d27.0	d26.0	d5.1	16.0	3.7	4.4
Net Income	[6] 568.0	[5] 801.0	[4] 714.0	744.0	[3] 767.6	[2] 684.6	[1] 547.8
Cash Flow	987.0	1,184.0	1,087.0	1,106.6	1,119.2	1,019.8	898.0
Average Shs. Outstg. (000)	175,500	178,700	181,500	187,800	202,000	211,900	212,600
BALANCE SHEET (IN MILLIONS):							
Cash & Cash Equivalents	158.0	128.0	129.0	69.6	105.6	62.1	111.9
Total Current Assets	3,062.0	2,660.0	2,584.0	2,296.4	2,275.5	2,168.2	2,025.9
Net Property	2,933.0	2,905.0	2,855.0	2,913.5	2,834.8	2,742.3	2,787.3
Total Assets	8,914.0	7,387.0	6,868.0	6,441.4	6,194.3	5,893.9	5,651.5
Total Current Liabilities	2,384.0	1,912.0	1,662.0	1,768.9	1,629.4	1,459.9	359.8
Long-Term Obligations	1,836.0	1,081.0	1,257.0	833.9	735.5	773.4	774.0
Net Stockholders' Equity	3,106.0	2,880.0	2,509.0	2,482.6	2,569.2	2,923.0	2,473.1
Net Working Capital	678.0	748.0	922.0	527.5	646.1	708.3	1,666.1
Year-end Shs. Outstg. (000)	173,988	175,000	117,826	183,215	194,450	206,988	213,682
STATISTICAL RECORD:							
Operating Profit Margin %	14.9	17.0	17.8	17.9	18.4	16.0	12.5
Net Profit Margin %	7.3	10.7	9.7	10.3	10.9	10.8	9.5
Return on Equity %	18.3	27.8	28.5	30.0	29.9	23.4	22.2
Return on Assets %	6.4	10.8	10.4	11.6	12.4	11.6	9.7
Debt/Total Assets %	20.6	14.6	18.3	12.9	11.9	13.1	13.7
Price Range	70 3/4-47 15/16	76 5/8-49 1/8	67 1/2-48 5/8	62 1/4-42 7/8	47 7/8-34 7/8	42 1/8-33 3/4	38 1/8-29 11/16
P/E Ratio	21.9-14.8	17.1-11.0	17.1-12.3	15.7-10.8	12.6-9.2	17.3-13.9	27.4-21.4
Average Yield %	2.6	2.3	2.3	2.4	2.9	3.0	3.1

Statistics are as originally reported. Adj for 2-1 split, 6/94. [1] Bef dr$363.2 mil acct adj & incl $126.4 mil restr. chg & $44.2 mil a-tx chg sale med elec bus. [2] Incl $51.9 mil a-tx chg dvst med elec bus. [3] Incl $24.2 mil a-tax nonrecur. gain. [4] Incl $102 mil nonrecur. p-tx chg & $59 mil p-tx gain. [5] Incl. $85.0 mill. p-tax gain fr. the sale of European flat & automotive glass bus. & $27.0 mill. p-tax restr. chg. and oth. chgs. [6] Incl. $110.0 mill. in p-tax chgs.

OFFICERS:
R. W. LeBoeuf, Chmn., C.E.O.
D. W. Kiener, Treas.

INVESTOR CONTACT: Douglas B. Atkinson, Dir. of Inv. Rel., (412) 434-3312

PRINCIPAL OFFICE: One PPG Place, Pittsburgh, PA 15272

TELEPHONE NUMBER: (412) 434-3131
FAX: (412) 434-2571
WEB: www.ppg.com
NO. OF EMPLOYEES: 32,500 (avg.)
SHAREHOLDERS: 31,595
ANNUAL MEETING: In Apr.
INCORPORATED: PA, Nov., 1883; reincorp., PA, Nov., 1920

INSTITUTIONAL HOLDINGS:
No. of Institutions: 396
Shares Held: 90,704,300
% Held: 52.2

INDUSTRY: Paints and allied products (SIC: 2851)

TRANSFER AGENT(S): ChaseMellon Shareholder Services, Ridgefield Park, NJ.

NYSE SYMBOL PG
Rec. Pr. 66½ (5/31/00)

PROCTER & GAMBLE COMPANY (THE)

YIELD 1.9%
P/E RATIO 25.7

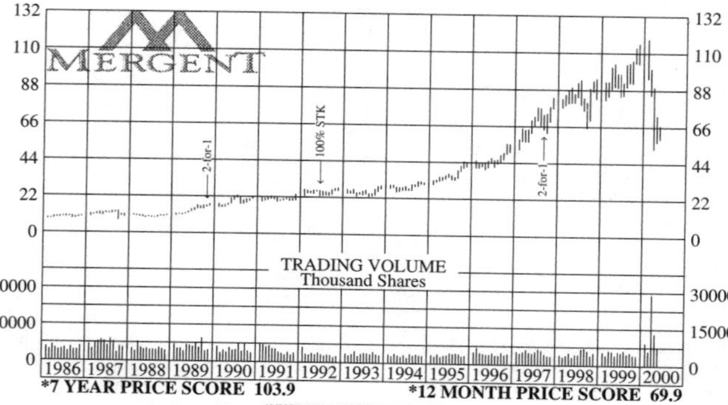

*7 YEAR PRICE SCORE 103.9 *12 MONTH PRICE SCORE 69.9

*NYSE COMPOSITE INDEX=100

INTERIM EARNINGS (Per Share):

Qtr.	Sept.	Dec.	Mar.	June
1996-97	0.70	0.68	0.63	0.43
1997-98	0.79	0.71	0.65	0.47
1998-99	0.80	0.78	0.72	0.29
1999-00	0.80	0.78	...	...

INTERIM DIVIDENDS (Per Share):

Amt.	Decl.	Ex.	Rec.	Pay.
0.285Q	4/13/99	4/21/99	4/23/99	5/14/99
0.32Q	7/13/99	7/21/99	7/23/99	8/16/99
0.32Q	10/12/99	10/20/99	10/22/99	11/15/99
0.32Q	12/30/99	1/19/00	1/21/00	2/15/00
0.32Q	4/12/00	4/18/00	4/20/00	5/15/00

Indicated div.: $1.28 (Div. Reinv. Plan)

CAPITALIZATION (6/30/99):

	($000)	(%)
Long-Term Debt	6,231,000	33.4
Deferred Income Tax	362,000	1.9
Preferred Stock	1,781,000	9.5
Common & Surplus	10,277,000	55.1
Total	18,651,000	100.0

DIVIDEND ACHIEVER STATUS:
Rank: 129 10-Year Growth Rate: 11.36%
Total Years of Dividend Growth: 46

RECENT DEVELOPMENTS: For the quarter ended 12/31/99, net income declined slightly to $1.13 billion from $1.14 billion in the year-earlier quarter. Results for fiscal 2000 included charges of $137.0 million related to PG's organization 2005 program. Net sales improved 6.6% to $10.59 billion. Net sales in the fabric and home care segment improved 10.0% to $3.17 billion, while net sales in the paper segment grew 1.0% to $3.18 billion.

PROSPECTS: PG should continue to post solid sales growth due mainly to its Organization 2005 program, strict cost management and new product introductions. Accordingly, PG expects to deliver sales growth of 7.0% to 8.0% for the second half of fiscal 2000. Meanwhile, the Company plans to launch four new products over the next few months and will launch ten to fifteen new products over the next year or two.

BUSINESS

THE PROCTER & GAMBLE COMPANY manufactures and markets 300 brands of consumer products including laundry, cleaning and personal-care products, pharmaceuticals, foods and beverages, and business and industrial products. Leading brands are: CHEER, SPIC & SPAN and TIDE cleansing compounds; CRISCO shortenings, CREST toothpastes, IVORY soaps, HEAD AND SHOULDERS and PANTENE PROV shampoos. Other products include VICK'S cough and cold remedies, CHARMIN toilet tissue, PAMPERS diapers, OIL OF OLAY skin products, OLD SPICE deodorants and fragrances, FOLGER'S coffee, HAWAIIAN PUNCH fruit drinks and PRINGLES potato chips. PG has operations in over 70 countries and markets to consumers in more than 140 countries. On 9/1/99, PG acquired The Iams Company, a global leader in pet nutrition.

REVENUES

(06/30/99)	($000)	(%)
Laundry & Cleaning	11,517,000	30.2
Paper	11,451,000	30.0
Beauty Care	7,115,000	18.7
Food & Beverage	4,381,000	11.5
Health Care	2,836,000	7.4
Corporate	825,000	2.2
Total	38,125,000	100.0

ANNUAL FINANCIAL DATA

	6/30/99	6/30/98	6/30/97	6/30/96	6/30/95	6/30/94	6/30/93
Earnings Per Share	[2] **2.59**	**2.56**	**2.43**	**2.15**	**1.86**	**1.55**	[1][2] **0.13**
Cash Flow Per Share	**4.09**	**3.67**	**3.60**	**3.21**	**2.84**	**2.45**	**1.04**
Tang. Book Val. Per Share	**2.62**	**2.55**	**4.59**	**4.05**	**2.99**	**2.29**	**1.25**
Dividends Per Share	**1.21**	**1.07**	**0.95**	**0.85**	**0.75**	**0.66**	**0.58**
Dividend Payout %	**46.7**	**42.0**	**39.3**	**39.6**	**40.4**	**42.7**	**467.6**
INCOME STATEMENT (IN MILLIONS):							
Total Revenues	38,125.0	37,154.0	35,764.0	35,284.0	33,434.0	30,296.0	30,433.0
Costs & Expenses	29,724.0	29,501.0	28,789.0	29,111.0	28,002.0	25,582.0	28,837.0
Depreciation & Amort.	2,148.0	1,598.0	1,487.0	1,358.0	1,253.0	1,134.0	1,140.0
Operating Income	6,253.0	6,055.0	5,488.0	4,815.0	4,179.0	3,580.0	[2] 456.0
Net Interest Inc./(Exp.)	d650.0	d548.0	d457.0	d484.0	d488.0	d482.0	d552.0
Income Before Income Taxes	5,838.0	5,708.0	5,249.0	4,669.0	4,000.0	3,346.0	349.0
Income Taxes	2,075.0	1,928.0	1,834.0	1,623.0	1,355.0	1,135.0	80.0
Net Income	[2] 3,763.0	3,780.0	3,415.0	3,046.0	2,645.0	2,211.0	[1][2] 269.0
Cash Flow	5,802.0	5,274.0	4,798.0	4,301.0	3,796.0	3,243.0	1,307.0
Average Shs. Outstg. (000)	1,446,800	1,465,500	1,360,000	1,372,000	1,372,000	1,366,000	1,360,000
BALANCE SHEET (IN MILLIONS):							
Cash & Cash Equivalents	2,800.0	2,406.0	3,110.0	2,520.0	2,178.0	2,656.0	2,628.0
Total Current Assets	11,358.0	10,577.0	10,786.0	10,807.0	10,842.0	9,988.0	9,975.0
Net Property	12,626.0	12,180.0	11,376.0	11,118.0	11,026.0	10,024.0	9,485.0
Total Assets	32,113.0	30,966.0	27,544.0	27,730.0	28,125.0	25,535.0	24,935.0
Total Current Liabilities	10,761.0	9,250.0	7,798.0	7,825.0	8,648.0	8,040.0	8,287.0
Long-Term Obligations	6,231.0	5,765.0	4,143.0	4,670.0	5,161.0	4,980.0	5,174.0
Net Stockholders' Equity	12,058.0	12,236.0	12,046.0	11,722.0	10,589.0	8,832.0	7,441.0
Net Working Capital	597.0	1,327.0	2,988.0	2,982.0	2,194.0	1,948.0	1,688.0
Year-end Shs. Outstg. (000)	1,319,800	1,337,400	1,360,000	1,372,000	1,374,000	1,368,000	1,364,000
STATISTICAL RECORD:							
Operating Profit Margin %	16.4	16.3	15.3	13.6	12.5	11.8	1.5
Net Profit Margin %	9.9	10.2	9.5	8.6	7.9	7.3	0.9
Return on Equity %	31.2	30.9	28.3	26.0	25.0	25.0	3.6
Return on Assets %	11.7	12.2	12.4	11.0	9.4	8.7	1.1
Debt/Total Assets %	19.4	18.6	15.0	16.8	18.4	19.5	20.7
Price Range	115 5/8-82	94 13/16-65 1/8	83 7/16-51 13/16	55 1/2-39 11/16	44 3/4-30 5/16	32 5/16-25 5/8	29 7/16-22 5/8
P/E Ratio	44.6-31.7	37.0-25.4	34.3-21.3	25.9-18.5	24.1-16.3	20.9-16.6	235.3-180.9
Average Yield %	1.2	1.3	1.4	1.8	2.0	2.3	2.2

Statistics are as originally reported. Adj. for stk. splits: 2-for-1, 9/97. [1] Bef. acctg. chrg. $925.0 mill. [2] Incl. non-recurr. chrg. $385.0 mill., 6/30/99; $2.7 mill., 6/30/93.

OFFICERS:
D. I. Jager, Chmn., Pres., C.E.O.
J. J. Johnson, Sr. V.P., Gen. Couns.

INVESTOR CONTACT: Jim Martis, Assoc. Dir., Inv. Rel. (513) 983-1100

PRINCIPAL OFFICE: One Procter & Gamble Plaza, Cincinnati, OH 45202

TELEPHONE NUMBER: (513) 983-1100
FAX: (513) 983-2062
WEB: www.pg.com

NO. OF EMPLOYEES: 110,000 (approx.)

SHAREHOLDERS: 278,245

ANNUAL MEETING: In Oct.

INCORPORATED: OH, May, 1905

INSTITUTIONAL HOLDINGS:
No. of Institutions: 1,028
Shares Held: 665,900,962
% Held: 50.7

INDUSTRY: Soap and other detergents (SIC: 2841)

TRANSFER AGENT(S): The Company, Cincinnati, OH.

PROGRESSIVE CORPORATION (THE)

YIELD 0.3%
P/E RATIO 23.8

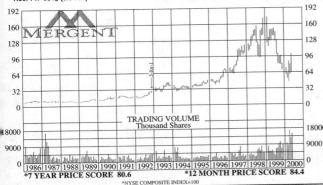

TRADING VOLUME
Thousand Shares

7 YEAR PRICE SCORE 80.6 *12 MONTH PRICE SCORE 84.4*
NYSE COMPOSITE INDEX=100

INTERIM EARNINGS (Per Share):

Qtr.	Mar.	June	Sept.	Dec.
1995	0.79	0.79	0.81	0.86
1996	0.82	1.01	1.08	1.23
1997	1.02	1.36	1.54	1.39
1998	1.58	1.61	1.81	1.05
1999	1.41	1.50	0.99	0.05

INTERIM DIVIDENDS (Per Share):

Amt.	Decl.	Ex.	Rec.	Pay.
0.065Q	12/30/99	6/09/99	6/11/99	6/30/99
0.065Q	8/27/99	9/08/99	9/10/99	9/30/99
0.065Q	10/22/99	12/08/99	12/10/99	12/31/99
0.065Q	2/07/00	3/08/00	3/10/00	3/31/00
0.065Q	4/24/00	6/07/00	6/09/00	6/30/00

Indicated div.: $0.26

CAPITALIZATION (12/31/99):

	($000)	(%)
Long-Term Debt	1,048,600	27.6
Common & Surplus	2,752,800	72.4
Total	3,801,400	100.0

DIVIDEND ACHIEVER STATUS:
Rank: 244   10-Year Growth Rate: 5.89%
Total Years of Dividend Growth: 30

RECENT DEVELOPMENTS: For the year ended 12/31/99, net income decreased 35.4% to $295.2 million compared with $456.7 million in the previous year. Total revenues were $6.12 billion, up 15.7% from $5.29 billion the year before. Net realized gains on security sales were $47.2 million and $11.4 million in 1999 and 1998, respectively. Net premiums written jumped 15.6% to $6.12 billion from $5.30 billion in the prior year.

PROSPECTS: Going forward, the Company will continue to focus on its strategy of achieving a 4.0% underwriting profit and growing at 15.0% in excess of the rate of inflation. Meanwhile, the Company expects difficulty in achieving its historic growth and profit margin targets over the next several quarters mainly due to reduced rates, higher loss trends and continued strong growth in the direct business.

BUSINESS

THE PROGRESSIVE CORPORATION is an insurance holding company that owns 82 subsidiaries and one mutual insurance company affiliate. PGR through its subsidiaries and affiliate provides personal automobile insurance and other specialty property-casualty insurance and related services throughout the United States. The Company's personal lines segment writes insurance for private passenger automobiles and recreation vehicles. The Company's property-casualty insurance products protect its customers against collision and physical damage to their motor vehicles and liability to others for personal injury or property damage arising out of the use of those vehicles. The Company's other lines of business include the commercial vehicle business unit, United Financial Casualty Company, Professional Liability Group and Motor Carrier business unit.

REVENUES

(12/31/99)	($000)	(%)
Premiums earned	5,683,600	92.81
Investment income	340,700	5.56
Net real gains on securs	47,200	0.77
Service revenues	47,500	0.78
Other income	5,200	0.08
Total	6,124,200	100.0

ANNUAL FINANCIAL DATA

	12/31/99	12/31/98	12/31/97	12/31/96	12/31/95	12/31/94	12/31/93
Earnings Per Share	3.96	6.11	5.31	4.14	3.26	3.59	3.59
Tang. Book Val. Per Share	32.96	31.14	25.95	20.65	16.79	12.70	10.89
Dividends Per Share	0.26	0.25	0.24	0.23	0.22	0.21	0.20
Dividend Payout %	6.6	4.1	4.5	5.6	6.7	5.8	5.6
INCOME STATEMENT (IN MILLIONS):							
Total Premium Income	5,683.6	4,948.0	4,189.5	3,199.3	2,727.2	2,191.1	1,668.7
Other Income	440.6	344.4	418.7	279.1	284.7	224.2	286.1
Total Revenues	6,124.2	5,292.4	4,608.2	3,478.4	3,011.9	2,415.3	1,954.8
Policyholder Benefits	4,256.4	3,376.3	2,967.5	2,236.1	1,943.8	1,397.3	1,028.0
Income Before Income Taxes	412.2	661.1	578.5	441.7	345.9	379.8	373.1
Income Taxes	117.0	204.4	178.5	128.0	95.4	105.5	105.8
Net Income	295.2	456.7	400.0	313.7	250.5	274.3	275.3
Average Shs. Outstg. (000)	74,600	74,700	75,300	74,200	74,200	74,000	71,800
BALANCE SHEET (IN MILLIONS):							
Cash & Cash Equivalents	243.2	460.5	432.7	175.1	319.0	292.5	239.5
Premiums Due	2,015.5	1,737.2	1,478.3	1,130.8	988.0	922.1	761.5
Invst. Assets: Fixed-term	4,532.7	4,219.0	3,891.4	3,409.2	2,772.9	2,424.6	2,101.7
Invst. Assets: Equities	1,243.6	636.9	620.8	540.1	310.0	106.2	453.9
Invst. Assets: Total	6,427.7	5,674.3	5,270.4	4,450.6	3,768.0	3,180.0	2,786.4
Total Assets	9,704.7	8,463.1	7,559.6	6,183.9	5,352.5	4,675.1	4,011.3
Long-Term Obligations	1,048.6	776.6	775.9	775.7	675.9	675.6	477.1
Net Stockholders' Equity	2,752.8	2,557.1	2,135.9	1,676.9	1,475.8	1,151.9	997.9
Year-end Shs. Outstg. (000)	73,100	72,500	72,300	71,500	72,100	71,200	72,100
STATISTICAL RECORD:							
Return on Revenues %	4.8	8.6	8.7	9.0	8.3	11.4	14.1
Return on Equity %	10.7	17.9	18.7	18.7	17.0	23.8	27.6
Return on Assets %	3.0	5.4	5.3	5.1	4.7	5.9	6.9
Price Range	174¼-68½	172-94	119¼-61½	72¼-40⅜	49½-34¾	40½-27¾	46⅛-27½
P/E Ratio	44.0-17.3	28.2-15.4	22.5-11.6	17.5-9.8	15.2-10.7	11.3-7.7	12.8-7.7
Average Yield %	0.2	0.2	0.3	0.4	0.5	0.6	0.5

Statistics are as originally reported.

OFFICERS:
P. B. Lewis, Chmn., Pres., C.E.O.
W. T. Forrester, C.F.O., Treas.
D. M. Schneider, Chief Legal Officer, Sec.

INVESTOR CONTACT: Shareholder's Services, (800) 879-7764

PRINCIPAL OFFICE: 6300 Wilson Mills Rd., Mayfield Village, OH 44143

TELEPHONE NUMBER: (440) 461-5000
FAX: (440) 446-7168
WEB: www.progressive.com

NO. OF EMPLOYEES: 18,753

SHAREHOLDERS: 3,877

ANNUAL MEETING: In Apr.

INCORPORATED: OH, Feb., 1965

INSTITUTIONAL HOLDINGS:
No. of Institutions: 227
Shares Held: 52,804,811
% Held: 72.4

INDUSTRY: Fire, marine, and casualty insurance (SIC: 6331)

TRANSFER AGENT(S): National City Bank, Cleveland, OH.

PROTECTIVE LIFE CORP.

YIELD 1.9%
P/E RATIO 12.0

TRADING VOLUME
Thousand Shares

| 1986|1987|1988|1989|1990|1991|1992|1993|1994|1995|1996|1997|1998|1999|2000 |

*7 YEAR PRICE SCORE 92.1   ***12 MONTH PRICE SCORE 84.5**

*NYSE COMPOSITE INDEX=100

INTERIM EARNINGS (Per Share):

Qtr.	Mar.	June	Sept.	Dec.
1996	0.36	0.39	0.32	0.40
1997	0.40	0.44	0.48	0.47
1998	0.47	0.52	0.52	0.53
1999	0.56	0.54	0.57	0.62

INTERIM DIVIDENDS (Per Share):

Amt.	Decl.	Ex.	Rec.	Pay.
0.12Q	4/26/99	5/12/99	5/14/99	6/01/99
0.12Q	8/02/99	8/11/99	8/13/99	9/01/99
0.12Q	11/01/99	11/09/99	11/12/99	11/29/99
0.12Q	2/07/00	2/16/00	2/18/00	3/01/00
0.13Q	5/01/00	5/10/00	5/12/00	6/01/00

Indicated div.: $0.52

CAPITALIZATION (12/31/99):

	($000)	(%)
Long-Term Debt	181,023	18.0
Deferred Income Tax	d37,828	-3.8
Common & Surplus	865,223	85.8
Total	1,008,418	100.0

DIVIDEND ACHIEVER STATUS:
Rank: 150   10-Year Growth Rate: 10.38%
Total Years of Dividend Growth: 10

RECENT DEVELOPMENTS: For the year ended 12/31/99, income was $153.1 million, before an extraordinary loss of $1.8 million, compared with net income of $130.8 million a year earlier. Results for 1999 included a $1.18 million realized loss on the sale of investments. The 1998 results included a realized gain of $3.1 million. Total revenues advanced 12.3% to $1.53 billion from $1.37 billion the year before. Premium and policy fees increased 15.8% to $1.30 million due to strong performances in the dental and acquisitions divisions. On 1/20/00, the Company acquired the Lydon Insurance Group, which markets specialty insurance products. On 2/23/00, the Company entered into an agreement with MassMutual Financial Group to sell its joint venture ownership in CRC Protective Life Insurance Company Limited in Hong Kong.

BUSINESS

PROTECTIVE LIFE CORP. is a holding company, that through its subsidiaries, provides financial services through the production, distribution and administration of insurance and investment products. The Company operates seven divisions whose strategic focuses can be grouped into three segments: life insurance, specialty insurance products and retirement savings and investment products. The life insurance segment includes the individual life, west coast and acquisitions divisions. The specialty insurance products segment includes the dental and consumer benefits and financial institutions divisions. The retirement savings and investment products include the stable value products and investment products division. In addition, the Company operates a corporate and other segment.

BUSINESS LINE ANALYSIS

(12/31/1999)	Rev(%)	Inc(%)
Individual Life	12.9	13.3
West Coast	6.7	10.8
Acquisitions	15.9	26.4
Dental & Consumer Benefit	27.7	16.3
Financial Institutions	10.4	9.1
Stable Value Products	13.7	11.9
Invest Prods, Corp & Othe	12.7	12.2
Total	100.0	100.0

ANNUAL FINANCIAL DATA

	12/31/99	12/31/98	12/31/97	12/31/96	12/31/95	12/31/94	12/31/93
Earnings Per Share	① 2.32	2.04	1.78	1.47	1.34	1.28	1.04
Tang. Book Val. Per Share	10.03	11.51	12.30	9.99	9.15	4.93	6.59
Dividends Per Share	0.47	0.43	0.39	0.35	0.31	0.28	0.25
Dividend Payout %	20.3	21.1	21.9	23.8	23.1	21.5	24.4
INCOME STATEMENT (IN MILLIONS):							
Total Premium Income	761.3	662.8	522.3	494.2	432.6	402.8	370.8
Net Investment Income	676.4	636.4	591.4	517.5	475.9	417.8	362.1
Other Income	96.2	67.2	33.6	26.4	13.4	27.9	26.7
Total Revenues	1,533.9	1,366.4	1,147.3	1,038.0	921.9	848.4	759.6
Income Before Income Taxes	255.8	220.7	179.4	139.7	121.0	106.2	85.0
Income Taxes	92.1	77.8	61.0	47.5	41.2	34.0	28.5
Equity Earnings/Minority Int.	d10.6	d12.1	d6.4	d3.2	d3.2	d1.8	...
Net Income	① 153.1	130.8	112.0	89.0	76.7	70.4	56.6
Average Shs. Outstg. (000)	66,161	64,088	62,850	61,608	57,320	54,953	54,764
BALANCE SHEET (IN MILLIONS):							
Cash & Cash Equivalents	165.3	225.7	123.6	235.3	65.0	64.0	27.1
Premiums Due	940.3	797.2	639.4	380.0	309.7	152.6	128.9
Invst. Assets: Fixed-term	6,311.8	6,437.8	6,374.3	4,686.1	3,892.0	3,493.6	3,051.3
Invst. Assets: Equities	36.4	12.3	15.0	35.3	38.7	45.0	40.6
Invst. Assets: Total	8,722.0	8,606.6	8,049.4	6,552.2	6,025.1	5,301.9	4,766.7
Total Assets	12,994.2	11,989.5	10,511.6	8,263.2	7,231.3	6,130.3	5,316.0
Long-Term Obligations	181.0	152.3	120.0	168.2	115.5	98.0	137.6
Net Stockholders' Equity	865.2	944.2	758.2	615.3	526.6	270.4	360.7
Year-end Shs. Outstg. (000)	64,502	64,435	61,642	61,608	57,550	54,852	54,772
STATISTICAL RECORD:							
Return on Revenues %	10.0	9.6	9.8	8.6	8.3	8.3	7.4
Return on Equity %	17.7	13.9	14.8	14.5	14.6	26.0	15.7
Return on Assets %	1.2	1.1	1.1	1.1	1.1	1.1	1.1
Price Range	40¾-27¹³⁄₁₆	41¼-28	32¾-18¹³⁄₁₆	20¹³⁄₁₆-15¹⁄₁₆	15¹¹⁄₁₆-10¹¹⁄₁₆	12³⁄₁₆-9¼	13⅛-6⅞
P/E Ratio	17.6-12.0	20.2-13.7	18.4-10.6	14.2-10.2	11.7-8.0	9.5-7.2	12.6-6.6
Average Yield %	1.4	1.2	1.5	2.0	2.4	2.6	2.5

Statistics are as originally reported. Adj. for 100% stk. split, 4/98, 2-for-1, 6/95. ① Bef. extraord. loss of $1.8 mill.

OFFICERS:
D. Nabers Jr., Chmn., C.E.O.
J. D. Johns, Pres., C.O.O.
A. S. Williams III, Exec. V.P., Treas.
D. J. Long, Sr. V.P., Gen. Couns., Sec.

INVESTOR CONTACT: Drayton Nabers, Jr., C.E.O., (205) 868-3515

PRINCIPAL OFFICE: 2801 Highway 280 South, Birmingham, AL 35223

TELEPHONE NUMBER: (205) 879-9230
FAX: (205) 868-3541
WEB: www.protective.com

NO. OF EMPLOYEES: 2,628 (approx.)

SHAREHOLDERS: 2,600 (approx.)

ANNUAL MEETING: In May

INCORPORATED: DE, Feb., 1981

INSTITUTIONAL HOLDINGS:
No. of Institutions: 168
Shares Held: 44,936,125
% Held: 69.7

INDUSTRY: Life insurance (SIC: 6311)

TRANSFER AGENT(S): Bank of New York, New York, NY

QUAKER CHEMICAL CORPORATION

YIELD 4.7%
P/E RATIO 9.5

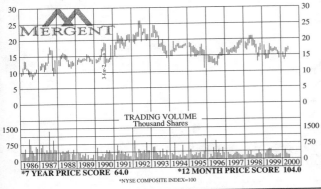

TRADING VOLUME
Thousand Shares

1986 1987 1988 1989 1990 1991 1992 1993 1994 1995 1996 1997 1998 1999 2000
*7 YEAR PRICE SCORE 64.0   ***12 MONTH PRICE SCORE 104.0**
*NYSE COMPOSITE INDEX=100

INTERIM EARNINGS (Per Share):

Qtr.	Mar.	June	Sept.	Dec.
1996	0.19	0.31	d0.68	d0.70
1997	0.30	0.54	0.38	0.23
1998	0.33	0.39	0.40	0.08
1999	0.34	0.42	0.48	0.51

INTERIM DIVIDENDS (Per Share):

Amt.	Decl.	Ex.	Rec.	Pay.
0.19Q	5/12/99	7/14/99	7/16/99	7/30/99
0.195Q	9/15/99	10/13/99	10/15/99	10/29/99
0.195Q	11/17/99	1/12/00	1/17/00	1/31/00
0.195Q	3/22/00	4/12/00	4/14/00	4/28/00
0.195Q	5/10/00	7/13/00	7/17/00	7/31/00

Indicated div.: $0.78

CAPITALIZATION (12/31/99):

	($000)	(%)
Long-Term Debt	25,122	21.2
Deferred Income Tax	3,949	3.3
Minority Interest	8,118	6.9
Common & Surplus	81,199	68.6
Total	118,388	100.0

DIVIDEND ACHIEVER STATUS:
Rank: 232   10-Year Growth Rate: 6.70%
Total Years of Dividend Growth: 28

RECENT DEVELOPMENTS: For the year ended 12/31/99, net income soared 47.0% to $15.7 million compared with $10.7 million in 1998. Results in 1999 and 1998 included an after-tax charge for repositioning and integration of $314,000 and $5.3 million, respectively. Net sales were $258.5 million, up from $257.1 million a year ago. Sales benefited from increases in the Brazil and Asia-Pacific metalworking process chemicals segment.

PROSPECTS: The Company expects results for 2000 will benefit from strategic business initiatives and global-industry reorganization despite the rise of raw material costs. During 1999, the Company announced an organization shift from geographically-based structure to global-industry structure. The change in the Company's structure is expected to enhance performance in the upcoming year through increased opportunities and improved results.

BUSINESS

QUAKER CHEMICAL CORPORATION develops, produces, and markets a broad range of custom-formulated chemical specialty products and is a provider of fluid management services for global manufacturers, primarily in the steel, automotive, aerospace, environmental, pulp and paper, and can industries. The Company's principal product lines include metal processing lubricants and coolants, corrosion preventives, hydraulic fluids, cleaners, surface treatment chemicals, and pulp and paper processing chemicals. Services include computer solutions that provide solutions in product tracking systems, quality systems, and production planning simulation software. Management services include custom-designed packages to clients to assist with reducing manufacturing costs, focusing on core businesses, and reducing liabilities.

ANNUAL FINANCIAL DATA

	12/31/99	12/31/98	12/31/97	12/31/96	12/31/95	12/31/94	12/31/93
Earnings Per Share	⑤ 1.74	⑤ 1.20	④ 1.45	③ d0.88	0.76	② 1.03	① d0.19
Cash Flow Per Share	2.52	2.00	2.28	0.13	1.77	1.89	0.63
Tang. Book Val. Per Share	7.30	7.01	7.01	6.00	8.52	9.15	8.32
Dividends Per Share	0.77	0.73	0.70	0.69	0.68	0.62	0.60
Dividend Payout %	44.0	60.8	48.6	...	89.5	60.2	...
INCOME STATEMENT (IN THOUSANDS):							
Total Revenues	258,461	257,100	241,534	240,251	229,128	196,929	196,425
Costs & Expenses	224,224	232,719	213,122	235,574	206,958	173,912	190,945
Depreciation & Amort.	6,956	7,111	7,264	8,708	8,647	7,250	7,566
Operating Income	27,281	17,270	21,148	d4,031	13,523	15,767	d2,086
Net Interest Inc./(Exp.)	d1,992	d1,589	d1,218	d1,474	d1,426	d846	d91
Income Before Income Taxes	27,151	16,797	19,735	d3,997	12,097	14,921	d2,177
Income Taxes	10,860	6,719	7,893	466	4,887	5,916	234
Equity Earnings/Minority Int.	d640	572	769	d3,136	d522	397	653
Net Income	⑤ 15,651	⑤ 10,650	④ 12,611	③ d7,599	6,688	② 9,402	① d1,758
Cash Flow	22,607	17,761	19,875	1,109	15,335	16,652	5,808
Average Shs. Outstg.	8,975	8,860	8,707	8,635	8,664	8,819	9,242
BALANCE SHEET (IN THOUSANDS):							
Cash & Cash Equivalents	8,677	10,213	18,416	8,525	7,230	11,345	20,293
Total Current Assets	96,241	96,068	98,126	86,552	86,718	83,400	84,387
Net Property	44,752	49,622	40,654	43,960	56,309	51,694	55,541
Total Assets	182,213	189,903	176,640	165,608	185,408	170,172	170,985
Total Current Liabilities	44,657	50,432	47,759	64,034	60,868	43,427	42,642
Long-Term Obligations	25,122	25,344	25,203	5,182	9,300	12,207	16,095
Net Stockholders' Equity	81,199	83,735	75,642	74,254	93,992	93,677	91,383
Net Working Capital	51,584	45,636	50,367	22,518	25,850	39,973	41,745
Year-end Shs. Outstg.	8,934	8,894	8,720	9,664	8,803	8,897	9,242
STATISTICAL RECORD:							
Operating Profit Margin %	10.6	6.7	8.8	...	5.9	8.0	...
Net Profit Margin %	6.1	4.1	5.2	...	2.9	4.8	...
Return on Equity %	19.3	12.7	16.7	...	7.1	8.9	...
Return on Assets %	8.6	5.6	7.4	...	3.6	5.5	...
Debt/Total Assets %	13.8	13.3	14.8	3.1	5.0	7.2	9.4
Price Range	18³⁄₈-13¹⁄₂	21-13	19¹³⁄₁₆-15	17¹⁄₄-11³⁄₄	... 19-11	19¹⁄₂-14³⁄₄	24⁵⁄₈-14¹⁄₄
P/E Ratio	10.6-7.8	17.5-10.8	13.7-10.3	...	25.0-14.5	18.9-14.3	...
Average Yield %	4.8	4.3	4.1	4.7	4.5	3.6	3.1

Statistics are as originally reported. ① Incl. $7.9 mill. reposit. chgs. ② Incl. $347.0 mill. reposit. chgs. ③ Incl. $16.9 mill. aft-tax spl. chg. ④ Incl. $1.7 mill. aft-tax gain fr. sale of Erpn bus. & $1.3 mill. aft-tax chg. for lit. ⑤ Incl. $5.3 mill. aft-tax chgs. for reposit. and integration, 1998; $314,000, 1999.

OFFICERS:
R. J. Naples, Chmn., C.E.O.
J. W. Bauer, Pres., C.O.O.
M. F. Barry, V.P., C.F.O., Treas.

INVESTOR CONTACT: Richard J. Fagan, Controller and Treasurer

PRINCIPAL OFFICE: Elm And Lee Streets, Conshohocken, PA 19428

TELEPHONE NUMBER: (610) 832-4000
FAX: (610) 832-8682
WEB: www.quakerchem.com

NO. OF EMPLOYEES: 923

SHAREHOLDERS: 936

ANNUAL MEETING: In May

INCORPORATED: PA, 1930

INSTITUTIONAL HOLDINGS:
No. of Institutions: 46
Shares Held: 3,594,727
% Held: 40.3

INDUSTRY: Lubricating oils and greases (SIC: 2992)

TRANSFER AGENT(S): American Stock Transfer & Trust Company, New York, NY.

QUESTAR CORPORATION

YIELD 3.3%
P/E RATIO 17.1

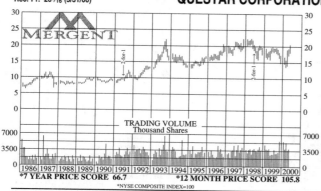

INTERIM EARNINGS (Per Share):

Qtr.	Mar.	June	Sept.	Dec.
1997	0.50	0.16	0.20	0.42
1998	0.50	0.19	0.10	0.14
1999	0.52	0.28	0.18	0.21

INTERIM DIVIDENDS (Per Share):

Amt.	Decl.	Ex.	Rec.	Pay.
0.165Q	5/18/99	5/26/99	5/28/99	6/21/99
0.17Q	8/10/99	8/18/99	8/20/99	9/13/99
0.17Q	10/28/99	11/17/99	11/19/99	12/13/99
0.17Q	2/08/00	2/16/00	2/18/00	3/13/00
0.17Q	5/16/00	5/24/00	5/26/00	6/19/00

Indicated div.: $0.68 (Div. Reinv. Plan)

CAPITALIZATION (12/31/99):

	($000)	(%)
Long-Term Debt	735,043	39.3
Deferred Income Tax	211,112	11.3
Common & Surplus	925,845	49.5
Total	1,872,000	100.0

TRADING VOLUME
Thousand Shares

*7 YEAR PRICE SCORE 66.7   *12 MONTH PRICE SCORE 105.8
*NYSE COMPOSITE INDEX=100

DIVIDEND ACHIEVER STATUS:
Rank: 288   10-Year Growth Rate: 3.55%
Total Years of Dividend Growth: 20

RECENT DEVELOPMENTS: For the year ended 12/31/99, net income increased 28.5% to $98.8 million from $76.9 million in the previous year. Results for 1998 included a $34.0 million write-down of oil and gas properties. Revenues climbed 2.0% to $924.2 million from $906.3 million the year before. Revenues were positively affected by increased natural gas production, higher selling prices and revenues from electronic commerce, which were largely offset by lower revenues from gas distribution.

PROSPECTS: Near-term results are promising as energy prices improve and production and reserves increase. Going forward, the Company should continue to benefit from its nonregulated lines of business. Meanwhile, Questar Exploration and Production Company expanded its operations in Canada by completing the acquisition of Canor. Canor owns more than 800 wells located primarily in Alberta. The acquisition expands Canadian reserves by 61.1 billion cubic feet equivalent.

BUSINESS

QUESTAR CORPORATION is an intergrated energy services holding company. Operations are conducted through two basic divisions: Market Resources and Regulated Services. The Market Resources division is engaged in energy development and production; gas gathering and processing; and wholesale gas, electricity and hydrocarbon liquids marketing and trading. Regulated Services conducts interstate gas transmission and storage activities and retail gas distribution services. Other operations include Questar InfoComm, a full-service provider of integrated information, communications and electronic measurement services and technologies.

ANNUAL FINANCIAL DATA

	12/31/99	12/31/98	12/31/97	12/31/96	12/31/95	12/31/94	12/31/93
Earnings Per Share	1.20	②0.93	1.26	1.20	1.03	①0.61	1.05
Cash Flow Per Share	2.95	2.48	2.82	2.55	2.28	1.82	2.20
Tang. Book Val. Per Share	11.37	10.62	10.30	9.41	8.76	8.08	7.49
Dividends Per Share	0.67	0.65	0.62	0.59	0.58	0.56	0.55
Dividend Payout %	55.8	70.2	49.2	49.8	56.6	93.4	51.9
INCOME STATEMENT (IN MILLIONS):							
Total Revenues	924.2	906.3	933.3	818.0	649.3	670.3	660.4
Costs & Expenses	599.6	644.8	634.6	536.4	406.2	418.1	420.9
Depreciation & Amort.	144.7	128.7	128.5	110.0	101.1	97.6	91.2
Operating Income	179.9	132.8	170.2	171.6	142.0	154.7	148.3
Net Interest Inc./(Exp.)	d53.9	d48.0	d43.8	d41.1	d42.8	d39.8	d34.0
Income Taxes	47.8	29.0	45.6	45.4	32.7	8.6	33.5
Net Income	98.8	②76.9	104.8	98.1	83.8	①49.4	84.5
Cash Flow	243.5	205.6	233.1	207.8	184.4	146.4	175.0
Average Shs. Outstg. (000)	82,676	82,817	82,668	81,656	81,104	80,584	79,990
BALANCE SHEET (IN MILLIONS):							
Gross Property	3,258.8	3,104.5	2,741.9	2,575.0	2,330.9	2,263.2	2,024.4
Accumulated Depreciation	1,471.9	1,356.9	1,210.7	1,097.6	1,020.8	955.5	871.7
Net Property	1,786.9	1,747.6	1,531.2	1,477.3	1,310.1	1,307.6	1,152.7
Total Assets	2,238.0	2,161.3	1,945.0	1,816.2	1,584.6	1,585.6	1,417.7
Long-Term Obligations	735.0	615.8	542.0	555.5	421.7	494.7	371.7
Net Stockholders' Equity	925.8	878.0	845.8	772.1	712.7	653.6	601.9
Year-end Shs. Outstg. (000)	81,419	82,632	82,142	82,050	81,396	80,858	80,338
STATISTICAL RECORD:							
Operating Profit Margin %	19.5	14.7	18.2	21.0	21.9	23.1	22.5
Net Profit Margin %	10.7	8.5	11.2	12.0	12.9	7.4	12.8
Net Inc./Net Property %	5.5	4.4	6.8	6.6	6.4	3.8	7.3
Net Inc./Tot. Capital %	5.3	4.5	6.5	6.4	6.3	3.8	7.4
Return on Equity %	10.7	8.8	12.4	12.7	11.8	7.6	14.0
Accum. Depr./Gross Prop. %	45.2	43.7	44.2	42.6	43.8	42.2	43.1
Price Range	19¹⁵/₁₆-14³/₄	22³/₈-15¹³/₁₆	22⁵/₁₆-17¹/₈	20¹¹/₁₆-15¹¹/₁₆	16⁷/₈-13³/₁₆	17⁵/₈-13⁵/₁₆	22-12¹¹/₁₆
P/E Ratio	16.6-12.3	24.1-17.0	17.7-13.6	17.3-12.9	16.5-12.7	29.1-22.0	21.0-12.1
Average Yield %	3.9	3.4	3.1	3.3	3.9	3.7	3.1

Statistics are as originally reported. Adj. for 2-for-1 stk. split, 6/98 ① Incls. non-recurr. chrg. 12/31/94, $38.1 mill. ($0.95/sh.). ② Incls. one-time chrg. of $20.3 mill.

OFFICERS:
R. D. Cash, Chmn., Pres., C.E.O.
S. E. Parks, V.P., Treas., C.F.O.
C. C. Holbrook, V.P., Corp. Sec.

INVESTOR CONTACT: C. C. Holbrook, V.P. & Sec., (801)324-5202

PRINCIPAL OFFICE: 180 East 100 South Street, Salt Lake City, UT 84145-0433

TELEPHONE NUMBER: (801) 324-5000
FAX: (801) 324-5483
WEB: www.questarcorp.com

NO. OF EMPLOYEES: 2,288 (avg.)

SHAREHOLDERS: 12,046

ANNUAL MEETING: In May

INCORPORATED: UT, Oct., 1984

INSTITUTIONAL HOLDINGS:
No. of Institutions: 174
Shares Held: 50,502,986
% Held: 61.3

INDUSTRY: Gas transmission and distribution (SIC: 4923)

TRANSFER AGENT(S): Questar Corp., Salt Lake City, UT; Bank One, Chicago, IL

RAVEN INDUSTRIES, INC.

YIELD	5.0%
P/E RATIO	10.4

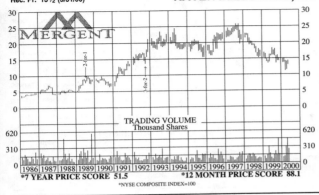

620
TRADING VOLUME
Thousand Shares

| 1986 | 1987 | 1988 | 1989 | 1990 | 1991 | 1992 | 1993 | 1994 | 1995 | 1996 | 1997 | 1998 | 1999 | 2000 |

*7 YEAR PRICE SCORE 51.5   ***12 MONTH PRICE SCORE 88.1**

*NYSE COMPOSITE INDEX=100

INTERIM EARNINGS (Per Share):

Qtr.	Apr.	July	Oct.	Jan.
1994-95	0.29	0.03	0.53	0.42
1995-96	0.32	0.23	0.41	0.34
1996-97	0.38	0.30	0.48	0.45
1997-98	0.44	0.33	0.33	0.55
1998-99	0.21	0.31	0.44	0.34
1999-00	0.31	0.40	0.52	0.31

INTERIM DIVIDENDS (Per Share):

Amt.	Decl.	Ex.	Rec.	Pay.
0.16Q	5/27/99	6/23/99	6/25/99	7/15/99
0.17Q	8/27/99	9/23/99	9/27/99	10/15/99
0.17Q	11/29/99	12/22/99	12/27/99	1/14/00
0.17Q	3/13/00	3/23/00	3/27/00	4/14/00
0.17Q	5/25/00	6/22/00	6/26/00	7/14/00

Indicated div.: $0.68 (Div. Reinv. Plan)

CAPITALIZATION (1/31/00):

	($000)	(%)
Long-Term Debt	3,024	5.3
Common & Surplus	54,519	94.7
Total	57,543	100.0

DIVIDEND ACHIEVER STATUS:
Rank: 77   10-Year Growth Rate: 14.35%
Total Years of Dividend Growth: 12

RECENT DEVELOPMENTS: For the year ended 1/31/00, net income totaled $6.8 million, an increase of 9.4% compared with $6.2 million in the previous year. Earnings for the 2000 period included a gain on the sale of Glasstite of $1.2 million. Net sales declined 3.2% to $147.9 million from $152.8 million the year before. Electronics segment sales climbed 5.6% to $48.9 million from $46.3 million a year earlier. Plastics segment sales fell slightly to $70.7 million from $70.8 million in 1999. Sewn products segment sales decreased 20.6% to $28.3 million from $35.7 million a year earlier. Gross profit as a percentage of net sales grew to 16.6% versus 16.2% in the prior year. Operating income advanced 9.4% to $10.6 million from $9.7 million a year ago. The Company has disposed of a non-strategic business and reduced its underperforming assets, in order to reposition its business in fiscal 2000.

BUSINESS

RAVEN INDUSTRIES, INC. supplies specialized products for a number of markets, including industrial, recreation, agriculture, automotive and defense. Many of these product lines are an extension of technology and production methods developed in the Company's original balloon business. The company has three business segments: Electronics, Plastics and Sewn Products. Assemblies manufactured by the Electronics segment include communication, computer and other products. Flow control devices, used primarily for precision farming applications, are designed and produced within this business segment. The segment also builds and installs automated control systems for use in feedmills. Products in the Plastics segment include heavy-duty sheeting for industrial and agricultural applications; fiberglass, polyethylene and dual-laminate tanks for industrial and agricultural use; high altitude balloons for public and commercial research; and pickup-truck toppers sold in the small truck aftermarket. The Sewn Products segment produces and sells outerwear for a variety of recreational activities, including skiing, hunting and fishing. The segment also manufactures sport balloons principally for recreational use.

ANNUAL FINANCIAL DATA

	1/31/00	1/31/99	1/31/98	1/31/97	1/31/96	1/31/95	1/31/94
Earnings Per Share	1.55	1.30	1.65	1.61	1.30	1.27	1.45
Cash Flow Per Share	2.66	2.38	2.70	2.58	2.18	2.02	2.05
Tang. Book Val. Per Share	11.61	13.27	12.76	11.36	10.05	9.30	8.64
Dividends Per Share	0.65	0.61	0.54	0.49	0.43	0.38	0.30
Dividend Payout %	41.9	46.9	32.7	30.4	33.5	29.5	20.7
INCOME STATEMENT (IN THOUSANDS):							
Total Revenues	147,906	152,798	149,619	139,441	120,444	121,720	121,468
Costs & Expenses	132,445	137,992	133,920	122,904	106,641	109,002	108,131
Depreciation & Amort.	4,884	5,133	5,137	4,566	4,242	3,582	2,897
Operating Income	10,577	9,673	10,562	11,971	9,561	9,136	10,440
Net Interest Inc./(Exp.)	d418	d474	d323	d310	d375	d323	d327
Income Before Income Taxes	10,503	9,649	12,540	11,915	9,566	9,372	10,638
Income Taxes	3,741	3,467	4,478	4,227	3,369	3,284	3,684
Equity Earnings/Minority Int.	...	...	...	...	...	300	350
Net Income	6,762	6,182	8,062	7,688	6,197	6,088	6,954
Cash Flow	11,646	11,315	13,199	12,254	10,439	9,670	9,851
Average Shs. Outstg.	4,372	4,757	4,891	4,755	4,782	4,791	4,796
BALANCE SHEET (IN THOUSANDS):							
Cash & Cash Equivalents	5,707	5,335	2,850	3,439	3,804	2,304	4,446
Total Current Assets	55,371	60,861	57,831	56,696	45,695	43,795	45,037
Net Property	15,068	19,563	19,817	18,142	18,069	18,510	13,371
Total Assets	74,047	83,674	82,590	80,662	67,553	65,636	60,597
Total Current Liabilities	14,702	16,792	19,375	20,016	14,771	15,078	16,088
Long-Term Obligations	3,024	4,572	1,128	3,181	2,816	4,179	2,539
Net Stockholders' Equity	54,519	62,293	61,563	56,729	49,151	45,526	41,100
Net Working Capital	40,669	44,069	38,456	36,680	30,924	28,717	28,949
Year-end Shs. Outstg.	4,694	4,694	4,824	4,836	4,716	4,735	4,694
STATISTICAL RECORD:							
Operating Profit Margin %	7.2	6.3	7.1	8.6	7.9	7.5	8.6
Net Profit Margin %	4.6	4.0	5.4	5.5	5.1	5.0	5.7
Return on Equity %	12.4	9.9	13.1	13.6	12.6	13.4	16.9
Return on Assets %	9.1	7.4	9.8	9.5	9.2	9.3	11.5
Debt/Total Assets %	4.1	5.5	1.4	3.9	4.2	6.4	4.2
Price Range	18¼-13½	22¾-15¼	25¾-19½	23-16	21-15½	24½-18	23½-18
P/E Ratio	11.8-8.7	17.5-11.7	15.6-11.8	14.3-9.9	16.2-11.9	19.3-14.2	16.2-12.4
Average Yield %	4.1	3.2	2.4	2.5	2.4	1.8	1.4

Statistics are as originally reported.

OFFICERS:
D. A. Christensen, Pres., C.E.O.
T. Iacarella, V.P., Fin., Treas., Sec.

INVESTOR CONTACT: T. Iacarella, V.P. Fin., Sec. & Treas., (605) 336-2750

PRINCIPAL OFFICE: 205 E. 6th St., P.O. Box 5107, Sioux Falls, SD 57117

TELEPHONE NUMBER: (605) 336-2750
FAX: (605) 335-0268
WEB: www.ravenind.com

NO. OF EMPLOYEES: 1,100 (approx.)

SHAREHOLDERS: 2,749

ANNUAL MEETING: In May

INCORPORATED: SD, Feb., 1956

INSTITUTIONAL HOLDINGS:
No. of Institutions: 19
Shares Held: 1,742,287
% Held: 43.0

INDUSTRY: Fabricated textile products, nec (SIC: 2399)

TRANSFER AGENT(S): Norwest Bank South Dakota, N.A., St. Paul, MN

RAYMOND JAMES FINANCIAL, INC.

YIELD 1.5%
P/E RATIO 8.4

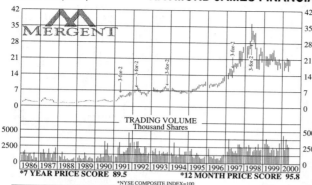

TRADING VOLUME Thousand Shares

7 YEAR PRICE SCORE 89.5   *12 MONTH PRICE SCORE 95.8*

*NYSE COMPOSITE INDEX=100

INTERIM EARNINGS (Per Share):

Qtr.	Dec.	Mar.	June	Sept.
1995-96	0.27	0.22	0.30	0.61
1996-97	0.37	0.79	0.35	0.53
1997-98	0.47	0.50	0.46	0.45
1998-99	0.36	0.45	0.49	0.46
1999-00	0.56	...	...	...

INTERIM DIVIDENDS (Per Share):

Amt.	Decl.	Ex.	Rec.	Pay.
0.07Q	5/21/99	6/14/99	6/16/99	7/01/99
0.07Q	8/25/99	9/14/99	9/16/99	10/05/99
0.075Q	11/19/99	12/10/99	12/14/99	1/10/00
0.075Q	2/14/00	3/17/00	3/21/00	4/05/00
0.075Q	5/25/00	6/16/00	6/20/00	7/05/00

Indicated div.: $0.30

CAPITALIZATION (9/24/99):

	($000)	(%)
Common & Surplus	558,486	100.0
Total	558,486	100.0

DIVIDEND ACHIEVER STATUS:
Rank: 5   10-Year Growth Rate: 26.68%
Total Years of Dividend Growth: 13

RECENT DEVELOPMENTS: For the quarter ended 12/31/99, net income advanced 53.4% to $26.8 million from $17.5 million in the prior-year period. Total revenues improved 45.1% to $383.9 million from $264.5 million a year earlier. Securities commissions and fees increased 48.6% to $244.0 million from $164.3 million in the previous year. Interest revenue grew 54.4% to $75.9 million compared with $49.2 million in the prior year.

PROSPECTS: Looking ahead, RJF expects continued growth in commissions, interest revenues, financial services fees and investment banking income. Separately, the Company introduced a mutual fund electronic order entry system for its financial advisors, which should reduce costs, alleviate processing problems and reduce errors. A series of additional support systems will be introduced to benefit RJF's clients and financial advisors throughout 2000.

BUSINESS

RAYMOND JAMES FINANCIAL, INC., with assets totaling $6.08 billion as of 3/31/00, is a Florida-based holding company that was incorporated in 1974 as a successor to its predecessor corporation founded in 1962. The Company, through its subsidiaries, is primarily engaged in investment and financial planning, including securities brokerage, investment banking and asset management; banking and cash management; trust services; and life insurance. The Company's two broker/dealer subsidiaries, Raymond James & Associates and Raymond James Financial Services, serve more than 1,000,000 individual and institutional accounts. The Company's asset management subsidiaries manage in excess of $17.00 billion in financial assets for individuals, pension plans and municipalities.

BUSINESS LINE ANALYSIS

(09/24/99)	Rev (%)	Inc (%)
Retail Distribution	68.8	65.9
Institutional Distribution	12.9	9.3
Investment Banking	2.9	2.6
Asset Management	7.7	15.7
Other Revenue	7.7	6.5
Total	100.0	100.0

ANNUAL FINANCIAL DATA

	9/24/99	9/25/98	9/26/97	9/27/96	9/29/95	9/30/94	9/24/93
Earnings Per Share	1.76	② 1.86	① 2.04	1.40	0.99	0.88	1.01
Cash Flow Per Share	2.17	2.18	2.32	1.63	1.20	1.02	1.12
Tang. Book Val. Per Share	11.08	10.56	8.87	6.67	5.74	4.65	4.29
Dividends Per Share	0.28	0.24	0.21	0.17	0.16	0.14	0.09
Dividend Payout %	15.9	12.9	10.2	12.1	16.1	16.3	9.4
INCOME STATEMENT (IN MILLIONS):							
Total Revenues	1,232.2	1,082.9	927.6	721.8	554.1	507.1	451.7
Costs & Expenses	1,074.6	916.4	753.8	601.9	469.9	432.9	366.5
Depreciation & Amort.	20.1	16.3	13.3	11.3	9.7	7.0	5.0
Operating Income	137.5	150.2	160.5	108.5	74.5	67.2	80.3
Income Before Income Taxes	137.5	150.2	160.5	108.5	74.5	67.2	80.3
Income Taxes	52.4	57.5	61.6	42.5	28.3	25.1	30.9
Net Income	85.1	② 92.7	① 98.9	66.0	46.1	42.1	49.3
Cash Flow	105.1	109.0	112.2	77.3	55.8	49.1	54.3
Average Shs. Outstg. (000)	48,449	49,951	48,387	47,306	46,586	48,058	48,652
BALANCE SHEET (IN MILLIONS):							
Cash & Cash Equivalents	1,353.8	1,243.5	888.8	735.3	454.4	295.6	208.2
Total Current Assets	4,259.8	3,223.7	2,769.2	2,152.1	1,739.2	1,456.3	1,322.4
Net Property	91.3	81.4	51.7	39.6	40.9	42.1	35.2
Total Assets	5,030.7	3,852.7	3,278.6	2,566.4	2,012.7	1,698.3	1,447.6
Total Current Liabilities	4,472.2	3,298.1	2,841.2	2,214.9	1,733.4	1,457.6	1,228.6
Long-Term Obligations	...	44.8	14.2	24.9	13.1	13.2	13.4
Net Stockholders' Equity	558.5	509.9	423.3	326.6	266.2	227.5	205.6
Net Working Capital	d212.4	d74.4	d72.0	d62.7	5.8	d1.3	93.8
Year-end Shs. Outstg. (000)	47,242	48,268	47,696	48,998	46,382	48,879	47,961
STATISTICAL RECORD:							
Operating Profit Margin %	11.2	13.9	17.3	15.0	13.4	13.3	17.8
Net Profit Margin %	6.9	8.6	10.7	9.1	8.3	8.3	10.9
Return on Equity %	15.2	18.2	23.4	20.2	17.3	18.5	24.0
Return on Assets %	1.7	2.4	3.0	2.6	2.3	2.5	3.4
Debt/Total Assets %	...	1.2	0.4	1.0	0.7	0.8	0.9
Price Range	25³⁄₁₆-16¹¹⁄₁₆	36½-16¾	26½-12¹¹⁄₁₆	13¹¹⁄₁₆-8⁷⁄₁₆	11¹⁄₄-6¹⁄₈	8⁵⁄₁₆-5¹³⁄₁₆	9-6¹⁄₁₆
P/E Ratio	14.3-9.5	19.6-9.0	13.0-6.1	9.8-6.1	11.3-6.2	9.5-6.7	8.9-6.0
Average Yield %	1.3	0.9	1.1	1.5	1.8	2.0	1.3

Statistics are as originally reported. Adj for 3-for-2 stock split, 4/98, 4/97 & 11/93. ① Incl. $30.6 mill. gain fr. the sale of Liberty Investment Management, Inc. & a $2.5 mill. gin fr. the sale of the Company's former headquarters building. ② Incl. $1.7 mill. gain related to the sale of the real estate portfolio and property management subsidiaries & $2.4 mill. gain from the sale of the Company's specialist operations on the Chicago Exchange.

OFFICERS:
T. A. James, Chmn., C.E.O.
R. F. Schuck, Vice-Chmn.
F. S. Godbold, Pres.
J. P. Julien, V.P., C.F.O.

INVESTOR CONTACT: Lawrence Silver, V.P., (727) 573-3800

PRINCIPAL OFFICE: 880 Carillon Parkway, St. Petersburg, FL 33716

TELEPHONE NUMBER: (727) 573-3800
FAX: (727) 573-8365
WEB: www.raymondjames.com

NO. OF EMPLOYEES: 4,480

SHAREHOLDERS: 11,000 (approx.)

ANNUAL MEETING: In Feb.

INCORPORATED: FL, 1974

INSTITUTIONAL HOLDINGS:
No. of Institutions: 113
Shares Held: 21,544,330
% Held: 46.2

INDUSTRY: Security brokers and dealers (SIC: 6211)

TRANSFER AGENT(S): ChaseMellon Shareholder Services, Ridgefield Park, NJ

REGIONS FINANCIAL CORPORATION

YIELD 4.8%
P/E RATIO 9.3

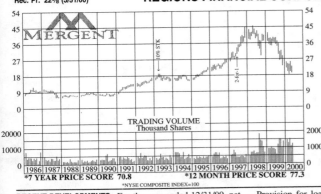

TRADING VOLUME
Thousand Shares

*7 YEAR PRICE SCORE 70.8   *12 MONTH PRICE SCORE 77.3
*NYSE COMPOSITE INDEX=100

INTERIM EARNINGS (Per Share):

Qtr.	Mar.	June	Sept.	Dec.
1996	0.43	0.50	0.41	0.52
1997	0.52	0.54	0.56	0.57
1998	0.56	0.59	0.23	0.57
1999	0.61	0.63	0.59	0.59

INTERIM DIVIDENDS (Per Share):

Amt.	Decl.	Ex.	Rec.	Pay.
0.25Q	5/20/99	6/15/99	6/17/99	7/01/99
0.25Q	7/21/99	9/13/99	9/15/99	10/01/99
0.25Q	11/17/99	12/14/99	12/16/99	1/03/00
0.27Q	1/19/00	3/15/00	3/17/00	4/03/00
0.27Q	5/16/00	6/14/00	6/16/00	7/03/00

Indicated div.: $1.08 (Div. Reinv. Plan)

CAPITALIZATION (12/31/99):

	($000)	(%)
Total Deposits	29,989,094	86.2
Long-Term Debt	1,750,861	5.0
Common & Surplus	3,065,112	8.8
Total	34,805,067	100.0

DIVIDEND ACHIEVER STATUS:
Rank: 154   10-Year Growth Rate: 10.02%
Total Years of Dividend Growth: 28

RECENT DEVELOPMENTS: For the year ended 12/31/99, net income advanced 24.6% to $525.4 million from $421.7 million in the previous year. Earnings for 1998 included merger-related charges of $121.4 million. The increase in earnings reflected acquisition activity and internal growth. Net interest income increased 7.6% to $1.43 billion from $1.32 billion in the prior year. Interest and fees on loans grew 6.3% to $2.20 billion from $2.07 billion a year earlier.

Provision for loan losses surged to $113.7 million versus $60.5 million in 1998. Total non-interest income increased 13.2% to $537.1 million. Service charges on deposit accounts rose 13.8% to $195.0 million. However, mortgage service fees declined 7.6% to $103.1 million, while gains on securities fell to $160,000 from $7.0 million the year before. Total non-interest expense declined 3.6% to $1.06 billion from $1.10 billion a year earlier.

BUSINESS

REGIONS FINANCIAL CORPORATON (formerly First Alabama Bancshares, Inc.) is a bank holding company with assets of $42.71 billion as of 12/31/99. The Company operates more than 760 full-service banking offices in Alabama, Arkansas, South Carolina, Texas, Tennessee, Florida, Louisiana and Georgia. RGBK offers commercial banking services and trust services in several locations. First Alabama Bank, the Company's principal banking subsidiary, operates 196 full-service banking offices throughout Alabama. Regions Bank of Florida, the Company's Florida banking affiliate, operates 64 full-service banking offices in northwest Florida. Supplementing the Company's banking operations are a mortgage banking company, credit-life insurance related companies and a registered broker/dealer firm. The Company also has real estate loan origination offices in Georgia, Tennessee, Mississippi and South Carolina.

ANNUAL FINANCIAL DATA

	12/31/99	12/31/98	12/31/97	12/31/96	12/31/95	12/31/94	12/31/93
Earnings Per Share	2.35	1.88	2.15	1.85	1.88	1.70	1.51
Tang. Book Val. Per Share	13.89	13.61	13.99	12.76	12.37	11.26	10.37
Dividends Per Share	0.98	0.89	0.78	0.69	0.65	0.58	0.49
Dividend Payout %	41.7	47.3	36.0	37.3	34.4	34.1	32.7
INCOME STATEMENT (IN MILLIONS):							
Total Interest Income	2,854.7	2,597.8	1,653.1	1,386.1	1,017.3	785.8	555.7
Total Interest Expense	1,428.8	1,273.0	824.2	685.7	520.0	350.1	213.6
Net Interest Income	1,425.9	1,324.8	828.9	700.5	497.3	435.6	342.1
Provision for Loan Losses	113.7	60.5	41.8	29.0	20.7	19.0	21.5
Non-Interest Income	537.1	474.7	258.6	220.7	159.8	143.4	132.0
Non-Interest Expense	1,064.3	1,103.7	600.3	553.8	378.0	343.1	287.0
Income Before Taxes	785.0	635.3	445.3	338.4	258.5	217.0	165.5
Net Income	525.4	421.7	299.7	229.7	172.8	145.9	112.0
Average Shs. Outstg. (000)	223,967	223,781	139,421	124,272	92,194	85,812	74,410
BALANCE SHEET (IN MILLIONS):							
Cash & Due from Banks	1,393.4	1,619.0	726.1	774.8	484.1	551.1	462.0
Securities Avail. for Sale	6,873.3	4,893.4	1,576.6	1,797.5	1,609.3	685.4	20.4
Total Loans & Leases	28,221.2	24,430.1	16,427.6	13,335.5	9,564.4	9,043.5	6,869.5
Allowance for Credit Losses	414.9	379.9	227.0	199.8	148.3	142.7	137.0
Net Loans & Leases	27,806.3	24,050.2	16,200.6	13,135.6	9,416.1	8,900.8	6,732.5
Total Assets	42,714.4	36,831.9	23,034.2	18,930.2	13,708.6	12,839.3	10,476.3
Total Deposits	29,989.1	28,350.1	17,750.9	15,048.3	10,896.1	10,093.1	8,770.7
Long-Term Obligations	1,750.9	571.0	400.2	447.3	552.6	519.2	462.9
Total Liabilities	39,649.3	33,831.5	21,121.4	17,331.4	12,583.4	11,825.5	9,625.4
Net Stockholders' Equity	3,065.1	3,000.4	1,912.9	1,598.7	1,125.1	1,013.9	851.0
Year-end Shs. Outstg. (000)	220,636	220,454	136,696	125,310	90,920	90,016	82,098
STATISTICAL RECORD:							
Return on Equity %	17.1	14.1	15.7	14.4	15.4	14.4	13.2
Return on Assets %	1.2	1.1	1.3	1.2	1.3	1.1	1.1
Equity/Assets %	7.2	8.1	8.3	8.4	8.2	7.9	8.1
Non-Int. Exp./Tot. Inc. %	54.2	61.3	55.2	60.1	57.5	59.2	60.5
Price Range	41⅝-23³¹⁄₁₆	45⅝-28⁷⁄₈	45-25¹¹⁄₁₆	27-20¹⁄₄	22½-15¹⁄₂	18⅜-14⁷⁄₈	19³⁄₁₆-14¹³⁄₁₆
P/E Ratio	17.7-9.9	24.3-15.4	20.9-11.9	14.6-10.9	12.0-8.3	10.8-8.7	12.7-9.8
Average Yield %	3.0	2.4	2.2	2.9	3.4	3.5	2.9

Statistics are as originally reported. Adj. for stk. splits: 2-for-1, 6/13/97; 10% div., 3/1/93

OFFICERS:
J. S. Mackin, Chmn.
R. D. Horsley, Vice-Chmn. & C.F.O.
C. E. Jones Jr., Pres. & C.E.O.
S. E. Upchurch Jr., Exec. V.P., Gen. Couns.

INVESTOR CONTACT: Ronald C. Jackson, Sr. V.P., (205) 326-7090

PRINCIPAL OFFICE: 417 North 20th Street, Birmingham, AL 35203

TELEPHONE NUMBER: (205) 326-7100
FAX: (205) 832-8419
WEB: www.regionsbank.com

NO. OF EMPLOYEES: 14,606

SHAREHOLDERS: 53,338

ANNUAL MEETING: In May

INCORPORATED: DE, June, 1970

INSTITUTIONAL HOLDINGS:
No. of Institutions: 224
Shares Held: 55,836,896
% Held: 24.9

INDUSTRY: National commercial banks (SIC: 6021)

TRANSFER AGENT(S): First Chicago Trust Company of New York, Jersey City, NJ

RELIASTAR FINANCIAL CORP.

YIELD 1.7%
P/E RATIO 18.1

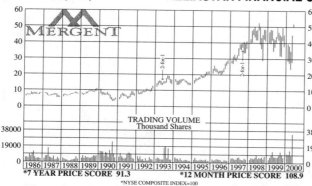

TRADING VOLUME
Thousand Shares

*7 YEAR PRICE SCORE 91.3   *12 MONTH PRICE SCORE 108.9
*NYSE COMPOSITE INDEX=100

INTERIM EARNINGS (Per Share):

Qtr.	Mar.	June	Sept.	Dec.
1995	0.98	1.15	1.10	1.13
1996	1.24	1.23	1.26	1.29
1997	0.63	0.64	0.66	0.62
1998	0.70	0.79	0.73	0.42
1999	0.71	0.81	0.53	0.80

INTERIM DIVIDENDS (Per Share):

Amt.	Decl.	Ex.	Rec.	Pay.
0.205Q	4/08/99	4/22/99	4/26/99	5/14/99
0.205Q	7/08/99	7/15/99	7/19/99	8/13/99
0.205Q	10/14/99	10/21/99	10/25/99	11/12/99
0.205Q	1/13/00	1/20/00	1/24/00	2/11/00
0.22Q	4/13/00	4/19/00	4/24/00	5/12/00

Indicated div.: $0.88 (Div. Reinv. Plan)

CAPITALIZATION (12/31/99):

	($000)	(%)
Long-Term Debt	803,600	26.9
Redeemable Pfd. Stock	242,600	8.1
Common & Surplus	1,945,700	65.0
Total	2,991,900	100.0

DIVIDEND ACHIEVER STATUS:
Rank: 148   10-Year Growth Rate: 10.49%
Total Years of Dividend Growth: 28

RECENT DEVELOPMENTS: For the year ended 12/31/99, net income totaled $253.6 million compared with income from continuing operations of $244.9 million in the previous year. Results included special after-tax charges of $1.9 million in 1999 and $34.3 million in 1998. Total revenues climbed 6.6% to $3.04 billion compared with $2.85 billion in the prior year. Premiums revenues jumped 17.6% to $1.19 billion versus $1.01 billion a year earlier.

PROSPECTS: During 2000, the personal financial services segment plans to introduce several Internet strategies designed to supplement existing distribution channels by generating leads, and providing agents with access to educational materials and retirement planning tools. Accordingly, the Company announced the launch of a new Internet marketing initiative, IHateFinancialPlanning.com. The new site should target approximately 17.6 million households.

BUSINESS

RELIASTAR FINANCIAL CORP. is a Minneapolis-based holding company whose subsidiaries specialize in providing life insurance and related financial services products. RLR operates in four reportable segments: Personal Financial Services, Worksite Financial Services, Tax-Sheltered and Fixed Annuities, and Reinsurance. The Company has four life insurance company subsidiaries, each of which is owned directly or indirectly by ReliaStar Life Insurance Company. These include ReliaStar Life, Northern Life Insurance Company, Security-Connecticut Life Insurance Company, and ReliaStar Life Insurance Company of New York. These subsidiaries provide and distribute individual life insurance and annuities, employee benefits products and services, retirement plans, life and health reinsurance, mutual funds and bank products.

ANNUAL FINANCIAL DATA

	12/31/99	12/31/98	12/31/97	12/31/96	12/31/95	12/31/94	12/31/93
Earnings Per Share	2.85	③ 2.64	2.55	2.52	② 2.18	① 1.65	1.32
Tang. Book Val. Per Share	21.89	23.85	22.25	17.71	18.28	11.85	12.02
Dividends Per Share	0.80	0.71	0.60	0.55	0.49	0.44	0.39
Dividend Payout %	28.1	26.9	23.7	21.7	22.4	26.5	29.8
INCOME STATEMENT (IN MILLIONS):							
Total Premium Income	1,192.8	1,014.1	887.9	836.9	851.5	726.9	659.6
Net Investment Income	1,115.9	1,116.9	1,025.0	940.7	891.1	618.3	635.0
Other Income	728.6	717.2	597.4	413.0	347.8	225.6	195.9
Total Revenues	3,037.3	2,848.2	2,510.3	2,190.6	2,090.4	1,570.8	1,490.4
Policyholder Benefits	1,715.2	1,552.0	1,372.0	1,287.7	1,321.2	1,025.3	1,006.3
Income Before Income Taxes	403.1	401.1	359.9	304.1	259.8	166.6	128.6
Income Taxes	136.3	143.0	127.5	106.1	90.7	58.4	46.1
Net Income	253.6	③ 244.9	222.0	193.0	② 169.1	① 107.7	82.5
Average Shs. Outstg. (000)	89,000	92,700	87,100	74,600	73,800	60,244	56,302
BALANCE SHEET (IN MILLIONS):							
Cash & Cash Equivalents	205.6	190.2	203.6	151.8	180.0	83.4	110.2
Premiums Due	940.0	705.4	541.9	370.0	328.2	226.8	197.0
Invst. Assets: Fixed-term	11,041.8	11,625.1	11,146.7	9,298.2	9,053.7	5,781.0	5,359.4
Invst. Assets: Equities	54.9	60.3	27.0	36.9	35.9	43.7	44.9
Invst. Assets: Loans	3,049.6	2,857.1	2,934.0	2,404.4	2,448.3	1,877.1	2,038.5
Invst. Assets: Total	14,463.2	14,909.1	14,420.5	11,996.3	11,814.2	7,918.2	7,716.3
Total Assets	24,926.9	22,608.7	21,000.8	16,707.0	15,519.2	10,366.8	9,912.9
Long-Term Obligations	803.6	509.4	593.5	407.5	422.3	194.6	230.3
Net Stockholders' Equity	1,945.7	2,120.2	2,011.0	1,417.7	1,420.1	798.5	800.6
Year-end Shs. Outstg. (000)	88,900	88,900	90,400	80,034	72,634	59,576	58,892
STATISTICAL RECORD:							
Return on Revenues %	8.3	8.6	8.8	8.8	8.1	6.9	5.5
Return on Equity %	13.0	11.6	11.0	13.6	11.9	13.5	10.3
Return on Assets %	1.0	1.1	1.1	1.2	1.1	1.0	0.8
Price Range	49¹³/₁₆-31¹¹/₁₆	52⁷/₁₆-29	41¹/₁₆-27	29³/₁₆-20	22¹/₄-14½	17¼-13½	19⅜-12³/₁₆
P/E Ratio	17.5-11.1	19.9-11.0	16.1-10.6	11.6-8.0	10.2-6.7	10.5-8.2	14.7-9.2
Average Yield %	2.0	1.7	1.8	2.2	2.7	2.8	2.5

Statistics are as originally reported. Adj. for 2-for-1 spl., 5/93 & 9/97. ① Bef. dr$2.6 mill. disc. op. ② Bef. dr$5.4 mill. disc. op. ③ Bef. disc. oper. loss $7.2 mill.

OFFICERS:
J. G. Turner, Chmn., C.E.O.
R. C. Salipante, Pres., C.O.O.
J. R. Miller, Sr. V.P., C.F.O., Treas.
R. R. Crowl, Sr. V.P., Gen. Couns., Sec.

INVESTOR CONTACT: Karen E. Glasgow, Dir., Investor Relations, (612) 342-3979

PRINCIPAL OFFICE: 20 Washington Ave. South, Minneapolis, MN 55401

TELEPHONE NUMBER: (612) 372-5432
FAX: (612) 342-3966
WEB: www.reliastar.com

NO. OF EMPLOYEES: 3,800 (avg.)

SHAREHOLDERS: 21,711

ANNUAL MEETING: In May

INCORPORATED: DE, 1988

INSTITUTIONAL HOLDINGS:
No. of Institutions: 239
Shares Held: 58,567,250
% Held: 66.2

INDUSTRY: Life insurance (SIC: 6311)

TRANSFER AGENT(S): Norwest Bank Minnesota, N.A., St. Paul, MN.

REYNOLDS & REYNOLDS COMPANY

YIELD 2.0%
P/E RATIO 13.9

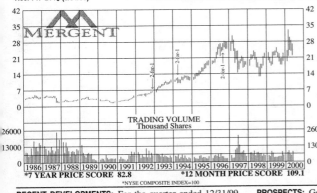

TRADING VOLUME
Thousand Shares

| 1986 | 1987 | 1988 | 1989 | 1990 | 1991 | 1992 | 1993 | 1994 | 1995 | 1996 | 1997 | 1998 | 1999 | 2000 |

*7 YEAR PRICE SCORE 82.8   ***12 MONTH PRICE SCORE 109.1**

*NYSE COMPOSITE INDEX=100

INTERIM EARNINGS (Per Share):

Qtr.	Dec.	Mar.	June	Sept.
1995-96	0.25	0.27	0.29	0.29
1996-97	0.30	0.31	0.09	Nil
1997-98	0.29	0.32	0.32	0.38
1998-99	0.29	0.38	0.39	0.40
1999-00	0.40	...	...	...

INTERIM DIVIDENDS (Per Share):

Amt.	Decl.	Ex.	Rec.	Pay.
0.10Q	8/10/99	8/20/99	8/24/99	9/10/99
0.11Q	11/16/99	12/15/99	12/17/99	1/13/00
0.11Q	2/10/00	3/20/00	3/22/00	4/13/00
0.11Q	5/09/00	5/22/00	5/24/00	6/13/00

Indicated div.: $0.44 (Div. Reinv. Plan)

CAPITALIZATION (9/30/99):

	($000)	(%)
Long-Term Debt	383,408	40.2
Deferred Income Tax	106,232	11.1
Common & Surplus	463,435	48.6
Total	953,075	100.0

DIVIDEND ACHIEVER STATUS:
Rank: 54   10-Year Growth Rate: 15.46%
Total Years of Dividend Growth: 10

RECENT DEVELOPMENTS: For the quarter ended 12/31/99, net income was $31.3 million, up 35.6% versus income from continuing operations of $23.1 million a year earlier. Net sales and revenues climbed 17.6% to $418.0 million from $355.6 million the previous year. Automotive division sales advanced 19.8% to $210.0 million, while sales in the Information Solutions division grew 16.0% to $198.3 million. Financial Services sales rose 4.2% to $9.8 million.

PROSPECTS: Going forward, revenue growth is expected to be driven by the introduction of new e-business services and continued growth of customer relationship management services. However, earnings are not expected to grow as rapidly as revenues due to increased research and development and related expenses stemming from the Company's efforts to expand its e-business offerings.

BUSINESS

REYNOLDS & REYNOLDS COMPANY operates principally in three business segments: the Automotive Group, the Information Solutions Group and Financial Services. The Automotive Group provides integrated computer systems products and services, customer relationship networking software, paper-based and electronic business forms for automotive retailers and manufacturers. The Information Solutions Group sells a mix of traditional forms and digital products for medium to large-sized organizations. Through its wholly-owned subsidiary, Reyna Capital Corporation, REY provides financing services to automotive retailers across North America who wish to invest in the acquisition of one of the Automotive Group's retail management systems.

REVENUES

(9/30/1999)	($000)	(%)
Automotive	793,309	50.7
Information Solutions	731,048	46.8
Financial Services	38,674	2.5
Total	1,563,031	100.0

ANNUAL FINANCIAL DATA

	9/30/99	9/30/98	9/30/97	9/30/96	9/30/95	9/30/94	9/30/93
Earnings Per Share	③ 1.46	③ 1.40	② 0.70	1.10	0.92	0.76	① 0.60
Cash Flow Per Share	2.04	2.13	1.43	1.62	1.36	1.16	0.89
Tang. Book Val. Per Share	3.88	3.12	2.50	2.50	1.99	1.83	1.50
Dividends Per Share	0.40	0.36	0.32	0.25	0.20	0.17	0.13
Dividend Payout %	27.4	25.7	45.7	22.7	21.7	21.9	21.7
INCOME STATEMENT (IN MILLIONS):							
Total Revenues	1,563.0	1,486.0	1,385.7	1,100.4	910.9	808.8	697.0
Costs & Expenses	1,310.4	1,223.0	1,199.0	891.3	736.5	675.8	580.8
Depreciation & Amort.	47.3	59.6	60.6	44.3	37.3	34.9	25.1
Operating Income	205.3	203.4	126.0	164.8	137.0	98.1	91.1
Net Interest Inc./(Exp.)	d6.2	d12.7	d8.1	d4.1	d2.1	d2.4	d2.0
Income Before Income Taxes	199.3	188.0	115.7	162.2	136.8	97.3	89.3
Income Taxes	82.3	74.5	56.5	68.5	58.2	31.1	36.8
Net Income	③ 116.9	③ 113.6	② 59.2	93.7	78.6	66.2	① 52.5
Cash Flow	164.3	173.1	119.9	138.1	115.9	101.1	77.6
Average Shs. Outstg. (000)	80,340	81,146	84,012	85,228	85,032	87,562	87,572
BALANCE SHEET (IN MILLIONS):							
Cash & Cash Equivalents	103.6	40.0	7.6	11.1	18.4	20.2	9.4
Total Current Assets	467.6	372.0	327.9	271.1	188.2	175.5	168.9
Net Property	187.8	174.2	188.5	167.7	128.5	117.5	111.2
Total Assets	1,262.1	1,157.7	1,102.5	923.6	755.5	634.7	570.6
Total Current Liabilities	212.0	198.2	208.6	167.3	125.8	90.0	83.4
Long-Term Obligations	383.4	372.1	368.5	246.5	173.1	145.4	127.7
Net Stockholders' Equity	463.4	404.5	364.2	373.0	332.6	293.0	263.3
Net Working Capital	255.6	173.8	119.3	103.8	62.4	85.5	85.5
Year-end Shs. Outstg. (000)	96,532	97,757	98,986	100,961	102,012	103,414	108,476
STATISTICAL RECORD:							
Operating Profit Margin %	13.1	13.7	9.1	15.0	15.0	12.1	13.1
Net Profit Margin %	7.5	7.6	4.3	8.5	8.6	8.2	7.5
Return on Equity %	25.2	28.1	16.3	25.1	23.6	22.6	19.9
Return on Assets %	9.3	9.8	5.4	10.1	10.4	10.4	9.2
Debt/Total Assets %	30.4	32.1	33.4	26.7	22.9	22.9	22.4
Price Range	25¹⁵/₁₆-17⁵/₁₆	24-12⁵/₈	30⁵/₈-14⅛	28¼-18³/₁₆	19¹³/₁₆-11⁷/₁₆	13⁵/₁₆-9⁷/₈	11½-6¹¹/₁₆
P/E Ratio	17.3-11.9	17.1-9.0	43.7-20.5	25.7-16.5	21.5-12.4	17.6-13.1	19.1-10.1
Average Yield %	1.9	2.0	1.4	1.1	1.3	1.4	1.5

Statistics are as originally reported. Adj. for 2-for-1 stk. split, 9/96 & 3/94. ① Bef. $19.1 mil ($0.22/sh) chg. for acctg. adj. ② Incl. $34.1 mil ($0.41/sh) non-recur. after-tax chg. ③ Bef. disc. oper. gain of $5.8 mil ($0.07/sh), 1999; loss $10.4 mill. ($0.13/sh.), 1998.

OFFICERS:
D. R. Holmes, Chmn., C.E.O.
L. G. Waterhouse, Pres., C.O.O.
D. L. Medford, V.P., C.F.O.
M. J. Gapinski, Treas., Asst. Sec.

INVESTOR CONTACT: Mitch Haws, Director of Investor Relations, (937) 485-4460

PRINCIPAL OFFICE: 115 South Ludlow Street, Dayton, OH 45402

TELEPHONE NUMBER: (937) 485-2000
FAX: (937) 449-4213
WEB: www.reyrey.com

NO. OF EMPLOYEES: 9,083 (avg.)

SHAREHOLDERS: 3,874 (Cl. A); 1 (Cl. B)

ANNUAL MEETING: In Feb.

INCORPORATED: OH, 1889

INSTITUTIONAL HOLDINGS:
No. of Institutions: 193
Shares Held: 57,390,969
% Held: 74.3

INDUSTRY: Manifold business forms (SIC: 2761)

TRANSFER AGENT(S): Norwest Bank Minnesota, N.A., South St. Paul, MN

NYSE SYMBOL RLI
Rec. Pr. 36 3/8 (5/31/00)

RLI CORP.

YIELD 1.6%
P/E RATIO 11.8

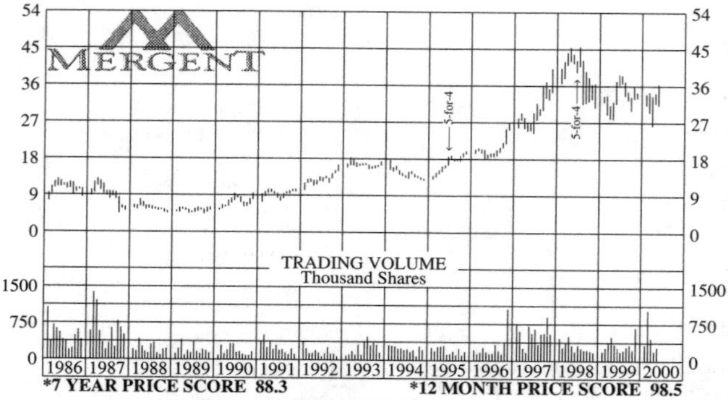

54
45
36
27
18
9
0
MERGENT
5-for-4
5-for-4
TRADING VOLUME
Thousand Shares
1500
750
0
1986 1987 1988 1989 1990 1991 1992 1993 1994 1995 1996 1997 1998 1999 2000

*7 YEAR PRICE SCORE 88.3 *12 MONTH PRICE SCORE 98.5

*NYSE COMPOSITE INDEX=100

INTERIM EARNINGS (Per Share):

Qtr.	Mar.	June	Sept.	Dec.
1995	0.54	0.56	d0.98	0.49
1996	0.50	0.57	0.60	0.62
1997	0.59	0.72	0.67	0.68
1998	0.65	0.71	0.53	0.77
1999	0.63	0.88	0.84	0.74

INTERIM DIVIDENDS (Per Share):

Amt.	Decl.	Ex.	Rec.	Pay.
0.14Q	5/07/99	6/28/99	6/30/99	7/15/99
0.14Q	8/30/99	9/28/99	9/30/99	10/15/99
0.14Q	12/14/99	12/29/99	12/31/99	1/14/00
0.14Q	3/10/00	3/29/00	3/31/00	4/14/00
0.15Q	5/04/00	6/28/00	6/30/00	7/14/00

Indicated div.: $0.60 (Div. Reinv. Plan)

CAPITALIZATION (12/31/99):

	($000)	(%)
Deferred Income Tax	41,662	12.4
Common & Surplus	293,069	87.6
Total	334,731	100.0

DIVIDEND ACHIEVER STATUS:
Rank: 190 10-Year Growth Rate: 8.59%
Total Years of Dividend Growth: 23

RECENT DEVELOPMENTS: For the year ended 12/31/99, net income advanced 11.3% to $31.5 million compared with $28.2 million in the previous year. Consolidated revenues jumped 34.3% to $225.8 million from $168.1 million the year before. Net premiums earned soared 37.2% to 195.3 million from $142.3 million in 1998. Net investment income rose 8.6% to $26.0 million from $23.9 million in the prior year. Net realized investment gains more than doubled to $4.5 million from $1.9 million a year earlier. Equity in earnings of unconsolidated investee increased 20.6% to $1.6 million from $1.3 million a year ago. In 2000, the Company will attempt to improve the top-line via the addition of underwriting talent in certain production lines, strategic alliances with producers on existing products, or through acquisition. The Company expects some leveling of difference in conditions premiums in 2000 despite a continued soft market.

BUSINESS

RLI CORP. is a holding company, which, through its subsidiaries, underwrites selected property and casualty insurance. RLI Insurance Group is composed primarily of four main insurance companies. RLI Insurance Company, the principal subsidiary, writes multiple lines of insurance on an admitted basis in all 50 states, the District of Columbia and Puerto Rico. Mt. Hawley Insurance Company, a subsidiary of RLI Insurance Company, writes surplus lines of insurance in all 50 states, the District of Columbia, Puerto Rico, the Virgin Islands and Guam. Other companies in the RLI Insurance Group include: Replacement Lens Inc., RLI Insurance Agency, Ltd., RLI Insurance Ltd. and Underwriters Indemnity General Agency, Inc. In December 1996, the Company merged its ophthalmic services subsidiary, RLI Vision Corp., with Hester Enterprises, Inc. The resulting organization operates under the name Maui Jim, Inc. As of 12/31/99, the Company maintained a 44% minority interest in Maui Jim, Inc. In January 1999, the Company announced that its subsidiary RLI Insurance Company acquired Underwriters Indemnity Holdings, Inc. for $40.7 million.

ANNUAL FINANCIAL DATA

	12/31/99	12/31/98	12/31/97	12/31/96	12/31/95	12/31/94	12/31/93
Earnings Per Share	**3.08**	**2.65**	**[1] 2.66**	**[1] 2.28**	**0.81**	**d0.49**	**[2] 1.60**
Cash Flow Per Share	**3.34**	**2.85**	**3.46**	**2.85**	**1.17**	**d0.19**	**1.89**
Tang. Book Val. Per Share	**26.23**	**28.44**	**34.70**	**20.46**	**16.16**	**13.37**	**14.60**
Dividends Per Share	**0.54**	**0.51**	**0.47**	**0.44**	**0.41**	**0.36**	**0.34**
Dividend Payout %	**17.5**	**19.2**	**17.7**	**19.3**	**50.6**	**...**	**21.3**
INCOME STATEMENT (IN THOUSANDS):							
Total Revenues	225,756	168,114	169,424	155,354	190,549	171,902	155,125
Costs & Expenses	177,567	127,380	125,015	115,082	175,434	177,149	132,052
Depreciation & Amort.	2,663	2,070	2,290	2,455	3,499	3,244	3,067
Operating Income	45,526	38,664	42,119	37,818	11,616	d8,491	20,005
Net Interest Inc./(Exp.)	d4,104	d2,280	d1,548	d2,808	d3,347	d3,431	d1,856
Income Before Income Taxes	43,035	37,721	41,522	35,240	8,268	d11,922	18,149
Income Taxes	11,584	9,482	11,351	9,544	319	cr6,921	4,017
Equity Earnings/Minority Int.	1,613	1,337	951	231	...	...	...
Net Income	31,451	28,239	[1] 30,171	[1] 25,696	7,950	d5,001	[2] 14,132
Cash Flow	34,114	30,309	32,461	28,150	11,449	d1,758	17,199
Average Shs. Outstg.	10,222	10,638	9,371	9,871	9,812	9,341	9,108
BALANCE SHEET (IN THOUSANDS):							
Cash & Cash Equivalents	64,092	51,917	18,697	40,824	25,072	60,864	54,248
Total Current Assets	384,210	273,302	217,474	248,844	267,331	302,076	232,928
Net Property	15,441	12,200	12,388	12,127	13,951	14,906	14,658
Total Assets	1,170,363	1,012,685	911,741	845,474	814,647	752,301	668,921
Total Current Liabilities	122,676	73,929	51,992	25,835	40,544	39,860	38,908
Long-Term Obligations	...	...	...	46,000	46,000	52,255	53,000
Net Stockholders' Equity	293,069	293,959	266,552	200,039	158,608	129,597	139,299
Net Working Capital	261,534	199,373	165,482	223,009	226,786	262,217	194,021
Year-end Shs. Outstg.	9,873	10,335	10,793	9,777	9,814	9,420	9,247
STATISTICAL RECORD:							
Operating Profit Margin %	20.2	23.0	24.9	24.3	6.1	...	12.9
Net Profit Margin %	13.9	16.8	17.8	16.5	4.2	...	9.1
Return on Equity %	10.7	9.6	11.3	12.8	5.0	...	10.1
Return on Assets %	2.7	2.8	3.3	3.0	1.0	...	2.1
Debt/Total Assets %	...	...	...	5.4	5.6	6.9	7.9
Price Range	38 13/16-27 7/8	45 5/8-30 11/16	40 3/16-24 3/8	26 13/16-17 7/8	20-13 1/16	17 3/4-12 3/4	18 5/16-15 7/16
P/E Ratio	12.6-9.0	17.2-11.6	12.1-7.3	10.3-6.9	24.7-16.1	...	11.8-10.0
Average Yield %	1.6	1.3	1.4	1.9	2.4	2.4	2.0

Statistics are as originally reported. Adjusted for 5-for-4 stock split 6/95, 6/98. [1] Incl. net realized gains of $0.21 per share, 1997; $0.07 per share, 1996. [2] Excl. $1.7 mill. gain from acctg. changes.

OFFICERS:
J. E. Dondanville, Vice Chmn,, C.F.O.
G. D. Stephens, Pres.

INVESTOR CONTACT: Mike Price, Treasurer, (309) 693-5880

PRINCIPAL OFFICE: 9025 North Lindbergh Drive, Peoria, IL 61615

TELEPHONE NUMBER: (309) 692-1000
FAX: (309) 692-1068
WEB: www.rlicorp.com
NO. OF EMPLOYEES: 394 full-time; 64 part-time
SHAREHOLDERS: 4,098
ANNUAL MEETING: In May
INCORPORATED: IL, 1965; reincorp., DE, 1984

INSTITUTIONAL HOLDINGS:
No. of Institutions: 63
Shares Held: 5,232,093
% Held: 52.7

INDUSTRY: Fire, marine, and casualty insurance (SIC: 6331)

TRANSFER AGENT(S): Norwest Bank Minnesota, N.A., St. Paul, MN.

ROHM & HAAS COMPANY

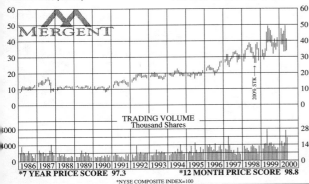

7 YEAR PRICE SCORE 97.3   **12 MONTH PRICE SCORE 98.8**
*NYSE COMPOSITE INDEX=100

TRADING VOLUME
Thousand Shares

2000¢ STK →

INTERIM EARNINGS (Per Share):

Qtr.	Mar.	June	Sept.	Dec.
1997	0.54	0.62	0.48	0.52
1998	0.58	0.96	0.50	0.44
1999	0.64	d0.06	0.26	0.41

INTERIM DIVIDENDS (Per Share):

Amt.	Decl.	Ex.	Rec.	Pay.
0.18Q	5/03/99	5/12/99	5/14/99	6/01/99
0.19Q	7/26/99	8/11/99	8/13/99	9/01/99
0.19Q	10/21/99	11/03/99	11/05/99	12/01/99
0.19Q	2/07/00	2/16/00	2/18/00	3/01/00
0.19Q	5/01/00	5/10/00	5/12/00	6/01/00

Indicated div.: $0.76

CAPITALIZATION (12/31/99):

	($000)	(%)
Long-Term Debt	3,122,000	39.8
Deferred Income Tax	1,231,000	15.7
Minority Interest	19,000	0.2
Common & Surplus	3,475,000	44.3
Total	7,847,000	100.0

DIVIDEND ACHIEVER STATUS:
Rank: 231   10-Year Growth Rate: 6.71%
Total Years of Dividend Growth: 22

RECENT DEVELOPMENTS: For the year ended 12/31/99, net earnings were $249.0 million compared with income before an extraordinary loss of $453.0 million in 1998. Results for 1999 included charges totaling $163.0 million. Results for 1998 included a gain of $131.0 million and excluded an extraordinary loss of $13.0 million. Net sales jumped 43.5% to $5.34 billion from $3.72 billion the year before. Results benefited from strong growth in the Company's core businesses and ongoing cost reduction efforts.

PROSPECTS: Future earnings may be hampered by an increase in raw material costs in the performance polymers segment. For the first quarter of 2000, raw material costs rose 7.0% compared with the fourth quarter of 1999. ROH expects earnings per share for the second quarter of 2000 will be 10.0% lower than the previous quarter if raw material costs continue to rise. Going forward, ROH expects the electronic materials division will continue to grow and benefit from improvements in operating efficiencies.

BUSINESS

ROHM & HAAS COMPANY is a multinational producer of specialty polymers and biologically active compounds. Products range from basic petrochemicals such as propylene, acetone and styrene to differentiated specialty products. It has developed acrylic plastics, a field which it pioneered with its development of Plexiglas (used in outdoor signs, industrial lighting, skylights, and boat windshields). Other products include polymers, resins and monomers geared toward a wide variety of industrial applications. The Company also manufactures agricultural and industrial chemicals. Contributions to sales in 1999 were as follows: performance polymers, 55.0%; chemical specialties, 23.2%; electronic materials, 14.1%; and salt, 7.7%. In January 1999, ROH acquired LeaRonal, an electronic materials firm, and in June 1999 acquired Morton International, a manufacturer of specialty chemicals and salt.

ANNUAL FINANCIAL DATA

	12/31/99	12/31/98	12/31/97	12/31/96	12/31/95	12/31/94	12/31/93
Earnings Per Share	[5] 1.27	[4] 2.52	2.13	[1] 1.82	[3] 1.41	1.26	[2] 0.58
Cash Flow Per Share	3.19	4.02	3.55	3.15	2.60	2.40	1.70
Tang. Book Val. Per Share	. . .	9.66	9.15	8.44	8.16	7.32	6.43
Dividends Per Share	0.74	0.69	0.63	0.57	0.52	0.48	0.45
Dividend Payout %	58.3	27.4	29.7	31.6	37.0	38.0	78.1
INCOME STATEMENT (IN MILLIONS):							
Total Revenues	5,339.0	3,720.0	3,999.0	3,982.0	3,884.0	3,534.0	3,269.0
Costs & Expenses	4,260.0	2,822.0	3,103.0	3,153.0	3,129.0	2,836.0	2,743.0
Depreciation & Amort.	451.0	276.0	279.0	262.0	242.0	231.0	226.0
Operating Income	628.0	622.0	617.0	567.0	513.0	467.0	300.0
Net Interest Inc./(Exp.)	d159.0	d34.0	d39.0	d32.0	d32.0	d39.0	d41.0
Income Before Income Taxes	464.0	700.0	611.0	530.0	441.0	407.0	194.0
Income Taxes	215.0	247.0	201.0	167.0	149.0	143.0	68.0
Equity Earnings/Minority Int.	7.0	2.0	11.0	d17.0	d3.0	. . .	d6.0
Net Income	[5] 249.0	[4] 453.0	410.0	[1] 363.0	[3] 292.0	264.0	[2] 126.0
Cash Flow	698.0	723.0	682.0	618.0	527.0	488.0	344.0
Average Shs. Outstg. (000)	218,981	179,700	192,300	196,200	202,500	203,100	202,857
BALANCE SHEET (IN MILLIONS):							
Cash & Cash Equivalents	57.0	16.0	40.0	11.0	43.0	127.0	35.0
Total Current Assets	2,497.0	1,287.0	1,397.0	1,456.0	1,421.0	1,440.0	1,200.0
Net Property	3,496.0	1,908.0	2,008.0	2,066.0	2,048.0	1,960.0	1,869.0
Total Assets	11,256.0	3,648.0	3,900.0	3,933.0	3,916.0	3,861.0	3,524.0
Total Current Liabilities	2,510.0	875.0	850.0	886.0	828.0	932.0	701.0
Long-Term Obligations	3,122.0	409.0	509.0	562.0	606.0	629.0	690.0
Net Stockholders' Equity	3,475.0	1,561.0	1,797.0	1,728.0	1,781.0	1,620.0	1,441.0
Net Working Capital	d13.0	412.0	547.0	570.0	593.0	508.0	499.0
Year-end Shs. Outstg. (000)	218,981	154,000	182,700	189,300	201,900	203,100	202,935
STATISTICAL RECORD:							
Operating Profit Margin %	11.8	16.7	15.4	14.2	13.2	13.2	9.2
Net Profit Margin %	4.7	12.2	10.3	9.1	7.5	7.5	3.9
Return on Equity %	7.2	29.0	22.8	21.0	16.4	16.3	8.7
Return on Assets %	2.2	12.4	10.5	9.2	7.5	6.8	3.6
Debt/Total Assets %	27.7	11.2	13.1	14.3	15.5	16.3	19.6
Price Range	49¼-28⅛	38⅞-26	33¾-23⁹⁄₁₆	27½-18⁵⁄₁₆	21⅝-16½	22¹³⁄₁₆-17¾	20¹¹⁄₁₆-15¾
P/E Ratio	38.8-22.1	15.4-10.3	15.8-11.1	15.1-10.1	15.4-11.7	18.1-14.1	35.6-27.2
Average Yield %	1.9	2.1	2.2	2.5	2.7	2.4	2.5

Statistics are as originally reported. Adj. for 3-for-1 split, 9/98. [1] Incl. $6.0 mill. aft-tax non-recur. chgs. [2] Bef. dr$19.0 mill. acct. adj. [3] Incl. $17.0 mill. chg. for environ. cleanup. [4] Excl. $13.0 mill. aft-tax extraord. loss fr. exting. of debt. [5] Incl. $105.0 mill. R&D chg., $22.0 mill. loss fr. disp. of jt. vent. & $36.0 mill. restr. chg.

OFFICERS:
R. L. Gupta, Chmn., C.E.O.
J. M. Fitzpatrick, Pres., C.O.O.

INVESTOR CONTACT: Laura L. Hadden, Mgr., Bus. & Fin. Comm., (215) 592-3092

PRINCIPAL OFFICE: 100 Independence Mall West, Philadelphia, PA 19106-2399

TELEPHONE NUMBER: (215) 592-3045
FAX: (215) 592-3377
WEB: www.rohmhaas.com

NO. OF EMPLOYEES: 21,512 (avg.)
SHAREHOLDERS: 9,462
ANNUAL MEETING: In May
INCORPORATED: DE, Apr., 1917

INSTITUTIONAL HOLDINGS:
No. of Institutions: 298
Shares Held: 163,020,442
% Held: 74.5

INDUSTRY: Plastics materials and resins (SIC: 2821)

TRANSFER AGENT(S): EquiServe, LP, Boston, MA.

RPM, INC.

YIELD 5.0%
P/E RATIO 15.7

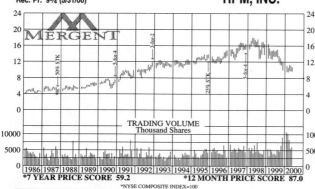

TRADING VOLUME
Thousand Shares

| 1986 | 1987 | 1988 | 1989 | 1990 | 1991 | 1992 | 1993 | 1994 | 1995 | 1996 | 1997 | 1998 | 1999 | 2000 |

*7 YEAR PRICE SCORE 59.2   ***12 MONTH PRICE SCORE 87.0**
*NYSE COMPOSITE INDEX=100

INTERIM EARNINGS (Per Share):

Qtr.	Aug.	Nov.	Feb.	May
1996-97	0.25	0.19	0.08	0.29
1997-98	0.29	0.22	0.06	0.33
1998-99	0.29	0.20	0.06	0.32
1999-00	0.07	0.19	0.04	...

INTERIM DIVIDENDS (Per Share):

Amt.	Decl.	Ex.	Rec.	Pay.
0.117Q	4/05/99	4/14/99	4/16/99	4/30/99
0.117Q	12/30/99	7/14/99	7/16/99	7/30/99
0.122Q	10/08/99	10/14/99	10/18/99	10/29/99
0.122Q	12/30/99	1/12/00	1/14/00	1/28/00
0.122Q	12/30/99	4/12/00	4/14/00	4/28/00

Indicated div.: $0.49

CAPITALIZATION (5/31/99):

	($000)	(%)
Long-Term Debt	582,109	42.2
Deferred Income Tax	53,870	3.9
Common & Surplus	742,876	53.9
Total	1,378,855	100.0

DIVIDEND ACHIEVER STATUS:

Rank: 211   10-Year Growth Rate: 7.72%
Total Years of Dividend Growth: 26

RECENT DEVELOPMENTS: For the quarter ended 2/29/00, net income declined 39.1% to $3.7 million compared with $6.1 million in the equivalent 1999 quarter. Net sales were $411.4 milion, up 10.3% from $373.0 million a year earlier. The decline in earnings was attributed to the seasonality of DAP's business, manufacturing and marketing caulks and sealants and other specialty adhesives in North America. However, the DAP acquisition accounted for approximately all of the sales increase.

PROSPECTS: The DAP acquisition is expected to recover its dilutive earnings in the fourth quarter. As anticipated, RPM's Dryvit subisidiary obtained final court approval of its settlement of the North Carolina class action lawsuit. Based upon the terms of the final settlement, the anticipated claims rate, the attorney fee award and the nearly two years of claims experience of another earlier settling EIFS supplier, RPM believes that Dryvit has adequate financial commitments and other insurance in place to cover its obligations under the settlement.

BUSINESS

RPM, INC. is a widely-diversified manufacturer of protective coatings, with manufacturing facilities in the United States, Belgium, Canada, China, South Africa, the Netherlands, Asia, South America, and Europe. The Company participates in two broad market categories worldwide: industrial and consumer. Brand names include Rust-Oleum®, Carboline®, Bondo®, Zinsser®, and Day-Glo®. Approximately 60% of the Company's sales are derived from the industrial market sectors, with the remainder in consumer products. The vast majority of RPM's specialty coatings, both consumer and industrial, protect existing goods or structures and are generally not affected by cyclical movements in the economy. On 8/31/99, RPM acquired DAP Products Inc. and DAP Canada Corp.

ANNUAL FINANCIAL DATA

	5/31/99	5/31/98	5/31/97	5/31/96	5/31/95	5/31/94	5/31/93
Earnings Per Share	0.86	0.84	0.80	0.72	0.86	0.74	0.66
Cash Flow Per Share	1.44	1.47	1.32	1.17	1.37	1.11	1.02
Tang. Book Val. Per Share	0.77	...	...	0.18	0.71	2.50	1.69
Dividends Per Share	0.45	0.42	0.39	0.36	0.34	0.31	0.29
Dividend Payout %	52.7	50.5	49.0	50.7	39.6	42.1	44.3
INCOME STATEMENT (IN MILLIONS):							
Total Revenues	1,712.2	1,615.3	1,350.5	1,136.4	1,017.0	815.6	625.7
Costs & Expenses	1,457.6	1,372.0	1,131.1	948.1	849.7	688.2	524.7
Depreciation & Amort.	62.1	57.0	51.1	42.6	36.9	25.9	21.4
Operating Income	192.4	186.3	168.3	145.7	130.3	101.5	79.5
Net Interest Inc./(Exp.)	d32.8	d36.7	d32.6	d25.8	d23.4	d13.4	d13.4
Income Before Income Taxes	159.6	149.6	135.7	119.9	106.9	88.1	66.1
Income Taxes	65.1	61.7	57.4	51.0	45.8	35.5	26.7
Net Income	94.5	87.8	78.3	68.9	61.1	52.6	39.4
Cash Flow	156.7	144.8	129.5	111.5	98.0	78.5	60.8
Average Shs. Outstg. (000)	108,731	98,527	97,894	95,685	71,554	70,896	59,486
BALANCE SHEET (IN MILLIONS):							
Cash & Cash Equivalents	19.7	40.8	37.4	34.3	28.0	25.4	24.8
Total Current Assets	705.4	672.5	720.3	465.1	421.3	334.5	280.7
Net Property	339.7	305.9	270.3	224.7	204.0	151.0	134.2
Total Assets	1,737.2	1,683.3	1,633.2	1,155.1	959.1	660.8	584.6
Total Current Liabilities	302.5	285.8	241.8	189.4	151.1	104.0	117.9
Long-Term Obligations	582.1	715.7	784.4	447.7	406.4	233.0	220.9
Net Stockholders' Equity	742.9	567.1	493.3	445.8	347.6	314.5	239.1
Net Working Capital	402.9	386.7	478.5	275.7	270.2	230.5	162.7
Year-end Shs. Outstg. (000)	109,443	100,254	98,029	96,811	71,196	70,939	59,153
STATISTICAL RECORD:							
Operating Profit Margin %	11.2	11.5	12.5	12.8	12.8	12.4	12.7
Net Profit Margin %	5.5	5.4	5.8	6.1	6.0	6.5	6.3
Return on Equity %	12.7	15.5	15.9	15.5	17.6	16.7	16.5
Return on Assets %	5.4	5.2	4.8	6.0	6.4	8.0	6.7
Debt/Total Assets %	33.5	42.5	48.0	38.8	42.4	35.3	37.8
Price Range	18-12¾	16¹³⁄₁₆-12½	14⅞-11½	13¹³⁄₁₆-11⅜	12⁹⁄₁₆-10⅜	12⅜-10³⁄₈	11¹³⁄₁₆-8¹⁄₁₆
P/E Ratio	20.9-14.8	20.0-14.9	18.6-14.4	19.2-15.8	14.7-12.1	16.7-14.0	17.8-12.1
Average Yield %	2.9	2.9	3.0	2.9	3.0	2.8	3.0

Statistics are as originally reported. Adj. for stk. splits: 5-for-4, 12/8/97; 25% div., 12/8/95.

OFFICERS:
T. C. Sullivan, Chmn., C.E.O.
J. A. Karman, Vice-Chmn.
F. C. Sullivan, Pres.
D. P. Reif, III, C.F.O., V.P.

PRINCIPAL OFFICE: 2628 Pearl Road, P.O.
Box 777, Medina, OH 44258

TELEPHONE NUMBER: (330) 273-5090
FAX: (330) 225-8743
WEB: www.rpminc.com
NO. OF EMPLOYEES: 7,537
SHAREHOLDERS: 47,515
ANNUAL MEETING: In Oct.
INCORPORATED: OH, May, 1947

INSTITUTIONAL HOLDINGS:
No. of Institutions: 178
Shares Held: 50,556,820
% Held: 46.8

INDUSTRY: Paints and allied products (SIC: 2851)

TRANSFER AGENT(S): Harris Trust and Savings Bank, Chicago, IL

S & T BANCORP, INC.

	YIELD	4.4%
	P/E RATIO	11.9

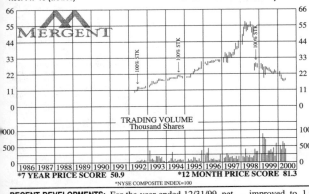

TRADING VOLUME
Thousand Shares

| 1986 | 1987 | 1988 | 1989 | 1990 | 1991 | 1992 | 1993 | 1994 | 1995 | 1996 | 1997 | 1998 | 1999 | 2000 |

*7 YEAR PRICE SCORE 50.9   ***12 MONTH PRICE SCORE 81.3**
*NYSE COMPOSITE INDEX=100

INTERIM EARNINGS (Per Share):

Qtr.	Mar.	June	Sept.	Dec.
1996	----------	1.05	----------	
1997	0.27	0.29	0.30	0.31
1998	0.33	0.34	0.34	0.35
1999	0.37	0.37	0.37	0.39

INTERIM DIVIDENDS (Per Share):

Amt.	Decl.	Ex.	Rec.	Pay.
0.18Q	3/16/99	3/30/99	4/01/99	4/23/99
0.19Q	6/21/99	6/29/99	7/01/99	7/23/99
0.19Q	9/20/99	9/29/99	10/01/99	10/25/99
0.20Q	12/21/99	12/29/99	12/31/99	1/25/00
0.20Q	3/21/00	3/29/00	3/31/00	4/25/00

Indicated div.: $0.80

CAPITALIZATION (12/31/99):

	($000)	(%)
Total Deposits	1,435,065	70.4
Long-Term Debt	364,062	17.9
Common & Surplus	239,700	11.8
Total	2,038,827	100.0

DIVIDEND ACHIEVER STATUS:
Rank: 25   10-Year Growth Rate: 20.20%
Total Years of Dividend Growth: 10

RECENT DEVELOPMENTS: For the year ended 12/31/99, net income advanced 9.1% to $41.4 million compared with $38.0 million in the previous year. Net interest income was $86.8 million, a 5.5% increase from $82.3 million in the previous year. Non-interest income fell 17.7% to $20.1 million from $24.4 million. Noninterest expense increased 3.6% to $43.5 million. The return on average assets improved to 1.95% from 1.90% in the prior year. The improvement was driven by increases in the investment portfolio combined with a strong year in commercial lending, which grew by $1.7 million for the year. Net interest margin fell to 4.61% from 4.55% in the prior year due to higher cost borrowings, a $25 million bank-owned life insurance investment and the share repurchase program.

BUSINESS

S&T BANCORP, INC. is a bank holding company with assets of $2.19 billion in assets as of 12/31/99. The Company has two wholly-owned subsidiaries, S&T Bank and S&T Investment Company, Inc. S&T Bank offers a variety of services including time and demand deposit accounts, secured and unsecured commercial and consumer loans, letters of credit, discount brokerage services, personal finance planning and credit card services. S&T Investment Company, Inc. is an investment holding company, which manages investments previously owned by the bank. The Company operates through a branch network of 38 offices in 7 counties of Pennsylvania. Commonwealth Trust Credit Life Insurance Company is a joint venture that reinsures credit life, accident and health insurance policies sold by S&T Bank.

LOAN DISTRIBUTION

(12/31/99)	($000)	(%)
Real Estate- Construction	94,786	6.3
Real Estate-Resid Mtge	466,881	31.2
Real Estate-Commer Mtge	527,970	35.3
Commercial & Industrial	302,877	20.3
Consumer Installment	103,763	6.9
Total	1,496,277	100.0

ANNUAL FINANCIAL DATA

	12/31/99	12/31/98	12/31/97	12/31/96	12/31/95	12/31/94	12/31/93
Earnings Per Share	1.51	1.35	1.17	1.05	0.91	0.82	0.73
Tang. Book Val. Per Share	8.88	9.38	9.20	7.96	7.42	6.28	5.38
Dividends Per Share	0.74	0.63	0.53	0.45	0.35	0.28	0.23
Dividend Payout %	49.0	46.7	45.3	42.9	38.5	35.0	32.4
INCOME STATEMENT (IN MILLIONS):							
Total Interest Income	156.7	151.4	141.1	111.4	107.0	92.7	86.9
Total Interest Expense	69.9	69.2	62.3	51.5	50.0	39.3	37.0
Net Interest Income	86.8	82.3	78.8	59.9	57.0	53.3	50.0
Provision for Loan Losses	4.0	10.6	5.0	4.3	3.8	3.5	3.6
Non-Interest Income	20.1	24.4	16.4	11.2	8.3	6.9	6.6
Non-Interest Expense	43.5	42.0	43.2	35.5	33.5	31.6	30.8
Income Before Taxes	59.4	54.2	47.1	31.3	28.0	25.1	22.2
Net Income	41.4	38.0	34.1	23.2	20.5	18.4	16.3
Average Shs. Outstg. (000)	27,367	28,055	28,618	22,146	22,486	22,568	22,470
BALANCE SHEET (IN MILLIONS):							
Cash & Due from Banks	38.7	48.7	36.0	33.3	39.9	38.8	32.9
Securities Avail. for Sale	558.0	565.1	521.1	353.8	315.3	118.9	142.7
Total Loans & Leases	1,496.3	1,365.9	1,273.8	1,046.1	976.8	924.4	796.7
Allowance for Credit Losses	27.1	26.7	20.4	17.0	15.9	14.3	13.5
Net Loans & Leases	1,469.1	1,339.2	1,253.3	1,029.1	960.9	910.1	783.2
Total Assets	2,194.1	2,069.6	1,920.3	1,495.9	1,400.7	1,293.7	1,194.0
Total Deposits	1,435.1	1,380.1	1,284.7	1,032.3	979.6	903.2	898.3
Long-Term Obligations	364.1	240.1	144.2	136.6	96.6	43.4	15.0
Total Liabilities	1,954.4	1,810.0	1,660.2	1,319.7	1,233.8	1,152.2	1,072.9
Net Stockholders' Equity	239.7	259.6	260.1	176.3	166.9	141.6	121.1
Year-end Shs. Outstg. (000)	26,999	27,676	28,282	22,150	22,486	22,532	22,520
STATISTICAL RECORD:							
Return on Equity %	17.3	14.6	12.8	13.2	12.3	13.0	13.5
Return on Assets %	1.9	1.8	1.7	1.6	1.5	1.4	1.4
Equity/Assets %	10.9	12.5	13.5	11.8	11.9	10.9	10.1
Non-Int. Exp./Tot. Inc. %	40.7	39.4	45.3	50.0	51.3	52.5	54.4
Price Range	29-19	57¾-24	44½-29½	31¾-28	30½-19½	21¼-17⅜	18⅞-13⅛
P/E Ratio	19.2-12.6	42.8-17.8	38.0-25.2	30.2-26.7	33.5-21.4	26.1-21.3	26.0-18.1
Average Yield %	3.1	1.5	1.4	1.5	1.4	1.5	1.5

Statistics are as originally reported. Adj. for 100% stk. split, 11/98 & 9/94.

OFFICERS:
R. D. Duggan, Chmn.
J. C. Miller, Pres., C.E.O.
R. E. Rout, Exec. V.P., C.F.O.
J. Barone, Exec. V.P., Sec., Treas.

INVESTOR CONTACT: Sandy Ingmire, (724) 465-1466

PRINCIPAL OFFICE: 800 Philadelphia Street, Indiana, PA 15701

TELEPHONE NUMBER: (724) 349-1800
FAX: (412) 465-1488
WEB: www.stbank.com

NO. OF EMPLOYEES: 662

SHAREHOLDERS: 3,218

ANNUAL MEETING: In April

INCORPORATED: PA, March, 1983

INSTITUTIONAL HOLDINGS:
No. of Institutions: 35
Shares Held: 5,406,489
% Held: 19.9

INDUSTRY: State commercial banks (SIC: 6022)

TRANSFER AGENT(S): American Stock Transfer & Trust Company, New York, NY

SAFECO CORPORATION

YIELD 6.0%
P/E RATIO 13.1

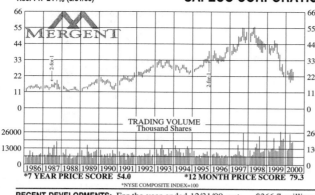

TRADING VOLUME
Thousand Shares

1986|1987|1988|1989|1990|1991|1992|1993|1994|1995|1996|1997|1998|1999|2000
*7 YEAR PRICE SCORE 54.0 *12 MONTH PRICE SCORE 79.3
*NYSE COMPOSITE INDEX=100

INTERIM EARNINGS (Per Share):

Qtr.	Mar.	June	Sept.	Dec.
1995	0.52	0.82	0.91	0.91
1996	0.90	0.82	0.92	0.84
1997	0.88	0.93	0.96	0.58
1998	0.79	0.49	0.54	0.70
1999	0.87	0.54	0.12	0.34

INTERIM DIVIDENDS (Per Share):

Amt.	Decl.	Ex.	Rec.	Pay.
0.37Q	5/05/99	7/07/99	7/09/99	7/26/99
0.37Q	8/04/99	10/06/99	10/08/99	10/25/99
0.37Q	11/03/99	1/05/00	1/07/00	1/24/00
0.37Q	2/02/00	4/05/00	4/07/00	4/24/00
0.37Q	5/03/00	7/05/00	7/07/00	7/24/00

Indicated div.: $1.48 (Div. Reinv. Plan)

CAPITALIZATION (12/31/99):

	($000)	(%)
Long-Term Debt	2,316,100	35.0
Common & Surplus	4,294,100	65.0
Total	6,610,200	100.0

DIVIDEND ACHIEVER STATUS:
Rank: 162   10-Year Growth Rate: 9.71%
Total Years of Dividend Growth: 24

RECENT DEVELOPMENTS:

RECENT DEVELOPMENTS: For the year ended 12/31/99, net income totaled $297.0 million, a decline of 25.2% compared with $396.8 million in the previous year. Results for 1998 included a write-off of deferred acquisition costs of $46.8 million. Earnings were negatively affected by property and casualty losses, partially offset by gains in SAFC's life, credit and asset management operations. Total revenue improved 4.1% to $6.72 billion from $6.45 billion in the prior year. Property and casualty operations reported a

$366.7 million underwriting loss versus a $109.4 million underwriting profit in 1998. Recently, SAFC formed a strategic alliance with Concur Technologies, Inc.™ of Redmond, Washington to deliver an e-Business solution for small and medium-sized businesses, and agreed to make an investment in Concur. In addition, the Company gained the right to market Netstock Direct Corp.'s ShareBuilder™ automatic stock buying service under the brand name, "SAFECO ShareBuilder."

BUSINESS

SAFECO CORPORATION owns operating subsidiaries in segments of insurance and other financially related businesses. Its insurance operations include property, casualty, life, and surety. Through independent agents, the Company's property and casualty subsidiaries write personal, commercial and surety lines of insurance. Coverages include automobile, homeowners, fire and allied lines, workers' compensation, commercial multiperil, miscellaneous casualty, surety and fidelity. SAFC offers individual and group insurance products, retirement services (pension) and annuity products. SAFC's products are marketed through professional agents in all states and the District of Columbia.

GEOGRAPHIC DATA

(12/31/1999)($000)	REV	INC
1st Quarter	1,666,300	118,500
2nd Quarter	1,666,300	73,100
3rd Quarter	1,672,200	16,100
4th Quarter	1,712,300	44,500

ANNUAL FINANCIAL DATA

	12/31/99	12/31/98	12/31/97	12/31/96	12/31/95	12/31/94	12/31/93
Earnings Per Share	1.90	☐ 2.51	☐ 3.31	3.48	3.17	2.50	3.39
Tang. Book Val. Per Share	22.80	30.94	29.24	32.58	31.61	22.47	22.04
Dividends Per Share	1.44	1.34	1.22	1.11	1.02	0.94	0.86
Dividend Payout %	75.8	53.4	36.9	31.9	32.2	37.6	25.4
INCOME STATEMENT (IN MILLIONS):							
Total Premium Income	4,743.8	4,561.7	3,106.8	2,541.3	2,423.7	2,330.2	2,235.7
Net Investment Income	1,585.1	1,518.9	1,244.7	1,116.7	1,075.3	991.6	951.8
Other Income	388.2	371.5	357.8	307.3	255.9	240.8	329.2
Total Revenues	6,717.1	6,452.1	4,709.3	3,965.4	3,754.9	3,562.6	3,516.7
Income Before Income Taxes	332.3	462.8	572.6	578.5	513.8	389.7	576.9
Income Taxes	35.3	66.0	127.8	139.5	114.8	75.4	151.0
Net Income	297.0	☐ 396.8	☐ 444.8	439.0	399.0	314.4	☐ 425.9
Average Shs. Outstg. (000)	132,800	139,900	129,800	126,074	125,961	125,944	125,758
BALANCE SHEET (IN MILLIONS):							
Cash & Cash Equivalents	488.3	390.8	526.1	161.4	134.3	165.1	176.9
Premiums Due	3,156.2	2,658.6	2,340.3	1,476.1	1,365.2	1,279.9	1,150.8
Invst. Assets: Fixed-term	19,564.0	20,576.5	19,851.8	14,424.6	13,972.7	11,562.2	10,721.0
Invst. Assets: Loans	861.8	629.8	584.3	506.1	472.4	472.3	452.6
Invst. Assets: Total	22,931.0	24,160.0	23,036.6	16,889.5	16,132.2	13,467.0	12,640.7
Total Assets	30,572.7	30,891.7	29,467.8	19,917.7	18,767.8	15,901.7	14,807.3
Long-Term Obligations	2,316.1	2,615.6	2,359.9	1,233.5	1,067.5	982.9	918.4
Net Stockholders' Equity	4,294.1	5,575.8	5,461.7	4,115.3	3,982.6	2,829.5	2,774.4
Year-end Shs. Outstg. (000)	128,900	136,300	141,200	126,308	125,979	125,904	125,864
STATISTICAL RECORD:							
Return on Revenues %	4.4	6.1	9.4	11.1	10.6	8.8	12.1
Return on Equity %	6.9	7.1	8.1	10.7	10.0	11.1	15.4
Return on Assets %	1.0	1.3	1.5	2.2	2.1	2.0	2.9
Price Range	46¾-21¹³⁄₁₆	56-38¼	55⅜-36½	42¼-30⅞	39¼-25⅛	29⅞-23⅜	33⅜-26¹⁵⁄₁₆
P/E Ratio	24.6-11.5	22.3-15.2	16.7-11.0	12.1-8.9	12.4-7.9	11.9-9.3	9.8-7.9
Average Yield %	4.2	2.8	2.7	3.0	3.2	3.5	2.9

Statistics are as originally reported. Adj. for stk. split: 2-for-1, 12/95 ☐ Incl. non-recurr. chrg. $46.8 mill. & excl. net distributions on capital securities of $44.9 mill. ☐ Incl. non-recurr. chrg. $60.0 mill. ($0.46/sh.) & excl. net distributions on capital securities $14.8 mill. ($0.11/sh.) ☐ Bef. acctg. change credit $2.9 mill. ($0.02/sh.)

OFFICERS:
R. H. Eigsti, Chmn., C.E.O.
B. A. Dickey, Pres., C.O.O.
R. A. Pierson, Sr. V.P., C.F.O., Sec.
J. W. Ruddy, Sr. V.P., Gen. Couns.
INVESTOR CONTACT: Rod A. Pierson, S.V.P. & C.F.O., (206) 545-5000
PRINCIPAL OFFICE: 4333 Brooklyn Ave. N.E., SAFECO Plaza, Seattle, WA 98185

TELEPHONE NUMBER: (206) 545-5000
FAX: (206) 545-5995
WEB: www.safeco.com
NO. OF EMPLOYEES: 13,000 (approx.)
SHAREHOLDERS: 3,900 (approx.)
ANNUAL MEETING: In May
INCORPORATED: WA, Jul., 1929

INSTITUTIONAL HOLDINGS:
No. of Institutions: 235
Shares Held: 83,561,446
% Held: 64.3

INDUSTRY: Fire, marine, and casualty insurance (SIC: 6331)

TRANSFER AGENT(S): Bank of New York, New York, NY

ST. JOSEPH LIGHT & POWER COMPANY

YIELD 4.7%
P/E RATIO 28.5

*7 YEAR PRICE SCORE 81.0   *12 MONTH PRICE SCORE 100.5
*NYSE COMPOSITE INDEX=100

INTERIM EARNINGS (Per Share):

Qtr.	Mar.	June	Sept.	Dec.
1996	0.28	0.32	0.67	0.06
1997	0.25	0.28	0.67	0.15
1998	0.30	0.25	0.64	0.13
1999	0.05	d0.02	0.65	0.06

INTERIM DIVIDENDS (Per Share):

Amt.	Decl.	Ex.	Rec.	Pay.
0.25Q	3/17/99	4/29/99	5/03/99	5/18/99
0.25Q	7/21/99	7/30/99	8/03/99	8/18/99
0.25Q	9/15/99	11/01/99	11/03/99	11/18/99
0.25Q	1/19/00	2/01/00	2/03/00	2/18/00
0.25Q	3/15/00	5/01/00	5/03/00	5/18/00

Indicated div.: $1.00 (Div. Reinv. Plan)

CAPITALIZATION (12/31/99):

	($000)	(%)
Long-Term Debt	68,597	34.1
Capital Lease Obligations..	2,697	1.3
Deferred Income Tax	32,610	16.2
Minority Interest	1,313	0.7
Common & Surplus	96,188	47.8
Total	201,405	100.0

DIVIDEND ACHIEVER STATUS:
Rank: 305   10-Year Growth Rate: 2.78%
Total Years of Dividend Growth: 19

RECENT DEVELOPMENTS: For the year ended 12/31/99, net income declined 42.6% to $6.1 million versus $10.7 million in 1998. Results included merger-related expenses of $3.1 million and $105,000 in 1999 and 1998, respectively. Total operating revenues declined 2.8% to $120.9 million from $124.4 million in the prior year. Operating income fell 25.4% to $16.6 million from $22.4 million in 1998.

PROSPECTS: Growth in retail electric revenues is being driven by commercial and industrial customers. Meanwhile, the Company's merger with UtiliCorp United is progressing on schedule. The Public Service Commission has set the merger application for hearing during July 2000. Based on this schedule, the PSC could approve the merger by the fall of 2000.

BUSINESS

ST. JOSEPH LIGHT & POWER COMPANY is engaged in the generation, transmission and distribution of electric energy to customers in its ten-county service territory in northwest Missouri. SAJ supplies this service in St. Joseph and 52 other incorporated communities and the intervening rural territory. The service area contains 3,300 square miles. SAJ provides electric energy to more than 61,000 customers in 74 cities. The Company supplies natural gas to 6,400 natural gas customers in Maryville, a town of about 10,000, and 14 other communities. SAJ also supplies industrial steam to six customers in St. Joseph. The Company owns SJLP Inc., a non-regulated subsidiary, which seeks acquisition, investment and partnership opportunities in undervalued businesses, which offer substantial investment returns along with a positive impact on the consolidated earnings of the company. Electric revenues accounted for 75.0% of 1999 total operating revenues.

ANNUAL FINANCIAL DATA

	12/31/99	12/31/98	12/31/97	12/31/96	12/31/95	12/31/94	12/31/93
Earnings Per Share	① 0.74	1.31	1.36	1.32	1.42	1.41	0.99
Cash Flow Per Share	2.27	2.83	2.79	2.65	2.70	2.65	2.18
Tang. Book Val. Per Share	11.63	11.76	11.34	10.87	10.41	9.93	9.54
Dividends Per Share	1.00	0.98	0.96	0.94	0.92	0.90	0.88
Dividend Payout %	135.1	74.8	70.6	71.2	65.0	64.1	88.9
INCOME STATEMENT (IN THOUSANDS):							
Total Revenues	120,949	124,374	116,165	95,869	93,521	90,782	88,539
Costs & Expenses	83,468	81,369	73,761	56,021	53,439	51,937	60,153
Depreciation & Amort.	12,611	12,346	11,440	10,474	10,022	9,834	9,514
Maintenance Exp.	8,312	8,472	7,976	8,446	9,788	8,262	8,186
Operating Income	16,558	22,187	22,988	15,693	15,713	15,538	12,248
Net Interest Inc./(Exp.)	d7,312	d6,787	d6,480	d5,807	d5,555	d4,460	d4,457
Income Taxes	3,705	5,512	6,214	5,235	4,559	5,211	cr1,562
Equity Earnings/Minority Int.	79	d71	106	...	...	...	...
Net Income	① 6,127	10,664	10,840	10,357	11,040	11,066	7,922
Cash Flow	18,738	23,010	22,280	20,831	21,062	20,900	17,436
Average Shs. Outstg.	8,247	8,129	7,996	7,868	7,814	7,884	8,016
BALANCE SHEET (IN THOUSANDS):							
Gross Property	360,086	348,667	333,979	313,590	301,089	283,707	276,444
Accumulated Depreciation	178,057	167,112	157,127	147,539	140,391	135,415	131,107
Net Property	182,029	181,555	176,852	166,051	160,698	148,292	145,337
Total Assets	261,326	251,255	243,769	227,250	219,330	199,699	180,985
Long-Term Obligations	71,294	76,417	71,837	76,371	75,612	55,627	55,642
Net Stockholders' Equity	96,188	95,805	91,168	86,170	81,394	77,592	76,462
Year-end Shs. Outstg.	8,268	8,147	8,042	7,926	7,816	7,816	8,018
STATISTICAL RECORD:							
Operating Profit Margin %	13.7	17.8	19.8	16.4	16.8	17.1	13.8
Net Profit Margin %	5.1	8.6	9.3	10.8	11.8	12.2	8.9
Net Inc./Net Property %	3.4	5.9	6.1	6.2	6.9	7.5	5.5
Net Inc./Tot. Capital %	3.0	5.2	5.6	5.4	5.9	6.9	5.1
Return on Equity %	6.4	11.1	11.9	12.0	13.6	14.3	10.4
Accum. Depr./Gross Prop. %	49.4	47.9	47.0	47.0	46.6	47.7	47.4
Price Range	21¼-15½	19⅜-17¼	17¹⁵/₁₆-15	17¾-13⅞	18¼-13⁹/₁₆	15⅛-12½	18¹⁵/₁₆-14⅜
P/E Ratio	28.7-20.9	14.8-13.2	13.2-11.0	13.4-10.5	12.9-9.6	10.8-8.9	19.1-14.5
Average Yield %	5.4	5.4	5.8	5.9	5.8	6.5	5.3

Statistics are as originally reported. Adj. for stk. splits: 2-for-1, 7/96. ① Incl. merger-related exp. of $3.1 mill.

OFFICERS:
T. F. Steinbecker, Pres., C.E.O.
L. J. Stoll, V.P., Fin., Treas., Asst. Sec.
G. L. Meyers, V.P., Gen. Couns., Sec.

INVESTOR CONTACT: Investor Relations, (800) 367-4562

PRINCIPAL OFFICE: 520 Francis Street, P.O. Box 998, St. Joseph, MO 64502-0998

TELEPHONE NUMBER: (816) 233-8888
FAX: (816) 387-6332
WEB: www.sjlp.com

NO. OF EMPLOYEES: 317 full-time; 4 part-time

SHAREHOLDERS: 4,688

ANNUAL MEETING: In May
INCORPORATED: MO, Nov., 1895

INSTITUTIONAL HOLDINGS:
No. of Institutions: 37
Shares Held: 1,234,174
% Held: 15.0

INDUSTRY: Electric and other services combined (SIC: 4931)

TRANSFER AGENT(S): Harris Trust & Savings Bank, Chicago, IL

ST. PAUL COMPANIES, INC.

YIELD 2.9%
P/E RATIO 12.2

TRADING VOLUME
Thousand Shares

*7 YEAR PRICE SCORE 70.2   *12 MONTH PRICE SCORE 108.7
*NYSE COMPOSITE INDEX=100

INTERIM EARNINGS (Per Share):

Qtr.	Mar.	June	Sept.	Dec.
1995	0.64	0.65	0.82	0.89
1996	0.75	0.76	0.75	0.93
1997	1.13	1.25	0.94	1.01
1998	0.76	d1.18	0.27	0.40
1999	0.68	0.90	0.56	0.93

INTERIM DIVIDENDS (Per Share):

Amt.	Decl.	Ex.	Rec.	Pay.
0.26Q	5/04/99	6/28/99	6/30/99	7/16/99
0.26Q	8/03/99	9/28/99	9/30/99	10/15/99
0.26Q	11/02/99	12/29/99	12/31/99	1/17/00
0.27Q	2/01/00	3/29/00	3/31/00	4/17/00
0.27Q	5/02/00	6/28/00	6/30/00	7/17/00

Indicated div.: $1.08 (Div. Reinv. Plan)

CAPITALIZATION (12/31/99):

	($000)	(%)
Long-Term Debt	1,466,000	17.5
Redeemable Pfd. Stock	425,000	5.1
Preferred Stock	24,000	0.3
Common & Surplus	6,448,000	77.1
Total	8,363,000	100.0

DIVIDEND ACHIEVER STATUS:
Rank: 229   10-Year Growth Rate: 6.72%
Total Years of Dividend Growth: 13

RECENT DEVELOPMENTS: For the year ended 12/31/99, income from continuing operations totaled $779.0 million compared with $199.0 million in the previous year. Results included realized investment gains of $277.0 million and $201.0 million in 1999 and 1998, respectively. Revenues were $7.57 billion, down 1.8% from $7.71 billion in the prior year. Premiums earned fell 4.7% to $5.29 billion compared with $5.55 billion in the prior year.

PROSPECTS: On 4/18/00, the Company completed the acquisition of MMI Companies, Inc., a health care risk services company, for approximately $192.3 million. Going forward, the Company will continue to focus on reducing operating expenses. Accordingly, the Company expects to reduce expenses by approximately $100.0 million in 2000. Also in 2000, the Company expects to realize annual savings of $260.0 million from the merger with USF&G.

BUSINESS

ST. PAUL COMPANIES, INC. is a management company principally engaged, through its subsidiaries, in two industry segments: property-liability insurance and investment banking/asset management. As a management company, SPC oversees the operations of its subsidiaries and provides those subsidiaries with capital, management and administrative services. The primary business of the Company is underwriting, which produced 67% of consolidated revenues in 1999. The Company's investment banking-asset management operations accounted for 33% of consolidated revenues in 1999. In May 1997, the Company sold its insurance brokerage operation, The Minet Group. In April 1998, SPC acquired USF&G Corporation.

ANNUAL FINANCIAL DATA

	12/31/99	12/31/98	12/31/97	12/31/96	12/31/95	12/31/94	12/31/93
Earnings Per Share	③ 3.19	② 0.32	① 4.20	① 3.25	3.00	2.56	2.46
Tang. Book Val. Per Share	26.42	25.79	25.09	22.87	20.76	14.57	16.06
Dividends Per Share	1.03	0.98	0.93	0.86	0.79	0.74	0.69
Dividend Payout %	32.3	307.7	22.0	26.5	26.3	28.8	28.3
INCOME STATEMENT (IN MILLIONS):							
Total Premium Income	5,290.0	6,944.6	4,616.5	4,448.2	3,971.3	3,412.1	3,178.3
Net Investment Income	1,557.0	1,585.0	886.2	807.3	771.6	694.6	661.1
Other Income	722.0	578.8	716.6	478.6	666.7	594.6	620.7
Total Revenues	7,569.0	9,108.4	6,219.3	5,734.2	5,409.6	4,701.3	4,460.2
Policyholder Benefits	3,720.0	5,603.6	3,345.2	3,318.3	2,864.3	2,461.7	2,303.7
Income Before Income Taxes	1,017.0	d46.3	1,018.7	699.1	656.2	563.6	522.6
Income Taxes	238.0	cr135.6	245.5	141.3	135.0	120.8	95.0
Net Income	④ 779.0	② 89.3	① 773.2	① 557.9	521.2	442.8	427.6
Average Shs. Outstg. (000)	246,000	238,682	184,522	168,838	170,798	169,632	170,432
BALANCE SHEET (IN MILLIONS):							
Cash & Cash Equivalents	1,583.0	1,209.2	552.9	470.6	1,223.6	1,092.8	1,056.5
Premiums Due	7,185.0	6,404.5	3,544.7	3,622.6	3,979.6	3,710.4	3,558.2
Invst. Assets: Fixed-term	19,329.0	21,056.3	12,449.8	11,944.1	10,372.9	8,828.7	9,148.0
Invst. Assets: Equities	1,618.0	1,258.5	1,033.9	808.3	711.5	531.0	548.7
Invst. Assets: Total	26,252.0	27,222.7	15,166.3	14,509.2	13,316.6	11,310.6	11,562.2
Total Assets	38,873.0	38,322.7	21,500.7	20,681.0	19,557.2	17,495.8	17,149.2
Long-Term Obligations	1,466.0	1,260.4	782.8	689.1	704.0	622.6	639.7
Net Stockholders' Equity	6,472.0	6,636.4	4,626.7	4,003.8	3,811.7	2,737.5	3,003.8
Year-end Shs. Outstg. (000)	224,830	233,750	167,456	167,032	167,952	168,404	169,430
STATISTICAL RECORD:							
Return on Revenues %	10.3	1.0	12.4	9.7	9.6	9.4	9.6
Return on Equity %	12.0	1.3	16.7	13.9	13.7	16.2	14.2
Return on Assets %	2.0	0.2	3.6	2.7	2.7	2.5	2.5
Price Range	37¹¹/₁₆-25³/₈	47³/₁₆-28¹/₁₆	42³/₄-28¹³/₁₆	30³/₈-25¹/₁₆	29¹¹/₁₆-21³/₄	22³/₄-18⁷/₈	24¹/₂-18³/₄
P/E Ratio	11.6-8.0	147.4-87.7	10.2-6.9	9.4-7.7	9.9-7.3	8.9-7.4	10.0-7.6
Average Yield %	3.3	2.6	2.6	3.1	3.1	3.5	3.2

Statistics are as originally reported. Adj. for stk. splits: 2-for-1, 5/98 & 6/94 ① Bef. disc. oper. loss 97: $67.8 mill.; 96: $107.8 mill. ② Incl. non-recurr. chrg. $221.0 mill. ③ Incl. the oper. of USF&G Corp., from the acquisition date. ④ Bef. acctg. change chrg. $30.0 mill. and excl. from disc. oper. $164.0 mill.

OFFICERS:
D. W. Leatherdale, Chmn., C.E.O.
J. E. Gustafson, Pres., C.O.O.
P. J. Liska, Exec. V.P., C.F.O.
T. E. Bergmann, V.P., Treas.
INVESTOR CONTACT: Sandra Utsaker Wiese, Stock Transfer, (612) 310-8506
PRINCIPAL OFFICE: 385 Washington St., St. Paul, MN 55102

TELEPHONE NUMBER: (651) 310-7911
FAX: (201) 222-4892
WEB: www.stpaul.com
NO. OF EMPLOYEES: 12,000 (approx.)
SHAREHOLDERS: 22,603
ANNUAL MEETING: In May
INCORPORATED: MN, May, 1853

INSTITUTIONAL HOLDINGS:
No. of Institutions: 336
Shares Held: 182,701,270
% Held: 80.4
INDUSTRY: Fire, marine, and casualty insurance (SIC: 6331)
TRANSFER AGENT(S): Norwest Bank Minnesota, N.A., St. Paul, MN.

SARA LEE CORPORATION

	YIELD	3.0%
	P/E RATIO	14.2

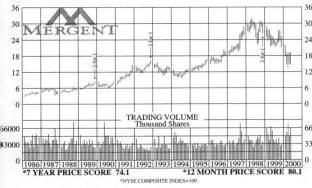

INTERIM EARNINGS (Per Share):

Qtr.	Sept.	Dec.	Mar.	June
1996-97	0.21	0.32	0.21	0.29
1997-98	0.23	d1.36	0.23	0.31
1998-99	0.35	0.34	0.26	0.31
1999-00	0.28	0.42	...	...

INTERIM DIVIDENDS (Per Share):

Amt.	Decl.	Ex.	Rec.	Pay.
0.125Q	6/24/99	8/30/99	9/01/99	10/01/99
0.135Q	10/28/99	11/29/99	12/01/99	1/03/00
0.135Q	1/27/00	2/28/00	3/01/00	4/03/00
0.135Q	5/25/00	5/30/00	6/01/00	7/03/00

Indicated div.: $0.54 (Div. Reinv. Plan)

CAPITALIZATION (7/3/99):

	($000)	(%)
Long-Term Debt	1,892,000	48.9
Deferred Income Tax	62,000	1.6
Minority Interest	613,000	15.9
Preferred Stock	33,000	0.9
Common & Surplus	1,266,000	32.7
Total	3,866,000	100.0

DIVIDEND ACHIEVER STATUS:
Rank: 139   10-Year Growth Rate: 10.76%
Total Years of Dividend Growth: 23

*7 YEAR PRICE SCORE 74.1   ***12 MONTH PRICE SCORE 80.1**
*NYSE COMPOSITE INDEX=100

RECENT DEVELOPMENTS: For the three months ended 1/1/00, net income advanced 20.8% to $389.0 million from $322.0 million the previous year. The prior-year results included a one-time pre-tax charge of $76.0 million stemming from a recall of certain packaged meat products. Net sales inched up to $5.33 billion from $5.29 billion the year before. Operating income totaled $599.0 million, up 1.9% versus $588.0 million a year earlier.

PROSPECTS: On 3/24/00, the Company reached an agreement to acquire Courtaulds Textiles plc, a U.K.-based apparel manufacturer and marketer with 1999 sales of $1.49 billion, for approximately $341.0 million in cash, including the assumption of $102.0 million of debt. The acquisition, expected to be modestly accretive to SLE's earnings in fiscal 2001, will help strengthen the Company's distribution of apparel in Europe.

BUSINESS

SARA LEE CORPORATION is a global manufacturer and marketer of brand-name foods and consumer products. Branded Apparel (37% of fiscal 1999 sales) is comprised of SLE's intimates, knit products, legwear and accessories businesses. Well-known brands include BALI, HANES HER WAY, PLAYTEX and COACH leather goods. Sara Lee Foods (26%) is comprised of the packaged meats segment, which includes such brands as HILLSHIRE FARM, JIMMY DEAN, BALL PARK, and BRYAN, and the bakery segment. Foodservice (14%) consists of PYA/Monarch, which is a foodservice distributor throughout the U.S. Coffee and Tea (13%) includes such brands as DOUWE EGBERTS, MARCILLA and PICKWICK. Household and Body Care (10%) is comprised of shoe care, body care, insecticides and air fresheners.

ANNUAL FINANCIAL DATA

	7/3/99	6/27/98	6/28/97	6/29/96	7/1/95	7/2/94	7/3/93
Earnings Per Share	② 1.26	③ d0.57	1.02	0.92	0.81	① 0.22	0.70
Cash Flow Per Share	1.83	0.09	1.71	1.57	1.44	0.81	1.24
Tang. Book Val. Per Share	...	...	0.35	0.46	0.02	...	0.27
Dividends Per Share	0.50	0.46	0.42	0.38	0.34	0.32	0.29
Dividend Payout %	39.7	...	41.4	41.5	42.0	145.4	41.4

INCOME STATEMENT (IN MILLIONS):

Total Revenues	20,012.0	20,011.0	19,734.0	18,624.0	17,719.0	15,536.0	14,580.0
Costs & Expenses	17,708.0	17,620.0	17,411.0	16,439.0	15,709.0	13,702.0	12,894.0
Depreciation & Amort.	553.0	618.0	680.0	634.0	606.0	568.0	522.0
Operating Income	1,751.0	1,773.0	1,643.0	1,551.0	1,404.0	1,266.0	1,164.0
Net Interest Inc./(Exp.)	d141.0	d176.0	d159.0	d173.0	d185.0	d145.0	d82.0
Income Before Income Taxes	1,671.0	1,853.0	1,484.0	1,378.0	1,219.0	389.0	1,082.0
Income Taxes	480.0	80.0	475.0	462.0	415.0	155.0	378.0
Net Income	② 1,191.0	③ d523.0	1,009.0	916.0	804.0	① 234.0	704.0
Cash Flow	1,732.0	81.0	1,663.0	1,523.0	1,382.0	778.0	1,200.0
Average Shs. Outstg. (000)	944,000	939,000	970,000	970,000	960,000	960,000	970,000

BALANCE SHEET (IN MILLIONS):

Cash & Cash Equivalents	279.0	273.0	272.0	243.0	202.0	189.0	325.0
Total Current Assets	4,987.0	5,220.0	5,391.0	5,081.0	4,928.0	4,469.0	3,976.0
Net Property	2,169.0	2,090.0	3,079.0	3,007.0	2,964.0	2,900.0	2,878.0
Total Assets	10,521.0	10,989.0	12,953.0	12,602.0	12,431.0	11,665.0	10,862.0
Total Current Liabilities	5,953.0	5,733.0	5,016.0	4,642.0	4,844.0	4,919.0	4,269.0
Long-Term Obligations	1,892.0	2,270.0	1,933.0	1,842.0	1,817.0	1,496.0	1,164.0
Net Stockholders' Equity	1,299.0	1,866.0	4,322.0	4,358.0	3,973.0	3,357.0	3,578.0
Net Working Capital	d966.0	d513.0	375.0	439.0	84.0	d450.0	d293.0
Year-end Shs. Outstg. (000)	883,783	921,328	960,554	970,110	961,312	961,530	970,756

STATISTICAL RECORD:

Operating Profit Margin %	8.7	8.9	8.3	8.3	7.9	8.1	8.0
Net Profit Margin %	6.0	...	5.1	4.9	4.5	1.5	4.8
Return on Equity %	94.1	...	23.3	21.0	20.2	7.0	19.7
Return on Assets %	11.3	...	7.8	7.3	6.5	2.0	6.5
Debt/Total Assets %	18.0	20.7	14.9	14.6	14.6	12.8	10.7
Price Range	28¾-21¹/₁₆	31¹³/₁₆-22³/₁₆	28¹⁵/₁₆-18¹/₄	20¼-14¹⁵/₁₆	16⁷/₈-12¹/₈	13-9¹¹/₁₆	15⁹/₁₆-10¹/₂
P/E Ratio	22.8-16.7	...	28.5-18.0	22.1-16.3	20.8-15.0	59.1-44.0	22.2-15.0
Average Yield %	2.0	1.7	1.8	2.2	2.3	2.8	2.2

Statistics are as originally reported. Adj. for 2-for-1 stk. split, 12/98. ① Bef. $35 mil ($0.04/sh) chg. for acctg. adj. & incl. $495 mil ($0.52/sh) net non-recur. chg. ② Incl. $50 mil ($0.05/sh) net chg. from product recall & incl. $97 mil ($0.10/sh) net gain on sale of int'l tobacco opers. ③ Incl. $1.60 bil ($1.72/sh) after-tax restr. chg.

OFFICERS:
J. H. Bryan, Chmn.
C. S. McMillan, Pres., C.E.O.
C. D. McMillan, C.F.O., Chief Admin. Off.

INVESTOR CONTACT: Janet Bergman, V.P., Inv. Rel. & Corp. Affairs, (312) 558-4966

PRINCIPAL OFFICE: Three First National Plaza, Suite 4600, Chicago, IL 60602-4260

TELEPHONE NUMBER: (312) 726-2600
FAX: (312) 558-4913
WEB: www.saralee.com

NO. OF EMPLOYEES: 138,000

SHAREHOLDERS: 83,200 (approx.)

ANNUAL MEETING: In Oct.

INCORPORATED: MD, Sept., 1941

INSTITUTIONAL HOLDINGS:
No. of Institutions: 597
Shares Held: 506,080,736
% Held: 56.6

INDUSTRY: Sausages and other prepared meats (SIC: 2013)

TRANSFER AGENT(S): Sara Lee Corporation, Company Office.

SBC COMMUNICATIONS, INC.

YIELD		2.3%
P/E RATIO		19.1

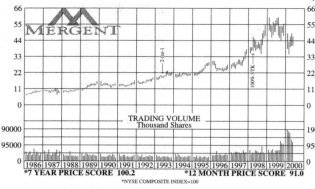

*7 YEAR PRICE SCORE 100.2			*12 MONTH PRICE SCORE 91.0	

*NYSE COMPOSITE INDEX=100

INTERIM EARNINGS (Per Share):

Qtr.	Mar.	June	Sept.	Dec.
1996	0.38	0.41	0.49	0.45
1997	0.43	d0.43	0.45	0.32
1998	0.49	0.52	0.65	2.05
1999	0.56	0.59	0.64	0.50

INTERIM DIVIDENDS (Per Share):

Amt.	Decl.	Ex.	Rec.	Pay.
0.244Q	3/26/99	4/07/99	4/10/99	5/03/99
0.244Q	6/25/99	7/07/99	7/10/99	8/02/99
0.244Q	8/31/99	9/07/99	9/09/99	11/01/99
0.244Q	12/17/99	1/06/00	1/10/00	2/01/00
0.254Q	3/31/00	4/06/00	4/10/00	5/01/00

Indicated div.: $1.01 (Div. Reinv. Plan)

CAPITALIZATION (12/31/99):

	($000)	(%)
Long-Term Debt	17,475,000	34.9
Deferred Income Tax	4,821,000	9.6
Redeemable Pfd. Stock	1,000,000	2.0
Common & Surplus	26,726,000	53.4
Total	50,022,000	100.0

DIVIDEND ACHIEVER STATUS:
Rank: 278   10-Year Growth Rate: 4.15%
Total Years of Dividend Growth: 15

RECENT DEVELOPMENTS: For the year ended 12/31/99, income of $6.57 billion, before an extraordinary gain and an accounting credit, fell 15.0% from income of $7.74 billion, before an extraordinary charge and an accounting credit, in 1998. Results for 1999 included costs of $866.0 million, while results for 1998 included non-recurring gains of $1.12 billion. Revenues rose 7.1% to $49.49 billion. Comparisons were made with restated 1998 figures.

PROSPECTS: SBC expects earnings growth of at least 15.0% and double-digit revenue growth beginning in 2001 from rapid progress in major business lines and initiatives, as well as cost savings from merger integration. Meanwhile, SBC and BellSouth Corporation announced they will combine their U.S. wireless operations, creating a new wireless company to compete nationwide in wireless voice and data businesses.

BUSINESS

SBC COMMUNICATIONS, INC. (formerly Southwestern Bell) is one of seven regional holding companies divested by AT&T in 1984. SBC has 90.4 million voice grade equivalent lines and 11.2 million wireless customers across the U.S., as well as investments in telecommunications businesses in 23 foreign countries. SBC offers wireline services in thirteen states. SBC offers a variety of services under the Southwestern Bell, Ameritech, Pacific Bell, SBC Telecom, SNET, Nevada Bell and Cellular One brands. The services and products that SBC offers include: local exchange services, wireless communications, long distance services, Internet services, cable and wireless television services, security monitoring, telecommunications equipment, messaging, paging, and directory advertising and publishing. On 4/1/97, SBC acquired Pacific Telesis Group. SBC completed its $61.00 billion acquisition of Ameritech Corp. on 10/8/99.

ANNUAL FINANCIAL DATA

	12/31/99	12/31/98	[1] 12/31/97	12/31/96	12/31/95	12/31/94	12/31/93
Earnings Per Share	[6] 1.90	[4] 2.05	[2][3] 0.80	1.73	1.55	1.37	[8][9] 1.20
Cash Flow Per Share	4.35	4.62	3.42	3.55	3.30	3.01	2.81
Tang. Book Val. Per Share	5.87	4.95	3.61	3.62	2.94	4.68	5.38
Dividends Per Share	0.96	0.93	0.89	0.85	0.82	0.78	0.75
Dividend Payout %	209.8	45.1	110.8	49.2	52.7	57.0	62.7

INCOME STATEMENT (IN MILLIONS):

Total Revenues	49,489.0	28,777.0	24,856.0	13,898.0	12,670.0	11,618.5	10,690.3
Costs & Expenses	29,423.0	16,786.0	16,845.0	8,134.0	7,505.0	6,851.0	6,369.5
Depreciation & Amort.	8,468.0	5,105.0	4,841.0	2,208.0	2,128.0	1,977.2	1,941.2
Operating Income	11,598.0	6,886.0	3,170.0	3,556.0	3,037.0	2,790.3	2,379.6
Net Interest Inc./(Exp.)	d1,430.0	d993.0	d947.0	d472.0	d515.0	d480.2	d496.2
Income Before Income Taxes	10,853.0	6,374.0	2,337.0	3,267.0	2,792.0	2,433.8	2,060.2
Income Taxes	4,280.0	2,306.0	863.0	1,166.0	903.0	785.1	625.0
Net Income	[6] 6,573.0	[4] 4,068.0	[2][3] 1,474.0	2,101.0	1,889.0	1,648.7	[8] 1,435.2
Cash Flow	15,041.0	9,173.0	6,315.0	4,309.0	4,017.0	3,625.9	3,376.4
Average Shs. Outstg. (000)	3,458,000	1,984,000	1,844,000	1,214,000	1,218,000	1,202,800	1,199,600

BALANCE SHEET (IN MILLIONS):

Cash & Cash Equivalents	495.0	460.0	398.0	242.0	490.0	364.6	618.4
Total Current Assets	11,930.0	7,538.0	7,062.0	3,912.0	3,679.0	3,493.3	3,619.8
Net Property	46,571.0	29,920.0	27,339.0	14,007.0	12,988.0	17,316.6	17,091.5
Total Assets	83,215.0	45,066.0	42,132.0	23,449.0	22,002.0	26,005.3	24,307.5
Total Current Liabilities	19,313.0	9,989.0	10,252.0	5,820.0	5,056.0	5,190.8	4,488.5
Long-Term Obligations	17,475.0	11,612.0	12,019.0	5,505.0	5,672.0	5,848.3	5,459.4
Net Stockholders' Equity	26,726.0	12,780.0	9,892.0	6,853.0	6,256.0	8,355.6	7,608.6
Net Working Capital	d7,383.0	d2,451.0	d3,190.0	d1,908.0	d1,377.0	d1,697.5	d868.7
Year-end Shs. Outstg. (000)	3,395,272	1,959,000	1,837,000	1,200,000	1,218,000	1,218,164	1,200,468

STATISTICAL RECORD:

Operating Profit Margin %	23.4	23.9	12.8	25.6	24.0	24.0	22.3
Net Profit Margin %	13.3	14.1	5.9	15.1	14.9	14.2	13.4
Return on Equity %	24.6	31.8	14.9	30.7	30.2	19.7	18.9
Return on Assets %	7.9	9.0	3.5	9.0	8.6	6.3	5.9
Debt/Total Assets %	21.0	25.8	28.5	23.5	25.8	22.5	22.5
Price Range	59 15/16-44 11/16	54 7/8-35	38 1/16-24 5/8	30 1/8-23	29 1/4-19 13/16	22 3/16-18 3/8	23 1/2-17 1/8
P/E Ratio	130.3-95.8	26.8-17.1	47.6-30.8	17.4-13.3	18.9-12.8	16.2-13.4	19.7-14.3
Average Yield %	1.9	2.1	2.8	3.2	3.3	3.9	3.7

Statistics are as originally reported. Adj. for stk. splits: 100%, 3/98, 2-for-1, 5/93. [1] Incls. Pacific Telesis Group, acq. 4/97. [2] Incls. non-recurr. chrgs. $1.89 bill. [3] Bef. extraord. chrg. 12/31/97: $2.82 bill.; chrg. 12/31/93: $153.0 mill. [4] Bef. extraord. loss $60.0 mill.; bef. acctg. credit $15.0 mill. [5] Bef. acctg. chrg. $2.13 bill. [6] Bef. extraord. gain $1.38 bill.; bef. acctg. credit $207.0 mill.; incl. non-recurr. chrgs. $866.0 mill.

OFFICERS:
E. E. Whitacre, Jr., Chmn., C.E.O.
R. S. Caldwell, Vice-Chmn., Pres.

INVESTOR CONTACT: Larry L. Soloman, (210) 351-3990

PRINCIPAL OFFICE: 175 E. Houston, P.O. Box 2933, San Antonio, TX 78205-2933

TELEPHONE NUMBER: (210) 821-4105
FAX: (210) 351-3553
WEB: www.sbc.com

NO. OF EMPLOYEES: 204,530 (avg.)

SHAREHOLDERS: 1,038,807

ANNUAL MEETING: In Apr.

INCORPORATED: DE, Oct., 1983

INSTITUTIONAL HOLDINGS:
No. of Institutions: 1,034
Shares Held: 1,581,441,626
% Held: 46.4

INDUSTRY: Holding companies, nec (SIC: 6719)

TRANSFER AGENT(S): First Chicago Trust Company of New York, Jersey City, NJ

NYSE SYMBOL SGP
Rec. Pr. 48 (5/31/00)

SCHERING-PLOUGH CORPORATION

YIELD 1.2%
P/E RATIO 32.4

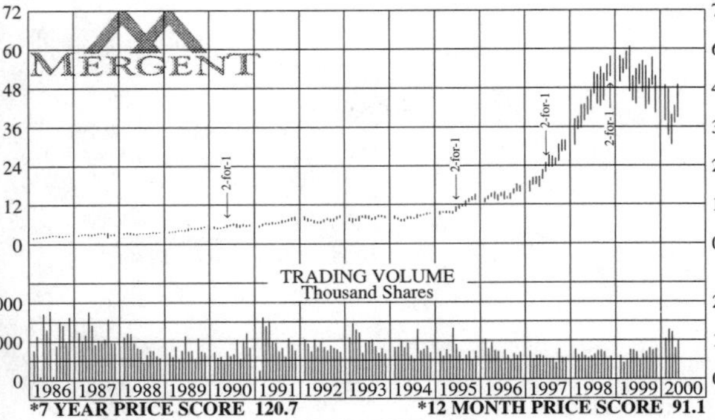

***7 YEAR PRICE SCORE 120.7** ***12 MONTH PRICE SCORE 91.1**

*NYSE COMPOSITE INDEX=100

INTERIM EARNINGS (Per Share):

Qtr.	Mar.	June	Sept.	Dec.
1995	0.19	0.19	0.17	0.17
1996	0.23	0.22	0.20	0.19
1997	0.26	0.26	0.24	0.24
1998	0.31	0.31	0.29	0.28
1999	0.36	0.37	0.35	0.34

INTERIM DIVIDENDS (Per Share):

Amt.	Decl.	Ex.	Rec.	Pay.
0.125Q	4/27/99	5/05/99	5/07/99	5/28/99
0.125Q	6/22/99	8/04/99	8/06/99	8/31/99
0.125Q	10/26/99	11/03/99	11/05/99	11/30/99
0.125Q	1/25/00	2/02/00	2/04/00	2/29/00
0.14Q	4/25/00	5/03/00	5/05/00	5/30/00

Indicated div.: $0.56 (Div. Reinv. Plan)

CAPITALIZATION (12/31/99):

	($000)	(%)
Deferred Income Tax	284,000	5.2
Common & Surplus	5,165,000	94.8
Total	5,449,000	100.0

DIVIDEND ACHIEVER STATUS:
Rank: 50 10-Year Growth Rate: 16.06%
Total Years of Dividend Growth: 14

RECENT DEVELOPMENTS: For the year ended 12/31/99, net income advanced 20.2% to $2.11 billion from $1.76 billion in the previous year. Net sales rose 13.6% to $9.18 billion from $8.08 billion, due to volume growth of 13.0% and price increases of 1.0%. Worldwide sales of allergy and respiratory products grew 14.0% to $3.85 billion from $3.38 billion, and worldwide sales of anti-infective and anticancer products jumped 37.6% to $1.74 billion.

PROSPECTS: Worldwide pharmaceuticals should continue to drive sales higher, with SGP's two largest therapeutic product categories, allergy/respiratory and anti-infective/anticancer, recording strong growth. SGP will continue to invest heavily in research and development with expenditures expected to be approximately 15.0% higher and total about $1.40 billion. Meanwhile, the Company anticipates earnings per share of $1.64 in 2000.

BUSINESS

SCHERING-PLOUGH CORPORATION is a global company primarily engaged in the discovery, development, manufacturing and marketing of pharmaceutical and consumer products. Pharmaceutical products include prescription drugs, over-the-counter medicines, vision-care products and animal health products promoted to the medical and allied professions. The healthcare product segment consists of over-the-counter foot care products, including DR SHOLLS, and sun care products, including COPPERTONE. Healthcare products are sold primarily in the United States. In 1999, contributions to sales were pharmaceutical products, 84.3%; and healthcare products, 15.7%.

QUARTERLY DATA

(12/31/99) ($000)	REV	INC
1st Quarter	2,186,000	539,000
2nd Quarter	2,451,000	547,000
3rd Quarter	2,236,000	518,000
4th Quarter	2,303,000	506,000

ANNUAL FINANCIAL DATA

	12/31/99	12/31/98	12/31/97	12/31/96	12/31/95	12/31/94	12/31/93
Earnings Per Share	**1.42**	**1.18**	**0.97**	**0.83**	**[1] 0.71**	**0.60**	**[2] 0.53**
Cash Flow Per Share	**1.60**	**1.34**	**1.11**	**0.94**	**0.82**	**0.71**	**0.62**
Tang. Book Val. Per Share	**3.11**	**2.33**	**1.60**	**1.41**	**1.11**	**1.06**	**0.90**
Dividends Per Share	**0.48**	**0.42**	**0.37**	**0.32**	**0.28**	**0.25**	**0.22**
Dividend Payout %	**34.2**	**36.0**	**37.9**	**38.8**	**39.4**	**41.0**	**41.1**
INCOME STATEMENT (IN MILLIONS):							
Total Revenues	9,176.0	8,077.0	6,778.0	5,656.0	5,104.0	4,657.1	4,341.3
Costs & Expenses	6,117.0	5,513.0	4,665.0	3,836.8	3,495.0	3,249.9	3,091.4
Depreciation & Amort.	264.0	238.0	200.0	173.2	157.0	157.6	142.4
Operating Income	2,795.0	2,326.0	1,913.0	1,646.0	1,452.0	1,249.6	1,107.5
Net Interest Inc./(Exp.)	...	...	...	...	...	d27.6	...
Income Before Income Taxes	2,795.0	2,326.0	1,913.0	1,606.0	1,395.0	1,213.2	1,078.4
Income Taxes	685.0	570.0	469.0	393.0	342.0	291.2	253.4
Net Income	2,110.0	1,756.0	1,444.0	1,213.0	[1] 1,053.0	922.0	[2] 825.0
Cash Flow	2,374.0	1,994.0	1,644.0	1,386.2	1,210.0	1,079.6	967.4
Average Shs. Outstg. (000)	1,486,000	1,488,000	1,480,000	1,470,800	1,478,800	1,530,400	1,560,800
BALANCE SHEET (IN MILLIONS):							
Cash & Cash Equivalents	1,876.0	1,259.0	714.0	535.1	321.4	160.6	429.4
Total Current Assets	4,909.0	3,958.0	2,920.0	2,364.6	1,956.3	1,739.1	1,900.5
Net Property	2,939.0	2,675.0	2,526.0	2,246.3	2,098.9	2,082.3	1,967.7
Total Assets	9,375.0	7,840.0	6,507.0	5,398.1	4,664.6	4,325.7	4,316.9
Total Current Liabilities	3,209.0	3,032.0	2,891.0	2,599.1	2,362.1	2,028.8	2,132.4
Long-Term Obligations	...	...	46.0	46.4	87.1	185.8	182.3
Net Stockholders' Equity	5,165.0	4,002.0	2,821.0	2,059.9	1,622.9	1,574.4	1,581.9
Net Working Capital	1,700.0	926.0	29.0	d234.5	d405.8	d289.7	d231.9
Year-end Shs. Outstg. (000)	1,472,000	1,472,000	1,466,000	1,461,468	1,456,800	1,488,112	1,548,440
STATISTICAL RECORD:							
Operating Profit Margin %	30.5	28.8	28.2	29.1	28.4	26.8	25.5
Net Profit Margin %	23.0	21.7	21.3	21.4	20.6	19.8	19.0
Return on Equity %	40.9	43.9	51.2	58.9	64.9	58.6	52.2
Return on Assets %	22.5	22.4	22.2	22.5	22.6	21.3	19.1
Debt/Total Assets %	...	...	0.7	0.9	1.9	4.3	4.2
Price Range	60 13/16-40 1/4	57 3/4-30 3/8	32-15 7/8	18 5/16-12 5/8	15 3/16-8 7/8	9 1/2-6 13/16	8 7/8-6 1/2
P/E Ratio	42.8-28.3	48.9-25.7	33.0-16.4	22.2-15.3	21.3-12.4	15.7-11.3	16.8-12.2
Average Yield %	1.0	1.0	1.5	2.1	2.3	3.0	2.8

Statistics are as originally reported. Adjusted for 2-for-1 stock split, 12/98, 8/97 & 6/95. [1] Bef. dis. opers. loss of $166.4 mill. [2] Bef. acctg. adj. loss of $94.2 mill.

OFFICERS:
R. J. Kogan, Chmn., C.E.O.
H. A. D'Andrade, Vice-Chmn., C.A.O.
R. E. Cesan, Pres., C.O.O.
J. L. Wyszomierski, Exec. V.P., C.F.O.

INVESTOR CONTACT: Geraldine U. Foster, Investor Relations, (973) 822-7410

PRINCIPAL OFFICE: One Giralda Farms, Madison, NJ 07940-1000

TELEPHONE NUMBER: (973) 822-7000
FAX: (973) 822-7048
WEB: www.sch-plough.com

NO. OF EMPLOYEES: 26,500 (approx.)

SHAREHOLDERS: 46,000 (approx.)

ANNUAL MEETING: In Apr.

INCORPORATED: NJ, Jul., 1970

INSTITUTIONAL HOLDINGS:
No. of Institutions: 900
Shares Held: 962,056,046
% Held: 65.5

INDUSTRY: Pharmaceutical preparations (SIC: 2834)

TRANSFER AGENT(S): The Bank of New York, New York, N.Y.

NASDAQ SYMBOL SHLM
Rec. Pr. $11\frac{13}{16}$ (5/31/00)

SCHULMAN (A.), INC.

YIELD 4.6%
P/E RATIO 7.7

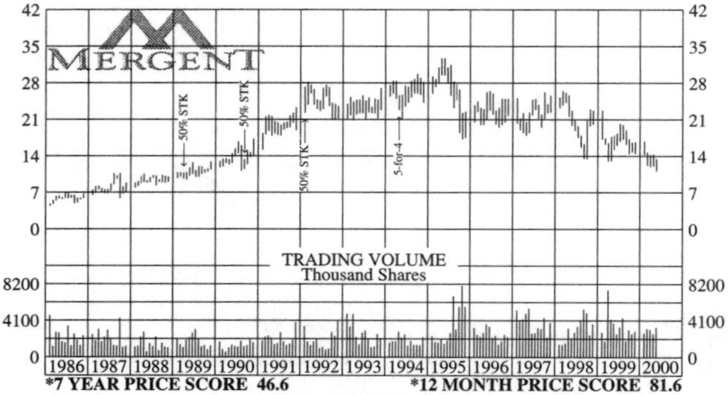

MERGENT
50% STK
50% STK
50% STK
5-for-4
TRADING VOLUME
Thousand Shares
1986 1987 1988 1989 1990 1991 1992 1993 1994 1995 1996 1997 1998 1999 2000

*7 YEAR PRICE SCORE 46.6 *12 MONTH PRICE SCORE 81.6

*NYSE COMPOSITE INDEX=100

INTERIM EARNINGS (Per Share):

Qtr.	Nov.	Feb.	May	Aug.
1996-97	0.32	0.26	0.37	0.42
1997-98	0.35	0.31	0.38	0.44
1998-99	0.40	0.27	0.36	0.48
1999-00	0.38	0.32	...	...

INTERIM DIVIDENDS (Per Share):

Amt.	Decl.	Ex.	Rec.	Pay.
0.125Q	7/09/99	7/23/99	7/27/99	8/05/99
0.125Q	10/07/99	10/21/99	10/25/99	11/03/99
0.135Q	1/13/00	1/25/00	1/27/00	2/04/00
0.135Q	4/12/00	4/24/00	4/26/00	5/05/00

Indicated div.: $0.54

CAPITALIZATION (8/31/99):

	($000)	(%)
Long-Term Debt	65,000	14.9
Deferred Income Tax	11,375	2.6
Minority Interest	3,394	0.8
Preferred Stock	1,069	0.2
Common & Surplus	355,177	81.5
Total	436,015	100.0

DIVIDEND ACHIEVER STATUS:
Rank: 87 10-Year Growth Rate: 13.40%
Total Years of Dividend Growth: 23

RECENT DEVELOPMENTS: For the second quarter ended 2/29/00, net income advanced 12.7% to $9.7 million from $8.6 million in the corresponding prior-year quarter. The 1999 results included a gain of $1.7 million from consideration recieved due to the demutualization of an insurance carrier in North America. Net sales increased 5.5% to $248.1 million from $235.2 million in the year-earlier period. Sales in North America grew 4.0% to $105.3 million, while sales from Europe grew 6.6% to $142.8 million. Cost of goods rose 5.9% to $207.2 million from $195.7 million a year ago. Gross profit as a percentage of net sales, which amounted to 16.5% from16.8%, were negatively affected by elevated costs of plastic resins and competitive pricing pressure. Operating income climbed 18.6% to $18.3 million compared with $15.4 million the year before.

BUSINESS

SCHULMAN (A.), INC. is a supplier of plastic compounds and resins. These materials are fabricated into a wide variety of end products by manufacturers around the world. The Company's principal product lines consist of engineered plastic compounds that are custom formulated to match specific customer product specifications. The Company also produces specialty color concentrates and additive masterbatches widely used in plastic products such as packaging films, fibers and various other applications. In addition, the Company's worldwide marketing organization serves as a distributor and merchant for various types of plastic materials manufactured by major polymer producers. The Company, with headquarters in Akron, Ohio, operates 13 manufacturing plants in North America, Europe, Mexico and the Asia-Pacific region. SHLM acquired J.M. Huber in February 1995 and operates this business as Texas Polymer Services, Inc.

ANNUAL FINANCIAL DATA

	8/31/99	8/31/98	8/31/97	8/31/96	8/31/95	8/31/94	8/31/93
Earnings Per Share	**1.51**	**1.48**	**1.37**	**1.12**	**1.43**	**1.19**	[1] **1.04**
Cash Flow Per Share	**2.16**	**1.98**	**1.85**	**1.60**	**1.83**	**1.58**	**1.44**
Tang. Book Val. Per Share	**11.41**	**10.97**	**10.83**	**11.43**	**10.48**	**9.21**	**7.84**
Dividends Per Share	**0.50**	**0.46**	**0.42**	**0.38**	**0.34**	**0.30**	**0.26**
Dividend Payout %	**33.1**	**31.1**	**30.7**	**33.9**	**23.8**	**25.0**	**24.6**
INCOME STATEMENT (IN MILLIONS):							
Total Revenues	988.3	996.5	1,001.4	982.8	1,034.6	756.2	693.2
Costs & Expenses	883.6	891.3	894.0	889.1	922.1	669.3	614.7
Depreciation & Amort.	20.8	17.8	17.8	18.1	16.8	14.7	14.7
Operating Income	84.0	87.3	89.5	75.6	95.6	72.2	63.8
Net Interest Inc./(Exp.)	d3.7	d1.9	d3.1	d4.2	d5.2	d1.2	d1.2
Income Before Income Taxes	78.0	86.3	86.3	71.0	89.8	70.4	62.5
Income Taxes	30.2	34.2	35.5	28.8	36.2	25.9	23.5
Equity Earnings/Minority Int.	d1.8	d0.7	d0.9	d0.4	d0.5	d0.4	d0.3
Net Income	47.8	52.2	50.7	42.2	53.6	44.6	[1] 38.9
Cash Flow	68.5	69.9	68.5	60.3	70.4	59.2	53.6
Average Shs. Outstg. (000)	31,680	35,275	37,125	37,585	38,579	37,438	37,326
BALANCE SHEET (IN MILLIONS):							
Cash & Cash Equivalents	56.8	60.8	71.9	150.5	144.3	121.8	113.5
Total Current Assets	408.1	395.5	403.7	466.8	491.1	399.4	312.7
Net Property	160.3	148.2	139.4	139.0	141.2	98.1	85.0
Total Assets	591.5	561.9	562.9	623.4	647.2	510.4	407.9
Total Current Liabilities	117.8	107.2	111.7	106.0	128.1	108.4	74.8
Long-Term Obligations	65.0	40.0	12.0	40.1	75.1	23.1	10.1
Net Stockholders' Equity	356.2	366.3	393.4	433.1	405.2	345.9	294.2
Net Working Capital	290.3	288.3	292.0	360.8	363.0	291.0	237.9
Year-end Shs. Outstg. (000)	31,130	33,279	36,230	37,806	38,579	37,459	37,389
STATISTICAL RECORD:							
Operating Profit Margin %	8.5	8.8	8.9	7.7	9.2	9.5	9.2
Net Profit Margin %	4.8	5.2	5.1	4.3	5.2	5.9	5.6
Return on Equity %	13.4	14.2	12.9	9.7	13.2	12.9	13.2
Return on Assets %	8.1	9.3	9.0	6.8	8.3	8.7	9.5
Debt/Total Assets %	11.0	7.1	2.1	6.4	11.6	4.5	2.5
Price Range	22¾-13	26½-13$\frac{7}{16}$	26¼-18	26½-19½	32¾-17¼	29¾-21	27-20$\frac{13}{16}$
P/E Ratio	15.1-8.6	17.9-9.1	19.2-13.1	23.7-17.4	22.9-12.1	25.0-17.6	26.0-20.0
Average Yield %	2.8	2.3	1.9	1.7	1.4	1.2	1.1

Statistics are as originally reported. Adj. for stk. split: 5-for-2, 4/94 [1] Bef. acctg. change chrg. $2.2 mill. ($0.06/sh.)

OFFICERS:
R. A. Stefanko, Chmn., Exec. V.P., C.F.O.
T. L. Haines, Pres., C.E.O.

INVESTOR CONTACT: Robert A. Stefanko, Chmn, Exec. V.P., C.F.O., (330) 666-3751

PRINCIPAL OFFICE: 3550 West Market Street, Akron, OH 44333

TELEPHONE NUMBER: (330) 666-3751
FAX: (330) 668-7204
WEB: www.aschulman.com

NO. OF EMPLOYEES: 2,400 (approx.)

SHAREHOLDERS: 971

ANNUAL MEETING: In Dec.

INCORPORATED: OH, 1928; reincorp., DE, Aug., 1969

INSTITUTIONAL HOLDINGS:
No. of Institutions: 121
Shares Held: 20,714,429
% Held: 66.7

INDUSTRY: Plastics materials and resins (SIC: 2821)

TRANSFER AGENT(S): First Chicago Trust Company, Jersey City, NJ

SCHWAB (CHARLES) CORPORATION

YIELD	0.1%
P/E RATIO	50.1

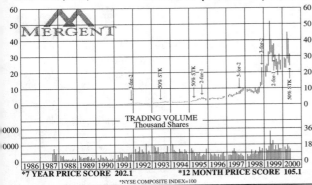

TRADING VOLUME
Thousand Shares

| 1986 | 1987 | 1988 | 1989 | 1990 | 1991 | 1992 | 1993 | 1994 | 1995 | 1996 | 1997 | 1998 | 1999 | 2000 |

*7 YEAR PRICE SCORE 202.1   ***12 MONTH PRICE SCORE 105.1**

*NYSE COMPOSITE INDEX=100

INTERIM EARNINGS (Per Share):

Qtr.	Mar.	June	Sept.	Dec.
1996	0.04	0.06	0.05	0.05
1997	0.06	0.05	0.07	0.05
1998	0.06	0.07	0.12	0.09
1999	0.11	0.12	0.10	0.13

INTERIM DIVIDENDS (Per Share):

Amt.	Decl.	Ex.	Rec.	Pay.
0.014Q	7/22/99	8/10/99	8/12/99	8/26/99
0.014Q	10/28/99	11/09/99	11/12/99	11/26/99
0.014Q	1/18/00	2/08/00	2/10/00	2/24/00
0.014Q	4/19/00	5/08/00	5/10/00	5/24/00
50% STK	5/03/00	5/31/00	5/12/00	5/30/00

Indicated div.: $0.04 (Adj.; Div. Reinv. Plan)

CAPITALIZATION (12/31/99):

	($000)	(%)
Long-Term Debt	455,000	16.7
Common & Surplus	2,273,935	83.3
Total	2,728,935	100.0

DIVIDEND ACHIEVER STATUS:

Rank: 3   10-Year Growth Rate: 34.00%
Total Years of Dividend Growth: 10

RECENT DEVELOPMENTS:

For the year ended 12/31/99, net income soared 69.0% to $588.9 million from $348.5 million in 1998. Total revenues advanced 44.2% to $3.94 billion from $2.74 billion the year before. Commissions revenue rose 42.3% to $1.86 billion. Mutual fund service fees improved 34.1% to $750.1 million. Net interest revenue increased 47.7% to $702.7 million, while principal transactions revenue rose 74.5% to $500.5 million.

PROSPECTS:

On 5/1/00, the Federal Reserve approved the Company's acquisition of U.S. Trust Corporation, scheduled to be completed by July 2000. Separately, SCH will introduce PocketBroker™, its first wireless product for U.S. investors. Meanwhile, SCH and Barclays PLC will develop and operate an automated foreign exchange facility that will enable the Company's non-U.S. customers to buy and sell securities in different foreign markets.

BUSINESS

THE CHARLES SCHWAB CORPORATION and its subsidiaries provide brokerage and related investment services to 6.9 million active investor accounts, with $823.00 billion in customer assets as of 5/00. The Company's principal subsidiary, Charles Schwab & Co. Inc., is a securities broker-dealer and is the United States' largest on-line brokerage firm. Mayer & Schweitzer, Inc., a market-maker in Nasdaq securities, provides trade-execution services to institutional clients and broker-dealers. With a network of 356 branch offices, SCH is represented in 48 states, Puerto Rico, Canada, the United Kingdom, the U.S. Virgin Islands, the Caymen Islands and Hong Kong.

REVENUES

(12/31/99)	($000)	(%)
Commissions	1,863,306	49.2
Mutual Fund Service Fees	750,141	19.0
Interest Revenue	702,677	17.8
Principal Transactions	500,496	12.7
Other	128,202	3.2
Total	3,944,822	100.0

ANNUAL FINANCIAL DATA

	12/31/99	12/31/98	12/31/97	12/31/96	12/31/95	12/31/94	12/31/93
Earnings Per Share	0.47	0.28	② 0.22	0.19	0.14	0.11	① 0.10
Cash Flow Per Share	0.59	0.39	0.32	0.28	0.20	0.16	0.14
Tang. Book Val. Per Share	1.81	1.15	0.90	0.66	0.47	0.38	0.30
Dividends Per Share	0.037	0.035	0.031	0.027	0.021	0.014	0.009
Dividend Payout %	8.0	12.7	14.1	13.8	14.4	12.1	9.1
INCOME STATEMENT (IN MILLIONS):							
Total Revenues	3,944.8	2,736.2	2,298.8	1,850.9	1,419.9	1,064.6	965.0
Costs & Expenses	2,816.9	2,021.2	1,726.8	1,358.5	1,074.0	785.7	714.3
Depreciation & Amort.	156.7	138.5	124.7	98.3	68.8	54.6	44.4
Operating Income	971.2	576.5	447.2	394.1	277.1	224.3	206.3
Income Before Income Taxes	971.2	576.5	447.2	394.1	277.1	224.3	206.3
Income Taxes	382.4	228.1	177.0	160.3	104.5	89.0	81.9
Net Income	588.9	348.5	② 270.3	233.8	172.6	135.3	① 124.4
Cash Flow	745.6	486.9	395.0	332.1	241.4	189.9	168.8
Average Shs. Outstg. (000)	1,264,635	1,234,515	1,226,589	1,169,591	1,204,713	1,182,641	1,203,863
BALANCE SHEET (IN MILLIONS):							
Cash & Cash Equivalents	10,544.7	11,398.9	7,571.5	7,869.3	5,855.9	4,587.1	3,956.1
Total Current Assets	28,087.5	21,379.3	15,590.1	13,113.0	9,944.1	7,597.0	6,581.0
Net Property	597.8	396.2	342.3	315.4	243.5	129.1	136.4
Total Assets	29,299.1	22,264.4	16,481.7	13,778.8	10,552.0	7,917.9	6,896.5
Total Current Liabilities	26,570.1	20,484.8	14,975.5	12,640.4	9,673.0	7,279.5	6,332.0
Long-Term Obligations	455.0	351.0	361.0	283.8	246.1	171.4	185.3
Net Stockholders' Equity	2,273.9	1,428.6	1,145.1	854.6	632.9	467.0	379.2
Net Working Capital	1,517.4	894.6	614.5	472.6	271.2	317.5	249.0
Year-end Shs. Outstg. (000)	1,233,374	1,205,649	1,204,599	1,181,709	1,174,716	1,153,548	1,153,548
STATISTICAL RECORD:							
Operating Profit Margin %	24.6	21.1	19.5	21.3	19.5	21.1	21.4
Net Profit Margin %	14.9	12.7	11.8	12.6	12.2	12.7	12.9
Return on Equity %	25.9	24.4	23.6	27.4	27.3	29.0	32.8
Return on Assets %	2.0	1.6	1.6	1.7	1.6	1.7	1.8
Debt/Total Assets %	1.6	1.6	2.2	2.1	2.3	2.2	2.7
Price Range	51¹¹/₁₆-16¹⁵/₁₆	22¹³/₁₆-6³/₁₆	9¹³/₁₆-4¹¹/₁₆	4⁷/₈-2¹¹/₁₆	4⁵/₁₆-1⁵/₈	1¹³/₁₆-1³/₁₆	1⁷/₈-0¹³/₁₆
P/E Ratio	110.7-36.3	80.6-21.8	44.7-20.4	25.2-13.8	29.8-11.4	16.0-10.3	18.4-8.0
Average Yield %	0.1	0.2	0.4	0.7	0.7	0.9	0.7

Statistics are as originally reported. Adj. for 2-for-1 split: 7/99 & 9/95; 3-for-2 split: 5/00, 12/98, 9/97, 3/95 & 6/93. ① Bef. extra. chg. of $6.7 mill. for early retire. of debt. ② Incl. $23.6 mill. chg. for settlement of market-maker litigation.

OFFICERS:

C. R. Schwab, Chmn., Co-C.E.O.
D. S. Pottruck, Pres., Co-C.E.O.
S. L. Scheid, Exec. V.P., C.F.O.

INVESTOR CONTACT: Barb Novak, (651) 450-4053

PRINCIPAL OFFICE: 120 Kearny St., San Francisco, CA 94104

TELEPHONE NUMBER: (415) 627-7000
FAX: (415) 627-8538
WEB: www.schwab.com

NO. OF EMPLOYEES: 18,100

SHAREHOLDERS: 9,996

ANNUAL MEETING: In May

INCORPORATED: DE, Nov., 1986

INSTITUTIONAL HOLDINGS:
No. of Institutions: 426
Shares Held: 543,849,917 (Adj.)
% Held: 44.2

INDUSTRY: Security brokers and dealers (SIC: 6211)

TRANSFER AGENT(S): Norwest Bank Minnesota, N.A., St. Paul, MN.

SEMCO ENERGY, INC.

YIELD 6.3%
P/E RATIO 13.2

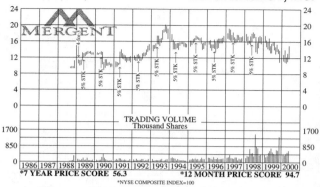

*7 YEAR PRICE SCORE 56.3   *12 MONTH PRICE SCORE 94.7

*NYSE COMPOSITE INDEX=100

INTERIM EARNINGS (Per Share):

Qtr.	Mar.	June	Sept.	Dec.
1995	0.54	0.02	d0.20	0.46
1996	0.65	0.01	d0.21	d1.09
1997	0.70	0.01	d0.23	0.61
1998	0.59	d0.18	d0.18	0.37
1999	0.60	0.01	d0.12	0.52

INTERIM DIVIDENDS (Per Share):

Amt.	Decl.	Ex.	Rec.	Pay.
0.05Sp	4/20/99	5/03/99	5/05/99	5/15/99
0.205Q	6/10/99	8/03/99	8/05/99	8/15/99
0.205Q	10/14/99	11/03/99	11/05/99	11/15/99
0.205Q	12/16/99	2/02/00	2/04/00	2/15/00
0.21Q	3/03/00	5/03/00	5/05/00	5/15/00

Indicated div.: $0.84 (Div. Reinv. Plan)

CAPITALIZATION (12/31/99):

	($000)	(%)
Long-Term Debt	170,000	50.3
Deferred Income Tax	25,774	7.6
Common & Surplus	142,340	42.1
Total	338,114	100.0

DIVIDEND ACHIEVER STATUS:
Rank: 263   10-Year Growth Rate: 4.94%
Total Years of Dividend Growth: 21

RECENT DEVELOPMENTS: On 1/11/00, the Company's common stock began trading on the New York Stock Exchange under the ticker symbol "SEN." For the year ended 12/31/99, the Company reported net income of $17.7 million compared with income of $8.8 million, before the cumulative effect of an accounting change, in 1999. Operating revenues totaled $384.7 million, a decline of 39.6% from $637.5 million a year earlier. Gas marketing revenues declined 75.2% to $96.9 million due to the sale of the business by the Company on 3/31/99. Engineering service revenues fell 63.8% to $14.8 million primarily due to lower revenues from turn-key projects and lower pipeline inspection revenues. Recently, the Company acquired Illinois-based KLP Construction Co., Inc., a provider of natural gas pipeline and fiber optic construction services, as well as certain assets of Lake Area Utilities.

BUSINESS

SEMCO ENERGY, INC. (formerly Southeastern Michigan Gas Company) operates four business segments: gas distribution, engineering services, pipeline construction services and propane, pipelines and storage. The Company's gas distribution business segment distributes and transports natural gas to approximately 250,000 customers within the state of Michigan. The engineering services segment has offices in New Jersey, Michigan, Louisiana and Texas and provides a variety of energy related engineering and quality assurance services in several states. The pipeline construction services business segment provides primarily pipeline construction services in Iowa, Kansas, Michigan, Missouri, Nebraska and Tennessee. The propane, pipelines and storage segment supplies propane to over 7,500 retail customers in Michigan's upper peninsula and northeast Wisconsin and operates natural gas transmission, gathering and storage facilities in Michigan.

ANNUAL FINANCIAL DATA

	12/31/99	12/31/98	12/31/97	12/31/96	12/31/95	12/31/94	12/31/93
Earnings Per Share	1.00	①②0.63	1.09	③d0.93	0.83	①0.80	①0.77
Cash Flow Per Share	2.13	1.52	2.06	0.17	1.71	1.70	1.83
Tang. Book Val. Per Share	...	7.61	6.82	6.33	8.00	7.86	7.28
Dividends Per Share	0.86	0.78	0.75	0.71	0.67	0.64	0.61
Dividend Payout %	86.5	123.9	69.3	...	81.4	80.5	80.0
INCOME STATEMENT (IN THOUSANDS):							
Total Revenues	384,763	637,485	775,932	547,630	335,538	372,430	288,963
Costs & Expenses	322,867	597,941	733,902	505,847	290,552	328,883	245,214
Depreciation & Amort.	20,006	15,349	12,863	11,317	12,035	11,549	12,468
Maintenance Exp.	...	...	...	...	4,337	4,503	4,253
Operating Income	41,890	24,195	29,167	30,466	28,614	27,495	27,028
Net Interest Inc./(Exp.)	d20,575	d14,811	d13,059	d11,053	d10,721	d10,775	d11,534
Income Taxes	7,012	6,320	8,469	6,371	6,188	5,204	5,598
Net Income	17,659	①②8,755	15,425	③d8,965	11,348	①11,296	①9,759
Cash Flow	37,665	24,104	28,288	2,352	23,366	22,827	22,208
Average Shs. Outstg.	17,697	15,906	13,703	13,668	13,697	13,440	12,155
BALANCE SHEET (IN THOUSANDS):							
Gross Property	603,939	408,370	360,022	342,778	314,602	287,414	272,571
Accumulated Depreciation	129,593	118,132	102,790	96,391	87,308	76,674	70,629
Net Property	474,346	290,238	275,462	255,972	240,177	226,755	218,299
Total Assets	815,183	489,662	505,487	478,238	378,523	371,698	348,813
Long-Term Obligations	170,000	170,000	163,548	106,468	105,858	104,910	97,884
Net Stockholders' Equity	142,340	135,483	97,771	89,813	112,783	110,667	88,947
Year-end Shs. Outstg.	17,909	17,382	13,864	13,671	13,703	13,688	11,766
STATISTICAL RECORD:							
Operating Profit Margin %	10.9	3.8	3.8	5.6	8.5	7.4	9.4
Net Profit Margin %	4.6	1.4	· 2.0	...	3.4	3.0	3.4
Net Inc./Net Property %	3.7	3.0	5.6	...	4.7	5.0	4.5
Net Inc./Tot. Capital %	5.2	2.7	5.6	...	4.8	4.8	4.8
Return on Equity %	12.4	6.5	15.8	...	10.1	10.2	11.0
Accum. Depr./Gross Prop. %	21.5	28.9	28.6	28.1	27.8	26.7	25.9
Price Range	17½-10¹⁵⁄₁₆	18³⁄₈-13¹⁄₈	19¼-15¹¹⁄₁₆	17⁷⁄₁₆-13½	17½-13¹³⁄₁₆	17¹³⁄₁₆-13	20³⁄₁₆-15⅜
P/E Ratio	17.5-10.9	29.2-20.8	17.7-14.5	...	21.1-16.9	22.3-17.5	26.4-17.8
Average Yield %	6.1	5.0	4.3	4.6	4.3	4.0	3.6

Statistics are as originally reported. Adj. for stk. splits: 5% div., 5/15/98; 5% div., 5/15/97; 5% div., 5/96; 5% div., 5/95; 5% div., 4/94; 5% div., 4/93 ① Bef. extraord. chrg. 12/31/98: $499,000; 12/31/94: $1.3 mill. ($0.10/sh.); 12/31/93: $177,000 ($0.01/sh.); 12/31/92: $901,000 ($0.08/sh.) ② Bef. acctg. change credit $1.8 mill. ③ Incl. non-recurr. chrg. $21.0 mill.

OFFICERS:
W. L. Johnson, Chmn., C.E.O.
C. W. Porter, Pres., C.O.O.
S. Coppola, Sr. V.P., C.F.O.
E. R. Mason Jr., Treas.
INVESTOR CONTACT: Edric R. Mason Jr., Director of Investor Relations, (800) 255-7647
PRINCIPAL OFFICE: 405 Water Street, Port Huron, MI 48060

TELEPHONE NUMBER: (810) 987-2200
FAX: (810) 987-4570
WEB: www.semcoenergy.com
NO. OF EMPLOYEES: 1,632 (approx.)
SHAREHOLDERS: 9,214 (common)
ANNUAL MEETING: In Apr.
INCORPORATED: MI, Nov., 1977

INSTITUTIONAL HOLDINGS:
No. of Institutions: 38
Shares Held: 1,862,304
% Held: 10.4

INDUSTRY: Natural gas distribution (SIC: 4924)

TRANSFER AGENT(S): Norwest Bank Minnesota, NA, St Paul, MN

NYSE SYMBOL SVM
Rec. Pr. 12¹³⁄₁₆ (5/31/00)

SERVICEMASTER COMPANY (THE)

YIELD 3.1%
P/E RATIO 22.9

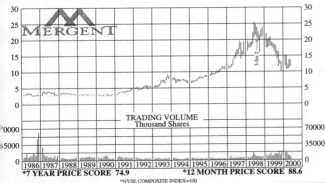

INTERIM EARNINGS (Per Share):

Qtr.	Mar.	June	Sept.	Dec.
1996	0.13	0.22	0.21	0.20
1997	0.14	0.27	0.27	0.14
1998	0.10	0.19	0.19	0.16
1999	0.12	0.06	0.21	0.17

INTERIM DIVIDENDS (Per Share):

Amt.	Decl.	Ex.	Rec.	Pay.
0.09Q	4/30/99	7/14/99	7/16/99	7/30/99
0.09Q	10/04/99	10/13/99	10/15/99	10/29/99
0.09Q	12/13/99	1/12/00	1/14/00	1/31/00
0.09Q	3/17/00	4/12/00	4/14/00	4/28/00
0.10Q	4/28/00	7/12/00	7/14/00	7/31/00

Indicated div.: $0.40 (Div. Reinv. Plan)

CAPITALIZATION (12/31/99):

	($000)	(%)
Long-Term Debt	1,697,582	58.5
Common & Surplus	1,205,716	41.5
Total	2,903,298	100.0

TRADING VOLUME
Thousand Shares

7 YEAR PRICE SCORE 74.9   **12 MONTH PRICE SCORE 88.6**
NYSE COMPOSITE INDEX=100

DIVIDEND ACHIEVER STATUS:
Rank: 267   10-Year Growth Rate: 4.50%
Total Years of Dividend Growth: 29

RECENT DEVELOPMENTS: For the year ended 12/31/99, net income declined 8.6% to $173.6 million versus $190.0 million in 1998. Operating revenues were $5.70 billion, up 20.7% from $4.72 billion a year earlier. Consumer and Commercial Services revenues increased 53.0% to $3.10 billion, reflecting growth in existing businesses and successful integration of acquisitions.

PROSPECTS: The Company and Kleiner Perkins Caufield & Byers announced the formation and initial funding of WeServeHomes.com, a separate Internet company that will provide comprehensive on-line solutions for home services, products and information. ServiceMaster will initially have an 84.0% ownership. WeServeHomes.com will be launched on a regional basis in the first half of 2000.

BUSINESS

THE SERVICEMASTER COMPANY (formerly ServiceMaster Limited Partnership), provides outsourcing services to more than 12 million customers in the United States and in 40 other countries. The core service capabilities of the Company include lawn care and landscaping, termite and pest control, plumbing, heating and air conditioning maintenance and repair, appliance maintenance and repair, cleaning, plant maintenance and supportive management. These services are provided through a network of over 5,800 Company-owned and franchised service centers and business units, operating under brands including TruGreen-ChemLawn, TruGreen-LandCare, Terminix, American Home Shield, Rescue Rooter, American Residential Services, ServiceMaster Residential and Commercial Services, Merry Maids, AmeriSpec, Furniture Medic and ServiceMaster Management Services.

ANNUAL FINANCIAL DATA

	12/31/99	12/31/98	12/31/97	12/31/96	12/31/95	12/31/94	12/31/93
Earnings Per Share	② 0.55	0.64	③ 0.55	0.76	0.64	0.33	① 0.56
Cash Flow Per Share	0.99	0.99	1.41	0.99	0.88	0.76	0.76
Dividends Per Share	0.36	0.33	0.31	0.29	0.28	0.27	0.26
Dividend Payout %	65.4	51.6	56.4	38.2	43.8	137.0	46.4
INCOME STATEMENT (IN MILLIONS):							
Total Revenues	5,703.5	4,724.1	3,961.5	3,458.3	3,202.5	2,985.2	2,758.9
Costs & Expenses	5,181.9	4,223.1	3,524.5	3,084.1	2,884.6	2,717.0	2,535.9
Depreciation & Amort.	138.4	104.6	93.1	79.0	66.0	54.2	50.0
Operating Income	383.2	396.4	343.9	295.2	251.9	214.0	173.0
Net Interest Inc./(Exp.)	d109.0	d92.9	d76.4	d38.3	d35.9	d31.5	d26.6
Income Before Income Taxes	296.2	318.8	274.3	252.4	177.6	142.6	148.1
Income Taxes	122.6	128.8	cr54.8	7.3	5.6	2.8	2.1
Equity Earnings/Minority Int.	. . .	. . .	d7.5	d14.7	d45.7	d45.2	d28.5
Net Income	② 173.6	190.0	329.1	245.1	172.0	139.9	① 145.9
Cash Flow	312.0	294.6	422.1	324.1	238.0	194.1	195.9
Average Shs. Outstg. (000)	314,406	298,887	299,640	326,403	270,275	255,650	259,355
BALANCE SHEET (IN MILLIONS):							
Cash & Cash Equivalents	114.2	120.4	124.1	114.4	49.4	34.4	32.7
Total Current Assets	959.2	670.2	594.1	499.3	393.2	331.0	291.3
Net Property	318.1	212.2	158.3	146.4	145.9	128.4	115.8
Total Assets	3,870.2	2,914.9	2,475.2	1,846.8	1,649.9	1,230.8	1,122.5
Total Current Liabilities	845.8	753.7	558.2	425.6	372.9	304.4	239.6
Long-Term Obligations	1,697.6	1,076.2	1,247.8	482.3	411.9	386.5	384.5
Net Stockholders' Equity	1,205.7	956.5	524.4	796.8	746.7	307.3	289.2
Net Working Capital	113.4	d83.5	35.9	73.8	20.3	26.6	51.7
Year-end Shs. Outstg. (000)	307,530	298,030	279,944	331,196	275,144	256,574	257,938
STATISTICAL RECORD:							
Operating Profit Margin %	6.7	8.4	8.7	8.5	7.9	7.2	6.3
Net Profit Margin %	3.0	4.0	8.3	7.1	5.4	4.7	5.3
Return on Equity %	14.4	19.9	62.7	30.8	23.0	45.5	50.5
Return on Assets %	4.5	6.5	13.3	13.3	10.4	11.4	13.0
Debt/Total Assets %	43.9	36.9	50.4	26.1	25.0	31.4	34.3
Price Range	22-10⅛	25½-16	19¹¹⁄₁₆-10¹⁵⁄₁₆	11¹³⁄₁₆-8⅝	9-6³⁄₈	8⁷⁄₁₆-6³⁄₈	9³⁄₁₆-5¼
P/E Ratio	40.0-18.4	39.8-25.0	35.9-20.0	15.7-11.4	14.0-9.9	25.5-19.3	16.3-9.3
Average Yield %	2.2	1.6	2.0	2.9	3.6	3.7	3.6

Statistics are as originally reported. Adj. for stk. splits: 3-for-2, 6/98, 6/97, 6/96, 6/93. ① Incl. non-recurr. credit $30.2 mill., 1993. ② Incl. non-recurr. chrg. $85.5 mill., 1999. ③ On 12/26/97, SVM converted from a publicly traded partnership to a taxable corporation. Prior to that date, net income was not subject to federal and state taxes.

OFFICERS:
C. W. Pollard, Chmn., C.E.O.
P. B. Rooney, Vice-Chmn., C.O.O.
C. W. Stair, Vice-Chmn.
C. H. Cantu, Pres., C.E.O.

INVESTOR CONTACT: Bruce Duncan, V.P., (630) 271-1300

PRINCIPAL OFFICE: One Servicemaster Way, Downers Grove, IL 60515-1700

TELEPHONE NUMBER: (630) 271-1300
FAX: (630) 271-2710
WEB: www. servicemaster.com

NO. OF EMPLOYEES: 72,000 (avg.)

SHAREHOLDERS: 41,000

ANNUAL MEETING: In April

INCORPORATED: DE, Oct., 1986

INSTITUTIONAL HOLDINGS:
No. of Institutions: 251
Shares Held: 88,110,424
% Held: 28.4

INDUSTRY: Management services (SIC: 8741)

TRANSFER AGENT(S): Harris Trust & Savings Bank, Chicago, IL

NYSE SYMBOL SHW
Rec. Pr. 23 1/4 (5/31/00)

SHERWIN-WILLIAMS COMPANY

YIELD 2.3%
P/E RATIO 12.9

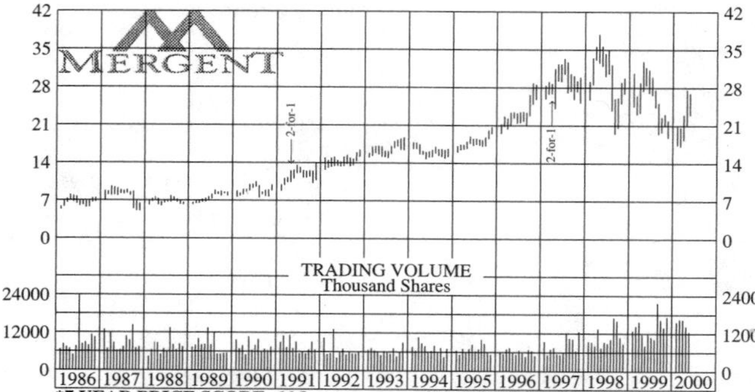

*7 YEAR PRICE SCORE 66.8 *12 MONTH PRICE SCORE 106.4

*NYSE COMPOSITE INDEX=100

INTERIM EARNINGS (Per Share):

Qtr.	Mar.	June	Sept.	Dec.
1996	0.16	0.48	0.51	0.23
1997	0.13	0.54	0.57	0.26
1998	0.14	0.57	0.58	0.28
1999	0.17	0.63	0.66	0.34

INTERIM DIVIDENDS (Per Share):

Amt.	Decl.	Ex.	Rec.	Pay.
0.12Q	4/28/99	5/26/99	5/28/99	6/11/99
0.12Q	7/21/99	8/18/99	8/20/99	9/03/99
0.12Q	10/25/99	10/28/99	11/01/99	11/15/99
0.135Q	2/02/00	2/24/00	2/28/00	3/13/00
0.135Q	4/26/00	5/24/00	5/26/00	6/09/00

Indicated div.: $0.54 (Div. Reinv. Plan)

CAPITALIZATION (12/31/99):

	($000)	(%)
Long-Term Debt[1]	624,365	26.9
Common & Surplus	1,698,532	73.1
Total	2,322,897	100.0

DIVIDEND ACHIEVER STATUS:
Rank: 143 10-Year Growth Rate: 10.62%
Total Years of Dividend Growth: 20

RECENT DEVELOPMENTS: For the year ended 12/31/99, net income increased 11.4% to $303.9 million compared with $272.9 million in 1998. Net sales were $5.00 billion, up 1.4% from $4.93 billion a year earlier. The Paint Stores' operating profit increased 8.6% to $376.8 million for the year primarily due to paint volume sales gains. Operating profits of the Consumer segment advanced 23.7% to $154.9 million. Operating profits for the Automotive Finishes segment increased 2.0% to $66.5 million.

PROSPECTS: Going forward, the Paint Stores segment plans to open approximately 80 new stores while investing in new sales territories and field technical personnel. Service levels should continue to improve through added investments in staffing, color matching equipment and other productivity improving equipment. During the fourth quarter of 1999, SHW purchased 850,000 shares, bringing the total treasury shares purchased for the year to 5.9 million.

BUSINESS

SHERWIN-WILLIAMS COMPANY is engaged in the manufacture, distribution and sale of coatings and related products. The Paint Stores' divisions sell products through more than 2,396 company-operated specialty paint stores located in the U.S., Canada, the Virgin Islands and Puerto Rico. The Consumer segment develops, manufactures and distributes architectural paints, stains, varnishes, industrial maintenance products, wood finishing products, paint applicators, corrosion inhibitors, and paint-related products in the U.S. and Canada. The Automotive Finishes segment develops, manufactures and distributes motor vehicle finish, refinish and touch-up products primarily throughout North and South America and the Caribbean Islands. The International Coatings segment develops, licenses, manufactures and distributes architectural paints, stains, varnishes, industrial maintenance products, product finishes, wood finishing products and paint-related products worldwide.

ANNUAL FINANCIAL DATA

	12/31/99	12/31/98	12/31/97	12/31/96	12/31/95	12/31/94	12/31/93
Earnings Per Share	**1.80**	**1.57**	**1.50**	**1.34**	**1.18**	**1.08**	**0.93**
Cash Flow Per Share	**2.72**	**2.42**	**2.30**	**1.92**	**1.62**	**1.51**	**1.31**
Tang. Book Val. Per Share	**2.32**	**1.76**	**0.70**	**3.65**	**5.85**	**5.39**	**4.96**
Dividends Per Share	**0.48**	**0.45**	**0.40**	**0.35**	**0.32**	**0.28**	**0.25**
Dividend Payout %	**26.7**	**28.7**	**26.8**	**26.1**	**27.1**	**25.9**	**27.0**
INCOME STATEMENT (IN MILLIONS):							
Total Revenues	5,003.8	4,934.4	4,881.1	4,132.9	3,273.8	3,100.1	2,949.3
Costs & Expenses	4,273.0	4,254.9	4,218.7	3,610.6	2,874.6	2,717.4	2,609.4
Depreciation & Amort.	155.7	147.9	139.2	103.6	77.9	73.7	68.8
Operating Income	575.1	531.6	523.2	418.6	321.3	308.9	271.1
Net Interest Inc./(Exp.)	d61.2	d72.0	d80.8	d24.5	d2.5	d3.2	d6.5
Income Before Income Taxes	490.1	440.1	427.3	371.1	318.5	298.5	264.4
Income Taxes	186.3	167.2	166.7	146.2	117.8	111.9	99.1
Net Income	303.9	272.9	260.6	224.9	200.7	186.6	165.2
Cash Flow	459.6	420.8	399.9	328.5	278.6	260.3	234.0
Average Shs. Outstg. (000)	169,026	173,536	174,032	171,117	171,487	172,151	178,872
BALANCE SHEET (IN MILLIONS):							
Cash & Cash Equivalents	18.6	19.1	3.5	1.9	269.5	251.4	269.8
Total Current Assets	1,597.4	1,547.3	1,532.3	1,416.2	1,238.9	1,188.6	1,151.1
Net Property	711.7	718.9	692.3	549.4	456.4	409.2	394.1
Total Assets	4,052.1	4,065.5	4,035.8	2,994.6	2,141.1	1,962.0	1,914.7
Total Current Liabilities	1,189.9	1,112.0	1,115.7	1,051.0	618.9	597.0	567.5
Long-Term Obligations	624.4	730.3	843.9	142.7	24.0	20.5	37.9
Net Stockholders' Equity	1,698.5	1,715.9	1,592.2	1,401.2	1,212.1	1,053.3	1,033.2
Net Working Capital	407.5	435.3	416.6	365.2	620.0	591.6	583.6
Year-end Shs. Outstg. (000)	165,664	171,033	172,907	171,831	170,910	169,652	177,012
STATISTICAL RECORD:							
Operating Profit Margin %	11.5	10.8	10.7	10.1	9.8	10.0	9.2
Net Profit Margin %	6.1	5.5	5.3	5.4	6.1	6.0	5.6
Return on Equity %	17.9	15.9	16.4	16.1	16.6	17.7	16.0
Return on Assets %	7.5	6.7	6.5	7.5	9.4	9.5	8.6
Debt/Total Assets %	15.4	18.0	20.9	4.8	1.1	1.0	2.0
Price Range	32 7/8-18 3/4	37 7/8-19 7/16	33 3/8-24 1/8	28 7/8-19 1/2	20 3/4-16	17 7/8-14 3/4	18 3/4-14 15/16
P/E Ratio	18.3-10.4	24.1-12.4	22.2-16.1	21.5-14.6	17.6-13.6	16.5-13.7	20.3-16.1
Average Yield %	1.9	1.6	1.4	1.4	1.7	1.7	1.5

Statistics are as originally reported. Adj. for stk. splits: 2-for-1, 3/97. [1] Incl. debentures conv. into common.

OFFICERS:
J. G. Breen, Chmn.
C. M. Connor, Vice-Chmn., C.E.O.
J. M. Scaminace, Pres., C.O.O.
L. J. Pitorak, Sr. V.P., C.F.O., Treas.

INVESTOR CONTACT: Conway G. Ivy, Investor Relations, (216) 566-2000

PRINCIPAL OFFICE: 101 Prospect Avenue N.W., Cleveland, OH 44115-1075

TELEPHONE NUMBER: (216) 566-2000
FAX: (216) 566-3310
WEB: www.sherwin.com

NO. OF EMPLOYEES: 25,697

SHAREHOLDERS: 11,412

ANNUAL MEETING: In Apr.

INCORPORATED: OH, July, 1884

INSTITUTIONAL HOLDINGS:
No. of Institutions: 308
Shares Held: 103,567,702
% Held: 62.4

INDUSTRY: Paints and allied products (SIC: 2851)

TRANSFER AGENT(S): The Bank of New York, New York, NY

NYSE SYMBOL SIG
Rec. Pr. 25½ (3/31/00)

SIGCORP, INC.

YIELD	5.0%
P/E RATIO	11.6

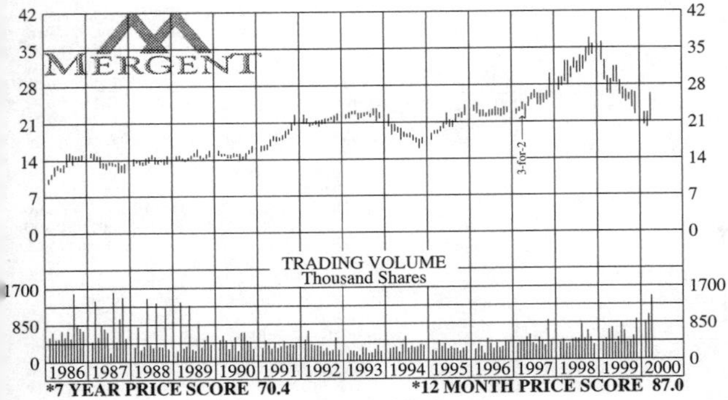

*7 YEAR PRICE SCORE 70.4   *12 MONTH PRICE SCORE 87.0

*NYSE COMPOSITE INDEX=100

INTERIM EARNINGS (Per Share):

Qtr.	Mar.	June	Sept.	Dec.
1996	0.56	0.37	0.67	0.22
1997	0.55	0.27	0.84	0.29
1998	0.70	0.38	0.75	0.30
1999	0.53	0.34	0.85	0.47

INTERIM DIVIDENDS (Per Share):

Amt.	Decl.	Ex.	Rec.	Pay.
0.31Q	1/21/99	2/17/99	2/19/99	3/20/99
0.31Q	4/28/99	5/19/99	5/21/99	6/21/99
0.31Q	7/23/99	8/18/99	8/20/99	9/20/99
0.31Q	10/19/99	11/17/99	11/19/99	12/20/99
0.318Q	1/21/00	2/16/00	2/18/00	3/20/00

Indicated div.: $1.27 (Div. Reinv. Plan)

CAPITALIZATION (12/31/99):

	($000)	(%)
Long-Term Debt	273,531	32.5
Deferred Income Tax	154,459	18.4
Redeemable Pfd. Stock	7,500	0.9
Preferred Stock	11,898	1.4
Common & Surplus	393,208	46.8
Total	840,596	100.0

DIVIDEND ACHIEVER STATUS:
Rank: 296   10-Year Growth Rate: 3.26%
Total Years of Dividend Growth: 40

RECENT DEVELOPMENTS: For the year ended 12/31/99, net income grew 3.1% to $52.1 million from $50.5 million in 1998, reflecting higher average unit sales to retail and municipal customers. Results for 1998 included an after-tax gain of $2.9 million. Total operating revenues grew 8.5% to $604.5 million from $557.1 million in 1998. Electric revenues rose 3.3% to $307.6 million. Energy services revenues and other operations increased 18.8% to $228.7 million.

PROSPECTS: On 3/31/00, SIG and Indiana Energy, Inc. completed a merger to form Vectren Corporation in a transaction valued at approximately $1.90 billion. Vectren Corporation began trading on the NYSE under the symbol VVC on 4/3/00. VVC plans to grow earnings per share at an average annual compounded rate of 10.0% over the next five years. The merger should generate cost savings of approximately $200.0 million in the next 10 years.

BUSINESS

SIGCORP, INC. merged with Indiana Energy on 3/31/00 to form Vectren Corp. Prior to the merger, SIGCORP, Inc. a holding company, through its public utility subsidiary, Southern Indiana Gas & Electric Co. and ten non-regulated subsidiaries, was engaged in the generation, transmission, distribution and sale of electricity, and the purchase of natural gas and its transportation, distribution, and sale in a service area that covers ten counties in Southwestern Indiana. SIG's electric business services approximately 126,605 customers in Evansville and 74 cities, towns, communities and adjacent areas. Additionally, wholesale electric service is supplied to another eight communities. The Company's gas business services approximately 109,388 customers in the Evansville area and 64 cities, towns and nearby communities and their environs.

ANNUAL FINANCIAL DATA

	12/31/99	12/31/98	12/31/97	12/31/96	12/31/95	12/31/94	12/31/93
Earnings Per Share	**2.19**	**② 2.12**	**1.95**	**1.83**	**① 1.63**	**1.69**	**1.63**
Cash Flow Per Share	**4.07**	**3.92**	**3.66**	**3.46**	**3.29**	**3.28**	**3.19**
Tang. Book Val. Per Share	**17.14**	**15.70**	**14.77**	**14.00**	**13.32**	**12.55**	**...**
Dividends Per Share	**1.24**	**1.21**	**1.18**	**1.15**	**1.13**	**1.10**	**1.07**
Dividend Payout %	**56.6**	**57.1**	**60.5**	**62.9**	**69.3**	**65.1**	**65.6**
INCOME STATEMENT (IN MILLIONS):							
Total Revenues	604.5	557.1	433.2	372.7	338.7	330.0	329.5
Costs & Expenses	435.7	390.7	278.1	219.4	195.3	190.3	195.9
Depreciation & Amort.	45.3	42.7	40.4	38.6	39.3	37.7	37.0
Maintenance Exp.	34.7	37.6	29.2	29.6	32.2	30.4	26.8
Operating Income	88.8	86.1	85.6	61.0	53.9	52.4	51.6
Net Interest Inc./(Exp.)	d18.7	d17.1	d17.6	d19.2	d19.5	d18.0	d17.6
Income Taxes	25.7	24.0	23.9	24.0	18.1	19.3	18.3
Net Income	52.1	② 50.5	46.1	43.3	① 38.5	39.9	38.5
Cash Flow	96.3	93.2	86.5	81.9	77.8	77.6	75.4
Average Shs. Outstg. (000)	23,724	23,765	23,631	23,633	23,633	23,633	23,633
BALANCE SHEET (IN MILLIONS):							
Gross Property	1,362.5	1,316.3	1,265.2	1,205.4	1,169.7	1,134.9	...
Accumulated Depreciation	623.6	593.9	557.6	524.1	490.3	456.9	...
Net Property	738.9	722.4	707.6	681.3	679.4	677.9	...
Total Assets	1,144.1	1,029.5	989.9	952.7	924.0	917.4	...
Long-Term Obligations	273.5	205.6	276.1	266.2	264.3	273.6	...
Net Stockholders' Equity	405.0	382.9	361.1	342.9	326.9	308.8	...
Year-end Shs. Outstg. (000)	23,631	23,631	23,631	23,633	23,634	23,633	...
STATISTICAL RECORD:							
Operating Profit Margin %	14.7	15.5	19.8	16.4	15.9	15.9	15.6
Net Profit Margin %	8.6	9.1	10.7	11.6	11.4	12.1	11.7
Net Inc./Net Property %	7.1	7.0	6.5	6.4	5.7	5.9	...
Net Inc./Tot. Capital %	6.2	6.8	5.8	5.7	5.3	5.6	...
Return on Equity %	12.9	13.2	12.8	12.6	11.8	12.9	...
Accum. Depr./Gross Prop. %	45.8	45.1	44.1	43.5	41.9	40.3	...
Price Range	36⅛-22 5/16	36⅞-26⅞	30⅛-21⅝	24 11/16-21 15/16	24¼-17 9/16	22 9/16-16	23 11/16-21¼
P/E Ratio	17.2-10.6	17.4-12.7	15.4-11.1	13.5-12.0	14.9-10.8	13.4-9.5	14.5-13.1
Average Yield %	4.2	3.8	4.6	5.0	5.4	5.7	4.8

Statistics are as originally reported. Adj. for stk. splits: 3-for-2, 3/97. ① Bef. acctg. change credit $6.3 mill. ② Incl. after-tax one-time gain of $2.9 mill. ($0.12/sh.)

OFFICERS:
R. G. Reherman, Chmn., C.E.O.
A. E. Goebel, Pres., C.O.O.
T. L. Burke, Sec., Treas.

INVESTOR CONTACT: Investor Relations, (800) 227-8625

PRINCIPAL OFFICE: 20 N. W. Fourth Street, Evansville, IN 47741-0001

TELEPHONE NUMBER: (812) 465-5300
FAX: (812) 464-4554
WEB: www.sigcorpinc.com

NO. OF EMPLOYEES: 1

SHAREHOLDERS: 8,407

ANNUAL MEETING: In Apr.

INCORPORATED: IN, Oct., 1994

INSTITUTIONAL HOLDINGS:
No. of Institutions: 84
Shares Held: 6,836,775
% Held: 28.9

INDUSTRY: Electric and other services combined (SIC: 4931)

TRANSFER AGENT(S): Continental Stock Transfer & Trust Company, New York, NY.

NASDAQ SYMBOL SIAL
Rec. Pr. 33⅜ (5/31/00)

SIGMA-ALDRICH CORPORATION

YIELD 0.9%
P/E RATIO 19.5

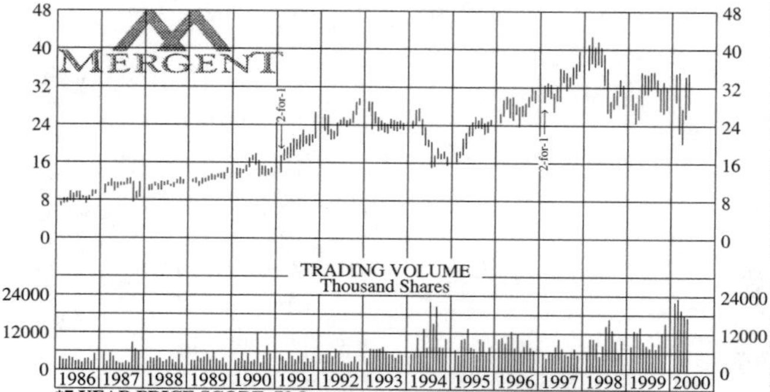

MERGENT
2-for-1
2-for-1
TRADING VOLUME
Thousand Shares
1986 1987 1988 1989 1990 1991 1992 1993 1994 1995 1996 1997 1998 1999 2000

*7 YEAR PRICE SCORE 72.8 *12 MONTH PRICE SCORE 99.6
*NYSE COMPOSITE INDEX=100

INTERIM EARNINGS (Per Share):

Qtr.	Mar.	June	Sept.	Dec.
1995	0.33	0.34	0.33	0.32
1996	0.37	0.37	0.37	0.37
1997	0.41	0.41	0.42	0.41
1998	0.43	0.41	0.41	0.39
1999	0.44	0.44	0.44	0.33

INTERIM DIVIDENDS (Per Share):

Amt.	Decl.	Ex.	Rec.	Pay.
0.072Q	5/05/99	5/27/99	6/01/99	6/15/99
0.072Q	8/10/99	8/30/99	9/01/99	9/15/99
0.077Q	11/09/99	12/13/99	12/15/99	1/03/00
0.077Q	2/15/00	2/28/00	3/01/00	3/15/00
0.077Q	5/02/00	5/30/00	6/01/00	6/15/00

Indicated div.: $0.31

CAPITALIZATION (12/31/99):

	($000)	(%)
Long-Term Debt	205	0.0
Common & Surplus	1,259,351	100.0
Total	1,259,556	100.0

DIVIDEND ACHIEVER STATUS:
Rank: 107 10-Year Growth Rate: 12.41%
Total Years of Dividend Growth: 18

RECENT DEVELOPMENTS: For the year ended 12/31/99, net income increased 2.6% to $148.6 million compared with $144.9 million in the previous year. Earnings included unusual items that resulted in a net gain of $2.6 million in 1999 and $4.1 million in 1998. Earnings for 1999 and 1998 excluded income from discontinued operations of $23.7 million and $21.5 million, respectively. Net sales rose 7.5% to $1.04 billion from $965.9 million in the prior year. Chemical sales benefited from price increases, new product introductions, acquisitions of Genosys Biotechnologies Inc. and Riedel-de-Haen, and the opening of new international sales offices. Metal sales increased 10.6% to $252.6 million. Gross margin slipped to 53.8% from 55.9% the year before. Comparisons were made with restated prior-year results. On 5/1/00, the Company completed the sale of its B-Line Systems business to Cooper Industries, Inc. for $425.0 million. The sale is part of the SIAL's strategic focus aimed at growing its life-science-based business.

BUSINESS

SIGMA-ALDRICH CORPORATION develops, manufactures and distributes a broad range of biochemicals, organic chemicals, chromatography products and diagnostic reagents. The Company is organized into four business units: Laboratory Products, Life Science Products, Diagnostics, and Fine Chemicals. The Laboratory and Life Science products are used by scientists in academia and industry performing research. The Company's Diagnostic Products are used to help diagnose and treat diseases. Fine Chemical products are used primarily by pharmaceutical companies to produce medicines. On 12/23/98, the Company acquired Genosys Biotechnologies Inc. for $39.5 million.

QUARTERLY DATA

(12/31/99)($000)	REV	INC
1st Quarter	272,300	39,100
2nd Quarter	256,400	38,800
3rd Quarter	257,100	38,000
4th Quarter	252,100	32,700

ANNUAL FINANCIAL DATA

	12/31/99	12/31/98	12/31/97	12/31/96	12/31/95	12/31/94	12/31/93
Earnings Per Share	**[2] [3] 1.47**	**1.64**	**1.62**	**1.48**	**1.32**	**1.11**	**[1] 1.08**
Cash Flow Per Share	**2.13**	**2.25**	**2.08**	**1.93**	**1.73**	**1.47**	**1.40**
Tang. Book Val. Per Share	**11.89**	**10.96**	**9.73**	**9.41**	**8.27**	**7.02**	**5.93**
Dividends Per Share	**0.29**	**0.28**	**0.25**	**0.22**	**0.18**	**0.17**	**0.14**
Dividend Payout %	**19.7**	**17.1**	**15.4**	**14.9**	**13.6**	**14.9**	**13.5**
INCOME STATEMENT (IN MILLIONS):							
Total Revenues	1,037.9	1,194.3	1,127.1	1,034.6	959.8	851.2	739.4
Costs & Expenses	767.3	889.9	826.3	759.7	714.8	644.2	541.3
Depreciation & Amort.	66.9	61.8	48.1	45.2	40.9	36.7	32.5
Operating Income	203.7	242.6	252.8	229.7	204.2	170.3	165.6
Income Before Income Taxes	203.7	242.6	252.8	229.7	204.2	170.3	165.6
Income Taxes	55.1	76.2	86.7	81.8	72.5	60.0	58.5
Net Income	[2] [3] 148.6	166.3	166.1	147.9	131.7	110.3	[1] 107.2
Cash Flow	215.5	228.2	214.1	193.1	172.6	147.0	139.7
Average Shs. Outstg. (000)	100,984	101,188	102,804	99,930	99,714	99,658	99,604
BALANCE SHEET (IN MILLIONS):							
Cash & Cash Equivalents	43.8	24.3	46.2	103.7	84.0	9.7	10.3
Total Current Assets	774.6	772.7	706.7	666.6	610.0	502.3	450.8
Net Property	481.7	518.7	438.9	379.1	327.9	302.7	257.3
Total Assets	1,432.0	1,432.8	1,243.8	1,100.0	985.2	852.0	753.4
Total Current Liabilities	105.6	142.4	119.5	110.3	108.0	105.0	111.4
Long-Term Obligations	0.2	0.4	0.6	3.8	13.8	14.5	17.3
Net Stockholders' Equity	1,259.4	1,216.4	1,060.3	942.3	824.7	699.5	591.1
Net Working Capital	669.0	630.3	587.2	556.3	502.0	397.3	339.4
Year-end Shs. Outstg. (000)	98,292	100,623	100,377	100,100	99,754	99,664	99,610
STATISTICAL RECORD:							
Operating Profit Margin %	19.6	20.3	22.4	22.2	21.3	20.0	22.4
Net Profit Margin %	14.3	13.9	14.7	14.3	13.7	13.0	14.5
Return on Equity %	11.8	13.7	15.7	15.7	16.0	15.8	18.1
Return on Assets %	10.4	11.6	13.4	13.4	13.4	13.0	14.2
Debt/Total Assets %	...	...	...	0.3	1.4	1.7	2.3
Price Range	35¼-24½	42¾-25¾	39⅝-26⅞	32 1/16-23¾	25⅞-16¼	27⅝-15	29-22¼
P/E Ratio	24.0-16.7	26.1-15.7	24.5-16.6	21.7-16.0	19.6-12.3	25.0-13.6	27.0-20.7
Average Yield %	1.0	0.8	0.8	0.8	0.9	0.8	0.6

Statistics are as originally reported. Adj. for stk. splits: 2-for-1, 1/2/97 [1] Bef. acctg. change chrg. $10.8 mill. ($0.11/sh.) [2] Bef. disc. oper. gain $23.7 mill. [3] Incl. non-recurr. net gain $2.6 mill.

OFFICERS:
C. T. Cori, Chmn.
D. R. Harvey, Pres. & C.E.O.
K. A. Richter, Treas.
M. R. Hogan, V.P., C.F.O., C.A.O., Sec.

INVESTOR CONTACT: Kirk Richter, Treas., (314) 286-8004

PRINCIPAL OFFICE: 3050 Spruce Street, St. Louis, MO 63103

TELEPHONE NUMBER: (314) 771-5765
FAX: (314) 286-7874
WEB: www.sigma-aldrich.com

NO. OF EMPLOYEES: 7,322

SHAREHOLDERS: 1,600

ANNUAL MEETING: In May

INCORPORATED: DE, May, 1975

INSTITUTIONAL HOLDINGS:
No. of Institutions: 284
Shares Held: 68,331,412
% Held: 67.7

INDUSTRY: Chemicals & allied products, nec (SIC: 5169)

TRANSFER AGENT(S): Harris Trust & Savings Bank, Chicago, IL

ASE SYMBOL SJW
Rec. Pr. 113 (5/31/00)

SJW CORP.

YIELD 2.2%
P/E RATIO 21.6

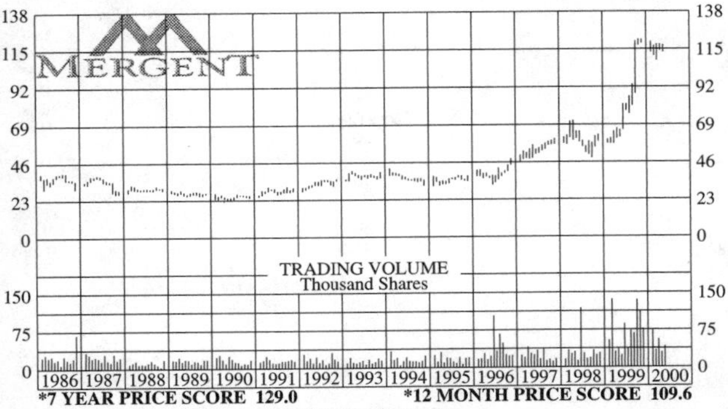

*7 YEAR PRICE SCORE 129.0 *12 MONTH PRICE SCORE 109.6

*NYSE COMPOSITE INDEX=100

INTERIM EARNINGS (Per Share):

Qtr.	Mar.	June	Sept.	Dec.
1996	0.46	1.21	3.26	0.82
1997	0.63	1.62	1.63	0.92
1998	0.48	1.64	1.83	1.10
1999	0.58	1.34	1.78	1.52

INTERIM DIVIDENDS (Per Share):

Amt.	Decl.	Ex.	Rec.	Pay.
0.60Q	4/22/99	4/28/99	5/01/99	6/01/99
0.60Q	7/22/99	7/29/99	8/02/99	9/01/99
0.60Q	10/28/99	11/04/99	11/08/99	12/01/99
0.615Q	1/27/00	2/04/00	2/08/00	3/01/00
0.615Q	4/20/00	4/27/00	5/01/00	6/01/00

Indicated div.: $2.46

CAPITALIZATION (12/31/99):

	($000)	(%)
Long-Term Debt	90,000	34.6
Deferred Income Tax	25,947	10.0
Common & Surplus	143,894	55.4
Total	259,841	100.0

DIVIDEND ACHIEVER STATUS:
Rank: 304 10-Year Growth Rate: 2.80%
Total Years of Dividend Growth: 33

RECENT DEVELOPMENTS: On 10/29/99, the Company signed an agreement to be acquired by American Water Works Company, Inc. for approximately $390.0 million in cash and the assumption of $90.0 million in debt. The acquisition is expected to be completed during the second half of 2000 following all required regulatory approvals. Shareholders of SJW approved the merger on 4/20/00. For the year ended 12/31/99, net income slipped to $15.9 million from $16.0 million in the prior year. Earnings for 1999 included merger costs of $1.6 million. Earnings for 1999 and 1998 included one-time net gains from the sale of a nonutility property of $3.1 million and $1.6 million, respectively. Operating revenue climbed 10.4% to $117.0 million from $106.0 million the year before. This increase was attributed to a 4.0% increase in water consumption and increased office rental business. Operating income grew 4.8% to $19.7 million versus $18.8 million a year earlier.

BUSINESS

SJW CORP. is a holding company with two wholly-owned subsidiaries, San Jose Water Company and SJW Land Company. San Jose Water Company is a public utility in the business of providing water service to a population of approximately 979,000 in an area comprising about 138 square miles in the metropolitan San Jose area. SJW Land Company owns and operates a 900-space surface parking facility located adjacent to the San Jose Water Company's service area. SJW also owns 1,099,952 shares of California Water Service Group (formerly California Water Service Company), acquired through the liquidation of Western Precision, Inc., formerly a wholly-owned subsidiary of the Company.

ANNUAL FINANCIAL DATA

	12/31/99	12/31/98	12/31/97	12/31/96	12/31/95	12/31/94	12/31/93
Earnings Per Share	**[1] [2] 5.20**	**[1] 5.05**	**[1] 4.80**	**[1] 5.75**	**3.55**	**3.05**	**3.64**
Cash Flow Per Share	**8.55**	**8.08**	**7.59**	**8.44**	**5.89**	**5.29**	**5.74**
Tang. Book Val. Per Share	**45.35**	**43.29**	**40.21**	**35.87**	**31.47**	**29.99**	**29.79**
Dividends Per Share	**2.40**	**2.34**	**2.28**	**2.22**	**2.16**	**2.10**	**2.04**
Dividend Payout %	**46.2**	**46.3**	**47.5**	**38.6**	**60.8**	**68.9**	**56.0**
INCOME STATEMENT (IN THOUSANDS):							
Total Revenues	117,001	106,010	110,084	102,593	97,385	99,422	95,045
Costs & Expenses	71,515	60,975	64,726	60,399	60,335	65,687	59,774
Depreciation & Amort.	10,235	9,594	8,847	8,671	7,626	7,292	6,823
Maintenance Exp.	6,638	6,909	7,087	6,851	6,342	6,289	5,417
Operating Income	19,739	18,847	19,314	17,606	15,314	13,767	14,960
Net Interest Inc./(Exp.)	d6,552	d5,629	d5,695	d5,892	d4,888	d5,082	d4,489
Income Taxes	8,874	9,685	10,110	9,066	7,768	6,387	8,071
Net Income	[1] [2] 15,884	[1] 16,018	[1] 15,216	[1] 18,560	11,535	9,902	11,767
Cash Flow	26,119	25,612	24,063	27,231	19,161	17,194	18,590
Average Shs. Outstg.	3,055	3,170	3,170	3,227	3,251	3,251	3,237
BALANCE SHEET (IN THOUSANDS):							
Gross Property	432,262	403,227	371,200	342,368	324,098	308,515	293,683
Accumulated Depreciation	129,828	122,809	114,851	107,584	100,000	95,083	90,030
Net Property	312,567	291,778	263,650	242,071	230,722	220,610	210,428
Total Assets	372,427	359,380	323,223	296,536	280,497	262,530	256,851
Long-Term Obligations	90,000	90,000	75,000	75,000	76,500	62,500	64,000
Net Stockholders' Equity	143,894	143,149	133,553	120,028	108,854	104,098	103,130
Year-end Shs. Outstg.	3,045	3,168	3,170	3,170	3,251	3,251	3,251
STATISTICAL RECORD:							
Operating Profit Margin %	16.9	17.8	17.5	17.2	15.7	13.8	15.7
Net Profit Margin %	13.6	15.1	13.8	18.1	11.8	10.0	12.4
Net Inc./Net Property %	5.1	5.5	5.8	7.7	5.0	4.5	5.6
Net Inc./Tot. Capital %	6.1	6.2	6.6	8.8	5.8	5.5	6.5
Return on Equity %	11.0	11.2	11.4	15.5	10.6	9.5	11.4
Accum. Depr./Gross Prop. %	30.0	30.5	30.9	31.4	30.9	30.8	30.7
Price Range	121-57¼	71½-48½	60½-46	48¼-32	37⅞-31¼	42½-31¾	41-34¾
P/E Ratio	23.3-11.0	14.2-9.6	12.6-9.6	8.4-5.6	10.7-8.8	13.9-10.4	11.3-9.5
Average Yield %	2.7	3.9	4.3	5.5	6.2	5.7	5.4

Statistics are as originally reported. [1] Incl. non-recurr. gain $3.1 mill., 12/99; $3.6 mill., 12/98; $9.4 mill., 12/97; $5.3 mill., 12/96; [2] Incl. merger. chrg. $1.6 mill.

OFFICERS:
J. W. Weinhardt, Chmn.
W. R. Roth, Pres., C.E.O.
A. Yip, C.F.O., Treas.
R. A. Loehr, Sec.

INVESTOR CONTACT: Angela Yip, Invest. Relations, (408) 279-7960

PRINCIPAL OFFICE: 374 West Santa Clara Street, San Jose, CA 95196

TELEPHONE NUMBER: (408) 279-7800
FAX: (408) 279-7934
WEB: www.sjwater.com

NO. OF EMPLOYEES: 285 (avg.)

SHAREHOLDERS: 993 (of record)

ANNUAL MEETING: In April

INCORPORATED: CA, Feb., 1985

INSTITUTIONAL HOLDINGS:
No. of Institutions: 33
Shares Held: 362,579
% Held: 11.9

INDUSTRY: Water supply (SIC: 4941)

TRANSFER AGENT(S): Boston Equiserve, Boston, MA

NYSE SYMBOL SLM
Rec. Pr. 33 11/16 (5/31/00)

SLM HOLDING CORPORATION

YIELD 1.9%
P/E RATIO 11.0

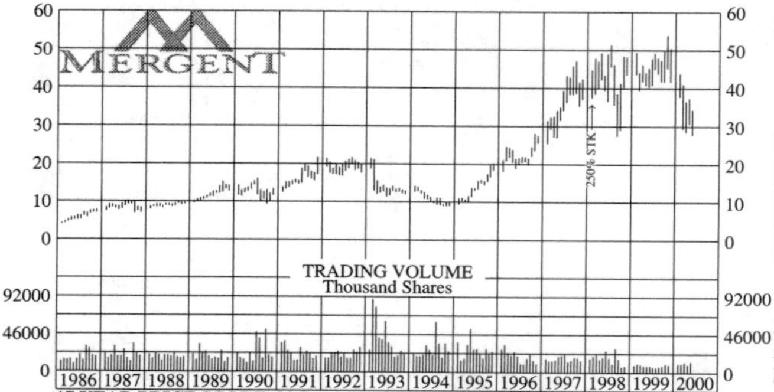

*7 YEAR PRICE SCORE 99.7 *12 MONTH PRICE SCORE 78.3

*NYSE COMPOSITE INDEX=100

INTERIM EARNINGS (Per Share):

Qtr.	Mar.	June	Sept.	Dec.
1995	0.33	0.34	0.35	0.48
1996	0.50	0.51	0.51	0.57
1997	0.62	0.63	0.79	0.75
1998	0.80	0.84	0.64	0.66
1999	0.69	0.76	0.75	0.87

INTERIM DIVIDENDS (Per Share):

Amt.	Decl.	Ex.	Rec.	Pay.
0.15Q	2/04/99	2/24/99	2/26/99	3/12/99
0.15Q	5/21/99	6/02/99	6/04/99	6/18/99
0.15Q	7/22/99	9/01/99	9/03/99	9/17/99
0.16Q	11/18/99	12/01/99	12/03/99	12/17/99
0.16Q	1/28/00	3/01/00	3/03/00	3/17/00

Indicated div.: $0.64

CAPITALIZATION (12/31/99):

	($000)	(%)
Long-Term Debt	4,496,267	81.0
Minority Interest	213,883	3.9
Preferred Stock	165,000	3.0
Common & Surplus	675,914	12.2
Total	5,551,064	100.0

DIVIDEND ACHIEVER STATUS:
Rank: 34 10-Year Growth Rate: 17.95%
Total Years of Dividend Growth: 19

RECENT DEVELOPMENTS: For the year ended 12/31/99, net income declined slightly to $500.8 million compared with $501.5 million in the previous year. Results for the current year included a gain on the sale of student loans of $27.2 million. Total interest income was $2.81 billion, an increase of 9.0% from $2.58 billion the year before. Total other income amounted to $450.8 million compared with $496.3 million in the prior year, a decrease of 9.2%.

PROSPECTS: Going forward, the Company should continue to benefit from the introduction of the Laureate loan delivery system. Laureate is currently being used by 80 colleges and universities on more than 100 campuses. In addition, the Company has retained servicing rights and signed long-term servicing agreements with four companies for new loan originations, which should boost long-term results.

BUSINESS

SLM HOLDING CORPORATION (formerly The Student Loan Marketing Association) is a state-chartered stockholder-owned corporation, which was created to provide liquidity, primarily through instituting a secondary market and warehousing facilities for insured student loans made under state-sponsored student loan programs. These programs include the Guaranteed Student Loan Program, which encompasses Stafford loans, ''PLUS'' loans and Supplemental Loans for Students loans, as well as the Health Education Assistance Loan Program. SLM provides financial services to financial institutions, educational institutions, state agencies, and students. The services include loan purchases, funding and operational support.

ANNUAL FINANCIAL DATA

	12/31/99	12/31/98	12/31/97	12/31/96	12/31/95	12/31/94	12/31/93
Earnings Per Share	**[3] 3.06**	**2.95**	**[2] 2.80**	**[2] 2.13**	**[1] [2] 2.14**	**[2] 2.01**	**[2] 2.56**
Tang. Book Val. Per Share	**4.29**	**3.98**	**3.67**	**3.63**	**6.01**	**4.06**	**5.07**
Dividends Per Share	**0.61**	**0.57**	**0.52**	**0.47**	**0.43**	**0.41**	**0.36**
Dividend Payout %	**19.9**	**19.3**	**18.5**	**22.0**	**20.2**	**20.2**	**13.9**
INCOME STATEMENT (IN MILLIONS):							
Total Interest Income	2,808.6	2,576.3	3,283.8	3,449.3	3,693.7	2,851.6	2,417.5
Total Interest Expense	2,114.8	1,925.0	2,526.2	2,582.9	3,020.6	2,142.5	1,480.7
Net Interest Income	693.8	662.7	757.7	866.4	673.0	709.1	936.8
Provision for Loan Losses	34.4	28.6	...	...	...	...	...
Non-Interest Income	450.8	477.0	500.9	146.9	...	...	...
Non-Interest Expense	358.6	360.9	493.8	405.7	160.6	130.4	109.4
Income Before Taxes	751.7	750.1	764.8	607.7	512.5	578.6	827.4
Equity Earnings/Minority Int.	d10.7	d10.7	d10.7	d10.7	...	...	...
Net Income	[3] 500.8	501.5	[2] 511.2	[2] 413.5	[1] [2] 371.2	[2] 412.1	[2] 567.4
Average Shs. Outstg. (000)	163,158	170,066	182,941	194,466	...	...	...
BALANCE SHEET (IN MILLIONS):							
Total Loans & Leases	35,879.3	31,005.6	32,764.3	38,016.3	39,513.5	39,351.2	35,543.7
Net Loans & Leases	35,879.3	31,005.6	32,764.3	38,016.3	39,513.5	39,351.2	35,543.7
Total Assets	44,024.8	37,210.0	39,908.8	47,629.9	50,001.7	53,361.3	46,855.5
Long-Term Obligations	4,496.3	8,810.6	14,541.3	22,606.2	30,082.6	34,319.4	30,925.4
Total Liabilities	43,183.9	36,556.4	39,234.2	46,795.9	48,920.5	51,489.6	45,228.6
Net Stockholders' Equity	840.9	653.6	674.6	833.9	1,081.2	1,471.2	1,280.1
Year-end Shs. Outstg. (000)	157,577	164,127	183,633	229,934	144,265	309,610	210,128
STATISTICAL RECORD:							
Return on Equity %	59.6	76.7	75.8	49.6	34.3	28.0	44.3
Return on Assets %	1.1	1.3	1.3	0.9	0.7	0.8	1.2
Equity/Assets %	1.9	1.8	1.7	1.8	2.2	2.8	2.7
Non-Int. Exp./Tot. Inc. %	31.3	32.0	39.2	40.0	23.9	18.4	11.7
Price Range	53 15/16-39 1/2	51 3/8-27 1/2	47 3/16-25 7/16	28 1/16-18 1/16	20 1/4-9 3/8	14 1/4-8 15/16	21 1/2-11 3/8
P/E Ratio	17.6-12.9	17.4-9.3	16.8-9.1	13.2-8.5	9.5-4.4	7.1-4.4	8.4-4.4
Average Yield %	1.3	1.4	1.4	2.0	2.9	3.5	2.2

Statistics are as originally reported. Adj. for stk. split: 7-for-2, 1/98 [1] Bef. acctg. change chrg. $130.1 mill. [2] Bef. charges on debt extinguished, $3.3 mill., 1997; $4.8 mill., 1996; $4.9 mill., 1995; $9.3 mill., 1994; $137.4 mill., 1993. [3] Incl. gain on the sale of student loans $27.2 mill.

OFFICERS:
E. A. Fox, Chmn.
A. L. Lord, Vice-Chmn., C.E.O.
M. G. Overend, C.F.O.

INVESTOR CONTACT: Jeffrey R. Heinz, Asst. V.P., Inv. Rel. (703) 810-7743

PRINCIPAL OFFICE: 11600 Sallie Mae Drive, Reston, VA 11600

TELEPHONE NUMBER: (703) 810-3000
FAX: (703) 810-5074
WEB: www.salliemae.com

NO. OF EMPLOYEES: 3,753 (avg.)

SHAREHOLDERS: 680 (approx.)

ANNUAL MEETING: In May

INCORPORATED: DE, Feb., 1997

INSTITUTIONAL HOLDINGS:
No. of Institutions: 277
Shares Held: 141,103,261
% Held: 88.7

INDUSTRY: Personal credit institutions (SIC: 6141)

TRANSFER AGENT(S): ChaseMellon Shareholder Services, L.L.C., Ridgefield Park, NJ

NYSE SYMBOL SON
Rec. Pr. $22\frac{1}{16}$ (5/31/00)

SONOCO PRODUCTS COMPANY

YIELD	3.6%
P/E RATIO	12.1

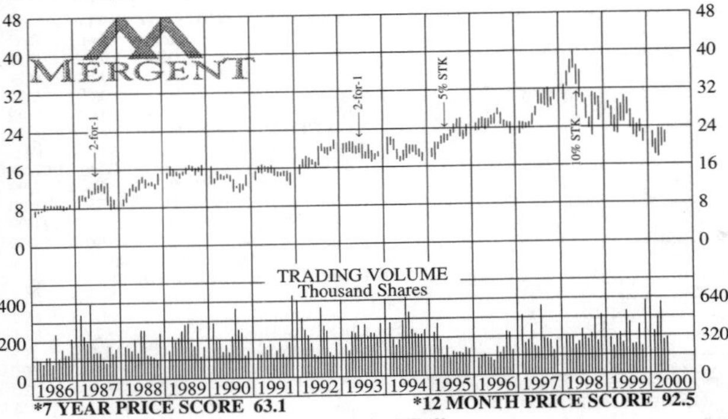

***7 YEAR PRICE SCORE 63.1** ***12 MONTH PRICE SCORE 92.5**

*NYSE COMPOSITE INDEX=100

INTERIM EARNINGS (Per Share):

Qtr.	Mar.	June	Sept.	Dec.
1996	0.41	0.45	0.38	0.40
1997	0.39	0.43	0.39	d1.20
1998	0.48	0.70	0.39	0.31
1999	0.43	0.46	0.44	0.50

INTERIM DIVIDENDS (Per Share):

Amt.	Decl.	Ex.	Rec.	Pay.
0.19Q	7/21/99	8/18/99	8/20/99	9/10/99
0.19Q	10/11/99	11/17/99	11/19/99	12/10/99
0.19Q	2/02/00	2/16/00	2/18/00	3/10/00
0.20Q	4/19/00	5/17/00	5/19/00	6/09/00

Indicated div.: $0.80 (Div. Reinv. Plan)

CAPITALIZATION (12/31/99):

	($000)	(%)
Long-Term Debt	819,540	47.6
Common & Surplus	901,220	52.4
Total	1,720,760	100.0

DIVIDEND ACHIEVER STATUS:
Rank: 202 10-Year Growth Rate: 7.90%
Total Years of Dividend Growth: 16

RECENT DEVELOPMENTS: For the year ended 12/31/99, net income declined 2.2% to $187.8 million compared with income of $192.0 million, before an extraordinary loss of $11.8 million, in 1998. Sales were $2.55 billion, down slightly from $2.56 billion a year earlier. Results included a gain on assets held for sale of $3.5 million in 1999 and $100.4 million in 1998.

PROSPECTS: SON raised prices on uncoated recycled paperboard by $30.00 per ton effective 4/3/00. SON initiated this increase as a partial pass-through of increasing costs in energy, freight, chemicals, repair parts and other vital supplies. Separately, the Company is experiencing healthy volume continuing in most of its businesses in January 2000 to date, coupled with ongoing productivity realization and pricing gains not yet fully realized.

BUSINESS

SONOCO PRODUCTS COMPANY is a major multinational manufacturer of industrial and consumer packaging products. The Company is also vertically integrated into paperboard production and recovered-paper collection. The paperboard utilized in SON's packaging products is produced substantially from recovered paper. SON operates 275 facilities in 32 countries and has subsidiaries in Europe, Canada, Mexico, South America, Australia and Asia, and affiliates in Canada, Japan and France. The consumer packaging segment (75% of 1999 sales) includes food and beverage processors and the personal and health care industries. The industrial packaging segment (25%) includes paper, textile and automotive manufacturers and chemical and pharmaceutical producers.

ANNUAL FINANCIAL DATA

	12/31/99	12/31/98	12/31/97	12/31/96	12/31/95	12/31/94	12/31/93
Earnings Per Share	**③ 1.83**	**② 1.84**	**① Nil**	**1.64**	**1.56**	**1.22**	**1.17**
Cash Flow Per Share	**3.25**	**3.24**	**1.43**	**3.08**	**2.82**	**2.34**	**2.12**
Tang. Book Val. Per Share	**6.37**	**6.40**	**6.69**	**3.49**	**3.34**	**3.00**	**2.73**
Dividends Per Share	**0.75**	**0.70**	**0.64**	**0.59**	**0.53**	**0.48**	**0.46**
Dividend Payout %	**41.0**	**38.2**	**...**	**35.8**	**33.9**	**39.4**	**39.3**
INCOME STATEMENT (IN MILLIONS):							
Total Revenues	2,546.7	2,557.9	2,847.8	2,788.1	2,706.2	2,300.1	1,947.2
Costs & Expenses	2,067.7	2,124.1	2,352.0	2,315.8	2,270.4	1,942.9	1,639.2
Depreciation & Amort.	145.8	145.7	153.5	142.9	125.8	112.8	95.7
Operating Income	333.2	288.1	342.3	329.4	309.9	244.4	212.2
Net Interest Inc./(Exp.)	d47.2	d48.9	d52.2	d49.3	d39.1	d33.5	d25.1
Income Before Income Taxes	289.6	339.6	63.7	280.1	270.8	210.9	192.9
Income Taxes	108.6	154.0	60.1	107.4	106.6	82.5	75.2
Equity Earnings/Minority Int.	6.8	6.4	d1.0	d1.8	0.4	1.4	1.1
Net Income	③ 187.8	② 192.0	① 2.6	170.9	164.5	129.8	118.8
Cash Flow	333.7	337.7	153.1	306.6	282.6	234.9	213.3
Average Shs. Outstg. (000)	102,780	104,275	107,350	99,564	100,253	100,590	100,850
BALANCE SHEET (IN MILLIONS):							
Cash & Cash Equivalents	36.5	57.2	53.6	71.3	61.6	28.4	25.9
Total Current Assets	723.1	661.4	873.0	737.6	661.8	570.7	513.1
Net Property	1,032.5	1,013.8	939.5	995.4	865.6	763.1	737.2
Total Assets	2,297.0	2,083.0	2,176.9	2,387.5	2,115.4	1,835.1	1,707.1
Total Current Liabilities	416.6	436.1	434.1	475.1	432.5	348.6	303.2
Long-Term Obligations	819.5	686.8	696.7	791.0	591.9	488.0	455.3
Net Stockholders' Equity	901.2	821.6	848.8	920.6	918.7	832.2	788.4
Net Working Capital	306.4	225.3	438.9	262.5	229.3	222.1	209.9
Year-end Shs. Outstg. (000)	101,448	101,683	105,417	98,850	100,229	100,378	101,001
STATISTICAL RECORD:							
Operating Profit Margin %	13.1	11.3	12.0	11.8	11.5	10.6	10.9
Net Profit Margin %	7.4	7.5	0.1	6.1	6.1	5.6	6.1
Return on Equity %	20.8	23.4	0.3	18.6	17.9	15.6	15.1
Return on Assets %	8.2	9.2	0.1	7.2	7.8	7.1	7.0
Debt/Total Assets %	35.7	33.0	32.0	33.1	28.0	26.6	26.7
Price Range	$30\frac{1}{2}$-$20\frac{11}{16}$	40-$22\frac{1}{8}$	$32\frac{1}{4}$-$22\frac{5}{8}$	$28\frac{1}{16}$-$22\frac{5}{8}$	$26\frac{1}{8}$-$17\frac{3}{8}$	$22\frac{5}{16}$-$17\frac{1}{8}$	$21\frac{9}{16}$-$17\frac{1}{8}$
P/E Ratio	16.7-11.3	21.7-12.0	...	17.1-13.8	16.7-11.1	18.3-14.0	18.4-14.6
Average Yield %	2.9	2.3	2.3	2.3	2.4	2.4	2.4

Statistics are as originally reported. Adj. for stk. splits: 2-for-1, 6/93; 5% div., 6/95; 10%, 6/98. ① Incl. non-recurr. after-tax chrg. $174.5 mill. for asset write-down. ② Bef. exraord. loss of $11.8 mill. and net gain on sale of divested assets of $85.4 mill. ③ Incl. gain on assets held for sale of $3.5 mill.

OFFICERS:
C. W. Coker, Chmn.
P. C. Browning, Pres., C.E.O.
F. T. Hill Jr., V.P., C.F.O.

INVESTOR CONTACT: Allan C. Cecil, V.P. Investor Relations & Corp. Affairs, (843) 383-7524

PRINCIPAL OFFICE: North Second Street, Hartsville, SC 29551-0160

TELEPHONE NUMBER: (843) 383-7000
FAX: (843) 383-7008
WEB: www.sonoco.com

NO. OF EMPLOYEES: 17,500 (approx.)

SHAREHOLDERS: 39,000 (approx.)

ANNUAL MEETING: In Apr.

INCORPORATED: SC, May, 1899

INSTITUTIONAL HOLDINGS:
No. of Institutions: 169
Shares Held: 41,580,551
% Held: 40.8

INDUSTRY: Paperboard mills (SIC: 2631)

TRANSFER AGENT(S): EquiServe, Boston, MA

NASDAQ SYMBOL SOTR
Rec. Pr. 27 1/16 (5/31/00)

SOUTHTRUST CORPORATION

YIELD 3.7%
P/E RATIO 10.3

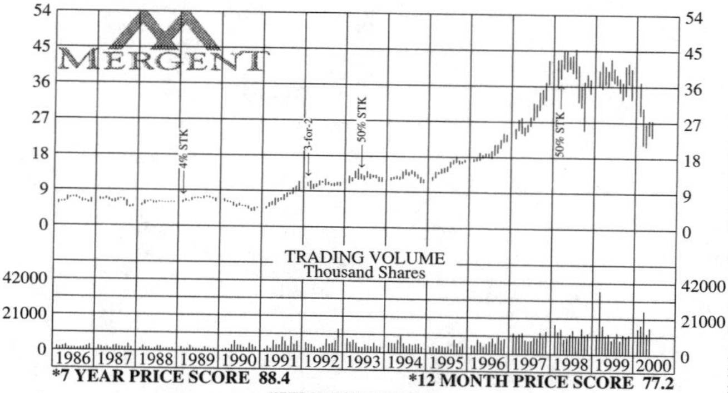

***7 YEAR PRICE SCORE 88.4** ***12 MONTH PRICE SCORE 77.2**

*NYSE COMPOSITE INDEX=100

INTERIM EARNINGS (Per Share):

Qtr.	Mar.	June	Sept.	Dec.
1996	0.43	0.44	0.45	0.47
1997	0.48	0.50	0.52	0.53
1998	0.54	0.55	0.57	0.59
1999	0.62	0.65	0.67	0.69

INTERIM DIVIDENDS (Per Share):

Amt.	Decl.	Ex.	Rec.	Pay.
0.22Q	4/21/99	5/26/99	5/28/99	7/01/99
0.22Q	7/15/99	8/25/99	8/27/99	10/01/99
0.22Q	10/20/99	11/23/99	11/26/99	1/01/00
0.25Q	1/19/00	2/23/00	2/25/00	4/03/00
0.25Q	4/19/00	5/24/00	5/26/00	7/03/00

Indicated div.: $1.00

CAPITALIZATION (12/31/99):

	($000)	(%)
Total Deposits	27,739,345	78.5
Long-Term Debt	4,655,807	13.2
Common & Surplus	2,927,429	8.3
Total	35,322,581	100.0

DIVIDEND ACHIEVER STATUS:
Rank: 116 10-Year Growth Rate: 11.91%
Total Years of Dividend Growth: 29

RECENT DEVELOPMENTS: For the year ended 12/31/99, net income advanced 20.2% to $443.2 million compared with $368.6 million in the prior year. Total interest income grew 13.6% to $2.91 billion from $2.56 billion the year before. Interest income benefited from fees generated from loans and securities, partially offset by a decline in income from short-term investments. Total interest expenses increased 11.1% to $1.54 billion. Total non-interest income, which increased 15.0% to $443.6 million, was driven by growth in service charges on deposit accounts, investment fees and bank owned life insurance. Total non-interest expense grew 10.5% to 1.01 billion. Provision for loan losses amounted to $141.2 million compared with $94.8 million in 1998. Return on average assets totaled 1.10% compared with 1.08%, while return on average equity improved to 15.75% versus 14.47% the year before.

BUSINESS

SOUTHTRUST CORPORATION, a multibank holding company with headquarters in Birmingham, Alabama, which owns and operates banks with 623 offices in Alabama, Florida, Georgia, Mississippi, North Carolina, South Carolina, Tennessee and Texas. Consolidated total assets as of 3/31/00 amounted to $43.87 billion. The Company has four reportable business segments: Commercial Banking, Regional Banking, Funds Management, and Other. The Commercial Banking segment derives its revenues from commercial, industrial and commercial real estate customers. This business segment also provides cash management, international and commercial leasing services. The Regional Banking segment generates revenues from retail lending, depository services, and regional commercial lending not underwritten by the Commercial Banking division. The Funds Management segment is responsible for the Company's asset and liability management. Other services segment include business segments such as non-bank subsidiaries and the Company's trust asset management division. These areas provide services such as mortgage banking, insurance, brokerage services, investment services.

ANNUAL FINANCIAL DATA

	12/31/99	12/31/98	12/31/97	12/31/96	12/31/95	12/31/94	12/31/93
Earnings Per Share	**2.63**	**2.25**	**2.03**	**1.79**	**1.58**	**1.43**	**1.29**
Tang. Book Val. Per Share	**17.44**	**16.38**	**14.28**	**12.03**	**10.85**	**9.29**	**8.83**
Dividends Per Share	**0.85**	**0.74**	**0.65**	**0.57**	**0.51**	**0.44**	**0.38**
Dividend Payout %	**32.3**	**32.7**	**31.9**	**32.0**	**32.5**	**30.7**	**29.7**
INCOME STATEMENT (IN MILLIONS):							
Total Interest Income	2,906.4	2,557.5	2,232.3	1,804.2	1,484.6	1,108.6	927.6
Total Interest Expense	1,539.5	1,386.3	1,186.1	938.2	791.4	501.1	397.7
Net Interest Income	1,366.9	1,171.2	1,046.2	866.0	693.2	607.5	529.8
Provision for Loan Losses	141.2	94.8	90.6	90.0	61.3	45.0	45.0
Non-Interest Income	443.6	386.1	270.5	254.8	208.7	184.8	174.7
Non-Interest Expense	1,010.5	914.4	748.2	643.3	536.5	486.0	435.0
Income Before Taxes	658.7	547.8	477.9	387.5	304.0	261.3	224.5
Net Income	443.2	368.9	306.7	254.7	199.0	173.0	150.5
Average Shs. Outstg. (000)	168,778	164,148	151,008	142,154	125,838	120,942	116,658
BALANCE SHEET (IN MILLIONS):							
Cash & Due from Banks	875.0	970.8	877.9	903.1	773.7	650.4	607.8
Securities Avail. for Sale	5,130.5	3,875.9	2,975.8	2,859.0	2,614.8	2,280.8	2,454.8
Total Loans & Leases	31,972.8	27,526.6	22,633.9	19,466.7	14,757.1	12,215.6	9,527.0
Allowance for Credit Losses	717.3	586.6	474.5	405.4	308.6	265.4	213.9
Net Loans & Leases	31,255.5	26,940.0	22,159.3	19,061.3	14,448.5	11,950.2	9,313.1
Total Assets	43,262.5	38,123.7	30,906.4	26,223.2	20,787.0	17,632.1	14,708.0
Total Deposits	27,739.3	24,839.9	19,586.6	17,305.5	14,575.1	12,801.2	11,515.3
Long-Term Obligations	4,655.8	3,935.3	3,888.8	2,727.4	1,187.3	640.7	470.0
Total Liabilities	40,335.1	35,395.5	28,711.8	24,488.3	19,356.2	16,496.8	13,656.2
Net Stockholders' Equity	2,927.4	2,738.3	2,194.6	1,734.9	1,430.9	1,135.3	1,051.8
Year-end Shs. Outstg. (000)	167,905	167,211	153,664	144,179	131,856	122,139	119,102
STATISTICAL RECORD:							
Return on Equity %	15.1	13.5	14.0	14.7	13.9	15.2	14.3
Return on Assets %	1.0	1.0	1.0	1.0	1.0	1.0	1.0
Equity/Assets %	6.8	7.2	7.1	6.6	6.9	6.4	7.2
Non-Int. Exp./Tot. Inc. %	55.8	58.7	56.8	57.4	59.5	61.3	61.7
Price Range	42 7/8-32 3/4	45 3/8-24 7/8	42 1/2-22 3/4	24 1/16-16 13/16	18 3/16-12	14 3/4-11 5/16	14 3/4-11 1/16
P/E Ratio	16.3-12.5	20.2-11.1	20.9-11.2	13.4-9.4	11.5-7.6	10.3-7.9	11.4-8.5
Average Yield %	2.2	2.1	2.0	2.8	3.4	3.4	3.0

Statistics are as originally reported. Adj. for stk. splits: 3-for-2, 2/26/98; 3-for-2, 5/20/93

OFFICERS:
W. D. Malone Jr., Chmn., Pres., C.E.O.
A. E. Yother, Sec., Treas., Contr.

INVESTOR CONTACT: C.H. Crouch, Jr., Sr. V.P., Inv. Rel., (205) 254-6868

PRINCIPAL OFFICE: 420 N. 20th St., Birmingham, AL 35203

TELEPHONE NUMBER: (205) 254-5000
FAX: (205) 254-5405
WEB: www.southtrust.com

NO. OF EMPLOYEES: 12,500

SHAREHOLDERS: 15,491 (approx.)

ANNUAL MEETING: In April

INCORPORATED: DE, 1968

INSTITUTIONAL HOLDINGS:
No. of Institutions: 259
Shares Held: 79,639,712
% Held: 47.5

INDUSTRY: National commercial banks (SIC: 6021)

TRANSFER AGENT(S): ChaseMellon Shareholder Services, L.L.C., Ridgefield Park, NJ

SOVEREIGN BANCORP, INC.

	YIELD	1.5%
	P/E RATIO	5.8

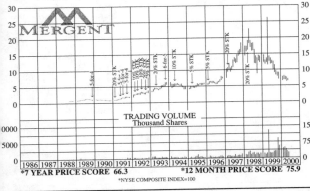

TRADING VOLUME
Thousand Shares

| 1986|1987|1988|1989|1990|1991|1992|1993|1994|1995|1996|1997|1998|1999|2000 |

*7 YEAR PRICE SCORE 66.3   ***12 MONTH PRICE SCORE 75.9**

*NYSE COMPOSITE INDEX=100

INTERIM EARNINGS (Per Share):

Qtr.	Mar.	June	Sept.	Dec.
1995	0.17	0.17	0.17	0.19
1996	0.18	0.20	Nil	0.22
1997	0.13	0.24	0.02	0.24
1998	0.09	0.27	0.22	0.27
1999	0.28	0.30	0.31	0.29

INTERIM DIVIDENDS (Per Share):

Amt.	Decl.	Ex.	Rec.	Pay.
0.025Q	3/18/99	4/28/99	4/30/99	5/17/99
0.025Q	6/18/99	7/28/99	7/30/99	8/16/99
0.025Q	9/17/99	10/27/99	10/29/99	11/16/99
0.025Q	12/17/99	1/27/00	1/31/00	2/15/00
0.025Q	3/24/00	4/25/00	4/27/00	5/15/00

Indicated div.: $0.10 (Div. Reinv. Plan)

CAPITALIZATION (12/31/99):

	($000)	(%)
Total Deposits	11,719,646	60.7
Long-Term Debt	5,760,724	29.8
Common & Surplus	1,821,495	9.4
Total	19,301,865	100.0

DIVIDEND ACHIEVER STATUS:

Rank: 6   10-Year Growth Rate: 26.16%
Total Years of Dividend Growth: 11

RECENT DEVELOPMENTS: For the year ended 12/31/99, net income advanced 31.4% to $179.3 million from $136.5 million in the previous year. Earnings for 1998 included merger-related charges of $49.9 million. Net interest income grew 24.5% to $614.7 million from $493.6 million in the prior year. This increase was attributed to commercial and consumer loan growth, recent acquisitions, an increase in average balances in investment securities available for sale and growth in core deposits. Total other income rose 23.9% to $130.3 million, reflecting growth in fees, partially offset by a decrease in sales from loans and securities. Total operating expenses increased 20.1% to $392.9 million versus $327.3 million a year earlier. On 9/3/99, the Company signed a definitive purchase and assumption agreement to acquire Sovereign Bank New England from FleetBoston.

BUSINESS

SOVEREIGN BANCORP, INCORPORATED is the holding company for Sovereign Bank, and is headquartered in Philadelphia, PA. Sovereign Bank is headquartered in Wyomissing, PA. At 12/31/99, the Company's consolidated assets, deposits, and stockholders' equity totaled $26.61 billion, $11.72 billion, and $1.82 billion, respectively. The Company's primary business consists of attracting deposits and originating commercial, consumer and residential mortgage loans from its network of community banking offices located in eastern and northcentral Pennsylvania, New Jersey and northern Delaware. The Company also has customers in New York and several New England States. On 9/3/99, the Company entered into a purchase and assumption agreement with FleetBoston Financial to acquire branch banking offices located in Connecticut, Massachusetts, New Hampshire and Rhode Island. The transaction includes about $12.00 billion in deposits, $8.00 billion in loans and approximately 279 retail banking offices and is anticipated to be completed in the second quarter of 2000.

ANNUAL FINANCIAL DATA

	12/31/99	12/31/98	12/31/97	12/31/96	12/31/95	12/31/94	12/31/93
Earnings Per Share	1.01	0.85	0.63	0.60	0.69	0.63	0.45
Tang. Book Val. Per Share	6.03	4.87	5.05	3.50	3.17	3.65	2.86
Dividends Per Share	0.10	0.08	0.067	0.0583	0.0581	0.0576	0.056
Dividend Payout %	9.9	9.4	10.6	9.7	8.4	9.1	12.4
INCOME STATEMENT (IN MILLIONS):							
Total Interest Income	1,607.3	1,355.4	960.7	616.3	493.0	354.1	256.7
Total Interest Expense	992.7	861.8	619.9	399.5	318.8	198.7	141.3
Net Interest Income	614.7	493.6	340.8	216.7	174.2	155.4	115.4
Provision for Loan Losses	30.0	28.0	37.2	2.5	1.0	4.1	8.1
Non-Interest Income	130.3	105.6	38.5	26.7	25.8	14.6	14.5
Non-Interest Expense	430.9	298.0	175.1	157.8	112.5	90.9	63.2
Income Before Taxes	268.6	211.2	130.0	83.0	85.9	74.9	51.1
Net Income	179.3	136.5	77.6	51.5	51.5	46.4	37.5
Average Shs. Outstg. (000)	178,167	161,211	122,947	86,160	81,504	74,016	...
BALANCE SHEET (IN MILLIONS):							
Cash & Due from Banks	374.0	471.1	189.1	99.7	130.8	110.3	73.2
Securities Avail. for Sale	8,030.2	6,662.4	1,029.5	484.3	889.5	87.1	1,322.3
Total Loans & Leases	14,226.5	11,285.8	9,923.5	6,156.3	4,674.4	4,350.9	2,726.0
Allowance for Credit Losses	133.0	133.8	90.9	33.8	34.9	36.3	31.7
Net Loans & Leases	14,093.6	11,152.0	9,832.6	6,122.5	4,639.5	4,314.6	2,694.3
Total Assets	26,607.1	21,913.9	14,336.3	9,433.2	8,078.3	6,564.1	4,495.4
Total Deposits	11,719.6	12,322.7	7,889.9	5,052.4	5,039.1	4,027.1	2,842.3
Long-Term Obligations	5,760.7	3,978.9	857.8	1,091.7	1,017.9	439.9	736.5
Total Liabilities	24,785.6	20,708.8	13,558.0	8,957.3	7,651.3	6,260.2	4,274.9
Net Stockholders' Equity	1,821.5	1,204.1	778.2	475.8	427.0	303.9	220.5
Year-end Shs. Outstg. (000)	230,274	159,727	112,133	76,450	65,470	65,616	66,483
STATISTICAL RECORD:							
Return on Equity %	9.8	11.3	10.0	10.8	13.2	15.3	17.0
Return on Assets %	0.7	0.6	0.5	0.5	0.7	0.7	0.8
Equity/Assets %	6.8	5.5	5.4	5.0	5.3	4.6	4.9
Non-Int. Exp./Tot. Inc. %	57.8	49.7	46.1	64.8	56.2	53.5	48.7
Price Range	26¼-7	22¾-8¾	18⁷/₁₆-7⁷/₁₆	8-5⁵/₁₆	5-4¹/₁₆	6⅜-4¹/₁₆	6⅜-3⅜
P/E Ratio	26.0-6.9	26.8-10.3	29.3-11.8	13.4-8.8	8.6-5.9	10.2-6.5	14.2-7.5
Average Yield %	0.6	0.5	0.5	0.9	1.2	1.1	1.1

Statistics are as originally reported. Adj. for stk. splits: 6-for-5, 1/22/98; 6-for-5, 1/16/97; 5% div., 2/15/96; 5% div., 4/11/95; 10% div., 5/16/94; 6-for-5, 11/17/93; 20% div., 5/17/93; 5% div., 2/16/93.

OFFICERS:
R. E. Mohn, Chmn.
J. S. Sidhu, Pres. & C.E.O.
D. Marlo, C.F.O. & Treas.
L. M. Thompson Jr., Chief Administrative Officer & Sec.
INVESTOR CONTACT: Linda Hagginbothom, Investor Relations Officer, (800) 628-2673
PRINCIPAL OFFICE: 1130 Berkshire Blvd., Wyomissing, PA 19610

TELEPHONE NUMBER: (610) 320-8400
FAX: (610) 320-8448
WEB: www.sovereignbank.com
NO. OF EMPLOYEES: 3,923 full-time; 573 part-time
SHAREHOLDERS: 17,098
ANNUAL MEETING: In April
INCORPORATED: PA, Dec., 1987

INSTITUTIONAL HOLDINGS:
No. of Institutions: 200
Shares Held: 104,408,738
% Held: 46.6

INDUSTRY: Federal savings institutions (SIC: 6035)

TRANSFER AGENT(S): ChaseMellon Shareholder Services, Pittsburgh, PA

STANLEY WORKS

	YIELD	3.3%
	P/E RATIO	16.1

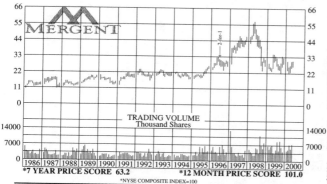

INTERIM EARNINGS (Per Share):

Qtr.	Mar.	June	Sept.	Dec.
1996	0.34	0.37	0.42	d0.03
1997	0.41	d0.72	d0.46	0.29
1998	0.40	0.47	0.37	0.29
1999	0.34	0.28	0.56	0.49

INTERIM DIVIDENDS (Per Share):

Amt.	Decl.	Ex.	Rec.	Pay.
0.215Q	5/19/99	6/03/99	6/07/99	6/28/99
0.22Q	7/13/99	9/02/99	9/07/99	9/28/99
0.22Q	...	11/23/99	11/26/99	12/27/99
0.22Q	1/27/00	3/02/00	3/06/00	3/24/00
0.22Q	5/30/00	6/01/00	6/05/00	6/30/00

Indicated div.: $0.88

CAPITALIZATION (1/1/00):

	($000)	(%)
Long-Term Debt	290,000	28.3
Common & Surplus	735,400	71.7
Total	1,025,400	100.0

DIVIDEND ACHIEVER STATUS:
Rank: 258   10-Year Growth Rate: 5.49%
Total Years of Dividend Growth: 32

TRADING VOLUME
Thousand Shares

*7 YEAR PRICE SCORE 63.2   *12 MONTH PRICE SCORE 101.0
*NYSE COMPOSITE INDEX=100

RECENT DEVELOPMENTS: For the year ended 1/1/00, net income advanced 8.9% to $150.0 million compared with $137.8 million in 1998. Net sales were $2.75 billion, up slightly from $2.73 billion a year earlier. Results for 1999 included a restructuring credit of $21.3 million. The Company experienced volume increases in excess of 5.0% from most of the products it sells through consumer channels.

PROSPECTS: On 3/29/00, SWK announced the signing of a strategic alliance agreement with TradeOut.com, a global Internet marketplace for business surplus assets, to provide Stanley customers with TradeOut.com's exchange capabilities. Under the terms of the agreement, SWK will bring certain of its excess inventories and other assets to TradeOut.com's pool of on-line buyers.

BUSINESS

STANLEY WORKS is a worldwide producer of tools and door products for professional, industrial and consumer use. The Tools segment manufactures and markets carpenters, mechanics, pneumatic and hydraulic tools as well as tool sets. SWK markets its carpenters tools under the Stanley®, IntelliTools™, Contractor Grade™, and Goldblatt® brands. The Doors segment manufactures and markets commercial and residential doors as well as closet doors and systems, home decor and door and consumer hardware. Products in the Doors segment include, residential insulated steel, reinforced fiberglass and wood entrance door systems. Door products are marketed under the Stanley®, Magic-Door®, Stanley-Acmetrack™, Monarch™ and Acme® brands. A substantial portion of SWK's products are sold through home centers and mass merchant distribution channels in the U.S.

ANNUAL FINANCIAL DATA

	1/1/00	1/2/99	1/3/98	12/28/96	12/30/95	12/31/94	1/1/94
Earnings Per Share	④ 1.67	③ 1.53	② d0.47	② 1.09	② 0.67	1.40	① 1.03
Cash Flow Per Share	2.62	2.41	0.34	1.93	1.58	2.31	1.93
Tang. Book Val. Per Share	6.19	5.32	5.67	7.68	6.79	6.52	5.70
Dividends Per Share	0.87	0.83	0.77	0.73	0.71	0.69	0.67
Dividend Payout %	52.1	54.2	...	67.0	106.8	49.3	65.0
INCOME STATEMENT (IN MILLIONS):							
Total Revenues	2,751.8	2,729.1	2,669.5	2,670.8	2,624.3	2,510.9	2,273.1
Costs & Expenses	2,410.0	2,397.8	2,577.2	2,377.1	2,385.7	2,162.6	1,984.6
Depreciation & Amort.	85.6	79.7	72.4	74.7	81.2	81.8	80.7
Operating Income	256.2	251.6	19.9	219.0	157.4	266.5	207.8
Net Interest Inc./(Exp.)	d27.9	d23.1	d16.6	d22.5	d30.3	d29.0	d25.2
Income Before Income Taxes	230.8	215.4	d18.6	174.2	112.8	201.8	148.0
Income Taxes	80.8	77.6	23.3	77.3	53.7	76.5	55.4
Net Income	④ 150.0	③ 137.8	② d41.9	② 96.9	② 59.1	125.3	① 92.6
Cash Flow	235.6	217.5	30.5	171.6	140.3	207.1	173.3
Average Shs. Outstg. (000)	89,887	90,193	89,469	88,824	88,720	89,550	89,870
BALANCE SHEET (IN MILLIONS):							
Cash & Cash Equivalents	88.0	110.1	152.2	84.0	75.4	69.3	43.7
Total Current Assets	1,091.0	1,086.4	1,005.3	910.9	915.1	888.5	758.6
Net Property	520.6	511.4	513.2	570.4	556.5	559.8	566.5
Total Assets	1,890.6	1,932.9	1,758.7	1,659.6	1,670.0	1,701.1	1,576.9
Total Current Liabilities	693.0	702.1	622.7	381.6	387.7	421.5	357.1
Long-Term Obligations	290.0	344.8	283.7	342.6	391.1	387.1	377.2
Net Stockholders' Equity	735.4	669.4	607.8	780.1	734.6	744.2	680.9
Net Working Capital	398.0	384.3	382.6	529.3	527.4	467.0	401.5
Year-end Shs. Outstg. (000)	88,945	88,772	88,788	88,720	88,758	88,898	89,392
STATISTICAL RECORD:							
Operating Profit Margin %	9.3	9.2	0.7	8.2	6.0	10.6	9.1
Net Profit Margin %	5.5	5.0	...	3.6	2.3	5.0	4.1
Return on Equity %	20.4	20.6	...	12.4	8.0	16.8	13.6
Return on Assets %	7.9	7.1	...	5.8	3.5	7.4	5.9
Debt/Total Assets %	15.3	17.8	16.1	20.6	23.4	22.8	23.9
Price Range	35-22	57¼-23½	47⅜-28	32¹³⁄₁₆-23⅝	26¹¹⁄₁₆-17¹³⁄₁₆	22⁷⁄₁₆-17⁷⁄₁₆	23¹³⁄₁₆-18¹⁵⁄₁₆
P/E Ratio	21.0-13.2	37.4-15.4	...	30.1-21.7	40.1-26.8	16.0-12.5	23.2-18.4
Average Yield %	3.1	2.1	2.0	2.6	3.2	3.5	3.1

Statistics are as originally reported. Adj. for stk. split: 2-for-1, 6/96. ① Incl. a gain of $29 mill. from sale of investment, Max, Co. Ltd.; a fine fee of $5.0 mill.; and a chrg. of $23 mill. for contingency reserves related to litigation & bef. acctg. change chrg. of $8.5 mill. ② Incl. pretax restruct chrgs. of $238.5 mill., 1997; $47.8 mill., 1996; & $85.8 mill., 1995. ③ Incl. restruct. chrg. of $27.8 mill. ④ Incl. restruct. credit of $21.3 mill.

OFFICERS:
J. M. Trani, Chmn., C.E.O.
J. M. Loree, V.P., C.F.O.
S. S. Weddle, V.P., Gen. Couns., Sec.

INVESTOR CONTACT: Gerad J. Gould, Dir., Investor Relations, (860) 827-3833

PRINCIPAL OFFICE: 1000 Stanley Dr., P. O. Box 7000, New Britain, CT 06053

TELEPHONE NUMBER: (860) 225-5111
FAX: (860) 827-3895
WEB: www.stanleyworks.com

NO. OF EMPLOYEES: 16,890

SHAREHOLDERS: 16,947

ANNUAL MEETING: In Apr.

INCORPORATED: CT, July, 1852

INSTITUTIONAL HOLDINGS:
No. of Institutions: 174
Shares Held: 51,381,810
% Held: 57.5

INDUSTRY: Hardware, nec (SIC: 3429)

TRANSFER AGENT(S): EquiServe, Boston, MA

NYSE SYMBOL STT
Rec. Pr. 111½ (5/31/00)

STATE STREET CORPORATION

YIELD 0.6%
P/E RATIO 28.2

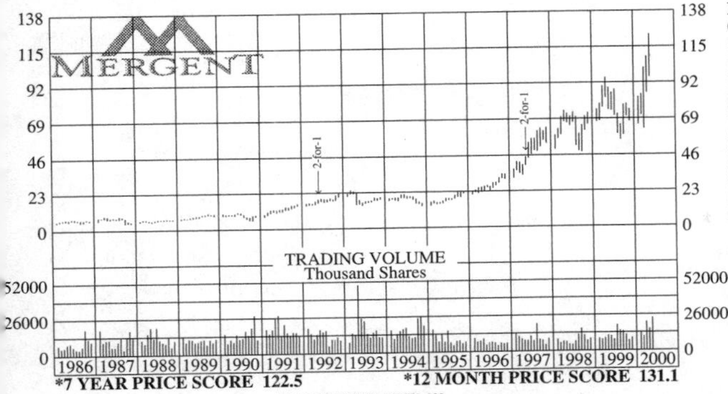

***7 YEAR PRICE SCORE 122.5** ***12 MONTH PRICE SCORE 131.1**

*NYSE COMPOSITE INDEX=100

INTERIM EARNINGS (Per Share):

Qtr.	Mar.	June	Sept.	Dec.
1996	0.42	0.44	0.45	0.48
1997	0.53	0.57	0.62	0.61
1998	0.64	0.66	0.68	0.68
1999	0.74	0.75	0.77	1.52

INTERIM DIVIDENDS (Per Share):

Amt.	Decl.	Ex.	Rec.	Pay.
0.14Q	3/18/99	3/30/99	4/01/99	4/15/99
0.15Q	6/17/99	6/29/99	7/01/99	7/15/99
0.15Q	9/16/99	9/29/99	10/01/99	10/15/99
0.16Q	12/16/99	12/30/99	1/03/00	1/18/00
0.16Q	3/16/00	3/30/00	4/03/00	4/17/00

Indicated div.: $0.64 (Div. Reinv. Plan)

CAPITALIZATION (12/31/99):

	($000)	(%)
Total Deposits	34,145,000	90.5
Long-Term Debt	921,000	2.4
Common & Surplus	2,652,000	7.0
Total	37,718,000	100.0

DIVIDEND ACHIEVER STATUS:
Rank: 64 10-Year Growth Rate: 14.87%
Total Years of Dividend Growth: 19

RECENT DEVELOPMENTS: For the year ended 12/31/99, net income advanced 42.0% to $619.0 million from $436.0 million in 1998. Earnings for 1999 included a pre-tax net gain of $282.0 million on the sale of STT's commercial banking business. Net interest revenue increased 4.8% to $781.0 million from $745.0 million the year before. Total fee revenue climbed 12.9% to $2.26 billion. Provision for loan losses was $14.0 million versus $17.0 million in 1998.

PROSPECTS: Going forward, the Company expects to generate strong revenue growth due to new business installed and high transaction volumes. STT will continue to focus on increasing revenues outside of the United States, particularly in Canada, Europe and Japan, as capital markets develop. On 5/4/00, the Company introduced FX Connect, an electronic foreign exchange trading system, to multiple counterparties, including Deutsche Bank.

BUSINESS

STATE STREET CORPORATION (formerly State Street Boston Corporation) is a $60.53 billion (3/31/00) bank holding company that conducts business worldwide principally through its subsidiary, State Street Bank and Trust Company. The Company has two lines of business: services for institutional investors and investment management. Services for Institutional Investors are primarily accounting, custody and other services for large pools of assets. Investment Management offers index and active equity strategies, short-term investment funds and fixed income products. On 10/1/99, the Company sold its commercial lending business.

LOAN DISTRIBUTION

(12/31/99)	($000)	(%)
Commercial & Fin-		
Domestic	1,908,000	44.4
Non-United States	843,000	19.7
Lease Financing-		
Domestic	418,000	9.7
Non-United States	1,124,000	26.2
Total	4,293,000	100.0

ANNUAL FINANCIAL DATA

	12/31/99	12/31/98	12/31/97	12/31/96	12/31/95	12/31/94	12/31/93
Earnings Per Share	**1 3.78**	**2.66**	**2.32**	**1.80**	**1.49**	**1.35**	**1.18**
Tang. Book Val. Per Share	**16.62**	**14.38**	**11.93**	**10.94**	**9.63**	**8.05**	**7.28**
Dividends Per Share	**0.58**	**0.50**	**0.42**	**0.37**	**0.33**	**0.29**	**0.25**
Dividend Payout %	**15.3**	**18.8**	**18.1**	**20.6**	**22.1**	**21.5**	**21.2**
INCOME STATEMENT (IN MILLIONS):							
Total Interest Income	2,437.0	2,237.0	1,755.0	1,443.0	1,336.6	904.7	698.9
Total Interest Expense	1,656.0	1,492.0	1,114.0	892.0	907.2	537.5	381.3
Net Interest Income	781.0	745.0	641.0	551.0	429.4	367.2	317.6
Provision for Loan Losses	14.0	17.0	16.0	8.0	8.0	11.6	11.3
Non-Interest Income	2,537.0	1,997.0	1,673.0	1,302.0	1,119.1	981.0	833.4
Non-Interest Expense	2,336.0	2,068.0	1,734.0	1,398.0	1,174.0	1,016.4	862.3
Income Before Taxes	968.0	657.0	564.0	447.0	366.5	320.3	277.5
Net Income	1 619.0	436.0	380.0	293.0	247.1	207.4	179.8
Average Shs. Outstg. (000)	163,751	163,927	163,789	163,266	166,116	153,702	152,386
BALANCE SHEET (IN MILLIONS):							
Cash & Due from Banks	2,930.0	1,365.0	2,411.0	1,623.0	1,421.9	1,004.9	1,469.4
Securities Avail. for Sale	15,489.0	10,072.0	10,580.0	9,642.0	6,039.2	3,754.2	1,376.5
Total Loans & Leases	4,293.0	6,309.0	5,562.0	4,713.0	3,986.1	3,233.2	2,680.2
Allowance for Credit Losses	48.0	84.0	83.0	73.0	63.5	58.2	54.3
Net Loans & Leases	4,245.0	6,225.0	5,479.0	4,640.0	3,922.7	3,175.0	2,625.9
Total Assets	60,896.0	47,082.0	37,975.0	31,524.0	25,785.2	21,729.5	18,720.1
Total Deposits	34,145.0	27,539.0	24,878.0	19,519.0	16,647.2	13,902.7	13,017.9
Long-Term Obligations	921.0	922.0	774.0	476.0	126.6	127.5	128.9
Total Liabilities	58,244.0	44,771.0	35,980.0	29,749.0	24,197.7	20,498.2	17,615.1
Net Stockholders' Equity	2,652.0	2,311.0	1,995.0	1,775.0	1,587.5	1,231.3	1,105.0
Year-end Shs. Outstg. (000)	159,590	160,695	167,223	162,308	164,776	152,950	151,748
STATISTICAL RECORD:							
Return on Equity %	23.3	18.9	19.0	16.5	15.6	16.8	16.3
Return on Assets %	1.0	0.9	1.0	0.9	1.0	1.0	1.0
Equity/Assets %	4.4	4.9	5.3	5.6	6.2	5.7	5.9
Non-Int. Exp./Tot. Inc. %	70.4	75.4	74.9	75.4	75.8	75.4	74.9
Price Range	95¼-55½	74 5/16-47⅞	63 11/16-31 5/16	34¼-20⅞	23⅛-14	21 9/16-13 13/16	24 9/16-14⅝
P/E Ratio	25.2-14.7	27.9-18.0	27.5-13.5	19.1-11.6	15.5-9.4	16.0-10.2	20.8-12.4
Average Yield %	0.8	0.8	0.9	1.3	1.8	1.6	1.3

Statistics are as originally reported. Adj. for 2-for-1 stock splits, 5/97. 1 Incl. pre-tax net gain on the sale of Co.'s commercial banking business of $282.0 mill.

OFFICERS:
M. N. Carter, Chmn.
J. R. Towers, Vice-Chmn., Chief Admin. Off.
N. A. Lopardo, Vice-Chmn.
D. A. Spina, Pres., C.E.O.

INVESTOR CONTACT: Karen A. Warren, Inv. Rel., (617) 664-2888

PRINCIPAL OFFICE: 225 Franklin Street, Boston, MA 02110

TELEPHONE NUMBER: (617) 786-3000
FAX: (617) 985-8055
WEB: www.statestreet.com

NO. OF EMPLOYEES: 16,769 full-time; 444 part-time

SHAREHOLDERS: 5,970

ANNUAL MEETING: In Apr.

INCORPORATED: MA, Oct., 1969

INSTITUTIONAL HOLDINGS:
No. of Institutions: 452
Shares Held: 107,542,704
% Held: 67.2

INDUSTRY: State commercial banks (SIC: 6022)

TRANSFER AGENT(S): State Street Bank and Trust Company, Boston, MA

STEPAN COMPANY

YIELD 3.0%
P/E RATIO 10.6

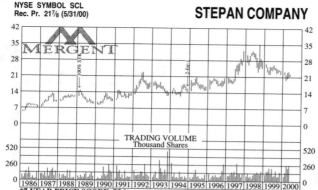

*7 YEAR PRICE SCORE 75.0   *12 MONTH PRICE SCORE 92.9
*NYSE COMPOSITE INDEX=100

INTERIM EARNINGS (Per Share):

Qtr.	March	June	Sept.	Dec.
1994	0.17	0.37	0.37	0.35
1995	0.55	0.49	d0.08	0.50
1996	0.57	0.46	0.38	0.50
1997	0.41	0.57	0.55	0.33
1998	0.52	0.64	0.45	0.51
1999	0.57	0.75	d0.02	0.76

INTERIM DIVIDENDS (Per Share):

Amt.	Decl.	Ex.	Rec.	Pay.
0.15Q	5/11/99	5/26/99	5/31/99	6/15/99
0.15Q	8/03/99	8/27/99	8/31/99	9/15/99
0.163Q	11/05/99	11/26/99	11/30/99	12/15/99
0.163Q	2/22/00	2/25/00	2/29/00	3/15/00
0.163Q	5/09/00	5/26/00	5/31/00	6/15/00

Indicated div.: $0.65

CAPITALIZATION (12/31/99):

	($000)	(%)
Long-Term Debt	107,420	35.3
Deferred Income Tax	41,975	13.8
Preferred Stock	19,575	6.4
Common & Surplus	135,489	44.5
Total	304,459	100.0

DIVIDEND ACHIEVER STATUS:

Rank: 186   10-Year Growth Rate: 8.74%
Total Years of Dividend Growth: 33

RECENT DEVELOPMENTS: For the year ended 12/31/99, net income decreased 5.6% to $22.1 million versus $23.5 million the previous year. Results for 1999 included an after-tax charge of $6.3 million related to a lawsuit settlement. Net sales were $666.8 million, up 9.2% from $610.5 million the year before. Sales from surfactants increased 10.6% to $525.0 million, reflecting increased sales volume due to rising demand for personal care and laundry and cleaning products. Polymers sales rose 4.3% to $121.4 million, benefiting from higher sales volume of polyurethane polyols. Specialty products sales grew 4.4% to $20.4 million due to higher selling prices. Going forward, SCL plans to grow earnings by at least 10.0% per year through the development of value-added products and efficient processes, acquisitions, strategic alliances, expansion of manufacturing locations, sales offices and laboratories.

BUSINESS

THE STEPAN COMPANY is a producer of specialty and intermediate chemicals that are sold to other manufacturers for use in a variety of end products. The Company operates in three business segments: surfactants, polymers, and specialty products. Surfactants are a principal ingredient in consumer and industrial cleaning products. Other applications include lubricating ingredients and emulsifiers for agricultural products and plastics and composites. The polymers product group includes phthalic anhydride (PA), polyurethane systems and polyurethane polyols. PA is used in construction materials and components of automotive, boating and other consumer products. Polyurethane systems provide thermal insulation and are sold to construction, industrial and appliance markets. Polyurethane polyols are used in manufacturing laminate board for the construction industry. Specialty products include flavors, emulsifiers and solubilizers used in the food and pharmaceutical industry.

BUSINESS LINE ANALYSIS

(12/31/1999)($000)	REV	INC
Surfactants	78.7	66.4
Polymers	18.2	27.9
Specialty Products	3.1	5.7
Total	100.0	100.0

ANNUAL FINANCIAL DATA

	12/31/99	12/31/98	12/31/97	12/31/96	12/31/95	12/31/94	12/31/93
Earnings Per Share	① 2.08	2.12	1.86	1.80	1.51	1.29	0.98
Cash Flow Per Share	5.79	5.51	5.08	5.12	4.66	4.31	3.89
Tang. Book Val. Per Share	14.28	13.24	12.16	11.38	10.25	9.18	8.56
Dividends Per Share	0.61	0.56	0.51	0.48	0.45	0.42	0.41
Dividend Payout %	29.4	26.5	27.6	26.5	29.6	32.9	41.3
INCOME STATEMENT (IN THOUSANDS):							
Total Revenues	666,784	610,451	581,949	536,635	528,218	443,948	438,825
Costs & Expenses	585,554	527,681	502,298	464,111	465,214	385,160	383,896
Depreciation & Amort.	39,452	37,347	35,281	32,138	30,384	28,935	27,679
Operating Income	41,778	45,423	44,370	40,386	32,620	29,853	27,250
Net Interest Inc./(Exp.)	d8,376	d7,453	d7,595	d7,243	d7,865	d7,136	d7,626
Income Before Income Taxes	34,829	38,766	34,874	32,261	24,991	22,512	19,624
Income Taxes	12,700	15,312	14,464	13,194	8,872	8,667	8,848
Net Income	① 22,129	23,454	20,410	19,067	16,119	13,845	10,776
Cash Flow	60,723	59,905	50,649	46,427	45,702	41,437	37,358
Average Shs. Outstg.	10,632	11,043	10,959	10,002	9,984	9,924	9,894
BALANCE SHEET (IN THOUSANDS):							
Cash & Cash Equivalents	3,969	983	5,507	4,778	3,148	2,452	1,515
Total Current Assets	166,660	149,758	146,482	153,698	150,154	129,371	119,160
Net Property	209,481	215,096	206,601	207,159	192,470	183,657	170,270
Total Assets	414,576	404,361	374,936	381,012	362,527	324,948	300,488
Total Current Liabilities	98,045	87,944	82,693	83,376	83,298	80,456	70,591
Long-Term Obligations	107,420	107,708	94,898	102,567	109,023	89,795	89,660
Net Stockholders' Equity	155,064	147,984	137,598	131,651	122,477	111,302	104,663
Net Working Capital	68,615	61,814	63,789	70,322	66,856	48,915	48,569
Year-end Shs. Outstg.	9,488	9,693	9,692	9,817	10,002	9,944	9,896
STATISTICAL RECORD:							
Operating Profit Margin %	6.3	7.4	7.6	7.5	6.2	6.7	6.2
Net Profit Margin %	3.3	3.8	3.5	3.6	3.1	3.1	2.5
Return on Equity %	14.3	15.8	14.8	14.5	13.2	12.4	10.3
Return on Assets %	5.3	5.8	5.4	5.0	4.4	4.3	3.6
Debt/Total Assets %	25.9	26.6	25.3	26.9	30.1	27.6	29.8
Price Range	26¹¹⁄₁₆-22³⁄₁₆	35⅛-23⅛	32⅜-18	20½-15¾	20⅞-14¾	17¹¹⁄₁₆-12⅜	18¹⁵⁄₁₆-12⁹⁄₁₆
P/E Ratio	12.8-10.7	16.6-10.9	17.4-9.7	11.4-8.7	13.8-9.8	13.7-9.6	19.3-12.8
Average Yield %	2.5	1.9	2.0	2.6	2.5	2.8	2.6

Statistics are as originally reported. Adj. for stk. splits: 2-for-1, 12/94 ① Incl. after-tax chrg. of $6.3 mill. related to a lawsuit settlement.

OFFICERS:
F. Q. Stepan, Chmn., C.E.O.
F. Q. Stepan Jr., Pres., C.O.O.
J. W. Bartlett, V.P., Sec., Gen. Couns.
INVESTOR CONTACT: Joan M. Kusher,
Investor Rel., (847) 501-2295
PRINCIPAL OFFICE: Edens & Winnetka
Road, Northfield, IL 60093

TELEPHONE NUMBER: (847) 446-7500
FAX: (847) 501-2443
WEB: www.stepan.com
NO. OF EMPLOYEES: 1,365 (avg.)
SHAREHOLDERS: 1,423
ANNUAL MEETING: In May
INCORPORATED: IL, Jan., 1940; reincorp., DE, 1959

INSTITUTIONAL HOLDINGS:
No. of Institutions: 31
Shares Held: 2,748,719
% Held: 28.9
INDUSTRY: Surface active agents (SIC: 2843)
TRANSFER AGENT(S): Harris Trust & Savings Bank, Chicago, IL

SUNTRUST BANKS, INC.

	YIELD	2.5%
	P/E RATIO	16.3

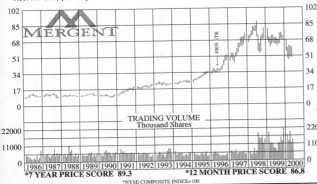

INTERIM EARNINGS (Per Share):

Qtr.	Mar.	Jun.	Sept.	Dec.
1996	0.67	0.68	0.70	0.72
1997	0.74	0.77	0.80	0.82
1998	0.85	0.88	0.91	0.49
1999	0.87	0.91	1.00	0.71

INTERIM DIVIDENDS (Per Share):

Amt.	Decl.	Ex.	Rec.	Pay.
0.345Q	4/20/99	5/27/99	6/01/99	6/15/99
0.345Q	8/10/99	8/30/99	9/01/99	9/15/99
0.345Q	11/09/99	11/29/99	12/01/99	12/15/99
0.37Q	2/08/00	2/28/00	3/01/00	3/15/00
0.37Q	4/18/00	5/30/00	6/01/00	6/15/00

Indicated div.: $1.48 (Div. Reinv. Plan)

CAPITALIZATION (12/31/99):

	($000)	(%)
Total Deposits	60,100,529	82.7
Long-Term Debt	4,967,346	6.8
Common & Surplus	7,626,862	10.5
Total	72,694,737	100.0

DIVIDEND ACHIEVER STATUS:
Rank: 86   10-Year Growth Rate: 13.47%
Total Years of Dividend Growth: 14

TRADING VOLUME Thousand Shares

*7 YEAR PRICE SCORE 89.3   *12 MONTH PRICE SCORE 86.8
*NYSE COMPOSITE INDEX=100

RECENT DEVELOPMENTS: For the year ended 12/31/99, STI reported income of $1.12 billion, before an extraordinary gain of $202.6 million, versus net income of $971.0 million in 1998. Earnings for 1999 and 1998 included pre-tax merger-related expenses of $45.6 million and $119.4 million, respectively. Net interest income advanced 7.4% to $3.15 billion from $2.93 billion a year earlier. Total non-interest income fell 3.3% to $1.66 billion.

PROSPECTS: In 2000, the Company estimates earnings per share of $4.41 or $4.42. STI expects continued double-digit earnings growth throughout 2000 and beyond, due to loan growth, expense control and the Company's significant presence in the Sunbelt region. In addition, STI intends to expand its Internet banking operations, which currently has 200,000 customers. The Company will use the Internet to encourage customers to utilize other banking services.

BUSINESS

SUNTRUST BANKS, INC. offers a full line of consumer and commercial banking services to more than 3.0 million customers through more than 1,100 branches and 1,900 ATMs across six states, including Alabama, Florida, Georgia, Maryland, Tennessee and Virginia, as well as the District of Columbia. STI's banking network also includes telephone and computer-based banking alternatives. At 3/31/00, SunTrust had total assets of $96.00 billion. The Company's primary businesses include traditional deposit and credit services as well as trust and investment services. Through various subsidiaries, SunTrust provides credit cards, mortgage banking, credit-related insurance, data processing and information services, discount brokerage and investment banking services.

LOAN DISTRIBUTION

(12/31/99)	($000)	(%)
Commercial	26,933,477	41.0
Construction	2,547,095	3.9
Residential Mortgages	19,619,353	29.6
Other Real Estate	7,794,942	11.7
Credit Card	77,364	.1
Other Consumer Loans	9,120,600	13.7
Total	66,002,831	100.0

ANNUAL FINANCIAL DATA

	12/31/99	12/31/98	12/31/97	12/31/96	12/31/95	12/31/94	12/31/93
Earnings Per Share	[1][2] 3.50	[1] 3.04	3.13	2.76	2.47	2.25	1.89
Tang. Book Val. Per Share	23.24	22.99	23.38	20.87	17.71	13.90	13.89
Dividends Per Share	1.38	1.00	0.93	0.82	0.74	0.66	0.58
Dividend Payout %	33.4	32.9	29.6	29.9	30.0	29.3	30.8
INCOME STATEMENT (IN MILLIONS):							
Total Interest Income	5,960.2	5,675.9	3,650.7	3,246.0	3,027.2	2,552.4	2,362.4
Total Interest Expense	2,814.8	2,746.8	1,756.4	1,461.8	1,350.8	932.5	790.7
Net Interest Income	3,145.5	2,929.1	1,894.4	1,784.2	1,676.4	1,619.9	1,571.7
Provision for Loan Losses	170.4	214.6	117.0	115.9	112.1	137.8	189.1
Non-Interest Income	1,660.0	1,716.2	934.2	818.0	713.1	699.9	726.5
Non-Interest Expense	2,939.4	2,932.4	1,685.6	1,583.1	1,451.5	1,400.0	1,408.4
Income Before Taxes	1,695.7	1,498.3	1,026.0	903.2	825.9	782.0	700.7
Net Income	[1][2] 1,124.0	[1] 971.0	667.3	616.6	565.5	522.7	473.7
Average Shs. Outstg. (000)	317,079	319,711	213,480	223,486	229,544	232,078	251,312
BALANCE SHEET (IN MILLIONS):							
Cash & Due from Banks	3,909.7	4,289.9	2,991.3	3,037.3	2,641.4	2,595.1	2,363.7
Securities Avail. for Sale	259.5	239.7	178.4	80.4	96.6	98.1	112.5
Total Loans & Leases	67,534.6	65,089.2	40,135.5	35,404.2	31,301.4	28,548.9	25,347.6
Allowance for Credit Losses	871.3	944.6	751.8	725.8	698.9	647.0	616.7
Net Loans & Leases	66,663.3	64,144.6	39,383.7	34,678.3	30,602.5	27,901.9	24,730.9
Total Assets	95,390.0	93,169.9	57,982.7	52,468.2	46,471.5	42,709.1	40,728.4
Total Deposits	60,100.5	59,033.3	38,197.5	36,890.4	33,183.2	32,218.4	30,485.8
Long-Term Obligations	4,967.3	4,757.9	3,171.8	1,565.3	1,002.4	930.4	630.4
Total Liabilities	87,763.1	84,991.3	52,783.4	47,588.3	42,201.9	39,255.8	37,118.8
Net Stockholders' Equity	7,626.9	8,178.6	5,199.4	4,880.0	4,269.6	3,453.3	3,609.6
Year-end Shs. Outstg. (000)	293,544	321,124	209,909	220,469	225,726	231,358	244,936
STATISTICAL RECORD:							
Return on Equity %	14.7	11.9	12.8	12.6	13.2	15.1	13.1
Return on Assets %	1.2	1.0	1.2	1.2	1.2	1.2	1.2
Equity/Assets %	8.0	8.8	9.0	9.3	9.2	8.1	8.9
Non-Int. Exp./Tot. Inc. %	61.2	63.1	59.6	60.8	60.7	60.3	61.3
Price Range	79¹³/₁₆-60⁷/₁₆	87¾-54	71¼-44¹/₈	52½-32⁵/₈	35⁷/₁₆-23⁵/₈	25¹¹/₁₆-21¾	24¹³/₁₆-20¹¹/₁₆
P/E Ratio	22.8-17.3	28.9-17.8	24.0-14.1	19.0-11.6	14.3-9.6	11.4-9.7	13.2-11.0
Average Yield %	2.0	1.4	1.5	2.0	2.5	2.8	2.5

Statistics are as originally reported. Adj. for 2-for-1 stk. split, 5/96. [1] Incl. pre-tax merger-related chrg.: $45.6 mill., 1999; $119.4 mill., 1998. [2] Bef. extraord. gain of $202.6 mill., 1999.

OFFICERS:
L. P. Humann, Chmn., Pres., C.E.O.
R. G. Tilghman, Vice-Chmn.
J. W. Spiegel, Exec. V.P., C.F.O.

INVESTOR CONTACT: Eugene S. Putnam, Sr. Vice Pres.-Inv. Rel. & Corp. Commun., (404) 658-4879

PRINCIPAL OFFICE: 303 Peachtree N.E., Atlanta, GA 30308

TELEPHONE NUMBER: (404) 588-7711
FAX: (404) 827-6173
WEB: www.SunTrust.com

NO. OF EMPLOYEES: 30,222

SHAREHOLDERS: 41,275

ANNUAL MEETING: In Apr.

INCORPORATED: GA, July, 1985

INSTITUTIONAL HOLDINGS:
No. of Institutions: 399
Shares Held: 154,120,109
% Held: 48.2

INDUSTRY: National commercial banks (SIC: 6021)

TRANSFER AGENT(S): SunTrust Bank Atlanta, Atlanta, GA

NYSE SYMBOL SUP
Rec. Pr. 27 15/16 (5/31/00)

SUPERIOR INDUSTRIES INTERNATIONAL, INC.

YIELD 1.4%
P/E RATIO 10.6

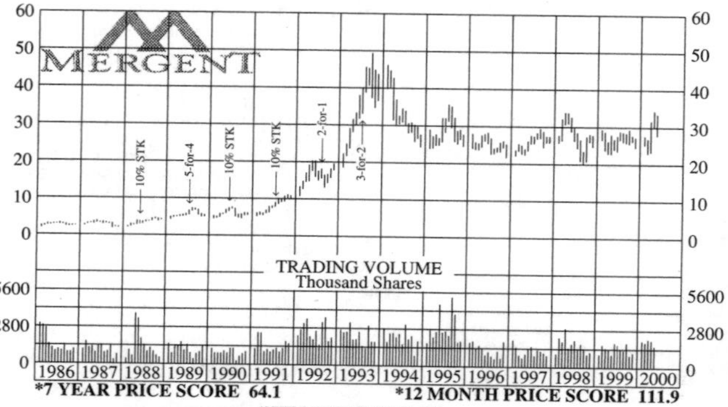

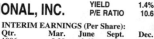

*7 YEAR PRICE SCORE 64.1 *12 MONTH PRICE SCORE 111.9

*NYSE COMPOSITE INDEX=100

INTERIM EARNINGS (Per Share):

Qtr.	Mar.	June	Sept.	Dec.
1996	0.30	0.48	0.40	0.45
1997	0.41	0.54	0.47	0.56
1998	0.46	0.44	0.28	0.71
1999	0.57	0.71	0.54	0.81

INTERIM DIVIDENDS (Per Share):

Amt.	Decl.	Ex.	Rec.	Pay.
0.09Q	5/06/99	6/30/99	7/02/99	7/16/99
0.09Q	7/27/99	10/06/99	10/08/99	10/22/99
0.09Q	10/25/99	1/06/00	1/10/00	1/24/00
0.09Q	3/20/00	4/05/00	4/07/00	4/21/00
0.10Q	5/12/00	6/28/00	6/30/00	7/14/00

Indicated div.: $0.40 (Div. Reinv. Plan)

CAPITALIZATION (12/31/99):

	($000)	(%)
Capital Lease Obligations..	340	0.1
Deferred Income Tax	6,932	1.9
Common & Surplus	353,086	98.0
Total	360,358	100.0

DIVIDEND ACHIEVER STATUS:
Rank: 46 10-Year Growth Rate: 16.50%
Total Years of Dividend Growth: 14

RECENT DEVELOPMENTS: For the year ended 12/31/99, net income grew 35.3% to $70.8 million from $52.3 million the year before. Net sales grew 6.0% to $571.8 million from $539.4 million a year earlier. OEM sales, which grew 8.9% to $551.0 million, benefited from a 10.5% unit increase in aluminum road wheels to automobile manufacturers. Sales of aftermarket products fell 37.6% to $20.8 million due to discontinuance of SUP's aftermarket road wheel business and aftermarket certain product accessories.

PROSPECTS: During 1999 and early 2000, the Company has been awarded new aluminum supply contracts valued at more than $350.0 million. These orders included new business contracts with Rover Group, Ltd. and Mitsubishi Motor Manufacturing of America, Inc. and a renewed contract with DaimlerChryler Corporation. Separately, the Company began accepting orders for aluminum suspension and related underbody components. Orders are scheduled to begin shipping in the fourth quarter of 2001.

BUSINESS

SUPERIOR INDUSTRIES INTERNATIONAL, INC. designs and manufactures automotive parts and accessories for original equipment manufacturers (OEMs) and for the automotive aftermarket. The OEM cast aluminum road wheels, the Company's primary product, are sold to Ford, Mazda, BMW, Volkswagen, Audi, Rover, Toyota, Nissan, Isuzu, Mitsubishi, DaimlerChrysler and General Motors for factory installation as optional or standard equipment on selected vehicle models. In addition, the Company manufactures and distributes aftermarket accessories including bed mats, exhaust extensions, license frames, lug nuts, springs and suspension products, steering wheel covers and other miscellaneous accessories. Aftermarket products are sold to customers, including Sears, Pep Boys, Wal-Mart and Western Auto. The Company operates 12 manufacturing facilities within the U.S., Mexico and Europe.

ANNUAL FINANCIAL DATA

	12/31/99	12/31/98	12/31/97	12/31/96	12/31/95	12/31/94	12/31/93
Earnings Per Share	**2.62**	**1.88**	**1.96**	**1.63**	**1.78**	**1.85**	**1.47**
Cash Flow Per Share	**3.67**	**2.84**	**2.92**	**2.58**	**2.70**	**2.73**	**2.18**
Tang. Book Val. Per Share	**13.35**	**11.42**	**10.30**	**8.87**	**7.89**	**6.76**	**5.88**
Dividends Per Share	**0.34**	**0.30**	**0.26**	**0.22**	**0.19**	**0.15**	**0.11**
Dividend Payout %	**13.0**	**16.0**	**13.3**	**13.5**	**10.7**	**8.1**	**7.5**
INCOME STATEMENT (IN THOUSANDS):							
Total Revenues	571,782	539,431	549,131	504,241	521,997	456,638	393,033
Costs & Expenses	438,051	432,387	434,030	395,129	400,449	337,869	296,761
Depreciation & Amort.	28,523	26,698	26,917	27,330	27,716	26,604	21,695
Operating Income	105,208	80,346	88,184	81,782	93,832	92,165	74,577
Net Interest Inc./(Exp.)	5,451	4,287	2,170	d326	d2,182	d1,022	d912
Income Before Income Taxes	108,518	80,801	86,208	74,071	84,918	90,304	72,640
Income Taxes	37,710	28,482	30,819	27,221	31,854	33,989	27,463
Net Income	70,808	52,319	55,389	46,850	53,064	56,315	45,177
Cash Flow	99,331	79,017	82,306	74,180	80,780	82,919	66,872
Average Shs. Outstg.	27,056	27,818	28,221	28,798	29,895	30,376	30,708
BALANCE SHEET (IN THOUSANDS):							
Cash & Cash Equivalents	108,081	86,566	73,693	42,103	11,179	27,042	36,588
Total Current Assets	263,740	235,886	199,846	164,080	142,659	160,771	141,219
Net Property	163,113	158,194	147,989	161,670	177,538	185,853	162,225
Total Assets	460,468	427,430	382,679	357,590	341,770	357,683	310,123
Total Current Liabilities	86,847	91,111	65,415	76,369	81,746	106,923	75,991
Long-Term Obligations	340	673	1,344	1,940	5,814	23,075	34,004
Net Stockholders' Equity	353,086	312,034	287,416	251,111	229,153	200,182	176,869
Net Working Capital	176,893	144,775	134,431	87,711	60,913	53,848	65,228
Year-end Shs. Outstg.	26,454	27,312	27,902	28,324	29,029	29,612	30,061
STATISTICAL RECORD:							
Operating Profit Margin %	18.4	14.9	16.1	16.2	18.0	20.2	19.0
Net Profit Margin %	12.4	9.7	10.1	9.3	10.2	12.3	11.5
Return on Equity %	20.1	16.8	19.3	18.7	23.2	28.1	25.5
Return on Assets %	15.4	12.2	14.5	13.1	15.5	15.7	14.6
Debt/Total Assets %	0.1	0.2	0.4	0.5	1.7	6.5	11.0
Price Range	29 3/8-22 3/4	33 7/8-20 1/16	29 1/2-22 1/8	28 3/8-21 5/8	35 3/4-23 7/8	46 1/4-24 1/4	49 3/8-18 9/16
P/E Ratio	11.2-8.7	18.0-10.7	15.1-11.3	17.4-13.3	20.1-13.4	25.0-13.1	33.6-12.6
Average Yield %	1.3	1.1	1.0	0.9	0.6	0.4	0.3

Statistics are as originally reported. Adj. for stk. split: 3-for-2, 7/93.

OFFICERS:
L. L. Borick, Chmn., Pres.
S. I. Ausman, Vice-Chmn.
R. J. Ornstein, V.P., C.F.O.
D. L. Levine, Corp. Sec., Treas.

INVESTOR CONTACT: Cathy Buccieri, Shareholder Rel., (818) 902-2701

PRINCIPAL OFFICE: 7800 Woodley Avenue, Van Nuys, CA 91406

TELEPHONE NUMBER: (818) 781-4973
FAX: (818) 780-3500
WEB: www.supind.com

NO. OF EMPLOYEES: 5,200 (approx.)

SHAREHOLDERS: 1,100 (approx.)

ANNUAL MEETING: In May

INCORPORATED: DE, June, 1969; reincorp., CA, June, 1994

INSTITUTIONAL HOLDINGS:
No. of Institutions: 119
Shares Held: 13,274,606
% Held: 49.8

INDUSTRY: Motor vehicle parts and accessories (SIC: 3714)

TRANSFER AGENT(S): Chase Mellon Shareholder Services, Los Angeles, CA

SUPERIOR UNIFORM GROUP, INC.

YIELD	5.8%
P/E RATIO	7.9

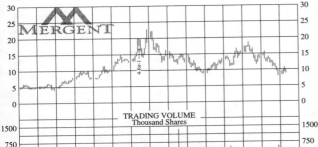

TRADING VOLUME
Thousand Shares

*7 YEAR PRICE SCORE 55.2   *12 MONTH PRICE SCORE 89.0
*NYSE COMPOSITE INDEX=100

INTERIM EARNINGS (Per Share):

Qtr.	Mar.	June	Sept.	Dec.
1994	0.23	0.32	0.29	0.33
1995	0.27	0.24	0.24	d0.30
1996	0.24	0.26	0.28	0.29
1997	0.22	0.29	0.30	0.32
1998	0.20	0.23	0.27	0.31
1999	0.23	0.28	0.28	0.38

INTERIM DIVIDENDS (Per Share):

Amt.	Decl.	Ex.	Rec.	Pay.
0.135Q	5/07/99	5/13/99	5/17/99	5/28/99
0.135Q	8/06/99	8/12/99	8/16/99	8/26/99
0.135Q	10/29/99	11/10/99	11/15/99	11/26/99
0.135Q	2/04/00	2/10/00	2/14/00	2/25/00
0.135Q	5/05/00	5/11/00	5/15/00	5/26/00

Indicated div.: $0.54 (Div. Reinv. Plan)

CAPITALIZATION (12/31/99):

	($000)	(%)
Long-Term Debt	19,473	18.8
Deferred Income Tax	1,655	1.6
Common & Surplus	82,718	79.7
Total	103,845	100.0

DIVIDEND ACHIEVER STATUS:

Rank: 85   10-Year Growth Rate: 13.67%
Total Years of Dividend Growth: 16

RECENT DEVELOPMENTS: For the year ended 12/31/99, net income increased 14.7% to $9.1 million versus $7.9 million in the previous year. Results for 1998 included a business process re-engineering charge of $3.5 million. Net sales rose 4.5% to $168.0 million from $160.7 million in 1998. The increase in sales was attributed to the continuation of new uniform programs as well as the April 1999 acquisition of The Empire Company and the January 1998 acquisition of Sope Creek. Cost of goods as a percentage of net sales decreased to 66.0% in 1999 compared with 66.3% in 1998. Earnings before taxes on income amounted to $14.3 million versus $12.5 million in the prior year.

BUSINESS

SUPERIOR UNIFORM GROUP. INC. (formerly Superior Surgical Mfg. Co., Inc.) through its marketing divisions, Fashion Seal Uniforms, Martin's, Empire, Appel, Worklon, Universal and Sope Creek, manufactures and sells a wide range of uniforms, corporate I.D., career apparel and accessories for the hospital and healthcare fields; hotels; fast food and other restaurants; and public safety, industrial, transportation and commercial markets, as well as corporate and resort embroidered sportswear. In 1999, uniforms and service apparel accounted for 90-95% of total sales. None of SGC's customers accounted for more than 10% of sales in 1999.

ANNUAL FINANCIAL DATA

	12/31/99	12/31/98	12/31/97	12/31/96	12/31/95	12/31/94	12/31/93
Earnings Per Share	⬚1.17	1.00	1.14	1.07	⬚0.45	1.17	⬚0.89
Cash Flow Per Share	1.71	1.57	1.69	1.61	0.90	1.50	1.17
Tang. Book Val. Per Share	9.75	9.91	9.74	9.11	8.45	8.38	7.78
Dividends Per Share	0.54	0.51	0.46	0.38	0.36	0.32	0.28
Dividend Payout %	46.1	51.0	39.9	35.5	80.0	27.3	31.5
INCOME STATEMENT (IN THOUSANDS):							
Total Revenues	168,006	160,718	144,607	141,421	135,198	135,067	130,127
Costs & Expenses	147,890	139,068	124,689	121,877	117,584	114,982	112,612
Depreciation & Amort.	4,214	4,544	4,427	4,354	3,748	2,865	2,504
Operating Income	15,902	17,106	15,491	15,189	13,866	17,221	15,011
Net Interest Inc./(Exp.)	d1,605	d1,116	d1,101	d1,295	d969	d960	d642
Income Before Income Taxes	14,296	12,516	14,390	13,894	8,647	16,261	12,119
Income Taxes	5,180	4,570	5,220	5,200	4,885	6,180	4,415
Net Income	⬚9,116	7,946	9,170	8,694	⬚3,762	10,081	⬚7,704
Cash Flow	13,331	12,490	13,597	13,049	7,510	12,946	10,208
Average Shs. Outstg.	7,794	7,966	8,062	8,125	8,321	8,646	8,693
BALANCE SHEET (IN THOUSANDS):							
Cash & Cash Equivalents	3,021	514	8,890	4,719	5,422	11,234	3,030
Total Current Assets	81,701	85,711	78,136	73,382	72,388	76,457	64,201
Net Property	29,460	27,934	26,772	28,995	30,735	26,235	20,873
Total Assets	122,852	119,039	108,355	105,659	106,134	104,864	87,168
Total Current Liabilities	19,007	18,671	14,371	13,139	17,306	12,161	11,105
Long-Term Obligations	19,473	17,600	13,467	15,733	18,000	18,600	4,200
Net Stockholders' Equity	82,718	80,503	78,117	74,156	69,518	70,938	68,568
Net Working Capital	62,694	67,040	63,765	60,243	55,082	64,296	53,097
Year-end Shs. Outstg.	7,595	7,847	7,937	8,054	8,134	8,364	8,703
STATISTICAL RECORD:							
Operating Profit Margin %	9.5	10.6	10.7	10.7	10.3	12.7	11.5
Net Profit Margin %	5.4	4.9	6.3	6.1	2.8	7.5	5.9
Return on Equity %	11.0	9.9	11.7	11.7	5.4	14.2	11.2
Return on Assets %	7.4	6.7	8.5	8.2	3.5	9.6	8.8
Debt/Total Assets %	15.9	14.8	12.4	14.9	17.0	17.7	4.8
Price Range	15¾-8	18⅝-11⅝	16¾-11	13½-8⅞	14¾-8¾	16-11¾	22¼-12⅜
P/E Ratio	13.5-6.8	18.6-11.6	14.7-9.6	12.6-8.3	32.8-19.4	13.7-10.0	25.0-13.9
Average Yield %	4.5	3.4	3.3	3.4	3.1	2.3	1.6

Statistics are as originally reported. ⬚ Incl. non-recurr. chrg. $3.5 mill., 12/99; $4.3 mill., 12/95; $2.3 mill., 12/93.

QUARTERLY DATA

(12/31/99)($000)	Rev	Inc
1st Quarter	37,504	1,811
2nd Quarter	42,826	2,189
3rd Quarter	42,133	2,173
4th Quarter	45,542	2,942

OFFICERS:
G. M. Benstock, Chmn., C.E.O.
A. D. DeMott Jr., Treas., Prin. Acctg. Off.

PRINCIPAL OFFICE: 10099 Seminole Blvd., Seminole, FL 33772-0002

TELEPHONE NUMBER: (727) 397-9611
FAX: (727) 391-5401
WEB: www.superioruniformgroup.com

NO. OF EMPLOYEES: 1,700 (approx.)

SHAREHOLDERS: 353

ANNUAL MEETING: In May

INCORPORATED: NY, 1922

INSTITUTIONAL HOLDINGS:
No. of Institutions: 23
Shares Held: 3,085,128
% Held: 39.9

INDUSTRY: Men's and boys' work clothing (SIC: 2326)

TRANSFER AGENT(S): First Union National Bank, Charlotte, NC

SUPERVALU INC.

	YIELD	2.6%
	P/E RATIO	11.2

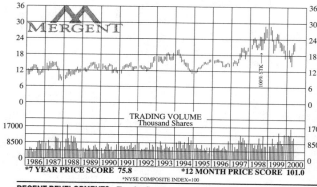

*7 YEAR PRICE SCORE 75.8   *12 MONTH PRICE SCORE 101.0
*NYSE COMPOSITE INDEX=100

INTERIM EARNINGS (Per Share):

Qtr.	May	Aug.	Nov.	Feb.
1996-97	0.34	0.27	0.30	0.40
1997-98	0.37	0.72	0.34	0.43
1998-99	0.43	0.33	0.37	0.45
1999-00	0.55	0.37	0.42	0.52

INTERIM DIVIDENDS (Per Share):

Amt.	Decl.	Ex.	Rec.	Pay.
0.135Q	6/30/99	8/11/99	8/13/99	9/15/99
0.135Q	10/13/99	11/29/99	12/01/99	12/15/99
0.135Q	12/08/99	2/28/00	3/01/00	3/15/00
0.135Q	4/12/00	5/30/00	6/01/00	6/15/00

Indicated div.: $0.54 (Div. Reinv. Plan)

CAPITALIZATION (2/26/00):

	($000)	(%)
Long-Term Debt	1,408,858	37.3
Capital Lease Obligations..	544,883	14.4
Deferred Income Tax	3,306	0.1
Common & Surplus	1,821,479	48.2
Total	3,778,526	100.0

DIVIDEND ACHIEVER STATUS:
Rank: 225   10-Year Growth Rate: 6.88%
Total Years of Dividend Growth: 27

RECENT DEVELOPMENTS: For the fiscal year ended 2/26/00, net earnings advanced 27.0% to $242.9 million from $191.3 million in the prior year. Net sales grew 16.8% to $20.34 billion from $17.42 billion a year earlier. Results in the recent period included a pre-tax gain of $163.7 million from the sale of Hazelwood Farms Bakeries, partially offset by restructuring and other charges totaling $103.6 million. Operating earnings were $624.2 million, up 39.1% versus $448.7 million the previous year.

PROSPECTS: Results are benefiting from the mid-1999 acquisition of Richfood Holdings Inc., growth in price superstores and limited assortment stores, cost control initiatives and a new supply agreement with Kmart. During the current fiscal year, the Company expects to generate synergistic savings from the Richfood acquisition of between $25.0 million and $35.0 million and plans to open between 20 to 25 new price superstores and up to 60 limited assortment stores.

BUSINESS

SUPERVALU INC. is a major food retailer and distributor to independently-owned retail food stores. The Company operates three principal store formats at retail and sells food and non-food products at wholesale. SVU operates 194 price superstores under the Cub Foods, Shop 'n Save, Shoppers Food Warehouse, Metro and bigg's banners and 838 limited assortment stores including 662 licensed locations under the Save-A-Lot banner, and 85 other supermarkets, under the names Farm Fresh, Laneco, Scott's Foods, and Hornbachers. Additionally, the Company is the primary supplier to approximately 3,500 supermarkets and a partial supplier to approximately 2,600 stores, including 1,350 Kmart locations.

REVENUES

(2/26/2000)	($000)	(%)
Retail Food	8,070	39.7
Food Distribution	12,269	60.3
Total	20,339	100.0

ANNUAL FINANCIAL DATA

	2/26/00	2/27/99	2/28/98	2/22/97	2/24/96	2/25/95	2/26/94
Earnings Per Share	③ 1.87	1.57	② 1.83	1.30	1.22	① 0.31	1.29
Cash Flow Per Share	4.06	3.45	3.64	3.03	2.82	1.70	2.59
Tang. Book Val. Per Share	1.58	6.09	5.80	6.06	5.27	4.79	5.84
Dividends Per Share	0.54	0.53	0.51	0.49	0.48	0.46	0.41
Dividend Payout %	28.9	33.4	27.9	38.1	39.3	149.1	32.2
INCOME STATEMENT (IN MILLIONS):							
Total Revenues	20,339.1	17,420.5	17,201.4	16,551.9	16,486.3	16,563.8	15,936.9
Costs & Expenses	19,531.0	16,772.7	16,565.9	15,939.3	15,900.5	16,255.2	15,381.6
Depreciation & Amort.	285.3	229.6	230.1	232.1	219.1	198.7	186.3
Operating Income	582.8	418.2	405.4	380.5	366.8	109.8	369.1
Net Interest Inc./(Exp.)	d135.4	d101.9	d114.0	d120.7	d116.7	d111.3	d89.8
Income Before Income Taxes	447.5	316.3	384.8	280.5	267.7	15.9	294.1
Income Taxes	204.5	124.9	154.0	105.5	101.3	cr27.4	108.8
Equity Earnings/Minority Int.	...	...	93.4	20.7	17.6	17.4	14.8
Net Income	③ 242.9	191.3	② 230.8	175.0	166.4	① 43.3	185.3
Cash Flow	528.3	421.0	460.8	407.1	385.5	242.1	371.5
Average Shs. Outstg. (000)	130,090	121,961	126,550	134,510	136,554	142,776	143,634
BALANCE SHEET (IN MILLIONS):							
Cash & Cash Equivalents	10.9	7.6	6.1	6.5	5.2	4.8	2.8
Total Current Assets	2,177.6	1,582.5	1,612.1	1,600.8	1,553.7	1,646.3	1,563.3
Net Property	2,168.2	1,699.0	1,589.6	1,648.5	1,600.2	1,571.3	1,410.1
Total Assets	6,495.4	4,265.9	4,093.0	4,283.3	4,183.5	4,305.1	4,042.4
Total Current Liabilities	2,509.6	1,521.9	1,457.2	1,369.1	1,326.7	1,447.1	1,224.4
Long-Term Obligations	1,953.7	1,246.3	1,260.7	1,420.6	1,445.6	1,459.8	1,263.0
Net Stockholders' Equity	1,821.5	1,305.6	1,201.9	1,307.4	1,216.2	1,193.2	1,275.5
Net Working Capital	d332.0	60.6	154.9	231.7	227.0	199.2	338.9
Year-end Shs. Outstg. (000)	134,662	120,109	120,368	133,764	134,886	140,348	144,118
STATISTICAL RECORD:							
Operating Profit Margin %	2.9	2.4	2.4	2.3	2.2	0.7	2.3
Net Profit Margin %	1.2	1.1	1.3	1.1	1.0	0.3	1.2
Return on Equity %	13.3	14.7	19.2	13.4	13.7	3.6	14.5
Return on Assets %	3.7	4.5	5.6	4.1	4.0	1.0	4.6
Debt/Total Assets %	30.1	29.2	30.8	33.2	34.6	33.9	31.2
Price Range	28⁷/₈-16¹³/₁₆	28¹⁵/₁₆-20³/₁₆	21¹/₈-14¹/₁₆	16¹/₂-13⁹/₁₆	16⁷/₈-11¼	20¹/₁₆-11	18¹⁵/₁₆-14³/₄
P/E Ratio	15.4-9.0	18.4-12.9	11.6-7.7	12.7-10.4	13.5-9.2	65.8-36.1	14.7-11.4
Average Yield %	2.4	2.1	2.9	3.3	3.5	2.9	2.5

Statistics are as originally reported. Adj. for 100% stk. div., 8/98. ① Incl. $244 mil total non-recur. chg. ② Incl. $53.7 mil ($0.43/sh.) non-recur net gain from sale of int. in ShopKo Stores, Inc. ③ Incl. $163.7 pre-tax gain on sale of Hazelwood Farms Bakeries & incl. $103.6 pre-tax restructuring chg.

OFFICERS:
M. W. Wright, Chmn., Pres., C.E.O.
P. K. Knous, Exec. V.P., C.F.O.
K. M. Erickson, Sr. V.P., Treas.

INVESTOR CONTACT: Investor Relations, (612) 828-4540

PRINCIPAL OFFICE: 11840 Valley View Road, Eden Prairie, MN 55344

TELEPHONE NUMBER: (612) 828-4000
FAX: (612) 828-8998
WEB: www.supervalu.com
NO. OF EMPLOYEES: 80,000 (approx.)
SHAREHOLDERS: 7,559
ANNUAL MEETING: In June
INCORPORATED: DE, Dec., 1925

INSTITUTIONAL HOLDINGS:
No. of Institutions: 259
Shares Held: 105,197,894
% Held: 75.4

INDUSTRY: Groceries, general line (SIC: 5141)

TRANSFER AGENT(S): Norwest Shareowner Services, St. Paul, MN

NASDAQ SYMBOL SUSQ
Rec. Pr. 13 9/16 (5/31/00)

SUSQUEHANNA BANCSHARES, INC.

YIELD 5.0%
P/E RATIO 11.6

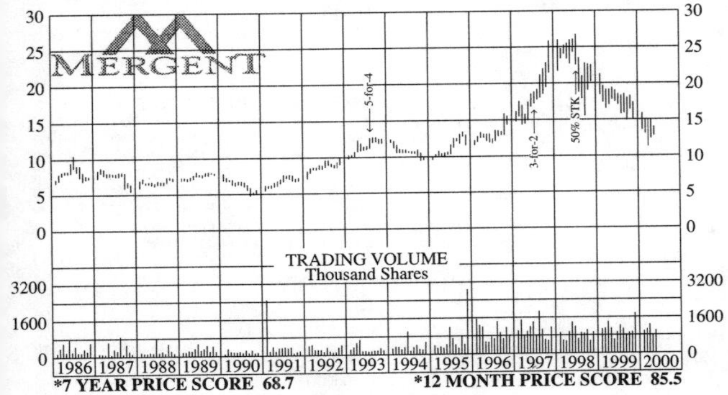

*7 YEAR PRICE SCORE 68.7 *12 MONTH PRICE SCORE 85.5

*NYSE COMPOSITE INDEX=100

INTERIM EARNINGS (Per Share):

Qtr.	Mar.	June	Sept.	Dec.
1995	0.20	0.24	0.28	0.27
1996	0.27	0.28	0.17	0.29
1997	0.29	0.27	0.32	0.33
1998	0.30	0.31	0.32	0.33
1999	0.32	0.33	0.40	0.12

INTERIM DIVIDENDS (Per Share):

Amt.	Decl.	Ex.	Rec.	Pay.
0.15Q	4/21/99	4/29/99	5/03/99	5/21/99
0.15Q	7/21/99	7/29/99	8/02/99	8/20/99
0.17Q	10/20/99	10/28/99	11/01/99	11/22/99
0.17Q	1/19/00	1/26/00	1/28/00	2/22/00
0.17Q	4/19/00	4/27/00	5/01/00	5/22/00

Indicated div.: $0.68 (Div. Reinv. Plan)

CAPITALIZATION (12/31/99):

	($000)	(%)
Total Deposits	3,180,520	86.4
Long-Term Debt	95,000	2.6
Common & Surplus	404,390	11.0
Total	3,679,910	100.0

DIVIDEND ACHIEVER STATUS:
Rank: 229 10-Year Growth Rate: 6.72%
Total Years of Dividend Growth: 29

RECENT DEVELOPMENTS: For the year ended 12/31/99, net income slipped 3.9% to $43.4 million from $45.2 million in the previous year. Earnings for 1999 included restructuring charges of $7.4 million. Total interest income slipped to $299.8 million from $300.8 million a year earlier, reflecting a decrease in interest on short-term investments and interest and fees on loans and leases. Total interest expenses decreased 2.7% to $138.8 million. Net interest income grew to $160.9 million from $158.1 million in 1998. Provision for loan and lease losses rose to $153.7 million from $152.8 million the year before. Total other income jumped 21.8% to $40.0 million from $31.2 million in the prior year. Non-interest income climbed 28.2% to $40.0 million from $31.2 million in 1998. Total other expenses rose 11.7% to $131.9 million compared with $118.1 million in 1998.

BUSINESS

SUSQUEHANNA BANCSHARES, INC. is a multi-state bank holding company that operates nine commercial banks, one federal savings bank, and two non-bank subsidiaries. These subsidiaries provide banking and banking-related services from 141 offices located in central, southeastern and southwestern Pennsylvania, Maryland and southern New Jersey. In addition, the Company operates two non-bank subsidiaries that provide leasing and insurance services. As of 12/31/99, the Company had assets of $4.31 billion, loans receivable of $2.96 billion and deposits of $3.18 billion.

ANNUAL FINANCIAL DATA

	12/31/99	12/31/98	12/31/97	12/31/96	12/31/95	12/31/94	12/31/93
Earnings Per Share	**1.17**	**1.26**	**1.20**	**1.01**	**0.99**	**[1] 0.94**	**[2] 0.91**
Tang. Book Val. Per Share	**10.92**	**10.91**	**10.25**	**9.87**	**9.38**	**8.29**	**8.42**
Dividends Per Share	**0.62**	**0.57**	**0.55**	**0.52**	**0.49**	**0.45**	**0.41**
Dividend Payout %	**53.0**	**45.2**	**45.6**	**51.3**	**49.3**	**48.3**	**45.2**
INCOME STATEMENT (IN MILLIONS):							
Total Interest Income	299.8	292.8	264.1	231.8	189.8	131.9	125.5
Total Interest Expense	138.8	138.6	118.4	103.1	82.6	46.4	46.2
Net Interest Income	160.9	154.2	145.7	128.7	107.2	85.6	79.3
Provision for Loan Losses	7.2	5.2	4.6	4.6	5.0	3.8	5.0
Non-Interest Income	40.0	30.9	23.8	21.3	16.1	13.1	12.4
Non-Interest Expense	131.9	113.2	106.0	100.8	80.9	64.1	57.6
Income Before Taxes	61.8	66.7	58.8	44.6	37.4	30.7	29.2
Net Income	43.4	45.6	40.2	30.0	26.0	[1] 22.0	[2] 20.7
Average Shs. Outstg. (000)	37,137	36,179	33,495	29,612	26,267	26,177	22,797
BALANCE SHEET (IN MILLIONS):							
Cash & Due from Banks	144.5	105.3	97.3	98.5	87.1	77.4	70.5
Securities Avail. for Sale	896.6	949.1	615.4	550.2	568.2	375.5	450.6
Total Loans & Leases	2,995.2	2,773.6	2,569.6	2,173.1	1,713.0	1,278.2	1,152.5
Allowance for Credit Losses	37.2	35.2	34.6	31.9	27.6	22.8	20.7
Net Loans & Leases	2,957.9	2,738.4	2,535.1	2,141.1	1,685.4	1,255.4	1,131.8
Total Assets	4,310.6	4,064.8	3,524.9	3,038.5	2,586.2	1,976.3	1,815.3
Total Deposits	3,180.5	3,124.3	2,851.2	2,493.5	2,116.0	1,687.3	1,536.0
Long-Term Obligations	95.0	370.2	181.9	115.4	86.3	17.9	28.9
Total Liabilities	3,906.2	3,673.6	3,178.1	2,745.8	2,312.8	1,781.8	1,618.2
Net Stockholders' Equity	404.4	391.2	346.7	292.7	273.4	194.5	197.1
Year-end Shs. Outstg. (000)	37,022	35,857	33,833	29,657	29,135	23,479	23,398
STATISTICAL RECORD:							
Return on Equity %	10.7	11.6	11.6	10.2	9.5	11.3	10.5
Return on Assets %	1.0	1.1	1.1	1.0	1.0	1.1	1.1
Equity/Assets %	9.4	9.6	9.8	9.6	10.6	9.8	10.9
Non-Int. Exp./Tot. Inc. %	65.6	61.2	62.6	67.2	65.6	65.0	62.8
Price Range	21 1/4-14 7/8	26 3/4-15 1/2	25 13/16-14 5/16	15 7/8-11 9/16	13 7/16-9 9/16	12 7/16-9 7/16	12 3/4-9 3/4
P/E Ratio	18.2-12.7	21.2-12.3	21.5-11.9	15.7-11.4	13.6-9.6	13.3-10.1	14.1-10.8
Average Yield %	3.4	2.7	2.7	3.8	4.3	4.1	3.6

Statistics are as originally reported. Adj. for stk. splits: 50% div., 7/1/98; 3-for-2, 7/2/97; 5-for-4, 8/27/93 [1] Bef. extraord. chrg. $732,000 [2] Bef. acctg. change credit $1.0 milll.

OFFICERS:
R. S. Bolinger, Chmn., C.E.O.
W. J. Reuter, Pres.
D. K. Hostetter, Sr. V.P., C.F.O., Treas.

INVESTOR CONTACT: Drew K. Hostetter, V.P., C.F.O., Treas. (717) 626-4721 ext. 400

PRINCIPAL OFFICE: 26 North Cedar St., Lititz, PA 17543

TELEPHONE NUMBER: (717) 626-4721
FAX: (717) 626-1874
WEB: www.susqbanc.com

NO. OF EMPLOYEES: 1,622 full-time; 300 part-time

SHAREHOLDERS: 6,700

ANNUAL MEETING: In May

INCORPORATED: PA, Sept., 1982

INSTITUTIONAL HOLDINGS:
No. of Institutions: 85
Shares Held: 8,508,988
% Held: 23.0

INDUSTRY: Bank holding companies (SIC: 6712)

TRANSFER AGENT(S): The Bank of New York, New York, NY

NYSE SYMBOL SNV
Rec. Pr. 20 (5/31/00)

SYNOVUS FINANCIAL CORPORATION

YIELD 2.2%
P/E RATIO 23.8

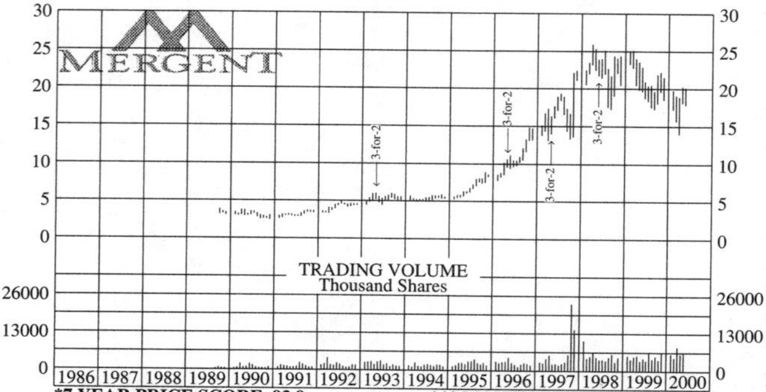

***7 YEAR PRICE SCORE 93.9** ***12 MONTH PRICE SCORE 99.9**

*NYSE COMPOSITE INDEX=100

INTERIM EARNINGS (Per Share):

Qtr.	Mar.	June	Sept.	Dec.
1997	0.13	0.15	0.16	0.17
1998	0.15	0.17	0.18	0.20
1999	0.18	0.19	0.21	0.22

INTERIM DIVIDENDS (Per Share):

Amt.	Decl.	Ex.	Rec.	Pay.
0.09Q	5/10/99	6/22/99	6/24/99	7/01/99
0.09Q	9/13/99	9/21/99	9/23/99	10/01/99
0.09Q	11/15/99	12/21/99	12/23/99	1/03/00
0.11Q	3/20/00	3/22/00	3/24/00	4/01/00
0.11Q	5/15/00	6/20/00	6/22/00	7/01/00

Indicated div.: $0.44

CAPITALIZATION (12/31/99):

	($000)	(%)
Total Deposits	9,440,087	85.4
Long-Term Debt	318,620	2.9
Minority Interest	64,285	0.6
Common & Surplus	1,226,669	11.1
Total	11,049,661	100.0

DIVIDEND ACHIEVER STATUS:
Rank: 30 10-Year Growth Rate: 18.44%
Total Years of Dividend Growth: 23

RECENT DEVELOPMENTS: For the year ended 12/31/99, net income increased 14.7% to $225.3 million compared with $196.5 million in 1998. Net interest income rose 12.8% to $513.3 million. Noninterest income grew 27.0% to $739.8 million. The increase in noninterest income resulted primarily from data processing revenues, which jumped 34.0% to $490.2 million, and other operating income, which advanced 15.8% to $143.1 million. Noninterest expense climbed 23.1% to $869.7 million.

PROSPECTS: In 2000, the Company estimates earnings per share of $0.92 and a return on equity of more than 20%, up from 19.33% in 1999. On 3/6/00, the Company announced an agreement to acquire ProCard, Inc., a provider of software and Internet tools designed to assist organizations with the management of purchasing, travel and fleet card programs. This acquisition will enable SNV to expand the services Total System Services offers to clients who want to enlarge their commercial card portfolios.

BUSINESS

SYNOVUS FINANCIAL CORPORATION, with assets of $13.05 billion as of 3/31/00, is a registered bank holding company engaged in two principal business segments: banking, which encompasses commercial banking, trust services, mortgage banking, credit card banking and certain securities brokerage operations, and bankcard data processing. The Company currently has 38 wholly-owned subsidiaries located in Georgia, Alabama, Florida and South Carolina. SNV and its subsidiaries offer a wide range of commercial banking services, including accepting customary types of demand and savings deposits; making individual, consumer, commercial, installment, first and second mortgage loans; offering money transfers, safe deposit services, trust, investment, IRA, and other fiduciary services.

LOAN DISTRIBUTION

(12/31/1999)	($000)	(%)
Commercial	6,788,782	74.8
Retail	2,288,644	25.2
Total	9,077,516	100.0

ANNUAL FINANCIAL DATA

	12/31/99	12/31/98	12/31/97	12/31/96	12/31/95	12/31/94	12/31/93
Earnings Per Share	**0.80**	**0.70**	**0.62**	**0.53**	**0.45**	**0.38**	**[1] 0.33**
Tang. Book Val. Per Share	**4.35**	**3.96**	**3.44**	**2.99**	**2.66**	**2.22**	**2.12**
Dividends Per Share	**0.34**	**0.28**	**0.23**	**0.19**	**0.15**	**0.13**	**0.11**
Dividend Payout %	**42.9**	**40.0**	**36.9**	**35.0**	**34.4**	**33.4**	**32.4**
INCOME STATEMENT (IN MILLIONS):							
Total Interest Income	888.0	769.2	725.7	663.3	615.8	429.4	389.3
Total Interest Expense	374.7	328.7	313.3	288.4	273.9	169.9	160.2
Net Interest Income	513.3	440.5	412.4	374.9	341.9	259.5	229.1
Provision for Loan Losses	34.0	26.7	32.3	31.8	25.8	22.1	23.5
Non-Interest Income	739.8	562.0	489.2	425.4	340.8	263.9	226.1
Non-Interest Expense	869.7	684.2	610.4	549.2	477.5	366.9	317.7
Income Before Taxes	349.3	291.6	258.9	219.3	179.5	134.5	114.0
Net Income	225.3	187.1	165.2	139.6	114.6	86.4	[1] 74.1
Average Shs. Outstg. (000)	283,355	269,151	265,665	261,299	258,647	226,942	224,870
BALANCE SHEET (IN MILLIONS):							
Cash & Due from Banks	466.5	348.4	388.1	405.0	...	290.8	292.9
Securities Avail. for Sale	1,716.7	1,514.1	1,325.0	1,276.1	1,106.3	763.1	800.9
Total Loans & Leases	9,077.5	7,420.5	6,615.6	6,075.5	5,528.8	4,330.5	3,848.5
Allowance for Credit Losses	136.8	119.4	108.8	104.9	96.2	81.0	78.2
Net Loans & Leases	8,940.7	7,301.2	6,506.8	5,970.5	5,432.6	4,249.5	3,770.3
Total Assets	12,547.0	10,498.0	9,260.3	8,612.3	7,545.8	6,115.4	5,627.4
Total Deposits	9,440.1	8,542.8	7,707.9	7,203.0	6,727.9	5,027.5	4,673.8
Long-Term Obligations	318.6	127.0	7.2	97.3	106.8	119.8	130.5
Total Liabilities	11,320.3	2,246.0	1,786.4	1,815.5	1,647.9	1,388.4	1,211.1
Net Stockholders' Equity	1,226.7	1,070.6	903.7	783.8	693.6	508.1	476.3
Year-end Shs. Outstg. (000)	282,014	270,218	262,808	261,779	260,665	228,499	225,137
STATISTICAL RECORD:							
Return on Equity %	18.4	17.5	18.3	17.8	16.5	17.0	15.5
Return on Assets %	1.8	1.8	1.8	1.6	1.4	1.4	1.3
Equity/Assets %	9.8	10.2	9.8	9.1	8.7	8.3	8.5
Non-Int. Exp./Tot. Inc. %	69.5	68.3	67.7	68.6	70.0	70.1	70.0
Price Range	25 1/8-17 1/4	25 15/16-17 1/4	22 7/16-13 1/8	14 13/16-7 3/4	8 7/8-5 1/4	5 7/8-4 15/16	6 1/16-4 7/16
P/E Ratio	31.4-21.6	37.0-24.6	36.2-21.1	27.8-14.6	20.0-11.8	15.4-12.9	18.3-13.5
Average Yield %	1.6	1.3	1.3	1.7	2.2	2.4	2.0

Statistics are as originally reported. Adj. for stk. splits: 3-for-2, 5/98; 4/97; 4/96 & 4/93
[1] Bef. acctg. change chrg. $2.9 mill.

OFFICERS:
J. H. Blanchard, Chmn., C.E.O.
J. D. Yancey, Pres., C.O.O.
T. J. Prescott, Exec. V.P., C.F.O.

INVESTOR CONTACT: Patrick A. Reynolds, Dir.-Inv. Rel., (706) 649-5220

PRINCIPAL OFFICE: One Arsenal Place, 901 Front Avenue, Suite 301, Columbus, GA 31901

TELEPHONE NUMBER: (706) 649-2387
FAX: (706) 649-2342
WEB: www.synovus.com

NO. OF EMPLOYEES: 9,221

SHAREHOLDERS: 33,648 (approx.)

ANNUAL MEETING: In Apr.

INCORPORATED: GA, Jun., 1972

INSTITUTIONAL HOLDINGS:
No. of Institutions: 168
Shares Held: 86,047,545
% Held: 30.8

INDUSTRY: National commercial banks (SIC: 6021)

TRANSFER AGENT(S): State Street Bank and Trust Company, Boston, MA

SYSCO CORPORATION

	YIELD	1.1%
	P/E RATIO	35.1

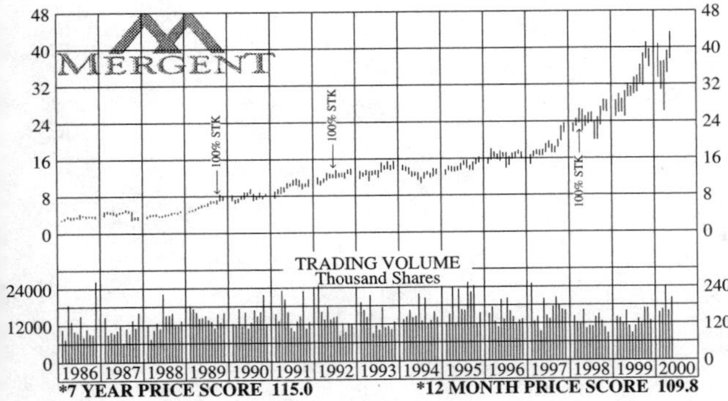

7 YEAR PRICE SCORE 115.0 **12 MONTH PRICE SCORE 109.8**
*NYSE COMPOSITE INDEX=100

INTERIM EARNINGS (Per Share):

Qtr.	Sept.	Dec.	Mar.	June
1996-97	0.21	0.22	0.18	0.26
1997-98	0.24	0.25	0.19	0.29
1998-99	0.26	0.26	0.22	0.35
1999-00	0.32	0.31	...	...

INTERIM DIVIDENDS (Per Share):

Amt.	Decl.	Ex.	Rec.	Pay.
0.10Q	9/03/99	9/29/99	10/01/99	10/22/99
0.12Q	11/05/99	1/05/00	1/07/00	1/28/00
0.12Q	2/09/00	4/05/00	4/07/00	4/28/00
0.12Q	5/10/00	7/05/00	7/07/00	7/28/00

Indicated div.: $0.48 (Div. Reinv. Plan)

CAPITALIZATION (7/3/99):

	($000)	(%)
Long-Term Debt	997,717	37.4
Deferred Income Tax	244,129	9.1
Common & Surplus	1,427,196	53.5
Total	2,669,042	100.0

DIVIDEND ACHIEVER STATUS:
Rank: 9   10-Year Growth Rate: 24.06%
Total Years of Dividend Growth: 23

RECENT DEVELOPMENTS: For the 13 weeks ended 1/1/00, net earnings advanced 17.9% to $101.9 million from $86.4 million the year before. Total sales climbed 9.5% to $4.65 billion from $4.25 billion a year earlier. Sales benefited from new acquisitions and increased customer acceptance of SYSCO® brand products, partially offset by lower prices for dairy and poultry products. Earnings before income taxes were $165.7 million, up 17.0% versus $141.6 million the previous year.

PROSPECTS: Near-term sales should benefit from the Company's acquisition activities. On 3/17/00, SYY completed the acquisition of FreshPoint Holdings, Inc., a Dallas, Texas-based foodservice and wholesale produce distributor with annual sales of approximately $750.0 million. On 1/26/00, the Company completed the acquisition of Watson Foodservice, Inc., a full-line foodservice distibutor located in Lubbock, Texas with annual revenues of more than $70.0 million.

BUSINESS

SYSCO CORPORATION is the largest marketer and distributor of foodservice products in America. Included among its customers are about 325,000 restaurants, hotels, hospitals, schools and other institutions. The Company distributes entree items, dry and canned foods, fresh produce, beverages, dairy products and certain nonfood products, including paper products and cleaning supplies. Through its SYGMA Network, Inc. subsidiary, the Company serves pizza, chicken, steak and hamburgers to fast-food chains and other limited menu chain restaurants. SYY has three Canadian facilities located in British Columbia and Ontario. In fiscal 1999, the foodservice sales breakdown was: 64% restaurants; 10% hospitals and nursing homes; 7% schools and colleges; 5% hotels and motels; and 14% other.

ANNUAL FINANCIAL DATA

	7/3/99	6/27/98	6/28/97	6/29/96	7/1/95	7/2/94	7/3/93
Earnings Per Share	1.08	① 0.95	0.85	0.76	0.69	0.59	0.54
Cash Flow Per Share	1.68	1.47	1.31	1.15	1.05	0.91	0.83
Tang. Book Val. Per Share	3.41	3.13	3.34	3.39	3.13	2.66	2.36
Dividends Per Share	0.40	0.35	0.30	0.26	0.22	0.18	0.14
Dividend Payout %	37.0	37.4	35.3	34.2	31.9	30.5	25.9
INCOME STATEMENT (IN MILLIONS):							
Total Revenues	17,422.8	15,327.5	14,454.6	13,395.1	12,118.0	10,942.5	10,021.5
Costs & Expenses	16,550.1	14,555.3	13,752.0	12,756.5	11,533.3	10,420.4	9,545.0
Depreciation & Amort.	205.0	181.2	160.3	144.7	130.8	120.0	107.7
Operating Income	667.7	591.0	542.3	494.0	454.0	402.1	368.8
Net Interest Inc./(Exp.)	d72.8	d58.4	d46.5	d41.0	d38.6	d36.3	d39.0
Income Before Income Taxes	593.9	532.5	496.0	453.9	417.6	367.6	332.0
Income Taxes	231.6	207.7	193.4	177.0	165.8	150.8	130.2
Net Income	362.3	① 324.8	302.5	276.9	251.8	216.8	201.8
Cash Flow	567.3	506.1	462.8	421.6	382.6	336.7	309.5
Average Shs. Outstg. (000)	336,797	343,440	354,470	365,198	365,560	368,678	373,492
BALANCE SHEET (IN MILLIONS):							
Cash & Cash Equivalents	149.3	110.3	117.7	107.8	133.9	86.7	68.8
Total Current Assets	2,408.8	2,180.1	1,964.4	1,922.3	1,789.4	1,599.6	1,419.7
Net Property	1,227.7	1,151.1	1,058.4	990.6	896.1	817.2	759.9
Total Assets	4,096.6	3,780.2	3,436.6	3,325.4	3,097.2	2,811.7	2,530.0
Total Current Liabilities	1,427.5	1,324.2	1,113.8	1,037.5	932.6	846.6	746.5
Long-Term Obligations	997.7	867.0	685.6	581.7	541.6	538.7	494.1
Net Stockholders' Equity	1,427.2	1,356.8	1,400.5	1,474.7	1,403.6	1,240.9	1,137.2
Net Working Capital	981.2	855.9	850.6	884.8	856.7	753.1	673.3
Year-end Shs. Outstg. (000)	329,672	335,009	344,876	360,826	365,730	366,138	368,914
STATISTICAL RECORD:							
Operating Profit Margin %	3.8	3.9	3.8	3.7	3.7	3.7	3.7
Net Profit Margin %	2.1	2.1	2.1	2.1	2.1	2.0	2.0
Return on Equity %	25.4	23.9	21.6	18.8	17.9	17.5	17.7
Return on Assets %	8.8	8.6	8.8	8.3	8.1	7.7	8.0
Debt/Total Assets %	24.4	22.9	20.0	17.5	17.5	19.2	19.5
Price Range	41⅛-24¹⁵/₁₆	28¹¹/₁₆-19¹⁵/₁₆	23⅝-14⅝	18⅛-13¹³/₁₆	16⁵/₁₆-12⁷/₁₆	14⅝-10⁹/₁₆	15½-11⅛
P/E Ratio	38.1-23.1	30.2-21.0	27.8-17.2	23.8-18.2	23.6-18.0	24.8-17.9	28.7-20.6
Average Yield %	1.2	1.5	1.6	1.6	1.5	1.4	1.1

Statistics are as originally reported. Adj. for 2-for-1 stk. split, 3/98. ① Bef. $28.1 mil ($0.08/sh) chg. for acctg. adj.

OFFICERS:
C. H. Cotros, Chmn., C.E.O.
R. J. Schnieders, Pres., C.O.O.
J. K. Stubblefield, Jr., Exec. V.P., C.F.O.

INVESTOR CONTACT: Toni R. Spigelmyer, Assistant V.P., (281) 584-1458

PRINCIPAL OFFICE: 1390 Enclave Parkway, Houston, TX 77077-2099

TELEPHONE NUMBER: (281) 584-1390
FAX: (281) 584-2880
WEB: www.syscosmart.com

NO. OF EMPLOYEES: 35,100 (approx.)

SHAREHOLDERS: 15,485

ANNUAL MEETING: In Nov.

INCORPORATED: DE, May, 1969

INSTITUTIONAL HOLDINGS:
No. of Institutions: 484
Shares Held: 221,968,261
% Held: 67.4

INDUSTRY: Groceries, general line (SIC: 5141)

TRANSFER AGENT(S): BankBoston N.A., Boston, MA

T. ROWE PRICE ASSOCIATES, INC.

YIELD 1.4%
P/E RATIO 20.6

INTERIM EARNINGS (Per Share):

Qtr.	Mar.	June	Sept.	Dec.
1996	0.17	0.20	0.21	0.22
1997	0.23	0.27	0.32	0.32
1998	0.32	0.34	0.33	0.35
1999	0.41	0.41	0.48	0.55

INTERIM DIVIDENDS (Per Share):

Amt.	Decl.	Ex.	Rec.	Pay.
0.10Q	3/10/99	3/23/99	3/25/99	4/09/99
0.10Q	6/03/99	6/21/99	6/23/99	7/08/99
0.10Q	9/09/99	9/22/99	9/24/99	10/08/99
0.13Q	12/16/99	12/23/99	12/28/99	1/12/00
0.13Q	3/10/00	3/22/00	3/24/00	4/07/00

Indicated div.: $0.52

CAPITALIZATION (12/31/99):

	($000)	(%)
Long-Term Debt	17,716	2.1
Minority Interest	60,220	7.1
Common & Surplus	770,184	90.8
Total	848,120	100.0

DIVIDEND ACHIEVER STATUS:
Rank: 14   10-Year Growth Rate: 22.52%
Total Years of Dividend Growth: 13

TRADING VOLUME
Thousand Shares

1986	1987	1988	1989	1990	1991	1992	1993	1994	1995	1996	1997	1998	1999	2000

*7 YEAR PRICE SCORE 110.4   ***12 MONTH PRICE SCORE 104.6**
*NYSE COMPOSITE INDEX=100

RECENT DEVELOPMENTS: On 4/11/00, TROW announced an agreement to acquire Robert Fleming Holdings, Ltd.'s 50% interest in Rowe Price-Fleming International, Inc. for $780.0 million. For the year ended 12/31/99, net income advanced 37.5% to $239.4 million compared with $174.1 million in the previous year. Revenues grew 17.0% to $801.6 million. Administrative fee revenues rose 13.8% to

$197.3 million, attributable to the Company's defined contribution retirement plan recordkeeping services; however, increased operating expenses partially offset these gains. Investment and other income revenue grew 31.5% to $37.5 million, primarily due to larger money market fund balances and increased venture capital investments.

BUSINESS

T. ROWE PRICE ASSOCIATES, INC. and its subsidiaries serve as investment adviser to the T. Rowe Price Mutual Funds, other sponsored investment portfolios, and private accounts of other institutional and individual investors primarily located in the United States, including defined benefit and defined contribution plans, endowments, foundations, trusts and other mutual funds including those which hold the assets of variable annuity insurance contracts. As of 12/31/99, total assets under management were $179.9 billion. The Company also provides investment advisory-related administrative services, including mutual fund transfer agent, accounting and shareholder services, participant recordkeeping and transfer agent services for defined contribution retirement plans, discount brokerage, and trust services.

REVENUES

(12/31/1999)	($000)	(%)
Investment Advisory Fees	588,014	77.9
Administrative Fees	144,906	19.2
Investment & Other	22,037	2.9
Total	754,957	100.0

ANNUAL FINANCIAL DATA

	12/31/99	12/31/98	12/31/97	12/31/96	12/31/95	12/31/94	12/31/93
Earnings Per Share	1.85	1.34	1.13	0.80	0.66	0.53	0.40
Cash Flow Per Share	2.11	1.59	1.35	0.94	0.79	0.62	0.48
Tang. Book Val. Per Share	6.41	5.11	4.12	3.00	2.39	1.89	1.68
Dividends Per Share	0.40	0.34	0.26	0.21	0.16	0.13	0.10
Dividend Payout %	21.6	25.4	23.0	26.4	24.2	24.5	26.4
INCOME STATEMENT (IN MILLIONS):							
Total Revenues	1,036.4	886.1	755.0	586.1	439.3	382.4	310.0
Costs & Expenses	589.0	540.7	461.2	380.5	282.3	251.1	209.2
Depreciation & Amort.	32.6	32.6	29.0	18.1	13.3	10.1	9.8
Operating Income	414.8	312.8	264.8	187.5	143.7	121.2	91.0
Income Before Income Taxes	414.8	312.8	264.8	187.5	143.7	121.2	91.0
Income Taxes	155.2	118.7	101.2	72.6	54.3	46.6	35.3
Equity Earnings/Minority Int.	d20.2	d20.0	d19.2	d16.4	d12.9	d13.5	d6.8
Net Income	239.4	174.1	144.4	98.5	76.5	61.2	48.9
Cash Flow	272.0	206.8	173.4	116.5	89.7	71.3	58.7
Average Shs. Outstg. (000)	129,200	129,952	128,073	123,884	114,200	115,500	122,460
BALANCE SHEET (IN MILLIONS):							
Cash & Cash Equivalents	358.5	283.8	200.4	114.6	81.4	60.0	73.9
Total Current Assets	480.1	384.5	287.2	187.8	137.3	106.7	117.0
Net Property	210.3	166.6	142.5	101.2	60.2	49.3	39.8
Total Assets	998.0	796.8	646.1	478.8	365.3	297.3	263.4
Total Current Liabilities	149.9	129.8	109.6	95.0	69.5	52.1	43.8
Long-Term Obligations	17.7	…	…	…	…	12.6	12.9
Net Stockholders' Equity	770.2	614.3	486.7	345.7	274.2	216.2	196.0
Net Working Capital	330.2	254.7	177.6	92.8	67.8	54.6	73.1
Year-end Shs. Outstg. (000)	120,108	120,183	118,195	115,146	114,660	114,276	116,380
STATISTICAL RECORD:							
Operating Profit Margin %	40.0	35.3	35.1	32.0	32.7	31.7	29.3
Net Profit Margin %	23.1	19.7	19.1	16.8	17.4	16.0	15.8
Return on Equity %	31.1	28.3	29.7	28.5	27.9	28.3	24.9
Return on Assets %	24.0	21.9	22.4	20.6	20.9	20.6	18.6
Debt/Total Assets %	1.8	…	…	…	…	4.2	4.9
Price Range	43¼-25⁷⁄₈	42⁷⁄₈-20⁷⁄₈	36⁷⁄₈-18¼	22¹³⁄₁₆-10¹¹⁄₁₆	14³⁄₁₆-6³⁄₄	9⁹⁄₁₆-6⁵⁄₁₆	8¼-5¹¹⁄₁₆
P/E Ratio	23.4-14.0	32.0-15.6	32.6-16.1	28.7-13.4	21.5-10.2	18.0-11.6	20.6-12.7
Average Yield %	1.2	1.1	0.9	1.3	1.5	1.7	1.6

Statistics are as originally reported. Adj. for 2-for-1 stock splits: 4/98, 12/96 & 11/93.

OFFICERS:
G. A. Roche, Chmn., Pres., C.F.O.
J. S. Riepe, Vice-Chmn.
M. D. Testa, Vice-Chmn.
J. P. Croteau, V.P., Treas., Contr.

INVESTOR CONTACT: Barbara A. Van Horn, Secretary, (410) 345-2000

PRINCIPAL OFFICE: 100 East Pratt Street, Baltimore, MD 21202

TELEPHONE NUMBER: (410) 345-2000
FAX: (410) 752-3477
WEB: www.troweprice.com

NO. OF EMPLOYEES: 3,700

SHAREHOLDERS: 3,600

ANNUAL MEETING: In Apr.

INCORPORATED: MD, Jan., 1947

INSTITUTIONAL HOLDINGS:
No. of Institutions: 234
Shares Held: 57,187,168
% Held: 47.8

INDUSTRY: Investment advice (SIC: 6282)

TRANSFER AGENT(S): Norwest Bank Minnesota, NA , South St. Paul, MN

TARGET CORPORATION

YIELD 0.6%
P/E RATIO 25.3

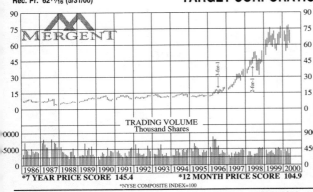

7 YEAR PRICE SCORE 145.4   **12 MONTH PRICE SCORE 104.9**
NYSE COMPOSITE INDEX=100

INTERIM EARNINGS (Per Share):

Qtr.	Apr.	July	Oct.	Jan.
1996-97	0.09	0.22	0.26	0.48
1997-98	0.28	0.31	0.40	0.76
1998-99	0.34	0.36	0.39	0.95
1999-00	0.41	0.49	0.52	1.06

INTERIM DIVIDENDS (Per Share):

Amt.	Decl.	Ex.	Rec.	Pay.
0.10Q	6/09/99	8/18/99	8/20/99	9/10/99
0.10Q	11/10/99	11/17/99	11/20/99	12/10/99
0.10Q	1/13/00	2/16/00	2/20/00	3/10/00
0.10Q	3/09/00	5/17/00	5/20/00	6/10/00
Indicated div.: $0.40 (Div. Reinv. Plan)				

CAPITALIZATION (1/29/00):

	($000)	(%)
Long-Term Debt	4,521,000	43.5
Common & Surplus	5,862,000	56.5
Total	10,383,000	100.0

DIVIDEND ACHIEVER STATUS:
Rank: 201   10-Year Growth Rate: 7.92%
Total Years of Dividend Growth: 28

RECENT DEVELOPMENTS: For the fiscal year ended 1/29/00, earnings of $1.19 billion, before an extraordinary charge, were up 23.2% compared with earnings of $962.0 million, before an extraordinary charge, the previous year. Total revenues rose 9.9% to $33.70 billion from $30.66 billion the year before. Comparable-store sales climbed 5.1% year-over-year, driven by a 6.7% comparable-store sales increase at Target stores. Revenues from Target stores increased 13.3% to $26.08 billion.

PROSPECTS: Going forward, revenue and earnings growth should be fueled by new store growth and by investments in e-commerce initiatives. During 2000, the Company anticipates opening approximately 80 new Target stores, concentrated primarily in the Mid-Atlantic and Northeast U.S. including locations in two new states, West Virginia and Connecticut. Also, TGT plans to essentially double the number of SuperTarget locations in 2000, by adding 15 new units.

BUSINESS

TARGET CORPORATION (formerly Dayton Hudson Corporation) is a diversified general merchandise retailer. As of 4/6/00, the Company operated 1,252 stores in 45 states including 921 Target stores, 267 Mervyn's stores and 64 Department Stores. Target is a national discount store chain offering low prices with stores selling hardlines and fashion softgoods; Mervyn's is a moderate-priced department store chain specializing in active and casual apparel and home softlines. The Department Store division operates three groups of full-service, full-line department stores under the names of Dayton's stores, Hudson's stores and Marshall Field Stores, offering moderate to better merchandise.

BUSINESS LINE ANALYSIS

(1/29/2000)	Rev(%)	Inc(%)
Target	78.4	80.2
Mervyn's	12.4	8.1
Department Stores	9.2	11.7
Total	100.0	100.0

ANNUAL FINANCIAL DATA

	1/29/00	1/30/99	1/31/98	2/3/97	2/3/96	1/28/95	1/29/94
Earnings Per Share	☐ 2.54	☐ 2.04	☐ 1.70	☐ 1.04	0.65	0.96	0.83
Cash Flow Per Share	4.38	3.73	3.22	2.57	2.09	2.27	2.06
Tang. Book Val. Per Share	12.86	11.41	9.55	8.11	7.28	6.75	6.34
Dividends Per Share	0.40	0.36	0.33	0.31	0.29	0.28	0.27
Dividend Payout %	15.7	17.6	19.4	29.6	44.6	29.2	32.0

INCOME STATEMENT (IN MILLIONS):

Total Revenues	33,702.0	30,951.0	27,757.0	25,371.0	23,516.0	21,311.0	19,233.0
Costs & Expenses	30,519.0	28,217.0	25,322.0	23,496.0	21,979.0	19,623.0	17,665.0
Depreciation & Amort.	854.0	780.0	693.0	650.0	594.0	548.0	515.0
Operating Income	2,329.0	1,954.0	1,742.0	1,225.0	943.0	1,140.0	1,053.0
Net Interest Inc./(Exp.)	d393.0	d398.0	d416.0	d442.0	d442.0	d426.0	d446.0
Income Before Income Taxes	1,936.0	1,556.0	1,326.0	783.0	501.0	714.0	607.0
Income Taxes	751.0	594.0	524.0	309.0	190.0	280.0	232.0
Net Income	☐ 1,185.0	☐ 962.0	☐ 802.0	☐ 474.0	311.0	434.0	375.0
Cash Flow	2,039.0	1,742.0	1,495.0	1,124.0	905.0	982.0	890.0
Average Shs. Outstg. (000)	465,700	467,300	463,700	437,400	433,600	432,000	432,000

BALANCE SHEET (IN MILLIONS):

Cash & Cash Equivalents	220.0	255.0	211.0	201.0	175.0	147.0	321.0
Total Current Assets	6,483.0	6,005.0	5,561.0	5,440.0	4,955.0	4,959.0	4,511.0
Net Property	9,899.0	8,969.0	8,125.0	7,467.0	7,294.0	6,385.0	5,947.0
Total Assets	17,143.0	15,666.0	14,191.0	13,389.0	12,570.0	11,697.0	10,778.0
Total Current Liabilities	5,850.0	5,057.0	4,556.0	4,111.0	3,523.0	3,390.0	3,075.0
Long-Term Obligations	4,521.0	4,452.0	4,425.0	4,808.0	4,959.0	4,488.0	4,279.0
Net Stockholders' Equity	5,862.0	5,311.0	4,460.0	3,790.0	3,403.0	3,193.0	2,737.0
Net Working Capital	633.0	948.0	1,005.0	1,329.0	1,432.0	1,569.0	1,436.0
Year-end Shs. Outstg. (000)	455,841	411,809	437,800	434,000	432,000	432,000	432,000

STATISTICAL RECORD:

Operating Profit Margin %	6.9	6.3	6.3	4.8	4.0	5.3	5.5
Net Profit Margin %	3.5	3.1	2.9	1.9	1.3	2.0	1.9
Return on Equity %	20.2	18.1	18.0	12.5	9.1	13.6	13.7
Return on Assets %	6.9	6.1	5.7	3.5	2.5	3.7	3.5
Debt/Total Assets %	26.4	28.4	31.2	35.9	39.5	38.4	39.7
Price Range	77-50¹/₁₆	54¹/₄-31⁷/₁₆	37-17¹⁵/₁₆	20⁵/₁₆-11¹/₂	13⁷/₁₆-10⁹/₁₆	14¹/₂-10³/₁₆	14³/₁₆-10⁷/₁₆
P/E Ratio	30.3-19.7	26.6-15.4	21.8-10.6	19.6-11.1	20.6-16.2	15.1-11.3	17.0-12.5
Average Yield %	0.6	0.8	1.2	1.9	2.4	2.2	2.2

Statistics are as originally reported. Adj. for 2-for-1 stk. split, 4/98 & 3-for-1 stk. split, 7/96. ☐ Bef. $41 mil ($0.09/sh) extraord. chg., 2000; $27 mil ($0.06/sh) extraord chg., 1999; $51 mil ($0.11/sh) extraord. chg. & incl. $45 mil pre-tax gain, 1998; bef. $11 mil extraord. chg. & incl. $134 mil pre-tax chg., 1997.

OFFICERS:
R. J. Ulrich, Chmn., C.E.O.
K. B. Woodrow, Vice-Chmn.
D. A. Scovanner, Exec. V.P., C.F.O.
J. T. Hale, Sr. V.P., Gen. Couns., Sec.

INVESTOR CONTACT: S. D. Kahn, V.P.-Invest. Rel., (612) 370-6736

PRINCIPAL OFFICE: 777 Nicollet Mall, Minneapolis, MN 55402-2055

TELEPHONE NUMBER: (612) 370-6948
FAX: (612) 370-5502
WEB: www.targetcorp.com

NO. OF EMPLOYEES: 281,000 (avg.)

SHAREHOLDERS: 13,883

ANNUAL MEETING: In May

INCORPORATED: MN, 1902

INSTITUTIONAL HOLDINGS:
No. of Institutions: 575
Shares Held: 360,240,517
% Held: 82.2

INDUSTRY: Variety stores (SIC: 5331)

TRANSFER AGENT(S): First Chicago Trust Company of New York, Jersey City, NJ

TECO ENERGY INC.

YIELD 6.3%
P/E RATIO 14.3

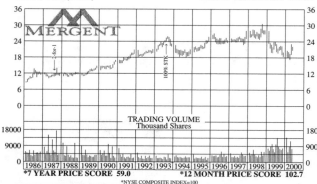

INTERIM EARNINGS (Per Share):

Qtr.	Mar.	June	Sept.	Dec.
1996	0.36	0.41	0.56	0.38
1997	0.37	0.39	0.51	0.31
1998	0.23	0.44	0.54	0.31
1999	0.37	0.39	0.42	0.32

INTERIM DIVIDENDS (Per Share):

Amt.	Decl.	Ex.	Rec.	Pay.
0.325Q	4/21/99	4/28/99	4/30/99	5/15/99
0.325Q	7/21/99	7/28/99	7/30/99	8/15/99
0.325Q	10/22/99	10/28/99	11/01/99	11/15/99
0.325Q	1/19/00	1/28/00	2/01/00	2/15/00
0.335Q	4/19/00	4/27/00	5/01/00	5/15/00

Indicated div.: $1.34 (Div. Reinv. Plan)

CAPITALIZATION (12/31/99):

	($000)	(%)
Long-Term Debt	1,207,800	38.5
Deferred Income Tax	509,400	16.2
Common & Surplus	1,417,800	45.2
Total	3,135,000	100.0

TRADING VOLUME
Thousand Shares

| 1986 | 1987 | 1988 | 1989 | 1990 | 1991 | 1992 | 1993 | 1994 | 1995 | 1996 | 1997 | 1998 | 1999 | 2000 |

*7 YEAR PRICE SCORE 59.0   *12 MONTH PRICE SCORE 102.7

*NYSE COMPOSITE INDEX=100

DIVIDEND ACHIEVER STATUS:
Rank: 254   10-Year Growth Rate: 5.57%
Total Years of Dividend Growth: 40

RECENT DEVELOPMENTS: For the year ended 12/31/99, income from continuing operations declined 1.6% to $200.9 million versus income from continuing operations of $204.2 million in 1998. Results for 1999 included nonrecurring charges of $19.6 million and excluded a loss of $14.8 million from discontinued operations. The 1998 results included nonrecurring charges of $19.6 million and excluded a net gain of $2.3 million from discontinued operations. Revenues improved 1.4% to $1.98 billion.

PROSPECTS: Tampa Electric and Peoples Gas should experience 2.5% sales growth and 4.0% customer growth in 2000. As a result of upcoming and existing projects, TECO Power Services is expected to double its 1999 annual earnings contributions in 2000. Although continued weakness in the export coal market is anticipated, TECO Transport is expected to grow 7.0% in 2000. The Company's objective for 2000 is to achieve earnings per share growth of 7.0%.

BUSINESS

TECO ENERGY, INC. is a diversified, energy-related holding company. Tampa Electric, which accounts for the majority of net income for TE, generates, purchases, transmits, distributes and sells electric energy to West Central Florida. The Peoples Gas System division purchases, distributes and markets natural gas for residential, commercial, industrial and electric power generation customers in Florida. TECO Transport Corp. transports, stores and transfers coal and other bulk dry commodities. TECO Coal Corp. owns mineral rights, owns or operates surface and underground mines, coal processing and loading facilities in Kentucky, Tennessee and Virginia. TECO Power Services Corp. is a wholesale power supplier that owns and operates independent power projects. TECO Coalbed Methane, Inc. produces natural gas from coalbeds. TECO Gas Services, Inc. provides gas management and marketing services. Bosek, Gibson and Associates, Inc. offer engineering and marketing services.

ANNUAL FINANCIAL DATA

	12/31/99	12/31/98	12/31/97	12/31/96	12/31/95	12/31/94	12/31/93
Earnings Per Share	③④ 1.53	②③ 1.52	③ 1.61	1.71	1.60	② 1.32	① 1.30
Cash Flow Per Share	3.37	3.31	3.37	3.34	3.14	2.87	2.77
Tang. Book Val. Per Share	11.19	11.42	11.04	10.73	10.00	8.65	8.89
Dividends Per Share	1.28	1.23	1.17	1.10	1.05	1.00	0.95
Dividend Payout %	84.0	80.6	72.4	64.6	65.5	75.6	72.9

INCOME STATEMENT (IN MILLIONS):

Total Revenues	1,983.0	1,958.1	1,862.3	1,473.0	1,392.3	1,350.9	1,283.9
Costs & Expenses	1,192.8	1,197.6	1,104.2	847.3	793.7	800.3	725.0
Depreciation & Amort.	241.3	236.1	231.3	190.6	179.6	179.7	169.5
Maintenance Exp.	125.3	128.9	114.2	92.2	101.3	101.1	98.9
Operating Income	423.6	395.5	412.6	342.9	317.7	269.8	290.5
Net Interest Inc./(Exp.)	d123.7	d104.3	d105.8	d86.9	d83.2	d77.1	d76.1
Income Taxes	87.0	81.0	94.7	71.4	59.1	45.8	55.0
Net Income	③④ 200.9	②③ 200.4	③ 211.4	200.7	186.1	② 153.2	① 150.3
Cash Flow	442.2	436.5	442.7	391.3	365.7	332.9	319.9
Average Shs. Outstg. (000)	131,200	131,700	131,200	117,200	116,500	115,923	115,340

BALANCE SHEET (IN MILLIONS):

Gross Property	6,064.4	5,600.5	5,359.5	4,721.6	4,490.5	4,095.7	3,846.1
Accumulated Depreciation	2,436.6	2,292.9	2,123.0	1,765.0	1,616.2	1,475.5	1,363.1
Net Property	3,627.8	3,307.6	3,236.5	2,956.6	2,874.3	2,620.3	2,483.0
Total Assets	4,690.1	4,179.3	3,960.4	3,560.7	3,473.4	3,312.2	3,127.8
Long-Term Obligations	1,207.8	1,279.6	1,080.2	996.3	994.9	1,023.9	1,043.2
Net Stockholders' Equity	1,417.8	1,507.8	1,444.7	1,282.1	1,221.7	1,060.1	1,082.5
Year-end Shs. Outstg. (000)	126,700	132,000	130,900	117,600	116,700	116,199	115,621

STATISTICAL RECORD:

Operating Profit Margin %	21.4	20.2	22.2	23.3	22.8	20.0	22.6
Net Profit Margin %	10.1	10.2	11.4	13.6	13.4	11.3	11.7
Net Inc./Net Property %	5.5	6.1	6.5	6.8	6.5	5.8	6.1
Net Inc./Tot. Capital %	6.4	6.1	7.1	7.4	7.1	6.2	6.0
Return on Equity %	14.2	13.3	14.6	15.7	15.2	14.4	13.9
Accum. Depr./Gross Prop. %	40.2	40.9	39.6	37.4	36.0	36.0	35.4
Price Range	28-18⅜	30⅝-24¾	28-22¾	27-23	25¾-20	22⅝-18⅛	25⅞-20³/₁₆
P/E Ratio	18.3-12.0	20.1-16.3	17.4-14.1	15.8-13.4	16.1-12.5	17.1-13.7	19.9-15.5
Average Yield %	5.5	4.4	4.6	4.4	4.6	4.9	4.1

Statistics are as originally reported. Adj. for stk. splits: 2-for-1, 8/93 ① Bef. acctg. credit $11.2 mill. ($0.10/sh.) ② Incl. non-recurr. chrg. $16.1 mill., 1999; $25.9 mill., 1998; $25.0 mill. ($0.13/sh.), 1994 ③ Bef. disc. oper. loss $14.8 mill., 1999; gain $6.1 mill., 1998; loss $9.5 mill. ($0.07/sh.), 1997 ④ Incl. after-tax nonrecurr. chrgs. of $19.6 mill. ($0.15/sh.)

OFFICERS:
R. D. Fagan, Chmn., Pres., C.E.O.
G. L. Gillette, V.P., Fin., C.F.O.
S. M. McDevitt, V.P., Gen. Couns.

INVESTOR CONTACT: Mark H. Tubb, Investor Relations, (800) 810-2032

PRINCIPAL OFFICE: Teco Plaza, 702 N. Franklin Street, Tampa, FL 33602

TELEPHONE NUMBER: (813) 228-4111
FAX: (813) 228-1670
WEB: www.tecoenergy.com

NO. OF EMPLOYEES: 5,487

SHAREHOLDERS: 26,031 (approx.)

ANNUAL MEETING: In April

INCORPORATED: FL, Jan., 1981

INSTITUTIONAL HOLDINGS:
No. of Institutions: 243
Shares Held: 50,415,238
% Held: 38.9

INDUSTRY: Electric services (SIC: 4911)

TRANSFER AGENT(S): BankBoston, N.A., Boston, MA

TELEFLEX INC.

YIELD	1.7%
P/E RATIO	13.8

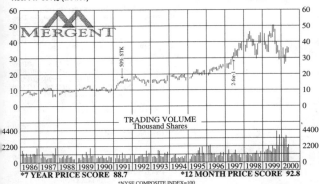

INTERIM EARNINGS (Per Share):

Qtr.	Mar.	June	Sept.	Dec.
1996	0.42	0.42	0.28	0.47
1997	0.45	0.49	0.36	0.56
1998	0.52	0.55	0.42	0.66
1999	0.60	0.67	0.49	0.71

INTERIM DIVIDENDS (Per Share):

Amt.	Decl.	Ex.	Rec.	Pay.
0.13Q	4/30/99	5/21/99	5/25/99	6/15/99
0.13Q	8/02/99	8/23/99	8/25/99	9/15/99
0.13Q	11/01/99	11/22/99	11/25/99	12/15/99
0.13Q	1/31/00	2/23/00	2/25/00	3/15/00
0.15Q	4/28/00	5/23/00	5/25/00	6/15/00

Indicated div.: $0.60 (Div. Reinv. Plan)

CAPITALIZATION (12/26/99):

	($000)	(%)
Long-Term Debt	246,191	29.0
Common & Surplus	602,564	71.0
Total	848,755	100.0

DIVIDEND ACHIEVER STATUS:
Rank: 102   10-Year Growth Rate: 12.66%
Total Years of Dividend Growth: 22

TRADING VOLUME
Thousand Shares

*7 YEAR PRICE SCORE 88.7   ***12 MONTH PRICE SCORE 92.8**
*NYSE COMPOSITE INDEX=100

RECENT DEVELOPMENTS: For the year ended 12/26/99, net income climbed 15.3% to $95.2 million versus $82.6 million in 1998. Revenues rose 11.4% to $1.60 billion from $1.44 billion in the prior year. Sales in the commercial products business segment grew 18.2% to $199.9 million, while sales in the medical products business segment climbed 8.8% to $97.9 million. Operating profit was $178.3 million, up 12.1% from $159.1 million the year before.

PROSPECTS: Telair International, a subsidiary of TFX, agreed to acquire Air Cargo Equipment Corporation. The acquisition should enhance Telair's container and narrow-body cargo systems product lines. The transaction is expected to close by the end of June 2000. Meanwhile, the Company acquired GFI Control Systems, Inc. TFX previously invested $8.7 million for a 50.0% interest in GFI and then purchased the remaining portion for $8.7 million.

BUSINESS

TELEFLEX INC. operates in three segments. Commercial Products (47.3% of 1999 sales and 42.5% of operating profit) designs and manufactures proprietary mechanical controls for the automotive market; mechanical, electrical and hydraulic controls, and electronics for the pleasure marine market; and proprietary products for fluid transfer and industrial applications. Medical Products (23.3%, 27.8%) manufactures and distributes a broad range of invasive disposable and reusable devices worldwide. Aerospace Products (29.4%, 29.7%) serves the aerospace and turbine engine markets. Its businesses design and manufacture precision controls and cargo systems for aviation; provide coating and repair services and manufactured components for users of both flight and land-based turbine engines.

ANNUAL FINANCIAL DATA

	12/26/99	12/27/98	12/28/97	12/29/96	12/31/95	12/25/94	12/26/93
Earnings Per Share	2.47	2.15	1.86	1.58	1.38	1.18	0.98
Cash Flow Per Share	4.22	3.71	3.13	2.65	2.43	2.12	1.79
Tang. Book Val. Per Share	15.85	14.21	12.49	11.30	10.28	8.94	7.90
Dividends Per Share	0.51	0.45	0.39	0.34	0.30	0.26	0.23
Dividend Payout %	20.6	20.7	20.8	21.5	21.8	22.1	23.1
INCOME STATEMENT (IN MILLIONS):							
Total Revenues	1,601.1	1,437.6	1,145.8	931.2	912.7	812.7	666.8
Costs & Expenses	1,373.2	1,235.7	977.0	791.8	782.7	698.3	571.9
Depreciation & Amort.	67.4	60.1	47.9	38.8	37.7	33.0	28.1
Operating Income	160.5	141.8	120.8	100.7	92.2	81.4	66.8
Net Interest Inc./(Exp.)	d17.7	d17.1	d14.4	d13.9	d18.6	d18.4	d14.5
Income Before Income Taxes	142.8	124.8	106.4	86.8	73.6	63.0	52.3
Income Taxes	47.5	42.2	36.3	29.6	24.7	21.8	18.6
Net Income	95.2	82.6	70.1	57.2	48.9	41.2	33.7
Cash Flow	162.6	142.7	118.0	95.9	86.6	74.2	61.8
Average Shs. Outstg. (000)	38,525	38,425	37,661	36,198	35,574	35,060	34,534
BALANCE SHEET (IN MILLIONS):							
Cash & Cash Equivalents	29.0	66.7	30.7	68.6	55.7	24.1	11.3
Total Current Assets	604.9	616.9	566.5	466.0	445.8	390.2	322.2
Net Property	465.9	431.8	364.0	291.8	271.8	264.3	261.4
Total Assets	1,263.4	1,215.9	1,079.2	857.9	785.2	710.8	640.6
Total Current Liabilities	329.4	311.5	294.9	196.7	193.2	169.7	150.9
Long-Term Obligations	246.2	275.6	237.6	195.9	196.8	190.5	183.5
Net Stockholders' Equity	602.6	534.5	463.8	409.2	355.4	309.0	269.8
Net Working Capital	275.5	305.5	271.6	269.4	252.7	220.5	171.4
Year-end Shs. Outstg. (000)	38,019	37,615	37,118	36,222	34,554	34,554	34,168
STATISTICAL RECORD:							
Operating Profit Margin %	10.0	9.9	10.5	10.8	10.1	10.0	10.0
Net Profit Margin %	5.9	5.7	6.1	6.1	5.4	5.1	5.1
Return on Equity %	15.8	15.4	15.1	14.0	13.8	13.3	12.5
Return on Assets %	7.5	6.8	6.5	6.7	6.2	5.8	5.3
Debt/Total Assets %	19.5	22.7	22.0	22.8	25.1	26.8	28.6
Price Range	50⁷/₁₆-28⁷/₈	46³/₈-29¹/₂	39³/₄-23³/₁₆	26¹/₄-18¹⁵/₁₆	22⁷/₈-17³/₁₆	20¹/₈-15⁷/₈	19¹/₈-13⁷/₈
P/E Ratio	20.4-11.7	21.6-13.7	21.4-12.5	16.5-12.0	16.6-12.5	17.1-13.5	19.6-14.2
Average Yield %	1.3	1.2	1.2	1.5	1.5	1.4	1.4

Statistics are as originally reported. Adj. for 2-for-1 split, 6/97.

OFFICERS:
L. K. Black, Chmn., C.E.O.
H. L. Zuber Jr., V.P., C.F.O.
T. M. Byrne, Asst. Treas.

INVESTOR CONTACT: Janine Dusossoit,
V.P., Investor Relations, (610) 834-6301

PRINCIPAL OFFICE: 630 W. Germantown Pike, Ste. 450, Plymouth Meeting, PA 19462

TELEPHONE NUMBER: (610) 834-6301
FAX: (610) 834-8228
WEB: www.teleflex.com

NO. OF EMPLOYEES: 14,700 (approx.)

SHAREHOLDERS: 1,300 (approx.)

ANNUAL MEETING: In Apr.

INCORPORATED: DE, Jun., 1943

INSTITUTIONAL HOLDINGS:
No. of Institutions: 166
Shares Held: 21,468,713
% Held: 56.5

INDUSTRY: Surgical and medical instruments (SIC: 3841)

TRANSFER AGENT(S): American Stock Transfer & Trust Company, New York, NY.

TELEPHONE AND DATA SYSTEMS, INC.

YIELD 0.5%
P/E RATIO 25.7

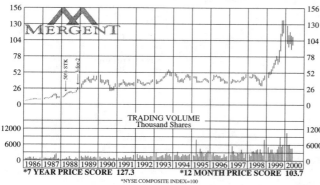

*7 YEAR PRICE SCORE 127.3

*12 MONTH PRICE SCORE 103.7

*NYSE COMPOSITE INDEX=100

INTERIM EARNINGS (Per Share):

Qtr.	Mar.	June	Sept.	Dec.
1997	0.15	0.11	0.14	d0.59
1998	1.20	d0.23	0.10	d0.05
1999	1.06	2.93	0.85	0.18

INTERIM DIVIDENDS (Per Share):

Amt.	Decl.	Ex.	Rec.	Pay.
0.115Q	5/24/99	6/11/99	6/15/99	6/30/99
0.115Q	8/24/99	9/13/99	9/15/99	9/30/99
0.115Q	11/05/99	12/13/99	12/15/99	12/31/99
0.125Q	2/25/00	3/13/00	3/15/00	3/31/00
0.125Q	5/24/00	6/13/00	6/15/00	6/30/00

Indicated div.: $0.50 (Div. Reinv. Plan)

CAPITALIZATION (12/31/99):

	($000)	(%)
Long-Term Debt	1,279,877	25.8
Deferred Income Tax	382,468	7.7
Minority Interest	509,658	10.3
Preferred Stock	309,005	6.2
Common & Surplus	2,483,101	50.0
Total	4,964,109	100.0

DIVIDEND ACHIEVER STATUS:

Rank: 246   10-Year Growth Rate: 5.87%
Total Years of Dividend Growth: 25

RECENT DEVELOPMENTS: For the year ended 12/31/99, income from continuing operations was $314.2 million compared with income from continuing operations of $201.4 million in 1998. Results included gains of $345.9 million in 1999 and $262.7 million in 1998 on the sale of of cellular and other investments. Revenues improved 18.9% to $1.96 billion from $1.65 billion the year before. U.S. Cellular operating revenues rose 21.9% to $1.42 billion,

while TDS Telecom operating revenues increased 11.8% to $545.9 million. Operating income advanced 43.0% to $370.4 million from $259.1 million in 1998. On 5/5/00, TDS announced the completion of the acquisition of VoiceStream Wireless Corporation and Aerial Communications. TDS acquired 35.6 million shares of VoiceStream common stock, becoming VoiceStream's second largest shareholder.

BUSINESS

TELEPHONE AND DATA SYSTEMS, INC. is a diversified telecommunications service company with local telephone, cellular telephone and personal communications service (PCS) operations. Local telephone operations are conducted through the Company's wholly-owned subsidiary, TDS Telecommunications Corporation, which operates 104 telephone subsidiaries serving 547,500 access lines in 28 states. Cellular operations are conducted through the Company's 80.7%-owned subsidiary, United States Cellular Corp., which provides cellular service to 2.6 million customers through 139 majority-owned and managed cellular systems. As of 12/31/99, telephone operations provided 27.8% of revenues and cellular operations 72.2%.

REVENUES

(12/31/99)	($000)	(%)
U.S. Cellular	1,417,181	72.2
TDS Telecom	545,917	27.8
Total	1,963,098	100.0

ANNUAL FINANCIAL DATA

	12/31/99	12/31/98	12/31/97	12/31/96	12/31/95	12/31/94	12/31/93
Earnings Per Share	☑5.02	1.03	☐d0.19	☑2.08	1.74	1.07	0.67
Cash Flow Per Share	10.62	7.74	4.82	5.89	5.19	4.07	3.36
Tang. Book Val. Per Share	39.81	36.58	32.49	33.23	32.94	30.73	24.15
Dividends Per Share	0.46	0.44	0.42	0.40	0.38	0.36	0.34
Dividend Payout %	9.2	42.7	...	19.2	21.8	33.6	50.7
INCOME STATEMENT (IN MILLIONS):							
Total Revenues	1,963.1	1,805.7	1,471.5	1,214.6	954.4	730.8	590.7
Costs & Expenses	1,239.4	1,417.2	1,173.7	829.0	621.3	460.2	393.5
Depreciation & Amort.	353.3	409.5	301.6	231.6	201.1	161.8	127.5
Operating Income	370.4	d20.9	d3.7	154.1	132.0	108.8	69.7
Net Interest Inc./(Exp.)	d104.2	d126.8	d76.1	d27.3	d37.8	d30.6	d29.4
Income Before Income Taxes	542.3	133.7	19.0	251.8	185.0	101.3	60.4
Income Taxes	228.2	69.3	28.6	123.6	81.0	40.7	26.5
Net Income	☑314.2	64.4	☐d9.5	☐128.1	104.0	60.5	33.9
Cash Flow	666.3	472.2	290.1	357.9	303.1	220.5	159.0
Average Shs. Outstg. (000)	62,736	60,982	60,211	60,732	58,356	54,197	47,266
BALANCE SHEET (IN MILLIONS):							
Cash & Cash Equivalents	116.0	60.4	75.6	119.3	80.9	44.6	73.4
Total Current Assets	508.0	405.4	408.3	346.1	256.1	185.9	179.6
Net Property	2,095.9	2,672.6	2,465.7	1,828.9	2,471.8	2,153.6	1,738.3
Total Assets	5,375.8	5,527.5	4,971.6	4,201.0	3,469.1	2,790.1	2,259.2
Total Current Liabilities	369.7	623.4	905.9	509.3	427.7	346.2	163.5
Long-Term Obligations	1,279.9	1,553.1	1,264.2	982.2	858.9	536.5	514.4
Net Stockholders' Equity	2,792.1	2,237.9	1,968.1	2,032.9	1,684.5	1,473.0	1,224.3
Net Working Capital	138.3	d217.9	d497.6	d163.2	d171.6	d160.3	16.0
Year-end Shs. Outstg. (000)	62,370	61,177	60,871	61,154	51,137	47,938	50,689
STATISTICAL RECORD:							
Operating Profit Margin %	18.9	...	...	12.7	13.8	14.9	11.8
Net Profit Margin %	16.0	3.6	...	10.5	10.9	8.3	5.7
Return on Equity %	11.3	2.9	...	6.3	6.2	4.1	2.8
Return on Assets %	5.8	1.2	...	3.1	3.0	2.2	1.5
Debt/Total Assets %	23.8	28.1	25.4	23.4	24.8	19.2	22.8
Price Range	137-44⅛	50⅛-30⅝	49¹⁵/₁₆-34½	48⅞-34¾	46⅜-35⅝	51½-35½	57-33¼
P/E Ratio	27.3-8.8	48.7-29.7	...	23.5-16.7	26.7-20.5	48.1-33.2	85.1-49.6
Average Yield %	0.5	1.1	1.0	1.0	0.9	0.8	0.8

Statistics are as originally reported. ☐ Incls. non-recurr. credit 12/31/97: $41.4 mill.; credit 12/31/96: $138.7 mill.; ☑ Bef. disc. oper. loss of $142.3 mill. & incl. gain of $345.9 mill.

OFFICERS:
L. T. Carlson, Chmn.
L. T. Carlson Jr., Pres., C.E.O.
S. L. Helton, Exec. V.P., C.F.O.
P. L. Sereda, Treas., V.P.

INVESTOR CONTACT: M. Steinkrauss, V.P., Corp. Rel., (312) 630-1900

PRINCIPAL OFFICE: 30 North Lasalle Street, Chicago, IL 60602

TELEPHONE NUMBER: (312) 630-1900
FAX: (312) 630-1908
WEB: www.teldta.com

NO. OF EMPLOYEES: 10,150

SHAREHOLDERS: 2,742

ANNUAL MEETING: In May

INCORPORATED: IA, Mar., 1968; reincorp., DE, May, 1998

INSTITUTIONAL HOLDINGS:
No. of Institutions: 231
Shares Held: 40,224,929
% Held: 73.4

INDUSTRY: Radiotelephone communications (SIC: 4812)

TRANSFER AGENT(S): Harris Trust and Savings Bank, Chicago, IL

TENNANT COMPANY

YIELD 2.1%
P/E RATIO 16.5

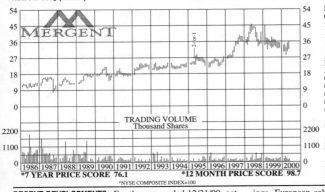

*7 YEAR PRICE SCORE 76.1 *12 MONTH PRICE SCORE 98.7

*NYSE COMPOSITE INDEX=100

INTERIM EARNINGS (Per Share):

Qtr.	Mar.	June	Sept.	Dec.
1995	0.39	0.53	0.47	0.59
1996	0.40	0.51	0.50	0.69
1997	0.44	0.64	0.60	0.75
1998	0.54	0.70	0.67	0.76
1999	0.53	0.66	0.35	0.61

INTERIM DIVIDENDS (Per Share):

Amt.	Decl.	Ex.	Rec.	Pay.
0.19Q	5/06/99	5/27/99	6/01/99	6/15/99
0.19Q	8/12/99	8/30/99	9/01/99	9/15/99
0.19Q	11/18/99	12/14/99	12/16/99	12/31/99
0.19Q	2/25/00	3/02/00	3/06/00	3/15/00
0.19Q	5/04/00	5/30/00	6/01/00	6/15/00

Indicated div.: $0.76 (Div. Reinv. Plan)

CAPITALIZATION (12/31/99):

	($000)	(%)
Long-Term Debt	16,003	10.5
Common & Surplus	135,915	89.5
Total	151,918	100.0

DIVIDEND ACHIEVER STATUS:
Rank: 295   10-Year Growth Rate: 3.29%
Total Years of Dividend Growth: 27

RECENT DEVELOPMENTS: For the year ended 12/31/99, net earnings decreased 22.2% to $19.7 million compared with $25.3 million in the prior year. Earnings for 1999 included restructuring charges of $6.7 million. Net sales grew 10.3% to $429.4 million from $389.4 million in the previous year. North American sales increased 6.1% to $311.7 million, driven by growth in the industrial and commercial equipment segments, partially offset by a decrease in floor coat-

ings. European sales climbed 35.0% to $82.2 million primarily due to the January 1999 acquisition of Paul Andra KG. Gross profit was $174.0 million, or 40.5% of sales, versus $163.2 million, or 41.9% of sales, the year before. Profit from operations declined 16.3% to $31.3 million from $37.3 million in the prior-year period, reflecting manufacturing inefficiencies and shipping delays related to closing facilities.

BUSINESS

TENNANT COMPANY specializes in the design, manufacture, and sale of non-residential floor maintenance equipment and related products. The equipment manufactured consisting mainly of motorized cleaning equipment and related products, including floor cleaning and preservation products, and are sold through a direct sales organization and independent distributors in more than 40 countries throughout the world. The Company has manufacturing operations in Holland, Michigan; Uden, The Netherlands; and Waldhausen, Germany. In January 1999, the Company acquired the business and assets of Paul Andra KG, a privately owned manufacturer of commercial floor maintenance equipment in Germany. Products are sold

QUARTERLY DATA

(12/31/1999)	REV(000)	INC(000)
First quarter	99,715	4,886
Second quarter	106,410	5,984
Third quarter	104,287	3,155
Fourth quarter	118,995	5,668

ANNUAL FINANCIAL DATA

	12/31/99	12/31/98	12/31/97	12/31/96	12/31/95	12/31/94	12/31/93
Earnings Per Share	① 2.15	2.67	2.41	2.10	1.98	1.60	① 0.93
Cash Flow Per Share	4.20	4.51	4.15	3.73	3.40	2.94	2.04
Tang. Book Val. Per Share	13.06	12.68	12.12	10.57	8.86	10.10	8.01
Dividends Per Share	0.76	0.74	0.72	0.69	0.68	0.65	0.64
Dividend Payout %	35.3	27.7	29.9	32.9	34.3	40.6	68.8
INCOME STATEMENT (IN THOUSANDS):							
Total Revenues	429,407	389,388	372,428	344,433	325,368	281,685	221,002
Costs & Expenses	379,478	334,489	318,872	296,415	281,096	244,440	198,682
Depreciation & Amort.	18,667	17,550	17,468	16,387	14,090	13,121	10,987
Operating Income	31,262	37,349	36,088	31,631	30,182	24,124	① 11,333
Net Interest Inc./(Exp.)	d1,097	1,479	2,678	1,768	1,492	2,130	3,074
Income Before Income Taxes	30,586	39,092	37,630	32,329	29,435	24,081	12,928
Income Taxes	10,893	13,767	13,425	11,302	9,773	8,346	3,802
Net Income	① 19,693	25,325	24,205	21,027	19,662	15,735	① 9,126
Cash Flow	38,360	42,875	41,673	37,414	33,752	28,856	20,113
Average Shs. Outstg.	9,140	9,500	10,032	10,021	9,916	9,826	9,836
BALANCE SHEET (IN THOUSANDS):							
Cash & Cash Equivalents	14,928	17,693	16,279	9,881	4,247	1,851	2,675
Total Current Assets	165,093	150,868	143,105	126,481	123,508	98,810	73,752
Net Property	66,306	66,640	65,111	65,384	63,724	56,552	46,622
Total Assets	257,533	239,098	233,870	219,180	215,750	182,834	128,634
Total Current Liabilities	74,999	60,809	56,115	49,588	61,723	66,065	30,847
Long-Term Obligations	16,003	23,038	20,678	21,824	23,149	6,300	1,103
Net Stockholders' Equity	135,915	131,267	134,086	128,860	114,131	96,249	84,093
Net Working Capital	90,094	90,059	86,990	76,893	61,785	32,745	42,905
Year-end Shs. Outstg.	8,989	9,123	9,699	9,965	9,952	9,839	9,826
STATISTICAL RECORD:							
Operating Profit Margin %	7.3	9.6	9.7	9.2	9.3	8.6	5.1
Net Profit Margin %	4.6	6.5	6.5	6.1	6.0	5.6	4.1
Return on Equity %	14.5	19.3	18.1	16.3	17.2	16.3	10.9
Return on Assets %	7.6	10.6	10.3	9.6	9.1	8.6	7.1
Debt/Total Assets %	6.2	9.6	8.8	10.0	10.7	3.4	0.9
Price Range	45-31⁷/₁₆	45³/₄-33	39⅝-26⅛	27½-21¼	29-22¼	24¼-20½	24¼-19¾
P/E Ratio	20.9-14.6	17.1-12.4	16.4-10.8	13.1-10.1	14.6-11.2	15.2-12.8	26.1-21.2
Average Yield %	2.0	1.9	2.2	2.8	2.7	2.9	2.9

Statistics are as originally reported. Adj. for stk. split: 2-for-1, 4/26/95 ① Incl. non-recurr. chrg. $6.7 mill, 12/99; $4.1 mill., 12/93

TOOTSIE ROLL INDUSTRIES, INC.

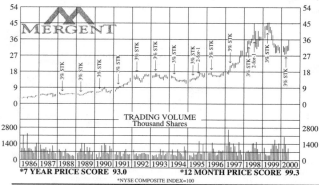

TRADING VOLUME
Thousand Shares

| 1986 | 1987 | 1988 | 1989 | 1990 | 1991 | 1992 | 1993 | 1994 | 1995 | 1996 | 1997 | 1998 | 1999 | 2000 |

*7 YEAR PRICE SCORE 93.0   *12 MONTH PRICE SCORE 99.3
*NYSE COMPOSITE INDEX=100

INTERIM EARNINGS (Per Share):

Qtr.	Mar.	June	Sept.	Dec.
1996	0.17	0.18	0.38	0.20
1997	0.18	0.24	0.49	0.27
1998	0.22	0.15	0.53	0.30
1999	0.24	0.29	0.58	0.30

INTERIM DIVIDENDS (Per Share):

Amt.	Decl.	Ex.	Rec.	Pay.
0.063Q	9/13/99	9/29/99	10/01/99	10/12/99
0.063Q	12/07/99	12/16/99	12/20/99	1/07/00
0.063Q	2/21/00	3/03/00	3/07/00	4/06/00
3% STK	2/21/00	3/03/00	3/07/00	4/19/00
0.07Q	5/30/00	6/15/00	6/19/00	7/10/00

Indicated div.: $0.28

CAPITALIZATION (12/31/99):

	($000)	(%)
Long-Term Debt	7,500	1.7
Deferred Income Tax	9,520	2.1
Common & Surplus	430,646	96.2
Total	447,666	100.0

DIVIDEND ACHIEVER STATUS:
Rank: 31   10-Year Growth Rate: 18.32%
Total Years of Dividend Growth: 36

RECENT DEVELOPMENTS: For the year ended 12/31/99, net earnings increased 5.6% to $71.3 million from $67.5 million in the previous year. Net sales inched up 2.1% to $396.8 million from $388.7 million due to promotional programs, line extensions, new products and seasonal packs. Gross margin climbed 1.6% to $204.2 million. Earnings from operations rose 3.2% to $104.5 million.

PROSPECTS: On 5/15/00, TR acquired the assets of Andes Candies, Inc., from Brach's Confections, Inc. Andes is a chocolatey mint known for its green creme de menthe center layer. TR expects this strong brand to contribute to its long-term success. Going forward, TR plans to increase revenues by expanding the sales of existing products, introducing new products and product line extensions.

BUSINESS

TOOTSIE ROLL INDUSTRIES, INC. is engaged in the manufacture and sale of candy. Major products include: TOOTSIE ROLL, TOOTSIE ROLL POPS, CHILDS PLAY, CARAMEL APPLE POPS, CHARMS, BLOW-POP and BLUE RAZZ. Other candy products include CELLAS, MASON DOTS, JUNIOR MINTS, CHARLESTON CHEW, SUGAR DADDY, SUGAR BABIES and ANDES. In September 1988, TR acquired Charms Co. for approximately $65.0 million. The Company has manufacturing facilities in Chicago, New York, Covington, Tennessee and Mexico City. TR celebrated its 100th anniversary in 1996.

GEOGRAPHIC DATA

(12/31/99)	($000)	(%)
United States	365,975	92.2
Mexico & Canada	30,775	7.8
Total	396,750	100.0

ANNUAL FINANCIAL DATA

	12/31/99	12/31/98	12/31/97	12/31/96	12/31/95	12/31/94	12/31/93
Earnings Per Share	1.42	1.33	1.19	0.91	0.78	0.74	0.70
Cash Flow Per Share	1.61	1.58	1.43	1.15	1.00	0.94	0.88
Tang. Book Val. Per Share	6.92	6.08	5.13	4.27	3.50	2.82	2.21
Dividends Per Share	0.22	0.17	0.14	0.12	0.10	0.08	0.07
Dividend Payout %	15.5	13.1	11.8	12.9	12.8	11.5	9.7
INCOME STATEMENT (IN THOUSANDS):							
Total Revenues	396,750	388,659	375,594	340,909	312,660	296,932	259,593
Costs & Expenses	282,252	274,587	272,688	257,309	240,463	226,466	197,262
Depreciation & Amort.	9,979	12,807	12,819	12,068	10,794	10,478	8,814
Operating Income	104,519	101,265	90,087	71,532	61,403	59,988	53,517
Net Interest Inc./(Exp.)	...	...	...	2,389	1,646	d361	1,333
Income Before Income Taxes	111,447	106,063	95,361	75,098	64,038	61,167	57,710
Income Taxes	40,137	38,537	34,679	27,891	23,670	23,236	22,268
Net Income	71,310	67,526	60,682	47,207	40,368	37,931	35,442
Cash Flow	81,289	80,333	73,501	59,275	51,162	48,409	44,256
Average Shs. Outstg.	50,443	50,966	51,217	51,392	51,392	51,392	50,268
BALANCE SHEET (IN THOUSANDS):							
Cash & Cash Equivalents	159,506	163,920	142,280	144,157	103,450	62,370	56,203
Total Current Assets	224,532	228,539	206,961	201,513	164,949	118,887	111,914
Net Property	95,897	83,024	78,364	81,687	81,999	85,648	86,699
Total Assets	529,416	487,423	436,742	391,456	353,816	310,083	303,940
Total Current Liabilities	56,109	53,384	53,606	48,184	55,306	26,261	50,862
Long-Term Obligations	7,500	7,500	7,500	7,500	7,500	27,500	27,500
Net Stockholders' Equity	430,646	396,457	351,163	312,881	272,186	240,461	212,343
Net Working Capital	168,423	175,155	153,355	153,329	109,643	92,626	61,052
Year-end Shs. Outstg.	49,959	49,271	50,776	51,392	50,294	50,303	50,268
STATISTICAL RECORD:							
Operating Profit Margin %	26.3	26.1	24.0	21.0	19.6	20.2	20.6
Net Profit Margin %	18.0	17.4	16.2	13.8	12.9	12.8	13.7
Return on Equity %	16.6	17.0	17.3	15.1	14.8	15.8	16.7
Return on Assets %	13.5	13.9	13.9	12.1	11.4	12.2	11.7
Debt/Total Assets %	1.4	1.5	1.7	1.9	2.1	8.9	9.0
Price Range	45⁹⁄₁₆-28¹⁄₂	45¹⁄₈-26⁵⁄₈	29¹⁵⁄₁₆-16⁹⁄₁₆	17¹⁵⁄₁₆-15¹⁄₁₆	17¹¹⁄₁₆-12⁷⁄₁₆	15¹¹⁄₁₆-11³⁄₁₆	16¹⁵⁄₁₆-13¹⁄₈
P/E Ratio	32.1-20.1	34.0-20.0	25.2-13.9	19.6-16.5	22.6-15.9	21.4-15.4	24.1-18.6
Average Yield %	0.6	0.5	0.6	0.7	0.7	0.6	0.5

Statistics are as originally reported. Adj. for all stk. splits and divs. through 4/99

OFFICERS:
M. J. Gordon, Chmn., C.E.O.
E. R. Gordon, Pres., C.O.O.
B. P. Bowen, Treas., Asst. Sec.
G. H. Ember Jr., V.P., Asst. Sec.

INVESTOR CONTACT: Investor Relations, (800) 851-9677

PRINCIPAL OFFICE: 7401 South Cicero Ave., Chicago, IL 60629

TELEPHONE NUMBER: (773) 838-3400
FAX: (773) 838-3534
WEB: www.tootsie.com

NO. OF EMPLOYEES: 1,750 (approx.)

SHAREHOLDERS: 5,800 (approx.)

ANNUAL MEETING: In May

INCORPORATED: VA, June, 1919

INSTITUTIONAL HOLDINGS:
No. of Institutions: 92
Shares Held: 9,831,380 (Adj.)
% Held: 28.1

INDUSTRY: Candy & other confectionery products (SIC: 2064)

TRANSFER AGENT(S): ChaseMellon Shareholder Services, LLC, Ridgefield Park, N.J.

TRUSTCO BANK CORP.

YIELD 4.9%
P/E RATIO 17.8

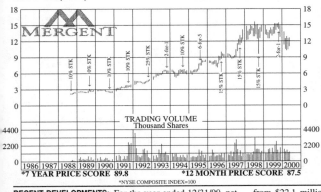

TRADING VOLUME
Thousand Shares

*7 YEAR PRICE SCORE 89.8   ***12 MONTH PRICE SCORE 87.5**
*NYSE COMPOSITE INDEX=100

INTERIM EARNINGS (Per Share):

Qtr.	Mar.	June	Sept.	Dec.
1996	0.12	0.13	0.14	0.14
1997	0.14	0.15	0.15	0.15
1998	0.15	0.16	0.17	0.16
1999	0.17	0.17	0.18	0.17

INTERIM DIVIDENDS (Per Share):

Amt.	Decl.	Ex.	Rec.	Pay.
0.275Q	8/17/99	9/01/99	9/03/99	10/01/99
2-for-1	8/17/99	11/15/99	10/22/99	11/12/99
0.15Q	11/16/99	12/08/99	12/10/99	1/03/00
0.15Q	2/15/00	3/08/00	3/10/00	4/03/00
0.15Q	5/16/00	6/07/00	6/09/00	7/03/00

Indicated div.: $0.60 (Div. Reinv. Plan)

CAPITALIZATION (12/31/99):

	($000)	(%)
Total Deposits	1,994,909	92.3
Common & Surplus	166,356	7.7
Total	2,161,265	100.0

DIVIDEND ACHIEVER STATUS:

Rank: 22   10-Year Growth Rate: 20.64%
Total Years of Dividend Growth: 23

RECENT DEVELOPMENTS: For the year ended 12/31/99, net income rose 9.1% to $38.2 million compared with $35.0 million in 1998. Results for 1999 benefited from TRST's effort in eliminating a significant portion of its high-cost deposits, while at the same time increasing its net interest margin. Interest income declined 3.9% to $167.2 million from $174.1 million in 1998. Interest expense fell 16.2% to $74.0 million from $88.3 million a year ago. Net interest income grew 8.7% to $93.2 million from $85.7 million in 1998. Noninterest income declined 30.3% to $15.4 million

from $22.1 million in the prior year. Net interest margin was 4.16% in 1999 versus 3.81% in 1998. Noninterest expenses fell 6.4% to $45.6 million from $48.8 million a year ago. Return on average assets improved to 1.58% compared with 1.44% in 1998. Return on average shareholders' equity rose to 22.52% from 21.47%. On 2/21/00, TRST agreed to acquire Landmark Financial Corp. and its subsidiary, Landmark Community Bank. The transaction is subject to approval and is expected to be completed in the third quarter of 2000.

BUSINESS

TRUSTCO BANK CORP. is a one-bank holding company for Trustco Bank, N.A. As of 12/31/99, assets totaled $2.36 billion. The bank provides a range of both personal and business banking services to individuals, partnerships, corporations, municipalities and governments of New York. The bank operates 53 banking offices and 33 automatic teller machines in Albany, Columbia, Greene, Rensselaer, Saratoga, Schenectady, Schoharie, Warren, and Washington counties of New York State. The largest part of such business consists of accepting deposits and making loans and investments.

LOAN DISTRIBUTION

(12/31/99)	($000)	(%)
Commercial	193,530	14.3
Construction	15,867	1.2
Residential Mortgage	980,141	72.6
Home Equity Credit Line	138,339	10.2
Installment	22,891	1.7
Total	1,350,768	100.0

ANNUAL FINANCIAL DATA

	12/31/99	12/31/98	12/31/97	12/31/96	12/31/95	12/31/94	12/31/93
Earnings Per Share	0.68	0.63	0.58	0.69	0.62	0.56	☐ 0.58
Tang. Book Val. Per Share	3.11	3.47	3.32	3.98	3.95	3.45	3.24
Dividends Per Share	0.55	0.48	0.42	0.36	0.32	0.26	0.21
Dividend Payout %	80.9	76.5	71.9	52.8	51.3	45.9	35.5
INCOME STATEMENT (IN MILLIONS):							
Total Interest Income	167.2	174.1	172.0	166.6	161.6	140.3	133.7
Total Interest Expense	74.0	88.3	86.5	82.3	80.2	60.7	61.6
Net Interest Income	93.2	85.7	85.5	84.3	81.4	79.6	72.0
Provision for Loan Losses	5.1	4.6	5.4	6.6	12.7	8.1	11.6
Non-Interest Income	15.4	22.1	17.2	10.3	14.1	4.6	19.2
Non-Interest Expense	45.6	48.8	46.2	42.0	44.4	40.6	43.5
Income Before Taxes	57.9	54.5	51.1	46.0	38.3	35.5	36.1
Net Income	38.2	35.0	32.2	28.7	25.5	22.9	☐ 23.6
Average Shs. Outstg. (000)	55,910	55,908	55,849	42,044	41,481	41,085	40,857
BALANCE SHEET (IN MILLIONS):							
Cash & Due from Banks	54.5	42.0	42.7	45.8	50.9	52.5	51.0
Securities Avail. for Sale	640.8	717.4	601.9	618.7	640.2	117.5	242.8
Total Loans & Leases	1,350.8	1,323.8	1,299.5	1,243.3	1,227.9	1,154.6	1,063.0
Allowance for Credit Losses	56.8	55.4	54.7	53.0	50.1	40.8	36.4
Net Loans & Leases	1,294.0	1,268.3	1,244.8	1,190.3	1,177.8	1,113.8	1,026.6
Total Assets	2,364.0	2,485.1	2,372.3	2,261.8	2,176.2	1,975.7	1,971.3
Total Deposits	1,994.9	2,107.4	2,021.9	1,953.1	1,930.6	1,789.8	1,794.2
Long-Term Obligations	. . .	. . .	. . .	. . .	. . .	3.6	2.8
Total Liabilities	2,197.7	2,299.2	2,193.4	2,099.4	2,016.1	1,836.4	1,841.4
Net Stockholders' Equity	166.4	185.8	178.8	162.4	160.1	139.3	129.9
Year-end Shs. Outstg. (000)	53,408	53,584	53,824	40,776	40,567	40,342	40,144
STATISTICAL RECORD:							
Return on Equity %	23.0	18.8	18.0	17.7	15.9	16.4	18.2
Return on Assets %	1.6	1.4	1.4	1.3	1.2	1.2	1.2
Equity/Assets %	7.0	7.5	7.5	7.2	7.4	7.0	6.6
Non-Int. Exp./Tot. Inc. %	40.0	45.6	44.9	42.4	46.7	43.6	51.2
Price Range	15⁷/₁₆-12½	15⅝-9⅝	14⅛-8¹¹/₁₆	10-7¹/₁₆	8¹¹/₁₆-5³/₄	6³/₄-5¼	6¹¹/₁₆-4⁷/₈
P/E Ratio	22.7-18.3	25.0-15.3	24.5-15.0	14.6-10.3	14.1-9.3	12.2-9.4	11.5-8.4
Average Yield %	3.9	3.8	3.6	4.2	4.4	4.3	3.6

Statistics are as originally reported. Adj. for stk. splits: 2-for-1, 11/99; 15% div., 1998; 15% div., 11/14/97; 15% div., 11/15/96; 6-for-5, 8/24/95; 10% div., 10/21/94; 2-for-1, 11/19/93 ☐ Bef. acctg. change chrg. $3.3 mill. ($0.14/sh.)

OFFICERS:
R. A. McCormick, Pres., C.E.O.
R. T. Cushing, V.P., C.F.O.
W. F. Terry, Sr. V.P., Sec.
INVESTOR CONTACT: William F. Terry, Sec., (518) 377-3311
PRINCIPAL OFFICE: 320 State Street, Schenectady, NY 12305-2356

TELEPHONE NUMBER: (518) 377-3311
FAX: (518) 381-3668
NO. OF EMPLOYEES: 451
SHAREHOLDERS: 11,517
ANNUAL MEETING: In May
INCORPORATED: NY, 1981

INSTITUTIONAL HOLDINGS:
No. of Institutions: 69
Shares Held: 10,501,309
% Held: 19.6
INDUSTRY: State commercial banks (SIC: 6022)
TRANSFER AGENT(S): Trustco Bank, Schenectady, NY

NASDAQ SYMBOL TRMK
Rec. Pr. 19 11/16 (5/31/00)

TRUSTMARK CORPORATION

YIELD 2.5%
P/E RATIO 14.5

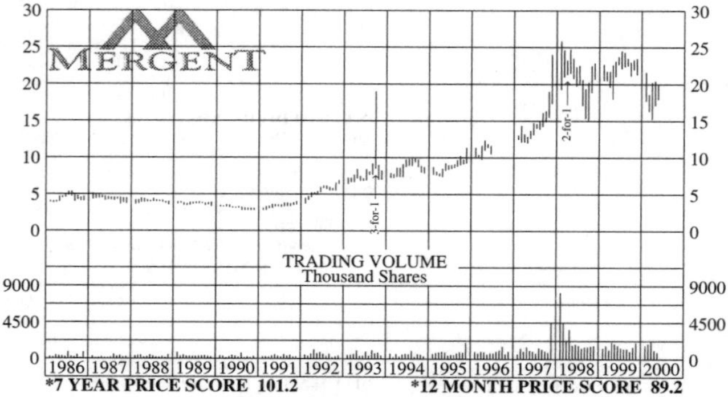

*7 YEAR PRICE SCORE 101.2 *12 MONTH PRICE SCORE 89.2

*NYSE COMPOSITE INDEX=100

INTERIM EARNINGS (Per Share):

Qtr.	Mar.	June	Sept.	Dec.
1995	0.20	0.21	0.23	0.22
1996	0.22	0.24	0.25	0.23
1997	0.24	0.24	0.25	0.25
1998	0.27	0.28	0.29	0.30
1999	0.33	0.34	0.35	0.34

INTERIM DIVIDENDS (Per Share):

Amt.	Decl.	Ex.	Rec.	Pay.
0.105Q	5/11/99	5/27/99	6/01/99	6/15/99
0.105Q	7/13/99	8/30/99	9/01/99	9/15/99
0.125Q	11/09/99	11/29/99	12/01/99	12/15/99
0.125Q	2/08/00	2/28/00	3/01/00	3/15/00
0.125Q	5/09/00	5/30/00	6/01/00	6/15/00

Indicated div.: $0.50 (Div. Reinv. Plan)

CAPITALIZATION (12/31/99):

	($000)	(%)
Total Deposits	3,924,796	85.7
Common & Surplus	655,756	14.3
Total	4,580,552	100.0

DIVIDEND ACHIEVER STATUS:
Rank: 141 10-Year Growth Rate: 10.70%
Total Years of Dividend Growth: 26

RECENT DEVELOPMENTS: For the year ended 12/31/99, net income increased 17.6% to $98.0 million compared with $83.3 million in the previous year. Total interest income jumped 6.8% to $448.5 million from $420.1 million a year ago. Net interest income totaled $243.4 million, an improvement of 6.7% from $228.2 million the year before. The increase in net interest income was attributed to a higher level of average interest-earning assets, partially offset by an increase in funding costs. Provision for loan losses advanced 16.7% to $9.1 million from $7.8 million in 1998. Total noninterest income rose 17.2% to $101.9 million from $87.0 million in the prior year. Total noninterest expenses increased 4.9% to $187.1 million from $178.3 million a year earlier, primarily due to an increase in salaries and employee benefits. Return on average assets climbed to 1.49% compared with 1.41% in the prior year, while return on average equity grew to 14.93% versus 13.53% in the 1998 period.

BUSINESS

TRUSTMARK CORPORATION is a one-bank holding company. The Company's primary business activities are conducted through its wholly-owned subsidiary, Trustmark National Bank and its wholly-owned nonbanking subsidiaries, Trustmark Financial Services, Inc. and Trustmark Insurance Agency, Inc. Through its subsidiaries, the Company operates as a statewide banking organization providing banking, investment and insurance services to corporate, institutional and individual customers within the state of Mississippi. TRMK engages in business through its three reportable segments: Retail Banking, Commercial Banking and Financial Services. Retail Banking provides a full range of financial products and services to individuals and small business customers through TRMK's 133 branch locations located in 50 Mississippi communities. Commercial Banking provides various financial products and services to corporate and middle market clients through the Company's Commercial Lending, Commercial Real Estate, Indirect Lending and Private Banking Groups. Financial Services includes trust and fiduciary services, discount brokerage services, insurance services, as well as, credit card and mortgage services.

ANNUAL FINANCIAL DATA

	12/31/99	12/31/98	12/31/97	12/31/96	12/31/95	12/31/94	12/31/93
Earnings Per Share	**1.36**	**1.14**	**0.98**	**0.93**	**0.86**	**0.79**	**[1] 0.81**
Tang. Book Val. Per Share	**8.39**	**8.29**	**7.61**	**6.95**	**6.32**	**5.48**	**5.10**
Dividends Per Share	**0.44**	**0.35**	**0.29**	**0.25**	**0.22**	**0.20**	**0.19**
Dividend Payout %	**32.4**	**30.9**	**29.8**	**26.9**	**25.9**	**25.8**	**23.6**
INCOME STATEMENT (IN MILLIONS):							
Total Interest Income	448.5	420.1	376.9	358.1	348.3	315.4	290.6
Total Interest Expense	205.1	191.9	172.9	164.0	162.7	124.3	109.0
Net Interest Income	243.4	228.2	204.0	194.1	185.6	191.2	181.6
Provision for Loan Losses	9.1	7.8	4.7	5.8	2.4	2.8	17.6
Non-Interest Income	101.9	89.1	75.6	67.0	59.5	48.7	45.4
Non-Interest Expense	187.1	180.4	167.9	157.8	151.3	152.8	139.6
Income Before Taxes	149.2	129.1	107.0	97.4	91.3	84.2	69.7
Net Income	98.0	83.3	71.1	65.1	59.8	55.0	[1] 48.6
Average Shs. Outstg. (000)	71,921	72,946	72,786	69,822	69,822	69,610	60,376
BALANCE SHEET (IN MILLIONS):							
Cash & Due from Banks	280.0	312.5	292.6	337.1	299.0	280.1	238.4
Securities Avail. for Sale	783.2	776.0	610.6	528.0	488.9	440.8	86.8
Total Loans & Leases	4,014.9	3,702.3	2,983.7	2,634.6	2,580.2	2,347.6	2,083.8
Allowance for Credit Losses	65.9	66.2	64.1	63.0	70.1	83.1	62.7
Net Loans & Leases	3,949.1	3,636.2	2,919.6	2,571.6	2,510.1	2,264.4	2,021.2
Total Assets	6,743.4	6,355.2	5,545.2	5,193.7	4,992.6	4,745.2	4,432.0
Total Deposits	3,924.8	3,946.4	3,818.9	3,597.4	3,530.0	3,449.2	3,189.2
Total Liabilities	6,087.6	5,703.3	4,951.5	4,669.5	4,513.8	4,342.4	4,073.4
Net Stockholders' Equity	655.8	651.9	593.6	524.2	478.8	421.0	358.6
Year-end Shs. Outstg. (000)	70,424	72,532	72,740	69,822	69,822	69,822	62,346
STATISTICAL RECORD:							
Return on Equity %	14.9	12.8	12.0	12.4	12.5	13.1	13.6
Return on Assets %	1.5	1.3	1.3	1.3	1.2	1.2	1.1
Equity/Assets %	9.7	10.3	10.7	10.1	9.6	8.9	8.1
Non-Int. Exp./Tot. Inc. %	54.2	56.9	60.1	60.5	61.7	63.7	61.5
Price Range	24 1/2-18	25 7/8-15 1/8	24-12	14-9 3/4	11 3/8-7 3/8	9 7/8-7 1/4	19-6 7/16
P/E Ratio	18.0-13.2	22.7-13.3	24.5-12.2	15.1-10.5	13.3-8.6	12.5-9.2	23.6-8.0
Average Yield %	2.1	1.7	1.6	2.1	2.4	2.4	1.5

Statistics are as originally reported. Adj. for stk. splits: 2-for-1, 3/30/98; 3-for-1, 10/12/93
[1] Bef. acctg. change credit $1.5 mill. ($0.03/sh.)

OFFICERS:
T. H. Kendall III, Chmn.
R. G. Hickson, Pres., C.E.O.
G. R. Host, Treas.
H. M. Walker, Sec.

INVESTOR CONTACT: Joseph Rein, V.P.-Investor Relations, (601) 949-6898

PRINCIPAL OFFICE: 248 East Capitol St., Jackson, MS 39201

TELEPHONE NUMBER: (601) 354-5111
FAX: (601) 949-2387
WEB: www.trustmark.com

NO. OF EMPLOYEES: 2,304

SHAREHOLDERS: 5,100 (approx.)

ANNUAL MEETING: In Mar.

INCORPORATED: MS, Aug., 1968

INSTITUTIONAL HOLDINGS:
No. of Institutions: 65
Shares Held: 9,890,062
% Held: 13.9

INDUSTRY: National commercial banks (SIC: 6021)

TRANSFER AGENT(S): Trustmark National Bank, Jackson, MS

NYSE SYMBOL TRW
Rec. Pr. 48½ (5/31/00)

TRW INC.

YIELD 2.7%
P/E RATIO 8.5

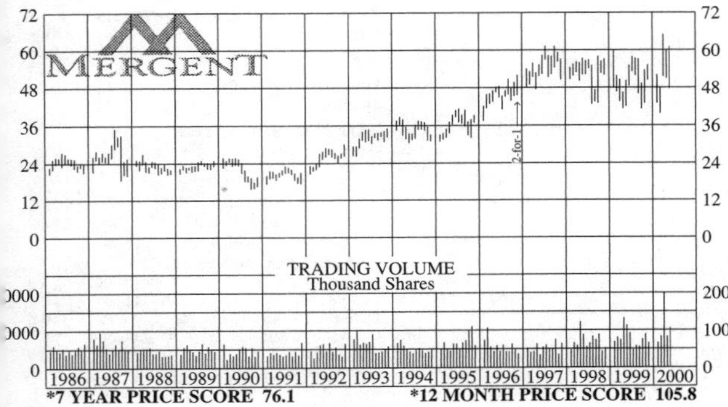

*7 YEAR PRICE SCORE 76.1 *12 MONTH PRICE SCORE 105.8

*NYSE COMPOSITE INDEX=100

INTERIM EARNINGS (Per Share):

Qtr.	Mar.	June	Sept.	Dec.
1996	0.87	0.98	d1.11	0.85
1997	0.93	1.05	0.86	d3.34
1998	1.03	1.00	0.85	0.96
1999	0.04	1.14	1.08	1.81

INTERIM DIVIDENDS (Per Share):

Amt.	Decl.	Ex.	Rec.	Pay.
0.33Q	7/28/99	8/11/99	8/13/99	9/15/99
0.33Q	10/27/99	11/09/99	11/12/99	12/15/99
0.33Q	12/08/99	2/09/00	2/11/00	3/15/00
0.005RR	12/08/99	2/09/00	2/11/00	3/15/00
0.33Q	4/26/00	5/10/00	5/12/00	6/15/00

Indicated div.: $1.32 (Div. Reinv. Plan)

CAPITALIZATION (12/31/99):

	($000)	(%)
Long-Term Debt	5,369,000	56.2
Deferred Income Tax	1,352,000	14.2
Minority Interest	113,000	1.2
Common & Surplus	2,712,000	28.4
Total	9,546,000	100.0

DIVIDEND ACHIEVER STATUS:
Rank: 271 10-Year Growth Rate: 4.38%
Total Years of Dividend Growth: 28

RECENT DEVELOPMENTS: For the year ended 12/31/99, net income fell 1.7% to $468.8 million compared with $476.8 million in the previous year. Earnings for 1999 included after-tax net nonrecurring charges of $99.6 million. Earnings for 1998 included nonrecurring charges of $2.7 million. Sales advanced 42.8% to $16.97 billion from $11.89 billion due to the LucasVarity acquisition. Total automotive sales increased 57.3% to $11.33 billion.

PROSPECTS: On 3/24/00, the Company was awarded a five-year, $3.10 billion contract from the Department of Energy. Under the contract, TRW will be the lead contractor to develop a site for spent U.S. nuclear fuel. On 3/8/00, the Company was awarded a $3.90 billion subcontract in connection with a public safety project in Britain. TRW will integrate an advanced digital communications service that will be used by British police forces.

BUSINESS

TRW INC. provides high technology products and services for automotive, aerospace and information technology markets worldwide. Automotive products (66.8% of 1999 sales) include steering, suspension, electronic and occupant restraint systems, engine valves and valve train parts, electromechanical assemblies, fasteners, and automotive electronic products. Aerospace and Information Technology (33.2%) designs and manufactures spacecraft and related equipment as well as software and systems engineering support services primarily for the U.S. Government. TRW has 200 automotive locations in 25 countries. On 3/25/99, TRW acquired LucasVarity Plc.

GEOGRAPHIC DATA

(12/31/99)	Rev(000)	Inc($000)
1st Quarter	3,097,000	(28,000)
2nd Quarter	4,785,000	139,000
3rd Quarter	4,462,000	134,000
4th Quarter	4,625,000	224,000

ANNUAL FINANCIAL DATA

	12/31/99	12/31/98	12/31/97	12/31/96	12/31/95	12/31/94	12/31/93
Earnings Per Share	**4 3.80**	**3.83**	**3 d0.40**	**2 1.37**	**3.35**	**2.53**	**1 1.70**
Cash Flow Per Share	**10.39**	**8.38**	**3.57**	**4.81**	**7.18**	**6.15**	**5.24**
Tang. Book Val. Per Share	**. . .**	**6.76**	**6.63**	**15.68**	**11.53**	**8.98**	**6.68**
Dividends Per Share	**1.32**	**1.26**	**1.24**	**1.14**	**1.02**	**0.97**	**0.94**
Dividend Payout %	**34.7**	**32.9**	**. . .**	**82.8**	**30.6**	**38.4**	**55.5**
INCOME STATEMENT (IN MILLIONS):							
Total Revenues	16,969.0	11,886.0	10,831.0	9,857.0	10,172.0	9,087.0	7,948.0
Costs & Expenses	14,873.0	10,497.0	10,029.0	8,949.0	8,849.0	7,962.0	7,002.0
Depreciation & Amort.	850.0	566.0	490.0	452.0	510.0	476.0	458.0
Operating Income	1,246.0	823.0	312.0	456.0	813.0	649.0	488.0
Net Interest Inc./(Exp.)	d477.0	d114.0	d75.0	d84.0	d95.0	d105.0	d138.0
Income Before Income Taxes	787.0	746.0	240.0	302.0	708.0	535.0	359.0
Income Taxes	318.0	269.0	289.0	120.0	262.0	202.0	139.0
Net Income	4 468.8	477.0	3 d49.0	2 182.0	446.0	333.0	1 220.0
Cash Flow	1,282.0	1,042.0	440.0	633.0	955.0	808.0	677.0
Average Shs. Outstg. (000)	123,500	124,400	123,700	131,700	133,200	131,600	129,400
BALANCE SHEET (IN MILLIONS):							
Cash & Cash Equivalents	228.0	83.0	70.0	386.0	59.0	109.0	79.0
Total Current Assets	5,199.0	2,703.0	2,435.0	2,781.0	2,336.0	2,215.0	1,994.0
Net Property	3,894.0	2,683.0	2,621.0	2,480.0	2,563.0	2,489.0	2,327.0
Total Assets	18,266.0	7,169.0	6,410.0	5,472.4	5,890.0	5,636.0	5,336.0
Total Current Liabilities	6,729.0	3,018.0	2,719.0	2,157.0	2,012.0	1,986.0	1,826.0
Long-Term Obligations	5,369.0	1,353.0	1,117.0	458.0	541.0	694.0	870.0
Net Stockholders' Equity	2,712.0	1,878.0	1,624.0	2,189.0	2,172.0	1,822.0	1,534.0
Net Working Capital	d1,530.0	d315.0	d284.0	624.0	324.0	229.0	168.0
Year-end Shs. Outstg. (000)	110,400	119,900	122,500	126,100	131,200	129,800	128,200
STATISTICAL RECORD:							
Operating Profit Margin %	7.3	6.9	2.9	4.6	8.0	7.1	6.1
Net Profit Margin %	2.8	4.0	. . .	1.8	4.4	3.7	2.8
Return on Equity %	17.3	25.4	. . .	8.3	20.5	18.3	14.3
Return on Assets %	2.4	6.7	. . .	3.3	7.6	5.9	4.1
Debt/Total Assets %	29.4	18.9	17.4	8.4	9.2	12.3	16.3
Price Range	59⅞-41³⁄₁₆	58-42¹¹⁄₁₆	61⁵⁄₁₆-47⅜	52-37⁷⁄₁₆	41⁵⁄₁₆-30⅞	38¾-30½	35⅛-26¼
P/E Ratio	15.8-10.8	15.1-11.1	. . .	38.0-27.3	12.4-9.2	15.3-12.1	20.7-15.5
Average Yield %	2.6	2.5	2.3	2.5	2.8	2.8	3.1

Statistics are as originally reported. Adj. for 2-for-1 stk. split, 12/96. 1 Incl. net gain of $2.1 mill. & bef. chrg. of $24.7 mill. for acct. adjs. 2 Incl. $382.7 mill. in pre-tax restruct. chrgs. & excl. after-tax gain of $297.7 mill. from the sale of its Information Services unit. 3 Incl. $547.9 mill. in R&D chrgs. 4 Incl. net non-recurr. chrg. $99.6 mill.

OFFICERS:
J. T. Gorman, Chmn., C.E.O.
D. M. Cote, Pres., C.O.O
C. G. Miller, Exec. V.P., C.F.O.

INVESTOR CONTACT: Joseph S. Cantle, Vice Pres.-Investor Relations, (216) 291-7506

PRINCIPAL OFFICE: 1900 Richmond Road, Cleveland, OH 44124-3760

TELEPHONE NUMBER: (216) 291-7000
FAX: (216) 291-7321
WEB: www.trw.com

NO. OF EMPLOYEES: 122,000 (approx.)

SHAREHOLDERS: 23,062

ANNUAL MEETING: In Apr.

INCORPORATED: OH, June, 1916

INSTITUTIONAL HOLDINGS:
No. of Institutions: 277
Shares Held: 73,563,795
% Held: 60.5

INDUSTRY: Motor vehicle parts and accessories (SIC: 3714)

TRANSFER AGENT(S): The Company & National City Bank, Cleveland, OH

TUSCARORA INCORPORATED

INTERIM EARNINGS (Per Share):

Qtr.	Nov.	Feb.	May	Aug.
1996-97	0.39	0.22	0.20	0.17
1997-98	0.40	d0.09	0.27	0.27
1998-99	0.41	0.20	0.31	0.30
1999-00	0.47	0.25	...	...

INTERIM DIVIDENDS (Per Share):

Amt.	Decl.	Ex.	Rec.	Pay.
0.11S	6/16/98	6/24/98	6/26/98	7/06/98
0.12S	12/16/98	12/23/98	12/28/98	1/08/99
0.12S	6/11/99	6/18/99	6/22/99	7/02/99
0.135S	12/15/99	12/22/99	12/27/99	1/06/00

Indicated div.: $0.27

CAPITALIZATION (8/31/99):

	($000)	(%)
Long-Term Debt	60,065	40.6
Deferred Income Tax	1,123	0.8
Common & Surplus	86,684	58.6
Total	147,872	100.0

DIVIDEND ACHIEVER STATUS:
Rank: 112   10-Year Growth Rate: 12.08%
Total Years of Dividend Growth: 10

*7 YEAR PRICE SCORE 59.6   *12 MONTH PRICE SCORE 107.6
*NYSE COMPOSITE INDEX=100

RECENT DEVELOPMENTS: For the second quarter ended 2/29/00, net income increased 22.6% to $2.3 million compared with $1.9 million in the prior-year period. Net sales totaled $61.3 million, an improvement of 14.3% from $53.6 million the year before. The improvement in net sales reflected increased demand for TUSC's products in virtually all end-user markets in North America, the successful integration of Berry Packaging, Inc. and Lane Container Company, and higher selling prices for many of its products. Gross profit grew 16.2% to $14.0 million from 12.0

million a year earlier. Recently, the Company purchased business and operating assets of Texas-based, Cushion Packaging Company, a custom fabricator of interior foam cushioning products used primarily for packaging and transporting fragile products, and California-based, Erickson Wood Products, a manufacturer of custom wood pallets and containers primarily used to transport sensitive electronic devices for high technology customers. Separately, TUSC opened a new facility in Guadalajara, Mexico, which will offer protective packaging products.

BUSINESS

TUSCARORA INCORPORATED designs and manufactures products made from expanded foam plastic materials. The Company molds and fabricates foam plastic for interior packaging and other protective applications, as well as for automotive and insulation components. The Company also integrates materials such as corrugated paperboard, thermoformed plastic, wood and aluminum into various packaging and material handling applications. The Company's customers include the high technology, consumer electronics, automotive and major appliance industries. The Company serves more than 3,600 customers located in the United States, Canada, Mexico and the United Kingdom, from 36 manufacturing locations.

ANNUAL FINANCIAL DATA

	8/31/99	8/31/98	8/31/97	8/31/96	8/31/95	8/31/94	8/31/93
Earnings Per Share	1.23	0.83	0.98	1.03	0.97	0.62	⊡ 0.43
Cash Flow Per Share	3.06	2.62	2.60	2.42	2.15	1.68	1.44
Tang. Book Val. Per Share	8.27	7.33	6.77	6.53	5.94	5.12	4.64
Dividends Per Share	0.24	0.22	0.19	0.17	0.15	0.13	0.12
Dividend Payout %	19.5	26.5	19.7	16.8	15.8	21.5	27.7
INCOME STATEMENT (IN THOUSANDS):							
Total Revenues	233,841	232,902	209,207	182,590	163,300	120,085	101,075
Costs & Expenses	193,005	197,605	174,302	150,797	134,624	99,859	85,046
Depreciation & Amort.	17,590	17,231	15,286	12,977	10,890	9,721	9,206
Operating Income	23,246	18,067	19,619	18,816	17,786	10,506	6,823
Net Interest Inc./(Exp.)	d4,619	d4,944	d3,741	d2,928	d2,603	d1,328	d1,307
Income Before Income Taxes	18,860	13,181	15,441	15,905	15,034	9,017	6,285
Income Taxes	7,130	5,149	6,146	6,253	6,054	3,314	2,336
Net Income	11,729	8,032	9,295	9,653	8,980	5,703	⊡ 3,949
Cash Flow	29,319	25,262	24,582	22,630	19,870	15,424	13,155
Average Shs. Outstg.	9,570	9,657	9,452	9,362	9,231	9,194	9,164
BALANCE SHEET (IN THOUSANDS):							
Cash & Cash Equivalents	6,090	5,452	5,095	3,380	2,660	3,671	2,030
Total Current Assets	64,434	61,806	56,594	46,913	45,594	35,635	26,835
Net Property	101,055	97,538	93,115	78,710	67,591	55,356	50,205
Total Assets	177,386	172,166	162,388	131,169	117,721	94,225	79,770
Total Current Liabilities	27,059	26,947	26,810	23,689	23,204	19,087	10,942
Long-Term Obligations	60,065	61,184	57,166	39,249	36,510	25,284	23,930
Net Stockholders' Equity	86,684	78,740	72,717	64,904	54,974	47,180	42,546
Net Working Capital	37,375	34,859	29,784	23,224	22,390	16,548	15,893
Year-end Shs. Outstg.	9,430	9,526	9,475	9,415	9,259	9,221	9,171
STATISTICAL RECORD:							
Operating Profit Margin %	9.9	7.8	9.4	10.3	10.9	8.7	6.8
Net Profit Margin %	5.0	3.4	4.4	5.3	5.5	4.7	3.9
Return on Equity %	13.5	10.2	12.8	14.9	16.3	12.1	9.3
Return on Assets %	6.6	4.7	5.7	7.4	7.6	6.1	5.0
Debt/Total Assets %	33.9	35.5	35.2	29.9	31.0	26.8	30.0
Price Range	14½-8½	17½-10	21⅜-14⅛	18⁹/₁₆-14	17-11³/₁₆	13⁵/₁₆-8¹¹/₁₆	12⁵/₁₆-7¹¹/₁₆
P/E Ratio	11.8-6.9	21.1-12.0	21.8-14.4	18.0-13.6	17.5-11.5	21.5-14.0	28.5-17.7
Average Yield %	2.1	1.6	1.1	1.1	1.1	1.2	1.2

Statistics are as originally reported. Adj. for stk. split: 3-for-2, 1/13/97 ⊡ Bef. acctg. change credit $321,218 ($0.03/sh.)

OFFICERS:
J. P. O'Leary Jr., Chmn., Pres., C.E.O.
B. C. Mullins, Sr. V.P., C.F.O., Treas.
D. C. O'Leary, Sr. V.P., C.O.O.

INVESTOR CONTACT: Brian C. Mullins, V.P. & Treas., (412) 843-8200

PRINCIPAL OFFICE: 800 Fifth Avenue, New Brighton, PA 15066

TELEPHONE NUMBER: (724) 843-8200
FAX: (724) 843-4402
WEB: www.tuscarora.com

NO. OF EMPLOYEES: 1,890

SHAREHOLDERS: 708

ANNUAL MEETING: In Dec.

INCORPORATED: PA, 1962

INSTITUTIONAL HOLDINGS:
No. of Institutions: 30
Shares Held: 3,044,398
% Held: 32.4

INDUSTRY: Plastics foam products (SIC: 3086)

TRANSFER AGENT(S): ChaseMellon Shareholder Services, Pittsburgh, PA

NYSE SYMBOL UGI
Rec. Pr. 22 1/8 (5/31/00)

UGI CORPORATION

YIELD 7.0%
P/E RATIO 11.3

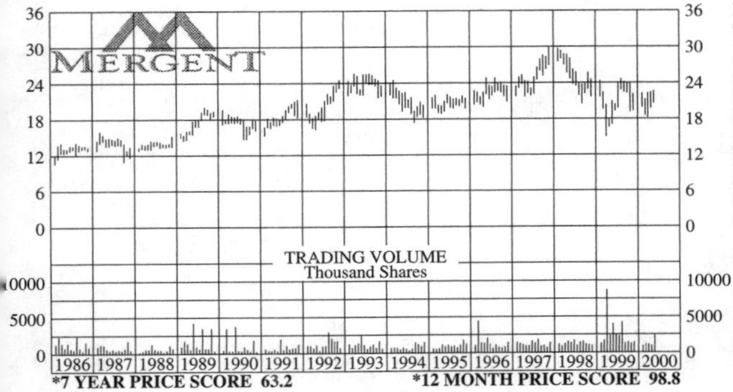

*7 YEAR PRICE SCORE 63.2 *12 MONTH PRICE SCORE 98.8

*NYSE COMPOSITE INDEX=100

INTERIM EARNINGS (Per Share):

Qtr.	Dec.	Mar.	June	Sept.
1996-97	0.84	1.08	d0.04	d0.32
1997-98	0.75	0.94	d0.12	d0.36
1998-99	0.55	1.14	0.36	d0.31
1999-00	0.77	...	...	...

INTERIM DIVIDENDS (Per Share):

Amt.	Decl.	Ex.	Rec.	Pay.
0.365Q	4/27/99	5/26/99	5/28/99	7/01/99
0.375Q	7/28/99	9/15/99	9/17/99	10/01/99
0.375Q	10/26/99	11/26/99	11/30/99	1/01/00
0.375Q	1/25/00	2/25/00	2/29/00	4/01/00
0.388Q	4/25/00	5/26/00	5/31/00	7/01/00

Indicated div.: $1.55 (Div. Reinv. Plan)

CAPITALIZATION (9/30/99):

	($000)	(%)
Long-Term Debt	989,600	60.2
Deferred Income Tax	174,300	10.6
Minority Interest	209,900	12.8
Redeemable Pfd. Stock	20,000	1.2
Common & Surplus	249,200	15.2
Total	1,643,000	100.0

DIVIDEND ACHIEVER STATUS:
Rank: 300 10-Year Growth Rate: 2.97%
Total Years of Dividend Growth: 12

RECENT DEVELOPMENTS: For the three months ended 12/31/99, net income increased 17.2% to $21.1 million from $18.0 million in the corresponding period of the previous year. Total revenues advanced 24.9% to $466.6 million from $373.7 million in the prior-year period. Total operating income increased 15.0% to $70.7 million from $61.5 million a year earlier. Total costs and expenses rose 26.8% to $395.9 million.

PROSPECTS: Results are being positively affected by investments made in the Company's core utility and propane businesses. In addition, the Company's investments in related and complementary businesses should prove similarly successful over time. Going forward, the Company plans to continue focusing on expanding its PPX® barbeque cylinder exchange program, acquiring profitable retailers and expanding its national accounts.

BUSINESS

UGI CORPORATION is a holding company that operates propane distribution, gas and electric utility, energy marketing and related businesses in Pennsylvania and distributing propane nationally. UGI carries out its business through UGI Utilities, which serves 326,000 customers in 14 counties, and AmeriGas which provides propane to 969,000 customers in 46 states. Gas throughput in 1999 was derived: 33% residential; 29% commercial/industrial; 11% motor fuel; 7% agricultural and 20% wholesale. Electric kilowatt-hour sales were broken down by residential 52%, commerical 35%, and industrial and other 13%. Revenues in 1999 were derived: 63.1% propane, 30.4% utilities and 6.5% other.

BUSINESS LINE ANALYSIS

(09/30/99)($000)	Rev	Inc
Propane	63.1	15.2
Gas Utility	25.0	52.5
Electric Utility	5.4	10.3
Energy Marketing	6.5	2.6
Other	0.2	(5.9)
Corporate	(0.2)	25.3
Total	100.0	100.0

ANNUAL FINANCIAL DATA

	9/30/99	9/30/98	9/30/97	9/30/96	9/30/95	9/30/94	[2] 9/30/93
Earnings Per Share	[3] 1.74	1.22	1.57	1.19	[1] 0.24	1.17	0.42
Cash Flow Per Share	4.54	3.87	4.17	3.79	2.10	2.47	1.39
Tang. Book Val. Per Share	...	...	...	...	...	5.54	5.12
Dividends Per Share	1.47	1.45	1.43	1.41	1.39	1.36	1.32
Dividend Payout %	84.5	118.8	91.1	118.5	578.9	116.2	314.2
INCOME STATEMENT (IN MILLIONS):							
Total Revenues	1,383.6	1,439.7	1,642.0	1,557.6	877.6	762.2	509.5
Costs & Expenses	1,118.0	1,181.7	1,356.0	1,311.9	738.4	603.5	411.5
Depreciation & Amort.	89.7	87.8	86.1	86.0	60.9	41.8	29.2
Operating Income	175.9	170.2	199.9	159.7	78.3	116.9	68.8
Net Interest Inc./(Exp.)	d84.6	d84.4	d83.1	d79.5	d59.3	d43.3	d32.6
Income Before Income Taxes	109.6	76.9	98.5	75.9	38.7	73.6	36.2
Income Taxes	43.2	34.4	43.6	33.6	22.7	33.6	18.2
Equity Earnings/Minority Int.	d10.7	d8.9	d18.3	d4.3	14.4	d1.0	d3.1
Net Income	[3] 55.7	40.3	52.1	39.5	[1] 7.9	37.7	12.8
Cash Flow	145.4	128.1	138.2	125.5	68.8	79.5	42.0
Average Shs. Outstg. (000)	32,016	33,123	33,132	33,142	32,710	32,200	30,300
BALANCE SHEET (IN MILLIONS):							
Cash & Cash Equivalents	55.6	148.4	129.4	97.1	132.7	77.4	125.3
Total Current Assets	290.9	350.6	403.9	381.6	367.3	179.0	213.3
Net Property	1,084.1	999.0	987.2	974.6	954.7	620.6	603.8
Total Assets	2,135.9	2,074.6	2,151.7	2,144.9	2,164.0	1,134.7	1,167.9
Total Current Liabilities	402.3	321.8	404.5	369.2	329.3	211.8	218.1
Long-Term Obligations	989.6	890.8	844.8	845.2	815.2	363.5	394.4
Net Stockholders' Equity	249.2	367.1	376.1	377.6	380.5	425.3	415.2
Net Working Capital	d111.4	28.8	d0.6	12.4	38.0	15.7	39.4
Year-end Shs. Outstg. (000)	27,270	32,823	33,199	33,136	32,917	32,393	31,938
STATISTICAL RECORD:							
Operating Profit Margin %	12.7	11.8	12.2	10.3	8.9	15.3	13.5
Net Profit Margin %	4.0	2.8	3.2	2.5	0.9	4.9	2.5
Return on Equity %	22.4	11.0	13.9	10.5	2.1	8.9	3.1
Return on Assets %	2.6	1.9	2.4	1.8	0.4	3.3	1.1
Debt/Total Assets %	46.3	42.9	39.3	39.4	37.7	32.0	33.8
Price Range	24 11/16-15	29 3/4-20 1/2	29 7/8-21 5/8	24 7/8-20	22 1/8-18 7/8	24 1/2-17 3/8	25 5/8-21 1/2
P/E Ratio	14.2-8.6	24.4-16.8	19.0-13.8	20.9-16.8	92.1-78.6	20.9-14.8	61.0-51.2
Average Yield %	7.4	5.8	5.6	6.3	6.8	6.5	5.6

Statistics are as originally reported. Incls. results of AP Propane on a consolidated basis. [1] Incls. non-recurr. chrgs. totaling $24.9 mill. [2] Fiscal Year end changed to 9/30 [3] Incls. non-recurr. chrg. of $1.6 mill.

OFFICERS:
L. R. Greenberg, Chmn., Pres., C.E.O.
A. J. Mendicino, C.F.O., V.P., Fin.
B. P. Bovaird, V.P., Gen. Coun.

INVESTOR CONTACT: Robert W. Krick, Asst. Treas., (610) 337-1000

PRINCIPAL OFFICE: 460 North Gulph Road, King of Prussia, PA 19406

TELEPHONE NUMBER: (610) 337-1000
FAX: (610) 992-3254
WEB: www.ugicorp.com

NO. OF EMPLOYEES: 6,720

SHAREHOLDERS: 11,711

ANNUAL MEETING: In Feb.

INCORPORATED: PA, 1991

INSTITUTIONAL HOLDINGS:
No. of Institutions: 99
Shares Held: 15,661,126
% Held: 49.3

INDUSTRY: Gas and other services combined (SIC: 4932)

TRANSFER AGENT(S): ChaseMellon Shareholder Services, Ridgefield Park, NJ

UNITED DOMINION REALTY TRUST, INC.

YIELD 10.0%
P/E RATIO 20.3

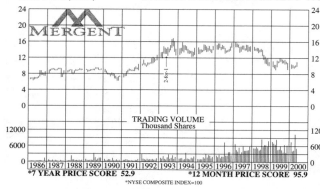

TRADING VOLUME
Thousand Shares

| 1986 | 1987 | 1988 | 1989 | 1990 | 1991 | 1992 | 1993 | 1994 | 1995 | 1996 | 1997 | 1998 | 1999 | 2000 |

*7 YEAR PRICE SCORE 52.9   ***12 MONTH PRICE SCORE 95.9**

*NYSE COMPOSITE INDEX=100

INTERIM EARNINGS (Per Share):

Qtr.	Mar.	June	Sept.	Dec.
1996	0.13	0.10	0.13	0.14
1997	0.17	0.13	0.20	0.11
1998	0.13	0.29	0.08	Nil
1999	0.10	0.30	0.10	0.03

INTERIM DIVIDENDS (Per Share):

Amt.	Decl.	Ex.	Rec.	Pay.
0.265Q	3/10/99	4/14/99	4/16/99	4/30/99
0.265Q	6/22/99	7/14/99	7/16/99	7/30/99
0.265Q	9/17/99	10/13/99	10/15/99	11/01/99
0.265Q	12/08/99	1/12/00	1/14/00	1/31/00
0.268Q	3/09/00	4/12/00	4/14/00	4/28/00

Indicated div.: $1.07

CAPITALIZATION (12/31/99):

	($000)	(%)
Long-Term Debt	2,176,059	60.8
Minority Interest	94,167	2.6
Preferred Stock	427,872	12.0
Common & Surplus	882,340	24.6
Total	3,580,438	100.0

DIVIDEND ACHIEVER STATUS:

Rank: 249   10-Year Growth Rate: 5.83%
Total Years of Dividend Growth: 14

RECENT DEVELOPMENTS: For the year ended 12/31/99, income before an extraordinary gain totaled $92.7 million versus income of $72.5 million, before an extraordinary loss, a year earlier. Results for 1999 included a $19.3 million impairment loss on real estate and investments. Results for 1998 included a $15.6 million loss on the termination of an interest rate risk management agreement. Results included gains on the sale of investments of $38.0 million

and $26.7 million in 1999 and 1998, respectively. Total revenues were $620.7 million, up 28.7% from $482.1 million in the prior year. Rental income soared 29.3% to $618.7 million from $478.7 million in the preceding year. Other non-property income declined 42.6% to $1.9 million compared with $3.4 million in the previous year. Income before gains on sales of investments, minority interests and extraordinary item jumped 27.5% to $60.4 million.

BUSINESS

UNITED DOMINION REALTY TRUST, INC. a self-administered equity real estate investment trust with activities related to the ownership, development, acquisition, renovation, management, marketing and strategic disposition of multifamily apartment communities nationwide. At 12/31/99, UDR's apartment portfolio included 301 communities having a total of 82,154 completed apartment homes. In addition, the Company had three new communities and three additional phases to existing communities with 1,622 apartment homes under development at 12/31/99. The Company's apartment communities consist primarily of upper and middle-income garden and townhouse communities that make up the broadest segment of the apartment market.

ANNUAL FINANCIAL DATA

	12/31/99	12/31/98	12/31/97	12/31/96	12/31/95	12/31/94	12/31/93
Earnings Per Share	①②0.54	①②0.49	①②0.60	①②0.49	0.50	①0.41	0.29
Tang. Book Val. Per Share	8.59	9.11	9.01	9.09	7.30	7.09	6.24
Dividends Per Share	1.06	1.04	1.00	0.94	0.87	0.76	0.69
Dividend Payout %	195.8	212.2	166.2	192.8	174.0	185.3	237.8
INCOME STATEMENT (IN MILLIONS):							
Rental Income	618.7	478.7	386.7	242.1	195.2	140.0	89.1
Total Income	620.7	482.1	387.8	243.8	195.2	140.0	89.1
Costs & Expenses	280.4	225.3	172.2	110.5	86.5	63.7	41.2
Depreciation	126.2	103.2	78.8	48.7	40.0	29.6	20.4
Interest Expense	153.7	106.2	79.0	50.8	40.6	28.3	16.9
Income Before Income Taxes	98.4	74.0	70.5	38.1	33.1	19.2	11.2
Equity Earnings/Minority Int.	d5.7	d1.5	d0.3	d0.1	...	...	...
Net Income	①92.7	①72.5	①70.2	①38.0	33.1	①19.2	11.2
Average Shs. Outstg. (000)	103,639	100,062	87,339	57,482	52,781	46,182	38,202
BALANCE SHEET (IN MILLIONS):							
Cash & Cash Equivalents	7.7	18.5	0.5	13.5	2.9	7.3	5.8
Total Real Estate Investments	3,204.7	3,362.6	2,080.9	1,834.3	1,001.6	887.3	490.8
Total Assets	3,688.3	3,755.4	2,313.7	1,966.9	1,080.6	911.9	505.8
Long-Term Obligations	2,176.1	2,167.5	1,192.9	1,044.8	530.3	526.7	72.9
Total Liabilities	2,378.1	2,381.3	1,255.4	1,116.5	564.2	554.9	245.9
Net Stockholders' Equity	1,310.2	1,374.1	1,058.4	850.4	516.4	357.0	260.0
Year-end Shs. Outstg. (000)	102,741	103,639	89,168	81,983	56,375	50,356	41,653
STATISTICAL RECORD:							
Net Inc.+Depr./Assets %	5.9	4.7	6.4	4.4	6.8	5.4	6.2
Return on Equity %	7.1	5.3	6.6	4.5	6.4	5.4	4.3
Return on Assets %	2.5	1.9	3.0	1.9	3.1	2.1	2.2
Price Range	12¹⁄₁₆-9¹⁄₁₆	14¹³⁄₁₆-10¹⁄₁₆	16-13⅜	15¹³⁄₁₆-13⅛	15⅜-13	15⅞-12¼	16⅞-11⅞
P/E Ratio	22.3-16.8	30.2-20.5	26.7-22.3	32.3-26.8	30.7-26.0	38.7-29.9	58.2-40.9
Average Yield %	10.0	8.4	6.8	6.5	6.1	5.4	4.8

Statistics are as originally reported. Adj. for stock split: 2-for-1, 5/5/93 ① Bef. extraord. gain, $927,000, 99; chrg. $138,000, 98; $50,000, 97; $23,000, 96; $89,000, 94. ② Incl. nonrecurr. chrg. $19.3 mill., 99; $15.6 mill., 98; $1.4 mill., 97; $290,000, 96.

UNITED FIRE & CASUALTY COMPANY

TRADING VOLUME
Thousand Shares

| 1986 | 1987 | 1988 | 1989 | 1990 | 1991 | 1992 | 1993 | 1994 | 1995 | 1996 | 1997 | 1998 | 1999 | 2000 |

*7 YEAR PRICE SCORE 52.4   ***12 MONTH PRICE SCORE 81.3**
*NYSE COMPOSITE INDEX=100

INTERIM EARNINGS (Per Share):

Qtr.	Mar.	June	Sept.	Dec.
1996	0.81	0.48	0.12	0.63
1997	0.69	0.48	0.33	1.18
1998	0.83	1.18	d0.19	0.41
1999	0.29	0.05	0.63	0.54

INTERIM DIVIDENDS (Per Share):

Amt.	Decl.	Ex.	Rec.	Pay.
0.17Q	2/19/99	3/03/99	3/02/99	3/16/99
0.17Q	5/19/99	5/27/99	6/01/99	6/15/99
0.17Q	8/20/99	8/30/99	9/01/99	9/15/99
0.17Q	11/19/99	12/13/99	12/15/99	1/05/00
0.17Q	2/23/00	2/28/00	3/01/00	3/15/00
	Indicated div.: $0.68			

CAPITALIZATION (12/31/99):

	($000)	(%)
Deferred Income Tax	7,430	3.0
Common & Surplus	237,793	97.0
Total	245,223	100.0

DIVIDEND ACHIEVER STATUS:
Rank: 218   10-Year Growth Rate: 7.25%
Total Years of Dividend Growth: 14

RECENT DEVELOPMENTS: For the year ended 12/31/99, net income fell 35.0% to $15.4 million compared with $23.7 million in the previous year. Results included realized investment gains and other income of $2.9 million and $22.8 million in 1999 and 1998, respectively. Total revenues improved 4.4% to $353.2 million from $338.3 million in the prior year. Net premium earned jumped 11.1% to $273.1 million versus $245.8 million a year earlier. Net

income reported for the Company's property and casualty segment declined 53.6% to $6.1 million from $13.1 million a year earlier. Net income reported for the life insurance segment dropped 12.2% to $9.3 million versus $10.6 million the year before. Revenue for the property and casualty segment grew 3.1% to $274.9 million versus $266.5 million a year ago. Revenue for the life insurance segment rose 9.0% to $78.3 million from $71.8 million in 1998.

BUSINESS

UNITED FIRE & CASUALTY COMPANY and its insurance subsidiaries are engaged in the business of property and casualty insurance and life insurance. The Company's property and casualty segment includes the following subsidiaries: Addison Insurance Company, a wholly owned property and casualty insurer; Addison Insurance Agency, a wholly owned general agency of Addison Insurance Company; Lafayette Insurance Company, a wholly owned property and casualty insurer; Insurance Brokers & Managers Inc., a wholly owned general agency of Lafayette Insurance Company; American Indemnity Financial Corporation, a wholly owned holding company; American Indemnity Company, a wholly owned property and casualty company of American Indemnity Financial Corporation and its subsidiaries: American Fire and Indemnity Company, Texas General Indemnity Company, American Computing Company, and the affiliate American Indemnity Lloyds, which is financially and operationally controlled by the Company. The Company's life insurance segment subsidiary is United Life Insurance Company, a wholly owned life insurance company.

ANNUAL FINANCIAL DATA

	12/31/99	12/31/98	12/31/97	12/31/96	12/31/95	12/31/94	12/31/93
Earnings Per Share	1.53	2.28	2.68	2.04	2.66	2.08	1.72
Tang. Book Val. Per Share	22.84	25.31	25.74	21.12	19.13	15.58	14.06
Dividends Per Share	0.68	0.66	0.62	0.60	0.49	0.48	0.44
Dividend Payout %	44.4	28.9	23.1	29.4	18.4	23.1	25.8
INCOME STATEMENT (IN MILLIONS):							
Total Premium Income	273.1	245.7	244.9	234.8	207.5	184.7	174.1
Other Income	80.2	92.5	66.2	65.5	57.1	49.1	43.8
Total Revenues	353.2	338.3	311.1	300.3	264.6	233.8	217.9
Income Before Income Taxes	17.2	28.4	38.2	27.4	38.1	28.7	22.2
Income Taxes	1.8	4.7	9.4	5.4	9.2	6.2	3.5
Net Income	15.4	23.7	28.7	22.0	28.8	22.5	18.6
Average Shs. Outstg. (000)	10,080	10,393	10,727	10,774	10,830	10,830	10,830
BALANCE SHEET (IN MILLIONS):							
Cash & Cash Equivalents	798.2	356.0	168.5	111.6	113.2	22.1	14.9
Premiums Due	82.2	61.5	58.5	56.6	55.6	58.1	46.5
Invst. Assets: Fixed-term	311.2	591.2	677.4	651.1	589.7	591.7	519.9
Invst. Assets: Equities	109.1	111.1	128.7	91.3	75.7	56.2	55.3
Invst. Assets: Loans	8.6	11.5	11.3	10.6	10.2	9.9	11.0
Invst. Assets: Total	1,230.7	1,084.1	995.9	860.2	790.4	676.8	595.1
Total Assets	1,467.7	1,250.6	1,157.9	1,024.8	943.1	828.1	733.0
Net Stockholders' Equity	237.8	256.3	277.2	227.9	208.8	170.7	154.6
Year-end Shs. Outstg. (000)	10,060	10,092	10,727	10,728	10,829	10,830	10,830
STATISTICAL RECORD:							
Return on Revenues %	4.4	7.0	9.2	7.3	10.9	9.6	8.6
Return on Equity %	6.5	9.2	10.4	9.6	13.8	13.2	12.1
Return on Assets %	1.0	1.9	2.5	2.1	3.1	2.7	2.5
Price Range	35½-19¼	46¼-32	47-29¾	40-27⁵/₁₆	29³/₁₆-17¹³/₁₆	20-16	19⅛-15⁷/₁₆
P/E Ratio	23.2-12.6	20.3-14.0	17.5-11.1	19.6-13.4	11.0-6.7	9.6-7.7	11.1-9.0
Average Yield %	2.5	1.7	1.6	1.8	2.1	2.7	2.6

Statistics are as originally reported. Adj. for stk. splits: 3-for-2, 1/5/96; 3-for-2, 1/5/95

OFFICERS:
S. Mclyntire Jr., Chmn.
J. A. Rife, Pres.
K. G. Baker, V.P., C.F.O.
G. E. Underwood, Treas.

INVESTOR CONTACT: Mary D. Schoop, Sec., (319) 399-5702

PRINCIPAL OFFICE: 118 Second Avenue, S.E., Cedar Rapids, IA 52407-3909

TELEPHONE NUMBER: (319) 399-5700
FAX: (319) 399-5499
WEB: www.unitedfiregroup.com

NO. OF EMPLOYEES: 727

SHAREHOLDERS: 939

ANNUAL MEETING: In May

INCORPORATED: IA, Jan., 1946

INSTITUTIONAL HOLDINGS:
No. of Institutions: 29
Shares Held: 3,452,339
% Held: 34.3

INDUSTRY: Fire, marine, and casualty insurance (SIC: 6331)

TRANSFER AGENT(S): Harris Trust and Savings Bank, Chicago, IL

ASE SYMBOL UTL
Rec. Pr. 26 (5/31/00)

UNITIL CORPORATION

YIELD 5.3%
P/E RATIO 14.9

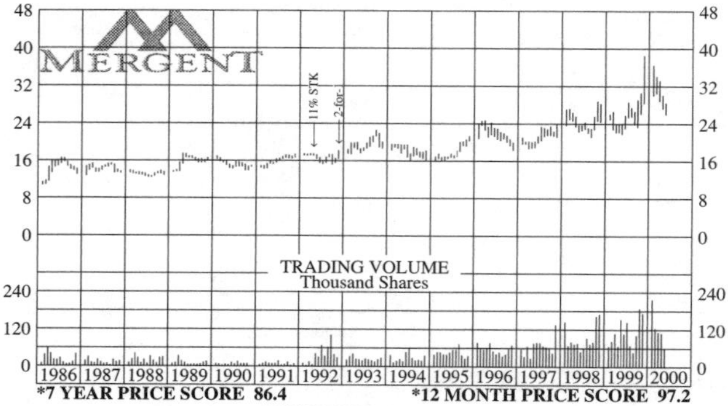

*7 YEAR PRICE SCORE 86.4 *12 MONTH PRICE SCORE 97.2

*NYSE COMPOSITE INDEX=100

INTERIM EARNINGS (Per Share):

Qtr.	3/31	6/30	9/30	12/31
1997	0.65	0.36	0.32	0.47
1998	0.56	0.30	0.36	0.50
1999	0.58	0.32	0.35	0.49

INTERIM DIVIDENDS (Per Share):

Amt.	Decl.	Ex.	Rec.	Pay.
0.345Q	3/18/99	4/28/99	4/30/99	5/14/99
0.345Q	6/24/99	7/28/99	7/30/99	8/13/99
0.345Q	9/23/99	10/28/99	11/01/99	11/15/99
0.345Q	1/19/00	1/28/00	2/01/00	2/15/00
0.345Q	3/16/00	4/27/00	5/01/00	5/15/00

Indicated div.: $1.38

CAPITALIZATION (12/31/99):

	($000)	(%)
Long-Term Debt	84,966	39.7
Capital Lease Obligations	3,860	1.8
Deferred Income Tax	42,634	19.9
Redeemable Pfd. Stock	3,757	1.8
Common & Surplus	78,675	36.8
Total	213,892	100.0

DIVIDEND ACHIEVER STATUS:
Rank: 285 10-Year Growth Rate: 3.95%
Total Years of Dividend Growth: 14

RECENT DEVELOPMENTS: For the year ended 12/31/99, net income increased 2.3% to $8.4 million from $8.2 million in the previous year. Operating revenues rose 3.4% to $172.4 million from $166.7 million the year before. Total electric kilowatt-hour (KWH) sales increased 4.4%, due primarily to system growth and a warmer summer season. Electric KWH sales to residential customers improved 5.6%, due to warmer summer weather and a 1.1% increase in the number of residential customers served. Electric KWH sales to commercial and industrial customers rose 3.8%, due to a continued strong regional economy. Meanwhile, total gas firm therm sales increased 0.5% in 1999 compared with the year before. Gas firm therm sales to residential customers decreased 5.8% to $11.0 million, while commerical and industrial firm therm sales increased 7.6% to $11.2 million.

BUSINESS

UNITIL CORPORATION is a public utility holding company primarily engaged in the retail sale and distribution of: electricity and related services in areas of New Hampshire; and both electricity and gas and related services in north-central Massachusetts. The Company's wholly-owned retail distribution utility subsidiaries include Concord Electric Company, Exeter & Hampton Electric Company and Fitchburg Gas & Electric. Unitil Power Corp., the Company's wholesale electric power utility subsidiary, provides all the electric power supply requirements to Concord Electric and Exeter & Hampton for resale at retail, and also engages in various other wholesale electric power services with affiliates and non-affiliates throughout the New England region. Other wholly-owned subsidiaries include: Unitil Realty Corp., Unitil Service Corp., and Unitil Resources Inc., the Company's wholly owned non-utility subsidiary engaged in the marketing of electricity, gas and other energy commodities in wholesale and retail markets.

REVENUES

(12/31/99)	($000)	(%)
Electric	154,077	89.4
Gas	18,116	10.5
Other Revenue	180	0.1
Total	172,373	100.0

ANNUAL FINANCIAL DATA

	12/31/99	12/31/98	12/31/97	12/31/96	12/31/95	12/31/94	12/31/93
Earnings Per Share	**1.74**	**1.72**	**1.76**	**1.94**	**1.88**	**1.83**	**1.75**
Cash Flow Per Share	**4.12**	**3.81**	**3.86**	**3.92**	**3.67**	**3.62**	**4.28**
Tang. Book Val. Per Share	**16.70**	**16.47**	**16.05**	**15.51**	**14.76**	**14.06**	**13.37**
Dividends Per Share	**1.38**	**1.36**	**1.34**	**1.32**	**1.28**	**1.24**	**1.15**
Dividend Payout %	**79.3**	**79.1**	**76.1**	**68.0**	**68.1**	**67.8**	**65.7**
INCOME STATEMENT (IN THOUSANDS):							
Total Revenues	172,373	166,678	169,738	170,846	156,670	153,416	151,609
Costs & Expenses	141,768	141,706	140,832	143,184	130,477	127,770	126,370
Depreciation & Amort.	11,150	9,666	9,178	8,776	7,834	7,735	7,478
Operating Income	15,408	15,306	19,728	18,886	18,359	17,911	17,761
Net Interest Inc./(Exp.)	d6,919	d6,901	d7,167	d6,171	d5,639	d5,798	d6,523
Income Taxes	4,047	3,710	4,166	4,613	4,135	4,137	457
Net Income	8,438	8,249	8,235	8,729	8,369	8,038	7,600
Cash Flow	19,320	17,641	17,025	17,090	15,789	15,335	17,913
Average Shs. Outstg.	4,693	4,634	4,413	4,354	4,299	4,234	4,181
BALANCE SHEET (IN THOUSANDS):							
Gross Property	219,838	209,462	219,475	207,544	190,177	178,777	171,540
Accumulated Depreciation	66,429	63,428	68,360	63,787	60,683	57,204	53,469
Net Property	158,460	146,034	151,157	143,800	129,537	121,711	118,208
Total Assets	363,527	376,835	237,977	232,108	211,702	204,521	201,509
Long-Term Obligations	88,826	78,334	68,629	65,547	65,944	68,666	59,160
Net Stockholders' Equity	78,675	75,351	71,644	67,974	63,895	59,997	56,234
Year-end Shs. Outstg.	4,712	4,575	4,464	4,384	4,330	4,268	4,205
STATISTICAL RECORD:							
Operating Profit Margin %	8.9	9.2	11.6	11.1	11.7	11.7	11.7
Net Profit Margin %	4.9	4.9	4.9	5.1	5.3	5.2	4.2
Net Inc./Net Property %	5.3	5.6	5.4	6.1	6.5	6.6	6.4
Net Inc./Tot. Capital %	3.9	4.1	4.5	4.9	4.8	4.6	6.7
Return on Equity %	10.7	10.9	11.5	12.8	13.1	13.4	13.5
Accum. Depr./Gross Prop. %	30.2	30.3	31.1	30.7	31.9	32.0	31.2
Price Range	38 9/16-21 3/4	28 13/16-21 1/8	24 1/8-18 5/8	24 3/4-18 1/4	21 3/8-16	19 5/8-15 7/8	22 5/8-17 3/8
P/E Ratio	22.2-12.5	16.8-12.3	13.7-10.6	12.8-9.4	11.4-8.5	10.7-8.7	12.9-9.9
Average Yield %	4.6	5.4	6.3	6.1	6.8	7.0	5.8

Statistics are as originally reported.

OFFICERS:
R. G. Schoenberg, Chmn., C.E.O.
M. J. Dalton, Pres., C.O.O.
A. Baratta, Sr. V.P., C.F.O.

INVESTOR CONTACT: Mark H. Collins, Treas., (603) 772-0775

PRINCIPAL OFFICE: 6 Liberty Lane West, Hampton, NH 03842-1720

TELEPHONE NUMBER: (603) 772-0775
FAX: (603) 772-4651
WEB: www.unitil.com

NO. OF EMPLOYEES: 328

SHAREHOLDERS: 2,700 (record)

ANNUAL MEETING: In April

INCORPORATED: NH, Sept., 1984

INSTITUTIONAL HOLDINGS:
No. of Institutions: 29
Shares Held: 679,884
% Held: 14.4

INDUSTRY: Electric and other services combined (SIC: 4931)

TRANSFER AGENT(S): BankBoston, Boston, MA

NYSE SYMBOL UVV
Rec. Pr. 23 3/16 (5/31/00)

UNIVERSAL CORPORATION

YIELD 5.3%
P/E RATIO 6.5

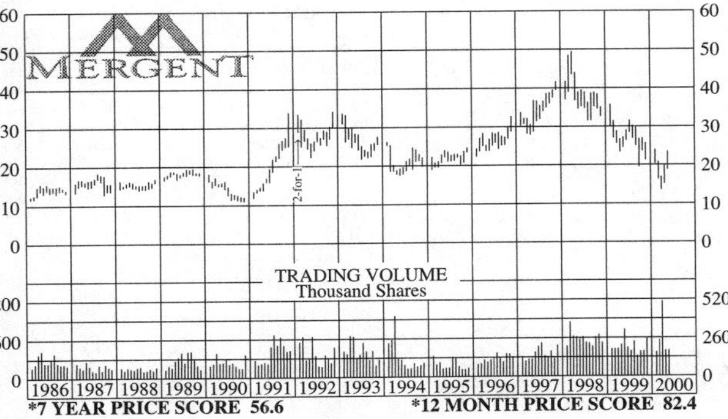

*7 YEAR PRICE SCORE 56.6 *12 MONTH PRICE SCORE 82.4

*NYSE COMPOSITE INDEX=100

INTERIM EARNINGS (Per Share):

Qtr.	Sept.	Dec.	Mar.	June
1996-97	0.57	0.90	0.79	0.63
1997-98	0.63	1.08	1.18	1.10
1998-99	0.78	1.23	0.88	0.91
1999-00	0.93	0.85	...	...

INTERIM DIVIDENDS (Per Share):

Amt.	Decl.	Ex.	Rec.	Pay.
0.30Q	5/05/99	7/08/99	7/12/99	8/09/99
0.30Q	8/05/99	10/06/99	10/11/99	11/08/99
0.31Q	12/02/99	1/06/00	1/10/00	2/14/00
0.31Q	2/03/00	4/06/00	4/10/00	5/08/00
0.31Q	5/03/00	7/06/00	7/10/00	8/14/00

Indicated div.: $1.24 (Div. Reinv. Plan)

CAPITALIZATION (6/30/99):

	($000)	(%)
Long-Term Debt	221,545	26.5
Deferred Income Tax	39,198	4.7
Minority Interest	36,389	4.4
Common & Surplus	539,036	64.5
Total	836,168	100.0

DIVIDEND ACHIEVER STATUS:
Rank: 257 10-Year Growth Rate: 5.54%
Total Years of Dividend Growth: 29

RECENT DEVELOPMENTS: For the second quarter ended 12/31/99, net income declined 36.9% to $26.1 million from $41.4 million in the corresponding period of the previous year. Sales and other operating revenues were $1.03 billion, a decline of 20.4% from $1.30 billion in the prior-year period. Operating income decreased 28.3% to $59.4 million from $82.9 million in the corresponding prior-year quarter.

PROSPECTS: UVV expects earnings per share for the fiscal year ending 6/30/00 to range between $3.45 to $3.65. This estimate includes the $7.0 million severance cost related to recently announced U.S. plant closures. Going forward, the uncertain environment in world tobacco markets may continue to negatively affect results; however, UVV's international tobacco operations should continue to perform well.

BUSINESS

UNIVERSAL CORPORATION has operations in tobacco, lumber and building products and agri-products. UVV's primary subsidiary, Universal Leaf, is the world's largest independent tobacco dealer, providing buying, processing, packing, storing and financing services for manufacturers of tobacco products. Lumber and building products operations involve distribution to the building and construction trade in Europe, and the manufacture of laminated wood products in the United States. Agri-products operations primarily involve the buying and selling of products such as rubber, tea, peanuts, sunflower seeds and vegetable oils.

BUSINESS LINE ANALYSIS

(06/30/99)	Rev (%)	Inc (%)
Tobacco	73.5	85.1
Lumber & Building Product	13.7	8.7
Agri-products	12.8	6.2
Total	100.0	100.0

ANNUAL FINANCIAL DATA

	6/30/99	6/30/98	6/30/97	6/30/96	6/30/95	6/30/94	6/30/93
Earnings Per Share	**[4] 3.80**	**3.99**	**2.88**	**[1] 2.04**	**[2] 0.73**	**[3] 1.09**	**2.39**
Cash Flow Per Share	**5.38**	**5.43**	**4.35**	**3.54**	**2.12**	**2.35**	**3.45**
Tang. Book Val. Per Share	**12.47**	**11.71**	**9.37**	**7.64**	**6.87**	**6.46**	**7.81**
Dividends Per Share	**1.20**	**1.12**	**1.06**	**1.02**	**1.00**	**0.96**	**0.88**
Dividend Payout %	**31.6**	**28.1**	**36.8**	**50.0**	**137.0**	**88.1**	**36.8**
INCOME STATEMENT (IN MILLIONS):							
Total Revenues	4,004.9	4,287.2	4,112.7	3,570.2	3,280.9	2,975.1	3,047.2
Costs & Expenses	3,697.6	3,957.7	3,824.3	3,325.2	3,106.9	2,828.0	2,847.2
Depreciation & Amort.	52.8	51.1	51.6	52.5	48.6	44.9	35.7
Operating Income	254.6	278.4	236.8	192.5	125.4	102.2	164.3
Net Interest Inc./(Exp.)	d56.8	d64.0	d64.9	d68.8	d69.6	d58.4	d46.1
Income Before Income Taxes	211.8	248.0	171.9	123.7	55.8	43.8	118.2
Income Taxes	76.0	98.7	68.8	49.5	24.9	11.8	43.5
Equity Earnings/Minority Int.	d8.5	d8.1	d2.3	d2.9	d5.3	6.5	5.5
Net Income	[4] 127.3	141.3	100.9	[1] 71.4	[2] 25.6	[3] 38.6	80.2
Cash Flow	180.0	192.3	152.4	123.9	74.3	83.4	115.9
Average Shs. Outstg. (000)	33,477	35,388	35,076	35,038	35,014	35,502	33,599
BALANCE SHEET (IN MILLIONS):							
Cash & Cash Equivalents	92.8	79.8	109.1	214.8	158.1	164.5	119.7
Total Current Assets	1,170.3	1,430.3	1,431.2	1,329.0	1,262.4	1,186.0	1,086.9
Net Property	348.3	329.8	309.7	320.4	334.4	269.2	277.8
Total Assets	1,823.1	2,056.7	1,982.0	1,889.5	1,808.0	1,667.0	1,562.0
Total Current Liabilities	898.5	1,101.5	1,083.7	1,029.2	997.6	868.0	786.4
Long-Term Obligations	221.5	263.1	291.6	309.5	284.9	298.1	281.8
Net Stockholders' Equity	539.0	547.9	469.6	417.3	390.0	377.5	417.9
Net Working Capital	271.8	328.8	347.5	299.8	264.7	318.0	300.5
Year-end Shs. Outstg. (000)	32,091	34,866	35,139	35,056	35,030	35,001	35,632
STATISTICAL RECORD:							
Operating Profit Margin %	6.4	6.5	5.8	5.4	3.8	3.4	5.4
Net Profit Margin %	3.2	3.3	2.5	2.0	0.8	1.3	2.6
Return on Equity %	23.6	25.8	21.5	17.1	6.6	10.2	19.2
Return on Assets %	7.0	6.9	5.1	3.8	1.4	2.3	5.1
Debt/Total Assets %	12.2	12.8	14.7	16.4	15.8	17.9	18.0
Price Range	35 3/4-19 7/16	49 1/2-31 1/2	41 11/16-27 7/8	32 3/4-22 1/4	24 5/8-18 7/8	26 1/4-17 1/2	33 3/4-21 3/4
P/E Ratio	9.4-5.1	12.4-7.9	14.5-9.7	16.1-10.9	33.7-25.9	24.1-16.1	14.1-9.1
Average Yield %	4.3	2.8	3.0	3.7	4.6	4.4	3.2

Statistics are as originally reported. [1] Bef. extraord. gain $900,000. [2] Incls. non-recurr. chrg. of $15.6 mill. [3] Bef. acctg. change chrg. $29.4 mill. and incls. non-recurr. chrg. of $11.8 mill [4] Incls. gain of $16.7 million from the sale of investment.

OFFICERS:
H. H. Harrell, Chmn., C.E.O.
A. B. King, Pres., C.O.O.
H. H. Roper, V.P., C.F.O.

INVESTOR CONTACT: Karen M. L. Whelan, V.P., Treas., (804) 254-8689

PRINCIPAL OFFICE: 1501 North Hamilton Street, Richmond, VA 23230

TELEPHONE NUMBER: (804) 359-9311
FAX: (804) 254-3594
WEB: www.universalcorp.com

NO. OF EMPLOYEES: 35,000 (approx.)

SHAREHOLDERS: 3,106

ANNUAL MEETING: In Oct.

INCORPORATED: VA, Jan., 1918

INSTITUTIONAL HOLDINGS:
No. of Institutions: 130
Shares Held: 22,239,272
% Held: 71.8

INDUSTRY: Farm-product raw materials, nec (SIC: 5159)

TRANSFER AGENT(S): Norwest Bank Minnesota, N.A., St. Paul, MN

UNIVERSAL HEALTH REALTY INCOME TRUST

YIELD 11.3%
P/E RATIO 10.5

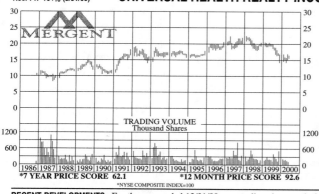

TRADING VOLUME
Thousand Shares

*7 YEAR PRICE SCORE 62.1   *12 MONTH PRICE SCORE 92.6
*NYSE COMPOSITE INDEX=100

INTERIM EARNINGS (Per Share):

Qtr.	Mar.	June	Sept.	Dec.
1996	0.40	0.40	0.39	0.39
1997	0.41	0.40	0.37	0.38
1998	0.40	0.39	0.39	0.42
1999	0.44	0.42	0.25	0.44

INTERIM DIVIDENDS (Per Share):

Amt.	Decl.	Ex.	Rec.	Pay.
0.45Q	6/02/99	6/11/99	6/15/99	6/30/99
0.455Q	9/01/99	9/13/99	9/15/99	9/30/99
0.455Q	12/01/99	12/14/99	12/16/99	12/31/99
0.455Q	3/10/00	3/15/00	3/17/00	3/31/00
0.46Q	6/01/00	6/13/00	6/15/00	6/30/00

Indicated div.: $1.84 (Div. Reinv. Plan)

CAPITALIZATION (12/31/99):

	($000)	(%)
Long-Term Debt	1,289	1.3
Minority Interest	75	0.1
Common & Surplus	99,675	98.7
Total	101,039	100.0

DIVIDEND ACHIEVER STATUS:
Rank: 313   10-Year Growth Rate: 2.17%
Total Years of Dividend Growth: 12

RECENT DEVELOPMENTS: For the year ended 12/31/99, net income decreased 2.5% to $14.0 million compared with $14.3 million in the previous year. Results for 1999 included a provision of $1.6 million for investment losses. Equity in income of limited liability companies amounted to $2.6 million in 1999 and $1.5 million in the prior year. Total revenues rose 2.7% to $23.9 million from $23.2 mil-

lion the year before. The increase in revenues reflected a 2.6% improvement in base rental revenues to $20.2 million and a 153.2% surge in interest revenues to $281,000. However, bonus rental revenues declined 1.7% to $2.9 million. For the quarter ended 12/31/99, net income totaled $4.0 million versus $3.8 million in 1998. Total revenues were $6.2 million versus $5.9 million the year before.

BUSINESS

UNIVERSAL HEALTH REALTY INCOME TRUST is an organized Maryland real estate investment trust (REIT). As of December 31, 1999, the Trust had investments in thirty-seven facilities located in fifteen states consisting of investments in healthcare and human service related facilities including acute care hospitals, behavioral healthcare facilities, rehabilitation hospitals, sub-acute care facilities, surgery centers, childcare centers and medical office buildings. Seven of the Trust's hospital facilities and two medical office buildings are leased to subsidiaries of Universal Health Services, Inc.

REVENUES

(12/31/99)	($000)	(%)
Base Rental-UHS		
Facils	13,828	57.9
Base Rental-Non Rel		
Party	6,844	28.7
Bonus Rental	2,912	12.2
Interest	281	1.2
Total	23,865	100.0

ANNUAL FINANCIAL DATA

	12/31/99	12/31/98	12/31/97	12/31/96	12/31/95	12/31/94	12/31/93
Earnings Per Share	① 1.56	1.60	1.56	1.58	1.52	1.60	1.45
Tang. Book Val. Per Share	11.09	11.32	11.47	11.62	11.74	11.90	11.96
Dividends Per Share	1.81	1.75	1.71	1.70	1.68	1.67	1.66
Dividend Payout %	116.0	109.7	109.3	107.3	110.5	104.1	114.5
INCOME STATEMENT (IN THOUSANDS):							
Rental Income	23,584	23,123	22,180	21,172	19,459	17,993	17,737
Interest Income	281	111	584	751	958	833	526
Total Income	23,865	23,234	22,764	21,923	20,417	18,826	18,263
Costs & Expenses	3,003	3,065	2,524	2,193	1,626	1,320	1,330
Depreciation	3,857	3,879	3,775	3,636	3,382	3,282	3,140
Interest Expense	4,004	3,490	2,943	2,565	1,825	1,146	1,905
Income Before Income Taxes	11,418	12,800	13,522	13,529	13,584	14,312	11,888
Equity Earnings/Minority Int.	2,554	1,537	445	629	...	...	...
Net Income	① 13,972	14,337	13,967	14,158	13,584	14,312	11,888
Average Shs. Outstg.	8,977	8,974	8,967	8,960	8,947	8,947	8,457
BALANCE SHEET (IN THOUSANDS):							
Cash & Cash Equivalents	852	572	1,238	137	139	2	44
Total Real Estate Investments	141,367	129,838	133,486	139,434	131,188	127,516	125,727
Total Assets	178,821	169,406	146,755	148,566	132,770	128,907	126,657
Long-Term Obligations	1,289	1,216	1,147	1,082	1,021	963	907
Total Liabilities	79,146	68,058	44,063	44,584	27,773	22,462	19,627
Net Stockholders' Equity	99,675	101,348	102,692	103,982	104,997	106,445	107,030
Year-end Shs. Outstg.	8,991	8,955	8,955	8,952	8,947	8,947	8,947
STATISTICAL RECORD:							
Net Inc.+Depr./Assets %	10.0	10.8	12.1	12.0	12.8	13.6	11.9
Return on Equity %	14.0	14.1	13.6	13.6	12.9	13.4	11.1
Return on Assets %	7.8	8.5	9.5	9.5	10.2	11.1	9.4
Price Range	20½-14¼	22½-17¹⁵/₁₆	22⅜-18⅜	20⅝-17⅜	17⅞-15¾	18-15¾	18⅞-14⅜
P/E Ratio	13.1-9.1	14.1-11.2	14.3-11.8	13.1-11.0	11.8-10.4	11.2-9.8	13.0-9.9
Average Yield %	10.4	8.7	8.4	8.9	10.0	9.9	10.0

Statistics are as originally reported. ① Incl. a provision of $1.6 mill. for investment losses.

OFFICERS:
A. B. Miller, Chmn., C.E.O.
K. E. Gorman, Pres., C.F.O., Sec.
C. K. Ramagano, V.P., Treas.

INVESTOR CONTACT: Cheryl K. Ramagano, V.P., Treas., (610) 265-0688

PRINCIPAL OFFICE: Universal Corporate Center, 367 South Gulph Road, King Of Prussia, PA 19406-0958

TELEPHONE NUMBER: (610) 265-0688
FAX: (610) 768-3336
WEB: www.uhrit.com

NO. OF EMPLOYEES: 0

SHAREHOLDERS: 885 (approx.)

ANNUAL MEETING: In June

INCORPORATED: MD, July, 1986

INDUSTRY: Real estate investment trusts (SIC: 6798)

TRANSFER AGENT(S): Boston EquiServe, L.P., Boston, Mass.

NYSE SYMBOL UNM
Rec. Pr. 22 11/16 (5/31/00)

UNUMPROVIDENT CORPORATION

YIELD 2.6%
P/E RATIO ...

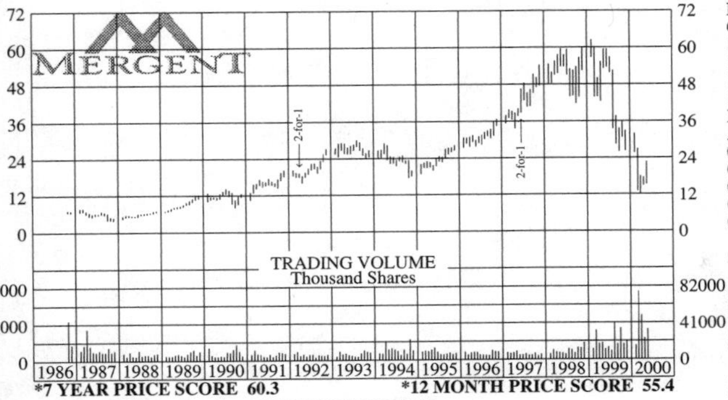

MERGENT
72
60
48
36
24
12
0
2-for-1
2-for-1
TRADING VOLUME
Thousand Shares
82000
41000
0
1986 1987 1988 1989 1990 1991 1992 1993 1994 1995 1996 1997 1998 1999 2000

*7 YEAR PRICE SCORE 60.3 — *12 MONTH PRICE SCORE 55.4

*NYSE COMPOSITE INDEX=100

INTERIM EARNINGS (Per Share):

Qtr.	Mar.	June	Sept.	Dec.
1996	0.50	0.51	0.30	0.33
1997	0.81	0.63	0.66	0.54
1998	0.66	0.70	0.74	0.47
1999	0.37	d0.80	d0.91	0.56

INTERIM DIVIDENDS (Per Share):

Amt.	Decl.	Ex.	Rec.	Pay.
0.147Q	3/12/99	4/22/99	4/26/99	5/21/99
0.147Q	7/28/99	8/04/99	8/06/99	8/20/99
0.147Q	9/10/99	11/03/99	11/05/99	11/19/99
0.147Q	1/21/00	1/27/00	1/31/00	2/18/00
0.147Q	4/12/00	4/19/00	4/24/00	5/19/00

Indicated div.: $0.59 (Div. Reinv. Plan)

CAPITALIZATION (12/31/99):

	($000)	(%)
Long-Term Debt	1,166,500	17.4
Deferred Income Tax	238,300	3.6
Preferred Stock	300,000	4.5
Common & Surplus	4,982,200	74.5
Total	6,687,000	100.0

DIVIDEND ACHIEVER STATUS:
Rank: 59 10-Year Growth Rate: 15.27%
Total Years of Dividend Growth: 12

RECENT DEVELOPMENTS: For the year ended 12/31/99, the Company reported a net loss of $182.9 million compared with net income of $617.4 million in the previous year. Results for 1999 included pre-tax special charges totaling $874.5 million in 1999 versus $103.2 million in 1998. In addition, results included realized investment gains of $87.1 million and $55.0 million in 1999 and 1998, respectively. Total revenues were $9.33 billion, up 9.5% from $8.52 billion in the prior year.

PROSPECTS: UNM has a number of initiatives underway to help restore sales momentum in the Employee Benefits segment, including targeted incentive plans, organizational changes, and enhanced communication with producers. Going forward, UNM will continue to implement organizational changes to focus on specific distribution channels to market Voluntary Benefits products. It is expected that revenue and income in UNM's other segment will decline over time as these business lines wind down.

BUSINESS

UNUMPROVIDENT CORPORATION (formerly UNUM Corporation), is a holding company for a group of insurance companies that collectively operate in all 50 states, the District of Columbia, Puerto Rico, and Canada. The Company was created from the merger between UNUM Corporation and Provident Companies, Inc. The Company's principal operating subsidiaries are Unum Life Insurance Company of America, Provident Life and Accident Insurance Company, The Paul Revere Life Insurance Company, and Colonial Life & Accident Insurance Company. The Company, through its subsidiaries, is the largest provider of group and individual disability insurance in North America, the United Kingdom, and Japan. It also provides a complementary portfolio of life insurance products, including long-term care insurance, life insurance, employer- and employee-paid group benefits, and related services.

REVENUES

(12/31/99)	($000)	(%)
Premium Income	6,843,200	73.4
Net Investment Income	2,059,700	22.1
Net Realized Invest Gains	87,100	0.9
Other Income	339,600	3.6
Total	9,329,600	100.0

ANNUAL FINANCIAL DATA

	12/31/99	[3] 12/31/98	12/31/97	12/31/96	12/31/95	12/31/94	12/31/93
Earnings Per Share	[4] d0.77	2.57	[1] 2.59	1.63	1.94	[1] 1.05	[2] 1.98
Tang. Book Val. Per Share	17.79	19.74	17.61	15.76	15.77	13.23	13.84
Dividends Per Share	0.59	0.58	0.56	0.55	0.52	0.46	0.38
Dividend Payout %	...	22.8	21.8	33.4	26.7	44.0	19.3
INCOME STATEMENT (IN MILLIONS):							
Total Premium Income	6,843.2	3,841.7	3,188.7	3,120.4	3,018.2	2,732.4	2,474.1
Other Income	2,486.4	799.7	888.0	922.3	1,104.7	891.3	922.9
Total Revenues	9,329.6	4,641.4	4,076.7	4,042.7	4,122.9	3,623.7	3,397.0
Policyholder Benefits	6,787.6	2,886.2	2,395.3	2,324.7	2,493.0	2,248.1	1,775.7
Income Before Income Taxes	d165.5	517.4	536.4	341.6	381.9	198.6	460.3
Income Taxes	17.4	154.0	166.1	103.6	100.8	43.9	148.3
Net Income	[4] d182.9	363.4	[1] 370.3	238.0	281.1	[1] 154.7	[2] 312.0
Average Shs. Outstg. (000)	239,081	141,400	142,923	146,000	145,354	148,316	157,558
BALANCE SHEET (IN MILLIONS):							
Cash & Cash Equivalents	613.9	296.7	147.6	200.4	939.2	328.0	90.4
Premiums Due	5,505.9	2,288.1	1,664.8	1,366.2	645.2	189.7	165.5
Invst. Assets: Fixed-term	22,356.7	7,896.9	7,310.9	6,942.7	9,135.4	7,867.8	7,432.7
Invst. Assets: Equities	38.4	31.0	30.7	31.3	25.2	627.9	730.0
Invst. Assets: Loans	3,595.0	1,441.0	1,259.5	1,365.0	1,382.6	1,417.3	1,611.1
Invst. Assets: Total	26,549.3	9,837.7	8,934.1	8,724.7	11,692.5	10,433.8	10,095.9
Total Assets	38,447.5	15,182.9	13,200.3	15,467.5	14,787.8	13,127.2	12,437.3
Long-Term Obligations	1,166.5	881.8	635.8	526.9	583.8	428.7	238.6
Net Stockholders' Equity	5,282.2	2,737.7	2,434.8	2,263.1	2,302.9	1,915.4	2,102.7
Year-end Shs. Outstg. (000)	240,339	138,709	138,272	143,600	146,016	144,826	151,962
STATISTICAL RECORD:							
Return on Revenues %	...	7.8	9.1	5.9	6.8	4.3	9.2
Return on Equity %	...	13.3	15.2	10.5	12.2	8.1	14.8
Return on Assets %	...	2.4	2.8	1.5	1.9	1.2	2.5
Price Range	62 1/2-26	60 1/16-41 3/4	54 1/4-33 5/8	36 3/4-27 3/8	28 1/4-18 13/16	29-17 9/16	30 1/16-23 7/8
P/E Ratio	...	23.4-16.2	20.9-13.0	22.5-16.8	14.6-9.7	27.7-16.8	15.2-12.1
Average Yield %	1.3	1.1	1.3	1.7	2.2	2.0	1.4

Statistics are as originally reported. Adj. for stk. splits: 2-for-1, 6/97. [1] Incl. non-recurr. chrg. 1997, $43.6 mill.; 1994, $134.5 mill. [2] Bef. acctg. change chrg. $12.1 mill. [3] Results through 1st quarter of 1999 are for UNUM Corp. only [4] Incl. pre-tax non-recurr. chrgs. $874.5 mill.

OFFICERS:
J. H. Chandler, Chmn., Pres., C.E.O.
F. D. Copeland, Exec. V.P., Gen. Couns.

INVESTOR CONTACT: Kent M. Mohnkern, V.P. Investor Relations, (207) 770-4330

PRINCIPAL OFFICE: 2211 Congress Street, Portland, ME 04122

TELEPHONE NUMBER: (207) 770-2211
FAX: (207) 770-4450
WEB: www.unum.com

NO. OF EMPLOYEES: 11,900 (approx.)

SHAREHOLDERS: 23,403

ANNUAL MEETING: In May

INCORPORATED: DE, Jan., 1985

INSTITUTIONAL HOLDINGS:
No. of Institutions: 333
Shares Held: 166,500,205
% Held: 69.4

INDUSTRY: Accident and health insurance (SIC: 6321)

TRANSFER AGENT(S): First Chicago Trust Company of New York, Jersey City, NJ

VALLEY RESOURCES, INC.

YIELD	3.2%
P/E RATIO	29.3

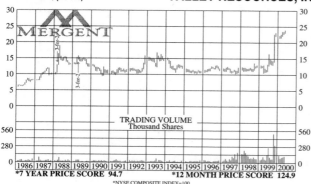

*7 YEAR PRICE SCORE 94.7   *12 MONTH PRICE SCORE 124.9

*NYSE COMPOSITE INDEX=100

INTERIM EARNINGS (Per Share):

Qtr.	Nov.	Feb.	May	Aug.
1995-96	d0.18	0.90	0.47	d0.25
1996-97	d0.18	0.76	0.46	d0.18
1997-98	d0.15	0.65	0.37	d0.14
1998-99	d0.13	0.66	0.47	d0.16
1999-00	d0.17	0.67	...	...

INTERIM DIVIDENDS (Per Share):

Amt.	Decl.	Ex.	Rec.	Pay.
0.188Q	3/15/99	3/29/99	3/31/99	4/15/99
0.188Q	6/15/99	6/28/99	6/30/99	7/15/99
0.188Q	9/09/99	9/28/99	9/30/99	10/15/99
0.188Q	12/14/99	12/29/99	12/31/99	1/15/00
0.188Q	3/21/00	3/29/00	3/31/00	4/15/00

Indicated div.: $0.75

CAPITALIZATION (8/31/99):

	($000)	(%)
Long-Term Debt	31,873	38.3
Capital Lease Obligations..	775	0.9
Deferred Income Tax	14,670	17.6
Common & Surplus	35,805	43.1
Total	83,124	100.0

DIVIDEND ACHIEVER STATUS:
Rank: 299   10-Year Growth Rate: 3.09%
Total Years of Dividend Growth: 19

RECENT DEVELOPMENTS: For the second quarter ended 2/29/00, net income increased 2.2% to $3.4 million versus $3.3 million in the corresponding quarter of the previous year. Total operating revenue advanced 12.5% to $32.8 million from $29.2 million in the year-earlier quarter. Utility revenue grew 14.3% to $26.7 million from $23.3 million in the prior year, reflecting increased gas throughput due to colder weather. Nonutility revenue increased 5.1%

to $6.2 million, primarily due to stronger commercial equipment sales. Cost of gas sold increased 16.4% to $15.2 million. Operating income increased 2.5% to $4.1 million compared with $4.0 million the year before. For the six months ended 2/29/00, net income slipped 4.3% to $2.5 million from $2.7 million in the corresponding 1999 period. Total operating revenue advanced 10.7% to $49.2 million versus $44.5 million the year before.

BUSINESS

VALLEY RESOURCES, INC. is a holding company with six active subsidiaries. Valley Gas Company and Bristol & Warren Gas Company are regulated natural gas distribution companies. Valley Appliance and Merchandising Company is a merchandising, appliance rental and service company. Valley Propane, Inc. is a propane sales and service company. Morris Merchants, Inc. is a wholesale distributor of franchised lines in plumbing and heating contractor supply and other energy-related business. Alternate Energy Corporation, 90.0% owned by the Company, sells, installs and designs natural gas conversion systems, natural gas refueling facilities and energy use control devices.

ANNUAL FINANCIAL DATA

	8/31/99	8/31/98	8/31/97	8/31/96	8/31/95	8/31/94	8/31/93
Earnings Per Share	0.84	0.73	0.86	0.94	0.61	0.91	0.89
Cash Flow Per Share	1.51	1.38	1.58	1.62	1.23	1.49	1.42
Tang. Book Val. Per Share	7.17	7.14	7.00	6.33	6.10	6.18	5.92
Dividends Per Share	0.75	0.749	0.74	0.73	0.71	0.69	0.67
Dividend Payout %	89.3	102.4	85.7	77.4	117.2	76.4	75.3
INCOME STATEMENT (IN THOUSANDS):							
Total Revenues	81,710	81,589	87,484	80,360	74,870	83,553	77,286
Costs & Expenses	69,775	70,333	76,152	68,931	64,956	73,138	67,445
Depreciation & Amort.	3,350	3,226	3,095	2,907	2,635	2,429	2,259
Maintenance Exp.	1,690	1,672	1,634	1,672	1,535	1,485	1,497
Operating Income ⊡	6,895	6,358	6,604	6,850	5,745	6,501	6,084
Net Interest Inc./(Exp.)	d3,008	d3,041	d3,368	d3,312	d3,305	d2,902	d2,610
Net Income	4,187	3,606	3,659	3,998	2,555	3,826	3,727
Cash Flow	7,537	6,832	6,754	6,906	5,190	6,255	5,987
Average Shs. Outstg.	4,980	4,966	4,267	4,259	4,223	4,206	4,203
BALANCE SHEET (IN THOUSANDS):							
Gross Property	86,446	82,965	79,729	76,535	72,760	67,680	63,489
Accumulated Depreciation	34,111	31,655	29,282	27,093	25,349	23,473	21,177
Net Property	58,053	57,719	56,536	55,954	52,971	50,163	48,042
Total Assets	100,223	98,481	97,697	96,689	92,338	91,069	80,795
Long-Term Obligations	32,648	33,566	35,827	27,589	25,871	28,782	29,427
Net Stockholders' Equity	35,805	35,223	34,307	27,092	25,993	26,036	24,943
Year-end Shs. Outstg.	4,993	4,933	4,900	4,280	4,261	4,213	4,213
STATISTICAL RECORD:							
Operating Profit Margin %	8.4	7.8	7.5	8.5	7.7	7.8	7.9
Net Profit Margin %	5.1	4.4	4.2	5.0	3.4	4.6	4.8
Net Inc./Net Property %	7.2	6.2	6.5	7.1	4.8	7.6	7.8
Net Inc./Tot. Capital %	5.0	4.3	4.4	5.9	4.0	5.8	6.3
Return on Equity %	11.7	10.2	10.7	14.8	9.8	14.7	14.9
Accum. Depr./Gross Prop. %	39.5	38.2	36.7	35.4	34.8	34.7	33.4
Price Range	23⅛-10½	13⅝-11	12½-10¼	13-10⅝	11⅞-10¼	15¼-10⅝	16⅞-12¼
P/E Ratio	27.5-12.5	18.7-15.1	14.5-11.9	13.8-11.3	19.5-16.8	16.8-11.7	19.0-13.8
Average Yield %	4.5	6.1	6.5	6.5	4.8	6.5	5.4	4.6

Statistics are as originally reported. ⊡ Incls. income taxes

OFFICERS:
A. P. Degen, Chmn., Pres., C.E.O.
S. Partridge, V.P., C.F.O., Treas., Sec.
P. A. Morrison, Asst. Sec.

INVESTOR CONTACT: Sharon Partridge,
V.P., C.F.O., Treas. & Sec., (401) 334-1188

PRINCIPAL OFFICE: 1595 Mendon Rd.,
Cumberland, RI 02864

TELEPHONE NUMBER: (401) 334-1188
FAX: (401) 333-3527
WEB: www.valleyresources.com

NO. OF EMPLOYEES: 249 (avg.)

SHAREHOLDERS: 2,062

ANNUAL MEETING: In Dec.

INCORPORATED: RI, Oct., 1979

INSTITUTIONAL HOLDINGS:
No. of Institutions: 9
Shares Held: 620,442
% Held: 12.4

INDUSTRY: Natural gas distribution (SIC: 4924)

TRANSFER AGENT(S): The Bank of New York, New York, NY

VALSPAR CORPORATION (THE)

YIELD	1.5%
P/E RATIO	18.0

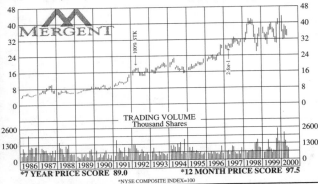

INTERIM EARNINGS (Per Share):

Qtr.	Jan.	Apr.	July	Oct.
1997	0.18	0.39	0.47	0.46
1998	0.20	0.45	0.50	0.48
1999	0.22	0.51	0.59	0.55
2000	0.26	...	...	...

INTERIM DIVIDENDS (Per Share):

Amt.	Decl.	Ex.	Rec.	Pay.
0.115Q	2/24/99	3/30/99	4/01/99	4/15/99
0.115Q	6/16/99	6/29/99	7/01/99	7/15/99
0.115Q	8/19/99	9/29/99	10/01/99	10/15/99
0.13Q	12/15/99	12/29/99	12/31/99	1/14/00
0.13Q	2/23/00	3/29/00	3/31/00	4/14/00

Indicated div.: $0.52 (Div. Reinv. Plan)

CAPITALIZATION (10/29/99):

	($000)	(%)
Long-Term Debt	298,874	42.5
Deferred Income Tax	11,148	1.6
Common & Surplus	393,756	55.9
Total	703,778	100.0

DIVIDEND ACHIEVER STATUS:
Rank: 56 10-Year Growth Rate: 15.38%
Total Years of Dividend Growth: 21

TRADING VOLUME
Thousand Shares

*7 YEAR PRICE SCORE 89.0   *12 MONTH PRICE SCORE 97.5
*NYSE COMPOSITE INDEX=100

RECENT DEVELOPMENTS: For the quarter ended 1/28/00, net income increased 17.9% to $11.5 million compared with $9.7 million in the equivalent 1999 quarter. Net sales were $323.7 million, up 21.8% from $265.8 million a year earlier. Income from operations rose 28.3% to $24.0 million versus $18.7 million in 1998. The Company benefited from the continued sales strength registered by its packaging, industrial coatings and resin product lines.

PROSPECTS: Although sales remain at strong levels, the Company continues to face new challenges from increased competition and pressure from higher raw material costs. VAL is responding to rising raw materials costs with selected price increases and a tight focus on cost controls. In addition, the restructuring activities associated with the acquired Dexter Packaging Coatings operations are continuing to improve the Company's global cost structure.

BUSINESS

THE VALSPAR CORPORATION is a multinational paint and coatings manufacturer that has two reportable segments: Coatings (90% of 1999 sales) and Coating Intermediates (10%). The Company manufactures and distributes a broad portfolio of coatings products. The Architectural, Automotive and Specialty product line includes interior and exterior decorative paints and aerosols, automotive and fleet refinish coatings and high performance floor coatings. The Packaging product line includes coatings and inks for rigid packaging containers. The Industrial product line includes decorative and protective coatings for metal, wood and plastic substrates. Coating Intermediates, primarily resins and colorants, are sold to the Company and to other coatings manufacturers.

ANNUAL FINANCIAL DATA

	10/29/99	10/30/98	10/31/97	10/25/96	10/27/95	10/28/94	10/29/93
Earnings Per Share	1.87	1.63	1.49	1.26	[2] 1.08	[1] 1.04	0.93
Cash Flow Per Share	2.78	2.32	2.07	1.76	1.54	1.48	1.40
Tang. Book Val. Per Share	4.07	5.70	5.68	5.79	4.82	4.03	4.57
Dividends Per Share	0.46	0.42	0.36	0.33	0.30	0.26	0.22
Dividend Payout %	24.6	25.8	24.2	26.2	27.9	25.0	23.8
INCOME STATEMENT (IN MILLIONS):							
Total Revenues	1,387.7	1,155.1	1,017.3	859.8	790.2	786.8	693.7
Costs & Expenses	1,202.9	1,002.7	879.5	742.5	687.2	688.8	603.7
Depreciation & Amort.	39.8	30.7	25.8	22.3	20.3	19.1	20.6
Operating Income	145.0	121.7	112.0	95.0	82.7	78.9	69.3
Net Interest Inc./(Exp.)	d19.1	d10.7	d5.3	d3.0	d4.2	d2.5	d1.6
Income Before Income Taxes	135.1	118.8	109.2	93.0	79.2	75.8	65.6
Income Taxes	52.9	46.7	43.3	37.2	31.7	30.3	25.5
Net Income	82.1	72.1	65.9	55.9	[2] 47.5	[1] 45.5	40.2
Cash Flow	121.9	102.9	91.6	78.2	67.8	64.6	60.8
Average Shs. Outstg. (000)	43,836	44,320	44,233	44,402	44,182	43,646	43,382
BALANCE SHEET (IN MILLIONS):							
Cash & Cash Equivalents	33.2	15.0	11.1	7.1	4.9	2.4	1.6
Total Current Assets	514.9	426.1	356.8	275.2	236.9	220.9	197.5
Net Property	312.1	233.5	185.7	153.8	130.4	107.0	103.1
Total Assets	1,110.7	801.7	615.5	486.4	398.2	363.4	336.8
Total Current Liabilities	374.7	268.0	259.4	179.1	145.9	134.8	113.5
Long-Term Obligations	298.9	164.8	35.8	31.9	21.7	35.3	7.9
Net Stockholders' Equity	393.8	340.2	295.1	253.7	212.1	174.1	196.5
Net Working Capital	140.2	158.1	97.4	96.1	91.0	86.1	84.0
Year-end Shs. Outstg. (000)	42,983	43,418	43,678	43,854	43,978	43,164	43,012
STATISTICAL RECORD:							
Operating Profit Margin %	10.4	10.5	11.0	11.0	10.5	10.0	10.0
Net Profit Margin %	5.9	6.2	6.5	6.5	6.0	5.8	5.8
Return on Equity %	20.9	21.2	22.3	22.0	22.4	26.1	20.4
Return on Assets %	7.4	9.0	10.7	11.5	11.9	12.5	11.9
Debt/Total Assets %	26.9	20.6	5.8	6.6	5.4	9.7	2.3
Price Range	41 7/16-29 1/4	42 1/8-25 3/4	33 11/16-26 13/16	29 5/16-20 15/16	22 5/16-16 11/16	22 15/16-15 1/4	20 3/4-15 3/16
P/E Ratio	22.4-15.6	25.8-15.8	22.2-18.0	23.3-16.6	20.8-15.5	22.1-14.7	22.4-16.4
Average Yield %	1.3	1.2	1.2	1.3	1.5	1.4	1.2

Statistics are as originally reported. Adj. for stk. splits: 2-for-1, 3/97. [1] Incl. pretax chrg. of $2.5 mill. from the writedown of a plant. [2] Reflects the acquisition of Sunbelt Coatings on a pooling of interests basis. [3] Incl. restruct. chrg. of $8.3 mill.

OFFICERS:
R. M. Rompala, Chmn., Pres., C.E.O.
P. C. Reyelts, Sr. V.P., Fin., C.F.O.
R. Engh, Sr. V.P., Gen. Couns.

INVESTOR CONTACT: Rolf Engh, Sr. V.P., Gen. Couns., (612) 332-7371

PRINCIPAL OFFICE: 1101 Third Street, South Minneapolis, MN 55415

TELEPHONE NUMBER: (612) 332-7371
FAX: (612) 375-7723
WEB: www.valspar.com

NO. OF EMPLOYEES: 4,500 (approx.)

SHAREHOLDERS: 1,808

ANNUAL MEETING: In Feb.

INCORPORATED: DE, Dec., 1934

INSTITUTIONAL HOLDINGS:
No. of Institutions: 103
Shares Held: 18,489,163
% Held: 42.8

INDUSTRY: Paints and allied products (SIC: 2851)

TRANSFER AGENT(S): ChaseMellon Shareholder Services, Ridgefield Park, NJ

VF CORPORATION

YIELD 3.1%
P/E RATIO 9.6

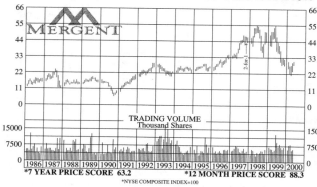

TRADING VOLUME
Thousand Shares

*7 YEAR PRICE SCORE 63.2   *12 MONTH PRICE SCORE 88.3
*NYSE COMPOSITE INDEX=100

INTERIM EARNINGS (Per Share):

Qtr.	Mar.	June	Sept.	Dec.
1995	0.45	0.51	0.54	d0.29
1996	0.43	0.54	0.71	0.64
1997	0.54	0.61	0.86	0.74
1998	0.62	0.69	0.96	0.84
1999	0.69	0.64	0.85	0.81

INTERIM DIVIDENDS (Per Share):

Amt.	Decl.	Ex.	Rec.	Pay.
0.21Q	4/20/99	6/04/99	6/08/99	6/18/99
0.21Q	7/20/99	9/08/99	9/10/99	9/20/99
0.22Q	10/20/99	12/08/99	12/10/99	12/20/99
0.22Q	2/08/00	3/08/00	3/10/00	3/20/00
0.22Q	4/25/00	6/07/00	6/09/00	6/19/00

Indicated div.: $0.88 (Div. Reinv. Plan)

CAPITALIZATION (1/1/00):

	($000)	(%)
Long-Term Debt	517,834	18.9
Redeemable Pfd. Stock	51,544	1.9
Common & Surplus	2,163,818	79.2
Total	2,733,196	100.0

DIVIDEND ACHIEVER STATUS:
Rank: 233   10-Year Growth Rate: 6.45%
Total Years of Dividend Growth: 27

RECENT DEVELOPMENTS: For the year ended 1/1/00, net income decreased 5.7% to $366.2 million from $388.3 million in the previous year. Net sales were $5.55 billion, up slightly from $5.48 billion in the prior year. Apparel sales increased 2.5% to $4.92 billion from $4.80 billion a year earlier. Other sales declined 7.1% to $634.6 million versus $682.8 million in the prior year. Operating income decreased 4.6% to $652.6 million.

PROSPECTS: The key to VFC's success lies in achieving stronger top-line performance. Going forward, the Company will focus on the launch of its Tommy Hilfiger and Nike licensed intimate apparel lines, a variety of innovative new products from its Lily of France and Vanity Fair brands, new marketing programs supporting its Lee Riveted and Mass jeans programs, and a new line of luggage from JanSport.

BUSINESS

VF CORPORATION designs, manufactures and markets branded jeanswear, intimate apparel, children's playwear, occupational apparel, knitwear and other apparel. Apparel is manufactured and marketed under the following brands: LEE, WRANGLER, RUSTLER, RIDERS, and BRITTANIA jeanswear; LEE CASUAL, and TIMBER CREEK BY WRANGLER casual/sportswear; VANITY FAIR, LILY OF FRANCE, OSCAR DE LA RENTA, and NIKE intimate apparel; RED KAP and BULWARK occupational apparel; JANTZEN and NIKE swimwear; and HEALTHTEX, LEE, and NIKE children's apparel. Jeanswear is manufactured and marketed internationally under the LEE, WRANGLER, MAVERICK and OLD AXE brands, and intimate apparel is marketed under various labels.

ANNUAL FINANCIAL DATA

	1/1/00	1/2/99	1/3/98	1/4/97	12/31/95	12/31/94	1/1/94
Earnings Per Share	2.99	3.10	2.70	2.32	1.21	2.10	1.90
Cash Flow Per Share	4.37	4.40	3.91	3.61	2.55	3.35	2.91
Tang. Book Val. Per Share	10.08	9.33	8.68	8.68	6.97	6.41	7.54
Dividends Per Share	0.85	0.81	0.77	0.73	0.69	0.65	0.61
Dividend Payout %	28.4	26.1	28.5	31.5	57.3	31.0	32.1
INCOME STATEMENT (IN MILLIONS):							
Total Revenues	5,551.6	5,478.8	5,222.2	5,137.2	5,062.3	4,971.7	4,320.4
Costs & Expenses	4,731.6	4,633.3	4,460.9	4,419.3	4,547.2	4,274.4	3,762.8
Depreciation & Amort.	167.4	161.4	156.3	160.6	167.7	158.5	125.8
Operating Income	652.6	684.2	605.1	557.3	347.4	538.8	431.8
Net Interest Inc./(Exp.)	d62.5	d55.9	d25.9	d49.4	d66.2	d71.0	d37.4
Income Before Income Taxes	595.6	631.6	585.9	508.4	284.1	455.7	400.0
Income Taxes	229.3	243.3	234.9	208.9	126.8	181.1	153.6
Net Income	366.2	388.3	350.9	299.5	157.3	274.5	246.4
Cash Flow	530.1	546.0	503.4	456.1	320.9	428.8	367.9
Average Shs. Outstg. (000)	122,258	124,995	129,720	127,292	127,486	129,240	128,022
BALANCE SHEET (IN MILLIONS):							
Cash & Cash Equivalents	79.9	63.2	124.1	270.6	84.1	59.7	151.6
Total Current Assets	1,877.4	1,848.2	1,601.5	1,706.3	1,667.6	1,551.2	1,500.2
Net Property	804.4	776.1	706.0	721.5	749.9	767.0	712.8
Total Assets	4,026.5	3,836.7	3,322.8	3,449.5	3,447.1	3,335.6	2,877.3
Total Current Liabilities	1,113.5	1,033.0	765.9	766.3	868.3	912.3	669.8
Long-Term Obligations	517.8	521.7	516.2	519.1	614.2	516.7	527.6
Net Stockholders' Equity	2,163.8	2,066.3	1,866.8	1,973.7	1,771.5	1,734.0	1,547.4
Net Working Capital	763.9	815.1	835.6	940.1	799.3	638.8	840.3
Year-end Shs. Outstg. (000)	116,205	119,466	121,225	127,816	126,878	128,330	128,978
STATISTICAL RECORD:							
Operating Profit Margin %	11.8	12.5	11.6	10.8	6.9	10.8	10.0
Net Profit Margin %	6.6	7.1	6.7	5.8	3.1	5.5	5.7
Return on Equity %	16.9	18.8	18.8	15.2	8.9	15.8	15.9
Return on Assets %	9.1	10.1	10.6	8.7	4.6	8.2	8.6
Debt/Total Assets %	12.9	13.6	15.5	15.0	17.8	15.5	18.3
Price Range	55-27 7/16	54 11/16-33 7/16	48 1/4-32 1/4	34 15/16-23 3/16	28 7/16-23 3/8	26 7/8-22 1/8	28 1/4-19 3/4
P/E Ratio	18.4-9.2	17.6-10.8	17.9-11.9	15.1-10.3	23.7-19.4	12.8-10.5	14.9-10.4
Average Yield %	2.1	1.8	1.9	2.5	2.7	2.7	2.5

Statistics are as originally reported. Adj. for stk. split: 2-for-1, 11/97

VIRCO MFG. CORPORATION

	YIELD	0.8%
	P/E RATIO	6.6

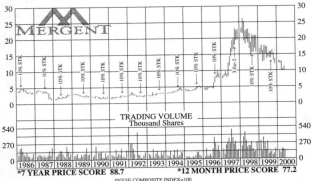

INTERIM EARNINGS (Per Share):

Qtr.	4/30	7/31	10/31	1/31
1995-96	-------------	0.48	-------------	
1996-97	d0.14	0.34	0.31	0.22
1997-98	0.05	0.38	0.61	0.21
1998-99	0.07	0.52	0.66	0.29
1999-00	d0.18	0.61	0.61	d0.08

INTERIM DIVIDENDS (Per Share):

Amt.	Decl.	Ex.	Rec.	Pay.
0.02Q	6/21/99	6/28/99	6/30/99	7/30/99
10% STK	8/24/99	9/01/99	9/03/99	9/30/99
0.02Q	8/24/99	10/06/99	10/11/99	10/29/99
0.02Q	12/09/99	12/29/99	12/31/99	1/31/00
0.02Q	2/18/00	3/29/00	3/31/00	4/28/00

Indicated div.: $0.08

CAPITALIZATION (1/31/00):

	($000)	(%)
Long-Term Debt	46,027	31.9
Deferred Income Tax	4,531	3.1
Common & Surplus	93,834	65.0
Total	144,392	100.0

DIVIDEND ACHIEVER STATUS:
Rank: 21   10-Year Growth Rate: 20.76%
Total Years of Dividend Growth: 17

7 YEAR PRICE SCORE 88.7   **12 MONTH PRICE SCORE 77.2**
*NYSE COMPOSITE INDEX=100

RECENT DEVELOPMENTS: For the year ended 1/31/00, net income totaled $10.2 million, a decrease of 42.3% compared with $17.6 million in the previous year. Net sales fell 2.6% to $266.6 million from $273.6 million a year earlier. The decrease in net sales was due to price competition from regional competitors and a decline in sales and orders of commercial furniture, partially offset by increases in sales to hospitality markets, convention centers, churches, and the Government Services Administration. Education sales declined slightly to $166.8 million from $168.2 million in 1999. Commercial sales dropped 5.3% to $99.8 million from $105.4 million the year before. Gross profit as a percentage of net sales grew to 34.3% versus 34.0% in the prior-year period. The increase resulted from a favorable product mix and stable material costs, partially offset by increased overhead costs.

BUSINESS

VIRCO MFG. CORPORATION is engaged in the design and production of furniture for contract and educational markets worldwide. The Company offers a broad product line of furniture for the K-12 market, as well as a variety of products for the preschool markets, and has recently developed products that are targeted for college, university, and corporate learning center environments. These products include student and teacher desks, computer stations, chairs, activity tables, and folding and stacking chairs for cafeteria and auditorium seating. The Company also produces a variety of tables, chairs and storage equipment designed for the hospitality market, convention centers, churches, and corporate and government facilities. The Company's manufacturing and distribution facilities are located in California and Arkansas.

QUARTERLY DATA

(1/31/2000)($000)	Rev	Inc
1st Quarter	37,479	(1,965)
2nd Quarter	88,224	6,527
3rd Quarter	93,895	6,414
4th Quarter	47,043	(810)

ANNUAL FINANCIAL DATA

	1/31/00	1/31/99	1/31/98	1/31/97	1/31/96	1/31/95	1/31/94
Earnings Per Share	0.96	1.60	1.26	0.85	0.48	0.46	① 0.40
Cash Flow Per Share	1.90	2.24	1.90	1.46	0.97	0.86	0.74
Tang. Book Val. Per Share	9.08	8.38	7.19	5.97	5.17	4.72	4.26
Dividends Per Share	0.075	0.068	0.063	0.061	0.022	0.020	0.018
Dividend Payout %	7.8	4.2	4.6	6.5	4.2	3.9	4.1
INCOME STATEMENT (IN THOUSANDS):							
Total Revenues	266,641	273,620	258,194	236,277	224,349	215,659	205,629
Costs & Expenses	237,364	236,315	226,208	211,528	208,481	200,563	193,768
Depreciation & Amort.	9,993	7,132	7,110	6,541	5,364	4,243	3,642
Operating Income	19,284	30,173	24,876	18,208	10,504	10,853	8,219
Net Interest Inc./(Exp.)	d2,385	d1,111	d1,794	d2,507	d3,130	d2,329	d2,156
Income Before Income Taxes	16,693	28,902	22,604	15,054	8,413	8,024	6,900
Income Taxes	6,527	11,272	8,752	5,728	3,204	3,023	2,598
Net Income	10,166	17,630	13,852	9,326	5,209	5,001	① 4,302
Cash Flow	20,159	24,762	20,962	15,867	10,573	9,244	7,944
Average Shs. Outstg.	10,583	11,048	11,050	10,899	10,845	10,799	10,729
BALANCE SHEET (IN THOUSANDS):							
Cash & Cash Equivalents	1,072	1,086	1,221	722	661	585	383
Total Current Assets	89,926	82,508	74,219	72,688	74,622	69,832	68,723
Net Property	87,937	59,320	39,369	37,478	36,955	31,318	23,716
Total Assets	190,863	151,380	122,015	118,020	119,225	115,008	97,164
Total Current Liabilities	38,503	35,103	30,187	27,545	23,302	27,052	21,685
Long-Term Obligations	46,027	21,344	9,459	21,513	35,909	32,577	24,667
Net Stockholders' Equity	93,834	88,923	77,325	63,965	55,461	50,466	45,637
Net Working Capital	51,423	47,405	44,032	45,143	51,320	42,780	47,038
Year-end Shs. Outstg.	10,330	10,608	10,753	10,719	10,719	10,701	10,701
STATISTICAL RECORD:							
Operating Profit Margin %	7.2	11.0	9.6	7.7	4.7	5.0	4.0
Net Profit Margin %	3.8	6.4	5.4	3.9	2.3	2.3	2.1
Return on Equity %	10.8	19.8	17.9	14.6	9.4	9.9	9.4
Return on Assets %	5.3	11.6	11.4	7.9	4.4	4.3	4.4
Debt/Total Assets %	24.1	14.1	7.8	18.2	30.1	28.3	25.4
Price Range	17¹³⁄₁₆-12	26⅛-14⁹⁄₁₆	23¹⁄₁₆-7½	9-3¹³⁄₁₆	5⁵⁄₁₆-3⅝	4⅞-2¹⁵⁄₁₆	3⅜-2³⁄₁₆
P/E Ratio	18.5-12.5	16.3-9.1	18.3-6.0	11.7-4.5	11.1-7.6	10.6-6.4	8.4-5.4
Average Yield %	0.5	0.3	0.4	0.8	0.4	0.5	0.6

Statistics are as originally reported. Adj. for all stk. splits and divs. thru 9/99. ① Bef. acctg. change chrg. $275,000 ($0.05/sh.)

OFFICERS:
R. A. Virtue, Chmn., Pres., C.E.O.
R. E. Dose, V.P., Fin., Treas., Sec.

PRINCIPAL OFFICE: 2027 Harpers Way. Torrance, CA 90501

TELEPHONE NUMBER: (310) 533-0474
FAX: (310) 782-6098
WEB: www.vicro-mfg.com
NO. OF EMPLOYEES: 2,600 (approx.)
SHAREHOLDERS: 372 (registered); 3,000 (approx. beneficial)
ANNUAL MEETING: In June
INCORPORATED: CA, Feb., 1950; reincorp., DE, Apr., 1984

INSTITUTIONAL HOLDINGS:
No. of Institutions: 21
Shares Held: 2,403,042
% Held: 22.0

INDUSTRY: Public building & related furniture (SIC: 2531)

TRANSFER AGENT(S): ChaseMellon Shareholder Services, Ridgefield Park, NJ

WACHOVIA CORPORATION

YIELD 3.1%
P/E RATIO 14.0

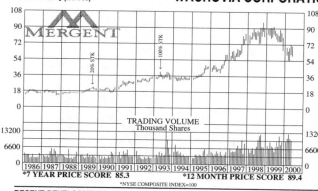

TRADING VOLUME
Thousand Shares

| 1986 | 1987 | 1988 | 1989 | 1990 | 1991 | 1992 | 1993 | 1994 | 1995 | 1996 | 1997 | 1998 | 1999 | 2000 |

*7 YEAR PRICE SCORE 85.3   *12 MONTH PRICE SCORE 89.4
*NYSE COMPOSITE INDEX=100

INTERIM EARNINGS (Per Share):

Qtr.	Mar.	June	Sept.	Dec.
1996	0.87	0.94	0.98	1.02
1997	0.99	1.01	1.04	0.02
1998	0.93	1.00	1.09	1.19
1999	1.18	1.19	1.25	1.28

INTERIM DIVIDENDS (Per Share):

Amt.	Decl.	Ex.	Rec.	Pay.
0.49Q	4/23/99	5/04/99	5/06/99	6/01/99
0.54Q	7/23/99	8/03/99	8/05/99	9/01/99
0.54Q	10/22/99	11/02/99	11/04/99	12/01/99
0.54Q	1/28/00	2/08/00	2/10/00	3/01/00
0.54Q	4/28/00	5/09/00	5/11/00	6/01/00

Indicated div.: $2.16 (Div. Reinv. Plan)

CAPITALIZATION (12/31/99):

	($000)	(%)
Total Deposits	41,786,418	75.6
Long-Term Debt	7,814,263	14.1
Common & Surplus	5,658,457	10.2
Total	55,259,138	100.0

DIVIDEND ACHIEVER STATUS:
Rank: 126   10-Year Growth Rate: 11.45%
Total Years of Dividend Growth: 22

RECENT DEVELOPMENTS: For the year ended 12/31/99, net income advanced 15.7% to $1.01 billion compared with $874.2 million in the previous year. Earnings for 1999 and 1998 included pre-tax merger-related charges of $19.3 million and $85.3 million, respectively. Net interest income increased 5.1% to $2.47 billion from $2.35 billion the year before. Non-interest income grew 29.8% to $1.62 billion, while non-interest expense rose 12.7% to $2.25 billion.

PROSPECTS: On 2/1/00, WB acquired the $1.99 billion credit card portfolio of Partners First Holdings LLC, the credit card subsidiary of Bankmont Financial, U.S. holding company of Bank of Montreal. The acquisition includes a five-year arrangement for WB to act as the credit card provider for Harris Bank, a $27.00 billion in assets subsidiary of Bankmont Financial. Separately, WB acquired B C Bankshares Inc., with assets of $412.1 million.

BUSINESS

WACHOVIA CORPORATION is one of the largest interstate bank holding companies in the Southeast, with $67.76 billion in assets (3/31/00). Wachovia operates more than 700 full-service offices and 1,300 Automatic Teller Machines (ATMs) throughout Florida, Georgia, North Carolina, South Carolina and Virginia. Wachovia offers full-service banking, investment banking, mortgage banking, trust, investment, insurance and several other services. At 12/31/99, the loan portfolio consisted of: commercial loans, 35.7%; retail, 20.6%; real estate, 35.9%; lease financing and foreign, 7.8%. On 4/1/99, WB completed its merger with Interstate/Johnson Lane, Inc.

LOAN DISTRIBUTION

(12/31/99)	($000)	(%)
Commercial	17,732,793	35.8
Retail	10,207,936	20.6
Real Estate	17,822,551	35.9
Lease Financing - net	2,597,271	5.2
Foreign	1,260,674	2.5
Total	49,621,225	100.0

ANNUAL FINANCIAL DATA

	12/31/99	12/31/98	12/31/97	12/31/96	12/31/95	12/31/94	12/31/93
Earnings Per Share	③ 4.90	② 4.18	② 2.94	3.81	① 3.50	3.13	2.83
Tang. Book Val. Per Share	28.04	26.30	25.13	22.96	22.15	19.23	17.61
Dividends Per Share	2.06	1.86	1.68	1.52	1.38	1.23	1.11
Dividend Payout %	42.0	44.5	57.1	39.9	39.4	39.3	39.2
INCOME STATEMENT (IN MILLIONS):							
Total Interest Income	4,666.8	4,665.2	4,262.4	3,227.3	3,019.7	2,362.3	2,122.8
Total Interest Expense	2,196.7	2,314.2	2,168.8	1,672.6	1,579.1	1,038.4	839.0
Net Interest Income	2,470.1	2,351.0	2,093.6	1,554.7	1,440.6	1,323.9	1,283.8
Provision for Loan Losses	298.1	299.5	264.9	149.9	103.8	71.8	92.7
Non-Interest Income	1,621.0	1,248.6	1,007.2	787.7	735.6	607.8	627.6
Non-Interest Expense	2,250.6	1,996.3	1,966.7	1,257.5	1,203.6	1,098.4	1,131.2
Income Before Taxes	1,542.4	1,303.8	869.1	934.9	868.9	761.5	687.5
Net Income	③ 1,011.2	② 874.2	② 592.8	644.6	① 602.5	539.1	492.1
Average Shs. Outstg. (000)	206,192	209,153	201,901	169,097	172,089	172,339	173,941
BALANCE SHEET (IN MILLIONS):							
Cash & Due from Banks	3,475.0	3,800.3	4,221.8	3,367.7	2,692.3	2,670.1	2,529.5
Securities Avail. for Sale	7,966.1	8,648.5	9,908.7	7,946.2	8,524.8	4,428.2	788.8
Total Loans & Leases	49,621.2	45,719.2	44,194.4	31,283.2	29,261.2	25,890.8	22,977.5
Allowance for Credit Losses	554.8	548.0	544.7	409.3	408.8	406.1	404.8
Net Loans & Leases	49,066.4	45,171.2	43,649.7	30,873.9	28,852.3	25,484.7	22,572.7
Total Assets	67,352.5	64,122.8	65,397.1	46,904.5	44,981.3	39,188.0	36,525.8
Total Deposits	41,786.4	40,994.7	42,653.8	27,250.1	26,368.8	23,069.3	23,352.4
Long-Term Obligations	7,814.3	7,596.7	5,934.1	6,466.9	5,423.0	4,790.5	2,960.5
Total Liabilities	61,694.1	58,784.6	60,222.8	43,142.7	41,207.6	35,901.5	33,507.8
Net Stockholders' Equity	5,658.5	5,338.2	5,174.3	3,761.8	3,773.8	3,286.5	3,017.9
Year-end Shs. Outstg. (000)	201,812	202,986	205,927	163,844	170,359	170,934	171,376
STATISTICAL RECORD:							
Return on Equity %	17.9	16.4	11.5	17.1	16.0	16.4	16.3
Return on Assets %	1.5	1.4	0.9	1.4	1.3	1.4	1.3
Equity/Assets %	8.4	8.3	7.9	8.0	8.4	8.4	8.3
Non-Int. Exp./Tot. Inc. %	55.2	55.8	63.5	53.8	56.8	57.0	60.0
Price Range	92⁵⁄₁₆-65⁷⁄₁₆	96¹³⁄₁₆-72³⁄₄	83¹⁵⁄₁₆-53½	60¼-39⅝	48¼-32	35⅜-30⅛	40½-31⅞
P/E Ratio	18.8-13.4	23.2-17.4	28.5-18.2	15.8-10.4	13.8-9.1	11.3-9.6	14.3-11.3
Average Yield %	2.6	2.2	2.4	3.0	3.4	3.8	3.1

Statistics are as originally reported. Adj. for 100% dividend 3/93. ① Incl. after-tax gain of $30.7 mill. from non-recurring items. ② Incl. pre-tax merger-related chgs.: $19.3 mill., 1999; $85.3 mill., 1998; $220.3 mill., 1997. ③ Incl. a pre-tax litigation charge of $20.0 mill.

OFFICERS:
L. M. Baker Jr., Chmn., C.E.O.
R. S. McCoy Jr., Vice-Chmn., C.F.O., Sr. Exec. V.P.
G. Prendergast, Pres., C.O.O.

INVESTOR CONTACT: H. J. Barlow, Vice-President, (336) 732-5787

PRINCIPAL OFFICE: 100 North Main Street, Winston-Salem, NC 27101

TELEPHONE NUMBER: (336) 770-5000
FAX: (336) 732-2281
WEB: www.wachovia.com

NO. OF EMPLOYEES: 21,294

SHAREHOLDERS: 52,178

ANNUAL MEETING: In Apr.

INCORPORATED: NC, July, 1985

INSTITUTIONAL HOLDINGS:
No. of Institutions: 399
Shares Held: 100,396,140
% Held: 49.6

INDUSTRY: National commercial banks (SIC: 6021)

TRANSFER AGENT(S): Wachovia Bank, N.A., Winston-Salem, NC

NYSE SYMBOL WMT
Rec. Pr. 58 (5/31/00)

WAL-MART STORES, INC.

YIELD 0.4%
P/E RATIO 46.4

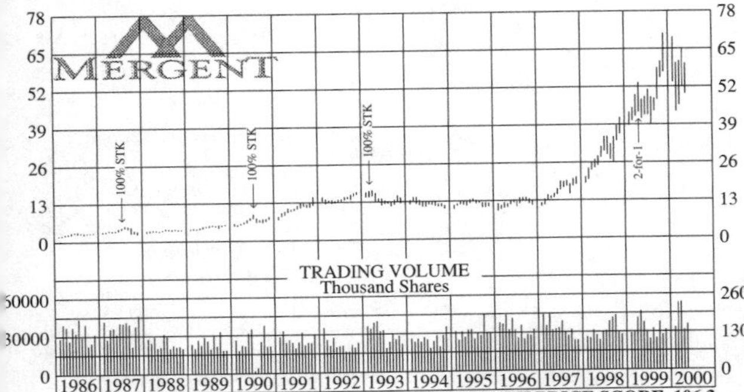

*7 YEAR PRICE SCORE 152.6   *12 MONTH PRICE SCORE 106.3

*NYSE COMPOSITE INDEX=100

INTERIM EARNINGS (Per Share):

Qtr.	Apr.	July	Oct.	Jan.
1996-97	0.13	0.16	0.15	0.24
1997-98	0.15	0.18	0.18	0.29
1998-99	0.19	0.23	0.23	0.35
1999-00	0.25	0.28	0.29	0.43

INTERIM DIVIDENDS (Per Share):

Amt.	Decl.	Ex.	Rec.	Pay.
2-for-1	3/03/99	4/20/99	3/19/99	4/19/99
0.05Q	6/03/99	6/16/99	6/18/99	7/12/99
0.05Q	8/12/99	9/15/99	9/17/99	10/12/99
0.05Q	11/11/99	12/15/99	12/17/99	1/10/00
0.06Q	3/02/00	3/15/00	3/17/00	4/10/00

Indicated div.: $0.24 (Div. Reinv. Plan)

CAPITALIZATION (1/31/00):

	($000)	(%)
Long-Term Debt	13,672,000	31.2
Capital Lease Obligations	3,002,000	6.9
Minority Interest	1,279,000	2.9
Common & Surplus	25,834,000	59.0
Total	43,787,000	100.0

DIVIDEND ACHIEVER STATUS:
Rank: 15   10-Year Growth Rate: 22.12%
Total Years of Dividend Growth: 18

RECENT DEVELOPMENTS: For the year ended 1/31/00, income before an accounting charge totaled $5.58 billion, up 25.8% compared with net income of $4.43 billion the previous year. Net sales climbed 19.8% to $166.81 billion from $139.21 billion the year before. Comparable-store sales grew 7.7% year-over-year. Operating profit in the Wal-Mart Stores segment, including Supercenters, advanced 19.0% to $8.42 billion, while operating profit in the Sam's Club segment rose 16.8% to $759.0 million.

PROSPECTS: During the current fiscal year, WMT anticipates opening approximately 40 new Wal-Mart stores and about 165 new Supercenters in the U.S. Relocations or expansions of existing discount stores will account for 107 of the Supercenters, while approximately 58 will be new locations. WMT also expects to open 19 new Sam's Clubs, including eight relocations, during the year. Internationally, the Company plans to develop or relocate 90 to 100 retail units.

BUSINESS

WAL-MART STORES, INC. operates 1,784 discount department stores, 753 Supercenters and 465 Sam's Clubs in the United States. WMT also operates 460 Wal-Mart stores in Mexico, 236 in the United Kingdom, 166 in Canada, 95 in Germany, 15 in Puerto Rico, 16 in Brazil, 10 in Argentina, and five in Korea. WMT also operates eight stores in China under joint venture agreements. WMT stores offer one-stop shopping by providing a wide assortment of merchandise to satisfy most of the clothing, home, recreational and convenience needs of the family. Supercenters combine food, general merchandise, and services including pharmacy, dry cleaning, portrait studios, photo finishing, hair salons, and optical shops. WMT also operates McLane and Western, a specialty distribution subsidiary, serving over 30,000 convenience stores and independent grocers.

BUSINESS LINE ANALYSIS

(1/31/00)	Rev(%)	Inc(%)
Wal-Mart Stores	65.9	83.3
SAM'S Club	15.0	7.5
International	13.8	8.1
Other	5.3	1.1
Total	100.0	100.0

ANNUAL FINANCIAL DATA

	1/31/00	1/31/99	1/31/98	1/31/97	1/31/96	1/31/95	1/31/94
Earnings Per Share	**[1] 1.25**	**0.99**	**0.78**	**0.67**	**0.60**	**0.59**	**0.51**
Cash Flow Per Share	**1.78**	**1.41**	**1.14**	**0.99**	**0.88**	**0.82**	**0.69**
Tang. Book Val. Per Share	**3.69**	**4.75**	**4.13**	**3.75**	**3.22**	**2.77**	**2.34**
Dividends Per Share	**0.189**	**0.15**	**0.128**	**0.104**	**0.096**	**0.08**	**0.062**
Dividend Payout %	**15.1**	**15.2**	**16.4**	**15.5**	**16.0**	**13.6**	**12.2**
INCOME STATEMENT (IN MILLIONS):							
Total Revenues	166,809.0	139,208.0	119,299.0	106,146.0	94,749.0	83,412.0	67,985.0
Costs & Expenses	154,329.0	129,216.0	111,162.0	98,988.0	88,211.0	77,374.0	62,928.0
Depreciation & Amort.	2,375.0	1,872.0	1,634.0	1,463.0	1,304.0	1,070.0	849.0
Operating Income	10,105.0	8,120.0	6,503.0	5,695.0	5,234.0	4,968.0	4,208.0
Net Interest Inc./(Exp.)	d1,022.0	d797.0	d784.0	d845.0	d888.0	d706.0	d517.0
Income Before Income Taxes	9,083.0	7,323.0	5,719.0	4,850.0	4,346.0	4,262.0	3,691.0
Income Taxes	3,338.0	2,740.0	2,115.0	1,794.0	1,606.0	1,581.0	1,358.0
Equity Earnings/Minority Int.	d170.0	d153.0	d78.0	...	...	...	...
Net Income	[1] 5,575.0	4,430.0	3,526.0	3,056.0	2,740.0	2,681.0	2,333.0
Cash Flow	7,950.0	6,302.0	5,160.0	4,519.0	4,044.0	3,751.0	3,182.0
Average Shs. Outstg. (000)	4,474,000	4,485,000	4,533,000	4,592,000	4,598,000	4,582,000	4,574,000
BALANCE SHEET (IN MILLIONS):							
Cash & Cash Equivalents	1,856.0	1,879.0	1,447.0	883.0	83.0	45.0	20.0
Total Current Assets	24,356.0	21,132.0	19,352.0	17,993.0	17,331.0	15,338.0	12,114.0
Net Property	35,969.0	25,973.0	23,606.0	20,324.0	18,894.0	15,874.0	13,176.0
Total Assets	70,349.0	49,996.0	45,384.0	39,604.0	37,541.0	32,819.0	26,441.0
Total Current Liabilities	25,803.0	16,762.0	14,460.0	10,957.0	11,454.0	9,973.0	7,406.0
Long-Term Obligations	16,674.0	9,607.0	9,674.0	10,016.0	10,600.0	9,709.0	7,960.0
Net Stockholders' Equity	25,834.0	21,112.0	18,503.0	17,143.0	14,756.0	12,726.0	10,753.0
Net Working Capital	d1,447.0	4,370.0	4,892.0	7,036.0	5,877.0	5,365.0	4,708.0
Year-end Shs. Outstg. (000)	4,457,000	4,448,000	4,482,000	4,570,000	4,586,000	4,594,000	4,598,000
STATISTICAL RECORD:							
Operating Profit Margin %	6.1	5.8	5.5	5.4	5.5	6.0	6.2
Net Profit Margin %	3.3	3.2	3.0	2.9	2.9	3.2	3.4
Return on Equity %	21.6	21.0	19.1	17.8	18.6	21.1	21.7
Return on Assets %	7.9	8.9	7.8	7.7	7.3	8.2	8.8
Debt/Total Assets %	23.7	19.2	21.3	25.3	28.2	29.6	30.1
Price Range	70 1/4-38 11/16	41 3/8-18 13/16	20-11	14 1/8-9 9/16	13 13/16-10 1/4	14 5/8-10 1/2	17 1/16-11 1/2
P/E Ratio	56.2-30.9	41.8-19.0	26.9-14.1	21.2-14.4	23.2-17.2	25.0-17.9	33.4-22.5
Average Yield %	0.3	0.5	0.8	0.9	0.8	0.6	0.4

Statistics are as originally reported. Adj. for 100% stk. div., 4/99. [1] Bef. $198.0 mil ($0.04/sh) acctg. chg.

OFFICERS:
S. R. Walton, Chmn.
D. G. Soderquist, Sr. Vice-Chmn.
H. L. Scott, Jr., Pres., C.E.O.
T. M. Schoewe, Exec. V.P., C.F.O.

PRINCIPAL OFFICE: 702 Southwest 8th Street, Bentonville, AR 72716

TELEPHONE NUMBER: (501) 273-4000
FAX: (501) 273-1986
WEB: www.wal-mart.com

NO. OF EMPLOYEES: 1,140,000 (avg.)

SHAREHOLDERS: 341,000 (approx.)

ANNUAL MEETING: In June

INCORPORATED: DE, Oct., 1969

INSTITUTIONAL HOLDINGS:
No. of Institutions: 966
Shares Held: 1,561,178,299
% Held: 35.1

INDUSTRY: Variety stores (SIC: 5331)

TRANSFER AGENT(S): First Chicago Trust Company of New York, Jersey City, NJ

WALGREEN COMPANY

YIELD	0.5%
P/E RATIO	41.7

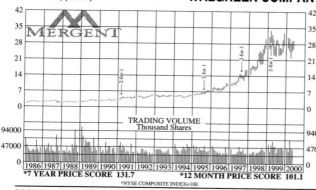

*7 YEAR PRICE SCORE 131.7 ***12 MONTH PRICE SCORE 101.1**
*NYSE COMPOSITE INDEX=100

INTERIM EARNINGS (Per Share):

Qtr.	Nov.	Feb.	May	Aug.
1996-97	0.08	0.15	0.11	0.11
1997-98	0.09	0.17	0.13	0.15
1998-99	0.11	0.20	0.16	0.16
1999-00	0.13	0.23	...	...

INTERIM DIVIDENDS (Per Share):

Amt.	Decl.	Ex.	Rec.	Pay.
0.033Q	7/14/99	8/18/99	8/20/99	9/11/99
0.034Q	10/13/99	11/10/99	11/15/99	12/11/99
0.034Q	1/13/00	2/16/00	2/18/00	3/11/00
0.034Q	4/12/00	5/17/00	5/19/00	6/12/00

Indicated div.: $0.14 (Div. Reinv. Plan)

CAPITALIZATION (8/31/99):

	($000)	(%)
Deferred Income Tax	74,800	2.1
Common & Surplus	3,484,300	97.9
Total	3,559,100	100.0

DIVIDEND ACHIEVER STATUS:
Rank: 126   10-Year Growth Rate: 11.45%
Total Years of Dividend Growth: 24

RECENT DEVELOPMENTS: For the three months ended 2/29/00, net earnings advanced 19.3% to $238.9 million from $200.2 million the previous year. Net sales totaled $5.61 billion, up 19.6% compared with $4.69 billion the year before. Higher sales were fueled by increased sales at existing stores coupled with added sales from the operation of 300 more stores than in the prior year. Comparable-store sales climbed 12.2% versus a year earlier.

PROSPECTS: The Company is partnering with other prominent retailers, initially eleven, to form the WorldWide Retail Exchange, a Web-based marketplace that will facilitate transactions between retailers and more than 100,000 suppliers, partners and distributors operating in the food, general merchandise, and drugstore industries. The World-Wide Retail Exchange is expected to begin operating in mid-2000.

BUSINESS

WALGREEN COMPANY operated 3,007 drugstores located in 41 states and Puerto Rico as of 4/4/00. The drugstores sell prescription and non-prescription drugs in addition to other products including general merchandise, cosmetics, toiletries, liquor and beverages, and tobacco. Customer prescription purchases can be made at the drugstores as well as through the mail, telephone and the Internet. WAG's retail drugstore operations are supported by nine distribution centers and a mail service facility located in Beaverton, Oregon. Prescription drugs comprised 52% of fiscal 1999 total sales; general merchandise, 28%; non-prescription drugs, 12%; and cosmetics and toiletries, 8%.

ANNUAL FINANCIAL DATA

	8/31/99	8/31/98	8/31/97	8/31/96	8/31/95	8/31/94	8/31/93
Earnings Per Share	0.62	② 0.54	0.44	0.38	0.33	0.29	① 0.25
Cash Flow Per Share	0.82	0.72	0.60	0.52	0.46	0.40	0.35
Tang. Book Val. Per Share	3.47	2.86	2.40	2.08	1.82	1.60	1.40
Dividends Per Share	0.131	0.126	0.12	0.11	0.10	0.09	0.08
Dividend Payout %	21.1	23.3	27.6	30.0	31.0	30.9	31.4
INCOME STATEMENT (IN MILLIONS):							
Total Revenues	17,838.8	15,307.0	13,363.0	11,778.4	10,395.1	9,235.0	8,294.8
Costs & Expenses	16,613.3	14,283.0	12,491.0	11,027.0	9,743.5	8,661.2	7,784.0
Depreciation & Amort.	210.1	189.0	164.0	147.3	131.5	118.1	104.7
Operating Income	1,015.4	835.0	708.0	604.1	520.0	455.6	406.2
Net Interest Inc./(Exp.)	11.9	5.0	4.0	2.9	3.7	2.8	0.3
Income Before Income Taxes	1,027.3	877.0	712.0	606.9	523.7	458.4	399.7
Income Taxes	403.2	340.0	276.0	235.2	203.0	176.5	154.4
Net Income	624.1	② 537.0	436.0	371.7	320.8	281.9	① 245.3
Cash Flow	834.2	726.0	600.0	519.1	452.3	400.0	349.9
Average Shs. Outstg. (000)	1,014,282	1,005,692	996,670	993,744	990,108	989,168	990,160
BALANCE SHEET (IN MILLIONS):							
Cash & Cash Equivalents	141.8	144.0	73.0	8.8	22.2	108.4	121.3
Total Current Assets	3,221.7	2,623.0	2,326.0	2,019.0	1,812.9	1,672.8	1,463.1
Net Property	2,593.9	2,144.0	1,754.0	1,448.4	1,249.0	1,085.5	927.3
Total Assets	5,906.7	4,902.0	4,207.0	3,633.6	3,252.6	2,908.7	2,535.2
Total Current Liabilities	1,923.8	1,580.0	1,439.0	1,182.0	1,077.8	1,050.7	883.5
Long-Term Obligations	...	...	...	10.1	10.3	...	...
Net Stockholders' Equity	3,484.3	2,849.0	2,373.0	2,043.1	1,792.6	1,573.6	1,378.8
Net Working Capital	1,297.9	1,043.0	887.0	837.1	735.2	622.1	579.6
Year-end Shs. Outstg. (000)	1,004,022	996,488	987,580	984,564	984,564	984,568	984,568
STATISTICAL RECORD:							
Operating Profit Margin %	5.7	5.5	5.3	5.1	5.0	4.9	4.9
Net Profit Margin %	3.5	3.5	3.3	3.2	3.1	3.1	3.0
Return on Equity %	17.9	18.8	18.4	18.2	17.9	17.9	17.8
Return on Assets %	10.6	11.0	10.4	10.2	9.9	9.7	9.7
Debt/Total Assets %	...	...	...	0.3	0.3	...	...
Price Range	33¹⁵/₁₆-22¹¹/₁₆	30¼-14¹³/₁₆	16¹³/₁₆-9⅝	10¹⁵/₁₆-7³/₁₆	7⅞-5⁷/₁₆	5¹¹/₁₆-4¼	5⁹/₁₆-4⁷/₁₆
P/E Ratio	54.7-36.6	56.5-27.6	38.2-21.9	29.1-19.4	24.1-16.6	19.9-14.8	22.6-17.9
Average Yield %	0.5	0.6	0.9	1.2	1.5	1.8	1.6

Statistics are as originally reported. Adj. for 2-for-1 stk. split, 2/99, 8/97 & 7/95. ① Bef. $23.6 mil chg. for acctg. adj. & incl. $4.2 mil non-recur. chg. ② Bef. $26.4 mil ($0.03/sh) chg. for acctg. adj. & incl. $23 mil ($0.03/sh) after-tax gain.

OFFICERS:
L. D. Jorndt, Chmn., C.E.O.
D. W. Bernauer, Pres., C.O.O.
R. L. Polark, Sr. V.P., C.F.O.
J. A. Rein, V.P., Treas.

INVESTOR CONTACT: John M. Palizza, Asst. Treas., (847) 940-2935

PRINCIPAL OFFICE: 200 Wilmot Rd., Deerfield, IL 60015

TELEPHONE NUMBER: (847) 940-2500
FAX: (847) 914-2654
WEB: www.walgreens.com

NO. OF EMPLOYEES: 71,000 full-time (approx.); 36,000 part-time (approx.)

SHAREHOLDERS: 85,264

ANNUAL MEETING: In Oct.

INCORPORATED: IL, Feb., 1909

INSTITUTIONAL HOLDINGS:
No. of Institutions: 601
Shares Held: 506,461,847
% Held: 50.4

INDUSTRY: Drug stores and proprietary stores (SIC: 5912)

TRANSFER AGENT(S): Harris Trust and Savings Bank, Chicago, IL

WALLACE COMPUTER SERVICES, INC.

YIELD 6.6%
P/E RATIO 6.1

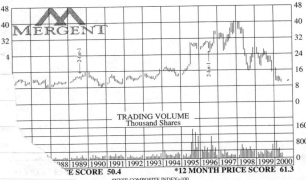

TRADING VOLUME
Thousand Shares

'88 1989 1990 1991 1992 1993 1994 1995 1996 1997 1998 1999 2000
'E SCORE 50.4   *12 MONTH PRICE SCORE 61.3
*NYSE COMPOSITE INDEX=100

INTERIM EARNINGS (Per Share):

Qtr.	Oct.	Jan.	Apr.	July
1996-97	0.48	0.50	0.45	0.45
1997-98	0.49	0.48	0.41	0.33
1998-99	0.40	0.45	0.49	0.46
1999-00	0.44	0.25	...	...

INTERIM DIVIDENDS (Per Share):

Amt.	Decl.	Ex.	Rec.	Pay.
0.16Q	6/03/99	8/30/99	9/01/99	9/20/99
0.165Q	9/08/99	11/29/99	12/01/99	12/20/99
0.165Q	11/03/99	2/28/00	3/01/00	3/20/00
0.165Q	3/15/00	5/30/00	6/01/00	6/20/00

Indicated div.: $0.66

CAPITALIZATION (7/31/99):

	($000)	(%)
Long-Term Debt	416,653	39.1
Deferred Income Tax	64,438	6.1
Common & Surplus	583,567	54.8
Total	1,064,658	100.0

DIVIDEND ACHIEVER STATUS:

Rank: 114   10-Year Growth Rate: 12.01%
Total Years of Dividend Growth: 28

ENTS: For the three months ended
' 45.9% to $10.3 million from $19.0
·sults were negatively affected by
·reased manufacturing expenses
·ment. Net sales grew 2.1% to
·llion the year before. Oper-
·illion.

PROSPECTS: The Company is implementing a number of cost-control initiatives, including the closing of four manufacturing facilities, workforce reductions of more than 300 positions, and the write-off of certain underutilized equipment and software. These restructuring efforts are expected to boost quarterly operating income up to $7.0 million beginning in the fourth quarter of the current fiscal year.

electronic business forms, the manufacture of both electronic data processing labels and prime labels, and the manufacture and distribution of a standard line of office products. The Integrated Graphics Segment includes the design and manufacture of high-color, high quality marketing and promotional materials, and the manufacture of direct response printing materials.

ANNUAL FINANCIAL DATA

	7/31/99	7/31/98	7/31/97	7/31/96	7/31/95	7/31/94	7/31/93
Per Share	② 1.80	1.71	1.88	② 1.60	1.23	① 1.07	0.92
· Per Share	3.58	3.26	3.01	2.59	2.06	1.81	1.60
. Val. Per Share	6.56	5.94	10.06	10.25	9.47	8.81	7.98
s Per Share	0.65	0.63	0.57	0.46	0.39	0.33	0.30
Payout %	35.8	36.5	30.6	28.9	31.3	31.2	32.3

STATEMENT (IN MILLIONS):

.evenues	1,530.5	1,356.1	906.3	862.3	712.8	588.2	545.3
& Expenses	1,299.1	1,143.8	722.0	700.3	590.5	483.5	454.1
.reciation & Amort.	75.4	67.5	49.2	45.0	37.3	33.0	30.3
.erating Income	155.9	144.7	135.1	116.9	85.0	71.6	60.9
Net Interest Inc./(Exp.)	d29.2	d21.4	d0.7	1.6	2.4	2.2	1.5
Income Before Income Taxes	126.8	123.4	134.4	118.5	87.5	73.9	62.4
Income Taxes	50.7	49.2	53.1	45.5	32.2	26.6	21.2
Net Income	② 76.1	74.2	81.3	② 73.0	55.3	① 47.3	41.2
Cash Flow	151.5	141.7	130.5	118.0	92.6	80.3	71.5
Average Shs. Outstg. (000)	42,375	43,397	43,322	45,582	44,980	44,386	44,696

BALANCE SHEET (IN MILLIONS):

Cash & Cash Equivalents	8.0	3.5	15.9	62.6	41.1	77.0	46.9
Total Current Assets	448.4	426.8	290.5	304.1	258.9	248.2	213.1
Net Property	437.0	454.4	301.5	288.9	256.5	232.9	227.9
Total Assets	1,297.7	1,257.5	720.4	695.9	592.7	538.6	480.7
Total Current Liabilities	191.9	189.9	141.3	97.9	65.7	64.8	55.2
Long-Term Obligations	416.7	428.2	24.5	30.6	25.6	23.5	25.2
Net Stockholders' Equity	583.6	547.5	493.2	510.4	456.1	410.1	368.1
Net Working Capital	256.5	236.9	149.2	206.2	193.2	183.4	157.9
Year-end Shs. Outstg. (000)	42,307	43,268	43,070	45,587	45,378	44,786	44,122

STATISTICAL RECORD:

Operating Profit Margin %	10.2	10.7	14.9	13.6	11.9	12.2	11.2
Net Profit Margin %	5.0	5.5	9.0	8.5	7.8	8.0	7.5
Return on Equity %	13.0	13.6	16.5	14.3	12.1	11.5	11.2
Return on Assets %	5.9	5.9	11.3	10.5	9.3	8.8	8.6
Debt/Total Assets %	32.1	34.1	3.4	4.4	4.3	4.4	5.2
Price Range	27¼-14¹⁵⁄₁₆	40-15⁷⁄₁₆	40⅜-25⅝	35⅝-25¼	30-13¾	18⅛-12¹⁵⁄₁₆	16¹⁵⁄₁₆-11⁷⁄₁₆
P/E Ratio	15.1-8.3	23.4-9.0	21.5-13.6	22.3-15.8	24.4-11.2	17.0-12.1	18.4-12.4
Average Yield %	3.1	2.3	1.7	1.5	1.8	2.1	2.1

Statistics are as originally reported. Adj. for 2-for-1 stk. split, 7/96. ① Bef. $663,000 ($0.03/sh) gain from acctg. adj. ② Incl. $1.6 mil ($0.02/sh) non-recur. chg. rel to inv. adj., 1999; & $6.2 mil ($0.14/sh) non-recur. chg. rel. to takeover exp., 1996.

OFFICERS:
N. E. Stearns, Jr., Chmn.
M. O. Duffield, Pres., C.O.O., Acting C.E.O.
S. K. Brandt, Treas.

INVESTOR CONTACT: Brad Samson, Dir., Investor Relations, (630) 588-5396

PRINCIPAL OFFICE: 2275 Cabot Drive, Lisle, IL 60532

TELEPHONE NUMBER: (630) 588-5000
FAX: (630) 449-1161
WEB: www.wallace.com

NO. OF EMPLOYEES: 8,464 (avg.)

SHAREHOLDERS: 2,995

ANNUAL MEETING: In Nov.

INCORPORATED: DE, June, 1963

INSTITUTIONAL HOLDINGS:
No. of Institutions: 140
Shares Held: 33,351,589
% Held: 78.7

INDUSTRY: Manifold business forms (SIC: 2761)

TRANSFER AGENT(S): Boston EquiServe, L.P., Boston, MA

WARNER-LAMBERT COMPANY

		YIELD	0.8%
		P/E RATIO	61.7

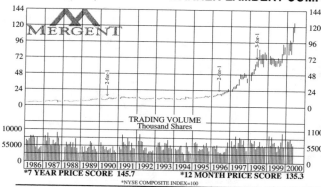

TRADING VOLUME
Thousand Shares

| 1986 | 1987 | 1988 | 1989 | 1990 | 1991 | 1992 | 1993 | 1994 | 1995 | 1996 | 1997 | 1998 | 1999 | 2000 |

*7 YEAR PRICE SCORE 145.7   ***12 MONTH PRICE SCORE 135.3**

*NYSE COMPOSITE INDEX=100

INTERIM EARNINGS (Per Share):

Qtr.	Mar.	June	Sept.	Dec.
1996	0.31	0.23	0.19	0.21
1997	0.25	0.29	0.24	0.28
1998	0.33	0.40	0.35	0.40
1999	0.45	0.51	0.47	0.55

INTERIM DIVIDENDS (Per Share):

Amt.	Decl.	Ex.	Rec.	Pay.
0.20Q	4/27/99	5/05/99	5/07/99	6/10/99
0.20Q	6/28/99	8/04/99	8/06/99	9/10/99
0.20Q	9/28/99	11/03/99	11/05/99	12/10/99
0.24Q	1/25/00	2/02/00	2/04/00	3/10/00
0.24Q	4/14/00	4/19/00	4/24/00	5/12/00

Indicated div.: $0.96 (Div. Reinv. Plan)

CAPITALIZATION (12/31/99):

	($000)	(%)
Long-Term Debt	1,249,500	16.1
Deferred Income Tax	1,405,200	18.1
Common & Surplus	5,098,300	65.8
Total	7,753,000	100.0

DIVIDEND ACHIEVER STATUS:

Rank: 81   10-Year Growth Rate: 14.13%
Total Years of Dividend Growth: 47

RECENT DEVELOPMENTS: For the year ended 12/31/99, net income jumped 20.3% to $1.73 billion in 1998. Net sales grew 20.3% to $12.93 billion. Worldwide sales in the Pharmaceutical products segment increased 30.0% to $8.00 billion. Worldwide sales in the Consumer Health Care products segment increased 10.0% to $3.00 billion. Comparisons were made with restated 1998 results, to reflect the Agouron Pharmaceuticals, Inc. acquisition.

PROSPECTS: The merger agreement between the Company and American Home Products (AMP) has been terminated, resulting in termination fees of $1.80 billion to be paid by WLA. On 2/7/00, WLA and Pfizer, Inc. entered into a definitive merger agreement valued at $90.00 billion or $98.31 per WLA share. Completion of the merger is expected by mid-2000. The combined company will have annual revenues of approximately $28.00 billion.

BUSINESS

WARNER-LAMBERT COMPANY develops, manufactures and markets ethical pharmaceuticals and biologicals, consumer health care products and confectionery products. The principal products of the Pharmaceutical products segment are biologicals, capsules and ethical pharmaceuticals sold under the trademarks and trade names of PARKEDAVIS and GOEDECKE. The principal products of the Consumer Health Care products segment are over-the-counter health care products, shaving products and pet care products such as BENADRYL anti-allergy medication, LUBRIDERM skin lotion, ROLAIDS antacid, EFFERDENT denture cleanser, LISTERINE mouthwash, SCHICK razors and blades and TETRA pet care products. The principal products of the Confectionery products segment are chewing gums, breath mints and cough/throat tablets such as TRIDENT and DENTYNE chewing gums, CERTS breath mints, and HALLS cough drops. In addition, the Company sells specialty candies and mints under the SAILA trademark.

ANNUAL FINANCIAL DATA

	12/31/99	12/31/98	12/31/97	12/31/96	12/31/95	12/31/94	12/31/93
Earnings Per Share	1.96	1.48	1.04	③ 0.97	② 0.91	0.86	① 0.35
Cash Flow Per Share	2.37	1.83	1.36	1.25	1.16	1.09	0.56
Tang. Book Val. Per Share	4.04	2.29	1.37	1.38	2.26	1.78	1.34
Dividends Per Share	0.80	0.64	0.51	0.46	0.43	0.41	0.38
Dividend Payout %	40.8	43.2	48.9	47.6	47.5	47.1	107.9
INCOME STATEMENT (IN MILLIONS):							
Total Revenues	12,928.9	10,213.7	8,179.8	7,231.4	7,039.8	6,416.8	5,793.7
Costs & Expenses	9,896.6	7,998.3	6,480.6	5,786.7	5,706.6	5,165.1	5,333.9
Depreciation & Amort.	362.8	296.3	275.5	230.8	201.9	181.4	170.4
Operating Income	2,669.5	1,919.1	1,423.7	1,213.9	1,131.3	1,070.3	289.4
Income Before Income Taxes	2,441.2	1,766.2	1,233.4	1,176.7	1,148.6	1,005.3	318.5
Income Taxes	708.0	512.2	363.9	321.2	279.1	219.1	33.5
Equity Earnings/Minority Int.	...	...	...	d69.0	d130.0	d92.2	...
Net Income	1,733.2	1,254.0	869.5	③ 786.5	② 739.5	694.0	① 285.0
Cash Flow	2,096.0	1,550.3	1,145.0	1,017.3	941.4	875.4	455.4
Average Shs. Outstg. (000)	884,643	849,076	839,190	813,660	810,129	804,600	810,000
BALANCE SHEET (IN MILLIONS):							
Cash & Cash Equivalents	1,943.2	911.3	773.2	492.3	563.2	465.1	...
Total Current Assets	5,690.1	4,102.3	3,297.0	2,784.8	2,778.0	2,515.3	1,778.2
Net Property	3,341.9	2,775.3	2,427.0	2,168.0	2,006.3	1,846.0	1,599.3
Total Assets	11,441.5	9,230.6	8,030.5	7,197.3	6,100.9	5,532.8	4,387.6
Total Current Liabilities	3,688.5	3,230.0	2,588.9	2,136.9	2,425.2	2,353.4	2,015.9
Long-Term Obligations	1,249.5	1,260.3	1,831.2	1,720.5	634.5	535.2	546.2
Net Stockholders' Equity	5,098.3	3,612.1	2,835.5	2,581.0	2,246.1	1,816.4	1,389.6
Net Working Capital	2,001.6	872.3	708.1	647.9	352.8	161.9	d237.7
Year-end Shs. Outstg. (000)	862,047	821,552	816,672	813,612	813,594	807,570	804,840
STATISTICAL RECORD:							
Operating Profit Margin %	20.6	18.8	17.4	16.8	16.1	16.7	5.0
Net Profit Margin %	13.4	12.3	10.6	10.9	10.5	10.8	4.9
Return on Equity %	34.0	34.7	30.7	30.5	32.9	38.2	20.5
Return on Assets %	15.1	13.6	10.8	10.9	12.1	12.5	6.5
Debt/Total Assets %	10.9	13.7	22.8	23.9	10.4	9.7	12.4
Price Range	93¹⁵/₁₆-60¹³/₁₆	85¹⁵/₁₆-39⅞	50¹³/₁₆-23¹¹/₁₆	26¹¹/₁₆-14⅞	16⁵/₁₆-12¼	14⁷/₁₆-10	12¾-9¹⁵/₁₆
P/E Ratio	47.9-31.0	58.1-26.6	49.1-22.3	27.6-15.4	17.9-13.4	16.8-11.6	36.2-28.3
Average Yield %	1.0	1.0	1.4	2.2	3.0	3.3	3.3

Statistics are as originally reported. Adj. for 3-for-1 stk. split, 5/98 & 2-for-1 stk. split, 5/96. ① Incl. after-tax restruct. chg. of $360.4 mill. & bef. acctg. adj. gain of $36.0 mill. ② Incl. an after-tax gain of $82.0 mill. ③ Incl. gain on sale of pharm. bus. & prov. for legal matters.

OFFICERS:
L. J. de Vink, Chmn., Pres., C.E.O.
E. J. Larini, Exec. V.P., Admin., C.F.O.
R. G. Paltiel, Sec.
G. L. Johnson, Sr. V.P., Gen. Couns.

INVESTOR CONTACT: George J. Shields, V.P. Inv. Rel., (973) 385-2000

PRINCIPAL OFFICE: 201 Tabor Rd., Morris Plains, NJ 07950-2693

TELEPHONE NUMBER: (973) 385-2000
FAX: (973) 385-3761
WEB: www.warner-lambert.com

NO. OF EMPLOYEES: 44,000 (approx.)

SHAREHOLDERS: 48,000 (approx.)

ANNUAL MEETING: In Apr.

INCORPORATED: DE, Nov., 1920

INSTITUTIONAL HOLDINGS:
No. of Institutions: 865
Shares Held: 585,880,088
% Held: 68.2

INDUSTRY: Pharmaceutical preparations (SIC: 2834)

TRANSFER AGENT(S): First Chicago Trust Company of New York, Jersey City, NJ

NYSE SYMBOL WGL
Rec. Pr. 26 5/8 (5/31/00)

WASHINGTON GAS LIGHT COMPANY

YIELD 4.7%
P/E RATIO 15.0

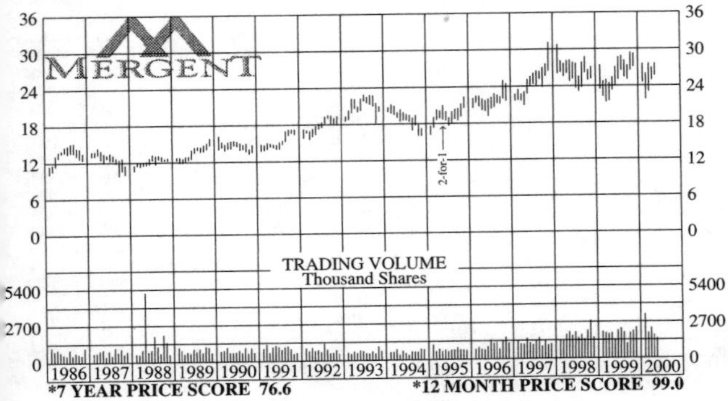
MERGENT
TRADING VOLUME
Thousand Shares
2-for-1
1986 1987 1988 1989 1990 1991 1992 1993 1994 1995 1996 1997 1998 1999 2000

***7 YEAR PRICE SCORE 76.6** ***12 MONTH PRICE SCORE 99.0**

*NYSE COMPOSITE INDEX=100

INTERIM EARNINGS (Per Share):

Qtr.	Dec.	Mar.	June	Sept.
1996-97	0.85	1.35	d0.02	d0.33
1997-98	0.87	1.22	d0.17	d0.38
1998-99	0.55	1.39	d0.15	d0.31
1999-00	0.85	...	...	...

INTERIM DIVIDENDS (Per Share):

Amt.	Decl.	Ex.	Rec.	Pay.
0.305Q	3/31/99	4/08/99	4/12/99	5/01/99
0.305Q	6/30/99	7/08/99	7/12/99	8/01/99
0.305Q	9/29/99	10/07/99	10/12/99	11/01/99
0.305Q	12/15/99	1/06/00	1/10/00	2/01/00
0.31Q	3/03/00	4/06/00	4/10/00	5/01/00

Indicated div.: $1.24 (Div. Reinv. Plan)

CAPITALIZATION (9/30/99):

	($000)	(%)
Long-Term Debt	506,084	36.8
Deferred Income Tax	156,495	11.4
Preferred Stock	28,420	2.1
Common & Surplus	684,034	49.7
Total	1,375,033	100.0

DIVIDEND ACHIEVER STATUS:
Rank: 310 10-Year Growth Rate: 2.28%
Total Years of Dividend Growth: 23

RECENT DEVELOPMENTS: For the quarter ended 12/31/99, net income grew 59.7% to $39.8 million compared with $24.9 million in the prior-year period. Results for 1998 included a nonrecurring loss of $3.3 million. Net revenues improved 5.2% to $133.9 million versus $127.4 million in the prior-year period. Revenues benefited from higher deliveries of natural gas to firm customers, which increased 9.0% to 353.5 million therms due to warmer temperatures.

PROSPECTS: On 3/3/00, WGL shareholders approved the Company's plan to reorganize under a holding company structure, WGL Holdings, Inc. Subject to final regulatory approval, WGL, as the regulated utility, and the subsidiaries it holds, would each operate as separate subsidiaries of the holding company. WGL plans to have the new structure in place by 7/1/00.

BUSINESS

WASHINGTON GAS LIGHT COMPANY distributes natural gas to Washington D.C. and adjoining areas through three divisions: District of Columbia Natural Gas, Maryland Natural Gas and Northern Virginia Natural Gas. WGL also has four active subsidiaries: Shenandoah Gas, Frederick Gas and Hampshire Gas, which provide gas service to areas in Virginia; Crab Run Gas, which is involved in the exploration and development of natural gas prospects; and Washington Resources Group, which conducts WGL's non-gas investments including real estate, energy-related services and equity holdings in emerging growth companies. The 1,537 million therms delivered in 1999 were derived as follows: 39% residential customers, 22% commercial and industrial, 39% gas delivered for others.

ANNUAL FINANCIAL DATA

	9/30/99	9/30/98	9/30/97	9/30/96	9/30/95	9/30/94	9/30/93
Earnings Per Share	**(3) 1.47**	**(2) 1.54**	**1.85**	**(1) 1.85**	**1.45**	**1.42**	**1.31**
Cash Flow Per Share	**2.88**	**2.90**	**3.13**	**3.09**	**2.65**	**2.56**	**2.32**
Tang. Book Val. Per Share	**14.72**	**13.83**	**13.48**	**12.79**	**11.95**	**11.51**	**11.04**
Dividends Per Share	**1.22**	**1.20**	**1.18**	**1.14**	**1.12**	**1.10**	**1.08**
Dividend Payout %	**82.6**	**77.6**	**63.8**	**61.3**	**77.1**	**78.1**	**82.8**
INCOME STATEMENT (IN MILLIONS):							
Total Revenues	1,112.2	1,040.6	1,055.8	969.8	828.7	914.9	894.3
Costs & Expenses	861.1	802.8	799.8	720.7	616.4	701.5	698.6
Depreciation & Amort.	65.2	59.4	55.9	53.5	51.3	48.0	41.7
Maintenance Exp.	35.6	38.5	36.9	33.1	31.3	35.8	33.5
Operating Income	107.8	140.0	163.1	162.4	129.7	129.6	120.6
Net Interest Inc./(Exp.)	d37.0	d37.7	d34.1	d30.6	d31.9	d32.1	d29.1
Income Taxes	42.5	38.0	47.9	49.4	37.5	37.3	34.6
Net Income	(3) 68.8	(2) 68.6	82.0	(1) 81.6	62.9	60.5	55.1
Cash Flow	132.6	126.7	136.6	133.8	112.9	107.1	95.4
Average Shs. Outstg. (000)	45,984	43,691	43,706	43,360	42,575	41,836	41,044
BALANCE SHEET (IN MILLIONS):							
Gross Property	2,114.1	1,992.8	1,846.5	1,722.0	1,608.5	1,516.2	1,405.3
Accumulated Depreciation	711.3	673.3	629.3	591.4	552.5	521.2	484.2
Net Property	1,402.7	1,319.5	1,217.1	1,130.6	1,056.1	995.0	921.1
Total Assets	1,766.7	1,682.4	1,552.0	1,464.6	1,360.1	1,333.0	1,194.7
Long-Term Obligations	506.1	428.6	431.6	353.9	329.1	342.3	347.7
Net Stockholders' Equity	712.5	636.2	617.5	587.2	541.5	514.0	486.6
Year-end Shs. Outstg. (000)	46,473	43,955	43,700	43,704	42,932	42,186	41,504
STATISTICAL RECORD:							
Operating Profit Margin %	9.7	13.5	15.5	16.8	15.7	14.2	13.5
Net Profit Margin %	6.2	6.6	7.8	8.4	7.6	6.6	6.2
Net Inc./Net Property %	4.9	5.2	6.7	7.2	6.0	6.1	6.0
Net Inc./Tot. Capital %	5.0	5.7	6.9	7.6	6.3	6.2	6.1
Return on Equity %	9.7	10.8	13.3	13.9	11.6	11.8	11.3
Accum. Depr./Gross Prop. %	33.6	33.8	34.1	34.3	34.3	34.4	34.5
Price Range	29 7/16-21 5/16	30 3/4-23 1/16	31 1/8-20 7/8	25-19 1/8	22 3/8-16 1/8	21 1/4-16	22 7/8-18 1/8
P/E Ratio	20.0-14.5	20.0-15.0	16.8-11.3	13.5-10.3	15.4-11.1	15.0-11.3	17.5-13.8
Average Yield %	4.8	4.4	4.5	5.1	5.8	5.9	5.3

Statistics are as originally reported. Adjusted for 2-for-1 stock split 5/95. (1) Incl. a nonrecurr. after-tax chg. $3.8 mill. assoc. with the Company's reorganization. (2) Incl. a net gain $1.6 mill. from the sale of invest. in venture capital funds. (3) Incl. a nonrecurr. gain $3.0 mill. from the sale of non-utility assets and a nonrecurr. chrg. $2.9 mill. fr. the sale of utility prop.

OFFICERS:
J. H. DeGraffenreidt Jr., Chmn., C.E.O.
J. M. Schepis, Pres., C.O.O.
F. M. Kline, V.P., C.F.O.
S. C. Jennings, Treas.

INVESTOR CONTACT: Craig Gilbert, Manager, Inv. Rel., (703) 624-6410

PRINCIPAL OFFICE: 1100 H. Street, N.W., Washington, DC 20080

TELEPHONE NUMBER: (703) 750-4440
FAX: (703) 624-6196
WEB: www.washgas.com

NO. OF EMPLOYEES: 2,117

SHAREHOLDERS: 21,565

ANNUAL MEETING: In Mar.

INCORPORATED: DC, Mar., 1957

INSTITUTIONAL HOLDINGS:
No. of Institutions: 152
Shares Held: 16,888,967
% Held: 36.3

INDUSTRY: Natural gas distribution (SIC: 4924)

TRANSFER AGENT(S): Bank of New York, New York, NY

WASHINGTON MUTUAL, INC.

YIELD 3.9%
P/E RATIO 8.9

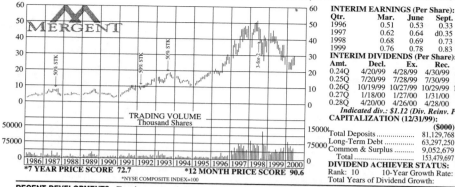

TRADING VOLUME
Thousand Shares

*7 YEAR PRICE SCORE 72.7   *12 MONTH PRICE SCORE 90.6
*NYSE COMPOSITE INDEX=100

INTERIM EARNINGS (Per Share):

Qtr.	Mar.	June	Sept.	Dec.
1996	0.51	0.53	0.33	d0.54
1997	0.62	0.64	d0.35	0.63
1998	0.68	0.69	0.73	0.27
1999	0.76	0.78	0.83	0.80

INTERIM DIVIDENDS (Per Share):

Amt.	Decl.	Ex.	Rec.	Pay.
0.24Q	4/20/99	4/28/99	4/30/99	5/14/99
0.25Q	7/20/99	7/28/99	7/30/99	8/13/99
0.26Q	10/19/99	10/27/99	10/29/99	11/15/99
0.27Q	1/18/00	1/27/00	1/31/00	2/15/00
0.28Q	4/20/00	4/26/00	4/28/00	5/15/00

Indicated div.: $1.12 (Div. Reinv. Plan)

CAPITALIZATION (12/31/99):

	($000)	(%)
Total Deposits	81,129,768	52.9
Long-Term Debt	63,297,250	41.2
Common & Surplus	9,052,679	5.9
Total	153,479,697	100.0

DIVIDEND ACHIEVER STATUS:
Rank: 10   10-Year Growth Rate: 23.52%
Total Years of Dividend Growth: 10

RECENT DEVELOPMENTS: For the year ended 12/31/99, net income increased 22.2% to $1.82 billion from $1.49 billion in the prior year. Net interest income advanced 3.7% to $4.45 billion from $4.29 billion a year earlier. Net interest margin fell to 2.63% from 2.88% the year before. Total non-interest income remained relatively flat at $1.51 billion compared with the year before. Total non-interest expense dropped 11.0% to $2.91 billion.

PROSPECTS: On 4/5/00, WM opened the first five of 21 new retail concept financial stores in Southern Nevada. The remaining sixteen stores will open by the end of Summer 2000. WM expects the stores to break even after one year of operation and to achieve a return on common equity of 20.0% by the end of the second year of operation. Separately, WM plans to increase its proportion of higher-margin loans, diversify revenues, and launch new services.

BUSINESS

WASHINGTON MUTUAL, INC. is a holding company for both banking and nonbanking subsidiaries. The Company's primary banking subsidiaries are Washington Mutual Bank, FA (formerly Washington Mutual Savings Bank), Washington Mutual Bank and Washington Mutual Bank fsb. These organizations provide consumer banking, full-service securities brokerage, mutual fund management, and travel and insurance underwriting services. As of 3/31/00, WM and its subsidiaries had assets of $188.61 billion and operated more than 2,000 offices nationwide. On 12/20/96, the Company acquired Keystone Holdings, Inc. and its subsidiary, American Savings Bank. Effective 7/1/97, WM acquired Great Western Financial Corporation. On 10/1/98, the Company acquired H.F. Ahmanson & Company.

LOAN DISTRIBUTION

(12/31/99)	($000)	(%)
SFR	80,628,424	70.4
SFR Construction	1,242,784	1.1
Second Mortgage & Other	8,527,303	7.4
Special Mortgage Finance	4,451,631	3.9
Commercial Business	1,451,505	1.3
Comercial Real Estate	18,237,507	15.9
Total	114,539,154	100.0

ANNUAL FINANCIAL DATA

	12/31/99	12/31/98	12/31/97	12/31/96	12/31/95	12/31/94	12/31/93
Earnings Per Share	3.16	⑤2.56	④1.24	③0.57	1.65	1.69	①②1.83
Tang. Book Val. Per Share	12.61	13.27	11.96	11.97	13.26	11.98	10.79
Dividends Per Share	0.98	0.82	0.71	0.60	0.51	0.47	0.33
Dividend Payout %	31.0	32.0	57.0	105.8	31.2	27.6	18.1
INCOME STATEMENT (IN MILLIONS):							
Total Interest Income	12,062.2	11,221.5	6,811.0	3,149.2	2,916.1	1,207.8	1,035.9
Total Interest Expense	7,610.4	6,929.7	4,154.5	1,958.2	1,923.4	636.6	506.5
Net Interest Income	4,451.8	4,291.7	2,656.5	1,191.0	992.6	571.2	529.4
Provision for Loan Losses	167.1	162.0	207.1	201.5	75.0	20.0	35.0
Non-Interest Income	1,509.0	1,577.0	750.9	259.3	208.3	107.8	143.9
Non-Interest Expense	2,909.6	3,337.3	2,299.1	1,025.3	700.5	384.3	369.3
Income Before Taxes	2,884.2	2,369.5	901.1	223.5	425.5	274.8	269.0
Equity Earnings/Minority Int.	...	...	...	d13.6	d15.8	...	...
Net Income	1,817.1	⑤1,486.9	④481.8	③114.3	289.9	172.3	①②175.3
Average Shs. Outstg. (000)	574,553	578,562	370,568	169,289	164,916	90,743	88,431
BALANCE SHEET (IN MILLIONS):							
Securities Avail. for Sale	34.7	39.1	23.4	1.6	0.2	0.6	1.1
Total Loans & Leases	113,745.7	107,612.2	67,810.7	30,694.2	24,428.1	12,534.6	11,006.3
Allowance for Credit Losses	1,041.9	1,067.8	670.5	590.8	319.0	128.0	115.2
Net Loans & Leases	112,703.7	106,544.4	67,140.2	30,103.4	24,109.1	12,406.6	10,891.1
Total Assets	186,513.6	165,493.3	96,981.1	44,551.9	41,471.4	18,457.7	15,827.2
Total Deposits	81,129.8	85,492.1	50,986.0	24,080.1	24,463.0	9,777.9	9,351.4
Long-Term Obligations	63,297.3	45,198.1	22,991.3	7,918.5	5,306.0	3,816.7	2,163.6
Total Liabilities	177,461.0	156,148.9	91,672.0	42,154.0	39,484.9	17,153.1	14,631.5
Net Stockholders' Equity	9,052.7	9,344.4	5,309.1	2,397.9	2,541.7	1,304.6	1,195.7
Year-end Shs. Outstg. (000)	571,589	593,408	386,340	189,213	179,532	92,957	90,137
STATISTICAL RECORD:							
Return on Equity %	20.1	15.9	9.1	4.8	11.4	13.2	14.7
Return on Assets %	1.0	0.9	0.5	0.3	0.7	0.9	1.1
Equity/Assets %	4.9	5.6	5.5	5.4	6.1	7.1	7.6
Non-Int. Exp./Tot. Inc. %	48.8	56.9	67.5	70.7	58.3	56.6	54.8
Price Range	45¾-24¹¹⁄₁₆	51¹¹⁄₁₆-26¾	48⁷⁄₁₆-28³⁄₁₆	30⁹⁄₁₆-17¹⁄₁₆	19¹¹⁄₁₆-11¹⁄₁₆	16¹¹⁄₁₆-10½	18¹⁵⁄₁₆-11¹⁵⁄₁₆
P/E Ratio	14.5-7.8	20.2-10.4	39.0-22.7	53.9-30.7	11.9-6.7	9.8-6.2	10.4-6.5
Average Yield %	2.8	2.1	1.8	2.5	3.3	3.4	2.1

Statistics are as originally reported. Adj. for stk. 3-for-2 splits: 6/98, 8/93. ① Bef. extraord. chrg.: $9.0 mill. ② Bef. acctg. credit $13.4 mill. ③ Incl. various pre-tax net exps. of $256.7 mill. ④ Incl. transact.-rel. exp. of $531.1 mill., $116.5 mill. in tax benefits, $20.8 mill. gain fr. the sale of subsid., & write-off of consult. fees of $9.9 mill. ⑤ Incl. net pre-tax non-recurr. gains of $316.0 mill. & a write-down of $52.9 mill. ⑥ Incl. trans.-rel. exp. of $95.7 mill.

OFFICERS:
K. K. Killinger, Chmn., Pres., C.E.O.
W. A. Longbrake, Vice-Chmn., C.F.O.

INVESTOR CONTACT: JoAnn DeGrande, First Vice-Pres., (206) 461-3186

PRINCIPAL OFFICE: 1201 Third Avenue, Seattle, WA 98101

TELEPHONE NUMBER: (206) 461-2000
FAX: (206) 554-2778
WEB: www.wamu.com

NO. OF EMPLOYEES: 28,509

SHAREHOLDERS: 36,861

ANNUAL MEETING: In Apr.

INCORPORATED: WA, Nov., 1994

INSTITUTIONAL HOLDINGS:
No. of Institutions: 461
Shares Held: 429,878,556
% Held: 74.5

INDUSTRY: Savings institutions, except federal (SIC: 6036)

TRANSFER AGENT(S): ChaseMellon Shareholder Services, L.L.C., Ridgefield Park, NJ

NYSE SYMBOL WRE
Rec. Pr. 16⅞ (5/31/00)

WASHINGTON REAL ESTATE INVESTMENT TRUST

YIELD 7.4%
P/E RATIO 13.5

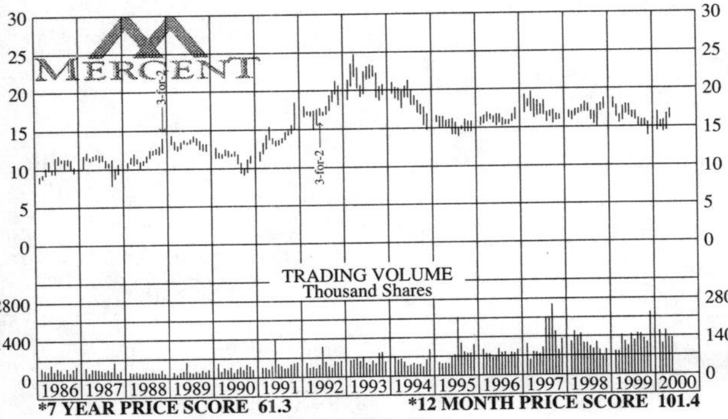

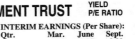

MERGENT
3-for-2
3-for-2
TRADING VOLUME
Thousand Shares
1986 1987 1988 1989 1990 1991 1992 1993 1994 1995 1996 1997 1998 1999 2000

*7 YEAR PRICE SCORE 61.3 *12 MONTH PRICE SCORE 101.4

*NYSE COMPOSITE INDEX=100

INTERIM EARNINGS (Per Share):

Qtr.	Mar.	June	Sept.	Dec.
1995	0.22	0.22	0.22	0.22
1996	0.22	0.22	0.22	0.22
1997	0.22	0.22	0.23	0.23
1998	0.40	0.23	0.23	0.28
1999	0.46	0.25	0.25	0.29

INTERIM DIVIDENDS (Per Share):

Amt.	Decl.	Ex.	Rec.	Pay.
0.292Q	5/20/99	6/11/99	6/15/99	6/30/99
0.292Q	8/24/99	9/13/99	9/15/99	9/29/99
0.292Q	11/24/99	12/09/99	12/13/99	12/30/99
0.292Q	2/22/00	3/14/00	3/16/00	3/30/00
0.313Q	5/18/00	6/13/00	6/15/00	6/29/00

Indicated div.: $1.25

CAPITALIZATION (12/31/99):

	($000)	(%)
Long-Term Debt	297,038	53.4
Minority Interest	1,522	0.3
Common & Surplus	257,189	46.3
Total	555,749	100.0

DIVIDEND ACHIEVER STATUS:

Rank: 259 10-Year Growth Rate: 5.46%

Total Years of Dividend Growth: 38

RECENT DEVELOPMENTS: For the year ended 12/31/99, net income climbed 7.9% to $44.3 million versus $41.1 million in 1999. Results included a gain on sale of investment of $7.9 million and $6.8 million in 1999 and 1998, respectively. Real estate rental revenue rose 14.8% to $119.0 million from $103.6 million a year earlier. The percentage increase in real estate rental revenue for office buildings, apartment buildings, retail centers, and industrial/flex properties was 20.0%, 8.0%, 40.0%, and 20.0%, respectively. Funds from operations were $56.0 million versus $49.7 million in 1999, an increase of 12.6%. On 2/16/00, WRE acquired an unoccupied retail/office building in Alexandria, Virginia and an adjoining parking lot for $1.35 billion in cash. WRE has entered negotiations with a national retailer to occupy the entire building by Spring 2000. On 5/8/00, WRE acquired Wayne Plaza, an occupied nine-story office building with two levels of underground parking located in Silverspring, Maryland for $7.7 million.

BUSINESS

WASHINGTON REAL ESTATE INVESTMENT TRUST is a self-administered qualified equity real estate investment trust. The Trust's business consists of the ownership of income-producing real estate properties principally in the Greater Washington, D.C.-Baltimore, MD area. Upon the purchase of a property, WRE begins a program of improving real estate to increase the value and to improve the operations with the goals of generating higher rental income and reducing expenses. As of 5/8/00, the Trust owned a diversified portfolio consisting of 11 neighborhood retail centers, 22 office buildings, nine apartment buildings, and 15 industrial distribution properties. WRE's principal objective is to invest in high quality, real estate in prime locations and to monitor closely the management of these properties, which includes active leasing and ongoing capital improvement programs.

BUSINESS LINE ANALYSIS

(12/31/99)	Rev (000s)	%
Office Buildings	61,657	51.9
Industrial/Flex Props.	16,196	13.6
Apartment Buildings	22,926	19.3
Retail Centers	18,196	15.2
Total	118,875	100.0

ANNUAL FINANCIAL DATA

	12/31/99	12/31/98	12/31/97	12/31/96	12/31/95	12/31/94	12/31/93
Earnings Per Share	[1] **1.24**	[1] **1.15**	**0.90**	**0.88**	**0.88**	**0.82**	**0.82**
Tang. Book Val. Per Share	**7.20**	**7.11**	**7.07**	**6.15**	**6.29**	**5.48**	**5.57**
Dividends Per Share	**1.16**	**1.11**	**1.07**	**1.03**	**0.99**	**0.92**	**0.89**
Dividend Payout %	**93.3**	**96.5**	**118.9**	**117.0**	**112.5**	**112.2**	**108.5**
INCOME STATEMENT (IN MILLIONS):							
Rental Income	119.0	103.6	79.4	65.5	52.6	45.5	39.4
Total Income	119.0	103.6	79.4	65.5	52.6	45.5	39.4
Costs & Expenses	41.5	37.7	29.7	25.0	20.0	17.3	14.7
Depreciation	19.6	15.4	10.9	7.8	5.1	3.9	3.6
Interest Expense	22.3	17.1	9.7	5.5	2.2	0.6	0.1
Income Before Income Taxes	44.3	41.1	30.1	28.0	26.1	23.1	23.2
Net Income	[1] 44.3	[1] 41.1	30.1	28.0	26.1	23.1	23.2
Average Shs. Outstg. (000)	35,700	35,700	33,400	31,800	29,787	28,239	28,223
BALANCE SHEET (IN MILLIONS):							
Cash & Cash Equivalents	4.7	4.6	7.9	1.7	3.5	2.7	18.0
Total Real Estate Investments	578.3	530.6	448.3	305.9	231.6	169.8	137.2
Total Assets	608.5	558.7	468.6	318.5	241.8	178.8	162.0
Long-Term Obligations	297.0	238.9	107.5	107.6	7.7	...	...
Total Liabilities	351.3	305.0	216.5	122.9	42.0	24.1	4.7
Net Stockholders' Equity	257.2	253.7	252.1	195.6	199.7	154.7	157.3
Year-end Shs. Outstg. (000)	35,721	35,692	35,678	31,803	31,752	28,243	28,228
STATISTICAL RECORD:							
Net Inc.+Depr./Assets %	10.5	10.1	8.8	11.2	12.9	15.1	16.6
Return on Equity %	17.2	16.2	12.0	14.3	13.1	15.0	14.8
Return on Assets %	7.3	7.3	6.4	8.8	10.8	12.9	14.3
Price Range	18¾-13 13/16	18¾-15 1/16	19⅝-15½	17½-15¼	16⅝-13⅞	21¼-14¾	24¾-18⅝
P/E Ratio	15.1-11.1	16.3-13.1	21.8-17.2	19.9-17.3	18.9-15.8	25.9-18.0	30.2-22.7
Average Yield %	7.1	6.6	6.1	6.3	6.5	5.1	4.1

Statistics are as originally reported. [1] Incl. gain on sale of investment, $7.9 mill., 1999, $6.8 mill., 1998.

OFFICERS:
A. A. Birney, Chmn.
E. B. Cronin Jr., Pres., C.E.O.
L. E. Finger, Sr. V.P., C.F.O.

PRINCIPAL OFFICE: 6110 Executive Boulevard, Suite 800, Rockville, MD 20852-3927

TELEPHONE NUMBER: (301) 984-9400
FAX: (301) 984-9610
WEB: www.washreit.com
NO. OF EMPLOYEES: 243
SHAREHOLDERS: 37,000 (approx.)
ANNUAL MEETING: In May
INCORPORATED: DC, Nov., 1960; reincorp., MD, June, 1996

INSTITUTIONAL HOLDINGS:
No. of Institutions: 92
Shares Held: 6,106,567
% Held: 17.1

INDUSTRY: Real estate investment trusts (SIC: 6798)

TRANSFER AGENT(S): American Stock Transfer & Trust Company, New York, NY

WAUSAU-MOSINEE PAPER MILLS CORPORATION

YIELD 3.7%
P/E RATIO 11.4

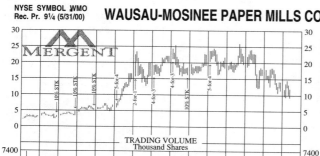

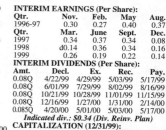

*7 YEAR PRICE SCORE 47.2   *12 MONTH PRICE SCORE 84.0

*NYSE COMPOSITE INDEX=100

TRADING VOLUME
Thousand Shares

INTERIM EARNINGS (Per Share):

Qtr.	Nov.	Feb.	May	Aug.
1996-97	0.30	0.27	0.40	0.37
Qtr.	Mar.	June	Sept.	Dec.
1997	0.34	0.37	0.34	0.08
1998	d0.14	0.36	0.34	0.16
1999	0.26	0.19	0.22	0.14

INTERIM DIVIDENDS (Per Share):

Amt.	Decl.	Ex.	Rec.	Pay.
0.08Q	4/22/99	4/29/99	5/03/99	5/17/99
0.08Q	6/01/99	7/29/99	8/02/99	8/16/99
0.08Q	10/21/99	10/28/99	11/01/99	11/15/99
0.08Q	12/16/99	1/27/00	1/31/00	2/14/00
0.085Q	4/20/00	5/01/00	5/03/00	5/17/00

Indicated div.: $0.34 (Div. Reinv. Plan)

CAPITALIZATION (12/31/99):

	($000)	(%)
Long-Term Debt	220,476	30.7
Deferred Income Tax	103,386	14.4
Common & Surplus	393,760	54.9
Total	717,622	100.0

DIVIDEND ACHIEVER STATUS:
Rank: 92   10-Year Growth Rate: 13.05%
Total Years of Dividend Growth: 15

RECENT DEVELOPMENTS: For the year ended 12/31/99, net income increased 4.0% to $42.4 million compared with $40.8 million in 1998. Results for 1998 included a restructuring charge of $42.8 million. Net sales were $944.6 million, down slightly from $946.1 million a year earlier. Although net sales were comparable for the twelve months ended 12/31/99 and 12/31/98, the tonnage shipped increased in 1999 by 13,000 tons, or 2.0%, to 844,800 tons. Overall, the selling prices for WMO's products began to increase late in 1999 following selling price declines in 1997, 1998 and part of 1999. The selling price declines experienced were due to competitive pressure on several products in WMO's printing and writing, specialty and towel and tissue grades. In 2000, the printing & writing group will focus on increasing premium paper sales. The increase will be sought through normal distribution channels as well as an expansion of the retail business. Meanwhile, the improvement of overall product mix will again be the focus for the Specialty Paper Group in the year 2000.

BUSINESS

WAUSAU-MOSINEE PAPER MILLS CORPORATION (formerly Wausau Paper Mills Company) manufactures, converts and sells paper. The Company competes in different markets within the paper industry. Each of its operating groups serves distinct market niches. The Company's eleven operating facilities are organized into three operating groups: the Specialty Paper Group; the Printing & Writing Group; and the Towel & Tissue Group. The Specialty Paper Group combines the Company's Mosinee, Sorg, Rhinelander, and Otis facilities to produce a wide variety of technical specialty papers. The Printing & Writing Group produces and converts two lines of paper products in five facilities. The Towel & Tissue Group produces a complete line of towel and tissue products which are marketed along with soap and dispensing system products for the industrial and commercial ''away-from-home'' market.

ANNUAL FINANCIAL DATA

	12/31/99	12/31/98	12/31/97	8/31/97	8/31/96	8/31/95	8/31/94
Earnings Per Share	0.81	② 0.73	② 1.13	1.34	1.12	0.85	① 1.13
Cash Flow Per Share	1.86	1.63	1.95	2.07	1.75	1.39	1.61
Tang. Book Val. Per Share	7.66	7.46	7.61	7.82	7.25	...	5.82
Dividends Per Share	0.31	0.27	0.25	0.25	0.22	0.20	0.17
Dividend Payout %	38.3	37.3	22.1	18.7	19.6	23.6	15.4

INCOME STATEMENT (IN THOUSANDS):

Total Revenues	944,629	946,127	933,127	570,258	542,669	515,743	426,504
Costs & Expenses	810,061	824,157	765,040	462,152	450,006	443,049	338,879
Depreciation & Amort.	55,012	49,825	47,259	26,586	23,140	19,940	17,635
Operating Income	79,646	72,145	120,828	81,520	69,523	52,754	69,990
Net Interest Inc./(Exp.)	d11,593	d7,280	d8,008	d3,348	d2,224	d1,449	d1,847
Income Before Income Taxes	68,017	65,801	113,589	78,399	66,829	50,851	68,052
Income Taxes	25,600	25,000	48,191	29,500	25,600	19,600	26,000
Net Income	42,327	② 40,801	② 65,398	48,899	41,229	31,251	① 42,052
Cash Flow	97,339	90,626	112,657	75,485	64,369	51,191	59,687
Average Shs. Outstg.	52,265	55,705	57,811	36,514	36,821	36,830	37,028

BALANCE SHEET (IN THOUSANDS):

Cash & Cash Equivalents	5,397	2,495	2,584	5,297	2,372	2,347	3,214
Total Current Assets	252,311	242,126	234,929	149,419	119,240	120,017	105,934
Net Property	653,823	625,065	604,930	386,466	330,536	292,191	247,072
Total Assets	936,462	900,149	872,064	555,615	467,028	434,686	361,389
Total Current Liabilities	111,489	160,720	108,276	62,305	59,053	52,751	46,056
Long-Term Obligations	220,476	127,000	140,500	83,510	53,119	68,623	30,270
Net Stockholders' Equity	393,760	396,586	440,160	303,554	264,711	236,689	214,818
Net Working Capital	140,822	81,406	126,653	87,114	60,187	67,266	59,878
Year-end Shs. Outstg.	51,417	53,164	57,802	38,840	36,513	29,464	36,930

STATISTICAL RECORD:

Operating Profit Margin %	8.4	7.6	12.9	14.3	12.8	10.2	16.4
Net Profit Margin %	4.5	4.3	7.0	8.6	7.6	6.1	9.9
Return on Equity %	10.7	10.3	14.9	16.1	15.6	13.2	19.6
Return on Assets %	4.5	4.5	7.5	8.8	8.8	7.2	11.6
Debt/Total Assets %	23.5	14.1	16.1	15.0	11.4	15.8	8.4
Price Range	18⁷/₁₆-10⁵/₈	24¹/₈-12¹/₈	26-17¹/₈	26-17¹/₈	24¹/₂-16¹/₄	22¹³/₁₆-16³/₁₆	25⁷/₁₆-15¹³/₁₆
P/E Ratio	22.8-13.1	33.0-16.6	23.0-15.2	19.4-12.8	21.9-14.5	28.9-20.5	27.4-17.0
Average Yield %	2.1	1.5	1.2	1.2	1.1	1.0	0.8

Statistics are as originally reported. Adj. for stk. splits: 5-for-4, 1/17/96; 10% div., 1/17/95; 4-for-3, 1/10/94; 4-for-3, 1/14/93. ① Bef. acctg. change credit of $1.0 mill. ($0.03/sh.), 8/94. ② Incl. restruct. chrg. of $13.5 mill., 1997; and $42.8 mill., 1998.

OFFICERS:
S. W. Orr, Jr., Chmn., C.E.O.
R. L. Radt, Vice-Chmn.
G. P. Peterson, Sr. V.P., Fin., Treas., Sec.
PRINCIPAL OFFICE: 1244 Kronenwetter Drive, P.O. Box 1408, Mosinee, WI 54455-9099

TELEPHONE NUMBER: (715) 693-4470
WEB: www.wausaumosinee.com
NO. OF EMPLOYEES: 3,400 (approx.)
SHAREHOLDERS: 3,000 (approx.); 8,500 (approx. beneficial)
ANNUAL MEETING: In Feb.
INCORPORATED: WI, June, 1899

INSTITUTIONAL HOLDINGS:
No. of Institutions: 104
Shares Held: 29,689,923
% Held: 57.7
INDUSTRY: Paper mills (SIC: 2621)
TRANSFER AGENT(S): Harris Trust and Savings Bank, Chaicgo, IL

WEIS MARKETS, INC.

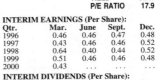

YIELD 3.2%
P/E RATIO 17.9

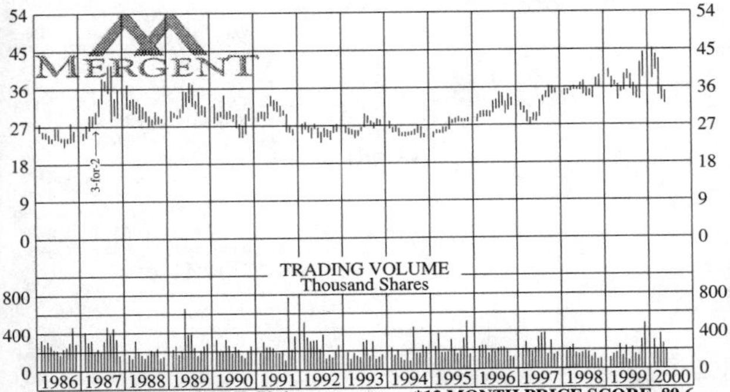

INTERIM EARNINGS (Per Share):

Qtr.	Mar.	June	Sept.	Dec.
1996	0.46	0.46	0.47	0.48
1997	0.43	0.46	0.46	0.52
1998	0.64	0.40	0.44	0.52
1999	0.51	0.46	0.46	0.48
2000	0.43	...	...	...

INTERIM DIVIDENDS (Per Share):

Amt.	Decl.	Ex.	Rec.	Pay.
0.26Q	7/12/99	8/04/99	8/06/99	8/20/99
0.26Q	10/26/99	11/03/99	11/05/99	11/19/99
0.26Q	1/31/00	2/09/00	2/11/00	2/25/00
0.26Q	4/13/00	5/03/00	5/05/00	5/19/00

Indicated div.: $1.04 (Div. Reinv. Plan)

CAPITALIZATION (12/25/99):

	($000)	(%)
Deferred Income Tax	18,904	2.0
Common & Surplus	918,477	98.0
Total	937,381	100.0

DIVIDEND ACHIEVER STATUS:
Rank: 240   10-Year Growth Rate: 6.18%
Total Years of Dividend Growth: 25

*7 YEAR PRICE SCORE 79.4   *12 MONTH PRICE SCORE 89.6
*NYSE COMPOSITE INDEX=100

RECENT DEVELOPMENTS: For the year ended 12/25/99, net income slid 4.7% to $79.7 million from $83.7 million in 1998. The 1999 results included a one-time pre-tax gain of $3.4 million from the sale of an investment. Prior-year results included a pre-tax gain of $30.4 million from the sale of two marketable securities, partially offset by a pre-tax charge of $5.6 million from closing several under performing SuperPetz units. Net sales grew 7.4% to $2.00 billion from $1.87 billion the year before.

PROSPECTS: WMK announced that it will sell its Weis Food Service subsidiary to Reinhart FoodService. The sale will help WMK sharpen its focus on operating its core retail food business. Going forward, WMK will continue to focus on implementing its strategic store expansion program in an effort to boost sales and increase market share. Over the next eighteen months, WMK anticipates investing up to $135.6 million in capital expenditures to open 17 new superstores and expand or remodel 20 others.

BUSINESS

WEIS MARKETS, INC. operates 168 supermarkets in Pennsylvania, New Jersey, New York, Maryland, Virginia and West Virginia. The Company supplies its retail stores from distribution centers in Sunbury, Northumberland, and Milton, PA. Many of WMK's private label products are supplied by the Company's ice cream manufacturing plant, fresh meat processing plant, and milk processing plant. The Company also owns and operates Weis Food Service, a supplier of frozen foods and grocery items to restaurants and institutions, and SuperPetz, an operator of 34 pet supply stores in 10 states.

ANNUAL FINANCIAL DATA

	12/25/99	12/26/98	12/27/97	12/28/96	12/30/95	12/31/94	12/25/93
Earnings Per Share	☐ 1.91	☐ 2.00	1.87	1.87	1.84	1.75	1.66
Cash Flow Per Share	3.02	3.11	2.91	2.77	2.61	2.45	2.33
Tang. Book Val. Per Share	22.03	21.33	20.28	19.47	18.61	17.53	16.85
Dividends Per Share	1.02	0.98	0.94	0.88	0.80	0.74	0.70
Dividend Payout %	53.4	49.0	50.3	47.1	43.5	42.3	42.2

INCOME STATEMENT (IN MILLIONS):

	12/25/99	12/26/98	12/27/97	12/28/96	12/30/95	12/31/94	12/25/93
Total Revenues	2,004.9	1,867.5	1,818.8	1,753.2	1,646.4	1,556.7	1,441.1
Costs & Expenses	1,865.6	1,744.8	1,690.2	1,624.5	1,527.1	1,446.1	1,332.5
Depreciation & Amort.	46.3	46.3	43.5	38.1	33.2	30.6	29.0
Operating Income	93.0	76.4	85.1	90.6	86.2	80.0	79.7
Income Before Income Taxes	124.0	134.5	118.6	120.7	121.7	117.2	113.7
Income Taxes	44.3	50.8	40.4	41.9	42.3	40.9	40.7
Equity Earnings/Minority Int.	...	...	...	...	0.2	...	...
Net Income	☐ 79.7	☐ 83.7	78.2	78.9	79.4	76.3	73.0
Cash Flow	126.0	130.0	121.7	117.0	112.6	106.9	101.9
Average Shs. Outstg. (000)	41,718	41,776	41,843	42,280	43,083	43,662	43,827

BALANCE SHEET (IN MILLIONS):

	12/25/99	12/26/98	12/27/97	12/28/96	12/30/95	12/31/94	12/25/93
Cash & Cash Equivalents	389.2	411.1	377.3	390.7	435.5	457.0	467.2
Total Current Assets	602.6	608.2	575.8	590.6	606.5	617.8	605.8
Net Property	439.4	398.4	365.2	343.9	286.0	245.3	225.3
Total Assets	1,058.2	1,029.2	971.8	966.3	923.0	892.1	844.5
Total Current Liabilities	120.8	118.7	104.3	127.4	115.3	112.3	92.6
Net Stockholders' Equity	918.5	890.6	847.3	818.5	791.6	762.4	738.1
Net Working Capital	481.7	489.5	471.6	463.3	491.1	505.4	513.2
Year-end Shs. Outstg. (000)	41,692	41,756	41,773	42,041	42,534	43,484	43,796

STATISTICAL RECORD:

	12/25/99	12/26/98	12/27/97	12/28/96	12/30/95	12/31/94	12/25/93
Operating Profit Margin %	4.6	4.1	4.7	5.2	5.2	5.1	5.5
Net Profit Margin %	4.0	4.5	4.3	4.5	4.8	4.9	5.1
Return on Equity %	8.7	9.4	9.2	9.6	10.0	10.0	9.9
Return on Assets %	7.5	8.1	8.0	8.2	8.6	8.5	8.6
Price Range	44⁵⁄₁₆-32⅞	38⅞-33¼	36¼-26⅞	34⅞-27¾		29-24	28-23⅞	29⅞-24
P/E Ratio	23.2-17.2	19.4-16.6	19.4-14.4	18.6-14.8	15.8-13.0	16.0-13.6	18.0-14.5
Average Yield %	2.6	2.7	3.0	2.8	3.0	2.9	2.6

Statistics are as originally reported. ☐ Incl. $3.4 mil pre-tax gain fr. sale of asset, 1999; $8.3 mil ($0.20/sh) after-tax gain from sale of stk., 1998.

QUARTERLY DATA

(12/25/99)($000)	Rev	Inc
1st Quarter	496,281	21,191
2nd Quarter	490,019	19,199
3nd Quarter	492,293	19,150
4rd Quarter	526,354	20,185

OFFICERS:
R. F. Weis, Chmn., Treas.
N. S. Rich, Pres.
W. R. Mills, V.P., Sec.

PRINCIPAL OFFICE: 1000 South Second Street, Sunbury, PA 17801-0471

TELEPHONE NUMBER: (570) 286-4571
FAX: (570) 286-3286
WEB: www.weismarkets.com

NO. OF EMPLOYEES: 20,100 (approx.)

SHAREHOLDERS: 7,172

ANNUAL MEETING: In June

INCORPORATED: PA, Dec., 1924

INSTITUTIONAL HOLDINGS:
No. of Institutions: 63
Shares Held: 17,163,793
% Held: 41.2

INDUSTRY: Grocery stores (SIC: 5411)

TRANSFER AGENT(S): American Stock Transfer & Trust Company, New York, NY

WELLS FARGO & COMPANY

YIELD	1.9%
P/E RATIO	19.6

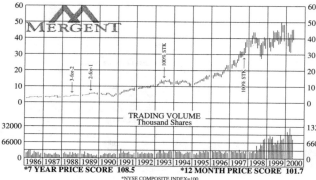

7 YEAR PRICE SCORE 108.5   **12 MONTH PRICE SCORE 101.7**

*NYSE COMPOSITE INDEX=100

TRADING VOLUME Thousand Shares

INTERIM EARNINGS (Per Share):

Qtr.	Mar.	June	Sept.	Dec.
1996	0.37	0.38	0.38	0.41
1997	0.42	0.43	0.45	0.46
1998	0.41	0.44	0.45	d0.12
1999	0.53	0.55	0.57	0.58

INTERIM DIVIDENDS (Per Share):

Amt.	Decl.	Ex.	Rec.	Pay.
0.20Q	4/27/99	5/05/99	5/07/99	6/01/99
0.20Q	7/27/99	8/04/99	8/06/99	9/01/99
0.20Q	10/25/99	11/03/99	11/05/99	12/01/99
0.22Q	1/25/00	2/02/00	2/04/00	3/01/00
0.22Q	4/25/00	5/03/00	5/05/00	6/01/00

Indicated div.: $0.88 (Div. Reinv. Plan)

CAPITALIZATION (12/31/99):

	($000)	(%)
Total Deposits	132,708,000	74.5
Long-Term Debt	23,375,000	13.1
Preferred Stock	344,000	0.2
Common & Surplus	21,787,000	12.2
Total	178,214,000	100.0

DIVIDEND ACHIEVER STATUS:

Rank: 60   10-Year Growth Rate: 15.24%
Total Years of Dividend Growth: 12

RECENT DEVELOPMENTS: For the year ended 12/31/99, net income advanced 92.2% to $3.75 billion from $1.95 billion in 1998. Results included a pre-tax net gain of $16.0 million in 1999 and a pre-tax net loss of $325.0 million in 1998, on dispositions of premises and equipment. Net interest income rose 4.1% to $9.36 billion from $8.99 billion a year earlier. Non-interest income increased 15.5% to $7.42 billion. Non-interest expense fell 7.5% to $9.78 billion.

PROSPECTS: WFC signed a definitive agreement to acquire First Security Corporation for approximately $3.20 billion. First Security, with $23.00 billion in assets, is the second-largest independent bank holding company in the western United States. The combined company will be the largest banking franchise in deposits in Utah, Nevada, New Mexico, and Idaho. The transaction is expected to close in the second half of 2000.

BUSINESS

WELLS FARGO & COMPANY (formerly Norwest Corporation), with $222.28 billion in assets as of 3/31/00, is a diversified financial services company providing banking, insurance, investments, mortgage and consumer finance from more than 5,300 financial services stores and the Internet across North America and elsewhere internationally. In early November 1998, the former Wells Fargo & Company merged with WFC Holdings, a subsidiary of Norwest Corp., with WFC Holdings as the surviving corporation. In connection with the merger, Norwest changed its name to Wells Fargo & Company.

ANNUAL FINANCIAL DATA

	12/31/99	12/31/98	12/31/97	12/31/96	12/31/95	12/31/94	12/31/93
Earnings Per Share	④ 2.23	③ 1.17	1.75	① 1.54	1.38	1.23	1.07
Tang. Book Val. Per Share	7.87	6.71	8.90	7.88	7.05	5.34	5.52
Dividends Per Share	0.79	0.70	0.61	0.53	0.45	0.38	0.32
Dividend Payout %	35.2	59.8	35.1	34.2	32.6	31.2	30.0
INCOME STATEMENT (IN MILLIONS):							
Total Interest Income	14,375.0	14,055.0	6,697.4	6,318.3	5,717.3	4,393.7	3,734.1
Total Interest Expense	5,020.0	5,065.0	2,664.0	2,617.0	2,448.0	1,590.1	1,358.0
Net Interest Income	9,355.0	8,990.0	4,033.4	3,701.3	3,269.3	2,803.6	2,376.1
Provision for Loan Losses	1,045.0	1,545.0	524.7	394.7	312.4	164.9	140.1
Non-Interest Income	7,420.0	6,427.0	2,962.3	2,564.6	1,865.0	1,638.3	1,542.5
Non-Interest Expense	9,782.0	10,579.0	4,421.3	4,089.7	3,399.1	3,096.4	2,840.8
Income Before Taxes	5,948.0	3,293.0	2,049.7	1,781.5	1,422.8	1,180.6	937.7
Net Income	④ 3,747.0	③ 1,950.0	1,351.0	① 1,153.9	956.0	800.4	653.6
Average Shs. Outstg. (000)	1,665,200	1,641,800	750,059	739,400	663,358	630,184	586,694
BALANCE SHEET (IN MILLIONS):							
Cash & Due from Banks	13,250.0	12,731.0	4,912.1	4,856.6	4,320.3	3,431.2	2,600.7
Securities Avail. for Sale	38,518.0	31,997.0	18,470.8	16,433.6	15,393.6	13,774.1	10,787.2
Total Loans & Leases	119,464.0	107,994.0	44,634.1	41,154.2	37,830.7	33,703.6	27,952.8
Allowance for Credit Losses	3,170.0	3,134.0	3,346.4	2,814.0	2,594.8	1,917.5	1,752.7
Net Loans & Leases	116,294.0	104,860.0	41,287.7	38,340.2	35,235.9	31,786.1	26,200.1
Total Assets	218,102.0	202,475.0	88,540.2	80,175.4	72,134.4	59,315.9	50,782.3
Total Deposits	132,708.0	136,788.0	55,457.1	50,130.2	42,028.8	36,424.0	32,573.2
Long-Term Obligations	23,375.0	19,709.0	12,766.7	13,082.2	13,676.8	9,186.3	6,802.4
Total Liabilities	195,971.0	181,716.0	81,518.0	74,111.2	66,822.3	55,469.5	47,213.9
Net Stockholders' Equity	22,131.0	20,759.0	7,022.2	6,064.2	5,312.1	3,846.4	3,568.4
Year-end Shs. Outstg. (000)	1,627,000	1,644,000	758,619	737,406	705,520	621,284	584,350
STATISTICAL RECORD:							
Return on Equity %	16.9	9.4	19.2	19.0	18.0	20.8	18.3
Return on Assets %	1.7	1.0	1.5	1.4	1.3	1.3	1.3
Equity/Assets %	10.1	10.3	7.9	7.6	7.4	6.5	7.0
Non-Int. Exp./Tot. Inc. %	58.3	68.6	63.2	65.3	66.2	69.7	72.5
Price Range	49¹⁵/₁₆-32³/₁₆	43⁷/₈-27¹/₂	39¹/₂-21³/₈	23⁷/₁₆-15¹/₄	17³/₈-11⁵/₁₆	14¹/₈-10¹/₂	14¹/₂-10⁵/₁₆
P/E Ratio	22.4-14.4	37.5-23.5	22.6-12.2	15.3-9.9	12.6-8.2	11.5-8.6	13.6-9.7
Average Yield %	1.9	2.0	2.0	2.7	3.1	3.1	2.6

Statistics are as originally reported. Adj. for 2-for-1 stock split, 10/97 & 6/93. ① Incl. one-time SAIF pre-tax chg. of $19.0 mill. ② Reflects 11/98 merger with Norwest Corp. & subsequent name change to Wells Fargo & Co. Years prior to 12/31/98 include the results of Norwest Corp. only. ③ Incl. $1.20 bill. in merger-related & other chgs., a $320.0 mill. prov. for loan losses, & a pre-tax net loss of $325.0 mill. on the disposition of premises & equip. ④ Incl. pre-tax net gain on dispositions of premises & equipment of $16.0 mill., 12/99.

OFFICERS:
P. Hazen, Chmn.
L. S. Biller, Vice-Chmn., C.O.O.
R. M. Kovacevich, Pres., C.E.O.

INVESTOR CONTACT: Robert S. Strickland, Investor Relations, (415) 396-0523

PRINCIPAL OFFICE: 420 Montgomery Street, San Francisco, CA 94163

TELEPHONE NUMBER: (800) 411-4932
FAX: (415) 677-9075
WEB: www.wellsfargo.com
NO. OF EMPLOYEES: 92,178
SHAREHOLDERS: 90,277
ANNUAL MEETING: In Apr.
INCORPORATED: DE, Jan., 1929

INSTITUTIONAL HOLDINGS:
No. of Institutions: 785
Shares Held: 1,011,902,996
% Held: 61.6

INDUSTRY: National commercial banks (SIC: 6021)

TRANSFER AGENT(S): Norwest Bank Minnesota, N.A., St. Paul, MN

WESBANCO, INC.

YIELD	3.9%
P/E RATIO	17.0

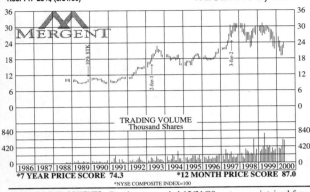

7 YEAR PRICE SCORE 74.3 **12 MONTH PRICE SCORE 87.0**
*NYSE COMPOSITE INDEX=100

INTERIM EARNINGS (Per Share):

Qtr.	Mar.	June	Sept.	Dec.
1996	0.35	0.37	0.33	0.33
1997	0.35	0.36	0.37	0.32
1998	0.36	0.37	0.36	0.29
1999	0.33	0.40	0.30	0.34

INTERIM DIVIDENDS (Per Share):

Amt.	Decl.	Ex.	Rec.	Pay.
0.22Q	5/19/99	6/09/99	6/11/99	7/01/99
0.22Q	8/19/99	9/08/99	9/10/99	10/01/99
0.22Q	11/17/99	12/08/99	12/10/99	1/03/00
0.22Q	2/17/00	3/08/00	3/10/00	4/01/00
0.225Q	5/17/00	6/07/00	6/09/00	7/01/00

Indicated div.: $0.90

CAPITALIZATION (12/31/99):

	($000)	(%)
Total Deposits	1,814,001	85.4
Long-Term Debt	41,588	2.0
Common & Surplus	269,664	12.7
Total	2,125,253	100.0

DIVIDEND ACHIEVER STATUS:
Rank: 174   10-Year Growth Rate: 9.22%
Total Years of Dividend Growth: 14

RECENT DEVELOPMENTS: For the year ended 12/31/99, net income decreased 2.5% to $27.6 million from $28.3 million in the prior year. Net interest income fell 2.5% to $86.6 million from $88.8 million in the previous year. On 1/14/00, WSBC restructured its banking and mortgage operations, merging all of its banking subsidiaries and its mortgage subsidiary into one state member banking corporation, WesBanco Bank, Inc. The corporation previously maintained four separate banking subsidiaries. In 1999, the Company consolidated its individual bank trust operations into a single operating division of its unit banking corporation under the name WesBanco Trust and Investment Services. The trust department is now one of the largest trust operations in West Virginia. As of 12/31/99, the market value of trust assets was approximately $3.1 billion.

BUSINESS

WESBANCO, INC. is a bank holding company. The Company offers a range of financial services including retail banking, corporate banking, personal and corporate trust services, brokerage, mortgage banking and insurance. The Company's primary business function is the operation of a commercial bank through 62 offices located in West Virginia and Eastern Ohio. Its subsidiary banking organization operates automated teller machines primarily under the name of MAC. The Company also offers services through its non-banking affiliates. WesBanco Insurance Services, Inc., which recently changed its name from Hunter Agency, Inc., is a multi-line insurance agency specializing in property, casualty and life insurance for personal and commercial clients. WesBanco Securities, Inc. is a full service broker-dealer which also offers discount brokerage services. WSBC also serves as investment adviser to a family of mutual funds under the name WesMark Funds, which include the WesMark Growth Fund, the WesMark Balanced Fund, the WesMark Bond Fund, and the WesMark West Virginia Municipal Bond Fund.

ANNUAL FINANCIAL DATA

	12/31/99	12/31/98	12/31/97	12/31/96	12/31/95	12/31/94	12/31/93
Earnings Per Share	1.37	1.36	1.40	1.39	1.42	1.21	1.48
Tang. Book Val. Per Share	13.63	14.35	15.58	14.42	13.34	12.27	12.69
Dividends Per Share	0.87	0.83	0.77	0.70	0.62	0.56	0.51
Dividend Payout %	63.5	61.0	55.2	50.5	43.7	46.4	34.2
INCOME STATEMENT (IN MILLIONS):							
Total Interest Income	155.9	162.7	124.5	112.9	97.9	92.0	73.9
Total Interest Expense	69.2	73.9	55.8	48.2	41.9	35.6	31.6
Net Interest Income	86.6	88.8	68.8	64.7	56.0	56.4	42.4
Provision for Loan Losses	4.3	4.4	4.3	4.3	2.8	6.1	2.7
Non-Interest Income	24.6	25.7	14.7	12.3	11.1	10.8	8.7
Non-Interest Expense	67.8	68.3	48.7	43.2	39.0	39.6	28.8
Income Before Taxes	39.1	41.8	30.4	29.5	25.4	21.5	19.6
Net Income	27.6	28.3	22.3	21.2	18.2	15.7	14.7
Average Shs. Outstg. (000)	20,230	20,867	15,868	15,254	12,705	12,887	9,893
BALANCE SHEET (IN MILLIONS):							
Cash & Due from Banks	67.2	63.0	56.4	58.8	49.0	47.6	32.2
Securities Avail. for Sale	354.7	465.7	342.5	276.2	172.1	202.7	...
Total Loans & Leases	1,513.7	1,363.7	1,021.3	1,026.4	858.4	786.2	566.8
Allowance for Credit Losses	19.8	19.1	15.5	15.5	20.6	21.4	10.9
Net Loans & Leases	1,493.9	1,344.6	1,005.7	1,010.8	837.8	764.8	555.9
Total Assets	2,269.7	2,242.7	1,789.3	1,677.8	1,371.8	1,351.0	1,038.9
Total Deposits	1,814.0	1,787.6	1,414.3	1,342.8	1,115.5	1,109.2	854.4
Long-Term Obligations	41.6	22.2	...	...	...	...	...
Total Liabilities	2,000.1	1,946.2	1,539.7	1,450.2	1,201.8	1,194.3	913.7
Net Stockholders' Equity	269.7	296.5	249.6	227.5	170.0	156.6	125.2
Year-end Shs. Outstg. (000)	19,790	20,660	16,016	15,783	12,744	12,765	9,867
STATISTICAL RECORD:							
Return on Equity %	10.2	9.5	8.9	9.3	10.7	10.0	11.7
Return on Assets %	1.2	1.3	1.2	1.3	1.3	1.2	1.4
Equity/Assets %	11.9	13.2	13.9	13.6	12.4	11.6	12.0
Non-Int. Exp./Tot. Inc. %	61.0	59.7	58.4	56.0	58.1	59.0	56.3
Price Range	31¼-21½	31⅛-22	31¼-21³⁄₁₆	21¹¹⁄₁₆-17³⁄₁₆	20-15³⁄₁₆	19¹¹⁄₁₆-15½	22¹³⁄₁₆-14¾
P/E Ratio	22.8-15.7	22.9-16.2	22.3-15.1	15.6-12.4	14.1-10.7	16.3-12.8	15.4-10.0
Average Yield %	3.3	3.1	3.0	3.6	3.5	3.2	2.7

Statistics are as originally reported. Adj. for stk. split: 3-for-2, 8/1/97; 2-for-1, 4/22/93.

OFFICERS:
J. C. Gardill, Chmn.
R. H. Martin, Vice-Chmn.
W. E. Mildren Jr., Vice-Chmn.
E. M. George, Pres., C.E.O.
P. M. Limbert, Exec. V.P., C.F.O.

PRINCIPAL OFFICE: 1 Bank Plaza,
Wheeling, WV 26003

TELEPHONE NUMBER: (304) 234-9000
FAX: (304) 232-9060
WEB: www.wesbanco.com

NO. OF EMPLOYEES: 1,096

SHAREHOLDERS: 5,739 (approximately)

ANNUAL MEETING: In Apr.

INCORPORATED: WV

INSTITUTIONAL HOLDINGS:
No. of Institutions: 39
Shares Held: 3,464,215
% Held: 17.4

INDUSTRY: National commercial banks
(SIC: 6021)

TRANSFER AGENT(S): American Stock
Transfer and Trust Company, New York,
NY

WESCO FINANCIAL CORPORATION

YIELD 0.5%
P/E RATIO 32.0

TRADING VOLUME
Thousand Shares

| 1986 | 1987 | 1988 | 1989 | 1990 | 1991 | 1992 | 1993 | 1994 | 1995 | 1996 | 1997 | 1998 | 1999 | 2000 |

*7 YEAR PRICE SCORE 81.4 *12 MONTH PRICE SCORE 87.1

*NYSE COMPOSITE INDEX=100

INTERIM EARNINGS (Per Share):

Qtr.	Mar.	June	Sept.	Dec.
1995	1.46	1.69	0.88	0.82
1996	1.20	0.92	1.10	1.08
1997	1.37	1.23	1.32	10.38
1998	1.24	6.65	1.32	0.87
1999	1.49	1.56	1.54	3.01

INTERIM DIVIDENDS (Per Share):

Amt.	Decl.	Ex.	Rec.	Pay.
0.295Q	3/25/99	5/03/99	5/05/99	6/09/99
0.295Q	7/22/99	8/02/99	8/04/99	9/08/99
0.295Q	9/16/99	11/01/99	11/03/99	12/08/99
0.305Q	1/20/00	2/07/00	2/09/00	3/08/00
0.305Q	3/23/00	5/01/00	5/03/00	6/07/00

Indicated div.: $1.22

CAPITALIZATION (12/31/99):

	($000)	(%)
Long-Term Debt	3,635	0.2
Common & Surplus	1,895,372	99.8
Total	1,899,007	100.0

DIVIDEND ACHIEVER STATUS:
Rank: 277   10-Year Growth Rate: 4.23%
Total Years of Dividend Growth: 28

RECENT DEVELOPMENTS: For the year ended 12/31/99, net income dropped 24.6% to $54.1 million from $71.8 million a year earlier. Results included net realized gains on securities and foreclosed property of $12.8 million and $52.7 million in 1999 and 1998, respectively. Net income for the insurance segment dropped 25.5% to $50.9 million from $68.3 million a year earlier. Net income for the industrial segment totaled $2.5 million, a decrease of 19.7% from

$3.2 million in the previous year. Total revenues declined 17.3% to $145.7 million from $176.2 million in the prior year. Sales and service revenues were $64.6 million, down 2.4% from $66.1 million in the prior year. Insurance premiums earned jumped 10.9% to $17.7 million from $15.9 million in the previous year. Dividend and interest income grew 22.5% to $49.7 million from $40.5 million the year before.

BUSINESS

WESCO FINANCIAL CORPORA-TION is engaged in two principal businesses: (1) the insurance business, through Wesco-Financial Insurance Company, which engages in the property and casualty insurance business, and The Kansas Bankers Surety Company, which provides specialized insurance coverages for banks; and (2) the steel service center business, through Precision Steel Warehouse, Inc. The Company's operations also include, through MS Property Company, the ownership and management of commercial real estate, and the development and liquidation of foreclosed real estate. Since 1973, the Company has been 80.1% owned by Blue Chip Stamps, a wholly owned subsidiary of Berkshire Hathaway Inc. In 2/00, WSC acquired CORT Business Services Corp., a provider of rental furniture, accessories and related services in the "rent-to-buy" segment of the furniture industry.

ANNUAL FINANCIAL DATA

	12/31/99	12/31/98	12/31/97	12/31/96	12/31/95	12/31/94	12/31/93
Earnings Per Share	7.60	10.08	14.30	4.30	4.85	2.66	①2.63
Tang. Book Val. Per Share	262.20	308.20	243.56	171.36	134.50	95.25	87.93
Dividends Per Share	1.18	1.14	1.10	1.06	1.02	0.98	0.94
Dividend Payout %	15.5	11.3	7.7	24.7	21.0	36.8	35.7
INCOME STATEMENT (IN MILLIONS):							
Total Premium Income	17.7	15.9	11.5	10.1	9.3	1.1	12.2
Net Investment Income	49.7	40.5	36.6	33.3	30.3	29.0	36.1
Other Income	78.4	119.7	171.0	64.6	71.5	65.3	69.1
Total Revenues	145.7	176.2	219.1	108.0	111.1	95.5	117.4
Income Before Income Taxes	74.8	102.3	152.8	39.5	45.0	20.8	23.7
Income Taxes	20.7	30.5	51.0	8.9	10.5	1.8	5.0
Net Income	54.1	71.8	101.8	30.6	34.5	19.0	①18.7
Average Shs. Outstg. (000)	7,120	7,120	7,120	7,120	7,120	7,120	7,120
BALANCE SHEET (IN MILLIONS):							
Cash & Cash Equivalents	66.3	320.0	10.7	23.0	88.0	15.8	5.2
Premiums Due	...	7.7	7.1	7.9	6.7	6.5	7.0
Invst. Assets: Equities	2,214.9	2,778.6	2,224.8	1,533.0	1,102.2	696.3	640.0
Invst. Assets: Total	2,524.9	2,847.5	2,509.8	1,725.7	1,240.8	902.8	872.0
Total Assets	2,652.2	3,228.4	2,588.1	1,818.4	1,365.7	961.8	915.2
Long-Term Obligations	3.6	33.6	33.6	37.2	37.4	37.6	37.9
Net Stockholders' Equity	1,895.4	2,223.8	1,764.3	1,251.0	957.6	678.1	626.1
Year-end Shs. Outstg. (000)	7,120	7,120	7,120	7,120	7,120	7,120	7,120
STATISTICAL RECORD:							
Return on Revenues %	37.2	40.8	46.5	28.3	31.1	19.9	15.9
Return on Equity %	2.9	3.2	5.8	2.4	3.6	2.8	3.0
Return on Assets %	2.0	2.2	3.9	1.7	2.5	2.0	2.0
Price Range	354-241½	395-280	343-180	194-155	192-113	136-104½	149¾-80
P/E Ratio	46.6-31.8	39.2-27.8	24.0-12.6	45.1-36.0	39.6-23.3	51.1-39.3	56.9-30.4
Average Yield %	0.4	0.3	0.4	0.6	0.7	0.8	0.8

Statistics are as originally reported.   ① Bef. acctg. change credit $1.0 mill.

OFFICERS:
C. T. Munger, Chmn., C.E.O.
R. H. Bird, Pres.
J. L. Jacobson, V.P., C.F.O.

PRINCIPAL OFFICE: 301 East Colorado Boulevard, Suite 300, Pasadena, CA 91101-1901

TELEPHONE NUMBER: (626) 585-6700

NO. OF EMPLOYEES: 263 (approx.)

SHAREHOLDERS: 700 (approx.); 5000 (approx. shares held in street name)

ANNUAL MEETING: In May

INCORPORATED: DE, Mar., 1959

INSTITUTIONAL HOLDINGS:
No. of Institutions: 45
Shares Held: 6,194,337
% Held: 87.0

INDUSTRY: Metals service centers and offices (SIC: 5051)

TRANSFER AGENT(S): ChaseMellon Shareholder Services, Los Angeles, CA

WESTAMERICA BANCORPORATION

YIELD 2.5%
P/E RATIO 14.7

TRADING VOLUME
Thousand Shares

| 1986 | 1987 | 1988 | 1989 | 1990 | 1991 | 1992 | 1993 | 1994 | 1995 | 1996 | 1997 | 1998 | 1999 | 2000 |

*7 YEAR PRICE SCORE 95.4   *12 MONTH PRICE SCORE 88.7
*NYSE COMPOSITE INDEX=100

INTERIM EARNINGS (Per Share):

Qtr.	Mar.	June	Sept.	Dec.
1996	0.31	0.32	0.33	0.35
1997	0.21	0.07	0.40	0.42
1998	0.41	0.42	0.44	0.46
1999	0.46	0.47	0.50	0.51

INTERIM DIVIDENDS (Per Share):

Amt.	Decl.	Ex.	Rec.	Pay.
0.16Q	4/22/99	4/28/99	4/30/99	5/14/99
0.16Q	7/22/99	7/28/99	7/30/99	8/13/99
0.18Q	10/28/99	11/03/99	11/05/99	11/19/99
0.18Q	1/27/00	2/02/00	2/04/00	2/18/00
0.18Q	4/27/00	5/03/00	5/05/00	5/19/00

Indicated div.: $0.72 (Div. Reinv. Plan)

CAPITALIZATION (12/31/99):

	($000)	(%)
Total Deposits	3,065,344	90.0
Long-Term Debt	41,500	1.2
Common & Surplus	300,592	8.8
Total	3,407,436	100.0

DIVIDEND ACHIEVER STATUS:
Rank: 38   10-Year Growth Rate: 17.35%
Total Years of Dividend Growth: 10

RECENT DEVELOPMENTS: For the year ended 12/31/99, net income advanced 3.6% to $76.1 million compared with $73.4 million in the previous year. Net interest income declined 0.6% to $179.2 million from $180.2 million the year before. Total interest income decreased 3.5% to $257.7 million from $266.8 million in the prior year. The decrease in income was primarily due to a decrease in earning-asset yields, a combination of lower loan yields and a decrease in investments yields. Total non-interest income climbed 6.2% to $40.2 million from $37.8 million, while total non-interest expense fell 1.3% to $100.1 million from $101.4 million a year ago. On 3/15/00, the Company and First Counties Bank announced the signing of a definitive merger agreement under which the Company will acquire all of the outstanding shares of common stock of First Counties Bank pursuant to a tax-free exchange of shares.

BUSINESS

WESTAMERICA BANCORPORA-TION is a bank holding company that provides a full range of banking services to individual and corporate customers. The Company is a regional community bank with over 80 branches in 21 Northern and Central California counties. The Company conducts its operations through its subsidiary banks, Westamerica Bank and Bank of Lake County. The Company offers a full range of products to individual and business customers such as checking and savings accounts, certificates of deposit, individual retirement accounts, credit cards, and loans. The Company also provides direct deposit, foreign exchange services, and electronic banking. Other services include payroll, cash and payment management services, real estate loans, letters of credit, and trust services. In addition, the Company has operations through its subsidiaries Westamerica Commercial Credit, Inc., and Community Banker Services Corporation.

ANNUAL FINANCIAL DATA

	12/31/99	12/31/98	12/31/97	12/31/96	12/31/95	12/31/94	12/31/93
Earnings Per Share	1.94	1.73	1.10	1.31	1.06	1.02	0.39
Tang. Book Val. Per Share	8.10	9.25	9.51	8.44	7.62	6.88	6.29
Dividends Per Share	0.66	0.52	0.36	0.30	0.25	0.21	0.18
Dividend Payout %	34.0	30.1	32.7	22.6	23.3	20.3	47.0
INCOME STATEMENT (IN MILLIONS):							
Total Interest Income	257.7	266.8	270.7	174.3	174.4	134.2	136.9
Total Interest Expense	78.5	86.7	88.1	60.9	58.6	41.1	42.3
Net Interest Income	179.2	180.2	182.6	113.3	115.8	93.1	94.6
Provision for Loan Losses	4.8	5.2	7.6	4.6	5.6	5.9	9.5
Non-Interest Income	40.2	37.8	37.0	22.0	21.5	19.4	23.9
Non-Interest Expense	100.1	101.4	137.9	75.6	86.3	71.1	96.6
Income Before Taxes	114.5	111.4	74.1	55.2	45.4	35.5	12.5
Net Income	76.1	73.4	48.1	37.7	31.4	24.7	9.5
Average Shs. Outstg. (000)	39,194	42,524	43,827	28,839	29,631	24,222	24,162
BALANCE SHEET (IN MILLIONS):							
Cash & Due from Banks	...	...	...	149.4	182.1	...	...
Securities Avail. for Sale	982.6	987.9	1,003.5	696.9	620.6	0.3	169.1
Total Loans & Leases	2,325.0	2,304.2	2,270.2	1,453.8	1,399.5	1,118.3	1,130.5
Allowance for Credit Losses	55.7	57.6	58.9	44.5	45.8	42.1	41.4
Net Loans & Leases	2,269.3	2,246.6	2,211.3	1,409.3	1,353.7	1,076.2	1,089.2
Total Assets	3,893.2	3,844.3	3,848.4	2,548.5	2,490.9	1,869.6	2,004.4
Total Deposits	3,065.3	3,189.0	3,078.5	2,081.4	2,049.5	1,688.9	1,731.2
Long-Term Obligations	41.5	47.5	52.5	42.5	20.0	25.5	36.4
Total Liabilities	3,592.6	3,475.7	3,441.3	2,309.5	2,267.0	1,864.0	1,852.0
Net Stockholders' Equity	300.6	368.6	407.2	238.9	223.9	166.2	152.4
Year-end Shs. Outstg. (000)	37,125	39,828	42,799	28,305	29,379	24,144	24,240
STATISTICAL RECORD:							
Return on Equity %	25.3	19.9	11.8	15.8	14.0	14.8	6.2
Return on Assets %	2.0	1.9	1.3	1.5	1.3	1.3	0.5
Equity/Assets %	7.7	9.6	10.6	9.4	9.0	8.9	7.6
Non-Int. Exp./Tot. Inc. %	45.6	46.5	62.8	55.9	62.9	63.2	81.5
Price Range	37½-26⅜	37¼-23⅝	35-18¹³/₁₆	19¾-14³/₁₆	14⁷/₁₆-9¹¹/₁₆	11¹/₁₆-8⁵/₈	10¹/₁₆-7³/₈
P/E Ratio	19.3-13.6	21.5-13.7	31.8-17.1	15.1-10.8	13.6-9.1	10.9-8.5	25.8-18.9
Average Yield %	2.1	1.7	1.3	1.7	2.0	2.1	2.1

Statistics are as originally reported. Adj. for 3-for-1 stk. split, 2/25/98.

OFFICERS:
D. L. Payne, Chmn., Pres., C.E.O.
J. F. Finger, Sr. V.P., C.F.O.
E. J. Bowler, Sr. V.P., Treas.

INVESTOR CONTACT: E. Joseph Bowler, (707) 863-6840

PRINCIPAL OFFICE: 1108 Fifth Ave., San Rafael, CA 94901

TELEPHONE NUMBER: (415) 257-8000
FAX: (415) 257-8013
WEB: www.westamerica.com

NO. OF EMPLOYEES: 1,094

SHAREHOLDERS: 8,710

ANNUAL MEETING: In Apr.

INCORPORATED: CA, Feb., 1972

INSTITUTIONAL HOLDINGS:
No. of Institutions: 108
Shares Held: 13,518,781
% Held: 35.9

INDUSTRY: National commercial banks (SIC: 6021)

TRANSFER AGENT(S): ChaseMellon Shareholder Services, Ridgefield Park, NJ.

NYSE SYMBOL WR
Rec. Pr. $15\frac{5}{8}$ (5/31/00)

WESTERN RESOURCES, INC.

YIELD 7.7%
P/E RATIO . . .

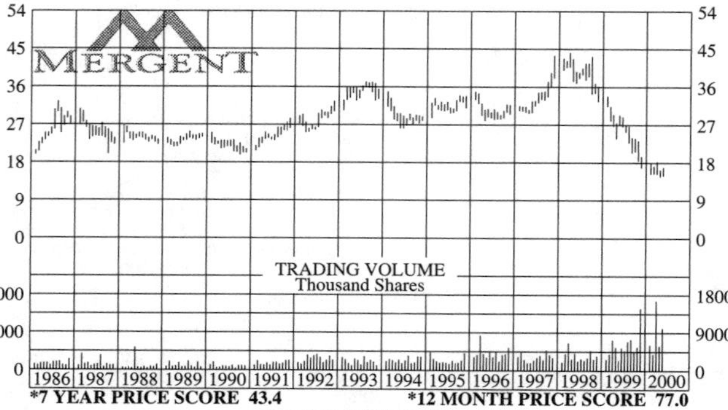

MERGENT
54
45
36
27
18
9
0
TRADING VOLUME
Thousand Shares
18000
9000
0
1986 1987 1988 1989 1990 1991 1992 1993 1994 1995 1996 1997 1998 1999 2000

*7 YEAR PRICE SCORE 43.4 *12 MONTH PRICE SCORE 77.0

*NYSE COMPOSITE INDEX=100

INTERIM EARNINGS (Per Share):

Qtr.	Mar.	June	Sept.	Dec.
1996	0.66	0.40	0.87	0.48
1997	0.61	0.36	7.77	d1.23
1998	0.45	0.50	1.10	d1.21
1999	0.31	0.27	0.72	d1.31

INTERIM DIVIDENDS (Per Share):

Amt.	Decl.	Ex.	Rec.	Pay.
0.535Q	7/21/99	9/07/99	9/09/99	10/01/99
0.535Q	11/17/99	12/07/99	12/09/99	1/03/00
0.535Q	1/26/00	3/07/00	3/09/00	4/03/00
0.30Q	5/17/00	6/07/00	6/09/00	7/03/00

Indicated div.: $1.20 (Div. Reinv. Plan)

CAPITALIZATION (12/31/99):

	($000)	(%)
Long-Term Debt	2,883,066	55.5
Minority Interest	193,499	3.7
Redeemable Pfd. Stock	220,000	4.2
Preferred Stock	24,858	0.5
Common & Surplus	1,875,466	36.1
Total	5,196,889	100.0

DIVIDEND ACHIEVER STATUS:
Rank: 318 10-Year Growth Rate: 2.03%
Total Years of Dividend Growth: 39

RECENT DEVELOPMENTS: For the year ended 12/31/99, income was $717,000, before an extraordinary gain of $11.7 million, versus income of $46.2 million, before an extraordinary gain of $1.6 million, in 1998. Results included net non-recurring charges of $88.1 million and $98.9 million in 1999 and 1998, respectively. Total sales rose slightly to $2.04 billion from $2.03 billion in 1998.

PROSPECTS: On 3/29/00, the Company announced plans to separate its electric utility business, to be called Westar Energy, from its non-electric business, which will be renamed later and until then referred to as ''Westar Capital.'' Both companies will be public entities. The separation is expected to be completed by year-end 2000 by means of a voluntary exchange offer.

BUSINESS

WESTERN RESOURCES INC. (formerly The Kansas Power and Light Company) is a publicly traded consumer services company. WR is engaged in the business of providing electric generation, transmission and distribution services to approximately 628,000 customers in Kansas and providing monitored services to approximately 1.6 million customers in North America, the United Kingdom and Continental Europe. The Company owns a 45% interest in ONEOK, Inc., a natural gas transmission and distribution company with approximately 1.4 million customers in Oklahoma and Kansas. Regulated electric service is provided by KPL, a division of the company, and Kansas Gas and Electric Company, a wholly-owned subsidiary. In addition, WR owns an 85.0% interest in Protection One, Inc., a security alarm company.

ANNUAL FINANCIAL DATA

	12/31/99	12/31/98	12/31/97	12/31/96	12/31/95	12/31/94	12/31/93
Earnings Per Share	**[1] [3] d0.01**	**[1] [3] 0.65**	**[1] 7.51**	**[1] 2.41**	**2.71**	**2.82**	**2.76**
Cash Flow Per Share	**5.88**	**4.92**	**11.45**	**5.77**	**5.65**	**5.59**	**5.86**
Tang. Book Val. Per Share	**11.47**	**11.38**	**17.73**	**25.14**	**24.71**	**23.93**	**23.08**
Dividends Per Share	**2.14**	**2.13**	**2.09**	**2.05**	**2.01**	**1.97**	**1.93**
Dividend Payout %	**. . .**	**327.6**	**27.8**	**85.1**	**74.2**	**69.9**	**69.9**
INCOME STATEMENT (IN MILLIONS):							
Total Revenues	2,036.2	2,034.1	2,151.8	2,046.8	1,572.1	1,617.9	1,909.4
Costs & Expenses	1,366.5	1,522.9	1,752.1	1,340.4	916.6	969.1	1,238.0
Depreciation & Amort.	395.2	280.7	256.7	214.2	182.9	170.4	183.5
Maintenance Exp.	. . .	. . .	. . .	99.1	108.6	113.2	117.8
Operating Income	274.5	230.5	142.9	304.0	275.4	269.5	292.1
Net Interest Inc./(Exp.)	d370.3	d226.1	d193.2	d149.3	d119.6	d116.0	d140.2
Income Taxes	cr33.4	14.6	378.6	89.1	88.5	95.6	78.0
Equity Earnings/Minority Int.	12.9	0.4	4.7	. . .	. . .	. . .	. . .
Net Income	[1] [3] 0.7	[1] [3] 46.2	[1] 494.1	[1] 169.0	181.7	187.4	177.4
Cash Flow	394.8	323.2	745.9	368.3	351.2	344.5	347.4
Average Shs. Outstg. (000)	67,080	65,634	65,128	63,834	62,157	61,618	59,294
BALANCE SHEET (IN MILLIONS):							
Gross Property	6,032.3	5,786.4	5,644.9	6,376.7	6,228.9	6,048.7	6,302.7
Accumulated Depreciation	2,170.9	2,030.8	1,899.1	2,058.6	1,926.5	1,790.3	1,821.7
Net Property	3,889.4	3,795.1	3,786.5	4,356.5	4,356.4	4,298.3	4,510.2
Total Assets	8,008.2	7,951.4	6,977.0	6,647.8	5,490.7	5,189.6	5,412.0
Long-Term Obligations	2,883.1	3,063.1	2,181.9	1,681.6	1,391.3	1,357.0	1,524.0
Net Stockholders' Equity	1,900.3	1,962.8	2,089.1	1,649.5	1,578.0	1,499.3	1,447.0
Year-end Shs. Outstg. (000)	67,402	65,909	65,410	64,625	62,856	61,618	61,618
STATISTICAL RECORD:							
Operating Profit Margin %	13.5	11.3	6.6	14.9	17.5	16.7	15.3
Net Profit Margin %	. . .	2.3	23.0	8.3	11.6	11.6	9.3
Net Inc./Net Property %	. . .	1.2	13.0	3.9	4.2	4.4	3.9
Net Inc./Tot. Capital %	. . .	0.8	10.6	3.6	4.1	4.7	4.3
Return on Equity %	. . .	2.4	23.7	10.2	11.5	12.5	12.3
Accum. Depr./Gross Prop. %	36.0	35.1	33.6	32.3	30.9	29.6	28.9
Price Range	$33\frac{7}{8}$-$16\frac{13}{16}$	$44\frac{3}{16}$-$32\frac{9}{16}$	$43\frac{7}{16}$-$29\frac{3}{4}$	$34\frac{7}{8}$-28	34-$28\frac{5}{8}$	$34\frac{7}{8}$-$26\frac{1}{8}$	$37\frac{1}{4}$-$30\frac{3}{8}$
P/E Ratio	. . .	68.0-50.1	5.8-4.0	14.5-11.6	12.5-10.6	12.4-9.3	13.5-11.0
Average Yield %	8.4	5.6	5.7	6.5	6.4	6.5	5.7

Statistics are as originally reported. [1] Incl. net non-recurr. chrgs. $88.1 mill., 12/99; $98.9 mill., 12/98; $776.1 mill., 12/97; $18.2 mill., 12/96. [3] Bef. extraord. gain $11.7 mill., 12/99; $1.6 mill., 12/98.

OFFICERS:
D. C. Wittig, Chmn., Pres., C.E.O.
W. B. Moore, Exec. V.P., C.F.O., Treas.
R. D. Terrill, Exec. V.P., Gen. Couns., Corp. Sec.

INVESTOR CONTACT: James A. Martin, V.P. Investor Relations & Strategic Planning, (785) 575-6549

PRINCIPAL OFFICE: 818 S. Kansas Avenue, P.O. Box 889, Topeka, KS 66601-0889

TELEPHONE NUMBER: (785) 575-6300
FAX: (785) 575-8061
WEB: www.wr.com

NO. OF EMPLOYEES: 7,049

SHAREHOLDERS: 50,680

ANNUAL MEETING: In June

INCORPORATED: KS, March, 1924

INSTITUTIONAL HOLDINGS:
No. of Institutions: 133
Shares Held: 24,002,727
% Held: 35.3

INDUSTRY: Electric and other services combined (SIC: 4931)

TRANSFER AGENT(S): Western Resources, Inc., Topeka, KS

WEYCO GROUP, INC.

YIELD 1.8%
P/E RATIO 9.6

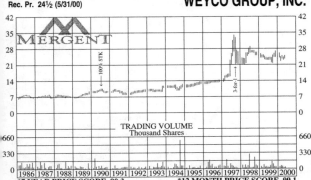

7 YEAR PRICE SCORE 90.3 **12 MONTH PRICE SCORE 99.1**
*NYSE COMPOSITE INDEX=100

INTERIM EARNINGS (Per Share):

Qtr.	Mar.	June	Sept.	Dec.
1996	1.10	0.95	1.67	1.25
1997	0.50	0.37	0.59	0.42
1998	0.55	0.41	0.49	0.62
1999	0.61	0.48	0.57	0.89

INTERIM DIVIDENDS (Per Share):

Amt.	Decl.	Ex.	Rec.	Pay.
0.10Q	4/27/99	5/27/99	6/01/99	7/01/99
0.10Q	7/26/99	8/30/99	9/01/99	10/01/99
0.10Q	11/01/99	11/29/99	12/01/99	1/01/00
0.10Q	1/31/00	3/02/00	3/06/00	4/01/00
0.11Q	4/25/00	5/30/00	6/01/00	7/01/00

Indicated div.: $0.44

CAPITALIZATION (12/31/99):

	($000)	(%)
Deferred Income Tax	1,916	2.8
Common & Surplus	67,751	97.2
Total	69,667	100.0

DIVIDEND ACHIEVER STATUS:
Rank: 160   10-Year Growth Rate: 9.74%
Total Years of Dividend Growth: 19

RECENT DEVELOPMENTS: For the year ended 12/31/99, net earnings rose 12.8% to $11.1 million compared with $9.8 million in the comparable year. Results for 1999 included a net gain of $496,000 on the sale of warehouse facilities. Net sales increased 5.1% to $133.5 million versus $127.1 million in the previous year. Wholesale division sales rose 5.3% to $126.6 million primarily due to the strong perform-

ance of the Stacy Adams division and customer acceptance of the "SAO by Stacy Adams" casual shoe product line. Retail division sales were $6.9 million, up slightly from $6.8 million the year before. Going forward, WEYS is well positioned to generate top and bottom line growth as all of its brands entered the new year with double-digit increases in their respective order backlogs.

BUSINESS

WEYCO GROUP, INC. and its subsidiaries engage in the manufacture, purchase and distribution of men's footwear. These shoes are sold under various brand names. The principal brands of shoes sold are NUNN BUSH, BRASS BOOT and STACY ADAMS. The Company's wholesale division, which generated approximately 95% of total sales in 1999, markets footwear through more than 8,000 shoe, clothing and department stores across the United States. The retail division consists of eleven Company-operated stores in the United States.

ANNUAL FINANCIAL DATA

	12/31/99	12/31/98	12/31/97	12/31/96	12/31/95	12/31/94	12/31/93
Earnings Per Share	② 2.55	2.07	1.88	1.66	1.21	0.99	① 0.77
Cash Flow Per Share	2.84	2.20	2.05	1.87	1.41	1.19	0.96
Tang. Book Val. Per Share	16.28	14.73	13.96	12.41	11.34	10.46	9.75
Dividends Per Share	0.38	0.34	0.30	0.29	0.273	0.267	0.25
Dividend Payout %	14.9	16.4	16.1	17.3	22.6	26.9	32.8
INCOME STATEMENT (IN THOUSANDS):							
Total Revenues	133,498	127,074	127,029	129,314	120,643	114,719	122,144
Costs & Expenses	117,033	112,647	113,561	116,605	110,907	104,100	113,809
Depreciation & Amort.	1,242	626	821	1,045	1,134	1,226	1,203
Operating Income	15,223	13,801	12,646	11,664	8,602	9,392	7,131
Net Interest Inc./(Exp.)	831	1,419	1,475	...	...	...	...
Income Before Income Taxes	16,958	15,255	14,133	12,790	10,810	10,066	7,716
Income Taxes	5,900	5,450	5,065	4,718	4,003	3,887	2,808
Net Income	② 11,058	9,805	9,068	8,072	6,807	6,179	① 4,908
Cash Flow	12,300	10,431	9,890	9,117	7,941	7,406	6,112
Average Shs. Outstg.	4,339	4,731	4,825	4,871	5,641	6,231	6,352
BALANCE SHEET (IN THOUSANDS):							
Cash & Cash Equivalents	8,704	13,094	10,684	15,017	23,925	32,694	26,536
Total Current Assets	53,093	48,051	42,912	47,813	59,494	62,454	64,996
Net Property	16,594	13,801	2,313	2,653	3,513	4,574	4,860
Total Assets	95,919	92,782	82,204	73,077	79,328	72,827	74,915
Total Current Liabilities	26,253	26,387	14,643	13,973	13,498	9,486	9,132
Net Stockholders' Equity	67,751	65,148	66,677	59,104	64,083	59,427	62,335
Net Working Capital	26,840	21,664	28,269	33,840	45,997	52,968	55,864
Year-end Shs. Outstg.	4,161	4,424	4,775	4,762	5,652	5,682	6,395
STATISTICAL RECORD:							
Operating Profit Margin %	11.4	10.9	10.0	9.0	7.1	8.2	5.8
Net Profit Margin %	8.3	7.7	7.1	6.2	5.6	5.4	4.0
Return on Equity %	16.3	15.0	13.6	13.7	10.6	10.4	7.9
Return on Assets %	11.5	10.6	11.0	11.0	8.6	8.5	6.6
Price Range	27-21⅝	29-21	34-13⁷/₁₆	14⁵/₁₆-12½	13¹¹/₁₆-11	12⁹/₁₆-9¹¹/₁₆	11¹³/₁₆-9³/₁₆
P/E Ratio	10.6-8.5	14.0-10.1	18.1-7.1	8.6-7.5	11.3-9.1	12.7-9.7	15.3-11.9
Average Yield %	1.6	1.4	1.3	2.1	2.2	2.4	2.4

Statistics are as originally reported. Adj. for stk. splits: 3-for-1 10/1/97. ① Bef. acctg. change credit $880,000 ($0.14/sh) ② Incl. after-tax gain of $496,000 on the sale of assets.

OFFICERS:
T. W. Florsheim, Chmn.
T. W. Florsheim Jr., Pres., C.E.O.
J. W. Florsheim, Exec. V.P., C.O.O., Asst. Sec.
J. F. Wittkowske, V.P., Fin., Sec.

INVESTOR CONTACT: Investor Relations, (414) 908-1600

PRINCIPAL OFFICE: 333 W. Estabrook Boulevard, Glendale, WI 53217

TELEPHONE NUMBER: (414) 908-1600
FAX: (414) 908-1601
WEB: www.stacyadams.com

NO. OF EMPLOYEES: 400 (approx.)

SHAREHOLDERS: 364 (approx.); 150 (Cl. B)

ANNUAL MEETING: In April

INCORPORATED: WI, June, 1906

INSTITUTIONAL HOLDINGS:
No. of Institutions: 19
Shares Held: 998,709
% Held: 30.5

INDUSTRY: Men's footwear, except athletic (SIC: 3143)

TRANSFER AGENT(S): American Stock Transfer & Trust Co., New York, NY

WILMINGTON TRUST CORPORATION

YIELD 3.5%
P/E RATIO 15.8

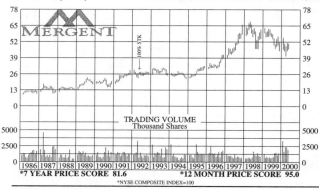

INTERIM EARNINGS (Per Share):

Qtr.	Mar.	June	Sept.	Dec.
1995	0.60	0.64	0.66	0.66
1996	0.66	0.70	0.73	0.74
1997	0.72	0.77	0.79	0.80
1998	0.79	0.82	0.86	0.87
1999	0.53	0.92	0.89	0.87

INTERIM DIVIDENDS (Per Share):

Amt.	Decl.	Ex.	Rec.	Pay.
0.42Q	7/15/99	7/29/99	8/02/99	8/16/99
0.42Q	10/22/99	10/28/99	11/01/99	11/15/99
0.42Q	1/21/00	1/28/00	2/01/00	2/16/00
0.45Q	4/20/00	4/27/00	5/01/00	5/15/00

Indicated div.: $1.80 (Div. Reinv. Plan)

CAPITALIZATION (12/31/99):

	($000)	(%)
Total Deposits	5,369,484	89.0
Long-Term Debt	168,000	2.8
Common & Surplus	498,231	8.3
Total	6,035,715	100.0

DIVIDEND ACHIEVER STATUS:
Rank: 137   10-Year Growth Rate: 10.83%
Total Years of Dividend Growth: 18

RECENT DEVELOPMENTS: For the year ended 12/31/99, net income declined 6.1% to $107.3 million. Results for 1999 included a one-time charge of $13.4 million related to the Company's plans to outsource certain back office data processing functions, check processing and core accounting processing for personal and institutional trust accounts. Including the charge, net profit margin was 24.5% in 1999 versus 27.1% in 1998. Net interest income rose 3.5% to $245.9 million from $237.7 million a year ago. Total inter-

est income increased 1.1% to $462.2 million from $456.9 million in the previous year. Total other expense climbed 12.2% to $258.2 million from $230.1 million a year ago. Total loans advanced 11.5% to $4.82 billion from $4.32 billion the year before. Total assets grew 14.3% to $7.20 billion from $6.30 billion a year earlier. Return on average assets was 1.60% versus 1.83% the previous year, while return on average stockholders' equity was 20.18% compared with 21.70% in the prior year.

BUSINESS

WILMINGTON TRUST CORPORATION and its subsidiaries, with assets of $7.20 billion as of 12/31/99, provide a full range of banking and related services to individual and corporate customers in the Delaware area. The Company operates branches in Delaware, Pennsylvania, Maryland, Nevada, New York, California and Florida. WILM offers a full range of trust, custody and investment services to institutions and individuals, including a family of mutual funds, portfolio management and precious metals storage. The bank also provides discount brokerage, insurance and travel services.

ANNUAL FINANCIAL DATA

	12/31/99	12/31/98	12/31/97	12/31/96	12/31/95	12/31/94	12/31/93
Earnings Per Share	☐ 3.21	3.34	3.08	2.83	2.56	2.37	2.24
Tang. Book Val. Per Share	10.34	12.14	15.03	13.71	13.09	11.80	10.88
Dividends Per Share	1.65	1.53	1.41	1.29	1.17	1.06	0.97
Dividend Payout %	51.4	45.8	45.8	45.6	45.7	44.7	43.5
INCOME STATEMENT (IN MILLIONS)							
Total Interest Income	462.2	456.9	430.6	402.9	377.3	307.9	291.0
Total Interest Expense	216.3	219.2	200.6	188.6	180.0	123.6	116.1
Net Interest Income	245.9	237.7	230.0	214.2	197.4	184.3	174.8
Provision for Loan Losses	17.5	20.0	21.5	16.0	12.3	4.6	9.5
Non-Interest Income	191.5	183.9	157.5	138.2	127.6	113.1	113.7
Non-Interest Expense	258.2	230.1	207.7	192.3	181.0	172.0	161.8
Income Before Taxes	161.7	171.5	158.4	144.1	131.7	120.8	117.2
Net Income	☐ 107.3	114.3	106.0	97.3	90.0	85.2	82.8
Average Shs. Outstg. (000)	33,383	34,275	34,466	34,399	35,213	35,990	37,029
BALANCE SHEET (IN MILLIONS)							
Cash & Due from Banks	225.1	204.6	239.4	231.2	252.8	203.5	186.3
Securities Avail. for Sale	1,686.3	1,298.7	1,316.4	798.5	910.2	253.2	21.8
Total Loans & Leases	4,821.6	4,324.4	4,004.8	3,783.9	3,527.6	3,283.0	3,039.8
Allowance for Credit Losses	78.4	76.7	74.6	66.8	55.6	51.6	53.6
Net Loans & Leases	4,743.2	4,247.7	3,930.1	3,717.1	3,472.0	3,231.4	2,986.2
Total Assets	7,201.9	6,300.6	6,122.4	5,564.4	5,372.2	4,742.4	4,637.8
Total Deposits	5,369.5	4,536.8	4,169.0	3,913.7	3,587.6	3,308.8	3,391.4
Long-Term Obligations	168.0	168.0	43.0	43.0	28.0	...	...
Total Liabilities	6,703.7	5,754.4	5,619.3	5,099.7	4,912.8	4,324.1	4,242.6
Net Stockholders' Equity	498.2	546.2	503.0	464.7	459.4	418.2	395.2
Year-end Shs. Outstg. (000)	32,353	33,329	33,478	33,893	35,090	35,449	36,308
STATISTICAL RECORD:							
Return on Equity %	21.5	20.9	21.1	20.9	19.6	20.4	20.9
Return on Assets %	1.5	1.8	1.7	1.7	1.7	1.8	1.8
Equity/Assets %	6.9	8.7	8.2	8.4	8.6	8.8	8.5
Non-Int. Exp./Tot. Inc. %	59.2	55.4	53.6	54.8	56.1	57.4	56.1
Price Range	63½-44¾	68½-46⅜	66-39¼	41¾-30¼	32½-22¾	28½-22	31-24¾
P/E Ratio	19.8-13.9	20.5-13.9	21.4-12.7	14.8-10.7	12.7-8.9	12.0-9.3	13.8-11.0
Average Yield %	3.0	2.7	2.7	3.6	4.2	4.2	3.5

Statistics are as originally reported. ☐ Incl. non-recurr. chrg. $13.4 mill.

OFFICERS:
T. T. Cecala, Chmn., C.E.O.
R. V. Harra Jr., Pres., C.O.O., Treas.
D. R. Gibson, Sr. V.P., C.F.O.

INVESTOR CONTACT: Ellen J. Roberts, V.P., Media & Investor Relations, (302) 651-8069

PRINCIPAL OFFICE: Rodney Square North, 1100 North Market St., Wilmington, DE 19890-0001

TELEPHONE NUMBER: (302) 651-1000
FAX: (302) 651-8010
WEB: www.wilmingtontrust.com

NO. OF EMPLOYEES: 2,434

SHAREHOLDERS: 9,617

ANNUAL MEETING: In May

INCORPORATED: DE, Mar., 1901

INSTITUTIONAL HOLDINGS:
No. of Institutions: 165
Shares Held: 12,198,505
% Held: 37.5

INDUSTRY: State commercial banks (SIC: 6022)

TRANSFER AGENT(S): Norwest Bank Minnesota, N.A., South St. Paul, MN

NYSE SYMBOL WEC
Rec. Pr. 21 1/8 (5/31/00)

WISCONSIN ENERGY CORPORATION

YIELD 7.4%
P/E RATIO 11.8

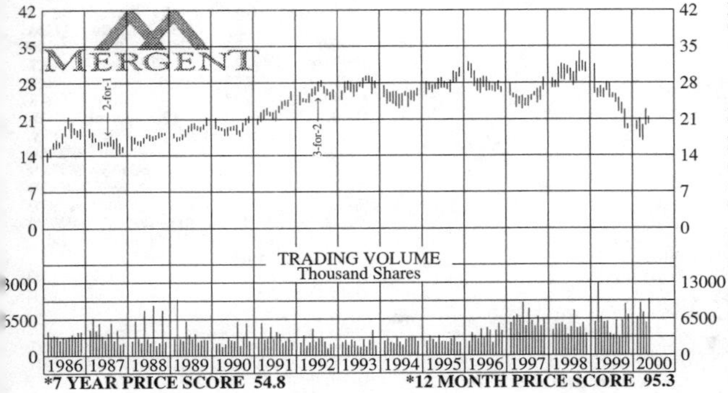

*7 YEAR PRICE SCORE 54.8 *12 MONTH PRICE SCORE 95.3

*NYSE COMPOSITE INDEX=100

INTERIM EARNINGS (Per Share):

Qtr.	Mar.	June	Sept.	Dec.
1996	0.57	0.41	0.48	0.51
1997	0.40	d0.09	0.21	0.02
1998	0.43	0.25	0.50	0.45
1999	0.46	0.42	0.59	0.32

INTERIM DIVIDENDS (Per Share):

Amt.	Decl.	Ex.	Rec.	Pay.
0.39Q	7/28/99	8/10/99	8/12/99	9/01/99
0.39Q	10/28/99	11/09/99	11/12/99	12/01/99
0.39Q	1/25/00	2/10/00	2/14/00	3/01/00
0.39Q	4/27/00	5/10/00	5/12/00	6/01/00

Indicated div.: $1.56 (Div. Reinv. Plan)

CAPITALIZATION (12/31/99):

	($000)	(%)
Long-Term Debt	2,134,636	42.7
Deferred Income Tax	624,864	12.5
Redeemable Pfd. Stock	200,000	4.0
Preferred Stock	30,450	0.6
Common & Surplus	2,007,744	40.2
Total	4,997,694	100.0

DIVIDEND ACHIEVER STATUS:
Rank: 287 10-Year Growth Rate: 3.68%
Total Years of Dividend Growth: 38

RECENT DEVELOPMENTS: For the year ended 12/31/99, net income increased 11.0% to $209.0 million versus $188.1 million the previous year. Results for 1999 included a $10.8 million after-tax charge related to the settlement of litigation. Total operating revenues advanced 11.4% to $2.27 billion from $2.04 billion. Utility revenues grew 3.5% to $2.05 billion. Operating income rose 21.8% to $456.4 million from $374.8 million in 1998.

PROSPECTS: On 4/26/00, the Company completed its acquisition of WICOR for a total cash consideration of approximately $1.20 billion. WEC will operate more than 16,500 miles of gas main and 30,000 miles of electrical transmission and distribution wires. The transaction is expected to increase growth oppotunities, provide earnings diversification and expansion, and enable the Company to take advantage of converging markets.

BUSINESS

WISCONSIN ENERGY CORPORATION is a Milwaukee-based holding company with subsidiaries in utility and non-utility businesses. The Company serves more than 1.0 million electric and 921,000 natural gas customers in Wisconsin and Michigan's Upper Peninsula through its subsidiaries, Wisconsin Electric, Wisconsin Gas and Edison Sault Electric. WEC's non-utility subsidiaries include energy services and development, pump manufacturing, waste-to-energy and real estate businesses. On 4/26/00, the Company acquired WICOR, a Milwaukee-based diversified holding company, for $1.20 billion in cash.

REVENUES

(12/31/1999)	($000)	(%)
Utility	2,050,218	90.2
Non-Utility	193,240	8.5
Other	29,181	1.3
Total	2,272,639	100.0

ANNUAL FINANCIAL DATA

	12/31/99	12/31/98	12/31/97	12/31/96	12/31/95	12/31/94	12/31/93
Earnings Per Share	**[3] 1.79**	**1.65**	**[2] 0.54**	**1.97**	**2.13**	**[1] 1.67**	**1.81**
Cash Flow Per Share	**4.51**	**4.14**	**2.90**	**4.19**	**4.21**	**3.71**	**3.75**
Tang. Book Val. Per Share	**16.89**	**16.46**	**16.51**	**17.42**	**16.89**	**16.01**	**15.67**
Dividends Per Share	**1.56**	**1.55**	**1.53**	**1.51**	**1.46**	**1.40**	**1.34**
Dividend Payout %	**87.1**	**94.2**	**284.2**	**76.5**	**68.3**	**83.6**	**74.1**
INCOME STATEMENT (IN MILLIONS):							
Total Revenues	2,272.6	1,980.0	1,789.6	1,773.8	1,770.5	1,742.2	1,643.7
Costs & Expenses	1,497.5	1,249.3	1,189.4	1,117.7	1,101.0	1,134.4	1,023.9
Depreciation & Amort.	318.8	284.7	265.6	247.2	228.1	220.0	202.0
Maintenance Exp.	...	169.3	135.1	103.0	112.4	124.6	155.2
Operating Income	456.4	276.7	199.5	305.8	329.0	263.3	262.6
Net Interest Inc./(Exp.)	d111.1	d92.1	d88.2	d88.4	d93.5	d90.5	d83.0
Income Taxes	111.1	cr2.6	cr26.8	cr1.3	cr2.5	cr1.2	cr0.3
Net Income	[3] 209.0	188.1	[2] 60.7	218.1	234.0	[1] 180.9	188.5
Cash Flow	527.8	472.8	326.3	465.3	462.1	400.8	390.4
Average Shs. Outstg. (000)	117,019	114,315	112,570	110,983	109,850	108,025	104,240
BALANCE SHEET (IN MILLIONS):							
Gross Property	6,814.2	6,435.6	5,925.2	5,552.3	5,271.3	5,155.2	4,838.2
Accumulated Depreciation	3,250.0	3,007.7	2,700.8	2,442.0	2,288.1	2,134.5	1,964.3
Net Property	3,846.6	3,515.6	3,314.6	3,185.8	3,042.5	3,077.4	2,926.6
Total Assets	6,233.1	5,361.8	5,037.7	4,810.8	4,560.7	4,408.3	4,223.1
Long-Term Obligations	2,134.6	1,749.0	1,532.4	1,416.1	1,367.6	1,283.7	1,286.2
Net Stockholders' Equity	2,038.2	1,933.6	1,893.4	1,975.8	1,901.7	1,775.0	1,686.5
Year-end Shs. Outstg. (000)	118,904	115,607	112,866	111,679	110,819	108,940	105,320
STATISTICAL RECORD:							
Operating Profit Margin %	20.1	14.0	11.1	17.2	18.6	15.1	16.0
Net Profit Margin %	9.2	9.5	3.4	12.3	13.2	10.4	11.5
Net Inc./Net Property %	5.4	5.4	1.8	6.8	7.7	5.9	6.4
Net Inc./Tot. Capital %	4.2	4.4	1.5	5.6	6.2	5.1	5.5
Return on Equity %	10.3	9.7	3.2	11.0	12.3	10.2	11.2
Accum. Depr./Gross Prop. %	47.7	46.7	45.6	44.0	43.4	41.4	40.6
Price Range	31 9/16-19 1/16	34-27	29 1/16-23	32-26	30 7/8-25 3/4	27 1/2-23 1/8	29 3/8-24 3/4
P/E Ratio	17.6-10.6	20.6-16.4	53.8-42.6	16.2-13.2	14.5-12.1	16.5-13.8	16.2-13.7
Average Yield %	6.2	5.1	5.9	5.2	5.1	5.5	5.0

Statistics are as originally reported. [1] Incl. non-recurr chrg. $190.1 mill. related to restructuring. [2] Incl. non-recurr chrg. $36.9 mill. [3] Incl. non-recurr. after-tax chrg. $10.8 mill. related to ligiation settlement.

OFFICERS:
R. A. Abdoo, Chmn., Pres., C.E.O.
C. H. Baker, Treas.
P. Donovan, Sr. V.P., C.F.O.

INVESTOR CONTACT: Jim Schubilske, Investor Relations Coordinator, (414) 221-2592

PRINCIPAL OFFICE: 231 West Michigan Street, P.O. Box 2949, Milwaukee, WI 53201

TELEPHONE NUMBER: (414) 221-2345
FAX: (414) 221-2172
WEB: www.wisenergy.com

NO. OF EMPLOYEES: 5,706 full-time; 171 part-time

SHAREHOLDERS: 91,062

ANNUAL MEETING: In June

INCORPORATED: WI, June, 1981

INSTITUTIONAL HOLDINGS:
No. of Institutions: 208
Shares Held: 55,848,522
% Held: 47.4

INDUSTRY: Electric and other services combined (SIC: 4931)

TRANSFER AGENT(S): Peter Sirko, Milwaukee, WI

WORTHINGTON INDUSTRIES, INC.

YIELD	5.3%
P/E RATIO	10.8

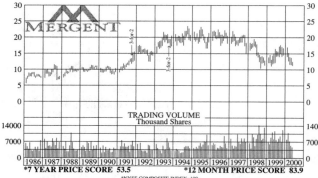

*7 YEAR PRICE SCORE 53.5   *12 MONTH PRICE SCORE 83.9

*NYSE COMPOSITE INDEX=100

TRADING VOLUME Thousand Shares

INTERIM EARNINGS (Per Share):

Qtr.	Aug.	Nov.	Feb.	May
1996-97	0.22	0.23	0.23	0.28
1997-98	0.24	0.23	0.23	0.26
1998-99	0.18	0.20	0.21	0.31
1999-00	0.27	0.28	0.26	...

INTERIM DIVIDENDS (Per Share):

Amt.	Decl.	Ex.	Rec.	Pay.
0.15Q	5/20/99	6/08/99	6/10/99	6/28/99
0.15Q	8/26/99	9/07/99	9/09/99	9/27/99
0.15Q	11/18/99	12/13/99	12/15/99	12/29/99
0.15Q	2/24/00	3/13/00	3/15/00	3/29/00
0.16Q	5/22/00	6/13/00	6/15/00	6/29/00

Indicated div.: $0.64

CAPITALIZATION (5/31/99):

	($000)	(%)
Long-Term Debt	365,802	29.8
Deferred Income Tax	124,444	10.1
Minority Interest	47,819	3.9
Common & Surplus	689,649	56.2
Total	1,227,714	100.0

DIVIDEND ACHIEVER STATUS:

Rank: 157   10-Year Growth Rate: 9.83%
Total Years of Dividend Growth: 17

RECENT DEVELOPMENTS: On 4/19/00, the Company begin trading on the New York Stock Exchange under the ticker symbol "WOR." The Company was previously traded on Nasdaq under the ticker symbol "WTHG." For the quarter ended 2/29/00, net earnings were $23.2 million compared with earnings from continuing operations of $19.1 million in the comparable prior-year quarter. Earnings for 1999 excluded a loss from discontinued operations of $16.9 million. Net sales advanced 15.3% to $486.5 million from

$422.1 million in the year-earlier quarter. Revenues were driven by growth from start-up facilities within the Processed Steel Products segment as well as acquisitions by the Pressure Cylinders segment. Processed Steel Products sales increased 17.3% to $313.1 million, while Metal Framing sales increased 10.6% to $85.2 million. Pressure Cylinders sales increased 13.4% to $86.6 million. Gross margin on sales slipped to 16.4% versus 17.1%, reflecting elevated steel and pressure cylinders material prices.

BUSINESS

WORTHINGTON INDUSTRIES, INC. is a diversified steel processor that focuses on steel processing and metals-related businesses. WOR operates 39 facilities through three business segments: Processed Steel Products, Metal Framing and Pressure Cylinders. The Processed Steel Products segment includes The Worthington Steel Company business unit and The Gerstenslager Company business unit. The Metal Framing segment is made up of Dietrich Industries, Inc. and the Pressure Cylinders segment consists of Worthington Cylinder Corporation. In addition, the Company holds an equity position in seven joint ventures.

ANNUAL FINANCIAL DATA

	5/31/99	5/31/98	5/31/97	5/31/96	5/31/95	5/31/94	5/31/93
Earnings Per Share	[1][2] 0.90	[1][3] 0.85	0.97	1.01	1.29	0.94	0.74
Cash Flow Per Share	1.74	1.48	1.50	1.44	1.66	1.30	1.06
Tang. Book Val. Per Share	6.74	7.08	6.38	6.32	6.50	5.56	4.81
Dividends Per Share	0.55	0.51	0.47	0.43	0.39	0.34	0.39
Dividend Payout %	61.1	60.0	48.4	42.6	30.2	36.5	53.1
INCOME STATEMENT (IN MILLIONS):							
Total Revenues	1,763.1	1,624.4	1,911.7	1,477.8	1,483.6	1,285.1	1,115.7
Costs & Expenses	1,538.4	1,427.5	1,706.1	1,312.5	1,295.6	1,133.3	977.9
Depreciation & Amort.	78.5	61.5	51.4	39.2	34.1	32.4	29.2
Operating Income	146.2	135.5	154.2	126.1	153.8	119.4	108.5
Net Interest Inc./(Exp.)	d43.1	d25.6	d18.4	d8.3	d6.0	d3.0	d3.4
Income Before Income Taxes	108.3	111.3	136.8	118.7	148.4	116.8	105.1
Income Taxes	49.1	48.3	57.2	56.5	70.0	50.8	38.9
Equity Earnings/Minority Int.	24.5	19.3	13.8	29.1	38.3	18.9	...
Net Income	[1][2] 83.6	[1][3] 82.3	93.3	91.3	116.7	84.9	66.2
Cash Flow	162.1	143.8	144.7	130.6	150.8	117.2	95.4
Average Shs. Outstg. (000)	93,106	96,949	96,557	90,812	90,730	90,378	89,699
BALANCE SHEET (IN MILLIONS):							
Cash & Cash Equivalents	7.6	3.8	7.2	19.0	2.0	13.3	17.6
Total Current Assets	624.3	643.0	594.1	476.0	451.9	413.1	364.0
Net Property	871.3	933.2	691.0	512.3	334.9	307.6	293.4
Total Assets	1,687.0	1,842.3	1,561.2	1,220.1	917.0	798.6	686.1
Total Current Liabilities	427.7	410.0	246.8	151.3	179.2	180.5	147.0
Long-Term Obligations	365.8	439.6	450.4	298.7	53.5	54.1	55.6
Net Stockholders' Equity	689.6	780.3	715.5	639.5	590.3	503.9	433.1
Net Working Capital	196.5	233.0	347.3	324.8	272.7	232.6	217.1
Year-end Shs. Outstg. (000)	89,949	96,657	96,711	90,830	90,840	90,561	90,113
STATISTICAL RECORD:							
Operating Profit Margin %	8.3	8.3	8.1	8.5	10.4	9.3	9.7
Net Profit Margin %	4.7	5.1	4.9	6.2	7.9	6.6	5.9
Return on Equity %	12.1	10.5	13.0	14.3	19.8	16.8	15.3
Return on Assets %	5.0	4.5	6.0	7.5	12.7	10.6	9.6
Debt/Total Assets %	21.7	23.9	28.8	24.5	5.8	6.8	8.1
Price Range	19⁹⁄₁₆-10⅜	22-15⅛	22¹⁄₂-17¹⁄₂	23¹⁄₄-16⅝	23¹⁄₂-17¹⁄₂	21¹¹⁄₁₆-15	17⁹⁄₁₆-12⁷⁄₁₆
P/E Ratio	21.7-11.5	25.9-17.8	23.2-18.0	23.0-16.5	18.2-13.6	23.0-16.0	23.8-16.8
Average Yield %	3.7	2.7	2.4	2.2	1.9	1.9	2.6

Statistics are as originally reported. Adj. for stk. splits: 3-for-2, 10/25/93 [1] Bef. disc. oper. loss 5/31/99: $20.9 mill. ($0.23/sh.); gain 5/31/98: $17.3 mill. ($0.18/sh.) [2] Bef. acctg. change chrg. $7.8 mill. ($0.08/sh.) [3] Bef. extraord. credit $18.8 mill. ($0.19/sh.)

OFFICERS:
J. P. McConnell, Chmn., C.E.O.
J. S. Christie, Pres., C.O.O.
J. T. Baldwin, V.P., C.F.O.

INVESTOR CONTACT: Allison McFerren
Sanders, Invest. Rel., (614)840-3133

PRINCIPAL OFFICE: 1205 Dearborn Drive,
Columbus, OH 43085

TELEPHONE NUMBER: (614) 438-3210
FAX: (614) 438-3256
WEB: www.worthingtonindustries.com
NO. OF EMPLOYEES: 7,500 (approx.)
SHAREHOLDERS: 11,408 (approx.)
ANNUAL MEETING: In Sept.
INCORPORATED: OH, June, 1955; reincorp.,
OH, Sept., 1998

INSTITUTIONAL HOLDINGS:
No. of Institutions: 189
Shares Held: 38,657,752
% Held: 43.4

INDUSTRY: Cold finishing of steel shapes
(SIC: 3316)

TRANSFER AGENT(S): BankBoston, NA,
Boston, MA

NYSE SYMBOL WPS
Rec. Pr. 31¼ (5/31/00)

WPS RESOURCES CORPORATION

YIELD 6.5%
P/E RATIO 14.0

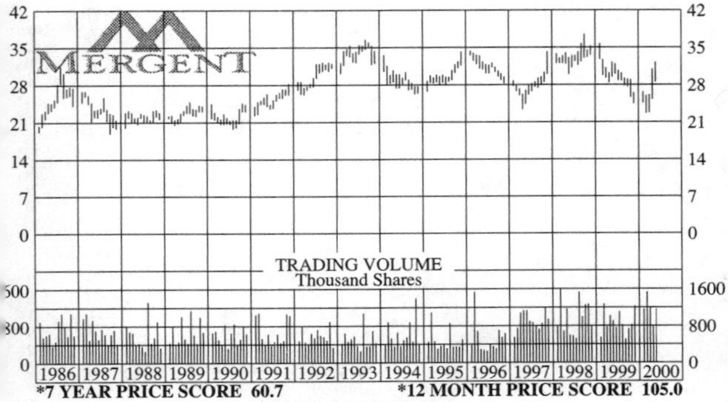

42
35
28
21
14
7
0
TRADING VOLUME
Thousand Shares
1600
800
0
1986 1987 1988 1989 1990 1991 1992 1993 1994 1995 1996 1997 1998 1999 2000

***7 YEAR PRICE SCORE 60.7** ***12 MONTH PRICE SCORE 105.0**

*NYSE COMPOSITE INDEX=100

INTERIM EARNINGS (Per Share):

Qtr.	Mar.	June	Sept.	Dec.
1996	0.98	0.42	0.43	0.17
1997	0.76	0.40	0.54	0.55
1998	0.72	0.41	0.45	0.24
1999	0.86	0.38	0.52	0.48

INTERIM DIVIDENDS (Per Share):

Amt.	Decl.	Ex.	Rec.	Pay.
0.505Q	7/08/99	8/27/99	8/31/99	9/20/99
0.505Q	10/14/99	11/26/99	11/30/99	12/20/99
0.505Q	2/10/00	2/25/00	2/29/00	3/20/00
0.505Q	4/13/00	5/26/00	5/31/00	6/20/00

Indicated div.: $2.02 (Div. Reinv. Plan)

CAPITALIZATION (12/31/99):

	($000)	(%)
Long-Term Debt	510,917	38.3
Capital Lease Obligations	73,585	5.5
Deferred Income Tax	111,092	8.3
Redeemable Pfd. Stock	50,000	3.8
Preferred Stock	51,193	3.8
Common & Surplus	536,300	40.2
Total	1,333,087	100.0

DIVIDEND ACHIEVER STATUS:
Rank: 311 10-Year Growth Rate: 2.26%
Total Years of Dividend Growth: 41

RECENT DEVELOPMENTS: For the year ended 12/31/99, net income jumped 27.7% to $59.6 million versus $46.6 million in 1998. The growth in earnings was attributed to higher sales volumes at WPSC, new Wisconsin retail electric and gas rates and the elimination of net trading losses at WPS Energy Services. Total operating revenues grew 3.3% to $1.10 billion from $1.06 billion the year before.

PROSPECTS: Expansion in wholesale gas, retail gas, and retail electric markets at WPS Energy Services, as well as the acquisition of additional generation facilities at WPS Power Development should have a favorable effect on results. Meanwhile, WPS Energy Services has agreed to purchase the production of a 37-megawatt renewable energy facility in Northern Maine.

BUSINESS

WPS RESOURCES CORPORATION (formerly Wisconsin Public Service Corp.) operates as a holding company with both regulated utility and non-regulated business units. The Company's principal wholly-owned subsidiaries are: Wisconsin Public Service Corporation (WPSC), a regulated electric and gas utility in Wisconsin and Michigan; Upper Peninsula Power Company, a regulated electric utility in Michigan; and WPS Energy Service, Inc. and WPS Power Development, Inc., both non-regulated subsidiaries. As of 12/31/99, WPSC, the Company's largest unit with 65.0% of 1999 sales, served 388,390 electric retail and 229,905 gas retail customers.

ANNUAL FINANCIAL DATA

	12/31/99	12/31/98	12/31/97	12/31/96	12/31/95	12/31/94	12/31/93
Earnings Per Share	**2.24**	**1.76**	**2.25**	**2.00**	**2.32**	**2.21**	**2.47**
Cash Flow Per Share	**2.79**	**1.83**	**6.11**	**5.93**	**6.46**	**5.77**	**6.16**
Tang. Book Val. Per Share	**20.03**	**19.51**	**20.00**	**19.56**	**19.39**	**18.69**	**18.18**
Dividends Per Share	**2.00**	**1.96**	**1.92**	**1.88**	**1.84**	**1.80**	**1.76**
Dividend Payout %	**89.3**	**111.4**	**85.3**	**94.0**	**79.3**	**81.4**	**71.3**
INCOME STATEMENT (IN MILLIONS):							
Total Revenues	1,098.5	1,063.7	878.3	858.3	719.8	673.8	680.6
Costs & Expenses	705.8	910.9	644.4	617.2	461.6	432.8	423.9
Depreciation & Amort.	98.7	102.5	92.2	93.9	99.1	85.2	88.3
Maintenance Exp.	60.6	52.8	41.7	48.8	50.8	50.0	51.6
Operating Income	119.7	100.0	100.1	98.3	108.4	105.8	83.7
Net Interest Inc./(Exp.)	d32.8	d27.1	d26.4	d25.0	d25.4	d25.1	d25.8
Income Taxes	29.7	23.4	29.3	24.4	30.8	29.5	32.5
Equity Earnings/Minority Int.	...	d0.6	0.8	0.3	...	...	...
Net Income	59.6	46.6	53.7	47.8	55.3	52.7	62.2
Cash Flow	272.0	48.4	145.9	141.6	154.5	137.9	147.2
Average Shs. Outstg. (000)	26,644	26,511	23,873	23,891	23,897	23,897	23,888
BALANCE SHEET (IN MILLIONS):							
Gross Property	2,429.2	2,197.6	1,899.4	1,825.8	1,760.0	1,690.8	1,626.9
Accumulated Depreciation	1,293.4	1,206.1	1,032.1	952.3	905.4	846.5	801.1
Net Property	1,150.9	1,010.2	886.4	892.9	868.9	863.8	843.9
Total Assets	1,816.5	1,510.4	1,299.6	1,330.7	1,266.7	1,217.3	1,198.8
Long-Term Obligations	584.5	343.0	304.0	305.8	306.6	309.9	314.2
Net Stockholders' Equity	587.5	568.4	529.0	518.7	514.6	497.7	485.7
Year-end Shs. Outstg. (000)	26,780	26,511	23,897	23,897	23,897	23,897	23,897
STATISTICAL RECORD:							
Operating Profit Margin %	10.9	9.4	11.4	11.5	15.1	15.7	12.3
Net Profit Margin %	5.4	4.4	6.1	5.6	7.7	7.8	9.1
Net Inc./Net Property %	5.2	4.6	6.1	5.3	6.4	6.1	7.4
Net Inc./Tot. Capital %	4.5	4.3	5.6	5.0	5.8	5.6	6.6
Return on Equity %	10.1	8.2	10.2	9.2	10.8	10.6	12.8
Accum. Depr./Gross Prop. %	53.2	54.9	54.3	52.2	51.4	50.1	49.2
Price Range	35¾-24 7/16	37½-29 15/16	34¼-23⅜	34⅜-28¼	34¼-26¾	33⅝-26¼	36½-30⅛
P/E Ratio	23.5-16.1	21.3-17.0	15.2-10.4	17.2-14.1	14.8-11.5	15.2-11.9	14.8-12.2
Average Yield %	6.6	5.8	6.7	6.0	6.0	1.5	5.3

Statistics are as originally reported.

OFFICERS:
L. L. Weyers, Chmn., Pres., C.E.O.
D. P. Bittner, Sr. V.P., C.F.O.
R. G. Baeten, V.P., Treas.
B. J. Wolf, Sec.

INVESTOR CONTACT: Ralph G. Baeten, V.P., Treas., (920) 433-1449

PRINCIPAL OFFICE: 700 North Adams Street, P.O. Box 19001, Green Bay, WI 54307-9001

TELEPHONE NUMBER: (920) 433-4901
FAX: (920) 433-1526
WEB: www.wpsr.com

NO. OF EMPLOYEES: 2,900

SHAREHOLDERS: 25,020

ANNUAL MEETING: In May

INCORPORATED: WI, July, 1883

INSTITUTIONAL HOLDINGS:
No. of Institutions: 103
Shares Held: 7,504,286
% Held: 28.0

INDUSTRY: Electric and other services combined (SIC: 4931)

TRANSFER AGENT(S): Firstar Bank Milwaukee, N.A., Milwaukee, WI

NYSE SYMBOL WWY
Rec. Pr. 80 1/16 (5/31/00)

WRIGLEY (WILLIAM) JR. CO.

YIELD 1.7%
P/E RATIO 30.1

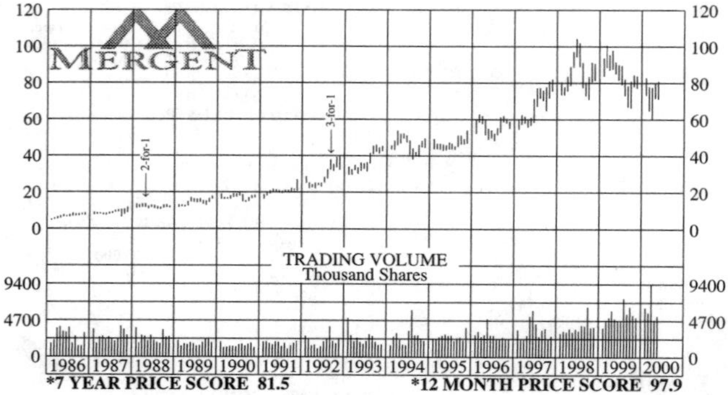

***7 YEAR PRICE SCORE 81.5** ***12 MONTH PRICE SCORE 97.9**

*NYSE COMPOSITE INDEX=100

INTERIM EARNINGS (Per Share):

Qtr.	Mar.	June	Sept.	Dec.
1996	0.50	0.49	0.53	0.47
1997	0.54	0.66	0.60	0.54
1998	0.66	0.73	0.63	0.61
1999	0.60	0.75	0.67	0.64

INTERIM DIVIDENDS (Per Share):

Amt.	Decl.	Ex.	Rec.	Pay.
0.22Q	8/23/99	10/13/99	10/15/99	11/01/99
0.47E	10/27/99	11/29/99	12/01/99	12/15/99
0.35Q	10/27/99	1/12/00	1/15/00	2/01/00
0.35Q	3/06/00	4/12/00	4/14/00	5/01/00
0.35Q	5/24/00	7/12/00	7/14/00	8/01/00

Indicated div.: $1.40 (Div. Reinv. Plan)

CAPITALIZATION (12/31/99):

	($000)	(%)
Deferred Income Tax	44,963	3.8
Common & Surplus	1,138,775	96.2
Total	1,183,738	100.0

DIVIDEND ACHIEVER STATUS:

Rank: 95 10-Year Growth Rate: 13.00%
Total Years of Dividend Growth: 19

RECENT DEVELOPMENTS: For the year ended 12/31/99, net earnings rose 1.2% to $308.2 million from $304.5 million in the previous year. Total revenues increased 2.8% to $2.08 billion from $2.02 billion in the prior year. North American net sales advanced 2.6% to $842.1 million from $820.4 million as a result of a favorable product mix due to the launch of Eclipse®, a sugar-free pellet gum, in 1999. International net sales increased by 8.0% due to higher unit volume, product mix and selected selling price increases.

PROSPECTS: Near-term prospects are promising. WWY's shipments increased during the second half of 1999 and the Company plans to use this momentum for new product intitiatives and new advertising efforts during 2000. WWY is also planning to expand its international presence in 2000. Meanwhile, WWY announced that it will launch two new products in the U.S. during the third quarter of 2000. WWY expects to begin shipping Extra Polar Ice® and Eclipse Polar Ice to retailers in July.

BUSINESS

WM. WRIGLEY JR. CO. is the world's largest chewing gum producer. Wrigley brands are produced in 15 factories around the world and sold in more than 140 countries. Main brands are WRIGLEYS SPEARMINT, DOUBLEMINT, JUICY FRUIT, WINTER FRESH, BIG RED, EXTRA, FREEDENT, ECLIPSE and HUBBA BUBBA bubble gum. All other businesses account for less than 10% of combined revenues, operating profit and assets. Wrigley operates three plants in the U.S. plus 12 others outside the U.S. WWY's three wholly-owned U.S. subsidiaries are Amurol Confections Co., L.A. Dreyfus Co. and Northwestern Flavors, Inc. Sales for 1999 were derived from North America, 40.8%; Europe, 43.9%; Asia/Pacific/Latin America, 14.4%; other, 1.0%. WWY's largest non-U.S. markets by shipments are Australia, Canada, China, France, Germany, Philippines, Poland, Russia, Taiwan and the United Kingdom.

BUSINESS LINE ANALYSIS

(12/31/99)	Rev(%)	Inc(%)
North America	40.8	46.3
Europe	43.9	46.1
Asia, Pacific & Other	14.4	13.6
All other	0.9	(0.6)
Total	100.0	100.0

ANNUAL FINANCIAL DATA

	12/31/99	12/31/98	12/31/97	12/31/96	12/31/95	12/31/94	12/31/93
Earnings Per Share	**2.66**	**[2] 2.63**	**[1] 2.34**	**[1] 1.99**	**1.93**	**[1] 1.98**	**1.50**
Cash Flow Per Share	**3.19**	**3.11**	**2.78**	**2.39**	**2.30**	**2.33**	**1.80**
Tang. Book Val. Per Share	**9.95**	**9.96**	**8.50**	**7.74**	**6.87**	**5.92**	**4.94**
Dividends Per Share	**1.33**	**1.30**	**1.17**	**1.02**	**0.96**	**0.90**	**0.75**
Dividend Payout %	**50.0**	**49.4**	**50.0**	**51.3**	**49.7**	**45.5**	**50.0**
INCOME STATEMENT (IN MILLIONS):							
Total Revenues	2,079.2	2,023.4	1,954.2	1,850.6	1,769.7	1,661.3	1,440.4
Costs & Expenses	1,572.9	1,536.5	1,505.2	1,423.7	1,373.8	1,265.4	1,125.5
Depreciation & Amort.	61.2	55.8	50.4	47.3	43.8	41.1	34.6
Operating Income	445.1	431.1	398.5	379.6	352.2	354.8	280.3
Net Interest Inc./(Exp.)	d0.7	d0.6	d1.0	d1.1	d2.0	d1.5	d1.5
Income Before Income Taxes	444.4	440.9	394.2	359.1	350.2	353.3	278.8
Income Taxes	136.2	136.4	122.6	128.8	126.5	122.7	103.9
Net Income	308.2	[2] 304.5	[1] 271.6	[1] 230.3	223.7	[1] 230.5	174.9
Cash Flow	369.4	360.3	322.1	277.6	267.5	271.6	209.5
Average Shs. Outstg. (000)	115,861	115,964	115,964	115,983	116,066	116,358	116,511
BALANCE SHEET (IN MILLIONS):							
Cash & Cash Equivalents	306.9	351.7	327.4	300.6	231.7	230.2	189.8
Total Current Assets	803.7	843.2	797.7	729.4	672.1	623.3	502.3
Net Property	559.1	520.1	430.5	388.1	347.5	289.4	239.9
Total Assets	1,547.7	1,520.9	1,343.1	1,233.5	1,099.2	978.8	815.3
Total Current Liabilities	251.8	218.6	225.8	218.2	213.4	209.9	159.2
Net Stockholders' Equity	1,138.8	1,157.0	985.4	897.4	796.9	688.5	575.2
Net Working Capital	551.9	624.5	571.9	511.3	458.7	413.4	343.1
Year-end Shs. Outstg. (000)	114,496	116,110	115,969	115,970	116,002	116,209	116,400
STATISTICAL RECORD:							
Operating Profit Margin %	21.4	21.3	20.4	20.5	19.9	21.4	19.5
Net Profit Margin %	14.8	15.0	13.9	12.4	12.6	13.9	12.1
Return on Equity %	27.1	26.3	27.6	25.7	28.1	33.5	30.4
Return on Assets %	19.9	20.0	20.2	18.7	20.4	23.6	21.5
Price Range	100 5/8-66 1/2	104 5/16-70 15/16	82 1/16-54 9/16	62 7/8-48 3/8	54-42 7/8	53 7/8-38 1/8	46 1/8-29 1/2
P/E Ratio	37.8-25.0	39.7-27.0	35.1-23.3	31.6-24.3	28.0-22.2	27.2-19.3	30.7-19.7
Average Yield %	1.6	1.5	1.7	1.8	2.0	2.0	2.0

Statistics are as originally reported. [1] Incls. non-recurring net chrg. 12/31/97: $3.3 mill.; chrg. 12/31/96: $13.0 mill.; credit 12/31/94: $24.8 mill. [2] Incls. one-time gain of $10.4 mill.

OFFICERS:
W. Wrigley Jr., Pres., C.E.O.
A. J. Schneider, Treas.
H. Malovany, Sec., Gen. Couns.

INVESTOR CONTACT: M. J. Foss, Stkhlder. Rel. Adm., (312) 645-4083

PRINCIPAL OFFICE: 410 North Michigan Avenue, Chicago, IL 60611

TELEPHONE NUMBER: (312) 644-2121
FAX: (312) 645-4083
WEB: www.wrigley.com

NO. OF EMPLOYEES: 9,300 (approx.)

SHAREHOLDERS: 38,138 (common); 3,594 (class B common)

ANNUAL MEETING: In March

INCORPORATED: DE, Oct., 1927

INSTITUTIONAL HOLDINGS:
No. of Institutions: 297
Shares Held: 37,884,051
% Held: 40.7

INDUSTRY: Chewing gum (SIC: 2067)

TRANSFER AGENT(S): First Chicago Trust Company, Jersey City, NJ